Milestone Documents of American Leaders

Exploring the Primary
Sources of Notable
American Leaders

MILESTONE DOCUMENTS OF AMERICAN LEADERS

Exploring the Primary
Sources of Notable
American Leaders

Second Edition

Volume 1
Abigail Adams to Frederick Douglass

Editors
Paul Finkelman
James A. Percoco
David Simonelli

SCHLAGER GROUP

GREY HOUSE PUBLISHING

Schlager Group, Inc.
325 N. Saint Paul, Suite 3425
Dallas, TX 75201
http://www.schlagergroup.com

Grey House Publishing
4919 Route 22, PO Box 56
Amenia, NY 12501
http://www.greyhouse.com

Milestone Documents, 2017, published by Grey House Publishing, Inc., Amenia, NY.

∞ The paper used in these volumes conforms to the American National Standard for Permanence of Paper for Printed Library Materials, Z39.48 1992 (R2009).

Publisher's Cataloging-In-Publication Data
(Prepared by The Donohue Group, Inc.)

Names: Finkelman, Paul, 1949- editor. | Percoco, James A., editor. | Simonelli, David, editor.

Title: Milestone documents of American leaders : exploring the primary sources of notable American leaders / editors, Paul Finkelman, James A. Percoco, David Simonelli.

Description: Second edition. | Dallas, TX : Schlager Group ; Amenia, NY : Grey House Publishing, [2017] | Includes bibliographical references and index. | Contents: Volume 1. Abigail Adams to Frederick Douglass — Volume 2. W.E.B. Du Bois to John Jay — Volume 3. Thomas Jefferson to James Polk — Volume 4. Adam Clayton Powell, Jr., to Brigham Young.

Identifiers: ISBN 978-1-68217-165-3 (set) | ISBN 978-1-68217-167-7 (v.1) | ISBN 978-1-68217-168-4 (v.2) | ISBN 978-1-68217-169-1 (v.3) | ISBN 978-1-68217-170-7 (v.4)

Subjects: LCSH: United States—History—Sources. | Statesmen—United States—Sources.

Classification: LCC E173 .M63 2017 | DDC 973—dc23

Contents

Volume 2: W.E.B. Du Bois to John Jay

Volume 3: Thomas Jefferson to James Polk

Volume 4: Adam Clayton Powell, Jr., to Brigham Young

Editor's Introduction

From the creation of the United States, written documents have shaped our national culture. Unlike almost every other country, the United States began with a written statement of purpose –Thomas Jefferson's Declaration of Independence – a "milestone" document that created the nation, providing its twin moral and political foundations. Jefferson, the primary author of the Declaration, first set out the theory of representative government on which the United States was built: that "governments are instituted among men, deriving their just powers from the consent of the governed." Jefferson then articulated the moral theory on which representation had to be based: that we are all "created equal" and endowed with the "inalienable rights of life, liberty, and the pursuit of happiness." This is one of the many "foundational" documents in this series. Others include Virginia's Declaration of Rights, drafted by George Mason, some of the Federalist Papers, and George Washington's farewell address.

Documents can also illuminate the cultural, economic and social principles on which the nation was founded, as securely as it was founded on political freedoms and representative government. For example, the United States is still one of the most religious nation-states on earth, based on church attendance. John Wesley, the founder of Methodism, was a major influence on the way many English-born American colonists thought of their relationship to the unknown, whether it be God or the environment they had settled into. While he opposed American independence, in his letter to Lord North (1775), Wesley at least showed that he understood how and why the colonists – many of them Methodists – would consider rebellion against the British metropole. Likewise, the US became a world leader in industry because its people were inventive and innovative – like Benjamin Banneker, an African-American whose journal entries on cicadas (1800) would introduce planning to eradicate locusts from American agricultural fields in the century to come. A century later, Andrew Carnegie would try to show how the acquisition of wealth by one could become the foundation of a better America for all. And the journals and autobiography of Davy Crockett introduced the myth of rugged individualism as central to the development of an American culture.

Since the writing of the Declaration of Independence, many documents have influenced the history of the United States –constitutional provisions, political speeches and manifestos, judicial opinions, legislative acts, essays, and other writings. Because the United States is a democracy, written and spoken words have been particularly important in the development of our political cultures and in stimulating social change. This collection includes numerous documents that illustrate social activism, such as Jane Addam's essay on the "Necessity for Social Settlements" (1892), Eugene V. Debs's essay on why he became a Socialist (1902), and Elizabeth Cady Stanton's Declaration of Sentiments presented at the Seneca Falls Convention of 1848. Speeches and essays by the key civil rights leaders and activists W. E. B. Du Bois, Ella Baker, Ida B. Wells, Frederick Douglass, Alain Locke, Malcolm X, and Martin Luther King, Jr., help us understand the civil rights movement from their perspectives. These documents are supplemented by political documents about civil rights, among them, President Lyndon Baines Johnson's address to a joint session of Congress in 1965 in support of voting rights legislations and Chief Justice Earl Warren's opinion in the pivotal anti-segregation case *Brown v. Board of Education of Topeka* (1954). On the other side of the issue are statements by those who opposed civil rights, like Samuel F.B. Morse's Biblical defense of slavery (1863), President Andrew Johnson's vetoes of the Freedmen's Bureau Bill (1866) and the Civil Rights Act (1866) and Senator Strom Thurmond's keynote address at the States' Rights Democratic Conference (1948), arguing against federal encroachment on states' authority (particularly with respect to segregation).

Great speeches and documents have often inspired Americans. Martin Luther King's "I have a dream" speech helped change the minds of millions of Americans about the fundamental injustice of segregation. Similarly, the addresses and writings of Susan B. Anthony and Elizabeth Cady Stanton helped build public support for extending the right to vote to women. Speeches, pamphlets and reports, when widely circulated and read, have created groundswells of opinion that have led to policy and cultural changes. Horace Mann and Catherine Beecher championed the development of a public school system with women in prominent roles as teachers; today that role has become positively stereotypical. John James Audubon and John Muir taught Americans to value their continent's environmental diversity, celebrate it, and protect it. At the same time, the pleas of Native American leaders such as Ely Parker and Chief John Ross, labor activists like Eugene V. Debs and César Chavez, and populists like Huey Long as well as anarchists like Emma Goldman remind us that even the most passionately voiced arguments have not always found a sympathetic audience ready to take up the cause.

Legal documents have also dramatically altered the way Americans have viewed their rights and the rights of others.

Salmon P. Chases' *Reclamation of Fugitives from Service* helped lead antebellum northerners to see the unfairness and wrongness of the fugitive slave laws. Chief Justice Earl Warren's opinion on *Miranda v. Arizona* had a somewhat different effect. Initially, Americans thought that the Supreme Court was being too lenient with criminals. Police officials were especially fearful that the new "Miranda warnings" would hamper law enforcement. But within a decade the nation's police forces came to accept the idea that even the accused had rights and that coercive police tactics were not consistent with democratic values.

Political life in America has always been tied to addresses in legislatures and assemblies, manifestos, essays, and public oratory. The events leading to the American Revolution included actions like the Boston Tea Party, but they also consisted of speeches, letters, and public pronouncements, like George Mason's letter to the Committee of Merchants in London (1766), Samuel Adams's instructions to Boston's representatives, and Patrick Henry's famous speech attacking the Intolerable Acts. The Boston massacre reflected public indignation at the presence of British troops in an American city, but John Hancock's Boston Massacre oration (1774) helped galvanize opposition to the British.

The interplay between the writings of different leaders illustrates the ebb and flow of political and social history. Abraham Lincoln's "house divided" speech had a profound effect on public sentiment and helped form the northern response to Chief Justice Roger Taney's opinion in *Dred Scott v. Sandford* (1857), which essentially denied citizenship status to slaves. A generation later, William Jennings Bryan's "cross of gold" speech dramatically affected the populist movement and national response to industrialization and the economic crisis of the 1890s. In the end, it did not carry the day, and Bryan lost the presidential race to William McKinley, whose speech in 1898 on intervention in Cuba set the stage for the Spanish-American War. In our own time, we have seen the clashing of ideas between George W. Bush's address to the nation on military operations in Iraq (2003) and Senator Robert Byrd's speech "The Emperor Has No Clothes" of the same year. Donald Trump's announcement of his candidacy for president in 2015 shows how disparate and fleeting the appeal of ideas can be to a voting public.

The war speeches of Presidents McKinley and Bush help us understand the role of foreign policy in American politics, as do James K. Polk's message to Congress on war with Mexico in 1846, Franklin D. Roosevelt's "four freedoms" message during World War II, and Harry S. Truman's report to the American people on Korea in 1951. These foreign policy speeches by presidents are supplemented by the documents of others who shaped our international relations, such as Henry Cabot Lodge's speech concerning President Woodrow Wilson's plan for a world peace (1917), George Kennan's "The Sources of Soviet Conduct" (1947), and Condoleezza Rice's "International Support for Iraqi Democracy"(2005). American priorities in foreign policy and maintenance of diplomats are highlighted in Hillary Rodham Clinton's speech to the Senate investigation of the terrorist attack in Benghazi (2015). But elected and appointed officials are not the only leaders to influence foreign policy. On the eve of World War II, Walter Reuther, a key leader of the labor movement, promised that the members of his United Automobile Workers could produce "500 planes a day" as Americans began to put in place the "arsenal of democracy."

Beyond foreign policy we have many other statements by senators, political leaders, and presidents. Americans often pay particular attention to the speeches and political position papers of politicians. Elected officials have used the podium –what President Theodore Roosevelt called the "bully pulpit" –to sway political opinion. In times of crisis presidential inaugural addresses have served to inspire the nation. Thomas Jefferson's first inaugural helped heal the wounds caused by the vicious election of 1800 and the partisan prosecutions under the Sedition Act of 1800 when he declared, "Every difference of opinion is not a difference of principle. We have called by different names brethren of the same principle. We are all Republicans, we are all Federalists."

Similarly, Abraham Lincoln's first inaugural –in the wake of the secession of seven southern states –was a long plea to the South to return to the Union. He spoke about a shared history and appealed to patriotism to head off the coming war, and he closed with the memorable words

> We are not enemies, but friends. We must not be enemies. Though passion may have strained it must not break our bonds of affection. The mystic chords of memory, stretching from every battlefield and patriot grave to every living heart and hearthstone over all this broad land, will yet swell the chorus of the Union, when again touched, as surely they will be, by the better angels of our nature.

The "better angels" would not return in Lincoln's lifetime, and his second inaugural was a masterpiece in explaining the carnage of four years of war and looking forward to the peace that would soon come. Having given moral meaning to the war and the huge loss of life, Lincoln closed by offering peace without vengeance. "With malice toward none, with charity for all, with firmness in the right as God gives us to see the right, let us strive on to finish the work we are in, to bind up the nation's wounds, to care for him who shall have borne the battle, and for his widow and his orphan, to do all which may achieve and cherish a just and lasting peace among ourselves and with all nations."

In the twentieth century we remember Franklin Delano Roosevelt's inspiration to a nation in the throes of the Great Depression, with at least a third of the nation out of work. At this point in history, Roosevelt told the nation, "The only thing we have to fear, is fear itself." This was not entirely true –many Americans on that day feared not having enough to eat the next day. But the speech helped reassure Americans that the new administration would be working from day one to save the nation and the economy. John Kennedy's inaugural was memorable for its soaring rhetoric urging a new commitment to a better world: "Ask

not what your country can do for you, ask what you can do for your country."

A short introduction to a large collection does not allow space to mention all of the leaders who have contributed to the key moments of American history or the words they spoke and wrote. Generals, labor leaders, social activist, and the wives of presidents all took an active role in political life. We have the speeches and writings of those who succeeded and those who failed. There are both prophetic statements and bold predictions that never came about. Taken together, the documents in these volumes offer guideposts to our past and help us to better understand our present. They are the building blocks of American history and American life. The speeches and documents in these volumes guide us through our history, helping us see how language and ideas shapes our past and created out present.

Paul Finkelman
President William McKinley Distinguished
Professor of Law and Public Policy
Albany Law School
Albany, New York

David Simonelli
Department of History
Youngstown State University
Youngstown, Ohio

Publisher's Note

Overview

Milestone Documents of American Leaders offers a unique biographical approach to the study of primary source documents. The 133 entries in the set cover notable Americans from the Revolutionary era to the twenty-first century, including presidents, senators, diplomats, Supreme Court justices, labor leaders, social activists, first ladies, presidential candidates, and religious figures Through two discrete components—an in-depth original essay and a section of primary document text—each entry highlights the writings and speeches that helped establish each person's place in history.

Organization

The set is organized alphabetically in four volumes:

- Volume 1: Abigail Adams to Frederick Douglass
- Volume 2: W. E. B. Du Bois to John Jay
- Volume 3: Thomas Jefferson to James Polk
- Volume 4: Adam Clayton Powell, Jr., to Brigham Young

Entry Format

The entries in *Milestone Documents of American* Leaders follow a uniform structure using the same standardized headings. Following is the full list of entry headings:

- **Overview** gives a summary of the leader's life and describes the person's place in American history and the sorts of documents he or she produced.
- **Time Line** chronicles key events in the leader's own life and events in American history during the person's lifetime.
- **Explanation and Analysis of Documents** consists of a detailed examination of each featured document text.
- **Impact and Legacy** examines the historical influence of the leader, discussing the legacy of the person and lasting impact of the documents.
- **Essential Quotes** offers a selection of key quotes from the documents.
- **Questions for Further Study** poses study questions for students related to the leader and the documents.
- **Key Sources** is an annotated bibliography of the subject's writings, including library and online archives, autobiographies and memoirs, and letters.
- **Further Reading** lists articles, books, and Web sites for further research.
- **Document Text** gives the actual text of each primary document, along with a glossary defining important, difficult, or unusual terms in the document text. Each entry features the byline of the scholar who wrote the analysis. Readers should note that in many entries the "Document Text" section gives abridged text of the primary source document—especially in the case of lengthy documents such as Supreme Court decisions, which generally contain several parts (majority opinion, concurring opinions, dissenting opinions). In all instances where the document text has been abridged, readers will find ellipses (...) to indicate the location of truncated text.

A Note about Primary Document Text

In most cases, we have reprinted the primary documents as they originally appeared in their own time. Thus, throughout this set, readers will find that some documents contain typographical errors, grammatical oddities, and unusual spellings. This is especially true of documents from the eighteenth and nineteenth centuries. In the case of speech transcripts, however, we have generally repaired obvious errors of transcription.

Features

In addition to the text of the 133 entries, the set features over 250 photographs and illustrations. The front matter of Volume 1 includes a Publisher's Note to introduce and describe the set and how it has been organized, the Editor's Introduction, and a section of interest to educators: "Teachers' Activity Guides." This section comprises

eight distinct guides, all of which are tied to the National History Standards and which make use of the documents covered in this set. This section was written by James A. Percoco. At the end of Volume 4, readers will find a "List of Documents by Category" and a cumulative "Subject Index."

Questions

We welcome questions and comments about the set. Readers may address all such comments to the following

MILESTONE DOCUMENTS OF AMERICAN LEADERS
Schlager Group Inc.
325 N. Saint Paul, Suite 3425
Dallas, TX 75201

Teachers' Activity Guides

The following activity guides correspond to the National History Standards as published by the National Center for History in the Schools. The documents in *Milestone Documents of American Leaders* relate to most, though not all, of the eras and standards found in the National History Standards.

Era 3: Revolution and the New Nation (1754–1820s)

Standard 1: The causes of the American Revolution, the ideas and interests involved in forging the Revolutionary movement, and the reasons for the American victory

Focus Question: How did the major players of the American Revolution guide the United States through a new application of Enlightenment philosophy and a war that secured not only victory but independence as well?

- Review with students the major ideas of Enlightenment thinking with regard to natural rights, republicanism, and the social contract.
- Provide students with copies of Patrick Henry's resolutions in opposition to the Stamp Act, speech to the First Continental Congress, and speech to the Virginia Revolutionary Convention in opposition to the Intolerable Acts; Thomas Jefferson's Declaration of Independence; George Mason's Fairfax County Resolves and Virginia Declaration of Rights; and George Washington's address to Congress on resigning his commission as well as his farewell address.
- Instruct students to examine these documents and determine how they align with Enlightenment philosophy, particularly as applied to national independence and republican forms of government.
- Ask students to review the two George Washington documents and determine how the actions associated with them— voluntarily resigning his positions as supreme military commander and president, respectively—reflect Enlightenment values concerning liberty and responsible government.
- Use the information derived from the sources to spark a discussion of civilian authority over the military and how Washington's actions created a tradition that has become a fundamental part of American political life.

Standard 2: The impact of the American Revolution on politics, economy, and society

Focus Question: What role did the leaders of the American Revolution play in shaping economic policy, putting the new nation on the road to a sound financial footing, and defining a framework for a national culture as applied to political and social interactions?

- Ask students to define in their own words the ideas of "sound financial footing" and "national culture."
- Next ask them to discuss ways in which the government charts economic policy and to consider what role (if any) government plays in defining national culture and identity.
- Provide students with copies of Abigail Adams's 1776 letter to her husband, John Adams's *Thoughts on Government*, and Alexander Hamilton's "First Report on Public Credit."
- Ask students to discuss how distinctions between public policy and private matters are established in these documents.
- Ask students to write a reply from John Adams to his wife in response to her letter.
- Have students create a compare-and-contrast list regarding John Adams's *Thoughts on Government* and Hamilton's "First Report on Public Credit" as to the role government plays in the lives of its citizens.

Standard 3: The institutions and practices of government created during the Revolution and how they were revised between 1787 and 1815 to create the foundation of the American political system based on the U.S. Constitution and Bill of Rights

Focus Question: How did the American concepts of individual rights evolve over the period between the end of the Revolutionary War and 1815, and how did these concepts extend the influence of Enlightenment principles into the nineteenth century?

- Have students undertake basic research on John Adams, Samuel Adams, Thomas Jefferson, James Madison, and George Mason with regard to their backgrounds, personalities, political beliefs, and positions on key issues of their time. Review the Bill of Rights with students.
- Provide students with copies of John Adams's *Report of a Constitution, or Form of Government, for the Commonwealth of Massachusetts*, Samuel Adams's comments to the Massachusetts Ratifying Convention,

Jefferson's Virginia Act for Establishing Religious Freedom, Madison's Virginia Resolutions, and Mason's Virginia Declaration of Rights.
- Have students role-play the different leaders, presenting their respective views on the idea of rights, with an emphasis on the influence of Enlightenment principles—particularly with regard to natural rights—on their own thinking.
- Have students write a persuasive essay either for or against the idea of an activist government that may deny citizens' individual rights in service to what its leaders regard as the greater public good.

Era 4: Expansion and Reform (1801–1861)

Standard 1: U.S. territorial expansion between 1801 and 1861 and how it affected relations with external powers and Native Americans

Focus Question: What effect did westward expansion have on the lives of American Indians? How did this expansion—combined with Americans' idea of Manifest Destiny—lead to a war with Mexico?

- Provide students with an introduction to the idea of Manifest Destiny. Refer them to the essays by the journalist John L. O'Sullivan in which the idea was first explicitly formulated—"The Great Nation of Futurity" (1839) and "Annexation" (1845).
- Show students an image of Emanuel Leutze's painting *Westward the Course of Empire Takes Its Way*.
- Review with students maps showing U.S. territorial expansion between 1801 and 1861. Be sure to point out the Louisiana Purchase, the Cherokee Trail of Tears, and the Mexican Cession.
- Provide students with copies of the following documents by John Ross: his memorial to Congress, his 1832 annual message to the Cherokee Nation, his letter to Martin Van Buren, and his addresses to the Cherokee Nation and to a general council of the Cherokee. Ask them to list three or four of Ross's main arguments with regard to federal treatment of the Cherokee people.
- Provide students with copies of Andrew Jackson's second annual message to Congress and ask them to identify its salient points regarding Indian removal. Next ask them to consider how Jackson's ideas fit within the tenets of Manifest Destiny.
- Provide students with copies of President James Polk's inaugural address and his message to Congress on war with Mexico as well as Henry Clay's letter to the editors of the *Washington National Intelligencer* on Texas annexation. Ask them to underline or identify phrases that support the belief in Manifest Destiny.
- Have students debate the merits of the Cherokee removal and the war with Mexico in terms of those actions' ultimate positive benefit or detriment to the United States.
- Have students write newspaper editorials either in support of or in opposition to Cherokee removal and the war with Mexico.

Standard 2: How the Industrial Revolution, increasing immigration, the rapid expansion of slavery, and the westward movement changed the lives of Americans and led toward regional tensions

Focus Question: What was the response of American leaders to the various pressures generated by change as the nation matured during the middle of the nineteenth century?

- Ask students to research, investigate, and prepare mini-presentations on the following topics with regard to their influence on social pressures in the mid-nineteenth century: German and Irish immigration; emerging American nationalism; the market revolution and capitalism; the need for internal improvements; and new inventions of the era, including the cotton gin, telegraph, sewing machine, and mechanical reaper.
- Discuss the impact these pressures had on the sectional tensions within the country.
- Ask students to research and present the major national ideas of the "American triumvirate": Henry Clay, John C. Calhoun, and Daniel Webster.
- Provide students with copies of Calhoun's "On the Reception of Abolition Petitions" (sometimes called "Slavery a Positive Good"), Clay's Senate speech on the Compromise of 1850 resolutions, Andrew Jackson's proclamation to the people of South Carolina regarding nullification, and Webster's second reply to Robert Hayne. Ask them to determine which elements of these documents reveal an underlying theme of nationalism in the face of rapid social and political change.
- Have students create original political cartoons that reflect their understanding of Clay, Calhoun, Webster, and Jackson within the context of either these documents or the social and sectional pressures exerted on the United States in the mid-nineteenth century.

Standard 3: The extension, restriction, and reorganization of political democracy after 1800

Focus Question: How did the John Marshall Court shape the relationship between the individual states and the federal government?

- Ask students to review the constitutional provisions that established the separation of powers and organized a federal republic.
- Ask students to research the life of John Marshall and explain why he was a fervent member of the Federalist Party and a supporter of Hamiltonian principles of a strong central government.

- Provide students with copies of Marshall's rulings in the cases of *Marbury v. Madison, McCulloch v. Maryland, and Gibbons v. Ogden.*
- Have students determine the specific aspects of these decisions that reflect the supremacy of the federal government over the states.
- Ask students to explain how Marshall's observation, in his *McCulloch* opinion, that "the power to tax is the power to destroy" embodies principles of a strong national government as exemplified by these three decisions of the Marshall Court.
- Have students write newspaper editorials against each of these decisions.

Standard 4: The sources and character of cultural, religious, and social reform movements in the antebellum period

Focus Question: How did leaders of the antislavery and women's movements come to be allies in the struggle for social justice in the United States between 1830 and 1860?

- Provide students with background on William Lloyd Garrison and Frederick Douglass.
- Divide students into three groups and have each examine one of these documents by Frederick Douglass: his letter "To My Old Master," the excerpt from the *Narrative of the Life of Frederick Douglass,* and his speech "What to the Slave Is the Fourth of July?" Have each group discuss the ways in which their document constitutes an indictment of slavery as an institution.
- Provide students with a copy of Wendell Phillips's essays "The Murder of Lovejoy" and "The Philosophy of the Abolition Movement." Ask them to list the similarities of sentiments between Douglass and Phillips.
- Provide students with copies of Elizabeth Cady Stanton's Declaration of Sentiments (her address to the 1848 Seneca Falls Convention) and her speech for the anniversary of the American Anti-Slavery Society. Have them list the various attitudes and opinions regarding both women's grievances and the institution of slavery.
- Provide students with a copy of William Lloyd Garrison's "To the Public" and compare this document with Stanton's Declaration of Sentiments, whose language likewise echoes that of the Declaration of Independence.
- Ask students to complete a Venn diagram comparing and contrasting the complaints and demands of abolitionists and advocates of women's rights in antebellum America.

Era 5: Civil War and Reconstruction (1850–1877)

Standard 1: The causes of the Civil War

Focus Question: What was the relationship of slavery to the cause of the American Civil War? How was that relationship expressed by President Abraham Lincoln?

- Have students research the period between the presidential election on November 6, 1860, and Lincoln's inauguration in March 4, 1861, with the aim of understanding the momentous events that took place over those four months.
- Provide students with Lincoln's "house divided" speech and his first inaugural address. Instruct them to list the points in each speech that reflect Lincoln's opposition to the extension of slavery. Have them discuss why he did not at that point seek the emancipation of slaves in states where slavery already existed.
- Have students compare and contrast the attitudes toward slavery and emancipation expressed by Lincoln in his first and second inaugural addresses.
- Have students compare and contrast the use of language in the Gettysburg address and the other Lincoln documents in this lesson plan.
- Have students conduct research on Lincoln's changing views regarding slavery and abolition and then write an essay on the evolution of his moral vision as it related to these issues.

Standard 4: The course and character of the Civil War and its effects on the American people

Focus Question: In what ways was the issue of "states' rights" a justification for the southern states to secede from the Union?

- Provide students with a copy of John C. Calhoun's address "To the People of the United States."
- Ask them to identify the main points of the speech as well as Calhoun's justification for secession. Remind students that this speech was delivered during the administration of Andrew Jackson, three decades before the Civil War.
- Provide students with copies of Jefferson Davis's resolutions to the U.S. Senate on the relations of states and his farewell address to the Senate. Have them prepare a Venn diagram comparing his remarks with those of Calhoun.
- Ask students to read Sam Houston's speech on his refusal to take an oath of loyalty to the Confederacy and list his objections to the formation of the breakaway republic.
- Using these documents as a basis, have students defend or refute the idea that the issue of states' rights was central to the existence of the Confederate States of America.

Standard 3: How various Reconstruction plans succeeded or failed

Focus Question: How successful was Reconstruction in securing economic, social, and political equality for African Americans?

- Introduce students to the basic issues regarding and competing plans for the reconstruction of the Union at the conclusion of the Civil War as well as the role that the Freedmen's Bureau was to play in the American South during the Reconstruction period.
- Explain the purposes of the Thirteenth, Fourteenth, and Fifteenth Amendments to the U.S. Constitution and how these amendments affected the legal status of African Americans.
- Provide students with copies of Andrew Johnson's first annual message to Congress and his vetoes of the Civil Rights Act and the Freedmen's Bureau Bill. Ask them to identify the major points in each and to consider what these documents say about his racial attitudes, particularly in light of his tolerance for the Black Codes and other efforts to limit the civil rights of African Americans in the former states of the Confederacy.
- Have students investigate Johnson's 1868 impeachment and the role Radical Republicans played in it. Have them draw original political cartoons depicting the event and its major players.
- Provide students with Ulysses S. Grant's first inaugural address, his special message to Congress announcing ratification of the Fifteenth Amendment, and his sixth annual message to Congress. Have them compare and contrast Grant's views and attitudes regarding Reconstruction with those of Andrew Johnson.
- Have students write an essay defending or rejecting the idea that Reconstruction was a success and beneficial to African Americans.

Era 6: The Development of the Industrial United States (1870–1900)

Standard 1: How the rise of corporations, heavy industry, and mechanized farming transformed the American people

Focus Question: How did industrialization and the growth of markets transform the public and private lives of Americans in the late nineteenth century?

- Have students research and report on the issue of bimetallism, which dominated much of the public dialogue over economic policy in the late nineteenth century. Ask them to contrast the views on the issue presented by William Jennings Bryan in his "cross of gold" speech and Grover Cleveland in his special message to Congress regarding the economic crisis of 1893.
- Discuss the issue of protectionism in the late nineteenth century. Provide students with copies of Bryan's speech on tariff reform and William McKinley's Home Market Club speech. Have them consider whether Bryan's anti- or McKinley's pro-tariff position would provide the greatest benefit to the greatest number of Americans.
- Give students copies of Cleveland's first inaugural address and Stephen J. Field's *Munn v. Illinois* opinion and his "Centenary of the Supreme Court of the United States." Ask them to explain how these documents reflect the changing relationship between the federal government and large corporations, especially railroads.
- Ask students to read Jane Addams's "Subjective Necessity for Social Settlements," Susan B. Anthony's "Status of Women, Past, Present, and Future," Elizabeth Cady Stanton's "Solitude of Self," and Victoria Woodhull's "And the Truth Shall Make You Free." Have them discuss how economic developments during the period helped change the status of women and encouraged the rise of social activism.
- Have students compare and contrast the relationship between economic and racial equality presented by W. E. B. Du Bois in "Strivings of the Negro People" and Booker T. Washington in his Atlanta Exposition speech.

Standard 2: Massive immigration after 1870 and how new social patterns, conflicts, and ideas of national unity developed among growing cultural diversity

Focus Question: How did the growth of immigration in the late nineteenth century help create new ideas of national identity? How did these ideas serve both to unite and to divide the American people?

- Instruct students to research and report on one of the large immigrant groups in late-nineteenth-century America: Irish and other western Europeans, particularly in the northeastern United States; Germans and other Central Europeans, especially in the Midwest; Eastern Europeans (paying special attention to the popular association of this group with anarchist and syndicalist organizations); and Asians, especially Chinese in California and other parts of the West.
- Ask students to examine Stephen J. Field's opinion in *Ho Ah Kow v. Nunan* and discuss what the Court's decision illustrates about changing views of cultural differences within the American legal framework.
- Provide students with copies of John Marshall Harlan's opinions in the Civil Rights Cases and *Plessy v. Ferguson*. Ask them to consider whether African Americans were being treated as "foreigners" within their own country and to contrast their situation with that of actual immigrants.

Standard 3: The rise of the American labor movement and how political issues reflected social and economic changes.

Focus Question: What role did labor unions play in protecting the rights and interests of American workers?

- Ask students to conduct research on the American labor movement of the late nineteenth and early twentieth centuries. Have them report on the major strikes and incidents of labor unrest from the era.
- Give students brief biographical sketches of Samuel Gompers and Eugene V. Debs.
- Provide students with Gompers's address to workers in Louisville, Kentucky, and his editorial on the Pullman strike and ask them to list his main points regarding the value of the American worker and the labor movement.
- Ask students to read Debs's "Liberty" and "How I Became a Socialist" and contrast his views on workers and the labor movement with those of Gompers. Have students read Wendell Phillips's "Foundation of the Labor Movement" and discuss the parallels and contrasts he draws between the situation of workers in the United States and that of their counterparts in England and other industrialized nations of Western Europe.
- Have students perform a dramatic exercise to illustrate the circumstances of labor in the late nineteenth century. Each member of the class can take on the role of a worker in manufacturing or associated industries such as coal mining, research the facts concerning that line of the work during the relevant period, and then talk to the rest of the group in the first person about what life was like for people in that industry.

Standard 4: Federal Indian policy and U.S. foreign policy after the Civil War

Focus Question: How did federal policy toward Native Americans and the foreign policy of the United States reflect common attitudes regarding the alleged superiority of whites over people of color?

- Distribute copies of Ely Parker's report on Indian affairs to the War Department, his annual report as commissioner of the Bureau of Indian Affairs, his letter of resignation as commissioner, and his letter to Harriett Maxwell Converse on Indian reform. Have students chart the sentiments expressed by Parker in each document and how they became progressively more negative with regard to U.S. Indian policy.
- Have students draw a political cartoon or write a newspaper editorial regarding the circumstances that brought about Parker's disillusionment with government policy toward Native Americans.
- Have students read Grover Cleveland's message to Congress on Hawaiian sovereignty and his fourth annual message to Congress (in which he addresses the growing crisis in Cuba) as well as William McKinley's message to Congress on intervention in Cuba and his "benevolent assimilation" speech. Ask them to compare and contrast the views expressed by each man regarding U.S. foreign policy.
- Ask students to write a response to Cleveland or McKinley from the standpoint of a Hawaiian, Cuban, or Philippine nationalist.

Era 7: The Emergence of Modern America (1890–1930)

Standard 1: How Progressives and others addressed problems of industrial capitalism, urbanization, and political corruption

Focus Question: How did African American reformers address the issues of racism during the Progressive Era?

- Play for students the Billie Holiday song "Strange Fruit" and explain its significance in terms of the horrors of the lynching of four thousand to five thousand people of color during the late nineteenth and early twentieth centuries.
- Explain to students that race relations between whites and blacks of the era were influenced by application of Darwin's theory of "survival of the fittest"—social Darwinism—to race, whereby blacks were viewed as inferior to whites.
- Instruct students to read Booker T. Washington's "Protest against Lynching" and Ida B. Wells's "Lynching: Our National Crime," "Eight Men Lynched," and "Lynching and the Excuse for It." Ask students to list the similarities between Washington's and Wells's arguments against lynching.
- Next, have students read Washington's Atlanta Exposition address and ask them to identify the main ideas, focusing on the quote "Cast down your bucket where you are." Define for students the term *accommodationist*, associated with Washington.
- Provide students with copies of W. E. B. Du Bois's "Agitation," "The Parting of the Ways," and "Strivings of the Negro People." Have students summarize Du Bois's attitudes on race relations in America. Explain to students that Du Bois was one of the founders of the National Association for the Advancement of Colored People and edited their newsletter, the *Crisis*.
- Have students read Wells's "Booker T. Washington and His Critics" and ask them to compare and contrast Wells, Du Bois, and Washington in their approaches to the racial issues of the era.
- Read to students the Dudley Randall poem "Booker T. and W.E.B." and have students pick out the ideas of both leaders.
- Ask students to write columns for the *Free Press*, of which Wells was editor and part owner.
- Have students research the 1906 case of Ota Benga, an African pygmy who was put on display in the Monkey House of the Bronx Zoo in New York City, and report on how this case reflected the ideas of social Darwinism as it applied to race relations during the time period.

- Have students research the continual failure of Congress and the presidency to support federal lynching laws.

Standard 2: The changing role of the United States in world affairs through World War I

Focus Question: What role did President Woodrow Wilson play in shaping America's role in the postwar world?

- Have students read George Washington's farewell address. Ask students to identify Washington's position on American foreign relations with European nations.
- Introduce the life of Woodrow Wilson to the students, explaining that he was raised with high moral and religious expectations that influenced his worldview.
- Have students examine Wilson's address in support of a World League for Peace, his second inaugural address, his war message to Congress, and his "fourteen points" speech.
- Have students summarize the main points of Wilson's speeches with regard to America's role in global affairs.
- Have students read the speech of Senator Henry Cabot Lodge opposing the League of Nations. Ask students to consider how Lodge's remarks reflect the ideas of Washington's farewell address.
- Ask students to research the meaning of the term *isolationism* within the context of American foreign policy and how the rejection of American participation in the League of Nations led to Warren G. Harding's 1920 presidential election campaign slogan "Return to Normalcy."
- Have students reflect on the lack of American participation in the League of Nations and consider whether it played a role in the rise of totalitarianism in the 1920s and 1930s, leading to World War II.

Standard 3: How the United States changed from the end of World War I to the eve of the Great Depression

Focus Question: How were women's rights extended in the years after World War I? What were some of the social changes as a result of that extension?

- Have students read Susan B. Anthony's essays "The Status of Woman, Past, Present, and Future" and "Is It a Crime for a Citizen of the United States to Vote?" Ask students to list her complaints.
- Have students read Victoria Woodhull's speech on the principles of social freedom and her lecture on constitutional equality. Ask students to list the similarities of Woodhull's concerns to those of Anthony.
- Provide students with a copy of the Nineteenth Amendment and ask them to consider how Anthony and Woodhull's arguments might have contributed to the eventual passage of this amendment.
- Present a brief lecture on the life of Margaret Sanger. Give students copies of Sanger's documents "Sexual Impulse— Part II," "The Prevention of Conception," and "Birth Control and Racial Betterment." Ask students to summarize Sanger's position on the value of birth control.
- Have students write an essay that argues that there is a correlation between the passage of the Nineteenth Amendment and the evolution of Sanger's ideas of birth control.
- Ask students to write essays in the voice of Anthony, Woodhull, or Sanger, summarizing what they might have to say about the current debate on abortion in the United States.

Era 8: The Great Depression and World War II (1929–1945)

Standard 1: The causes of the Great Depression and how it affected American society

Focus Question: What circumstances brought about the Great Depression, and how did it permanently change the character of American life?

- Lead students in researching and discussing the causes of the economic crisis that brought about the Great Depression. Begin by explaining the nature, purpose, and functioning of the stock market, including the use of the Dow Jones Industrial Average as an index of market growth. Encourage the class to consider ways in which the crisis might have been averted or at least minimized.
- Introduce students to Huey Long through his "Every Man a King," "Share Our Wealth," and "Our Growing Calamity" speeches and through his fictional alter-ego Willie Stark in Robert Penn Warren's *All the King's Men*. Have the class discuss reasons behind Long's appeal, and ask them to consider how they might have responded to his message if they had lived during the dark days of the 1930s.
- Make use of materials from a variety of media to present a vivid image of the 1930s for students. Such materials might include John Steinbeck's *The Grapes of Wrath* and the 1940 film adaptation, the Dust Bowl photographs of Dorothea Lange, and any number of radio broadcasts or songs such as "Brother, Can You Spare a Dime?" by Jay Gorney and E. Y. Harburg. Then have students write about whether and how exposure to these works helped them gain a better understanding of the era.

Standard 2: How the New Deal addressed the Great Depression, transformed American federalism, and initiated the welfare state.

Focus Question: How were New Deal policies shaped by Franklin Roosevelt and his advisers?

- Have students read Franklin D. Roosevelt's first inaugural address and list the hopes voiced by President Roosevelt about how to get the United States back on its feet economically.
- Divide students into two groups. Ask group 1 to research the successes of the New Deal between 1932 and 1936 and group 2 to research the failures of the New Deal in those years. Both groups should focus on "alphabet soup" agencies and how these programs related to relief, recovery, and reform.
- Have students present their findings to the class and compare student research with the aspirations of President Roosevelt, as noted in his speeches.
- Provide students with a copy of Frances Perkins's radio address on "social insurance." Have students research the implications of Social Security on American life.
- Divide students into two groups and hold a debate about whether the long-term implications of the New Deal have been positive or negative for American life.

Era 9: Postwar United States (1945 to the early 1970s)

Standard 1: The economic boom and social transformation of the postwar United States

Focus Question: To what extent did race relations change after World War II?

- Discuss with students the 1896 case of *Plessy v. Ferguson* and how that decision legitimized segregation.
- Distribute copies of President Harry Truman's inaugural address and his address before the National Association for the Advancement of Colored People. Have students identify the purposes, goals, and methods to reach the goals proposed by Truman. How did these statements and actions serve as a corrective against the abuses associated with the Jim Crow culture of segregation in America?
- Distribute copies of Strom Thurmond's Southern Manifesto and ask students to list how Thurmond's position on race compares with that of Truman and how Thurmond's ideas reinforce a Jim Crow mentality.
- Provide students with Earl Warren's opinion in the case of *Brown v. Board of Education of Topeka*. Ask students to consider how this case undermined the Jim Crow culture.
- Discuss the benefits generated by this landmark case.

Standard 2: How the cold war and conflicts in Korea and Vietnam influenced domestic and international politics

Focus Question: To what extent was the Vietnam War a reflection of the policy of containment?

- Give students a brief lecture on the Truman Doctrine.
- Distribute copies of George C. Marshall's Marshall Plan speech and George Kennan's article "The Sources of Soviet Conduct" and his "Long Telegram." Have students work in pairs to determine the main tenants of these documents with respect to the policy of containment of Communism.
- Have students research President Dwight Eisenhower's "domino theory" and report their findings to the class the next day.
- Distribute copies of Lyndon Johnson's remarks on the Tonkin Gulf incident. Ask students to research the background of the Gulf of Tonkin Resolution.
- The following day, have students debate the merits of the Gulf of Tonkin Resolution and whether it was an appropriate response to Communist aggression in Southeast Asia.
- Have students write newspaper editorials either in favor of or against the Gulf of Tonkin Resolution as a means for blunting the spread of Communism.

Standard 3: Domestic policies after World War II

Focus Question: To what extent did Senator Joseph McCarthy's behavior heighten domestic cold war tensions with his senatorial committee investigating Communist infiltration of the U.S. government?

- Instruct students to investigate the actions, beliefs, accomplishments, failures, criticisms, or supporters of Senator Joseph McCarthy.
- Share research findings and discuss the career of Senator McCarthy.
- Distribute copies of Senator McCarthy's "enemies from within" speech delivered at Wheeling, West Virginia. Have students read the speech and list McCarthy's main points.
- Discuss with students the definition of the word *paranoia*.
- Share with students the fact that McCarthy never produced or was asked for the list of names that he claimed to have had.
- Show students relevant clips from the original science fiction film *Invasion of the Body Snatchers* and discuss with students the subtext of this film.
- Ask students to write an essay discussing whether the red scare of the 1950s was based on fact or fiction.

Standard 4: The struggle for racial and gender equality and the extension of civil liberties

Focus Question: How did Martin Luther King, Jr.'s philosophy of nonviolent direct action as well as his belief in Christian principle influence the civil rights movement?

- Provide students with one of the following documents from Martin Luther King, Jr.: his "I have a dream" speech," the "Letter from a Birmingham Jail," and

his speech opposing the Vietnam War. Have students identify the main themes of these documents within the context of nonviolent direct action and Christianity and consider the connection he makes between his work for civil rights and his opposition to the war.
- Provide students with copies of Lyndon Johnson's University of Michigan commencement speech and his address to Congress on civil rights. Have students list the ways in which Johnson's speeches reflect King's influence on his policy decisions.
- Distribute Robert Kennedy's Indianapolis remarks on the death of King. Ask students to identify the ways in which Kennedy was influenced by the life of King.
- Have students write an essay or debate the role that religion plays in generating change in a secular nation. Students may consider the role religion played in the abolition movement, the woman's rights movement, or the temperance movement.

Era 10: Contemporary United States (1968 to the present)

Standard 1: Recent developments in foreign and domestic politics

Focus Question: How effective was President George W. Bush's decision to invade Iraq in waging a war on terrorism?

- Direct students to gather information on the terrorist attacks of September 11, 2001, on the United States.
- Distribute copies of Bush's address to the nation concerning military operations in Iraq and his second inaugural address and ask students to identify the arguments made by President Bush for attacking Iraq as part of a global war on terrorism.
- Distribute copies of Colin Powell's remarks to the UN Security Council. Have students determine the connection between Powell's remarks and those of President Bush.
- Discuss whether the speeches and remarks are effective in communicating the reality of the perceived threats to U.S. security.
- Have students debate the merits of the war in Iraq as part of the global war on terror.

Standard 2: Economic, social, and cultural developments in the contemporary United States

Focus Question: How did Americans' attitudes toward their government and their fellow citizens change in the late twentieth and early twenty-first centuries?

- Have students research the facts behind Watergate. Supply them with Warren Burger's majority opinion in *United States v. Nixon*, Barbara Jordan's remarks on the constitutional basis for impeachment, and Nixon's own resignation speech. Have students stage a dramatic portrayal of events, with various members of the class taking the roles of key players— not only Richard Nixon and his associates but also opponents in politics and the media.
- Provide students with Ronald Reagan's 1976 convention speech and first inaugural address, Al Gore's "From Red Tape to Results," and Bill Clinton's remarks on signing the 1996 Personal Responsibility and Work Opportunity Reconciliation Act. Lead the class in a discussion regarding the ability of the federal government to solve the problems facing Americans.
- Discuss with students the emerging role of minority and female figures in American public life, using as resources the following documents: Shirley Chisholm's speech in favor of the Equal Rights Amendment, Susan Gushee O'Malley's interview "Ella Baker: Organizing for Civil Rights," César Chávez's "wrath of grapes" speech, Jesse Jackson's 1988 speech on the civil rights struggle, Barbara Jordan's 1992 address to the Democratic National Convention, and Condoleezza Rice's 2000 address to the Republican National Convention.
- Poll students concerning their opinions on abortion rights. Then divide the class into pro-life and pro-choice groups. Ask students to argue for the opposing side: Those who are pro-life will debate from a pro-choice position and vice versa. Use the following documents as reference points for the debate: Harry Blackmun's majority opinion in *Roe v. Wade and his dissent in Beal v. Doe* and Sandra Day O'Connor's concurrence in *Webster v. Reproductive Health Services*.
- Lead the class in a discussion regarding the role of religion in modern public life, using the following documents as resources: Ronald Reagan's "evil empire" speech, Bill Clinton's remarks at the 1998 prayer breakfast, and Billy Graham's "When Life Turns against Us" and "A Final Word from Billy Graham."

Milestone Documents of American Leaders

Exploring the Primary
Sources of Notable
American Leaders

Mrs. Abigail Smith Adams – 1766 Portrait by Benjamin Blythe

Abigail Adams: Original Analysis

Wife of the Second President of the United States

1744–1818

Overview

Abigail Adams, the wife of the second president of the United States, was never a leader of any kind during her lifetime, except in the circle of her devoted family. But a generation after her death, Americans began to see her as a paragon of domestic patriotism during the Revolution. By the late nineteenth century she was widely regarded as one of America's finest letter writers. In the late twentieth century she took on a new role as a feminist heroine, and her current reputation—as a fully engaged patriotic wife and mother, as an accomplished literary correspondent, and as a powerful voice for all women in the pre-modern era—stands higher than ever.

Nearly every brushstroke in this striking portrait would have astonished Abigail Adams, although perhaps not her admiring husband, John. Born Abigail Smith in Weymouth, Massachusetts, in November 1744, to the town's leading pastor, the Reverend William Smith, and the well-born Elizabeth Quincy, she was raised in a modest but comfortable home. Although her parents were not wealthy, her father's profession and her mother's prominent family placed her squarely in the small upper-middle class of eastern Massachusetts's largely rural, agrarian society. Like nearly all eighteenth-century colonial women, Abigail was not schooled outside her home, but as the daughter of a learned minister with a large personal library, she was not only fully literate but relatively well read by her teens in literature and history, and she continued her reading in her lawyer husband's large library for more than two decades after her marriage.

Raised to be a dutiful wife and devoted mother, Abigail took on both roles without complaint or regret during her twenties and remained her husband's strongest supporter and closest confidant through every victory and defeat in his long career, until her death. Yet quietly, in her private letters to John, to her sisters, and to a few close friends, she gradually became an effective critic of eighteenth-century American society and particularly of the role that married women were forced to play in that traditional world. It was this critique, fused with a strong pride in New England's social virtues, that brought her letters to the attention of nineteenth-century American readers, both men and women, and commanded an even higher regard from twentieth-century women as they sought to recover an American past from which they could take both pleasure and instruction.

The course of Adams's life was fairly straightforward. A few facts are of the first importance in understanding her letters. In October 1764, just before her twentieth birthday, she married John Adams, an aspiring young Harvard-educated lawyer nine years her senior, and moved about five miles to neighboring Braintree, Massachusetts, the hometown of both her husband and her mother. She and John had four children who reached adulthood: Abigail (1765), John Quincy (1767), Charles (1770), and Thomas Boylston (1772). Adams lived mostly in Braintree, with shorter stays in Boston, until her voyage to Europe in 1784 to join her diplomat husband in France and then in England; and after their return in 1788, she resided seasonally in New York and Philadelphia and briefly in Washington, again to accompany John during his vice presidency and presidency, before their long retirement in Quincy (formerly Braintree), Massachusetts. She died there in October 1818, shortly before her seventy-fourth birthday, survived by her husband and her sons John Quincy (later the sixth president of the United States) and Thomas Boylston.

Explanation and Analysis of Documents

As a thoroughly domestic person throughout her life, Abigail Adams wrote no formal documents of any kind, but her private correspondence with every member of her family and with several prominent contemporaries, including Thomas Jefferson, was voluminous. Her sharp wit and discerning political and social observations, her paraphrases and quotations from her extensive reading in history and literature, and her deeply felt beliefs as a wife, a mother, and a woman appear in hundreds of passages throughout these letters. At their center is her correspondence with John Adams, beginning during their courtship in the early 1760s, when she was in her teens, and extending through more than a thousand exchanged letters before John's retirement in 1801.

Although the contents of Adams's letters to John, her children, other relatives, and friends, were wide ranging—from farm management and Braintree gossip to international news—she always regarded her entire correspondence as strictly private. Adams wrote for her own comfort and to both comfort and inform her husband, family, and other intimate acquaintances, and never for the public world. Adams always feared that any miscarriage or misplacement of her letters might place her and her family uncomfortably in the public gaze. As early as September 1774 she

instructed John to burn her letters lest they should fall into others' hands. Some twenty years later, after harshly criticizing Alexander Hamilton in a letter to her husband, she reiterated her plea to burn the letter. John Adams, however, had his own ideas about Abigail's correspondence. To the great benefit of his countrymen and countrywomen of later generations, John Adams apparently never destroyed a single letter from his wife.

Virtually all of Adams's letters remained closed to the public, who scarcely guessed at their existence, until 1840, when her admiring grandson, Charles Francis Adams, published a selection from her family correspondence. In 1848 he followed this with dozens of his grandfather John's letters to Abigail, a massive edition of John Adams's published works and more public letters in the 1850s, and finally a Revolutionary centennial edition of Abigail's and John's correspondence in 1876. Since the 1960s the editors of the Adams Papers project at the Massachusetts Historical Society have published annotated texts of virtually all of Abigail's letters up to 1789 and several of her best letters, without notes, from the 1790s. The five letters chosen for inclusion here, to four different correspondents, show her reacting to a range of historical and domestic challenges facing her and her immediate family.

♦ Letter to John Adams (1774)

Following her lively courtship correspondence in the 1760s, Abigail Adams wrote few letters to her husband until his first travel outside New England in 1774 forced her to develop her patience and skill as a long-distance correspondent. John Adams was elected a Massachusetts delegate to the First Continental Congress in June 1774 and departed for Philadelphia with his cousin, Samuel Adams, and two other delegates on August 10. In her letter to John of August 19, Abigail artfully blends her longing for him with her own musings on the sacrifices demanded of all lovers of liberty.

Her immediate concern was for her ability to endure her husband's long absence, but she was not entirely unfamiliar with this challenge. From the first year of their marriage, John Adams, like other ambitious lawyers, had traveled to the several county seats of eastern and central Massachusetts to attend court days and represent any clients there who wished to employ his services. His journeys to far-off Maine, then a part of Massachusetts, were the most tedious for both Adamses, but John apparently did not write to Abigail until his last northern journey early in the summer of 1774, and Abigail, not knowing just where he would be and when, did not reply.

In August 1774, however, Abigail knew that John would be in Philadelphia for weeks, and she began sending letters with that mix of wifely anxiety, domestic concern, and often deep loneliness that would fill many of her letters to John for the next eight years. In this letter, however, Abigail also reveals another dimension of her character that would appear throughout her correspondence and for which she would later become famous—her ardent patriotism. Educated to revere the political virtues of the ancient Greeks and Romans, she immediately connects the crises faced by

Time Line

1744	November 22	■ Abigail Smith is born in Weymouth, Massachusetts.
1764	October 25	■ Abigail marries John Adams and moves to Braintree, Massachusetts.
1774		■ John Adams is elected to Congress and travels to Philadelphia; he serves in Congress until 1777, while Abigail stays in Braintree to raise the children and manage the farm and the family's finances.
1774	August 19	■ Adams writes to her husband, who had traveled to Philadelphia as a delegate to the First Continental Congress; she blends her longing for him with musings on the sacrifices demanded of all lovers of liberty.
1776	March 31	■ In a letter to John Adams, the most celebrated in her correspondence, Adams argues forcefully for equal marital rights for women.
1780	January 12	■ Adams writes to her son John Quincy in Europe concerning the opportunities and temptations of foreign travel.
1784		■ Adams and her daughter sail to England and travel to France to join John at his diplomatic post in Paris.
1784	September 5	■ Adams writes to her niece, Lucy Cranch, from Europe, criticizing France and the French.
1796	November 8	■ In a letter to her son Thomas Boylston, Adams speaks of America's partisan political divisions and of her husband's qualifications for the office of president.
1797–1799		■ Adams, quite ill, is a largely absent first lady during the presidency of John Adams but briefly visits Philadelphia as her health allows.

Time Line

1800–1801		■ Adams resides in the newly built White House in Washington, D.C., during the last months of John's presidency, after which John and Abigail retire to Quincy to enjoy the companionship that public life had denied them.
1818	October 28	■ Adams dies in Quincy at age seventy-three.

several Greek city-states challenged by the conqueror Philip of Macedon (father of Alexander the Great) and later faced by Sparta, as they all struggled to preserve their ancient liberties, to America's challenge, under the leadership of the First Continental Congress, to defend its own liberty. She further connects them to what she saw as Britain's last chance, like Rome at the time of Caesar's assassination, to hold on to its liberties by heeding Congress's appeal for reconciliation.

♦ Letter to John Adams (1776)

Abigail's letter to John written on March 31, 1776, sometimes referred to simply by its most famous phrase, "Remember the ladies," is the most celebrated in her entire correspondence. Half its length is devoted to her reaction to news already familiar to John—the Revolutionary conflict in Virginia—and to fresher news that he was just beginning to hear of the evacuation of Boston by the British army on March 17. The most distinctive passages, however, are Abigail's argument that America's struggle for liberty from Britain was incompatible with its retention of racial slavery; her feeling of relief that Britain has finally left Massachusetts in peace; and, above all, her extended passage on the severely restricted rights of women within marriage.

Abigail's ringing defense of women, extending from the sentence, "I long to hear that you have declared an independency," to the letter's end, has sometimes been misunderstood. She was not arguing for equal electoral rights—for the suffrage—for all or, indeed, any women, even though in the passage "we … will not hold ourselves bound by any laws in which we have no voice or representation," she seems to assume that women deserve this right. She is instead tackling the greatest obstacle to independence for women in eighteenth-century America: the powerful legal tradition of denying women control over their own property or even their own persons within marriage.

Abigail's model for a civilized marriage was her own marriage, in which she felt that John was not her "master"—which he was under the law—but her "friend." However, because so many husbands preferred inflicting emotional and even physical abuse to accepting this "more tender and endearing" role, she called for vigorous legal action. The new nation should legislate marital equality. Elsewhere in her correspondence Abigail stated her conviction that a woman's proper place was in the home but that home must be for her a place of honor and security. Nineteenth-century America did see the rise of a suffrage movement; but long before women's suffrage became a reality, women began to achieve in law what Abigail had envisioned: the first foundations of equality in marriage, the control of their own property and respect for their security.

John Adams's humorous but dismissive reply to Abigail's appeal for sensitivity to the rights of women in his letter of April 14, 1776, disappointed Abigail, who complained of it to her good friend and a highly accomplished woman author, Mercy Otis Warren. But John's unresponsiveness did not dampen Abigail's concern for the role of women in American culture and society. In June 1778 she wrote a long letter to John, who was then in Paris, in which she responded to her husband's praise of French ladies by lamenting the limited and circumscribed education of women in America. For Abigail, education was the solution to the low status of American women, both within marriage and in the larger society.

♦ Letter to John Quincy Adams (1780)

Abigail wrote many letters across several decades to all four of her children, but she wrote most often to her eldest son, John Quincy, to whom she seems to have been closest. Perhaps because he was the first to leave home, journeying with his father to Europe in February 1778, and again in November 1779, and stayed away the longest, on several different European assignments, he was often in Abigail's thoughts.

Adams's letter to her son, written on January 12, 1780, is characteristic of several that Abigail wrote to him from 1778 to 1783, when she felt that he, as a raw youth exposed to the temptations of Europe, was in the greatest need of her moral exhortations. But as this letter shows, Abigail's concern for her son's good character was fully equaled by her conviction that he had a rare opportunity to see the wider world and to learn and profit from it. Moreover, he was seeing the world at a most advantageous moment in history, for "these are times in which a genius would wish to live." Young John must ever be mindful of this blessing. He would be challenged in his travels by adversity as few youth ever were, but if he met those challenges he would be greatly rewarded. Appealing again to the lessons of Roman history and the struggles of its great patriot orator Cicero, Abigail declares: "Great necessities call out great virtues."

John Quincy Adams greatly admired his mother, but he did not always appreciate her anxious concern for his moral welfare or her ardent encouragement of his worldly career. In his mid-teens, while living in Holland, Russia, and France, he cut back on writing letters home and drew Abigail's sharp rebuke. As late as his forties, when he was serving as America's first diplomatic minister to Russia, he still had occasion to resent what he saw as Abigail's interference in his career. But mother and son remained close over several decades, and John Quincy Adams would in time become the very model of the moral, upright statesman that Abigail hoped he would be.

♦ Letter to Lucy Cranch (1784)

In the summer of 1784, Abigail, who had never traveled outside eastern Massachusetts, left her two younger sons with relatives and sailed with her daughter Abigail (called Nabby in the family) to England to join her husband and her eldest son, John Quincy. In August the Adamses made the journey to France, described in a letter to her niece Lucy Cranach, so that John could join Benjamin Franklin and Thomas Jefferson in negotiating commercial treaties for America. The family occupied a large, elegant house in Auteuil, then a village four miles west of Paris where several French intellectuals and writers made their homes. They remained there until May 1785, when John Quincy returned to America to prepare for college and Abigail, John, and Nabby moved to London so John could began his service as America's first diplomatic minister to Great Britain.

Abigail's letter of September 5, 1784, to Lucy was one of her earliest from France and is one of her most critical of that nation, castigating both the countryside and Paris, the general population and polite society, and even the horses. Within a few months, she would learn to tolerate Paris, to love the French theater, and to admire at least a few French women of a less eccentric and flamboyant character than Madame Helvétius, the rich, noble widow she had met at Franklin's home and whom she describes in her letter. But this letter is one of Abigail's most colorful and reveals much of her own character. In some twenty years as a correspondent to husband, family, and friends, she had seldom judged another woman in anything but the most positive terms, but when suddenly thrust, for the first time in her rather sheltered life, into the most foreign surroundings, she felt compelled to declare how a proper woman should behave.

It would be easy to dismiss this letter as the cranky complaint of a provincial New England minister's daughter, but in expressing her distaste so vividly Abigail powerfully conveys her idea of what a proper society and a healthy, prosperous nation should look like. In her nine months in Auteuil, Abigail would write some twenty long, detailed letters to her sisters and nieces in Massachusetts, and with each passing month France would appear in a more positive light. But neither the country nor its people ever won Abigail's heart; in her view, England was far superior. In the great bulk of her letters, however, America itself was better yet; if she did not find it perfect—and she never did—she always hoped for its improvement.

♦ Letter to Thomas Boylston Adams (1796)

In September 1796, President George Washington announced in a Philadelphia newspaper (in what came to be called his farewell address) that he did not want to serve a third term. America's first contested presidential election began at once, and in a field of several candidates from several states the most prominent were Vice President John Adams and the former secretary of state Thomas Jefferson. By the date of the following letter the election had already begun, but it would be about seven weeks before the final results—John Adams's election as America's second president and Jefferson's as vice president—were known.

In November 1796, Abigail's eldest son, John Quincy, was at The Hague as America's diplomatic minister to the Netherlands, and her youngest son, Thomas Boylston, was serving as his brother's secretary. Both the date and her correspondent prompted Abigail to devote a long letter, written on November 8 of that year, to one of her favorite subjects, national politics. Abigail makes no attempt to disguise her ardent support for her husband or her fear that America's growing partisan divisions might become even worse if he were defeated. She had not the slightest doubt that John Adams would make a better president than Jefferson or any other candidate. But in this and other letters of this year, she was at a loss to know whether it would be better for John to win the election and suffer four years of sharp partisan attacks to which even Washington, with all of his advantages (which she enumerates), had not been immune or to lose and enjoy a well-earned peaceful retirement in Quincy. This letter shows her struggling with the question, one that was nearly as interesting to her sons in Europe as it was to her.

Impact and Legacy

Abigail Adams achieved a quite different kind of historical significance from that of most American leaders, whether men or women. She was never a political leader or the head of any kind of social or cultural organization, and she never enjoyed, or sought, any social visibility beyond her family and town until the 1790s, when she occasionally shined, between serious bouts of illness, as a gracious hostess in Philadelphia during her husband's vice presidency and presidency. Yet as a wife and then as a mother, she exerted a greater influence on the course of American politics than any other woman born before the nineteenth century and perhaps before the twentieth century as well. This is no mere idle assertion. We cannot know whether John Adams would have triumphed as a congressman and diplomat and finally reached the presidency with some other wife or without a wife, but John himself was deeply grateful for Abigail's sacrifices for his public career and full of admiration for her penetrating political observations during the Revolution. No other presidential wife in any century has equaled both Abigail's influence on her husband throughout his career and the depth of her political perception. Again, we cannot know how John Quincy Adams would have fared as a public servant without his mother's steady advice and exhortations to excel, but her devotion to his success combined with his father's advice and example make the strongest political legacy passed on by any American couple to a son who sought a career in public service.

In the twentieth century, Abigail Adams's literary legacy began to affect directly America's other gender, an audience that was closed to her in her lifetime and for many years thereafter. As more of her letters appeared in print, American women discovered an exemplary traditional New England matron who had looked closely at America's domestic patriarchy and found it wanting. Abigail's proposed remedy

for abusive husbands and dependent wives was radical in her day, but she always saw a woman's primary role as domestic. Still, by asserting that women were morally equal to men, she assured later generations of women, married and single, that equality for women was the natural state of things, even in a society where the nuclear family remained the central pillar of the social order. For a quiet Braintree farmwife who carefully avoided any public role, Abigail Adams's influence on her country, through her husband, her son, and her superb letters, has been remarkable and has yet to run its course.

Key Sources

The bulk of Abigail Adams's letters and of those written to her are in the Adams Family Papers collection at the Massachusetts Historical Society in Boston. The American Antiquarian Society in Worcester, Massachusetts, has a substantial body of letters from Abigail to her sister, Mary Cranch, and a few to other Cranch relatives. The fullest edition of Abigail's letters appears in *Adams Family Correspondence*, edited by Lyman Butterfield and his successors at the Adams Family Papers editorial project at the Massachusetts Historical Society. This edition, still in progress, currently extends to eight volumes, published between 1963 and 2006, and includes virtually all of Abigail's letters through 1789. Two shorter compilations of her letters by editors at the Adams Family Papers project are quite useful: L.H. Butterfield et al., eds., *The Book of Abigail and John: Selected Letters of the Adams Family, 1762–1784* (1975), and Margaret A. Hogan and C. James Taylor, eds., *My Dearest Friend: Letters of Abigail and John Adams* (2007).

Essential Quotes

"Did ever any kingdom or state regain its liberty, when once it was invaded, without bloodshed?"

(Letter to John Adams, 1774)

"The passion for liberty cannot be equally strong in the breasts of those who have been accustomed to deprive their fellow-creatures of theirs."

(Letter to John Adams, 1776)

"I long to hear that you have declared an independency. And, by the way, in the new code of laws which I suppose it will be necessary for you to make, I desire you would remember the ladies and be more generous and favorable to them than your ancestors. Do not put such unlimited power into the hands of the husbands. Remember, all men would be tyrants if they could. If particular care and attention is not paid to the ladies, we are determined to foment a rebellion, and will not hold ourselves bound by any laws in which we have no voice or representation."

(Letter to John Adams, 1776)

Essential Quotes

"These are times in which a genius would wish to live. It is not in the still calm of life, or the repose of a pacific station, that great characters are formed."

(Letter to John Quincy Adams, 1780)

"Great necessities call out great virtues. When a mind is raised and animated by scenes that engage the heart, then those qualities, which would otherwise lie dormant, wake into life and form the character of the hero and the statesman."

(Letter to John Quincy Adams, 1780)

"You inquire of me how I like Paris. Why, they tell me I am no judge, for that I have not yet seen it. One thing, I know, and that is that I have smelt it."

(Letter to Lucy Cranch, 1784)

"I feel anxious for the fate of my country. If the administration should get into hands which would depart from the system under which we have enjoyed so great a share of peace, prosperity, and happiness, we should soon be involved in the wars and calamities which have deluged other nations in blood. We should soon become a divided and a miserable people."

(Letter to Thomas Boylston Adams, 1796)

Further Reading

■ Articles

Gelles, Edith B. "The Abigail Industry." *William and Mary Quarterly*, 3d Series, 45 (1988): 656–683.

Ryerson, Richard Alan. "The Limits of a Vicarious Life: Abigail Adams and Her Daughter." *Proceedings of the Massachusetts Historical Society* 100 (1988): 1–14.

■ Books

Akers, Charles W. *Abigail Adams: An American Woman*. New York: Pearson/Longman, 2006.

Gelles, Edith B. *Portia: The World of Abigail Adams*. Bloomington: Indiana University Press, 1992.

Levin, Phyllis Lee. *Abigail Adams*. New York: St. Martin's Press, 1987.

Nagel, Paul C. *The Adams Women: Abigail and Louisa, Their Sisters and Daughters*. New York: Oxford University Press, 1987.

Withey, Lynne. *Dearest Friend: A Life of Abigail Adams*. New York: Free Press, 1981.

—*Richard Ryerson*

Questions for Further Study

1. Adams's letter of August 19, 1774, to her husband is an excellent example of her ability to communicate thoughtfully while drawing on a variety of concepts that only a highly educated person of her time (let alone the present) would understand. Hence her references to events described nearly two millennia earlier by the Greek historian Polybius in his *Histories*. Research Polybius and his work, particularly with regard to the events Adams mentions in this letter, and discuss how her reading of this ancient classic influenced her thinking as expressed in this or other communications.

2. Discuss the arguments for the rights of women that Adams made in her most famous letter, addressed to her husband and dated March 31, 1776. What do you think were some of the factors that made her capable of holding these beliefs and presenting a reasoned case for them at a time when women had few rights? Compare her argument that women should not be bound by laws that exclude them with the same theme as developed a century later by Susan B. Anthony in her speech "Is It a Crime for a Citizen of the United States to Vote?" Do you agree with Adams's claim that "all men would be tyrants if they could"? Finally, consider her development of an overall philosophical and perhaps literary theme in the letter, which begins and ends with the subject of vassals.

3. Do you think the assessment of France and the French people offered in Adams's letter to Lucy Cranch is too harsh? Show examples to support your position.

4. Another great example of Adams's wide-ranging knowledge is her 1796 letter to her son Thomas, in which she quotes from several poets and poems. Using an online search engine, seek out the works she cites and discuss what they mean as well as what they may have meant to Adams (based on her character as displayed in her writings).

Document Text

LETTER TO JOHN ADAMS

1774

Braintree, 19 August, 1774

The great distance between us makes the time appear very long to me. It seems already a month since you left me. The great anxiety I feel for my country, for you, and for our family, renders the day tedious, and the night unpleasant. The rocks and quicksands appear upon every side. What course you can or will take is all wrapped in the bosom of futurity. Uncertainty and expectation leave the mind great scope. Did ever any kingdom or state regain its liberty, when once it was invaded, without bloodshed? I cannot think of it without horror. Yet we are told, that all the misfortunes of Sparta were occasioned by their too great solicitude for present tranquility, and, from an excessive love of peace, they neglected the means of making it sure and lasting. They ought to have reflected, says Polybius, that, "as there is nothing more desirable or advantageous than peace, when founded in justice and honor. So there is nothing more shameful, and at the same time more pernicious, when attained by bad measures, and purchased at the price of liberty." I have received a most charming letter from our friend Mrs. Warren. She desires me to tell you that her best wishes attend you through your journey, both as a friend and a patriot, —hopes you will have no uncommon difficulties to surmount, or hostile movements to impede you, —but, if the Locrians should interrupt you, she hopes that you will beware, that no future annals may say you chose an ambitious Philip for your leader, who subverted the noble order of the American Amphictyons, and built up a monarchy on the ruins of the happy institution.

I have taken a very great fondness for reading Rollin's Ancient History since you left me. I am determined to go through with it, if possible, in these my days of solitude. I find great pleasure and entertainment from it, and I have persuaded Johnny to read me a page or two every day, and hope he will, from his desire to oblige me, entertain a fondness for it. We have had a charming rain, which lasted twelve hours, and has greatly revived the dying fruits of the earth.

I want much to hear from you. I long impatiently to have you upon the stage of action. The first of September, or the month of September, perhaps, may be of as much importance to Great Britain, as the Ides of March were to Caesar. I wish you every public, as well as private blessing, and that wisdom which is profitable both for instruction and edification, to conduct you in this difficult day. The little flock remember papa, and kindly wish to see him; so does your most affectionate

Abigail Adams

Glossary

Amphictyons:	the Amphictyonic League, a loose collection of city-states in archaic, or pre-classical, Greece
as the Ides of March were to Caesar:	Julius Caesar was murdered on the Ides of March, or March 15, 44 BCE
Johnny:	John Quincy Adams
Locrians:	an ancient tribe said to have entered the region of present-day Greece sometime in the second millennium BCE and who were among the ancestors of the Greeks of the classical era
Mrs. Warren:	a mutual acquaintance who was the wife of General James Warren
Philip V:	Macedonian king (ruled 238–179 BCE), heir to the throne once held by Alexander the Great, who fought to control Sparta and other Greek city-states

Glossary

Polybius:	Greek historian (230–120 BCE), whose *Histories* discuss the Macedonian Wars (215–148 BCE) in the context of Rome's Mediterranean conquests
Rollin's Ancient History:	a book by the French historian Charles Rollin, published in the 1730s
subverted:	overthrew
wrapped in the bosom of futurity:	not for us to know, but to find out in the future

Document Text

Letter to John Adams

1776

Braintree, 31 March 1776

I wish you would ever write me a letter half as long as I write you, and tell me, if you may, where your fleet are gone; what sort of defense Virginia can make against our common enemy; whether it is so situated as to make an able defense. Are not the gentry lords, and the common people vassals? Are they not like the uncivilized natives Britain represents us to be? I hope their riflemen, who have shown themselves very savage and even blood-thirsty, are not a specimen of the generality of the people. I am willing to allow the colony great merit for having produced a Washington; but they have been shamefully duped by a Dunmore.

I have sometimes been ready to think that the passion for liberty cannot be equally strong in the breasts of those who have been accustomed to deprive their fellow creatures of theirs. Of this I am certain, that it is not founded upon that generous and Christian principle of doing to others as we would that others should do unto us.

Do not you want to see Boston? I am fearful of the small-pox, or I should have been in before this time. I got Mr. Crane to go to our house and see what state it was in. I find it has been occupied by one of the doctors of a regiment; very dirty, but no other damage has been done to it. The few things which were left in it are all gone. I look upon it as a new acquisition of property—a property which one month ago I did not value at a single shilling, and would with pleasure have seen it in flames.

The town in general is left in a better state than we expected; more owing to a precipitate fight than any regard to the inhabitants; though some individuals discovered a sense of honor and justice, and have left the rent of the houses in which they were, for the owners, and the furniture unhurt, or, if damaged, sufficient to make it good. Others have committed abominable ravages. The mansion-house of your President is safe, and the furniture unhurt; while the houses and furniture of the Solicitor General have fallen a prey to their own merciless party. Surely the very fiends feel a reverential awe for virtue and patriotism, whilst they detest the parricide and traitor.

I feel very differently at the approach of spring from what I did a month ago. We knew not then whether we could plant or sow with safety, whether when we had tilled we could reap the fruits of our own industry, whether we could rest in our own cottages or whether we should be driven from the seacoast to seek shelter in the wilderness; but now we feel a temporary peace, and the poor fugitives are returning to their deserted habitations.

Though we felicitate ourselves, we sympathize with those who are trembling lest the lot of Boston should be theirs. But they cannot be in similar circumstances unless pusillanimity and cowardice should take possession of them. They have time and warning given them to see the evil and shun it.

I long to hear that you have declared an independency. And, by the way, in the new code of laws which I suppose it will be necessary for you to make, I desire you would remember the ladies and be more generous and favorable to them than your ancestors. Do not put such unlimited power into the hands of the husbands. Remember, all men would be tyrants if they could. If particular care and attention is not paid to the ladies, we are determined to foment a rebellion, and will not hold ourselves bound by any laws in which we have no voice or representation.

That your sex are naturally tyrannical is a truth so thoroughly established as to admit of no dispute; but such of you as wish to be happy willingly give up the harsh title of master for the more tender and endearing one of friend. Why, then, not put it out of the power of the vicious and the lawless to use us with cruelty and indignity with impunity? Men of sense in all ages abhor those customs which treat us only as the vassals of your sex; regard us then as beings placed by Providence under your protection, and in imitation of the Supreme Being make use of that power only for happiness.

Abigail Adams

Glossary

felicitate ourselves:	congratulate ourselves
parricide:	a person who kills his or her father, mother, or another close relative
pusillanimity:	excessive timidity
vassals:	completely dependent subjects

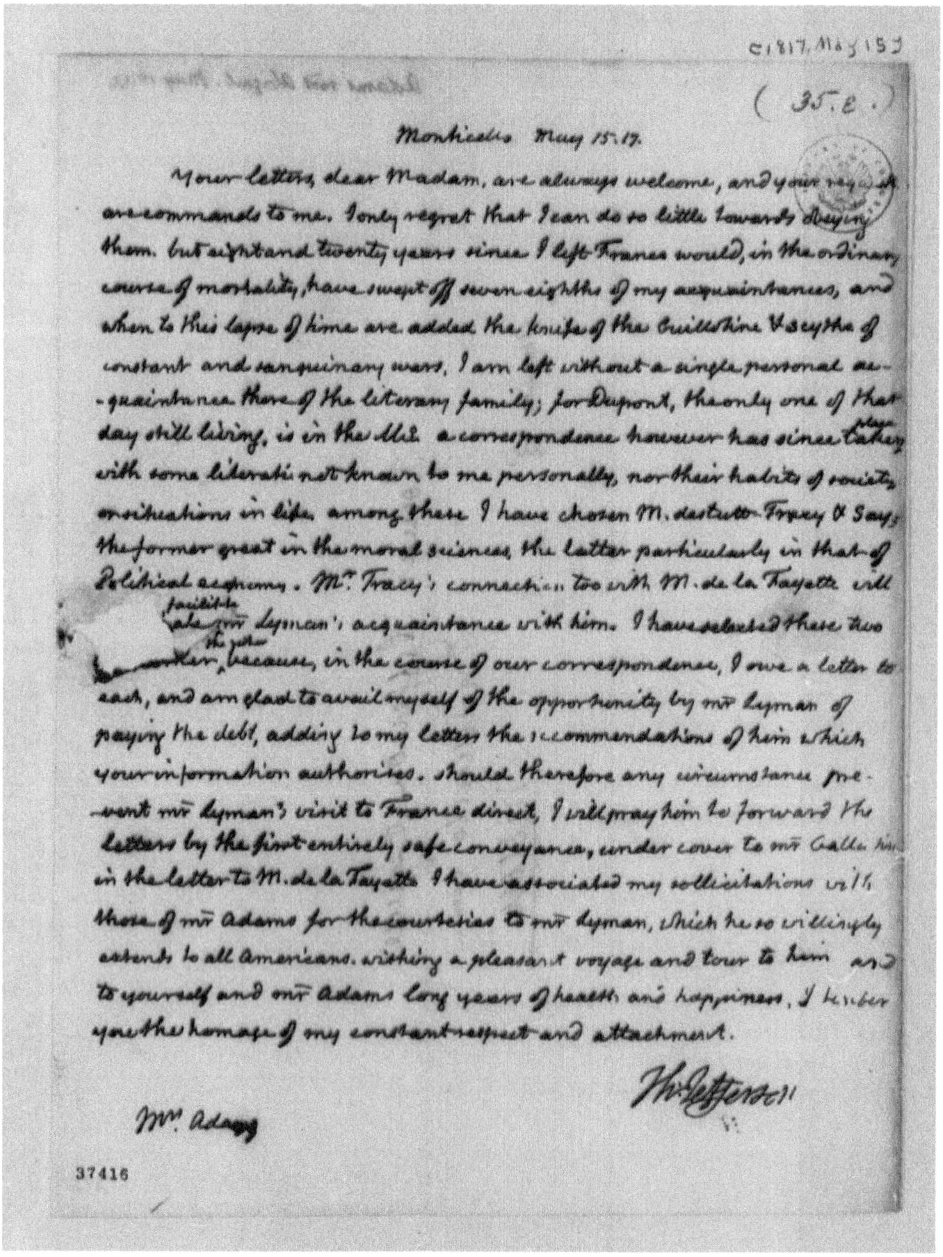

[1817 May 15]

(35. E.)

Monticello May 15. 17.

Your letters, dear Madam, are always welcome, and your requests are commands to me. I only regret that I can do so little towards obeying them. but eight and twenty years since I left France would, in the ordinary course of mortality, have swept off seven eighths of my acquaintances, and when to this lapse of time are added the knife of the Guillotine & scythe of constant and sanguinary wars, I am left without a single personal acquaintance there of the literary family; for Dupont, the only one of that day still living, is in the US. a correspondence however has since taken place with some literati not known to me personally, nor their habits of society or situations in life. among these I have chosen M. Destutt Tracy & Say; the former great in the moral sciences, the latter particularly in that of Political economy. Mr. Tracy's connection too with M. de la Fayette will facilitate mr Lyman's acquaintance with him. I have selected these two the rather, because, in the course of our correspondence, I owe a letter to each, and am glad to avail myself of the opportunity by mr Lyman of paying the debt, adding to my letters the recommendations of him which your information authorises. should therefore any circumstance prevent mr Lyman's visit to France direct, I will pray him to forward the letters by the first entirely safe conveyance, under cover to mr Gallatin. in the letter to M. de la Fayette I have associated my sollicitations with those of mr Adams for the courtesies to mr Lyman, which he so willingly extends to all Americans. wishing a pleasant voyage and tour to him and to yourself and mr Adams long years of health and happiness, I tender you the homage of my constant respect and attachment.

Th: Jefferson

Mrs. Adams

37416

One of last letters sent by Thomas Jefferson at Monticello to Abigail Adams, May 1817

Document Text

Letter to John Quincy Adams

1780

12 January 1780

My dear son,

I hope you have had no occasion, either from enemies or the dangers of the sea, to repent your second voyage to France. If I had thought your reluctance arose from proper deliberation, or that you were capable of judging what was most for your own benefit, I should not have urged you to accompany your father and brother when you appeared so averse to the voyage.

You, however, readily submitted to my advice, and I hope, will never have occasion yourself, nor give me reason, to lament it. Your knowledge of the language must give you greater advantages now than you could possibly have reaped whilst ignorant of it; and as you increase in years, you will find your understanding opening and daily improving.

Some author, that I have met with, compares a judicious traveler to a river, that increases its stream the further it flows from its source; or to certain springs, which, running through rich veins of minerals, improve their qualities as they pass along. It will be expected of you, my son, that, as you are favored with superior advantages under the instructive eye of a tender parent, your improvement should bear some proportion to your advantages. Nothing is wanting with you but attention, diligence, and steady application. Nature has not been deficient.

These are times in which a genius would wish to live. It is not in the still calm of life, or the repose of a pacific station, that great characters are formed. Would Cicero have shone so distinguished an orator if he had not been roused, kindled, and inflamed by the tyranny of Catiline, Verres, and Mark Anthony? The habits of a vigorous mind are formed in contending with difficulties. All history will convince you of this, and that wisdom and penetration are the fruit of experience, not the lessons of retirement and leisure. Great necessities call out great virtues. When a mind is raised and animated by scenes that engage the heart, then those qualities, which would otherwise lie dormant, wake into life and form the character of the hero and the statesman. War, tyranny, and desolation are the scourges of the Almighty, and ought no doubt to be deprecated. Yet it is your lot, my son, to be an eyewitness of these calamities in your existence of their invaded liberties, and who, aided by a generous and powerful ally, with the blessing of Heaven, will transmit this inheritance to ages yet unborn. Nor ought it to be one of the least of your incitements towards exerting every power and faculty of your mind, that you have a parent who has taken so large and active a share in this contest, and discharged the trust reposed in him with so much satisfaction as to be honored with the important embassy which at present calls him abroad.

I cannot fulfill the whole of my duty towards you, if I close this Letter, without reminding you of a failing which calls for a strict attention and watchfull care to correct. You must do it for yourself. You must curb that impetuosity of temper, for which I have frequently chid you, but which properly directed may be productive of great good. I know you capable of these exertions, with pleasure I observed my advice was not lost upon you. If you indulge yourself in the practise of any foible or vice in youth, it will gain strength with your years and become your conqueror.

The strict and inviolable regard you have ever paid to truth, gives me pleasing hopes that you will not swerve from her dictates, but add justice, fortitude, and every manly virtue which can adorn a good citizen, do honor to your country, and render your parents supremely happy, particularly your ever affectionate mother.

A. A.

Glossary

Catiline, Verres, and Mark Anthony:	Both Catiline and Mark Anthony attempted to overthrow the Roman Republic, and Verres was a corrupt Roman governor of Sicily.
chid:	rebuked
Cicero:	Roman statesman (106–43 BCE)
deprecated:	held in high disapproval
pacific:	peaceful

Letter to Lucy Cranch

1784

Auteuil, 5 September, 1784

My dear Lucy,

I promised to write to you from the Hague, but your uncle's unexpected arrival at London prevented me. Your uncle purchased an excellent travelling coach in London, and hired a post-chaise for our servants. In this manner we travelled from London to Dover, accommodated through England with the best of horses, positions, and good carriages; clean, neat apartments, genteel entertainment, and prompt attendance. But no sooner do you cross from Dover to Calais, than every thing is reversed, and yet the distance is very small between them.

The cultivation is by no means equal to that of England; the villages look poor and mean, the houses all thatched, and rarely a glass window in them; their horses, instead of being handsomely harnessed, as those in England are, have the appearance of so many old cart-horses. Along you go, with seven horses tied up with ropes and chains, rattling like trucks; two ragged postilions, mounted, with enormous jackboots, add to the comic scene. And this is the style in which a duke or count travels through this kingdom. You inquire of me how I like Paris. Why, they tell me I am no judge, for that I have not seen it yet. One thing, I know, and that is that I have smelt it. If I was agreeably disappointed in London, I am as much disappointed in Paris. It is the very dirtiest place I ever saw. There are some buildings and some squares, which are tolerable; but in general the streets are narrow, the shops, the houses, inelegant and dirty, the streets full of lumber and stone, with which they build. Boston cannot boast so elegant public buildings; but, in every other respect, it is as much superior in my eyes to Paris, as London is to Boston. To have had Paris tolerable to me, I should not have gone to London. As to the people here, they are more given to hospitality than in England, it is said. I have been in company with but one French lady since I arrived; for strangers here make the first visit, and nobody will know you until you have waited upon them in form.

This lady [Madame Helvétius] I dined with at Dr. Franklin's. She entered the room with a careless, jaunty air; upon seeing ladies who were strangers to her, she bawled out, "Ah! mon Dieu, where is Franklin? Why did you not tell me there were ladies here?" You must suppose her speaking all this in French. "How I look!" said she, taking hold of a chemise made of tiffany, which she had on over a blue lutestring, and which looked as much upon the decay as her beauty, for she was once a handsome woman; her hair was frizzled; over it she had a small straw hat, with a dirty gauze half-handkerchief round it, and a bit of dirtier gauze, than ever my maids wore, was bowed on behind. She had a black gauze scarf thrown over her shoulders. She ran out of the room; when she returned, the Doctor entered at one door, she at the other; upon which she ran forward to him, caught him by the hand, "Helas! Franklin" then gave him a double kiss, one upon each cheek, and another upon his forehead. When we went into the room to dine, she was placed between the Doctor and Mr. Adams. She carried on the chief of the conversation at dinner, frequently locking her hand into the Doctor's and sometimes spreading her arms upon the backs of both the gentleman's chairs, then throwing her arm carelessly upon the Doctor's neck.

I should have been greatly astonished at this conduct, if the good Doctor had not told me that in this lady I should see a genuine Frenchwoman, wholly free from affectation or stiffness of behavior, and one of the best women in the world. For this I must take the Doctor's word; but I should have set her down for a very bad one, although sixty years of age, and a widow. I own I was highly disgusted, and never wish for an acquaintance with any ladies of this cast. After dinner she threw herself upon a settee, where she showed more than her feet. She had a little lap-dog, who was, next to the Doctor, her favorite. This she kissed, and when he wet the floor she wiped it up with her chemise. This is one of the Doctor's most intimate friends, with whom he dines once every week, and she with him. She is rich, and

Document Text

is my near neighbour; but I have not yet visited her. Thus you see, my dear, that manners differ exceedingly in different countries. I hope, however, to find amongst the French ladies manners more consistent with my ideas of decency, or I shall be a mere recluse.

You must write to me, and let me know all about you; marriages, births, and preferments; every thing you can think of Give my respects to the Germantown [a part of Braintree] family. I shall begin to get letters for them by the next vessel.

Good night. Believe me
Your most affectionate aunt,
A. A.

Glossary

bowed:	tied in a bow
cast:	type
the Doctor:	Benjamin Franklin
Helas:	a cheery exclamation of greeting, like "Hey!"
London to Dover:	a distance of 73 miles (117 kilometers)
lute-string:	a type of silk used for ribbons in female fashions of the time
mean:	shabby
post-chaise:	a small carriage for pleasure rides
postilions:	persons who ride one of the horses pulling a coach and drive the entire team
preferments:	advances in society or government
tiffany:	a gauze-like variety of silk

Letter to Thomas Boylston Adams

Quincy, 8 November, 1796

My dear son,

I have just received your letter sent by the *General Green,* Capt. Sheldon, via Rhode Island, dated August 27th. I believe I have scarcely lost a letter from you or your brother, notwithstanding the many hazards and chances to which they have been liable. Accept my thanks for your last communications.

I rejoice at the return of your health, strength and spirits and most sincerely wish that your connections may be mended by the ordeal you have passed.

I have much upon my mind which I could say to you; prudence forbids my committing it to writing. At this eventful period, I can judge of your solicitude to learn, through a channel upon which you could depend, whatever affects the interests of your country.

In a quotation from the Chronicle you cannot expect truth. Falsehood and malevolence are its strongest features. It is the offspring of faction, and nursed by the sedition, the adopted bantling of party. It has been crying monarchy and aristocracy, and vociferating anathemas against the "Defense," as favouring monarchy; and making quotations of detached sentences as the atheist endeavoured to prove from scripture that "there is no God," by omitting, "the fool hath said in his heart."

One writer asserts, that "Mr. Adams has immortalized himself as an advocate for hereditary government, as much as Mr. Jefferson has distinguished himself, in and out of office, as a true republican. Mr. Adams has sons placed in high offices, and who are, no doubt, understood to be what he calls the well-born, and who, following his own principle, may as he hopes, one time become the neighbors or lords of this country. Mr. Jefferson has daughters only, and had he the wish, has no male successor."

By such false and glaring absurdities do these miserable beings endeavour to deceive and delude the people into a distrust of their most disinterested friends, the real guardians of their liberties and defenders of their privileges.

I feel anxious for the fate of my country. If the administration should get into hands which would depart from the system under which we have enjoyed so great a share of peace, prosperity and happiness, we should soon be involved in the wars and calamities which have deluged other nations in blood. We should soon become a divided and a miserable people. I have been too long a witness to the scenes which have been acted for years past, and know too well what must be endured, to have any other sensations, when I look to an elevated seat, than painful solicitude and anxiety. It is a mark at which envy, pride and malevolence will shoot their envenomed arrows. Joy dwells in these dear silent shades at Quincy; and domestic pleasures, in peace and tranquility. If I should be called to quit you, with what regret shall I part from you.

I feel perhaps too keenly the abuse of party. Washington endured it; but he had the support of the people and their undiminished confidence to the hour of his resignation, and a combination of circumstances which no other man can look for. First, a unanimous choice. Secondly, personally known to more people by having commanded the armies, than any other man. Thirdly, possessed of a large landed estate. Fourthly, refusing all emoluments of office both in his military and civil capacity. Take his character all together, and we shall not look upon his like again; notwithstanding which, he was reviled and abused, his administration perplexed, and his measures impeded. What is the expected lot of a successor? He must be armed as Washington was with integrity, with firmness, with intrepidity. These must be his shield and his wall of brass; and religion too, or he never will be able to stand sure and steadfast. Dr. Priestley, in a dedication of some sermons which he delivered last winter, and which he dedicated to the Vice President of the United States, observes to him, "that religion is of as much use to a statesman as to any individual whatever; for Christian principles will best enable men to devote their time, their lives, their talents, and what is often a greater sacrifice, their characters, to the public good; and in public life, he observes, this will often be in a great measure necessary. Let a man attain to eminence of any kind, and by whatever means, even the most honorable, he will be exposed to envy and jealousy. And of course he must expect to meet with calumny and abuse. What principles can enable a man to consult the real good of his fellow citizens

Document Text

without being diverted from his generous purpose by a regard to their opinion concerning him, like those of the Christian who can be satisfied with the approbation of his own mind, and who, though not insensible to due praise, can despise calumny, and steadily overlooking every thing which is intermediate, patiently wait for the day of final retribution?"

Thus says the Poet;

"Fame for good deeds is the reward of virtue;
Thirst after fame is given us by the gods
Both to excite our minds to noble acts,
And give a proof of some immortal state,
Where we shall know that Fame we leave behind,
That highest blessing which the gods bestow."

As I consider it one of my chief blessings to have sons worthy of the confidence of their country, so I hope, in imitation of their father, they will serve it with honor and fidelity, and with consciences void of offence; and though they may sometimes meet with ingratitude, they will have

"The soul's calm sunshine and the heart-felt joy."

Adieu, my dear son, I hope to see you in the course of another year. Time, which improves youth, every year furrows the brow of age.

"Our years
As life declines, speed rapidly away;
And not a year but pilfers, as he goes,
Some youthful grace that age would gladly keep,
A tooth or auburn lock."

Thus, my son, in the course of three years absence, you will find many depredations of time upon those whom you left advanced in life, and in none more, perhaps, than in your mother, whose frequent indispositions hasten its strides and impair a frail fabric. But neither time, absence nor sickness have lessened the warmth of her affection for her dear children, which will burn with undiminished fervor until the lamp of life is extinguished together with the name of

Abigail Adams.

Glossary

anathemas:	denunciations
bantling:	a young child
be called to quit you:	die
calumny:	hostilities
Chronicle:	a London newspaper that ran from 1757 to 1823
Dr. Priestley:	a prominent minister and family friend
emoluments:	benefits
landed estate:	inherited lands
making quotations of detached sentences:	quoting things out of context
Poet:	Shakespeare
seignours:	a term, used here in a derogatory fashion, for midlevel nobility under the feudal system of medieval times
a true republican:	a genuine supporter of government by the people under the authority of the law, rather than a hereditary monarchy
to prove from scripture that "there is no God":	a reference to Psalm 14:1
vociferating:	speaking loudly

Official Presidential portrait of John Adams by John Trumbull

John Adams: Original Analysis

Second President of the United States

1735–1826

Overview

A successful Boston lawyer, leading member of both Continental Congresses, and prominent diplomat, John Adams concluded his public service as the first vice president and then second president of the United States. His career in national public office, extending from 1774 to 1801, was the longest of any prominent early leader of the American Revolution. Yet Adams had a second, parallel political career that was just as important as his first and of even longer duration. From 1763 until 1814 he wrote newspaper essays, pamphlets, and a multivolume historical study, all devoted to political, constitutional, and diplomatic questions, in addition to an elaborate framework for his state's government. The quantity of Adams's published work far exceeds that of any other Revolutionary leader, and at the height of his intellectual powers in the 1770s his conceptual originality made him the leading penman of the Revolution.

John Adams was born in October 1735 in Braintree, Massachusetts, the eldest son of an established farmer and local officeholder. He attended Harvard College, graduating in 1755, and three years later began practicing law in Braintree and Boston. In 1764 he married Abigail Smith and within a decade had five children, including his oldest son, John Quincy Adams, later the sixth president of the United States. By 1770 Adams was one of the most successful and certainly the most learned lawyers in Massachusetts.

The principles and conduct of politics fascinated Adams from his early twenties, and he soon began addressing the issues of the day in Boston newspapers. In 1765 he wrote his first essays destined for fame, published as his *Dissertation on the Canon and the Feudal Law*, which celebrated the moral and political superiority of New England over the mother country. In 1766 he began two terms as a Braintree selectman and wrote essays praising the British constitution. Beginning in the spring of 1771, Adams took a break from all political activity and began thinking deeply about liberty and power, about America and Britain. At the beginning of 1773 he agreed to draft the Massachusetts House of Representatives' reply to Governor Thomas Hutchinson's argument that the British parliament must reign supreme over the whole empire. Writing anonymously for the House, Adams responded that the colony owed no allegiance to Parliament but only to the king, a daring argument that no American legislature had ever advanced. At the end of the year, when local Patriots ignited the series of events that led quickly to rebellion against Britain by throwing taxed East India Company tea into Boston Harbor, Adams praised the Boston Tea Party and declared his confidence that it would open a new era for America.

In June 1774, upon learning that he had been elected by the Massachusetts House to the First Continental Congress, Adams had one last moment of doubt, not in the justice of America's cause but in the ability of some two million unsophisticated colonials to face down the world's most powerful empire. But after he reached Philadelphia, Adams never looked back. His personal diary is the only surviving source for what many delegates actually said in support of the momentous resolves reported so dryly in Congress's journals. When Adams returned to Massachusetts at the end of the year and saw Congress roundly attacked in the Boston press by anonymous Loyalist writers, he leapt to the defense. His "Letters of Novanglus," published in 1775, was the longest and most learned argument for colonial autonomy mounted anywhere in America.

When the Second Continental Congress convened in May 1775, Adams moved quickly into the top leadership. In the meetings to advise the several colonies on restructuring their governments, Adams was quickly recognized as a constitutional authority and asked by one congressman and then another to write a letter that each delegate could send to friends and supporters back home. By the spring of 1776, tiring of this duplication, Adams wrote his shortest and most effective pamphlet, *Thoughts on Government*. In the fall of 1777 Adams resigned from Congress to resume his law practice. Shortly after his return to Braintree, however, Congress appointed him to join Benjamin Franklin and Arthur Lee on America's three-man diplomatic commission in Paris. Adams brought much-needed order to the commission's daily business, but he could not persuade the French government to increase its naval activity in American waters. In early 1779 word reached Paris that Congress had appointed Franklin to succeed the commission. Adams, cut adrift with no new assignment, returned to Massachusetts, deeply discouraged.

As Adams again sought to resume his law practice, Braintree elected him to the state's constitutional convention, and by September he was drafting the constitution for that body. Before he even finished this task, Congress appointed him America's sole commissioner to negotiate peace with Britain. In November, Adams departed again for Europe. In two years of energetic lobbying in the Netherlands, Adams

won recognition of America, then a loan, and finally a treaty of amity and commerce (October 1782). He followed up his triumph by returning to Paris to join Benjamin Franklin and John Jay in negotiating a highly advantageous preliminary peace with Britain (November 1782), which became the Peace of Paris in September 1783.

Adams's constitutional thought had appeared in many publications from as early as the 1760s. During his brief return home from Europe in 1779, Adams, elected to his state's constitutional convention, was delegated to draft Massachusetts's new frame of government. In October 1779, he completed the longest, most detailed, and most carefully structured of America's early constitutions—and the most durable. The Massachusetts Constitution of 1780, although repeatedly and substantially amended, has never been superseded; it is the oldest written constitution in the world still in operation. For the next five years Adams's diplomatic obligations took precedence, but in 1786 he began writing *A Defence of the Constitutions of Government of the United States of America* in defense of republican forms of government.

In the spring of 1788, stymied by Britain's refusal to negotiate a commercial treaty, Adams returned home. As the most senior and accomplished Revolutionary leader after Washington who was still young enough for public service, he was well positioned to secure the new office of vice president. Yet Adams's eight years at this post (1789–1797) would become the most tedious chapter in his long public career. He steadfastly supported George Washington by casting more tie-breaking votes in the small Senate chamber than any of his successors, but he found the obligation to preside over that body without taking part in its deliberations highly frustrating.

In September 1796 Washington announced his intention to retire from public office, and America's first contested presidential election began. Adams and his old, now-estranged friend Thomas Jefferson soon emerged as the front-runners. In December, Adams was elected America's second president, with Jefferson, under provisions of the Constitution in effect at that time, taking the vice presidency. At his inauguration in March 1797, Adams delivered an address in which he briefly recounted America's embrace of republican government, expressed his admiration for the Constitution, and pledged to follow the policies of Washington during his term in office. During Washington's second term, national politics had grown increasingly polarized, pitting merchants against planters, New England against Virginia, and the supporters of close relations with traditional Britain against the ardent admirers of revolutionary France, which went to war with Britain in 1793. The first of each pair had coalesced as Federalists, and the second as Republicans (also called Democratic-Republicans) by the mid-1790s, and both Washington and Adams, while sincerely deploring factionalism, supported most Federalist positions. In leaning more toward Great Britain, America had alienated France, and by Adams's inauguration the French government had dismissed Amer-

Time Line

1735	October 30	■ John Adams born in Braintree (later Quincy), Massachusetts.
1755		■ Adams graduates from Harvard College and moves to Worcester to teach and to study law.
1758		■ Adams begins to practice law in Braintree, Massachusetts.
1773		■ Adams writes the Massachusetts legislature's reply to Governor Thomas Hutchinson's assertions of the authority of the British Parliament.
1774	September–October	■ Adams serves in the First Continental Congress.
1775	January–April	■ Adams writes "Letters of Novanglus."
	May	■ Adams begins his service in the Second Continental Congress.
1776	March–April	■ Adams writes *Thoughts on Government.*
	July	■ Adams leads Congress to approve independence.
1778		■ Adams travels to Paris to serve as a diplomat with Benjamin Franklin and Arthur Lee.
1779	September–October	■ Adams returns to America and writes the Massachusetts Constitution; that year he wrote *The Report of a Constitution, or Form of Government, for the Commonwealth of Massachusetts.*
1780		■ Adams travels back to Europe as commissioner to negotiate peace with Britain.
1782	October 8	■ Adams negotiates commercial treaty with the Netherlands.
1783	September 3	■ Adams concludes and signs the Peace of Paris with Great Britain.

Time Line		
1785–1788		■ Adams serves as America's first diplomatic minister to Great Britain.
1787–1788		■ Adams publishes *A Defence of the Constitutions of Government of the United States of America.*
1789–1797		■ Adams serves as America's first vice president.
1797	March 4	■ Adams delivers his inaugural address as second president of the United States.
1800		■ Adams is defeated for reelection.
1826	July 4	■ Adams dies in Quincy, Massachusetts.

ica's diplomatic minister and began seizing American ships trading with Britain.

For the next four years, the crisis with France shaped the chief executive's every move. The Quasi War with France, an undeclared naval war in which France attacked American naval and merchants shipping, extended through most of Adams's presidency. In 1799 Adams saw a new opening for diplomacy in France, and his envoy signed a peace accord with that country in October 1800. For Adams himself, however, peace came too late. In the fall of 1800 he lost his bid for reelection, and in March 1801 he turned the executive chair over to Thomas Jefferson. Some two centuries later most historians have concluded that in skillfully avoiding a full-scale war with France, Adams was in fact one of America's stronger and better chief executives.

In his long retirement, Adams continued to write, defending his public career in letters to the *Boston Patriot* and resuming his long-suspended correspondence with Jefferson. This correspondence is a national treasure, full of perceptive pronouncements on politics, culture, and society. John Adams lived long enough to see his son John Quincy Adams become president in 1825 and to outlive every other signer of the Declaration of Independence except Maryland's Charles Carroll. He died on July 4, 1826, the fiftieth anniversary of Congress's approval of the Declaration, the same day as Jefferson himself.

Explanation and Analysis of Documents

Adams's long public career and longer life naturally generated a large body of written material, especially letters of many kinds and scores of official documents. But these were only part of Adams's rich literary legacy. As the most prolific published author of America's founding generation, he penned his first newspaper essay when he was twenty-seven and his last book when he was seventy-eight, a fifty-one-year span that produced pamphlets in English, French, and Dutch; series of newspaper essays in several American and European cities; and a three-volume study of republican constitutions from ancient Greece to eighteenth-century western Europe. All of Adams's work falls into two broad categories: addresses, letters, and essays arising directly out of his official duties as a congressman, diplomat, and president; and newspaper essays, pamphlets, and his multivolume study, all written in support of the larger political ideas and causes to which he had become committed. The five documents selected to illustrate Adams's career as a public leader and influential thinker are drawn from both classes of his work. They address, directly or indirectly, the central issue of his entire career: the nature of republican government.

♦ "Letters of Novanglus"

Adams's letters signed with the pseudonym Novanglus ("New Englander") arose in part out of his public service; he began this long series of newspaper essays in reply to a Massachusetts author who was critical of the authority and policy of the First Continental Congress, in which Adams had just served. But his Novanglus letters say virtually nothing about Congress. Instead they launch into an examination of the last fifteen troubled years in Massachusetts and move on to a broad assertion of the province's autonomy and of the autonomy of all North American colonies within the British Empire, based on the writings of ancient and modern political writers. They go on to construct a detailed legal history of England and its dominions over the past several hundred years.

In December 1774, Adams began reading essays by "Massachusettensis" (Daniel Leonard) in Boston's *Massachusetts Gazette*. He expected some other penman to oppose this spirited attack on the Patriot movement; when no one stepped forward, Adams placed his first Novanglus letter in the *Boston Gazette* on January 23, 1775. Eleven more learned essays, replete with historical details and citations to colonial and British proclamations, laws, and court decisions running back for centuries, appeared in the same journal, the last on April 17, and Adams had another essay ready for the next issue when the battles of Lexington and Concord on April 19 abruptly ended polite exchanges in the local press. Taken together, the twelve serially published "Letters of Novanglus," running to nearly two hundred pages, comprised Adams's longest composition before his three-volume *Defence of the Constitutions of Government of the United States of America*. The letters appeared anonymously and were first published under his name in a collected edition in 1784.

The first four letters recount in detail the struggles between Massachusetts Whigs (Patriots) and Tories (later, Loyalists) since 1760. In the fifth letter, dated March 6, 1775, Adams characterizes the Patriots' opposition to

tyrannical government as lawful resistance, not rebellion, and examines both the Massachusetts and British constitutions. In the brief excerpt reproduced here, he comments on the word *rebellion*, arguing that the colonists' opposition to "usurpation and lawless violence" is not rebellion; rebellion is resistance to lawful authority. Although Adams wrote the Novanglus letters primarily in response to Massachusettensis, he also wrote in response to an anonymous pamphlet published in 1774 titled *Letter from a Veteran to the Officers of the Army Encamped at Boston*, possibly written by Robert A. Prescott. Like Massachusettensis, the "Veteran" wrote from a Tory—that is, Loyalist—perspective. In the pamphlet the "Veteran" notes that in war even the word *rebel* is a convertible term, suggesting that the word can have opposite connotations, one negative and one positive, depending on whose perspective is taken.

Adams's argument reaches its climax in the seventh letter, dated March 27, 1775. Here he extends the claim of autonomy he makes for Massachusetts to several other American colonies. He begins his argument for American autonomy by first pointing out that the colonies were established before the "British empire" came into being during the reign of Queen Anne by an act of Parliament that united England and Scotland. On this ground Adams argues that any concept that "the colonies are a part of the British empire" is dubious. He goes on to raise a number of questions about the relationship between a colony and a mother country. If a colony is to be regarded as "a part of the state," then its inhabitants should enjoy "equal right, powers, and privileges, as well as equal protection" as the citizens of the mother country. Adams, however, suggests that America has not been made part of the British realm, principally because it does not have representation in Parliament.

Adams then agrees with the principle that "two supreme and independent authorities cannot exist in the same state." To Adams, the logical conclusion of this principle is that the provincial legislature should reign supreme in the colonies. In what could be considered a note of defiance, Adams acknowledges that "Parliament has our consent to assume a jurisdiction" over the seas that separate Britain and the Americas. Finally, Adams argues that the American colonies cannot be part of a "British empire" because no such entity exists. Rather, he points out, Britain is a "limited monarchy," and he declares that "the British constitution is much more like a republic than an empire" because it is "a government of laws, and not of men." A republic, he argues, is a government controlled by laws and providing for the active participation of the whole people. Within those limits, it may be constructed in several different ways, even around an inherited monarchy. Adams's countrymen would never follow him to this last conclusion, but he would defend it again at great length in his *Defence of the Constitutions of Government of the United States of America.*

♦ Thoughts on Government

Thoughts on Government is both a product of Adams's public service and a personal statement of his constitutional beliefs. The genesis of the essay lay in his participation in congressional deliberations over the best advice to give the colonies as they sought to restructure their governments to function effectively in the rebellion against Britain. The specific impetus to publish this pamphlet came from congressional colleagues who sought his constitutional expertise for their home colonies. But the act of issuing his wise counsel in a general publication was voluntary and broadened Adams's audience from small clusters of colonial legislators to the whole American political public.

The core idea of *Thoughts on Government* was first expressed in Adams's letters of advice to congressional colleagues from Virginia, New Jersey, and North Carolina, beginning in November 1775. By the spring of 1776 he had expanded his argument to the point where his text was very close to that of *Thoughts on Government*. At this point publication seemed easier than continued copying for yet more congressmen. The pamphlet first appeared in Philadelphia in April 1776. Adams's good friend Benjamin Rush first identified him as its author in the spring of 1777. *Thoughts on Government* was the first American pamphlet to present a clear plan for organizing new governments on republican principles. Adams's generic model enabled any British colony to preserve its traditional liberties while waging a rebellion against British authority and was well suited for the anticipated state of total independence from the British Empire.

The essay's success rested on three features: its brevity, its simplicity, and its flexibility. By paring away all the historical and philosophical considerations that had filled the pages of his "Letters of Novanglus," Adams produced an effective republican blueprint in just nine pages. Adams's architecture, too, was simple; he listed the minimum ingredients that he thought were essential for republican government: an executive, a two-house legislature, and an independent judiciary. Because he was addressing men who lived in several different colonies with different habits and traditions, he largely ignored the mechanics of nominations and elections, insisting that it was the larger republican idea, the vital principle of resting the government on the whole people and bringing them into the political process, that was crucial to the successful remodeling of authority in America's new political environment.

Adams's recommendations on republican architecture clearly derive from his intimate knowledge of Massachusetts's government, but he presents his advice in such a generalized way that most of the rebelling thirteen colonies could easily attend his lesson. He first states that the end of government is "the happiness of society" and that only a government founded on promoting human virtue can achieve this. All English political philosophers, he continues, agree that "there is no good government but what is republican." Adams then identifies a representative assembly that is "an exact portrait of the people at large" as the core of any republic. A fully competent republic, however, must vest executive power in one person (a governor), establish an independent judiciary, and create a council (an upper

legislative house) to mediate between the people's assembly and the executive. The rest of his pamphlet discusses various mechanisms for choosing the council, the governor, and other officers and concedes that several different electoral devices and roles may be effective. He closes with a deep appreciation of America's bright prospects: "How few of the human race have ever enjoyed an opportunity of making an election [a choice] of government, more than of air, soil, or climate, for themselves and their children."

Thoughts on Government was one of Adams's most important political works. It immediately influenced the writing of new republican constitutions for New Jersey, Virginia, and North Carolina, and later in New Hampshire and New York; by 1777 this brief essay had come to embody the orthodox concept of American republicanism. Over time, Adams's model republic appeared in several more American guises, first in his own Massachusetts Constitution of 1780, then in the U.S. Constitution, and finally in both the revised constitutions of several old states and the first constitutions of many new states that entered the Union over the next two centuries.

♦ The Report of a Constitution, or Form of Government, for the Commonwealth of Massachusetts

The committee report of the Massachusetts Constitution of 1780 (October 1779) is an official working document. It was distributed in print exclusively to the members of the Massachusetts Constitutional Convention for their use in debating proposed changes and giving it their final approval, and it survives only in printed form. The report was nominally the work of the convention's thirty-member drafting committee, which received the rough draft from a three-man subcommittee, but over 90 percent of the text is Adams's work. The only paragraphs that he did not compose appear in Article III of the "Declaration of Rights," which perpetuated Massachusetts's religious establishment, and in chapter VI, section I, which guaranteed the rights of Harvard College. Because no manuscript text of this draft constitution has ever been found, however, there is no direct evidence to either confirm or refute Adams's claim that his committee colleagues changed no more than a few single lines of his prose before it was printed. Adams had the report published in London and Paris in 1780, but it was not made directly available to the American public until Charles Francis Adams included it in his edition of Adams's works in 1851.

In the report, Adams introduced a major innovation in constitutional architecture. In every prior constitution and in all American colonial charters extending back to the seventeenth century, the texts were quite unarticulated by clearly labeled sections and, in some cases, even by paragraphs. Adams, however, cast his document in an entirely new form. He carefully divided his text into sections and chapters, with every sentence part of an enumerated article that occupied a logical place in the entire structure. This textual articulation greatly aided the study of the document by the convention members in 1779–1780 and by ensuing generations of legislators, governors, judges, lawyers, and the general public. And it did something more; by structuring his text so carefully, Adams invited everyone to visualize republican government and perceive how all of its parts related to the whole.

This first example was persuasive. When the framers of the U.S. Constitution in Philadelphia produced their finished draft in September 1787, they employed a quite similar architectural design, thereby giving both constitutional thought and constitutional law an enhanced structure that they have retained to this day. Adams's constitution, revised in convention in 1779–1780, has acquired more than one hundred amendments over some two hundred years, but it remains in effect in Massachusetts. The selections, taken from the general "Preamble," the "Declaration of Rights," and the opening statement of the "Frame of Government," convey the essence of John Adams's political philosophy.

Of all of Adams's major political works, his draft *The Report of a Constitution* is the easiest to summarize because of the care he took to organize and title each of its several parts. Adams begins with a "Preamble" that blends his introductory rhetoric from *Thoughts on Government* with Massachusetts's distinctive Puritan political convictions. Its essence is the statement "The end of the institution … of government is to secure the existence of the body-politic," which Adams defines as "a voluntary association of individuals … a social compact." He then sets out a "Declaration of Rights of the Inhabitants of Massachusetts" in thirty-one articles, several of which he freely borrowed from similar constitutional declarations in Pennsylvania, Virginia, and other states. Nearly four-fifths of the report, however, is taken up with its "Frame of Government." Opening with a celebrated pledge to observe the strict separation of governmental powers, the frame proceeds through five broad chapters devoted to the powers of the bicameral legislature; the powers of the executive (with its distinctive governor's council); the judiciary power; the choosing of delegates to Congress and the formal granting of commissions; and the preservation of Massachusetts's moral and cultural life by protecting Harvard Collage and encouraging local education.

♦ A Defence of the Constitutions of Government of the United States of America

A Defence of the Constitutions of Government of the United States of America, Against the Attack of M. Turgot, in His Letter to Dr. Price, Dated the Twenty-Second Day of March, 1778, which swelled to three long volumes published in 1787–1788, was originally intended as an answer to a recently published letter by the late French *philosophe* and government minister Anne-Robert Turgot. This letter criticized America's state constitutions for their separation of powers, checks and balances, and two-house legislatures—the very features of America's governments of which Adams was most proud. The *Defence* itself, however, devotes few pages to addressing Turgot's critique and even fewer to defending any American state constitution. Instead, Adams

surveys dozens of republican constitutions from ancient Athens to contemporary European nations and reviews political writers from Plato and Polybius to Machiavelli and Montesquieu, all to prove that only balanced governments that incorporate checks and balances could ensure the stability and survival of any republic.

The *Defence* is Adams's longest work and has certain features in common with the "Letters of Novanglus." Like that work, the *Defence* lacks any comprehensive organization and shows unmistakable evidence that Adams did not carefully structure his text in advance but mostly carpentered it together as he went along. It is not at all certain that Adams, when he began to write, intended to produce more than a single volume. It seems more likely that as his vision of his subject grew, so did his ambition. This work also has a more unusual feature. Of all Adams's writings, only the *Defence of the Constitutions of Government of the United States* (that is to say, a defense of America's state constitutions framed since 1776) bears a title that seems to be so disconnected from its contents. At no point in its three volumes does Adams discuss any American state constitution, even that of Massachusetts. Instead, he chooses to defend America's constitutions by asserting—without making explicit comparisons—that they resembled the other republican constitutions he does discuss, past and present, that succeeded, and differed from yet others that failed. In the last paragraph of his final volume, written just after he had read the new federal Constitution, he briefly praises that document as demonstrating the validity of his entire work, but without making a single concrete observation on it.

Yet Adams's *Defence* was a remarkable achievement. It is the most learned study of comparative republican governments by any American in the eighteenth century and the last important work of political science written in the classical republican tradition that had begun with the Italian writer Niccolò Machiavelli nearly three centuries earlier. The two selections, from the "Recapitulation" of his opening chapters in volume 1 and from his general "Conclusion" at the end of volume 3, together give a sense of his commitment to the separation and balance of powers as the key to the durability of republican governments.

The greater part of the *Defence* is devoted to comparative republican history. In over two-thirds of volume 1, all of volume 2, and over half of volume 3, Adams closely examines some four dozen modern, medieval, and ancient republics of widely varying character. He interrupts these investigations only twice, to consider several political writers in volume 1 and one more writer toward the end of volume 3. The most distinctive feature of volume 1 is its classification of twenty-five eighteenth-century governments into three categories, as democratic, aristocratic, or monarchical republics, in its first three chapters. In the "Recapitulation," then, he summarizes the characteristics of successful republican governments, noting that they all have a "first magistrate," a senate, a house of representatives, checks and balances among the branches of government, "orders" of offices but not of men, and flourishing arts and sciences. Then, following three chapters on the political opinions of three "philosophers" (all recent or contemporary writers), four "writers on government" (from Machiavelli to Montesquieu), and six "historians" (from Plato to David Hume), Adams turns to sixteen ancient republics, again arranging them into democratic, aristocratic, and monarchical categories. It was this first volume, with its praise of England's monarchical constitution as the finest of all republics outside America, which so disturbed many of Adams's countrymen upon its appearance in the spring of 1787. Adams's second and third volumes, devoted entirely to medieval Italian republics and to the seventeenth-century English writer Marchemont Nedham, had far less impact in America.

♦ Inaugural Address

When he took the oath of office as America's second president, Adams's particular political liabilities prompted him to give a somewhat longer inaugural address than Washington had done in 1789. In entering a new office in a new government, Washington could defer discussing any and all specific issues that might arise during his presidency until they did arise. By 1797, however, the young republic had a track record of contested issues, declarations, treaties, and laws. Adams had a track record, too, including certain propositions advanced in his *Defence of the Constitutions* that had prompted many Americans to suspect he might not be sufficiently republican for their new government. In his address, Adams was at some pains to set the record straight.

He begins with a brief look back to the Revolutionary War and the Articles of Confederation, which had both taught Americans the need for national unity. He then turns to the Constitution, which he endorses in the strongest terms, praising it as arising from the "usual good sense" of the American people. To confront rumors that he had not been entirely happy with certain parts of the document, he declares that he had thoroughly approved the Constitution upon first reading it in England, and he denies that he had ever objected to it for not making "the Executive and Senate … more permanent" (which was true of his public statements, although not, at least regarding the executive, of his private correspondence). A decade later, Adams could now assert, in this address, that "the operation of [the Constitution] has equaled the most sanguine expectations of its friends." He concludes his general praise by asking "What other form of government can so well deserve our esteem and love?"

Adams then advances a brief summary of the virtues of republican government, repeatedly stressing its intimate relationship with an enlightened people, before turning to the dire perils that even this best of governments could face.

The worst, he declares, would be any corruption "of our free, fair, virtuous, and independent elections," which faced their greatest challenge from the "flattery or menaces" of foreign nations. In the midst of such dangers America had been most fortunate to have had, as its chief executive, Adams's prudent, just, and patriotic predecessor, whom he felt no need to name. After making several promises to treat all citizens impartially and to seek peace with honor with belligerent France, he pledges to follow Washington's example, and he concludes, much as had Washington in 1789, with an appeal to divine providence to bless the nation and his administration.

Impact and Legacy

Adams was a leader of the first rank during the American Revolution and the early national period. Yet both his thought and behavior were as controversial and at times as paradoxical as those of any prominent American of his generation. As a public servant he was seldom popular, and several of his most prominent contemporaries, including Franklin, Alexander Hamilton, Jefferson, and James Madison, severely criticized his performance and even his character at some point in his career. But many other colleagues in public service, as well as Jefferson in the 1770s and 1780s, admired Adams's character and found his political and diplomatic efforts indispensable. In the Continental Congress he was a leader, and a workhorse, without equal, earning him the nickname "the Atlas of Independence." In his long public career, he was second only to Franklin as an accomplished diplomat and second only to Washington as a national leader. It would be hard to write the history of the Revolutionary and early national eras, whether in the 1770s, the 1780s, or 1790s, without taking account of Adams.

As a political writer and thinker, Adams was even more remarkable and more paradoxical. In the 1770s he was America's leading authority on the construction of republican constitutions. When Adams first tackled constitutional issues in Massachusetts in 1773, writers in every British North American colony were largely ignorant of constitutional history beyond their own provincial charters and, with the exception of John Locke's *Second Treatise on Government*, quite unfamiliar with the subtleties of the republican tradition in Western political thought. When he finished drafting the Massachusetts Constitution in 1779, he presented his country with a detailed constitutional blueprint that would expand and endure for over two centuries. Yet in the late 1780s Adams quixotically sought to expand the definition of republics to include monarchical and aristocratic elements that Americans could not admire and that many Europeans were trying to escape. Thereafter, the reasoning that Americans embraced to understand republican constitutions, embodied most effectively in Hamilton's and Madison's Federalist Papers, took a different path, even as the mechanics of the nation's constitutions remained much as Adams had left them.

Thomas Jefferson instructed that his tombstone should record three achievements: the Declaration of Independence, Virginia's Statute for Religious Freedom, and the University of Virginia—but not his presidency. Had Adams cared to design his tombstone he might have done something rather similar, listing his role as Congress's "Atlas of Independence," his authorship of the Massachusetts Constitution, and his proposal that his Massachusetts countrymen establish the American Academy of Arts and Sciences, which they did in 1780. One suspects that he would have been no more eager than Jefferson to remember most of his presidency. But the man who named his Quincy home "Peacefield" might have been tempted to list his concluding peace with Britain in 1783 and with France in 1800 as worthy legacies to America.

Key Sources

Most of the several thousand letters and other documents that John Adams wrote or received have survived in good order. The great bulk of his personal papers and many of his public papers, including his original diary, dozens of letter books recording nearly all of his own letters, and thousands of loose letters to him, form a major part of the massive Adams Papers Collection at the Massachusetts Historical Society in Boston, Massachusetts. Hundreds of other Adams documents are in archives in several American cities and in London, Paris, Amsterdam, and other European capitals. Adams's personal library, numbering nearly three thousand volumes, also survives largely intact in the Rare Book Room of the Boston Public Library. Many of Adams's writings, both public and private, have been carefully edited and published beginning as early as the 1840s. Since the 1960s the ongoing Adams Papers editorial project at the Massachusetts Historical Society has produced some thirty volumes of material by and to John Adams and his family. The major editions are Charles Francis Adams, ed., *The Works of John Adams*, 10 vols. (1850–1856); Lyman H. Butterfield, ed., *Diary and Autobiography of John Adams*, 4 vols. (1961); Lyman H. Butterfield et al., eds., *Adams Family Correspondence*, 8 vols. (1963–); Kinvin Wroth and Hiller Zobel, eds., *The Legal Papers of John Adams*, 3 vols. (1965); and Robert Taylor et al., eds., *The Papers of John Adams*, 14 vols. (1977–). Also useful are two volumes of selections from his family letters edited by members of the Adams Papers staff: Lyman H. Butterfield, ed., *The Book of Abigail and John: Selected Letters of the Adams Family, 1762–1784* (1975), and Margaret Hogan and C. James Taylor, eds., *My Dearest Friend: The Letters of Abigail and John Adams* (2007).

Essential Quotes

"Our provincial legislatures are the only supreme authorities in our colonies.... And here is a line fairly drawn between the rights of Britain and the rights of the colonies, namely, the banks of the [Atlantic] ocean."

("Letters of Novanglus")

"The British constitution is nothing more nor less than a republic, in which the king is first magistrate. This office being hereditary ... is no objection to the government being a republic, as long as it is bound by fixed laws, which the people have a voice in making, and a right to defend."

("Letters of Novanglus")

"The form of government which communicates ease, comfort, security, or, in one word, happiness, to the greatest number of persons, and in the greatest degree, is best."

(*Thoughts on Government*)

"There is no good government but what is republican.... The only valuable part of the British constitution is so; because the very definition of a republic is 'an empire of laws, and not of men.'"

(*Thoughts on Government*)

"The end of the institution ... of government, is to secure the body-politic; to protect it; and to furnish the individuals who compose it, with the power of enjoying, in safety and tranquility, their natural rights, and the blessings of life."

(*The Report of a Constitution, or Form of Government, for the Commonwealth of Massachusetts*)

"In the government of the Commonwealth of Massachusetts, the legislative, executive, and judicial power, shall be placed in separate departments, to the end that it might be a government of laws and not of men."

(*The Report of a Constitution, or Form of Government, for the Commonwealth of Massachusetts*)

Essential Quotes

"The body politic cannot subsist, any more than the animal body, without a head."

(*A Defence of the Constitutions of Government of the United States of America*)

"It is now in our power to bring this work to a conclusion with unexpected dignity.... The deliberate union of so great and various a people in such a plan [the U.S. Constitution] is, without all partiality or prejudice, the greatest single effort of national deliberation that the world has ever seen."

(*A Defence of the Constitutions of Government of the United States of America*)

"What other form of government, indeed, can so well deserve our esteem and love?"

(Inaugural Address)

"With this great example [of Washington] before me, with the sense and spirit ... of the American people, pledged to support the Constitution of the United States, I entertain no doubt of its continuance in all its energy; and my mind is prepared ... to support it to the utmost of my power."

(Inaugural Address)

Milestone Documents

Further Reading

■ Articles

Ferling, John. "Cliffhanger: The Election of 1800." *Smithsonian* 35, no. 8 (2004): 44–55.

■ Books

Ferling, John. *John Adams: A Life*. Knoxville: University of Tennessee Press, 1992.

Haraszti, Zoltán. *John Adams and the Prophets of Progress*. Cambridge, Mass.: Harvard University Press, 1952.

McCullough, David G. *John Adams*. New York: Simon and Schuster, 2001.

Ryerson, Richard Alan, ed. *John Adams and the Founding of the Republic*. Boston: Massachusetts Historical Society, 2001.

Shaw, Peter. *The Character of John Adams*. Chapel Hill: University of North Carolina Press, 1976.

Thompson, C. Bradley. *John Adams and the Spirit of Liberty*. Lawrence: University Press of Kansas, 1998.

—Richard Ryerson

Questions for Further Study

1. On what basis does John Adams claim that the American colonies were autonomous, that is, independent from Great Britain?

2. Throughout his writings Adams argues that a republican form of government is best. What does Adams mean by "republican" in this context? What are the features of a republican government? To what extent were such features incorporated into the U.S. Constitution?

3. In much of his writing, Adams makes extensive reference to historical persons, including philosophers, religious leaders, poets, and political figures. Why did Adams include these learned references? What did these historical allusions add to his arguments?

4. Adams earned the nickname "the Atlas of Independence." Who was Atlas, and why did Adams's colleagues and early Americans refer to Adams in that manner?

5. Compare those portions of Adams's *Report of a Constitution, or Form of Government, for the Commonwealth of Massachusetts* that have a bearing on religion with Thomas Jefferson's Bill for Establishing Religious Freedom. How do the points of view of the two documents differ? Do the two documents express any common beliefs?

6. Based on John Adams's inaugural address and George Mason's "Objections to This Constitution of Government," imagine a conversation between the two men about the Constitution. How might Adams have responded to Mason's objections?

THOUGHTS ON GOVERNMENT

1776

My dear Sir,—If I was equal to the task of forming a plan for the government of a colony, I should be flattered with your request, and very happy to comply with it; because, as the divine science of politics is the science of social happiness, and the blessings of society depend entirely on the constitutions of government, which are generally institutions that last for many generations, there can be no employment more agreeable to a benevolent mind than a research after the best.

Pope flattered tyrants too much when he said,

"For forms of government let fools contest,
That which is best administered is best."

Nothing can be more fallacious than this. But poets read history to collect flowers, not fruits; they attend to fanciful images, not the effects of social institutions. Nothing is more certain, from the history of nations and nature of man, than that some forms of government are better fitted for being well administered than others.

We ought to consider what is the end of government, before we determine which is the best form. Upon this point all speculative politicians will agree, that the happiness of society is the end of government, as all divines and moral philosophers will agree that the happiness of the individual is the end of man. From this principle it will follow, that the form of government which communicates ease, comfort, security, or, in one word, happiness, to the greatest number of persons, and in the greatest degree, is the best.

All sober inquirers after truth, ancient and modern, pagan and Christian, have declared that the happiness of man, as well as his dignity, consists in virtue. Confucius, Zoroaster, Socrates, Mahomet, not to mention authorities really sacred, have agreed in this.

If there is a form of government, then, whose principle and foundation is virtue, will not every sober man acknowledge it better calculated to promote the general happiness than any other form?

Fear is the foundation of most governments; but it is so sordid and brutal a passion, and renders men in whose breasts it predominates so stupid and miserable, that Americans will not be likely to approve of any political institution which is founded on it.

Honor is truly sacred, but holds a lower rank in the scale of moral excellence than virtue. Indeed, the former is but a part of the latter, and consequently has not equal pretensions to support a frame of government productive of human happiness.

The foundation of every government is some principle or passion in the minds of the people. The noblest principles and most generous affections in our nature, then, have the fairest chance to support the noblest and most generous models of government.

A man must be indifferent to the sneers of modern Englishmen, to mention in their company the names of Sidney, Harrington, Locke, Milton, Nedham, Neville, Burnet, and Hoadly. No small fortitude is necessary to confess that one has read them. The wretched condition of this country, however, for ten or fifteen years past, has frequently reminded me of their principles and reasonings. They will convince any candid mind, that there is no good government but what is republican. That the only valuable part of the British Constitution is so; because the very definition of a republic is "an empire of laws, and not of men." That, as a republic is the best of governments, so that particular arrangement of the powers of society, or, in other words, that form of government which is best contrived to secure an impartial and exact execution of the laws, is the best of republics.

Of republics there is an inexhaustible variety, because the possible combinations of the powers of society are capable of innumerable variations.

As good government is an empire of laws, how shall your laws be made? In a large society, inhabiting an extensive country, it is impossible that the whole should assemble to make laws. The first necessary step, then, is to depute power from the many to a few of the most wise and good. But by what rules shall you choose your representatives? Agree upon the number and qualifications of persons who shall have the benefit of choosing, or annex this privilege to the inhabitants of a certain extent of ground.

The principal difficulty lies, and the greatest care should be employed, in constituting this representative assembly. It should be in miniature an exact portrait of the people at large. It should think, feel, reason, and act like them. That it may be the interest of this assembly to do strict justice at all times, it

should be an equal representation, or, in other words, equal interests among the people should have equal interests in it. Great care should be taken to effect this, and to prevent unfair, partial, and corrupt elections. Such regulations, however, may be better made in times of greater tranquillity than the present; and they will spring up themselves naturally, when all the powers of government come to be in the hands of the people's friends. At present, it will be safest to proceed in all established modes, to which the people have been familiarized by habit.

A representation of the people in one assembly being obtained, a question arises, whether all the powers of government, legislative, executive, and judicial, shall be left in this body? I think a people cannot be long free, nor ever happy, whose government is in one assembly. My reasons for this opinion are as follow:—

1. A single assembly is liable to all the vices, follies, and frailties of an individual; subject to fits of humor, starts of passion, flights of enthusiasm, partialities, or prejudice, and consequently productive of hasty results and absurd judgments. And all these errors ought to be corrected and defects supplied by some controlling power.
2. A single assembly is apt to be avaricious, and in time will not scruple to exempt itself from burdens, which it will lay, without compunction, on its constituents.
3. A single assembly is apt to grow ambitious, and after a time will not hesitate to vote itself perpetual. This was one fault of the Long Parliament; but more remarkably of Holland, whose assembly first voted themselves from annual to septennial, then for life, and after a course of years, that all vacancies happening by death or otherwise, should be filled by themselves, without any application to constituents at all.
4. A representative assembly, although extremely well qualified, and absolutely necessary, as a branch of the legislative, is unfit to exercise the executive power, for want of two essential properties, secrecy and despatch.
5. A representative assembly is still less qualified for the judicial power, because it is too numerous, too slow, and too little skilled in the laws.
6. Because a single assembly, possessed of all the powers of government, would make arbitrary laws for their own interest, execute all laws arbitrarily for their own interest, and adjudge all controversies in their own favor.

But shall the whole power of legislation rest in one assembly? Most of the foregoing reasons apply equally to prove that the legislative power ought to be more complex; to which we may add, that if the legislative power is wholly in one assembly, and the executive in another, or in a single person, these two powers will oppose and encroach upon each other, until the contest shall end in war, and the whole power, legislative and executive, be usurped by the strongest.

The judicial power, in such case, could not mediate, or hold the balance between the two contending powers, because the legislative would undermine it. And this shows the necessity, too, of giving the executive power a negative upon the legislative, otherwise this will be continually encroaching upon that.

To avoid these dangers, let a distinct assembly be constituted, as a mediator between the two extreme branches of the legislature, that which represents the people, and that which is vested with the executive power.

Let the representative assembly then elect by ballot, from among themselves or their constituents, or both, a distinct assembly, which, for the sake of perspicuity, we will call a Council. It may consist of any number you please, say twenty or thirty, and should have a free and independent exercise of its judgment, and consequently a negative voice in the legislature.

These two bodies, thus constituted, and made integral parts of the legislature, let them unite, and by joint ballot choose a governor, who, after being stripped of most of those badges of domination, called prerogatives, should have a free and independent exercise of his judgment, and be made also an integral part of the legislature....

You and I, my dear friend, have been sent into life at a time when the greatest lawgivers of antiquity would have wished to live. How few of the human race have ever enjoyed an opportunity of making an election of government, more than of air, soil, or climate, for themselves or their children! When, before the present epocha, had three millions of people full

Document Text

power and a fair opportunity to form and establish the wisest and happiest government that human wisdom can contrive? I hope you will avail yourself and your country of that extensive learning and indefatigable industry which you possess, to assist her in the formation of the happiest governments and the best character of a great people. For myself, I must beg you to keep my name out of sight; for this feeble attempt, if it should be known to be mine, would oblige me to apply to myself those lines of the immortal John Milton, in one of his sonnets:—

> "I did but prompt the age to quit their clogs
> By the known rules of ancient liberty,
> When straight a barbarous noise environs me
> Of owls and cuckoos, asses, apes, and dogs."

Glossary

Confucius, Zoroaster, Socrates, Mahomet:	Confucius (551–479 BCE), the founder of Chinese Confucianism; Zoroaster (dates unknown; Latinized version of Zarathushtra), an ancient Iranian poet and prophet who founded the religion called Zoroastrianism; Socrates (469–399 BCE), classical Greek philosopher and author of *Republic*; Mahomet (ca. 570–662; Western variant of Muhammad), founder of Islam
despatch:	speed, efficiency ("dispatch" in modern English)
divines:	theologians and ministers
indefatigable:	tireless, incapable of being fatigued
Locke:	John Locke (1632–1704), English Enlightenment philosopher
Long Parliament:	session of the British Parliament called by Charles I in 1640 that, through an act of Parliament, could be dissolved only by agreement of the members, which did not occur until 1660
Milton:	John Milton (1608–1674), English poet; the quotation at the end of the document is from his Sonnet XII, whose title is the first line of the quotation
Nedham:	Marchmont Nedham (1620–1678), English journalist and propagandist
Pope:	Alexander Pope (1688–1744), a prominent English poet; the quotation is from his *Essay on Man* (1733–1734)

Document Text

"Letters of Novanglus"

1775

No. V

We are told: "It is a universal truth that he that would excite a rebellion, is at heart as great a tyrant as ever wielded the iron rod of oppression." Be it so. We are not exciting a rebellion. Opposition, nay, open, avowed resistance by arms, against usurpation and lawless violence, is not rebellion by the law of God or the land. Resistance to lawful authority makes rebellion. Hampden, Russell, Sidney, Somers, Holt, Tillotson, Burnet, Hoadly, & c. were no tyrants nor rebels, although some of them were in arms, and the others undoubtedly excited resistance against the tories. Do not beg the question, Mr. Massachusettensis, and then give yourself airs of triumph. Remember the frank Veteran acknowledges, that "the word rebel is a convertible term."...

No. VII

Then we are told, "that the colonies are a part of the British empire." But what are we to understand by this? Some of the colonies, most of them, indeed, were settled before the kingdom of Great Britain was brought into existence. The union of England and Scotland was made and established by act of parliament in the reign of Queen Anne, and it was this union and statute which erected the kingdom of Great Britain. The colonies were settled long before, in the reigns of the Jameses and Charleses. What authority over them had Scotland? Scotland, England, and the colonies were all under one king before that; the two crowns of England and Scotland united on the head of James I., and continued united on that of Charles I., when our first charter was granted. Our charter, being granted by him, who was king of both nations, to our ancestors, most of whom were, born after the union of the two crowns, and consequently, as was adjudged in Calvin's case, free, natural subjects of Scotland, as well as England,—had not the king as good a right to have governed the colonies by his Scottish, as by his English parliament, and to have granted our charters under the seal of Scotland, as well as that of England?...

"The best writers upon the law of nations tell us, that when a nation takes possession of a distant country, and settles there, that country, though separated from the principal establishment, or mother country, naturally becomes a part of the state, equal with its ancient possessions." We are not told who these "best writers" are. I think we ought to be introduced to them. But their meaning may be no more, than that it is best they should be incorporated with the ancient establishment by contract, or by some new law and institution, by which the new country shall have equal right, powers, and privileges, as well as equal protection, and be under equal obligations of obedience, with the old. Has there been any such contract between Britain and the colonies? Is America incorporated into the realm? Is it a part of the realm? Is it a part of the kingdom? Has it any share in the legislative of the realm? The constitution requires that every foot of land should be represented in the third estate, the democratical branch of the constitution. How many millions of acres in America, how many thousands of wealthy landholders, have no representatives there?

But let these "best writers" say what they will, there is nothing in the law of nations, which is only the law of right reason applied to the conduct of nations, that requires that emigrants from a state should continue, or be made, a part of the state....

I agree, that "two supreme and independent authorities cannot exist in the same state," any more than two supreme beings in one universe; and, therefore, I contend, that our provincial legislatures are the only supreme authorities in our colonies. Parliament, notwithstanding this, may be allowed an authority supreme and sovereign over the ocean, which may be limited by the banks of the ocean, or the bounds of our charters; our charters give us no authority over the high seas. Parliament has our consent to assume a jurisdiction over them. And here is a line fairly drawn between the rights of Britain and the rights of the colonies, namely, the banks of the ocean, or low-water mark; the line of division between common law, and civil or maritime law....

"If, then, we are a part of the British empire, we must be subject to the supreme power of the state, which is vested in the estates in parliament."

Here, again, we are to be conjured out of our senses by the magic in the words "British empire," and "supreme power of the state." But, however it may sound, I say we are not a part of the British empire; because the British government is not an

Document Text

empire. The governments of France, Spain, & c. are not empires, but monarchies, supposed to be governed by fixed fundamental laws, though not really. The British government is still less entitled to the style of *an empire*. It is a limited monarchy. If Aristotle, Livy, and Harrington knew what a republic was, the British constitution is much more like a republic than an empire. They define a republic to be a *government of laws, and not of men*. If this definition be just, the British constitution is nothing more nor less than a republic, in which the king is first magistrate. This office being hereditary, and being possessed of such ample and splendid prerogatives, is no objection to the government's being a republic, as long as it is bound by fixed laws, which the people have a voice in making, and a right to defend.

Glossary

Aristotle, Livy, and Harrington:	the Greek philosopher Aristotle (384–322 BCE), author of *Politics*; the Roman historian Livy (59 BCE–17 CE); and the English political theorist James Harrington (also spelled Harington; 1611–1677), who wrote about republicanism in *The Commonwealth of Oceana* (1656)CE
Calvin:	John Calvin (1509–1564), Protestant reformer whose views were held by many early Pilgrims and Puritans
Charles I:	king of England, Scotland, and Ireland (1600–1649)
Hampden, Russell, Sidney, Somers, Holt, Tillotson, Burnet, Hoadly:	references to John Hampden, Lord William Russell, Algernon Sidney, John Somers, Lord Chief Justice John Holt, Archbishop John Tillotson, Gilbert Burnet, and Benjamin Hoadly, all regarded as seventeenth-century English political and religious rebels
James I:	king of England and Ireland and, as James VI, king of Scotland (1566–1625)
post nati:	Latin for "born after"; generally applied to immigrants to the United States after the Declaration of Independence
prerogatives:	privileges
Queen Anne:	queen of England and Scotland (1665–1714)
third estate:	the legislature, which Adams calls "the democratical branch of the constitution"

Thoughts on Government

1776

My dear Sir,—If I was equal to the task of forming a plan for the government of a colony, I should be flattered with your request, and very happy to comply with it; because, as the divine science of politics is the science of social happiness, and the blessings of society depend entirely on the constitutions of government, which are generally institutions that last for many generations, there can be no employment more agreeable to a benevolent mind than a research after the best.

Pope flattered tyrants too much when he said,

> "For forms of government let fools contest,
> That which is best administered is best."

Nothing can be more fallacious than this. But poets read history to collect flowers, not fruits; they attend to fanciful images, not the effects of social institutions. Nothing is more certain, from the history of nations and nature of man, than that some forms of government are better fitted for being well administered than others.

We ought to consider what is the end of government, before we determine which is the best form. Upon this point all speculative politicians will agree, that the happiness of society is the end of government, as all divines and moral philosophers will agree that the happiness of the individual is the end of man. From this principle it will follow, that the form of government which communicates ease, comfort, security, or, in one word, happiness, to the greatest number of persons, and in the greatest degree, is the best.

All sober inquirers after truth, ancient and modern, pagan and Christian, have declared that the happiness of man, as well as his dignity, consists in virtue. Confucius, Zoroaster, Socrates, Mahomet, not to mention authorities really sacred, have agreed in this.

If there is a form of government, then, whose principle and foundation is virtue, will not every sober man acknowledge it better calculated to promote the general happiness than any other form?

Fear is the foundation of most governments; but it is so sordid and brutal a passion, and renders men in whose breasts it predominates so stupid and miserable, that Americans will not be likely to approve of any political institution which is founded on it.

Honor is truly sacred, but holds a lower rank in the scale of moral excellence than virtue. Indeed, the former is but a part of the latter, and consequently has not equal pretensions to support a frame of government productive of human happiness.

The foundation of every government is some principle or passion in the minds of the people. The noblest principles and most generous affections in our nature, then, have the fairest chance to support the noblest and most generous models of government.

A man must be indifferent to the sneers of modern Englishmen, to mention in their company the names of Sidney, Harrington, Locke, Milton, Nedham, Neville, Burnet, and Hoadly. No small fortitude is necessary to confess that one has read them. The wretched condition of this country, however, for ten or fifteen years past, has frequently reminded me of their principles and reasonings. They will convince any candid mind, that there is no good government but what is republican. That the only valuable part of the British Constitution is so; because the very definition of a republic is "an empire of laws, and not of men." That, as a republic is the best of governments, so that particular arrangement of the powers of society, or, in other words, that form of government which is best contrived to secure an impartial and exact execution of the laws, is the best of republics.

Of republics there is an inexhaustible variety, because the possible combinations of the powers of society are capable of innumerable variations.

As good government is an empire of laws, how shall your laws be made? In a large society, inhabiting an extensive country, it is impossible that the whole should assemble to make laws. The first necessary step, then, is to depute power from the many to a few of the most wise and good. But by what rules shall you choose your representatives? Agree upon the number and qualifications of persons who shall have the benefit of choosing, or annex this privilege to the inhabitants of a certain extent of ground.

The principal difficulty lies, and the greatest care should be employed, in constituting this

representative assembly. It should be in miniature an exact portrait of the people at large. It should think, feel, reason, and act like them. That it may be the interest of this assembly to do strict justice at all times, it should be an equal representation, or, in other words, equal interests among the people should have equal interests in it. Great care should be taken to effect this, and to prevent unfair, partial, and corrupt elections. Such regulations, however, may be better made in times of greater tranquillity than the present; and they will spring up themselves naturally, when all the powers of government come to be in the hands of the people's friends. At present, it will be safest to proceed in all established modes, to which the people have been familiarized by habit.

A representation of the people in one assembly being obtained, a question arises, whether all the powers of government, legislative, executive, and judicial, shall be left in this body? I think a people cannot be long free, nor ever happy, whose government is in one assembly. My reasons for this opinion are as follow:—

1. A single assembly is liable to all the vices, follies, and frailties of an individual; subject to fits of humor, starts of passion, flights of enthusiasm, partialities, or prejudice, and consequently productive of hasty results and absurd judgments. And all these errors ought to be corrected and defects supplied by some controlling power.
2. A single assembly is apt to be avaricious, and in time will not scruple to exempt itself from burdens, which it will lay, without compunction, on its constituents.
3. A single assembly is apt to grow ambitious, and after a time will not hesitate to vote itself perpetual. This was one fault of the Long Parliament; but more remarkably of Holland, whose assembly first voted themselves from annual to septennial, then for life, and after a course of years, that all vacancies happening by death or otherwise, should be filled by themselves, without any application to constituents at all.
4. A representative assembly, although extremely well qualified, and absolutely necessary, as a branch of the legislative, is unfit to exercise the executive power, for want of two essential properties, secrecy and despatch.
5. A representative assembly is still less qualified for the judicial power, because it is too numerous, too slow, and too little skilled in the laws.
6. Because a single assembly, possessed of all the powers of government, would make arbitrary laws for their own interest, execute all laws arbitrarily for their own interest, and adjudge all controversies in their own favor.

But shall the whole power of legislation rest in one assembly? Most of the foregoing reasons apply equally to prove that the legislative power ought to be more complex; to which we may add, that if the legislative power is wholly in one assembly, and the executive in another, or in a single person, these two powers will oppose and encroach upon each other, until the contest shall end in war, and the whole power, legislative and executive, be usurped by the strongest.

The judicial power, in such case, could not mediate, or hold the balance between the two contending powers, because the legislative would undermine it. And this shows the necessity, too, of giving the executive power a negative upon the legislative, otherwise this will be continually encroaching upon that.

To avoid these dangers, let a distinct assembly be constituted, as a mediator between the two extreme branches of the legislature, that which represents the people, and that which is vested with the executive power.

Let the representative assembly then elect by ballot, from among themselves or their constituents, or both, a distinct assembly, which, for the sake of perspicuity, we will call a Council. It may consist of any number you please, say twenty or thirty, and should have a free and independent exercise of its judgment, and consequently a negative voice in the legislature.

These two bodies, thus constituted, and made integral parts of the legislature, let them unite, and by joint ballot choose a governor, who, after being stripped of most of those badges of domination, called prerogatives, should have a free and independent exercise of his judgment, and be made also an integral part of the legislature....

You and I, my dear friend, have been sent into life at a time when the greatest lawgivers of antiquity would have wished to live. How few of the human race have ever enjoyed an opportunity of making an election of government, more than of air, soil, or climate, for themselves or their children! When, before the present epocha, had three millions of people full power and a fair opportunity to form and establish the wisest and happiest government that human wisdom can contrive? I hope you will avail yourself

Document Text

and your country of that extensive learning and indefatigable industry which you possess, to assist her in the formation of the happiest governments and the best character of a great people. For myself, I must beg you to keep my name out of sight; for this feeble attempt, if it should be known to be mine, would oblige me to apply to myself those lines of the immortal John Milton, in one of his sonnets:—

"I did but prompt the age to quit their clogs
By the known rules of ancient liberty,
When straight a barbarous noise environs me
Of owls and cuckoos, asses, apes, and dogs."

Glossary

Confucius, Zoroaster, Socrates, Mahomet:	Confucius (551–479 BCE), the founder of Chinese Confucianism; Zoroaster (dates unknown; Latinized version of Zarathushtra), an ancient Iranian poet and prophet who founded the religion called Zoroastrianism; Socrates (469–399 BCE), classical Greek philosopher and author of *Republic*; Mahomet (ca. 570–662; Western variant of Muhammad), founder of Islam
despatch:	speed, efficiency ("dispatch" in modern English)
divines:	theologians and ministers
indefatigable:	tireless, incapable of being fatigued
Locke:	John Locke (1632–1704), English Enlightenment philosopher
Long Parliament:	session of the British Parliament called by Charles I in 1640 that, through an act of Parliament, could be dissolved only by agreement of the members, which did not occur until 1660
Milton:	John Milton (1608–1674), English poet; the quotation at the end of the document is from his Sonnet XII, whose title is the first line of the quotation
Nedham:	Marchmont Nedham (1620–1678), English journalist and propagandist
Pope:	Alexander Pope (1688–1744), a prominent English poet; the quotation is from his *Essay on Man* (1733–1734)

The Report of a Constitution, or Form of Government, for the Commonwealth of Massachusetts

1779

Preamble

The end of the institution, maintenance and administration of government, is to secure the existence of the body-politic; to protect it; and to furnish the individuals who compose it, with the power of enjoying, in safety and tranquility, their natural rights, and the blessings of life: And whenever these great objects are not obtained, the people have a right to alter the government, and to take measures necessary for their safety, happiness and prosperity.

The body politic is formed by a voluntary association of individuals: It is a social compact, by which the whole people covenants with each citizen, and each citizen with the whole people, that all shall be governed by certain laws for the common good. It is the duty of the people, therefore, in framing a Constitution of Government, to provide for an equitable mode of making laws, as well as for an impartial interpretation; and a faithful execution of them, that every man may, at all times, find his security in them....

Chapter I

A DECLARATION of the RIGHTS of the Inhabitants of the Commonwealth of Massachusetts

Article I. All men are born equally free and independent, and have certain natural, essential, and unalienable rights: among which may be reckoned the right of enjoying and defending their lives and liberties; that of acquiring, possessing, and protecting their property; in fine, that of seeking and obtaining their safety and happiness.

Article II. It is the duty of all men in society, publicly, and at stated seasons, to worship the SUPREME BEING, the great creator and preserver of the universe. And no subject shall be hurt, molested, or restrained, in his person, liberty, or estate, for worshiping GOD in the manner most agreeable to the dictates of his own conscience; or for his religious profession or sentiments; provided he doth not disturb the public peace, or obstruct others in their religious worship.

Article III. Good morals being necessary to the preservation of civil society; and the knowledge and belief of the being of GOD, His providential government of the world, and of a future state of rewards and punishment, being the only true foundation of morality, the legislature hath therefore a right, and ought, to provide at the expence of the subject, if necessary, a suitable support for the public worship of GOD, and of the teachers of religion and morals; and to enjoin upon all the subjects an attendance upon their instructions, at stated times and seasons: Provided there be any such teacher, on whose ministry they can conscientiously and conveniently attend.

All monies, paid by the subject to the support of public worship, and of the instructors in religion and morals, shall, if he requires it, be uniformly applied to the support of the teacher or teachers of his own religious denomination, if there be such, whose ministry he attends upon: otherwise it may be paid to the teacher or teachers of the parish or precinct where he usually resides.

Article IV. The people of this commonwealth have the sole and exclusive right of governing themselves, as a free, sovereign, and independent state; and do, and forever hereafter shall, exercise and enjoy every power, jurisdiction, and right, which are not, or may not hereafter, be by them expressly delegated to the United States of America, in Congress assembled.

Article V. All power residing originally in the people, and being derived from them, the several magistrates and officers of government, vested with authority, whether legislative, executive or judicial, are their substitutes and agents, and are at all times accountable to them.

Article VI. No man, nor corporation or association of men, have any other title to obtain advantages, or particular and exclusive privileges, distinct from those of the community, than what arises from the consideration of services rendered to the public; and this title being in nature neither hereditary, nor transmissible to children, or descendants, or relations by blood, the idea of a man born a magistrate, law-giver, or judge, is absurd and unnatural.

Document Text

Article VII. Government is instituted for the common good; for the protection, safety, prosperity and happiness of the people; and not for the profit, honor, or private interest of any one man, family, or class of men: Therefore the people alone have an incontestable, unalienable, and indefeasible right to institute government; and to reform, alter, or totally change the same, when their protection, safety, prosperity and happiness require it.

Article VIII. In order to prevent those who are vested with authority from becoming oppressors, the people have a right, at such periods and in such manner as may be delineated in their frame of government, to cause their public officers to return to private life, and to fill up vacant places by certain and regular elections....

Article XII. No subject shall be held to answer for any crime or offence, untill the same is fully and plainly, substantially and formally, described to him: He cannot be compelled to accuse himself, or to furnish evidence against himself; and every subject shall have a right to be fully heard in his defence, by himself or his council, at his election; to meet the witnesses against him face to face, to produce all proofs that may be favourable to him; to require a speedy and public trial by an impartial jury of the country, without whose unanimous consent, or his own voluntary confession, he cannot finally be declared guilty, or sentenced to loss of life, liberty or property....

Article XV. Every man has a right to be secure from all unreasonable searches and seizures of his person, his houses, his papers, and all his possessions. All warrants, therefore, are contrary to this right, if the cause or foundation of them be not previously supported by oath or affirmation; and if the order in the warrant to a civil officer, to make search in suspected places, or to arrest one or more suspected persons, or to seize their property, be not accompanied with a special designation of the persons or objects of search, arrest or seizure; and no warrant ought to be issued but in cases and with the formalities prescribed by the laws....

Article XVII. The people have a right to the freedom of speaking, writing and publishing their sentiments: The liberty of the press therefore ought not to be restrained.

Article XVIII. The people have a right to keep and to bear arms for the common defence. And as in time of peace standing armies are dangerous to liberty, they ought not to be maintained without the consent of the legislature; and the military power shall always be held in an exact subordination to the civil authority, and be governed by it....

Chapter II

The Frame of Government

The people inhabiting the territory heretofore called the Province of Massachusetts-Bay, do hereby solemnly and mutually agree with each other, to form themselves into a free, sovereign, and independent body-politic or state, by the name of THE COMMONWEALTH OF MASSACHUSETTS.

In the government of the Commonwealth of Massachusetts, the legislative, executive, and judicial power, shall be placed in separate departments, to the end that it might be a government of laws and not of men.

Glossary

body-politic:	the people and their government considered as a collective unit
Commonwealth:	the official designation of four U.S. states: Kentucky, Pennsylvania, Virginia, and Pennsylvania
indefeasible:	incapable of being undone or voided

A Defence of the Constitutions of Government of the United States of America

Recapitulation

As we have taken a cursory view of those countries in Europe where the government may be called, in any reasonable construction of the word, republican, let us now pause a few moments, and reflect upon what we have seen.

Among every people, and in every species of republics, we have constantly found *a first magistrate, a head, a chief*, under various denominations, indeed, and with different degrees of authority, with the title of stadtholder, burgomaster, avoyer, doge, gonfaloniero, president, syndic, mayor, alcalde, capitaneo, governor, or king; in every nation we have met with a distinguished officer. If there is no example, then, in any free government, any more than in those which are not free, of a society without a principal personage, we may fairly conclude that the body politic cannot subsist, any more than the animal body, without a head. If M. Turgot had made any discovery which had escaped the penetration of all the legislators and philosophers who have lived before him, he ought at least to have communicated it to the world for their improvement; but as he has never hinted at any such invention, we may safely conclude that he had none; and, therefore, that the Americans are not justly liable to censure for instituting *governors*.

In every form of government we have seen a *senate*, or *little council*, a composition, generally, of those officers of state who have the most experience and power, and of a *few* other members selected from the highest ranks and most illustrious reputations. On these lesser councils, with the first magistrate at their head, generally rests the principal burden of administration, a share in the legislative, as well as executive and judicial authority of government. The admission of such senates to a participation of these three kinds of power, has been generally observed to produce in the minds of their members an ardent aristocratical ambition, grasping equally at the prerogatives of the first magistrate, and the privileges of the people, and ending in the nobility of a few families, and a tyrannical oligarchy. But in those states, where the senates have been debarred from all executive power, and confined to the legislative, they have been observed to be firm barriers against the encroachments of the crown, and often great supporters of the liberties of the people. The Americans, then, who have carefully confined their senates to the legislative power, have done wisely in adopting them.

We have seen, in every instance, another and a larger assembly, composed of the body of the people, in some little states; of representatives chosen by the people, in others; of members appointed by the senate, and supposed to represent the people, in a third sort; and of persons appointed by themselves or the senate, in certain aristocracies; to prevent them from becoming oligarchies. The Americans, then, whose assemblies are the most adequate, proportional, and equitable representations of the people, that are known in the world, will not be thought mistaken in appointing houses of representatives.

In every republic,—in the smallest and most popular, in the larger and more aristocratical, as well as in the largest and most monarchical,—we have observed a multitude of curious and ingenious inventions to balance, in their turn, all those powers, to check the passions peculiar to them, and to control them from rushing into those exorbitancies to which they are most addicted. The Americans will then be no longer censured for endeavoring to introduce an equilibrium, which is much more profoundly meditated, and much more effectual for the protection of the laws, than any we have seen, except in England. We may even question whether that is an exception.

In every country we have found a variety of *orders*, with very great distinctions. In America, there are different orders of *offices*, but none of *men*. Out of office, all men are of the same species, and of one blood; there is neither a greater nor a lesser nobility. Why, then, are the Americans accused of establishing different orders of men? To our inexpressible mortification, we must have observed, that the people have preserved a share of power, or an existence in the government, in no country out of England, except upon the tops of a few inaccessible mountains, among

rocks and precipices, in territories so narrow that you may span them with a hand's breadth, where, living unenvied, in extreme poverty, chiefly upon pasturage, destitute of manufactures and commerce, they still exhibit the most charming picture of life, and the most dignified character of human nature.

Wherever we have seen a territory somewhat larger, arts and sciences more cultivated, commerce flourishing, or even agriculture improved to any great degree, an aristocracy has risen up in a course of time, consisting of a few rich and honorable families, who have united with each other against both the people and the first magistrate; who have wrested from the former, by art and by force, all their participation in the government; and have even inspired them with so mean an esteem of themselves, and so deep a veneration and strong attachment to their rulers, as to believe and confess them a superior order of beings....

We have seen no one government in which is a distinct separation of the legislative from the executive power, and of the judicial from both, or in which any attempt has been made to balance these powers with one another, or to form an equilibrium between the one, the few, and the many, for the purpose of enacting and executing equal laws, by common consent, for the general interest, excepting in England.

Shall we conclude, from these melancholy observations, that human nature is incapable of liberty, that no honest equality can be preserved in society, and that such forcible causes are always at work as must reduce all men to a submission to despotism, monarchy, oligarchy, or aristocracy?

By no means. We have seen one of the first nations in Europe, possessed of ample and fertile territories at home and extensive dominions abroad, of a commerce with the whole world, immense wealth, and the greatest naval power which ever belonged to any nation, which has still preserved the power of the people by the equilibrium we are contending for, by the trial by jury, and by constantly refusing a standing army. The people of England alone, by preserving their share in the legislature, at the expense of the blood of heroes and patriots, have enabled their king to curb the nobility, without giving him a standing army.

After all, let us compare every constitution we have seen with those of the United States of America, and we shall have no reason to blush for our country. On the contrary, we shall feel the strongest motives to fall upon our knees, in gratitude to heaven for having been graciously pleased to give us birth and education in that country, and for having destined us to live under her laws! We shall have reason to exult, if we make our comparison with England and the English constitution. Our people are undoubtedly sovereign; all the landed and other property is in the hands of the citizens; not only their representatives, but their senators and governors, are annually chosen; there are no hereditary titles, honors, offices, or distinctions; the legislative, executive, and judicial powers are carefully separated from each other; the powers of the one, the few, and the many are nicely balanced in the legislatures; trials by jury are preserved in all their glory, and there is no standing army; the *habeas corpus* is in full force; the press is the most free in the world. Where all these circumstances take place, it is unnecessary to add that the laws alone can govern....

It is now in our power to bring this work to a conclusion with unexpected dignity. In the course of the last summer, two authorities have appeared, greater than any that have been before quoted, in which the principles we have attempted to defend have been acknowledged.

The first is, an Ordinance of Congress, of the thirteenth of July, 1787, for the Government of the Territory of the United States, Northwest of the River Ohio.

The second is, the Report of the Convention at Philadelphia, of the seventeenth of September, 1787.

The former confederation of the United States was formed upon the model and example of all the confederacies, ancient and modern, in which the federal council was only a diplomatic body. Even the Lycian, which is thought to have been the best, was no more. The magnitude of territory, the population, the wealth and commerce, and especially the rapid growth of the United States, have shown such a government to be inadequate to their wants; and the new system, which seems admirably calculated to unite their interests and affections, and bring them to an uniformity of principles and sentiments, is equally well combined to unite their wills and forces as a single nation. A result of accommodation cannot be supposed to reach the ideas of perfection of any one; but the conception of such an idea, and the deliberate union of so great and various a people in such a plan, is, without all partiality or prejudice, if not the greatest exertion of human understanding, the greatest single effort of national deliberation that

Document Text

the world has ever seen. That it may be improved is not to be doubted, and provision is made for that purpose in the report itself. A people who could conceive, and can adopt it, we need not fear will be able to amend it, when, by experience, its inconveniences and imperfections shall be seen and felt.

Glossary

habeas corpus: legal action by which a person seeks relief from unlawful arrest; among the Founders, a crucial guarantee of freedom against arbitrary state action

Lycian: pertaining to Lycia, a confederation of ancient cities in what is now Turkey and the world's first confederation with democratic principles, similar to those enshrined in the U.S. Constitution

oligarchy: a form of government in which power is concentrated in the hands of a small number of elite people

Adams' birthplace in Quincy, Massachusetts

Inaugural Address

When it was first perceived, in early times, that no middle course for America remained between unlimited submission to a foreign legislature and a total independence of its claims, men of reflection were less apprehensive of danger from the formidable power of fleets and armies they must determine to resist, than from those contests and dissensions, which would certainly arise, concerning the forms of government to be instituted, over the whole, and over the parts of this extensive country. Relying, however, on the purity of their intentions, the justice of their cause, and the integrity and intelligence of the people, under an overruling Providence, which had so signally protected this country from the first, the representatives of this nation, then consisting of little more than half its present numbers, not only broke to pieces the chains which were forging, and the rod of iron that was lifted up, but frankly cut asunder the ties which had bound them, and launched into an ocean of uncertainty.

The zeal and ardor of the people during the revolutionary war, supplying the place of government, commanded a degree of order, sufficient at least for the temporary preservation of society. The confederation, which was early felt to be necessary, was prepared from the models of the Batavian and Helvetic confederacies, the only examples which remain, with any detail and precision, in history, and certainly the only ones which the people at large had ever considered. But, reflecting on the striking difference in so many particulars between this country and those where a courier may go from the seat of government to the frontier in a single day, it was then certainly foreseen by some, who assisted in Congress at the formation of it, that it could not be durable.

Negligence of its regulations, inattention to its recommendations, if not disobedience to its authority, not only in individuals but in States, soon appeared, with their melancholy consequences; universal languor, jealousies, rivalries of States; decline of navigation and commerce; discouragement of necessary manufactures; universal fall in the value of lands and their produce; contempt of public and private faith; loss of consideration and credit with foreign nations; and, at length, in discontents, animosities, combinations, partial conventions, and insurrection; threatening some great national calamity.

In this dangerous crisis the people of America were not abandoned by their usual good sense, presence of mind, resolution, or integrity. Measures were pursued to concert a plan to form a more perfect union, establish justice, ensure domestic tranquillity, provide for the common defence, promote the general welfare, and secure the blessings of liberty. The public disquisitions, discussions, and deliberations, issued in the present happy constitution of government.

Employed in the service of my country abroad, during the whole course of these transactions, I first saw the Constitution of the United States in a foreign country. Irritated by no literary altercation, animated by no public debate, heated by no party animosity, I read it with great satisfaction, as a result of good heads, prompted by good hearts; as an experiment better adapted to the genius, character, situation, and relations of this nation and country, than any which had ever been proposed or suggested. In its general principles and great outlines, it was conformable to such a system of government as I had ever most esteemed, and in some States, my own native State in particular, had contributed to establish. Claiming a right of suffrage in common with my fellow-citizens, in the adoption or rejection of a constitution, which was to rule me and my posterity as well as them and theirs, I did not hesitate to express my approbation of it on all occasions, in public and in private. It was not then nor has been since any objection to it, in my mind, that the Executive and Senate were not more permanent. Nor have I entertained a thought of promoting any alteration in it, but such as the people themselves, in the course of their experience, should see and feel to be necessary or expedient, and by their representatives in Congress and the State legislatures, according to the Constitution itself, adopt and ordain.

Returning to the bosom of my country, after a painful separation from it for ten years, I had the honor to be elected to a station under the new order of things, and I have repeatedly laid myself under the most serious obligations to support the Constitution.

Document Text

The operation of it has equalled the most sanguine expectations of its friends; and, from an habitual attention to it, satisfaction in its administration, and delight in its effect upon the peace, order, prosperity, and happiness of the nation, I have acquired an habitual attachment to it, and veneration for it.

What other form of government, indeed, can so well deserve our esteem and love?…:

In the midst of these pleasing ideas, we should be unfaithful to ourselves, if we should ever lose sight of the danger to our liberties, if any thing partial or extraneous should infect the purity of our free, fair, virtuous, and independent elections. If an election is to be determined by a majority of a single vote, and that can be procured by a party, through artifice or corruption, the government may be the choice of a party, for its own ends, not of the nation, for the national good. If that solitary suffrage can be obtained by foreign nations, by flattery or menaces; by fraud or violence; by terror, intrigue, or venality; the government may not be the choice of the American people, but of foreign nations. It may be foreign nations who govern us, and not we, the people, who govern ourselves. And candid men will acknowledge, that, in such cases, choice would have little advantage to boast of over lot or chance.

Such is the amiable and interesting system of government (and such are some of the abuses to which it may be exposed), which the people of America have exhibited, to the admiration and anxiety of the wise and virtuous of all nations, for eight years; under the administration of a citizen, who, by a long course of great actions regulated by prudence, justice, temperance, and fortitude, conducting a people, inspired with the same virtues, and animated with the same ardent patriotism and love of liberty, to independence and peace, to increasing wealth and unexampled prosperity, has merited the gratitude of his fellow-citizens, commanded the highest praises of foreign nations, and secured immortal glory with posterity.…

With this great example before me, with the sense and spirit, the faith and honor, the duty and interest of the same American people, pledged to support the Constitution of the United States, I entertain no doubt of its continuance in all its energy; and my mind is prepared without hesitation, to lay myself under the most solemn obligations to support it to the utmost of my power.

And may that Being, who is supreme over all, the patron of order, the fountain of justice, and the protector, in all ages of the world, of virtuous liberty, continue his blessing upon this nation and its government, and give it all possible success and duration, consistent with the ends of his providence!

Glossary

Batavian:	a reference to the republican government introduced into Amsterdam, Holland, by the French in 1795
Helvetic:	the name given to the confederation of Swiss republics under Napoleonic rule

John Quincy Adams by Gilbert Stuart, 1818

John Quincy Adams: Original Analysis

Sixth President of the United States

1767–1848

Overview

John Quincy Adams was born in Braintree (now Quincy), Massachusetts, on July 11, 1767. His father, John Adams, was a stalwart of the Revolutionary movement and the second president of the United States. Both his father and his mother, Abigail Smith Adams, instilled in John Quincy a commitment to moral perfectionism and public service. That service began when he accompanied his father on a diplomatic mission to Europe at ten years of age, and it was made official when he became secretary to the American minister designate to Russia four years later. He graduated from Harvard College in 1787 and began the practice of law.

The first significant phase of Adams's career was as a diplomat. George Washington appointed him minister to the Netherlands; his father made him the minister to Prussia. After one term as a U.S. senator from Massachusetts, from 1803 to 1808, during which Adams displayed an increasing political independence, President James Madison appointed him minister to Russia in 1809. Adams served as the key negotiator for the Treaty of Ghent, ending the War of 1812. Following a brief stint as the minister to Great Britain, Adams became President James Monroe's secretary of state. In this position Adams used his considerable experience to define and extend the nation's boundaries. His extensive diaries provide a good sense of the evolution of his thinking and negotiations. With Great Britain he obtained valuable fishing rights and the northern border of the Louisiana Purchase at the 49th parallel. He manipulated Andrew Jackson's unauthorized invasion of Florida in 1818 into the Adams-Onís Treaty (also called the Transcontinental Treaty) of 1819. The United States not only acquired Florida and extended the western boundary of the Louisiana Purchase but also removed Spanish claims to the Pacific Northwest north of the 42nd parallel. With James Monroe, Adams helped devise the Monroe Doctrine in 1823, which increased the nation's prestige in the Western Hemisphere and established a fundamental piece of future American foreign policy. Many scholars recognize John Quincy Adams as the nation's greatest secretary of state.

No one secured a majority of Electoral College votes in the presidential election of 1824, such that it was the House of Representatives that elected Adams in February 1825. His thoughtful policies for national growth are contained in his presidential messages to Congress. In a nation fragmented into many political factions, Adams failed to negotiate significant measures through Congress other than commercial trade treaties. The contrast between his presidential and diplomatic years could not be starker.

Adams is the only former president to serve in the House of Representatives. Elected in 1830, Adams used his office to promote his nationalistic goals. He worked with the Whig Party in opposition to the Jacksonian Democrats, but his sense of morality often led him to follow a distinctive political course. He demanded higher tariff and land sales revenues to finance internal improvements. He claimed the role of protector of liberty from the autocratic slaveholders of the South, who, he felt, stunted the nation's progress in placing the interests of slavery over all else. His attacks on the "gag rule" that prevented the acceptance of antislavery petitions in the House of Representatives led admirers to call him "Old Man Eloquent." In 1841, before the Supreme Court, Adams delivered a biting sarcastic oration against the slave trade and for the freedom of the slaves who had rebelled aboard the Spanish ship *Amistad*. For all his moral sense, Adams was an inept politician, refusing to compromise and alienating potential allies. His last major crusade was one of opposition to the Mexican-American War. It was at his seat in the House in 1848 that he suffered a fatal stroke.

Explanation and Analysis of Documents

The career of John Quincy Adams had three distinct phases, such that the documents that best reveal his thinking and accomplishments are different for each time period. As a diplomat, Adams often expressed his goals in conversations with his superiors, fellow cabinet officers, and foreign diplomats. These are meticulously recounted in his diaries. The entries bring to light the formulation of the Adams-Onís Treaty and of the Monroe Doctrine. As president, Adams sought through his public messages to persuade a factionalized Congress to pursue an ambitious national program of development. His first annual message captures his presidential philosophy. Finally, Adams's actions as a congressman are best revealed through his debates in Congress and his appeals to his constituents. The address to the New York Historical Society celebrating the Constitution, his part in the congressional debate over the motion for his censure, and his speech to the voters in his hometown in September 1842 give readers a sense of how the people and his political colleagues saw him.

♦ Diary Entries on the Adams-Onís Treaty

When General Andrew Jackson exceeded his orders to patrol the border with Florida by invading the Spanish colony in 1818, condemnation came from many quarters. The Spanish demanded an explanation and apology for Jackson's capture of two garrisons at St. Marks and Pensacola. President Monroe and most of the cabinet were also appalled. Secretary of State Adams, however, not only refused to apologize but additionally saw an opportunity to convince the Spanish that their presence in Florida was untenable. He also initiated a discussion about the vague western border of the 1803 Louisiana Purchase.

In the entry dated February 3, 1819, Adams reports his conversation with Andrew Jackson over an issue that would loom large twenty years later. Significantly, these two future adversaries agreed about the relative importance of Florida and Texas. By accepting the Sabine River (the current border of Louisiana and Texas) and not the Rio Grande ("Rio del Norte" in the diary) as marking the extent of American territory, the United States was conceding its tenuous claim to Texas. Adams and Jackson concurred that acquiring Florida took priority.

In the following weeks Adams used Jean-Guillaume, the baron Hyde de Neuville, the French minister to the United States, as an intermediary between himself and Luis de Onís, the Spanish minister. Rather than claim Texas, Adams vigorously pushed Onís and the Spanish to cede lands north of present-day Texas. Furthermore, Adams wanted to eliminate Spanish claims to the Pacific Northwest. Thus he insisted on "latitude forty-two, from the source of the Arkansas [River] to the South Sea [Pacific Ocean]." At a late stage in the negotiations Onís expressed second thoughts, though Spanish records indicate that he had the authority to make the deal outlined in this entry. Adams's obstinacy was significant for two reasons. First, his unusual demand for the boundary to be at rivers' edges reflected his confidence that American growth would be such that the nation "would have extensive settlements upon them in a very few years." Second, Adams's European experience told him that Spain could be pushed around. Spain not only was dealing with revolts in its South American colonies but also was weak and had no European allies willing to offer assistance. Spain could not afford to confront a hostile United States at the same time. This insight would likewise be important for the formulation of the Monroe Doctrine.

Adams justly takes pride in the completion of the Adams-Onís Treaty. Although there are indications that Adams could have secured even more territory, he far exceeded the expectations of President Monroe and the cabinet in his negotiations. Clearly the path to the Pacific was a major accomplishment. In his diary twenty-five years later, on September 27, 1844, Adams proudly states, "The Florida Treaty was the most important incident in my life, and the most successful negotiation ever consummated by the Government of this Union" (*Memoirs*, vol. 12, p. 78).

Time Line

1767	July 11	■ John Quincy Adams is born in Braintree (now Quincy), Massachusetts.
1787	July 16	■ Adams graduates from Harvard College.
1794		■ President George Washington appoints Adams minister to the Netherlands.
1797		■ President John Adams appoints his son minister to Prussia.
1803		■ Massachusetts legislature elects John Quincy Adams to the U.S. Senate.
1807		■ Adams supports President Thomas Jefferson's Embargo Act, alienating him from the Federalist Party.
1809		■ President James Madison appoints Adams minister to Russia.
1814	December 24	■ Adams concludes negotiations on the Treaty of Ghent, ending the War of 1812.
1815		■ President Madison appoints Adams minister to Great Britain.
1817		■ Adams becomes secretary of state in the James Monroe administration.
1818		■ Adams negotiates the Convention of 1818 with Great Britain.
1819	February 22	■ Adams concludes negotiation of the Adams-Onís Treaty (or Transcontinental Treaty) with Spain.
1823	December 2	■ President Monroe issues the Monroe Doctrine in his annual message to Congress.
1825	February 9	■ The House of Representatives elects Adams president of the United States.
	December 6	■ Adams issues his first annual message to Congress.
1828	November	■ Andrew Jackson defeats Adams in his bid for reelection.

Time Line		
1830	November	■ Adams is elected to the House of Representatives.
1836	May	■ Adams unsuccessfully opposes the first "gag rule" prohibiting petitions regarding slavery.
1839	April 30	■ Adams delivers his jubilee of the Constitution address in New York City on the fiftieth anniversary of Washington's inauguration.
1841	February 24–March 1	■ Adams advocates the freedom of the *Amistad* slaves in the U.S. Supreme Court.
1842	February 3	■ Adams fights a motion in the House of Representatives to censure him for presenting a petition to dissolve the Union.
	September 17	■ In an address at Braintree, Massachusetts, Adams defends his actions to his constituents and speaks against the southern plan to acquire Texas as a way to preserve slavery.
1844	December	■ Adams helps defeat renewal of the "gag rule."
1846	May 11	■ Adams votes against the declaration of war against Mexico.
1848	February 23	■ Adams dies of a stroke in Washington, D.C.

♦ Diary Entries on the Monroe Doctrine

Spain's inability to retain its continental American empire in the early 1820s created a new set of opportunities and challenges for the United States and Secretary of State Adams. The nation extended formal recognition to Mexico, Peru, Colombia, and others but was wary that Spain's allies in the Holy Alliance, which included Austria, Russia, and France, might try to restore the colonies and militarily challenge the United States if it attempted to oppose them. Great Britain, however, presented the greater obstacle to recolonization as new trading partners emerged in Central and South America. The British invited the United States to stand with them in opposition to Spain's reconquest. The unilateral response of the United States was ultimately announced in President James Monroe's annual message of December 2, 1823, three paragraphs of which became known as the Monroe Doctrine.

As early as July 1823 Adams notes in his diary that he had made it clear to the Russian ambassador Baron de Tuyll van Serooskerken that the United States had decided that the time for colonization in the Western Hemisphere was over. In asserting the principle of noncolonization, Adams was blunter than President Monroe felt comfortable with. Adams sent similar instructions to the American minister to Great Britain.

A second principle of the ultimate Monroe Doctrine is apparent in Adams's report of conversation with the president and cabinet in November 1823. Adams followed the policies of George Washington and succeeding presidents by advocating staying out of the affairs of Europe. President Monroe and others in the cabinet, however, were interested in supporting the Greek revolution for independence from Turkey. Secretary of State Adams on November 22 tells of urging restraint to the president, who would ultimately agree. Adams, however, would take the policy further. The third principle of the Monroe Doctrine would stress that Europe should not only abandon colonization but also cease to interfere in the affairs of independent American nations.

Both Monroe and Adams agreed that the United States should not become a weak partner with Great Britain, but the question of whether the three principles of the Monroe Doctrine could be sustained caused some anxiety. Again, it was Adams who had the key insight. He feared the Holy Alliance much less than did Secretary of War John C. Calhoun and saw England as the more important player. But, as he argues on November 25, it was in England's economic interest to defend the Monroe Doctrine even if the United States issued it unilaterally. If Monroe were to assert the three principles "promptly and decisively," the nation could augment its reputation and lend moral support to Latin America while letting the British supply the military component if necessary. Events proved Adams right.

♦ First Annual Message to Congress

The election of 1824 displayed the lack of a national political focus. Andrew Jackson received a plurality of Electoral College votes but not a majority. The Constitution's provisions eliminated Henry Clay, the fourth-place finisher, and placed the election in the hands of the House of Representatives. There, Adams narrowly defeated Jackson and Secretary of Treasury William H. Crawford. Clay's support for Adams proved crucial. Undeterred by his narrow margin of victory, President Adams presented his nationalistic ideals to Congress when they met on December 6, 1825.

The concluding part of his message is a strident call for improvement, physical and moral, on a national scale. Adams's sense of the power of government was broad, and his argument for improvement is unequivocal. Using his foreign experience, he places the United States in an international context and offers a statesmanlike program for national greatness. The key agent in raising America will be the federal government.

Adams renews George Washington's request for a national university and additional support for the military academy at West Point. He calls for a thorough exploration

of the Pacific Northwest coast, anticipating a time when the United States and Great Britain would end their joint occupation. The federal government, in Adams's opinion, should encourage scientific exploration by devising a system of weights and measures and should promote astronomy. In a particularly unfortunate phrase, Adams calls for "light-houses of the skies," or astronomical observatories. In this and other scientific research, the United States would inevitably exceed the achievements of Europe.

A grand concept that Adams repeatedly stresses is that government has the power and the "sacred" responsibility for "the progressive improvement of the condition of the governed." Although he warns Congress not to transcend its constitutional powers, failure to pursue the president's plan "would be treachery to the most sacred of trusts." In a most revealing phrase, Adams praises the governmental system and emphasizes that "liberty is power." The federal government should use that power for the benefit of all.

The tragedy of Adams's presidency was that neither Congress nor the country was willing to embrace his far-sighted program. His first annual message was the product of a lifetime of scholarship and an international education, but the United States was not prepared for it. While many ridiculed the "light-houses of the skies," many more feared the augmentations to government power. Localism and self-centered personal ambitions dominated perspectives. Several in the cabinet, especially the politically astute Secretary of State Henry Clay and Attorney General William Wirt, warned the president that such would be the case, but to no avail. Further complicating matters was the circumstance that Adams, despite his sincere devotion to the Union, was not a good politician. His relationship with Congress deteriorated, and his pleas for improvement went largely unheeded. By the election of 1828 the Jacksonian Democrats were poised to capture and dominate the presidency for most of the next thirty years.

♦ Jubilee of the Constitution Address

John Quincy Adams was the only former president to serve in the House of Representatives. It would be too simplistic to categorize his service as an increasingly bitter attempt to redeem his presidential legacy or to exact revenge on his enemies. The speech he made on the fiftieth anniversary of George Washington's inauguration, April 30, 1839, is a reminder of the high-minded principles and goals Adams fervently held.

With Washington's accession to the presidency, the Constitution finally went into effect, an event that in Adams's view represented the fruition of the Declaration of Independence. Through the comprehension of the primacy of the Declaration, he asserts, the promise of America can be achieved. The people, through their representatives, had broken with the British nation. Individual states were not independent as separate states; rather, the former colonists formed one union composed of thirteen states. Throughout Adams's address the concept of state sovereignty is subordinated to the collective interests of the people. He argues that when the nation has deviated from that principle, it has faced disaster. The flawed Articles of Confederation were rooted in "the grossly immoral and dishonest doctrine of despotic state sovereignty." In contrast, the Constitution was an act by representatives of the people, not the states. The people, not the states, ratified it. The new Constitution reaffirmed rights of the people proclaimed by the Declaration. At great length Adams argues that President Washington brilliantly established the executive branch and generally eliminated the state sovereignty concept, which had "brought the union itself to the verge of dissolution."

Adams makes sure his listeners understand that recent state sovereignty arguments revolving around nullification and secession are illegitimate in light of the origins of the Constitution and the Declaration of Independence. He does not attack the South or discuss issues of the late 1830s or even of his presidency. Rather, Adams encourages his listeners to apply the lessons of history, as he defines them, to current events. Adams acknowledges that his perceptions of the nature of the Constitution are not shared by all. Indeed, his idiosyncratic political course made others hesitant to accept the full implication of his views. The ideals in this address, however, were precursors of those enunciated by later leaders, perhaps most notably by Abraham Lincoln in the late 1850s and particularly as president.

♦ Congressional Debate over Motion for Censure

As a representative from Massachusetts, Adams was motivated by the ideals of the Declaration of Independence and by anger toward southern congressmen who too often seemed to undermine them. At times it was difficult to determine whether Adams knew which was more important. Similarly, it was unclear whether he hated slavery more than the constitutional provision that counted slaves as three-fifths persons and gave the South disproportionate representation in the House and Electoral College. Certainly his disgust at the "gag rule" that restricted the acceptance of constituent petitions about slavery was immediate and sincere. Adams, however, deliberately antagonized the rule's proponents and snarled House proceedings. One such incident occurred on January 24, 1842, when he presented a petition from forty-six citizens of Haverhill, Massachusetts, asking that the Union be dissolved because the South was an excessive economic drain. Representatives Thomas Marshall of Kentucky and Thomas Gilmer and Henry Wise of Virginia took the bait, calling for Adams to be censured by the House and removed from the chairmanship of the Foreign Affairs Committee.

For more than two weeks debate raged, with Adams vigorously defending himself. His remarks of February 3 are typical. He places the right of petition, whatever

the subject, in the context of other irrevocable rights. He also pits the North against the South and threatens the censurers with a public uprising. In truth, some southerners and Adams's fellow Whigs wanted an end to the debate. On February 7, a deal was struck whereby Adams agreed to suspend his defense if the censure resolution was tabled forever. It is difficult to assess whether these proceedings bore a measurable impact on public opinion. Abolitionists, particularly William Lloyd Garrison and his followers, did adopt a new slogan of "No Union with Slaveholders." The House still refused to accept the petition from Haverhill.

♦ Address to Constituents at Braintree

Congressional reapportionment affected a significant portion of Adams's district, and his soon-to-be former constituents invited "Old Man Eloquent" to address them one last time. The majority of Adams's remarks on this occasion consist of an attack on President John Tyler. Adams broadens his assault by suggesting that there is a "conflict between freedom and slavery" and that the South's (and Tyler's) interests are not those of the nation. Adams withholds nothing in labeling slaveholders as hypocrites, double-dealers, and frauds. To preserve slavery, southern officeholders sought the acquisition of Texas, from which "ten slave-spotted" new states would be created to guarantee "the dominion of the slave-ridden over the free." Rights, such as to petition, would be compromised; money from land sales would be wasted; tariff revenues would be reduced. All of the improvements that Adams pushed for in his first annual message would forever be starved for money.

For five and a half more years Adams served in the House, growing increasingly bitter, as his Braintree address suggests. The annexation of Texas and subsequent war with Mexico only confirmed to Adams the notion that the presence of the Slave Power, the political leverage of the southern slaveholding class, compromised the nation's future and the principles of the Declaration of Independence.

Impact and Legacy

John Quincy Adams's words and writings had the greatest impact on the nation as produced in his roles of diplomat and secretary of state. His keen insights persuaded superiors such as President Monroe and compelled foreign diplomats to retreat. Although his diary entries must be treated carefully and read as self-serving, it is clear that Adams held sway in one-on-one negotiations and in cabinet meetings. The diaries also reveal a powerful intellect enhanced by a truly international education that was dedicated to the future greatness of the United States.

When Adams reached out as president to Congress and the nation, his words were far less effective. The intellect and patriotism remained, but the ideas did not usually resonate with the interests of the people and their representatives. As president, he could not adapt his goals to mesh with those of a parochial public. As congressman and former president Adams was deeply respected, but again he failed to fashion a message that congressmen, even those in the Whig Party, could rally around. As his frustration grew, he became revered by a minority for his attacks on slaveholders.

In assessments of his legacy, Adams's contributions to America's growth after the near-disastrous War of 1812 are unquestioned. He correctly gauged how to gain respect from European nations. The tragedy is that Adams's vision of American greatness and the articulate respect he paid to the Declaration of Independence were muddied by his bitter, divisive tirades. Had he been more adept at the give-and-take of antebellum partisan politics, his words and unique perspective might have been used for more constructive purposes, although it is doubtful that Adams himself would have ever been satisfied. Instead, his congressional speeches and addresses usually inspired abolitionists in the North while inciting sectional extremists in the South. His failures as a president and congressional leader have sadly led Americans to forget his most noble sentiments for his countrymen.

Key Sources

The Adams Family Papers manuscript collection is located at the Massachusetts Historical Society in Boston. The invaluable diaries are available in digital form from the Massachusetts Historical Society Web site (http://www.masshist.org/jqadiaries). An edited version is Charles Francis Adams, ed., *Memoirs of John Quincy Adams, Comprising Portions of His Diary from 1795 to 1848*, 12 vols. (1874–1877). Worthington C. Ford, ed., *Writings of John Quincy Adams*, 7 vols. (1913–1917), includes works by Adams through 1823, and additional writings are in Walter LaFeber, ed., *John Quincy Adams and American Continental Empire: Letters, Papers and Speeches*. Treaties and presidential messages are found in *American State Papers*, which are online at the Library of Congress (http://memory.loc.gov/ammem/amlaw/lwsp.html) and in print in James D. Richardson, ed., *A Compilation of the Messages and Papers of the Presidents, 1789–1897*, vol. 2 (1896–1899). Records of Adams's service as secretary of state and in various postings are among the records of the Department of State in the National Archives. Papers of President James Monroe at the Library of Congress and at the New York Public Library also contain important material from his service as secretary of state. The *Congressional Globe* contains records of Adams's activities in the House, and the supplement volumes contain several of his revised speeches.

Essential Quotes

"I rejoined that it was notorious that the Floridas had always been a burden instead of a benefit to Spain; that, so far as her interest was concerned, to obtain five millions of dollars for them would be a bargain for Onis to boast of, instead of being ashamed."

(Diary Entries on the Adams-Onís Treaty)

"I told him specially that we should contest the right of Russia to any territorial establishment on this continent, and that we should assume distinctly the principle that the American continents are no longer subjects for any new European colonial establishments."

(Diary Entries on the Monroe Doctrine)

"The great object of the institution of civil government is the improvement of the condition of those who are parties to the social compact."

(First Annual Message to Congress)

"Let us not be unmindful that liberty is power; that the nation blessed with the largest portion of liberty must in proportion to its numbers be the most powerful nation upon earth."

(First Annual Message to Congress)

"The Declaration of Independence proclaims the natural rights of man, and the constituent power of the people to be the only sources of legitimate government. State sovereignty is a mere argument of power, without regard to right—a mere reproduction of the omnipotence of the British parliament in another form, and therefore not only inconsistent with, but directly in opposition to, the principles of the Declaration of Independence."

(Jubilee of the Constitution Address)

"That the Constitution of the United States was a return to the principles of the Declaration of Independence, and the exclusive constituent power of the people. That it was the work of the ONE PEOPLE of the United States; and that those United States, though doubled in numbers, still constitute as a nation, but ONE PEOPLE."

(Jubilee of the Constitution Address)

Essential Quotes

"If he had withdrawn the petition, he would consider himself as having sacrificed the right of petition; as having sacrificed the right of habeas corpus; as having sacrificed the right of trial by jury; as having sacrificed the sacred confidence of the post office; as having sacrificed the freedom of the press; as having sacrificed the freedom of speech; as having sacrificed every element of liberty that was enjoyed by his fellow-citizens."

(Congressional Debate over Motion for Censure)

"Are not fraud and hypocrisy the religion of the man who calls himself a democrat, and holds his fellow-man in bondage?"

(Address to Constituents at Braintree)

Milestone Documents

Further Reading

Books

Bemis, Samuel Flagg. *John Quincy Adams and the Foundations of American Foreign Policy*. New York: Knopf, 1949.

———. *John Quincy Adams and the Union*. New York: Knopf, 1956.

Hargreaves, Mary W. M. *The Presidency of John Quincy Adams*. Lawrence: University Press of Kansas, 1985.

Howe, Daniel Walker. *What Hath God Wrought: The Transformation of America, 1815–1848*. New York: Oxford University Press, 2007.

Lewis, James E., Jr. *John Quincy Adams: Policymaker for the Union*. Wilmington, Del.: Scholarly Resources, 2001.

Miller, William Lee. *Arguing about Slavery: The Great Battle in the United States Congress*. New York: Knopf, 1996.

Nagel, Paul C. *John Quincy Adams: A Public Life, A Private Life*. New York: Knopf, 1997.

Richards, Leonard L. *The Life and Times of Congressman John Quincy Adams*. New York: Oxford University Press, 1986.

Wood, Gary V. *Heir to the Fathers: John Quincy Adams and the Spirit of Constitutional Government*. Lanham, Md.: Lexington Books, 2004.

Web Sites

"John Quincy Adams (1767–1848)." Miller Center of Public Affairs "American President: An Online Reference Resource" Web site. http://millercenter.org/academic/americanpresident/jqadams.

—M. Philip Lucas

Questions for Further Study

1. Although it was named after President James Monroe, under whom Adams served as secretary of state, the Monroe Doctrine was largely the creation of Adams. A statement of principle regarding U.S. foreign policy in relation to European powers and the New World, the Monroe Doctrine consists of three points: a prohibition against recolonization of former European possessions in the Western Hemisphere, a promise that the United States will stay out of European affairs, and a demand that Europe cease interference in the countries of North and South America and the Caribbean. Discuss these three points in terms of their cause (events, ideas, and examples that influenced Adams in arriving at these principles) and their effect, particularly with regard to how the United States applied the Monroe Doctrine in the years immediately following its adoption.

2. Consider a few of the critical moments in later U.S. history when the Monroe Doctrine was applied. Examples might include the discovery of the infamous Zimmermann telegram, in which Germany attempted to court an alliance with Mexico against the United States, thereby provoking a U.S. declaration of war in 1917; the Cuban missile crisis of 1962; or the Grenada invasion of 1983, sparked by a Soviet-backed revolution. How is it that a document created in 1823, with Great Britain, France, and Spain in mind, has continued to be relevant in later years, as the nation faced opposition from imperial and later Nazi Germany, Soviet Russia, and Soviet satellites in the New World?

3. The elections of 1824 and 2000 offer strange parallels: Both pitted the son of a former president (Adams and George W. Bush) against a prominent Tennessean (Andrew Jackson and Al Gore), and in both the declared winner failed to capture a clear numerical majority over his rival. Additionally, like Gore many years later, Adams became a leading opponent of the party in power once he lost to Jackson in 1828. Discuss the comparisons and contrasts between the two elections and between Adams and both Bush and Gore.

4. Adams has often been ridiculed for a passage from his first annual message to Congress in which he calls for the establishment of astronomical observatories, or "light-houses of the skies." Despite this poor analogy between lighthouses and observatories, just how wrong was Adams in his call for increased investment in science on the part of the U.S. government? Compare and contrast his ideas with those of John F. Kennedy and Lyndon B. Johnson in supporting the space program or of Al Gore and others who encouraged government involvement in the Internet.

Document Text

Diary Entries on the Adams-Onés Treaty

1819

February 3.—General Jackson came to my house this morning, and I showed him the boundary line which has been offered to the Spanish Minister.... He said there were many individuals who would take exception to our receding so far from the boundary of the Rio del Norte, which we claim, as the Sabine, and the enemies of the Administration would certainly make a handle of it to assail them: but the possession of the Floridas was of so great importance to the southern frontier of the United States, and so essential even to their safety, that the vast majority of the nation would be satisfied with the western boundary as we propose, if we obtain the Floridas....

February 15....A more formidable objection was made by Mr. Onis to my third article, containing the boundary line westward of the Mississippi. After a long and violent struggle, he had agreed to take longitude one hundred, from the Red River to the Arkansas, and latitude forty-two, from the source of the Arkansas to the South Sea. But he insisted upon having the middle of all the rivers for the boundary, and not, as I proposed, the western and southern banks; and he also insisted upon the free navigation of the rivers to be common to both nations. De Neuville urged these demands with great earnestness, and thought it was a point of honor which Onis could not abandon without humiliation....

I told him that I could see no humiliation in it. We were to agree upon a boundary, for which purpose the bank of a river was more simple and less liable to occasion future controversy than the middle of the river. It was extremely difficult to ascertain where the middle of a river throughout its course was. It would take a century to settle the middle of the Sabine, Red, and Arkansas Rivers, and to which of the parties every island in them would belong.... It was of no importance to Spain, who never would have any settlements on these rivers. But the United States would have extensive settlements upon them within a very few years....

He said Onis was exceedingly anxious upon this article, and fearful that he would be blamed in Spain for having sold the Floridas for five millions of dollars. He said there were difficulties to get over in the King's Council at Madrid as well as in the Senate of the United States. There was an influence of priests in the council, which was always counteracting the policy of the Ministers....

I rejoined that it was notorious that the Floridas had always been a burden instead of a benefit to Spain; that, so far as her interest was concerned, to obtain five millions of dollars for them would be a bargain for Onis to boast of, instead of being ashamed—as a mere pecuniary bargain, it would be a hard one to us; that as to the priests, if Onis signed the treaty without transcending his powers, it would be too late when it should reach Madrid for them to resist its ratification—and he himself had told me that he had unlimited powers....

February 22....The acquisition of the Floridas has long been an object of earnest desire to this country. The acknowledgment of a definite line of boundary to the South Sea forms a great epoch in our history. The first proposal of it in this negotiation was my own, and I trust it is now secured beyond the reach of revocation. It was not even among our claims by the Treaty of Independence with Great Britain. It was not among our pretensions under the purchase of Louisiana—for that gave us only the range of the Mississippi and its waters. I first introduced it in the written proposal of 31st October last, after having discussed verbally both with Onis and De Neuville. It is the only peculiar and appropriate right acquired by this treaty in the event of its ratification.

Glossary

Arkansas: the Arkansas River, a Mississippi tributary that flows in an easterly and southeasterly direction from present-day Colorado

De Neuville: Jean-Guillaume, baron Hyde de Neuville (1776–1857), French ambassador to the United States from 1816 to 1821

Glossary

the Floridas:	present-day Florida, at that time divided into the provinces of East and West Florida
Red River:	a tributary of the Mississippi on the border between Texas and Oklahoma
Rio del Norte:	the Rio Grande river
Sabine:	the Sabine River, on the border between present-day Texas and Louisiana
South Sea:	the Pacific Ocean
Spanish Minister:	Luis de Onés Gonzalez Vara (1762–1827), Spanish foreign minister to the United States from 1809 to 1819

Document Text

Diary Entries on the Monroe Doctrine

1823

July 17, 1823.—At the office, Baron Tuyl came, enquired if he might inform his Government that instructions would be forwarded by Mr. Hughes to Mr. Middleton for negotiating on the Northwest Coast question.... I told him specially that we should contest the right of Russia to *any* territorial establishment on this continent, and that we should assume distinctly the principle that the American continents are no longer subjects for *any* new European colonial establishments....

November 22.... I left with the President my draft for a second dispatch to R. Rush on South American affairs. And I spoke to him again urging him to abstain from everything in his message which the Holy Allies could make a pretext for construing into aggression upon them.... The ground that I wish to take is that of earnest remonstrance against the interference of European powers by force with South America, but to disclaim all interference on our part with Europe; to make an American cause, and adhere inflexibly to that....

November 25. :... I replied that, at all events, nothing that we should now do would commit us to absolute war; that Great Britain was already committed more than we; that the interest of no one of the allied powers would be promoted by the restoration of South America to Spain; that the interest of each of them was against it, and that if they could possibly agree among themselves upon a partition principle, the only possible bait they could offer to Great Britain for acceding to it was Cuba, which neither they nor Spain would consent to give her; that my reliance upon the co-operation of Great Britain rested not upon her principles, but her interest—this I thought was clear; but that my paper came in conflict with no principle which she would dare to maintain. We avowed republicanism, but we disclaimed propagandism; we asserted national independence, to which she was already fully pledged. We disavowed all interference with European affairs....

November 26.... There was another point of view, which the President had in part suggested, and which I thought highly important. Suppose the Holy Allies should attack South America, and Great Britain should resist them alone and without our cooperation. I thought this not an improbable contingency, and I believed in such a struggle the allies would be defeated and Great Britain would be victorious, by her command of the sea. But, as the independence of the South Americans would then be only protected by the guarantee of Great Britain, it would throw them completely into her arms, and in the result make them her Colonies instead of those of Spain. My opinion was, therefore, that we must act promptly and decisively.

Glossary

avowed republicanism:	supported the establishment of a government by elected leaders, as opposed to a monarchy
Baron Tuyl:	Baron Tuyl (sometimes rendered as Tuyll) van Serooskerken, Russian ambassador to the United States in 1823
Holy Allies:	Russia, Austria, and Prussia, which together formed the Holy Alliance in 1815 in an effort to preserve peace and prevent the spread of revolution in Europe
Mr. Hughes:	Christopher Hughes, American diplomat
Mr. Middleton:	Henry Middleton (1770–1846), South Carolina governor and minister to Russia (1820–1830)
Northwest Coast:	the present-day Pacific Northwest
R. Rush:	Richard Rush (1780–1859), U.S. minister to Great Britain (1817–1825)

Document Text

First Annual Message to Congress

1825

Upon this first occasion of addressing the Legislature of the Union, with which I have been honored, in presenting to their view the execution so far as it has been effected of the measures sanctioned by them for promoting the internal improvement of our country, I can not close the communication without recommending to their calm and persevering consideration the general principle in a more enlarged extent. The great object of the institution of civil government is the improvement of the condition of those who are parties to the social compact, and no government, in whatever form constituted, can accomplish the lawful ends of its institution but in proportion as it improves the condition of those over whom it is established. Roads and canals, by multiplying and facilitating the communications and intercourse between distant regions and multitudes of men, are among the most important means of improvement. But moral, political, intellectual improvement are duties assigned by the Author of Our existence to social no less than to individual man. For the fulfillment of those duties governments are invested with power, and to the attainment of the end—the progressive improvement of the condition of the governed—the exercise of delegated powers is a duty as sacred and indispensable as the usurpation of powers not granted is criminal and odious. Among the first, perhaps the very first, instrument for the improvement of the condition of men is knowledge, and to the acquisition of much of the knowledge adapted to the wants, the comforts, and enjoyments of human life public institutions and seminaries of learning are essential. So convinced of this was the first of my predecessors in this office, now first in the memory, as, living, he was first in the hearts, of our countrymen, that once and again in his addresses to the Congresses with whom he cooperated in the public service he earnestly recommended the establishment of seminaries of learning, to prepare for all the emergencies of peace and war—a national university and a military academy....

Looking back to the history only of the half century since the declaration of our independence, and observing the generous emulation with which the Governments of France, Great Britain, and Russia have devoted the genius, the intelligence, the treasures of their respective nations to the common improvement of the species in these branches of science, is it not incumbent upon us to inquire whether we are not bound by obligations of a high and honorable character to contribute our portion of energy and exertion to the common stock?... We have been partakers of that improvement and owe for it a sacred debt, not only of gratitude, but of equal or proportional exertion in the same common cause. Of the cost of these undertakings, if the mere expenditures of outfit, equipment, and completion of the expeditions were to be considered the only charges, it would be unworthy of a great and generous nation to take a second thought....

In inviting the attention of Congress to the subject of internal improvements upon a view thus enlarged it is not my design to recommend the equipment of an expedition for circumnavigating the globe for purposes of scientific research and inquiry. We have objects of useful investigation nearer home, and to which our cares may be more beneficially applied. The interior of our own territories has yet been very imperfectly explored. Our coasts along many degrees of latitude upon the shores of the Pacific Ocean, though much frequented by our spirited commercial navigators, have been barely visited by our public ships. The River of the West, first fully discovered and navigated by a countryman of our own, still bears the name of the ship in which he ascended its waters, and claims the protection of our armed national flag at its mouth. With the establishment of a military post there or at some other point of that coast, recommended by my predecessor and already matured in the deliberations of the last Congress, I would suggest the expediency of connecting the equipment of a public ship for the exploration of the whole northwest coast of this continent.

The establishment of an uniform standard of weights and measures was one of the specific objects contemplated in the formation of our Constitution, and to fix that standard was one of the powers delegated by express terms in that instrument to Congress. The Governments of Great Britain and France have scarcely ceased to be occupied with inquiries and speculations on the same subject since the existence of our Constitution....

Document Text

Connected with the establishment of an university, or separate from it, might be undertaken the erection of an astronomical observatory, with provision for the support of an astronomer, to be in constant attendance of observation upon the phenomena of the heavens, and for the periodical publication of his observations. It is with no feeling of pride as an American that the remark may be made that on the comparatively small territorial surface of Europe there are existing upward of 130 of these light-houses of the skies, while throughout the whole American hemisphere there is not one. If we reflect a moment upon the discoveries which in the last four centuries have been made in the physical constitution of the universe by the means of these buildings and of observers stationed in them, shall we doubt of their usefulness to every nation? And while scarcely a year passes over our heads without bringing some new astronomical discovery to light, which we must fain receive at second hand from Europe, are we not cutting ourselves off from the means of returning light for light while we have neither observatory nor observer upon our half of the globe and the earth revolves in perpetual darkness to our unsearching eyes?...

The Constitution under which you are assembled is a charter of limited powers. After full and solemn deliberation upon all or any of the objects which, urged by an irresistible sense of my own duty, I have recommended to your attention should you come to the conclusion that, however desirable in themselves, the enactment of laws for effecting them would transcend the powers committed to you by that venerable instrument which we are all bound to support, let no consideration induce you to assume the exercise of powers not granted to you by the people.... If these powers and others enumerated in the Constitution may be effectually brought into action by laws promoting the improvement of agriculture, commerce, and manufactures, the cultivation and encouragement of the mechanic and of the elegant arts, the advancement of literature, and the progress of the sciences, ornamental and profound, to refrain from exercising them for the benefit of the people themselves would be to hide in the earth the talent committed to our charge—would be treachery to the most sacred of trusts.

The spirit of improvement is abroad upon the earth. It stimulates the hearts and sharpens the faculties not of our fellow-citizens alone, but of the nations of Europe and of their rulers. While dwelling with pleasing satisfaction upon the superior excellence of our political institutions, let us not be unmindful that liberty is power; that the nation blessed with the largest portion of liberty must in proportion to its numbers be the most powerful nation upon earth, and that the tenure of power by man is, in the moral purposes of his Creator, upon condition that it shall be exercised to ends of beneficence, to improve the condition of himself and his fellow-men. While foreign nations less blessed with that freedom which is power than ourselves are advancing with gigantic strides in the career of public improvement, were we to slumber in indolence or fold up our arms and proclaim to the world that we are palsied by the will of our constituents, would it not be to cast away the bounties of Providence and doom ourselves to perpetual inferiority?...

Finally, fellow-citizens, I shall await with cheering hope and faithful cooperation the result of your deliberations, assured that, without encroaching upon the powers reserved to the authorities of the respective States or to the people, you will, with a due sense of your obligations to your country and of the high responsibilities weighing upon yourselves, give efficacy to the means committed to you for the common good.

Glossary

Author of Our existence:	God
career:	pursuit
common stock:	humanity in general
fain:	preferably
mechanic and ... elegant arts:	art with a practical purpose as well as art created merely for enjoyment
name of the ship:	*the Columbia Redidiva*, of which Robert Gray (1755–1806) was captain

Glossary

palsied:	paralyzed
River of the West:	the Columbia River, which flows through present-day British Columbia and Washington State
the sciences, ornamental and profound:	purely speculative or theoretical science, as well as science with a practical application
social compact:	an agreement between individuals to form a government for their mutual protection and safety
that venerable instrument:	the Constitution

Jubilee of the Constitution Address

1839

Independence was declared. The colonies were transformed into States. Their inhabitants were proclaimed to be *one people*, renouncing all allegiance to the British crown; all co-patriotism with the British nation; all claims to chartered rights as Englishmen. Thenceforth their charter was the Declaration of Independence. Their rights, the natural rights of mankind. Their government, such as should be instituted by themselves, *under the solemn mutual pledges of perpetual union*, founded on the self-evident truths proclaimed in the Declaration....

The dissolution of allegiance to the British crown, the severance of the Colonies from the British empire, and their actual existence as Independent States, thus declared of *right*, were definitively established *in fact*, by war and peace. The independence of each separate State had never been declared of *right*. It never existed *in fact*. Upon the principles of the Declaration of Independence, the dissolution of the ties of allegiance, the assumption of sovereign power, and the institution of civil government, are all acts of transcendant authority, which the people *alone* are competent to perform—and accordingly, it is in the name and by the authority of the people, that two of these acts—the dissolution of allegiance, with the severance from the British empire, and the declaration of the United Colonies, as free and independent States, were performed by that instrument.

But there still remained the last and crowning act, which *the People* of the Union alone were competent to perform—the institution of civil government, for that compound nation, the United States of America....

There was thus no congeniality of principle between the Declaration of Independence and the Articles of Confederation. The foundation of the former were a superintending Providence—the rights of man, and the constituent revolutionary power of the people. That of the latter was the sovereignty of organized power, and the independence of the separate or dis-united States....

The Declaration of Independence proclaims the natural rights of man, and the constituent power of the people to be the *only* sources of legitimate government. State sovereignty is a mere argument of power, without regard to right—a mere reproduction of the omnipotence of the British parliament in another form, and therefore not only inconsistent with, but directly in opposition to, the principles of the Declaration of Independence....

The revolution itself was a work of thirteen years—and had never been completed until that day. The Declaration of Independence and the Constitution of the United States, are parts of one consistent whole, founded upon one and the same theory of government, then new, not as a theory, for it had been working itself into the mind of man for many ages, and been especially expounded in the writings of Locke, but had never before been adopted by a great nation in practice.

There are yet, even at this day, many speculative objections to this theory. Even in our own country, there are still philosophers who deny the principles asserted in the Declaration, as self-evident truths—who deny the natural equality and inalienable rights of man—who deny that the people are the only legitimate source of power—who deny that all just powers of government are derived from the *consent* of the governed. Neither your time, nor perhaps the cheerful nature of this occasion, permit me here to enter upon the examination of this anti-revolutionary theory, which arrays state sovereignty against the constituent sovereignty of the people, and distorts the Constitution of the United States into a league of friendship between confederate corporations. I speak to matters of fact. There is the Declaration of Independence, and there is the Constitution of the United States—let them speak for themselves. The grossly immoral and dishonest doctrine of despotic state sovereignty, the exclusive judge of its own obligations, and responsible to no power on earth or in heaven, for the violation of them, is not there....

Now the *virtue* which had been infused into the Constitution of the United States, and was to give to its vital existence the stability and duration to which it was destined, was no other than the concretion of those abstract principles which had been first proclaimed in the Declaration of Independence—namely, the self-evident truths of the natural and unalienable rights of man, of the indefeasible constituent and dissolvent sovereignty of the people, always subordinate to a rule of right and wrong, and always

Document Text

responsible to the Supreme Ruler of the universe for the *rightful* exercise of that sovereign, constituent, and dissolvent power.

This was the platform upon which the Constitution of the United States had been erected. Its VIRTUES, its republican character, consisted in its conformity to the principles proclaimed in the Declaration of Independence, and as its administration must necessarily be always pliable to the fluctuating varieties of public opinion; its stability and duration by a like overruling and irresistible necessity, was to depend upon the stability and duration in the hearts and minds of the people of that virtue, or in other words, of those principles, proclaimed in the Declaration of Independence, and embodied in the Constitution of the United States....

In the calm hours of self-possession, the right of a State to nullify an act of Congress, is too absurd for argument, and too odious for discussion. The right of a state to secede from the Union, is equally disowned by the principles of the Declaration of Independence....

It has been my purpose, Fellow-Citizens, in this discourse to show:—

1. That this Union was formed by a spontaneous movement of *the people* of thirteen English Colonies....
5. That this one people did not immediately institute a government for themselves. But instead of it, their delegates in Congress, by authority from their separate state legislatures, without voice or consultation of the people, instituted a mere confederacy.
6. That this confederacy totally departed from the principles of the Declaration of Independence, and substituted instead of the constituent power of the people, an assumed sovereignty of each separate state, as the source of all its authority.
7. That as a primitive source of power, this separate state sovereignty, was not only a departure from the principles of the Declaration of Independence, but directly contrary to, and utterly incompatible with them.
8. That the tree was made known by its fruits. That after five years wasted in its preparation, the confederacy dragged out a miserable existence of eight years more, and expired like a candle in the socket, having brought the union itself to the verge of dissolution.
9. That the Constitution of the United States was a return to the principles of the Declaration of Independence, and the exclusive constituent power of the people. That it was the work of the ONE PEOPLE of the United States; and that those United States, though doubled in numbers, still constitute as a nation, but ONE PEOPLE.

And now the future is all before us, and Providence our guide.

Glossary

Articles of Confederation:	the constitution for the thirteen original U.S. states from 1777 until 1787, when it was replaced by the Constitution
concretion of those abstract principles:	the realization or establishment, in actual and physical form, of ideas
confederate corporations:	organizations or governments joined in a loose alliance
declared of *right* ... definitively established *in fact*:	rights that were given to the colonies by nature, in Adams's view, were later won through war and then made into law
Locke:	John Locke (1632–1704), English philosopher whose political ideas strongly influenced the Declaration of Independence and the U.S. Constitution
nullify:	refuse to accept the legal authority of
primitive:	not based on principles or ideals but simply on strength

Glossary

republican:	referring to a political system in which the people elect their rulers, as opposed to a monarchy or dictatorship
sovereignty of organized power:	legal rights of a nation or other state that come not from natural law but from the ability to enforce those rights by the strength of police or armies
state sovereignty:	the power of a political entity, such as a nation, to govern itself
that instrument:	the Declaration of Independence
the tree was made known by its fruits:	a reference to a statement made by Jesus in Matthew 12:33, meaning that the effects of something help to identify its cause

Document Text

Congressional Debate over Motion for Censure

1842

He [Adams] did not know how many plans they [southern congressmen] had got for excluding petitions. But that was not enough. Until gentlemen [southerners] could bring it to a point where it might bear on the members of this House, and intimidate them from the performance of their duty in presenting petitions, they could not be satisfied nor gratified. No. But if the gentlemen could get a solemn vote of this House censuring members for presenting petitions, then, they thought, this question would be settled; they thought the freemen of the North would not send petitions on any subject they thought proper to oppose. When gentlemen had got their chains on the members of the North—when the language was held to them, Ay, present your petitions, but you do it under the penalty of violating the privileges of the House—then, they thought, the matter would be ended. But he [Adams] promised them that it would *not* be ended; he promised them that they would have the people coming here (to use the expression of a sublime and lofty poet of England) "besieging, not beseeching."

If he [Adams] had withdrawn the petition, he would consider himself as having sacrificed the right of petition; as having sacrificed the right of habeas corpus; as having sacrificed the right of trial by jury; as having sacrificed the sacred confidence of the post office; as having sacrificed the freedom of the press; as having sacrificed the freedom of speech; as having sacrificed every element of liberty that was enjoyed by his fellow-citizens; because, if he had proved craven in his trust under the intimidation of the charges of the gentleman from Albemarle [Thomas Gilmer], and the gentleman from Kentucky [Thomas Marshall], never more would the House have seen a petition presented from the people of the Union, expressing their grievances in a manner that might not be pleasing to the members of the "peculiar institution," until at length the people should teach them the lesson that, however their representatives might be intimidated from the discharge of their duty, they (the people) would be their own champions, and the defenders of their own rights. *There* was the deadly character of the attempt made to put him down—to charge him as a criminal for presenting a petition. Did the gentleman from Albemarle think that *that* was the way to appease dissatisfaction and discord? Let him look to the public presses of the North upon this very transaction—from New York, or even from Philadelphia, northward—and see the opinions which they had already expressed as to the manner in which he [Adams] had been persecuted. And if that gentleman and the gentleman from Kentucky thought that this censure upon him, (Mr. A.) produced as they were attempting to produce it, would appease discord and silence discussion, they would find very different sentiments prevailing.

Glossary

Albemarle [Thomas Gilmer]:	a native of Albemarle County, Virginia, Gilmer (1802–1844), served in Congress from 1841 to 1844
besieging, not beseeching:	a play on words, meaning "attacking, not begging"
censuring:	reprimanding
habeas corpus:	Latin for "present the body"; the legal right of an accused person not to be held or detained without the opportunity of being formally charged for specific crimes
"peculiar institution":	a term often used for the practice of slavery, "peculiar" meaning unusual, distinct, or individual
sublime:	great, beautiful, and pure
Thomas Marshall:	nephew of John Marshall, chief justice of the United States; represented his Kentucky district in Congress from 1841 to 1843

Document Text

Address to Constituents at Braintree

1842

Are you incredulous of the possibility that the free representation of the North should be wheedled into the support of a system, so diametrically opposite to the first elements of true Democracy, and to the clearest interests of their own section? Mr. [Nathan] Appleton has apprised you of the charm by which New Hampshire has been converted into an anti-tariff State; and the same spell which has been of potency sufficient to fasten the Atherton gag upon the sacred right of petition, will find her equally ready to sacrifice all the inalienable rights of man to the Moloch of slavery, and to fasten, from the plunder of Mexico, ten slave-spotted States upon the Union, to settle for all time, and beyond the possibility of redemption, the preponderancy of Southern slavery over the democracy and the freedom of the North....

It is then the *sectional* division of parties, or in other words, the conflict between freedom and slavery, which constitutes the axle round which the administration of your National Government revolves. All its measures of foreign and domestic policy, are but radiations from that centre. John Tyler is a Virginian slaveholder. All the affections of his soul are bound up in the system of supporting, spreading, and perpetuating the peculiar institutions of the South. The *political* division of parties with him, and with all Southern statesmen of his stamp, is a mere instrument of power, to purchase auxiliary support to the cause of slavery, even from the freemen of the North. Democracy! Why upon what foundation can Democracy find a foothold to stand, but upon the rights of man; upon the self-evident truths of the Declaration of Independence? Democracy and Slavery?... Is not the brand of double-dealer stamped on the forehead of every democratic slaveholder? Are not fraud and hypocrisy the religion of the man who calls himself a democrat, and holds his fellow-man in bondage?

Fellow Citizens, I have opened and exposed to your view the dark chambers of the motive of Andrew Jackson, who first broached the doctrine of giving away those public lands to speculating adventurers, or to the States in which they are situated, and of John Tyler, for adhering, with such unrelenting tenacity, to the system of squandering the whole of this exhaustless treasure in the current annual expenditures of the National Administration; in doubling armies, quadrupling navies, and filching funds to buy up popular newspapers, and hungry sycophants, to pander for presidential electioneering. The motive is one, though the means are not the same. It comes from the store-house of Nullification.... It is of the same family with the war against Mexico for the annexation of Texas; with the war against England for the Island of Cuba; or to burn at the stake the self-emancipators of the Creole. Its most dreaded foes are the self-evident truths, the right of petition, the panoply of the habeas corpus, the trial by jury, the freedom of speech, of the press, and of legislative debate. The first founder of the family is SLAVERY. Its ultimate aspiration of destiny is, the dominion of the slave-ridden over the free. Its antipathy to the African slave-trade is for the monopoly of the market in human flesh. Its fearful but remorseless foreboding of the future, is the freedom of all mankind—and its abhorrence of all internal improvement by the mighty arm of the Union, is to rivet forever the manacles and fetters of the slave.

Glossary

Creole:	people of French or Spanish descent born and raised in the New World
habeas corpus:	Latin for "present the body"; the legal right of an accused person not to be held or detained without the opportunity of being formally charged for specific crimes
her:	New Hampshire
manacles and fetters:	handcuffs and ankle chains

Glossary

Moloch:	in the Old Testament, a god worshipped by Israel's neighbors through the sacrificing of children to him and thus a name used for anything that demands extreme sacrifice
Mr. [Nathan] Appleton:	a native of New Hampshire (1779–1861) who in 1842 represented a Massachusetts district in Congress, where he was known for his support of high tariffs
Nullification:	refusal by a U.S. state to enforce the laws of the federal government
pander:	to appeal to someone in a dishonorable manner
panoply:	protective armor
preponderancy:	numerical superiority
self-emancipators:	liberators
speculating adventurers:	investors whose aim is to increase their profits without regard to law or principles
stamp:	type
sycophants:	flatterers, hangers-on
tariff:	a tax or duty on imported goods
war against England for the Island of Cuba:	England won control of Cuba from Spain in 1762, but traded it for Florida in the following year.
wheedled:	influenced by pressure or nagging

Légation des Etats Unis d'Amérique
EN ANGLETERRE.
PASSEPORT.
No. 89

Signalement
Age 41 Ans
Taille 5 Pieds 8½ Pouces Anglois
Front haut
Yeux bleus
Nez droit
Bouche moyenne
Menton rond
Cheveux blonds
Teint clair
Visage rond
Signature
W Story

Le Soussigné Envoyé Extraordinaire et Ministre Plénipotentiaire des Etats Unis d'Amérique, à la Cour du Royaume Uni de la Grande Bretagne et de L'Irlande, prie tous ceux qui sont à prier de laisser surement et librement passer, et en cas de besoin de donner aide et protection à William Story allant en France

Citoyen des Etats Unis

Donné sous ma Signature, et l'Empreinte du Sceau de la Légation à Londres le 24 Juillet 1815 l'An 40. de l'Indépendance des Etats Unis.

John Quincy Adams.

LEGATION OF THE UNITED STATES OF AMERICA TO GREAT BRITAIN

1815 US passport issued by John Quincy Adams at London

In this c. 1772 portrait by John Singleton Copley, Adams points at the Massachusetts Charter, which he viewed as a constitution that protected the peoples' rights.

Samuel Adams: Original Analysis

Politician, Statesman, and Founding Father

1722–1803

Overview

Samuel Adams was born in Boston on September 16, 1722. He entered the Massachusetts House of Representatives in 1765. He became a member of the Continental Congress in 1774, signed the Declaration of Independence, and was an architect of the Articles of Confederation. He helped draft Massachusetts's 1780 Constitution. Upon retiring from Congress in 1782, he served as a state senator until becoming Massachusetts lieutenant governor in 1789. He attended the 1788 Massachusetts convention that ratified the proposed U.S. Constitution. Adams became governor upon the death of John Hancock in 1793 and was elected governor in his own right in 1794. He served as governor until 1797, when he retired from public life. He died in Boston on October 2, 1803.

Adams's lengthy political career demonstrates that eighteenth-century American politicians need not be great orators. It was his 1764 written instructions to Boston's representatives, not speeches, that helped propel Adams into the Massachusetts House. There he became famous for crafting powerful documents. As his "CANDIDUS" essay shows, he, like other politically active Americans, placed writings in newspapers to try to influence people's political decisions. And in an age when political letters regularly appeared in newspapers or were passed from hand to hand, Adams consciously fashioned letters to push his political agenda. Excerpts from speeches he gave at the Massachusetts ratifying convention show why he was noted for directness, not flowery oratory. As governor of Massachusetts, Adams used annual addresses to underscore his political ideals and to champion political programs.

The documents that Adams fashioned to attack British policies reveal a skilled politician using language to try to awaken people to what Adams once called the threat of the lurking serpent. His writings, especially those dealing with American government, show a pragmatic politician at work. Adams accepted the old adage that "politics is the art of compromise." He embraced compromise in part because he believed humans are fallible; thus, even their best political formulations will be flawed. Nevertheless, his pragmatism was always tempered by a guiding principle: One must steadfastly defend the people's natural and constitutional rights.

Explanation and Analysis of Documents

Samuel Adams's emergence as a prominent crafter of political documents began in 1764, when Britain placed direct taxes on Americans. From 1764 on, Adams consistently labored to persuade his fellow colonists to resist Britain's efforts to reshape the empire. He supported using economic boycotts to oppose the Stamp Act (1765) and the Townshend duties (1767). He seethed when Britain introduced troops into Boston in 1768 and soon decided that only independence could protect Americans' rights. Once the Revolutionary War began in 1775, Adams gave special attention to fashioning and defending central and state governments that were approved by the people and that protected their liberties.

♦ Instructions to Boston's Representatives

In 1764 the British prime minister, George Grenville, decided that the American colonists should be taxed to help the economically strapped mother country. When the Boston Town Meeting approved Adams's instructions to Boston's representatives on May 24, 1764, it became the first American governmental body to challenge Grenville's policy. The instructions are important because Adams states core arguments that many colonists were soon voicing against Britain's imperial policies.

Adams, who often repeats themes and key words in his writings, asserts that the representatives' most important task is to protect the people's fundamental *rights*. As Adams puts it, and British politicians agreed, taxes are "free Grants" from the people or their representatives. British politicians would also accept his assertion that the people must be represented in the legislature. There the agreement stopped. British politicians claimed the colonists were virtually represented. Adams insists the colonists cannot legally be taxed because they are not *directly* represented in Parliament. Following his dictum to put one's enemy in the wrong, Adams says parliamentary taxation "annihilates our Charter Right to govern & tax ourselves—It strikes at our Brittish Privileges." Underscoring the long-term dangers, Adams asks: "If our Trade may be taxed why not our Lands? Why not the Produce of our Lands & every thing we possess or make use of?" Invoking imagery that soon became commonplace in colonial writings, Adams asks: "If Taxes are laid upon us in any shape without our having a legal Representation where they are laid, are we not reduced from the Character of free Subjects to the miserable State of tributary Slaves?"

Anticipating what became another contentious issue, Adams maintains that Britain might subvert the Massachusetts judicial system. As it then worked, monarchs appointed colonial judges, but the colonial legislatures paid their salaries. Adams alludes to this point by saying that "as the Judges of the Land do depend upon the free Grants of the General Assembly for Support; It is incumbent upon you at all times to give your Voice for their honorable Maintenance." This statement not only stresses that the representatives have the power of the purse when it comes to paying judges but also raises the specter that the British might—as they later did—strip that power away.

Colonists offered pragmatic as well as philosophical attacks on Britain's taxing policy. Adams showed the way by depicting the new taxing plan as economically counterproductive. His argument rests on the assertion, which many in Britain accepted, that "it is the Trade of the Colonys, that renders them beneficial to the Mother Country." Certainly Britain's manufacturers benefit mightily because colonists buy their wares. But, says Adams, the new taxing policy will likely render the colonists unable to purchase Britain's manufactured goods. Adams's comments subtly imply that the colonists might wage economic warfare by refusing to buy British merchandise. That implied threat soon became reality. From 1765 on, colonists repeatedly used economic boycotts to attack British imperial policy.

Adams closes the instructions to the representatives by openly calling for a unified colonial resistance. Saying that all the northern colonies faced the same problems, Adams calls for "united Applications" from the colonies so that "All may happily obtain Redress." Beginning with the 1765 Stamp Act Congress, the colonial resistance movement did emphasize the need to take unified action.

♦ "CANDIDUS"

Responding to the colonists' economic boycott, Parliament repealed the Stamp Act on March 18, 1766. Parliament, however, passed the Declaratory Act the same day. It said that Parliament had and always had had the right to bind the colonies in all cases whatsoever. By 1766 the issue was less about the government's need for revenue than it was about establishing a clear precedent for such taxation. If the colonists voluntarily paid *any* tax it levied, Parliament could cite that tax as precedent, as justification for placing additional taxes on the colonists. That is why Adams applauded using an economic boycott against the 1768 Townshend duties. The effort was partially successful. In March 1770, Parliament decided to repeal every Townshend duty except one. By retaining the tea duty, Parliament effectively issued a second Declaratory Act. Given his concern about precedents, Adams wanted the boycott continued until *all* the taxes were repealed.

In the spring of 1770 there was reason to believe that Americans would be particularly concerned about protecting their rights. Responding to Boston's resistance to its imperial policies, in 1768 Britain sent soldiers to police, not protect, Boston. From the day troops arrived on October 1, Bostonians feared they would kill civilians. It happened on

Time Line

1722	September 16	■ Samuel Adams is born in Boston.
1740		■ Adams graduates from Harvard College.
1756		■ Adams becomes a Boston tax collector and serves in this post until 1765.
1764	May 24	■ In his instructions to Boston's representatives, Adams states his core arguments against Britain's new imperial policies.
1765	September 27	■ Adams is elected to the Massachusetts House.
1766	May 28	■ Adams becomes clerk of the Massachusetts House.
1771	August 19	■ In his continuing effort to stir his fellow colonists to political action, Adams writes his fifth essay under the pen name "CANDIDUS."
1774	September–October	■ Adams attends the First Continental Congress.
1775	May 10	■ Adams joins the Second Continental Congress.
1776	January 7	■ In a letter to James Warren, Adams emphasizes his belief that a standing army endangers liberties.
1780		■ Adams serves in the Massachusetts constitutional convention.
1781	April	■ Adams retires from the Confederation Congress.
1782	February 20	■ Adams becomes president of the Massachusetts Senate.
1784	April 30	■ Writing to Noah Webster in support of Congress's vote to extend full pay to army officers for five years, Adams stresses that in a free America the rule of law must prevail.

Time Line

1787	December 3	■ In a letter to Richard Henry Lee, Adams gives some of the reasons why he (and other Americans) disliked the proposed new constitution that had been drafted by the Constitutional Convention.
1788	January–February	■ Adams attends the Massachusetts ratifying convention.
1788	February 1 and 6	■ Adams speaks to the Massachusetts ratifying convention in support of a compromise to the passage of the new constitution, whereby amendments to the constitution would limit the power of the central government and protect people's basic liberties.
	December	■ Adams loses his race to become a member of the U.S. House of Representatives.
1789	May 27	■ Adams becomes lieutenant governor of Massachusetts.
1793	October 8	■ Adams becomes governor of Massachusetts upon the death of John Hancock.
1794	May	■ Adams is elected governor of Massachusetts.
1795	January 16	■ As governor, Adams gives a state of the commonwealth address in which he states his core political ideals and emphasizes his commitment to protect constitutional governments that rest on the authority of the citizens.
1797	May	■ Adams retires from the governorship.
1803	October 2	■ Adams dies in Boston.

March 5, 1770, when British soldiers fired into a crowd. Three civilians were killed; eight were wounded, and two of them later died. Although it seemed that resistance to Britain would escalate in the wake of this "Boston Massacre," just the opposite happened. The boycott collapsed; the resistance movement withered.

Adams employed newspapers, the American media of the eighteenth century, to try to awaken his fellow colonists from their political lethargy. He adopted the clever pen name "CANDIDUS" for one of the many series of essays he produced for the *Boston Gazette*. The fifth "CANDIDUS" essay appeared on August 19, 1771. It illustrates how Adams used recent history. He praises an influential Boston crowd action of August 14, 1765, that forced the resignation of the man scheduled to distribute stamps in Massachusetts under the Stamp Act. "The *People* shouted; and their shout was heard to the distant end of this Continent." All true Americans should, says Adams, remember that these heroes were "animated with a zeal for their country then upon the brink of destruction, and resolved, at once to save her." The message is clear: People can protect their rights by taking bold, direct action.

Adams also underscores the importance of precedent. If the people "are voluntarily silent while the single duty on tea is continued," then "we are in extreme hazard; if ever we are so distracted as to consent to it, we are undone." By alluding to Britain's responses to earlier petitions, Adams calls for bolder action than petitioning: "When we petition'd, and remonstrated our grievances: What was the Consequence? Still further indignity; and finally a formal invasion of this town by a fleet and army in the memorable year 1768." In spite of such arguments and Adams's continuing efforts, the resistance movement did not again gain real strength until Parliament made the mistake of passing the Tea Act of May 1773, which raised the specter that Great Britain would destroy American business through the creation of monopolies.

♦ Letter to James Warren

Eighteenth-century politicians steeped in British political traditions agreed that a standing army endangered liberty. Adams repeatedly emphasized this view in his writings. As he put it in a January 7, 1776, letter to James Warren, a political ally and Massachusetts legislator who was one of the leading supporters of the independence movement in the state, "A standing Army, however necessary it may be at some times, is always dangerous to the Liberties of the People." Clearly, 1776 was a time when America needed a standing army, but that reality did not lessen the danger. Adams uses the letter to Warren to explain why a standing army is dangerous and to suggest how Americans can counter the threat.

A standing army is dangerous, says Adams, because "soldiers are apt to consider themselves as a Body distinct from the rest of the Citizens." Soldiers have weapons, are tightly controlled, and usually do whatever their officers command them to do. In sum, soldiers often develop a military way of thinking. It follows that soldiers "should be watchd with a jealous Eye." Adams stresses that if the war against Britain is lengthy, even American soldiers might "lose the Spirit and Feeling of Citizens."

Adams offers an antidote to a standing army. That antidote is a militia system. Adams maintains that because they are "free Citizens" militiamen would not use their military

power to destroy their own rights. And free citizens would never allow others to attack their rights. For Adams, it follows that the militia is a free country's "natural Strength."

Adams suggests how Massachusetts can do even more to protect America from the military mindset. Young Massachusetts men with military potential should be "instructed in the Art of War." But, at the same time, they should be "taught the Principles of a free Government, and deeply impressd with a Sense of the indispensible Obligation which every member is under to the whole Society." Although Adams's plan was not enacted, it, like his praise for a militia system, reveals his technique of using letters to explain his ideals and to push a political agenda.

♦ Letter to Noah Webster

By 1784 Americans had won independence and established a central government under the Articles of Confederation. In addition, each state had its own constitution. Adams always said that he became a Revolutionary to protect the people's established constitutional and natural rights. He always insisted that unless tyranny forced them to do otherwise, the people must follow the rule of law. So, in 1784, he saw himself not as a Revolutionary but as a defender of America's constitutional governments. On April 30, 1784, writing to Noah Webster, a Connecticut educator and staunch supporter of the American Revolution, Adams explains why he supports Congress's controversial vote to give army officers full pay for five years. Because Adams originally opposed giving officers special pay, some guessed that he would oppose Congress's action. But Adams argues that since the pledge "was made in behalf of the United States by their Representative authorizd to do it, each State was bound in Justice & Honor to comply with it." Thus Adams emphasizes that in a free America the rule of law must prevail.

Adams's desire to protect the rule of law led him to comment on the way some people challenged Congress's vote on officers' pay. Protestors formed popular committees and conventions, the very instruments Adams had employed against the British in the 1760s and 1770s. Adams defends the earlier committees and conventions because they protected constitutional rights. The modern committees and conventions are, he holds, fundamentally different. By promoting "Discord & Animosity," they can undermine constitutional government. The people should watch public officials carefully. "Such Attention is the Peoples great Security. But there is Decency & Respect due to Constitutional Authority, and those Men, who under any Pretence or by any Means whatever, would lessen the Weight of Government lawfully exercised, must be Enemies to our happy Revolution & the Common Liberty."

♦ Letter to Richard Henry Lee

The Articles of Confederation, approved in 1781, were designed to prevent the central government from threatening the people's liberties. That is why the Articles declared that each state retained its sovereignty and that Congress could exercise only those powers "expressly" given to it. Adams did not want to see these aspects of the Articles changed. Still, like most political leaders, Adams soon conceded that Congress needed additional powers. However, he opposed the idea of creating a new constitution because he feared it would contain vague language. Vague wording, he warned in 1785, might allow those individuals who wanted a consolidated national government to achieve their goal. When the Constitutional Convention of 1787 issued its proposed constitution, Adams did not like what he read. Using the established procedure of crafting letters for political purposes, he wrote to Richard Henry Lee of Virginia on December 3, 1787. Lee and Adams, who had served together in the Continental Congress and were old friends, wanted to strengthen, not destroy, the Articles.

Adams's letter provides some of the reasons why approximately half of the American people opposed the proposed constitution. Adams was especially bothered by the proposed government's national, not state, focus. That is why he opens by writing: "I confess, as I enter the Building I stumble at the Threshold. I meet with a National Government, instead of a Federal Union of Sovereign States." Reflecting what was then a common political theory, Adams argues that the Union is physically too large and too diverse to have one national legislature. He warns that one all-powerful national legislature would "be highly dangerous, and destructive of the Peace Union and Safety of the Nation."

The proposed constitution is, says Adams, the culmination of an ongoing conspiracy. As he speaks of the conspiracy and pleads with the people to oppose it, Adams uses a powerfully pejorative term—"aristocracy." In today's parlance, Adams plays the aristocracy card. In sentences crafted for wide circulation, Adams claims that "the Seeds of Aristocracy began to spring even before the Conclusion of our Struggle for the natural Rights of Men, Seeds which like a Canker Worm lie at the Root of free Governments." He warns that "the few haughty Families, think *They* must govern. The Body of the People tamely consent & submit to be their Slaves." The protection of individual state sovereignty enshrined in the Articles must be defended, says Adams, to stop the few from destroying the liberties of the many.

♦ Massachusetts Ratifying Convention Speeches

Samuel Adams clearly disliked the proposed constitution. That is why its supporters expressed dismay when he was elected to the Massachusetts ratifying convention that began deliberations in January 1788. Although he had reservations about the proposed constitution, Adams also believed that the central government must have more power, lest the Union disintegrate. So he agreed to a compromise. Adams and John Hancock, president of the convention, agreed to vote for ratification so that a more vigorous government could soon be in place. For their part, the constitution's advocates promised to work to add amendments, a Bill of Rights, once the new government began functioning. Adams argued that if Massachusetts ratified based on such

a promise, other states would follow suit. They, too, would ratify with recommendations for adding amendments that would protect the people's liberties. That is what happened.

On February 1, Adams supported the compromise only because he anticipated getting an amendment limiting the central government to those powers "expressly" stated in the constitution. Adams wanted that wording because of his fear, which turned out to be well founded, that politicians would use vague wording in the constitution to increase the national government's power.

On February 6, Adams tried to do even more to protect basic liberties. He offered a list of basic rights—such as "the just liberty of the press" and "the rights of conscience"—that would be protected. When some convention members balked, Adams withdrew his proposal. Still, a comparison of Adams's recommendations and the amendments added to the Constitution in 1791 is revealing. It shows that Adams listed many of the rights and liberties eventually incorporated into the Bill of Rights.

♦ Address to the Massachusetts Legislature

As executives traditionally do, Governor Adams used annual addresses to express ideals and advocate specific programs. His state of the commonwealth address on January 16, 1795, emphasizes many of Adams's core political ideals and trumpets, in particular, his commitment to protect constitutional governments that rest on the authority of the citizens.

Long before 1795 Adams proclaimed that voting was not just a right but a duty. Asserting that "elections are the immediate acts of the people's sovereignty," Adams repeats an argument he had made time and again: People should vote thoughtfully and for the public good. Adams underscores the importance of elections in a free country by saying that "the purity of the government, and consequently the safety and welfare of the citizens" depends "upon free and unbiased elections."

Adams had also long asserted that education played a vital role in maintaining a republican form of government. He spoke of supporting education in each of his annual addresses. In this address he both paraphrases and quotes from the Massachusetts constitution he helped draft. Adams reminds the legislators that they should establish "such modes of education as tend to inculcate in the minds of youth, the feelings and habits of 'piety, religion and morality,' and to lead them to the knowledge and love of those truly Republican principles upon which our civil institutions are founded."

The 1795 address is particularly significant because of how Adams responded to the Whiskey Rebellion. In 1794 people living in western Pennsylvania resorted to violence to stop collection of the onerous 25 percent tax on the production of whiskey. They assaulted tax collectors, stopped mail deliveries, and disrupted courts. The national government sent several thousand soldiers to quell the violence. By the time they arrived, the Whiskey Rebellion had evaporated. All of these events happened at a time when national political parties were emerging in America. The Federalist Party controlled the national government. The Democratic Republicans, who drew strength from areas such as western Pennsylvania, were headed by Thomas Jefferson; Samuel Adams was a leader of the party in Massachusetts. Jefferson called the Whiskey Rebellion insignificant. Adams did not. He stresses that Americans have a ready constitutional remedy for any perceived grievance; they can vote. Given this power, "What excuse then can there be for forcible opposition to the laws?" Having pointed out the danger, Adams expresses optimism about the future of America's republicanism. "The virtuous and enlightened citizens of this Commonwealth, and of all united America," says Adams, "have understanding and firmness, sufficient to support those Constitutions of Civil Government which they have themselves formed, and which have done them so much honor in the estimation of the world."

Impact and Legacy

Samuel Adams's contemporaries, both friend and foe, considered him one of the principal leaders of the movement that made America independent. They also agreed that his writings and determination, rather than his oratorical skills, made him so important. He was praised—or damned—for his ability to craft powerful political missives that uncompromisingly championed what were considered the colonists' fundamental rights. In an era when flowery language was common in political discourse, Adams produced a clearer, often simpler prose. Adams used history, including recent history, to convey a sense of immediacy. Because Adams believed that people would take bold action only if they thought their rights were being violated, his documents offered telling phrases that emphasized what he called first principles. Adams's writings reveal that he was a politician who tried, albeit unsuccessfully, to persuade or shame his fellow colonists into being politically consistent in their opposition to Britain.

Adams has been called America's first modern politician in part because he was especially adept at using the eighteenth-century media to emphasize what were "hot button" issues. Indeed, one of the reasons Adams's writings were considered powerful is, as he liked to say, that he put and kept his enemy in the wrong. During the movement for independence, Adams's political opponents routinely moaned about his ability to savage their reputations. Modern politicians who specialize in the typically hated, but often effective, technique of slinging mud continue a practice at which Adams excelled.

Adams's political writings have a special legacy because they remind us of some timeless realities of American government. His desire to limit the power of the central government and to accentuate the power of the states still resonates with many Americans. His often-stated view that the people should protect liberty by keeping a watchful eye on their elected officials is as relevant today as it was in the

eighteenth century. Equally relevant is his denunciation of the use of violence to challenge laws that can be changed by voting. And there is a timelessness to his argument that there is a "Decency & Respect due to Constitutional Authority." Adams's writings reveal that his ultimate legacy is this: He was one of the leaders of America's greatest generation—the generation that achieved American independence and created written constitutions for the states and nation that made the ideal of republican government a living reality.

Key Sources

The major collection of Adams manuscripts, the Samuel Adams Papers housed in the New York Public Library, are available on microfilm. Harry A. Cushing, ed., *The Writings of Samuel Adams*, 4 vols. (1904–1908), is essential but less than complete. The last three Cushing volumes can be accessed online at http://onlinebooks.library.upenn.edu/webbin/gutbook/author?name=Adams%2C%20Samuel%2C%201722-1803.

Essential Quotes

"It is the Trade of the Colonys, that renders them beneficial to the Mother Country."

(Instructions to Boston's Representatives)

"If Taxes are laid upon us in any shape without our having a legal Representation where they are laid, are we not reduced from the Character of free Subjects to the miserable State of tributary Slaves?"

(Instructions to Boston's Representatives)

"The People *shouted; and their shout was heard to the distant end of this Continent."*

("CANDIDUS")

"A standing Army, however necessary it may be at some times, is always dangerous to the Liberties of the People."

(Letter to James Warren)

"It is prudent for the People to keep a watchful Eye over the Conduct of all those who are entrusted with Publick Affairs. Such Attention is the Peoples great Security. But there is Decency & Respect due to Constitutional Authority, and those Men, who under any Pretence or by any Means whatever, would lessen the Weight of Government lawfully exercised, must be Enemies to our happy Revolution & the Common Liberty."

(Letter to Noah Webster)

Essential Quotes

"I confess, as I enter the Building I stumble at the Threshold. I meet with a National Government, instead of a Federal Union of Sovereign States."

(Letter to Richard Henry Lee)

"So great is the Wickedness of some Men, & the stupid Servility of others, that one would be almost inclined to conclude that Communities cannot be free. The few haughty Families, think They *must govern. The Body of the People tamely consent & submit to be their Slaves. This unravels the Mystery of Millions being enslaved by the few!"*

(Letter to Richard Henry Lee)

"I have long considered the watchfulness of the people over the conduct of their rulers, the strongest guard against the encroachments of power; and I hope the people of this country will always be thus watchful."

(Massachusetts Ratifying Convention Speeches)

"All elections ought to be free, and every qualified elector who feels his own independence as he ought, will act his part according to his best, and most enlightened judgment. Elections are the immediate acts of the people's sovereignty, in which no foreigners should be allowed to intermeddle. Upon free and unbiased elections, the purity of the government, and consequently the safety and welfare of the citizens, may I not say altogether depend."

(Address to the Massachusetts Legislature)

"No people can be more free under a Constitution established by their own voluntary compact, and exercised by men appointed by their own frequent suffrages. What excuse then can there be for forcible opposition to the laws? If any law shall prove oppressive in its operation, the future deliberations of a freely elective Representative, will afford a constitutional remedy."

(Address to the Massachusetts Legislature)

Further Reading

Books

Alexander, John K. *Samuel Adams: America's Revolutionary Politician*. Lanham, Md.: Rowman & Littlefield, 2002.

Brown, Richard D. *Revolutionary Politics in Massachusetts: The Boston Committee of Correspondence and the Towns, 1772–1774*. Cambridge, Mass.: Harvard University Press, 1970.

Fowler, William M., Jr. *Samuel Adams: Radical Puritan*. New York: Longman, 1997.

Miller, John C. *Sam Adams: A Pioneer in Propaganda*. Boston: Little, Brown, 1936.

Wells, William V. *The Life and Public Services of Samuel Adams*. 3 vols. Boston: Little, Brown, 1865.

—John K. Alexander

Questions for Further Study

1. In numerous writings, most notably his 1776 letter to James Warren, Adams maintained that a standing army—that is, a military force composed of professional soldiers rather than civilian draftees or volunteers—posed a threat to liberty. Rather than a standing army, Adams recommended the establishment of militias, or armies composed of citizen volunteers. What are the merits of this argument? Consider, for instance, the experience of ancient Rome, whose government was often under threat from politically ambitious men, such as Julius Caesar, who manipulated standing armies for their own purposes by appealing to soldiers' greed. Also notable are modern examples from various countries in Africa, Latin America, and Asia, where the political independence of the military has often assisted dictators in seizing power. On the other hand, what are the disadvantages of *not* having a standing army?

2. Although Adams did not coin the phrases "No taxation without representation" or "Taxation without representation is tyranny," those statements are very much in line with the political philosophy he expressed in numerous writings, including his instructions to Boston's representatives. Examine Adams's arguments on this issue, and consider the effects that he claimed would result from taxation without representation—not just popular discontent with British rule but a situation in which colonists would be unable to afford manufactured goods from Britain. Many modern critics of the federal government blame Washington for taxing the American people without genuinely representing their interests. How valid is this argument?

3. Because of his ability to make use of the news media that existed in his time, Adams has been called the first modern politician in American history. This is particularly notable because he was not known as an especially powerful speaker. Compare and contrast his use of media (which in his time consisted primarily of newspapers) with that of a modern politician's. Pay special attention to the technique of "putting and keeping his enemy in the wrong," which Adams himself noted as one of his greatest rhetorical strengths.

Instructions to Boston's Representatives

1764

Your being chosen by the Freeholders & Inhabitants of the Town of Boston to represent them in the General Assembly the ensuing year, affords you the strongest Testimony of that Confidence which they place in your Integrity & Capacity. By this Choice they have delegated to you the Power of acting in their publick Concerns in general as your own Prudence shall direct you; always reserving to themselves the constitutional Right of expressing their mind & giving you fresh Instruction upon particular Matters as they at any time shall judge proper.

We therefore your Constituents take this opportunity to declare our just Expectations from you.

That you will constantly use your Power & Influence in maintaining the invaluable Rights & Privileges of the Province, of which this Town is so great a Part: As well those Rights which are derivd to us by the royal Charter, as those which being prior to & independent on it, we hold essentially as free born Subjects of Great Brittain. …

As the Preservation of Morals as well as Property & Right, so much depends upon the impartial Distribution of Justice, agreable to good & wholesom Law: and as the Judges of the Land do depend upon the free Grants of the General Assembly for Support; It is incumbent upon you at all times to give your Voice for their honorable Maintenance so long as they, having in their minds an Indifference to all other Affairs, shall devote themselves wholly to the Duties of their own Department, and the further Study of the Law, by which their Customs Precedents Proceedings & Determinations are adjusted & limited.

You will joyn in any Proposals which may be made for the better cultivating the Lands & improving the Husbandry of the Province: And as you represent a Town which lives by its Trade we expect in a very particular Manner that you make it the Object of your Attention, to support our Commerce in all its just Rights, to vindicate it from all unreasonable Impositions & promote its Prosperity—Our Trade has for a long time labord under great Discouragements; & it is with the deepest Concern that we see such further Difficultys coming upon it as will reduce it to the lowest Ebb, if not totally obstruct & ruin it. We cannot help expressing our Surprize, that when so early Notice was given by the Agent of the Intentions of the Ministry to burthen us with new Taxes, so little Regard was had to this most interesting Matter, that the Court was not even called together to consult about it till the latter end of ye Year; the Consequence of which was, that Instructions could not be sent to the Agent, tho sollicited by him, till the Evil had got beyond an easy Remedy. There is now no Room for further Delay: We therefore expect that you will use your earliest Endeavors in the Genl Assembly, that such Methods may be taken as will effectually prevent these Proceedings against us. By a proper Representation we apprehend it may easily be made to appear that such Severitys will prove detrimental to Great Brittain itself; upon which Account we have Reason to hope that an Application, even for a Repeal of the Act, should it be already passd, will be successfull. It is the Trade of the Colonys, that renders them beneficial to the Mother Country: Our Trade, as it is now, & always has been conducted, centers in Great Brittain, & in Return for her Manufactures affords her more ready Cash, beyond any Comparison, than can possibly be expected by the most sanguine Promoters of these extraordinary Methods. We are in short ultimately yielding large Supplys to the Revenues of the Mother Country, while we are laboring for a very moderate Subsistence for ourselves. But if our Trade is to be curtaild in its most profitable Branches, & Burdens beyond all possible Bearing, laid upon that which is sufferd to remain, we shall be so far from being able to take off the manufactures of Great Brittain, that it will be scarce possible for us to earn our Bread.—But what still heightens our apprehensions is, that these unexpected Proceedings may be preparatory to new Taxations upon us: For if our Trade may be taxed why not our Lands? Why not the Produce of our Lands & every thing we possess or make use of? This we apprehend annihilates our Charter Right to govern & tax ourselves—It strikes at our Brittish Privileges, which as we have never forfeited them, we hold in common with our Fellow Subjects who are Natives of Brittain: If Taxes are laid upon us in any shape without our having a legal Representation where they are laid, are we not reduced from the Character of free Subjects to the miserable State of tributary Slaves?

Document Text

We therefore earnestly recommend it to you to use your utmost Endeavors, to obtain in the Genl Assembly all necessary Instructions & Advice to our Agent at this most critical Juncture; that while he is setting forth the unshaken Loyalty of this Province & this Town—its unrivald Exertions in supporting His Majestys Governmt & Rights in this part of his Dominions—its acknowlegd Dependence upon & Subordination to Great Brittain, & the ready Submission of its Merchants to all just & necessary Regulations of Trade, he may be able in the most humble & pressing Manner to remonstrate for us all those Rights & Privileges which justly belong to us either by Charter or Birth.

As His Majestys other Northern American Colonys are embarkd with us in this most important Bottom, we further desire you to use your Endeavors, that their Weight may be added to that of this Province: that by the united Applications of all who are aggrievd, All may happily obtain Redress—

Glossary

apprehend:	understand
Bottom:	underlying aim or principle
burthen:	burden
Constituents:	persons represented by another, particularly in politics
curtaild:	curtailed, or reduced
free Grants:	voluntary support
Freeholders:	landowners
General Assembly:	the Massachusetts legislature
Genl:	general
Governmt:	government
Husbandry:	agriculture
Indifference to all other Affairs:	lack of personal stake or interest in anything other than the law
royal Charter:	the document that established Massachusetts as a British colony in 1691
sanguine:	enthusiastic
sufferd:	suffered, or allowed
the Province:	Massachusetts
their honorable Maintenance:	the support of judges appointed by the General Assembly
tho sollicited:	though solicited, or sought
united applications of all who are aggrievd:	collective requests or demands of all who feel that they have been wronged
vindicate it from all unreasonable Impositions:	protect it from all unfair demands
ye:	archaic form of "the"

"Candidus"

1771

For my own part, I cannot but at present be of opinion, and "*I have reason to believe* " that my opinion is well founded, that the measures of the British administration of the colonies, are still as disgustful and *odious* to the inhabitants of this respectable metropolis in general, as they ever have been: And I will venture further to add, that nothing, in my opinion, can convey a more unjust idea of the spirit of a true American, than to suppose he would even compliment, much less make an *adulating address* to any person sent here to trample on the Rights of his Country; or that he would ever condescend to kiss the hand which is ready prepared to rivet his own fetters—There are among us, it must be confess'd, needy expectants and dependents; and a few others of sordid and base minds, form'd by nature to bend and crouch even to *little* great men:—But whoever thinks, that by the most refined art and assiduous application of the most ingenious *political* oculist, the "public eye" can yet look upon the chains which are forg'd for them, or upon those detestable men who are employ'd to put them on, without abhorrence and indignation, are very much mistaken—I only wish that my Countrymen may be upon their guard against being led by the artifices of the tools of Administration, into any indiscreet measures, from whence they may take occasion to give such a coloring.hellip;

We cannot surely have forgot the accursed designs of a most detestable set of men, to destroy the Liberties of America as with one blow, by the Stamp-Act; nor the noble and successful efforts we then made to divert the impending stroke of ruin aimed at ourselves and our posterity. The Sons of Liberty on the 14th of August 1765, a Day which ought to be for ever remembered in America, animated with a zeal for their country then upon the brink of destruction, and resolved, at once to save her, or like *Samson,* to perish in the ruins, exerted themselves with such distinguished vigor, as made the house of *Dogon* to shake from its very foundation; and the hopes of the *lords of the Philistines* even while *their hearts were merry,* and when they were anticipating the joy of plundering this continent, were at that very time buried in the pit they had digged. The *People* shouted; and their shout was heard to the distant end of this Continent. In each Colony they deliberated and resolved, and every *Stampman* trembled; and swore by his Maker, that he would never execute a commission which he had so *infamously* received.

We cannot have forgot, that at the very Time when the stamp-act was repealed, another was made in which the Parliament of Great-Britain declared, that they had right and authority to make any laws whatever binding on his Majesty's subjects in America— How far this declaration can be consistent with the freedom of his Majesty's subjects in America, let any one judge who pleases—In consequence of such right and authority claim'd, the commons of Great Britain very soon fram'd a bill and sent it up to the Lords, wherein they pray'd his Majesty to accept of *their grant* of such a part as they were then pleas'd, by virtue of the right and authority *inherent* in them to make, of the property of his Majesty's subjects in America, by a duty upon paper, glass, painter's colours and tea. And altho' these duties are in part repeal'd, there remains enough to answer the purpose of administration, which was *to fix the precedent* . We remember the policy of Mr. Grenville, who would have been content for the present with *a pepper corn establish'd as a revenue in America* : If therefore we are voluntarily silent while the single duty on tea is continued, or do any act, however innocent, *simply considered,* which may be construed by the tools of administration, (some of whom appear to be fruitful in invention) as an acquiescence in the measure, we are in extreme hazard; if ever we are so distracted as to consent to it, we are undone.

Nor can we ever forget the indignity and abuse with which America in general, and this province and town in particular, have been treated, by the servants & officers of the crown, for making a manly resistance to the arbitrary measures of administration, in the representations that have been made to the men in power at home, who have always been dispos'd to believe every word as infallible truth. For opposing a *threatned Tyranny,* we have been not only called, but in effect adjudged *Rebels & Traitors* to the best of Kings, who has sworn to maintain and defend the *Rights* and *Liberties* of his Subjects—We have been

Document Text

represented as inimical to our fellow subjects in Britain, because we have boldly asserted those Rights and Liberties, wherewith they, as Subjects, are made free.—When we complain'd of this injurious treatment; when we petition'd, and remonstrated our grievances: What was the Consequence? Still further indignity; and finally a formal invasion of this town by a fleet and army in the memorable year 1768.

Glossary

acquiescence in the measure:	the act of giving in to a policy
animated:	given life
answer the purpose of administration:	serve the needs of government
artifices:	clever deceptions
Candidus:	a pen name making reference to a Latin word meaning "clear"
coloring:	a response or opinion
commons:	the House of Commons, which along with the House of Lords makes up the British parliament
Dogon:	a deity, sometimes known as Dagon, worshipped by enemies of Israel in the Old Testament
duty:	tax
execute a commission:	perform a job
fix the precedent:	establish a response to a particular situation that will serve as a guide to dealing with future occurrences of the same situation
forg'd:	forged, or given form; typically used in reference to metals
fruitful in invention:	capable of twisting facts
Mr. Grenville:	the British prime minister George Grenville (1712–1770)
painter's colours:	paint, especially that used for practical purposes such as painting a house
a pepper corn establish'd as a revenue:	a very small tax
Philistines:	a nation with whom the Israelites were frequently at war in the Old Testament
remonstrated our grievances:	made our complaints known
rivet:	fasten or attach
Samson:	judge or leader of Israel, known for his physical strength, whose story is told in the biblical book of Judges
sordid and base:	scandalous and low-minded
Stampman:	tax collector for the British in colonial America
undone:	finished or destroyed

Document Text

Letter to James Warren

1776

MY DEAR SIR—

I verily believe the Letters I write to you are three, to one I receive from you—however I consider the Multiplicity of Affairs you must attend to in your various Departments, and am willing to make due Allowance. Your last is dated the 19th of December. It contains a List of very important Matters lying before the General Assembly. I am much pleased to find that there is an End to the Contest between the two Houses concerning the Establishment of the Militia—and that you are in hopes of making an effectual Law for that Purpose. It is certainly of the last Consequence to a free Country that the Militia, which is its natural Strength, should be kept upon the most advantageous Footing. A standing Army, however necessary it may be at some times, is always dangerous to the Liberties of the People. Soldiers are apt to consider themselves as a Body distinct from the rest of the Citizens. They have their Arms always in their hands. Their Rules and their Discipline is severe. They soon become attachd to their officers and disposd to yield implicit Obedience to their Commands. Such a Power should be watchd with a jealous Eye. I have a good Opinion of the principal officers of our Army. I esteem them as Patriots as well as Soldiers. But if this War continues, as it may for years yet to come, we know not who may succeed them. Men who have been long subject to military Laws and inured to military Customs and Habits, may lose the Spirit and Feeling of Citizens. And even Citizens, having been used to admire the Heroism which the Commanders of their own Army have displayd, and to look up to them as their Saviors may be prevaild upon to surrender to them those Rights for the protection of which against Invaders they had employd and paid them. We have seen too much of this Disposition among some of our Countrymen. The Militia is composd of free Citizens. There is therefore no Danger of their making use of their Power to the destruction of their own Rights, or suffering others to invade them. I earnestly wish that young Gentlemen of a military Genius (& many such I am satisfied there are in our Colony) might be instructed in the Art of War, and at the same time taught the Principles of a free Government, and deeply impressd with a Sense of the indispensible Obligation which every member is under to the whole Society. These might be in time fit for officers in the Militia, and being thorowly acquainted with the Duties of Citizens as well as soldiers, might be entrusted with a Share in the Command of our Army at such times as Necessity might require so dangerous a Body to exist.

Glossary

Disposition:	attitude
inured:	accustomed
last Consequence:	greatest importance
Militia:	an army composed of citizens rather than professional soldiers
Multiplicity:	a great number
standing Army:	a full-time, professional army, as opposed to one composed of draftees called up on short notice
suffering:	allowing
thorowly:	thoroughly
verily:	honestly or truly

Letter to Noah Webster

1784

SIR

...Some time in the Month of September last, a Gentleman in Connecticutt requested me to give him my Opinion of a Subject, perhaps too much altercated in that State as well as this, The Commutation of half Pay granted by Congress to the Officers of the late Army for Life for full Pay during the Term of five years. I did not hesitate to say in Return, that in my Opinion Congress was, in the Nature of their Appointment, the sole Judge of the necessary Means of supporting the late Army raised for the Defence of our Common Rights against the Invasions of Great Britain; and if, upon their own deliberate Councils & the repeated Representations of the Commander in Chiefe of the Army, they judgd that the Grant of half Pay for Life was a Measure absolutely necessary for the Support of a disciplined Army for the Purpose before mentiond, they had an undoubted Right to make it; and as it was made in behalf of the United States by their Representative authorizd to do it, each State was bound in Justice & Honor to comply with it, even tho it should seem to any to have been an ill judgd Measure; because States & Individual Persons are equally bound to fulfill their Obligations, and it is given as Characteristick of an honest Man, that "though he sweareth (or promiseth) to his own hurt he changeth not." I moreover acquainted him, that although I was never pleasd with the Idea of half Pay for Life, for Reasons which appeard satisfactory to myself, some of which I freely explaind to him, yet I had always thought, that as the Opportunities of the Officers of the Army of acquiring moderate Fortunes or making such Provision for their Families as Men generally wish to make, were not equal to those of their Fellow Citizens at home, it would be but just & reasonable, that an adequate Compensation should be made to them at, or as soon as conveniently might be after, the End of the War; and that he might therefore conclude, that the Commutation, if it be an adequate Compensation had fully coincided with my Ideas of Justice & Policy.

Nothing was mentiond in his Letter to me, of the Nature or the Proceedings of County Conventions, & therefore I made no Observation upon them. I hope it will not be in the Power of any designing Men, by imposing upon credulous tho' well meaning Persons long to keep this Country, who may be happy if they will, long in a State of Discord & Animosity. We may see, from the present State of Great Britain, how rapidly such a Spirit will drive a Nation to destruction. It is prudent for the People to keep a watchful Eye over the Conduct of all those who are entrusted with Publick Affairs. Such Attention is the Peoples great Security. But there is Decency & Respect due to Constitutional Authority, and those Men, who under any Pretence or by any Means whatever, would lessen the Weight of Government lawfully exercised, must be Enemies to our happy Revolution & the Common Liberty. County Conventions & popular Committees servd an excellent Purpose when they were first in Practice. No one therefore needs to regret the Share he may then have had in them. But I candidly own it is my Opinion, with Deferrence to the Opinions of other Men, that as we now have constitutional & regular Governments and all our Men in Authority depend upon the annual & free Elections of the People, we are safe without them. To say the least, they are become useless. Bodies of Men, under any Denomination whatever, who convene themselves for the Purpose of deliberating upon & adopting Measures which are cognizable by Legislatures only will, if continued, bring Legislatures to Contempt & Dissolution. If the publick Affairs are illy conducted, if dishonest or incapable Men have crept unawares into Government, it is happy for us, that under our American Constitutions the Remedy is at hand, & in the Power of the great Body of the People. Due Circumspection & Wisdom at the next Elections will set all right, without the Aid of any self Created Conventions or Societies of Men whatever. While we retain those simple Democracies in all our Towns which are the Basis of our State Constitutions, and make a good Use of them, it appears to me we cannot be enslaved or materially injured. It must however be confessd, that Imperfection attends all human affairs.

Glossary

altercated:	fought over
attends:	is part of, or associated with
candidly own:	honestly maintain or believe
Commutation:	substitution
Denomination:	number or grouping

Document Text

Letter to Richard Henry Lee

1787

MY DEAR SIR:

...The Session of our General Court which lasted six Weeks, and my Station there requiring my punctual & constant Attendance, prevented my considering the *new* Constitution as it is already called, so closely as was necessary for me before I should venture an Opinion. I confess, as I enter the Building I stumble at the Threshold. I meet with a National Government, instead of a Federal Union of Sovereign States. I am not able to conceive why the Wisdom of the Convention led them to give the Preference to the former before the latter. If the several States in the Union are to become one entire Nation, under one Legislature, the Powers of which shall extend to every Subject of Legislation, and its Laws be supreme & controul the whole, the Idea of Sovereignty in these States must be lost. Indeed I think, upon such a Supposition, those Sovereignties ought to be eradicated from the Mind; for they would be Imperia in Imperio justly deemd a Solecism in Politicks, & they would be highly dangerous, and destructive of the Peace Union and Safety of the Nation. And can this National Legislature be competent to make Laws for the *free* internal Government of one People, living in Climates so remote and whose "Habits & particular Interests" are and probably always will be so different. Is it to be expected that General Laws can be adapted to the Feelings of the more Eastern and the more Southern Parts of so extensive a Nation? It appears to me difficult if practicable. Hence then may we not look for Discontent, Mistrust, Disaffection to Government and frequent Insurrections, which will require standing Armies to suppress them in one Place & another where they may happen to arise. Or if Laws could be made, adapted to the local Habits, Feelings, Views & Interests of those distant Parts, would they not cause Jealousies of Partiality in Government which would excite Envy and other malignant Passions productive of Wars and fighting. But should we continue distinct sovereign States, confederated for the Purposes of mutual Safety and Happiness, each contributing to the federal Head such a Part of its Sovereignty as would render the Government fully adequate to those Purposes and *no more,* the People would govern themselves more easily, the Laws of each State being well adapted to its own Genius & Circumstances, and the Liberties of the United States would be more secure than they can be, as I humbly conceive, under the proposed new Constitution. You are sensible, Sir, that the Seeds of Aristocracy began to spring even before the Conclusion of our Struggle for the natural Rights of Men, Seeds which like a Canker Worm lie at the Root of free Governments. So great is the Wickedness of some Men, & the stupid Servility of others, that one would be almost inclined to conclude that Communities cannot be free. The few haughty Families, think *They* must govern. The Body of the People tamely consent & submit to be their Slaves. This unravels the Mystery of Millions being enslaved by the few!

Glossary

Canker Worm:	a type of destructive parasite
confederated:	brought together in a loose association
controul:	control
eradicated:	removed
Imperia in Imperio:	sovereignties (independent powers) within a larger sovereignty
Jealousies of Partiality:	conflicting demands
malignant:	destructive

Glossary

productive of:	causing
Servility:	slavishness
Solecism:	mistake
Sovereignty:	independent power or self-rule
standing Armies:	full-time, professional armies, as opposed to ones composed of draftees called up on short notice

Document Text

Massachusetts Ratifying Convention Speeches

1788

Your Excellency's first proposition is, "that it be explicitly declared, that all powers not expressly delegated to Congress, are reserved to the several States, to be by them exercised." This appears to my mind to be a summary of a bill of rights, which gentlemen are anxious to obtain; it removes a doubt which many have entertained respecting the matter, and gives assurance that, if any law made by the Federal government shall be extended beyond the power granted by the proposed Constitution, and inconsistent with the Constitution of this State, it will be an error, and adjudged by the courts of law to be void. It is consonant with the second article in the present Confederation, that each State retains its sovereignty, freedom, and independence, and every power, jurisdiction, and right, which is not, by this Confederation, expressly delegated to the United States in Congress assembled. I have long considered the watchfulness of the people over the conduct of their rulers, the strongest guard against the encroachments of power; and I hope the people of this country will always be thus watchful.

February 6, 1788...[Adams makes a motion]... "that it be explicitly declared, that all powers not expressly delegated to Congress are reserved to the several states, to be by them exercised" [be expanded to say] "And that the said Constitution never be construed to authorize Congress to infringe the just liberty of the press, or the rights of conscience; or to prevent the people of the United States, who are peaceful citizens, from keeping their own arms; to raise standing armies, unless when necessary for the defence of the United States, or of some one or more of them; or to prevent the people from petitioning, in a peaceful and orderly manner, the federal legislature, for a redress of grievances; or to subject the people to unreasonable searches and seizures of their persons, papers or possessions."

Glossary

Confederation: a loose alliance of separate entities; more specifically, the organization of the thirteen original states under the Articles of Confederation (1777–87)

consonant with: in agreement with

the United States in Congress assembled: the federal government, as represented by the elected members of Congress

void: lacking legal validity or power

Document Text

Address to the Massachusetts Legislature

1795

The people of this Commonwealth, in their declaration of rights, have recorded their own opinion, that the Legislature ought frequently to assemble for the redress of grievances, correcting, strengthening and confirming the Laws, and making new Laws, as the common good may require.—The Laws of the Commonwealth are intended to secure to each and all the Citizens, their own rights and liberties, and the property which they honestly possess. If there are any instances wherein the Laws in being, are inadequate to these great and capital ends, your eye will discern the evil, and your wisdom will provide a suitable remedy....

I cannot but recommend to your consideration, whether it may not be necessary more effectually to guard the elections of public agents and officers against illegal practices. All elections ought to be free, and every qualified elector who feels his own independence as he ought, will act his part according to his best, and most enlightened judgment. Elections are the immediate acts of the people's sovereignty, in which no foreigners should be allowed to intermeddle. Upon free and unbiased elections, the purity of the government, and consequently the safety and welfare of the citizens, may I not say altogether depend.

If we continue to be a happy people, that happiness must be assured by the enacting and executing of reasonable and wise laws, expressed in the plainest language, and by establishing such modes of education as tend to inculcate in the minds of youth, the feelings and habits of "piety, religion and morality," and to lead them to the knowledge and love of those truly Republican principles upon which our civil institutions are founded. We have solemnly engaged ourselves, fellow citizens, to support the Constitution of the United States, and the Constitution of this Commonwealth. This must be reconcileable in the mind of any man, who judiciously considers the sovereign rights of the one as limited to federal purposes, and the sovereign rights of the other, as acting upon and directing the internal concerns of our own Republic....

Those who wish to persuade the world to believe, that a free representative Republic cannot be supported, will no doubt make use of every art to injure, and by degrees to alter, and finally to eradicate the principles of our free Constitutions: But the virtuous and enlightened citizens of this Commonwealth, and of all united America, have understanding and firmness, sufficient to support those Constitutions of Civil Government which they have themselves formed, and which have done them so much honor in the estimation of the world.

It is with pain that I mention the insurrection which has lately taken place in a sister state. It was pointed more immediately at an act of the Federal Government. An act of that government, as well as of the governments in the Union, is constitutionally an act of the people, and our Constitutions provide a safe and easy method to redress any real grievances. No people can be more free under a Constitution established by their own voluntary compact, and exercised by men appointed by their own frequent suffrages. What excuse then can there be for forcible opposition to the laws? If any law shall prove oppressive in its operation, the future deliberations of a freely elective Representative, will afford a constitutional remedy. But the measures adopted by The President of the United States, supported by the virtue of citizens of every description, in that, and the adjacent states, have prevailed, and there is an end of the insurrection. Let the glory be given to Him, who alone governs all events, while we express the just feelings of respect and gratitude due to all those, whom He honours as instruments to carry into effect his gracious designs.

Glossary

afford:	allow or make possible
art:	means or method
the Commonwealth:	Massachusetts
compact:	agreement
inculcate:	influence
insurrection … sister state:	a reference to the Whiskey Rebellion, a 1794 uprising in Pennsylvania
intermeddle:	interfere
Republican:	referring to a system of government in which the citizens elect their leaders, as opposed to a monarchy or dictatorship
sovereignty:	power of self-rule
suffrages:	votes or choices

Adams as portrayed by Paul Revere. 1774. Yale University Art Gallery

Sociologist, suffragette, social worker, philosopher, and Nobel Peace Prize winner Jane Addams, in 1924 or 1926 by Bain News Service Restoration by Adam Cuerden

Jane Addams: Original Analysis

Social Activist and Reformer

1860–1935

Overview

Jane Addams, the eighth of nine children, was born on September 6, 1860, in Cedarville, Illinois, into a wealthy family of Quaker background. Addams was a member of the first generation of American women to attend college. She graduated in 1881 from Rockford Female Seminary, in Illinois, which the following year became Rockford College for Women, allowing Addams to obtain her bachelor's degree. In the 1880s Addams began studying medicine at the Women's Medical College of Philadelphia, but she had to suspend her studies because of poor health. Throughout the decade Addams also suffered from depression owing to her father's sudden death in 1881. Her physical and mental conditions, however, did not prevent her from traveling extensively in Europe. During one of her voyages, Addams visited London's original settlement house of Toynbee Hall, established in 1884, with her companion, Ellen Gates Starr. The visit led the two women to establish the Chicago settlement house of Hull House in 1889, the second such house to be established in America. (Dr. Stanton Coit and Charles B. Stover had founded the first American settlement house, the Neighborhood Guild of New York City, in 1886.) Through Hull House, Addams found a vocation for her adult life, overcoming the sense of uselessness that had besieged her for most of the 1880s.

Addams campaigned for every major reform issue of her era, such as fairer workplace conditions for men and women, tenement regulation, juvenile-court law, women's suffrage, and women's rights. She worked closely with social workers, politicians, and labor and immigrant groups to achieve her purposes, and she was not afraid to take controversial stances, as when she decided to campaign against U.S. entry into World War I. While in the first part of her life Addams was mainly involved in social work in Hull House, in the twentieth century she used her notoriety to advance political causes and became a well-known public figure. In 1910 she was the first woman president of the National Conference of Social Work, and in 1912 she actively campaigned for the Progressive presidential candidate, Theodore Roosevelt, becoming the first woman to give a nominating speech at a party convention. Addams was also a founding member of the National Association for the Advancement of Colored People.

In conjunction with her antiwar efforts, she became the president of the Woman's Peace Party in 1915 and chaired the International Women's Congress for Peace and Freedom at The Hague, Netherlands. That congress led to the foundation of the Women's International League for Peace and Freedom, which Addams chaired until 1929, when she was made honorary president for the remainder of her life. Americans were not unanimous in their praise for Addams's campaigning for peace. On the contrary, she was bitterly attacked by the press and was expelled from the Daughters of the American Revolution. In 1931, however, Addams's antiwar efforts won her the Nobel Peace Prize, which she shared with Nicholas Murray Butler. Because of her declining health, she was unable to collect the prize in person. Addams died in Chicago on May 21, 1935, three days after being diagnosed with cancer.

Addams's life, speeches, and writings are typical of middle-class reformers at the turn of the century. She was widely acknowledged as a pioneer social worker, and she spoke vigorously in favor of social reform. Her addresses and public interventions show her to have been idealistic yet committed to concrete action. Like other Progressive thinkers, such as John Dewey, Herbert Croly, Walter Lippmann, and Charlotte Perkins Gilman, Addams was deeply concerned with the changing nature of human ties and the meaning of community in an increasingly industrialized and urbanized world. Taking a critical stance toward the laissez-faire capitalism that had characterized the Gilded Age, a period of excessive displays of wealth in the late nineteenth century, Progressives like Addams expanded the authority to solve private and public problems to include not only the individual but also the government. They charged the state with the task of intervening in social and economic matters when appropriate, to defeat self-interest in the name of the common good.

Explanation and Analysis of Documents

Jane Addams was part of the Progressive movement, a broad and diverse middle-class coalition that, at the turn of the twentieth century, tried to reform American society and reconcile democracy with capitalism. The steady industrialization and urbanization of the 1880s and 1890s had deeply transformed American society, spurring harsh conflicts between labor and management. The middle class had supported the process of industrialization by espousing the Victorian values of laissez-faire individualism, domesticity, and self-control. Yet by the 1890s, it was apparent that these values had trapped the middle class between the warring

demands of big business and the working classes. Growing consumerism, a new wave of immigration, and tensions between the sexes further challenged bourgeois existence. In the face of these confrontations, the Progressives tried to reform the American capitalist system and its institutions from within, seeking to strike a compromise between radical demands and the preservation of established interests. Addams's concern with the major issues of Progressivism and her own agenda for social reform clearly emerge from four documents: her illustration of the beliefs and convictions that led to the foundation of Hull House, her defense of the Pullman strike, her condemnation of military ideals in the conception of an effective model of social control and efficient management for economic and political institutions, and her passionate endorsement of women's suffrage.

♦ "The Subjective Necessity for Social Settlements"

Like many other young, middle-class Progressives, Addams felt an urge to be useful and to find a vocation to occupy her adult life. For eight years following her father's death, Addams was unable to act and find such a purpose in her life: "During most of that time," she recalls in her autobiography, *Twenty Years at Hull-House*, "I was absolutely at sea so far as any moral purpose was concerned." This period of personal and professional insecurity ended when she found a way to couple her idealism with concrete action through the establishment of Hull House in Chicago's slum neighborhood around Halsted Street. The settlement house was one of the most ambitious aspects of urban reform movements. Settlement houses were located in slum neighborhoods densely populated by immigrants and were mainly directed by women. Young middle-class people worked in settlements to improve the living conditions of slum dwellers, encouraging them to improve their education, jobs, and housing as well as their understanding of American society and culture. Settlement workers soon became the leading personalities of the movement for social reform, progressively broadening their focus to campaign for school nurses, public playgrounds, and better working conditions.

As with other Progressive causes, the political relevance of the settlement movement should not obscure its middle-class basis. Such a basis clearly emerges in Addams's 1892 speech "The Subjective Necessity for Social Settlements," delivered at the summer school of the Ethical Culture Societies at Plymouth, Massachusetts, and later reprinted as the sixth chapter of *Twenty Years at Hull-House*. Addams makes clear that the settlement serves as a political solution to the personal malaise of young middle-class professionals who needed to find "an outlet for that sentiment of universal brotherhood" and must "give tangible expression to the democratic ideal." Settlements like Hull House, Addams indicates, thus benefit both the slum dwellers they aim to serve and the middle-class people, particularly women, who work in them, allowing them to find an outlet for their talents and compassions. Without the settlement houses, such talents would largely remain untapped by society, and those unable to work in such houses would feel a sense of aimlessness.

Time Line

1860	September 6	■ Laura Jane Addams is born in Cedarville, Illinois.
1881		■ Addams graduates from Rockford Female Seminary.
1888		■ Addams visits the London settlement of Toynbee Hall.
1889	September 18	■ Addams and Ellen G. Starr found the Hull House settlement in Chicago.
1892	Summer	■ Addams delivers the speech "The Subjective Necessity for Social Settlements" at the summer school of the Ethical Culture Societies at Plymouth, Massachusetts.
1896		■ Addams's address to the Chicago Woman's Club, "A Modern Lear," defends the Pullman strike.
1907		■ Addams publishes *Newer Ideals of Peace*, which includes the chapter "Passing of the War Virtues," an indictment of the military ideals that are still at the core of American government.
1910		■ Addams becomes the first woman to receive an honorary degree from Yale and publishes her autobiography, *Twenty Years at Hull-House*.
1910	January	■ Addams publishes the editorial "Why Women Should Vote" in the *Ladies' Home Journal*.
1912	November 2	■ "A Modern Lear" is published in *Survey*.
1915–1929		■ Addams chairs the Women's International League for Peace and Freedom.
1931	December 10	■ Addams is awarded the Nobel Peace Prize.
1935	May 21	■ Addams dies of cancer in Chicago.

Building directly on her own experience, Addams indicts the domestic values of American Victorian culture for their negative impact on the lives of many women. Society restrains the desire to act to alleviate suffering that is part of the social obligation that human beings feel. While the aim of this culture may be to give women a life full of pleasure and free of worries, the corresponding social attitudes only make them unhappy. Addams claims that in America "a fast-growing number of cultivated young people … have no recognized outlet for their active faculties." To Addams, the fate of these young people who lack purpose is as pitiful as that of the destitute masses who occupy America's urban slums. Settlement houses can provide a medium of communication between the two groups and benefit both. Settlements are based on solidarity and the Christian impulse to better the lives of the poor.

The last part of the speech defines Hull House also as an experiment in urban sociology, designed to "relieve, at the same time, the overaccumulation at one end of society and the destitution at the other." According to Addams, this stark imbalance in the distribution of wealth is typical of the modern conditions of life in a great city. The activities of the settlement should be shaped by the conviction that solutions to urban problems can be achieved through cooperative efforts and reform. Settlement workers should have "a scientific patience in the accumulation of facts" about human life and should be tolerant, flexible, and keen to experiment with approaches. The goal of Hull House is not to highlight differences; on the contrary, the settlement should be built upon what workers and slum dwellers share. In Addams's conception, Hull House offers common ground where the working class and the middle class can meet and learn from one another.

♦ "A Modern Lear"

By the 1880s the status of labor in the United States had undergone dramatic changes. The introduction of technological innovations and a more mechanized production reduced the process of manufacturing to series of specific, time-determined, and standardized tasks. Workers could no longer consider themselves as actual producers and increasingly felt slaves to machines. The laissez-faire capitalism that prevailed during the Gilded Age, which lasted through the late nineteenth century until the depression-causing Panic of 1893, prevented the passage of effective protective legislation for workers. Anxious over their loss of independence in the production process and their inability to obtain better wages and working conditions, workers began to form unions such as the Knights of Labor and the American Federation of Labor. The conflicts between labor and the capitalist imperative became harsher as a severe economic depression materialized in the late 1880s and through the 1890s. Just like the Haymarket riot in Chicago, where at the end of a rally a bomb thrown at police led to fatal gunfire and capital punishment, the Pullman strike of 1894 represented the dramatic and irreconcilable clash between the interests of management and labor.

The Pullman Palace Car Company adopted a paternalistic policy toward its workers that Addams compares in her essay on the strike to the attitude of Shakespeare's King Lear toward his daughters. The company owned a town near Chicago where it housed its workers, providing them with accommodation and services but also exercising a high degree of social control over them. Pullman workers could never negotiate their wages. When the company was struck by the economic recession in 1893, workers' wages were cut by up to 40 percent while rents and prices in the so-called model town remained unaltered. Led by the charismatic Eugene V. Debs, the workers voted in favor of the strike. George Pullman refused to negotiate with union leaders and, thanks to U.S. Attorney General Richard Olney, obtained a court ruling to prevent the strikers from obstructing the railways and interrupting the delivery of mail. This, in turn, led President Grover Cleveland to send troops to Chicago. Although the stated task of the troops was to protect the mail, they were effectively used to suppress the strike, which ended within a month.

The opening of Addams's speech expresses her grief over "the barbaric instinct to kill, roused on both sides" and "the sharp division into class lines" caused by the Pullman strike. Here, Addams tries to position herself as mediating between the warring demands of the workers and the response of the employer. Yet, although the last part of the essay is devoted to what Addams sees as the shortcomings of the workers' strategy in the incident, it is clear that her sympathies lie with the strikers. The main body of the essay is devoted to criticism of Pullman's paternalistic attitude toward his employees, an attitude that the author finds strikingly similar to that of King Lear toward his daughters. Addams finds that "the relation of Lear to his children was archaic and barbaric, holding in it merely the beginnings of a family life, since developed." She claims that in the future we may come to see the industrial dynamics of American society at the turn of the century as being "quite as incomprehensible and selfish, quite as barbaric and undeveloped, as was the family relationship between Lear and his daughters." As Lear was at heart unable to listen to his children, in spite of his magnanimous offer, so Pullman, with his model town and ostentatious philanthropy, was unwilling to hear the demands of his employees.

Like Lear, Pullman had so thought of himself as noble and indulgent that he lost the capacity to perceive himself to be wrong. To Addams, Pullman's initial intentions were actually well meaning, as he "began to build his town from an honest desire to give his employees the best surroundings." Yet, as the outside world began to heap praise on Pullman for his philanthropic efforts, such external praise became more important, and he ceased to consider the usefulness of his benevolence "by the standard of the men's needs." Locked within the walls of his model town, Pullman lost touch with the development of the labor movement and his workers' evolving demands. Pullman believed his definition of what was good for his workers ("cleanliness, decency of living, and above all, thrift and temperance")

to be universal and timeless. He was therefore unable to understand his employees' striving for "the ultimate freedom ... from the conditions under which they now labor."

Addams praises the strikers' movement, however "ill-directed,... ill-timed and disastrous in results," for its "unselfish impulse." To the contrary, Pullman's stubbornness in refusing arbitration was rooted in his attitude of "consulting first its own personal and commercial ends," which led him to neglect the widespread demands for social improvements. Pullman is therefore representative of those philanthropists who are cut off from the social developments of their times and from "the great moral life" deriving from "common experiences." These philanthropists, "so long as they are'good to people,' rather than 'with them,'... are bound to accomplish a large amount of harm."

The last part of Addams's speech balances the criticism of Pullman with criticism of the strikers' movement. Just as Cordelia in *King Lear* does not escape censure for her coldness and lack of tenderness, the workingmen's conception of emancipation was too narrow, as it did not include their employer. To Addams, the doctrine of workers' emancipation rather must become part of a universal movement whose "fusing power" can "touch those who think they lose, as well as those who think they gain." In the end, Pullman occupies center stage in Addams's conclusion: learning from his dramatic failure could serve to avert similar industrial tragedies in the future.

♦ "Passing of the War Virtues"

One of the chief concerns of Progressives was the establishment of effective institutions that could replace the notions of individualism and unrestrained commercialism that had characterized the Gilded Age. In chapter 8 of her book *Newer Ideals of Peace* (1907), entitled "Passing of the War Virtues," Addams claims that a fairer society can be achieved only if the older military values that are considered founding virtues of the American social order are replaced by "the growth of that beneficent and progressive patriotism which we need for the understanding and healing of our current national difficulties." The chapter is a logical anticipation of Addams's involvement in the movement against U.S. entry into World War I. Although Addams credits the war spirit of the past with having brought men together, she claims that the changing times require a new type of spirit, one that seeks "the construction of means" by "industrial action" rather than "the destruction of obstacles" by "military action."

In an effort to appeal also to the most conservative sector of American society, Addams states that the quintessentially American faith in material progress itself discords with military virtues. American prosperity, she asserts, rests on "constructive labor and material progress, both of them in striking contrast to warfare." Military values lead to the establishment of an exploitative society and encourage younger people to "forget that civilization is the substitution of law for war." Addams is careful not to espouse a vision of society based merely on the accumulation of wealth, however. Consistent with the Progressive tenets that the government should intervene in social and economic affairs and that forms of social control are needed to protect the common good, Addams claims that one should be wary of "unrestricted commercialism," which is "an excellent preparation for governmental aggression." This line of thought is typical of Addams's strategy to mediate between those with more radical demands and those who want to preserve society as is. She begins by expressing her faith in the American ideal of material progress, yet she leads the reader to question the individualistic notions that hard work necessarily translates into economic success and that the poor have only themselves to blame.

Addams cites the urban poor and the immigrant as examples of citizens who are helping to develop the world peace movement: "Their sense of pity, their clamor for personal kindness, their insistence upon the right to join in our progress, can no longer be disregarded." The fight against poverty can stimulate "the latent fellowship between man and man"; thus, the quest for a fairer society can replace the war virtues to unite human beings across national borders. Like other Progressive reformers, Addams also stresses the importance of efficient industrial management. She holds that the fight against "degrading poverty, disease and intellectual weakness" will result in the improvement of industrial efficiency. Addams thus frames the replacement of military values and the fight against poverty within the Progressives' quest for proficient administration in economic, social, and political institutions. "Passing of the War Virtues" is revealing of Addams's beliefs that the present system of government was inadequate in a complex industrial age and that public officials should eliminate inefficiency and exploitation.

Another important dimension of the fight against poverty in this era was its international significance. Addams clearly emphasizes the importance of extending human fellowship beyond national interests, stating that the fight against social injustices can become a common element for nations. In accordance with its international dimension, the chapter ends with a description of the International Peace Conference held in Boston in 1904. Addams refers to it as a "huge meeting" at which influential thinkers from all over the world "gave reasons for their belief in the passing of war." Citing "the address which was read from the prophet Isaiah," Addams speaks of the prophet's vision of peace as being attainable only if men forsake "the gains of oppression" and respond "to the cause of the poor." She ends her chapter affirming that "an enlightened industrialism" would help to define peace not only in negative terms as "an absence of war" but also as "the unfolding of worldwide processes making for the nurture of human life." Once again Addams tries to strike a compromise between the demands of labor and management; the phrase "enlightened industrialism" positions the author, like the majority of the Progressives, as functioning within the capitalist economy. Addams's reformist creed did not target the system to overthrow it; on the contrary, it sought to prevent conflicts and promote a more harmonious society.

♦ "Why Women Should Vote"

Addams's essay on women's suffrage, "Why Women Should Vote," published as an editorial in the *Ladies' Home Journal* in January 1910, inscribes itself in the intense debate on the topic that took place at the beginning of the twentieth century in America. The women's movement was a crucial part of Progressivism, and one of its most pressing questions was how women could attain equality with men and reform a society dominated by them. Many women's rights advocates claimed that voting was essential for women to achieve their reformist goals. Addams shared this belief. Yet, contrary to other women's rights campaigners, she rooted her support for female suffrage within the values of domesticity. While many within the movement argued that suffrage would be instrumental in helping women move beyond the narrow boundaries of the home, Addams begins her essay by situating women's place firmly within the home. She finds that no social change will release women from their domestic obligations. However, for women to fulfill such obligations, it is crucial that they can vote so that they can "take part in the slow upbuilding of that code of legislation which is alone sufficient to protect the home from the dangers incident to modern life."

In that the essay apparently embraces the traditional domestic role that Victorian society ascribed to women, Addams was criticized by her contemporaries as bowing to the popular and conservative perceptions of gender and womanhood. Yet, as Victoria Bissell Brown has pointed out, "Why Women Should Vote" is indicative of Addams's "unusual ability to weave [her] concern [for economic and political democracy] with her own mediating temperament, diplomatic style, and genuine respect for domesticity into a pro-suffrage argument that appealed to mainstream sensibilities" (http://www.pbs.org/wgbh/amex/wilson/filmmore/fr_addams.html). Addams's rhetorical ability is apparent not only in what she includes in her essay but also in what she leaves out. While many pro-suffrage writings took direct issue with arguments against women's voting rights, Addams never once cites her adversaries in her speech, such that her style comes across as completely nonconfrontational.

To Addams, the quest for women's suffrage represents an opportunity to hear women's voices in matters that are fundamental to the improvement of family life and to the struggle against urban vices. In its focus on the enhancement of living conditions within the urban environment, "Why Women Should Vote" ties the question of women's suffrage to the larger Progressive agenda, clearly stating that the two mutually reinforce each other. Because women have deep knowledge of the needs of youth, they can provide unique insights into effective ways "on the one hand to control and on the other hand to provide recreational facilities for its young people." Defining voting rights for women as a potential service toward the entire community, the essay is typical of the Progressives' affirmation of collective over individual concerns. As Brown writes, Addams assigns domesticity a crucial place in women's life not to "placate the patriarchs," but "because her daily experience taught her that domesticity was … a utilitarian reality for her working-class neighbors, and one that could be powerful if deployed in the political arena against America's individualistic patriarchs" (http://www.pbs.org/wgbh/amex/wilson/filmmore/fr_addams.html).

Impact and Legacy

Jane Addams's speeches and writings, her key role in the foundation of America's most famous urban settlement house, and her involvement in all the major reform causes of the era made her one of the most influential social reformers in American history. Her commitment to immigrant communities, as through her efforts to improve the urban environment and the conditions of the working class within both the home and the workplace, helped pioneer social work and sociological observation in the United States. Her active contribution to the world peace movement also accounted for her reputation as one of the first internationalists. Her most enduring legacy is her vision of a more supportive and communitarian society based on the extension of democratic and civil rights to all groups and peoples.

Although her activism against America's entry into World War I temporarily damaged her reputation, Addams's death prompted a vast outburst of public grief. Following the various references to the Great Emancipator in her writings, many compared her to Abraham Lincoln. Despite her support for social reforms, Addams was committed to improving the capitalist system from within, not overthrowing it, just like the majority of Progressives. Her middle-class status and her attempts to observe life from the point of view of the less privileged have sometimes been challenged as mutually exclusive and anachronistic, but Addams's life is exemplary of how to combine idealism and concrete actions to foster social reciprocity through experience.

Key Sources

Jane Addams's papers are housed at the Swarthmore College Peace Collection, in Swarthmore, Pennsylvania. In *Democracy and Social Ethics* (1902), Addams argues that morality has a public rather than a merely personal dimension and conceives democracy not only as a basis for legislation but also as an obligation to establish new and fairer relationships between different social groups (http://www.gutenberg.org/etext/15487).). In *The Spirit of Youth and the City Streets* (1909), Addams discusses the restlessness of youth in the city and claims that the energies of young men and women should be given a clear direction by city officials and social workers (http://www.gutenberg.org/etext/16221). In her autobiography, *Twenty Years at Hull-House* (1910), Addams writes about her motivations for the founding of Hull House and describes her work with immigrant and working-class families in Chicago's West Side slums (http://www.gutenberg.org/etext/1325). In *A New Conscience and an Ancient Evil* (1912), Addams analyzes the fate of many young women who emigrated from rural to urban America and were forced to become prostitutes (http://www.gutenberg.org/etext/15221).

Essential Quotes

"This paper is an attempt to analyze the motives which underlie a movement based, not only upon conviction, but upon genuine emotion, wherever educated young people are seeking an outlet for that sentiment for universal brotherhood, which the best spirit of our times is forcing from an emotion into a motive."

("The Subjective Necessity for Social Settlements")

"The Settlement then, is an experimental effort to aid in the solution of the social and industrial problems which are engendered by the modern conditions of life in a great city. It insists that these problems are not confined to any one portion of a city. It is an attempt to relieve, at the same time, the overaccumulation at one end of society and the destitution at the other; but it assumes that this overaccumulation and destitution is most sorely felt in the things that pertain to social and educational privileges."

("The Subjective Necessity for Social Settlements")

"The president of the [Pullman] company desired that his employees should possess the individual and family virtues, but did nothing to cherish in them those social virtues which his own age demanded. He rather substituted for that sense of responsibility to the community, a feeling of gratitude to himself, who had provided them with public buildings, and had laid out for them a simulacrum of public life."

("A Modern Lear")

"We shall not have made any genuine advance until we have grown impatient of a patriotism founded upon military prowess and defence, because this really gets in the way and prevents the growth of that beneficent and progressive patriotism which we need for the understanding and healing of our current national difficulties."

("Passing of the War Virtues")

Essential Quotes

"To turn the administration of our civic affairs wholly over to men may mean that the American city will continue to push forward in its commercial and industrial development, and continue to lag behind in those things which make a city healthful and beautiful. After all, woman's traditional function has been to make her dwelling-place both clean and fair."

("Why Women Should Vote")

Milestone Documents

Further Reading

Books

Brown, Victoria Bissell. *The Education of Jane Addams.* Philadelphia: University of Pennsylvania Press, 2004.

Davis, Allen F. *American Heroine: The Life and Legend of Jane Addams.* New York: Oxford University Press, 1973.

Knight, Louise W. *Citizen: Jane Addams and the Struggle for Democracy.* Chicago: University of Chicago Press, 2005.

Spears, Timothy B. *Chicago Dreaming: Midwesterners and the City, 1871–1919.* Chicago: University of Chicago Press, 2005.

Web Sites

Brown, Victoria Bissell. "An Introduction to 'Why Women Should Vote.'" Public Broadcasting Service "American Experience" Web site. http://www.pbs.org/wgbh/amex/wilson/filmmore/fr_addams.html.

"Jane Addams: The Nobel Peace Prize 1931." Nobel Prize Web site. http://nobelprize.org/nobel_prizes/peace/laureates/1931/addams-bio.html.

—*Luca Prono*

Questions for Further Study

1. In "Why Women Should Vote" and other writings, Addams maintains that gaining suffrage, or the right to vote, would help women fulfill their domestic obligations—that is, their responsibilities as wives and mothers. Do you agree or disagree? Consider the opposing viewpoint as well and examine the arguments for it. Is the consideration of women's domestic obligations itself justified? In other words, should Addams have even been concerned that women maintain their position in the home, or should she have focused purely on securing the vote and other rights for women?

Questions for Further Study

2. Addams lived during a period that saw the rise of numerous political movements opposed to the capitalism represented by George Pullman and others. These movements ranged from labor groups purely interested in securing better wages and working conditions to liberals, progressives, Socialists, anarchists, and Communists. One of the few such movements to win political power was the extremist Bolshevik wing of Russia's Social Democratic Party, which imposed an increasingly rigid dictatorship after seizing control of a popular uprising in 1917. Contrast Addams's views—particularly her position that capitalism could and should be maintained and reformed rather than destroyed—with those of other leaders and movements in her time, especially V. I. Lenin, founder of the Soviet Communist state.

3. In her critique of the 1894 Pullman strike and its effects, Addams makes an extended family analogy, comparing George Pullman to King Lear and the workers to his daughter Cordelia. How useful is such an analogy? Discuss the plot of Shakespeare's *King Lear* and address the question of how valid Addams's comparisons—between the players in the strike and the characters in the play—truly were.

4. Despite the optimism expressed in her speech on the transformation of "war virtues" to peacetime purposes, war certainly continued in Addams's lifetime and beyond. She lived to see World War I, the greatest conflict the world had yet known, and at the time of her death in the 1930s the stage was being set for an even worse conflict, World War II. In view of these facts, was Addams's optimism about peace simply a case of being naive? Or is their more depth in her argument? What are some of the merits in her belief that "war virtues" could be turned to peaceful uses?

"The Subjective Necessity for Social Settlements"

1892

This paper is an attempt to analyze the motives which underlie a movement based, not only upon conviction, but upon genuine emotion, wherever educated young people are seeking an outlet for that sentiment for universal brotherhood, which the best spirit of our times is forcing from an emotion into a motive. These young people accomplish little toward the solution of this social problem, and bear the brunt of being cultivated into unnourished, oversensitive lives. They have been shut off from the common labor by which they live which is a great source of moral and physical health. They feel a fatal want of harmony between their theory and their lives, a lack of coördination between thought and action. I think it is hard for us to realize how seriously many of them are taking to the notion of human brotherhood, how eagerly they long to give tangible expression to the democratic ideal....

"It is true that there is nothing after disease, indigence and a sense of guilt, so fatal to health and to life itself as the want of a proper outlet for active faculties." I have seen young girls suffer and grow sensibly lowered in vitality in the first years after they leave school. In our attempt then to give a girl pleasure and freedom from care we succeed, for the most part, in making her pitifully miserable.... There is a heritage of noble obligation which young people accept and long to perpetuate. The desire for action, the wish to right wrong and alleviate suffering haunts them daily. Society smiles at it indulgently instead of making it of value to itself....

We have in America a fast-growing number of cultivated young people who have no recognized outlet for their active faculties. They hear constantly of the great social maladjustment, but no way is provided for them to change it, and their uselessness hangs about them heavily.... These young people have had advantages of college, of European travel, and of economic study, but they are sustaining this shock of inaction.... They tell their elders with all the bitterness of youth that if they expect success from them in business or politics or in whatever lines their ambition for them has run, they must let them consult all of humanity; that they must let them find out what the people want and how they want it. It is only the stronger young people, however, who formulate this. Many of them dissipate their energies in so-called enjoyment. Others not content with that, go on studying and go back to college for their second degrees; not that they are especially fond of study, but because they want something definite to do, and their powers have been trained in the direction of mental accumulation. Many are buried beneath this mental accumulation with lowered vitality and discontent....

This young life, so sincere in its emotion and good phrases and yet so undirected, seems to me as pitiful as the other great mass of destitute lives. One is supplementary to the other, and some method of communication can surely be devised. Mr. Barnett, who urged the first Settlement—Toynbee Hall, in East London,—recognized this need of outlet for the young men of Oxford and Cambridge, and hoped that the Settlement would supply the communication. It is easy to see why the Settlement movement originated in England, where the years of education are more constrained and definite than they are here, where class distinctions are more rigid.... We are fast feeling the pressure of the need and meeting the necessity for Settlements in America. Our young people feel nervously the need of putting theory into action, and respond quickly to the Settlement form of activity....

The Settlement then, is an experimental effort to aid in the solution of the social and industrial problems which are engendered by the modern conditions of life in a great city. It insists that these problems are not confined to any one portion of a city. It is an attempt to relieve, at the same time, the overaccumulation at one end of society and the destitution at the other; but it assumes that this overaccumulation and destitution is most sorely felt in the things that pertain to social and educational privileges.... The only thing to be dreaded in the Settlement is that it lose its flexibility, its power of quick adaptation, its readiness to change its methods as its environment may demand. It must be open to conviction and must have a deep and abiding sense of tolerance. It must be hospitable and ready for experiment.... Its residents must be emptied of all conceit of opinion and all self-assertion, and ready to arouse and interpret the public opinion of their neighborhood. They must be content to live quietly side by side with their neighbors, until they grow into a sense of relationship and

Document Text

mutual interests.... In short, residents are pledged to devote themselves to the duties of good citizenship and to the arousing of the social energies which too largely lie dormant in every neighborhood given over to industrialism. They are bound to regard the entire life of their city as organic, to make an effort to unify it, and to protest against its over-differentiation

It is always easy to make all philosophy point one particular moral and all history adorn one particular tale; but I may be forgiven the reminder that the best speculative philosophy sets forth the solidarity of the human race; that the highest moralists have taught that without the advance and improvement of the whole, no man can hope for any lasting improvement in his own moral or material individual condition; and that the subjective necessity for Social Settlements is therefore identical with that necessity, which urges us on toward social and individual salvation.

Glossary

emptied of all conceit of opinion:	forced to give up one's own beliefs and preferences
Mr. Barnett:	Samuel Barnett (1844–1919), who with his wife, Henrietta, founded the world's first settlement house in 1884
social settlements:	settlement houses, or community centers that offer a variety of services in an economically disadvantaged area

Document Text

"A Modern Lear"

1896

Those of us who lived in Chicago during the summer of 1894 were confronted by a drama which epitomized and, at the same time, challenged the code of social ethics under which we live, for a quick series of unusual events had dispelled the good nature which in happier times envelopes the ugliness of the industrial situation. It sometimes seems as if the shocking experiences of that summer, the barbaric instinct to kill, roused on both sides, the sharp division into class lines, with the resultant distrust and bitterness, can only be endured if we learn from it all a great ethical lesson....

In the midst of these discussions the writer found her mind dwelling upon a comparison which modified and softened all her judgments. Her attention was caught by the similarity of ingratitude suffered by an indulgent employer and an indulgent parent. King Lear came often to her mind. We have all shared the family relationship and our code of ethics concerning it is somewhat settled. We also bear a part in the industrial relationship, but our ethics concerning that are still uncertain. A comparative study of these two relationships presents an advantage, in that it enables us to consider the situation from the known experience toward the unknown. The minds of all of us reach back to our early struggles, as we emerged from the state of self-willed childhood to a recognition of the family claim....

Historically considered, the relation of Lear to his children was archaic and barbaric, holding in it merely the beginnings of a family life, since developed. We may in later years learn to look back upon the industrial relationships in which we are now placed as quite as incomprehensible and selfish, quite as barbaric and undeveloped, as was the family relationship between Lear and his daughters....

The president of the Pullman company doubtless began to build his town from an honest desire to give his employees the best surroundings. As it developed it became a source of pride and an exponent of power, that he cared most for when it gave him a glow of benevolence. Gradually, what the outside world thought of it became of importance to him and he ceased to measure its usefulness by the standard of the men's needs....

Was not the grotesque situation of the royal father and the philanthropic employer to perform so many good deeds that they lost the power of recognizing good in beneficiaries? Were not both so absorbed in carrying out a personal plan of improvement that they failed to catch the great moral lesson which their times offered them? This is the crucial point to the tragedies and may be further elucidated....

Without pressing the analogy too hard may we not compare the indulgent relation of this employer to his town to the relation which existed between Lear and Cordelia? He fostered his employees for many years, gave them sanitary houses and beautiful parks, but in their extreme need,... he lost his touch and had nothing wherewith to help them.... He had been ignorant of their gropings toward justice. His conception of goodness for them had been cleanliness, decency of living, and above all, thrift and temperance. He had provided them means for all this; had ... given them opportunities for enjoyment and comradeship. But he suddenly found his town in the sweep of a world-wide moral impulse. A movement had been going on about him and through the souls of his workingmen of which he had been unconscious.... The men who consorted with him at his club and in his business had spoken but little of it, and when they had discussed it had contemptuously called it the "Labor Movement," headed by deadbeats and agitators. Of the force and power of this movement, of all the vitality within it, of that conception of duty which induces men to go without food and to see their wives and children suffer for the sake of securing better wages for fellow-workmen whom they have never seen, this president had dreamed absolutely nothing....

Outside the ken of this philanthropist, the proletariat had learned to say in many languages that "the injury of one is the concern of all." Their watchwords were brotherhood, sacrifice, the subordination of individual and trade interests to the good of the working class; and their persistent strivings were toward the ultimate freedom of that class from the conditions under which they now labor.

Compared to these watchwords the old ones which the philanthropic employer had given his town were negative and inadequate....

Document Text

That the movement was ill-directed, that it was ill-timed and disastrous in results, that it stirred up and became confused in the minds of the public with the elements of riot and bloodshed, can never touch the fact that it started from an unselfish impulse....

The president of this company desired that his employees should possess the individual and family virtues, but did nothing to cherish in them those social virtues which his own age demanded. He rather substituted for that sense of responsibility to the community, a feeling of gratitude to himself, who had provided them with public buildings, and had laid out for them a simulacrum of public life.

Is it strange that when the genuine feeling of the age struck his town this belated and almost feudal virtue of personal gratitude fell before it?...

In so far as philanthropists are cut off ... from the code of ethics which rule the body of men, from the great moral life springing from our common experiences, so long as they are "good to people," rather than "with them," they are bound to accomplish a large amount of harm. They are outside of the influence of that great faith which perennially springs up in the hearts of the people, and re-creates the world.

In spite of the danger of overloading the tragedies with moral reflections, a point ought to be made on the other side. It is the weakness in the relation of the employees to the employer, the fatal lack of generosity in the attitude of workmen toward the company under whose exactions they feel themselves wronged.

In reading the tragedy of King Lear, Cordelia does not escape our censure. Her first words are cold, and we are shocked by her lack of tenderness. Why should she ignore her father's need for indulgence, and be so unwilling to give him what he so obviously craved?...

As the vision of the life of Europe caught the sight and quickened the pulses of Cordelia, so a vision of the wider life has caught the sight of workingmen. After the vision has once been seen it is impossible to do aught but to press toward its fulfillment.... We are all practically agreed that the social passion of the age is directed toward the emancipation of the wage-worker;...

The doctrine of emancipation preached to the wage-workers alone runs an awful risk of being accepted for what it offers them, for the sake of fleshpots, rather than for the human affection and social justice which it involves. This doctrine must be strong enough in its fusing power to touch those who think they lose, as well as those who think they gain. Only thus can it become the doctrine of a universal movement....

If only a few families of the English speaking race had profited by the dramatic failure of Lear, much heart-breaking and domestic friction might have been spared. Is it too much to hope that some of us will carefully consider this modern tragedy, if perchance it may contain a warning for the troublous times in which we live? By considering the dramatic failure of the liberal employer's plans for his employees we may possibly be spared useless industrial tragedies in the uncertain future which lies ahead of us.

Glossary

aught:	anything
Cordelia:	youngest of King Lear's three daughters and her father's favorite, who alone remained loyal to the king throughout his troubles
fleshpots:	purely material, as opposed to spiritual, satisfactions
his town:	Pullman, Illinois, founded in the 1880s for Pullman company workers and later annexed to the city of Chicago
ken:	understanding
King Lear:	principal character in William Shakespeare's play by that name, whose vanity and foolishness ultimately cost him both his kingdom and his family
president of the Pullman company:	George Pullman (1831–1897), inventor of the Pullman sleeping car, which made overnight travel more comfortable

Glossary

proletariat:	the working class, particularly industrial workers
the royal father and the philanthropic employer:	Lear and Pullman, respectively
simulacrum:	imitation or copy
summer of 1894:	the time (May 11, 1894) when three thousand Pullman Palace Car workers staged a strike to protest a 25 percent decrease in wages
tragedies:	a reference to Shakespeare's tragedies in general and *King Lear* in particular
vision of the life of Europe:	a reference to Cordelia's exile from Britain to France, whose king she married

Delegation to the Women's Suffrage Legislature Jane Addams (left) **and Miss Elizabeth Burke of the University of Chicago, 1911 by Chicago Daily News**

Document Text

"Passing of the War Virtues"

1907

Let us by all means acknowledge and preserve that which has been good in warfare and in the spirit of warfare; let us gather it together and incorporate it in our national fibre. Let us, however, not be guilty for a moment of shutting our eyes to that which for many centuries must have been disquieting to the moral sense, but which is gradually becoming impossible, not only because of our increasing sensibilities, but because great constructive plans and humanized interests have captured our hopes and we are finding that war is an implement too clumsy and barbaric to subserve our purpose. We have come to realize that the great task of pushing forward social justice could be enormously accelerated if primitive methods as well as primitive weapons were once for all abolished....

Warfare in the past has done much to bring men together. A sense of common anger and the stirring appeal to action for a common purpose, easily open the channels of sympathy through which we partake of the life about us. But there are certainly other methods of opening those channels. A social life to be healthy must be consciously and fully adjusted to the march of social needs, and as we may easily make a mistake by forgetting that enlarged opportunities are ever demanding an enlarged morality, so we will fail in the task of substitution if we do not demand social sympathy in a larger measure and of a quality better adapted to the contemporaneous situation. Perhaps the one point at which this undertaking is most needed is in regard to our conception of patriotism, which, although as genuine as ever before, is too much dressed in the trappings of the past and continually carries us back to its beginnings in military prowess and defence....

Unless our conception of patriotism is progressive, it cannot hope to embody the real affection and the real interest of the nation. We know full well that the patriotism of common descent is the mere patriotism of the clan—the early patriotism of the tribe—and that, while the possession of a like territory is an advance upon that first conception, both of them are unworthy to be the patriotism of a great cosmopolitan nation. We shall not have made any genuine advance until we have grown impatient of a patriotism founded upon military prowess and defence, because this really gets in the way and prevents the growth of that beneficent and progressive patriotism which we need for the understanding and healing of our current national difficulties....

We come at last to the practical question as to how these substitutes for the war virtues may be found. How may we, the children of an industrial and commercial age, find the courage and sacrifice which belong to our industrialism. We may begin with August Comte's assertion that man seeks to improve his position ... by the destruction of obstacles and by the construction of means, or, designated by their most obvious social results, if his contention is correct, by military action and by industrial action....

Then we find ourselves asking what may be done to make more picturesque those lives which are spent in a monotonous and wearing toil, compared to which the camp is exciting and the barracks comfortable. How shall it be made to seem as magnificent patiently to correct the wrongs of industrialism as to do battle for the rights of the nation? This transition ought not to be so difficult in America, for to begin with, our national life in America has been largely founded upon our success in invention and engineering, in manufacturing and commerce. Our prosperity has rested upon constructive labor and material progress, both of them in striking contrast to warfare....

We ignore the fact that war so readily throws back the ideals which the young are nourishing into the mold of those which the old should be outgrowing. It lures young men not to develop, but to exploit; it turns them from the courage and toil of industry to the bravery and endurance of war, and leads them to forget that civilization is the substitution of law for war....

It remains to be seen whether or not democratic rule will diminish war. Immoderate and uncontrolled desires are at the root of most national as well as of most individual crimes, and a large number of persons may be moved by unworthy ambitions quite as easily as a few. If the electorate of a democracy accustom themselves to take the commercial view of life, to consider the extension of trade as the test of a national prosperity, it becomes comparatively easy for mere extension of commercial opportunity to assume a moral aspect and to receive the moral sanction. Unrestricted commercialism is an excellent preparation for governmental aggression. The nation which is accustomed to condone the questionable business methods of a rich man because of his success, will find no difficulty in obscuring the moral issues involved in any undertaking that is successful. It becomes easy to deny the moral basis of self-government and to substitute militarism....

Document Text

The advance of constructive labor and the subsidence and disappearance of destructive warfare is a genuine line of progression....

To some of us it seems clear that marked manifestations of [the] movement [for world peace] are found in the immigrant quarters of American cities. The ... survey of the immigrant situation would indicate that all the peoples of the world have become part of the American tribunal, and that their sense of pity, their clamor for personal kindness, their insistence upon the right to join in our progress, can no longer be disregarded. The burdens and sorrows of men have unexpectedly become intelligent and urgent to this nation, and it is only by accepting them with some magnanimità that we can develop the larger sense of justice which is becoming world-wide and is lying in ambush, as it were, to manifest itself in governmental relations. Men of all nations are determining upon the abolition of degrading poverty, disease, and intellectual weakness, with their resulting industrial inefficiency, and are making a determined effort to conserve even the feeblest citizen to the State. To join in this determined effort is to break through national bonds and to unlock the latent fellowship between man and man.... It is but necessary to make this fellowship wider, to extend its scope without lowering its intensity. Those emotions which stir the spirit to deeds of self-surrender and to high enthusiasm, are among the world's most precious assets. That this emotion has so often become associated with war, by no means proves that it cannot be used for other ends. There is something active and tangible in this new internationalism, although it is difficult to make it clear, and in our striving for a new word with which to express this new and important sentiment, we are driven to the rather absurd phrase of "cosmic patriotism." Whatever it may be called, it may yet be strong enough to move masses of men out of their narrow national considerations and cautions into new reaches of human effort and affection....

The International Peace Conference held in Boston in 1904 was opened by a huge meeting in which men of influence and modern thought from four continents, gave reasons for their belief in the passing of war. But none was so modern, so fundamental and so trenchant, as the address which was read from the prophet Isaiah.... He contended that peace could be secured only as men abstained from the gains of oppression and responded to the cause of the poor; that swords would finally be beaten into plowshares and pruning-hooks, not because men resolved to be peaceful, but because all the metal of the earth would be turned to its proper use when the poor and their children should be abundantly fed. It was as if the ancient prophet foresaw that under an enlightened industrialism peace would no longer be an absence of war, but the unfolding of worldwide processes making for the nurture of human life. He predicted the moment which has come to us now that peace is no longer an abstract dogma but has become a rising tide of moral enthusiasm slowly engulfing all pride of conquest and making war impossible.

Glossary

the American tribunal:	a court of law, but here suggesting a larger and more informal community of shared ideals
August Comte:	French social philosopher and reformer (1798–1857)
the camp:	the military life
conserve:	preserve the existence of
enlarged morality:	a matured and maturing sense of right and wrong
intelligent:	understood
Isaiah:	Israelite prophet of the 700s bc for whom one of the most significant books in the Old Testament is named
magnanimità:	Italian version of the word *magnanimity*, meaning generosity of spirit
the march:	the changing nature
patriotism of common descent:	loyalty to one's nation that comes simply from having been born there, as opposed to loyalty based on principles

Document Text

"Why Women Should Vote"

1910

For many generations it has been believed that woman's place is within the walls of her home, and it is indeed impossible to imagine the time when her duty there shall be ended or to forecast any social change which shall release her from that paramount obligation....

Many women today are failing to discharge their duties to their own households properly simply because they do not perceive that as society grows more complicated it is necessary that woman shall extend her sense of responsibility to many things outside of her own home if she would continue to preserve the home in its entirety.... A woman's simplest duty, one would say, is to keep her house clean and wholesome and to feed her children properly. Yet if she lives in a tenement house ... she cannot fulfill these simple obligations by her own efforts because she is utterly dependent upon the city administration for the conditions which render decent living possible. Her basement will not be dry, her stairways will not be fireproof, her house will not be provided with sufficient windows to give light and air, nor will it be equipped with sanitary plumbing, unless the Public Works Department sends inspectors who constantly insist that these elementary decencies be provided. Women who live in the country sweep their own dooryards and may either feed the refuse of the table to a flock of chickens or allow it innocently to decay in the open air and sunshine. In a crowded city quarter, however, if the street is not cleaned by the city authorities no amount of private sweeping will keep the tenement free from grime; if the garbage is not properly collected and destroyed a tenement-house mother may see her children sicken and die of diseases from which she alone is powerless to shield them, although her tenderness and devotion are unbounded. She cannot even secure untainted meat for her household, she cannot provide fresh fruit, unless the meat has been inspected by city officials, and the decayed fruit, which is so often placed upon sale in the tenement districts, has been destroyed in the interests of public health. In short, if woman would keep on with her old business of caring for her house and rearing her children she will have to have some conscience in regard to public affairs lying quite outside of her immediate household. The individual conscience and devotion are no longer effective....

In other words, if women would effectively continue their old avocations they must take part in the slow upbuilding of that code of legislation which is alone sufficient to protect the home from the dangers incident to modern life....

The more extensively the modern city endeavors on the one hand to control and on the other hand to provide recreational facilities for its young people the more necessary it is that women should assist in their direction and extension. After all, a care for wholesome and innocent amusement is what women have for many years assumed. When the reaction comes on the part of taxpayers women's votes may be necessary to keep the city to its beneficent obligations toward its own young people....

Ever since steam power has been applied to the processes of weaving and spinning woman's traditional work has been carried on largely outside of the home. The clothing and household linen are not only spun and woven, but also usually sewed, by machinery; the preparation of many foods has also passed into the factory and necessarily a certain number of women have been obliged to follow their work there, although it is doubtful, in spite of the large numbers of factory girls, whether women now are doing as large a proportion of the world's work as they used to do. Because many thousands of those working in factories and shops are girls between the ages of fourteen and twenty-two there is a necessity that older women should be interested in the conditions of industry. The very fact that these girls are not going to remain in industry permanently makes it more important that someone should see to it that they shall not be incapacitated for their future family life because they work for exhausting hours and under insanitary conditions.

If woman's sense of obligation had enlarged as the industrial conditions changed she might naturally and almost imperceptibly have inaugurated the movements for social amelioration in the line of factory legislation and shop sanitation. That she has not done so is doubtless due to the fact that her conscience is slow to recognize any obligation outside of her own family circle, and because she was so absorbed in her own household that she failed to see what the conditions outside actually were. It would be interesting to know how far the

Document Text

consciousness that she had no vote and could not change matters operated in this direction. After all, we see only those things to which our attention has been drawn, we feel responsibility for those things which are brought to us as matters of responsibility. If conscientious women were convinced that it was a civic duty to be informed in regard to these grave industrial affairs, and then to express the conclusions which they had reached by depositing a piece of paper in a ballot box, one cannot imagine that they would shirk simply because the action ran counter to old traditions....

To turn the administration of our civic affairs wholly over to men may mean that the American city will continue to push forward in its commercial and industrial development, and continue to lag behind in those things which make a city healthful and beautiful. After all, woman's traditional function has been to make her dwelling-place both clean and fair. Is that dreariness in city life, that lack of domesticity which the humblest farm dwelling presents, due to a withdrawal of one of the naturally cooperating forces? If women have in any sense been responsible for the gentler side of life which softens and blurs some of its harsher conditions, may they not have a duty to perform in our American cities?

In closing, may I recapitulate that if woman would fulfill her traditional responsibility to her own children; if she would educate and protect from danger factory children who must find their recreation on the street; if she would bring the cultural forces to bear upon our materialistic civilization; and if she would do it all with the dignity and directness fitting one who carries on her immemorial duties, then she must bring herself to the use of the ballot—that latest implement for self government. May we not fairly say that American women need this implement in order to preserve the home?

Glossary

dooryards: small front yards

incident to: related to, or following from

tenement house: a slum dwelling

this implement: the vote

Susan B. Anthony

Susan B. Anthony: Original Analysis

Woman's Rights Activist

1820–1906

Overview

Susan Brownell Anthony, who devoted more than a half century to women's suffrage and other social issues, was born in Adams, Massachusetts, on February 15, 1820. She received her education at a Quaker boarding school in Philadelphia, where she trained as a teacher, an occupation she pursued for three years beginning in 1846. After the family moved to Rochester, New York, in 1845, she became active in a range of social causes, including abolition of slavery, temperance, the rights of labor, education reform, and particularly women's rights. She signed the Declaration of Sentiments produced by the 1848 Seneca Falls Convention in New York, the first women's rights convention held in the United States. In the early 1850s she met her lifelong friend and fellow suffragist, Elizabeth Cady Stanton—although in later years some tension emerged between the two, with Stanton adopting a more radical approach to women's rights and Anthony a more moderate position.

After the Civil War and the abolition of slavery, Anthony, Stanton, and other suffragist leaders were hopeful that the Fifteenth Amendment to the Constitution, which granted voting rights to African Americans, would extend the same rights to women—and were bitterly disappointed that it did not. In response, the two founded the American Equal Rights Association in 1866 and, in 1869, the National Woman Suffrage Association. In 1890 the latter organization merged with a third organization, the American Woman Suffrage Association, to become the National American Woman Suffrage Association. In 1868 Anthony launched a weekly journal called the *Revolution* under the motto "The true republic—men, their rights and nothing more; women, their rights and nothing less." For the next four decades Anthony devoted her life to writing and speaking in support of women's rights, particularly the right to vote.

After Anthony and several other women cast ballots in Rochester in the 1872 presidential election, she was arrested, tried, found guilty, and fined, though she never paid the fine and was never jailed. In response to her arrest, Anthony launched a statewide speaking tour in 1873, during which she delivered the address "Is It a Crime for a Citizen of the United States to Vote?" During the legal proceedings, she recorded her reactions in various letters she wrote in 1872 and 1873. Throughout the final decades of the nineteenth century, Anthony wrote articles and delivered speeches on issues affecting women and the suffragist cause. Her article "The Status of Woman, Past, Present, and Future" appeared in the *Arena* magazine in May 1897.

Anthony is often regarded as the author of the Nineteenth Amendment to the U.S. Constitution recognizing the right of women to vote. She originally wrote the amendment in 1877, using the Fifteenth Amendment ("The right of citizens of the United States to vote shall not be denied or abridged by the United States or by any State on account of race, color, or previous condition of servitude") as a model. The amendment, which came to be referred to as the Anthony Amendment, was submitted to Congress by a sympathetic senator, Aaron Sargent, and while Congress did not act on it, it was submitted in every session of Congress until 1919. Just one month before her death on March 13, 1906, Anthony concluded her last public speech, delivered at a meeting of the National American Women Suffrage Association, with the words "Failure is impossible"—her final public utterance and a phrase that survived as a rallying cry for women's rights proponents throughout the twentieth century. Her words proved to be prophetic, for Congress approved the Nineteenth Amendment in 1919, and the amendment was ratified in 1920.

Explanation and Analysis of Documents

In all her writings and speeches, Susan B. Anthony displayed her single-minded devotion to the cause of women's rights, and particularly the right to vote. Over the years she honed her arguments until the success of the cause of suffrage and women's rights became inevitable. This major shift in public opinion was the result in large part of Anthony's carefully crafted arguments.

♦ Letters concerning Casting a Vote in the 1872 Federal Election

On November 5, 1872, Anthony cast a vote in that year's presidential election—presumably voting for Ulysses S. Grant, since Anthony acknowledged voting a straight Republican Party ticket. (She did not vote for Victoria Woodhull, who ran under the banner of the Equal Rights Party and was the first woman ever nominated for the presidency.) Two weeks later, on November 18, a deputy U.S. marshal arrested Anthony for voting illegally. Seven months later she was found guilty and fined $100. She never paid

the fine, and she was never jailed for refusing to pay the fine. Accordingly, she was never able to appeal the conviction to a higher court.

Anthony's letters from the period following her casting of a vote in the 1872 presidential election take the reader into the details of her life at that time. Their prose, filled with abbreviations, dashes, eccentric punctuation, and obscure phrasing convey a sense of her excitement over having taken action with regard to women's suffrage. The first of these letters is addressed to her lifelong friend and fellow activist, Elizabeth Cady Stanton. In this letter she records that she has "gone & done it" by voting in the election, and she expresses her hope that other women around the country have done so as well. Twice she makes reference to Rhoda DeGarmo, a fellow Quaker who in the early decades of the century had been active in the abolition movement but, beginning in the 1850s, had devoted her energies to the rights of women. DeGarmo, too, voted in the election, though as a Quaker, she refused to "swear or affirm" but instead asserted that she would "tell the truth." Anthony also makes reference to the attorney Henry R. Selden, who was a founding member of the Republican Party in 1856 in New York—and who never billed Anthony for defending her at her trial.

Anthony's letter to Sarah Huntington of Connecticut is an example of the voluminous correspondence she carried on with women (and men) all over the country. Huntington had registered to vote, but her name was omitted from the county's list of registered voters, so her attempt to vote was rejected. What Anthony could not have known was that her statement that only women in Norwalk, Connecticut, and Rochester, New York, had voted or attempted to vote was incorrect. In the same election, a number of women throughout the country had voted or tried to vote, and earlier in 1872 numerous women had registered or tried to register to vote. Among them were women in Ohio, Michigan (where, in Battle Creek, Sojourner Truth tried to register and vote), Kansas, Oregon, Massachusetts, and in other locations in Connecticut and New York State.

The third letter is written to Benjamin Franklin Butler, a congressional representative from Massachusetts. The purpose of the letter is to inquire about the status of a U.S. Supreme Court case. The petitioner in the case was Myra Bradwell, a staunch supporter of women's rights who in 1890 became the first woman admitted to the bar to practice law in Illinois, but not before encountering obstacles. In 1869 she passed the Illinois bar examination, but the state denied her a license because of her gender. Her case went to the Illinois Supreme Court, which ruled that the Illinois law denying her admission to the bar did not violate her Fourteenth Amendment rights. In 1873 the U.S. Supreme Court upheld this decision, but the case was still pending when Anthony solicited Butler's support. The "Convention" Anthony refers to was most likely the New York State constitutional convention held in May 1873.

Time Line

1820		■ Susan Brownell Anthony is born on February 15 in Adams, Massachusetts.
1845		■ Anthony's family moves to Rochester, New York, where their home is opened to abolitionists such as Frederick Douglass.
1846		■ Anthony begins a three-year career as a teacher; she lobbies for reform, since male teachers' salaries were about four times that of women teachers.
1854		■ Anthony gathers petitions calling for married women's property rights and the ballot.
1856		■ The American Anti-Slavery Society appoints Anthony as an agent.
1866		■ Anthony and Elizabeth Cady Stanton found the American Equal Rights Association.
1868	January 8	■ Anthony begins publication of the journal the *Revolution*.
1869	May	■ Anthony and Stanton found the National Woman Suffrage Association.
1872	November 18	■ Anthony is arrested for voting in the presidential election.
1872–1873		■ Anthony records her reactions to the legal proceedings following her arrest in letters and diary entries.
1873		■ Anthony begins a speaking tour delivering the address "Is It a Crime for a Citizen of the United States to Vote?"
1877		■ Anthony writes a constitutional amendment that would grant women the right to vote; the "Anthony Amendment" would eventually become the Nineteenth Amendment to the Constitution.

Time Line		
1881–1902		■ Anthony, Stanton, and Matilda Gage publish four volumes of *History of Woman Suffrage*.
1897	May	■ Anthony publishes "The Status of Woman, Past, Present, and Future" in the *Arena* journal.
1906	February 15	■ Anthony delivers her final public address, known as the "failure is impossible" speech, at the National American Woman Suffrage Association.
1906	March 13	■ Anthony dies in her home in Rochester.
1920		■ The Nineteenth Amendment to the Constitution, recognizing the right of women to vote, is ratified.

♦ "Is It a Crime for a Citizen of the United States to Vote?"

In response to her arrest and trial for voting in the 1872 presidential election, Anthony launched a speaking tour throughout New York State. The address she delivered and that is included in the records of the trial is titled "Is It a Crime for a Citizen of the United States to Vote?" The address falls roughly into three parts. The first is an appeal to the nation's foundational documents, particularly the Declaration of Independence and the Constitution. The second is an appeal to the language of law as it applies to citizenship and other matters. In the third part, Anthony draws an analogy between women's suffrage and the issue of slavery.

In the opening paragraphs of her address, Anthony expresses the view that as a citizen of the United States, living under a "democratic-republican" form of government, she possesses a "natural right" to participate in the nation's political affairs by voting. (The terms *democratic* and *republican* in this context do not refer to modern political parties but to forms of government; *democratic* means that power is vested in the people through their elected representatives, *republican* means that the nation is ruled not by a monarch but by an elected head of state.) Anthony thus draws a distinction between rights that are granted by the state and those that any human being possesses by virtue of being a citizen.

The concept of natural rights represents a philosophical tradition from the eighteenth-century Age of Enlightenment that was articulated by such British philosophers as Thomas Hobbes and John Locke. In support of her view, Anthony cites the Declaration of Independence, which enshrines the Enlightenment concept of natural rights with its statement that "life, liberty and the pursuit of happiness" are "inalienable rights"—that is to say, rights that cannot be alienated, or taken away. Rights, then, are not granted by the state, nor can the state deny to citizens their full enjoyment of their rights. People possess rights by virtue of being human. In passing, she notes that the Quaker church into which she was born—she later affiliated herself with the liberal wing of Quakerism but was not a particularly religious person—had always been in the vanguard in acknowledging the rights of women. Indeed, Anthony's own home life, where she was the oldest of seven children, granted her and her mother and sisters a degree of freedom and independent thought that was uncharacteristic of the time. She goes on to say that the Declaration's avowal of the "right of the people to alter or abolish" a government that is "destructive of these ends" clearly implies the right to vote. Voting is the only civilized way to form and alter governments; the only alternative is brute force. Disenfranchising half of the population—women—compels them to obey laws to which they have never consented.

Anthony then cites the U.S. Constitution, noting that it begins with the words "We, the people," not "we, the white male citizens" or "we, the male citizens." This was a glancing reference to her bitter disappointment that the Fifteenth Amendment extending suffrage to freed slaves did not also extend suffrage to women, a failure that led to a rift between civil rights activists and women's rights activists in the final decades of the century. She notes that even James Madison, who earlier in his career had expressed fear of the rabble, came around to a belief in universal suffrage, a view that he expressed in the 1787 debates at the Constitutional Convention and that Anthony quotes.

Anthony refers to the first article of the Constitution, which, her opponents asserted, disenfranchised women because it turned over to the states the power to regulate elections. Anthony replies to this view by noting that all the Constitution does is prescribe what are in effect procedural matters to ensure that electors are qualified; these stipulations in no way imply that half the population is to be disenfranchised. She then turns to the distinction between a democratic republic and a monarchy. She argues that disenfranchisement on the basis of sex amounts to a "bill of attainder." This phrase is a reference to English common law, which said that a legislature or monarch could declare persons or classes of persons guilty of violating a law without giving them the benefit of a trial. A person thus found guilty was "attainted"—that is, "tainted"—and forfeited his or her civil rights, including the right to own and pass property and to vote. She notes that under current U.S. law, a "monarchy," or at best an "oligarchy" of males rules females, in direct violation of the Constitution, which requires every state to guarantee to its citizens a "republican" form of government, with the concomitant right to vote.

On this basis, Anthony takes up the issue of the language of the law, in the process making an ingenious argument. She notes that laws routinely use the pronouns *he* and *his*, suggesting that women are excluded, just as they

are excluded from the voting booth. If that is the case, then, women should be exempted from *all* laws in which *he* and *his* are used, including criminal laws and laws applying to taxation. Anthony extends her discussion of the language of the law to the indiscriminant use of words such as "persons, people, inhabitants, electors," and "citizens" and raises the question of who is included in these terms. She notes that under the Fourteenth Amendment, all "persons" who are born or naturalized in the United States are "citizens." If "persons" are "citizens," and if the under the Fourteenth Amendment "No State shall make or enforce any law which shall abridge the privileges or immunities of citizens of the United States," and further if women are "persons," then denying women the right to vote is a violation of the federal Constitution.

Anthony cites examples and goes on to elucidate by pointing out that women by law carry the penalties and burdens of government and therefore should also be allowed to enjoy its privileges. She notes that even citizenship laws, including the section of the federal code that deals with the naturalization of citizens, grants women citizenship without the concurrence of their husbands, even in cases where the husband has applied for citizenship but dies before it is granted. If a naturalized woman is entitled to all the rights and privileges of citizenship, should not, Anthony asks, women born in the United States enjoy the same rights and privileges?

Making a transition to the third major argument of her address, Anthony draws an analogy between the status of African Americans and that of women. In the early decades of the nineteenth century the issues of abolition and women's rights were often closely linked. Anthony herself was active in the abolition movement and served as a local agent for the American Anti-Slavery Society. It was thought that the condition of women and that of African Americans was similar, particularly because both were denied the franchise. The belief among many reformers was that women and African Americans, as natural allies, could make common cause in asserting their rights, though the passage of the Fifteenth Amendment, a victory for African Americans, left the cause of women's rights bereft.

Nevertheless, Anthony continues to make the argument that the law as it applies to black men should also apply to women. She begins with a reference to the Fourteenth Amendment, one of the three so-called Civil War Amendments, or Reconstruction Amendments, passed in the wake of the Civil War. The authors of the amendment were John A. Bingham, an Ohio congressman (who as a judge also presided over the trial of the Abraham Lincoln assassination conspirators and over the impeachment trial of Andrew Johnson), and Jacob Howard, a senator also from Ohio. Section 1 of the amendment reads:

All persons born or naturalized in the United States, and subject to the jurisdiction thereof, are citizens of the United States and of the State wherein they reside. No State shall make or enforce any law which shall abridge the privileges or immunities of citizens of the United States; nor shall any State deprive any person of life, liberty, or property, without due process of law; nor deny to any person within its jurisdiction the equal protection of the laws.

Although Section 1 of the amendment does not mention race, the effect of the amendment was to make African Americans "citizens," deny to the states the right to "abridge" the rights of any citizens, and give all citizens due process and equal protection under the law. Anthony makes the argument that the earlier Thirteenth Amendment, which banned slavery, in effect already made African Americans citizens of the nation, giving them the right to vote. The Fourteenth Amendment, Anthony suggests, was unnecessary, except for the purpose of granting African Americans equal protection under the law, among other provisions. She concludes the argument by stating:

Clearly, then if the Fourteenth Amendment was not to secure to black men their right to vote it did nothing for them, since they possessed everything else before. But if it was intended to prohibit the states from denying or abridging their right to vote, then it did the same for all persons, white women included, born or naturalized in the United States; for the amendment does not say that all male persons of African descent, but that all persons are citizens.

Anthony turns to the Fifteenth Amendment, which specifically states that the right to vote cannot be denied or abridged on the basis of "race, color, or previous condition of servitude," the last of the three items prohibiting states from denying the vote to former slaves. She notes that one of the motives behind the Fifteenth Amendment was to coerce the states of the former Confederacy into extending the franchise to newly freed blacks, thus ensuring that Ulysses S. Grant would win reelection in the 1872 election (the Republican Party, the party of Lincoln, at that time being identified as the antislavery party).

Then Anthony makes yet another ingenious argument. Her key point is that women, like African Americans, lived under the condition of servitude. She points out, for example, that a woman, like a slave, had no "control" over her person and could be corrected if she offended her master, though she presumably could not be corrected with a "cat-o'-nine-tails"—that is, a knotted whip. Similarly, just as a slave was not entitled to retain his earnings from labor, so, too, any earnings a woman might have were the property of her husband. A corollary to this was that if the wife was guilty of some offense, it was her husband, not her, who was sued, based on the principle that the wife did not own anything that the person who sues could collect; at the same time, a wife could not sue another, but a husband could file suit on her behalf. Put simply, then, women lived under the condition of servitude, holding a position little different from that of slaves. If the Fifteenth Amendment granted the right to vote despite "previous condition of servitude," then it granted women the right to vote.

♦ "The Status of Woman, Past, Present, and Future"

By 1897 Anthony was in a position to look back on decades of activity in the pursuit of women's rights. She was engaged in the writing and publication of the four-volume *History of Woman Suffrage* and was collaborating with Ida Husted

Harper in a three-volume biography, *The Life and Work of Susan B. Anthony*. She was in a unique position, then, to reflect on the status of women and how it had changed during her lifetime. The fact that the *Arena* journal asked her to write the article suggests that already Anthony was regarded as an icon of women's rights.

In the opening paragraph, Anthony begins by focusing on the past status of women, noting that a half century earlier a woman "was without a recognized individuality in any department of life." Women rarely if ever enjoyed the benefits of education, and the nation boasted few women of letters. A person such as Margaret Fuller was an exception. Fuller was associated with the Transcendental movement of Ralph Waldo Emerson, edited the movement's journal, the *Dial*, and was hired as a correspondent by Horace Greeley of the *New York Tribune*. Her most important work was *Woman in the Nineteenth Century*. "Channing" is a reference to William Henry Channing, also associated with the Transcendental movement and a prominent Unitarian minister and socialist reformer.

Anthony then present a grim picture of the status of women earlier in the century. The details of the picture are clear. Young women worked at domestic tasks, while their brothers were educated. Women had no opportunities to pursue a career. Young men received income from their fathers; women enjoyed no such privilege. Women were in effect the property of their fathers and then were turned over to husbands. If a woman earned wages outside the home, the wages were paid to the husband. Fathers willed their property to sons, generally not their daughters; in the few cases when women inherited property, that property became her husband's on marriage. Even widows were left in a dependent position through a "widow's dower." A widow generally retained an interest in a third of her deceased husband's property until she died, when the property would pass to a son. Anthony makes reference to English common law, which allowed husbands to beat their wives without fear of prosecution; *common law* refers to law developed through court decisions rather than statutes. Louisiana, because of its French roots, applies a system of statutory law rather than common law.

Women fifty years earlier could pursue few occupations outside the home. Teaching was perhaps the most attractive option, except that women were paid a fraction of what men were for the same work. Worse, women teachers remained dependent on members of their community for bed and board, while male teachers were given extra stipends for their room and board. Unmarried women had no social standing. They were dependent for a home on a married sibling. Women who worked outside the home were regarded as peculiar, as bitter spinsters, and were excluded from social gatherings.

Anthony paints a picture of significant improvement in the status of women. She marks the beginning of this improvement with the women's rights convention at Seneca Falls, New York, in 1848—though she also notes that the issue of women's rights had begun to percolate with the 1792 publication of *Vindication of the Rights of Woman* by Mary Wollstonecraft and with the agitation of the Scottish reformer and freethinker Frances Wright. Paulina Wright Davis was a vigorous antislavery and women's rights activist and writer, as were Ernestine Rose and Lucy Stone, who was the first woman in Massachusetts ever to hold a college degree (from Ohio's Oberlin College, the nation's first college to admit women, in 1837). In the intervening five decades, Anthony is happy to report, most of the proposals made in the Seneca Falls convention's "Declaration of Sentiments" have become a reality. Women can pursue occupations outside the home, girls are being educated, household drudgery has been lessened, and women have opportunities to become more self-supporting. In particular, Anthony notes that institutions of higher learning are now open to women, although Anthony's picture is perhaps rosier than the reality. While land-grant colleges and universities in the Midwest and West were among the first to open their doors to women, higher education for women was regarded as secondary to that of men, designed to outfit women for their roles as wives to a growing number of college-educated men, and as mothers to children who would also pursue educational goals.

Anthony speaks of improvements in the legal status of women. She says that women can now own their own property and businesses. They can retain ownership of property they have inherited. They can testify in court and sue; perversely, they can also be sued, suggesting that now they have a measure of wealth that a plaintiff can claim. Anthony points out, though, that wives have no claim on their husband's earnings, putting them at a disadvantage in divorce—though she also notes that courts are becoming more lenient in their treatment of women.

Anthony then turns to her all-consuming issue, that of the ballot, noting that for all the successes women have enjoyed, they still do not have the vote. She does, though, state that even in this matter the "steady pressure" of women has led to some success. Women can vote on school matters in twenty-five states. In some states, women can vote on other local matters. And four states have already acknowledged the right of women to vote in all elections, including federal ones. (Those states were Wyoming, Utah, Colorado, and Idaho.) Additionally, women are writing about political affairs, joining civic organizations, and holding state, county, and municipal posts. Women, Anthony says, have been among delegates sent to national political conventions and have been appointed electors in their states. Other women have won office as legislators—all without causing "domestic earthquakes."

In the final paragraphs of the article, Anthony strikes a note of optimism about the future. She points out the existence of such organizations as the National American Women Suffrage Association, whose efforts are buttressed by those of other women who are working for legislation favorable to women. At the state level, proponents of women's rights are working on amendments to state constitutions and lobbying legislatures for equal rights. She comments that the states of South Dakota and Washington are submitting women's suffrage amendments to their

legislatures, and with suffrage already a reality in the Rocky Mountain states, she expresses optimism that the remainder of the West and Northwest will follow their example. In paragraph 13, Anthony calls for a Sixteenth Amendment to the Constitution to give women the right to vote; she could not have known that such an amendment would be the Nineteenth. In the final paragraph, Anthony expresses optimism that sooner or later women will be granted the right to vote: "The day will come when man will recognize woman as his peer, not only at the fireside, but in the councils of the nation."

♦ Nineteenth Amendment

Anthony is usually credited with authorship of the Nineteenth Amendment. She wrote a version of the amendment in 1877, basing its wording on the Fifteenth Amendment, which said that the right to vote could not be denied on the basis of race, color, or previous condition of servitude (that is, slavery). A sympathetic California senator, Aaron Sargent, submitted the amendment to the U.S. Congress, which refused to take action on it. As the proposal was resubmitted in every session of Congress in the decades that followed, it came to be referred to as the Anthony Amendment.

After Anthony's death in 1906, pressure for passage of the amendment began to mount. It culminated in 1917 after the United States entered World War I. Early that year, the so-called Silent Sentinels, a group of suffragists led by Alice Paul, among others, began a two-and-a-half-year picket (with Sundays off) of the White House, urging President Woodrow Wilson to support a suffrage amendment. Public opinion began to sway in favor of the suffragists when it was learned that many of the picketers had been arrested and sentenced to jail, usually on thin charges of obstructing traffic, and that the conditions the jailed women endured were often brutal. Alice Paul, in particular, was subjected to inhuman treatment and launched a hunger strike in protest until she and the other protestors were released after a court of appeals ruled the arrests illegal.

Finally, on January 9, 1918, Wilson announced that he supported the amendment. On January 10, 1918, the House of Representatives narrowly passed the amendment, but the Senate refused to consider the matter until October, when the measure failed by just three votes. In response, the newly formed National Women's Party, led by Alice Paul, mounted a campaign against legislators who supported the Democratic Party's resistance to bringing the suffrage amendment to a vote in Congress and were up for reelection—as she and her supporters had done in 1914. These efforts, along with efforts to mold public opinion, were successful, for on May 21, 1919, after the House of Representatives passed the measure by a vote of 304 to 89, the Senate, on June 4, passed it by a vote of fifty-six to twenty-five. The amendment was then submitted to the states for ratification. The first state to ratify it was Illinois. Thirty-six states needed to ratify the amendment for it to become part of the Constitution. That number was reached on August 18, 1920, when Tennessee, following contentious debate and two deadlocked roll calls, ratified it after one legislator, Harry Burn, changed his vote on the urging of his mother. Oddly, several states throughout the South initially rejected the amendment and were quite slow to ratify it later, the last being Mississippi in 1984.

The language of the amendment is simple and straightforward. A preface notes that the resolution, dated May 1919, is before the first session of the Sixty-sixth Congress in Washington, D.C. The preface is followed by a description of the resolution and the process of approving it, including congressional approval and ratification by the states. In particular, it says that the resolution has to be approved by a two-thirds majority in both the House of Representatives and the Senate and that it must be ratified, or approved, by three fourths of the states—at that time, thirty-six states (out of forty-eight). The third part of the document is the text of the amendment itself, stating that citizens cannot be denied the right to vote on the basis of sex and that Congress has the power to enforce the amendment by legislation.

Impact and Legacy

It is difficult to overstate the impact of Susan B. Anthony and her ability, through her writings, speeches, and correspondence, to galvanize Americans in the pursuit of women's rights. She recognized, for example, that women could not achieve equal rights until they achieved economic independence and the education they needed for such independence. As long as women were under the economic control of men, legislators had no reason to grant them the right to vote or any other right, for they did not form a constituency. While numerous women in the middle decades of the nineteenth century were proponents of women's rights—and at the same time opposed to slavery—Anthony, along with such other towering figures as Elizabeth Cady Stanton and Lucretia Mott, was able to forge a sustained political movement that led to a series of successes ranging from the landmark 1860 Married Women's Property Act in New York to, eventually, the Nineteenth Amendment. She was able to focus attention by forging alliances with other women's groups, including, for example, the Woman's Christian Temperance Union, along with civic groups, college women, and women's clubs.

Most important, Anthony was able to bridge the gaps that had evolved in the women's movement. After the Civil War and the failure of the Reconstruction amendments to secure women the vote, she and Stanton broke with their former abolitionist allies. Many women's groups opposed this move, and the result was tension in the suffrage movement. But as the century wore on, the power of Anthony's influence overcame these tensions, and by the turn of the new century, the cause of woman suffrage and the name of "Miss Anthony" were almost synonymous. The nineteenth century featured numerous important women's rights activists, but in the twentieth century and beyond it is Susan B. Anthony's name that survives.

Key Sources

Many of Anthony's papers and addresses can be found in the four published volumes of *The Selected Papers of Elizabeth Cady Stanton and Susan B. Anthony*, edited by Ann D. Gordon (1997–2006). Two additional volumes are forthcoming. Gordon has also edited *Travels for Reform: The Early Work of Susan B. Anthony and Elizabeth Cady Stanton, 1852–1861*, available online at the Rutgers University Elizabeth Cady Stanton and Susan B. Anthony Papers Project (http://ecssba.rutgers.edu/pubs/EEtravels.html). Project Gutenberg publishes online "An Account of the Proceedings on the Trial of Susan B. Anthony, on the Charge of Illegal Voting" (http://www.gutenberg.org/etext/18281). Excerpts from Anthony's *History of Woman Suffrage* are reprinted in *The Concise History of Woman Suffrage: Selections from History of Woman Suffrage*, edited by Mari Jo Buhle and Paul Buhle (2005).

Essential Quotes

"Well I have been & gone & done it!!—positively voted the Republican ticket."

(Letter to Elizabeth Cady Stanton)

"Our democratic-republican government is based on the idea of the natural right of every individual member thereof to a voice and a vote in making and executing the laws."

("Is It a Crime for a Citizen of the United States to Vote?")

"I submit the question, if the deprivation by law of the ownership of one's own person, wages, property, children, the denial of the right as an individual to sue and be sued and testify in the courts, is not a condition of servitude most bitter and absolute, even though under the sacred name of marriage?"

("Is It a Crime for a Citizen of the United States to Vote?")

"The day will come when man will recognize woman as his peer, not only at the fireside, but in the councils of the nation."

("The Status of Woman, Past, Present, and Future")

Further Reading

■ Books

Baker, Jean H. *Sisters: The Lives of America's Suffragists*. New York: Hill and Wang, 2005.

———. *Votes for Women: The Struggle for Suffrage Revisited*. New York: Oxford University Press, 2002.

Clift, Eleanor. *Founding Sisters and the Nineteenth Amendment*. Hoboken, N.J.: Wiley, 2003.

DuBois, Ellen. *Woman Suffrage and Women's Rights*. New York: New York University Press, 1998.

Flexner, Eleanor, and Ellen Fitzpatrick. *Century of Struggle: The Woman's Rights Movement in the United States*, 2nd ed. Cambridge, Mass.: Harvard University Press, 1996.

Harper, Ida Husted. *The Life and Work of Susan B. Anthony*, 3 vols. Indianapolis: Bowen-Merrill, 1898–1908.

Kraditor, Aileen S. *The Ideas of the Woman Suffrage Movement: 1890–1920*. New York: W. W. Norton, 1981.

Lutz, Alma. *Susan B. Anthony: Rebel, Crusader, Humanitarian*. 1959. Reprint Charleston, S.C.: BiblioBazaar, 2007.

Sherr, Lynn. *Failure Is Impossible: Susan B. Anthony in Her Own Words*. New York: Three Rivers Press, 1996.

Stalcup, Brenda, ed. *Susan B. Anthony*. San Diego, Calif.: Greenhaven Press, 2001.

Ward, Geoffrey C., and Ken Burns. *Not for Ourselves Alone: The Story of Elizabeth Cady Stanton and Susan B. Anthony*. New York: Knopf, 2001.

—*Michael J. O'Neal*

Questions for Further Study

1. Anthony, who died in 1906, would no doubt be amazed if she came back today and observed all the progress made on behalf of women. Imagine that you are she and write a letter, using the style of her correspondence on the 1872 election, about what you see in the world today. Include not only positives but any negatives as Anthony might view them.

2. In her address called "Is It a Crime for a Citizen of the United States to Vote?" Anthony makes a number of interesting arguments. Particularly notable are her observations on the use of male pronouns (*he, him*) in the Constitution and other legal documents. Taking issue with those who claimed that this proved voting rights were only for men, she suggests that this logic, taken to its conclusion, means that women should not be subject to any laws. Critique her logic and discuss it with regard to other situations in which people are placed under a particular restriction without a corresponding right. (For example, there is the matter of "taxation without representation" that figured heavily into the Founders' resentment against British rule or the fact that a young person might be called up for military service at age seventeen, allowed to vote at eighteen, but not permitted to drink alcohol until age twenty-one.)

3. Discuss the history of the Nineteenth Amendment with a focus on Anthony's efforts toward its passage. Note that she referred to the proposed amendment as the Sixteenth, not knowing that three others would be passed in the years between her time and the ratification of the female voting amendment in 1920.

Letters concerning Casting a Vote in the 1872 Federal Election

1872–1873

♦ To Elizabeth Cady Stanton

Rochester Nov 5th 1872

Dear Mrs Stanton

Well I have been & gone & done it!!—positively voted the Republican ticket—strait this a.m. at 7 Oclock—& swore my vote in at that—was registered on Friday & 15 other women followed suit in this ward—then on Sunday others some 20 or thirty other women tried to register, but all save two were refused—all my three sisters voted—Rhoda De Garmo too—Amy Post was rejected & she will immediately bring action for that—similar to the Washington action—& Hon Henry R. Selden will be our Counsel—he has read up the law & all of our arguments & is satisfied that we [are] right & ditto the Old Judge Selden—his elder brother. so we are in for a fine agitation in Rochester on the question—I hope the morning's telegrams will tell of many women all over the country trying to vote—It is splendid that without any concert of action so many should have moved here so impromptu—... Haven't we wedged ourselves into the work pretty fairly & fully—& now that the Repubs have taken our votes—for it is the Republican members of the Board—The Democratic paper is out against us strong & that scared the Dem's on the registry board—How I wish you were here to write up the funny things said & done—Rhoda De Garmo told them that she wouldn't swear or affirm—"but would tell the truth"—& they accepted that When the Democrat said my vote should not go in the box—one Republican said to the other—What do you say Marsh!—I say put it in!—So do I said Jones—and "we'll fight it out on this line if it takes all winter"... If only now—all the women suffrage women would work to this end of enforcing the existing constitution—supremacy of national law over state law—what strides we might make this winter—But I'm awful tired—for five days I have been on the constant run—but to splendid purpose—So all right—I hope you voted too.

Affectionately,
Susan B. Anthony

♦ To Sarah Huntington

Rochester Nov 11th 1872.

My Dear Mrs Huntington

I rejoice to see your attempt to vote in old Connecticut.... Hoped hundreds of women throughout the country would make the attempt but thus far none are reported save in Norwalk Ct. and Rochester N.Y. You will have seen that about fifty presented their names here—16 were registered in the 8th Ward—1 in the 14th and 1 in the 4th—refused in the 1st—3rd—6th—7th—10th. Our city has 14 wards—thus you see women in 8 out of the 14 wards attempted to register—& that without the slightest preconcert of action—the votes of those in the 14th and 4th wards were rejected though duly registered—only the 8th Ward received and counted the votes—no mistake—for we waited & saw them distributed in the several boxes—Our papers are discussing the pro & con every day since—

I am hope[ful] you will persevere & bring action against your inspectors & Judges of election. We shall at once do so against ours who refused.... I tell them all that we me[a]n to find out if we have law enough & enforce it & if we have not already enough we mean soon to get it To vote is our wish & will....

Hastily yours—
Susan B. Anthony

♦ To Representative Benjamin F. Butler

Rochester April 27/73

Hon B. F. Butler Dear Sir

Will you give me your word on the decision of the Supreme Court of the U.S. on Mrs. Myra Bradwells case—to be read at our coming convention May 6th in New York?

The whole Democratic Press is Jubilant over this ... interpretation of the amendments—while not a Republican paper that I have seen has dared to declare the amendments mean just what they—say all persons & c —It is virtual concession of all we fought for in the late War—the supremacy of the National Gov't to protect the rights of all persons—all citizens—against the states attempts to deny or abridge—opinion of the decision—whatever it is—

My trial is to be the 13th of May—the week following the N.Y. meeting—I have just closed a canvass of this county—from which my jurors are to be drawn—and I rather guess the U.S. District Attorney—who is very bitter—will hardly find twelve men

Document Text

so ignorant on the citizen's rights—as to agree on a verdict of Guilty....

The right word spoken at our Convention—will greatly help my trial the week following—I find Judges & Courts are influenced by popular opinion—not a little—Hoping for the letter—sure—

Respectfully yours
Susan B. Anthony

Glossary

abridge:	limit
Amy Post:	a prominent Quaker suffragist and abolitionist in the period from the 1840s to the 1880s
canvass:	speaking tour
Marsh ... Jones:	Edwin T. Marsh and Beverly W. Jones (a man) were both inspectors of elections in Rochester, New York, where Anthony voted
preconcert of action:	a plan to work together
strait:	straight, meaning entirely
suffrage:	the right to vote
to splendid purpose:	with a very positive effect
ward:	an electoral district within a city or town

"Is It a Crime for a Citizen of the United States to Vote?"

1873

Friends and Fellow-citizens: I stand before you under indictment for the alleged crime of having voted at the last presidential election, without having a lawful right to vote. It shall be my work this evening to prove to you that in thus voting, I not only committed no crime, but instead simply exercised my citizen's right, guaranteed to me and all United States citizens by the National Constitution beyond the power of any State to deny.

Our democratic-republican government is based on the idea of the natural right of every individual member thereof to a voice and a vote in making and executing the laws. We assert the province of government to be to secure the people in the enjoyment of their inalienable rights. We throw to the winds the old dogma that governments can give rights. No one denies that before governments were organized each individual possessed the right to protect his own life, liberty and property. When 100 or 1,000,000 people enter into a free government, they do not barter away their natural rights; they simply pledge themselves to protect each other in the enjoyment of them through prescribed judicial and legislative tribunals. They agree to abandon the methods of brute force in the adjustment of their differences and adopt those of civilization. Nor can you find a word in any of the grand documents left us by the fathers which assumes for government the power to create or to confer rights. The Declaration of Independence, the United States Constitution, the constitutions of the several states and the organic laws of the territories, all alike propose *to protect* the people in the exercise of their God-given rights. Not one of them pretends to bestow rights.

"All men are created equal, and endowed by their Creator with certain inalienable rights. Among these are life, liberty and the pursuit of happiness. That to secure these [rights], governments are instituted among men, deriving their just powers from the consent of the governed."

Here is no shadow of government authority over rights, or exclusion of any class from their full and equal enjoyment. Here is pronounced the right of all men, and "consequently," as the Quaker preacher said, "of all women," to a voice in the government. And here, in this very first paragraph of the declaration, is the assertion of the natural right of all to the ballot; for how can "the consent of the governed" be given, if the right to vote be denied. Again:

"Whenever any form of government becomes destructive of these ends, it is the right of the people to alter or abolish it, and to institute a new government, laying its foundations on such principles, and organizing its powers in such forms as to them shall seem most likely to effect their safety and happiness."

Surely, the right of the whole people to vote is here clearly implied. For however destructive to their happiness this government might become, a disfranchised class could neither alter nor abolish it, nor institute a new one, except by the old brute force method of insurrection and rebellion. One-half of the people of this nation today are utterly powerless to blot from the statute books an unjust law, or to write there a new and a just one....

The preamble of the federal constitution says:

"We, the people of the United States, in order to form a more perfect union, establish justice, insure domestic tranquility, provide for the common defence, promote the general welfare and secure the blessings of liberty to ourselves and our posterity, do ordain and established this Constitution for the United States of America."

It was we, the people, not we, the white male citizens, nor we, the male citizens; but we, the whole people, who formed this Union. We formed it not to give the blessings of liberty but to secure them; not to the half of ourselves and the half of our posterity, but to the whole people—women as well as men. It is downright mockery to talk to women of their enjoyment of the blessings of liberty while they are denied the only means of securing them provided by this democratic-republican government—the ballot....

James Madison said;

"Under every view of the subject, it seems indispensable that the mass of the citizens should not be without a voice in making the laws which they are to obey, and in choosing the magistrates who are to administer them.... Let it be remembered, finally, that it has ever been the pride and the boast of America that the rights for which she contended were the rights of human nature."

Document Text

These assertions by the framers of the United States Constitution of the equal and natural right of all the people to a voice in the government, have been affirmed and reaffirmed by the leading statesmen of the nation, throughout the entire history of our government....

The clauses of the United States Constitution cited by our opponents as giving power to the States to disfranchise any classes of citizens they shall please are contained in Sections 2 and 4 of Article I. The second says:

"The House of Representatives shall be composed of members chosen every second year by the people of the several States; and the electors in each State shall have the qualifications requisite for electors of the most numerous branch of the State legislature."

This cannot be construed into a concession to the States of the power to destroy the right to become an elector, but simply to prescribe what shall be the qualification, such as competency of intellect, maturity of age, length of residence, that shall be deemed necessary to enable them to make an intelligent choice of candidates. If, as our opponents assert, the last clause of this section makes it the duty of the United States to protect citizens in the several States against higher or different qualifications for electors for representatives in Congress than for members of the Assembly, then it must be equally imperative for the national government to interfere with the States, and forbid them from arbitrarily cutting off the right of one-half of the people to become electors altogether. Section 4 says:

"The times, places and manner of holding elections for senators and representatives shall be prescribed in each State by the legislature thereof; but Congress may at any time, by law, make or alter such regulations, except as to the places of choosing Senators."

Here is conceded to the States the power only to prescribe times, places and manner of holding the elections; and even with these Congress may interfere in all excepting the mere place of choosing senators. Thus, you see, there is not the slightest permission in either section for the States to discriminate against the right of any class of citizens to vote. Surely, to regulate cannot be to annihilate; to qualify cannot be wholly to deprive....

For any State to make sex a qualification, which must ever result in the disfranchisement of one entire half of the people, is to pass a bill of attainder, or an ex post facto law, and is therefore a violation of the supreme law of the land. By it, the blessings of liberty are forever withheld from women and their female posterity. For them, this government has no just powers derived from the consent of the governed. For them this government is not a democracy. It is not a republic. It is the most odious aristocracy ever established on the face of the globe. An oligarchy of wealth, where the rich govern the poor; an oligarchy of learning, where the educated govern the ignorant; or even an oligarchy of race, where the Saxon rules the African, might be endured; but this oligarchy of sex, which makes father, brothers, husband, sons, the oligarchs over the mother and sisters, the wife and daughters of every household; which ordains all men sovereigns, all women subjects, carries dissension, discord and rebellion into every home of the nation. This most odious aristocracy exists, too, in the face of Section 4, of Article IV, which says: "The United States shall guarantee to every State in the Union a republican form of government."

What, I ask you, is the distinctive difference between the inhabitants of a monarchical and those of a republican form of government, save that in the monarchical the people are subjects, helpless, powerless, bound to obey laws made by political superiors—while in the republican, the people are citizens, individual sovereigns, all clothed with equal power, to make and unmake both their laws and law makers. The moment you deprive a person of his right to a voice in the government, you degrade him from the status of a citizen of the republic to that of a subject. It matters very little to him whether his monarch be an individual tyrant, as is the Czar of Russia, or a 15,000,000 headed monster, as here in the United States; he is a powerless subject, serf or slave; not in any sense a free and independent citizen.

It is urged that the use of the masculine pronouns *he, his* and *him,* in all the constitutions and laws, is proof that only men were meant to be included in their provisions. If you insist on this version of the letter of the law, we shall insist that you be consistent, and accept the other horn of the dilemma, which would compel you to exempt women from taxation for the support of the government and from penalties for the violation of laws....

Though the words persons, people, inhabitants, electors, citizens, are all used indiscriminately in the national and State constitutions, there was always a conflict of opinion, prior to the war, as to whether they were synonymous terms, but whatever there was for a doubt, under the old regime, the adoption of the Fourteenth Amendment settled that question forever, in its first sentence: "All persons born or naturalized

in the United States and subject to the jurisdiction thereof, are citizens of the United States and of the state wherein they reside."

The second settles the equal status of all citizens: "No State shall make or enforce any law which shall abridge the privileges or immunities of citizens of the United States; nor shall any State deprive any person of life, liberty or property, without due process of law, nor deny to any person within its jurisdiction the equal protection of the laws."

The only question left to be settled, now, is: Are women persons? I scarcely believe any of our opponents will have the hardihood to say they are not. Being persons, then, women are citizens, and no State has a right to make any new law, or to enforce any old law, which shall abridge their privileges or immunities. Hence, every discrimination against women in the constitutions and laws of the several States, is today null and void, precisely as is every one against negroes....

If the Fourteenth Amendment does not secure to all citizens the right to vote, for what purpose was the grand old charter of the fathers lumbered with its unwieldy proportions? The Republican party, and Judges Howard and Bingham, who drafted the document, pretended it was to do something for black men; and if that something were not to secure them in their right to vote and hold office, what could it have been? For, by the Thirteenth Amendment, black men had become people, and hence were entitled to all the privileges and immunities of the government, precisely as were the women of the country, and foreign men not naturalized....

Thus, you see, those newly-freed men were in possession of every possible right, privilege and immunity of the government, except that of suffrage, and hence, needed no constitutional amendment for any other purpose. What right in this country has the Irishman the day after he receives his naturalization papers that he did not possess the day before, save the right to vote and hold office? The Chinamen now crowding our Pacific coast are in precisely the same position. What privilege or immunity has California or Oregon the right to deny them, save that of the ballot? Clearly, then if the Fourteenth Amendment was not to secure to black men their right to vote it did nothing for them, since they possessed everything else before. But if it was intended to prohibit the states from denying or abridging their right to vote, then it did the same for all persons, white women included, born or naturalized in the United States; for the amendment does not say that all male persons of African descent, but that all persons are citizens.

However much the doctors of the law may disagree, as to whether people and citizens, in the original Constitution, were one and the same, or whether the privileges and immunities in the Fourteenth Amendment include the right of suffrage, the question of the citizen's right to vote is forever settled by the Fifteenth Amendment. "The right of citizens of the United States to vote shall not be denied or abridged by the United States or by any State on account of race, color, or previous condition of servitude." How can the State deny or abridge the right of the citizen, if the citizen does not possess it? There is no escape from the conclusion that to vote is the citizen's right, and the specifications of race, color, or previous condition of servitude can in no way impair the force of the emphatic assertion that the citizen's right to vote shall not be denied or abridged.

The political strategy of the second section of the Fourteenth Amendment, failing to coerce the rebel States into enfranchising their negroes, and the necessities of the Republican party demanding their votes throughout the South, to ensure the re-election of Grant in 1872, that party was compelled to place this positive prohibition of the Fifteenth Amendment upon the United States and all the States thereof....

If, however, you will insist that the Fifteenth Amendment's emphatic interdiction against robbing United States citizens of their suffrage "on account of race, color, or previous condition of servitude" is a recognition of the right of either the United States or any State to deprive them of the ballot for any or all other reasons, I will prove to you that the class of citizens for whom I now plead are by all the principles of our government, and many of the laws of the States, included under the term "previous condition of servitude."

Consider first married women and their legal status. What is servitude? "The condition of a slave." What is a slave? "A person who is robbed of the proceeds of his labor; a person who is subject to the will of another." By the laws of Georgia, South Carolina, and all the States of the South, the negro had no right to the custody and control of his person. He belonged to his master. If he were disobedient, the master had the right to use correction. If the negro did not like the correction and ran away, the master had a right to use coercion to bring him back. By the laws of almost every State in this Union today, North as well as South, the married woman has no right to the custody and control of her person. The wife

Document Text

belongs to the husband; and if she refuse obedience, he may use moderate correction, and if she do not like his moderate correction and leave his "bed and board," the husband may use moderate coercion to bring her back. The little word "moderate," you see, is the saving clause for the wife, and would doubtless be overstepped should her offended husband administer his correction with the "cat-o'-nine-tails," or accomplish his coercion with blood-hounds.

Again, the slave had no right to the earnings of his hands, they belonged to his master; no right to the custody of his children, they belonged to his master; no right to sue or be sued, or to testify in the courts. If he committed a crime, it was the master who must sue or be sued....

I submit the question, if the deprivation by law of the ownership of one's own person, wages, property, children, the denial of the right as an individual to sue and be sued and testify in the courts, is not a condition of servitude most bitter and absolute, even though under the sacred name of marriage?

Glossary

Assembly:	the legislature
Chinamen:	a term for Asians in general and persons of Chinese origin in particular common at the time and not considered a racial slur
disfranchised:	often rendered as *disenfranchised* and referring to having been denied the vote
doctors of the law:	lawyers
electors:	elected representatives from each state whose vote, in the Electoral College, decides presidential elections
enfranchising:	giving people the vote
ex post facto:	Latin for "after the fact," a term for a retroactive law, or a law that changes the consequences for specific acts that occurred prior to the time the law was adopted
the fathers:	the Founding Fathers
the grand old charter of the fathers:	the Constitution
hardihood:	audacity or daring
horn of the dilemma:	the position of being forced to choose between two equally unacceptable alternatives
interdiction:	prohibition
letter of the law:	the provisions of the law as written, without any attempt to interpret it in light of particular situations
lumbered with its unwieldy proportions:	cluttered up so much that it became too wordy to be useful or effective
magistrates:	government officials
the most numerous branch of the State legislature:	in most cases, the "lower house," equivalent to the House of Representatives in Congress

Glossary

odious aristocracy:	a terrible system of rule by the wealthy and powerful
old regime:	the U.S. government prior to the Civil War and the freeing of slaves
oligarchy:	a government in which a small group of people exercise dictatorial control
organic laws:	original, fundamental laws
prescribed … tribunals:	legally and formally chosen courts of review
privileges or immunities:	rights of citizens to enjoy the same constitutional freedoms in any state of the United States, as provided in Article IV of the Constitution
province:	responsibility
suffrage:	the right to vote

Document Text

1897

"The Status of Woman, Past, Present, and Future"

Fifty years ago woman in the United States was without a recognized individuality in any department of life. No provision was made in public or private schools for her education in anything beyond the rudimentary branches. An educated woman was a rarity, and was gazed upon with something akin to awe. The women who were known in the world of letters, in the entire country, could be easily counted upon the ten fingers. Margaret Fuller, educated by her father, a Harvard graduate and distinguished lawyer, stood preeminently at the head, and challenged the admiration of such men as Emerson, Channing, and Greeley.

In those days the women of the family were kept closely at home, carding, spinning, and weaving, making the butter and cheese, knitting and sewing, working by day and night, planning and economizing, to educate the boys of the family. Thus the girls toiled so long as they remained under the home roof, their services belonging to the father by law and by custom. Any kind of career for a woman was a thing undreamed of. Among the poorer families the girls might go about among the neighbors and earn a miserable pittance at housework or sewing. When the boy was twenty-one, the father agreed to pay him a fixed sum per annum, thenceforth, for his services, or, in default of this, he was free to carry his labor where it would receive a financial reward. No such agreement ever was made with the girls of the family. They continued to work without wages after they were twenty-one, exactly as they did before. When they married, their services were transferred to the husband, and were considered to be bountifully rewarded by food, shelter, and usually a very scanty supply of clothes. Any wages the wife might earn outside of the home belonged by law to the husband. No matter how drunken and improvident he might be; no matter how great her necessities and those of the children, if the employer paid the money to her he could be prosecuted by the husband and compelled to pay it again to him.

Cases were frequent where fathers willed all of their property to the sons, entirely cutting the daughters out. Where, however, the daughters received property, it passed directly into the sole possession of the husband, and all the rents and profits belonged to him to use as he pleased. At his death he could dispose of it by will, dispose of it by will, depriving the wife of all but what was called the "widow's dower," a life interest in one-third of that which was by right her own property. She lost not only the right to her earnings and her property, but also the right to the custody of her person and her children. The husband could apprentice the children at an early age, in spite of the mother's protest, and at his death could dispose of the children by will, even an unborn child. The wife could neither sue nor be sued, nor testify in the courts. The phrase in constant use in legal decisions was, "The wife is dead in law," or, "Husband and wife are one, and that one the husband." According to the English common law, which then prevailed in every State in the Union except Louisians, a man might beat his wife up to the point of endangering her life, without being liable to prosecution.

Fifty years ago no occupations were open to women except cooking, sewing, teaching, and factory work. Very few women were sufficiently educated to teach, but those who could do so received from $4 to $8 a month and "boarded 'round," while men, for exactly the same service, received $30 a month and board. Every woman must marry, either with or without love, for the sake of support, or be doomed to a life of utter dependence, living, after the death of parents, in the home of a married brother or sister, the druge and burden-bearer of the family, without any financial recompense, and usually looked upon with disrespect by the children. Women might work like galley slaves for their own relatives, receiving only their board and clothes, and hold their social position in the community; but the moment they stepped outside of the home and became wage-earners, thus securing pecuniary independence, they lost caste and were rigidly barred out from the quilting bees, the apple-parings, and all the society functions of the neighborhood. Is it any wonder that a sour and crabbed disposition was universally ascribed to spinsterhood, or that those women should be regarded as most unfortunate, doomed to a loveless, aimless, and dependent existence,—universally considered as having made a failure of life?…

Such was the helpless, dependent, fettered condition of women when the first Women"s Rights

Convention was called just forty-nine years ago, at Seneca Falls, N. Y., by Elizabeth Cady Stanton and Lucretia Mott. Half a century before this, Mary Wollstonecraft had written her "Vindication of the Rights of Women," that matchless plea for the equality of the sexes. A quarter of century before, Frances Wright, in connection with addresses upon other subjects, demanded equal rights for women. In 1835, Ernestine L. Rose and Paulina Wright Davis circulated the first petition for property rights for women, and during the next ten years Mrs. Rose addressed the New York Legislature a number of times asking political equality. Mrs. Stanton also had circulated petitions and addressed the Legislature during this period. In 1847, Lucy Stone, on her return from Oberlin College, made her first women's rights address in her brother's church in Gardner, Mass.

While there had been individual demands, from time to time, the first organized body to formulate a declaration of the rights of women was the one which met at Seneca Falls, July 19–20, 1848, and adjourned to meet at Rochester two weeks later. In the Declaration of Sentiments and the Resolutions there framed, every point was covered that, down to the present day, has been contended for by the advocates of equal rights for women. Every inequality of the existing laws and customs was carefully considered and a thorough and complete readjustment demanded. The only resolution that was not unanimously adopted was the one urging the elective franchise for women. Those who opposed it did so only because they feared it would make the movement ridiculous. But Mrs. Stanton and Frederick Douglass, seeing that the power to make laws and choose rulers was the right by which all others could be secured, persistently advocated the resolution and at last carried it by a good majority....

There is not space to follow the history of the last fifty years and study the methods by which these victories have been gained, but there is not one foot of advanced ground upon which women stand to-day that has not been obtained through the hard-fought battles of other women. The close of this nineteenth century finds every trade, vocation, and profession open to women, and every opportunity at their command for preparing themselves to follow these occupations. The girls as well as the boys of a family now fit themselves for such careers as their tastes and abilities permit. A vast amount of the household drudgery, that once monopolized the whole time and strength of the mother and daughters, has been taken outside and turned over to machinery in vast establishments. A money value is placed upon the labor of women. The ban of social ostracism has been largely removed from the woman wage-earner. She who can make for herself a place of distinction in any line of work receives commendation instead of condemnation. Woman is no longer compelled to marry for support, but may herself make her own home and earn her own financial independence.

With but few exceptions, the highest institutions of learning in the land are as freely opened to girls as to boys, and they may receive their degrees as legal, medical, and theological colleges, and practise their professions without hindrance. In the world of literature and art women divide the honors with men; and our civil-service rules have secured for them many thousands of remunerative positions under the Government....

There has been a radical revolution in the legal status of women. In most States the old common law has been annulled by legislative enactment, through which partial justice, at least, has been done to married women. In nearly every State they may retain and control property owned at marriage and all they may receive by gift or inheritance thereafter, and also their earnings outside the home. They may sue and be sued, testify in the courts, and carry on business in their own name, but in no State have wives any ownership in the joint earnings. In six or seven State have equal guardianship of the children. While in most States the divorce laws are the same for men and women, they never can bear equally upon both while all the property earned during marriage belongs wholly to the husband. There has been such a modification in public sentiment, however, that, in most cases, courts and juries show a marked leniency toward women.

The department of politics has been slowest to give admission to women. Suffrage is the pivotal rights, and if it could have been secured at the beginning, women would not have been half a century in gaining the privileges enumerated above, for privileges they must be called so long as others may either give or take them away. If women could make the laws or elect those who make them, they would be in the position of sovereigns instead of subjects. Were they the political peers of man they could command instead of having to beg, petition, and pray. Can it be possible it is for this reason that men have been so determined in their opposition to grant to women political power?

But even this stronghold is beginning to yield to the long and steady pressure. In twenty-five States

women possess suffrage in school matters; in four States they have a limited suffrage in local affairs; in one State they have municipal suffrage; in four States they have full suffrage, local, State, and national. Women are becoming more and more interested in political questions and public affairs. Every campaign sees greater numbers in attendance at the meetings, and able woman speakers are now found upon the platforms of all parties. Especial efforts are made by politicians to obtain the support of women, and during the last campaign one of the Presidential candidates held special meetings for women in the large cities throughout the country. Some of the finest political writing in the great newspapers of the day is done by women, and the papers are extensively read by women of all classes. In many of the large cities women have formed civic clubs and are exercising a distinctive influence in municipal matters. In most of the States of the Union woman are eligible for many offices, State and County Superintendents, Registers of Deeds, etc. They are Deputies to State, County, and City officials, notaries public, State Librarians, and enrolling and engrossing clerks in the Legislatures.

It follows, as a natural result, that in the States where women vote they are eligible to all offices. They have been sent as delegates to National Conventions, made Presidential electors, and are sitting to-day as members in both the Upper and Lower Houses of the Legislatures. In some towns all the offices are filled by women. These radical changes have been effected without any social upheaval or domestic earthquakes, family relations have suffered no disastrous changes, and the men of the States where women vote furnish the strongest testimony in favor of woman suffrage.…

From that little convention at Seneca Falls, with a following of a handful of women scattered through half-a-dozen different States, we have now the great National Association, with headquarters in New York City, and auxiliaries in almost every State in the Union. These State bodies are effecting a thorough system of county and local organizations for the purpose of securing legislation favorable to women, and especially to obtain amendments to their State Constitutions. As evidence of the progress of public opinion, more than half of the Legislatures in session, during the past winter, have discussed and voted upon bills for the enfranchisement of women, and in most of them they were adopted by one branch and lost by a very small majority in the other. The Legislatures of Washington and South Dakota have submitted woman-suffrage amendments to their electors for 1898, and vigorous campaigns will be made in those States during the next two years. For a quarter of a century Wyoming has stood as a conspicuous object-lesson in woman suffrage, and is now reinforced by the three neighboring States of Colorado, Utah, and Idaho. With this central group, standing on the very crest of the Rocky Mountains, the spirit of justice and freedom for women cannot fail to descend upon all the Western and Northwestern States. No one who makes a careful study of this question can help but believe that, in a very few years, all the States west of the Mississippi river will have enfranchised their women.

While the efforts of each State are concentrated upon its own Legislature, all of the States combined in the national organization are directing their energies toward securing a Sixteenth Amendment to the Constitution of the United States. The demands of this body have been received with respectful and encouraging attention from Congress. Hearings have been granted by the Committees of both Houses, resulting, in a number of instances, in favorable reports. Upon one occasion the question was brought to a discussion in the Senate, and received the affirmative vote of one-third of the members.

Until woman has obtained "that right protective of all other rights—the ballot," this agitation must still go on, absorbing the time and the energy of our best and strongest women. Who can measure the advantages that would result if the magnificent abilities of these women could be devoted to the needs of government, society, home, instead of being consumed in the struggle to obtain their birthright of individual freedom? Until this be gained we can never know, we cannot even prophesy, the capacity and power of woman for the uplifting of humanity. It may be delayed longer than we think, it may be here sooner than we expect, but the day will come when man will recognize woman as his peer, not only at the fireside, but in the councils of the nation. Then, and not until then, will there be the perfect comradeship, the ideal union between the sexes, that shall result in the highest development of the race. What this shall be we may not attempt to define, but this we know, that only good can come to the individual or the nation through the rendering of exact justice.

Glossary

boarded 'round:	sent to live in other households
carding:	brushing fabric in order to disentangle fibers
common law:	law based primarily on past legal judgments, rather than on statutes passed by a legislative body such as the U.S. Congress
crabbed:	irritable, crabby
elective franchise:	the right to vote
electors:	elected representatives from each state whose vote, in the Electoral College, decides presidential elections
enfranchisement:	provision of the right to vote
engrossing:	preparing official documents according to precise legal procedures
improvident:	unwilling or incapable of providing for the needs of those under one's care
Mary Wollstonecraft:	prominent English feminist (1759–1797) whose daughter, Mary Wollstonecraft Shelley, wrote *Frankenstein*
notaries public:	persons legally authorized to witness the signing of documents, administer oaths, and perform other duties
per annum:	per year
spinsterhood:	a term, common in the time before the sexual revolution of the 1960s, for the situation of a woman who will never be married
suffrage:	the right to vote
the race:	not a reference to "race" as it is commonly understood today but rather to the human race
the world of letters:	the world of literature
Upper and Lower Houses of the Legislature:	common divisions within parliamentary democracies such as the United States, in which the Senate and House of Representatives are the upper and lower house, respectively

Document Text

NINETEENTH AMENDMENT

1920

Section 1. The right of the citizens of the United States to vote shall not be denied or abridged by the United States or by any State on account of sex.

Section 2. Congress shall have power to enforce this article by appropriate legislation.

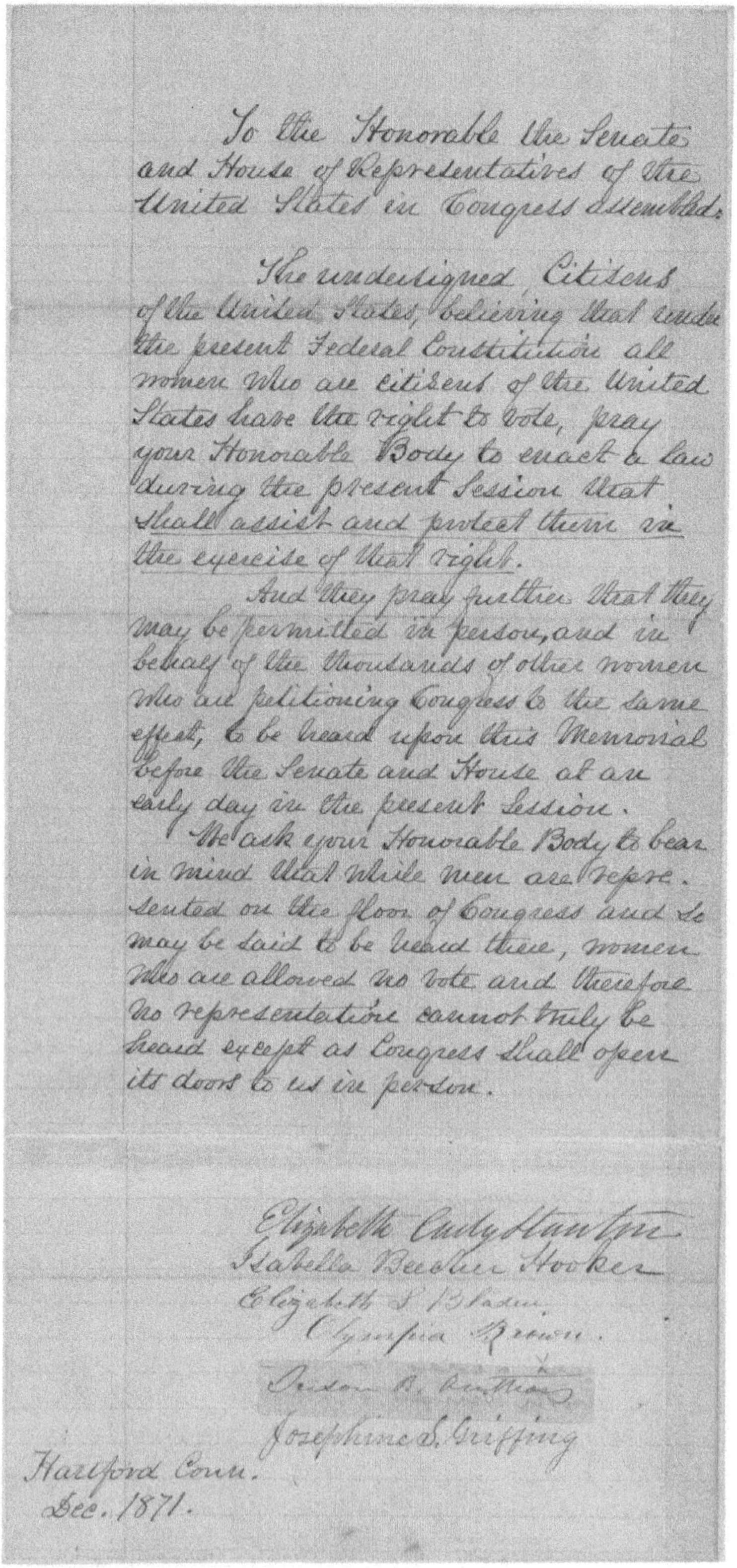

To the Honorable the Senate and House of Representatives of the United States in Congress Assembled:

The undersigned Citizens of the United States, believing that under the present Federal Constitution all women who are citizens of the United States have the right to vote, pray your Honorable Body to enact a law during the present Session that shall assist and protect them in the exercise of that right.

And they pray further that they may be permitted in person, and in behalf of the thousands of other women who are petitioning Congress to the same effect, to be heard upon this Memorial before the Senate and House at an early day in the present Session.

We ask your Honorable Body to bear in mind that while men are represented on the floor of Congress and so may be said to be heard there, women who are allowed no vote and therefore no representation cannot truly be heard except as Congress shall open its doors to us in person.

Elizabeth Cady Stanton
Isabella Beecher Hooker
Elizabeth L. Bladen
Olympia Brown
Susan B. Anthony
Josephine S. Griffing

Hartford Conn.
Dec. 1871.

Letter by Susan B. Anthony to US Congress in favor of Women's Suffrage

Engraving of Arnold, by H. B. Hall, after John Trumbull Artist (U.S. National Archives and Records Administration)

Benedict Arnold: Original Analysis

Continental Army officer

1741–1801

Overview

Benedict Arnold was born January 14, 1741, and grew up in the eastern Connecticut town of Norwich. He moved to New Haven as an adult and had found work as the captain of a merchant ship. Arnold built a reputation there as an untrustworthy troublemaker, dishonest, money-grubbing, quick to feel slighted and willing to express his anger in duels.

As the political crisis in the colonies grew, Arnold joined a militia in New Haven and found he had a talent for officering soldiers. When the American War for Independence started in 1775, Arnold's militia joined the Continental Army and quickly captured Fort Ticonderoga and Crown Point on Lake Champlain, commandeering its ammunition and cannon for the forces in Boston. For the next two years, he led campaigns in Quebec which, while not victorious, tied down British armies better deployed against George Washington's main colonial force to the south. Arnold assumed status as perhaps the colonists' most able military officer and one of the Revolutionary War's biggest colonial heroes.

In October 1777, Arnold led an army under the command of General Horatio Gates into battle, outside the New York town of Saratoga at Freeman's Farm. He fought for an unconventional and brilliant victory that directly convinced the French monarchy to join with the colonists as an ally in a war that seemed winnable by the colonists for the first time. At the end of the battle, a Hessian soldier shot and killed Arnold's horse out from under him; the horse's body fell and pinned Arnold's leg, crushing it. Arnold barely escaped with his life and his leg, and would walk with a pronounced limp for the rest of his life; Arnold's leg actually has a monument dedicated to it at Freeman's Farm today. More than one historian has speculated that if Benedict Arnold had died at Freeman's Farm, he might well be remembered as one of the United States' first military heroes, a martyr to the cause of the American Revolution.

Yet Arnold did not die. Instead, by the time of Saratoga he had also built a reputation for himself in the army and with the Continental Congress as a smarmy, grasping glory-seeker, determined to gain promotion to major general and to achieve a status in the continental forces vaguely akin to that of George Washington, his most ardent defender. He had offended numerous superiors with his arrogance and thin-skinned sense of outrage at a lack of recognition for his many military accomplishments. At one point, when another officer questioned his credentials as a naval commander, Arnold kicked him. Before Saratoga, he had been summoned to meet with the Continental Congress to answer to various charges of insubordination. Even after his promotion to major general in January 1778, Arnold still seethed over his lack of reimbursement from the Continental Congress for clothing and arming his soldiers.

In June 1778 Washington appointed Arnold as military commander of Philadelphia. There, he lived a lavish and spendthrift lifestyle, and directed smuggling operations in and out of the city for his own profit. He fell in love with Peggy Shippen, the nineteen year old daughter of a merchant who was still loyal to the British crown. Yet when the Continental Congress questioned the obvious incongruity of a colonial military governor hobnobbing with enemy sympathizers, Arnold expressed his rage at their disapproval of his conduct. He resigned as military governor in March 1779. A month later he married Peggy Shippen; a month after his marriage, he offered his services as a spy to the British military leadership in New York City.

Between 1779 and 1780, Benedict Arnold served as a traitorous resource for the British forces in North America, supplying them with information on colonial troop movements, fortifications and supplies. In return, he hoped for a vast monetary reward that would finally secure his finances, not to mention future status as a hero of the British Empire once the North American rebellion was put down, in what he now considered the colonists' best interest. When Washington appointed him the commander of West Point, the most important fortress securing the colonial position in New York City from the north, he offered to surrender West Point to a British attack force in return for £20,000, roughly $4.1 million.

In September 1780, British Major John André traveled in disguise to West Point to collect Arnold's terms and the plans for West Point. On the way back to British headquarters, Andre was captured by American militiamen, and revealed himself as a British officer. Arnold's plans and letters were discovered, and he fled for the British lines. Andre was hanged as a spy, but Arnold managed to escape Washington's anguish and wrath.

Upon joining the British army in North America, Arnold received his old title of brigadier general, a £6300 reward for his services and a lifelong pension of £360 a year. He became a raider, leading ferocious amphibious attacks on colonial forces in the Chesapeake Bay area and

New London, Connecticut. With Cornwallis' surrender at Yorktown in October 1781, he sailed with Peggy Shippen and the rest of the British military forces to England. He spent the rest of his life involving himself in colonial military ventures in the Caribbean, launching failed businesses, and begging for more money from the crown. He died in London on July 14, 1801.

Explanation and Analysis of Documents

Arnold began his career as a spy in May 1779. After resigning his position as military commander of Philadelphia, he asked a local loyalist sympathizer, Joseph Stansbury, to mediate with the British commander in chief in North America, General Sir Henry Clinton. Arnold's British contact, Major John Andre, was a former suitor of Arnold's new wife, Peggy Shippen, and may well have suggested Andre as a contact. Andre, who was quartered in the house of another loyalist in New York, Jonathan Odell, promised a substantial reward for Arnold's information. For more than a year, Arnold's letters provided information on where American armies were located, how well they were armed, how many soldiers they had, and who and where their French allies were.

♦ Letter to John Andre, July 12, 1780

Arnold believed his usefulness as a spy had reached a climax in the summer of 1780, as revealed in this letter, transcribed by Andre's friend Odell. First Arnold referred back to an earlier correspondence he had sent along to Captain George Beckwith, the aide-de-camp of Clinton's second-in-command, General William Knyphausen. At the time, Washington and Lafayette were planning to arouse panic amongst the British command by circulating a leaflet in Canada promising a coming invasion by the Continental Army, and asking ethnically French colonists there to rise up and join with the cause of their homeland to defeat the British Empire. The ruse was foiled by Arnold, who took the leaflet and gave a copy of it to Stansbury to bring to Andre in New York.

More important, however, was the news that he was to leave Philadelphia to take command at West Point, an appointment Arnold claimed he accepted because of its usefulness to his correspondents. Arnold wanted to meet with a British officer in person to plan for the turnover of the fortress to the British. He suggested the meeting could take place by having the officer captured near West Point, the terms of the surrender determined, and the soldier sent back to the British command as part of a prisoner exchange. Time was of the essence, as Washington expected 30, 000 French troops to land soon at Newport, Rhode Island, and combine with the colonists to attack New York City.

Time Line

1741	January 14	■ Benedict Arnold born
1766		■ Arnold joins New Haven Sons of Liberty
1774		■ Arnold appointed an officer in New Haven militia
1775	April	■ American War for Independence begins at Lexington and Concord
	May	■ Arnold, Ethan Allen and 400 troops capture Fort Ticonderoga and Crown Point on Lake Champlain
1776		■ Quebec campaign
1777	October	■ Battles of Saratoga
1778	June	■ Arnold appointed military commander in Philadelphia
1779	March	■ Arnold resigns as governor
	April	■ Marriage to Margaret (Peggy) Shippen
	May	■ Arnold offers to spy for the British forces in North America
1780	August	■ Appointed as commander of West Point
	September	■ Plot with Major John Andre to turn West Point over to British forces
	October	■ Arnold becomes brigadier general with British Army
1781	October	■ British surrender at Yorktown; Arnold evacuates to England
1801	July 14	■ Benedict Arnold dies

Arnold apparently believed the loss of West Point would be so discouraging to a flagging colonial morale that the colonists would soon give up and return to British rule. He also believed the loss of West Point was worth a lot of pounds in his pocket, and gave his financial terms for the surrender in a separate document. Yet after his signature ("J. Moore"), he also questioned the reliability of Stansbury, and asked for a two hundred guinea (guinea = one pound + one shilling) down payment for his services. Arnold was becoming uncomfortable with his position as responses from Clinton's command did not seem to match up to what Arnold had said in earlier correspondences. In reality, Stansbury was not unreliable – Clinton never saw the letters because he was fighting in Charleston, South Carolina, and would therefore correspond without knowing what information he had already received from Arnold.

♦ Benedict Arnold to George Washington, September 25, 1780

The plan to turn over West Point was ruined when Andre was captured on his way back to New York City with Arnold's plans. The leader of the local garrison in Tarrytown, where Andre was caught, sent a letter to his own commander – Arnold – asking what to do with the British spy his men had detained. Arnold, scheduled to breakfast with Washington that very morning, instead fled to the British ship on which Andre had been transported up the Hudson, the *Vulture*. The same day, September 25, 1780, Arnold wrote this letter, asking Washington to extend leniency to his wife and family, whom he claimed had nothing to do with his own actions. Arnold opened by defending his actions, claiming he acted out of a change in heart over the causes of the revolt, and that he did not expect "the World" to understand his actions or condone them. Nor did he expect the colonial government to show him any sort of favor; it says much of Arnold's ambitions and character that he accused them of continuing "ingratitude" for his earlier services.

On the other hand, Arnold had great faith in Washington's character, and asked him to protect his wife – whom he falsely claimed was innocent of any treasonous activity herself – by sending her home to Philadelphia or to be reunited with Arnold across enemy lines. He enclosed a personal letter to her, and asked that his personal effects be sent to him as well. In the event, Washington sent Peggy Shippen Arnold home to Philadelphia, where her involvement in the plot was better known and understood, and she was run out of town to meet up with Arnold in New York City. Finally, Arnold asked that his personal aides, Colonel Richard Varick and Major David Franks, be excused from any punishment as they were innocent of his actions: they were. Arnold also claimed that the owner of the house in which he had met with Andre, Joshua Hett Smith, was innocent as well. Smith was not innocent, and in fact fled to join British forces in New York City after losing a trial for treason in a civil court.

Washington asked for a prisoner exchange, to send the comparatively honest and courageous Andre back to British lines in exchange for the treasonous Arnold, but Clinton did not accept the deal, possibly because he did not think the colonists would execute Andre. Because he was wearing civilian clothes behind enemy lines, however, Andre was declared a spy as opposed to a major officer in the British army, and was hanged in October 1780. Military and political men in the know on both sides believed Arnold should have been exchanged and then executed for his treachery, but his information and military prowess were too useful to the British to give him up. Thus started the process of Arnold's vilification in American history, regardless of his repeatedly declared motives.

Impact and Legacy

To the end of his life, Arnold maintained he had become a spy because he had changed his mind on the causes of the war of independence, claiming that he believed the colonies would be better off remaining in the British Empire. His ability to convince people of his position was better summarized by Washington's reaction to Arnold's defection – the general turned to his French aide, the Marquis de Lafayette, and said "Whom can we trust now?" Historically, Arnold's name became American slang for any sort of turncoat, and in Britain he was socially ostracized. In the colonies at the time, though, Arnold's actions may have awoken rebel colonists to a new level of seriousness and willingness to put aside personal causes for the cause of the revolt, a cause which succeeded despite Arnold's betrayal in 1783. His correspondence at the time of his betrayal reveals his compromised integrity and efforts to shore up his reputation, while simultaneously trying to obtain the rewards he expected for his services.

Key Sources

The colony of New Haven is where Arnold spent his prewar years, and the New Haven Colony Historical Society had records of his time there. The New York Historical Society's Patricia D. Klingenstein Library holds images and papers relating to Arnold and his life. The Library of Congress is the repository for George Washington's papers. The University of Michigan's William L. Clements Library has an online collection of "Spy Letters of the American Revolution", with an entire section dedicated to "The Infamous Benedict Arnold".

Essential Quotes

"I have accepted the command at W[est]. P[oint]. As a Post in which I can render the most essential Services, and which will be in my disposal."

"The mass of the People are heartily tired of the War, and wish to be on their former footing - They are promised great events from this year's exertion -- If - disappointed - you have only to persevere and the contest will soon be at an end. The present Struggles are like the pangs of a dying man, violent but of a short duration--- "

"As Life and fortune are risked by serving His Majesty, it is Necessary that the latter shall be secured as well as the emoluments I give up, and a compensation for Services agreed on and a Sum advanced for that purpose - which I have mentioned in a letter which accompanies this, which Sir Henry will not, I believe, think unreasonable."

"The Heart which is Conscious of its Own rectitude, Cannot attempt to paliate a Step, which the World may Censure as wrong; I have ever acted from a Principle of Love to my Country, since the Commencement of the present unhappy Contest between Great Britain and the Colonies, the same principle of Love to my Country Actuates my present Conduct, however it may appear Inconsistent to the World: who very Seldom Judge right of any Mans Actions."

Further Reading

Books

Brandt, Clare. *The Man in the Mirror: A Life of Benedict Arnold.* New York: Random House, 1994.

Martin, James Kirby. *Benedict Arnold, Revolutionary Hero: An American Warrior Reconsidered.* New

York: New York University Press, 1997.

Philbrick, Nathaniel. *Valiant Ambition: George Washington, Benedict Arnold, and the Fate of the American Revolution.* New York: Viking, 2016.

Wilson, Barry K. *Benedict Arnold: A Traitor in Our Midst.* Montreal : McGill-Queen's University Press, 2001.

Web Sites

Shy, John. "Arnold, Benedict (1741–1801)". *Oxford Dictionary of National Biography*, Oxford University

Press, 2004 http://www.oxforddnb.com/view/article/675 (accessed 20 Aug 2016).

"Stories of Spies and Letters". *Spy Letters of the American Revolution*, Clement Library, University of

Michigan http://clements.umich.edu/exhibits/online/spies/stories.html (accessed 20 Aug 2016).

—David Simonelli, PhD

Questions for Further Study

1. What were the issues that divided colonial opinion during the American Wars of Independence? Benedict Arnold asserted that he had changed his opinions of the rebellion, that he believed it was in the colonists' best interest to return to the British Empire. He made it apparent that he expected to be seen as a future hero for coming to this conclusion – what body of opinion was he appealing to?

2. Personality plays a major role in history, moreso in the modern era of mass media, but even back in the eighteenth century. Benedict Arnold had a reputation in the colonies as a hero through the Battles of Saratoga – at the same time, he was a continuing irritation to the Continental Congress, and only his military talents and relationship with George Washington saved him from a court martial for insubordination. Try to think of a modern political, military or cultural figure who might be considered in a more positive fashion if we knew only of his or her public actions as opposed to private conflicts. During a war, when trying to rally opinion, would it have been better or worse for people to know more about Benedict Arnold as a public figure, before his betrayal?

I Benedict Arnold Major General 5
do acknowledge the UNITED STATES of AMERICA to be Free, Independent and Sovereign States, and declare that the people thereof owe no allegiance or obedience to George the Third, King of Great-Britain; and I renounce, refuſe and abjure any allegiance or obedience to him; and I do Swear that I will, to the utmoſt of my power, ſupport, maintain and defend the ſaid United States againſt the ſaid King George the Third, his heirs and ſucceſſors, and his or their abettors, aſſiſtants and adherents, and will ſerve the ſaid United States in the office of Major General which I now hold, with fidelity, according to the beſt of my ſkill and underſtanding.

Sworn before me this 30th. May 1778 at the Artillery Park Valley Forge H Knox B G Arty

B Arnold

Benedict Arnold's oath of allegiance, May 30, 1778

Letter to John Andre

July 12, 1780

[Decoded letter in Jonathan Odell's hand]
I wrote to Captn B[eckwith]-on the 7th of June, that a F[rench]--- fleet and army / were expected to act in conjunction with the A[merican]--- army. At the same time / I gave Mr. S[tansbury]-a manifesto intended to be published in C[anad]---a, and have / from time to time communicated to him such intelligence as I thought / interesting, which he assures me he has transmitted to you. I have / received no answer from my Letter, or any verbal Message - I expect soon / to command W[est] P[oin]t and most seriously wish an interview with some / intelligent officer in whom a mutual confidence could be placed. The / necessity is evident to arrange and to cooperate - An officer might / be taken Prisoner near that Post and permitted to return on parole, / or some officer on Parole sent out to effect an exchange.

General W[ashington]--- expects on the arrival of the F[rench]--- Troops to collect / 30,000 Troops to act in conjunction; if not disappointed, N[ew]. York is fixed / on as the first Object, if his numbers are not sufficient for that Object, / Can-a- is the second; of which I can inform you in time, as well as of / every other design. I have accepted the command at W[est]. P[oint]. As a Post in which / I can render the most essential Services, and which will be in my disposal. / The mass of the People are heartily tired of the War, and wish to be on / their former footing - They are promised great events from this / year's exertion -- If - disappointed - you have only to persevere / and the contest will soon be at an end. The present Struggles are / like the pangs of a dying man, violent but of a short duration---

As Life and fortune are risked by serving His Majesty, it is / Necessary that the latter shall be secured as well as the emoluments / I give up, and a compensation for Services agreed on and a Sum / advanced for that purpose - which I have mentioned in a letter / which accompanies this, which Sir Henry will not, I believe, think / unreasonable. I am Sir, your humble Servant. / July 12, 1780 J. Moore / Mr. Jn Anderson / P.S. I have great confidence in the Bearer, but beg Sir Henry / will threaten him with his resentment in case he abuses the con- / fidence placed in him, which will bring ruin on me. / The Bearer will bring me 200 Guineas, and pay the remainder to / Captn A----- who us requested to receive the deposit for Mr. Moore

[coded letter]
293.9.7 to C_t. B. 103.8.2. the 7th 152.9.17. that , a F__ 112.9.17. and 22.8.29 were 105.9.50 to / 4 9.71 in 62.8.20 with , 163.8.19 A 22.8.19 at with 230.8.13. 263.8.17 I gave Mr. S---y a 164.8.16 / 147.8.261 to be 209.9.216 in C----a and have from 163.8.17 to .163.8.17 .58.8.27 to him. / Such 147.8.21 as I 164.9.5 147.9.16 s which he 24.9.125 me has 169.9.23'd to you / I 129.8.7 .46.9.22'd no 19.8.29 to 175.9.17 . 158.8.8 - or any 177.8.13. 168.9.13 . ------- / I 105.9.5. soon to 57.9.7 .at 288.9.8 , 198.9.26, and most . 230.8.12. by --- / 291.8.27 an 149.8.27 with ---255.9.11 . 148.8.22, 182.4.28 in whom a 175.9.12 / 67.8.28 could be .196.9.16 --- the 177.8.8 is .103.8.19 to 22.9.3, and / to 66.8.15 -- are 182.8.28, 169.8.25 be . 260.8.5 , 205.9.3 near / that 209.9.18. --- and 192.9.9'd to 224.9.9 on ,188.8.13 or some ---- / 182.8.28 on 188.8.13 sent 185.6.24 to 95.9.124 an .104.8.1

120.9.7, W------- 105.9.5's on the .22.9.14.---- / of 163.8.19 F----- 172.8.7s to 56.9.8 |30.000| 172.8.70 to 11.94. in / 62.8.20. If 179.8.25, 84.8.9'd, 177.9.28. N---- is 111.9.27.'d on / 23.8.10. the 111.9.13, 180.9.19 if his 180.8.21 an .179.8.25., 255.8.17. for / that, 180.9.19, 44.8.9 --a-- is the 234.8.14 of 189.8.17. I --- / 44.8.9, 145.8.17, 294.9.12, in 266.8.17 as well as, 103.8.11, 184.9.15.---- / 80.4.20. ---- I149.8.7, 10.8.22'd the 57.9.71 at 288.9.9, 198.9.26, as, a / 100.4.18 in 189.8.19-- I can 221.8.6 the 173.8.19, 102.8.26, 236.8.21's- -- / and 289.8.17 will be in 175.9.7, 87.8.7--- the 166.8.11, of the .191.9.16 / are .129.19.21 'of --- 266.9.14 of the .286.8.20, and 291.8.27 to be an ---163.9.4 / 115.8.16 -'a .114.8.25ing --- 263.9.14. are 207.8.17ed, 125.8.15, 103.8.60--- / from this 294.8.50, 104.9.26 -- If 84.8.9ed -- 294.9.12, 129.8.7. only / to 193.8.3 and the 64.9.5, 290.9.20, 245.8.3 be at an, 99.8.14 . / the .204.8.2, 253.8.7s are 159.8.10 the 187.8.11 of a 94.9.9ing / 164.8.24, 279.8.16, but of a .238.8.25, 93.9.28.

As 158.9.25 and 115.9.12 are 226.9.3'd by. / 236.8.20ing , 131.9.21, 163.9.6 -- it is 177.8.6 that the 156.8.11'z / 236.9.28. be 234.9.3ed as well as the .98.8.22s I 128.9.25 up, / and a 159.8.5 for 236.8.21's 149.27 'on, and a 255.9.11.-- / 13.8.6'd for that 211.8.14 ----- which I have 168.8.20ed, in / a 158.8.8, 189.6.17, 10.9.9. This .189.8.17 Sir

Document Text

.300.8.4 / 290.9.20 7 not, I 31.9.13 think 282.9.12. / 152.12.12th.80--- / I am Sir, / Your Humble Servant,

Mr. John Anderson / 172.9.12---- / P.S. I have 125.8.15, 61.8.28. in the 30.8.8er, but / 30.8.8. S. 300.8.4 will 264.9.26 him with 231.9.27 / 223.8.1 in 116.8.19 He 14.8.9's the 61.8.28, 196.9.16. in / him 189.8.17, 294.9.29, 39.4.24, 48.8.19, 228.8.23 / 183.8.2. me. The 30.8.8'er .290.9.20 .39.9.24 / me |200| 126.9.141s, and .190.8.11 the .220.8.50. to 45.8.10 / A----- s, who is 222.9.15ed, to 216.9.22. the 80.8.8 for / Mr. 172.9.12 / 172.9.12

Document Text

Letter to George Washington

1780

On Board the Vulture Sepr 25th 1780

Sir

The Heart which is Concious of its Own rectitude, Cannot attempt to paliate a Step, which the world may Censure as wrong; I have ever acted from a Principle of Love to my Country, since the Commencement of the present unhappy Contest between Great Britian and the Colonies, the same principle of Love to my Country Actuates my present Conduct, however it may appear Inconsistent to the World: who very Seldom Judge right of any Mans Actions.

I have no favor to ask for myself, I have too often experienced the Ingratitude of my Country to Attempt it: But from the known humanity of your Excellence I am induced to ask your protection For Mrs Arnold from every Insult and Injury that the mistaken Vengence of my Country may expose Her to: It ought to fall only on me She is as good, and as Inocent as an Angel, and is Incapable of doing Wrong. I beg She may be permitted to return to Her Friends in Philada or to come to me as She may choose; from your Excellencey I have no fears on Her Account, but She may Suffer from the mistaken fury of The Country.

I have to request that the Inclosd Letter may be delivered to Mrs Arnold, and She permitted to write to me.

I have also to Ask that my Cloths & Baggage which are of little Consequence may be Sent to me, If required their Value shall be paid in Money. I have the honor to be With great reguard & Esteem Your Excellencys Most Obedt Hble Servt

B. Arnold

N. B. In Justice to the Gentlemen of my Family Colonel Varick & Major Franks, I think myself in honor bound to declare, that they as well as Joshua Smith Esqr. (who I know is suspected) are totally Ignorant of any transactions of mine that they had reason to believe were Injurious to the Public.

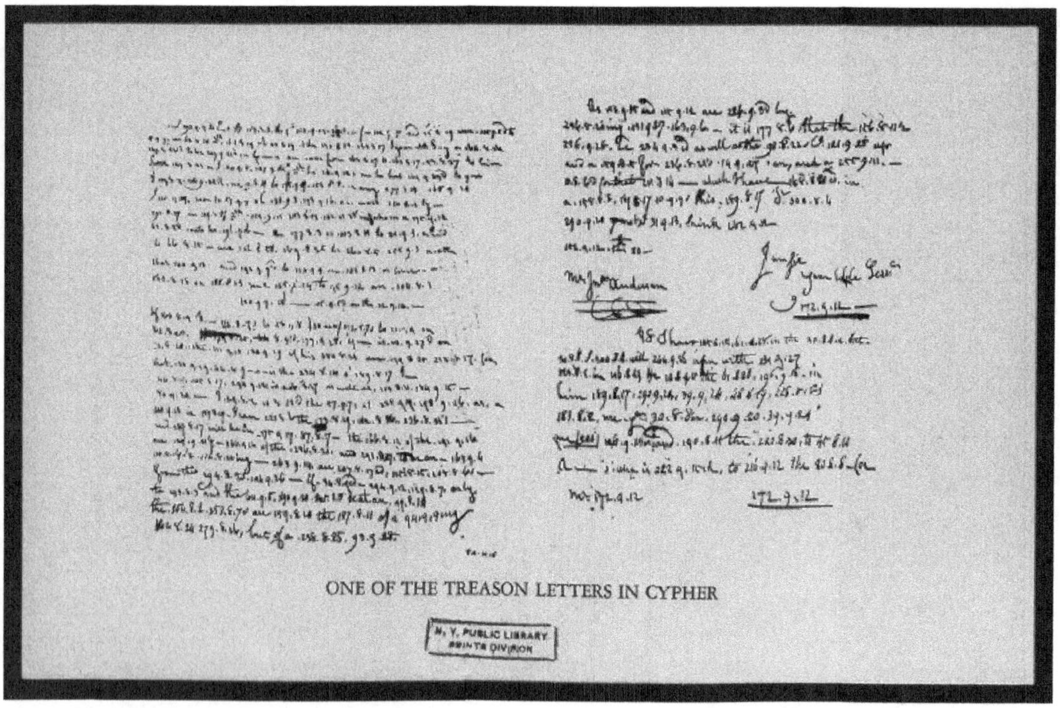
ONE OF THE TREASON LETTERS IN CYPHER
N. Y. PUBLIC LIBRARY PRINTS DIVISION

This is a reproduction of one of Benedict Arnold's coded communications with the British while he was negotiating what eventually became a failed attempt to surrender the fort at West Point in 1780. Lines of text written by his wife, Peggy Shippen Arnold, are interspersed with coded text (originally written in invisible ink) **written by Arnold.**

John James Audubon 1826

John James Audubon: Original Analysis

Artist, Naturalist, Author

1785–1851

Overview

John James Audubon was born in the French colony of Saint Domingue, modern-day Haiti, on April 26, 1785. His father sent him to France as the colony seemed on the verge of a slave revolt, and he was educated there by a woman whom the young "Jean-Jacques" regarded as a stepmother. To avoid being drafted into Napoleon's armies, in 1803 Jean-Jacques' father sent him to manage a farm that the family had inherited outside of Philadelphia, Pennsylvania, and Audubon thus ended up in the United States. There he became a bird enthusiast and simultaneously indulged in his love of art. He failed at several business enterprises, moved to Louisville, Kentucky, and actually was thrown in jail for defaulting on his debts. Through it all, Audubon continued to draw the wildlife he saw around him, especially the birds he loved. In 1820, with the encouragement of his family and his business partner, Audubon decided to publish a book of his paintings of American bird life.

Looking for subject matter meant life on the road, and Audubon left his family behind to travel throughout the American south, painting birds. He was often accompanied by other artists who would provide him with backgrounds to accompany his figure studies. He discovered he had rivals who wanted to produce their own books of American bird paintings in the United States, and thus concluded that he would have to look in Europe for a publisher. Earning money for the overseas passage through teaching, he collaborated with engravers in Edinburgh and London to create a huge picture book, three feet by two feet, which he named *Birds of America*.

Birds of America was produced in four volumes over eleven years, from 1827 to 1838. Audubon traveled from Europe to America and back repeatedly over the period, variously painting birds, lecturing on them to interested audiences and soliciting subscriptions. A subscriber would receive five prints a month from Audubon's engravers, to be mounted in a bound cover, and eventually *Birds of America* totaled 435 prints. The book came with only the prints, no captions or text; it was renowned enough that Audubon agreed to publish another, smaller version of his paintings with an accompanying explanatory text, called *Ornithological Biography*. In the end, only exceedingly wealthy people could afford the actual *Birds of America* subscription, and estimates are that only 200 full editions of *Birds of America* were ever produced. Yet its fame meant many people demanded cheaper versions of the picture book and its added text, so smaller editions sold well over the course of the 1840s and 1850s.

Audubon moved his family into a new home in New York City in 1842. He had already started a new publishing project, a chronicle of the mammals of North America called *The Viviparous Quadrupeds of North America*. This time, his expertise was not so extensive, so he worked with a collaborator, John Bachman. Bachman wrote the text, and Audubon painted the animals, many of which he found by sailing up and down the Missouri River into what was then native American territory within the Louisiana Purchase. As he was now nearing sixty, however, Audubon's eyesight was failing, and he left much of the later paintings to his sons, one of whom, John Woodhouse Audubon, created about half of the book's pictures. Audubon had a stroke in 1847, and his sons published the last volume of *The Viviparous Quadrupeds of North America* in 1848. Their father died on January 27, 1851, famous as the most successful chronicler of North American wildlife to that time.

Explanation and Analysis of Documents

Audubon decided on his book project while in Cincinnati, and any such project meaning to document as many birds as possible in North America would obviously require travel. Therefore, he recruited a background artist, Joseph Mason, to join him on the trip. He also picked up a friend and engineer named Samuel Cummings, who planned to make the trip in pursuit of a book of his own, mapping the Ohio and Mississippi Rivers for safe sailing channels. They booked passage on a barge run by Captain Jacob Aumack, who allowed them to pay for their passage by working as deck hands and hunters. Along the way, starting in October 1820, Audubon decided to keep a journal of his voyage, very little of which is still in existence. It is largely a story of hardship, conveying the difficulties the men had to go through to produce one of the most celebrated books of the nineteenth century.

♦ Journal of John James Audubon 1820-1821: Travels along the Mississippi

Audubon shot many birds along the voyage, both for eating and as still-life objects of portraiture. Many of his paintings have since become notorious for posing birds in impossible positions, the better to see their plumage; this was possible because Audubon painted them after he had gotten the opportunity to adjust their bodies for optimal display.

In December 1820, the travelers were close to a trading post up the Arkansas River a short way past its connection with the Mississippi. The climate on the barge had gotten tense; Captain Aumack often let his passengers know that he tired of their company, and Audubon complained that he wanted to "Leave the Boat I am now in if there is What the Kentuckians Term a 'half Chance'" because Aumack's behavior was becoming insufferable.

The next day, the party landed the barge at the mouth of the Arkansas and, with the help of a local French homesteader, made their way seven miles upriver to the trading post. Upon arriving, they took a meal at a local tavern where they ate like "4 Wolfs taring an old Carcass". After sleeping, Audubon hoped to see the Osage tribe that lived in the area, to gauge what birds he might find nearby. The Osage were unavailable, having joined a scouting party that was plotting out what would become the city of Little Rock farther up the Arkansas. Audubon was disappointed until, by happenstance, he ran into an old acquaintance from Pittsburgh, "Mr. Thomas", who had engaged with a botanist named Nutall recently in the same area. Nutall had seen many birds in Osage country and Thomas encouraged Audubon to make a later trip up the Arkansas to find birds he would likely have never seen before. Audubon liked the Osages; in the prevailing Romantic mood of the time, he considered them what might be called "noble savages", happy for their lack of civilization – in this case, clothes.

He described many of the birds he saw: mallard ducks, cranes, pelicans, hawks hunting sparrows, brown eagles. He also noted an abundance of fish at the confluence of the rivers. Interestingly, Audubon described the region around the trading post, whose people were exceedingly poor (an earthquake had just ravaged the area), but whose land might well support a general store supplying "Fresh Flour Whiskey, Candles, Cheese, Apples, Porter, Cider, Butter Onions, Tow Linen and Blankets ...Powder Lead, Flint, [and] Butchers Knives, Rifles, and blue Shrouds for the Indians." He opened the description by saying "I here feel Inclined to tell you" – clearly he intended his journal to be read.

Impact and Legacy

Audubon would later take a similar trip in the 1840s, this time accompanied by his sons, to record the four-legged fauna of North America for his next folio of engravings. While rendering America invaluable service as the first serious recorder of its animals, Audubon was also a quintessential frontiersman, sometimes actually wishing he could ditch his beloved family for the open spaces and rivers of the Midwest and south. He never did, of course, and the works he used to support his family made his name synonymous with the environment and its conservation in the United States.

Key Sources

What there is of Audubon's two surviving journals – the 1820-1821 journal and the 1840-1843 journals – were given to the Museum of Comparative Zoology at Harvard University. His many pictures are easily found on the internet. The original plates of *Ornithological Biography* are scattered about the country, some held at the American Museum of Natural History in New York City, others at the Audubon Memorial Museum in Henderson, Kentucky. The original paintings for *Birds of America* and *The Viviparous Quadrupeds of North America* are at the New-York Historical Society in New York City.

Time Line

1785	April 26	■ John James Audubon born in Saint Domingue
1803		■ Audubon emigrates to Philadelphia
1807		■ Moves to Louisville, Kentucky
1820		■ Conceives of publication of book on North American birds
1820–1834		■ Audubon travels the United States and its territories hunting and painting birds
1827–1838		■ Subscription publication of four volumes of *Birds of America*
1834–1840		■ Subscription publication of five volumes of *Ornithological Biography*
1840–1848		■ Subscription publication of *The Viviparous Quadrupeds of North America*
1842		■ Audubon and family move to New York City
1847		■ Audubon has stroke; sons take over production of *The Viviparous Quadrupeds of North America*
1851	January 27	■ John James Audubon dies

Essential Quotes

"I Hope to see the fort of Arkansas tomorrow and Hope to Leave the Boat I am now in if there is What the Kentuckians Term a 'half Chance'\ Our Commanders Looks and acting are so strange that I have become quite Sickened—"

"I here feel Inclined to tell you that an opportunity of Good; Fresh Flour Whiskey, Candles, Cheese, Apples, Porter, Cider, Butter Onions, Tow Linen and Blankets would meet with advantageous Sales during Winter, accompanied by Powder Lead, Flint, [and] Butchers Knives, Rifles, and blue Shrouds for the Indians."

Milestone Documents

Further Reading

■ Books

Plain, Nancy. *This Strange Wilderness: The Life and Art of John James Audubon*. Lincoln: University of

Nebraska Press, 2015.

Rhodes, Richard. *John James Audubon: The Making of an American*. New York: Alfred A. Knopf, 2004.

Souder, William. Under a Wild Sky: John James Audubon and the Making of the Birds of America. New York: North Point Press, 2004.

■ Web Sites

John J. Audubon's Birds of America. National Audubon Society http://www.audubon.org/birds-of-america [accessed September 19, 2016].

Viviparous Quadrupeds of North America. Digital Collections. The New-York Public Library http://digitalcollections.nypl.org/collections/viviparous-quadrupeds-of-north-america#/?tab=about&scroll=77 [accessed September 20, 2016].

—David Simonelli, PhD

Questions for Further Study

1. *Birds of America* was a cultural sensation when it came out - few could afford it, but many wanted some sort of access, which eventually made Audubon a wealthy man. Why would the depiction of the bird life of North America have occasioned so much interest in the mid-nineteenth century? Culturally, environmentally, how do you think most westerners viewed the US and its vast wilderness?

2. Who do you think Audubon's journal was addressed to? Why didn't Audubon publish it himself? His family actually destroyed much of the journal after he died - for what purpose, would you guess?

Document Text

Travels along the Mississippi

1820–1821

Saturday 8th December 1820

I have nothing to say for this day. I drew a little [today,] seeing a Green Briar with seeds on—Wrote to My Lucy and Lived on Sweet Potatoes—how Surly the Looks of ill fortune are to the poor. I Hope to see the fort of Arkansas tomorow and Hope to Leave the Boat I am now in if there is What the Kentuckians Term a "half Chance"\ Our Commanders Looks and acting are so strange that I have become quite Sickened—the Weather quite rough, all day, cleared at night, the Flat Boats passed us this evening—We have made a bad Landing according to my Ideals—

Sunday l0th December 1820

We floated down to the Caledonian point or Petite Landing about 4 Mile above the real mouth of White River here it was Concluded that Mr Aumack should walk to the old Post of Arkansas of course I & Joseph prepared and having made Enquiries concerning the road we determined to go by Watter to the mouth of the Cut off and then walk the remainder; Anthony joined us, and the Skiff doubled oared was taken; We left at 10 o'clock with Light hearts. Small Bottle of Whiskey a few Biscuits, and the determination of Reaching the Post that Night—

At the Entrance of White River we discovered that that stream Was full and Run Violently, the Watter a Dull Red Clay Color; We soon found ourselves forced to Land to Make a Natural Cordel of several Grape Vines and pull up by it—the distance to the Cutt off is Seven Miles that appeared at Least lo to us: here We Met 2 Canoes of Indians from the Osage Nation, Landed our Skiff on the opposite side of White River Which we here found a beautifull Clear Stream and Backed by the Watters of Arkansas running through the Cut off; We Walked through a Narrow Path often so thickly beset with green Briars that We Would be forced to give back and go round—this followed through Cypress Swamps and round Pounds and Cane Breaks untill We reached the first Settlement owned by a Frenchman Called Monsr Duval, this friendly Man about going to bed offered us his assistance put on shoes & clothing and Lead us 7 Miles through Mud & Watter to the Post; and at 9 o'clock P. M. We Entered the Only Tavern in the Country—Wearied, Muddy, Wet, & hungry—the Supper Was soon calld for, and soon served, and to see 4 Wolfs taring an old Carcass would not give you a bad Idea of our Manners while helping Ourselves the Bright Staring Eyes of the Land Ladies Notwithstanding

however I found Mrs Montgomery a handsome Woman of good Manners and rather superior to those in her rank of Life—to Bed and to sleep sound was the next Wish for 32 Miles in such a Country May be Calculated as a full dose for any Pedestrian per day—Led into a Large Building that formerly perhaps saw the great Concils of Spanish Dons we saw 3 Beds containing 5 men, Yet, all was arrangd in a few moments and as the Breaches were Coming off our Legs, Mr Aumack & Anthony sHded by into one and Joseph & myself into Another, to force Acquaintance with the strangers being of course necessary a Conversation ensued that Lulled Me a Sleep, and Nothing but the Want of Blankets Kept Me. from Resting Well, for I soon found a Place between the Tugs that Supported about lo lbs of Wild Turkey Feathers to save (?), My roundest Parts from the Sharp Edges of An Homespun Bedstead—

The Morning broke and with it, Mirth all about us, the Cardinals, the Iowa Buntings, the Meadow Larks and Many Species of Sparrows, clearing the approach of a Benevolent sun Shining day—dressed and about to take a View of all things in this Place, Met a Mr Thomas known formerly when in the Paragon Steam Boat—he introduced Me generally to the Medley Circle, around, and from thence took Me to a Keel Boat to receive the Information I Wanted about the Upper Countries through Which this Noble Stream Meanders—think of My Surprise at seeing here a Man who 1 3 years ago gave me Letters of Introduction at Pittsburgh (Penn) for Men

in Kentucky—this Was Mr. Barbour the former Partner of Cromwell—he Met Me with great Cordiality, told me of the absence of the Governor, the Indian agent and also that the Osage Missionaries had proceeded about 150 miles up to a Place called the Rocky Point. the Cadsaw is beyond that where a New town, the seat of Govemt was expected to be situated.

Disapointed to the utmost in Not Meeting those who I supposed Would of Course give me the best Information I requested of Mr Thomas to give the Governor My Letters and beg of him to Write Me a few Lines at New Orleans to the Care of Governor Robertson—[the Gentleman—] Mr Barbour told Me that he had for Several years past gone up to the Osage Nation about 900 Miles and that his Last Voyage he fell in with Nutall the Botanist and had him on board for 4 Months—that Many species of Birds were in that Country unknown in this and that the Navigation Was an agreable One, at the same time that it was rendered profitable by the enormous profits derived from the Trade with the Indians, whom he represented as friendly and Honorouble in all there dealings—that he would be extremely Happy of My Company and that of My Companions and that if I did not go with him at present that he Hoped I would Meet him when coming down the Arkansas Next Spring or Summer for he is about 6 Months employd each Voyage—The Post of Arkansas is Now a poor. Nearly deserted Village, it flourished in the time that the Spaniards & French kept it, and One 100 years passed it could have been called and agreable Small Town—at present, the decripid Visages of the Worn out Indian Traders and a few American famillies are all that gives it Life, the Natural situation is a handsome One, on a high Bank formerly the Edge of a Prairie, but rendered extremely sickly by the Back Neighborhood of Many Overflowing Lakes & Swamps.—

I was assured that only Two frosts had been felt here this Season and that the Ice in the River never Stopped the Navigation—the Town now Prospering at Point Rock is high healthy and in the Center of a Rich tract of [Land] Wood & Prairie Lands—and probably may flourish—the Arkansas River flows a Thick Current of red Clay & Sand, and if not for its coloring would have much of the appearance of the Mississippi—Cotton is raised here With some advantage—Corn grows Well, game & Fish are plenty—

I here feel Inclined to tell you that an oportunit of Good; Fresh Flour Whiskey, Candles, Cheese, Apples, Porter, Cider, Butter Onions, Tow Linen and Blankets would meet with advantageous Sales during Winter, accompanied by Powder Lead, Flint, [and] Butchers Knives, Rifles, and blue Shrouds for the Indians.

After Breakfast We Left the Post of Arkansas with a Wish to see the Country above, and so Strong is My Anthusiasm to Enlarge the Ornithological Knowledge of My Country that I felt as if I wish Myself in V-- again and thereby able to Leave My familly for a Couple of Years—here I saw a French Gentleman who but a few Weeks passed had Killed a Hawk of a Large size perfectly White except the Tail Which Was a bright red. Unfortunately, no remains of its Skin Legs or Bill were to be found—We travelled fast—reachd the Cutt off and Landd our Skiff, having Killed 5 Crows for their Quills, Never before did I see these Birds so easily approachd and in fact all the Birds We saw, 2 Hawks I did not know hovered high over us—the Indians still at their Canoes, We Hailed, and gave them a Drachem of Whiskey, and as they could not speak either french or English, I Drew a Deer with a stroke across its hind parts, [—] and thereby Made them Know our Wants of Venaison hams—they brought 2 We gave them [—] and a Couple Loads of Gun Powder to each, brought out smiles, and a Cordial Shaking of Hands—a Squaw with them a Handsome Woman waded to us as Well as the Men and drank freely—[Never do I] Whenever I meet Indians I feel the greatness of our Creator in all its Splendor, for there I see the Man Naked from his Hand and yet free from Acquired Sorrow = in White River We saw a great number of Geese Malards and Some Blue Cranes—also Two Large Flocks of these unknown Divers or Pelicans—reached our Boats about 6 in the afternoon fatigued but Contented a good Supper, Merry Chat—and good Looks all round—Went to bed all Well before I leave the Trip to the Arkansas Post I think I will give you More of it—We saw there a Velocipede

Document Text

Judge how fast the Arts & Sciences Improved in this Southwestern Country—I want also to tell you that the Squaw on White River While Wading out to us Craked a Large Louse taken from under her arm—

The Intrepid Hawks are extremely plenty along the Banks of the Mississipi where the feed abound-antly on the Swamp Sparrows as also on the Sturnus depradatorius; some of these are so strong and daring that they Will attack some Ducks on the Wing and often carry them off several hundreds of yards to the Sand Bars—

The Brown Eagles that were so plenty on the Ohio have entirely disapeared and nothing by White Head-ed Ones are to be seen—

The Lakes found in the Interior are stored with the finest of Fishes Such as Pikes, Salmons—Rock, Bass Sun Perches &c and the bottom covered with Thousands of Muskle Shells and Perrywinkles of many species—those Latter of Course find their Way while the Spring floods are so so general—the Bot-tom of Most of these Lakes is firm and Level—

American flamingo, John J. Audubon, Brooklyn Museum

Mural on the wall of row houses in Philadelphia. The artist is Parris Stancell, sponsored by the Freedom School Mural Arts Program. By Tony Fischer ("We Who Believe in Freedom Cannot Rest")

Ella Baker: Original Analysis

Civil Rights Activist

1903–1986

Overview

Ella Baker, born in Norfolk, Virginia, in 1903, was an enigmatic figure. She spent most of her career working behind the scenes, helping to organize the National Association for the Advancement of Colored People (NAACP), the Southern Christian Leadership Conference (SCLC), the Student Nonviolent Coordinating Committee (SNCC), and other civil rights groups, yet she was a charismatic public speaker. She had an ordinary childhood in a middle-class family, but when she went to live in the Harlem neighborhood of New York City, she was exposed to much of the leftist thought that was then popular among many African American intellectuals. She studied the works of Karl Marx, the nineteenth-century Socialist and economic theorist, and adapted the rhetoric of Marxism to her speeches. It is likely that her numerous conversations with other leftists helped her form the notion that society should be changed to suit people, instead of insisting that people adapt to society. As her career in the civil rights movement developed, she dropped much of her commitment to Socialism, even though she continued occasionally to use Marxist terminology in her speeches. Indeed, her belief that power should build from the bottom up instead of the top down put her in a long tradition of American political thought dating back to before the Revolutionary War. Much of her work helped bring closer to realization the ideals held by many of those who fought that war and who eventually wrote the Constitution.

When Baker graduated from college in April 1927, she wanted to become a missionary or social worker, but she could not afford the additional education she needed to get a job as one or the other, so she moved to New York City to look for opportunities. By 1930 she was involved in the management of the Young Negroes' Cooperative League and served as its national director for about four years. The league was part of an international movement in which people pooled their resources to provide food and other necessities for themselves; with mostly poor African Americans in the league, Baker developed her skills in the grassroots organizing of people who had little money and often had never voted.

The Great Depression of the 1930s was difficult for Baker, and during that decade she learned how to work with little money as well as how to motivate people with her speeches. During these years she worked as a publicist for the National Negro Congress and as a teacher and project supervisor for the federal government's Works Progress Administration. Her work from 1938 to 1946 for the NAACP—and with the New York Urban League beginning in 1946—had much to do with the NAACP's growth and success, and during that period she honed her motivational speaking skills into the style found in "The Black Woman in the Civil Rights Struggle." During the 1950s and 1960s, Baker tried to work quietly behind the scenes to organize civil rights workers; she did so because she wanted people themselves, and not outsiders, to make important choices about their lives. By the 1970s she was a respected figure among civil rights leaders but not well known outside the civil rights movement. This changed when historians began recognizing her achievements, and Baker was sought out by interviewers who wished to record her views of the civil rights movement.

Explanation and Analysis of Documents

Much of what Baker said and wrote has been lost. She did not write her speeches down, so the only way for them to survive was for someone to take notes or tape Baker as she spoke. She wrote many letters that offer glimpses behind the scenes of civil rights organizations, but they are scattered in many collections. "Bigger Than a Hamburger" is the best known of her documents and a rare instance of her committing her thoughts to the printed word. In it, she explains the broad social implications of the small acts of civil disobedience of sit-ins by African American college students at whites-only dining counters or tables. "The Black Woman in the Civil Rights Struggle," one of few remaining records of her many speeches, has historical significance because it provides an example of her remarkable ability to galvanize audiences with her speeches. The topic of this speech was one of her preoccupations: the contributions of women to the civil rights movement. Although she gave many interviews in the 1970s and 1980s, only a few have been published, including "Developing Community Leadership" and "Ella Baker: Organizing for Civil Rights." They offer insights into her thinking and her priorities during the time she organized local civil rights groups, sometimes at the risk of her life.

♦ "Bigger Than a Hamburger"

Although Baker had been important in organizing the SCLC, she had been frustrated by the role she and other women played in the organization. While women were doing much of the work behind the scenes to make the organization a powerful force in the civil rights movement, they were denied opportunities to shine. Then, on February 1, 1960, a Woolworth's store in Greensboro, North Carolina, became the starting place for a new movement when four African American college students sat at a whites-only dining counter and refused to leave until they were served. After several days of sit-ins, the Woolworth's began serving African Americans at the whites-only counter. College students through much of the South staged their own sit-ins, and gradually restaurants that had excluded African Americans began serving them. Baker recognized the potential of the sit-ins; she brought her formidable skills to bear on what was a disorganized movement of random protests and gave them organization, allowing the participants to form an effective social movement with broader consequences. "Bigger Than a Hamburger" derived from Baker's experience at a gathering of college students. The title of the article reflects her view that the sit-ins could have wide-ranging social consequences.

At the start of her article, Baker pointedly mentions white as well as black students. There had been disagreement among African Americans over the issue of inviting white students to participate in what became the SNCC. Although Baker often said she wanted the students to run their organization their way, she prodded the organizers into inviting white students to participate in the SNCC's projects, especially voter-registration drives. Hence her emphatic assertion "Whatever may be the difference in approach to their goal, the Negro and white students, North and South, are seeking to rid America of the scourge of racial segregation and discrimination—not only at lunch counters, but in every aspect of life." This statement served two important purposes. First, it gave the SNCC greater moral authority than it otherwise would have had by making the organization's efforts appeal to everyone rather than just to one segment of society. Second, it gave the SNCC universal authority because, as Baker points out, it addressed a profound moral problem that affects all of humanity. She had long sought to broaden the civil rights movement beyond African Americans into one in which everyone had a stake.

For most of her career Baker had made a point of soliciting the views of people who rarely had a say in how a civil rights organization was run. Her skill at making people comfortable enough to tell her what they really wanted worked well with college students, and she wanted to be emphatic that the decisions of the members of the SNCC came from the members themselves, although the very process of creating a "democratic" organization meant that Baker was impressing her own views about "group-centered leadership" on the new organization. She asserts that participation in decisions is important for young people who may not have had the education that taught them leadership;

Time Line

1903	December 13	■ Ella Baker was born in Norfolk, Virginia.
1927	April	■ Baker graduates from Shaw University in Raleigh, North Carolina.
1931–1934		■ Baker works as national director of the Young Negroes' Cooperative League.
1938		■ Baker joins the National Association for the Advancement of Colored People.
1941–1943		■ Baker is the field secretary for the National Association for the Advancement of Colored People.
1943	April 15	■ Baker becomes the director of branches for the National Association for the Advancement of Colored People, serving until July 15, 1946.
1954		■ Baker is elected president of the New York chapter of the National Association for the Advancement of Colored People.
1958		■ Baker helps establish the Southern Christian Leadership Conference in Atlanta, Georgia.
1960		■ Baker helps found the Student Nonviolent Coordinating Committee.
	June	■ Baker's article "Bigger Than a Hamburger" is published in *Southern Patriot*.
1969		■ Baker delivers her speech "The Black Woman in the Civil Rights Struggle" to the Institute for the Black World in Atlanta, Georgia.

Time Line		
1973		■ Gerda Lerner's December 1970 interview of Baker, "Developing Community Leadership," is published in *Black Women in White America: A Documentary History*.
1980		■ Ellen Cantarow and Susan Gushee O'Malley's interview of Baker, "Ella Baker: Organizing for Civil Rights," is published in *Moving the Mountain: Women Working for Social Change*.
1986	December 13	■ Baker dies in New York City.
1994	September 24	■ Baker is posthumously inducted into the National Women's Hall of Fame.

the dynamics of the group would give them the experience they needed to think for themselves. Even though Baker sometimes used such Marxist concepts and wording as "his highest potential for the benefit of the group," her belief in the primary importance of individuals was antithetical to Marxism and fit into a traditional line of American thought. She calls "unhealthy" the imposition of well-meaning adult leadership on students, because it would harm them by taking away their opportunities to make their own decisions and deal with the consequences. This is a warning to the leaders of the SNCC, who were debating among themselves how they might take over the student-led movement and subordinate its activities to their own organization.

♦ "The Black Woman in the Civil Rights Struggle"

Eyewitness accounts indicate that Baker was an inspirational speaker who drew her audiences into her themes by recounting unfamiliar history. She then would move to a statement of objectives and outline what she thought could be done. A theme that became ever more central to her thinking was that of the role of women in the civil rights movement. She believed that women were not being given their due for their work and the risks they took.

What makes this speech special is not so much its timing or its audience—probably students at a conference—but that it was tape-recorded. Her voice was deep, which surprised some listeners. Her pattern of speech and accent sounded educated, and she made no attempt to imitate the speaking patterns of her audiences, preferring to use her normal pattern of speaking. She often said that if she spoke like the person she was—educated and raised in a middle-class family—her audiences would have no trouble understanding her; she, in turn, had no trouble understanding them because she listened carefully to them.

Her remark "I have existed much longer than you" suggests that Baker was addressing an audience of young people. Baker mentions Vincent Harding and Bernice Reagon. Harding worked with Baker in the 1960s and in the 1980s became a noted historian; Reagon was Baker's longtime friend. Baker first touches on the plight of African American slaves, noting forms of resistance that were open to women. One was to pretend to be too sick to work; another was to commit infanticide to prevent their children from growing up as slaves. "There is a story of a woman in Kentucky," she says, "who had borne thirteen children and strangled each of them with her own hands rather than have them grow up as slaves." As a rhetorical device, this has shock value: It tends to rivet one's attention on the speaker while one wonders what other horrors may be in the offing. It also serves to emphasize the point that Baker wanted to make—that the lives of slaves were severely circumscribed, leaving them little opportunity to express their frustration and anger. Further, Baker lays out the notion that commitment to freedom and resentment of unjust treatment were part of the lives of African American women even among those who were slaves and, in fact, stood behind such dire acts as infanticide.

Baker and her own generation knew of many African American women who were also committed to freedom and who resented the restricted lives brought about by the laws and customs of segregation. Baker saw herself as born into the era in which African Americans were selectively educated, with the educated intended to become leaders of the uneducated. This was a subject near to Baker's heart because she believed that it embodied a wrongheaded approach to civil rights. To her mind, educating anyone to become a leader was intended to make African Americans conform to standards of behavior favored by their oppressors rather than to actually benefit those who most needed help in obtaining their rights. Although she cites the 1960s as the era for the emergence of a new idea, actually she had been advocating that very idea at least since the time she joined the NAACP: that liberation would come when the people being helped were helping themselves. To her, the civil rights movement's organizations should listen to what average African Americans wanted and then help them realize their hopes. Much of her life was spent listening to even the poorest of the poor because she believed a lack of formal education did not prevent people from thinking about their lives and understanding what they most needed.

In her account of the history of the shift from conforming to society to reshaping society, Baker perhaps gives too short shrift to what she calls "legalism"—the effort to eliminate segregation through courts of law. For instance, the outlawing by the U.S. Supreme Court of racial segregation in education was a momentous event in the civil rights movement, changing how money was spent on

education and who benefited from public education. Her misgivings about legalism stemmed from her belief that legal fighting was a top-down affair, with an African American social elite guiding the process on the assumption that they knew better than other African Americans what would be best for them. She hoped that the 1960s marked a shift to what she called "indigenous leaders," meaning people who were members of the communities they represented rather than outsiders telling the communities what was best for them.

Notable in this speech is Baker's introduction of feminist ideas. She had been asked to speak about African American women, so the presence of a feminist outlook is no surprise, but it is unclear whether Baker thought of herself as a feminist. She had long chafed under restrictions she believed had been placed on her only because she was a woman, and she had sometimes expressed her resentment of such restrictions. She suggests that the subordination of African American women may be ending. In her discussion of the roles of women, she gives a definition of the word *radical* that is indeed accurate: "I use the term radical in its original meaning—getting down to and understanding the root cause. It means facing a system that does not lend itself to your needs and devising means by which you change the system." That it is her personal definition of the word is revealing, because she used the word on other occasions to describe herself and her objectives.

Although Baker had been heavily influenced by Marxists during her early years in New York, she had long been shifting away from Marxist dogma. The Marxist phrase *masses of the people* was becoming antiquated even by 1969, perhaps because of its vagueness. Her use of the word *cadres* in her conclusion is likely a relic from her youth, meant to refer to organized groups of local people who would be committed to a universal course of action.

♦ "Developing Community Leadership"

Interviews with Baker often seem more like essays she has thoughtfully composed, perhaps because she had delivered so many speeches that she had already organized in her memory what she wanted to say and how she wanted to say it. In this interview, she discusses why organizing on a community-by-community basis is important for the civil rights movement. Baker mentions the psychologist Kenneth Clark, who conducted a study on the self-esteem of African American schoolchildren that points out the ill effects of segregated education on children. This study was used by the NAACP in the *Brown v. Board of Education* case (1954), in which the U.S. Supreme Court ruled that segregated education was inherently unequal and therefore unconstitutional. Clark and his wife, Mamie Phipps Clark, influenced Baker's approach to organizing local community-based civil rights groups.

Baker discusses the ramifications of the Supreme Court decision and the ways in which it affected the civil rights movement. She believed that the movement had to shift from battling in courts to organizing the people most in need of legal protections but least likely to receive them. Hence, Baker mentions de facto segregation—that is, segregation that is not embodied in law but is nonetheless practiced in society. Her example is the integration of New York schools and the discomfort caused by her suggestion that African American children live in white communities in order to integrate schools in those communities. She believed that there had to be a change in how Americans thought about race and segregation in order for the Supreme Court ruling of 1954 to have its fullest effect.

Baker explains why she did not believe strong central leadership could bring about the changes needed for people to fully realize their civil rights. As she put it, "I've never believed that the people who control things really were willing and able to pay the price of integration." In her works, she often makes pointed references to such charismatic leaders as Martin Luther King, Jr. She regarded their work as mostly grandstanding, with leaders like King becoming beholden to the news media that made them household names. "The charismatic leader usually becomes a leader because he has found a spot in the public limelight," she says. "The media made him, and the media may undo him." She explains that top-down leadership can result in large gaps between what ordinary people want and what their leaders try to achieve. Thus, Baker spent most of her career talking to individual community members in many different parts of the country, asking them what they wanted and discovering that no matter how uneducated they might have been, they had strong ideas about what would help them the most. Baker says she sought out the opinions of people who were not traditionally considered leaders. Her goal was to help generate a movement based on the everyday needs of people and that attracted a broad base of support among those who had an important stake in the success of civil rights organizations, such as the NAACP. Further, she hoped that by participating in community-based organizing, educated people would stop seeing themselves as an elite.

♦ "Ella Baker: Organizing for Civil Rights"

In this interview Baker combines both theory and practice to explain how she pursued her work as a social activist. Her first objective was to break down the social distance between educated people and uneducated ones, between well-to-do people and poor ones. She notes how people will create excuses for not caring about the violation of civil rights and say that those whose rights were violated deserved their mistreatment. Baker indicates the pragmatic course her comments will take by suggesting that the underprivileged not be insulted or otherwise denigrated. Instead, a civil rights organizer should try to show how the lives of the privileged few and the underprivileged many have much in common. Baker is practical enough to note that this effort to educate the privileged few does not always work, but she insists that an organizer must try.

In addition to the theme of how to organize civil rights groups, Baker takes up the topic of violence. Here she

gives an example of what middle-class African Americans might have in common with poor African Americans. She paints the picture starkly when she describes, for example, middle-class communities in Tampa, Florida, where homes were burned and where men protected their families and property with guns. "Disease doesn't have such a long barrier between us," she says. "As long as the violations of the rights of Tom Jones could take place with impunity, you are not secure." It would be easy to pigeonhole Baker by believing that her philosophy was one of nonviolence, but it would be untrue. Often armed men and women protected her, and during her speeches in the South guards with rifles frequently stood at the entrances to the meeting hall or church where she was speaking. She believed that people had the right to use violence to combat violence. Although she helped the SNCC, she regarded students' commitment to nonviolence to be naive and foolish; she believed that African Americans sometimes had to protect themselves against racist violence. She thought that the idea of African Americans protecting their lives and property with guns was appropriate and a matter of being pragmatic in a violent world.

To draw people into a civil rights organization, Baker insists that they should be talked with as equals, that condescension in behavior or speech would be detected and would be a barrier between an organizer and those she hoped to organize. This offers insight into what Baker actually did, as one story indicates. She eloquently describes the way in which she was able to reach across the divide at a church in St. Petersburg, Florida: "One lady came and all she could say was how my dress was the same as hers. Now, she didn't know how to deal with issues. But she identified. And she joined." Although Baker had a great career as an organizer, she never earned much money. To wear the same kind of clothes as rank-and-file members of a group would wear came naturally to her. She concludes by arguing that recruiting from disenfranchised people results in an organization that is strong at its base, with its members doing their own recruiting in their communities among people they knew and who knew them; this would be good for the long-term health of a civil rights organization.

Impact and Legacy

For most of her life, Baker was well known among people who participated in the civil rights movement but not among the general public; this seems to have irritated her, and she enjoyed the recognition she received near the end of her life. The civil rights movement might have been very different had she not participated in it. Her work for the NAACP helped broaden its base of support and helped enrich it enough that it could afford the often costly court battles it waged to win civil rights for African Americans. To hear her tell it, the SCLC would not have existed at all had she not organized it; history may affirm her view, because the SCLC does not seem to have become an organization until after she went to Atlanta and worked with King and other leaders of the group. She was not the creator of sit-ins—college students came up with the idea on their own—but the SNCC might not have been formed had she not helped organize it and build its membership. She indirectly had a hand in almost every success of the civil rights movement of the 1950s because she had helped provide civil rights activists with the means to strive for their goals. She drew people by the thousands, and through those thousands perhaps millions of others, to the civil rights movement through her many speeches, often given to small groups under fearful conditions. These people have continued her work to involve the rank and file in making decisions and to reshape society to meet the needs of its populace.

Key Sources

The Ella Baker Papers (1926) collection is held in the Schomburg Center for Research in Black Culture at the New York Public Library. Baker participated in the oral history project "Documenting the American South"; her interview "Oral History Interview with Ella Baker" (September 4, 1974), can be found online at http://docsouth.unc.edu/sohp/G-0007/. *Fundi: The Story of Ella Baker* is a 1981 documentary about her life.

Essential Quotes

"Whatever may be the difference in approach to their goal, the Negro and white students, North and South, are seeking to rid America of the scourge of racial segregation and discrimination—not only at lunch counters, but in every aspect of life."

("Bigger Than a Hamburger")

"Wherever there has been struggle, black women have been identified with that struggle."

("The Black Woman in the Civil Rights Struggle")

"I use the term radical in its original meaning—getting down to and understanding the root cause. It means facing a system that does not lend itself to your needs and devising means by which you change the system."

("The Black Woman in the Civil Rights Struggle")

"I've never believed that the people who control things really were willing and able to pay the price of integration."

("Developing Community Leadership")

"Every time I see a young person who has come through the system to a stage where he could profit from the system and identify with it, but who identifies more with the struggle of black people who have not had his chance, every time I find such a person I take new hope. I feel a new life as a result of it."

("Developing Community Leadership")

"If you got it, if you really *identify with him, what you wear won't make a damn bit of difference. But if you talk differently, and somehow talk down to people, they can sense it. They can feel it. And they know whether you are talking* with *them, or talking* at *them, or talking* about *them."*

("Ella Baker: Organizing for Civil Rights")

Further Reading

Articles

James, Joy. "Ella Baker: 'Black Women's Work' and Activist Intellectuals." *Black Scholar* 24 (1994): 8–15.

Books

Cantarow, Ellen, et al. *Moving the Mountain: Women Working for Social Change*. New York: Feminist Press, 1980.

Carson, Clayborne. *In Struggle: SNCC and the Black Awakening of the 1960s*. Cambridge, Mass.: Harvard University Press, 1981.
———et al., eds. *The Eyes on the Prize Civil Rights Reader: Documents, Speeches, and Firsthand Accounts from the Black Freedom Struggle, 1954–1990*. New York: Penguin Books, 1991.

Dallard, Shyrlee. *Ella Baker: A Leader behind the Scenes*. Englewood Cliffs, N.J.: Silver Burdett Press, 1990.

Grant, Joanne. *Ella Baker: Freedom Bound*. New York: John Wiley, 1998.

Lerner, Gerda. *Black Women in White America: A Documentary History*. New York: Vintage Books, 1992.

Ransby, Barbara. *Ella Baker and the Black Freedom Movement: A Radical Democratic Vision*. Chapel Hill: University of North Carolina Press, 2003.

—Kirk H. Beetz

Questions for Further Study

1. In "Bigger Than a Hamburger," Baker argues that white people should be included in the movement to establish civil rights for all Americans. This is part of an overall message of inclusion as she goes on to urge participation of people from different regions and age groups. What points does she use to make her case? Do you agree or disagree with her approach and why?

2. Baker's speech on black women in the civil rights struggle highlights the unique role of African American females in resisting racial oppression. In what ways has the struggle been different for black women than for black men?

3. Although she did not mention Martin Luther King, Jr., by name in her interview on the subject of developing community leadership, Baker often referred to him and other civil rights leaders with a degree of skepticism. Particularly notable in this document is the fourth paragraph, in which she discusses the pitfalls of "depend[ing] so largely upon a … charismatic leader." Examine the issue as Baker expresses it and critique her viewpoint. What have been the advantages and disadvantages of relying on such leadership in the civil rights movement? Have the advantages outweighed the disadvantages or vice versa?

Document Text

"Bigger than a Hamburger"

1960

The Student Leadership Conference made it crystal clear that current sit-ins and other demonstrations are concerned with something much bigger than a hamburger or even a giant-sized Coke.

Whatever may be the difference in approach to their goal, the Negro and white students, North and South, are seeking to rid America of the scourge of racial segregation and discrimination—not only at lunch counters, but in every aspect of life.

In reports, casual conversations, discussion groups, and speeches, the sense and the spirit of the following statement that appeared in the initial newsletter of the students at Barber-Scotia College, Concord, N.C., were re-echoed time and again:

We want the world to know that we no longer accept the inferior position of second-class citizenship. We are willing to go to jail, be ridiculed, spat upon and even suffer physical violence to obtain First Class Citizenship.

By and large, this feeling that they have a destined date with freedom, was not limited to a drive for personal freedom, or even freedom for the Negro in the South. Repeatedly it was emphasized that the movement was concerned with the moral implications of racial discrimination for the "whole world" and the "Human Race."

This universality of approach was linked with a perceptive recognition that "it is important to keep the movement democratic and to avoid struggles for personal leadership."

It was further evident that desire for supportive cooperation from adult leaders and the adult community was also tempered by apprehension that adults might try to "capture" the student movement. The students showed willingness to be met on the basis of equality, but were intolerant of anything that smacked of manipulation or domination.

This inclination toward *group-centered leadership,* rather than toward a *leader-centered group pattern of organization,* was refreshing indeed to those of the older group who bear the scars of the battle, the frustrations and the disillusionment that come when the prophetic leader turns out to have heavy feet of clay.

However hopeful might be the signs in the direction of group-centeredness, the fact that many schools and communities, especially in the South, have not provided adequate experience for young Negroes to assume initiative and think and act independently accentuated the need for guarding the student movement against well-meaning, but nevertheless unhealthy, over-protectiveness.

Here is an opportunity for adult and youth to work together and provide genuine leadership—the development of the individual to his highest potential for the benefit of the group.

Many adults and youth characterized the Raleigh meeting as the greatest or most significant conference of our period.

Whether it lives up to this high evaluation or not will, in a large measure, be determined by the extent to which there is more effective training in and understanding of non-violent principles and practices, in group dynamics, and in the re-direction into creative channels of the normal frustrations and hostilities that result from second-class citizenship.

Glossary

Barber-Scotia College:	a historically black institution, founded as a "seminary for women" in Concord, North Carolina, in 1867
Negro:	at that time, this word, though usually considered offensive today, was the most common and "politically correct" term for African Americans
Raleigh meeting:	a conference for youth activists, hosted by the Southern Christian Leadership Conference at Shaw University, Baker's alma mater, in Raleigh, North Carolina, over Easter weekend 1960
Student Leadership Conference:	a reference to what became the Student Nonviolent Coordinating Committee

"The Black Woman in the Civil Rights Struggle"

1969

I think that perhaps because I have existed much longer than you and have to some extent maintained some degree of commitment to a goal of freedom that this is the reason Vincent Harding invited me to come down as an exhibit of what might possibly be the goal of some of us to strive toward—that is, to continue to identify with the struggle as long as the struggle is with us.

I was a little bit amazed as to why the selection of a discussion on the role of black women in the world. I just said to Bernice Reagon that I have never been one to feel great needs in the direction of setting myself apart as a woman. I've always thought first and foremost of people as individuals ... [but] wherever there has been struggle, black women have been identified with that struggle. During slavery there was a tremendous amount of resistance in various forms. Some were rather subtle and some were rather shocking. One of the subtle forms was that of feigning illness.... One of the other forms of resistance which was perhaps much more tragic and has not been told to a great extent is the large number of black women who gave birth to children and killed them rather than have them grow up as slaves. There is a story of a woman in Kentucky who had borne thirteen children and strangled each of them with her own hands rather than have them grow up as slaves. Now this calls for a certain kind of deep *commitment* and *resentment*. *Commitment* to freedom and deep *resentment* against slavery.

I would like to divide my remaining comments into two parts. First, the aspect that deals with the struggle to get into the society, the struggle to be a part of the American scene. Second, the struggle for a different kind of society. The latter is the more radical struggle. In the previous period, the period of struggling to be accepted, there were certain goals, concepts, and values such as the drive for the "Talented Tenth." That, of course, was the concept that proposed that through the process of education black people would be accepted in the American culture and they would be accorded their rights in proportion to the degree to which they qualified as being persons of learning and culture....

[There was] an assumption that those who were trained were not trained to be *part* of the community, but to be *leaders* of the community. This carried with it another false assumption that being a leader meant that you were separate and apart from the masses, and to a large extent people were to look up to you, and that your responsibility to the people was to *represent* them. This means that the people were never given a sense of their own values.... Later, in the 1960s, a different concept emerged: the concept of the right of the people to participate in the decisions that affected their lives. So part of the struggle was the struggle toward intellectualism [which] so often separated us so far from the masses of people that the gulf was almost too great to be bridged.

The struggle for being a part of the society also led to another major phase of the civil rights struggle. That was the period in which legalism or the approach to battling down the barriers of racial segregation through the courts [which] was spearheaded by the National Association for the Advancement of Colored People.... We moved from the question of equal educational opportunity in terms of teachers' salaries into another phase: equality in travel accommodations.... One of the young persons who was part of the first efforts to test [segregated travel] was Pauli Murray. Pauli Murray and I were part of a committee that was organized to try to go into the South to test Jim Crow in bus travel. But the decision was made that only the men could go.... I had just finished a tour of duty with the NAACP and had ridden a lot of Jim Crow buses and wanted very much to go, but I guess it was decided that I was too frail to make such a journey.

I think the period that is most important to most of us now is the period when we began to question whether we really wanted in. Even though the sit-in movement started off primarily as a method of getting in, it led to the concept of questioning whether it was worth trying to get in. The first effort was to be able to sit down at the lunch counters. When you look back and think of all the tragedy and suffering that the first sit-iners went through you begin to wonder, Why pay a price like that for the privilege of eating at lunch counters? There were those who saw from the beginning that it was part of the struggle for full dignity as a human being. So out of that came two things that to me are very significant. First, there

Document Text

was the concept of the trained finding their identity with the masses. Another thing that came out of it at a later period was that of leadership training. As the young people moved out into the community and finally were able to be accepted, they began to discover indigenous leaders....

Around 1965 there began to develop a great deal of questioning about what is the role of women in the struggle. Out of it came a concept that black women had to bolster the ego of the male. This implied that the black male had been treated in such a manner as to have been emasculated both by the white society and black women because the female was the head of the household. We began to deal with the question of the need of black women to play the subordinate role. I personally have never thought of this as being valid because it raises the question as to whether the black man is going to try to be a man on the basis of his capacity to deal with issues and situations rather than be a man because he has some people around him who claim him to be a man by taking subordinate roles.

I don't think you could go through the Freedom Movement without finding that the backbone of the support of the Movement were women. When demonstrations took place and when the community acted, usually it was some woman who came to the fore....

I think at this stage the big question is, What is the American society? Is it the kind of society that ... permits people to grow and develop according to their capacity, that gives them a sense of value, not only for themselves, but a sense of value for other human beings? Is this the kind of society that is going to permit that? I think there is a great question as to whether it can become that kind of society....

In order for us as poor and oppressed people to become a part of a society that is meaningful, the system under which we now exist has to be radically changed. This means that we are going to have to learn to think in *radical* terms. I use the term radical in its original meaning—getting down to and understanding the root cause. It means facing a system that does not lend itself to your needs and devising means by which you change the system. That is easier said than done. But one of the things that has to be faced is, in the process of wanting to change the system, how much have we got to do to find out who we are, where we have come from and where we are going? About twenty-eight years ago I used to go around making speeches, and I would open up my talk by saying that there was a man who had a health problem and he was finally told by the doctor that they could save his sight or save his memory, but they couldn't save both. They asked him which did he want and he said, "Save my sight because I would rather see where I am going than remember where I have been." I am saying as you must say, too, that in order to see where we are going, we not only must remember where we've been, but *we must understand where we have been*. This calls for a great deal of analytical thinking and evaluation of methods that have been used. We have to begin to think in terms of where do we really want to go and how we want to get there.

Finally, I think it is also to be said that it is not a job that is going to be done by all the people simultaneously. Some will have to be in cadres, the advanced cadres, and some will have to come later. But one of the guiding principles has to be that we cannot lead a struggle that involves masses of people without getting the people to understand what their potentials are, what their strengths are.

Glossary

cadres:	groups of trained leaders
feigning:	pretending
Jim Crow:	a term, based on an African American character in a stage show, for the system of legalized segregation that prevailed in the southern United States from 1876 to 1965

"Developing Community Leadership"

1970

Black people who were living in the South were constantly living with violence. Part of the job was to help them to understand what that violence was and how they in an organized fashion could help to stem it. The major job was getting people to understand that they had something within their power that they could use, and it could only be used if they understood what was happening and how group action could counter violence even when it was perpetrated by the police or, in some instances, the state. My basic sense of it has always been to get people to understand that in the long run they themselves are the only protection they have against violence or injustice. If they only had ten members in the NAACP at a given point, those ten members could be in touch with twenty-five members in the next little town, with fifty in the next and throughout the state as a result of the organization of state conferences, and they, of course, could be linked up with the national. People have to be made to understand that they cannot look for salvation anywhere but to themselves....

When the 1954 Supreme Court decision on school desegregation came, I was serving as chairman of the Educational Committee of the New York branch [of the NAACP]. We began to deal with the problems of *de facto* segregation, and the results of the *de facto* segregation which were evidenced largely in the achievement levels of black children, going down instead of going up after they entered public school. We had called the first committee meeting and Kenneth Clark became the chairman of that committee [the Intergroup Committee]. During that period, I served on the Mayor's Commission on School Integration, with the subdivision on zoning. In the summer of 1957, I gave time to organizing what we called Parents in Action for Quality Education.

I've never believed that the people who control things really were willing and able to pay the price of integration. From a practical standpoint, anyone who looked at the Harlem area knew that the potential for integration *per se* was basically impossible unless there were some radically innovative things done. And those innovative things would not be acceptable to those who ran the school system, nor to communities, nor even to the people who call themselves supporters of integration. I did a good deal of speaking, and I went to Queens, I went to the Upper West Side, and the people very eagerly said they wanted school integration. But when you raised the question of whether they would permit or would welcome blacks to live in the same houses with them, which was the only practical way at that stage to achieve integration, they squirmed. Integration certainly had to be pushed concurrently with changing the quality of education that the black children were getting, and changing the attitudes of the educational establishment toward the black community...

I have always felt it was a handicap for oppressed peoples to depend so largely upon a leader, because unfortunately in our culture, the charismatic leader usually becomes a leader because he has found a spot in the public limelight. It usually means he has been touted through the public media, which means that the media made him, and the media may undo him. There is also the danger in our culture that, because a person is called upon to give public statements and is acclaimed by the establishment, such a person gets to the point of believing that he *is* the movement. Such people get so involved with playing the game of being important that they exhaust themselves and their time, and they don't do the work of actually organizing people.

For myself, circumstances frequently dictated what had to be done as I saw it. For example, I had no plans to go down and set up the office of SCLC. But it seemed unless something were done whatever impetus had been gained would be lost, and nobody else was available who was willing or able to do it. So I went because to me it was more important to do what was a potential for all of us than it was to do what I might have done for myself. I knew from the beginning that as a woman, an older woman, in a group of ministers who are accustomed to having women largely as supporters, there was no place for me to have come into a leadership role. The competition wasn't worth it.

The movement of the '50s and '60s was carried largely by women, since it came out of church groups. It was sort of second nature to women to play a supportive role. How many made a conscious decision on the basis of the larger goals, how many on the basis of habit pattern, I don't know. But it's true that

Document Text

the number of women who carried the movement is much larger than that of men. Black women have had to carry this role, and I think the younger women are insisting on an equal footing.

I don't advocate anybody following the pattern I followed, unless they find themselves in a situation where they think that the larger goals will be shortchanged if they don't. From the standpoint of the historical pattern of society, which seems to assume that this is the best role for women, I think that certainly the young people who are challenging this ought to be challenging it, and it ought to be changed. But I also think you have to have a certain sense of your own value, and a sense of security on your part, to be able to forgo the glamour of what the leadership role offers. From the standpoint of my work and my own self-concepts, I don't think I have thought of myself largely as a woman. I thought of myself as an individual with a certain amount of sense of the need of people to participate in the movement. I have always thought what is needed is the development of people who are interested not in being leaders as much as in developing leadership among other people. Every time I see a young person who has come through the system to a stage where he could profit from the system and identify with it, but who identifies more with the struggle of black people who have not had his chance, every time I find such a person I take new hope. I feel a new life as a result of it.

Glossary

***de facto*:**	in fact, even if not established as a formal theory or law
NAACP:	the National Association for the Advancement of Colored People, a civil rights organization founded in 1909
the national:	the national leadership of the NAACP
***per se*:**	in and of itself

Document Text

"Ella Baker: Organizing for Civil Rights"

1980

On what basis do you seek to organize people? Do you start to try to organize them on the fact of what *you* think, or what they are first interested in? You start where the *people* are. Identification with people. There's always this problem in the minority group that is escalating up the ladder in this culture, I think. Those who have gotten some training and those who have gotten some material gains, it's always the problem of their not understanding the possibility of being divorced from those who are not in their social classification. Now, there were those who felt they had made it, would be embarrassed by the fact that some people would get drunk and get in jail, and so they wouldn't be concerned too much about whether they were brutalized in jail. 'Cause he was a *drunk!* He was a so-and-so. Or she was a streetwalker. We get caught in that bag. And so you have to help break that down without alienating them at the same time. The gal who has been able to buy her minks and whose husband is a professional, they live well. You can't insult her, you never go and tell her she's a so-and-so for taking, for *not* identifying. You try to point out where her interest lies in identifying with that other one across the tracks who doesn't have minks.

How do you do that? You don't always succeed, but you try. You'd point out what had happened, in certain cases, where whole communities were almost destroyed by police brutality on a large scale. They went and burned the better homes. In Tampa, Florida, I met some of those people whose homes were burned down. These were people I'd call middle class. The men got the guns, and they carried their womenfolk and the children into the woods. And they stood guard. Some stood guard over the people in the woods, and they stood guard over their homes and property, ready to shoot. So what you do is to cite examples that had taken place somewhere else. You had to be persuasive on the basis of fact. You cite it, you see. This can happen to *you* . Sometimes you're able to cite instances of where there's been a little epidemic, or an outbreak of the more devastating kinds of disease. You point out that those of us who live across the railroad track and are in greater filth or lack of sanitation can have an effect on you who live on the other side, 'cause disease doesn't have such a long barrier between us, you see. As long as the violations of the rights of Tom Jones could take place with impunity, you are not secure. So you helped to reestablish a sense of identity of each with the struggle.

Of course, your success depended on both your disposition and your capacity to sort of stimulate people—and how you carried yourself, in terms of not being above people. And see, there were more people who were not economically secure than there were economically secure people. I didn't *have* any mink—I don't have any now—but you don't go into a group where minks are prohibitive in terms of getting them and carry your minks and throw 'em around. Why, they can't get past *that* . They can't get past the fact that you got minks and they don't have mink. And see, I had no problems 'cause I didn't have none. Nor did I have aspirations for these things.

I remember one place I got a contribution for a life membership in the NAACP, which was five-hundred dollars then, was from a longshoremen's union. They remembered somebody who had been there before from the NAACP, with a mink coat. When they gave this five-hundred dollar membership, somebody mentioned it. See, they had resented the mink coat. I don't think it was the mink coat that they resented. It was the *barrier* they could sense between them and the person in the coat. See, you can have a mink coat on and you can identify with the man who is working on the docks. If you got it, if you *really* identify with him, what you wear won't make a damn bit of difference. But if you talk differently, and somehow talk down to people, they can sense it. They can feel it. And they know whether you are talking *with* them, or talking *at* them, or talking *about* them.

If you feel that you are part of them and they are part of you, you don't say "I'm-a-part-of-you." What you really do is, you point out something. Especially the lower-class people, the people who'd felt the heel of oppression, see, they *knew* what you were talking about when you were speaking about when you talked about working at a job, doing the same work, and getting a differential in pay. And if your sense of being a part of them got over to them, they appreciated that. Somebody would get the point. Somebody would come out and say, "I'm gon' join that darn organization." As an example, I remember in someplace out

Document Text

of St. Petersburg, Florida, the first time I'd ever been to the Holy and Sanctified church. We had a good response. One lady came and all she could say was how my dress was the same as hers. Now, she didn't know how to deal with issues. But she identified. And she joined.

And then you have to recognize what people *can* do. There're some people in my experience, especially "the little people" as some might call them, who never could explain the NAACP as such. But they had the knack of getting money from John Jones or somebody. They might walk up to him: "Gimme a dollar for the NAACP." And maybe because of what they had done in relationship to John Jones, he'd give the dollar. They could never tell anybody what the program of the Association was. So what do you do about that? You don't be demeaning them. You say, well here is Mrs. Jones, Mrs. Susie Jones, and remember last year Sister Susie Jones came in with so much. And Sister Susie Jones would go on *next* year and get this money. Now, somewhere in the process she may learn some other methods, and she may learn to articulate some of the program of the Association. But whether she does or not, she *feels* it. And she transmits it to those she can talk to. And she might end up just saying, "You ain't doin' nothin' but spendin' your money down at that so-and-so place." She may shame him. Or she may say, "Boy, I know your mama." And so you start talkin' about what the mothers would like for them to do. So you do it because there's mama, mama's callin'. See, somewhere down the line this becomes important to them. At least these are the ways I saw it. And I think they respond.

Glossary

Holy and Sanctified church: a reference to a denomination associated with the Pentecostal movement in Protestant Christianity

NAACP: the National Association for the Advancement of Colored People, a civil rights organization founded in 1909

prohibitive: having the quality of creating a barrier to acceptance or use

Tampa: referring to the city in Florida where race riots broke out on June 11, 1967

Tom Jones ... John Jones: generic names, similar to John Doe

Image of Ella Baker, an African American civil rights and human rights activist. Retrieved from the The Ella Baker Center for Human Rights.

Woodcut portrait of Benjamin Bannaker (Banneker) **in title page of a Baltimore edition of his 1795 Pennsylvania, Delaware, Maryland, and Virginia Almana**

Benjamin Banneker: Original Analysis

Scientist and farmer

1731–1806

Overview

Benjamin Banneker was born on November 9, 1731, the son of a freed black slave and free black woman. His grandmother had some education and taught Benjamin to read and write; he also attended a Quaker school for a short period of time. Living in the British North American colonies – the most literate part of the world at the time – in the midst of the Enlightenment, Benjamin Banneker learned about science and mathematics along with reading the Bible and history, and soon demonstrated talent in math and science. When he was twenty years old, he built a wooden clock, gears, pendulum, bell and all, after merely having read about how one worked; he had never seen one because no one had ever built one in British North America. The clock kept perfect time until Banneker's death, and became a local attraction, as people came from miles around to see it.

Banneker took over his family's tobacco farm when his father died in 1759, and tobacco farming became his source of income. In 1771, when Banneker was forty, the Ellicott family started a wheat farm and milling industry next door to Banneker's farm. The Ellicott brothers and their children were scientifically inclined themselves, and George Ellicott taught him some of the principles of astronomy. By 1773 Banneker had made his first astronomical calculations for almanacs, for which he would later become famous.

In 1789, George Ellicott gave Banneker his own telescope. Using it, Banneker calculated the positions of various objects in the sky according to a calendar, and even predicted a solar eclipse. The success of these calculations convinced Banneker to give up his farm and try writing almanacs for a living. Abolitionist societies agreed to put up the costs for publishing *Benjamin Banneker's Pennsylvania, Delaware, Maryland and Virginia Almanack and Ephemeris.* The almanacs included a biography of Banneker written by Maryland Senator James McHenry, making Banneker a symbol in opposition to the evils of slavery. Unfortunately, the money dried up within five years and Banneker was unable to make a living off his almanacs. Instead, he sold off some of his land and rented the rest out, and he survived off a pension provided to him by the Ellicott family.

In 1791, George Washington located the nation's capital on the border of Virginia and Maryland along the Potomac River, and Major Andrew Ellicott was assigned the project of surveying the site. Banneker was Ellicott's first assistant on the project. He was placed in charge of locating the latitude of the site according to the stars and provided Ellicott with calculations necessary to calibrate the field clock that was used to survey the city. Then Pierre L'Enfant, the architect Washington hired, walked off the job. Since he took the plans for the city with him, Banneker reproduced them, from memory, in two days – there would be no Washington DC, with its famous spokes-in-a-wheel design, without Benjamin Banneker.

Returning home, Banneker sent the first version of his almanac to Thomas Jefferson. Jefferson had written *Notes on the State of Virginia*, in which he denied the intelligence of African-Americans and their ability to become full citizens of the United States. Banneker refuted this with a righteous but respectful anger, and received a sheepish reply from Jefferson that did little to boost his own argument. The two letters were attached to the publication of Banneker's almanacs as a pamphlet, to help sales.

As he entered his seventies, Banneker wrote essays on bees and "locusts" (actually cicadas), and became a regular commentator on the abolition of slavery. He died in his sleep on October 25, 1806. George Ellicott was conducting Banneker's burial service on his farm, when, by terrible coincidence, Banneker's cabin caught fire and burned to the ground. Destroyed were all his experiments and inventions, including his famous wooden clock. Nevertheless, Banneker's achievements made him an early hero to Enlightenment thinkers and abolitionists alike.

Explanation and Analysis of Documents

♦ Benjamin Banneker, *Journal*, April 1800

The significance of Banneker's writings came not just from what he wrote but from who he was. An African-American scientist in the eighteenth century was an anomaly, so far as white Americans were concerned. Banneker was remarkable not just in his inventions, writings and discoveries, but for his ability to get people, mostly abolitionists and others besides, to take him seriously. His essay on "locusts", really Brood X cicadas, has been justly famous for the fact that he was the first American to identify the insects' seventeen year gestation cycle. He lived through four different emergences of the cicadas, and having identified three of them, correctly identified the fact that the cicadas would return in 1800 in this passage. While this observation might seem like a

study of science for science's sake in 1800, the fact that the cicadas did not eat crops meant that identifying them and controlling their emergence might keep farmers from taking unnecessary or dangerous steps to maintain their harvests.

Impact and Legacy

Benjamin Banneker was a man of his time, the Enlightenment, and a hero to African-Americans besides. His almanacs were read as far away as France, and the calculations of the stars in them were usually more accurate than those of any other almanac of the time. He was an example for the abolitionist movement of the potential of African-Americans as contributing citizens to the US.

Key Sources

The first biography of Banneker was written by the man who provided the introduction to his almanac, Maryland Senator James McHenry. "A Letter from Mr. James McHenry ...Containing Particulars Reflecting Benjamin Banneker, a Free Negro" served as that introduction and can be found in McHenry's papers in the Library of Congress. The Library of Congress also has digitized collections of a scattered collection of papers about Banneker and by Banneker, included in the papers of George Washington and Thomas Jefferson especially. The New-York Public Library has also microformed Banneker's almanacs in a collection with the poems of John Greenleaf Whittier, which can be found in some university libraries.

Time Line

1731	November 9	■ Benjamin Banneker born
1753		■ Banneker makes wooden clock, first in British North America
1771		■ Ellicott family moves into adjacent farmland
1788		■ Banneker predicts positions of celestial bodies and solar eclipse
1791	February	■ Banneker assists Major Andrew Ellicott in survey of Washington DC region
	April	■ Returns to farm in Ellicott City
1792-1797		■ *Benjamin Banneker's Almanacs* published
1793		■ Correspondence with Thomas Jefferson; published with almanacs
1806	October 9	■ Benjamin Banneker dies

Essential Quotes

...[Th]e [cicadas] may be expected again in the year 1800, which is Seventeen years since their third appearance to me. So that if I may venture So to express it, their periodical return is Seventeen years, but they, like the Comets, make but a short stay with us[.] (Journal)

Further Reading

■ Books

Bedini, Silvio. *The Life of Benjamin Banneker.* New York: Charles Scribner's Sons, 1972.

Cerami, Charles A. Benjamin Banneker: Surveyor, Astronomer, Publisher, Patriot. New York: John Wiley & Sons, 2002.

■ Web Sites

"His Story". *Benjamin Banneker: A Memorial to America's First Black Man of Science*. Benjamin Banneker Memorial , Washington Interdependence Council (2016) http://www.bannekermemorial.org/ history.htm (accessed September 11, 2016).

"People and Events: Benjamin Banneker (1731-1806)". *Africans in America*, Part 2: Revolution (1750-

1805). PBS.org http://www.pbs.org/wgbh/aia/part2/2p84.html (accessed September 11, 2016).

—David Simonelli, PhD

Questions for Further Study

1. Benjamin Banneker was a successful scientist; most of his experiments and calculations were based on the sort of statistics that went into almanacs. Why do you think it was so important to have the skills and knowledge that went into almanacs in the eighteenth century? Why did Banneker expect to be able to earn a living with those skills?

Document Text

Observations on the Seventeen-Year Locust

1800

April 1800

The first great Locust year that I can Remember was 1749. I was then about Seventeen years of age when thousands of them came and was creeping up the trees and bushes, I then imagined they came to eat and destroy the fruit of the Earth, and would occation a famine in the land. I therefore began to kill and destroy them, but soon saw that my labor was in vain, therefore gave over my pretension. Again in the year 1766, which is Seventeen years after the first appearance, they made a Second, and appeared to me to be full as numerous as the first. I then, being about thirty-four years of age had more sense than to endeavor to destroy them, knowing they were not so pernicious to the fruit of the Earth as I did immagine they would be. Again in the year 1783 which was Seventeen years since their second appearance to me, they made their third; and they may be expected again in the year 1800, which is Seventeen years since their third appearance to me. So that if I may venture So to express it, their periodical return is Seventeen years, but they, like the Comets, make but a short stay with us–The female has a Sting in her tail as sharp and hard as a thorn, with which she perforates the branches of the trees, and in them holes lays eggs. The branch soon dies and fall, then the egg by some Occult cause immerges a great depth into the earth and there continues for the Space of Seventeen years as aforesaid.

I like to forgot to inform, that if their lives are Short they are merry, they begin to Sing or make a noise from the first they come out of Earth till they die, the hindermost part rots off, and it does not appear to be any pain to them for they still continue on Singing till they die

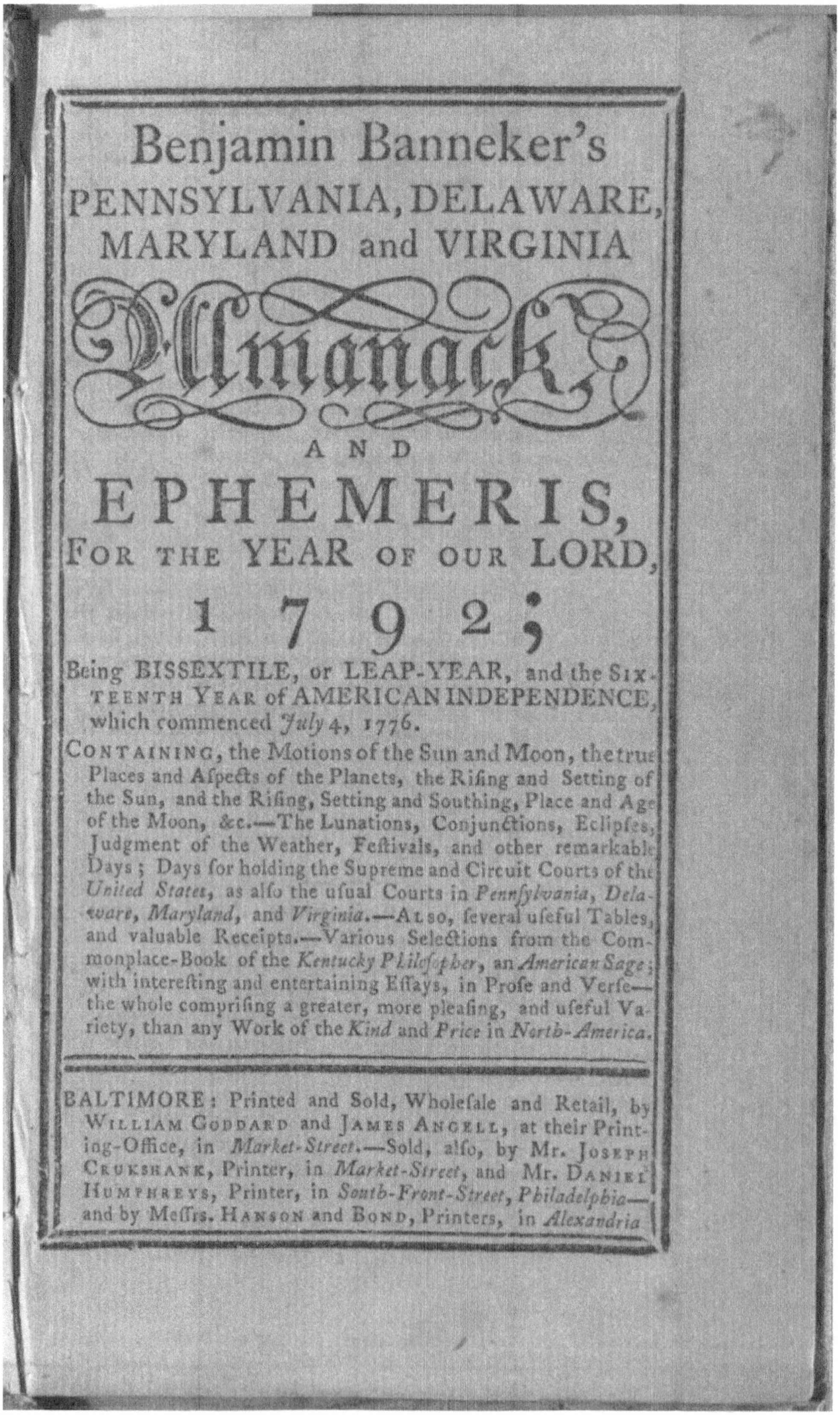
Benjamin Banneker's
PENNSYLVANIA, DELAWARE, MARYLAND and VIRGINIA
Almanack,
AND
EPHEMERIS,
FOR THE YEAR OF OUR LORD,
1792;
Being BISSEXTILE, or LEAP-YEAR, and the SIXTEENTH YEAR of AMERICAN INDEPENDENCE, which commenced *July* 4, 1776.

CONTAINING, the Motions of the Sun and Moon, the true Places and Aspects of the Planets, the Rising and Setting of the Sun, and the Rising, Setting and Southing, Place and Age of the Moon, &c.—The Lunations, Conjunctions, Eclipses, Judgment of the Weather, Festivals, and other remarkable Days; Days for holding the Supreme and Circuit Courts of the *United States*, as also the usual Courts in *Pennsylvania*, *Delaware*, *Maryland*, and *Virginia*.—ALSO, several useful Tables, and valuable Receipts.—Various Selections from the Commonplace-Book of the *Kentucky Philosopher*, an *American Sage*; with interesting and entertaining Essays, in Prose and Verse—the whole comprising a greater, more pleasing, and useful Variety, than any Work of the *Kind* and *Price* in *North-America*.

BALTIMORE: Printed and Sold, Wholesale and Retail, by WILLIAM GODDARD and JAMES ANGELL, at their Printing-Office, in *Market-Street*.—Sold, also, by Mr. JOSEPH CRUKSHANK, Printer, in *Market-Street*, and Mr. DANIEL HUMPHREYS, Printer, in *South-Front-Street*, *Philadelphia*—and by Messrs. HANSON and BOND, Printers, in *Alexandria*.

Title page of an edition of Banneker's 1792 almanac.

Catharine Beecher.

Catharine Beecher: Original Analysis

Author, Educator, Feminist

Overview

Catharine resolved to become a teacher – a profession mostly occupied by men at the time. In the nineteenth century, very few women received an education, and those that did usually were trained in the "domestic arts", learning art or sewing or to play the piano, and just enough knowledge to attract a man by being able to hold a conversation. Catharine argued that women held a role as disseminators of Christian morality in the home, and were thus well-placed not just to learn, but to educate children. The rapid growth of the US' population gave her opportunities to practice what she preached.

In 1832 the Beecher family moved to Cincinnati, and Catharine Beecher took up the cause of expanding public education on the American frontier. In 1841, she published *A Treatise on Domestic Economy*, a book defining the role of women as the moral centers of households and thus uniquely attuned to becoming teachers in public school systems. To that end, she founded the American Woman's Educational Association in 1852, a society promoting teacher education and placement for women, particularly out in the frontier states of Illinois, Wisconsin and Iowa. To Catharine Beecher, being a housewife and being a teacher were intimately entwined: making a domestically proper home was directly equivalent to controlling an educationally nurturing classroom, and vice versa – in fact, teaching was best done by single women as practice for the household they would create when they got married.

In deference to the memory of her lost fiancée, Catharine Beecher never established a household of her own with children – she never married. She died in Elmira, New York in 1878, at the home of her half-brother Thomas. She had championed the idea of public education for every child in the United States, and did more than anyone else to make the role of public school teacher seem like one which belonged to women. The modern public school system and the concept of the "Normal School", where teachers learn the norms of education, are in her debt.

Explanation and Analysis of Documents

Catharine Beecher became a major intellectual voice in the United States at the very beginning of what would be referred to as the Victorian age. Queen Victoria attained the throne in Britain in 1837, the very year that Beecher wrote *An Essay on Slavery and Abolitionism*. Victoria herself became a model of upright behavior in her time, bearing nine children, maintaining a healthy relationship with her consort, Prince Albert, and reigning over the world's largest empire besides. Over the course of her sixty years on the throne, Victoria symbolized the virtues prized by middle class women all over the western world: faith, charity, propriety, decorum, knowing her place as subordinate to her husband within the confines of marriage at the same time that she held sway over an ever-larger swathe of the world's geography and population. Victoria was admired by millions around the globe, and Catharine Beecher was surely one of them – mainly because, to paraphrase a modern quotation, Catharine was "Victorian when Victorian wasn't cool."

Beecher was outspoken in her advocacy of women's natural affinity for directing a household in a moral and upright fashion. On the other hand, she was exceedingly rigid in her belief as to how far that affinity could extend and to what it might apply.

♦ *An Essay on Slavery and Abolitionism with Reference to the Duty of American Females*

In this essay, Beecher posed the idea that made her particularly radical in her time: that the best use of a "common" – later public – school would be made if it was seen as an extension of the home, where children acquired morality, decency and Christian virtues, not to mention knowledge. And women would therefore make the best teachers, since they held the same sort of moral command around the house. Angelina Grimke provided Catharine Beecher with a solid foil to which she might compare her ideas.

Grimke had written her own essay, a letter meant for publication, calling for free women of conscience in the American southern states to oppose the institution of slavery on moral grounds. Grimke shared Catharine Beecher's conception of women as the moral centers of any given household, and also called upon northern women to second her position and join in the abolitionist movement. Beecher's essay opens with her own public response to this appeal, which she perceived as "unwise and inexpedient".

The essay goes on to state that women should avoid getting involved in the abolitionist movement, especially because the violence that it incited should be abhorrent to any self-respecting Christian woman in the US. Women

were out of their element as social actors in public – their realm was the home. This did not mean that northern women were tolerant, acceptant or indifferent to slavery: on the contrary, Beecher believed most women saw the institution as "a trade now ranked as piracy among all civilized nations." Yet beyond women's role in the home, the violence occasioned when abolitionists marched, published or held public meetings was worse for women to experience than any moral uplift the cause might provide them. Beecher considered Christianity to be the organizing principle behind American society, and in Christian terms, women were to be subordinate out in society, motivated by and representative of "the kindly, generous, peaceful and benevolent principles."

It is important to understand that Catharine Beecher not a crusty conservative in this belief – in fact, much of the point of her setting up such discussion was based on her desire to assert women's superior place in the home, to whom men would "yield not only willingly but proudly". She backs up her claim more than once in the essay by using a quote from the King James Bible, in the Book of James 3:17, that women's knowledge and power within the family should be "gentle, and easy to be entreated". She also references the story of Esther, Jewish queen of the Persians in the Book of Esther. Esther gambled her status with her king by admitting that she was Jewish and imploring him to allow the Jewish people to survive after the king falsely believed that they had plotted against him. (The festival of Purim is in celebration of Esther's heroism.) Beecher acknowledges that Esther set a good example for when an entire people's existence was at stake, but anything less than that made Esther a poor example. The passage says much about Beecher's limited sense of the disasters of slavery in the US – she clearly did not believe that the enslavement of Africans potentially constituted a similar type of ethnic cleansing.

This led her to discuss her real purpose in this essay, one of her first to be widely circulated in the US. What she was truly interested in was finding a way of making her criticism of Grimke lead to an appeal for the recruitment of female elementary school teachers. Such women could not and should not be swayed by arguments for their involvement in the abolitionist movement. The moral education of American children was more important, and would in the long run lead to slavery's decline and fall as children grew up to become moral and upright adults.

Impact and Legacy

Catharine Beecher would spend the four decades after writing *An Essay on Slavery and Abolitionism with Reference to the Duty of American Females* using any and every women's cause she could find as a platform for her ideas on women's role in education. In the process, she angered several of her siblings, who hated her opposition to women's suffrage. In the longer history of American intellectualism, her insistence on women's utter subordination outside the home became ridiculously outdated within mere years after her death. Yet she should also be remembered for her championing of the role of the homemaker as being worthy of the same respect accorded to breadwinners, and her advocacy of women as teachers in the elementary school classroom, providing many women with a level of professionalism and pride at a time when the prevailing chauvinism would have denied such pride to them.

Time Line

1800	September 1	■ Catharine Beecher born
1816		■ Mother dies
1821		■ Catharine resolves to become a teacher
1822		■ Alexander Fisher (fiancée) dies
1831-32		■ Beecher family moves to Cincinnati Ohio
1837		■ *An Essay on Slavery and Abolitionism* published
1841		■ *A Treatise on Domestic Economy* published
1852		■ Foundation of American Woman's Educational Association
1860s		■ Opposition to women's suffrage movement
1878	May 12	■ Catharine Beecher dies

Key Sources

Catharine Beecher's essays are still readily available in larger American library systems, particularly in universities. Among those not mentioned in this analysis are *Evils Suffered by American Women and Children: The Causes and the Remedy* (1846) and *True Remedy for the Wrongs of Women* (1851). Her family's correspondence and writings are collected at Yale University's Sterling Library and the Cincinnati Historical Society.

Milestone Documents

Essential Quotes

"I know not where to look for northern Christians, who would deny that ...the holding of our fellow men as property, or the withholding any of the rights of freedom, for mere purposes of gain, is a sin, and ought to be immediately abandoned."

"... In this arrangement of the duties of life, Heaven has appointed to one sex the superior, and to the other the subordinate station. ... It is Christianity that has given to woman her true place in society. And it is the peculiar trait of Christianity alone that can sustain her therein. "
"[T]he children, the little children of this nation must, to a wide extent, be taught by females, or remain untaught."

Further Reading

■ Books

Boydston, Jeanne, Mary Kelley and Anne Margolis. *The Limits of Sisterhood: The Beecher Sisters on Women's Rights and Woman's Sphere*. Chapel Hill : University of North Carolina Press, 1988.

Sklar, Kathryn Kish. *Catharine Beecher: A Study in American Domesticity*. New haven: Yale University Press, 1973.

White, Barbara A. *The Beecher Sisters*. New Haven: Yale University Press, 1973.

■ Web Sites

"Catharine Beecher (1800-1878)". *Only a Teacher: Schoolhouse Pioneers*. PBS.org http://www.pbs.org/onlyateacher/beecher.html (accessed September 15, 2016).

"Catharine E. Beecher (1800 – 1878)". *Portraits of American Women Writers That Appeared in Print before 1861*. The Library Company of Philadelphia http://www.librarycompany.org/women/portraits/beecher.htm (accessed September 19, 2016).

—David Simonelli, PhD

Questions for Further Study

How might Catharine Beecher be perceived as a radical in her time? How might she be perceived as a radical today? What are modern attitudes toward housewives and their role in society? Toward teachers and their role in society?

An Essay on Slavery and Abolitionism, with Reference to the Duty of American Females

1837

MY DEAR FRIEND,

Your public address to Christian females at the South has reached me, and I have been urged to aid in circulating it at the North. I have also been informed, that you contemplate a tour, during the ensuing year, for the purpose of exerting your influence to form Abolition Societies among ladies of the non-slave-holding States.

Our acquaintance and friendship give me a claim to your private ear; but there are reasons why it seems more desirable to address you, who now stand before the public as an advocate of Abolition measures, in a more public manner.

The object I have in view, is to present some reasons why it seems unwise and inexpedient for ladies of the non-slave-holding States to unite themselves in Abolition Societies; and thus, at the same time,

to exhibit the inexpediency of the course you propose to adopt.

I would first remark, that your public address leads me to infer, that you are not sufficiently informed in regard to the feelings and opinions of Christian females at the North. Your remarks seem to assume, that the principles held by Abolitionists on the subject of slavery, are peculiar to them, and are not generally adopted by those at the North who oppose their measures. In this you are not correctly informed. In the sense in which Abolitionists explain the terms they employ, there is little, if any, difference between them and most northern persons. Especially is this true of northern persons of religious principles. I know not where to look for northern Christians, who would deny that …the holding of our fellow men as property, or the withholding any of the rights of freedom, for mere purposes of gain, is a sin, and ought to be immediately abandoned… .

I do not suppose there is one person in a thousand, at the North, who would dissent from these principles. …As this is the state of public opinion at the North, there is no necessity for using any influence with northern ladies, in order that they may adopt your principles on the subject of slavery; for they hold them in common with yourself, and it would seem unwise, and might prove irritating, to approach them as if they held opposite sentiments. …

To appreciate more fully [my true] objections, it will be necessary to recur to some general views in relation to the place woman is appointed to fill by the dispensations of heaven.

It has of late become quite fashionable in all benevolent efforts, to shower upon our sex an abundance of compliments, not only for what they have done, but also for what they can do; and so injudicious and so frequent, are these oblations, that while I feel an increasing respect for my countrywomen, that their good sense has not been decoyed by these appeals to their vanity and ambition, I cannot but apprehend that there is some need of inquiry as to the just bounds of female influence, and the times, places, and manner in which it can be appropriately exerted.

It is the grand feature of the Divine economy, that there should be different stations of superiority and subordination, and it is impossible to annihilate this beneficent and immutable law. On its first entrance into life, the child is a dependent on parental love, and of necessity takes a place of subordination and obedience. … In this arrangement of the duties of life, Heaven has appointed to one sex the superior, and to the other the subordinate station, and this without any reference to the character or conduct of either. It is therefore as much for the dignity as it is for the interest of females, in all respects to conform to the duties of this relation. And it is as much a duty as it is for the child to fulfill similar relations to parents, or subjects to rulers. But while woman holds a subordinate relation in society to the other sex, it is not because it was designed that her duties or her influence should be any the less important, or all-pervading. But it was designed that the mode of gaining influence and of exercising power should be altogether different and peculiar.

It is Christianity that has given to woman her true place in society. And it is the peculiar trait of Christianity alone that can sustain her therein. "Peace on earth and good will to men" is the character of all the

rights and privileges, the influence, and the power of woman. A man may act on society by the collision of intellect, in public debate; he may urge his measures by a sense of shame, by fear and by personal interest; he may coerce by the combination of public sentiment; he may drive by physical force, and he does not outstep the boundaries of his sphere. But all the power, and all the conquests that are lawful to woman, are those only which appeal to the kindly, generous, peaceful and benevolent principles.

Woman is to win every thing by peace and love; by making herself so much respected, esteemed and loved, that to yield to her opinions and to gratify her wishes, will be the free-will offering of the heart. But this is to be all accomplished in the domestic and social circle. There let every woman become so cultivated and refined in intellect, that her taste and judgment will be respected; so benevolent in feeling and action, that her motives will be reverenced;--so unassuming and unambitious, that collision and competition will be banished;--so "gentle and easy to be entreated," as that every heart will repose in her presence; then, the fathers, the husbands, and the sons, will find an influence thrown around them, to which they will yield not only willingly but proudly. A man is never ashamed to own such influences, but feels dignified and ennobled in acknowledging them. But the moment woman begins to feel the promptings of ambition, or the thirst for power, her ægis of defence is gone. …

A woman may seek the aid of co-operation and combination among her own sex, to assist her in her appropriate offices of piety, charity, maternal and domestic duty; but whatever, in any measure, throws a woman into the attitude of a combatant, either for herself or others—whatever binds her in a party conflict--whatever obliges her in any way to exert coercive influences, throws her out of her appropriate sphere. If these general principles are correct, they are entirely opposed to the plan of arraying females in any Abolition movement; because it enlists them in an effort to coerce the South by the public sentiment of the North; because it brings them forward as partisans in a conflict that has been begun and carried forward by measures that are anything rather than peaceful in their tendencies; because it draws them forth from their appropriate retirement, to expose themselves to the ungoverned violence of mobs, and to sneers and ridicule in public places; because it leads them into the arena of political collision, not as peaceful mediators to hush the opposing elements, but as combatants to cheer up and carry forward the measures of strife.

If it is asked, "May not woman appropriately come forward as a suppliant for a portion of her sex who are bound in cruel bondage?" It is replied, that, the rectitude and propriety of any such measure, depend entirely on its probable results. If petitions from females will operate to exasperate; if they will be deemed obtrusive, indecorous, and unwise, by those to whom they are addressed; if they will increase, rather than diminish the evil which it is wished to remove; if they will be the opening wedge, that will tend eventually to bring females as petitioners and partisans into every political measure that may tend to injure and oppress their sex, in various parts of the nation, and under the various public measures that may hereafter be enforced, then it is neither appropriate nor wise, nor right, for a woman to petition for the relief of oppressed females.

The case of Queen Esther is one often appealed to as a precedent. When a woman is placed in similar circumstances, where death to herself and all her nation is one alternative, and there is nothing worse to fear, but something to hope as the other alternative, then she may safely follow such an example. But when a woman is asked to join an Abolition Society, or to put her name to a petition to congress, for the purpose of contributing her measure of influence to keep up agitation in congress, to promote the excitement of the North against the iniquities of the South, to coerce the South by fear, shame, anger, and a sense of odium to do what she has determined not to do, the case of Queen Esther is not at all to be regarded as a suitable example for imitation.

In this country, petitions to congress, in reference to the official duties of legislators, seem, IN ALL CASES, to fall entirely without the sphere of female duty. Men are the proper persons to make appeals to the rulers whom they appoint, and if their female friends, by arguments and persuasions, can induce them to petition, all the good that can be done by such measures will be secured. But if females cannot influence their nearest friends, to urge forward a public measure in this way, they surely are out of their place, in attempting to do it themselves.

There are some other considerations, which should make the American females peculiarly sensitive in reference to any measure, which should even <u>seem</u> to draw them from their appropriate relations in society.

Document Text

It is allowed by all reflecting minds, that the safety and happiness of this nation depends upon having the children educated, and not only intellectually, but morally and religiously. There are now nearly two millions of children and adults in this country who cannot read, and who have no schools of any kind. To give only a small supply of teachers to these destitute children, who are generally where the population is sparse, will demand thirty thousand teachers; and six thousand more will be needed every year, barely to meet the increase of juvenile population. But if we allow that we need not reach this point, in order to save ourselves from that destruction which awaits a people, when governed by an ignorant and unprincipled democracy; if we can weather the storms of democratic liberty with only one-third of our ignorant children properly educated, still we need ten thousand teachers at this moment, and an addition of two thousand every year. Where is this army of teachers to be found? ...Men will be educators in the college, in the high school, in some of the most honourable and lucrative common schools, but the children, the little children of this nation must, to a wide extent, be taught by females, or remain untaught. The drudgery of education, as it is now too generally regarded, in this country, will be given to the female hand. ...

The result will be, that America will be distinguished above all other nations, for well-educated females, and for the influence they will exert on the general interests of society. But if females, as they approach the other sex, in intellectual elevation, begin to claim, or to exercise in any manner, the peculiar prerogatives of that sex, education will prove a doubtful and dangerous blessing. But this will never be the result. For the more intelligent a woman becomes, the more she can appreciate the wisdom of that ordinance that appointed her subordinate station, and the more her taste will conform to the graceful and dignified retirement and submission it involves. ...

But it may be asked, is there nothing to be done to bring this national sin of slavery to an end? Must the internal slave-trade, a trade now ranked as piracy among all civilized nations, still prosper in our bounds? Must the very seat of our government stand as one of the chief slave-markets of the land; and must not Christian females open their lips, nor lift a finger, to bring such a shame and sin to an end?

In the present aspect of affairs among us, when everything seems to be tending to disunion and distraction, it surely has become the duty of every female instantly to relinquish the attitude of a partisan, in every matter of clashing interests, and to assume the office of a mediator, and an advocate of peace. And to do this, it is not necessary that a woman should in any manner relinquish her opinion as to the evils or the benefits, the right or the wrong, of any principle or practice. But, while quietly holding her own opinions, and calmly avowing them, when conscience and integrity make the duty imperative, every female can employ her influence, not for the purpose of exciting or regulating public sentiment, but rather for the purpose of promoting a spirit of candour, forbearance, charity, and peace.

[O]f peace and charity, ... it is in the power of the females of our country to advocate, both by example and by entreaties. These are the principles which alone can protect and preserve the right of free discussion, the freedom of speech, and liberty of the press. And with our form of government, and our liabilities to faction and party-spirit, the country will be safe and happy only in proportion to the prevalence of these maxims among the mass of the community. There probably will never arrive a period in the history of this nation, when the influence of these principles will be more needed, than the present. The question of slavery involves more pecuniary interests, touches more private relations, involves more prejudices, is entwined with more sectional, party, and political interests, than any other which can ever again arise. It is a matter which, if discussed and controlled without the influence of these principles of charity and peace, will shake this nation like an earthquake, and pour over us the volcanic waves of every terrific passion. The trembling earth, the low murmuring thunders, already admonish us of our danger; and if females can exert any saving influence in this emergency, it is time for them to awake. ...

It is by urging these considerations, and by exhibiting and advocating the principles of charity and peace, that females may exert a wise and appropriate influence, and one which will most certainly tend to bring to an end, not only slavery, but unnumbered other evils and wrongs. No one can object to such an influence, but all parties will bid God speed to every woman who modestly, wisely and benevolently attempts it.

Only remaining image of the Hartford Female Seminary, from an 1896 diploma.

Supreme Court Justice Hugo La Fayette Black by Harris & Ewing photography firm,

Hugo Black: Original Analysis

Supreme Court Justice

1886–1971

Overview

Hugo Black was one of the most vivid and controversial personalities ever to occupy a seat on the Supreme Court bench. A one-time Ku Klux Klan member, he would seem an unlikely defender of the First Amendment, and yet Black became the very embodiment of a black-letter, literalist jurist, with his commitment to the rights established in the first eight amendments to the Constitution making him into one of the Court's intellectual leaders. He carried a dog-eared copy of the Constitution around in his right coat pocket and referred to it often. "That Constitution is my legal bible," he would declare. "I cherish every word of it from the first to the last" (Schwartz, p. 239). No part of the Constitution was more sacred to Black than the First Amendment, which, as he frequently—and pointedly—noted, begins with the words "Congress shall make no law." For Black the framers of the Constitution meant what they wrote, and he demanded proof that laws being scrutinized by the Court were not in violation of any of the prohibitions that follow these words.

Hugo Lafayette Black was a son of the South, born in rural Harlan, Alabama, and raised in the town of Ashland, Alabama. His early legal career gave little indication of promise before politics afforded him a means of raising himself in the world. After holding a few local offices, Black decided to run for the U.S. Senate. The tactics he employed to get there were both practical and opportunistic. As a means of widening his base of support, Black used a populist orientation to appeal to organized labor, an alliance that led to him being called a "Bolshevik." During this same period, when acting as defense counsel during a notorious murder trial, Black appealed to racial and religious bias to win his client's acquittal. In 1923 he joined the Ku Klux Klan because, as he said later, most Alabama jurors were Klansmen. It was a decision he came to regret, and he resigned from the Klan two years later. But Black's election to the Senate in 1926 was clearly aided by Klan support.

In the Senate, Black pursued a populist agenda, vigorously investigating improper ties between government and business and pushing for a thirty-hour workweek. His ardent support for the New Deal—and, in particular, for Franklin Delano Roosevelt's plan to pack the Supreme Court with devotees as a means of ousting the old guard—attracted the president's attention. In 1937 Black himself became one of Roosevelt's Court nominees. Black's nomination was approved handily, but it was followed almost immediately by public revelation of his history with the Klan. Black confronted the issue head on by making a public confession over the radio, declaring that he had had no connection with the Klan for more than a dozen years and that he had no intention of having any further association with the organization.

Soon Roosevelt had appointed enough justices to make a "second," more liberal Court than the one Chief Justice Charles Evans Hughes had led since 1930. Joined by such like-minded individuals as William O. Douglas and Frank Murphy, Black began his ascent as one of the Court's leading liberal thinkers by voting with a new coalition that upheld important New Deal legislation and emphasized individual rights, as in *Johnson v. Zerbst* (1938), a Sixth Amendment right-to-counsel case for which Black wrote the opinion of the Court. Black went on to lead the Court's so-called due process revolution, although one of the most significant cases for which he is remembered gave civil libertarians fresh reason to doubt his liberal credentials: He wrote the opinion of the Court in *Korematsu v. United States* (1944), the case upholding the internment of Japanese Americans during World War II.

Black's commitment to individual rights was an almost inevitable consequence of his fealty to the Bill of Rights. When his customary literalist approach to constitutional interpretation proved inapposite to certain aspects of his agenda, he turned instead to what the historical record could tell him about original intent. In *Adamson v. California* (1947), for example, Black famously argued in dissent that his reading of the Fourteenth Amendment's adoption indicated that the framers intended to incorporate the Bill of Rights, thus making these protections binding at the state as well as the federal level. Black refused, on the other hand, to support rights others read into the Constitution without literal, written evidence to support their position. He was, for example, ardently opposed to the majority's extension of a broad right of marital privacy in *Griswold v. Connecticut* (1965). Although he did support the right of the *New York Times* to publish the Pentagon Papers in *New York Times Co. v. United States* (1971), other opinions dating from the later period of his career reflect the same restraint and conservatism one detects in Black's vigorous *Griswold* dissent. Black always maintained that his was a consistent, disciplined approach to constitutional analysis. By the mid-1960s, Black had no stomach for the

increasingly expansive reading of equal protection by the Court as headed by Earl Warren. The revolution he had set in motion seemed to have taken on a life of its own and passed him by. Black nonetheless hung on almost to the end. When he retired in 1971 after thirty-four years, he did so as one of the longest-serving justices the Court has ever known.

Explanation and Analysis of Documents

Hugo Black's contributions to the Supreme Court and to the nation through his majority opinions and dissents alike cannot be overestimated. Although *Korematsu* is universally considered one of the Court's worst moments, Black's pronouncement that "all legal restrictions which curtail the rights of a single racial group are immediately suspect" contains the seeds of a vital aspect of the Court's increasing emphasis on civil rights, the "strict scrutiny" test developed to assess when government action violates equal protection. The majority rejected Black's reasoning in *Adamson*, and the Court has continued to reject Black's total incorporation thesis, but subsequent to that decision the Court overruled a number of prior decisions holding parts of the Bill of Rights inapplicable at the state level. Eventually, the incorporation doctrine was used to make most of the guarantees of the Bill of Rights binding upon state governments. Black's opinion in the Steel Seizure Case reaffirmed the balance of powers and, in doing so, set a powerful precedent for disallowing claims of inherent presidential power. And although Black's dim view of unstated constitutional rights, such as the right to privacy he decries in *Griswold*, seemed out of step with the times in 1965, that opinion has since found favor with many who have been obliged to revisit one of the nation's most hotly contested issues: abortion.

♦ *Korematsu v. United States*

The Japanese attack on the U.S. Pacific Fleet at Pearl Harbor, Hawaii, on December 7, 1941, pushed the United States to enter World War II. Sentiment against the Japanese—even against Japanese Americans—ran high, and on February 19, 1942, President Franklin Roosevelt issued Executive Order 9066, permitting parts of the country to be declared military areas from which anyone could be excluded, which led to the internment of some one hundred twelve thousand Japanese Americans—both native born and immigrants. One of those affected by the order was Fred Korematsu, an American-born descendant of Japanese immigrants who grew up and lived in the San Francisco Bay Area. Health issues resulted in Korematsu's rejection from military service, but he was working in the defense industry when he became subject to the internment order. Because he did not want to be indefinitely separated from his Italian American girlfriend, Korematsu moved to a nearby town, changed his name, and underwent minor facial surgery in an effort to disguise himself as Mexican American. He was

Time Line

1886	February 27	■ Hugo Black is born in Harlan, Alabama.
1906		■ Black graduates from the University of Alabama School of Law.
1911		■ Black is appointed a part-time police court judge.
1914		■ Black is elected as a prosecuting attorney for Jefferson County, Alabama.
1917–1919		■ Black serves in the U.S. Army during and after World War I.
1923		■ Black joins the Ku Klux Klan.
1925		■ Black resigns from the Klan.
1926		■ Black is elected to the U.S. Senate.
1937	August 12	■ President Franklin Roosevelt nominates Black to the U.S. Supreme Court.
	August 19	■ Black takes the Supreme Court oath of office.
	October 1	■ Black delivers a national radio address concerning his Ku Klux Klan membership, admitting it but disavowing the Klan.
1944	December 18	■ Black writes the opinion for the Court majority in *Korematsu v. United States.*
1947	June 23	■ Black dissents in *Adamson v. California.*
1952	June 2	■ Black writes the opinion for the Court majority in *Youngstown Sheet & Tube Co. v. Sawyer*, also known as the Steel Seizure Case.
1963	March 18	■ Black writes the opinion for the Court majority in *Gideon v. Wainwright.*

Time Line		
1965	June 7	■ Black dissents in *Griswold v. Connecticut*.
1971	September 17	■ Black retires from the Court.
	September 25	■ Black dies in Washington, D.C., after suffering a stroke.

eventually arrested, convicted, paroled, and sent to a relocation camp in Utah.

Korematsu challenged his conviction, arguing that the exclusion order was unconstitutional because it authorized powers beyond those granted Congress, the president, or the military and because it was applied on a racially discriminatory basis. The government countered that such measures were necessary to prevent and counteract espionage and sabotage in a time of war. The government won in the lower courts, whereupon Korematsu appealed to the Supreme Court.

Korematsu, argued in October 1944, was one of a number of cases concerning Japanese internment that came before the Court after the enactment of Executive Order 9066. The Court had handed down its opinion in *Hirabayashi v. United States* on June 21 of the previous year, citing the demands of wartime as reasons for upholding the appellant's conviction for violating a curfew and failing to report to a detention center. Racial discrimination resulting from wartime legislation might be a necessary consequence of the need for national security. Faced with a similar set of facts in *Korematsu*, Black addresses the discrimination issue directly, stating unqualifiedly that all legal restrictions negatively affecting the rights of a racial group are inherently suspect and must be subject to "the most rigid scrutiny." Having said as much, Black goes on to uphold Korematsu's conviction for the same reason put forth by the Court in *Hirabayashi*: the need to protect the American people outweighs the need to protect the rights of any individual or any racial group. Thus, since some Japanese Americans refused to swear loyalty to the United States, the military, which was charged with enforcing the intent of Executive Order 9066 but was unable to expediently segregate the loyal from the disloyal, was obliged to apply exclusion regulations to the whole group. Korematsu was excluded from the off-limits military area not because of his race, Black asserts, but because of the nation's being at war with the Japanese Empire.

Korematsu is the only case in the history of the Supreme Court in which a restrictive law subjected to the "rigid scrutiny" test was deemed constitutional. In 1980 Fred Korematsu once again challenged his conviction in court. In 1984 the U.S. District Court for the Northern District of California overturned Korematsu's earlier conviction on the ground that the government had willingly suppressed evidence concerning the military necessity for interning Japanese Americans during the war. The second *Korematsu* case, however, merely addressed its particular facts, leaving the law of the 1944 case in place. In 1988 Congress authorized payments of $20,000 each to survivors of the internment camps after the government issued an official apology, but *Korematsu v. United States* has never been explicitly overturned and remains on the books as "good law."

♦ *Adamson v. California*

A long-simmering debate between Black and some of his brethren on the Court (Felix Frankfurter, in particular) about the application of the Bill of Rights at the state level surfaced publicly in *Adamson v. California*. The appellant, Adamson, had been convicted of murder and sentenced to death in California, where a prosecutor could legally make reference before a jury to a defendant's unwillingness to testify at trial. Such was the case with Adamson, and he appealed his conviction on the ground that California law violated the Fifth Amendment's prohibition against compulsory self-incrimination. By a vote of five to four, the Court upheld Adamson's conviction while admitting that the prosecutor's comments at Adamson's trial would have been reversed had the trial taken place in federal court. Relying on Supreme Court precedent, Stanley F. Reed, writing for the majority, declared that the due process clause of the Fourteenth Amendment does not automatically transfer all the protections of the Bill of Rights to state venues.

Black had long believed that the precedent in question, *Twining v. New Jersey* (1908), was misguided or worse. For Black, due process was a blunt instrument which, when wielded by judges lacking essential self-discipline, resulted in inconsistent and even capricious decisions that bypassed the legislative process and subverted the public will. In his powerful dissent in *Adamson*, Black likens the constitutional theory behind *Twining* to fashion, which can expand and contract at will to accommodate "what at a particular time constitutes 'civilized decency' and 'fundamental principles of liberty and justice.'" What is more, he says, *Twining* rested on decisions that have been discredited or undermined by subsequent decisions.

Searching for support for his own theory that due process encompasses all the specific prohibitions of the Bill of Rights, Black next plunges into a detailed account of the concept's history. The people demanded that a bill of rights be incorporated into the Constitution to protect them from governmental overreaching. The Fifth, Sixth, and Eighth Amendments, in particular, were intended to curb the powers of courts—particularly criminal courts, which were wont to arbitrarily exercise their powers to suppress speech, press, and religion. As such, Black reasons, these amendments are in essence supplements to the First Amendment. The first eight amendments were not, however, made to apply at the state level, and with the 1833 *Barron v. Baltimore* decision, the Court transformed this lacuna into law. Black's own research into the legislative history of the Fourteenth Amendment, however, convinced him that one of the drafters' primary motives in writing

the due process clause of this amendment was to override *Barron* and make the Bill of Rights applicable to the states. None of the cases cited as precedent for the majority's opinion in *Adamson* appraised the historical evidence for this incorporation motive, instead relying on previous, equally uninformed decisions.

Thus, according to Black's *Adamson* dissent, *Twining* embodies the unconstitutional evils that evolved from the Court's unwillingness to come to terms with the Fourteenth Amendment's origins: It affirmed the states' power to disregard the Bill of Rights and also consolidated the power the Court had assumed owing to its exercise of the due process clause to invalidate state and even federal laws. Black contends that to rely upon *Twining* and hold, as the majority does in *Adamson*, that the Court can determine which, if any, provisions of the Bill of Rights apply to the states frustrates the "great design of a written Constitution."

The Court never adopted Black's "total incorporation" theory, but over time it has employed "selective incorporation" to make nearly all of the protections of the Bill of Rights applicable at the state level. *Twining v. New Jersey* was explicitly reversed in 1964 by *Malloy v. Hogan*, while *Adamson* was overruled the following year in *Griffin v. California* (1948). Such can be the power of a well-crafted dissent.

♦ *Youngstown Sheet & Tube Co. v. Sawyer*

The cold war that succeeded World War II suddenly waxed hot when North Korea invaded South Korea in June 1950. President Harry S. Truman sent troops into combat there without a formal declaration of war. Despite its downplayed status as a "police action," the Korean War generated inflation in the United States, where wage and price controls ensued. The contract between the nation's steelmakers and the steelworkers belonging to the Congress of Industrial Organizations expired at the end of 1951. When little progress was made toward a new agreement, the steelworkers threatened to strike.

Truman made an attempt to reconcile the two sides of the labor dispute by asking the federal Wage Stabilization Board to recommend new wages and steel prices, but when these recommendations were rejected, a strike seemed inevitable. Truman feared that such a labor action, which would inevitably lead to a shortage of ammunition, threatened the welfare of American troops on the battlefield in Korea as well as the outcome of the war. It was, needless to say, his job as commander in chief to see that American forces had what they needed to bring the action to a successful conclusion. For primarily political reasons, Truman declined to invoke the 1947 Taft-Hartley Act to buy time (that is, an eighty-day cooling-off period) or to ask Congress to pass new legislation to resolve the impasse. Instead, Truman took the suggestion offered in a memo drafted by his former attorney general, Tom Clark, that he use his "inherent" powers as president to seize control of the steel mills.

Truman was probably encouraged to take this action by the fact that Tom Clark was by this time a member of the Supreme Court. The president was surely also encouraged by his friend Chief Justice Fred Vinson, who assured Truman that the seizure was legal. On April 8, 1952, one day before the strike deadline, Truman issued Executive Order 10340, authorizing his secretary of commerce, Charles Sawyer, to take control of the mills and run them in the government's name until labor and management had come to terms. Truman put Congress on notice, but it took no action. The steelmakers did act, however, obtaining a temporary injunction restraining Sawyer from carrying out Truman's order. The case was still before the federal appellate court when the Supreme Court agreed to hear it. Following an expedited schedule, the Court heard oral arguments less than a month later and issued its opinion after little more than two weeks of deliberation.

Like many other members of the Court, Hugo Black was a personal friend of Truman's, but he was also the most senior justice voting with the six-member majority to declare the president's action unconstitutional. As such, he had authority to select the author of the opinion of the Court, and he selected himself. For Black, what became known as the Steel Seizure Case was an easy one. In just eight brief paragraphs he works through the logic supporting the district court's injunction. For Black, the Constitution is absolutely clear on the subject of separation of powers, and any official who exercises powers that exceed those spelled out in that document is acting unconstitutionally. The president's power to issue an order such as Truman's must stem either from the Constitution itself or from an act of Congress, the body empowered to pass enabling legislation. No such law was on the books. Furthermore, Black points out, the executive did not even claim to be relying on statute, instead relying on "implied" authority arising from the aggregate of constitutionally granted powers: "Particular reliance is placed on provisions in Article II which say that 'The executive Power shall be vested in a President …'; that 'he shall take Care that the Laws be faithfully executed'; and that he 'shall be Commander in Chief of the Army and Navy of the United States.'"

For Black, such reasoning simply does not hold water. Although the concept of a battlefield is flexible, there is nothing in the Constitution to support the notion that the commander in chief has the wartime authority to seize private industry in order to prevent a strike from stopping production. As for the president's executive power, his office's mandate merely gives him the authority to recommend laws he thinks wise and veto those he finds bad. With Executive Order 10340, the president was not attempting to ensure the proper execution of a law as Congress intended it be executed; rather, the order was intended to ensure that presidential policy be carried out as he wished. Congress certainly has the authority to pass legislation enabling a presidential order to become law, whether to prescribe the taking of private property for public use, to govern labor relations, or to fix wages and working conditions. Congress can do all these things without subjecting such decisions to the control or supervision of

the president or the military. In this case, however, Congress elected to remain silent.

In conference, Justice Felix Frankfurter expressed his wish that each of the nine justices write a separate opinion in the Steel Seizure Case, and he almost got his wish: each of the five other justices in the majority wrote a separate concurring opinion, while Chief Justice Vinson wrote a dissenting opinion that was joined by Stanley Reed and Sherman Minton. Robert Jackson's concurring opinion, in particular, has been used subsequently to resist attempts to read inherent presidential powers into areas such as executive privilege, electronic surveillance, and national security. But it is Black's opinion, brief, eloquent, and unadorned, that has come down as perhaps the final word on the necessity for restraining presidential power within the parameters afforded by the Constitution.

♦ *Gideon v. Wainwright*

The factual background of *Gideon v. Wainwright* reads like a film script, and in fact, in 1980 the case was transformed into a made-for-television drama titled *Gideon's Trumpet* (the title borrowed from a 1964 book on the subject written by Anthony Lewis), starring Henry Fonda, José Ferrer, and John Houseman. Clarence Gideon, a semiliterate drifter with a history of petty crime, was picked up in Panama City, Florida, on the morning of June 4, 1961, on suspicion of burglary. The night before, a nearby pool hall had been broken into and robbed. A witness reported having seen Gideon in the pool room around 5:30 the next morning.

Gideon was indigent, but when he asked that the trial court assign him an attorney, his request was rejected. The Sixth Amendment requires that all indigent defendants being tried in federal courts be assigned a legal representative, but at the time state courts were required to provide lawyers only for defendants accused of capital crimes. Gideon was obliged to defend himself, and, not surprisingly, he performed poorly. Found guilty of the felony of breaking and entering, he was sentenced to serve five years in prison. While there, Gideon began to study law, and his study led him to believe that he had a right to petition the Florida Supreme Court for review of his case under a writ of habeas corpus, arguing that because he had been denied counsel, he had been illegally imprisoned. The Florida Supreme Court rejected Gideon's petition, after which Gideon drafted a handwritten petition for a writ of certiorari and forwarded it to the U.S. Supreme Court, asking the highest court in the land to review his case. The Court granted Gideon's wish—and even assigned him a lawyer, the future justice Abe Fortas.

The question before the Court in *Gideon v. Wainwright* (at the time, Louie L. Wainwright was secretary of the Florida Department of Corrections) was whether to uphold its own precedent, *Betts v. Brady* (1942), wherein the Court had found that the Fourteenth Amendment did not make the Sixth Amendment right to counsel applicable to all state criminal proceedings. Justice Black had written a dissent for the minority in that case, and now, in *Gideon*, he had the opportunity to right what he clearly thought a wrong—and in so doing to write the opinion for a unanimous Court. Black, an advocate of what came to be known as the total incorporation theory, believed that the drafters of the Fourteenth Amendment had intended their work to incorporate all of the protections in the Bill of Rights, thus making the first eight amendments applicable at the state level. After reviewing those aspects of the Bill of Rights that the Court had already applied to the states, Black says that in *Gideon* the Court takes at face value the *Betts* assumption that, owing to the Fourteenth Amendment, state courts must observe any provision of the Bill of Rights that is "fundamental and essential to a fair trial." Unlike the *Betts* Court, however, the *Gideon* Court believes that the guarantee of counsel is a fundamental right. Black finds plenty of support for this proposition in other Court opinions, making the case that *Betts* is an anomaly that must be overturned.

Gideon contributed mightily to the due process revolution expanding individual rights. The public defender program was greatly expanded nationwide. The Court, in turn, expanded *Gideon* in *Argersinger v. Hamlin* (1972), making the right to counsel applicable to misdemeanor defendants facing the prospect of incarceration. Before long, the right to counsel was being read to imply a right to effective counsel. Still other cases drew on *Gideon* when addressing the issue of when in the course of legal proceedings a lawyer must be assigned. More recently, legal associations have been urging courts to assign attorneys to impoverished litigants pursuing civil actions concerning such matters as housing, health care, and child care.

♦ *Griswold v. Connecticut*

Griswold concerned an 1879 Connecticut statute making it a crime for any person to use any drug or device to prevent conception. The law was used to convict Estelle Griswold, the executive director of the Planned Parenthood League of Connecticut, and Dr. C. Lee Buxton, a physician and Yale University professor, after the two opened a birth-control clinic in the state in order to test the validity of the statute. Like the other justices, Hugo Black thought the Connecticut law offensive and unwise. Unlike the seven-member majority, however, he did not think the statute unconstitutional. He disagreed with the notion that the statute violated the First Amendment, for what was at issue in the case was not speech but conduct. And he would not buy into the notion that just as the First Amendment had been expanded to suggest a freedom of association not spelled out in the Constitution, other amendments implied a right to privacy. In his dissent Black expresses distaste for the majority's endorsement of a newfound right forged as an "emanation" from some conglomeration of enumerated rights, a point he drives home by stating baldly, "I like my privacy as well as the next one, but I am nevertheless compelled to admit that government has a right to invade it unless prohibited by some specific constitutional provision."

Black reserves his most withering criticism for the due process, Ninth Amendment, and natural law arguments

advanced in concurring opinions signed by Justices John Marshall Harlan, Byron White, and Arthur Goldberg. The various lines of argument are, Black says, essentially the same and suffer from the same fatal flaw: all are too broad, bereft of specificity. More to the point, the adoption of any of these arguments would lead to the Court's appropriation of the lawmaking power: "Surely it has to be admitted that no provision of the Constitution specifically gives such blanket power to courts to exercise such a supervisory veto over the wisdom and value of legislative policies and to hold unconstitutional those laws which they believe unwise or dangerous."

Finally, Black addresses those who argue for new rights as a means of keeping the Constitution up to date. He is not opposed to the idea that the nation's foundational document be changed from time to time—indeed, the Founders themselves provided a mechanism for making such changes. But the process of adopting amendments is not for the Court but for the people to manage.

Impact and Legacy

Black's slight stature and soft southern accent belied his enormous will and self-assertiveness. Indeed, he embodied contradiction. Born into a racist society that condoned, even encouraged his membership in the Ku Klux Klan, once on the Supreme Court, he was largely responsible for the due process revolution that would contribute so much to the civil rights era. Once on the Court, the wily, practical politician became committed to a vision of America rooted in strict construction, resulting in what amounted to a social revolution.

Much has been made of the "conservatism" Black's jurisprudence displayed late in his career. Black's own view was that when he joined the Court in 1937, he was obliged to fight against a conservative bloc of justices using substantive due process to substitute their own social and economic values for those of the American people and their elected representatives. In the 1960s he opposed what he saw as an analogous threat originating on the left, whereby natural law and substantive equal protection were being employed to create new rights that he felt the framers of the Constitution would neither recognize nor approve. For Black, the words of the Constitution as set down by the nation's Founders contained all that the court of last resort ever needed to settle matters of public policy.

Key Sources

Justice Black left instructions that his personal notes on and for judicial conferences be burned upon his death, and that request was honored. The Library of Congress, however, houses the Hugo Lafayette Black Papers, a collection of correspondence, unfiled opinions, annotated drafts of subsequently published opinions, and Court memoranda. Black published personal statements about law and the Constitution in *New York University Law Review* (April 1960) and in his volume *A Constitutional Faith* (1968). Black also wrote two published autobiographical pieces: "Reminiscences," for the *Alabama Law Review* (Fall 1965), and, with his wife, *Mr. Justice and Mrs. Black: The Memoirs of Hugo L. Black and Elizabeth Black* (1986).

Essential Quotes

"It should be noted, to begin with, that all legal restrictions which curtail the civil rights of a single racial group are immediately suspect. That is not to say that all such restrictions are unconstitutional. It is to say that courts must subject them to the most rigid scrutiny. Pressing public necessity may sometimes justify the existence of such restrictions; racial antagonism never can."

(*Korematsu v. United States*)

"I cannot consider the Bill of Rights to be an outworn 18th Century 'strait jacket' as the Twining opinion did. Its provisions may be thought outdated abstractions by some. And it is true that they were designed to

meet ancient evils. But they are the same kind of human evils that have emerged from century to century wherever excessive power is sought by the few at the expense of the many. In my judgment the people of no nation can lose their liberty so long as a Bill of Rights like ours survives and its basic purposes are conscientiously interpreted, enforced and respected so as to afford continuous protection against old, as well as new, devices and practices which might thwart those purposes."

(*Adamson v. California*)

"The Founders of this Nation entrusted the lawmaking power to the Congress alone in both good and bad times. It would do no good to recall the historical events, the fears of power and the hopes for freedom that lay behind their choice. Such a review would but confirm our holding that this seizure order cannot stand."

(*Youngstown Sheet & Tube Co. v. Sawyer*)

"The right of one charged with crime to counsel may not be deemed fundamental and essential to fair trials in some countries, but it is in ours. From the very beginning, our state and national constitutions and laws have laid great emphasis on procedural and substantive safeguards designed to assure fair trials before impartial tribunals in which every defendant stands equal before the law. This noble ideal cannot be realized if the poor man charged with crime has to face his accusers without a lawyer to assist him."

(*Gideon v. Wainwright*)

"'Privacy' is a broad, abstract and ambiguous concept which can easily be shrunken in meaning but which can also, on the other hand, easily be interpreted as a constitutional ban against many things other than searches and seizures. I have expressed the view many times that First Amendment freedoms, for example, have suffered from a failure of the courts to stick to the simple language of the First Amendment in construing it, instead of invoking multitudes of words substituted for those the Framers used."

(*Griswold v. Connecticut*)

Essential Quotes

"I realize that many good and able men have eloquently spoken and written, sometimes in rhapsodical strains, about the duty of this Court to keep the Constitution in tune with the times. The idea is that the Constitution must be changed from time to time and that this Court is charged with a duty to make those changes. For myself, I must with all deference reject that philosophy. The Constitution makers knew the need for change and provided for it. Amendments suggested by the people's elected representatives can be submitted to the people or their selected agents for ratification. That method of change was good for our Fathers, and being somewhat old-fashioned I must add it is good enough for me."

(*Griswold v. Connecticut*)

Further Reading

Books

Ball, Howard. *Hugo L. Black: Cold Steel Warrior.* New York: Oxford University Press, 1996.

Black, Hugo L., Jr. *My Father: A Remembrance.* New York: Random House, 1975.

Freyer, Tony. *Hugo L. Black and the Dilemma of American Liberalism.* 2nd ed. New York: Pearson Longman, 2008.

Marcus, Maeva. *Truman and the Steel Seizure Case: The Limits of Presidential Power.* Durham, N.C.: Duke University Press, 1994.

Newman, Roger K. *Hugo Black: A Biography.* New York: Fordham University Press, 1997.

Schwartz, Bernard. *A History of the Supreme Court.* New York: Oxford University Press, 1993.

Simon, James F. *The Antagonists: Hugo Black, Felix Frankfurter and Civil Liberties in Modern America.* New York: Touchstone, 1990.

Yarbrough, Tinsley E. *Mr. Justice Black and His Critics.* Durham, N.C.: Duke University Press, 1988.

—*Lisa Paddock*

Questions for Further Study

1. The *Korematsu* case arose from controversy over the methods of dealing with individuals who were believed to be a threat to national security. In that particular situation, those individuals were Japanese Americans, whose racial heritage connected them to an enemy of the United States in World War II and caused them to be regarded as a liability. Compare and contrast *Korematsu* with rulings on the status of detainees at Guantánamo Bay, Cuba, in the aftermath of the September 11, 2001, terrorist attacks.

2. Black is widely known for his interpretation of the Fourteenth Amendment as extending the rights of the Fifth Amendment to the states, meaning that no state law could legally deny citizens their rights under the Fifth Amendment to the Constitution. This view, known as "incorporation," has become the prevailing one in legal circles—so much so that it seems a matter of common sense—but before Black's time the idea of this connection between the two amendments was not firmly fixed. Discuss the ideas and convictions that led him to this viewpoint and their effect on later legal rulings.

3. *Griswold v. Connecticut*, itself a landmark Supreme Court ruling, paved the way for an even more important case eight years later, *Roe v. Wade*. A major issue in both cases was the idea that the Constitution granted U.S. citizens a "right to privacy"—a concept with which Black himself strongly disagreed. Examine the issue from both sides: On the one hand, as Black noted, the phrase "right to privacy" is never explicitly stated in the Constitution; on the other hand, the spirit of the document itself could be interpreted to imply that such a right exists. How far should such a right, if indeed it is guaranteed by the Constitution, be extended?

Korematsu v. United States

The petitioner, an American citizen of Japanese descent, was convicted in a federal district court for remaining in San Leandro, California, a "Military Area," contrary to Civilian Exclusion Order No. 34 of the Commanding General of the Western Command, U.S. Army, which directed that, after May 9, 1942, all persons of Japanese ancestry should be excluded from that area. No question was raised as to petitioner's loyalty to the United States. The Circuit Court of Appeals affirmed, and the importance of the constitutional question involved caused us to grant certiorari.

It should be noted, to begin with, that all legal restrictions which curtail the civil rights of a single racial group are immediately suspect. That is not to say that all such restrictions are unconstitutional. It is to say that courts must subject them to the most rigid scrutiny. Pressing public necessity may sometimes justify the existence of such restrictions; racial antagonism never can. …

In the light of the principles we announced in the *Hirabayashi* case, we are unable to conclude that it was beyond the war power of Congress and the Executive to exclude those of Japanese ancestry from the West Coast war area at the time they did. True, exclusion from the area in which one's home is located is a far greater deprivation than constant confinement to the home from 8 p.m. to 6 a.m. Nothing short of apprehension by the proper military authorities of the gravest imminent danger to the public safety can constitutionally justify either. But exclusion from a threatened area, no less than curfew, has a definite and close relationship to the prevention of espionage and sabotage. The military authorities, charged with the primary responsibility of defending our shores, concluded that curfew provided inadequate protection and ordered exclusion. They did so, as pointed out in our *Hirabayashi* opinion, in accordance with Congressional authority to the military to say who should, and who should not, remain in the threatened areas.

In this case the petitioner challenges the assumptions upon which we rested our conclusions in the *Hirabayashi* case. He also urges that by May 1942, when Order No. 34 was promulgated, all danger of Japanese invasion of the West Coast had disappeared. After careful consideration of these contentions we are compelled to reject them.

Here, as in the *Hirabayashi* case, … "we cannot reject as unfounded the judgment of the military authorities and of Congress that there were disloyal members of that population, whose number and strength could not be precisely and quickly ascertained. We cannot say that the war-making branches of the Government did not have ground for believing that in a critical hour such persons could not readily be isolated and separately dealt with, and constituted a menace to the national defense and safety, which demanded that prompt and adequate measures be taken to guard against it."

Like curfew, exclusion of those of Japanese origin was deemed necessary because of the presence of an unascertained number of disloyal members of the group, most of whom we have no doubt were loyal to this country. It was because we could not reject the finding of the military authorities that it was impossible to bring about an immediate segregation of the disloyal from the loyal that we sustained the validity of the curfew order as applying to the whole group. In the instant case, temporary exclusion of the entire group was rested by the military on the same ground. The judgment that exclusion of the whole group was for the same reason a military imperative answers the contention that the exclusion was in the nature of group punishment based on antagonism to those of Japanese origin. That there were members of the group who retained loyalties to Japan has been confirmed by investigations made subsequent to the exclusion. Approximately five thousand American citizens of Japanese ancestry refused to swear unqualified allegiance to the United States and to renounce allegiance to the Japanese Emperor, and several thousand evacuees requested repatriation to Japan.

We uphold the exclusion order as of the time it was made and when the petitioner violated it.… In doing so, we are not unmindful of the hardships imposed by it upon a large group of American citizens. But hardships are part of war, and war is an aggregation

of hardships. All citizens alike, both in and out of uniform, feel the impact of war in greater or lesser measure. Citizenship has its responsibilities as well as its privileges, and in time of war the burden is always heavier. Compulsory exclusion of large groups of citizens from their homes, except under circumstances of direst emergency and peril, is inconsistent with our basic governmental institutions. But when under conditions of modern warfare our shores are threatened by hostile forces, the power to protect must be commensurate with the threatened danger....

We are thus being asked to pass at this time upon the whole subsequent detention program in both assembly and relocation centers, although the only issues framed at the trial related to petitioner's remaining in the prohibited area in violation of the exclusion order. Had petitioner here left the prohibited area and gone to an assembly center we cannot say either as a matter of fact or law that his presence in that center would have resulted in his detention in a relocation center. Some who did report to the assembly center were not sent to relocation centers, but were released upon condition that they remain outside the prohibited zone until the military orders were modified or lifted. This illustrates that they pose different problems and may be governed by different principles. The lawfulness of one does not necessarily determine the lawfulness of the others. This is made clear when we analyze the requirements of the separate provisions of the separate orders. These separate requirements were that those of Japanese ancestry (1) depart from the area; (2) report to and temporarily remain in an assembly center; (3) go under military control to a relocation center there to remain for an indeterminate period until released conditionally or unconditionally by the military authorities. Each of these requirements, it will be noted, imposed distinct duties in connection with the separate steps in a complete evacuation program. Had Congress directly incorporated into one Act the language of these separate orders, and provided sanctions for their violations, disobedience of any one would have constituted a separate offense....

Since the petitioner has not been convicted of failing to report or to remain in an assembly or relocation center, we cannot in this case determine the validity of those separate provisions of the order. It is sufficient here for us to pass upon the order which petitioner violated. To do more would be to go beyond the issues raised, and to decide momentous questions not contained within the framework of the pleadings or the evidence in this case. It will be time enough to decide the serious constitutional issues which petitioner seeks to raise when an assembly or relocation order is applied or is certain to be applied to him, and we have its terms before us....

It is said that we are dealing here with the case of imprisonment of a citizen in a concentration camp solely because of his ancestry, without evidence or inquiry concerning his loyalty and good disposition towards the United States. Our task would be simple, our duty clear, were this a case involving the imprisonment of a loyal citizen in a concentration camp because of racial prejudice. Regardless of the true nature of the assembly and relocation centers—and we deem it unjustifiable to call them concentration camps with all the ugly connotations that term implies—we are dealing specifically with nothing but an exclusion order. To cast this case into outlines of racial prejudice, without reference to the real military dangers which were presented, merely confuses the issue. Korematsu was not excluded from the Military Area because of hostility to him or his race. He was excluded because we are at war with the Japanese Empire, because the properly constituted military authorities feared an invasion of our West Coast and felt constrained to take proper security measures, because they decided that the military urgency of the situation demanded that all citizens of Japanese ancestry be segregated from the West Coast temporarily, and finally, because Congress, reposing its confidence in this time of war in our military leaders—as inevitably it must—determined that they should have the power to do just this. There was evidence of disloyalty on the part of some, the military authorities considered that the need for action was great, and time was short. We cannot—by availing ourselves of the calm perspective of hindsight—now say that at that time these actions were unjustified.

Glossary

concentration camp:	a detention center in which a group of people are gathered together or "concentrated," usually characterized by extremely harsh treatment of prisoners
exclusion order:	Executive Order 9066, issued by President Franklin Roosevelt on February 19, 1942, whereby persons considered to be a military threat could be excluded from certain areas
***Hirabayashi* case:**	*Hirabayashi v. United States,* in which the Supreme Court had upheld the constitutionality of the exclusion order
instant:	present
imperative:	requirement
pass:	judge or rule
petitioner:	one who brings a case before a court
reposing:	resting
sanctions:	punishments

Adamson v. California

1947

[Black dissent]

This decision reasserts a constitutional theory spelled out in *Twining v. New Jersey* ... that this Court is endowed by the Constitution with boundless power under "natural law" periodically to expand and contract constitutional standards to conform to the Court's conception of what at a particular time constitutes "civilized decency" and "fundamental principles of liberty and justice." Invoking this *Twining* rule, the Court concludes that although comment upon testimony in a federal court would violate the Fifth Amendment, identical comment in a state court does not violate today's fashion in civilized decency and fundamentals and is therefore not prohibited by the Federal Constitution as amended.

The *Twining* case was the first, as it is the only decision of this Court, which has squarely held that states were free, notwithstanding the Fifth and Fourteenth Amendments, to extort evidence from one accused of crime. I agree that if *Twining* be reaffirmed, the result reached might appropriately follow. But I would not reaffirm the *Twining* decision. I think that decision and the "natural law" theory of the Constitution upon which it relies, degrade the constitutional safeguards of the Bill of Rights and simultaneously appropriate for this Court a broad power which we are not authorized by the Constitution to exercise. Furthermore, the *Twining* decision rested on previous cases and broad hypotheses which have been undercut by intervening decisions of this Court....My reasons for believing that the *Twining* decision should not be revitalized can best be understood by reference to the constitutional, judicial, and general history that preceded and followed the case....

The first 10 amendments were proposed and adopted largely because of fear that Government might unduly interfere with prized individual liberties. The people wanted and demanded a Bill of Rights written into their Constitution. The amendments embodying the Bill of Rights were intended to curb all branches of the Federal Government in the fields touched by the amendments—Legislative, Executive, and Judicial. The Fifth, Sixth, and Eighth Amendments were pointedly aimed at confining exercise of power by courts and judges within precise boundaries, particularly in the procedure used for the trial of criminal cases. Past history provided strong reasons for the apprehensions which brought these procedural amendments into being and attest the wisdom of their adoption. For the fears of arbitrary court action sprang largely from the past use of courts in the imposition of criminal punishments to suppress speech, press, and religion. Hence the constitutional limitations of courts' powers were, in the view of the Founders, essential supplements to the First Amendment, which was itself designed to protect the widest scope for all people to believe and to express the most divergent political, religious, and other views.

But these limitations were not expressly imposed upon state court action. In 1833, *Barron v. Baltimore* was decided by this Court. It specifically held inapplicable to the states that provision of the Fifth Amendment which declares: "nor shall private property be taken for public use, without just compensation." In deciding the particular point raised, the Court there said that it could not hold that the first eight amendments applied to the states. This was the controlling constitutional rule when the Fourteenth Amendment was proposed in 1866.

My study of the historical events that culminated in the Fourteenth Amendment, and the expressions of those who sponsored and favored, as well as those who opposed its submission and passage, persuades me that one of the chief objects that the provisions of the Amendment's first section, separately, and as a whole, were intended to accomplish was to make the Bill of Rights, applicable to the states. With full knowledge of the import of the Barron decision, the framers and backers of the Fourteenth Amendment proclaimed its purpose to be to overturn the constitutional rule that case had announced. This historical purpose has never received full consideration or exposition in any opinion of this Court interpreting the Amendment....

For this reason, I am attaching to this dissent, an appendix which contains a resume, by no

means complete, of the Amendment's history. In my judgment that history conclusively demonstrates that the language of the first section of the Fourteenth Amendment, taken as a whole, was thought by those responsible for its submission to the people, and by those who opposed its submission, sufficiently explicit to guarantee that thereafter no state could deprive its citizens of the privileges and protections of the Bill of Rights. Whether this Court ever will, or whether it now should, in the light of past decisions, give full effect to what the Amendment was intended to accomplish is not necessarily essential to a decision here. However that may be, our prior decisions, including *Twining,* do not prevent our carrying out that purpose, at least to the extent of making applicable to the states, not a mere part, as the Court has, but the full protection of the Fifth Amendment's provision against compelling evidence from an accused to convict him of crime. And I further contend that the "natural law" formula which the Court uses to reach its conclusion in this case should be abandoned as an incongruous excrescence on our Constitution. I believe that formula to be itself a violation of our Constitution, in that it subtly conveys to courts, at the expense of legislatures, ultimate power over public policies in fields where no specific provision of the Constitution limits legislative power. And my belief seems to be in accord with the views expressed by this Court, at least for the first two decades after the Fourteenth Amendment was adopted....

The *Twining* decision, rejecting the compelled testimony clause of the Fifth Amendment, and indeed rejecting all the Bill of Rights, is the end product of one phase of this philosophy. At the same time, that decision consolidated the power of the Court assumed in past cases by laying broader foundations for the Court to invalidate state and even federal regulatory legislation. For the *Twining* decision, giving separate consideration to "due process" and "privileges or immunities," went all the way to say that the "privileges or immunities" clause of the Fourteenth Amendment "did not forbid the states to abridge the personal rights enumerated in the first eight Amendments...." And in order to be certain, so far as possible, to leave this Court wholly free to reject all the Bill of Rights as specific restraints upon state actions, the decision declared that even if this Court should decide that the due process clause forbids the states to infringe personal liberties guaranteed by the Bill of Rights, it would do so, not "because those rights are enumerated in the first eight Amendments, but because they are of such a nature that they are included in the conception of due process of law."

At the same time that the *Twining* decision held that the states need not conform to the specific provisions of the Bill of Rights, it consolidated the power that the Court had assumed under the due process clause by laying even broader foundations for the Court to invalidate state and even federal regulatory legislation. For under the *Twining* formula, which includes nonregard for the first eight amendments, what are "fundamental rights" and in accord with "canons of decency," as the Court said in *Twining,* and today reaffirms, is to be independently "ascertained from time to time by judicial action ...; "what is due process of law depends on circumstances." Thus the power of legislatures became what this Court would declare it to be at a particular time independently of the specific guarantees of the Bill of Rights such as the right to freedom of speech, religion and assembly, the right to just compensation for property taken for a public purpose, the right to jury trial or the right to be secure against unreasonable searches and seizures. Neither the contraction of the Bill of Rights safeguards nor the invalidation of regulatory laws by this Court's appraisal of "circumstances" would readily be classified as the most satisfactory contribution of this Court to the nation. In 1912, four years after the *Twining* case was decided, a book written by Mr. Charles Wallace Collins gave the history of this Court's interpretation and application of the Fourteenth Amendment up to that time. It is not necessary for one fully to agree with all he said in order to appreciate the sentiment of the following comment concerning the disappointments caused by this Court's interpretation of the Amendment. "It was aimed at restraining and checking the powers of wealth and privilege. It was to be a charter of liberty for human rights against property rights. The transformation has been rapid and complete. It operates today to protect the rights of property to the detriment of the rights of man. It has become the Magna Charta of accumulated and organized capital."...

It seems rather plain to me why the Court today does not attempt to justify all of the broad *Twining* discussion. That opinion carries its own refutation on what may be called the factual issue the Court resolved. The opinion itself shows, without resort to the powerful argument in the dissent of Mr. Justice Harlan, that outside of Star Chamber practices and influences, the "English-speaking" peoples have for centuries abhorred and feared the practice of compelling people to convict themselves of crime....

Document Text

I cannot consider the Bill of Rights to be an outworn 18th Century "strait jacket" as the *Twining* opinion did. Its provisions may be thought outdated abstractions by some. And it is true that they were designed to meet ancient evils. But they are the same kind of human evils that have emerged from century to century wherever excessive power is sought by the few at the expense of the many. In my judgment the people of no nation can lose their liberty so long as a Bill of Rights like ours survives and its basic purposes are conscientiously interpreted, enforced and respected so as to afford continuous protection against old, as well as new, devices and practices which might thwart those purposes. I fear to see the consequences of the Court's practice of substituting its own concepts of decency and fundamental justice for the language of the Bill of Rights as its point of departure in interpreting and enforcing that Bill of Rights.... I would follow what I believe was the original purpose of the Fourteenth Amendment—to extend to all the people of the nation the complete protection of the Bill of Rights. To hold that this Court can determine what, if any, provisions of the Bill of Rights will be enforced, and if so to what degree, is to frustrate the great design of a written Constitution. Conceding the possibility that this Court is now wise enough to improve on the Bill of Rights by substituting natural law concepts for the Bill of Rights, I think the possibility is entirely too speculative to agree to take that course. I would therefore hold in this case that the full protection of the Fifth Amendment's proscription against compelled testimony must be afforded by California. This I would do because of reliance upon the original purpose of the Fourteenth Amendment.

It is an illusory apprehension that literal application of some or all of the provisions of the Bill of Rights to the States would unwisely increase the sum total of the powers of this Court to invalidate state legislation. The Federal Government has not been harmfully burdened by the requirement that enforcement of federal laws affecting civil liberty conform literally to the Bill of Rights. Who would advocate its repeal? It must be conceded, of course, that the natural-law-due-process formula, which the Court today reaffirms, has been interpreted to limit substantially this Court's power to prevent state violations of the individual civil liberties guaranteed by the Bill of Rights. But this formula also has been used in the past and can be used in the future, to license this Court, in considering regulatory legislation, to roam at large in the broad expanses of policy and morals and to trespass, all too freely, on the legislative domain of the States as well as the Federal Government.

Glossary

abstractions:	mere ideas, as opposed to principles based on actual experience
afforded:	provided
apprehensions:	concerns or misgivings
book written by Mr. Charles Wallace Collins:	*The Fourteenth Amendment and the States* (1912), written by the American jurist and legal scholar Collins (1879–1964)
canons:	laws
comment upon testimony:	the act of informing the jury in a particular trial that the accused has refused to testify
due process:	the due process of law, whereby an individual accused of a crime has a right to be formally charged and tried
excrescence:	a deformed growth
extort:	force someone to surrender something
infringe:	limit

Glossary

intervening:	occurring between one time or event and a later time or event
Magna Charta:	Also called Magna Carta, "Great Charter," a document signed by King John of England in 1215, which granted specific rights to citizens and required the king to obey the law
Mr. Justice Harlan:	John Marshall Harlan, associate justice of the Supreme Court (1955–1971)
natural law:	the idea, which underlies the U.S. Constitution, that certain human rights are justified by nature itself and not granted by governments
privileges or immunities:	rights and freedoms, particularly from unfair prosecution, which are explicitly granted in the Fourteenth Amendment
proscription:	prohibition
resume:	summary
Star Chamber:	a secret court

YOUNGSTOWN SHEET & TUBE CO. v. SAWYER

1952

The President's power, if any, to issue the order must stem either from an act of Congress or from the Constitution itself. There is no statute that expressly authorizes the President to take possession of property as he did here. Nor is there any act of Congress to which our attention has been directed from which such a power can fairly be implied. Indeed, we do not understand the Government to rely on statutory authorization for this seizure. There are two statutes which do authorize the President to take both personal and real property under certain conditions. However, the Government admits that these conditions were not met and that the President's order was not rooted in either of the statutes. The Government refers to the seizure provisions of one of these statutes (201 (b) of the Defense Production Act) as "much too cumbersome, involved, and time-consuming for the crisis which was at hand."

Moreover, the use of the seizure technique to solve labor disputes in order to prevent work stoppages was not only unauthorized by any congressional enactment; prior to this controversy, Congress had refused to adopt that method of settling labor disputes. When the Taft-Hartley Act was under consideration in 1947, Congress rejected an amendment which would have authorized such governmental seizures in cases of emergency. Apparently it was thought that the technique of seizure, like that of compulsory arbitration, would interfere with the process of collective bargaining. Consequently, the plan Congress adopted in that Act did not provide for seizure under any circumstances. Instead, the plan sought to bring about settlements by use of the customary devices of mediation, conciliation, investigation by boards of inquiry, and public reports. In some instances temporary injunctions were authorized to provide cooling-off periods. All this failing, unions were left free to strike after a secret vote by employees as to whether they wished to accept their employers' final settlement offer.

It is clear that if the President had authority to issue the order he did, it must be found in some provision of the Constitution. And it is not claimed that express constitutional language grants this power to the President. The contention is that presidential power should be implied from the aggregate of his powers under the Constitution. Particular reliance is placed on provisions in Article II which say that "The executive Power shall be vested in a President ..."; that "he shall take Care that the Laws be faithfully executed"; and that he "shall be Commander in Chief of the Army and Navy of the United States."

The order cannot properly be sustained as an exercise of the President's military power as Commander in Chief of the Armed Forces. The Government attempts to do so by citing a number of cases upholding broad powers in military commanders engaged in day-to-day fighting in a theater of war.... Even though "theater of war" be an expanding concept, we cannot with faithfulness to our constitutional system hold that the Commander in Chief of the Armed Forces has the ultimate power as such to take possession of private property in order to keep labor disputes from stopping production. This is a job for the Nation's lawmakers, not for its military authorities.

Nor can the seizure order be sustained because of the several constitutional provisions that grant executive power to the President. In the framework of our Constitution, the President's power to see that the laws are faithfully executed refutes the idea that he is to be a lawmaker. The Constitution limits his functions in the lawmaking process to the recommending of laws he thinks wise and the vetoing of laws he thinks bad. And the Constitution is neither silent nor equivocal about who shall make laws which the President is to execute. The first section of the first article says that "All legislative Powers herein granted shall be vested in a Congress of the United States...." After granting many powers to the Congress, Article I goes on to provide that Congress may "make all Laws which shall be necessary and proper for carrying into Execution the foregoing Powers, and all other Powers vested by this Constitution in the Government of the United States, or in any Department or Officer thereof."

The President's order does not direct that a congressional policy be executed in a manner prescribed by Congress—it directs that a presidential policy be

Document Text

executed in a manner prescribed by the President. The preamble of the order itself, like that of many statutes, sets out reasons why the President believes certain policies should be adopted, proclaims these policies as rules of conduct to be followed, and again, like a statute, authorizes a government official to promulgate additional rules and regulations consistent with the policy proclaimed and needed to carry that policy into execution. The power of Congress to adopt such public policies as those proclaimed by the order is beyond question. It can authorize the taking of private property for public use. It can make laws regulating the relationships between employers and employees, prescribing rules designed to settle labor disputes, and fixing wages and working conditions in certain fields of our economy. The Constitution does not subject this lawmaking power of Congress to presidential or military supervision or control.

It is said that other Presidents without congressional authority have taken possession of private business enterprises in order to settle labor disputes. But even if this be true, Congress has not thereby lost its exclusive constitutional authority to make laws necessary and proper to carry out the powers vested by the Constitution "in the Government of the United States, or any Department or Officer thereof."

The Founders of this Nation entrusted the lawmaking power to the Congress alone in both good and bad times. It would do no good to recall the historical events, the fears of power and the hopes for freedom that lay behind their choice. Such a review would but confirm our holding that this seizure order cannot stand.

Glossary

collective bargaining:	organized negotiation between workers and employers
mediation:	settlement of disputes
the order:	Executive Order 10340 (April 8, 1952), which allowed the federal government to take temporary control of steel mills that had been closed owing to strikes
promulgate:	officially put into legal effect
statutory:	referring to statutes or laws
Taft-Hartley Act:	a measure sponsored by Senators Robert Taft and Fred Hartley and passed into law over President Harry Truman's veto, which greatly restricted the rights of labor unions

Document Text

GIDEON V. WAINWRIGHT

1963

The Sixth Amendment provides, "In all criminal prosecutions, the accused shall enjoy the right ... to have the Assistance of Counsel for his defence." We have construed this to mean that in federal courts counsel must be provided for defendants unable to employ counsel unless the right is competently and intelligently waived.

We accept *Betts v. Brady* 's assumption, based as it was on our prior cases, that a provision of the Bill of Rights which is "fundamental and essential to a fair trial" is made obligatory upon the States by the Fourteenth Amendment. We think the Court in *Betts* was wrong, however, in concluding that the Sixth Amendment's guarantee of counsel is not one of these fundamental rights.

In light of these and many other prior decisions of this Court, it is not surprising that the *Betts* Court, when faced with the contention that "one charged with crime, who is unable to obtain counsel, must be furnished counsel by the State," conceded that "[e]xpressions in the opinions of this court lend color to the argument...." The fact is that in deciding as it did—that "appointment of counsel is not a fundamental right, essential to a fair trial"—the Court in *Betts v. Brady* made an abrupt break with its own well-considered precedents. In returning to these old precedents, sounder we believe than the new, we but restore constitutional principles established to achieve a fair system of justice. Not only these precedents but also reason and reflection require us to recognize that in our adversary system of criminal justice, any person haled into court, who is too poor to hire a lawyer, cannot be assured a fair trial unless counsel is provided for him. This seems to us to be an obvious truth. Governments, both state and federal, quite properly spend vast sums of money to establish machinery to try defendants accused of crime. Lawyers to prosecute are everywhere deemed essential to protect the public's interest in an orderly society. Similarly, there are few defendants charged with crime, few indeed, who fail to hire the best lawyers they can get to prepare and present their defenses. That government hires lawyers to prosecute and defendants who have the money hire lawyers to defend are the strongest indications of the widespread belief that lawyers in criminal courts are necessities, not luxuries. The right of one charged with crime to counsel may not be deemed fundamental and essential to fair trials in some countries, but it is in ours. From the very beginning, our state and national constitutions and laws have laid great emphasis on procedural and substantive safeguards designed to assure fair trials before impartial tribunals in which every defendant stands equal before the law. This noble ideal cannot be realized if the poor man charged with crime has to face his accusers without a lawyer to assist him.

Glossary

adversary system of criminal justice:	a legal system in which individuals have the right to bring cases before a court
the Assistance of Counsel:	the help of a lawyer or other legal representative
but:	only
haled:	forced
impartial:	fair and unbiased
lend color:	give validity or believability
precedents:	legal rulings in response to a particular situation that will serve as a guide to dealing with future occurrences of the same situation
procedural and substantive:	relating to both the procedure by which cases are brought to trial, and the methods by which the facts or substance will be reviewed in that trial
sounder:	more sound, or logically justifiable

The Hugo L. Black United States Courthouse in Birmingham, Alabama by US Federal Judiciary

GRISWOLD V. CONNECTICUT

1965

[Black dissent]
I agree with my Brother STEWART'S dissenting opinion. And like him I do not to any extent whatever base my view that this Connecticut law is constitutional on a belief that the law is wise or that its policy is a good one....

Had the doctor defendant here, or even the nondoctor defendant, been convicted for doing nothing more than expressing opinions to persons coming to the clinic that certain contraceptive devices, medicines or practices would do them good and would be desirable, or for telling people how devices could be used, I can think of no reasons at this time why their expressions of views would not be protected by the First and Fourteenth Amendments, which guarantee freedom of speech.... But speech is one thing; conduct and physical activities are quite another.... Strongly as I desire to protect all First Amendment freedoms, I am unable to stretch the Amendment so as to afford protection to the conduct of these defendants in violating the Connecticut law....

The Court talks about a constitutional "right of privacy" as though there is some constitutional provision or provisions forbidding any law ever to be passed which might abridge the "privacy" of individuals. But there is not. There are, of course, guarantees in certain specific constitutional provisions which are designed in part to protect privacy at certain times and places with respect to certain activities. Such, for example, is the Fourth Amendment's guarantee against "unreasonable searches and seizures." But I think it belittles that Amendment to talk about it as though it protects nothing but "privacy." To treat it that way is to give it a niggardly interpretation, not the kind of liberal reading I think any Bill of Rights provision should be given. The average man would very likely not have his feelings soothed any more by having his property seized openly than by having it seized privately and by stealth. He simply wants his property left alone. And a person can be just as much, if not more, irritated, annoyed and injured by an unceremonious public arrest by a policeman as he is by a seizure in the privacy of his office or home.

One of the most effective ways of diluting or expanding a constitutionally guaranteed right is to substitute for the crucial word or words of a constitutional guarantee another word or words, more or less flexible and more or less restricted in meaning. This fact is well illustrated by the use of the term "right of privacy" as a comprehensive substitute for the Fourth Amendment's guarantee against "unreasonable searches and seizures." "Privacy" is a broad, abstract and ambiguous concept which can easily be shrunken in meaning but which can also, on the other hand, easily be interpreted as a constitutional ban against many things other than searches and seizures. I have expressed the view many times that First Amendment freedoms, for example, have suffered from a failure of the courts to stick to the simple language of the First Amendment in construing it, instead of invoking multitudes of words substituted for those the Framers used.... For these reasons I get nowhere in this case by talk about a constitutional "right of privacy" as an emanation from one or more constitutional provisions. I like my privacy as well as the next one, but I am nevertheless compelled to admit that government has a right to invade it unless prohibited by some specific constitutional provision. For these reasons I cannot agree with the Court's judgment and the reasons it gives for holding this Connecticut law unconstitutional....

I have no doubt that the Connecticut law could be applied in such a way as to abridge freedom of speech and press and therefore violate the First and Fourteenth Amendments. My disagreement with the Court's opinion holding that there is such a violation here is a narrow one, relating to the application of the First Amendment to the facts and circumstances of this particular case. But my disagreement with Brothers HARLAN, WHITE and GOLDBERG is more basic. I think that if properly construed neither the Due Process Clause nor the Ninth Amendment, nor both together, could under any circumstances be a proper basis for invalidating the Connecticut law. I discuss the due process and Ninth Amendment arguments together because on analysis they turn out to be the same thing merely using different words to claim for this Court and the federal judiciary power to invalidate any legislative act which the judges find irrational, unreasonable or offensive.

The due process argument which my Brothers HARLAN and WHITE adopt here is based, as their

opinions indicate, on the premise that this Court is vested with power to invalidate all state laws that it considers to be arbitrary, capricious, unreasonable, or oppressive, or on this Court's belief that a particular state law under scrutiny has no "rational or justifying" purpose, or is offensive to a "sense of fairness and justice." If these formulas based on "natural justice," or others which mean the same thing, are to prevail, they require judges to determine what is or is not constitutional on the basis of their own appraisal of what laws are unwise or unnecessary. The power to make such decisions is of course that of a legislative body. Surely it has to be admitted that no provision of the Constitution specifically gives such blanket power to courts to exercise such a supervisory veto over the wisdom and value of legislative policies and to hold unconstitutional those laws which they believe unwise or dangerous. I readily admit that no legislative body, state or national, should pass laws that can justly be given any of the invidious labels invoked as constitutional excuses to strike down state laws. But perhaps it is not too much to say that no legislative body ever does pass laws without believing that they will accomplish a sane, rational, wise and justifiable purpose. While I completely subscribe to the holding of *Marbury v. Madison* and subsequent cases, that our Court has constitutional power to strike down statutes, state or federal, that violate commands of the Federal Constitution, I do not believe that we are granted power by the Due Process Clause or any other constitutional provision or provisions to measure constitutionality by our belief that legislation is arbitrary, capricious or unreasonable, or accomplishes no justifiable purpose, or is offensive to our own notions of "civilized standards of conduct." Such an appraisal of the wisdom of legislation is an attribute of the power to make laws, not of the power to interpret them. The use by federal courts of such a formula or doctrine or whatnot to veto federal or state laws simply takes away from Congress and States the power to make laws based on their own judgment of fairness and wisdom and transfers that power to this Court for ultimate determination—a power which was specifically denied to federal courts by the convention that framed the Constitution....

My Brother GOLDBERG has adopted the recent discovery that the Ninth Amendment as well as the Due Process Clause can be used by this Court as authority to strike down all state legislation which this Court thinks violates "fundamental principles of liberty and justice," or is contrary to the "traditions and [collective] conscience of our people." He also states, without proof satisfactory to me, that in making decisions on this basis judges will not consider "their personal and private notions." One may ask how they can avoid considering them. Our Court certainly has no machinery with which to take a Gallup Poll. And the scientific miracles of this age have not yet produced a gadget which the Court can use to determine what traditions are rooted in the "[collective] conscience of our people." Moreover, one would certainly have to look far beyond the language of the Ninth Amendment to find that the Framers vested in this Court any such awesome veto powers over lawmaking, either by the States or by the Congress. Nor does anything in the history of the Amendment offer any support for such a shocking doctrine. The whole history of the adoption of the Constitution and Bill of Rights points the other way, and the very material quoted by my Brother GOLDBERG shows that the Ninth Amendment was intended to protect against the idea that "by enumerating particular exceptions to the grant of power" to the Federal Government, "those rights which were not singled out, were intended to be assigned into the hands of the General Government [the United States], and were consequently insecure." That Amendment was passed, not to broaden the powers of this Court or any other department of "the General Government," but, as every student of history knows, to assure the people that the Constitution in all its provisions was intended to limit the Federal Government to the powers granted expressly or by necessary implication. If any broad, unlimited power to hold laws unconstitutional because they offend what this Court conceives to be the "[collective] conscience of our people" is vested in this Court by the Ninth Amendment, the Fourteenth Amendment, or any other provision of the Constitution, it was not given by the Framers, but rather has been bestowed on the Court by the Court. This fact is perhaps responsible for the peculiar phenomenon that for a period of a century and a half no serious suggestion was ever made that the Ninth Amendment, enacted to protect state powers against federal invasion, could be used as a weapon of federal power to prevent state legislatures from passing laws they consider appropriate to govern local affairs. Use of any such broad, unbounded judicial authority would make of this Court's members a day-to-day constitutional convention.

I repeat so as not to be misunderstood that this Court does have power, which it should exercise, to hold laws unconstitutional where they are forbidden by the Federal Constitution. My point is that there is no provision of the Constitution which either expressly or impliedly vests power in this Court to sit as a supervisory agency over acts of duly constituted legislative bodies and set aside their laws because of the Court's

Document Text

belief that the legislative policies adopted are unreasonable, unwise, arbitrary, capricious or irrational. The adoption of such a loose, flexible, uncontrolled standard for holding laws unconstitutional, if ever it is finally achieved, will amount to a great unconstitutional shift of power to the courts which I believe and am constrained to say will be bad for the courts and worse for the country. Subjecting federal and state laws to such an unrestrained and unrestrainable judicial control as to the wisdom of legislative enactments would, I fear, jeopardize the separation of governmental powers that the Framers set up and at the same time threaten to take away much of the power of States to govern themselves which the Constitution plainly intended them to have.

I realize that many good and able men have eloquently spoken and written, sometimes in rhapsodical strains, about the duty of this Court to keep the Constitution in tune with the times. The idea is that the Constitution must be changed from time to time and that this Court is charged with a duty to make those changes. For myself, I must with all deference reject that philosophy. The Constitution makers knew the need for change and provided for it. Amendments suggested by the people's elected representatives can be submitted to the people or their selected agents for ratification. That method of change was good for our Fathers, and being somewhat old-fashioned I must add it is good enough for me. And so, I cannot rely on the Due Process Clause or the Ninth Amendment or any mysterious and uncertain natural law concept as a reason for striking down this state law. The Due Process Clause with an "arbitrary and capricious" or "shocking to the conscience" formula was liberally used by this Court to strike down economic legislation in the early decades of this century, threatening, many people thought, the tranquility and stability of the Nation.... That formula, based on subjective considerations of "natural justice," is no less dangerous when used to enforce this Court's views about personal rights than those about economic rights. I had thought that we had laid that formula, as a means for striking down state legislation, to rest once and for all....

So far as I am concerned, Connecticut's law as applied here is not forbidden by any provision of the Federal Constitution as that Constitution was written, and I would therefore affirm.

Glossary

affirm:	agree; in the language of the Supreme Court, to affirm is to agree with the disputed judgment of a lower court
agents:	elected representatives
construing:	interpreting
Due Process Clause:	a guarantee in the Fifth and Fourteenth Amendments that an individual accused of a crime has a right to be formally charged and tried
emanation:	something that comes from something else
HARLAN, WHITE and GOLDBERG:	John Marshall Harlan (1899–1911), Byron White (1917–2002), and Arthur Goldberg (1908–1990); served as associate justices of the Supreme Court, 1955–1971, 1962–1993, and 1962–1965, respectively
insecure:	not guaranteed
liberal reading:	open-minded interpretation
my Brother STEWART:	Potter Stewart (1915–1985), associate justice of the Supreme Court from 1958 to 1981; "brother" being a term used to refer to colleagues on the Court
niggardly:	stingy, small-minded
Ninth Amendment:	the amendment that guarantees that the listing of specific rights in the Constitution does not mean that other rights are denied to citizens
rhapsodical strains:	tones of overwhelming and unthinking excitement

Justice Blackmun

Harry Blackmun: Original Analysis

Supreme Court Justice

1908–1999

Overview

Harry Andrew Blackmun was the ninety-ninth justice appointed to the U.S. Supreme Court. He was appointed by President Richard M. Nixon and sat on the Court from 1970 until 1994. Raised in Saint Paul, Minnesota, Blackmun attended Harvard University on partial scholarship, graduating with a degree in mathematics. After graduating from Harvard Law School, he returned to Minnesota, where he clerked for Judge John Benjamin Sanborn of the Eight Circuit Court of Appeals. He later worked for the firm of Driscoll, Fletcher, Dorsey, and Barker in Minneapolis, practicing tax law and becoming a junior partner in 1939. In 1950 he accepted the position of resident counsel at the Mayo Clinic in Rochester, Minnesota, and in 1959 he was appointed to the Eighth Circuit Court of Appeals.

Blackmun was a childhood friend of Chief Justice Warren Burger, a conservative jurist who was already sitting on the Supreme Court when Blackmun was appointed. They were immediately dubbed the "Minnesota Twins" by the press. However, it soon became apparent that Blackmun was not voting in lockstep with the chief justice. Their relationship later deteriorated.

Blackmun is best known for the majority opinion he wrote in the seminal case *Roe v. Wade*, which struck down state laws criminalizing abortion. Although six justices joined him in the opinion, he has always been personally associated with the ruling and was the target of protests and even death threats for the remainder of his life. Over the course of his tenure, he filed several dissenting opinions defending *Roe* and lamenting that later decisions by the Court essentially rendered moot the rights recognized in *Roe*. His dissents in the abortion cases as well as other civil rights cases often urged the Court to remember the "little people" and the world "out there." Blackmun is also remembered for a dissent he filed in a death-penalty case a few months before retiring from the Court in 1994. The dissent stated his conviction that capital punishment was abhorrent as well as unconstitutional.

Explanation and Analysis of Documents

During his tenure on the Supreme Court, Blackmun along with his clerks worked long hours. More often than not, he worked in the justices' library, where he could research and write alone and without being disturbed by the telephone. When he first came to the Court, he tried to draft all of his legal opinions himself without the assistance of his law clerks. However, he, as well as most of the other justices with whom he served, soon realized that such a practice was not realistic, given the Court's heavy caseload. From that point on, his law clerks wrote most of the first drafts of his opinions. The degree to which he edited the drafts reportedly varied, but he was known as a heavy-handed editor and a stickler for proper grammar. In any case, Blackmun's humility and intellect come through clearly in his judicial writing. His opinions, particularly his dissenting opinions, often try to remind the Court about the realities of the world outside of the Supreme Court.

♦ *Roe v. Wade*

Blackmun's majority opinion in *Roe v. Wade* is his most well-known opinion. The case was a challenge to a Texas statute that made it a crime to have an abortion unless the abortion was performed to save the life of the pregnant woman. As noted in Blackmun's opinion, the majority of the states at the time had similar statutes on their books.

Roe was brought by Norma McCorvey, using the pseudonym Jane Roe, a young unmarried woman who had become pregnant as the result of a rape and who had been unable to obtain an abortion in Texas; Dr. James Hubert Hallford, a licensed physician who had been arrested for allegedly violating the Texas statute; and John and Mary Doe, a married couple also using a pseudonym. By the time the Court heard the first oral arguments in the case in December 1971, the issue of abortion was controversial and divisive. Blackmun was not initially committed to finding the Texas statute unconstitutional but knew that the opinion would be scrutinized. He reportedly spent five months drafting the opinion, including two weeks during the summer of 1971 spent in the Mayo Clinic library in Rochester, Minnesota, researching the history of abortion. In his draft of the opinion circulated to the other justices in May 1972, he avoided the issue of whether privacy rights should be extended by invalidating the statute as unconstitutionally vague. However, several justices urged that the Court rule on the "core" issue of whether all abortion laws should be struck down.

The second oral arguments were held in October 1972, and the opinion was announced on January 22, 1973. The Court struck down the Texas statute by a vote of seven to two, with Blackmun drafting the opinion. Blackmun begins by acknowledging that the issue is emotional and controversial while maintaining that the court's task is to determine

the constitutionality of the statute without emotion. To that end, the opinion provides a lengthy history of medical and nonmedical practices and attitudes toward abortion in the United States and internationally.

After finding that only Jane Roe had standing to bring the complaint in question, the opinion examines the history of abortion and the reasons for enactment of criminal abortion laws. The survey of the history of abortion addresses attitudes and practices in the ancient world, in common law, in recent English law, and in American law. It concludes that women in the United States had less of a right to abortion at the present than women had when the Constitution was adopted and throughout most of the nineteenth century.

The opinion then traces the history of the American Medical Association and its positions on abortion, concluding with descriptions of 1970 preambles and resolutions adopted by its House of Delegates. The judgments and moral principles of physicians that are emphasized in the preambles and resolutions are contrasted with the idea that women should be provided with abortions whenever they want. The opinion also notes that the American Public Health Association had adopted standards for abortion services and that the American Bar Association's House of Delegates had adopted a Uniform Abortion Act, setting forth standards for performing abortions.

The opinion proceeds to set forth three historical reasons that have been used to support the criminalization of abortion. The first is that such laws are meant to discourage sex outside of marriage. The second reason is the fact that when most of these criminal statutes were enacted in the nineteenth century abortions were dangerous for women and the mortality rate was high. The third reason is that the government has an interest "in protecting prenatal life."

The opinion finds that, although the drafters of the Constitution did not include an explicit right to privacy, the Constitution protects rights to personal privacy and rights to privacy within certain areas or zones. It notes that the privacy right of a woman to determine whether to terminate her pregnancy exists whether it is in the Ninth Amendment, as found by the lower court, or in the Fourteenth Amendment's concept of personal liberty and restrictions upon state action, as the Court finds it is. The opinion acknowledges that maternity may force a woman into poverty and a hopeless future and may cause psychological and physical harm to the woman and her family.

The opinion finds that the right to an abortion is not absolute and that the government has countervailing interests in protecting "health, medical standards, and prenatal life." It declines to decide when life begins, noting that experts in medicine, philosophy, and theology are divided on the issue. However, the opinion then provides a short historical survey indicating that there has always been strong support for the stance that life does not begin until actual birth. It concludes that the unborn have never been historically recognized in law as persons and are not included in the term *person* as used in the Fourteenth Amendment.

Time Line

1908	November 12	■ Harry Blackmun is born in Nashville, Illinois.
1932		■ After graduating from Harvard Law School, Blackmun begins an eighteen-month clerkship for Judge John Benjamin Sanborn on the Eighth Circuit Court of Appeals.
1934		■ Blackmun begins as an associate at Driscoll, Fletcher, Dorsey, and Barker in Minneapolis, becoming a junior partner in 1939 and general partner in 1943.
1950		■ Blackmun becomes resident counsel of the Mayo Clinic in Rochester, Minnesota.
1959		■ Blackmun is appointed to the Eighth Circuit Court of Appeals.
1970	April 4	■ Blackmun is nominated as associate justice of the U.S. Supreme Court by President Richard M. Nixon.
	June 9	■ Blackmun is sworn in as Supreme Court justice.
1973	January 22	■ The Supreme Court issues its opinion in *Roe v. Wade*.
1977	June 20	■ The Supreme Court issues its opinion in *Beal v. Doe*, with Blackmun dissenting.
1986	June 30	■ *Bowers v. Hardwick* is decided, with Blackmun dissenting; the case would be overruled by *Lawrence v. Texas* (2003).
1989	February 22	■ Blackmun dissents in *DeShaney v. Winnebago County Department of Social Services.*
1994	February 22	■ Blackmun issues his renowned dissent in the death-penalty case *Callins v. Collins.*
	August 3	■ Blackmun retires from the Supreme Court.

Time Line		
1994–1995		■ Harold Koh conducts interviews with Blackmun to produce an oral history.
1997		■ Blackmun appears in the film *Amistad* in the role of Justice Joseph Story.
1999	March 4	■ Blackmun dies in Arlington, Virginia.

The opinion concludes that the state has an important and legitimate interest in preserving and protecting the health of pregnant women as well as a separate and distinct, albeit important and legitimate, interest in protecting the fetus. Each interest becomes compelling at a particular point during pregnancy. The state's interest in protecting the health of the woman becomes compelling "at approximately the end of the first trimester"; its interest in potential life becomes compelling at viability, at which point the fetus has "the capability of meaningful life outside the mother's womb."

Thus, the opinion sets forth the now infamous trimester framework, whereby during the first trimester, the decision whether to perform an abortion is reached solely through the medically informed judgment of the woman's physician. For abortions during the second trimester, the state may "regulate the abortion procedure in ways that are reasonably related to maternal health." Only during the third trimester may the state "regulate, and even proscribe, abortion except where it is necessary, in appropriate medical judgment, for the preservation of the life or health of the mother."

Over the years, legal scholars have criticized the *Roe* opinion as weak and judicial lawmaking. One of the first and most critical reactions was a law review article written by John Hart Ely, a Yale Law School professor. Some legal scholars contend that the core of Blackmun's decision is the right of physicians to make medical decisions free from state regulation and that he only later developed a commitment to the rights of women. Others insist that *Roe* is indeed grounded in women's rights.

The decision was immediately controversial outside the legal community as well. Blackmun personally became the target and focus of antiabortion activists. He received boxes of mail on the issue throughout his life and was continually picketed. In 1985, after a bullet came through the window of his apartment, the Supreme Court police insisted that he no longer drive himself to work. Although the shot was later deemed random, Blackmun was driven to the Court for the remainder of his career.

Over the years, abortion cases meant to whittle away, if not overturn, *Roe* regularly appeared on the Court's docket. Blackmun often dissented and defended that opinion. In 1989, in *Webster v. Reproductive Health Services*, the Court found most of a highly restrictive Missouri law constitutional. Justice Sandra Day O'Connor argued that the law did not conflict with *Roe*. Justice Antonin Scalia urged that *Webster* be used to overturn *Roe*. In his concurrence/dissent, Blackmun cautions that although the fundamental constitutional right of women to abortion as recognized in *Roe* survives, it is not secure. He warns:

Today's decision involves the most politically divisive domestic legal issue of our time. By refusing to explain or to justify its proposed revolutionary revision in the law of abortion, and by refusing to abide not only by our precedents, but also by our canons for reconsidering those precedents, the plurality invites charges of cowardice and illegitimacy to our door. I cannot say that these would be undeserved. For today, at least, the law of abortion stands undisturbed. For today, the women of this Nation still retain the liberty to control their destinies. But the signs are evident and very ominous, and a chill wind blows. (*Webster v. Reproductive Health Services*, 492 U.S. 490, 559–60; 1989)

In 1992 in *Planned Parenthood v. Casey*, *Roe* again survived, but only barely. In a decision in which five separate opinions were filed, *Roe*'s trimester framework was deemed to be unessential to the holding of *Roe* and was replaced with an "undue burden" test: "An undue burden exists, and therefore a provision of law is invalid, if its purpose or effect is to place substantial obstacles in the path of a woman seeking an abortion before the fetus attains viability." Blackmun filed a separate opinion concurring in part and dissenting in part, with a warning that at eighty-three years old, he would not remain on the Court forever. He notes that the distance between the approach in *Roe* and the "undue burden" test set forth in *Casey* is one vote—his and then that of his successor will be the deciding vote in the future. He expresses his regret that the confirmation process of his successor "may be exactly where the choice between the two worlds will be made" (*Planned Parenthood of Southeastern Pennsylvania v. Casey*, 505 U.S. 833, 943; 1992).

♦ *Beal v. Doe*

Beal v. Doe was one in a trio of cases argued before the Court in January 1977 that addressed whether states and local authorities were required to pay for abortions for poor women. *Maher v. Roe* was a challenge to a Connecticut regulation that denied abortions to indigent women in the first trimester unless they were deemed to be necessary for medical reasons. In *Poelker v. Doe*, a municipal hospital sought to refuse nontherapeutic abortions to indigent women. In *Beal v. Doe*, the issue was whether states participating in federal Medicaid had to pay for abortions for indigent women that were not medically necessary. In all three cases, the Court decided that the government did not have an obligation to pay for the abortions for poor women. Blackmun's dissent in *Beal* was applicable to all three cases.

The five-paragraph dissent laments the impact of these decisions on real people. It observes that

the Court concedes the existence of a constitutional right but denies the realization and enjoyment of that right on the ground that existence and realization are separate

and distinct. For the individual woman concerned, indigent and financially helpless, as the Court's opinions in the three cases concede her to be, the result is punitive and tragic. Implicit in the Court's holdings is the condescension that she may go elsewhere for her abortion. I find that disingenuous and alarming, almost reminiscent of: "Let them eat cake."

The following paragraphs argue that the Court's ruling means that politicians, elected by a majority, now have the power to determine whether a minority will have access to nontherapeutic abortions. Blackmun dismisses the Court's financial argument as "specious," as abortions are cheaper than the costs of childbirth and the subsequent welfare costs of indigent care. The dissent ends with Blackmun's suspicion that the majority of the Court is refusing to recognize that there is another world outside the Supreme Court that the Court is either choosing to ignore or is afraid to acknowledge.

This dissent is one of the first opinions in which Blackmun urges the Court to remember the common people. In 1980 he filed a dissent in *Harris v. McRae*, another case addressing government funding of abortions, in which he stated that his dissent in *Beal* was applicable and quoted parts of that earlier opinion.

♦ *Bowers v. Hardwick*

Following *Roe v. Wade*, the Court was confronted with numerous cases seeking to define and expand the privacy right recognized by *Roe*. *Bowers* was one such case. Michael Hardwick was a gay man who had been charged with violating Georgia's criminal sodomy law for actions taken in his home. Although the criminal prosecution against him was eventually dropped, he challenged the law in federal court. The Court's opinion characterizes the case as about whether homosexuals have the constitutional right to engage in sodomy. It declares itself unwilling to find such a constitutional right. It finds that the cases involving reproduction and family issues are not relevant to homosexual conduct and sets forth a historical survey meant to demonstrate that homosexual sodomy has been illegal since ancient times.

Blackmun's dissent relies on the privacy rights recognized in the abortion cases as well as in other cases. It opens with the statement that, contrary to the majority's characterization, the case is about the right to be left alone and not about a fundamental constitutional right to engage in homosexual sodomy. Therefore, Blackmun contends, Hardwick's claim must be analyzed according to the constitutional right to privacy. That means that Georgia must come forward with more of a countervailing interest than its opinion that homosexual sodomy is an "'abominable crime not fit to be named among Christians.'" The dissent finds that the case implicates both lines of privacy cases—those recognizing that individuals, not the state, have the right to make certain decisions and those recognizing that certain places are more private.

Blackmun gives short shrift to Georgia's defense that homosexual sodomy in a private home interferes with any rights Georgia and the country have to maintain a moral society. He cites *Roe* with regard to his unwillingness to agree that the length of time a majority has held an opinion or its passions can immunize statutes from the Court's scrutiny. In his opinion, by denying individuals the right to decide how to conduct their intimate relationships, the Court betrays the deeply rooted values of the country. He states his hope that the Court will soon realize and correct its mistake. Blackmun's hope was realized seventeen years later: In 2003 *Bowers* was overruled by the Supreme Court in the case of *Lawrence v. Texas*.

♦ *DeShaney v. Winnebago County Department of Social Services*

Legal scholars have noted that Blackmun became increasingly vocal about the people "out there" in the later years of his tenure on the Supreme Court. His dissent in *DeShaney* is a frequently quoted example and is recognized as an unusual expression of emotion by a Supreme Court justice.

Joshua DeShaney was a four-year-old boy whose father had been awarded custody in his parents' divorce. In January 1982 the county authorities learned that he might be the victim of abuse in the hands of his father. The father denied the accusations, and the Department of Social Services (DSS) did not pursue the case. Joshua was hospitalized a year later with many bruises and abrasions. The hospital suspected child abuse and notified DSS. DSS recommended to the court that Joshua remain with his father but that his father was to comply with certain requirements. The court awarded custody to the father, and a month later Joshua was again admitted to the hospital with suspicious injuries. Over the following six months, the caseworker noted her suspicions that Joshua was being abused but did nothing. Finally, Joshua fell into a life-threatening coma. Brain surgery indicated that his head had been repeatedly beaten. He was expected to remain in an institution for the profoundly retarded. His father was convicted of child abuse.

Joshua and his mother sued the county and DSS claiming that they knew or should have known that his father was violent and that therefore they had violated Joshua and his mother's constitutional rights through their failure to intervene to protect Joshua from the risk that he would be subjected to abuse by his father. The Supreme Court disagreed, finding that the government's failure to protect Joshua from his father did not violate his constitutional rights.

Blackmun wrote a separate dissent that focuses on Joshua's plight. In Blackmun's view, the Fourteenth Amendment is broad enough to protect those such as Joshua. The short dissent ends with a passionate plea:

Poor Joshua! Victim of repeated attacks by an irresponsible, bullying, cowardly, and intemperate father, and abandoned by respondents who placed him in a dangerous predicament and who knew or learned what was going on, and yet did essentially nothing except, as the Court revealingly observes,... "dutifully recorded these incidents in [their] files."

While Blackmun was criticized for personalizing the constitutional issue, he explained that he added this lament because nobody seemed to care very much that the little boy had been horribly abused. He felt that the majority of the Court had set aside their feelings and retreated into sterile legal formalism to such an extent that they failed to apply the proper legal rules to the case.

♦ *Callins v. Collins*

A few months before his retirement from the Court, Blackmun used the case of *Callins v. Collins* to state his intention to never again vote in favor of capital punishment. While sitting on the Eighth Circuit and the Supreme Court he had registered his personal objections to capital punishment but had deferred to the states. However, in 1993 he and his clerks began drafting an opinion renouncing the death penalty as unconstitutional. He used it in *Callins*.

Bruce Callins had killed a person during a robbery of a bar in Texas and had petitioned the Court for review of his death sentence. On February 22, 1994, the Court announced its denial of his petition in the face of his scheduled execution at one o'clock the following morning. Blackmun filed a lone twenty-two-page dissent. The opinion begins with a graphic description of how Callins was scheduled to die by lethal injection the next morning. It then surveys the Court's efforts, deemed unsuccessful by Blackmun, to regulate the death penalty so that its use would be fair and consistent. The opinion ends with Blackmun's declaration that "from this day forward, I no longer shall tinker with the machinery of death." He explains that throughout his judicial career, he had struggled to delineate rules and procedures that would make the death penalty constitutional, but "the death penalty experiment has failed." In his opinion, no combination of rules and regulations can fix the fact that the death penalty is unconstitutional. Conservative pundits immediately latched on to Justice Scalia's concurrence, in which he dismisses Blackmun's dissent as emotional and having no legal consequence. However, Blackmun's dissent remains one of the most quoted objections to capital punishment by courts as well as by those who are not lawyers. Callins was not executed until the following May. His lawyer wrote Blackmun, enclosing a letter from Callins expressing his gratitude. Blackmun in turn thanked the lawyer but not the inmate.

Impact and Legacy

Although *Roe v. Wade* was decided by a seven-justice majority, Blackmun remains personally associated with the Court's decision legalizing abortion. He continued throughout his tenure not only to defend the rights of women to choose abortion but also to recognize individual rights in other areas, including immigration and sexuality. His dissent in *Callins* just before his retirement took the focus off *Roe*. It caused much discussion—a result with which Blackmun was happy.

Blackmun was appointed by President Nixon with the expectation that he would participate in a conservative push to unravel many of the opinions that had been issued by the liberal Earl Warren Court. While some argue that Blackmun became more liberal with time, that assessment is probably too simple. He believed, rather, that he had been consistent over the years and that the Court had become more conservative. He said that he always tried to remember the "little" people and to not lose sight of how the Court's opinions would affect individuals. Often described as shy, remote, and aloof, he is also remembered for his humility.

One of his most lasting legacies is the collection of papers he left to the Library of Congress. The papers were opened to the public in 2004, only five years after his death. The extensive collection of notes, drafts, phone messages, and other papers from his years on the Court provide not only background on Blackmun himself but also a privileged window into the workings of the Court for a quarter of a century.

Key Sources

Blackmun's opinions for the Supreme Court can be found in many places, including *United States Supreme Court Reports* and online legal resources. Blackmun donated his extensive collection of papers to the Library of Congress. The papers span the years 1913 to 2001, with the bulk of the material coming from his years on the Eighth Circuit Court of Appeals and the Supreme Court. There are 530,800 items in the collection, including his diary of "important events" (which he began as a child) as well as draft opinions, internal Supreme Court messages and notes, and videotapes. Many of the papers of Harry A. Blackmun can be viewed online in the manuscript division of the Library of Congress (http://www.loc.gov/rr/mss/blackmun/); also provided are transcripts of interviews conducted between July 6, 1994, and December 13, 1995, by Harold H. Koh, a former Blackmun law clerk who is now the dean of Yale Law School (http://lcweb2.loc.gov/diglib/blackmun-public/series.html?ID=D09). Judge Gerald W. Heaney prepared excerpts ("Reflections of Justice Blackmun") from Blackmun's comments at the 1990 Judicial Conference of the Eighth Circuit Court of Appeals as an article for *Bench & Bar of Minnesota* (August 2001). Philippa Strum conducted interviews with Blackmun, published as "Change and Continuity on the Supreme Court: Conversations with Harry S. Blackmun" in the *University of Richmond Law Review* (March 2000). Upon Justice Blackmun's retirement in 1994 and his death in 1999, many law school journals dedicated issues in tribute and to his memory, including *Yale Law Journal* (October 1994), *Harvard Law Review* (November 1994), *Stanford Law Review* (November 1994), *American University Law Review* (Spring 1994), *Columbia Law Review* (October 1999), and *Harvard Law Review* (November 1999).

Essential Quotes

"A state criminal abortion statute of the current Texas type, that excepts from criminality only a life-saving procedure on behalf of the mother, without regard to pregnancy stage and without recognition of the other interests involved, is violative of the Due Process Clause of the Fourteenth Amendment."

(*Roe v. Wade*)

"There is another world 'out there,' the existence of which the Court, I suspect, either chooses to ignore or fears to recognize. And so the cancer of poverty will continue to grow. This is a sad day for those who regard the Constitution as a force that would serve justice to all evenhandedly and, in so doing, would better the lot of the poorest among us."

(*Beal v. Doe*)

"I believe we must analyze Hardwick's claim in the light of the values that underlie the constitutional right to privacy. If that right means anything, it means that, before Georgia can prosecute its citizens for making choices about the most intimate aspects of their lives, it must do more than assert that the choice they have made is an '"abominable crime not fit to be named among Christians."'... Only the most willful blindness could obscure the fact that sexual intimacy is 'a sensitive, key relationship of human existence, central to family life, community welfare, and the development of human personality.'"

(*Bowers v. Hardwick*)

"From this day forward, I no longer shall tinker with the machinery of death."

(*Callins v. Collins*)

Further Reading

■ Books

Greenhouse, Linda. *Becoming Justice Blackmun: Harry Blackmun's Supreme Court Journey*. New York: Henry Holt, 2005.

Hutchinson, Dennis J. "Aspen and the Transformation of Harry Blackmun." In *Supreme Court Review*, eds. Dennis J. Hutchinson, David A. Strauss, and Geoffrey R. Stone. Chicago: University of Chicago Press, 2006.

Woodward, Bob, and Scott Armstrong. *The Brethren: Inside the Supreme Court*. New York: Simon and Schuster, 1979.

Yarbrough, Tinsley E. *Harry A. Blackmun: The Outsider Justice*. New York: Oxford University Press, 2008.

—*Renee C. Redman*

Questions for Further Study

1. Blackmun became widely known for his use of emotion in making legal arguments, as for example in the case of Joshua DeShaney. The situation of "Poor Joshua," as Blackmun calls him—a child whose father beat him so badly that he caused permanent brain damage—would likely move all but the most hard-hearted observer; nevertheless, does emotion have a place in legal proceedings? Discuss the pros and cons, paying notice to the many instances in which Blackmun, particularly toward the latter part of his career, urged his colleagues to keep "the common people" in mind.

2. In *Roe v. Wade*, Blackmun established a now-famous distinction regarding the three trimesters, or three-month periods, of a normal human pregnancy. In Blackmun's view, the mother and her physician should have full legal right to abort a fetus in the first trimester, whereas the power of the state to prevent an abortion increased with the two subsequent trimesters. How valid is this distinction? One's answer to this will most likely depend on one's opinion as to when life actually begins: at conception, at birth, or somewhere in between. In discussing this matter, consider the issue of viability, or the point at which the fetus would be capable of living outside its mother's womb; is viability itself an appropriate standard for deciding the point at which an abortion might take place?

3. *Beal v. Doe* and two other cases involved the question of whether a state or local government was required to pay for an abortion on behalf of a woman who could not afford one. In all three cases the Court dismissed the idea that governments had an obligation to pay in these circumstances, and in all three Blackmun dissented. Discuss the specifics of his dissent, which centered on the idea that refusing to provide the means of fulfilling a right was the same as denying that right. Do you agree or disagree? Consider his opinion in relation to later cases that involved state funding for controversial artwork. In a number of those situations, the artists and their supporters maintained that refusal to fund such works constituted denial of First Amendment rights. Does Blackmun's logic in *Beal* apply to such cases? Why or why not?

4. It has often been noted that most people take apparently contradictory opinions on abortion and the death penalty: Usually those who oppose the former support the latter or vice versa, as in Blackmun's case. Is the more typical dual position on abortion and capital punishment actually inconsistent, or is there a deeper logic that unites seemingly opposite positions? Consider this particularly in light of Blackmun's support for abortion rights in *Roe v. Wade* and *Beal v. Doe*, in contrast with his opposition to the death penalty, which culminated in his *Callins v. Collins* dissent.

Roe v. Wade

We forthwith acknowledge our awareness of the sensitive and emotional nature of the abortion controversy, of the vigorous opposing views, even among physicians, and of the deep and seemingly absolute convictions that the subject inspires. One's philosophy, one's experiences, one's exposure to the raw edges of human existence, one's religious training, one's attitudes toward life and family and their values, and the moral standards one establishes and seeks to observe, are all likely to influence and to color one's thinking and conclusions about abortion.

In addition, population growth, pollution, poverty, and racial overtones tend to complicate and not to simplify the problem.

Our task, of course, is to resolve the issue by constitutional measurement, free of emotion and of predilection. We seek earnestly to do this, and, because we do, we have inquired into, and in this opinion place some emphasis upon, medical and medical-legal history and what that history reveals about man's attitudes toward the abortion procedure over the centuries. We bear in mind, too, Mr. Justice Holmes' admonition in his now-vindicated dissent in *Lochner v. New York* ...

"(The Constitution) is made for people of fundamentally differing views, and the accident of our finding certain opinions natural and familiar, or novel, and even shocking, ought not to conclude our judgment upon the question whether statutes embodying them conflict with the Constitution of the United States."

I

The Texas statutes that concern us here ... make it a crime to "procure an abortion," as therein defined, or to attempt one, except with respect to "an abortion procured or attempted by medical advice for the purpose of saving the life of the mother." Similar statutes are in existence in a majority of the States.

Texas first enacted a criminal abortion statute in 1854.... This was soon modified into language that has remained substantially unchanged to the present time.... The final article in each of these compilations provided the same exception, as does the present Article 1196, for an abortion by "medical advice for the purpose of saving the life of the mother....

V

The principal thrust of appellant's attack on the Texas statutes is that they improperly invade a right, said to be possessed by the pregnant woman, to choose to terminate her pregnancy. Appellant would discover this right in the concept of personal "liberty" embodied in the Fourteenth Amendment's Due Process Clause; or in personal marital, familial, and sexual privacy said to be protected by the Bill of Rights ... or among those rights reserved to the people by the Ninth Amendment,... Before addressing this claim, we feel it desirable briefly to survey, in several aspects, the history of abortion, for such insight as that history may afford us, and then to examine the state purposes and interests behind the criminal abortion laws.

VI

It perhaps is not generally appreciated that the restrictive criminal abortion laws in effect in a majority of States today are of relatively recent vintage. Those laws, generally proscribing abortion or its attempt at any time during pregnancy except when necessary to preserve the pregnant woman's life, are not of ancient or even of common-law origin. Instead, they derive from statutory changes effected, for the most part, in the latter half of the 19th century....

VII

Three reasons have been advanced to explain historically the enactment of criminal abortion laws in the 19th century and to justify their continued existence.

It has been argued occasionally that these laws were the product of a Victorian social concern to discourage illicit sexual conduct. Texas, however, does not advance this justification in the present case, and it appears that no court or commentator has taken

the argument seriously. The appellants and amici contend, moreover, that this is not a proper state purpose at all and suggest that, if it were, the Texas statutes are overbroad in protecting it since the law fails to distinguish between married and unwed mothers.

A second reason is concerned with abortion as a medical procedure. When most criminal abortion laws were first enacted, the procedure was a hazardous one for the woman. This was particularly true prior to the development of antisepsis.... Abortion mortality was high.... Thus, it has been argued that a State's real concern in enacting a criminal abortion law was to protect the pregnant woman, that is, to restrain her from submitting to a procedure that placed her life in serious jeopardy.

Modern medical techniques have altered this situation. Appellants and various amici refer to medical data indicating that abortion in early pregnancy, that is, prior to the end of the first trimester, although not without its risk, is now relatively safe. Mortality rates for women undergoing early abortions, where the procedure is legal, appear to be as low as or lower than the rates for normal childbirth. Consequently, any interest of the State in protecting the woman from an inherently hazardous procedure, except when it would be equally dangerous for her to forgo it, has largely disappeared. Of course, important state interests in the areas of health and medical standards do remain. The State has a legitimate interest in seeing to it that abortion, like any other medical procedure, is performed under circumstances that insure maximum safety for the patient. This interest obviously extends at least to the performing physician and his staff, to the facilities involved, to the availability of after-care, and to adequate provision for any complication or emergency that might arise. The prevalence of high mortality rates at illegal "abortion mills" strengthens, rather than weakens, the State's interest in regulating the conditions under which abortions are performed. Moreover, the risk to the woman increases as her pregnancy continues. Thus, the State retains a definite interest in protecting the woman's own health and safety when an abortion is proposed at a late stage of pregnancy,

The third reason is the State's interest ... in protecting prenatal life. Some of the argument for this justification rests on the theory that a new human life is present from the moment of conception. The State's interest and general obligation to protect life then extends, it is argued, to prenatal life. Only when the life of the pregnant mother herself is at stake, balanced against the life she carries within her, should the interest of the embryo or fetus not prevail. Logically, of course, a legitimate state interest in this area need not stand or fall on acceptance of the belief that life begins at conception or at some other point prior to life birth. In assessing the State's interest, recognition may be given to the less rigid claim that as long as at least potential life is involved, the State may assert interests beyond the protection of the pregnant woman alone.

Parties challenging state abortion laws have sharply disputed in some courts the contention that a purpose of these laws, when enacted, was to protect prenatal life. Pointing to the absence of legislative history to support the contention, they claim that most state laws were designed solely to protect the woman. Because medical advances have lessened this concern, at least with respect to abortion in early pregnancy, they argue that with respect to such abortions the laws can no longer be justified by any state interest. There is some scholarly support for this view of original purpose. The few state courts called upon to interpret their laws in the late 19th and early 20th centuries did focus on the State's interest in protecting the woman's health rather than in preserving the embryo and fetus. Proponents of this view point out that in many States, including Texas, by statute or judicial interpretation, the pregnant woman herself could not be prosecuted for self-abortion or for cooperating in an abortion performed upon her by another. They claim that adoption of the "quickening" distinction through received common law and state statutes tacitly recognizes the greater health hazards inherent in late abortion and impliedly repudiates the theory that life begins at conception.

It is with these interests, and the weight to be attached to them, that this case is concerned.

VIII

The Constitution does not explicitly mention any right of privacy. In a line of decisions, however, going back perhaps as far as *Union Pacific R. Co. v. Botsford*,... the Court has recognized that a right of personal privacy, or a guarantee of certain areas or zones of privacy, does exist under the Constitution.... These decisions make it clear that only personal rights that can be deemed "fundamental" or "implicit in the concept of ordered liberty,"... are included in this guarantee of personal privacy. They also make

it clear that the right has some extension to activities relating to marriage,... procreation,... contraception,... family relationships,... and child rearing and education....

This right of privacy ... is broad enough to encompass a woman's decision whether or not to terminate her pregnancy. The detriment that the State would impose upon the pregnant woman by denying this choice altogether is apparent. Specific and direct harm medically diagnosable even in early pregnancy may be involved. Maternity, or additional offspring, may force upon the woman a distressful life and future. Psychological harm may be imminent. Mental and physical health may be taxed by child care. There is also the distress, for all concerned, associated with the unwanted child, and there is the problem of bringing a child into a family already unable, psychologically and otherwise, to care for it. In other cases, as in this one, the additional difficulties and continuing stigma of unwed motherhood may be involved. All these are factors the woman and her responsible physician necessarily will consider in consultation.

On the basis of elements such as these, appellant and some amici argue that the woman's right is absolute and that she is entitled to terminate her pregnancy at whatever time, in whatever way, and for whatever reason she alone chooses. With this we do not agree. Appellant's arguments that Texas either has no valid interest at all in regulating the abortion decision, or no interest strong enough to support any limitation upon the woman's sole determination, are unpersuasive. The Court's decisions recognizing a right of privacy also acknowledge that some state regulation in areas protected by that right is appropriate.... A State may properly assert important interests in safeguarding health, in maintaining medical standards, and in protecting potential life. At some point in pregnancy, these respective interests become sufficiently compelling to sustain regulation of the factors that govern the abortion decision. The privacy right involved, therefore, cannot be said to be absolute. In fact, it is not clear to us that the claim asserted by some amici that one has an unlimited right to do with one's body as one pleases bears a close relationship to the right of privacy previously articulated in the Court's decisions. The Court has refused to recognize an unlimited right of this kind in the past....

We, therefore, conclude that the right of personal privacy includes the abortion decision, but that this right is not unqualified and must be considered against important state interests in regulation.

We note that those federal and state courts that have recently considered abortion law challenges have reached the same conclusion....

Although the results are divided, most of these courts have agreed that the right of privacy, however based, is broad enough to cover the abortion decision; that the right, nonetheless, is not absolute and is subject to some limitations; and that at some point the state interests as to protection of health, medical standards, and prenatal life, become dominant. We agree with this approach.

Where certain "fundamental rights" are involved, the Court has held that regulation limiting these rights may be justified only by a "compelling state interest,"... and that legislative enactments must be narrowly drawn to express only the legitimate state interests at stake....

IX

A. The appellee and certain amici argue that the fetus is a "person" within the language and meaning of the Fourteenth Amendment. In support of this, they outline at length and in detail the well-known facts of fetal development. If this suggestion of personhood is established, the appellant's case, of course, collapses, for the fetus' right to life would then be guaranteed specifically by the Amendment. The appellant conceded as much on reargument. On the other hand, the appellee conceded on reargument that no case could be cited that holds that a fetus is a person within the meaning of the Fourteenth Amendment.

The Constitution does not define "person" in so many words. Section 1 of the Fourteenth Amendment contains three references to "person." The first, in defining "citizens," speaks of "persons born or naturalized in the United States."... "Person" is used in other places in the Constitution.... But in nearly all these instances, the use of the word is such that it has application only postnatally. None indicates, with any assurance, that it has any possible prenatal application.

All this, together with our observation ... that throughout the major portion of the 19th century prevailing legal abortion practices were far freer than they are today, persuades us that the word "person," as used in the Fourteenth Amendment, does not include the unborn. This is in accord with the results reached in those

few cases where the issue has been squarely presented.... Indeed, our decision in *United States v. Vuitch* ... inferentially is to the same effect, for we there would not have indulged in statutory interpretation favorable to abortion in specified circumstances if the necessary consequence was the termination of life entitled to Fourteenth Amendment protection.

This conclusion, however, does not of itself fully answer the contentions raised by Texas, and we pass on to other considerations.

B. The pregnant woman cannot be isolated in her privacy. She carries an embryo and, later, a fetus, if one accepts the medical definitions of the developing young in the human uterus.... The situation therefore is inherently different from marital intimacy, or bedroom possession of obscene material, or marriage, or procreation, or education, with which Eisenstadt and Griswold, Stanley, Loving, Skinner and Pierce and Meyer were respectively concerned. As we have intimated above, it is reasonable and appropriate for a State to decide that at some point in time another interest, that of health of the mother or that of potential human life, becomes significantly involved. The woman's privacy is no longer sole and any right of privacy she possesses must be measured accordingly.

Texas urges that, apart from the Fourteenth Amendment, life begins at conception and is present throughout pregnancy, and that, therefore, the State has a compelling interest in protecting that life from and after conception. We need not resolve the difficult question of when life begins. When those trained in the respective disciplines of medicine, philosophy, and theology are unable to arrive at any consensus, the judiciary, at this point in the development of man's knowledge, is not in a position to speculate as to the answer....

X

In view of all this, we do not agree that, by adopting one theory of life, Texas may override the rights of the pregnant woman that are at stake. We repeat, however, that the State does have an important and legitimate interest in preserving and protecting the health of the pregnant woman, whether she be a resident of the State or a non-resident who seeks medical consultation and treatment there, and that it has still another important and legitimate interest in protecting the potentiality of human life. These interests are separate and distinct. Each grows in substantiality as the woman approaches term and, at a point during pregnancy, each becomes "compelling."

With respect to the State's important and legitimate interest in the health of the mother, the "compelling" point, in the light of present medical knowledge, is at approximately the end of the first trimester. This is so because of the now-established medical fact, referred to above ... that until the end of the first trimester mortality in abortion may be less than mortality in normal childbirth. It follows that ... a State may regulate the abortion procedure to the extent that the regulation reasonably relates to the preservation and protection of maternal health. Examples of permissible state regulation in this area are requirements as to the qualifications of the person who is to perform the abortion; as to the licensure of that person; as to the facility in which the procedure is to be performed, that is, whether it must be a hospital or may be a clinic or some other place of less-than-hospital status; as to the licensing of the facility; and the like.

This means, on the other hand, that, for the period of pregnancy prior to this "compelling" point, the attending physician, in consultation with his patient, is free to determine, without regulation by the State, that, in his medical judgment, the patient's pregnancy should be terminated. If that decision is reached, the judgment may be effectuated by an abortion free of interference by the State.

With respect to the State's important and legitimate interest in potential life, the "compelling" point is at viability. This is so because the fetus then presumably has the capability of meaningful life outside the mother's womb. State regulation protective of fetal life after viability thus has both logical and biological justifications. If the State is interested in protecting fetal life after viability, it may go so far as to proscribe abortion during that period, except when it is necessary to preserve the life or health of the mother.

Measured against these standards, Art. 1196 of the Texas Penal Code, in restricting legal abortions to those "procured or attempted by medical advice for the purpose of saving the life of the mother," sweeps too broadly. The statute makes no distinction between abortions performed early in pregnancy and those performed later, and it limits to a single reason, "saving" the mother's life, the legal justification for the procedure. The statute, therefore, cannot survive the constitutional attack made upon it here....

Document Text

XI

To summarize and to repeat:

1. A state criminal abortion statute of the current Texas type, that excepts from criminality only a life-saving procedue on behalf of the mother, without regard to pregnancy stage and without recognition of the other interests involved, is violative of the Due Process Clause of the Fourteenth Amendment.
   (a) For the stage prior to approximately the end of the first trimester, the abortion decision and its effectuation must be left to the medical judgment of the pregnant woman's attending physician.
   (b) For the stage subsequent to approximately the end of the first trimester, the State, in promoting its interest in the health of the mother, may, if it chooses, regulate the abortion procedure in ways that are reasonably related to maternal health.
   (c) For the stage subsequent to viability, the State in promoting its interest in the potentiality of human life may, if it chooses, regulate, and even proscribe, abortion except where it is necessary, in appropriate medical judgment, for the preservation of the life or health of the mother....

This holding, we feel, is consistent with the relative weights of the respective interests involved, with the lessons and examples of medical and legal history, with the lenity of the common law, and with the demands of the profound problems of the present day. The decision leaves the State free to place increasing restrictions on abortion as the period of pregnancy lengthens, so long as those restrictions are tailored to the recognized state interests. The decision vindicates the right of the physician to administer medical treatment according to his professional judgment up to the points where important state interests provide compelling justifications for intervention. Up to those points, the abortion decision in all its aspects is inherently, and primarily, a medical decision, and basic responsibility for it must rest with the physician. If an individual practitioner abuses the privilege of exercising proper medical judgment, the usual remedies, judicial and intra-professional, are available.

Glossary

amici:	plural of *amicus*, as in *amicus curiae*, referring to persons who are invited to advise a court of law on a case in which they are not directly involved
answer:	satisfy
antisepsis:	a method of destroying microorganisms that cause infection
appellant:	the party appealing a case before a higher court—in this case, the Supreme Court
appellee:	the party against whom a case is brought by an appellant
Due Process Clause:	a guarantee, in the Fifth and Fourteenth Amendments, that an individual accused of a crime has a right to be formally charged and tried
excepts from criminality:	protects from criminal prosecution
holding:	judgment of a court
inferentially:	by inference, or implied understanding
lenity:	the quality of being lenient, or merciful
***Lochner v. New York*:**	a 1905 Supreme Court decision that upheld the idea that the right to freely engage in contracts was guaranteed by the due process clause
Mr. Justice Holmes:	Oliver Wendell Holmes (1841–1935), noted Supreme Court justice, who served on the Court from 1902 to 1932

Glossary

Ninth Amendment:	the amendment that guarantees that the listing of specific rights in the Constitution does not mean that other rights are denied to citizens
received common law:	judicial opinions based on past legal judgments rather than on laws passed by legislative bodies such as the U.S. Congress
statutory:	referring to statutes, or laws
***Union Pacific R. Co. v. Botsford*:**	an 1891 Supreme Court case
unqualified:	without restriction
viability:	the point at which a fetus is capable of living outside the womb

Document Text

Beal v. Doe

1977

[Blackmun dissent]

The Court today, by its decisions in these cases, allows the States, and such municipalities as choose to do so, to accomplish indirectly what the Court in *Roe v. Wade*,... and *Doe v. Bolton*,... by a substantial majority and with some emphasis, I had thought said they could not do directly. The Court concedes the existence of a constitutional right but denies the realization and enjoyment of that right on the ground that existence and realization are separate and distinct. For the individual woman concerned, indigent and financially helpless, as the Court's opinions in the three cases concede her to be, the result is punitive and tragic. Implicit in the Court's holdings is the condescension that she may go elsewhere for her abortion. I find that disingenuous and alarming, almost reminiscent of: "Let them eat cake."

The result the Court reaches is particularly distressing in *Poelker v. Doe,* where a presumed majority, in electing as mayor one whom the record shows campaigned on the issue of closing public hospitals to nontherapeutic abortions, punitively impresses upon a needy minority its own concepts of the socially desirable, the publicly acceptable, and the morally sound, with a touch of the devil-take-the-hindmost. This is not the kind of thing for which our Constitution stands.

The Court's financial argument, of course, is specious. To be sure, welfare funds are limited and welfare must be spread perhaps as best meets the community's concept of its needs. But the cost of a nontherapeutic abortion is far less than the cost of maternity care and delivery, and holds no comparison whatsoever with the welfare costs that will burden the State for the new indigents and their support in the long, long years ahead.

Neither is it an acceptable answer, as the Court well knows, to say that the Congress and the States are free to authorize the use of funds for nontherapeutic abortions. Why should any politician incur the demonstrated wrath and noise of the abortion opponents when mere silence and nonactivity accomplish the results the opponents want?

There is another world "out there," the existence of which the Court, I suspect, either chooses to ignore or fears to recognize. And so the cancer of poverty will continue to grow. This is a sad day for those who regard the Constitution as a force that would serve justice to all evenhandedly and, in so doing, would better the lot of the poorest among us.

Glossary

devil-take-the-hindmost: an expression meaning "every man for himself"—suggesting, in other words, that the last, or hindmost, will be taken by the devil

disingenuous: pretending not to know something

"Let them eat cake": a statement supposedly made by Marie Antoinette (1755–1793), wife of King Louis XVI of France, when she was told that the poor had no bread

lot: situation

specious: seemingly true, but actually false

BOWERS V. HARDWICK

1986

[Blackmun dissent]

This case is no more about "a fundamental right to engage in homosexual sodomy," as the Court purports to declare,... than *Stanley v. Georgia* ... was about a fundamental right to watch obscene movies, or *Katz v. United States* ... was about a fundamental right to place interstate bets from a telephone booth. Rather, this case is about "the most comprehensive of rights and the right most valued by civilized men," namely, "the right to be let alone."...

The statute at issue ... denies individuals the right to decide for themselves whether to engage in particular forms of private, consensual sexual activity. The Court concludes that § 16-6-2 is valid essentially because "the laws of ... many States ... still make such conduct illegal and have done so for a very long time."... But the fact that the moral judgments expressed by statutes like § 16-6-2 may be "'natural and familiar ... ought not to conclude our judgment upon the question whether statutes embodying them conflict with the Constitution of the United States.'"... Like Justice Holmes, I believe that "it is revolting to have no better reason for a rule of law than that so it was laid down in the time of Henry IV. It is still more revolting if the grounds upon which it was laid down have vanished long since, and the rule simply persists from blind imitation of the past."... I believe we must analyze Hardwick's claim in the light of the values that underlie the constitutional right to privacy. If that right means anything, it means that, before Georgia can prosecute its citizens for making choices about the most intimate aspects of their lives, it must do more than assert that the choice they have made is an "'abominable crime not fit to be named among Christians.'"...

Only the most willful blindness could obscure the fact that sexual intimacy is "a sensitive, key relationship of human existence, central to family life, community welfare, and the development of human personality,"... The fact that individuals define themselves in a significant way through their intimate sexual relationships with others suggests, in a Nation as diverse as ours, that there may be many "right" ways of conducting those relationships, and that much of the richness of a relationship will come from the freedom an individual has to choose the form and nature of these intensely personal bonds....

In a variety of circumstances we have recognized that a necessary corollary of giving individuals freedom to choose how to conduct their lives is acceptance of the fact that different individuals will make different choices. For example, in holding that the clearly important state interest in public education should give way to a competing claim by the Amish to the effect that extended formal schooling threatened their way of life, the Court declared: "There can be no assumption that today's majority is 'right' and the Amish and others like them are 'wrong.' A way of life that is odd or even erratic but interferes with no rights or interests of others is not to be condemned because it is different."... The Court claims that its decision today merely refuses to recognize a fundamental right to engage in homosexual sodomy; what the Court really has refused to recognize is the fundamental interest all individuals have in controlling the nature of their intimate associations with others....

I cannot agree that either the length of time a majority has held its convictions or the passions with which it defends them can withdraw legislation from this Court's scrutiny.... As Justice Jackson wrote so eloquently for the Court in *West Virginia Board of Education v. Barnette*,... "we apply the limitations of the Constitution with no fear that freedom to be intellectually and spiritually diverse or even contrary will disintegrate the social organization.... Freedom to differ is not limited to things that do not matter much. That would be a mere shadow of freedom. The test of its substance is the right to differ as to things that touch the heart of the existing order."... It is precisely because the issue raised by this case touches the heart of what makes individuals what they are that we should be especially sensitive to the rights of those whose choices upset the majority....

It took but three years for the Court to see the error in its analysis in *Minersville School District v. Gobitis*,... and to recognize that the threat to national cohesion posed by a refusal to salute the flag was vastly outweighed by the threat to those same values posed by compelling such a salute.... I can only hope that here, too, the Court soon will reconsider its analysis and conclude that depriving individuals

Document Text

of the right to choose for themselves how to conduct their intimate relationships poses a far greater threat to the values most deeply rooted in our Nation's history than tolerance of nonconformity could ever do. Because I think the Court today betrays those values, I dissent.

Glossary

the Amish:	a religious sect noted for its members' separation from modern society
consensual:	by mutual agreement
Henry IV:	English king who ruled from 1399 to 1413
Justice Holmes:	Oliver Wendell Holmes (1841–1935), noted Supreme Court justice, who served on the Court from 1902 to 1932
Justice Jackson:	Robert H. Jackson (1892–1954), Supreme Court justice from 1941 to 1954
sodomy:	specifically, anal sex; more generally, any form of sexual activity deemed immoral or unnatural by prevailing opinion

Document Text

DeShaney v. Winnebago County Department of Social Services

1989

[Blackmun dissent]

Poor Joshua! Victim of repeated attacks by an irresponsible, bullying, cowardly, and intemperate father, and abandoned by respondents who placed him in a dangerous predicament and who knew or learned what was going on, and yet did essentially nothing except, as the Court revealingly observes,... "dutifully recorded these incidents in [their] files." It is a sad commentary upon American life, and constitutional principles—so full of late of patriotic fervor and proud proclamations about "liberty and justice for all"—that this child, Joshua DeShaney, now is assigned to live out the remainder of his life profoundly retarded. Joshua and his mother, as petitioners here, deserve—but now are denied by this Court—the opportunity to have the facts of their case considered in the light of the constitutional protection that 42 U.S.C. § 1983 is meant to provide.

Glossary

petitioners: persons who bring a case, or petition, before a court

respondents: parties against whom a case has been brought

Document Text

Callins v. Collins

1994

[Blackmun dissent]

On February 23, 1994, at approximately 1:00 a.m., Bruce Edwin Callins will be executed by the State of Texas. Intravenous tubes attached to his arms will carry the instrument of death, a toxic fluid designed specifically for the purpose of killing human beings. The witnesses, standing a few feet away, will behold Callins, no longer a defendant, an appellant, or a petitioner, but a man, strapped to a gurney, and seconds away from extinction...

From this day forward, I no longer shall tinker with the machinery of death. For more than 20 years I have endeavored—indeed, I have struggled—along with a majority of this Court, to develop procedural and substantive rules that would lend more than the mere appearance of fairness to the death penalty endeavor. Rather than continue to coddle the Court's delusion that the desired level of fairness has been achieved and the need for regulation eviscerated, I feel morally and intellectually obligated simply to concede that the death penalty experiment has failed. It is virtually self-evident to me now that no combination of procedural rules or substantive regulations ever can save the death penalty from its inherent constitutional deficiencies. The basic question—does the system accurately and consistently determine which defendants "deserve" to die?—cannot be answered in the affirmative. It is not simply that this Court has allowed vague aggravating circumstances to be employed..., relevant mitigating evidence to be disregarded,... and vital judicial review to be blocked.... The problem is that the inevitability of factual, legal, and moral error gives us a system that we know must wrongly kill some defendants, a system that fails to deliver the fair, consistent, and reliable sentences of death required by the Constitution.

Glossary

appellant:	a party appealing a decision by a lower court
coddle:	humor or permit in a condescending way, as one might treat a child
eviscerated:	robbed of essential parts
mitigating:	making less bad; opposite of aggravating
petitioner:	a person who brings a case, or petition, before a court
substantive:	relating to the methods by which the facts, or substance, will be reviewed in a trial

Harry Blackmun wrote the Court's opinion for Roe v. Wade by Robert S. Oakes

Louis Brandeis by Harris & Ewing

Louis D. Brandeis: Original Analysis

Supreme Court Justice

1856–1941

Overview

During his long life, Louis Dembitz Brandeis had four related but distinct careers. After graduating from Harvard Law School and practicing law for a year in St. Louis, Missouri, he became a highly successful attorney in Boston, Massachusetts, and a pioneer in several aspects of legal practice, including that of donating services, without fee, on behalf of public causes. Then, beginning in the mid-1890s, he devoted increasing efforts to various reform crusades, to emerge as one of the country's leading progressive reformers. In August 1914 he assumed the leadership of American Zionism, successfully shaping a tiny and impotent organization into an efficient and effective social movement aimed at securing a Jewish homeland in Palestine. Finally, from 1916 until his retirement in 1939, Brandeis served as one of the most respected and venerated associate justices in the history of the Supreme Court. His work in any one of those four fields would have entitled him to a place in U.S. history; his prominence in all of them merits his recognition as one of America's most accomplished and influential figures.

Brandeis was born on November 13, 1856, in Louisville, Kentucky. His parents were Bohemian-Jewish immigrants who were part of a group of related families who left Europe after the failure of the liberal revolutions of 1848. They were well educated, cultivated, and nonreligious. Brandeis attended Louisville public schools, but in the early 1870s, when the American depression crippled his father's business, the family moved to Europe. They returned in 1875, and Brandeis entered Harvard Law School. He compiled a legendary record at Harvard, graduating at the age of twenty at the head of his class. Settling in Boston after an unhappy year in St. Louis, he soon built a successful legal firm and became a prominent, if sometimes controversial attorney. In 1891 he married Alice Goldmark, a second cousin from the group of families who had come to America together.

With growing financial independence Brandeis embarked upon a series of reform ventures. Beginning in Massachusetts, he worked to control public franchises, achieved a compromise on behalf of consumers of natural gas in Boston, devised and implemented a new system of life insurance for Massachusetts workers, and battled tirelessly for seven years to defeat a scheme to monopolize New England's transportation system. Somehow he found time to defend, before the Supreme Court, several state laws regulating workers' hours and wages; in one such case—*Muller v. Oregon* (1908)—he invented a new sort of legal argument (thereafter called the "Brandeis brief") by relying as much on sociological evidence as on legal precedent to justify state regulatory legislation. By 1910 Brandeis had emerged on the national stage with a reputation as "the people's attorney." He plunged into numerous reform activities, encompassing fields as diverse as conservation, railroad rates, labor relations, and antitrust. During the presidential campaign of 1912, he met and greatly impressed the Democratic candidate, Woodrow Wilson; when Wilson won the election, Brandeis became a close adviser and an architect of some of the principal reform legislation in Wilson's first term. It was also during this period that he undertook the leadership of the American Zionist movement and virtually revolutionized its operations, reputation, and activities.

In January 1916, Wilson nominated Brandeis to the Supreme Court. There followed an extremely bitter and protracted Senate hearing that lasted for months. Brandeis's opponents charged that he was a "radical" who lacked the judicial temperament. No doubt the opposition was in part caused by the fact that no Jew had ever served on the Court, and some Americans were wary of that possibility. He was eventually confirmed on a largely party-line vote in the Senate. For the next twenty-three years he performed the functions of a judge, becoming well known for some of his dissents with fellow justice Oliver Wendell Holmes, Jr., and for his pathbreaking opinions in the realms of free speech, labor, federal jurisdiction, and the right to privacy. By the time he retired, in 1939, he was universally recognized as one of the most distinguished justices in the Court's history. Some of his dissents have become standard legal doctrine, and he continues to be commonly regarded as one of the greatest judges to sit on an American bench.

In early October 1941, Brandeis—retired from the Court for almost three years but still living in Washington—suffered a heart attack. He died a few days later, on October 5. His ashes were placed at the entrance of the University of Louisville's law school, which is now named in his honor.

Explanation and Analysis of Documents

In each of his careers, Brandeis relied on the written and spoken word, and he left behind a wealth of documents. These include thousands of personal letters, several scholarly articles in legal journals, dozens of more popular books and essays furthering one of his numerous crusades, many

speeches to various audiences, and hundreds of written opinions in cases that came before the Supreme Court while he was on the bench. Naturally, the style he employed in these documents varied, depending upon the audience he wanted to reach and the cause he was attempting to advance. But almost all of his written and spoken expressions—whether put forward in letters, articles, speeches, or judicial opinions—had several things in common. First, they were meant to persuade and educate readers and listeners, to win them over to some cause, social ideal, or legal principle. Second, because he was set on convincing and teaching, he put great emphasis on clarity, directness, and simplicity of language; he was a careful craftsman of the written and spoken word, and his works were often the result of laborious effort and numerous preliminary drafts. And, third, he had enormous respect for facts; he based his arguments on painstaking research and had little tolerance for airy speculation that failed to rest on concrete factual or statistical evidence. He was himself capable of endless hours of concentrated research into materials that many others thought too detailed or uninteresting. He once remarked that as a young lawyer he had been tripped up in court by not knowing a matter of fact and that he resolved never to let that happen again. Brandeis's ability to painstakingly and effectively argue his perspective is evidenced in the documents presented.

♦ "The Opportunity in the Law"

On the evening of May 4, 1905, Brandeis crossed the river from Boston to Cambridge to deliver a speech at the Harvard Ethical Society about the legal profession and its relation to ethics. He had been practicing law in Boston since the late 1870s and was known as a skilled practitioner and litigator. He had also begun combining his professional career with important ventures into the realm of public affairs. Thus far he was not widely known outside Boston, but that would change as his reformist activities soon multiplied and began to take place on the national stage.

At the turn of the century, the legal profession in America was going through a period of intense self-examination. Elderly practitioners of the law could remember a time when lawyers enjoyed high status, independence, and general admiration. The attorney was among the most respected professionals in every American town, an individual respected for learning, judgment, and civic leadership. But by the beginning of the twentieth century, lawyers across the country felt that both their independence and their prestige were slipping. Increasingly, they were becoming servants of the great corporations that were dominating the American economy. Instead of striding into court and eloquently defending a client, lawyers were now relegated to advising corporate executives about how to circumvent regulations, avoid litigation, take advantage of loopholes in the law, and maximize profits.

In this speech Brandeis wanted to convince his listeners—Harvard undergraduates and law students—that the legal profession still offered great opportunities for personal satisfaction and service to the community. Because of their unique training, their respect for facts, and their reliance on reason, logic, and judgment, their skills would be needed more than ever. But their services were not needed as appendages of corporations. In the ongoing, unequal contest between private greed and everyday citizens, the forces of private wealth and corporate power have had the best

Time Line

1856	November 13	■ Louis D. Brandeis is born in Louisville, Kentucky.
1877	June	■ Brandeis graduates first in his class from Harvard Law School.
1879	July	■ Brandeis and Samuel Warren open a law practice in Boston.
1905	May 4	■ Brandeis delivers his speech "The Opportunity in the Law" to the Harvard Ethical Society.
1906	December 20	■ Brandeis publishes "The Greatest Life Insurance Wrong" in the *Independent.*
1912	August 28	■ Brandeis meets Woodrow Wilson.
1914	August 31	■ Brandeis assumes leadership of the American Zionist movement.
1915	June	■ Brandeis gives a speech entitled "The Jewish Problem: How to Solve It."
1916	January 28	■ Wilson nominates Brandeis to the Supreme Court.
1916	June 1	■ Brandeis is confirmed by the Senate, by a vote of forty-seven to twenty-two.
1927	May 16	■ Brandeis writes a concurring opinion in *Whitney v. California.*
1928	June 4	■ Brandeis dissents in *Olmstead v. United States*
1939	February 13	■ Brandeis resigns from the Supreme Court.
1941	October 5	■ Brandeis dies in Washington, D.C.

legal assistance available; the common people have generally been represented (when represented at all) by lawyers of mediocre ability. This is where the great opportunity in the law presently resides, Brandeis tells his audience: in defending the interests of the citizenry against the great concentrations of economic power. He ends with a solemn warning: If circumstances continue as they are and power keeps gravitating into the hands of fewer and fewer wealthy and powerful Americans, the people will certainly revolt, and their anger will lead them to extremes—revolution rather than evolution. Lawyers who enlist their talents on behalf of the people will help to avoid that potential catastrophe because they will secure greater justice and equality than currently exists.

It is impossible to know what all of Brandeis's listeners thought of this speech. But one of them, a young law student named Felix Frankfurter, was deeply moved by Brandeis's words. After graduating, he gave up a lucrative career in private practice and entered public service and distinguished teaching; he, too, eventually became a justice of the Supreme Court. He and Brandeis were to become extremely close in the years ahead, and Frankfurter always gave much credit for his views to this talk he heard as a young man.

♦ "The Greatest Life Insurance Wrong"

This article, which may be taken as typical of the numerous articles that Brandeis wrote on behalf of the various reform causes in which he engaged, was published in the *Independent* magazine in December 1906. It appeared in the midst of Brandeis's long campaign to establish the system of Savings Bank Life Insurance in Massachusetts. He had become interested in the insurance industry when he agreed to serve, without pay, as the lawyer for a group of policyholders in the wake of a scandal involving the affairs of the Equitable Life Assurance Society of New York. The New York legislature's Armstrong Committee had uncovered shocking abuses in the insurance business, and the worst of those abuses involved so-called industrial insurance—life insurance policies sold door to door by salesmen on commission. The targets of these salesmen were working men and women who were often struggling to keep themselves and their families afloat on meager wages. The huge profits from this branch of the business accounted for a large portion of the tremendous profits that the big insurance companies were making. As was typical of Brandeis, he began an exhaustive study of the insurance companies and was soon an expert in the intricacies of the business. That hard-won expertise is reflected in the mastery of facts and figures that he presents to his readers in this article.

Brandeis begins by describing the appalling records of the big companies in their industrial insurance operations. He dwells on the huge extent of that branch of the industry, the enormous profitability to the companies, and the reasons why a worker was ill advised to buy such a policy under the conditions presently imposed by the companies. Then he argues that the reason for this sorry situation is the fact that the big companies are not interested in the welfare of working American men and women who are desperately trying to provide some security for their loved ones in case they should die; the companies are interested, instead, in wringing large profits out of them to benefit the company, pay the large salaries of its officers, and pay healthy dividends to its stockholders. He dwells especially on the frightening lapse rates for these policies, as many workers find themselves unable to keep up with the premiums. In view of these abuses and the unwillingness of the big companies to reform themselves, Brandeis ends the first part of his article with the bold assertion that the solution to these difficulties must be "radical."

The solution to the problem of providing affordable life insurance to working men and women, Brandeis contends, lies in expanding the functions of a particular preexisting institution. Nonprofit "savings banks"—neighborhood institutions controlled by unpaid trustees and designed to encourage savings and provide modest interest—were functioning in both New York and Massachusetts. Such institutions had a record of community service, a history of very low operating expenses, and a reputation for honesty that the for-profit banks and private insurance companies could only envy. Brandeis proposes that these institutions be allowed to open insurance departments, whereby workers could take out modest policies without having to bear the expenses of big company salesmen, high executive salaries, advertising, and stockholder dividends. He argues that insurance is not a complicated business and does not require expertise beyond the understanding of actuarial statistics, such that the functions of insurance could easily be added to the duties of these savings banks without impairing their other functions or in any way risking their soundness.

By midsummer 1907, as a result of a tireless campaign of organizing the public, persuading officials, and lobbying the legislature, Brandeis was able to overcome the determined and powerful resistance of the insurance companies and establish the system of Savings Bank Life Insurance in Massachusetts. For the rest of his life he was attentive to the affairs of the system and extremely proud of its record of growth, low surrender rates, and service to working men and women. The system exists and thrives to this day.

♦ "The Jewish Problem: How to Solve It"

The modern Zionist movement, devoted to securing a homeland for the Jewish people in Palestine, began with the work of the European journalist Theodore Herzl in the late 1890s. The movement spread rapidly among European Jews but was relatively weak and disorganized in the United States. With the outbreak of World War I in August 1914, the World Zionist Organization was suddenly thrown into chaos; some Zionist leaders were active in England, Russia, and France, while others could be found on the opposite side of the battle lines in Germany and Austria. In this situation, communication was nearly impossible, and support was precarious for the dozens of small Jewish settlements already located in Palestine. In this crisis, a group of Ameri-

can Zionists met in New York City and formed a "provisional" executive committee for Zionist affairs. They chose Brandeis to be their leader.

He was in several respects an odd choice for this role. In the first place, the Brandeis family was made up of westernized Jews, cultured and German speaking; the overwhelming majority of Zionists were poor Eastern European Jews and Yiddish speakers. In addition, Brandeis was a complete stranger to Judaism. There is no record that he ever attended a Jewish religious service or observed Jewish holidays or customs. Many rank-and-file Zionists, by contrast, were deeply religious Jews, and a large number were strictly Orthodox. It was clear that Brandeis was chosen to head the organization because of his stature in American secular society—he was easily the best-known Jew in the United States in 1914—and because it was thought that his friendship with President Woodrow Wilson might prove useful. Undoubtedly, it was assumed that Brandeis would serve as a figurehead leader, not as a Zionist activist in any major way.

To the surprise of many veteran American Zionists, Brandeis seized immediate control of the movement. With his usual attention to facts, he made himself a master both of Zionist organizational politics and financial affairs and of conditions in Palestine. He single-handedly transformed the New York office into an efficient headquarters, spearheaded enormous fund-raising and membership drives, and shaped the movement into an effective voice for Zionism. In pursuit of these objectives, he wrote hundreds of letters to his lieutenants, demanded daily reports of progress, and worked ceaselessly to increase numbers and finances. He remained intensely active in the movement (while at the same time actively pursuing numerous social reform initiatives in Washington, D.C.) until his appointment to the Supreme Court in 1916. From 1916 until 1921 Brandeis was a behind-the-scenes policy maker and counselor to the movement he had so invigorated. In 1921 the Brandeis faction of the movement was ousted by Eastern European Jews, who followed the leadership of the English Zionist Chaim Weizmann. Then, in 1931, when the organization was once again suffering from disorganization and low morale, Brandeis's followers were recalled to leadership, and Justice Brandeis, by then in his late seventies, resumed a diminished role as an adviser to the movement and a serious student of Palestinian affairs.

This document is a speech that Brandeis delivered to the Eastern Council of Reform Rabbis in 1915; it was quickly reprinted and very widely distributed. In the speech Brandeis articulates his personal vision of the mission of Zionism and its role not only for Jews but also for the betterment of civilization. His main purpose is to convince his audience that there is absolutely no contradiction between loyalty to America and an allegiance to the Zionist purpose—indeed, that the two loyalties reinforced each other and could never be in conflict. Reform Jews, in particular, tended to resist Zionism, contending that America, not Palestine, was the "promised land" and that Zionism might arouse suspicions among other Americans that Jews were not fully committed citizens of the United States. Brandeis, whose brand of Zionism owed a great deal to his commitment to and experience in American progressive social reform, reflects these concerns in this document. His heavy emphasis on democracy and freedom and his apparent indifference to Zionism as a religious cause indicate his own views; his words are calculated to appeal to both relatively secular and thoroughly Americanized Jews.

♦ *Whitney v. California*

The celebrated case of *Whitney v. California* was argued before the Supreme Court in October 1925 and then reargued in March 1926. Anita Whitney, then in her early fifties, was a member of a prominent California family—one of her uncles was a former Supreme Court justice, and her father was a member of the state legislature. In 1919 she helped organize the Communist Labor Party of California. Because that party sanctioned the use of violence in the pursuit of its political and economic goals (though Whitney herself opposed the use of violence), she was convicted of violating California's Criminal Syndicalism Act of 1919, which declared participation in such activity illegal. On May 16, 1927, the Court handed down a unanimous opinion upholding Whitney's conviction.

The moment in American history when the events leading to this case occurred is sometimes called by historians the "first red scare" (to distinguish it from Senator Joseph McCarthy's hunt for Communists in the early 1950s). The Russian Revolution of October 1917, combined with continuing suspicion of nonconformity carried over from World War I and what many Americans saw as a heightened threat of anarchism, led several states to pass laws like California's. The federal government was also active in the prosecution and deportation of radicals in 1919–1920.

Seven members of the Court joined the opinion of Justice Edward Sanford to uphold the conviction. For some years the Court had been applying the test first enunciated by Justice Oliver Wendell Holmes in 1919, namely, that speech could be regulated only if its utterance constituted a "clear and present danger" of bringing about an evil that the Congress had the right to prevent. The Court's majority believed that, in this case, the California legislature's judgment—that the speech used by the Communist Labor Party satisfied the clear-and-present-danger test—had to be given great weight.

In his concurring opinion (in which he was joined by Justice Holmes), Brandeis makes arguments that expanded the freedom of speech. First, he points out that the Court had never fully defined what established a clear and present danger. Moreover, the Court was not obliged to accept the definition of the California legislature but could decide the matter on the basis of its own criteria. Brandeis then tries to define what should be meant by "present" danger—the danger, he said, should be imminent, close at hand. A radical speech advocating a course of action that could not possibly occur until years into the future, therefore, is

too remote to be regulated and so is protected by the First Amendment. Indeed, if there is time to answer the false ideas of an utterance with contrary ideas, the danger is not so imminent as to warrant that speech's punishment.

Brandeis was not particularly known for eloquence; that was Holmes's specialty. Brandeis rather had a strong reputation for using clear, simple, matter-of-fact language and for crafting arguments based on the careful marshaling of facts. But in this case, he gave voice to one of the greatest defenses of the freedom of speech in American history. By connecting the right to free and generally unrestrained speech both to the unafraid views of the nation's founders and to the responsibility of the citizen to hear and weigh arguments and by then attaching that process to the healthy functioning of democracy itself, Brandeis laid the groundwork for the broadest exercise of freedom of expression. This was an instance when the minority opinion received greater attention and respect than that of the majority, and eventually Brandeis's concurrence became the dominant precedent in speech cases coming before the Supreme Court. The governor of California referred to Brandeis's concurrence when he issued a pardon for Anita Whitney, and in another Supreme Court case, in 1969, the verdict in *Whitney* was explicitly overruled.

Although Brandeis obviously disagreed with the views of his brethren in this case, he nonetheless felt obliged to concur in their judgment. Whitney's lawyers had attacked the constitutionality of California's act, but they had not raised, in the lower courts, the question of "clear and present danger" regarding her activity. On that ground he would have probably voted to overturn the verdict, but he did not feel able to decide a case on the basis of an argument that had not been made.

♦ *Olmstead v. United States*

The United States adopted Prohibition through the Eighteenth Amendment, which was ratified by the needed number of states in January 1919; the manufacture, sale, or transportation of liquor was henceforth to be a crime. That ban gave rise to a lively and illegal bootlegging business that flouted the law and soon evolved into large-scale organized crime. Roy ("Big Boy") Olmstead of Seattle was a major smuggler of alcohol. Undercover agents of the U.S. government detected the activities of Olmstead and his associates (around fifty of them) and placed secret wiretaps on their telephones. For almost half a year they listened to all their phone calls, taking nearly eight hundred pages of notes. On the basis of the evidence they gathered by this method, the government arrested and convicted Olmstead and some seventy others.

The question before the Supreme Court was straightforward: Did the use of evidence obtained by secretly wiretapping telephones violate the Fourth and Fifth Amendments to the Constitution? The Fourth Amendment reads, in part, "The right of the people to be secure in their persons, houses, papers, and effects, against unreasonable searches and seizures, shall not be violated." The Fifth Amendment stipulates due process in criminal cases and protects citizens against self-incrimination. A slim majority of five justices, speaking through Chief Justice William Howard Taft, upheld the conviction, arguing that wiretapping did not contravene the Fourth Amendment's prohibition of unreasonable searches and seizures because it did not involve actual physical entry. Nor was the Fifth Amendment's protection against self-incrimination held to be violated by words spoken over the telephone. Four justices dissented, each writing a separate opinion, but the spirited dissent of Brandeis was the most prominent; two of the other dissenters explicitly mentioned in their opinions that they largely agreed with Brandeis's views.

No one who knew Brandeis could have been surprised at his dissent. Back in 1890 Brandeis and his law partner, Samuel Warren, had published a pathbreaking article in the *Harvard Law Review* entitled "The Right to Privacy." Roscoe Pound, the illustrious dean of Harvard Law School, later said of that article that had added a chapter to the law. To this day, appeals to a right to privacy must be traced back to that pioneering article. To Brandeis and Warren, it was one of the principal marks of a civilized society that every individual deserved to be protected from unwanted invasions of privacy.

In this dissent, Brandeis reminds readers that a living constitution must be flexible enough to change with new inventions and discoveries, especially innovations that the Founding Fathers could not possibly have foreseen. The fact that the word *wiretap* is not mentioned in the Fourth Amendment did not excuse the Court from weighing the intentions of the amendment and applying it to the modern world. But Brandeis's main thrust in his dissent is that the government must always be a scrupulous follower of legal and ethical practice, that the end (in this case, a conviction of Olmstead and his friends) cannot justify morally questionable means (such as wiretapping). The government must serve as a teacher of ethical behavior and a model of legal practice because citizens take behavioral cues from what they see the government doing. Justice Holmes, in his dissent, after writing that Brandeis had summed up his own view, added, "We have to choose, and for my part I think it a less evil that some criminals should escape than that the government should play an ignoble part."

This was another case in which the dissents (particularly Brandeis's) were more noteworthy than the majority's view. In 1934 Congress passed a law outlawing the use of wiretapping, and a series of Supreme Court cases since then have taken the dissenters' views about a fundamental right to privacy.

Impact and Legacy

In each of the fields that Brandeis entered he made important contributions, and these contributions not only touched the society in which he lived and worked but also in many cases extended down to succeeding generations

of Americans. As a practicing attorney Brandeis became, in several respects, a model for a certain class of socially active lawyers. Legal service rendered by attorneys without fee is called pro bono publico, "for the good of the public." Countless lawyers have followed Brandeis's pioneering example in performing pro bono work in nonprofit, legal aid, and civil liberties efforts. The American Bar Association now recommends that lawyers contribute at least fifty hours a year to such work. Before Brandeis's well-publicized example, such efforts were extremely rare. Only a very few lawyers have since carried his example to the extremes that he did. (Brandeis eventually adopted the practice of actually paying his own law firm for the time he spent doing pro bono work because he did not think it right for his partners to suffer a loss for the time he spent engaged in public causes.) In addition to the example he set in donating so large a percentage of his time to pro bono service, Brandeis called attention to the extent to which everyday Americans were often unrepresented or poorly represented in struggles with large and powerful corporate entities bent on private profit, often at the expense of the general public. Since his time, a number of lawyers—perhaps too small a number—have sought to follow his example as "the people's attorney." Brandeis became famous (and, indeed, relatively wealthy) as a lawyer for the extent to which he entered into the detailed affairs of his business clients, often laboriously learning their most intricate enterprises until he understood them as well as the owners themselves. He believed that only by doing this could he fully represent their interests in the legal arena—but he also used this intimate knowledge to suggest improvements in clients' business operations (such as how to ensure regularity of employment for workers). Finally, in defending—as a lawyer arguing before the Supreme Court—state experiments in fixing the hours and wages of workers, Brandeis virtually invented an entirely new way of presenting arguments. The so-called Brandeis brief, which relies on sociological, psychological, medical, and economic evidence, has become a standard way of arguing cases in the American judicial system.

The legacies of Brandeis as a social reformer are almost too numerous to mention. He played an important part, in the Wilson administration, in helping to draft both the Federal Reserve Act (1913) and the Clayton Antitrust Act (1914). He pioneered the rate-fixing functions of the Interstate Commerce Commission, working closely with (and for) the commission both before and during the Wilson administration. He practically invented the "sliding scale" that ties the raising of stockholders' dividends to the providing of consumer benefits, and he did invent Savings Bank Life Insurance for workers in Massachusetts and New York. No one in America was better known for spirited resistance to trusts and monopolies, and his articles on "the money trust," which were eventually published as a popular book, *Other People's Money and How the Bankers Use It* (1914), led to an awakened public awareness of the abuses of high finance. His work on behalf of management-labor mediation (most famously in the garment workers' strike of 1910) established a widely copied model for industrial cooperation. His conduct of the Pinchot-Ballinger conservation hearings before a joint House-Senate investigating committee brought attention to the issue of preserving natural resources for future generations. In some of these crusades he was the innovator and prime mover; in others he merely joined with like-minded reformers. But in every case his presence in the effort led to wider and more favorable publicity, greater effectiveness, and lasting change.

Brandeis's legacies as a Zionist and communal leader of American Jewry are also notable. Because of his stature in American life, he made it "respectable," in a sense, for American Jews to become part of the Zionist movement—no one could question the loyalty or patriotism of the "people's attorney," a friend and close adviser of the president of the United States and, after 1916, an esteemed member of the Supreme Court. He was thus able to enlist in the movement many who had been inclined to hang back for fear of appearing to harbor divided loyalties or of provoking an outbreak of European-style anti-Semitism. His modernization of the American Zionist movement, moreover, transformed it into a powerful lobby, and his personal intervention on behalf of the Jews of Palestine with both Woodrow Wilson and Franklin Roosevelt resulted in some official actions by the United States on behalf of world Jewry. (For example, Brandeis helped to persuade Wilson to endorse Britain's Balfour Declaration of 1917, supporting the establishment of a Jewish homeland in Palestine.) His expertise in Palestinian economic, social, and agricultural affairs shaped the forms of support that Zionists provided for pioneering Jewish settlers (with the campaign to rid the land of malaria, for example, largely due to his effort). Perhaps above all, Brandeis, more than anyone else, democratized the communal life of American Jews. He rejected and struggled against the tradition of having Jewish concerns represented by the American Jewish Committee, a group of aristocratic German Jews in New York City who used their behind-the-scenes contacts to influence American policy on Jewish matters. Instead, Brandeis and others organized the American Jewish Congress, a body representative of everyday American Jews that deliberated policy openly and took public positions in a way more in accordance with the American political process.

That Brandeis was the first Jew ever to serve on the U.S. Supreme Court is, in itself, an important breakthrough; there have been very few times since 1916 when there has not been at least one Jewish justice on the Court. But that fact is the most unimportant of Brandeis's achievements as an American judge. His opinions, both when he spoke for the majority and when he dissented, have often proved to be landmarks in American jurisprudence. His decisions were particularly important in the areas of civil liberties, the rights of labor, the freedom of individual states to experiment in social and economic legislation, the dangers of excessive bigness in both economic institutions and the federal government, the sanctity of democratic procedures, and the right to privacy. His opinions were notable for their

meticulous research into the underlying factual underpinnings of particular cases, and he was among the earliest of Supreme Court justices to cite academic and law journal articles in his opinions, now a common practice. Throughout his twenty-three-year career on the Court, Brandeis was a forceful spokesperson for judicial restraint, the view that judges should not make law on the basis of their own social views but should adhere strictly to the limitations of their function. At the same time, he believed that the U.S. Constitution was a living document and that it had to be applied in accordance with the ever-changing needs of the modern world. Although some opposed Brandeis's appointment to the Court in 1916 on the ground that he lacked a judicial temperament, nearly every expert ranking of American judges lists Louis Brandeis as among the most astute and influential practitioners of jurisprudence in U.S. history.

Key Sources

The major depository of the papers of Louis Brandeis is the enormous collection at the Louis D. Brandeis School of Law at the University of Louisville. There is an additional collection of Supreme Court–related papers at Harvard Law School, in Cambridge, Massachusetts. A sizable collection of his Zionist papers can be found at the American Jewish Archives in Cincinnati, Ohio. Portions of all of these collections are available on microfilm. Two excellent bibliographies of Brandeis's writings and speeches are Roy M. Mersky, *Louis Dembitz Brandeis, 1856–1941: A Bibliography* (1958), and Gene Teitelbaum, *Justice Louis D. Brandeis: A Bibliography of Writings and Other Materials on the Justice* (1988). Fine published collections of his works are Philippa Strum, ed., *Brandeis on Democracy* (1995), and Osmond K. Fraenkel, ed., *The Curse of Bigness: Miscellaneous Papers of Louis D. Brandeis* (1934). For a large selection of his letters, see Melvin I. Urofsky and David W. Levy, eds., *Letters of Louis D. Brandeis*, 5 vols. (1971–1978), and Melvin I. Urofsky and David Levy, eds., *"Half Brother, Half Son": The Letters of Louis D. Brandeis to Felix Frankfurter* (1991). All of his opinions and dissents as a justice of the Supreme Court are readily available in the official *U.S. Supreme Court Reports*.

Essential Quotes

"Instead of holding a position of independence, between the wealthy and the people, prepared to curb the excesses of either, able lawyers have, to a large extent, allowed themselves to become adjuncts of great corporations.... We hear much of the 'corporation lawyer,' and far too little of the 'people's lawyer.'"

("The Opportunity in the Law")

"The extraordinary wastefulness of the present system of industrial insurance is due in large part to the fact that the business ... is carried on for the benefit of others than the policy-holders. The needs and financial inexperience of the wage-earner are exploited for the benefit of stockholders or officials."

("The Greatest Life Insurance Wrong")

"Let no American imagine that Zionism is inconsistent with Patriotism. Multiple loyalties are objectionable only if they are inconsistent.... There is no inconsistency between loyalty to America and loyalty to Jewry. The

Essential Quotes

Jewish spirit, the product of our religion and experiences, is essentially modern and essentially American."

("The Jewish Problem: How to Solve It")

"Those who won our independence believed that the final end of the State was to make men free to develop their faculties.... They valued liberty both as an end and as a means. They believed liberty to be the secret of happiness and courage to be the secret of liberty. They believed that freedom to think as you will and to speak as you think are means indispensable to the discovery and spread of political truth."

(*Whitney v. California*)

"Our Government is the potent, the omnipresent teacher. For good or for ill, it teaches the whole people by its example. Crime is contagious. If the Government becomes a lawbreaker, it breeds contempt for law; it invites every man to become a law unto himself; it invites anarchy. To declare that, in the administration of the criminal law, the end justifies the means—to declare that the Government may commit crimes in order to secure the conviction of a private criminal—would bring terrible retribution."

(*Olmstead v. United States*)

Further Reading

■ Books

Mason, Alpheus T. *Brandeis: A Free Man's Life*. New York: Viking Press, 1946.

Paper, Lewis J. *Brandeis*. Englewood Cliffs, N.J.: Prentice-Hall, 1983.

Strum, Philippa. *Louis D. Brandeis: Justice for the People*. Cambridge, Mass: Harvard University Press, 1984.

Urofsky, Melvin I. *Brandeis*. New York: Basic Books, 2009.

—*David Levy*

Questions for Further Study

1. If Brandeis were on the Court today would he be regarded as a liberal or a conservative? Certainly he was considered a liberal in his time and is often cited as a liberal hero, but he also believed strongly in judicial restraint, a position today associated more with conservatism. Make an argument, using examples from his writings, for Brandeis as a liberal or a conservative—keeping in mind that these terms need not be understood rigidly but as general descriptions of the two prevailing movements in American political life.

2. What were Brandeis's most significant achievements and contributions, and which of these do you think had the most lasting impact?

3. Examine Brandeis's arguments on behalf of the Zionist cause. Although he did not live long enough to see the full effects of the Nazi Holocaust, how much would his ideas have been influenced if he had? How might he have regarded later events in Palestine, which brought about hostile relations between Jewish and Arab residents that persist to the present day?

4. Discuss the ways Brandeis develops some of his most celebrated ideas and themes in his *Whitney* and *Olmstead* opinions. The first involves the concept of clear and present danger and the second the impact of new inventions and discoveries, while both are concerned with the right to privacy. In what ways, and with what degree of success, does Brandeis develop these principles in these writings?

Document Text

"The Opportunity in the Law"

1905

I assume that in asking me to talk to you on the Ethics of the Legal Profession, you do not wish me to enter upon a discussion of the relation of law to morals, or to attempt to acquaint you with those detailed rules of ethics which lawyers have occasion to apply from day to day in their practice. What you want is this: Standing not far from the threshold of active life, feeling the generous impulse for service which the University fosters, you wish to know whether the legal profession would afford you special opportunities for usefulness to your fellowmen....

The whole training of the lawyer leads to the development of judgment. His early training—his work with books in the study of legal rules—teaches him patient research and develops both the memory and the reasoning faculties. He becomes practiced in logic.... The lawyer's processes of reasoning, his logical conclusions, are being constantly tested by experience. He is running up against facts at every point. Indeed it is a maxim of the law: Out of the facts grows the law; that is, propositions are not considered abstractly, but always with reference to facts....

Your chairman said: "People have the impression to-day that the lawyer has become mercenary." It is true that the lawyer has become largely a part of the business world.... The ordinary man thinks of the Bar as a body of men who are trying cases, perhaps even trying criminal cases. Of course there is an immense amount of litigation going on; and a great deal of the time of many lawyers is devoted to litigation. But by far the greater part of the work done by lawyers is done not in court, but in advising men on important matters, and mainly in business affairs. In guiding these affairs industrial and financial, lawyers are needed, not only because of the legal questions involved, but because the particular mental attributes and attainments which the legal profession develops are demanded in the proper handling of these large financial or industrial affairs....

It is true that at the present time the lawyer does not hold as high a position with the people as he held seventy-five or indeed fifty years ago; but the reason is not lack of opportunity. It is this: instead of holding a position of independence, between the wealthy and the people, prepared to curb the excesses of either, able lawyers have, to a large extent, allowed themselves to become adjuncts of great corporations and have neglected the obligation to use their powers for the protection of the people. We hear much of the "corporation lawyer," and far too little of the "people's lawyer." The great opportunity of the American Bar is and will be to stand again as it did in the past, ready to protect also the interests of the people.

The leading lawyers of the United States have been engaged mainly in supporting the claims of the corporation; often in endeavoring to evade or nullify the extremely crude laws by which legislators sought to regulate the power or curb the excesses of corporation.

Such questions as the regulation of trusts, the fixing of railway rates, the municipalization of public utilities, the relation between capital and labor, call for the exercise of legal ability of the highest order. Up to the present time the legal ability of a high order which has been expended on those questions has been almost wholly in opposition to the contention of the people. The leaders of the Bar, without any preconceived intent on their part, and rather as an incident to their professional standing, have, with rare exceptions, been ranged on the side of the corporations, and the people have been represented, in the main, by men of very meager legal ability.

If these problems are to be settled right, this condition cannot continue. Our country is, after all, not a country of dollars, but of ballots. The immense corporate wealth will necessarily develop a hostility from which much trouble will come to us unless the excesses of capital are curbed, through the respect for law, as the excesses of democracy were curbed seventy-five years ago. There will come a revolt of the people against the capitalists, unless the aspirations of the people are given some adequate legal expression; and to this end cooperation of the abler lawyers is essential.

For nearly a generation the leaders of the Bar have, with few exceptions, not only failed to take part in constructive legislation designed to solve in the public interest our great social, economic and industrial problems; but they have failed likewise to oppose legislation prompted by selfish interests....

Here, consequently, is the great opportunity in the law. The next generation must witness a continuing

Document Text

and ever-increasing contest between those who have and those who have not. The industrial world is in a state of ferment. The ferment is in the main peaceful, and, to a considerable extent, silent; but there is felt to-day very widely the inconsistency in this condition of political democracy and industrial absolutism. The people are beginning to doubt whether in the long run democracy and absolutism can co-exist in the same community; beginning to doubt whether there is a justification for the great inequalities in the distribution of wealth, for the rapid creation of fortunes, more mysterious than the deeds of Aladdin's lamp. The people have begun to think; and they show evidences on all sides of a tendency to act.... The people's thought will take shape in action; and it lies with us, with you to whom in part the future belongs, to say on what lines the action is to be expressed; whether it is to be expressed wisely and temperately, or wildly and intemperately; whether it is to be expressed on lines of evolution or on lines of revolution. Nothing can better fit you for taking part in the solution of these problems, than the study and preeminently the practice of law. Those of you who feel drawn to that profession may rest assured that you will find in it an opportunity for usefulness which is probably unequalled. There is a call upon the legal profession to do a great work for this country.

Glossary

absolutism: complete control by a ruler

adjuncts: extra parts; appendages

the Bar: the legal profession

capital and labor: business, particularly factory, owners as opposed to the people doing the physical work

mercenary: accepting pay to do work that is less than honorable

municipalization: placing under the control of a city government

trusts: large corporations with a total or near-total control in their areas of business

Document Text

"The Greatest Life Insurance Wrong"

1906

Industrial insurance, the workingman's life insurance, is simply life insurance in small amounts, on which the premiums are collected weekly at the homes of the insured. It includes both adult and child insurance. The regular premium charge for such insurance is about double that charged by the Equitable, the New York Life, or the Mutual Life of New York, for ordinary life insurance.... So heavy are the burdens cast upon those least able to bear them....

In the fifteen years ending December 31, 1905, the workingmen of Massachusetts paid to the so-called industrial life insurance companies an aggregate of $61,294,887 in premiums, and received back in death benefits, endowments, or surrender values an aggregate of only $21,819,606. The insurance reserve arising from these premiums still held by the insurance companies does not exceed $9,838,000. It thus appears that, in addition to interest on invested funds, about one-half of the amount paid by the workingmen in premiums has been absorbed in the expenses of conducting the business and in dividends to the stockholders of the insurance companies.

If this $61,294,887, instead of being paid to the insurance companies, had been deposited in Massachusetts savings banks, and the depositors had withdrawn from the banks an amount equal to the aggregate of $21,819,606 which they received from the insurance companies during the fifteen years, the balance remaining in the savings banks [on] December 31, 1905, with the accumulated interest, would have amounted to $49,931,548.35....

Perhaps the appalling sacrifice of workingmen's savings through this system of insurance can be made more clear by the following illustration:

The average expectancy of life in the United States of a man 21 years old is, according to Meech's Table of Mortality, 40.25 years. In other words, take any large number of men who are 21 years old, and the average age which they will reach is 61¼ years.

If a man, beginning with his 21st birthday, pays throughout life 50 cents a week into Massachusetts savings banks and allows these deposits to accumulate for his family, the survivors will, in case of his death at this average age of 61¼ years, inherit $2,265.90 if an interest rate of 3½ per cent a year is maintained.

If this same man should, beginning at the age of 21, pay throughout his life 50 cents a week to the Prudential Insurance Company as premiums on a so-called "industrial" life policy for the benefit of his family, the survivors would be legally entitled to receive, upon his death at the age of 61¼ years, only $820.

If this same man, having made his weekly deposit in a savings bank for 20 years, should then conclude to discontinue his weekly payments and withdraw the money for his own benefit, he would receive $746.20. If, on the other hand, having made for 20 years such weekly payments to the Prudential Insurance Company, he should then conclude to discontinue payments and surrender his policy, he would be legally entitled to receive only $165....

The extraordinary wastefulness of the present system of industrial insurance is due in large part to the fact that the business, whether conducted by stock or by mutual companies, is carried on for the benefit of others than the policy-holders. The needs and financial inexperience of the wage earner are exploited for the benefits of stockholders of officials....

But the excessive amounts paid in dividends or in salaries to the favored officials account directly for only a small part of the terrible shrinkage of the workingmen's savings. The main cause of waste lies in the huge expense of soliciting insurance, taken in connection with the large percentage of lapses, and in the heavy expenses incident to a weekly collection of premiums at the homes of the insured. The commission of the insurance solicitor is from ten to twenty times the amount of the first premium. The cost of collecting the premiums varies from one-fifth to one-sixth of the amount collected....

And only a small percentage of industrial policies survive the third year. A majority of the policies lapse within the first year. In 1905, the average payments on a policy in the Metropolitan so lapsing continued little more than six weeks. The aggregate number of such lapses in a single year reaches huge figures. In 1905, 1,253,635 Metropolitan and 951,704 Prudential policies lapsed....

Document Text

The supporters of the present system of industrial insurance declare that a reduction of expenses and of lapses is impossible. They insist that the loss to the insured and the heavy burden borne by the persisting policy-holders from lapses, as well as from the huge cost of premium collection, must all be patiently borne as being the inevitable incidents of the beneficial institution of life insurance, when applied to the workingman. It is obvious that remedy cannot come from men holding such views—from men who refuse to recognize that the best method of increasing the demand for life insurance is not eloquent persistent persuasion, but to furnish a good article at a low price.... To attain satisfactory results the change of system must be radical.

The saving banks established on the plan prevailing in New York and generally through the New England states are managed upon principles and under conditions upon which alone a satisfactory system of life insurance for workingmen can be established. These savings banks have no stockholders, being operated solely for the benefit of the depositors. They are managed by trustees, usually men of large business experience and high character, who serve without pay, recognizing that the business of collecting and investing the savings of persons of small means is a quasi-public trust, which should be conducted as a beneficent, and not as money-making institution. The trustees, the officers, and the employees of the savings banks have been trained in the administration of these saving to the practice of the strictest economy. While the expenses of managing the industrial departments of the Metropolitan, the Prudential and the John Hancock companies have, excluding taxes, exceeded 40 per cent of the year's premiums, the expenses of management in 1905 (exclusive of taxes on surplus) of the 130 New York Saving banks, holding $1,292,358,866 of deposits, was only 0.28 of 1 per cent of the average assets, or 1 per cent of the year's deposits; and the $662,000,000 of deposits held in 1905 in the 189 Massachusetts savings banks were managed at an expenses of 0.23 of 1 per cent of the average assets, or 1.36 per cent of the year's deposits.

Saving institutions so managed offer adequate means of providing insurance to the workingman. With a slight enlargement of their powers, these savings banks can, at a minimum of expense, fill the great need of cheaper life insurance in small amounts....

The insurance department of the savings banks would, of course, be kept entirely distinct as a matter of accounting from the savings department; but it would be conducted with the same plant and the same officials, without any large increase of clerical force or incidental expense, except such as would be required if the deposits of the bank were increased. On the other hand, the insurance department of savings banks would open with an extensive and potent good-will, and under the most favorable conditions for teaching the value of life insurance—a lesson easily learned when insurance is offered at about half the premium exacted by the industrial companies....

The safety of saving banks, would, of course, be in no way imperiled by extending their functions to life insurance. Life insurance rests upon substantial certainty, differing in this respect radically from fire, accident, and other kinds of insurance. Since practical experience has given to the world the mortality tables upon which life insurance premiums rest and the reserves for future needs are calculated, no life insurance company has ever failed which complied with the law governing the calculation, maintenance, and investment of the legal reserve. The causes of failure of life insurance companies have been excessive expenses, unsound investment, or dishonest management. From these abuses our saving banks have been practically free, and that freedom affords strong reason for utilizing them as the urgent need arises to supply the kindred service of life insurance.

Glossary

aggregate: combined total

distinct as a matter of accounting: completely separate, in terms of financial records and reporting, so as to avoid any opportunity for misuse of funds

dividends: payments to shareholders, based on the company's profits

Glossary

lapses:	insurance accounts that have been lost by the policyholders owing to failure to maintain payments
life insurance rests upon substantial certainty:	the business of life insurance has a great deal to do with statistical predictions based on data compiled from experience
Meech's Table of Mortality:	a reference work of the time that provided statistics on life expectancy and other factors important to calculating insurance costs
plant:	facility
reserve:	money set aside by an insurance company, under law, so as to pay future claims from policyholders
surrender values:	the refund value of a life insurance policy if the policyholder chose to cash it in before dying

"The Jewish Problem: How to Solve It"

1915

The suffering of the Jews due to injustices continuing throughout nearly twenty centuries is the greatest tragedy in history. Never was the aggregate of such suffering larger than today. Never were the injustices more glaring. Yet the present is preeminently a time for hopefulness. The current of world thought is at last preparing the way for our attaining justice. The war is developing opportunities which make possible the solution of the Jewish problem.…

For us the Jewish Problem means this: How can we secure for Jews, wherever they may live, the same rights and opportunities enjoyed by non-Jews? How can we secure for the world the full contribution which Jews can make, if unhampered by artificial limitations?…

Deeply imbedded in every people is the desire for full development, the longing, as Mazzini phrased it, "To elaborate and express their idea, to contribute their stone also to the pyramid of history." Nationality like democracy has been one of the potent forces making for man's advance during the past hundred years. The assertion of nationality has infused whole peoples with hope, manhood and self-respect. It has ennobled and made purposeful millions of lives. It offered them a future, and in doing so revived and capitalized all that was valuable in their past.…

W. Allison Phillips recently defined nationality as, "An extensive aggregate of persons, conscious of a community of sentiments, experiences, or qualities which make them feel themselves a distinct people."…

Can it be doubted that we Jews, aggregating 14,000,000 people, are "an extensive aggregate of persons"; that we are "conscious of a community of sentiments, experiences and qualities which make us feel ourselves a distinct people," whether we admit it or not?…

Conscious community of sentiments, common experiences, common qualities are equally, perhaps more, important. Religion, traditions and customs bound us together, though scattered throughout the world. The similarity of experience tended to produce similarity of qualities and community of sentiments. Common suffering so intensified the feeling of brotherhood as to overcome largely all the influences making for diversification. The segregation of the Jews was so general, so complete, and so long continued as to intensify our "peculiarities" and make them almost ineradicable.…

While every other people is striving for development by asserting its nationality, and a great war is making clear the value of small nations, shall we voluntarily yield to anti-Semitism, and instead of solving our "problem" end it by noble suicide? Surely this is no time for Jews to despair. Let us make clear to the world that we too are a nationality striving for equal rights to life and to self-expression.…

Standing against this broad foundation of nationality, Zionism aims to give it full development. Let us bear clearly in mind what Zionism is, or rather what it is not.

It is not a movement to remove all the Jews of the world compulsorily to Palestine. In the first place there are 14,000,000 Jews, and Palestine would not accommodate more than one-third of that number. In the second place, it is not a movement to compel anyone to go to Palestine. It is essentially a movement to give to the Jew more, not less freedom; it aims to exercise the same right now exercised by practically every other people in the world: To live at their option either in the land of their fathers or in some other country.…

Zionism seeks to establish in Palestine, for such Jews as choose to go and remain there and for their descendants, a legally secured home, where they may live together and lead a Jewish life, where they may expect ultimately to constitute a majority of the population, and may look forward to what we should call home rule. The Zionists seek to establish this home in Palestine because they are convinced that the undying longing of Jews for Palestine is a fact of deepest significance; that it is a manifestation in the struggle for existence by an ancient people which has established its right to live, a people whose three thousand years of civilization has produced a faith, culture and individuality which enable it to contribute largely in the future, as it has in the past, to the advance of civilization; and that it is not a right merely but a duty of the Jewish nationality to survive and develop. They believe that only in Palestine can the Jewish spirit reach its full and natural development; and that by securing for those Jews who wish to settle there

Document Text

the opportunity to do so, not only those Jews, but all other Jews will be benefited, and that the long perplexing Jewish Problem will, at last, find solution....

Let no American imagine that Zionism is inconsistent with Patriotism. Multiple loyalties are objectionable only if they are inconsistent. A man is a better citizen of the United States for being also a loyal citizen of his state, and of his city; for being loyal to his family, and to his profession or trade; for being loyal to his college or his lodge. Every Irish American who contributed towards advancing home rule was a better man and a better American for the sacrifice he made. Every American Jew who aids in advancing the Jewish settlement in Palestine, though he feels that neither he nor his descendants will ever live there, will likewise be a better man and a better American for doing so....

There is no inconsistency between loyalty to America and loyalty to Jewry. The Jewish spirit, the product of our religion and experiences, is essentially modern and essentially American. Not since the destruction of the Temple have the Jews in spirit and in ideals been so fully in harmony with the noblest aspirations of the country in which they lived.

America's fundamental law seeks to make real the brotherhood of man. That brotherhood became the Jewish fundamental law more than twenty-five hundred years ago. America's insistent demand in the twentieth century is for social justice. That also has been the Jews' striving for ages. Their affliction as well as their religion has prepared the Jews for effective democracy. Persecution broadened their sympathies. It trained them in patience and endurance, in self-control, and in sacrifice. It made them think as well as suffer. It deepened the passion for righteousness.

Indeed, loyalty to America demands rather that each American Jew become a Zionist. For only through the ennobling effect of its strivings can we develop the best that is in us and give to this country the full benefit of our great inheritance. The Jewish spirit, so long preserved, the character developed by so many centuries of sacrifice, should be preserved and developed further, so that in America as elsewhere the sons of the race may in future live lives and do deeds worthy of their ancestors....

Since the Jewish Problem is single and universal, the Jews of every country should strive for its solution. But the duty resting upon us of America is especially insistent. We number about 3,000,000, which is more than one fifth of all the Jews in the world, a number larger than comprised within any other country except the Russian Empire.... We are ourselves free from civil or political disabilities; and are relatively prosperous. Our fellow-Americans are infused with a high and generous spirit, which insures approval of our struggle to ennoble, liberate, and otherwise improve the condition of an important part of the human race; and their innate manliness makes them sympathize particularly with our efforts at self-help.... And a conflict between American interests or ambitions and Jewish aims is not conceivable. Our loyalty to America can never be questioned.

Let us therefore lead, earnestly, courageously and joyously, in the struggle for liberation. Let us all recognize that we Jews are a distinctive nationality of which every Jew, whatever his county, his station or shade of belief, is necessarily a member. Let us insist that the struggle for liberty shall not cease until equality of opportunity is accorded to nationalities as to individuals. Let us insist also that full equality of opportunity cannot be obtained by Jews until we, like members of other nationalities, shall have the option of living elsewhere or returning to the land of our forefathers.

Glossary

aggregate: combined total

destruction of the Temple: the destruction of the Temple of Jerusalem by the Romans in 70 ce, a key event in bringing the history of ancient Israel to an end with the scattering of the Jews throughout the world

ineradicable: incapable of being erased

Mazzini: Italian politician and philosopher Giuseppe Mazzini (1805–1872)

station: position in life

Whitney v. California

1927

[Brandeis concurrence]

Miss [Anita] Whitney was convicted of the felony of assisting in organizing, in the year 1919, the Communist Labor Party of California, of being a member of it, and of assembling with it. These acts are held to constitute a crime, because the party was formed to teach criminal syndicalism. The statute which made these acts a crime restricted the right of free speech and of assembly theretofore existing. The claim is that the statute, as applied, denied to Miss Whitney the liberty guaranteed by the Fourteenth Amendment.…

The mere act of assisting in forming a society for teaching syndicalism, of becoming a member of it, or assembling with others for that purpose is given the dynamic quality of crime. There is guilt although the society may not contemplate immediate promulgation of the doctrine. Thus the accused is to be punished, not for attempt, incitement or conspiracy, but for a step in preparation, which, if it threatens the public order at all, does so only remotely.…

But, although the rights of free speech and assembly are fundamental, they are not in their nature absolute. Their exercise is subject to restriction, if the particular restriction proposed is required in order to protect the state from destruction or from serious injury, political, economic or moral. That the necessity which is essential to a valid restriction does not exist unless speech would produce, or is intended to produce, a clear and imminent danger of some substantive evil which the state constitutionally may seek to prevent has been settled.…

This court has not yet fixed the standard by which to determine when a danger shall be deemed clear; how remote the danger may be and yet be deemed present; and what degree of evil shall be deemed sufficiently substantial to justify resort to abridgment of free speech and assembly as the means of protection.… Those who won our independence believed that the final end of the State was to make men free to develop their faculties, and that in its government the deliberative forces should prevail over the arbitrary. They valued liberty both as an end and as a means. They believed liberty to be the secret of happiness and courage to be the secret of liberty. They believed that freedom to think as you will and to speak as you think are means indispensable to the discovery and spread of political truth; that without free speech and assembly discussion would be futile; that with them, discussion affords ordinarily adequate protection against the dissemination of noxious doctrine; that the greatest menace to freedom is an inert people; that public discussion is a political duty; and that this should be a fundamental principle of the American government. They recognized the risks to which all human institutions are subject. But they knew that order cannot be secured merely through fear of punishment for its infraction; that it is hazardous to discourage thought, hope and imagination; that fear breeds repression; that repression breeds hate; that hate menaces stable government; that the path of safety lies in the opportunity to discuss freely supposed grievances and proposed remedies; and that the fitting remedy for evil counsels is good ones. Believing in the power of reason as applied through public discussion, they eschewed silence coerced by law—the argument of force in its worst form. Recognizing the occasional tyrannies of governing majorities, they amended the Constitution so that free speech and assembly should be guaranteed.

Fear of serious injury cannot alone justify suppression of free speech and assembly. Men feared witches and burnt women. It is the function of speech to free men from the bondage of irrational fears. To justify suppression of free speech there must be reasonable ground to fear that serious evil will result if free speech is practiced. There must be reasonable ground to believe that the danger apprehended is imminent. There must be reasonable ground to believe that the evil to be prevented is a serious one.… But even advocacy of violation [of the law], however reprehensible morally, is not a justification for denying free speech where the advocacy falls short of incitement and there is nothing to indicate that the advocacy would be immediately acted on. The wide difference between advocacy and incitement, between preparation and attempt, between assembling and conspiracy, must be borne in mind. In order to support a finding of clear and present danger it must be shown either that immediate serious violence was to be expected or was advocated, or that the past conduct furnished reason to

Document Text

believe that such advocacy was then contemplated. Those who won our independence by revolution were not cowards. They did not fear political change. They did not exalt order at the cost of liberty. To courageous, self-reliant men, with confidence in the power of free and fearless reasoning applied through the processes of popular government, no danger flowing from speech can be deemed clear and present, unless the incidence of the evil apprehended is so imminent that it may befall before there is opportunity for full discussion. If there be time to expose through discussion the falsehood and fallacies, to avert the evil by the processes of education, the remedy to be applied is more speech, not enforced silence. Only an emergency can justify repression. Such must be the rule if authority is to be reconciled with freedom. Such, in my opinion, is the command of the Constitution. It is therefore always open to Americans to challenge a law abridging free speech and assembly by showing that there was no emergency justifying it.

Moreover, even imminent danger cannot justify resort to prohibition of these functions essential to effective democracy, unless the evil apprehended is relatively serious. Prohibition of free speech and assembly is a measure so stringent that it would be inappropriate as the means for averting a relatively trivial harm to society.... The fact that speech is likely to result in some violence or in destruction of property is not enough to justify its suppression. There must be the probability of serious injury to the State. Among free men, the deterrents ordinarily to be applied to prevent crime are education and punishment for violations of the law, not abridgment of the rights of free speech and assembly....

Whenever the fundamental rights of free speech and assembly are alleged to have been invaded, it must remain open to a defendant to present the issue whether there actually did exist at the time a clear danger, whether the danger, if any, was imminent, and whether the evil apprehended was one so substantial as to justify the stringent restriction interposed by the Legislature....

Whether in 1919, when Miss Whitney did the things complained of, there was in California such clear and present danger of serious evil, might have been made the important issue in the case. She might have required that the issue be determined either by the court or the jury. She claimed below that the statute as applied to her violated the federal Constitution; but she did not claim that it was void because there was no clear and present danger of serious evil, nor did she request that the existence of these conditions of a valid measure thus restricting the rights of free speech and assembly be passed upon by the court of a jury.... Under these circumstances the judgment of the State court cannot be disturbed.... We lack here the power occasionally exercised on review of judgments of lower federal courts to correct in criminal cases vital errors, although the objection was not taken in the trial court.... Because we may not inquire into the errors now alleged I concur in affirming the judgment of the state court.

Glossary

eschewed:	refused, avoided
syndicalism:	a radical political movement based on rule by political unions

OLMSTEAD V. UNITED STATES

1928

[Brandeis dissent]

The defendants were convicted of conspiring to violate the National Prohibition Act. Before any of the persons now charged had been arrested or indicted, the telephones by means of which they habitually communicated with one another and with others had been tapped by federal officers. To this end, a lineman of long experience in wiretapping was employed on behalf of the Government and at its expense. He tapped eight telephones, some in the homes of the persons charged, some in their offices. Acting on behalf of the Government and in their official capacity, at least six other prohibition agents listened over the tapped wires and reported the messages taken. Their operations extended over a period of nearly five months. The typewritten record of the notes of conversations overheard occupies 775 typewritten pages. By objections seasonably made and persistently renewed, the defendants objected to the admission of the evidence obtained by wiretapping on the ground that the Government's wiretapping constituted an unreasonable search and seizure in violation of the Fourth Amendment, and that the use as evidence of the conversations overheard compelled the defendants to be witnesses against themselves in violation of the Fifth Amendment.

The Government ... relies on the language of the Amendment, and it claims that the protection given thereby cannot properly be held to include a telephone conversation.

"We must never forget," said Mr. Chief Justice Marshall in *McCulloch v. Maryland,* 4 Wheat. 316, 407, "that it is a constitution we are expounding." Since then, this Court has repeatedly sustained the exercise of power by Congress, under various clauses of that instrument, over objects of which the Fathers could not have dreamed.... Clauses guaranteeing to the individual protection against specific abuses of power must have a similar capacity of adaptation to a changing world....

When the Fourth and Fifth Amendments were adopted, "the form that evil had theretofore taken" had been necessarily simple. Force and violence were then the only means known to man by which a Government could directly effect self-incrimination.... Protection against such invasion of "the sanctities of a man's home and the privacies of life" was provided in the Fourth and Fifth Amendments by specific language.... But "time works changes, brings into existence new conditions and purposes." Subtler and more far-reaching means of invading privacy have become available to the Government. Discovery and invention have made it possible for the Government, by means far more effective than stretching upon the rack, to obtain disclosure in court of what is whispered in the closet....

The progress of science in furnishing the Government with means of espionage is not likely to stop with wiretapping. Ways may someday be developed by which the Government, without removing papers from secret drawers, can reproduce them in court, and by which it will be enabled to expose to a jury the most intimate occurrences of the home. Advances in the psychic and related sciences may bring means of exploring unexpressed beliefs, thoughts and emotions....

The evil incident to invasion of the privacy of the telephone is far greater than that involved in tampering with the mails. Whenever a telephone line is tapped, the privacy of the persons at both ends of the line is invaded and all conversations between them upon any subject, and, although proper, confidential and privileged, may be overheard. Moreover, the tapping of one man's telephone line involves the tapping of the telephone of every other person whom he may call or who may call him. As a means of espionage, writs of assistance and general warrants are but puny instruments of tyranny and oppression when compared with wiretapping....

The protection guaranteed by the Amendments is much broader in scope. The makers of our Constitution undertook to secure conditions favorable to the pursuit of happiness. They recognized the significance of man's spiritual nature, of his feelings, and of his intellect. They knew that only a part of the pain, pleasure and satisfactions of life are to be found in material things. They sought to protect Americans in their beliefs, their thoughts, their emotions and their sensations. They conferred, as against the Government, the right to be let alone—the most comprehensive of rights, and the right most valued by civilized men. To protect that right, every unjustifiable intrusion by the Government upon the privacy of the

Document Text

individual, whatever the means employed, must be deemed a violation of the Fourth Amendment. And the use, as evidence in a criminal proceeding, of facts ascertained by such intrusion must be deemed a violation of the Fifth.

Applying to the Fourth and Fifth Amendments the established rule of construction, the defendants' objections to the evidence obtained by wiretapping must, in my opinion, be sustained. It is, of course, immaterial where the physical connection with the telephone wires leading into the defendants' premises was made. And it is also immaterial that the intrusion was in aid of law enforcement. Experience should teach us to be most on our guard to protect liberty when the Government's purposes are beneficent. Men born to freedom are naturally alert to repel invasion of their liberty by evil-minded rulers. The greatest dangers to liberty lurk in insidious encroachment by men of zeal, well meaning but without understanding.

Independently of the constitutional question, I am of the opinion that the judgment should be reversed. By the laws of Washington, wiretapping is a crime. To prove its case, the Government was obliged to lay bare the crimes committed by its officers on its behalf. A federal court should not permit such a prosecution to continue....

Here, the evidence obtained by crime was obtained at the Government's expense, by its officers, while acting on its behalf; the officers who committed these crimes are the same officers who were charged with the enforcement of the Prohibition Act; the crimes of these officers were committed for the purpose of securing evidence with which to obtain an indictment and to secure a conviction. The evidence so obtained constitutes the warp and woof of the Government's case.... There is literally no other evidence of guilt on the part of some of the defendants except that illegally obtained by these officers. As to nearly all the defendants (except those who admitted guilt), the evidence relied upon to secure a conviction consisted mainly of that which these officers had so obtained by violating the state law....

And if this Court should permit the Government, by means of its officers' crimes, to effect its purpose of punishing the defendants, there would seem to be present all the elements of a ratification. If so, the Government itself would become a lawbreaker.

Will this Court, by sustaining the judgment below, sanction such conduct on the part of the Executive? The governing principle has long been settled. It is that a court will not redress a wrong when he who invokes its aid has unclean hands....

Decency, security and liberty alike demand that government officials shall be subjected to the same rules of conduct that are commands to the citizen. In a government of laws, existence of the government will be imperiled if it fails to observe the law scrupulously. Our Government is the potent, the omnipresent teacher. For good or for ill, it teaches the whole people by its example. Crime is contagious. If the Government becomes a lawbreaker, it breeds contempt for law; it invites every man to become a law unto himself; it invites anarchy. To declare that, in the administration of the criminal law, the end justifies the means—to declare that the Government may commit crimes in order to secure the conviction of a private criminal—would bring terrible retribution. Against that pernicious doctrine this Court should resolutely set its face.

Glossary

anarchy: a political state without government or laws

construction: legal interpretation

incident to: occurring in conjunction with, not necessarily causally related

pernicious: harmful

seasonably: regularly

stretching upon the rack: an especially cruel form of torture in which a person's joints are dislocated and eventually separated (along with muscles and cartilage)

Glossary

warp and woof:	the structure of something, drawn from terms in weaving—*warp* for threads running lengthwise and *woof* for the threads running across
writs of assistance:	legal documents used by the British as search warrants during the American Revolution

Louis Brandeis, 1915

William J. Brennan, Jr.

William J. Brennan, Jr.: Original Analysis

Supreme Court Justice

1906–1997

Overview

William Brennan, U.S. Supreme Court justice, was one of the architects of the constitutional revolution that radically changed American life in the second half of the twentieth century. As Chief Justice Earl Warren's right-hand man, Brennan was responsible for crafting majority opinions such as *Baker v. Carr*, which helped to establish the principle of "one person, one vote" and which Warren always referred to as the most important decision handed down during his momentous tenure on the Court. Brennan, whose politics placed him squarely at the Warren Court's center, was also responsible for crafting majorities for opinions such as the one he wrote in *New York Times Co. v. Sullivan*, which managed to greatly expand the First Amendment while avoiding his more liberal colleagues' wish to make criticism of public officials immune to libel suits. During the Warren years (1953–1969), Brennan was the justice least likely to dissent from the majority's views; but later, during the tenures of Chief Justices Warren Burger and William Rehnquist, he frequently played the role of passionate dissenter, most notably in death penalty cases. Nonetheless, as late as a year before he retired from an increasingly conservative Court, Brennan marshaled a majority in *Texas v. Johnson* and engineered an opinion that expanded the definition of protected speech. It is no accident that Brennan is remembered not only for the law he made but also for his skills as a coalition builder.

Born in Newark, New Jersey, on April 25, 1906, the son of Irish working-class parents, William Joseph Brennan, Jr., could be said to have inherited the social activism he later exhibited on the high bench. His father worked as coal stoker at a brewery, hard labor that prompted him to become, first, a leader of the local labor union and, later, a reformer as member of the Newark Board of Commissioners. William, Jr., shared many of his father's attitudes, but not—at least not overtly—his father's taste for politics. After graduating with an advanced business degree from the Wharton School at the University of Pennsylvania, Brennan attended Harvard Law School. He practiced law privately for only a short while before commencing a campaign to reform the New Jersey court system. Within a few years, he was sitting on the state supreme court bench, where, seemingly anticipating the role he would later play in connection to Earl Warren, Brennan became New Jersey Chief Justice Arthur Vanderbilt's closest associate.

Brennan arrived at the U.S. Supreme Court on October 16, 1956, appointed by President Dwight D. Eisenhower when Congress was in recess. When the Senate reconvened and voted on Brennan's appointment, only one voice was raised against him: that of Joseph McCarthy, who presumably objected not to Brennan's jurisprudence but to the latter's onetime comparison of McCarthy's Communist-hunting tactics with those employed at the Salem witch trials. Later, Eisenhower would come to regret his choice. Asked if he had made any mistakes as president, he responded, "Yes, two, and they are both sitting on the Supreme Court" (qtd. in Abraham, p. 246). Eisenhower grew to dislike Brennan's liberality on the Court almost as much as he disliked Warren's. And, indeed, Warren and Brennan worked together closely throughout Warren's tenure, meeting together privately to discuss strategies for bringing the other justices around to their view of current cases before each weekly judicial conference. Warren valued Brennan not only for his ability to parse and articulate a legal argument but also for his persuasiveness. Achieving unanimity—or, barring that, the clearest majority possible—was of the utmost importance to Warren, who sought to make his Court's precedents stick. Brennan was, in every sense, Warren's ambassador.

During the subsequent tenures of Chief Justices Burger and Rehnquist (respectively, 1969–1986 and 1986–2005), the politics of the Court shifted steadily rightward, and Brennan eventually lost both his leadership role and some of his optimism. Increasingly, he found himself in the minority, and whereas he had written few dissents during the Warren years, after 1969 the number rose steadily. Brennan's closest associate became Thurgood Marshall, one of the few other remaining members of the liberal voting bloc that had been responsible for so many of the Warren Court's momentous decisions. Brennan and Marshall frequently voted together—and they always voted together against imposing the death penalty, which both men believed to be inherently unconstitutional. In later years Brennan was, nonetheless, still an influential figure, drafting important opinions for the Court on gender discrimination and affirmative action, as well as First Amendment freedoms. He retired on July 20, 1990, having written 1,360 opinions, a number bested only by his fellow Warren Court liberal, William O. Douglas.

Time Line

1906	April 25	■ William J. Brennan, Jr., is born in Newark, New Jersey.
1931	May	■ Brennan graduates from Harvard Law School.
1942	July	■ Brennan is commissioned as a major in the U.S. Army, eventually receiving the Legion of Merit for helping to resolve labor disputes related to wartime conversion of private industry.
1949	February	■ Brennan is appointed to the New Jersey Superior Court.
1950	August	■ Brennan advances to the Appellate Division of the New Jersey Superior Court.
1952	March 13	■ Brennan is sworn in as an associate justice of the New Jersey Supreme Court.
1956	October 16	■ Brennan takes the oath as an associate justice of the United States Supreme Court.
1962	March 26	■ *Baker v. Carr* is decided, with Brennan's opinion for the Court paving the way for the principle of "one man, one vote."
1964	March 9	■ Brennan's opinion for a unanimous Court in *New York Times Co. v. Sullivan* greatly expands First Amendment rights.
1976	December 20	■ *Craig v. Boren,* a landmark gender-equality decision for which Brennan writes the majority opinion, is handed down.
1989	June 21	■ Brennan's next-to-last opinion for the Court, *Texas v. Johnson,* extends First Amendment coverage to "expressive conduct," such as flag burning.
1990	July 20	■ Following a series of health crises Brennan retires from the Court.
1997	July 24	■ Brennan dies in Washington, D.C.

Explanation and Analysis of Documents

During more than three decades on the high bench, William J. Brennan, Jr., was responsible for some of the most significant decisions the Court has ever known. The vast majority of these fall under the rubric of expansion of individual liberties. *Baker v. Carr*, for example, is known as the case that jump-started the movement toward social equality by, as it were, enfranchising the franchise with the principle of "one person, one vote." *New York Times Co. v. Sullivan*, by constraining libel laws, managed to extend both the First Amendment and civil rights. *Craig v. Boren* had an analogous effect on equal protection and gender equality. And in *Texas v. Johnson*, one of the last opinions he would write, Brennan returned to the familiar territory of the First Amendment, shoring up this perpetual bulwark of our democracy by supporting those who choose to attack the flag—our most cherished symbol of liberty.

♦ *Baker v. Carr*

Although *Baker v. Carr* did not establish the principle of "one person, one vote," (which would come the following year with William O. Douglas's opinion in *Gray v. Sanders*), Brennan's opinion for the Court certainly set the stage for what came to be known as the "reapportionment revolution." Prior to *Baker*, state-mandated legislative districts had continued to favor rural voters, even after populations had shifted to urban areas. In *Baker*, for example, residents of Memphis, Nashville, and Knoxville, Tennessee, sued Joe C. Carr, the Tennessee secretary of state, to force him to redraw the state's existing legislative districts. The boundaries of these districts had remained unchanged since 1901. As a result, the votes of those inhabiting rural districts carried more weight, individually and collectively, than did those of their more numerous urban counterparts.

The plaintiffs, believing that only a federal forum could bring redress, brought their suit in federal district court, asking that the Tennessee apportionment act, which required reapportionment of the state's ninety-five counties only every ten years (a directive that had plainly been disregarded) be declared unconstitutional and that state officials be enjoined from conducting further elections under the existing act. The district court, citing the principle requiring that so-called legal questions were for legislatures, rather than courts to decide, dismissed the case. The plaintiffs then appealed directly to the U.S. Supreme Court, claiming, as they had in the lower court, that their right to equal protection under the laws, granted by the Fourteenth Amendment, had been violated,

The ostensible issue before the high bench was whether federal courts could mandate equality among legislative districts. At its core, however, *Baker* concerned the scope and power of the Supreme Court itself. Seventeen years earlier, in *Colegrove v. Green* (1946), Justice Felix Frankfurter had written a plurality opinion for a seven-member Court (one justice was absent, and a recent vacancy had not been filled) declaring that the high court had no

authority to entertain cases concerning apportionment of state legislatures. Now, in the last opinion he would write before retiring from the Court, Frankfurter—always the advocate for judicial restraint—dissented from the majority, once again warning against the Court's entry into a "political thicket." *Colegrove* had been decided by a vote of three to three to one, with Justice Wiley B. Rutledge concurring in the result but not with Frankfurter's reasoning. Because of the unusual circumstances surrounding its decision, the status of *Colegrove* as precedent had always been shaky. Brennan's opinion for the Court in *Baker* destroyed that status entirely.

The appellants in *Baker* had appealed to the Supreme Court for a writ of certiorari, meaning that Court review was discretionary and requiring the justices to vote first on the issue of hearing the case. When this vote was taken, a bare majority of the justices (five) supported Frankfurter's contention that *Baker* was a political case outside Court jurisdiction. Only four justices are required to grant certiorari, however, and the Court agreed to hear the case. After two days of oral argument, on April 19 and 20, 1961, the Court was still split four to four on the merits of the appeal, with Justice Potter Stewart still undecided. Chief Justice Earl Warren, cognizant of *Baker*'s significance and potential for overturning *Colegrove*, held the case over for reargument in the next Court term. When *Baker* was reargued on October 9, 1961, neither side introduced anything new, and afterward Frankfurter attacked the plaintiffs' case with a sixty-page memorandum written to his colleagues. Only Brennan responded in kind, and his lengthy memo, addressing the injustice of malapportionment but asking only that Tennessee be obliged to defend its apportionment system (and intending to convince the still recalcitrant Stewart), carried the day. For his part, Warren, too, was convinced by Brennan's argument, and he assigned Brennan to write an opinion for what would eventually be a six-member majority (two justices dissented, and one did not participate) to overturn *Colegrove* and grant the Tennessee plaintiffs their day in court.

Brennan's opinion, though ultimately supporting the appellants' contention that Tennessee had acted unconstitutionally, comes at the matter tangentially. After rehearsing the facts of the case, Brennan addresses more technical matters. The court below had dismissed the case on grounds that federal courts lacked jurisdiction and that *Baker* presented a question that could not be resolved by judicial means. Brennan carefully distinguishes between these two arguments: Whereas a case that is nonjusticiable can still be considered by a court up to the point of decision, the court is barred from entertaining a case over which it lacks jurisdiction. In *Baker* the complaint clearly sets forth a case that arises under the Constitution; therefore, the district court unquestionably has jurisdiction. What is more, the appellants have sufficient interest in the value of their votes to be granted standing to sue. Justiciability presents a knottier problem for Brennan, who nonetheless succeeds in distinguishing this case, which concerns a question of federalism, from one raising a political question about the relationship among the three branches of government. The appellants, Brennan concludes, have a cause of action, and he sends their case back to the lower court "for further proceedings consistent with this opinion."

Baker was decided on very narrow grounds, but it was nonetheless hard fought. Justice Charles Whittaker found the pressure put on him by some of his colleagues during the Court's consideration of the case too much to bear. He was hospitalized for exhaustion before *Baker* was decided, and he took no part in its decision. A week after *Baker* was handed down on March 26, 1962, Whittaker resigned from the Court. Frankfurter, embittered by his defeat, suffered a debilitating stroke a few weeks later. On August 28, 1962, he, too, resigned from the Court. For urban residents of Tennessee—and other states—*Baker* had a happier aftermath. Within a year of its decision, thirty-six other states were involved in reapportionment suits. A string of Supreme Court cases that followed effectively declared the apportionment of every state legislature unconstitutional. Soon population equality was required of virtually all electoral districts, and even state senate seats were apportioned on the basis of population.

Earl Warren often referred to *Baker v. Carr* as the most interesting and important case decided during his tenure. Because the case succeeded in transferring political power from the largely landowning, largely conservative rural population to the more heterogeneous populace of the cities, *Baker* can be said to have opened the door to the major social restructuring America underwent during the Warren era as well as, perhaps, the conservative backlash that ensued decades later.

♦ *New York Times Co. v. Sullivan*

New York Times Co. v. Sullivan grew out of an advertisement concerning the struggle for civil rights that appeared in the *Times* on March 29, 1960. L.B. Sullivan, the city commissioner of Montgomery, Alabama, sued the newspaper as well as four African American clergymen affiliated with the Committee to Defend Martin Luther King and the Struggle for Freedom in the South, the organization behind the ad. Despite the fact that Sullivan was not named in the piece, he claimed that he had been libeled by the ad's assertion that truckloads of armed police—men his office was charged with overseeing—had circled the Alabama State University campus in Montgomery. In addition, as the defendants readily admitted, the ad contained a number of minor errors—for example, the statement that protesting students had sung "My Country, 'Tis of Thee" on the steps of the capitol, when in fact they had sung "The Star-Spangled Banner." These errors, Sullivan claimed, were indicative of the falsity of the ad. The state trial court bought this argument, calling the advertisement's claims false and misleading and the *Times* irresponsible. Sullivan was awarded $500,000 in damages against each of the defendants, a verdict upheld by the Alabama Supreme Court.

Prior to *Sullivan*, libel had been a matter of state rather than federal law. The U.S. Supreme Court nonetheless granted the newspaper's application for reconsideration of the state courts' decision. After the case was argued before the Court on January 6, 1964, a majority of the justices felt that the libel verdict could be dismissed on narrow ground: Because the advertisement had not named Sullivan, he had not been libeled. What is more, Sullivan had failed to demonstrate how the statements in the ad had harmed him. Justice Brennan, however, approached the case differently. The Court had an opportunity to preserve the constitutional ideals enshrined in the First Amendment by making the test of libel more rigorous. A mere showing of factual error should not, in itself, provide a cause of action for libel; what was required was proof of "actual malice" behind the error. Chief Justice Earl Warren assigned Brennan to write the opinion for what would in the end be a unanimous Court.

Brennan begins by quickly disposing of Sullivan's legalistic but misguided arguments, first that the Fourteenth Amendment does not mandate that the First Amendment be applied to a civil rather than a state action and, second, that even if the First Amendment applies, the protections afforded to free speech and press freedom do not, because the alleged libel appeared in a "commercial" advertisement. Brennan is also obliged to dispense with the Court's prior holdings that libel is not an essential part of any expression of ideas and is not constitutionally protected speech. He does so by arguing that libel is not in a category by itself, with "talismanic immunity" from constitutional restraints; libel must, in fact, be measured against the requirements of the First Amendment. The background of this case is of the utmost importance, for it involves a national debate on public issues that needs to be uninhibited. Such debate can involve unpleasant attacks in public. Like the long discredited Sedition Act of 1798, the civil law of libel as applied by the Alabama court has been invalidated by "the court of history," owing to the undue restrictions it imposes on criticism of the government and public officials.

The state rule of law cannot be saved just because it allows for a defense of truthfulness. Such a defense does not simply deter false speech but leads instead to the kind of self-censorship that is especially damaging to public debate. As such, the law is at odds with the intent of the First Amendment, even as it applies to the states through the Fourteenth Amendment. What the Constitution requires is a law that permits a public official to recover damages for an allegedly libelous statement not merely because it is false but also because he is able to prove that it was made with "reckless disregard" for whether or not it was false.

Sullivan revolutionized the law of libel, making it less dependent upon formulaic, often fine distinctions between protected and unprotected speech and upon muddy distinctions between truth and untruth. What mattered henceforth were the defendant's intent and, more important, the framers' intent as embodied in the First Amendment. *Sullivan* left unanswered the question of whether or not the actual malice standard extended to other libel plaintiffs. A few years later, in *Curtis Publishing Co. v. Butts* (1966) and *Associated Press v. Walker* (1967), the Court extended the standard to cases involving movie stars, athletes, high-profile business executives, and other individuals well known to the public. A decade after *Sullivan*, however, in *Gertz v. Robert Welch, Inc.*, the Court limited its prior holdings, ruling that the actual malice standard did not apply to cases brought by private individuals, even when the alleged libel concerned matters of public concern.

Sullivan cannot be properly understood unless it is viewed in the context of the times in which it was decided. As numerous commentators have noted, the case is as much about civil rights as it is about free speech. As previously applied, the law of libel had been used to curtail the civil rights movement; if the Warren Court had refused to hear *Sullivan* or had left the Alabama courts' argument unanswered, not only free speech but also racial equality would have been curtailed. *Sullivan* is one of those landmark cases that truly changed history.

♦ *Craig v. Boren*

On its face, *Craig v. Boren* seems an unlikely case to cite for its important role in Supreme Court—and U.S.—history. As Ruth Bader Ginsburg (later a Supreme Court justice herself but at the time a litigator for the Women's Rights Project of the American Civil Liberties Union) remarked tongue in cheek to appellants' counsel, "Delighted to see the Supreme Court is interested in beer drinkers" (http://www.supremecourthistory.org/05_learning/subs/05_e03.html). *Craig* concerned an Oklahoma statute permitting eighteen-year-old women to purchase beer with an alcohol content of 3.2 percent but requiring that men who wished to purchase 3.2 percent beer be at least twenty-one years old. Mark Walker, then an eighteen-year-old college freshman, decided to challenge the statute in court. Concerned that he might have difficulty demonstrating damages and thus obtaining standing to sue, his attorney recommended that Walker add a vendor of 3.2 percent beer as a plaintiff. Carolyn Whitener was accordingly added. As the case wended its way to court, Walker turned twenty-one, and a third plaintiff, then-eighteen-year-old Curtis Craig, became a third co-plaintiff.

The federal district court that tried *Craig* dismissed it out of hand, declaring the statute a valid exercise of Oklahoma's right under the Twenty-first Amendment to regulate commerce in alcoholic beverages. Plaintiffs then appealed to the U.S. Supreme Court. By the time the case reached the high court, however, Curtis Craig, too, had attained the age of majority, leaving Carolyn Whitener the only appellant with standing. In his opinion for the Court, Brennan addresses this oddity first, declaring that Whitener can rely upon the equal protection claims of affected eighteen- to twenty-year-old males, whose rights would be affected should her claim fail. Brennan's treatment of the state's Twenty-first Amendment argument is similarly direct: The Twenty-first Amendment, which repealed the Eighteenth

Amendment and legalized the sale of alcoholic beverages, was intended to effect interstate commerce in alcohol, not individual rights.

The heart of the case, however, concerned the appropriate standard of review for determining the constitutionality, under the equal protection clause of the Fourteenth Amendment, of a state law having a disparate impact on men and women. Was gender, like income, a "non-suspect" category subject only to the so-called rational basis test, whereby the state had to show only that its statute was reasonably related to a legitimate government interest? The Oklahoma law, which the state declared protected the populace from drunk drivers, might be said to fall under this rubric. Brennan, however, did not find the state's statistics convincing: "Suffice to say that the showing offered by the appellees does not satisfy us that sex represents a legitimate, accurate proxy for the regulation of drinking and driving." While Oklahoma could demonstrate that 0.18 percent of females versus 2 percent of males aged eighteen to twenty had been arrested for alcohol-related driving offenses, what of the 98 percent of young men who were not guilty of such transgressions? What is more, says Brennan, ever since deciding *Reed v. Reed* (a decision mandating that estate executors be appointed in a gender-neutral manner) in 1971, in order to withstand an equal protection challenge, states had been required to show something more than a rational basis for non-gender-neutral laws. Here, however, "the relationship between gender and traffic safety becomes far too tenuous to satisfy Reed's requirement that the gender-based difference be substantially related to achievement of the statutory objective."

Brennan goes on to enunciate the standard for determining the constitutionality of sex-based classifications in state laws. Although the strict scrutiny trained on suspect classifications such as race might not be appropriate, ordinary scrutiny was not rigorous enough when applied to statutes like the one in question. Gender-specific statutes "must serve important governmental objectives and be substantially related to achievement of those objectives" in order to pass constitutional muster. This standard, he avers, is the same one pronounced in *Reed*. As other justices pointed out in a multiplicity of concurring opinions, this last statement was inaccurate. In fact, Brennan—perhaps influenced by the burgeoning feminist movement and the contemporaneous drive for an equal rights amendment to the Constitution—had elaborated on *Reed* to develop a new standard. Ever since *Craig*, the Court has employed Brennan's "intermediate scrutiny" test to assess government actions based on gender.

♦ *Texas v. Johnson*

Coming near the end of Brennan's tenure on the Court, *Texas v. Johnson* was not a milestone in the sense that many of his earlier opinions were, but it was the most publicly controversial decision of his long career. The case concerned a radical demonstrator, Gregory Lee Johnson, who chose a particularly dramatic means of expressing his criticism of Republican policies during the 1984 Republican National Convention in Dallas: He burned the American flag. Within a half hour, police had arrested Johnson for violating a Texas statute barring violation of venerated objects. A trial jury found Johnson guilty, sentencing him to a year in prison and a $2,000 fine, but the Texas Court of Criminal Appeals overturned his conviction on the ground that Johnson was exercising his right of political dissent. Texas then appealed to the U.S. Supreme Court, confident that the Court's new conservative majority would uphold the state antidesecration statute.

The state of Texas did not, however, understand the power of precedent. While it is true that the Court had not yet ruled definitively on the constitutionality of flag desecration, as Brennan points out in his opinion for the Court, in *West Virginia State Board of Education v. Barnette* (1943) the Court had indicated that failure to demonstrate respect for the flag—in this case, by refusing to salute it—was a permissible exercise of the First Amendment right to express political dissent. For Brennan, such political "statements" made with respect to the flag, itself a symbol, were obviously symbolic. But are they speech of the sort protected by the First Amendment? The Court had found in the past that various forms of expressive conduct were equivalent to protected speech. For example, the Court had upheld as protected symbolic conduct the wearing of black armbands to protest military involvement in Vietnam and a sit-in by blacks in a "whites only" area to protest racial segregation.

Not every act intended as political dissent—even among those involving flag desecration—is protected, since government may have an overriding interest to protect. Such was the case in *United States v. O'Brien* (1968), where draft-card burning was considered to have combined speech and nonspeech elements and where the government was found to have a legitimate interest—protecting its ability to raise and support an army—that trumped the defendant's right to communicate his antiwar beliefs. When considering expressive conduct, Brennan notes, the Court has always taken context into account. At trial, Johnson had stated the reason for his actions this way: "The American Flag was burned as Ronald Reagan was being renominated as President. And a more powerful statement of symbolic speech, whether you agree with it or not, couldn't have been made at that time." While it is true that the Court has greater latitude in restricting expressive conduct than it does in curtailing words per se, for Brennan, Johnson's rationale certainly supersedes the state's claim that Johnson's arrest was aimed at preventing breaches of the peace. And he is unequivocal in dismissing the state's claim that its statute must be upheld because it is intended to preserve the flag's status as a symbol of nationhood: "If there is a bedrock principle underlying the First Amendment, it is that the government may not prohibit the expression of an idea simply because society finds the idea itself offensive or disagreeable."

Johnson provoked immediate public controversy. In Brennan's home state of New Jersey, residents of Hudson

County, where Brennan had begun his judicial career, circulated a petition to stop the creation of a statue honoring the justice. Only a few months after the Court passed down the *Johnson* decision, Congress passed the Flag Protection Act of 1989, which attempted to overrule the case by legislation. The next year, in *United States v. Eichman* (for which Brennan also wrote the majority opinion), the Court declared that this federal law, like the Texas statute at issue in *Johnson*, violated the First Amendment. Subsequently, Congress has made several attempts to pass a constitutional amendment prohibiting flag desecration, one of which failed in the Senate by one vote in 2006.

Impact and Legacy

When Justice Brennan left the high bench in 1990, he had served longer than all but two other justices; his lengthy tenure, his talent for forming coalitions, and his appetite for work combined to make him one of the most powerful influences on the Supreme Court and—by extension—modern American society. Always a liberal, he nonetheless managed, unlike his contemporaries Hugo Black and William O. Douglas, to refrain from overstatement and, in doing so, to convince other, more conservative justices to endorse his judgments—even if they did not agree with his reasoning. Chief Justice Earl Warren, who recognized the value of unanimous or near-unanimous endorsement of opinions issuing from the Court, trusted Brennan's diplomacy and legal skills and consequently assigned the associate to responsibility for majority opinions Warren himself could have written. Some others on the Court, jealous of the special relationship between Warren and Brennan, accused the latter of manipulation, but without Brennan and his considerable conciliatory powers, many of the last century's most important decisions on political speech, pornography, racial desegregation, gender equality, and application of the Bill of Rights at the state level might never have come about.

Brennan, who had been a little-known state jurist before his elevation to the high court, has been called the original "stealth" nominee. It was not long, however, before the Republican President Eisenhower was publicly bemoaning his choice, as Brennan issued one landmark decision after another. Beginning with *Baker v. Carr* in 1956, arguably the most important case of the Warren era, Brennan was responsible for drafting a series of opinions that moved American society decidedly leftward. In 1969 President Richard M. Nixon nominated Warren Burger as Earl Warren's successor. Burger's express mission was to roll back the "excesses" of the Warren Court, but owing largely to Brennan's continued presence the Burger years proved—at least initially—to be a continuation and consolidation of Warren Court initiatives. As more and more conservatives were nominated to the Court, and as—not coincidentally—the nation moved to the right, Brennan's power waned. His authority as a champion of the First Amendment, however, never did—as can be seen by the pair of flag-burning case opinions, in *Texas v. Johnson* (1989) and in *United States v. Eichman* (1990), Brennan authored at the end of his career.

At Harvard Law School, Brennan had been a student of Felix Frankfurter. On the Court, Brennan repeatedly challenged Justice Frankfurter's advocacy of judicial restraint—nowhere more so than in *Baker*, which overturned *Colegrove v. Green* (1946), the decision Frankfurter prized above all others. Brennan's critics then and now argue that Brennan embodied the spirit of unrestrained judicial arrogance, undermining the power of the people's elected representatives and their control over their daily lives. Brennan, for his part, saw his duty as evolutionary rather than revolutionary, interpreting the Constitution to suit contemporary social necessities but not prevailing, temporary political winds. For him the nation's foundation document was not fixed but rather constantly changing, a condition mandating flexibility and reconciliation between past ideals and present realities. Therein lay its genius—and his legacy.

Key Sources

Papers dating from William J. Brennan's years on the U.S. Supreme Court are located in the Library of Congress's Manuscript Division in Washington, D.C.

Essential Quotes

"Like insurrection, contempt, advocacy of unlawful acts, breach of the peace, obscenity, solicitation of legal business, and the various other formulae for the repression of expression that have been challenged in this court, libel can claim no talismanic immunity from constitutional limitations. It must be measured by standards that satisfy the First Amendment."

(*New York Times Co. v. Sullivan*)

"We consider this case against the background of a profound national commitment to the principle that debate on public issues should be uninhibited, robust, and wide-open, and that it may well include vehement, caustic, and sometimes unpleasantly sharp attacks on government and public officials."

(*New York Times Co. v. Sullivan*)

"Erroneous statement is inevitable in free debate, and … it must be protected if the freedoms of expression … are to have the 'breathing space' that they 'need … to survive.'"

(*New York Times Co. v. Sullivan*)

"A rule compelling the critic of official conduct to guarantee the truth of all his factual assertions … leads to a comparable 'self-censorship.' Allowance of the defense of truth, with the burden of proving it on the defendant, does not mean that only false speech will be deterred.… The constitutional guarantees require, we think, a federal rule that prohibits a public official from recovering damages for a defamatory falsehood relating to his official conduct unless he proves that the statement was made … with 'actual malice'—that is, with knowledge that it was false or with reckless disregard of whether it was false or not."

(*New York Times Co. v. Sullivan*)

Essential Quotes

"To withstand constitutional challenge … classifications by gender must serve important governmental objectives and must be substantially related to achievement of those objectives."

(*Craig v. Boren*)

"Pregnant with expressive content, the flag as readily signifies this Nation as does the combination of letters found in 'America.'"

(*Texas v. Johnson*)

"If there is a bedrock principle underlying the First Amendment, it is that the government may not prohibit the expression of an idea simply because society finds the idea itself offensive or disagreeable."

(*Texas v. Johnson*)

Further Reading

Books

Abraham, Henry J. *Justices and Presidents: A Political History of Appointments to the Supreme Court*. New York: Oxford University Press, 1974.

Clark, Hunter R. *Justice Brennan: The Great Conciliator*. Secaucus, N.J.: Carol Publishing Group, 1995.

Eisler, Kim Isaac. *A Justice for All: William J. Brennan, Jr., and the Decisions That Transformed America*. New York: Simon & Schuster, 1993.

Goldman, Roger, and David Gallen. *William J. Brennan, Jr.: Freedom First*. New York : Carroll & Graf Publishers, 1994.

Hasen, Richard. *The Supreme Court and Election Law: Judging Equality from Baker v. Carr to Bush v. Gore*. New York: New York University Press, 2006.

Rosenkranz, E. Joshua, and Bernard Schwartz, eds. *Reason and Passion: Justice Brennan's Enduring Influence*. New York: W. W. Norton, 1997.

Marion, David E. *The Jurisprudence of Justice: William J. Brennan, Jr.: The Law and Politics of a "Libertarian Dignity"*. Lanham, Md.: Rowman & Littlefield, 1997.

Michelman, Frank I. *Brennan and Democracy*. Princeton, N.J.: Princeton University Press, 1999.

Woodward, Bob, and Scott Armstrong. *The Brethren: Inside the Supreme Court* New York: Simon & Schuster, 1979.

Web Sites

"Supreme Court Decisions & Women's Rights." The Supreme Court Historical Society Learning Center Web site. http://www.supremecourthistory.org/05_learning/subs/05_e03.html.

—*Lisa Paddock*

Questions for Further Study

1. Brennan's opinion in *Baker v. Carr* draws on subtle reasoning with regard to the matter of a particular court's jurisdiction in a given situation. How does he make his point, and what does he conclude regarding the question under review in the case?

2. To what degree is Brennan's opinion in *Sullivan* about freedom of speech and to what degree is it about civil rights? Which is more important in the case itself?

3. *Texas v. Johnson* raises interesting questions about the expression of ideas and the difference between actions that are simply ends in themselves and those intended to prove a point. Had Johnson been burning a mere piece of cloth in a public place, this would have been at worst a case of arson and at best a nuisance. But since the piece of cloth in question was an American flag, burned as a political statement, the action was in an entirely different legal category. Discuss the reasoning involved and the distinction between acts that are symbolic and those with little or no symbolic purpose.

Baker v. Carr

1962

The District Court was uncertain whether our cases withholding federal judicial relief rested upon a lack of federal jurisdiction or upon the inappropriateness of the subject matter for judicial consideration—what we have designated "nonjusticiability." The distinction between the two grounds is significant. In the instance of nonjusticiability, consideration of the cause is not wholly and immediately foreclosed; rather, the Court's inquiry necessarily proceeds to the point of deciding whether the duty asserted can be judicially identified and its breach judicially determined, and whether protection for the right asserted can be judicially molded. In the instance of lack of jurisdiction the cause either does not "arise under" the Federal Constitution, laws or treaties (or fall within one of the other enumerated categories of Art. III, 2), or is not a "case or controversy" within the meaning of that section; or the cause is not one described by any jurisdictional statute. Our conclusion ... that this cause presents no nonjusticiable "political question" settles the only possible doubt that it is a case or controversy....

It is clear that the cause of action is one which "arises under" the Federal Constitution. The complaint alleges that the 1901 statute effects an apportionment that deprives the appellants of the equal protection of the laws in violation of the Fourteenth Amendment. Dismissal of the complaint upon the ground of lack of jurisdiction of the subject matter would, therefore, be justified only if that claim were "so attenuated and unsubstantial as to be absolutely devoid of merit."... Since the complaint plainly sets forth a case arising under the Constitution, the subject matter is within the federal judicial power defined in Art. III, 2, and so within the power of Congress to assign to the jurisdiction of the District Courts....

The appellees refer to *Colegrove v. Green* ... as authority that the District Court lacked jurisdiction of the subject matter. Appellees misconceive the holding of that case. The holding was precisely contrary to their reading of it. Seven members of the Court participated in the decision. Unlike many other cases in this field which have assumed without discussion that there was jurisdiction, all three opinions filed in *Colegrove* discussed the question....

We hold that the District Court has jurisdiction of the subject matter of the federal constitutional claim asserted in the complaint....

Have the appellants alleged such a personal stake in the outcome of the controversy as to assure that concrete adverseness which sharpens the presentation of issues upon which the court so largely depends for illumination of difficult constitutional questions? This is the gist of the question of standing. It is, of course, a question of federal law....

We hold that the appellants do have standing to maintain this suit.... These appellants seek relief in order to protect or vindicate an interest of their own, and of those similarly situated. Their constitutional claim is, in substance, that the 1901 statute constitutes arbitrary and capricious state action, offensive to the Fourteenth Amendment in its irrational disregard of the standard of apportionment prescribed by the State's Constitution or of any standard, effecting a gross disproportion of representation to voting population. The injury which appellants assert is that this classification disfavors the voters in the counties in which they reside, placing them in a position of constitutionally unjustifiable inequality vis-a-vis voters ... in irrationally favored counties. A citizen's right to a vote free of arbitrary impairment by state action has been judicially recognized as a right secured by the Constitution....

It would not be necessary to decide whether appellants' allegations of impairment of their votes by the 1901 apportionment will, ultimately, entitle them to any relief, in order to hold that they have standing to seek it. If such impairment does produce a legally cognizable injury, they are among those who have sustained it.... They are entitled to a hearing and to the District Court's decision on their claims....

In holding that the subject matter of this suit was not justiciable, the District Court relied on *Colegrove v. Green* .... We understand the District Court to have read the cited cases as compelling the conclusion that since the appellants sought to have a legislative apportionment held unconstitutional, their suit presented a "political question" and was therefore nonjusticiable. We hold that this challenge to an apportionment presents no nonjusticiable "political question."...

Document Text

We come, finally, to the ultimate inquiry whether our precedents as to what constitutes a nonjusticiable "political question" bring the case before us under the umbrella of that doctrine.... The question here is the consistency of state action with the Federal Constitution. We have no question decided, or to be decided, by a political branch of government coequal with this Court. Nor do we risk embarrassment of our government abroad, or grave disturbance at home if we take issue with Tennessee as to the constitutionality of her action here challenged. Nor need the appellants, in order to succeed in this action, ask the Court to enter upon policy determinations for which judicially manageable standards are lacking. Judicial standards under the Equal Protection Clause are well developed and familiar, and it has been open to courts since the enactment of the Fourteenth Amendment to determine, if on the particular facts they must, that a discrimination reflects no policy, but simply arbitrary and capricious action.

We conclude that the complaint's allegations of a denial of equal protection present a justiciable constitutional cause of action upon which appellants are entitled to a trial and a decision. The right asserted is within the reach of judicial protection under the Fourteenth Amendment.

The judgment of the District Court is reversed and the cause is remanded for further proceedings consistent with this opinion.

Glossary

appellants:	persons bringing a case on appeal to the Supreme Court
appellees:	persons against whom a case is appealed to the Supreme Court
holding:	the Supreme Court's ruling
judicial relief:	the means by which a court applies a judicial remedy–that is, a solution to the problem presented to it by a given case
offensive to:	in violation of
relief:	judicial relief
remanded:	sent back to a lower court
standing:	legal right to bring a lawsuit, which in the United States requires, among other things, clear proof that the party bringing the suit is directly and materially affected by the issue at hand

New York Times Co. v. Sullivan

The question before us is whether this rule of liability, as applied to an action brought by a public official against critics of his official conduct, abridges the freedom of speech and of the press that is guaranteed by the First and Fourteenth Amendments.

Respondent relies heavily, as did the Alabama courts, on statements of this Court to the effect that the Constitution does not protect libelous publications. Those statements do not foreclose our inquiry here. None of the cases sustained the use of libel laws to impose sanctions upon expression critical of the official conduct of public officials.... In deciding the question now, we are compelled by neither precedent nor policy to give any more weight to the epithet "libel" than we have to other "mere labels" of state law.... Like insurrection, contempt, advocacy of unlawful acts, breach of the peace, obscenity, solicitation of legal business, and the various other formulae for the repression of expression that have been challenged in this court, libel can claim no talismanic immunity from constitutional limitations. It must be measured by standards that satisfy the First Amendment.

The general proposition that freedom of expression upon public questions is secured by the First Amendment has long been settled by our decisions. The constitutional safeguard, we have said, "was fashioned to assure unfettered interchange of ideas for the bringing about of political and social changes desired by the people."... Thus we consider this case against the background of a profound national commitment to the principle that debate on public issues should be uninhibited, robust, and wide-open, and that it may well include vehement, caustic, and sometimes unpleasantly sharp attacks on government and public officials.... The present advertisement, as an expression of grievance and protest on one of the major public issues of our time, would seem clearly to qualify for the constitutional protection. The question is whether it forfeits that protection by the falsity of some of its factual statements and by its alleged defamation of respondent.

That erroneous statement is inevitable in free debate, and ... it must be protected if the freedoms of expression ... are to have the "breathing space" that they "need ... to survive."... Injury to official reputation affords no more warrant for repressing speech that would otherwise be free than does factual error.... Criticism of their official conduct does not lose its constitutional protection merely because it is effective criticism and hence diminishes their official reputations.

If neither factual error nor defamatory content suffices to remove the constitutional shield from criticism of official conduct, the combination of the two elements is no less inadequate. This is the lesson to be drawn from the great controversy over the Sedition Act of 1798, 1 Stat. 596, which first crystallized a national awareness of the central meaning of the First Amendment.

These views reflect a broad consensus that the Act, because of the restraint it imposed upon criticism of government and public officials, was inconsistent with the First Amendment.

There is no force in respondent's argument that the constitutional limitations implicit in the history of the Sedition Act apply only to Congress and not to the States.

What a State may not constitutionally bring about by means of a criminal statute is likewise beyond the reach of its civil law of libel. The fear of damage awards under a rule such as that invoked by the Alabama courts here may be markedly more inhibiting than the fear of prosecution under a criminal statute....

A rule compelling the critic of official conduct to guarantee the truth of all his factual assertions—and to do so on pain of libel judgments virtually unlimited in amount—leads to a comparable "self-censorship." Allowance of the defense of truth, with the burden of proving it on the defendant, does not mean that only false speech will be deterred. Even courts accepting this defense as an adequate safeguard have recognized the difficulties of adducing legal proofs that the alleged libel was true in all its factual particulars.... Under such a rule, would-be critics of official conduct may be deterred from voicing their criticism, even though it is believed to be true and even though it is in fact true, because of doubt whether it can be proved in court or fear of the expense of having to do so. They tend to make only statements which "steer far wider of the unlawful zone."... The

Document Text

rule thus dampens the vigor and limits the variety of public debate. It is inconsistent with the First and Fourteenth Amendments.

The constitutional guarantees require, we think, a federal rule that prohibits a public official from recovering damages for a defamatory falsehood relating to his official conduct unless he proves that the statement was made … with "actual malice"—that is, with knowledge that it was false or with reckless disregard of whether it was false or not.

We conclude that such a privilege is required by the First and Fourteenth Amendments.

Glossary

defamation:	the communication of demonstrably false information concerning a party, thus giving that party legal standing to bring a lawsuit on the issue
foreclose:	bring an end to
libelous:	characterized by a demonstrable effort to bring libel, or the issuing, in the form of writing or some other physical representation, of deliberately false information about another party
precedent:	a past case whose outcome provides a model for dealing with similar cases in the future
respondent:	the party against whom a lawsuit is brought by another party, the petitioner
Sedition Act of 1798:	one of the four Alien and Sedition Acts, a body of legislation issued under President John Adams that became notorious for its assault on civil liberties as a means of stifling disagreement with the administration
talismanic immunity:	a legal "free pass" or "get-out-of-jail-free card"

Craig v. Boren

1976

Analysis may appropriately begin with the reminder that [*Reed v.*] *Reed* emphasized that statutory classifications that distinguish between males and females are "subject to scrutiny under the Equal Protection Clause."... To withstand constitutional challenge, previous cases establish that classifications by gender must serve important governmental objectives and must be substantially related to achievement of those objectives....

Reed v. Reed has also provided the underpinning for decisions that have invalidated statutes employing gender as an inaccurate proxy for other, more germane bases of classification.... In light of the weak congruence between gender and the characteristic or trait that gender purported to represent, it was necessary that the legislatures choose either to realign their substantive laws in a gender-neutral fashion, or to adopt procedures for identifying those instances where the sex-centered generalization actually comported with fact....

In this case, too, "*Reed,* we feel, is controlling...." We turn then to the question whether, under *Reed,* the difference between males and females with respect to the purchase of 3.2% beer warrants the differential in age drawn by the Oklahoma statute. We conclude that it does not....

We accept for purposes of discussion the District Court's identification of the objective underlying 241 and 245 as the enhancement of traffic safety. Clearly, the protection ... of public health and safety represents an important function of state and local governments. However, appellees' statistics in our view cannot support the conclusion that the gender-based distinction closely serves to achieve that objective and therefore the distinction cannot under *Reed* withstand equal protection challenge.... Even were this statistical evidence accepted as accurate, it nevertheless offers only a weak answer to the equal protection question presented here. The most focused and relevant of the statistical surveys, arrests of 18–20-year-olds for alcohol-related driving offenses, exemplifies the ultimate unpersuasiveness of this evidentiary record. Viewed in terms of the correlation between sex and the actual activity that Oklahoma seeks to regulate–driving while under the influence of alcohol–the statistics broadly establish that .18% of females and 2% of males in that age group were arrested for that offense. While such a disparity is not trivial in a statistical sense, it hardly can form the basis for employment of a gender line as a classifying device. Certainly if maleness ... is to serve as a proxy for drinking and driving, a correlation of 2% must be considered an unduly tenuous "fit."... Moreover, the statistics exhibit a variety of other shortcomings that seriously impugn their value to equal protection analysis. Setting aside the obvious methodological problems, the surveys do not adequately justify the salient ... features of Oklahoma's gender-based traffic-safety law. None purports to measure the use and dangerousness of 3.2% beer as opposed to alcohol generally, a detail that is of particular importance since, in light of its low alcohol level, Oklahoma apparently considers the 3.2% beverage to be "non-intoxicating."... Moreover, many of the studies, while graphically documenting the unfortunate increase in driving while under the influence of alcohol, make no effort to relate their findings to age-sex differential as involved here. Indeed, the only survey that explicitly centered its attention upon young drivers and their use of beer–albeit apparently not of the diluted 3.2% variety–reached results that hardly can be viewed as impressive in justifying either a gender or age classification.

There is no reason to belabor this line of analysis. It is unrealistic to expect either members of the judiciary or state officials to be well versed in the rigors of experimental or statistical technique. But this merely illustrates that proving broad sociological propositions by statistics is a dubious business, and one that inevitably is in tension with the normative philosophy that underlies the Equal Protection Clause. Suffice to say that the showing offered by the appellees does not satisfy us that sex represents a legitimate, accurate proxy for the regulation of drinking and driving. In fact, when it is further recognized that Oklahoma's statute prohibits only the selling of 3.2% beer to young males and not their drinking the beverage once acquired (even after purchase by their 18–20-year-old female companions), the relationship between gender and traffic safety becomes far

Document Text

too tenuous to satisfy *Reed* 's requirement that the gender-based difference be substantially related to achievement of the statutory objective.

We hold, therefore, that under *Reed,* Oklahoma's 3.2% beer statute invidiously discriminates against males 18–20 years of age.

Glossary

appellee: the party against whom a case is appealed by another party (the appellant) in front of a higher court

controlling: carrying the ultimate authority for dealing with a particular legal situation

normative: offering a prescription as to standards

proxy: substitute

substantive: defining rights and duties

Texas v. Johnson

Johnson was convicted of flag desecration for burning the flag rather than for uttering insulting words. This fact somewhat complicates our consideration of his conviction under the First Amendment.... We must first determine whether Johnson's burning of the flag constituted expressive conduct, permitting him to invoke the First Amendment in challenging his conviction.... If his conduct was expressive, we next decide whether the State's regulation is related to the suppression of free expression.... If the State's regulation is not related to expression, then the less stringent standard we announced in *United States v. O'Brien* for regulations of noncommunicative conduct controls.... If it is, then we are outside of *O'Brien* 's test, and we must ask whether this interest justifies Johnson's conviction under a more demanding standard....

The First Amendment literally forbids the abridgment only of "speech," but we have long recognized that its protection does not end at the spoken or written word. While we have rejected "the view that an apparently limitless variety of conduct can be labeled 'speech' whenever the person engaging in the conduct intends thereby to express an idea," ... we have acknowledged that conduct may be "sufficiently imbued with elements of communication to fall within the scope of the First and Fourteenth Amendments."...

In deciding whether particular conduct possesses sufficient communicative elements to bring the First Amendment into play, we have asked whether "[a]n intent to convey a particularized message was present, and [whether] the likelihood was great that the message would be understood by those who viewed it."...

Especially pertinent to this case are our decisions recognizing the communicative nature of conduct relating to flags.... That we have had little difficulty identifying an expressive element in conduct relating to flags should not be surprising. The very purpose of a national flag is to serve as a symbol of our country; it is, one might say, "the one visible manifestation of two hundred years of nationhood."... Pregnant with expressive content, the flag as readily signifies this Nation as does the combination of letters found in "America."

We have not automatically concluded, however, that any action taken with respect to our flag is expressive. Instead, in characterizing such action for First Amendment purposes, we have considered the context in which it occurred.... The State of Texas conceded for purposes of its oral argument in this case that Johnson's conduct was expressive conduct.... Johnson burned an American flag as part—indeed, as the culmination—of a political demonstration that coincided with the convening of the Republican Party and its renomination of Ronald Reagan for President. The expressive, overtly political nature of this conduct was both intentional and overwhelmingly apparent. At his trial, Johnson explained his reasons for burning the flag as follows: "The American Flag was burned as Ronald Reagan was being renominated as President. And a more powerful statement of symbolic speech, whether you agree with it or not, couldn't have been made at that time. It's quite a just position [juxtaposition]. We had new patriotism and no patriotism."... In these circumstances, Johnson's burning of the flag was conduct "sufficiently imbued with elements of communication" ... to implicate the First Amendment.

The government generally has a freer hand in restricting expressive conduct than it has in restricting the written or spoken word.... It may not, however, proscribe particular conduct because it has expressive elements.... It is, in short, not simply the verbal or nonverbal nature of the expression, but the governmental interest at stake, that helps to determine whether a restriction on that expression is valid.

Thus, although we have recognized that where "'speech' and 'nonspeech' elements are combined in the same course of conduct, a sufficiently important governmental interest in regulating the nonspeech element can justify incidental limitations on First Amendment freedoms,"... we have limited the applicability of *O'Brien* 's relatively lenient standard to those cases in which "the governmental interest is unrelated to the suppression of free expression."

In order to decide whether *O'Brien* 's test applies here, therefore, we must decide whether Texas has asserted an interest in support of Johnson's conviction that is unrelated to the suppression of expression. If we find that an interest asserted by the State

is simply not implicated on the facts before us, we need not ask whether *O'Brien* 's test applies.... The State offers two separate interests to justify this conviction: preventing breaches of the peace and preserving the flag as a symbol of nationhood and national unity. We hold that the first interest is not implicated on this record and that the second is related to the suppression of expression.... The only evidence offered by the State at trial to show the reaction to Johnson's actions was the testimony of several persons who had been seriously offended by the flag burning.

The State's position, therefore, amounts to a claim that an audience that takes serious offense at particular expression is necessarily likely to disturb the peace and that the expression may be prohibited on this basis. Our precedents do not countenance such a presumption. On the contrary, they recognize that a principal "function of free speech under our system of government is to invite dispute. It may indeed best serve its high purpose when it induces a condition of unrest, creates dissatisfaction with conditions as they are, or even stirs people to anger."... Thus, we have not permitted the government to assume that every expression of a provocative idea will incite a riot, but have instead required careful consideration of the actual circumstances surrounding such expression, asking whether the expression "is directed to inciting or producing imminent lawless action and is likely to incite or produce such action."...

The State also asserts an interest in preserving the flag as a symbol of nationhood and national unity. In *Spence,* we acknowledged that the government's interest in preserving the flag's special symbolic value "is directly related to expression in the context of activity."... We are equally persuaded that this interest is related to expression in the case of Johnson's burning of the flag. The State, apparently, is concerned that such conduct will lead people to believe either that the flag does not stand for nationhood and national unity, but instead reflects other, less positive concepts, or that the concepts reflected in the flag do not in fact exist, that is, that we do not enjoy unity as a Nation. These concerns blossom only when a person's treatment of the flag communicates some message, and thus are related "to the suppression of free expression" within the meaning of *O'Brien* . We are thus outside of *O'Brien* 's test altogether.

It remains to consider whether the State's interest in preserving the flag as a symbol of nationhood and national unity justifies Johnson's conviction.

As in *Spence,* "[w]e are confronted with a case of prosecution for the expression of an idea through activity," and "[a]ccordingly, we must examine with particular care the interests . . . advanced by [petitioner] to support its prosecution."... Johnson was not, we add, prosecuted for the expression of just any idea; he was prosecuted for his expression of dissatisfaction with the policies of this country, expression situated at the core of our First Amendment values....

Whether Johnson's treatment of the flag violated Texas law thus depended on the likely communicative impact of his expressive conduct.... Johnson's political expression was restricted because of the content of the message he conveyed....

If there is a bedrock principle underlying the First Amendment, it is that the government may not prohibit the expression of an idea simply because society finds the idea itself offensive or disagreeable....

We have not recognized an exception to this principle even where our flag has been involved.... Nothing in our precedents suggests that a State may foster its own view of the flag by prohibiting expressive conduct relating to it. To bring its argument outside our ... precedents, Texas attempts to convince us that even if its interest in preserving the flag's symbolic role does not allow it to prohibit words or some expressive conduct critical of the flag, it does permit it to forbid the outright destruction of the flag. The State's argument cannot depend here on the distinction between written or spoken words and nonverbal conduct. That distinction, we have shown, is of no moment where the nonverbal conduct is expressive, as it is here, and where the regulation of that conduct is related to expression, as it is here....

Texas' focus on the precise nature of Johnson's expression, moreover, misses the point of our prior decisions: their enduring lesson, that the government may not prohibit expression simply because it disagrees with its message, is not dependent on the particular mode in which one chooses to express an idea. If we were to hold that a State may forbid flag burning wherever it is likely to endanger the flag's symbolic role, but allow it wherever burning a flag promotes that role—as where, for example, a person ceremoniously burns a dirty flag—we would be saying that when it comes to impairing the flag's physical integrity, the flag itself may be used as ... a symbol—as a substitute for the written or spoken word or a "short cut from mind to mind"—only in one direction. We would be permitting a State to "prescribe what shall be orthodox" by saying that one may burn the flag to convey one's attitude toward it and its referents only if one does not endanger the flag's representation of nationhood and national unity.

We never before have held that the Government may ensure that a symbol be used to express only one view of that symbol or its referents.... To conclude that the government may permit designated symbols to be used to communicate only a limited set of messages would be to enter territory having no discernible or defensible boundaries. Could the government, on this theory, prohibit the burning of state flags? Of copies of the Presidential seal? Of the Constitution? In evaluating these choices under the First Amendment, how would we decide which symbols were sufficiently special to warrant this unique status? To do so, we would be forced to consult our own political preferences, and impose them on the citizenry, in the very way that the First Amendment forbids us to do....

There is, moreover, no indication—either in the text of the Constitution or in our cases interpreting it—that a separate juridical category exists for the American flag alone.

Document Text

Indeed, we would not be surprised to learn that the persons … who framed our Constitution and wrote the Amendment that we now construe were not known for their reverence for the Union Jack. The First Amendment does not guarantee that other concepts virtually sacred to our Nation as a whole—such as the principle that discrimination on the basis of race is odious and destructive—will go unquestioned in the marketplace of ideas.… We decline, therefore, to create for the flag an exception to the joust of principles protected by the First Amendment.

It is not the State's ends, but its means, to which we object. It cannot be gainsaid that there is a special place reserved for the flag in this Nation, and thus we do not doubt that the government has a legitimate interest in making efforts to "preserv[e] the national flag as an unalloyed symbol of our country."… We reject the suggestion, urged at oral argument by counsel for Johnson, that the government lacks "any state interest whatsoever" in regulating the manner in which the flag may be displayed.… To say that the government has an interest in encouraging proper treatment of the flag, however, is not to say that it may criminally punish a person for burning a flag as a means of political protest.…

We are fortified in today's conclusion by our conviction that forbidding criminal punishment for conduct such as Johnson's will not endanger the special role played by our flag or the feelings it inspires. To paraphrase Justice Holmes, we submit that nobody can suppose that this one gesture of an unknown man will change our Nation's attitude towards its flag.… We are tempted to say, in fact, that the flag's deservedly cherished place in our community will be strengthened, not weakened, by our holding today. Our decision is a reaffirmation of the principles of freedom and inclusiveness that the flag best reflects, and of the conviction that our toleration of criticism such as Johnson's is a sign and source of our strength. Indeed, one of the proudest images of our flag, the one immortalized in our own national anthem, is of the bombardment it survived at Fort McHenry. It is the Nation's resilience, not its rigidity, that Texas sees reflected in the flag—and it is that resilience that we reassert today.

The way to preserve the flag's special role is not to punish those who feel differently about these matters. It is to persuade them that they are wrong.… And, precisely because it is our flag that is involved, one's response to the flag … burner may exploit the uniquely persuasive power of the flag itself. We can imagine no more appropriate response to burning a flag than waving one's own, no better way to counter a flag burner's message than by saluting the flag that burns, no surer means of preserving the dignity even of the flag that burned than by—as one witness here did—according its remains a respectful burial. We do not consecrate the flag by punishing its desecration, for in doing so we dilute the freedom that this cherished emblem represents.

Johnson was convicted for engaging in expressive conduct. The State's interest in preventing breaches of the peace does not support his conviction because Johnson's conduct did not threaten to disturb the peace. Nor does the State's interest in preserving the flag as a symbol of nationhood and national unity justify his criminal conviction for engaging in political expression.

Glossary

desecration: an act of showing disrespect toward an object normally accorded a much higher degree of respect

expressive conduct: actions intended to illustrate a point rather than as an end in themselves

Fort McHenry: a Baltimore military facility where British and American ships fought a naval battle in September 1814, inspiring Francis Scott Key, who observed it firsthand, to write "The Star-Spangled Banner"

gainsaid: denied

implicated on: dependant on

joust of principles: a battle between competing ideas

Glossary

juridical:	relating to the law
moment:	importance or significance
noncommunicative conduct:	conduct that does not serve to express a political meaning
pregnant with expressive content:	filled with symbolic meaning
proscribe:	prohibit
referents:	those things to which a symbol refers

On November 30, 1993, Justice Brennan was presented with the Presidential Medal of Freedom by President Bill Clinton

William Jennings Bryan, 1902

William Jennings Bryan: Original Analysis

Congressman, Secretary of State, and U.S. Presidential Candidate

1860–1925

Overview

William Jennings Bryan was born in Salem, Illinois, in 1860. He graduated at the top of his class in 1883 from Illinois College and earned a law degree from Union College of Law in Chicago two years later. In 1890 he won a surprising victory in a congressional election and became the first Democratic congressional representative in Nebraska history. He served two terms in the House of Representatives by exploiting an alliance with Nebraska Populists and many of their proposals, including tariff reform, a graduated income tax, and, eventually, free silver. His 1892 speech on the tariff in the House of Representatives is an early, though excellent, example of his rhetorical attempt to appeal to rural voters and common folk in economic distress. In 1894 he campaigned actively for the U.S. Senate, but the members of the Republican-dominated Nebraska state legislature chose a candidate from their own ranks despite Bryan's obvious popularity. Not surprisingly, he remained an impassioned supporter of direct election of U.S. senators until the ratification of the Seventeenth Amendment made it the law.

Although Bryan never held elective office again, he ran unsuccessfully as the Democratic nominee for the presidency three times: 1896, 1900, and 1908. The most celebrated and competitive of those candidacies was that of 1896, when he was the nominee of both the Democratic Party and the insurgent Populists (People's Party), who regarded Bryan's endorsement of free silver, a graduated income tax, and tariff reform as an adequate, though somewhat restrained, version of their own views. His "cross of gold" speech from the 1896 Democratic National Convention highlights all three of these issues and their importance to Bryan's political career.

Bryan revolutionized presidential campaigning by being among the first candidates to actively pursue voters through personal appearances at hundreds of rallies. His campaigns were, however, woefully underfunded, and he was seldom able to attract widespread support outside the West and the South. Among his contemporaries, his only peer in campaign style was Theodore Roosevelt, whose personal charisma and oratorical skill rivaled those of the "Great Commoner," as Bryan was widely known. But he also had a vast network of personal relationships, which he had formed as a wildly popular lecturer and through his magazine, the *Commoner*.

Bryan was instrumental in changing the nature and appeal of the Democratic Party. Perhaps second only to Franklin D. Roosevelt, Bryan was responsible for repackaging the Democrats as the party of the people instead of the party of urban bosses, eastern business conservatives, and unregenerate southern rebels. Bryan was a master at translating rather complicated economic issues, like free silver and tariff reform, into simplistic slogans and shibboleths with which common people could identify. He was also the most popular spokesperson for a stronger and more intrusive national government dedicated to solving the economic problems of ordinary citizens. Occasionally his politics flirted with agrarian radicalism, as when he championed government ownership of railroads, an issue close to the heart of many farmers, who were convinced that railroad freight rates blatantly discriminated against small shippers. Usually, however, he had a knack for staying close enough to mainstream sentiment to protect his reputation as a simple man of the people. Even after his failed political campaigns, Bryan used his enormous personal popularity to influence the content of Democratic platforms as a persuasive member of the party's platform committee for many years.

Bryan spent the last decade of his life on the fringes of party politics but at the center of controversial social issues like Prohibition and women's suffrage—both of which he supported—and the teaching of evolution in public schools, which he adamantly opposed. Creationism was his last great crusade, which was best symbolized by his 1925 participation in the prosecution of John T. Scopes, who was accused of breaking the Tennessee law against teaching evolutionary theory in public schools. Although Bryan's performance at the Scopes trial is often cited as evidence of closed-minded religious fundamentalism, his rhetorical style of championing ordinary citizens from the heartland against outsiders was remarkably consistent with his lifelong defense of the common man.

Explanation and Analysis of Documents

William Jennings Bryan was at the peak of his political career during a time when industrialization threatened to drive a permanent wedge between the most affluent and poorest elements of American society. Bryan was certainly

not the first politician to argue that an unregulated economy was a threat to traditional virtue and social stability, but he was clearly among the most popular to do so. Despite the fact that Bryan served only four years in elective office and lost three major presidential campaigns, he was critical to the debate about the direction of American national politics and that of his own party. Part of his influence derived from his impressive career as a public speaker for more than twenty years and from his editorial writings, which found their way into thousands of homes via his own magazine, the *Commoner*, and other popular journals. Indeed, from the middle of the 1890s until his death, Bryan supported himself, his family, and his political career largely through a steady income generated from speaking and writing to mass audiences. Three documents, all public speeches, illustrate the style, content, and appeal of Bryan's political and social rhetoric: his 1892 speech in Congress supporting tariff reform, his sensational 1896 "cross of gold" oration advocating free silver to the Democratic National Convention, and his famous remarks against the teaching of evolution at the trial of John T. Scopes in Dayton, Tennessee, in 1925.

♦ Speech to Congress on Tariff Reform

Twenty-first-century Americans have had only limited exposure to the issue of protectionism and tariff reform, principally through the debates surrounding the North American Free Trade Agreement, but the issue a hundred years or so ago was framed in different language and sometimes with considerably more passion. Originally designed to "protect" American manufactured goods against European competition by taxing imports, high tariff rates came under increasing criticism in the late nineteenth century from those who argued that most domestic industries were strong enough to survive on their own. Bryan capitalized on the long-standing suspicion among farmers, workers, and small businessmen that the tariff discriminated against the masses by forcing them to pay artificially high prices for manufactured products. He made the tariff a central issue in all of his political campaigns by insisting that high tariff rates amounted to an unnecessary subsidy for big business at the expense of ordinary citizens. In doing so, he frequently framed the issue as a battle against elite eastern industrial interests who placed their own economic self-interest above the interests of the common people of the heartland. His opponents, both Republicans and conservative Democrats, argued that tariffs actually promoted economic growth, which helped enrich the entire economy.

His detractors were quick to complain that although Bryan was an eloquent speaker, he had very little real understanding of economics. In short, they argued that his style bordered on demagoguery fed by widespread ignorance. Tariff reform remained a staple in Bryan's arsenal in the war on industrialists for almost two decades. In this speech, given during his first term in Congress, he demonstrates his skill at making his case that a high protective tariff—protectionism, he called it—was a threat to economic opportunity and even a potential danger to core American values.

Time Line

1860	March 19	■ William Jennings Bryan is born in Salem, Illinois.
1883		■ Bryan graduates from Illinois College at the top of his class.
1885		■ Bryan finishes Union College of Law in Chicago, Illinois.
1887		■ Bryan begins a law practice in Lincoln, Nebraska.
1890		■ Bryan is elected to Congress as a Democrat from Nebraska.
1892	March 16	■ Bryan gives his first major speech against high protective tariffs on the floor of Congress.
	November	■ Bryan is reelected to Congress for a second term.
1896	July 9	■ Bryan delivers his famous "cross of gold" speech at the Democratic National Convention and is nominated for president on the fifth ballot.
	November	■ Bryan loses the general election to William McKinley.
1898		■ Bryan accepts a commission as a colonel in the Third Nebraska Infantry in the Spanish-American War, but neither he nor his unit ever sees battlefield action.
1900	May	■ The Populists nominate Bryan for president.
	July 4–6	■ At the Democratic National Convention, the party nominates Bryan for the presidency.
	November	■ Bryan loses the presidential election by a wider margin than his relatively close defeat in 1896.
1901		■ Bryan launches his widely distributed magazine, the *Commoner*, which eventually reaches tens of thousands of homes.

Time Line

1908		■ Bryan accepts his party's nomination for president for the third time.
	November	■ Bryan is defeated by William Howard Taft for the presidency.
1912		■ Bryan swings his support to Woodrow Wilson for the Democratic nomination and campaigns vigorously for Wilson in the general election.
1913		■ Wilson appoints Bryan as secretary of state.
1915		■ Bryan resigns as secretary of state.
1920		■ Bryan declines an offer from the Prohibition Party to be its candidate for president.
1924		■ Bryan is instrumental in writing the Democratic platform at the party's convention and plays a formative role in rejecting a proposed resolution to condemn the Ku Klux Klan; he campaigns for the Democratic ticket, which includes his brother as the vice presidential nominee.
1925	July	■ Bryan and his son assist the prosecution in the case against John Scopes in Dayton, Tennessee.
	July 26	■ Bryan dies in Dayton two days after the Scopes trial adjourns.

The original speech was three hours long and in printed form fills almost eighty pages, much of which is occupied with statistical evidence, but its most memorable lines are those with which he concluded his remarks, a notable characteristic of his oratory.

In this speech, Bryan attacks pro-tariff Republicans for claiming to protect infant industries from competition, but, in fact, they ignore the most infant and vulnerable industry of all, the American family. So, in a speech that begins as a statistical tour de force, Bryan reduces the argument to a single point, stating that a high protective tariff that raises prices on consumer goods is antithetical to home life. Thus, a young married couple cannot afford the basic necessities: furniture, kitchenware, rugs, even the lumber and paint from which they hope to build their first house. Quite literally, he argues, greedy industrialists and their congressional lackeys (in the Republican Party) are laying siege to the homes of America, by attempting to price them out of existence.

Part of Bryan's unstated message is also that homes, particularly those in the rural hinterlands, are economic units—a kind of business too—and are just as deserving of protection as wealthy industrialists. It is important to know that Bryan is borrowing the term *home market* from the protectionist vocabulary. In fact, one of the most effective protectionist lobbying groups was the Home Market Club. Bryan's solution to this threat to American values is to support the Democratic Party's tariff reduction plan, which warns protectionists to "let that home industry live." His conclusion foreshadows a theme of egalitarianism that he used to great advantage in some of his most famous oratory, including the magnificent "cross of gold" speech four years later. His final lines had his colleagues in the House on their feet when he intoned that someday "Congress will meet here to pass laws for the benefit of all the people" and "Democracy will be king! Long live the king!"

Bryan was still in his first term (and barely thirty years old) when he gave these remarks, and although he had managed to wangle a seat on the powerful Ways and Means Committee, he was not yet a force in his party or in Congress. But this speech served notice that his oratorical skills were prodigious. Like-minded Democrats hailed the speech as brilliant, and even a few Republicans grudgingly acknowledged that Bryan was an impressive—albeit wildly partisan—performer; one even admitted that it was the best speech on the tariff issue that he had ever heard. Conservative members of his own party were less effusive, but virtually everyone, even casual observers in the House gallery, sensed that he had revived and recast the tariff controversy in compelling ways.

♦ "Cross of Gold" Speech

The "cross of gold" speech is legendary in American politics and is often cited as the most famous piece of political oratory in U.S. history. Bryan first delivered these remarks at the Democratic National Convention in Chicago in 1896 but gave several versions of it later; there even exists a commercially recorded copy made more than twenty years after the fact. By 1896 Bryan had been a supporter of free silver for several years. In Nebraska he had a close working alliance with the Populist Party and even supported their 1892 presidential nominee and silverite James B. Weaver. Bryan had several major speeches on the House floor—one of over three hours' duration—on free silver to his credit, so that by the time of the convention he had honed his text to a fine point, and he had succeeded in making the complexities of an inflated currency seem understandable. As he saw it, basing the national currency on silver as well as gold would have the effect of cheapening an expensive and inflexible money supply, which would, among other things, make

debts easier to repay. Free silver would also, he thought, provide the kind of managed inflation that would stimulate economic growth. The widespread economic depression of 1893 doubtless added a sense of urgency to his case and clearly made free silver more popular. By the time of the Democratic Convention, in fact, the arcane details of free silver were less important to most than its symbolic promise of assisting the downtrodden.

Although this speech is mostly about free silver, Bryan also touches on two other issues that were central to his political career. One of those was the graduated income tax, which would fall heaviest on those with high incomes and lightest on those with low incomes. In his view, the income tax would help redistribute wealth by demanding that the rich pay their fair share and help reverse the effects of the protective tariff on the struggling masses. Congress had actually enacted a version of the income tax, but the Supreme Court had struck it down in a recent decision, a fact to which he refers here. The other issue to which Bryan gives lip service in this speech is tariff reform, an issue that had served him well in Congress and would continue to be part of his political agenda during this campaign and even those of 1900 and 1908. But, as he makes clear, free silver had now surpassed both these issues for primacy in his struggle for economic opportunity. It is also significant that Bryan was speaking as a member of the platform committee of the Democratic Party in an effort to convince the assembled delegates that free silver ought to be the centerpiece of the party's platform. At this moment Bryan was as conscious of defeating the opponents of free silver in his own party as he was of campaigning against Republicans in the general election.

Barely of constitutional age (thirty-five) to be a presidential candidate, Bryan was not at this point in the convention an announced candidate for the nomination, although he was working hard behind the scenes to promote his career. He understood clearly that this speech at this particular moment had the potential to propel him to national attention. He begins by reviewing the history of the free silver movement in the party, which he asserts had its origin only a year earlier. In fact, however, the silver Democrats had been agitating for years against the more conservative, pro-gold, and largely eastern urban and mercantile branch of the party. Bryan's statement that "old leaders have been cast aside" is a clear allusion to the fact that the Democrats were sharply divided on the money question and that in part the struggle was over which faction would control the party's future. In vintage rhetoric, Bryan casts the issue as a moral struggle of the common citizen against wealthy interests. Free silver, as Bryan pictured it, was more than an economic issue. It was a way of life under siege. In the second-most-quoted passage of the speech, he returns to his agrarian theme that family farms were at the heart of American culture: "But destroy our farms and the grass will grow in the streets of every city in the country." The concluding words of the speech, cloaked in Christian symbolism and rhythmic intonation, are among the most quoted in modern history: "You shall not crucify mankind upon a cross of gold."

Bryan's speech was twenty minutes long, short by his standards. But the convention exploded in response. Both shouts of joy and tears were everywhere, and the demonstration that followed was unprecedented. Contrary to myth, however, the "cross of gold" speech did not deliver the nomination to Bryan immediately. His followers were ecstatic; no one had ever articulated their case for free silver as eloquently, and no one would do so ever again. Nevertheless, on the first nominating ballot the next day, Bryan was fully a hundred votes behind the leader, Richard Bland of Missouri. But as favorite sons began to drop out of the race on the second ballot, Bryan closed in on Bland's lead. By the fifth canvass, Bryan had not only overtaken the Missourian but also had secured enough delegates to clinch the nomination. He was, at thirty-six, the youngest nominee of a major party in the country's history.

♦ Speech at the Scopes Trial

Historians have not been altogether sympathetic with Bryan's late career. Although most admit that Bryan was an important contributor to national politics at the turn of the century, they are less impressed with his work after he left active politics in 1915. Increasingly out of touch with mainstream issues, Bryan appeared to take more interest in conservative evangelical causes like Prohibition and creationism. In fact, in many ways he seemed to be a self-appointed lay minister who tried to hold the line against godless modernism in the name of evangelical Protestantism. While there is some evidence to support this interpretation, it should be pointed out that it was in this period that Bryan also championed women's suffrage and even a primitive form of gender equality. He continued to support government regulation of railroads, and he embraced publicly financed political campaigns and opposed the death penalty, issues that some thought brought him close to political radicalism. But he was best known at the end of his life for his opposition to the teaching of evolution in public schools. The trial of John T. Scopes in 1925 for violating a newly enacted Tennessee law that made it illegal to teach evolution gave Bryan an opportunity to articulate his own ideas about creationism.

Bryan was indeed in the twilight of his influence by 1925. His health was failing (he suffered from advanced diabetes), and he had not practiced law in almost three decades. The trial itself was a publicity stunt that local businessmen hoped would put their town of Dayton, Tennessee, on the map. A local coach and substitute teacher, John T. Scopes, agreed to be the defendant in a trial that would test the legality of a Tennessee statute that made it a crime to teach evolution in the public schools. The Dayton boosters succeeded beyond their wildest dreams. Reporters descended on the hamlet in droves, and at least part of the trial was broadcast on the radio. Bryan's role in the

proceedings was that of an orator rather than a prosecutor. He called no witnesses, nor did he cross-examine any. He planned to give two speeches to the court, one on the fifth day and a summation on the last day of the trial. Bryan gave only the first, although he hoped to polish the second for public distribution. He died in Dayton two days after the trial, while in the midst of revising his second speech. His other appearance in the Dayton courtroom was as a witness on the infallibility of the Bible in a famous and sometimes embarrassing exchange with the skillful and notorious defense attorney Clarence Darrow.

Bryan's hope was that these remarks to the judge and jury—though clearly he had in mind a much larger audience—would win the battle for public opinion. Ironically, there was no need to convince the jury, because both defense and prosecution agreed that Scopes was guilty of violating Tennessee's 1925 anti-evolution law by teaching Darwinian theory in his biology class. Bryan had plenty of admirers in the audience and even more in Dayton and beyond, but his courtroom opponents—including Clarence Darrow—were among the most formidable that he had ever faced.

Bryan begins his summation by admitting that he has so far been silent in the courtroom. He points out that he is moved in this instance to speak because "the question involved is not confined to local questions, but is the broadest that will possibly arise." For this reason, he says, "I have felt justified in submitting my views on the case for the consideration of the court." For Bryan, the notion that outsiders could tamper with local decisions is at odds with both democratic practice and theory. The minority, he concludes, should not override the will of the majority. In his younger days, Bryan had attacked the distant and usually urban economic experts who had argued for high tariffs and the gold standard against the common people of the hinterlands, and here in the Scopes trial he calls on the same kind of language: "We do not need any experts in science," he roars. "Every member of the jury is as good an expert on the Bible." Bryan even introduced Scopes's biology textbook into evidence as proof that the experts were not in touch with the reality of local affairs or even with common sense. Evolution, he kept reminding the court, was no more than a theory expounded by those hell-bent on weaning the culture away from Christian principles.

Bryan was perilously close to engaging in pure demagoguery in his assault on outside experts, especially since he was one himself. It was a rhetorical tactic that had worked for him many times before, and his remarks were interrupted with a fair number voicing "Amen." His conclusion that taxpayers ought to be allowed to control what is taught in the schools they helped finance met with great applause. What is substantively different in his oratory at the Scopes trial, however, is his defense of a literal reading of the Bible as revealed truth and his contention that evolutionary theory is incompatible with Christianity, a position that could have made more moderate Protestants uneasy. Doubtless many agreed with Bryan on this point, but it left him open to the argument that not every Christian embraced a literal interpretation of the Bible, an issue that the prosecution exploited in its rebuttal.

Largely because of this kind of rhetoric, many see Bryan's last years as verging on bigotry and intolerance. By the time of this speech, of course, Bryan had been giving talks for several days in Dayton, some of them in local churches where the trial jurors and even the judge were sometimes in attendance. In short, he had already prepared his courtroom audience for much of what he had to say on the record; his hope was to influence a much larger audience through media coverage of the proceedings. The most dramatic moments were not all his, however. The defense's response to this speech—given by a former Bryan staffer at the State Department—was probably the most brilliant oration of the trial and was also greeted with great applause, perhaps even greater than that given to Bryan. Then, too, there was Clarence Darrow's devastating examination, which exposed the shallowness of Bryan's literalist Christian views and did as much as anything to discredit his fundamentalism.

Impact and Legacy

William Jennings Bryan was enormously influential in national politics for at least twenty years from the mid-1890s until World War I, and he was arguably significant for almost another decade after that. Despite the fact that he lost three presidential elections, he dictated much of the content of the Democratic Party's platform into the 1920s and in so doing helped transform the party into one that sought to use government authority to regulate great wealth to the betterment of all. To that extent he was among the most progressive politicians of his time. He was, in fact, sometimes labeled a Socialist, even though he was forever loyal to the party of Jefferson and Jackson.

That part of Bryan that is most difficult to understand in the twenty-first century was his devotion to evangelical Protestantism and its potential as an agent of political and social change. He frequently used the vocabulary of religious fervor to advocate causes, and perhaps that rhetorical style has kept many from seeing him as a true progressive reformer. Too, there were sometimes gaps in his vision for equity and fairness, the most obvious of which was his inability to see African Americans as among those most deserving of uplift. Many, both inside and outside the Democratic Party, were also unimpressed by Bryan's intellect, but virtually everyone admired and sometimes feared his ability to move voters to action. To be sure, he could be doctrinaire in his sense of self-righteousness and dogmatic in his devotion to party, but he could also be an effective broker of ideas and strategies when necessary. He was a man of extraordinary energy and dedication in his own time, but he is largely without defenders in ours.

Key Sources

The most extensive collection of Bryan manuscripts is in the Library of Congress in Washington, D.C. The Nebraska and Illinois Historical Societies and Occidental College in California have smaller holdings of Bryan's papers. *The Memoirs of William Jennings Bryan by Himself and His Wife, Mary Baird Bryan* (1925) contains many of Bryan's early speeches. Other speeches appear in his *Speeches of William Jennings Bryan* (1909). Bryan's account of his first presidential campaign is in his *First Battle: A Story of the Campaign of 1896* (1896). The official transcript of the Scopes trial is in *The World's Most Famous Court Trial, Tennessee Evolution Case* (1925).

Essential Quotes

"We cannot afford to destroy the peasantry of this country. We cannot afford to degrade the common people of this land, for they are the people who in time of prosperity and peace produce the wealth of the country, and they are also the people who in time of war bare their breasts to a hostile fire in defense of the flag."

(Speech to Congress on Tariff Reform)

"The day will come, Mr. Chairman, when those who annually gather about this Congress seeking to use the taxing power for private purposes will find their occupation gone, and the members of Congress will meet here to pass laws for the benefit of all the people. That day will come, and in that day, to use the language of another, 'Democracy will be king! Long live the king!'"

(Speech to Congress on Tariff Reform)

"The income tax is a just law. It simply intends to put the burdens of government justly upon the backs of the people. I am in favor of an income tax. When I find a man who is not willing to pay his share of the burden of the government which protects him, I find a man who is unworthy to enjoy the blessings of a government like ours."

("Cross of Gold" Speech)

Essential Quotes

"There are two ideas of government. There are those who believe that if you just legislate to make the well-to-do prosperous, that their prosperity will leak through on those below. The Democratic idea has been that if you legislate to make the masses prosperous their prosperity will find its way up and through every class that rests upon it."

("Cross of Gold" Speech)

"Having behind us the commercial interests and the laboring interests and all the toiling masses, we shall answer their demands for a gold standard by saying to them, you shall not press down upon the brow of labor this crown of thorns. You shall not crucify mankind upon a cross of gold."

("Cross of Gold" Speech)

"No, my friends, no court of the law, and no jury, great or small, is going destroy the issue between the believer and the unbeliever. The Bible is the Word of God; the Bible is the only expression of man's hope of salvation."

(Speech at the Scopes Trial)

Further Reading

Books

Coletta, Paolo E. *William Jennings Bryan*. 3 vols. Lincoln: University of Nebraska Press, 1964–1969.

Glad, Paul. *The Trumpet Soundeth: William Jennings Bryan and His Democracy, 1896–1912*. Lincoln: University of Nebraska Press, 1960.

Kazin, Michael. *A Godly Hero: The Life of William Jennings Bryan*. New York: Knopf, 2006.

Koenig, Louis W. *Bryan: A Political Biography of William Jennings Bryan*. New York: Putnam, 1971.

Levine, Lawrence W. *Defender of the Faith: William Jennings Bryan: The Last Decade, 1915–1925*. Cambridge, Mass.: Harvard University Press, 1987.

Web Sites

"1896: The Grand Realignment." University of Virginia Institute for Advanced Technology in the Humanities Web site. http://www.iath.virginia.edu/seminar/unit8/home.htm.

"William Jennings Bryan (1860–1925)." University of Missouri, Kansas City, Law School Web site. http://www.law.umkc.edu/faculty/projects/ftrials/scopes/bryanw.htm.

—*Charles Orson Cook*

Questions for Further Study

1. A number of issues that dominated Bryan's career remain relevant in present times—for instance, the questions surrounding free trade, protectionism, and tariffs addressed in his speech on tariff reform. How are debates over international trade in the late twentieth and early twenty-first centuries similar to those in the late nineteenth century? How are they different? Consider the North American Free Trade Agreement under President Clinton. Note the fact that Bryan and many other Democrats favored free trade, whereas Republicans tended to be protectionist; a century later, the sides had reversed.

2. In his speech on tariffs Bryan notes that trade protectionism hurts working people because it increases prices. Similar arguments have been raised with regard to international trade in the early twenty-first century, but the problem has become more complicated. Thanks to increasingly open global trade, consumers can purchase goods produced overseas (most notably in China) for much less than comparable items would cost if they were produced in America, yet the low price of goods produced overseas has brought about a sharp decline in American industry, with a corresponding loss of jobs and wages. Is the trade-off worth it? Take a position for or against free trade, using Bryan's speech to Congress as a reference point.

3. Although many of the problems that concerned Bryan are familiar to us today, the debate over bimetallism seems little more than a historical curiosity. Nevertheless, in his time it was the hottest of political topics, and Bryan, as a leader of the "free silver" movement, was a key player in the debate. Indeed, his "cross of gold" speech is among the most important pieces of political oratory in U.S. history. Discuss the issues leading up to his speech, including the "free silver" movement, bimetallism, and the gold standard. Contrast his views with those of his fellow Democrat Grover Cleveland, paying special attention to the role the Sherman Silver Act and the resulting drop in silver prices played in bringing on the financial crisis of 1893.

4. Near the end of his life, Bryan again became embroiled in a major debate when he joined the prosecution in the Scopes "monkey" trial. At issue was the question of whether scientific evolution could be taught to students in a community whose taxpayers overwhelmingly opposed evolutionary teaching in favor of the biblical Creation story. Evaluate the arguments on either side, taking into consideration several key issues. For example, does religion have a place in public education? Do the members of a community, as taxpayers, have a right to determine what should and should not be taught? Is the teaching of evolution, a theory overwhelmingly accepted by scientists, comparable to other teachings that might offend religiously based morals—for example, sex education?

5. To some political observers, there is an inconsistency between Bryan's early career and his later work, most notably his role in the Scopes trial. According to this view, the man who started his career as a left-wing progressive advocating the rights of the working class ultimately became a conservative reactionary. It can also be argued that there is a common theme to his apparently varying political positions: that Bryan remained a "man of the people," regardless of the labels that might be attached to his actions. Evaluate Bryan's stance on tariffs, bimetallism, and the issues raised in the Scopes trial—as well as other topics on which he took a major stand—and discuss whether you think he was consistent.

Speech to Congress on Tariff Reform

1892

When some young man selects a young woman who is willing to trust her future to his strong right arm, and they start to build a little home, that home which is the unit of society and upon which our government and our prosperity must rest—when they start to build this little home, and the man who sells the lumber reaches out his hand to collect a tariff upon that; then the man who sells paint and oil wants a tariff upon them; the man who furnishes the carpets, tablecloths, knives, forks, dishes, furniture, spoons, everything that enters into the construction and operation of that home—when all these hands, I say, are stretched out from every direction to lay their blighting weight upon that cottage, and the Democratic party says "Hands off, and let that home industry live," it is protecting the grandest home industry that this or any other nation ever had.

And I am willing that you, our friends on the other side, shall have what consolation you may from the protection of those "home industries" which have crowned with palatial residences the hills of New England, if you will simply give us the credit of being the champions of the homes of this land. It would seem that if any appeal could find a listening ear in this legislative hall it ought to be the appeal that comes up from those co-tenants of earth's only paradise; but your party has neglected them; more, it has spurned and spit open them. When they asked for bread you gave them a stone, and when they asked for a fish you gave them a serpent. You have laid upon them burdens grievous to be borne. You have filled their days with toil and their nights with anxious care, and when they cried aloud for relief you were deaf to their entreaties....

We have heard from that side of the House twice, I think, recently that "truth is eternally triumphant." That is true; and while the proposition may describe the success of the Democratic party in 1890 and give us encouragement to hope that that success will continue, I want to suggest to our friends over there a quotation that is far more appropriate to describe the condition of the Republican party. It is this: Though justice has leaden feet, it has an iron hand. You rioted in power. You mocked the supplication of the people, you denied their petitions and now you have felt their wrath. At last justice has overtaken you, and now you are suffering the penalty that must sooner or later overtake the betrayer of public trust....

Mr. Clarkson, a high Republican authority, has told us that the young men of the country are becoming Democrats. Why? Because we are right. And when you find where the young men of the country are going, you can rest assured that that party is going to succeed. Why are we right? Because, Mr. Chairman, we are demanding for this people equal and exact justice to every man, woman, and child. We desire that the laws of this country shall not be made, as they have been, to enable some men to get rich while many get poor....

We cannot afford to destroy the peasantry of this country. We cannot afford to degrade the common people of this land, for they are the people who in time of prosperity and peace produce the wealth of the country, and they are also the people who in time of war bare their breasts to a hostile fire in defense of the flag. Go to Arlington or to any of the national cemeteries, see there the plain white monuments which mark the place "where rest the ashes of the nation's countless dead," those of whom the poet has so beautifully written....

On Fame's eternal camping-ground
Their silent tents are spread.

Who were they? Were they the beneficiaries of special legislation? Were they the people who are every clamoring for privileges?... No; the people who fight the battles are largely the poor, the common people of the country; those who have little to save but their honor, and little to lose but their lives. These are the ones, and I say to you, sir, that the country cannot afford to lose them....

That, Mr. Chairman, is a noble sentiment and points the direction to the true policy for a free people.... A free government must find its safety in happy and contented citizens, who, protected in their rights and free from unnecessary burdens, will be willing to die that the blessings which they enjoy may be transmitted to their posterity....

That is the inspiration of the Democratic party; that is its aim and object. If it comes, Mr. Chairman, into power in all the departments of this Government it will not destroy industry; it will not injure labor; but it will save to the men who produce the

Document Text

wealth of the country a larger portion of that wealth. It will bring prosperity and joy and happiness, not to a few, but to everyone without regard to station or condition.... The day will come, Mr. Chairman, when those who annually gather about this Congress seeking to use the taxing power for private purposes will find their occupation gone, and the members of Congress will meet here to pass laws for the benefit of all the people. That day will come, and in that day, to use the language of another, "Democracy will be king! Long live the king!"

Glossary

1890:	the year in which, thanks in large part to the unpopularity of Republican protectionism, Democrats won a three-quarters majority in the House following the elections
blighting:	destroying
co-tenants:	people who live in the same area
earth's only paradise:	America
home industry:	referring both to the work that goes on in homes and to the "home industries" of the United States
Mr. Clarkson:	James S. Clarkson (1842–1918), a major figure in the Republican Party but one who held no elective public office
"On fame's eternal camping ground ...":	a quotation from Theodore O'Hara's "Bivouac of the Dead," portions of which are inscribed on placards at Arlington National Cemetery
our friends on the other side:	Republicans as well as those Democrats who opposed Bryan on the tariff issue
protectionism:	a policy of "protecting" industry in one country by imposing high tariffs on imports, thus removing any competitive price advantage for foreign-made goods
tariff:	a tax on imports

"Cross of Gold" Speech

1896

On the 4th of March, 1895, a few Democrats, most of them members of Congress, issued an address to the Democrats of the nation asserting that the money question was the paramount issue of the hour; asserting also the right of a majority of the Democratic Party to control the position of the party on this paramount issue; concluding with the request that all believers in free coinage of silver in the Democratic Party should organize and take charge of and control the policy of the Democratic Party. Three months later, at Memphis, an organization was perfected, and the silver Democrats went forth openly and boldly and courageously proclaiming their belief and declaring that if successful they would crystallize in a platform the declaration which they had made; and then began the conflict with a zeal approaching the zeal which inspired the crusaders who followed Peter the Hermit. Our silver Democrats went forth from victory unto victory, until they are assembled now, not to discuss, not to debate, but to enter up the judgment rendered by the plain people of this country.

But in this contest, brother has been arrayed against brother, and father against son. The warmest ties of love and acquaintance and association have been disregarded. Old leaders have been cast aside when they refused to give expression to the sentiments of those whom they would lead, and new leaders have sprung up to give direction to this cause of freedom. Thus has the contest been waged, and we have assembled here under as binding and solemn instructions as were ever fastened upon the representatives of a people....

When you come before us and tell us that we shall disturb your business interests, we reply that you have disturbed our business interests by your action. We say to you that you have made too limited in its application the definition of a businessman. The man who is employed for wages is as much a businessman as his employer. The attorney in a country town is as much a businessman as the corporation counsel in a great metropolis. The merchant at the crossroads store is as much a businessman as the merchant of New York. The farmer who goes forth in the morning and toils all day, begins in the spring and toils all summer, and by the application of brain and muscle to the natural resources of this country creates wealth, is as much a businessman as the man who goes upon the Board of Trade and bets upon the price of grain. The miners who go 1,000 feet into the earth or climb 2,000 feet upon the cliffs and bring forth from their hiding places the precious metals to be poured in the channels of trade are as much businessmen as the few financial magnates who in a backroom corner the money of the world.

We come to speak for this broader class of businessmen. Ah. my friends, we say not one word against those who live upon the Atlantic Coast; but those hardy pioneers who braved all the dangers of the wilderness, who have made the desert to blossom as the rose—those pioneers away out there, rearing their children near to nature's heart, where they can mingle their voices with the voices of the birds—out there where they have erected schoolhouses for the education of their children and churches where they praise their Creator, and the cemeteries where sleep the ashes of their dead—are as deserving of the consideration of this party as any people in this country.

It is for these that we speak. We do not come as aggressors. Our war is not a war of conquest. We are fighting in the defense of our homes, our families, and posterity. We have petitioned, and our petitions have been scorned. We have entreated, and our entreaties have been disregarded. We have begged, and they have mocked when our calamity came.

We beg no longer; we entreat no more; we petition no more. We defy them!...

They say we passed an unconstitutional law. I deny it. The income tax was not unconstitutional when it was passed. It was not unconstitutional when it went before the Supreme Court for the first time. It did not become unconstitutional until one judge changed his mind; and we cannot be expected to know when a judge will change his mind.

The income tax is a just law. It simply intends to put the burdens of government justly upon the backs of the people. I am in favor of an income tax. When I find a man who is not willing to pay his share of the burden of the government which protects him, I find a man who is unworthy to enjoy the blessings of a government like ours....

We say in our platform that we believe that the right to coin money and issue money is a function of

government. We believe it. We believe it is a part of sovereignty and can no more with safety be delegated to private individuals than can the power to make penal statutes or levy laws for taxation....

Now, my friends, let me come to the great paramount issue. If they ask us here why it is we say more on the money question than we say upon the tariff question, I reply that if protection has slain its thousands the gold standard has slain its tens of thousands. If they ask us why we did not embody all these things in our platform which we believe, we reply to them that when we have restored the money of the Constitution, all other necessary reforms will be possible, and that until that is done there is no reform that can be accomplished....

We go forth confident that we shall win. Why? Because upon the paramount issue in this campaign there is not a spot of ground upon which the enemy will dare to challenge battle. Why, if they tell us that the gold standard is a good thing, we point to their platform and tell them that their platform pledges the party to get rid of a gold standard and substitute bimetallism. If the gold standard is a good thing, why try to get rid of it? If the gold standard, and I might call your attention to the fact that some of the very people who are in this convention today and who tell you that we ought to declare in favor of international bimetallism and thereby declare that the gold standard is wrong and that the principles of bimetallism are better—these very people four months ago were open and avowed advocates of the gold standard and telling us that we could not legislate two metals together even with all the world....

Here is the line of battle. We care not upon which issue they force the fight. We are prepared to meet them on either issue or on both. If they tell us that the gold standard is the standard of civilization, we reply to them that this, the most enlightened of all nations of the earth, has never declared for a gold standard, and both the parties this year are declaring against it. If the gold standard is the standard of civilization, why, my friends, should we not have it? So if they come to meet us on that, we can present the history of our nation. More than that, we can tell them this, that they will search the pages of history in vain to find a single instance in which the common people of any land ever declared themselves in favor of a gold standard. They can find where the holders of fixed investments have.

Mr. Carlisle said in 1878 that this was a struggle between the idle holders of idle capital and the struggling masses who produce the wealth and pay the taxes of the country; and my friends, it is simply a question that we shall decide upon which side shall the Democratic Party fight. Upon the side of the idle holders of idle capital, or upon the side of the struggling masses? That is the question that the party must answer first; and then it must be answered by each individual hereafter. The sympathies of the Democratic Party, as described by the platform, are on the side of the struggling masses, who have ever been the foundation of the Democratic Party.

There are two ideas of government. There are those who believe that if you just legislate to make the well-to-do prosperous, that their prosperity will leak through on those below. The Democratic idea has been that if you legislate to make the masses prosperous their prosperity will find its way up and through every class that rests upon it.

You come to us and tell us that the great cities are in favor of the gold standard. I tell you that the great cities rest upon these broad and fertile prairies. Burn down your cities and leave our farms, and your cities will spring up again as if by magic. But destroy our farms and the grass will grow in the streets of every city in the country.

My friends, we shall declare that this nation is able to legislate for its own people on every question without waiting for the aid or consent of any other nation on earth, and upon that issue we expect to carry every single state in the Union....

If they dare to come out in the open field and defend the gold standard as a good thing, we shall fight them to the uttermost, having behind us the producing masses of the nation and the world. Having behind us the commercial interests and the laboring interests and all the toiling masses, we shall answer their demands for a gold standard by saying to them, you shall not press down upon the brow of labor this crown of thorns. You shall not crucify mankind upon a cross of gold.

Glossary

avowed:	self-proclaimed
bimetallism:	the idea that the value of the dollar should be based on that of two metals, gold and silver
capital:	wealth that can be used to produce more wealth
Peter the Hermit:	one of the most successful recruiters for the First Crusade (1095–1099)
free coinage of silver:	the right to coin U.S. dollars in silver as well as gold—an economic benefit to western states, where large silver deposits had been discovered
gold standard:	a system in which the value of a nation's currency is tied to that of gold, a principle abandoned by the United States in the early 1930s
magnates:	extremely wealthy and powerful individuals
money question:	the debate regarding whether gold or silver should be used as the basis for the value of the dollar—one of the key political issues in late nineteenth-century America
Mr. Carlisle:	John Griffin Carlisle, one of Bryan's principal rivals within the Democratic Party
protection:	the policy of imposing high tariffs (taxes) on imports so as to "protect" domestic industry by giving it the price advantage over foreign-made goods
slain its thousands …:	a reference to 1 Samuel 18:7 in the Old Testament
sovereignty:	self-rule

Speech at the Scopes Trial

1925

If the court please we are now approaching the end of the first week of this trial and I haven't thought it proper until this time to take part in the discussions that have been dealing with phases of this question, or case, where the state laws and the state rules of practice were under discussion and I feel that those who are versed in the law of the state and who are used to the customs of the court might better take the burden of the case, but today we come to the discussion of a very important part of this case, a question so important that upon its decision will determine the length of this trial. If the court holds, as we believe the court should hold, that the testimony that the defense is now offering is not competent and not proper testimony, then I assume we are near the end of this trial and because the question involved is not confined to local questions, but is the broadest that will possibly arise, I have felt justified in submitting my views on the case for the consideration of the court.…

Mr. Hays says that before he got here he read that I said this was to be a duel to the death, between science—was it? and revealed religion. I don't know who the other duelist was, but I was representing one of them and because of that they went to the trouble and the expense of several thousand dollars to bring down their witnesses.… We do not need any expert to tell us what that law means. An expert cannot be permitted to come in here and try to defeat the enforcement of a law by testifying that it isn't a bad law and it isn't—I mean a bad doctrine—no matter how these people phrase the doctrine—no matter how they eulogize it. This is not the place to try to prove that the law ought never to have been passed.… And, my friends, if the people of Tennessee were to go into a state like New York—the one from which this impulse comes to resist this law, or go into any state—if they went into any state and tried to convince the people that a law they had passed ought not to be enforced, just because the people who went there didn't think it ought to have been passed, don't you think it would be resented as an impertinence?… The people of this state passed this law, the people of this state knew what they were doing when they passed the law, and they knew the dangers of the doctrine—that they did not want it taught to their children, and my friends, it isn't—Your Honor, it isn't proper to bring experts in here to try to defeat the purpose of the people of this state by trying to show that this thing that they denounce and outlaw is a beautiful thing that everybody ought to believe in.… These people want to come here with experts to make Your Honor believe that the law should never have been passed and because in their opinion it ought not to have been passed, it ought not to be enforced. It isn't a place for expert testimony. We have sufficient proof in the book—doesn't the book state the very thing that is objected to, and outlawed in this state? Who has a copy of that book?

The Court—Do you mean the Bible?

Mr. Bryan—No, sir; the biology. (Laughter in the courtroom.)

A Voice—Here it is; Hunter's Biology.

Mr. Bryan—No, not the Bible, you see in this state they cannot teach the Bible. They can only teach things that declare it to be a lie, according to the learned counsel. These people in the state—Christian people—have tied their hands by their constitution. They say we all believe in the Bible for it is the overwhelming belief in the state, but we will not teach that Bible, which we believe even to our children through teachers that we pay with our money. No, no, it isn't the teaching of the Bible, and we are not asking it. The question is can a minority in this state come in and compel a teacher to teach that the Bible is not true and make the parents of these children pay the expenses of the teacher to tell their children what these people believe is false and dangerous? Has it come to a time when the minority can take charge of a state like Tennessee and compel the majority to pay their teachers while they take religion out of the heart of the children of the parents who pay the teachers?…

So, my friends, if that were true, if man and monkey were in the same class, called primates, it would mean they did not come up from the same order. It might mean that instead of one being the ancestor of the other they were all cousins. But it does not mean that they did not come up from the lower animals, if this is the only place they could come from, and the Christian believes man came from above, but the evolutionist believes he must have come from below.…

Document Text

Your Honor, I want to show you that we have evidence enough here, we do not need any experts to come in here and tell us about this thing. Here we have Mr. Hunter. Mr. Hunter is the author of this biology and this is the man who wrote the book Mr. Scopes was teaching. And here we have the diagram....

There is that book! There is the book they were teaching your children that man was a mammal and so indistinguishable among the mammals that they leave him there with thirty-four hundred and ninety-nine other mammals....

He tells the children to copy this, copy this diagram. In the notebook, children are to copy this diagram and take it home in their notebooks. To show their parents that you cannot find man. That is the great game to put in the public schools to find man among animals, if you can.

Tell me that the parents of this day have not any right to declare that children are not to be taught this doctrine? Shall not be taken down from the high plane upon which God put man? Shall be detached from the throne of God and be compelled to link their ancestors with the jungle, tell that to these children? Why, my friend, if they believe it, they go back to scoff at the religion of their parents! And the parents have a right to say that no teacher paid by their money shall rob their children of faith in God and send them back to their homes, skeptical, infidels, or agnostics, or atheists....

Mr. Bryan—Your Honor, we first pointed out that we do not need any experts in science. Here is one plain fact, and the statute defines itself, and it tells the kind of evolution it does not want taught, and the evidence says that this is the kind of evolution that was taught, and no number of scientists could come in here, my friends, and override that statute or take from the jury its right to decide this question, so that all the experts that they could bring would mean nothing. And, when it comes to Bible experts, every member of the jury is as good an expert on the Bible as any man that they could bring, or that we could bring.... We have a book here that shows everything that is needed to make one understand evolution, and to show that the man violated the law. Then why should we prolong this case? We can bring our experts here for the Christians; for every one they can bring who does not believe in Christianity, we can bring more than one who believes in the Bible and rejects evolution, and our witnesses will be just as good experts as theirs on a question of that kind. We could have a thousand or a million witnesses, but this case as to whether evolution is true or not, is not going to be tried here, within this city; if it is carried to the state's courts, it will not be tried there, and if it is taken to the great court at Washington, it will not be tried there. No, my friends, no court or the law, and no jury, great or small, is going to destroy the issue between the believer and the unbeliever. The Bible is the Word of God; the Bible is the only expression of man's hope of salvation.... That Bible is not going to be driven out of this court by experts who come hundreds of miles to testify that they can reconcile evolution, with its ancestor in the jungle, with man made by God in His image, and put here for purposes as a part of the divine plan.... Your court is an office of this state, and we who represent the state as counsel are officers of the state, and we cannot humiliate the great state of Tennessee by admitting for a moment that people can come from anywhere and protest against the enforcement of this state's laws on the ground that it does not conform with their ideas, or because it banishes from our schools a thing that they believe in and think ought to be taught in spite of the protest of those who employ the teacher and pay him his salary.

The facts are simple, the case is plain, and if those gentlemen want to enter upon a larger field of educational work on the subject of evolution, let us get through with this case and then convene a mock court for it will deserve the title of mock court if its purpose is to banish from the hearts of the people the Word of God as revealed.

Glossary

class ... order: terms of biological classification used here more generally to say that humans could not have descended from apes

counsel: legal representative

Glossary

diagram:	an illustration in Hunter's *Civic Biology,* showing in very broad terms what was then known about evolutionary family trees
mock court:	a court whose rulings have no force of law, suggesting that such a court in this instance would be a mockery of justice
Mr. Hays:	Arthur Garfield Hays, an attorney for the defense
Mr. Hunter:	George William Hunter, whose *Civic Biology,* originally published in 1914, was the textbook from which Scopes had taught his classes on evolution
revealed religion:	religions such as Christianity, Judaism, and Islam that involve a direct personal relationship with a god whose nature is "revealed" through scriptures
statute: law	
they cannot find man:	The diagram in Hunter's biology textbook showed mammals as a group but had no special designation for *Homo sapiens* within that group

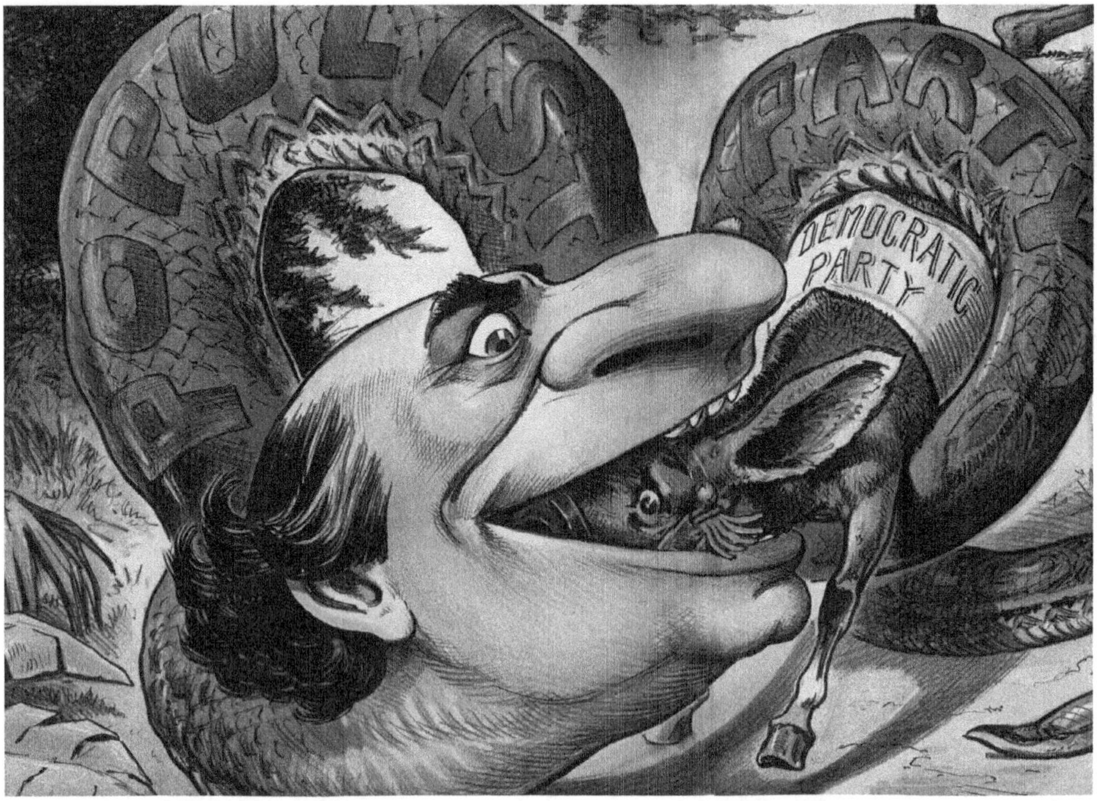

Bryan depicted as a Populist snake swallowing the Democratic Party; 1896 cartoon from the pro-GOP magazine Judge.

James Buchanan (cropped from the original image) **From Brady daguerreotype** (Mathew Brady).

James Buchanan: Original Analysis

Fifteenth President of the United States

Overview

Born in 1791, James Buchanan grew up in rural Pennsylvania. He graduated from Dickinson College in 1809. After moving to Lancaster, Pennsylvania, he studied law and gained admission to the bar in 1812. Two years later he was elected to the state assembly as a Federalist and then won election to the House of Representatives in 1820. During the 1820s he shifted from Federalist to Democratic ranks as an early supporter of Andrew Jackson. After declining to stand for reelection to Congress in 1830, he spent two years as minister to Russia (1832–1834) before returning to the United States to serve in the U.S. Senate for the next eleven years. He soon showed himself a staunch supporter of the South when it came to the defense of slavery's constitutionality, as his January 1836 remarks to Congress suggest. As secretary of state during the administration of James Polk (1845–1849) he oversaw negotiations leading to the settlement of the Oregon question (an agreement over the boundary between the western United States and Canada) and advised the president during the Mexican-American War. He retired to private life in 1849, but he accepted an appointment as minister to England in 1853 during the Franklin Pierce administration. In June 1856 he beat out Pierce and Illinois senator Stephen A. Douglas for the Democratic presidential nomination and defeated Republican John C. Frémont and Know Nothing Millard Fillmore in the fall contest.

In his inaugural address, Buchanan once more urged the nation to accept slavery's constitutionality as the first step to quell agitation of the issue. Two days after he took office, the Supreme Court issued its decision in *Dred Scott v. Sandford*, complete with Chief Justice Roger B. Taney's finding that neither Congress nor territorial governments could bar the expansion of slavery into the territories. Far from settling the issue of slavery in the territories, the Court's decision added more kindling to a fire that had been raging since 1854. When Buchanan backed a proposed constitution for the Kansas Territory framed by proslavery forces meeting at Lecompton, Douglas broke with the administration, claiming that the constitution was the result of fraud. The president went so far as to try to disrupt Douglas's bid for reelection to the Senate in 1858: in turn Douglas blocked Senate passage of the Lecompton proposal, ending slaveholders' bid to have Kansas enter the Union as a slave state.

Republicans achieved significant gains in the congressional elections of 1858, owing in part to Buchanan's efforts to lower the protective tariff and his failure to respond to an economic crisis, the burden of which was especially felt in the North, including Buchanan's own Pennsylvania. In 1859 the sectional crisis escalated anew, most notably when John Brown seized the federal armory at Harpers Ferry, Virginia, as the first step in his attempt to ignite a slave insurrection. Many Deep South Democrats joined advocates of secession in splitting the Democratic Party in 1860, ensuring that Republicans would elect Abraham Lincoln president.

Buchanan opposed secession but doubted that he could do much to prevent it. His last annual message pleaded with both sides to step back from the abyss of disunion and possible war, calling on northerners to cease agitating on the issue of slavery and southerners to abandon secession. Neither side heeded his words. By the time he left office, seven southern states had formed a new Confederate States of America, with several other slaveholding states still deliberating whether they would remain in the Union, join the new republic, or chart some middle course. Retiring to his beloved Wheatland, just outside Lancaster, Buchanan spent the remainder of his life defending his administration.

Explanation and Analysis of Documents

Throughout his career Buchanan argued that the Constitution protected slavery where it existed, and he offered no objection to its expansion. He willingly offered concession after concession to protect white southerners' feelings on this issue. In turn, Democrats found him to be completely trustworthy on the issue, which served to advance his political ambitions. Although they were offered twenty-one years apart, his remarks on efforts to seek the abolition of slavery in the District of Columbia in 1836 found their echo in his inaugural address in 1857. Nearly four years later, as his term drew to a close amid the opening of the secession crisis, he sounded the same themes once more, although now he also argued that secession also violated the Constitution. That same commitment to the document's wording, however, also led him to conclude that as president he could do little to resist secession should it take place.

♦ Remarks to Congress on Slavery

Buchanan had risen through the ranks of the Democratic Party of Pennsylvania, exploiting his early support of Andrew Jackson to gain an appointment as minister to Russia in 1832. Some two years later he was elected to the U.S. Senate and took his seat at the end of 1834. The following year the United States witnessed a wave of violent outbreaks across the country attributed to the agitation of the slavery question by abolitionists. In Washington, D.C., there had been riots on the heels of news that a slave, intoxicated by alcohol and abolitionist propaganda, had attempted to murder his owner, a prominent Washington widow. President Jackson ordered his postmaster general to intercept abolitionist literature sent through the mails; when Congress met that December, its members debated how it should handle the avalanche of abolitionist petitions arriving in Washington, some calling for a complete end to slavery and others urging Congress at least to abolish slavery in the District of Columbia. As newspapers across the nation reprinted congressional proceedings, considering these petitions in open session amounted to giving them free publicity throughout the Republic.

Buchanan addressed the threat posed by the mails campaign in December 1835. He argued that prudent and wise northerners would do whatever was necessary to suppress the circulation of literature that assailed southern sentiments or promised to arouse hostility and inspire violence, including a slave insurrection. For the moment, however, he advised the Senate not to act on any measure to explore the issue by establishing a select committee, lest it draw unwarranted attention to it. Several weeks later, on January 7, 1836, he rose again, this time to respond to a petition entrusted to him by Pennsylvania Quakers, who called for an end to slavery and the slave trade in the District of Columbia.

Buchanan admits that he is at pains to distinguish Quakers from abolitionists, whom he believed were intent upon disrupting southern society and inspiring insurrection. Still, he disagrees with their views. "If any one principle of constitutional law can, at this day, be considered as settled, it is, that Congress has no right, no power, over the question of slavery within those states where it exists," he declares, adding that Congress had recognized that principle back in 1790. Moreover, he adds, "the Union will be dissolved, and incalculable evils will rise from its ashes, the moment any such attempt is seriously made by the free States in Congress." Abolitionists, those "ignorant enthusiasts," promise to incite insurrection; in response, slaveholders would reinforce the bonds of enslavement. To abolish slavery in the District of Columbia would simply establish a place of refuge and encourage such terrible scenes. At the moment he does not reject receiving such petitions, but he wants them referred to a special committee or the Committee on the District of Columbia. He finds the notion of abolishing slavery in the District of Columbia extremely unwise and potentially dangerous, for it would establish a refuge for slaves who sought to escape their owners, especially from Virginia and Maryland, which bordered the District.

Time Line

1791	April 23	■ James Buchanan is born near Mercersburg, Pennsylvania.
1809		■ Buchanan graduates from Dickinson College.
1814		■ Buchanan is elected to the state assembly as a Federalist and serves two terms.
1820		■ Buchanan is elected to the U.S. House of Representatives, serving for five terms.
1832–1834		■ Buchanan serves as minister to Russia.
1834		■ Buchanan is elected to the U.S. Senate, serving until 1845.
1836	January 7	■ Buchanan delivers remarks in Congress on the issue of slavery.
1845		■ Buchanan is named secretary of state in the James Polk administration.
1853		■ Buchanan is appointed minister to England.
1856		■ Buchanan is elected president of the United States.
1857	March 4	■ Buchanan delivers his inaugural address.
1860	December 3	■ Buchanan delivers his fourth annual message to Congress.
1861		■ Buchanan retires to Wheatland, outside Lancaster, Pennsylvania.
1868	June 1	■ Buchanan dies at Wheatland.

The next month Buchanan rose again to remind his fellow senators that he had no problem with receiving such petitions and then rejecting them outright or burying them by referring them to a committee. He understood that to refuse to receive such petitions would simply exacerbate the debate over slavery. He maintained his determined opposition to abolitionists, accusing them of seeking to incite insurrection, but he also maintained that it would violate the civil rights of Americans to reject their petitions. In taking this position Buchanan sought to remind white

southerners that he sided with them on the issues of policy contained in the petitions while hastening to reassure northerners that he would not compromise their civil rights. In the case of the Quaker petition, he prevailed. When it came to the circulation of abolitionist publications through the mails, however, Buchanan argued that the federal government was well within its rights to prohibit the mailing of any material deemed to be incendiary, and he found that abolitionist literature fit his definition of incendiary.

♦ Inaugural Address

Between 1836 and 1856 Buchanan maintained his position of defending slavery as consistent with his interpretation of the Constitution. He declared that he had no interest in interfering with the institution where it already existed and that the Constitution forbade such interference. He identified his public career (and his prospects for political advancement) with maintaining that position. He refused to debate the merits of slavery as an institution, preferring to view it in constitutional terms; when it came to abolition, however, Buchanan raised again and again the specter of a possible slave insurrection, adding that abolitionists tended to stiffen and intensify southern support for slavery.

Having reassured southern whites of his position, Buchanan offered his views on the expansion of slavery. At first he believed that it would be best to extend the Missouri Compromise line of 36°30' all the way to the Pacific Ocean to cover the new lands acquired as a result of the Mexican-American War. He argued that in practice this would not result in the expansion of slavery, because he believed that the lands of the Mexican Cession would not prove hospitable to slavery: Between the dry heat and the arid regions, there was little prospect that plantation slavery would prove profitable. That slave labor could be used for other reasons seems not to have occurred to him. In taking this position, however, Buchanan asserted that Congress had the right to determine the fate of slavery in the territories; he hoped it would do so without promoting the agitation of the issue by abolitionists. However, he also believed that the principle of popular sovereignty espoused by Michigan senator Lewis Cass and Illinois senator Stephen Douglas, whereby the settlers of these territories should be left to decide for themselves whether to allow slavery in their territories, promised to perpetuate controversy and competition between pro-slavery and antislavery forces.

Buchanan attributed the controversy over slavery to abolitionist agitation, an assessment that could not but please slave-owning white southerners. He endorsed the Compromise of 1850 as a suitable settlement of the issue of slavery in the territories. However, after failing in his bid to secure the Democratic presidential nomination in 1852, Buchanan left the country the next year as minister to England. While he was overseas he missed the explosion caused by Douglas's 1854 introduction of a bill to organize the territories of Kansas and Nebraska according to the principle of popular sovereignty, although according to the Missouri Compromise, which included Kansas and Nebraska, slavery was previously barred from both territories. That same year, in framing the Ostend Manifesto, which called for the acquisition of Cuba from Spain, Buchanan seemed to be looking toward the Caribbean and Central America as possible future additions to the United States where plantation slavery might well prove profitable.

In 1856 Buchanan returned to the United States and prepared a new presidential bid. This time he was successful. In winning the Democratic nomination, he might have found it ironic that after years of reassuring white southerners of his position on slavery, it was Douglas who claimed a majority of the southern delegates at the convention until he withdrew in favor of Buchanan. In the fall contest he beat out the Republican candidate John C. Frémont and Know Nothing standard bearer Millard Fillmore.

As he prepared to become the fifteenth president of the United States, Buchanan hoped for an end to sectional conflict. This conflict had exploded into open bloodshed and violence in Kansas and on the floor of the U.S. Senate, where South Carolina congressman Preston S. Brooks had assaulted Massachusetts senator Charles Sumner with a cane in revenge for the senator's caustic remarks about Brooks's kinsman, South Carolina senator Andrew P. Butler. Looking for an end to such debate, Buchanan learned that the Supreme Court was preparing to rule on the fate of Dred Scott, a slave who was suing for freedom on the ground that he had resided in both a free state (Illinois) and a free territory (Wisconsin, later to become Minnesota). Buchanan urged associate Supreme Court justices John Catron and Robert Grier to ensure that the forthcoming decision could be treated as definitive.

At the time he took the oath of office on March 4, 1857, Buchanan knew that the Supreme Court's decision in Scott's case was imminent, and he believed it would prove decisive. With that in mind he reminds Americans that slavery is protected under the Constitution, adding that the Supreme Court would soon have something to say that would prove to be the last word on the issue of slavery in the territories. At the same time, he outlines his understanding of the situation in Kansas, pledging himself to support the principle of popular sovereignty. With those two issues out of the way, he believes that there would be no need for further agitation of the slavery question: "Most happy will it be for the country when the public mind shall be diverted from this question to others of more pressing and practical importance." It is also time to put an end to talk of secession, Buchanan believes, for disunion is an unpleasant prospect that will "involve all in one common ruin."

Unfortunately for Buchanan, the Supreme Court's decision in *Dred Scott v. Sandford*, issued just two days after Buchanan took office, not only failed to settle the issue of slavery once and for all but indeed served to make things worse. In denying that Congress could legislate on the issue of slavery in the territories or delegate that authority to the residents of the territory, the Court destroyed the viability of popular sovereignty and declared unconstitutional Republican efforts to contain slavery by prohibiting its expansion. Before long Buchanan made things even worse. He decided to support the efforts of the pro-slavery forces meeting in

Lecompton, Kansas, to offer for a vote two different versions of a state constitution, one providing for Kansas to open its doors to the future importation of more slaves, the other restricting slavery to its present strength. The delegates refused to allow for an up-or-down vote on the document as a whole and did not permit voters to bar slavery altogether.

Aware that between Lecompton and the *Dred Scott* decision his theory of popular sovereignty was in mortal danger, Douglas informed Buchanan that he would have to oppose the proposed constitution. Enraged, Buchanan reminded Douglas of the fate suffered by those Democrats who had once defied Andrew Jackson. Douglas replied by reminding Buchanan that Jackson was dead. The implication was that Buchanan was no Jackson. Although he did what he could to secure the passage of the Lecompton Constitution and the admission of Kansas as a slave state, in the end Buchanan had to admit defeat.

♦ Fourth Annual Message to Congress

Aside from the fiascos of *Dred Scott* and Lecompton, the Buchanan administration suffered a series of setbacks during its first three years. In 1857 a major economic panic resulted in a serious depression. Republicans achieved major gains in the elections of 1858, to the point that if they could hold on to those gains in 1860, they could claim the presidency. As if fulfilling Buchanan's prophecy of an insurrection, John Brown swept down on the federal armory at Harpers Ferry, Virginia, in October 1859, with the intention of inciting a slave revolt. His capture and later execution did little to reassure those southern whites who were already questioning whether slavery was better protected inside or outside the Union. Republicans launched a series of investigations into the activities of the administration, portraying Buchanan as the willing tool of the southern slave owners, eager to do whatever it took to protect the cause of slavery.

Disaster struck Democratic fortunes in 1860. In April the party convention at Charleston, South Carolina, collapsed when a group of southern delegates walked out. They had no interest in supporting Stephen A. Douglas's bid for the presidency. Each wing of the party nominated its own candidate, with Douglas the nominee of the northern Democrats while Buchanan's own vice president, John C. Breckenridge, headed the southern Democratic ticket. The Republicans nominated Abraham Lincoln of Illinois. Lincoln had battled Douglas to a standstill in 1858 and looked to be best suited to hold on to the party's gains in 1858, which he did against Douglas, Breckenridge, and John Bell of Tennessee, the nominee of the hastily cobbled-together Constitutional Union party. As Lincoln claimed victory, more and more white southerners publicly weighed the prospect of secession in order to protect slavery.

It was in these circumstances that Buchanan delivered his last annual message to Congress in December 1860. Once more he blames "the incessant and violent agitation of the slavery question throughout the North" for the resulting crisis, asserting that it "has at length produced its malign influence on the slaves, and inspired them with vague notions of freedom." In the discussion that follows one can hear echoes of his speeches of 1836 during the petition controversy. Indeed, he makes explicit reference to that controversy. In order to restore peace, he argues, it is necessary to leave the slave states alone, "permitted to manage their domestic institutions in their own way." Still, the crisis of the union is at hand: Buchanan sees fit to remind everyone, "I have long foreseen and often forewarned my countrymen of the now impending danger." Indeed he had. Only by ceasing abolitionist agitation over slavery and recognizing that it is constitutionally protected can a crisis be averted.

However, if the Constitution protects slavery, it does not sanction secession. Buchanan rejects outright the notion that Lincoln's mere election justified disunion, reminding listeners that the Republican candidate's election is perfectly in accord with the process laid out by the Constitution. There exists no cause for secession, no reason for revolution. The federal government has committed no transgression justifying such an extreme step. To claim that such violations are in the offing is unreasonable. Even efforts by northern state legislatures to curtail violations of the Fugitive Slave law of 1850 have no legal viability, as the Supreme Court showed in 1859 when it struck down Wisconsin's efforts to handcuff the recovery of fugitive slaves in *Ableman v. Booth*. However, if secession violates the Constitution, Buchanan confesses that his reading of the document does not allow him as president to challenge those proceedings by law or by force (a suggestion that General Andrew Jackson was indeed dead, as Jackson never would have reached that conclusion). For the moment Buchanan is reduced to warning Americans of the possible impact of the impending crisis, especially a war that would render a true sectional reconciliation "impossible." It is time to step back from the abyss and recall the need to preserve the republic of the founders. Buchanan's advice proved unavailing. By the time he left office in March 1861 seven southern states had seceded and formed their own republic. Six weeks later the war came.

Impact and Legacy

Many Americans today recall James Buchanan as nothing more than a failed president who floundered in the years leading to the secession crisis of 1860–1861. A few will recall that he was the only bachelor president, and fewer still may know that he is the only Pennsylvanian to hold the nation's highest office. In truth, Buchanan was one of the most politically experienced individuals ever to serve as president, and his election in 1856 capped more than four decades of public service at home and abroad. During that time he established credentials as a reliable Jacksonian Democrat whom white southerners found safe when it came to the issue of slavery, a fact that contributed to the advancement of his political fortunes. Once president, he struggled to achieve an enduring resolution of the slavery issue in ways that would satisfy white southerners, but he succeeded only in alienating northern Democrats and splitting his party along sectional lines. In the end, his concessions to white southern sensibilities proved useless in

preventing the growth of sectional division, while the actions of his administration helped pave the way for the Republican victory in the presidential contest of 1860. Unable to devise a more active response to the secession crisis than a stance of wait and see, Buchanan handed over a divided Union to his successor, Abraham Lincoln, and returned to Lancaster, where he spent his retirement attempting to justify his actions as president.

Buchanan built his political career upon his adherence to the notion that the Constitution protected slavery. Although he initially entered politics as a Federalist even as that party was in its decline, he soon shifted to supporting Andrew Jackson and became a prime proponent of Democratic ideology. Had he wanted to remain a power in Pennsylvania politics, he need not have done anything else. However, Buchanan clearly desired to rise to national office, in part because of his interest in foreign policy. He embraced the expansion of the boundaries of the United States across the North American continent. Realizing that the only way a northern Democrat could rise to national leadership was by currying favor among southern Democrats, he became a staunch supporter of southern interests, including slavery. He steadfastly insisted that the Constitution barred federal interference with slavery. He denounced abolitionists for agitating the issue, charging them with fomenting insurrection and driving white southerners into an overtly defensive posture.

Buchanan entered the presidency hoping that the Supreme Court's decision in *Dred Scott v. Sandford* would put an end to the controversy over slavery's westward expansion. Instead, disagreement over the decision divided Democrats and outraged Republicans. In his effort to secure congressional approval of the pro-slavery constitution framed by delegates meeting at Lecompton, Kansas, Buchanan made things worse. The pro-slavery delegates who met at Lecompton did not allow Kansas voters to reject either slavery or the document as a whole, restricting their choices to approving one of two versions of the proposed constitution that differed only over whether to allow the further importation of slaves into Kansas. Such a process made a mockery of Stephen A. Douglas's concept of popular sovereignty, which called for voters in a territory to decide whether they wanted to allow slavery. The Illinois senator broke with the president, a sign of the divisions in the Democratic Party that ripped the party apart in the 1860 presidential contest.

Key Sources

Buchanan's papers are concentrated in two major collections at the Library of Congress and the Historical Society of Pennsylvania. John Bassett Moore edited *The Works of James Buchanan* in twelve volumes (1908–1911).

Essential Quotes

"If any one principle of constitutional law can, at this day, be considered as settled, it is, that Congress has no right, no power, over the question of slavery within those States where it exists."

(Remarks to Congress on Slavery)

"These fanatics, instead of benefiting the slaves who are the objects of their regard, have inflicted serious injuries upon them."

(Remarks to Congress on Slavery)

"A difference of opinion has arisen in regard to the point of time when the people of a Territory shall decide this question for themselves. This is, happily, a matter of but little practical importance. Besides, it is a judicial question, which legitimately belongs to the Supreme Court of the United States, before whom it is now pending, and will, it is understood, be speedily and finally settled."

(Inaugural Address)

Essential Quotes

"The whole Territorial question being thus settled upon the principle of popular sovereignty—a principle as ancient as free government itself—everything of a practical nature has been decided. No other question remains for adjustment, because all agree that under the Constitution slavery in the States is beyond the reach of any human power except that of the respective States themselves wherein it exists."

(Inaugural Address)

"It is an evil omen of the times that men have undertaken to calculate the mere material value of the Union."

(Inaugural Address)

"The long-continued and intemperate interference of the Northern people with the question of slavery in the Southern States has at length produced its natural effects. The different sections of the Union are now arrayed against each other, and the time has arrived, so much dreaded by the Father of his Country, when hostile geographical parties have been formed."

(Fourth Annual Message to Congress)

"How easy would it be for the American people to settle the slavery question forever and to restore peace and harmony to this distracted country! They, and they alone, can do it. All that is necessary to accomplish the object, and all for which the slave States have ever contended, is to be let alone and permitted to manage their domestic institutions in their own way."

(Fourth Annual Message to Congress)

"The fact is that our Union rests upon public opinion, and can never be cemented by the blood of its citizens shed in civil war. If it can not live in the affections of the people, it must one day perish."

(Fourth Annual Message to Congress)

Further Reading

■ Books

Baker, Jean H. *James Buchanan*. New York: Times Books, 2004.

Binder, Frederick M. *James Buchanan and the American Empire*. Selinsgrove, Penn.: Susquehanna University Press, 1994.

Birkner, Michael J., ed. *James Buchanan and the Political Crisis of the 1850s*. Selinsgrove, Penn.: Susquehanna University Press, 1996.

Klein, Philip S. *President James Buchanan: A Biography*. University Park: Pennsylvania State University Press, 1970.

Nichols, Roy F. *The Disruption of American Democracy*. New York: Free Press, 1967.

Smith, Elbert B. *The Presidency of James Buchanan*. Lawrence: University Press of Kansas, 1975.

—*Brooks D. Simpson*

Questions for Further Study

1. Identify and evaluate Buchanan's various arguments for doing nothing to halt the continuation or spread of slavery. For example, he claimed that neither the president nor Congress possessed authority in the situation, but is this true according to the Constitution? Likewise he condemned the controversy over slavery as a conflict between regions, but was this the sort of regional conflict against which George Washington had warned his countrymen?

2. Discuss some of the ways in which Buchanan reinforces his support for the slaveholding states by his use of language—for example, the unequal blame he assigns to abolitionists as opposed to supporters of slavery or his use of the term *confederacy* to describe the United States. (Note that there was a historical basis for this usage, both in the Articles of Confederation and in the pre–Civil War states' view of themselves as semiautonomous entities in a relatively loose alliance. At the time of Buchanan's speeches, the southern states had not yet formed the Confederate States of America, so the term "confederacy" did not have the same implication that it does now.)

3. Was Buchanan correct in asserting, as he did before Congress in 1836, that slavery would not be a threat in the territories of the western United States because it would prove economically unworkable in that region? Give evidence to support your point of view. Furthermore, was he correct in assuming that economic considerations should be a factor in determining the future legality of the institution of slavery?

Remarks to Congress on Slavery

1836

If any one principle of constitutional law can, at this day, be considered as settled, it is, that Congress has no right, no power, over the question of slavery within those States where it exists. The property of the master in his slave existed in full force before the Federal Constitution was adopted. It was a subject which then belonged, as it still belongs, to the exclusive jurisdictions of the several States. These States, by the adoption of the Constitution, never yielded to the General Government any right to interfere with the question. It remains where it was previous to the establishment of our Confederacy.

The Constitution has, in the clearest terms, recognized the right of property in slaves. It prohibits any State into which a slave may have fled from passing any law to discharge him from slavery, and declares that he shall be delivered up by the authorities of such State to his master. Nay, more; it makes the existence of slavery the foundation of political power, by giving to those States in which it exists Representatives in Congress not only in proportion to the whole number of free persons, but also in proportion to three fifths of the number of slaves.

An occasion very fortunately arose in the first Congress to settle this question forever. The Society for the Abolition of Slavery in Pennsylvania brought it before that Congress, by a memorial which was presented on 11th day of February, 1790. After the subject had been discussed for several days, and after solemn deliberation, the House of Representatives, in Committee of the Whole on the 23rd day of March, 1790, resolved—

> "That Congress have no authority to interfere in the emancipation of slaves or in the treatment of them within any of the States; it remaining with the several States alone to provide any regulations therein which humanity and true policy may require."

I have thought it would be proper to present this decision, which was made almost half a century ago, distinctly to the view of the American people. The language of the resolution is clear, precise, and definite. It leaves the question where the Constitution left it and where, so far as I am concerned, it ever shall remain. The Constitution of the United States never would have been called into existence—instead of the innumerable blessings which have flowed from our happy Union, we should have had anarchy, jealousy, and civil war among the sister republics of which our Confederacy is composed—had not the free States abandoned all control over this question. For one, whatever may be my opinions upon the abstract question of slavery—and I am free to confess they are those of the people of Pennsylvania—I shall never attempt to violate this fundamental concept. The Union will be dissolved, and incalculable evils will rise from its ashes, the moment any such attempt is seriously made by the free States in Congress.

What, then, are the circumstances under which these memorials are now presented? A number of fanatics, led on by foreign incendiaries, have been scattering "arrows, firebrands, and death" throughout the southern States. The natural tendency of their publications is to produce dissatisfactions and revolt among the slaves, and to incite their wild passions to vengeance. All history, as well as the present condition of the slaves, proves that there can be no danger of the final result of a servile war. But, in the mean time, what dreadful action may be enacted before such an insurrection, which would spare neither age nor sex, could be suppressed! What agony of mind must be suffered, especially by the gentler sex, in consequence of these publications! Many a mother clasps her infant to her bosom, when she retires to rest, under dreadful apprehensions that she may be aroused from her slumbers by the savage yells of the slaves by whom she is surrounded. These are the works of the Abolitionists. That their motives may be honest, I do not doubt; but their zeal is without knowledge. The history of the human race presents numerous examples of ignorant enthusiasts, the purity of whose intentions cannot be doubted, who have spread devastation and bloodshed over the face of the earth.

These fanatics, instead of benefiting the slaves who are the objects of their regard, have infected serious injuries upon them. Self-preservation is the first law of nature. The masters, for the sake of their wives and children—for the sake of all that is near and dear to them on earth—must tighten the reins of authority over their slaves. They must thus

Document Text

counteract the efforts of the Abolitionists. The slaves are denied many indulgences which their masters would otherwise cheerfully grant; they must be kept in such a state of bondage as effectually to prevent their rising. These are the injurious effects produced by the Abolitionists upon the slave himself. Whilst, on the one hand, they render his condition miserable by presenting to his mind vague notions of freedom never to be realized, on the other, they make it doubly miserable by compelling the master to be severe, in order to prevent any attempts at insurrection. They thus render it impossible for the master to treat his slave according to the dictates of his heart and his feelings.

Besides, do not the abolitionists perceive that the sprit which is thus roused must protract to an indefinite period the emancipation of the slave? The necessary effect of their efforts is to render desperate those to whom the power of emancipation exclusively belongs. I believe most conscientiously, in whatever light this subject can be viewed, that the best interests of the slave require that the question should be left, where the Constitution has left it, to the slaveholding States themselves, without foreign interference.

Glossary

exclusive jurisdictions:	separate legal powers
foreign:	outside, but not necessarily "foreign" in the sense of being or coming from outside the United States
memorial:	petition
our Confederacy:	the United States
the property of the master in his slave:	the fact, in Buchanan's opinion, that a slave was the property of his or her master
rising:	revolting

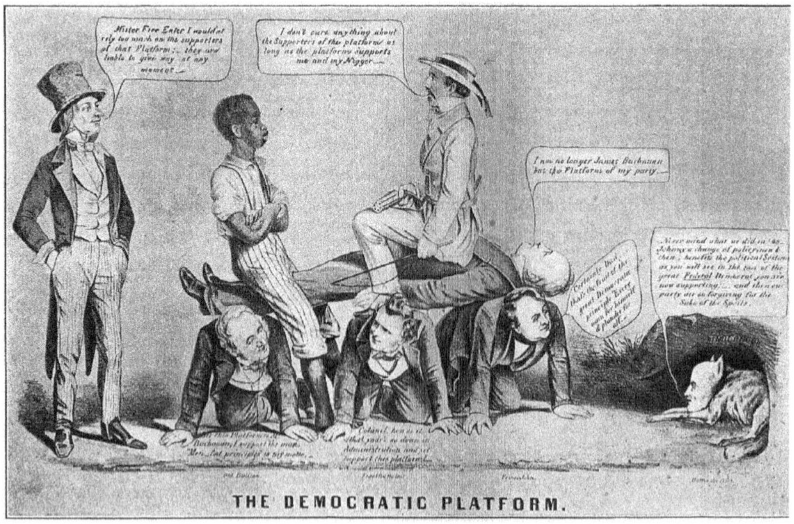

An anti-Buchanan political cartoon from the 1856 election

Inaugural Address

Fellow-Citizens:

I appear before you this day to take the solemn oath "that I will faithfully execute the office of President of the United States and will to the best of my ability preserve, protect, and defend the Constitution of the United States."

In entering upon this great office I must humbly invoke the God of our fathers for wisdom and firmness to execute its high and responsible duties in such a manner as to restore harmony and ancient friendship among the people of the several States and to preserve our free institutions throughout many generations. Convinced that I owe my election to the inherent love for the Constitution and the Union which still animates the hearts of the American people, let me earnestly ask their powerful support in sustaining all just measures calculated to perpetuate these, the richest political blessings which Heaven has ever bestowed upon any nation. Having determined not to become a candidate for reelection, I shall have no motive to influence my conduct in administering the Government except the desire ably and faithfully to serve my country and to live in grateful memory of my countrymen.

We have recently passed through a Presidential contest in which the passions of our fellow-citizens were excited to the highest degree by questions of deep and vital importance; but when the people proclaimed their will the tempest at once subsided and all was calm.

The voice of the majority, speaking in the manner prescribed by the Constitution, was heard, and instant submission followed. Our own country could alone have exhibited so grand and striking a spectacle of the capacity of man for self-government.

What a happy conception, then, was it for Congress to apply this simple rule, that the will of the majority shall govern, to the settlement of the question of domestic slavery in the Territories. Congress is neither "to legislate slavery into any Territory or State nor to exclude it therefrom, but to leave the people thereof perfectly free to form and regulate their domestic institutions in their own way, subject only to the Constitution of the United States."

As a natural consequence, Congress has also prescribed that when the Territory of Kansas shall be admitted as a State it "shall be received into the Union with or without slavery, as their constitution may prescribe at the time of their admission." A difference of opinion has arisen in regard to the point of time when the people of a Territory shall decide this question for themselves.

This is, happily, a matter of but little practical importance. Besides, it is a judicial question, which legitimately belongs to the Supreme Court of the United States, before whom it is now pending, and will, it is understood, be speedily and finally settled. To their decision, in common with all good citizens, I shall cheerfully submit, whatever this may be, though it has ever been my individual opinion that under the Nebraska-Kansas act the appropriate period will be when the number of actual residents in the Territory shall justify the formation of a constitution with a view to its admission as a State into the Union. But be this as it may, it is the imperative and indispensable duty of the Government of the United States to secure to every resident inhabitant the free and independent expression of his opinion by his vote. This sacred right of each individual must be preserved. That being accomplished, nothing can be fairer than to leave the people of a Territory free from all foreign interference to decide their own destiny for themselves, subject only to the Constitution of the United States.

The whole Territorial question being thus settled upon the principle of popular sovereignty—a principle as ancient as free government itself—everything of a practical nature has been decided. No other question remains for adjustment, because all agree that under the Constitution slavery in the States is beyond the reach of any human power except that of the respective States themselves wherein it exists. May we not, then, hope that the long agitation on this subject is approaching its end, and that the geographical parties to which it has given birth, so much dreaded by the Father of his Country, will speedily become extinct? Most happy will it be for the country when the public mind shall be diverted from this question to others of more pressing and practical importance. Throughout the whole progress of this agitation, which has scarcely known any intermission for more than twenty years, whilst it has been

Document Text

productive of no positive good to any human being it has been the prolific source of great evils to the master, to the slave, and to the whole country. It has alienated and estranged the people of the sister States from each other, and has even seriously endangered the very existence of the Union. Nor has the danger yet entirely ceased. Under our system there is a remedy for all mere political evils in the sound sense and sober judgment of the people. Time is a great corrective. Political subjects which but a few years ago excited and exasperated the public mind have passed away and are now nearly forgotten. But this question of domestic slavery is of far graver importance than any mere political question, because should the agitation continue it may eventually endanger the personal safety of a large portion of our countrymen where the institution exists. In that event no form of government, however admirable in itself and however productive of material benefits, can compensate for the loss of peace and domestic security around the family altar. Let every Union-loving man, therefore, exert his best influence to suppress this agitation, which since the recent legislation of Congress is without any legitimate object.

It is an evil omen of the times that men have undertaken to calculate the mere material value of the Union. Reasoned estimates have been presented of the pecuniary profits and local advantages which would result to different States and sections from its dissolution and of the comparative injuries which such an event would inflict on other States and sections. Even descending to this low and narrow view of the mighty question, all such calculations are at fault. The bare reference to a single consideration will be conclusive on this point. We at present enjoy a free trade throughout our extensive and expanding country such as the world has never witnessed. This trade is conducted on railroads and canals, on noble rivers and arms of the sea, which bind together the North and the South, the East and the West, of our Confederacy. Annihilate this trade, arrest its free progress by the geographical lines of jealous and hostile States, and you destroy the prosperity and onward march of the whole and every part and involve all in one common ruin. But such considerations, important as they are in themselves, sink into insignificance when we reflect on the terrific evils which would result from disunion to every portion of the Confederacy—to the North, not more than to the South, to the East not more than to the West. These I shall not attempt to portray, because I feel an humble confidence that the kind Providence which inspired our fathers with wisdom to frame the most perfect form of government and union ever devised by man will not suffer it to perish until it shall have been peacefully instrumental by its example in the extension of civil and religious liberty throughout the world.

Glossary

consideration:	example
our Confederacy:	the United States
popular sovereignty:	the principle that citizens in the territories had the right to decide for themselves, on a state-by-state basis, whether to allow slavery in their borders
Providence:	God's guidance and love
suffer:	allow

Fourth Annual Message to Congress

1860

Fellow-Citizens of the Senate and House of Representatives:

Throughout the year since our last meeting the country has been eminently prosperous in all its material interests. The general health has been excellent, our harvests have been abundant, and plenty smiles throughout the land. Our commerce and manufactures have been prosecuted with energy and industry, and have yielded fair and ample returns. In short, no nation in the tide of time has ever presented a spectacle of greater material prosperity than we have done until within a very recent period.

Why is it, then, that discontent now so extensively prevails, and the Union of the States, which is the source of all these blessings, is threatened with destruction?

The long-continued and intemperate interference of the Northern people with the question of slavery in the Southern States has at length produced its natural effects. The different sections of the Union are now arrayed against each other, and the time has arrived, so much dreaded by the Father of his Country, when hostile geographical parties have been formed.

I have long foreseen and often forewarned my countrymen of the now impending danger. This does not proceed solely from the claim on the part of Congress or the Territorial legislatures to exclude slavery from the Territories, nor from the efforts of different States to defeat the execution of the fugitive-slave law. All or any of these evils might have been endured by the South without danger to the Union … in the hope that time and reflection might apply the remedy. The immediate peril arises not so much from these causes as from the fact that the incessant and violent agitation of the slavery question throughout the North for the last quarter of a century has at length produced its malign influence on the slaves and inspired them with vague notions of freedom. Hence a sense of security no longer exists around the family altar. This feeling of peace at home has given place to apprehensions of servile insurrections. … Should this apprehension of domestic danger, whether real or imaginary, extend and intensify itself until it shall pervade the masses of the Southern people, then disunion will become inevitable. Self-preservation is the first law of nature, and has been implanted in the heart of man by his Creator for the wisest purpose; and no political union, however fraught with blessings and benefits in all other respects, can long continue if the necessary consequence be to render the homes and the firesides of nearly half the parties to it habitually and hopelessly insecure. Sooner or later the bonds of such a union must be severed. It is my conviction that this fatal period has not yet arrived, and my prayer to God is that He would preserve the Constitution and the Union throughout all generations.

But let us take warning in time and remove the cause of danger. It can not be denied that for five and twenty years the agitation at the North against slavery has been incessant. In 1835 pictorial handbills and inflammatory appeals were circulated extensively throughout the South of a character to excite the passions of the slaves,… This agitation has ever since been continued by the public press, by the proceedings of State and county conventions and by abolition sermons and lectures. The time of Congress has been occupied in violent speeches on this never-ending subject, and appeals, in pamphlet and other forms, indorsed by distinguished names, have been sent forth from this central point and spread broadcast over the Union.

How easy would it be for the American people to settle the slavery question forever and to restore peace and harmony to this distracted country! They, and they alone, can do it. All that is necessary to accomplish the object, and all for which the slave States have ever contended, is to be let alone and permitted to manage their domestic institutions in their own way. As sovereign States, they, and they alone, are responsible before God and the world for the slavery existing among them. For this the people of the North are not more responsible and have no more fight to interfere than with similar institutions in Russia or in Brazil.

Upon their good sense and patriotic forbearance I confess I still greatly rely. Without their aid it is beyond the power of any President, no matter what may be his own political proclivities, to restore peace and harmony among the States.…

And this brings me to observe that the election of any one of our fellow-citizens to the office of

President does not of itself afford just cause for dissolving the Union. This is more especially true if his election has been effected by a mere plurality, and not a majority of the people, and has resulted from transient and temporary causes, which may probably never again occur. In order to justify a resort to revolutionary resistance, the Federal Government must be guilty of "a deliberate, palpable, and dangerous exercise" of powers not granted by the Constitution.

The late Presidential election, however, has been held in strict conformity with its express provisions. How, then, can the result justify a revolution to destroy this very Constitution?... It is said, however, that the antecedents of the President-elect have been sufficient to justify the fears of the South that he will attempt to invade their constitutional rights. But are such apprehensions of contingent danger in the future sufficient to justify the immediate destruction of the noblest system of government ever devised by mortals?... The stern duty of administering the vast and complicated concerns of this Government affords in itself a guaranty that he will not attempt any violation of a clear constitutional right....

It is alleged as one cause for immediate secession that the Southern States are denied equal rights with the other States in the common Territories. But by what authority are these denied? Not by Congress, which has never passed, and I believe never will pass, any act to exclude slavery from these Territories; and certainly not by the Supreme Court, which has solemnly decided that slaves are property, and, like all other property, their owners have a right to take them into the common Territories and hold them there under the protection of the Constitution.

So far then, as Congress is concerned, the objection is not to anything they have already done, but to what they may do hereafter. It will surely be admitted that this apprehension of future danger is no good reason for an immediate dissolution of the Union....

The most palpable violations of constitutional duty which have yet been committed consist in the acts of different State legislatures to defeat the execution of the fugitive-slave law. It ought to be remembered, however, that for these acts neither Congress nor any President can justly be held responsible. Having been passed in violation of the Federal Constitution, they are therefore null and void. All the courts, both State and national, before whom the question has arisen have from the beginning declared the fugitive-slave law to be constitutional.... The validity of this law has been established over and over again by the Supreme Court of the United States with perfect unanimity. It is rounded upon an express provision of the Constitution, requiring that fugitive slaves who escape from service in one State to another shall be "delivered up" to their masters. Without this provision it is a well-known historical fact that the Constitution itself could never have been adopted by the Convention. In one form or other, under the acts of 1793 and 1850, both being substantially the same, the fugitive-slave law has been the law of the land from the days of Washington until the present moment. Here, then, a clear case is presented in which it will be the duty of the next President, as it has been my own, to act with vigor in executing this supreme law against the conflicting enactments of State legislatures. Should he fail in the performance of this high duty, he will then have manifested a disregard of the Constitution and laws, to the great injury of the people of nearly one-half of the States of the Union.... Let us wait for the overt act. The fugitive-slave law has been carried into execution in every contested case since the commencement of the present Administration, though often, it is to be regretted, with great loss and inconvenience to the master and with considerable expense to the Government. Let us trust that the State legislatures will repeal their unconstitutional and obnoxious enactments. Unless this shall be done without unnecessary delay, it is impossible for any human power to save the Union.

The Southern States, standing on the basis of the Constitution, have right to demand this act of justice from the States of the North. Should it be refused, then the Constitution, to which all the States are parties, will have been willfully violated by one portion of them in a provision essential to the domestic security and happiness of the remainder. In that event the injured States, after having first used all peaceful and constitutional means to obtain redress, would be justified in revolutionary resistance to the Government of the Union....

In order to justify secession as a constitutional remedy, it must be on the principle that the Federal Government is a mere voluntary association of States, to be dissolved at pleasure by any one of the contracting parties. If this be so, the Confederacy is a rope of sand, to be penetrated and dissolved by the first adverse wave of public opinion in any of the States.... By this process a Union might be entirely broken into fragments in a few weeks which cost our forefathers many years of toil, privation, and blood to establish....

It may be asked, then, Are the people of the States without redress against the tyranny and oppression

of the Federal Government? By no means. The right of resistance on the part of the governed against the oppression of their governments can not be denied. It exists independently of all constitutions, and has been exercised at all periods of the world's history. Under it old governments have been destroyed and new ones have taken their place. It is embodied in strong and express language in our own Declaration of Independence. But the distinction must ever be observed that this is revolution against an established government, and not a voluntary secession from it by virtue of an inherent constitutional right. In short, let us look the danger fairly in the face. Secession is neither more nor less than revolution. It may or it may not be a justifiable revolution, but still it is revolution.

What, in the meantime, is the responsibility and true position of the Executive? He is bound by solemn oath, before God and the country, "to take care that the laws be faithfully executed," and from this obligation he can not be absolved by any human power. But what if the performance of this duty, in whole or in part, has been rendered impracticable by events over which he could have exercised no control? Such at the present moment is the case throughout the State of South Carolina so far as the laws of the United States to secure the administration of justice by means of the Federal judiciary are concerned.... We no longer have a district judge, a district attorney, or a marshal in South Carolina. In fact, the whole machinery of the Federal Government necessary for the distribution of remedial justice among the people has been demolished, and it would be difficult, if not impossible, to replace it....

Apart from the execution of the laws, so far as this may be practicable, the Executive has no authority to decide what shall be the relations between the Federal Government and South Carolina.... He possesses no power to change the relations heretofore existing between them, much less to acknowledge the independence of that State. This would be to invest a mere executive officer with the power of recognizing the dissolution of the confederacy among our thirty-three sovereign States.... Any attempt to do this would, on his part, be a naked act of usurpation....

Without descending to particulars, it may be safely asserted that the power to make war against a State is at variance with the whole spirit and intent of the Constitution. Suppose such a war should result in the conquest of a State; how are we to govern it afterwards? Shall we hold it as a province and govern it by despotic power? In the nature of things, we could not by physical force control the will of the people and compel them to elect Senators and Representatives to Congress and to perform all the other duties depending upon their own volition and required from the free citizens of a free State as a constituent member of the Confederacy.

But if we possessed this power, would it be wise to exercise it under existing circumstances? The object would doubtless be to preserve the Union. War would not only present the most effectual means of destroying it, but would vanish all hope of its peaceable reconstruction. Besides, in the fraternal conflict a vast amount of blood and treasure would be expended, rendering future reconciliation between the States impossible. In the meantime, who can foretell what would be the sufferings and privations of the people during its existence?

The fact is that our Union rests upon public opinion, and can never be cemented by the blood of its citizens shed in civil war. If it can not live in the affections of the people, it must one day perish. Congress possesses many means of preserving it by conciliation, but the sword was not placed in their hand to preserve it by force.

But may I be permitted solemnly to invoke my countrymen to pause and deliberate before they determine to destroy this the grandest temple which has ever been dedicated to human freedom since the world began?... The Union has already made us the most prosperous, and ere long will, if preserved, render us the most powerful, nation on the face of the earth. In every foreign region of the globe the title of American citizen is held in the highest respect.... Surely when we reach the brink of the yawning abyss we shall recoil with horror from the last fatal plunge.

By such a dread catastrophe the hopes of the friends of freedom throughout the world would be destroyed, and a long night of leaden despotism would enshroud the nations. Our example for more than eighty years would not only be lost, but it would be quoted as a conclusive proof that man is unfit for self-government.

It is not every wrong ... which can justify a resort to such a fearful alternative. This ought to be the last desperate remedy of a despairing people, after every other constitutional means of conciliation had been exhausted. We should reflect that under this free Government there is an incessant ebb and flow in public opinion. The slavery question, like everything human, will have its day. I firmly believe that it has reached and passed the culminating point. But if in the midst of the existing excitement the Union shall perish, the evil may then become irreparable.

Glossary

absolved:	pardoned, excused
the acts of 1793 and 1850:	the original Fugitive Slave Act and its replacement, by the same name, under the Compromise of 1850
apprehensions of servile insurrections:	fears of slave revolts
the common Territories:	areas, primarily in the West, that had not yet become states and thus had not fully settled the slavery question
the Confederacy:	the United States
despotic:	dictatorial
ere:	before
the Executive:	the presidency
intemperate:	uncontrolled
invest:	formally and legally grant
late:	recent
pictorial handbills:	printed announcements or messages, an important means of communication at that time
plenty smiles:	evidence of financial well-being is everywhere
plurality:	a proportion of the votes that, while not a majority, is still larger than that of any other candidate or party
privation:	need, suffering
rounded upon:	built around
without descending to particulars:	without getting into too much detail

Chief Justice Warren Burger

Warren E. Burger: Original Analysis

Fifteenth Chief Justice of the United States

1907–1995

Overview

Warren Earl Burger was the fifteenth chief justice of the United States and enjoyed the fourth-longest tenure as head of the Supreme Court. Coming from a working-class family of modest means in Saint Paul, Minnesota, Burger took work at an early age to help out with his family's finances. He was a good student and won a scholarship to Princeton, which he declined because it would not have paid for all of his expenses. While selling insurance, Burger attended evening school, taking extension courses at the University of Minnesota from 1925 to 1927. He worked as an accountant while attending Saint Paul College of Law (now William Mitchell College of Law), from which he graduated magna cum laude in 1931.

For over twenty years Burger worked for the Saint Paul law firm of Boyesen, Otis & Faricy (1931–1953), where he became a named partner in 1935. He worked primarily in the fields of probate, real estate, and corporate law, meanwhile gaining experience in political matters. His active role in Republican politics in Minnesota resulted in his leading the delegation that sought to nominate the Minnesota governor Harold Stassen for president at the 1952 Republican National Convention. It was Burger who ultimately announced the transfer of the delegation's votes from Stassen to General Dwight D. Eisenhower, which gave the latter enough votes to win the nomination. Eisenhower proceeded to win the presidential election. Before the end of the year, Burger was named assistant attorney general in charge of the Justice Department's Claims Division (later the Civil Division). Burger did not have the type of practice, national reputation as a lawyer, or past experience in government that would have warranted his appointment; although his general competency as a lawyer was no doubt confirmed, Burger's role in the 1952 convention was what brought him to the attention of the Eisenhower administration.

Burger's role within the Claims Division, similarly, was not that of a brilliant trial lawyer who won cases others could not have won, nor was it that of an incisive intellectual who developed creative legal theories that led to victories in the appellate courts. Rather, Burger's role was primarily that of an administrator of a large government office. His role was to supervise the legal work of his office's attorneys, who were often younger than he was, and ensure that the legal positions taken by his office were consistent with the policy preferences of the Eisenhower administration. Burger's administrative ability and political loyalty led President Eisenhower to appoint Burger to the U.S. Court of Appeals for the District of Columbia Circuit in 1956, where he served for thirteen years.

On an appeals court that was often divided over decisions in criminal cases, Burger led the judges opposed to expanding the rights of criminal defendants—that is, persons who were charged with crimes and whose guilt or innocence was to be determined by a jury or court. Burger wanted to give more deference to trial judges, prosecutors, and the police in the proving of guilt and to provide fewer protections for defendants. By taking this position, he established a reputation as a conservative "law and order" judge. He also notably remained untainted by any ethical scandal. In 1969 President Richard Nixon nominated Burger for the position of chief justice of the United States. It was not Burger's legal brilliance that brought him to the attention of President Nixon; rather, it was his speeches—which might be referred to as political speeches—on limiting the rights of defendants. Nixon's nomination of Burger fulfilled a campaign promise to counter the Court's judicial activism under Earl Warren by appointing justices who, in his view, followed conservative philosophy. Burger was confirmed by the U.S. Senate by a vote of seventy-four to three.

Chief Justice Burger served on the Supreme Court for over seventeen years and during that time wrote more than 250 opinions. Under Chief Justice Warren, the Court had extended protections for those charged with crimes and decided cases abolishing school segregation and protecting the right to vote. Burger came to disappoint those who wanted a wholesale repudiation of the Warren Court era. He helped slow the rate at which change took place and in some cases diluted the effects of prior decisions, but he did little to overrule the decisions that had spurred political debate. The Burger Court did take a more limited view of the rights of those accused of crimes and was also more deferential to the states, under the banner of federalism. But it also recognized new rights and expanded others in the areas of welfare, abortion, gender-based discrimination, and affirmative action. This approach continued for Burger's entire term as chief justice. At times he continued the course of the Warren Court, as illustrated by his opinion in segregation cases like *Swann v. Charlotte-Mecklenburg Board of Education* (1971). Yet he also refused to extend the remedy for segregation to surrounding schools districts in *Milliken v. Bradley* (1974). In other cases, like

his dissent in *Bivens vs. Six Unknown Named Agents*, Burger tried to stem the expansion of judicial remedies but was unable to muster a majority on the Court. He served as chief justice until 1986, when he resigned to serve as chair of the Commission on the Bicentennial of the U.S. Constitution. Burger died in 1995 in Washington, D.C.

Explanation and Analysis of Documents

Burger's judicial philosophy and contributions to the U.S. Supreme Court can be illustrated by three opinions. *Bivens v. Six Unknown Named Agents* (1971) reflects Burger's basic conservatism, which included a willingness to defer to the legislative branch of government to make decision that others thought should be made by the courts. At the same time, *Bivens* reflects Burger's weakness due to his lack of actual experience in criminal matters, his reliance upon his own political theories, and his failure to carefully analyze cases. *United States v. Nixon* (1974) was undoubtedly Burger's most important case and shows the author in a most favorable light. Although he had been made chief justice by President Nixon, Burger's opinion in this case led directly to Nixon's resignation. Known for his concern about separation of powers, Burger crafted an opinion that articulated a very deferential view of the president's right to executive privilege and yet found that right inapplicable to the present claims made by Nixon. The Court's decision spared the nation the agony of going through a presidential impeachment. *Milliken v. Bradley* (1974) was decided the following day. Although Burger had been widely expected to "roll back" the decisions of the Warren Court, his decisions mainly stopped the expansion of Warren Court doctrines and consolidated that Court's gains. This was especially true in the areas of criminal law and criminal procedure, but it was also true in other areas; in *Milliken v. Bradley*, the Burger Court refused to expand the Warren Court's 1954 decision banning school segregation in *Brown v. Board of Education* to include interdistrict remedies but nevertheless preserved *Brown*'s basic holding.

♦ *Bivens v. Six Unknown Named Agents of the Federal Bureau of Narcotics*

When Burger selected thirty-eight of his most memorable Supreme Court opinions to be published by the Philippine Bar Association, he chose only one dissent: *Bivens v. Six Unknown Named Agents of the Federal Bureau of Narcotics* (1971). The *Bivens* case stemmed from allegations that federal agents had entered Webster Bivens's apartment and conducted a very extensive search of the apartment without a warrant and without probable cause, as required by the Fourth Amendment to the Constitution. In addition, Bivens claimed that the agents used unreasonable force and manacled him in front of his wife and children, meanwhile threatening to arrest his entire family. Bivens was arrested for a narcotics offense; he also claimed that after being interrogated, he was subjected to a visual strip search at the jail. The majority interpreted his claim for money damages

Time Line

1907	September 17	■ On Constitution Day, Warren Burger is born in Saint Paul, Minnesota.
1925		■ Burger begins two years of attending evening school at the University of Minnesota.
1931		■ Having attended law school in the evening while working daily as an accountant, Burger receives a law degree magna cum laude from Saint Paul College of Law (now William Mitchell College of Law).
1934		■ Burger helps organize the Minnesota Young Republicans.
1938		■ Burger works on the first of three consecutive successful campaigns by Harold Stassen to become governor of Minnesota.
1948		■ In Stassen's effort to win the Republican presidential nomination, Burger serves as floor manager.
1952		■ At the Republican National Convention, Burger, again serving as floor manager in Stassen's campaign for the presidential nomination, announces the transfer of Minnesota's votes from Stassen to Dwight Eisenhower, who thus wins the nomination.
		■ Eisenhower's selected attorney general, Herbert Brownell, appoints Burger to be assistant attorney general in charge of the Justice Department's Claims Division.
1956		■ President Eisenhower nominates Burger to be a judge on the U.S. Court of Appeals for the District of Columbia Circuit.
1969	June 23	■ Having been nominated by President Richard Nixon, Burger is sworn in as chief justice of the United States.

Time Line		
1971	June 21	■ The Supreme Court decides *Bivens v. Six Unknown Named Agents*, with Burger dissenting.
1974	July 24	■ The Court decides *United States v. Nixon*, with Burger authoring the unanimous opinion.
	July 25	■ Burger delivers the majority opinion in *Milliken v. Bradley*, decided by the Court by a five-to-four vote.
1986	September 26	■ Burger resigns his position as chief justice to become chair of the Commission on the Bicentennial of the U.S. Constitution.
1995	June 25	■ Burger dies in Washington, D.C.

to include the allegations that the search and arrest were unjustified and that he suffered humiliation and mental suffering.

Justice William J. Brennan wrote the opinion for the five-member majority, with whom Justice John Marshall Harlan concurred, finding that petitioners could sue for damages to their Fourth Amendment rights based directly on the Constitution and that no statutory provision allowing for such a suit was necessary. Burger dissented on the ground that any such course of legal remedy should be explicitly legislated by Congress, not simply created by the judiciary. He also used the case as a forum for attacking the rule that illegal evidence should be suppressed and for advocating alternative remedies.

In some ways, the chief justice's *Bivens* dissent parallels his reputation as a conservative administrator and reformer. Throughout the nation's history the Supreme Court has seen debate and disagreement over whether provisions of the U.S. Constitution are directly enforceable or require enforcement statutes analogous to those that exist under the Fourteenth Amendment. Chief Justice Burger here takes the view that enforcement statutes are required, a legally justified position. He also argues, consistently with his judicial philosophy, that if a direct remedy is to be recognized, it should be established by legislative action of the Congress and not by the Supreme Court.

Burger then proceeds beyond these core arguments, using the occasion to advance his hostile view of the exclusionary rule, which excludes illegally seized evidence from court proceedings. As he did throughout his judicial career, he adopts a trusting attitude toward the government and minimizes the significance of the illegal police activity in question, referring to such an act as a "blunder," or mistake. In turn, he neglects to cite any empirical evidence to support his point of view. Burger furthermore makes the philosophical point that the exclusionary rule is ineffectual because it renders the original lawbreaker inculpable while doing nothing to punish the illegally acting law-enforcement officer. But he turns a blind eye to the fact that before the exclusionary rule there was incentive for law-enforcement officers to violate the law in seeking to prosecute suspected criminals; this incentive was largely negated when the exclusionary rule came to be enforced.

As exemplified here, Burger's approach offers an interesting contrast to that of his predecessor, Earl Warren. Burger had no experience in law enforcement and so based his views upon his political philosophy and, presumably, his experience as a judge. Having been a county prosecutor and attorney general of California, Warren had grown more familiar with the intricacies of crime and law enforcement; on a very personal level, his own father's murder remained an unsolved crime. Warren's experiences taught him that the criminal justice system needed checks and balances, while Burger thought such checks unnecessary.

In his *Bivens* dissent, taking an approach similar to that of an administrator or legislator, Burger suggests to Congress general principles under which a sort of court of claims could be established to punish perpetrators of illegal searches. He cites law reform efforts with the same goal and provides a bibliography of articles opposed to the exclusionary rule. Nevertheless, the exclusionary rule continued to be applied, and Congress never saw fit to accept Chief Justice Burger's advice.

♦ United States v. Nixon

From a historical and political standpoint, *United States v. Nixon* (1974) was Burger's most important decision. While the Supreme Court ruled against the president, and the decision is thought to have ultimately resulted in Nixon's resignation, the Court did recognize for the first time a presumptive executive privilege of presidential communications. A landmark in the political and judicial history of the country, the case arose in a very troubled and stormy time for the nation. President Nixon was the first president since Grover Cleveland to have two of his nominees for the Supreme Court rejected by the Senate. Moreover, for the first time in history, a vice president of the United States, Spiro Agnew, had been indicted on a variety of charges of corruption. Agnew ultimately made a plea-bargain agreement under which he pleaded no contest to the charge of failure to report income and pay taxes and resigned from the office of vice president—the first ever to do so.

Nixon had won the presidential election with promises that included the ending of the Vietnam War. Although he reduced American troops and shifted their roles to the South Vietnamese, the North Vietnamese responded with more military attacks in the south. President Nixon, in turn, responded by expanding the aerial bombing campaign to Cambodia and Laos, which resulted in increased nationwide antiwar protests. During this time, the *New York Times*

obtained copies of a classified analysis of the war that became known as the Pentagon Papers. The Nixon administration was unsuccessful in trying to prevent the publication of these papers; meanwhile, a group known as the "plumbers" was created by the White House to fix leaks of confidential or classified information. Among other activities, certain people working for the plumbers broke into the headquarters of the Democratic National Committee at the Watergate apartment complex. The case *United States v. Nixon* grew out of the Watergate break-in and an attempt by a special prosecutor to secure records from President Nixon that were relevant to the prosecution of four Nixon aides. Refusing the prosecutor's demands, President Nixon publicly stated that he would abide only by a definitive decision of the Supreme Court. Although his remark was ambiguous, many people believed that Nixon would not feel bound even by a majority decision if a significant number of justices dissented.

From President Nixon's point of view, there was indeed some hope that the decision would be less than unanimous. After all, Nixon himself had appointed four members of his own political party to the Court: Burger, Harry A. Blackmun, Lewis F. Powell, Jr., and William H. Rehnquist. Furthermore, Justice Rehnquist had served in the attorney general's office during Nixon's presidency. (However, Rehnquist duly excused himself from the case.) It was not unreasonable for the president to think that if his counsel advanced a plausible argument, in a close case, at least some of his appointees might take his side. Still, if Nixon had been emboldened by dissenters to defy a majority of the Supreme Court, it would have almost surely resulted in impeachment and removal from office. Immediately after the trial, between July 27 and 30, 1974, the House Judiciary Committee would approve four articles of impeachment. Further proceedings to impeach the president would have produced widespread political turmoil and presented a crisis to the nation.

But the ruling handed down by the Supreme Court on July 24 was unanimous. Chief Justice Burger assumed the role of writing the opinion, which ordered President Nixon to honor the subpoena and produce the evidence sought by the special prosecutor. For the first time in history the Court held that there was a constitutional basis for the claim of executive privilege. Its rationale was that "the privilege can be said to be derived from the supremacy of each branch [of government] within its own assigned area of constitutional duties." Nevertheless, the Court found that President Nixon's generalized claim of confidentiality had to be weighed against the more specific duty of the federal courts to ensure that justice was done in a criminal proceeding, the right to call witnesses under the Sixth Amendment, and right to due process of law under the Fifth Amendment. Emphasizing that Nixon had made no claim that the evidence at issue involved any military, diplomatic, or sensitive national security secrets, the Court held that the president's "generalized interest in confidentiality" did not outweigh the "fundamental demands of due process of law in the fair administration of criminal justice."

The Court's unanimous decision indeed led Nixon to turn over the evidence sought by the subpoena, and among the evidence submitted was the proverbial "smoking gun" revealing that the president had been involved in the conspiracy to cover up the crime. Sixteen days after the opinion was announced, Nixon resigned, the only president to do so in the nation's history. There was a certain irony in the fact that Chief Justice Burger's opinion helped lead to the resignation of the very president who had nominated him for the Court. Notably, although Burger's early judicial advancement was based upon his political actions, his role in this case was not influenced by politics.

In many ways, *United States v. Nixon* shows Burger at his best. The opinion was unanimous on an issue of great national importance and was straightforward and easy to understand. While Burger ultimately rules against President Nixon's' "generalized claim" of privilege, he nevertheless goes out of his way in the decision to support more specific claims of privilege, to recognize the unique status of the president when subpoenaed, and to protect for future presidents the claim of a robust reading of executive privilege.

A deeper inquiry into this opinion reveals Burger's weaknesses. An examination of the memoranda and draft opinions circulated among the justices reveals that a significant part of the opinion was actually drafted by Justices Potter Stewart, Byron White, and Brennan, with a major initial contribution by Justice William O. Douglas. While a review of the memoranda and drafts of opinions exchanged by the justices before the final decision suggests that all eight participating justices agreed upon the final result from the outset, the unanimous opinion was achieved only by Burger's giving up his own views and language in deference to those of the other justices.

♦ *Milliken v. Bradley*

In the unanimous 1954 opinion in *Brown v. Board of Education*, authored by Earl Warren, the Supreme Court held that legally enforced segregation of schools by race was a violation of the equal protection clause of the Fourteenth Amendment. In a second opinion in the same case, commonly referred to as *Brown II*, the Court considered ways to remedy past segregation but, while outlining various considerations, decided to leave those matters to the district courts that would conduct local trials. Under Burger, the Court preserved *Brown* and generally carried forward its mandate. For example, in *Swann v. Charlotte-Mecklenburg Board of Education* (1971), the Court unanimously affirmed the decision of the district court that required the redrawing of school attendance zones and the use of busing as a remedy to create a racial mix at each school approximating the district's racial composition.

In *Milliken*, however, the Court denied a plan involving multiple school districts that intended to remedy wrongful

segregation within the school system of the city of Detroit. *Milliken v. Bradley* (1974) can be read in two ways, and those readings correspond to the two possibilities presented in the title question of a book edited by Bernard Schwartz: *The Burger Court: Counter-revolution or Confirmation?* This decision can be seen as confirming while in a sense consolidating the decision in *Brown*. Having found that past *Brown*-related cases involved only remedies within the segregated school districts in question, Chief Justice Burger presented his opinion as simply refusing to extend *Brown* to allow or require an interdistrict remedy. From this point of view, Burger's opinion was both a consolidation of the past Warren Court decisions and a refusal to extend the guiding principle in *Brown* to new situations.

The *Milliken* decision can also be viewed a second way. In each of the prior *Brown*-related decisions, the Court had limited the remedy to a single district based not upon the Constitution or law but rather upon the facts of the case. As such, the question of whether to extend the *Brown* remedy to interdistrict circumstances was a new legal issue that could have legitimately been decided in the contrary manner. Indeed, the fact that this was a five-to-four decision highlights the lack of inevitability to the Burger Court's majority opinion and validates the notion that a supportable decision could have been crafted with the opposite conclusion.

The dissenters in *Milliken* make the point that *Brown* required that the effects of segregation be remedied "root and branch," and the Burger Court's opinion did not do this. Indeed, while Burger accused the four dissenters of wanting to crudely balance the school system wholesale by numbers, he never convincingly responded to their claim that the only remedies left to the school district by his decision simply would not accomplish the "root and branch" solution mandated by *Brown II*. Further, as a practical matter, the *Milliken* plaintiffs were surely right that the "state," in the broadest sense of the term, had taken several actions or failed to take actions that led to the segregation of the district schools. As illustrated by the four dissenting justices, a different justice with a different point of view could have used this analysis to create a more effective remedy.

The chief justice refused to consider the entire picture of state actions, in part because he accepted the state argument that it should be allowed to compartmentalize itself into school districts. Burger so valued local school systems and local control that these priorities seemed to trump the duty imposed by *Brown* to provide a "root and branch" remedy. In the long run, then, *Milliken* not only curtailed the mandate of *Brown II* but also led to the resegregation of schools. In this sense, Burger's opinion was not a confirmation of *Brown* but rather a counterrevolution that foreshadowed the resegregation of schools nationwide.

Burger did not always produce such narrow readings of the relevant constitutional and statutory provisions in matters involving claims of racial discrimination. In *Fullilove v. Klutznick* (1980), Burger wrote an opinion upholding the requirement that 10 percent of public works funding be set aside for minority businesses. Similarly, in *Bob Jones University v. United States* (1983) he held that the Internal Revenue Service had the authority to deny tax exemptions to private religious schools that discriminated on the basis of race, a position that was contrary to the views of the Reagan administration.

Impact and Legacy

Burger's legacy is by and large a positive one, as shored up by his integrity, good work ethic, and administrative reform efforts. While he lacked the skill of John Marshall or Earl Warren in building majorities and consensus, he was a steady, if not brilliant, chief justice. His decisions proved beneficial in policing the boundaries necessary for the separation of powers, a doctrine that many hold as essential to American democracy. By using his decisions to maintain the balance between the branches, Burger helped prevent the accumulation of unwarranted power by any one branch. It was perhaps as an administrator and public spokesman for the judicial branch, however, that Burger enjoyed his greatest success. Commentators often analogized his role with that of Chief Justice William Taft, who was very active in the administration of the Court and in lobbying Congress for judicial reform. Administratively, Burger reduced oral arguments from one hour to one-half hour per side, allowed attorneys to be admitted to the Supreme Court bar by mail, changed the practice of reading full opinions from the bench to one of reading summaries of the opinions, and brought copy machines and computers into the Court's chambers. He also worked with outside organizations to try to aid in prison reform, the improvement of the legal profession, and other causes. As chief justice, Burger proved an incremental, conservative reformer who helped move the Supreme Court forward into the modern age.

Key Sources

The Warren E. Burger papers are held by the Earl Gregg Swem Library of the College of William and Mary but will not be available to researchers until 2026. An accounting of speeches delivered by Burger is in Evalyn Greene and Andrew H. Smith, "Chief Justice Burger's Administrative Agenda: A Chronology of His Speeches Made Available through Legal Publications and the Media, with Noteworthy Reponses: 1969–1986," *Law Library Journal* (1988). Burger himself authored a volume on the nation's founding document, titled *It Is So Ordered: A Constitution Unfolds* (1995).

Essential Quotes

"I dissent from today's holding which judicially creates a damage remedy not provided for by the Constitution and not enacted by Congress. We would more surely preserve the important values of the doctrine of separation of powers—and perhaps get a better result—by recommending a solution to the Congress as the branch of government in which the Constitution has vested the legislative power. Legislation is the business of the Congress, and it has the facilities and competence for that task."

(*Bivens v. Six Unknown Named Agents of the Federal Bureau of Narcotics*)

"The deterrence theory underlying the … exclusionary rule, has a certain appeal.… Notwithstanding its plausibility, many judges and lawyers and some of our most distinguished legal scholars have never quite been able to escape the force of Cardozo's statement of the doctrine's anomalous result: 'The criminal is to go free because the constable has blundered.'"

(*Bivens v. Six Unknown Named Agents of the Federal Bureau of Narcotics*)

"We conclude that when the ground for asserting privilege as to subpoenaed materials sought for use in a criminal trial is based only upon the generalized interest in confidentiality, it cannot prevail over the fundamental demands of due process of law in the fair administration of criminal justice."

(*United States v. Nixon*)

"Absent a claim of need to protect military, diplomatic, or sensitive national security secrets, we find it difficult to accept the argument that even the very important interest in confidentiality of Presidential communications is significantly diminished by production of such material for in camera inspection with all the protection that a district court will be obliged to provide."

(*United States v. Nixon*)

"No single tradition in public education is more deeply rooted than local control over the operation of schools; local autonomy has long been thought essential both to the maintenance of community concern and support for public schools and to quality of the educational process."

(*Milliken v. Bradley*)

Essential Quotes

"It is obvious from the scope of the interdistrict remedy itself that absent a complete restructuring of the laws of Michigan relating to school districts the District Court will become first, a de facto 'legislative authority' to resolve these complex questions, and then the 'school superintendent' for the entire area. This is a task which few, if any, judges are qualified to perform and one which would deprive the people of control of schools through their elected representatives."

(*Milliken v. Bradley*)

Milestone Documents

Further Reading

Articles

Howard, A. E. Dick. "Chief Enigma." *American Bar Association Journal* 81 (October 1995): 66–69.

"In Memoriam: Warren E. Burger." *Texas Law Review* 74, no. 2 (1995): 207–236.

Lamb, Charles M., and Lisa K. Parshall. " *United States v. Nixon* Revisited: A Case Study in Supreme Court Decision-Making." *University of Pittsburgh Law Review* 58, no. 1 (Fall 1996): 71–108.

Books

Cushman, Clare, ed. *The Supreme Court Justices: Illustrated Biographies, 1789–1993*. Washington, D.C.: Congressional Quarterly, 1993.

Lamb, Charles M., and Stephen C. Halpern, eds. *The Burger Court: Political and Judicial Profiles*. Urbana: University of Illinois Press, 1991.

Maltz, Earl M. *The Chief Justiceship of Warren Burger, 1969–1986*. Columbia: University of South Carolina Press, 2000.

Schwartz, Bernard. *The Ascent of Pragmatism: The Burger Court in Action*. Reading, Mass.: Addison-Wesley, 1990.

———, ed. *The Burger Court: Counter-revolution or Confirmation?* New York: Oxford University Press, 1998.

Web Sites

"The Burger Court: 1969–1986." Supreme Court Historical Society Web site. http://www.supremecourthistory.org/02_history/subs_history/02_c15.html.

"Warren Earl Burger: Chief Justice of the United States Supreme Court." Arlington National Cemetery Web site. http://www.arlingtoncemetery.net/weburger.htm.

—*Richard L. Aynes*

Questions for Further Study

1. Warren Burger was regarded as a conservative "law and order" judge. How do his decisions in both the *Bivens* case (involving a criminal defendant) and the *Nixon* case (involving the U.S. president) lend support to that view?

2. Burger often uses the word *deference* in his judicial opinions. What is deference, and to whom or what does the Court owe deference? Why?

3. How persuasive do you find Burger's arguments with regard to executive privilege—that is, the claim of presidents to keep documents and other forms of communication out of the public eye because they might contain sensitive information? What might be some of the unintended effects of restricting executive privilege?

4. Why was *Milliken v. Bradley* a significant case in the history of school desegregation? Did the ruling in the case set back the cause of school desegregation, or was it a reasonable response to the facts presented in the case? Explain.

Bivens v. Six Unknown Named Agents of the Federal Bureau of Narcotics

1971

[Burger dissent]

I dissent from today's holding which judicially creates a damage remedy not provided for by the Constitution and not enacted by Congress. We would more surely preserve the important values of the doctrine of separation of powers—and perhaps get a better result—by recommending a solution to the Congress as the branch of government in which the Constitution has vested the legislative power. Legislation is the business of the Congress, and it has the facilities and competence for that task—as we do not....

This case has significance far beyond its facts and its holding. For more than 55 years this Court has enforced a rule under which evidence of undoubted reliability and probative value has been suppressed and excluded from criminal cases whenever it was obtained in violation of the Fourth Amendment.... The rule has rested on a theory that suppression of evidence in these circumstances was imperative to deter law enforcement authorities from using improper methods to obtain evidence.

The deterrence theory underlying the ... exclusionary rule, has a certain appeal.... Notwithstanding its plausibility, many judges and lawyers and some of our most distinguished legal scholars have never quite been able to escape the force of Cardozo's statement of the doctrine's anomalous result: "The criminal is to go free because the constable has blundered."...

The plurality opinion in *Irvine v. California* ... (1954), catalogued the doctrine's defects:

"Rejection of the evidence does nothing to punish the wrong-doing official, while it may, and likely will, release the wrong-doing defendant. It deprives society of its remedy against one lawbreaker because he has been pursued by another. It protects one against whom incriminating evidence is discovered, but does nothing to protect innocent persons who are the victims of illegal but fruitless searches."...

I do not question the need for some remedy to give meaning and teeth to the constitutional guarantees against unlawful conduct by government officials. Without some effective sanction, these protections would constitute little more than rhetoric. Beyond doubt the conduct of some officials requires sanctions as cases like *Irvine* indicate. But the hope that this objective could be accomplished by the exclusion of reliable evidence from criminal trials was hardly more than a wistful dream.... This is illustrated by the paradox that an unlawful act against a totally innocent person such as petitioner claims to be—has been left without an effective remedy, and hence the Court finds it necessary now—55 years later—to construct a remedy of its own....

Today's holding seeks to fill one of the gaps of the suppression doctrine—at the price of impinging on the legislative and policy functions that the Constitution vests in Congress. Nevertheless, the holding serves the useful purpose of exposing the fundamental weaknesses of the suppression doctrine....

Judges cannot be faulted for being offended by arrests, searches, and seizures that violate the Bill of Rights or statutes intended to regulate public officials. But we can and should be faulted for clinging to an unworkable and irrational concept of law. My criticism is that we have taken so long to find better ways to accomplish these desired objectives....

Instead of continuing to enforce the suppression doctrine inflexibly, rigidly, and mechanically, we should view it as one of the experimental steps in the great tradition of the common law and acknowledge its shortcomings. But in the same spirit we should be prepared to discontinue what the experience of over half a century has shown neither deters errant officers nor affords a remedy to the totally innocent victims of official misconduct.

I do not propose, however, that we abandon the suppression doctrine until some meaningful alternative can be developed. In a sense our legal system has become the captive of its own creation. To overrule *Weeks* and *Mapp*, even assuming the Court was now prepared to take that step, could raise yet new problems. Obviously the public interest would be poorly served if law enforcement officials were suddenly to gain the impression, however erroneous, that all constitutional restraints on police had somehow been removed—that an open season on "criminals" had been declared. I am concerned lest some such mistaken impression might be fostered by a flat overruling of the suppression doctrine cases.

Reasonable and effective substitutes can be formulated if Congress would take the lead, as it did

Document Text

for example in 1946 in the Federal Tort Claims Act. I see no insuperable obstacle to the elimination of the suppression doctrine if Congress would provide some meaningful and effective remedy against unlawful conduct by government officials.

The problems of both error and deliberate misconduct by law enforcement officials call for a workable remedy. Private damage actions against individual police officers concededly have not adequately met this requirement, and it would be fallacious to assume today's work of the Court in creating a remedy will really accomplish its stated objective. There is some validity to the claims that juries will not return verdicts against individual officers except in those unusual cases where the violation has been flagrant or where the error has been complete, as in the arrest of the wrong person or the search of the wrong house....

I conclude, therefore, that an entirely different remedy is necessary but it is one that in my view is as much beyond judicial power as the step the Court takes today. Congress should develop an administrative or quasi-judicial remedy against the government itself to afford compensation and restitution for persons whose Fourth Amendment rights have been violated. The venerable doctrine of respondeat superior in our tort law provides an entirely appropriate conceptual basis for this remedy.

Glossary

Cardozo:	Benjamin Cardozo (1870–1938), U.S. Supreme Court justice from 1932 to 1938
common law:	law that evolves through court cases, as opposed to statutory law, which is based on codes passed by the legislature
holding:	a legal term that refers to a court's main legal principle in a case
insuperable:	insurmountable
probative:	tending to prove; in a legal case, evidence is probative if it would tend to prove an accused's guilt
respondeat superior:	literally, "let the master answer" in Latin; the legal doctrine that an employer is responsible for the acts of employees in the course of their duties
tort law:	the branch of law that deals with civil wrongs or breaches of duty, as opposed to crimes
***Weeks* and *Mapp* :**	references to *Weeks v. United States* (1914) and *Mapp v. Ohio* (1961), Court cases that were important in the development of the exclusionary rule

United States v. Nixon

1974

The first contention is a broad claim that the separation of powers doctrine precludes judicial review of a President's claim of privilege. The second contention is that if he does not prevail on the claim of absolute privilege, the court should hold as a matter of constitutional law that the privilege prevails over the subpoena duces tecum.

In the performance of assigned constitutional duties each branch of the Government must initially interpret the Constitution, and the interpretation of its powers by any branch is due great respect from the others.... Many decisions of this Court, however, have unequivocally reaffirmed the holding of *Marbury v. Madison* ... that "(i)t is emphatically the province and duty of the judicial department to say what the law is."...

Since this Court has consistently exercised the power to construe and delineate claims arising under express powers, it must follow that the Court has authority to interpret claims with respect to powers alleged to derive from enumerated powers....

Notwithstanding the deference each branch must accord the others, the "judicial Power of the United States" vested in the federal courts by Art. III, §1, of the Constitution can no more be shared with the Executive Branch than the Chief Executive, for example, can share with the Judiciary the veto power, or the Congress share with the Judiciary the power to override a Presidential veto. Any other conclusion would be contrary to the basic concept of separation of powers and the checks and balances that flow from the scheme of a tripartite government....

In support of his claim of absolute privilege, the President's counsel urges two grounds.... The first ground is the valid need for protection of communications between high Government officials and those who advise and assist them in the performance of their manifold duties; the importance of this confidentiality is too plain to require further discussion.... Whatever the nature of the privilege of confidentiality of Presidential communications in the exercise of Art. II powers, the privilege can be said to derive from the supremacy of each branch within its own assigned area of constitutional duties. Certain powers and privileges flow from the nature of enumerated powers; the protection of the confidentiality of Presidential communications has similar constitutional underpinnings.

The second ground asserted by the President's counsel in support of the claim of absolute privilege rests on the doctrine of separation of powers. Here it is argued that the independence of the Executive Branch within its own sphere ... insulates a President from a judicial subpoena in an ongoing criminal prosecution, and thereby protects confidential Presidential communications.

However, neither the doctrine of separation of powers, nor the need for confidentiality of high-level communications, without more, can sustain an absolute, unqualified Presidential privilege of immunity from judicial process under all circumstances. The President's need for complete candor and objectivity from advisers calls for great deference from the courts. However, when the privilege depends solely on the broad, undifferentiated claim of public interest in the confidentiality of such conversations, a confrontation with other values arises. Absent a claim of need to protect military, diplomatic, or sensitive national security secrets, we find it difficult to accept the argument that even the very important interest in confidentiality of Presidential communications is significantly diminished by production of such material for in camera inspection with all the protection that a district court will be obliged to provide.

The impediment that an absolute, unqualified privilege would place in the way of the primary constitutional duty of the Judicial Branch to do justice in criminal prosecutions would plainly conflict with the function of the courts under Art. III. In designing the structure of our Government and dividing and allocating the sovereign power among three co-equal branches, the Framers of the Constitution sought to provide a comprehensive system, but the separate powers were not intended to operate with absolute independence....

To read the Art. II powers of the President as providing an absolute privilege as against a subpoena essential to enforcement of criminal statutes on no more than a generalized claim of the public interest in confidentiality of nonmilitary and nondiplomatic discussions would upset the constitutional balance of

"a workable government" and gravely impair the role of the courts under Art. III....

Since we conclude that the legitimate needs of the judicial process may outweigh Presidential privilege, it is necessary to resolve those competing interests in a manner that preserves the essential functions of each branch....

A President and those who assist him must be free to explore alternatives in the process of shaping policies and making decisions and to do so in a way many would be unwilling to express except privately. These are the considerations justifying a presumptive privilege for Presidential communications. The privilege is fundamental to the operation of Government and inextricably rooted in the separation of powers under the Constitution.... We agree with Mr. Chief Justice Marshall's observation, therefore, that "(i) n no case of this kind would a court be required to proceed against the president as against an ordinary individual."...

But this presumptive privilege must be considered in light of our historic commitment to the rule of law. This is nowhere more profoundly manifest than in our view that "the twofold aim (of criminal justice) is that guilt shall not escape or innocence suffer."... The ends of criminal justice would be defeated if judgments were to be founded on a partial or speculative presentation of the facts. The very integrity of the judicial system and public confidence in the system depend on full disclosure of all the facts, within the framework of the rules of evidence. To ensure that justice is done, it is imperative to the function of courts that compulsory process be available for the production of evidence needed either by the prosecution or by the defense.

Only recently the Court restated the ancient proposition of law, albeit in the context of a grand jury inquiry rather than a trial, that "the public ... has a right to every man's evidence," except for those persons protected by a constitutional, common-law, or statutory privilege.... Whatever their origins, these exceptions to the demand for every man's evidence are not lightly created nor expansively construed, for they are in derogation of the search for truth....

The right to the production of all evidence at a criminal trial similarly has constitutional dimensions. The Sixth Amendment explicitly confers upon every defendant in a criminal trial the right "to be confronted with the witnesses against him" and "to have compulsory process for obtaining witnesses in his favor." Moreover, the Fifth Amendment also guarantees that no person shall be deprived of liberty without due process of law. It is the manifest duty of the courts to vindicate those guarantees, and to accomplish that it is essential that all relevant and admissible evidence be produced.

In this case we must weigh the importance of the general privilege of confidentiality of Presidential communications in performance of the President's responsibilities against the inroads of such a privilege on the fair administration of criminal justice....

On the other hand, the allowance of the privilege to withhold evidence that is demonstrably relevant in a criminal trial would cut deeply into the guarantee of due process of law and gravely impair the basic function of the courts. A President's acknowledged need for confidentiality in the communications of his office is general in nature, whereas the constitutional need for production of relevant evidence in a criminal proceeding is specific and central to the fair adjudication of a particular criminal case in the administration of justice. Without access to specific facts a criminal prosecution may be totally frustrated. The President's broad interest in confidentiality of communications will not be vitiated by disclosure of a limited number of conversations preliminarily shown to have some bearing on the pending criminal cases.

We conclude that when the ground for asserting privilege as to subpoenaed materials sought for use in a criminal trial is based only on the generalized interest in confidentiality, it cannot prevail over the fundamental demands of due process of law in the fair administration of criminal justice. The generalized assertion of privilege must yield to the demonstrated, specific need for evidence in a pending criminal trial....

Affirmed.

Glossary

Chief Justice Marshall:	John Marshall (1755–1835), the highly influential fourth chief justice of the United States from 1801 to 1835
derogation:	the taking away of the effectiveness of a law
enumerated powers:	in Article I, Section 8, of the Constitution, the list of specific powers held by Congress
express powers:	powers specifically granted (to the president or Congress, for example) by the U.S. Constitution
in camera:	in chambers (a judge's chambers), as opposed to in open court
***Marbury v. Madison*:**	a landmark Supreme Court case in 1803 that established the principle of judicial review, that is, that the judicial branch of government has the power to annul acts of the legislature and the executive
subpoena duces tecum:	a Latin legal term referring to a command to produce documents
vitiated:	diminished, eroded

Milliken v. Bradley

1974

We granted certiorari in these consolidated cases to determine whether a federal court may impose a multidistrict, areawide remedy to a single-district de jure segregation problem absent any finding that the other included school districts have failed to operate unitary school systems within their districts....

Ever since *Brown v. Board of Education* ... (1954), judicial consideration of school desegregation cases has begun with the standard:

"(I)n the field of public education the doctrine of 'separate but equal' has no place. Separate educational facilities are inherently unequal."...

The target of the *Brown* holding was clear and forthright: the elimination of state-mandated or deliberately maintained dual school systems with certain schools for Negro pupils and others for white pupils....

In *Brown v. Board of Education* ... (*Brown II*), the Court's first encounter with the problem of remedies in school desegregation cases, the Court noted:

"In fashioning and effectuating the decrees, the courts will be guided by equitable principles. Traditionally, equity has been characterized by a practical flexibility in shaping its remedies and by a facility for adjusting and reconciling public and private needs."...

While specifically acknowledging that the District Court's findings of a condition of segregation were limited to Detroit, the Court of Appeals approved the use of a metropolitan remedy largely on the grounds that it is

"impossible to declare 'clearly erroneous' the District Judge's conclusion that any Detroit only segregation plan will lead directly to a single segregated Detroit school district overwhelmingly black in all of its schools, surrounded by a ring of suburbs and suburban school districts overwhelmingly white in composition in a State in which the racial composition is 87 per cent white and 13 per cent black."...

Both [the District Court and the Court of Appeals] proceeded on an assumption that the Detroit schools could not be truly desegregated—in their view of what constituted desegregation—unless the racial composition of the student body of each school substantially reflected the racial composition of the population of the metropolitan area....

Here the District Court's approach to what constituted "actual desegregation" raises the fundamental question, not presented in *Swann,* as to the circumstances in which a federal court may order desegregation relief that embraces more than a single school district. The court's analytical starting point was its conclusion that school district lines are no more than arbitrary lines on a map drawn "for political convenience." Boundary lines may be bridged where there has been a constitutional violation calling for interdistrict relief, but the notion that school district lines may be casually ignored or treated as a mere administrative convenience is contrary to the history of public education in our country. No single tradition in public education is more deeply rooted than local control over the operation of schools; local autonomy has long been thought essential both to the maintenance of community concern and support for public schools and to quality of the educational process....

The Michigan educational structure involved in this case, in common with most States, provides for a large measure of local control, and a review of the scope and character of these local powers indicates the extent to which the interdistrict remedy approved by the two courts could disrupt and alter the structure of public education in Michigan. The metropolitan remedy would require, in effect, consolidation of 54 independent school districts historically administered as separate units into a vast new super school district.... Entirely apart from the logistical and other serious problems attending large-scale transportation of students, the consolidation would give rise to an array of other problems in financing and operating this new school system....

It may be suggested that all of these vital operational problems are yet to be resolved by the District Court, and that this is the purpose of the Court of Appeals' proposed remand. But it is obvious from the scope of the interdistrict remedy itself that absent a complete restructuring of the laws of Michigan relating to school districts the District Court will become first, a de facto "legislative authority" to resolve these complex questions, and then the "school superintendent" for the entire area. This is a task which few, if any, judges are qualified to perform and one

which would deprive the people of control of schools through their elected representatives.

Of course, no state law is above the Constitution. School district lines and the present laws with respect to local control, are not sacrosanct and if they conflict with the Fourteenth Amendment federal courts have a duty to prescribe appropriate remedies.... But our prior holdings have been confined to violations and remedies within a single school district. We therefore turn to address, for the first time, the validity of a remedy mandating cross-district or interdistrict consolidation to remedy a condition of segregation found to exist in only one district.

The controlling principle consistently expounded in our holdings is that the scope of the remedy is determined by the nature and extent of the constitutional violation.... Before the boundaries of separate and autonomous school districts may be set aside by consolidating the separate units for remedial purposes or by imposing a cross-district remedy, it must first be shown that there has been a constitutional violation within one district that produces a significant segregative effect in another district. Specifically, it must be shown that racially discriminatory acts of the state or local school districts, or of a single school district have been a substantial cause of interdistrict segregation. Thus an interdistrict remedy might be in order where the racially discriminatory acts of one or more school districts caused racial segregation in an adjacent district, or where district lines have been deliberately drawn on the basis of race. In such circumstances an interdistrict remedy would be appropriate to eliminate the interdistrict segregation directly caused by the constitutional violation. Conversely, without an interdistrict violation and interdistrict effect, there is no constitutional wrong calling for an interdistrict remedy....

With no showing of significant violation by the 53 outlying school districts and no evidence of any interdistrict violation or effect, the court ... mandated a metropolitan area remedy. To approve the remedy ordered by the court would impose on the outlying districts, not shown to have committed any constitutional violation, a wholly impermissible remedy based on a standard not hinted at in *Brown I* and *II* or any holding of this Court.

In dissent, Mr. Justice WHITE and Mr. Justice MARSHALL undertake to demonstrate that agencies having statewide authority participated in maintaining the dual school system found to exist in Detroit.... But the remedy is necessarily designed, as all remedies are, to restore the victims of discriminatory conduct to the position they would have occupied in the absence of such conduct. Disparate treatment of white and Negro students occurred within the Detroit school system, and not elsewhere, and on this record the remedy must be limited to that system....

The constitutional right of the Negro respondents residing in Detroit is to attend a unitary school system in that district.... The view of the dissenters, that the existence of a dual system in Detroit can be made the basis for a decree requiring cross-district transportation of pupils, cannot be supported on the grounds that it represents merely the devising of a suitably flexible remedy for the violation of rights already established by our prior decisions. It can be supported only by drastic expansion of the constitutional right itself, an expansion without any support in either constitutional principle or precedent....

We recognize that the ... record ... contains language and some specific incidental findings thought by the District Court to afford a basis for interdistrict relief. However, these comparatively isolated findings and brief comments concern only one possible interdistrict violation and are found in the context of a proceeding that, as the District Court conceded, included no proof of segregation practiced by any of the 85 suburban school districts surrounding Detroit. The Court of Appeals, for example, relied on five factors which, it held, amounted to unconstitutional state action with respect to the violations found in the Detroit system....

We conclude that the relief ordered by the District Court and affirmed by the Court of Appeals was based upon an erroneous standard and was unsupported by record evidence that acts of the outlying districts effected the discrimination found to exist in the schools of Detroit....

Reversed and remanded.

Glossary

***Brown I* and *II*:**	reference to the original *Brown v. Board of Education* case (*Brown I*) and a later case, *Brown II,* in which the Court, to implement *Brown I,* assigned to district courts the task of desegregating schools "with all deliberate speed"
certiorari:	a demand by a higher court that a lower court release its records relating to a particular case
de jure:	Latin for "in law," meaning that something is established or required by statute, as opposed to de facto, or "in fact," meaning that something exists independent of the law
remand:	the act of sending a case back to a lower court for reconsideration
***Swann*:**	*Swann v. Charlotte-Mecklenburg County* (1971), a key case in the controversy surrounding busing of students to achieve racial desegregation

With Betty Ford between them, Chief Justice Burger swears in President Gerald Ford following the resignation of President Richard Nixon. By Robert L. Knudsen, White House Press Office.

Portrait of Aaron Burr (1756-1836); **Collection of the New Jersey Historical Society. Attributed to Gilbert Stuart**

Aaron Burr: Original Analysis

Politician, Revolutionary War Hero, and Third Vice President of the United States

1756–1836

Overview

Aaron Burr was more a man of deeds than a man of letters. He had no overarching political theory by which his political views were organized; one of the reasons he and Thomas Jefferson clashed when Burr was vice president of the United States was that Burr treated politics as a game of strategy, whereas Jefferson regarded politics as among the most serious concerns of human life. Thus, when Burr wrote, he rarely discussed his views about the experiment of American democracy or about serious issues of national survival. He rarely thought far ahead, preferring to focus on immediate activities. He proved himself a brilliant political organizer when focusing on an election to occur in the near future, but he rarely contemplated organizing for the distant future. It was for his ability to direct such basic tasks as getting out the vote for his political party that he was chosen by the Democratic-Republicans to be Jefferson's vice president.

In his writings Burr sometimes seems to be two different men, and the contradictions are part of what make him a mysterious personality. In some instances he calls the Constitution too fragile to survive, while in others he hails the importance of the Constitution's protection of civil rights. When given the opportunity, he argues eloquently for the import of the application of those rights to all Americans at all times, as he does in his courtroom arguments from his trial for treason. In many of his writings, he suggests that he ought to be a monarch ruling a vast territory in North America—he is not picky about where in America, just so long as he would be a strongman ruling a nation. He even invites Spain, Britain, and France, in different instances, to aid him in taking land from the United States. Yet in other writings, he speaks of the robust vitality of American democracy and of how people are free to participate in the running of government and society. He is a pessimist one moment, stating his certainty that the United States is doomed to fall into fragments, but then in another moment he is an optimist, envisioning his grandson's future as one of unlimited possibilities because of American democracy. He may well have advocated treason in some of his writings, but he also applied the Constitution to the practice of law in a way that enhanced the rights of all Americans.

Explanation and Analysis of Documents

Burr was not a good writer, and he was not inclined to formulating explanations of his political views. A result of this is a paucity of public documents; most of what survives of his writings are letters. A further complication in researching Burr's documents is that the most significant ones are more paraphrases than his own words. His most important speech, his farewell to the U.S. Senate, survives only as recalled from the memories of those who heard it. His presentations at his federal trial for treason, in turn, were paraphrased by court recorders, who sometimes used his exact words and other times summarized his arguments. His journal of 1808 to 1812 is written in his true voice, as to his daughter.

♦ Farewell Address to the U.S. Senate

Three accounts of his farewell to the Senate survive. One was written by William Plumer, senator from New Hampshire, who kept notes on the activities of the Senate from 1803 to 1807 that were published in 1923 as *William Plumer's Memorandum of Proceedings in the United States Senate, 1803–1807*. This account is a short summary. Another account was written by John Quincy Adams in his diary; it is longer than Plumer's version and gives a sense of the power of Burr's delivery. The third and most complete account was compiled by the *Washington Federalist*, a newspaper, and was published on March 13, 1805, eleven days after the speech was delivered. This is the account most often reprinted in textbooks and accounts of Burr's life. It is more complete than the other two, and it was the version on which the reputation of the speech rested. Journalists spent about a week interviewing those who had been present in the Senate when the speech was delivered, and from those interviews the speech was recreated. According to the *Federalist*, those who heard the speech universally regarded it as the most impressive one they had ever heard. Further, the newspaper noted that the entire Senate was reduced to tears for half an hour—though other records disagree somewhat with this, noting that two senators wept for about half an hour but others recovered much sooner. Without doubt, all were deeply moved by Burr's words.

It is likely that Burr had not intended to speak about more than the "rules and orders of the house"—that is, of the Senate—but he ended up speaking extemporaneously about his views on how the Senate ought to conduct itself.

He spoke in a dignified manner, as was his custom, but he spoke from his emotions, which elevated his speech far above mere intellectual analysis. It was as if he were having a quiet, honest conversation with each individual senator. Burr's remark that "if the Constitution be destined ever to perish by the sacrilegious hands of the Demagogue or the Usurper, which God avert, its expiring agonies will be witnessed on this floor" would have called to the minds of his listeners the recent impeachment trial of the associate Supreme Court justice Samuel Chase. Chase's conduct of his duties had occasionally been deplorable, as when he would openly proclaim his political views from the bench, while the Supreme Court as a whole had sometimes thwarted the Jefferson administration's policies by ruling them unconstitutional. The administration hoped to start removing offending justices by beginning with Chase, whose evident misconduct made him vulnerable. Several members of the administration had courted Vice President Burr in the days after the House of Representatives had indicted Chase, probably hoping to influence his opinion because he would be the presiding judge during the Senate's trial of Chase. During the February 1805 trial, Burr conducted himself as a truly impartial judge, not favoring either side and allowing all perspectives to be heard. He won praise for his handling of the trial, which ended on March 1 with Chase's acquittal, and he may very well have helped to preserve the Constitution's balance of powers by refusing to use his position to dictate the outcome of the trial.

♦ Deciphered Letter to General James Wilkinson

The most controversial of all of Burr's documents is the letter he sent to General James Wilkinson in New Orleans in the midst of what came to be known as the Burr conspiracy. While he was still vice president of the United States, Burr began communications with Great Britain's ambassador to the United States, asking the ambassador to transmit to his government Burr's notions about the future of North America. The ambassador told his government that Burr believed that the people of the western territories were restive and unhappy with their government and wanted to form their own independent country. With military aid from Great Britain, Burr believed that he could form a new nation out of America's western states and the Louisiana Territory. Thus, even while still serving as vice president, Burr was already contemplating his conspiracy.

Burr did not choose to explain his actions publicly, other than to deny that he had intended treason. The bare facts are that he recruited well-to-do young men for a possible military adventure. His letters of the period contain enough lies to muddy his actual intentions. His recruits were to meet at Blennerhassett's Island in Ohio and travel downriver in boats specially built for the purpose, meeting recruits from western states on their way and eventually meeting General James Wilkinson, the military commander of New Orleans. They were then to settle on land Burr had purchased, invade Spanish holdings, or wage war on the United States, with the aims of splitting the Louisiana and Mississippi territories away from America and uniting

Time Line

1756	February 6	■ Aaron Burr, Jr., is born in Newark, New Jersey.
1772		■ Burr graduates from the College of New Jersey, later to become Princeton University.
1775		■ Burr joins the Continental army, staying on until 1779.
1782		■ Burr enters the New York bar, setting up his practice in Albany, New York.
1784		■ Burr is elected to the New York State Assembly, which he would leave in 1785.
1789		■ Burr begins a year of service as New York's attorney general.
1791	March 4	■ Burr becomes a U.S. senator representing New York.
1797	March 3	■ Burr finishes his Senate tenure, having lost his bid for reelection.
1798		■ Burr again serves in the New York State Assembly, leaving the following year.
1800		■ Burr and Thomas Jefferson achieve a draw in the presidential election, with seventy-three Electoral College votes each.
1801		■ Burr serves as president of New York State's constitutional convention.
1801		■ Burr becomes vice president of the United States, remaining so until 1805.
1804	July 11	■ Burr shoots and kills Alexander Hamilton in a duel in Weehawken, New Jersey.
1805	March 2	■ Burr delivers his farewell address to the U.S. Senate.

Time Line		
1806	July 29	■ Burr writes a coded letter supposedly about the Burr conspiracy to General James Wilkinson.
1807	March 31	■ Burr points out to the federal court that he has already been found innocent of treason in two states.
	September 1	■ In his trial for treason in Richmond, Virginia, Burr is found not guilty.
	August 20	■ Burr moves that prosecution evidence be limited only to the specific charges against him.
1808	June	■ Burr begins his journal addressed to his daughter Theodosia and boards a ship to go into exile in Europe.
1812	June 8	■ Burr returns to New York City to practice law.
1836	September 14	■ Burr dies in Port Richmond, New York.

them with Spain's North American colonies after capturing Mexico City. The plan may seem to have been absurd, but with Great Britain raiding American shipping and with Spain harboring people hostile to the United States, Americans were already worried about the outbreak of a new war.

General Wilkinson had befriended Burr, and Burr enlisted him in the conspiracy. Wilkinson has been alternately portrayed as a dishonorable villain or as a true patriot by historians. What is likely is that he was tempted by Burr but eventually chose his country over personal glory; he translated Burr's ciphered letter and sent a copy of it to President Jefferson, who was outraged.

At least two versions of the letter were written, about seven days apart, both of which survive. Burr may have dictated the letters, because they were not in his hand. Most historians recognize the handwriting as that of Charles Willie, a German immigrant who was Burr's personal secretary. The Burr biographer Milton Lomask claims that the handwriting is that of Burr's friend Jonathan Dayton, who had been Speaker of the House of Representatives from 1795 to 1799. The letter as sent by Wilkinson to Jefferson had a significant problem: It had been transcribed into plain English by Wilkinson, who was thought by some to have altered the letter's meaning to falsely imply that Burr was up to no good. On the other hand, if Burr was conducting perfectly legitimate business, his use of a secret code would seem pointless.

Once the original copy of the letter was made public, it presented another problem. It refers to Burr sometimes in the first person and sometimes in the third person. Lomask suggests that the passages in the first person were actually composed by Burr, while those in the third person were added by Dayton without Burr's knowledge, perhaps to enhance Burr's typically plain style. The problem becomes more complex because Burr did occasionally write of himself in the third person, and sometimes, as in parts of his journal, he switched back and forth between the first and the third person. The ciphered letter was an important element in generating the public's belief that Burr was a traitor, but its confusing language rendered it too ambiguous as evidence in Burr's trial.

♦ Address to the Court on Innocence of Treason

Burr was an outstanding lawyer. When speaking in court, he delivered his words in concise phrases; he sought to cut to the heart of an issue and lay its essentials bare. He participated in his defense in his federal trial, often asking questions of witnesses. His regard for the Constitution was ambiguous. When he was in Europe after his trial, he would say that it was fatally flawed and could not survive, yet he had expressed admiration for it on other occasions. In this address to the court, he refers to the clause in the Constitution forbidding double jeopardy, whereby no one who has been tried once and found not guilty may ever again be tried for the same crime.

While Burr was traveling in the western United States after the conspiracy came to light, he was arrested and brought to trial twice and was found not guilty twice. He holds in this address that the federal government should not have the right to try him after two state courts had found him not guilty based on the same evidence that resulted in his federal indictment. He further suggests that he is not receiving a swift trial, as guaranteed by the Constitution. Three months after his arrest by federal authorities, the prosecution was not ready to take the case to trial, and Burr implies that such was the case because there was insufficient evidence to try him. He had been in jail for a long time, and he notes that he had been forbidden pen and paper for communicating with the outside world, including his lawyers. He had been wrongly kept from aiding in the preparation of his defense, yet he was ready to proceed immediately, while the prosecution was not. He should therefore be freed, he argues, because there obviously was not enough evidence to hold him. Further, he insists that his trying to flee the authorities in the western territories of the United States should not be held against him, because he had reason to fear for his life: He believed that troops under the command of Wilkinson would kill him in order to silence him.

Burr's frequent references to himself in the third person may cause more confusion in this document than any other. The court clerk who recorded events during a trial would often reconstruct what was said from shorthand notes. The opening statement concerning "Col. Burr" indicates that the court clerk is reporting on Burr's remarks in

the third person, but if the entire document is the clerk's wording, then the clerk had a style that was more vigorous than would reasonably be expected from a clerk, as in this passage: "If he was to be prosecuted for such breach, he wished to know why he was brought to this place?... Why had he been debarred the use of pen, ink, and paper, and not even permitted to write to his daughter?" These seem much more likely to be Burr's own words than those of the clerk; it is possible that the clerk used Burr's own words for most of this document, while retaining a third-person point of view in keeping with his opening.

♦ Motion to the Court to Limit Prosecution Evidence

The trial's judge, Chief Justice John Marshall, had already presided over the treason trial of two of Burr's associates, Erich Bollman and Samuel Swartwout, who had carried letters for Burr. Of the many crimes that can be legally charged in the United States, treason is the only one defined in the Constitution. The Constitution limits the sorts of crimes that may be part of law, but the work of defining those other than treason is left to statutes. The writers of the Constitution were very familiar with the practice of European governments of extending treason to thoughts, spoken words, and associations with traitors. Almost anyone could be pulled off the street, charged with disrespecting a monarch, and then hanged. The Founding Fathers wanted the definition of treason to be severely limited, so that freedom of thought and political opinion would be protected. A traitor was someone who participated in an armed attack on the United States or who aided a foreign power in harming the United States. In the case of Bollman and Swartwout, Marshall had the opportunity to rule on what was required for a conviction of treason: The accused traitors had to have actively participated in a military force that either attacked the nation or its representatives or that was about to attack the United States, or they had to have materially aided a foreign power to harm the nation. In the case of Bollman and Swartwout, neither had done more than talk and write about the possibility of creating a new nation in the west, and thinking about treason was not treason. They were acquitted. In his opinion, Marshall made an aside that a person who helped equip or organize a military force could be considered a part of such a force if it ever assembled, even if he or she remained far from the action.

It was on this last point that prosecutors made their case against Burr: He was a traitor for organizing a military force intended to attack Americans. Further, they charged that he had also broken a statutory law that forbade Americans from privately waging war on a nation with which America was at peace—in this case Spain. Burr wanted the court to limit testimony to address only the specific charges against him. He notes that 135 witnesses had already been called and that the prosecution was planning to call hundreds more. According to Marshall's previous ruling in the Bollman and Swartwout case, two unimpeachable witnesses to the act of treason had to testify that they saw firsthand the acts of treason. The prosecution had produced witnesses who suggested Burr had thought about some sort of military adventure, but the gathering of young men in Ohio had featured far more in the way of food and camping equipment than weapons, and no one ever saw them assemble into a military formation in preparation for attacking someone. Essentially, Burr is arguing that the prosecution is trying him through character assassination, which he suggests is associated more with despotic practices under English common law than with the dictates of the Constitution. He contends that habeas corpus means that only evidence of the specific crime at issue should be presented to the court. The prosecution asserted that its countless witnesses were laying a foundation for evidence of the specific crimes with which Burr was charged. Marshall had accepted this explanation from the prosecution much earlier in the trial, when it became clear that witnesses were repeating the same stories over and over, with the requirement that the prosecution limit itself to only a few witnesses for each event. At this juncture he ruled in favor of Burr, and the precedent was established that only evidence related to the specific crimes charged could be presented by the prosecution in a criminal trial.

Again, Burr creates some confusion by referring to himself in both the first and third person, seeming to shift to the third person when discussing himself as his own client, as happens in the opening paragraph. The clerk who set down the text does a good job of distinguishing the voices of the various speakers, so that there is little doubt who is speaking at a given moment; the document captures some of the atmosphere of the complex debate that occurred in the courtroom during the trial. Those passages not identified as coming from George Hay (the chief prosecutor), John Wickham (a defense attorney), or Luther Martin (a defense attorney) are Burr's voice. Burr and his lawyers seek to narrow the question of treason to whether there is any evidence that the assembly of people on Blennerhassett's Island could be shown to be a military force, rather than just settlers gathering before making a voyage to their new homesteads, and whether Burr could be said to be involved in any activity on the island when he was far away in New York when the supposedly treasonous events transpired.

♦ The Private Journal of Aaron Burr

Burr often lied about his intentions. When he went to Europe to avoid being lynched by mobs in the United States, he tried to enlist first Great Britain and then France in his schemes to become monarch of a new nation in North America. He told the British government how he would aid it against France, and he told the French government how he would aid it against Great Britain, suggesting several different schemes, including invading Canada and making it into his new kingdom. Both governments kept written records of his proposals, but neither took him seriously. In one passage in his journal, he notes his efforts to claim to be a subject of the Crown, which he thought legitimate because he had been a British subject before the Revolutionary War.

Irrespective of his Machiavellian schemes, Burr had friends and family who loved him, and there were many

stories of his personal kindness. He was not a monster but a sad man who had let greatness slip from his grasp. His journal is written as if it were one long letter to his daughter Theodosia. He was probably closer to her than to any other person in his life. He took great pride in her high intelligence, and he often suggested subjects that she might research and write about. He devoted much time to her education and upbringing when she was a child, and it is perhaps forgivable that he should tell his daughter what she should do to raise her son. It is one of the mysteries of his personality that he could seem to lecture his daughter and yet come across as a doting man; he speaks to her in his customarily direct manner partly because he regards her as his intellectual equal. In his discussion of how to prepare her son for life in a democracy, one may discern a glimmer of what his preoccupations may have been had he become president in 1801. His vision is of a robust society in which citizens freely participate in the vital activities of civil life. Soon after writing this passage, he returned to the United States and set up a law practice in New York. Within a day of hanging out his sign, he had hundreds of clients, and thereafter his practice was very successful.

♦ Impact and Legacy

Burr is generally regarded as one of the foremost villains in American history, ranking not far below Benedict Arnold. Overall, his own writings condemn him as petty, envious, vengeful, and treasonous. The Burr conspiracy terrified many Americans, and his bizarre plans to set up settlements in the west, even to wage war, caused many Americans to detest him. His killing of Alexander Hamilton in a duel also damaged his reputation; between the two men, Hamilton contributed much more to American democracy, and many people resented Burr, as the lesser man, for being the one who survived the duel. For some historians, Burr was a brash rebel whose independent spirit made those who wished to be comfortable in their rule of the United States very uncomfortable; he forced them to defend their principles. Less recognized but more substantial was his effect on American law. Whether he intended to or not, he established the principle that even the most loathed of men must have a fair trial and that the Constitution applies equally to every American. Perhaps the most hated person in the United States in 1807, with even some jurors at his federal trial despising him, he was found not guilty because he used his skills to persuade Justice Marshall to require that the prosecution prove its exact charges, an issue that has become essential to criminal law in America.

Key Sources

The principal collection of Burr's political writings is *Political Correspondence and Public Papers of Aaron Burr* (1983), 2 vols., edited by Mary-Jo Kline and Joanne Wood Ryan. The Library of Congress and the Georgetown University Library have microfilm copies of Burr's papers; the Library of Congress additionally has some of Burr's manuscripts related to his travels in western territories as well as records of his trial for treason. Copies of the documents from Burr's trial are also kept in the National Archives. The Huntington Library, in San Marino, California, has a collection of Burr's papers. Some of Burr's papers are in the archives of the Missouri History Museum. Mathew L. Davis, Burr's literary executor, included some of Burr's letters in his *Memoirs of Aaron Burr: With Miscellaneous Selections from His Correspondence*, 2 vols. (1836–1837). There are two editions of Burr's journal: *The Private Journal of Aaron Burr, during His Residence of Four Years in Europe: With Selections from His Correspondence* (1838), edited by Matthew L. Davis, and *The Private Journal of Aaron Burr* (1903), edited by William K. Bixby.

Essential Quotes

"But he [Burr] challenged their [the senators'] attention to considerations more momentous than any which regarded merely their personal honor and character: the preservation of the Law, of Liberty and the Constitution—this house, said he, is a sanctuary and a citadel of law, of order, of liberty—and it is here—it is here—in this exalted refuge—here, if any where will resistance be made to the storms of popular phrenzy and the silent arts of corruption:—and if the Constitution be destined ever to perish by the sacrilegious hands of the Demagogue or the Usurper, which God avert, its expiring agonies will be witnessed on this floor."

(Farewell Address to the U.S. Senate)

Essential Quotes

"Burr guarantees the result with his life and honor—the lives, the honor and fortunes of hundreds, the best blood of our country."

(Deciphered Letter to General James Wilkinson)

"The people of the country to which we are going are prepared to receive us—their agents now with Burr say that if we will protect their religion, and will not subject them to a foreign power, that in three weeks all will be settled. The gods invite to glory and fortune—it remains to be seen whether we deserve the boon."

(Deciphered Letter to General James Wilkinson)

"The nature of his equipments clearly evinced that his object was purely peaceable and agricultural;... this fact alone ought to overthrow the testimony against him;... his designs were honorable, and would have been useful to the United States."

(Address to the Court on Innocence of Treason)

"He demanded the interposition of the civil authority;... it was from military despotism, from the tyranny of a military escort, that he wished to be delivered, not from an investigation into his conduct, or from the operation of the laws of his country."

(Address to the Court on Innocence of Treason)

"If, said he, the gentlemen mean or expect to prove an overt act; if they mean to prove that I am the source of the whole transaction, and that there was anything like an act of violence on Blennerhassett's Island, and that there was actual war waged, actual exertion of force used, a collision of arms, or the like, then to be sure the case will have a right to go on to that point; but even then there would be an absurdity, because of my being absent at that time, at a distance where I could not take a part in it."

(Motion to the Court to Limit Prosecution Evidence)

Milestone Documents

Essential Quotes

"I was desirous that the court, the jury, and the country should know what was charged against me; this has been done, and it has been found that I cannot be connected with the facts. I demand the opinion of the court on these points."

(Motion to the Court to Limit Prosecution Evidence)

"Besides, it is now that he [Aaron Burr Alston] should begin to imbibe that knowledge of the world so essential in democratic governments, and which can only be acquired by mingling with his equals on equal terms."

(*Private Journal of Aaron Burr*)

Further Reading

Articles

Prince, Carl E. "The Passing of the Aristocracy: Jefferson's Removal of the Federalists, 1801–1805." *Journal of American History* 57 (December 1970): 563–575.

Books

Daniels, Jonathan. *Ordeal of Ambition: Jefferson, Hamilton, Burr*. Garden City, N.Y.: Doubleday, 1970.

Fleming, Thomas. *Duel: Alexander Hamilton, Aaron Burr, and the Future of America*. New York: Basic Books, 1999.

Lomask, Milton. *Aaron Burr*. Vol. 1: *The Years from Princeton to Vice President, 1756–1805*. New York: Farrar, Strauss & Giroux, 1979; Vol. 2: *The Conspiracy and Years of Exile, 1805–1836*. New York: Farrar, Strauss & Giroux, 1982.

Melton, Buckner F., Jr. *Aaron Burr: Conspiracy to Treason*. New York: Wiley, 2002.

Rogow, Arnold A. *A Fatal Friendship: Alexander Hamilton and Aaron Burr*. New York: Hill and Wang, 1998.

—*Kirk H. Beetz*

Questions for Further Study

1. What does his writing style tell us about Aaron Burr's personality? Think, for example, of the way he switches back and forth from first to third person. What does his use of the third person say about his views of himself and the world?

2. Does Burr make a convincing plea for his innocence on charges of treason? Why or why not? Show how he responded—or failed to respond—to the evidence, including the communication with General Wilkinson.

3. What does Burr's *Private Journal* and the way in which he used it to provide training for his daughter Theodosia, say about Burr? Is it surprising that a man so given to troubles in his relations with the outside world should have apparently been a kind and loving father, especially in an era when society typically regarded girls as inferior to boys? Or is his warm relationship with Theodosia evidence of other qualities to his character? How are those qualities demonstrated in these samples of his writings?

Document Text

Farewell Address to the U.S. Senate

1805

Mr. Burr began by saying that he had intended to pass the day with them, but the increase of a slight indisposition ... had determined him then to take his leave of them. He touched lightly on some of the rules and orders of the house, and recommended in one or two points alterations of which he briefly explained the reasons and principles.

He then said he was sensible that he must at times, have wounded the feelings of individual members. He had ever avoided entering into any explanations at the time; because a moment of irritation was not the moment for explanation—because his position (being in the chair) rendered impossible to enter into explanations without obvious danger of consequences which might hazard the dignity of the Senate, or prove disagreeable and injurious in more than one point of view—That he had therefore preferred to leave to their reflections his justification, that on his part he had no injuries to complain of—If any had been done or attempted, he was ignorant of the authors: and if he had ever heard he had forgotten; for he thanked God he had no memory for injuries. He doubted not but that they had found occasion to observe, that to be prompt was not therefore to be precipitate, and that error was often to be preferred to indecision—that his errors, whatever they might have been, were those of rule and principle, and not of caprice—That it could not be deemed arrogance in him to say that in his official conduct he had known no party—no cause—no friend. That if in the opinion of any the discipline which had been established approached to rigor, they would at least admit that it was uniform and indiscriminate.

He further remarked that the ignorant and unthinking affected to treat as unnecessary and fastidious, a rigid attention to rules and decorum; but he thought nothing trivial which touched, however remotely, the dignity of that body; and he appealed to their experience for the justice of this sentiment, and urged them in language the most impressive, and in a manner the most commanding, to avoid the smallest relaxation of the habits which he had endeavored to indicate and establish.

But he challenged their attention to considerations more momentous than any which regarded merely their personal honor and character: the preservation of the *Law,* of *Liberty* and the Constitution—this house, said he, is a sanctuary and a citadel of law, of order, of liberty—and it is here—it is here—in this exalted refuge—here, if any where will resistance be made to the storms of popular phrenzy and the silent arts of corruption:—and if the Constitution be destined ever to perish by the sacrilegious hands of the Demagogue or the Usurper, which God avert, its expiring agonies will be witnessed on this floor.

He then adverted to those afflicting sensations which attended a final separation—a dissolution, perhaps forever, of those associations which he hoped had been mutually satisfactory. He consoled himself, however, and them with the reflections, that, though separated, they would be engaged in the common cause of disseminating principles of that body with interest and with solicitude—he should feel for their honor and the national honor so intimately connected with it—and took his leave with expressions of personal respect and with prayers and wishes.

Glossary

adverted:	called attention to
affected:	pretended
approached to rigor:	came close to being an extreme form of discipline
being in the chair:	a reference to Burr's role as vice president, making him president of the Senate
caprice:	thoughtless, ill-considered action
decorum:	correct actions
phrenzy:	frenzy
sensible:	aware
Usurper:	one who seizes power

Alexander Hamilton fights his fatal duel with Vice President Aaron Burr. From a painting by J. Mund.

Document Text

Letter to General James Wilkinson

1806

Yours postmarked 13th May is received. I have obtained funds, and have actually commenced the enterprise. Detachments from different points under different pretences will rendezvous on the Ohio, 1st November—everything internal and external favors views—protection of England is secured. T [Thomas Truxton] is gone to Jamaica to arrange with the admiral on that station, and will meet at the Mississippi—England—Navy of the United States are ready to join, and final orders are given to my friends and followers—it will be a host of choice spirits. Wilkinson shall be second to Burr only—Wilkinson shall dictate the rank and promotion of his officers. Burr will proceed westward 1st August, never to return: with him go his daughter—the husband will follow in October with a corps of worthies. Send forthwith an intelligent and confidential friend with whom Burr may confer. He shall return immediately with further interesting details—this is essential to concert and harmony of the movement. Send a list of all persons known to Wilkinson west of the mountains, who could be useful, with a note delineating their characters. By your messenger send me four or five of the commissions of your officers, which you can borrow under any pretence you please. They shall be returned faithfully. Already are orders to the contractor given to forward six months' provisions to points Wilkinson may name—this shall not be used until the last moment, and then under proper injunctions: the project is brought to the point so long desired: Burr guarantees the result with his life and honor—the lives, the honor and fortunes of hundreds, the best blood of our country. Burr's plan of operations is to move rapidly from the falls on the 15th of November, with the first five hundred or one thousand men, in light boats now constructing for that purpose—to be at Natchez between the 5th and 15th of December—then to meet Wilkinson—then to determine whether it will be expedient in the first instance to seize on or pass by Baton Rouge. On receipt of this send Burr an answer—draw on Burr for all expenses, &c. The people of the country to which we are going are prepared to receive us—their agents now with Burr say that if we will protect their religion, and will not subject them to a foreign power, that in three weeks all will be settled. The gods invite to glory and fortune—it remains to be seen whether we deserve the boon. The bearer [Samuel Swartwout] of this goes express to you—he will hand a formal letter of introduction to you from Burr, a copy of which is hereunto subjoined. He is a man of inviolable honor and perfect discretion—formed to execute rather than project—capable of relating facts with fidelity, and incapable of relating them otherwise. He is thoroughly informed of the plans and intentions of Burr, and will disclose to you as far as you inquire, and no further—he has imbibed a reverence for your character, and may be embarrassed in your presence—put him at ease and he will satisfy you—29th July.

Glossary

& c:	etc.
concert:	unified action; teamwork
the contractor:	the supplier
formed to execute rather than project:	trained to carry out orders rather than suggest his own ideas
imbibed a reverence:	formed a feeling of admiration
hereunto subjoined:	attached to this
a host of choice spirits:	a gathering of very good men
Samuel Swartout:	an associate of Burr's who was also tried for treason
Thomas Truxton:	also rendered as *Truxtun*, prominent American naval officer (1755–1822)
worthies:	reliable men

Address to the Court on Innocence of Treason

1807

Col. Burr then addressed the court, not, as he said, to remedy any omission of his counsel, who had done great justice to the subject, but to state a few facts, and repel some observations of a personal nature. The present inquiry involved a simple question of treason or misdemeanor. According to the Constitution, treason consisted in acts; whereas, in this case, his honor was invited to issue a warrant based upon mere conjecture. Alarms existed without cause. Mr. Wilkinson alarmed the President, and the President alarmed the people of Ohio. He appealed to historical facts. No sooner did he understand that suspicions were entertained in Kentucky of the nature and design of his movements, than he hastened to meet an investigation. The prosecution not being prepared, he was discharged. That he then went to Tennessee. While there he heard that the attorney for the district of Kentucky was preparing another prosecution against him; that he immediately returned to Frankfort, presented himself before the court, and again was honorably discharged; that what happened in the Mississippi Territory was equally well known; that there he was acquitted by the grand jury, but they went farther, and censured the conduct of the government; and if there had really been any cause of alarm, it must have been felt by the people of that part of the country; that the manner of his descent down the river was a fact which put at defiance all rumors about treason and misdemeanor; that the nature of his equipments clearly evinced that his object was purely peaceable and agricultural; that this fact alone ought to overthrow the testimony against him; that his designs were honorable, and would have been useful to the United States.

His flight, as it was termed, had been mentioned as evidence of guilt. He asked, at what time did he fly? In Kentucky, he invited inquiry, and that inquiry terminated in a firm conviction of his innocence; that the alarms were first great in the Mississippi Territory, and orders had been issued to seize and destroy the persons and property of himself and party; that he endeavored to undeceive the people, and convince them that he had no designs hostile to the United States, but that twelve hundred men were in arms for a purpose not yet developed; the people could not be deceived; and he was acquitted, and promised the protection of government; but the promise could not be performed; the arm of military power could not be resisted; that he knew there were military orders to seize his person and property, and transport him to a distance from that place; that he was assured by the officer of an armed boat, that it was lying in the river ready to receive him on board. Was it his duty to remain there thus situated? That he took the advice of his best friends, pursued the dictates of his own judgment, and abandoned a country where the laws ceased to be the sovereign power; that the charge stated in a handbill, that he had forfeited his recognizance, was false; that he had forfeited no recognizance; if he had forfeited any recognizance, he asked why no proceedings had taken place for the breach of it?

If he was to be prosecuted for such breach, he wished to know why he was brought to this place? Why not carry him to the place where the breach happened? That more than three months had elapsed since the order of the government had issued to seize and bring him to that place; yet it was pretended that sufficient time had not been allowed to adduce testimony in support of the prosecution. He asked why the guard who conducted him to that place avoided every magistrate along the way, unless from a conviction that they were acting without lawful authority? Why had he been debarred the use of pen, ink, and paper, and not even permitted to write to his daughter? That in the state of South Carolina, where he had happened to see three men together, he demanded the interposition of the civil authority; that it was from military despotism, from the tyranny of a military escort, that he wished to be delivered, not from an investigation into his conduct, or from the operation of the laws of his country. He concluded that there were three courses that might be pursued,—an acquittal; or a commitment for treason, or for a misdemeanor; that no proof existed in support of either but what was contained in the affidavits of Eaton and Wilkinson, abounding in crudities and absurdities.

Glossary

adduce:	present as an example
affidavits:	sworn statements
civil authority:	the civilian government, as opposed to the military authorities
commitment:	prison sentence
debarred:	prohibited
Eaton:	William Eaton, a general whom Burr tried unsuccessfully to enlist in his plot and who testified for the government and against Burr at his trial
evinced:	displayed or demonstrated
forfeited his recognizance:	posted bail by paying a nonrefundable fee
in arms:	armed and prepared for battle
magistrate:	judge
meet an investigation:	appear before the legal authorities to answer any questions
put at defiance:	showed the untruth of
repel some observations of a personal nature:	respond to personal attacks
to remedy any omission of his counsel:	to make up for anything his legal representatives had failed to mention
Wilkinson:	James Wilkinson, a general and co-conspirator of Burr's, who later betrayed his plot

Motion to the Court to Limit Prosecution Evidence

1807

Before the gentleman proceeds with his evidence, I will suggest that it has appeared to me that there would be great advantage and propriety in establishing a certain principle founded upon the facts which have been presented to the court. He [Burr?] said the facts which had been presented were to be taken for granted; and yet they utterly failed to prove that any overt act of war had been committed; and it was admitted that he was more than one hundred miles distant from the place where the overt act is charged to have been committed. He denied that any evidence was admissible to connect him with other persons, in acts done by them in his absence, and even done without his knowledge; or that facts brought from distant places could be connected with those done at Blennerhassett's Island, to give to the acts done there the name of treason, when no overt act of war was committed at that place. He commented upon the opinion of the supreme court in the Case of *Bollman and Swartwout,* and said that it had been totally misunderstood by the counsel for the prosecution. The defence had the right here to call upon the attorney for the United States to say whether an assemblage of men merely can be called, or in any way tortured into an act of "levying war." This point must be inevitably determined at some stage of the examination, and therefore they had the right to require of the prosecutor to show that every witness will give testimony tending to prove an overt act of war, or his testimony would be irrelevant and immaterial.

Another point was, whether a person not present, remote, in another district, can be considered, in any possible legal construction, to be present, and concerned in the transaction, so as to make him a principal in the guilt of it. If not, then the necessity of examining the remainder of these 135 witnesses is done away, because their testimony can have no bearing on the case. If, said he, the gentlemen mean or expect to prove an overt act; if they mean to prove that I am the source of the whole transaction, and that there was anything like an act of violence on Blennerhassett's Island, and that there was actual war waged, actual exertion of force used, a collision of arms, or the like, then to be sure the case will have a right to go on to that point; but even then there would be an absurdity, because of my being absent at that time, at a distance where I could not take a part in it. The gentlemen who are engaged with me as my counsel will enlarge on these points, and, if I am not mistaken, they will prove that this is the moment when the argument and decision will be most applicable, because upon the result will rest the future fate of the case.

Now, if my ideas are right, the gentlemen mean to argue that a bare assemblage of men, coupled with previous treasonable declarations, is treason. I understand that they mean to contend further, that a person not being present, but absent from the place where the treason is laid, he having counseled and advised the operations, should be denominated a principal in the treason. But this, I shall contend, is a species of constructive treason. Again: I shall ask what an accessory means, and prove that if it means what they think it does, resort must be had to the exploded common law of England. These questions, sir, will demand some attention from the court, and will be extremely interesting to the country at large, because every man might be affected by them. Gentlemen ought to come forward and say that they mean to charge me upon the common law: that though there was no force used in reality, yet by construction there was force used; that though I was not personally present, yet that by construction I was present; that though there really was no military array, yet by construction there was military array. Now, sir, we totally deny all these things, upon the soundest principles, and it is full time that it should be known what is, and what is not, the law on the subject.

Mr. Hay said he had no objection to any fair inquiry into these principles; but the motion was premature. He believed testimony would be introduced, and that presently, which would give a very different aspect to the transactions on Blennerhassett's Island to what had appeared. Although there was not on that island what Mr. Lee had called "open war," no "collision of arms," or "hard knocks," they would prove that there was "military array"; that the men were collected for military purposes, and that a military object was in

view. It was impossible then to tell in what precise light the transactions on Blennerhassett's Island would ultimately appear, because new light was every moment coming in. He asked if the court after all that had been exposed, and with the uncertainty as to what might be brought to view, would undertake to say that an overt act of treason had not been proved. That was a fact to be ascertained by the jury. It was their province, and theirs only, to say whether the act has or has not been committed. The object of the motion was not to save time, but it was to prevent the public from seeing what they ought to see. He denied that there was any privilege or authority in this court, or in the courts of Great Britain, to arrest inquiry and tell the jury that the act had not been proved, and therefore there was an end to the case. When the whole of the testimony should be laid before the court, it would then be in the power of the accused to address to the court a motion to instruct the jury on any point of law which the circumstances of the case might require. It would then become the duty of the court to take up the subject and say what is the law upon the case; and the jury would take the facts under their views, and regulate their verdict agreeably to the law and the facts that may appear. He did not understand what the common law had to do with any inquiry before our courts, except it was any part of it adopted by statute. He was willing to steer clear of the common law, and go entirely upon the principles of statutory law and common sense. The case was a charge for an overt act of treason in levying war. Would common sense say, or would our statutes or constitution require that the person who had produced all this commotion should be present when the battle was fought, or even when the troops were collected for the enterprise? He conceived the question to be, whether the accused was principally concerned with it—whether he did project and carry it on with a design to complete it? And how could this be ascertained, unless the prosecution were permitted to go on with the evidence?

Mr. Wickham, in answer to the allegation that it was not a proper time to bring forward such a motion, denied that, during the whole three days that had been occupied in the examination of witnesses, there had been a single word, by any one witness, that could tend in the least to support the indictment. It is proved, (said he,) and the attorney for the United States declares, that Colonel Burr was not present at the time and place charged. Now we declare that it is absolutely necessary to prove the fact of presence at once: we say the indictment must inevitably fail without it. The counsel for the accused propose now to go into this question, and I trust the court will hear them. He would give an intimation to the counsel for the prosecution, that they should take a wide and extensive range on the subject, and by which they were convinced there would be a stop put to the case at once.

Mr. Burr added: The gentlemen were about to proceed to connect me with the act. I deny, sir, that they can do so. They admit that I was not there, and therefore let the nature of the transaction be what it may, it cannot affect me. Again: I deny that there was war, at all, and no testimony can be brought to prove that there was war; and surely the article war is of imperious necessity in the charge of treason. Now, if this be true, will the court go on week after week, discovering nothing that can affect me? I was desirous that the court, the jury, and the country should know what was charged against me; this has been done, and it has been found that I cannot be connected with the facts. I demand the opinion of the court on these points.

Mr. Martin spoke of the great length of time that the trial would probably last, if the prosecutor was permitted to go on in his own way. It was a very sickly season, and the probability of sickness among some of the jury or the court was very great, which would prevent the case going on. If one of the jurors should die, however far the case may have progressed, the trial must begin anew.

The CHIEF JUSTICE said that there was no doubt that the court must hear the objections to the admissibility of the evidence; it was a right, and gentlemen might insist on it. But as some of the transactions on Blennerhassett's Island remained yet to be gone into, he suggested whether it would not be as well to postpone the motion till that evidence was gone through.

Mr. Burr.—I have no objection to that, if they do confine themselves to Blennerhassett's Island, and strictly to transactions on that island; if so, we will hear it.

Glossary

arrest:	put a stop to
aspect to:	interpretation or understanding of
common law:	a system of law based primarily on past legal judgments rather than formal statutes passed by a legislative body
counsel:	legal representatives
denominated:	regarded as
exploded common law of England:	an extended, overly interpreted version of the English common law
Mr. Hay:	George Hay, chief prosecutor
imperious:	intensely compelling
Mr. Lee:	Charles Lee, a defense attorney
levying:	bringing into action
Mr. Martin:	Luther Martin, a defense attorney
military array:	a gathering of armed men for the purpose of making war
presently:	very soon
species of constructive treason:	an attempt to define treason by far-fetched reasoning
statutory law:	a legal system based primarily on laws formally passed by a legislative body
tortured:	construed or interpreted according to strained logic
very sickly season:	a time of year when people were likely to get sick
Mr. Wickham:	John Wickham, a defense attorney

The Private Journal of Aaron Burr

He [John Reeves] showed me a letter from Colonel Jenkinson about my pretensions as a British subject. Dampier has given opinion that I may resume at pleasure, the Lord Chancellor, [earl of] Eldon, that I cannot, and am forever an alien....

London, May 9, 1812

If there should be war, and national honour and national interest loudly demand it, I advise your husband [Joseph Alston] to apply for a military commission. He has extraordinary talents in that line, and may never have another opportunity to display them. If he would succeed, he must apply in person; he would assuredly have the support of your governor, whoever he may be, and of the members from the state. I think he would easily obtain a regiment.

I am not content with the exclusive domestic education which you give the boy [Aaron Burr Alston]. It imposes on him a dreary labour, enough to benumb his faculties, and which will have that effect. None of the sports of youth to enliven his leisure hours! No emulation! no example! no associate in his labours! Besides, it is now that he should begin to imbibe that knowledge of the world so essential in democratic governments, and which can only be acquired by mingling with his equals on equal terms. It is high time that he commence this apprenticeship.

Think, also, of the moral effects which your mode will produce. I mean, its influence on his temper, his cast of mind, and his future views and projects. I could write an essay on this subject, but you can do it just as well; nay, better, for you will say all I could say and something more. So, madame, set about it forthwith. Keep in mind, in composing your essay, the difference, in this particular, between a republic and a despotism.

As to the controversy, so long subsisting, about the preference due to public or private education, all that I have read on the subject is little better than downright nonsense. There are those who can never agree about the sort of public or the sort of domestic education; nor about the destination of their pupil. I would unite the advantages of both, thus: So soon as I shall be settled in New-York, send me the boy and his tutor. They must both live with me. The college in New-York has excellent teachers in every branch, good mathematical instruments, philosophical apparatus, and library. The boy shall there try his strength in the arena of competition, where he shall have fair play, but no favour. I shall superintend his studies and his pursuits of every kind (for which I shall have abundant leisure, proposing to abstract myself from all political concerns), awaken his genius, and keep every faculty on the stretch.

Is it not manifest that, in this way, he would in one year acquire more, and with an ardour, an animation, and enthusiasm to which he has hitherto been a stranger, than he would in your way in four years of monotonous and gloomy toil? But the difference in the quantity of literary acquirements is of infinitely less moment than that which will be produced in his character, and in the invigoration of his faculties and the expansion of his mind. If, indeed, it be resolved that he is to do nothing in this world but drive negroes and plant rice, the present plan may do well enough; but even then I should pity the poor little fellow, for all the dull, irksome, unsatisfactory drudgery he must undergo....

The United States' charge des affaires here, Jonathan Russell, and the consuls, have done all in their power to keep me here. They, at least the consuls, and supposed under the influence of Russell, have menaced masters of vessels with the displeasure of government if they should dare to take me out. Whether this be by instructions from the government or of their private malice, I know not; but it has put me to great trouble and expense, and you and the boy will suffer for it, for I have been obliged to sell all the pretty things I had bought for you at Paris. Don't cry, dear little soul, pappy will buy thee more! But, in truth, I do not think either of you will much grudge the sacrifice of your watches, and trinkets, and cambrics, and ribands, when you know that the object was to get me out, and that there was no other way. Now I tell you that I shall get out in spite of them, and very soon.

Milestone Documents

Glossary

abstract myself:	remove myself
the boy [Aaron Burr Alston]:	Burr's grandson
cambrics:	items of an expensive white linen fabric
Colonel Jenkinson:	younger brother of Robert Banks Jenkinson, Lord Hawkesbury, who served in the Home Office and was in charge of aliens living in Great Britain
charge des affaires:	or chargé d'affaires, an official who runs an embassy or consulate when the ambassador is not present
consuls:	officials with responsibilities akin to those of ambassadors, though with an emphasis on trade and economic matters
Dampier:	Henry Dampier, a government functionary assigned to be a liaison between Aaron Burr and the British government while Burr resided in England
despotism:	dictatorship
exclusive domestic education:	homeschooling
forthwith:	immediately
functionary:	official
He [John Reeves]:	British government functionary
infinitely less moment:	far less importance
keep every faculty on the stretch:	keep all of his abilities finely tuned
the Lord Chancellor … Eldon:	John Scott (1751–1838), first earl of Eldon, who held the position of chancellor, second only to the prime minister in the British parliamentary government
pretensions as:	efforts to become
republic:	government by elected officials
ribands:	decorative ribbons
subsisting:	continuing
your husband [Joseph Alston]:	Burr's son-in-law

Official photograph portrait of former U.S. President George W. Bush. White house photo by Eric Draper.

George W. Bush: Original Analysis

Forty-third President of the United States

1946–

Overview

George W. Bush was born in 1946 in Connecticut but grew up in Texas. His father, George H. W. Bush, was a career politician who served in a variety of posts, including both vice president and president of the United States. After a business career as an oilman and owner of the Texas Rangers baseball team, the younger Bush was elected governor of Texas in 1994 and was reelected in 1998. He gained the Republican presidential nomination in 2000 based on a campaign that emphasized "compassionate conservatism," a new, more moderate approach to social and domestic issues. Bush won the 2000 election in one of the closest contests in U.S. history. His Democratic opponent, Al Gore, won the majority of the popular vote, but Bush won the electoral vote after controversy surrounding recounts in Florida. Bush achieved some initial successes in his domestic policy, including the bipartisan No Child Left Behind Act and a series of tax cuts; however, his presidency came to be defined by the terrorist attacks of September 11, 2001, and the subsequent U.S.-led "war on terror," as Bush referred to it. He was reelected in 2004.

Following the 2001 terrorist attacks by al Qaeda, Bush developed a coalition of nations and invaded Afghanistan, where U.S. and allied Afghan forces overthrew the Taliban regime and disrupted the al Qaeda network in the country. The United States then launched a variety of covert missions and financial operations against terrorist groups around the world. For its part, Congress enacted new domestic security measures, including the USA Patriot Act, which expanded the government's security powers. In the largest government reorganization since the 1940s, Bush created the Department of Homeland Security to coordinate the disparate agencies involved in domestic law enforcement and intelligence. In 2002 Bush instituted a new security doctrine to replace the cold war emphasis on containment and deterrence. The new strategy embraced preemptive war as a means to preventing future terrorist attacks against the United States. The first invocation of the new doctrine came in 2003, when the United States invaded Iraq under the pretext of the larger war on terror. The invasion led both to prolonged conflict in Iraq and to deep divisions between the United States and some of its closest allies, such as France, Germany, and Turkey. Bush's refusal to adopt the Kyoto Protocol on global warming and unilateralist actions such as the withdrawal from the 1972 Anti-Ballistic Missile Treaty added to tensions between the United States and other nations.

The president's security policies were initially very popular, and Bush's approval ratings soared above 90 percent. Bush's public appeal helped Republicans build sizable majorities in both houses of Congress in 2002 and 2004. However, his popularity was undermined by the administration's slow response to the devastation of Hurricane Katrina in New Orleans and the growing unpopularity of the war in Iraq. In addition, partially owing to increased security spending, the administration developed a substantial budget deficit. Democrats regained control of both chambers of Congress in 2006 for the first time since 1994. Faced with a hostile Congress, Bush was then unable to make progress on other domestic priorities, including an effort to reform Social Security.

Explanation and Analysis of Documents

Bush was not considered a great orator, but several of his addresses were widely praised for rallying the nation in the aftermath of the terrorist attacks of September 11, 2001. Indeed, Bush was initially hailed for his strong leadership, but in his second term, his resoluteness was increasingly perceived as stubbornness and an unwillingness to listen to alternative viewpoints. One result was that Bush was often condemned for pursuing unilateralist foreign policy by domestic and foreign detractors alike. When he first entered office, Bush laid out an ambitious domestic agenda. Part of that agenda is revealed in a short address on tax cuts that outlines his philosophy on the scope of government and federal spending. The majority of speeches and documents for which Bush will be remembered, however, deal with foreign policy and national security, including his address on the attacks of September 11; the "axis of evil" speech, in which he first articulated the doctrine of preemption; and his address on the war with Iraq, in which he announced the commencement of hostilities between the United States and Saddam Hussein's regime in Iraq. In his second inaugural address Bush articulated a renewed commitment for democracy around the globe.

♦ Remarks on Signing the Economic Growth and Tax Relief Reconciliation Act

One of President Bush's first priorities on entering office was the reform of the nation's tax code. Like other conservatives, Bush believed that the tax system placed an undue

burden on the middle class and stifled investors and small businesses, which, in turn, slowed economic growth. Bush crafted a bipartisan reform effort that brought together Republicans and moderate and conservative Democrats. The resulting legislation cut taxes for most Americans, including through reductions in the marginal tax rates, the estate tax, and the capital gains tax. The lowest tax rate was reduced from 15 percent to 10 percent, while the tax credit for children was doubled. The new law also simplified and reformed the regulations governing retirement plans. Most of the individual components of the tax measure were temporary, to expire in ten years absent Congress's renewal of the legislation.

When he signed the tax reform act on June 7, 2001, Bush issued a short address. He begins his comments by noting how the tax cuts would benefit an individual family, citing the case of the Ramoses of Pennsylvania. The president declares, "Today we're beginning to make life for the Ramos' a lot easier. Today we start to return some of the Ramos' money and not only their money but the money of everybody who paid taxes." Bush notes that major tax reforms of this nature had occurred only twice since World War II, once under President John F. Kennedy and then under Ronald W. Reagan. He then states, "Now it's happening for the third time, and it's about time."

Bush goes on to note the difficulty of enacting the measure, pointing out that most believed the effort would be impossible when he initially proposed the reforms. The president cites the bipartisan nature of the new law and specifically thanks leading congressional Republicans and Democrats for working together to produce the legislation. He also cites his appreciation for members of the administration who worked with Congress. Bush states that the bipartisan nature of the reform and the speed with which it was enacted signal a new era of cooperation in Washington. The president then cites both specific and general advantages that the tax cuts would bring to individual Americans and their families and to the business community. For instance, he notes that the per-child tax credit was doubled to $1,000. In addition, most American families would receive a $600 tax rebate as a result of the reduced tax rates. Bush then strongly argues that the new tax system removed economic obstacles and would be more just to Americans. He states that the new measure reflects the people's desire that the tax system be "fair and not penalize them for making good choices, good choices such as marriage and raising a family."

Bush cites the longstanding belief within the Republican Party that tax relief stimulates the economy by allowing people to spend or save more of their own money. He counters arguments that the tax reform would undermine the surplus by asserting that the surplus was really the people's money and that the government did not have a right to keep or spend more than it budgeted. Bush emphatically declares that "the surplus is not the Government's money. The surplus is the people's money, and we ought to trust them with their own money."

Time Line

1946	July 6	■ George Walker Bush is born in New Haven, Connecticut.
1975		■ Bush graduates from Harvard Business School.
1978		■ Bush unsuccessfully runs for the U.S. House of Representatives from Texas.
1994	November 8	■ Bush is elected governor of Texas for the first of two terms.
2000	November 7	■ In the U.S. presidential election, Al Gore wins the popular vote, but Bush wins more electoral votes; the results are contested in Florida.
	December 12	■ In *Bush v. Gore*, the Supreme Court halts the Florida recounts, and Bush is named president-elect.
2001	June 7	■ Bush delivers remarks in connection with his enactment of tax cuts.
	September 11	■ Terrorists use passenger jets to conduct a series of attacks on civilian targets in the United States, killing nearly three thousand.
	September 20	■ Bush addresses the nation in response to the terrorist attacks.
	November–December	■ U.S.-led coalition overthrows the Taliban regime in Afghanistan.
2002	January 29	■ Bush delivers his second State of the Union address, to be known as the "axis of evil" speech.
2003	March 19	■ Bush speaks to the nation about the impending military campaign against the regime of Saddam Hussein; the United States launches the invasion of Iraq the following day.
2005	January 20	■ Bush delivers his second inaugural address.

Time Line		
	August 29	■ Hurricane Katrina devastates New Orleans and the Mississippi Gulf Coast; the administration is criticized for its response to the disaster.
2006	November 7	■ The Democrats regain control of both houses of Congress for the first time in twelve years.
2009	January 20	■ Bush leaves the office of the presidency.

The 2001 tax cuts were followed by two additional measures that further altered the tax code. The resultant reduction in federal revenues, combined with an economic downturn and the increased security spending after September 2001, created significant annual budget shortfalls, which peaked in 2004 at $413 billion. The cuts also led to the defection of Senator Jim Jeffords of Vermont from the Republican Party in 2001. Jeffords became an independent who caucused with the Democrats, who thus gained control of the Senate for the first time since 1994.

♦ Address on the Terrorist Attacks of September 11

In probably the most important and most stirring speech of his career, Bush addressed the nation on September 20, 2001, in the aftermath of the al Qaeda terrorist attacks on the United States. The address was crafted by a team of speechwriters, including Michael J. Gerson and John Gibson. All involved in preparing the address understood its historic importance. The attacks killed 2,998 people (not including the terrorists who perpetrated the strikes) and injured more than six thousand. The attacks also shut down U.S. air traffic and destroyed a significant portion of Manhattan's financial district. The stock market suffered its largest single-week decline in its history in the week after September 11, and the economic costs of the attacks were estimated to be more than $500 billion.

In the address, the president assures the American people of the government's preparedness to take strong action against those who planned and conducted the attacks. In one of the most memorable lines, Bush declares, "Whether we bring our enemies to justice, or bring justice to our enemies, justice will be done." He goes on to point out that, with the exception of the attack on Pearl Harbor in 1941, the United States had fought its wars on foreign soil since the end of the Civil War.

There was initially a great deal of uncertainty about who perpetrated the attacks, and in his address Bush uses the occasion to present the case against al Qaeda. He emphatically lays the blame for the strikes on al Qaeda, noting that the same group had been responsible for past incidents, including the 1998 bombings of the U.S. embassies in Kenya and Tanzania and the attack on the U.S.S. *Cole* in Yemen in 2000. The president explains that al Qaeda was headquartered in Afghanistan, where it had close ties with the Taliban regime. He then issues a series of demands to the Taliban. First, the group is challenged to surrender the leadership of al Qaeda to the United States and dismantle terrorist training camps in the country. Second, the Taliban is ordered to provide the United States with access to the terrorist facilities in the country. Third, Bush demands that the Taliban release all foreign aid workers, journalists, and others who had been detained. The president states clearly that "these demands are not open to negotiation or discussion" and that the Taliban regime would have to turn over the al Qaeda terrorists or "share in their fate." Bush goes on to inform the American people and his global audience that action against al Qaeda and the Taliban would be part of a larger, global struggle against terrorism. He claims that the new "war on terror" would "not end until every terrorist group of global reach has been found, stopped and defeated."

Bush then endeavors to explain why the terrorist groups had targeted the United States. He argues that they hated the freedoms and liberties that marked American politics and society. The president ties al Qaeda to past antidemocratic and totalitarian regimes, including those of the Nazis and other authoritarian governments of the twentieth century. Just as the previous struggles against Fascism and Communism had not been concluded by a single battle or encounter, the new war on terror would be "a lengthy campaign." In wording that was popular at the time but has since been criticized, Bush casts the war as one of stark contrasts in which countries would be either allied with the United States and its partners or opposed to the antiterror coalition; he dramatically states, "Either you are with us, or you are with the terrorists." The administration has since been criticized for continuing strategic and diplomatic relationships with countries such as Pakistan, where al Qaeda and the Taliban established new bases after the U.S. invasion of Afghanistan.

Bush shifts from a discussion of the implications of the attacks for U.S. foreign policy to address how the strikes would change America's domestic security policies. He tells the nation of his creation of a new agency, the Office of Homeland Security, which will be responsible for coordinating domestic intelligence and security operations. The president warns Americans to be vigilant but not to unfairly target Muslims within the country. Bush also calls on Americans to continue going about their lives, since this would be the best way to demonstrate the nation's resolve and to help the economy rebound.

Bush concludes in a stirring fashion by asserting that the United States will provide global leadership in the war on terror. He states that the United States will "rally the world to this cause by our efforts, by our courage." He then declares, "We will not tire, we will not falter, and we will not fail." Bush's determination and confidence during the address rallied the American people and bolstered public support for the incipient war on terror and his domestic security initiatives.

♦ Second State of the Union Address

Bush's most controversial major speech was his State of the Union address of January 29, 2002, commonly known as the "axis of evil" speech. In the address, Bush identifies Iran, Iraq, and North Korea as members of an "axis of evil" that threatened world peace, and he promises to take preemptive action to prevent terrorist strikes against the United States. The president reminds the nation of the accomplishments made since the attacks of September 11, 2001, including the overthrow of the Taliban regime and the installation of a pro-Western, democratic government in Afghanistan. He pledges that the United States will continue to be a partner in Afghanistan's transition. The president also discusses the continuing threat posed to the United States and other nations by global terrorism and highlights some of the operations that the nation and its allies were undertaking to counter the danger. While Bush trumpets cooperative U.S. efforts, he also declares that "some governments will be timid in the face of terror" and that the United States would undertake unilateral action if those regimes did not take steps to destroy terrorist networks.

Bush then discourses for some time on the dangers posed by Iran, Iraq, and North Korea. He notes that each of the three had a history of pursuing weapons of mass destruction. He accuses North Korea of attempting to gain such weapons "while starving its citizens." Iran and Iraq are likewise accused of endeavoring to acquire such weapons and of supporting international terrorism. Bush also notes that the regime in Iraq had defied weapons inspections by the United Nations and had used chemical weapons against its own people.

In the next section of the speech, Bush speaks of the efforts undertaken by the United States to work with other countries to deter terrorism, but he again raises the possibility of unilateral American action to prevent terrorist attacks. The president states, "I will not wait on events, while dangers gather." Bush warns the American people that the war on terror was not expected to be a quick or short campaign. Instead, it would be an ongoing struggle that would likely not be finished during his presidency. Bush reminds Americans that the nation was no longer protected by the "vast oceans," such that only better domestic and foreign security policies could ameliorate the threat of international terrorism. He discusses the changes in national security policy and the increased spending on homeland security that had been implemented since the 2001 attacks. The president assures Americans that the government would spend whatever would be needed to improve security and protect the nation's interests and the lives of its citizens; he points out that his defense budget contained the largest increase in more than twenty years. Bush contends that some alterations in homeland security policy would have multiple benefits. For instance, enhanced border security would not only deter terrorists but would also constrain the import of illicit drugs. Bush concludes his address by speaking about the character of the American people. He dismisses contentions that Americans were self-centered or materialistic, instead arguing that the 2001 attacks had brought out the "true character" of the nation and that Americans had "responded magnificently, with courage and compassion, strength and resolve."

The "axis of evil" speech was delivered at a time when Bush enjoyed extraordinarily high levels of public support. The address was frequently interrupted by applause and was one of the most widely viewed State of the Union addresses in American history. Over the next year, the Bush administration drew ever closer to war with Iraq. In September 2002 the administration issued its updated version of *The National Security Strategy of the United States of America*, which codified the nation's new security priorities and polices and formally embraced the preemption doctrine as a means to countering immediate threats to the United States. The preemption strategy came to be known as the Bush Doctrine. In October 2002, Congress voted overwhelmingly to allow Bush to use force against Iraq; the vote in the House was 296 in favor to 133 opposed, while the Senate voted seventy-seven to twenty-three. That November, positive public perceptions of Bush's leadership in the war on terror led Republicans to reverse historic trends and gain seats in the midterm elections, which increased their majority in the House and allowed the president's party to regain control of the Senate.

♦ Address to the Nation on Military Operations in Iraq

Following the terrorist attacks of September 2001, the Bush administration accused the Iraqi regime of Saddam Hussein of having an ongoing program for weapons of mass destruction, of supporting terrorism, and of violating a range of United Nations (UN) Security Council resolutions enacted in the aftermath of the 1991 Gulf War. American leaders also decried the dictatorial nature of the regime and its brutal suppression of the Iraqi people. Through the fall of 2002 the administration conducted a diplomatic offensive to gain international support for military action to depose Hussein. The administration's efforts resulted in the unanimous passage of UN Security Resolution 1441, which affirmed that Iraq had been in "material breach" of past resolutions and initiated a new weapons inspection program. Through the winter, the inspectors met with mixed compliance and evasion by the regime. Efforts to gain a second UN resolution to explicitly authorize the use of force failed, though some members of the Bush administration argued that previous violations by Iraq made an additional UN resolution unnecessary. The diplomatic effort created fissures with some of America's closest allies, although domestically, polls indicated that support for military action against Iraq reached more than 70 percent in 2003.

On March 19, 2003, Bush went on television to explain to the American people why the United States was launching military strikes against Iraq, which officially began the following day. Bush opens the address by declaring that the war was being initiated "to disarm Iraq, to free its people and to defend the world from grave danger." To counter criticism that the conflict lacked international support, Bush notes that the U.S.-led anti–Saddam Hussein

coalition included thirty-five nations (although at first only the United States, Australia, Poland, and the United Kingdom contributed troops to the invasion force).

For several lines, the commander in chief speaks directly to the men and women of the U.S. military. He praises the professionalism of the military and its dedication to the principles that marked the ideology of the United States. Bush tells the men and women of the service that "the peace of a troubled world and the hopes of an oppressed people now depend on you." He assures the American people that every effort would be undertaken to prevent the unnecessary loss of civilian life. He further declares that the United States had no territorial ambitions in Iraq. Rather, the United States sought only to remove a tyrannical regime and bring freedom to the Iraqi people. The president pledges to use overwhelming force to end the conflict quickly.

The address was short and direct. Bush appeared somber and delivered the speech in a determined yet measured fashion. The U.S.-led coalition indeed quickly overran the country and toppled the Iraqi regime. On May 1, 2003, from the flight deck of an aircraft carrier, the USS *Abraham Lincoln*, Bush declared an end to major combat operations in Iraq. However, an anti-U.S. insurgency was spreading through many areas of the country. While only 140 U.S. troops were killed in the initial invasion (through May), by 2008 more than four thousand U.S. servicemen and servicewomen had been killed in Iraq. Meanwhile, the war became increasingly unpopular in the United States. Many criticized Bush for declaring an end to combat far too early and for underestimating the number of troops needed to conclude the conflict. Furthermore, subsequent inspections failed to produce any Iraqi weapons of mass destruction, undermining one of the central justifications for the invasion. By 2008 only about one-third of Americans continued to support the war.

♦ Second Inaugural Address

Bush's second inaugural address was a marked departure from his first in 2001 and from most of his other speeches. It was far more rhetorical and laced with symbolism, and it contained numerous religious references and allusions. It clearly was designed for history. Written by Gerson, Matthew Scully, and John McConnell, the speech was considered by many as one of Bush's best statements of his views on foreign affairs and on the role of the United States as a global leader. In many ways, the speech marked the high-water point of Bush's presidency. He had just been reelected with 51 percent of the vote to his opponent's 48 percent (making him the first president to receive more than 50 percent of the popular vote since 1988). In addition, Republicans increased their majorities in both chambers of Congress. Flushed from the apparent success of the war on terror and the overthrow of the regime of Saddam Hussein, Bush delivered a second inaugural address that focused primarily on foreign policy. Its central theme was U.S. support for democracy and a renewed commitment to spreading democracy throughout the world. Bush hoped to use a combination of U.S. military creditability and expanded diplomacy to promote democratic reforms. Bush and his advisers believed that democracy would be the best means to countering terrorism and international instability.

Bush begins this address by reminding Americans that for most of the past century, the United States was engaged in a succession of struggles to defend democracy and freedom. He asserts that the demise of Soviet Communism ushered in "years of repose, years of sabbatical," which were superseded by the war on terror. The United States was now again engaged in a global struggle, and Bush asserts that the only way to ensure freedom in the United States will be to extend liberty around the world. He pledges to support democratic movements anywhere in the world while assuring Americans that such efforts would not be conducted mainly through military action. Instead, a variety of economic, diplomatic, and social efforts would be coordinated to pressure antidemocratic regimes. The president promises that the United States would "not impose our own style of government on the unwilling" but would try to aid other nations in the development of governments and political systems that would match their individual cultural and historical backgrounds. The president notes that any attempt to expand democracy would be a multiyear process. Like the war on terror, the campaign to spread democracy would likely continue after the end of his presidency.

Bush undertook a number of steps to fulfill the sentiments of his second inaugural address. The United States supported democratic movements in Georgia, Ukraine, and Lebanon. On the other hand, the administration continued to support antidemocratic regimes such as that of Pakistan. Meanwhile, U.S. actions toward Georgia and Ukraine exacerbated tensions with Russia. Within the administration, Bush's foreign and security policy team changed dramatically after the 2004 election. Secretary of State Colin Powell was replaced by the former national security adviser Condoleezza Rice, and Michael Chertoff took the place of the first Homeland Security secretary, Tom Ridge. In 2006, Secretary of Defense Donald Rumsfeld resigned, and Bush appointed Robert Gates to take his place. These changes in leadership and Bush's declining stature both domestically and on the international stage further undermined the ability of the United States to fulfill Bush's pledge to expand democracy.

Impact and Legacy

As president, Bush's approval ratings in turn ranked among both the highest and lowest in modern American history. He enjoyed significant public approval during his first term but lost support during his second. Bush was not a great public speaker; however, he demonstrated an ability to rally the American people, especially following the terrorist attacks of September 11, 2001. He appeared unwavering in the face of threats to U.S. security and projected an image as a confident and capable leader. His strong and often sharp rhetoric initially resonated well with domestic audiences. Internationally, Bush was the focus of increasing criticism

for portraying a "cowboy" persona. Phrases such as "Either you are with us, or you are with the terrorists" and "axis of evil" were demonstrative of the type of language that some found too uncompromising. However, after the 2003 invasion of Iraq, Bush did pursue a more multilateral foreign policy that included negotiations with North Korea, one of the members of the so-called axis of evil, to end the country's programs for weapons of mass destruction.

Opposition to Bush united the Democratic Party and the political left in the United States. Democratic control of Congress after 2006 and the continuing unpopularity of the war in Iraq constrained Bush's domestic agenda during his final two years in office. Initiatives such as comprehensive immigration reform and efforts to privatize social security failed. Bush had pledged to unite the nation after the contentious 2000 election, but throughout his presidency his policies proved to be divisive.

Key Sources

The only significant collection of Bush's papers available as of 2008 is the *Public Papers of the Presidents of the United States: George W. Bush*, published by the National Archives and Records Administration. Documents from the collection are available online through the Government Printing Office (http://www.gpoaccess.gov/pubpapers/gwbush.html).

Essential Quotes

"Tax relief expands individual freedom."

(Remarks on Signing the Economic Growth and Tax Relief Reconciliation Act)

"We recognize, loud and clear, the surplus is not the Government's money. The surplus is the people's money, and we ought to trust them with their own money."

(Remarks on Signing the Economic Growth and Tax Relief Reconciliation Act)

"Whether we bring our enemies to justice, or bring justice to our enemies, justice will be done."

(Address on the Terrorist Attacks of September 11)

"We will rally the world to this cause by our efforts, by our courage. We will not tire, we will not falter, and we will not fail."

(Address on the Terrorist Attacks of September 11)

"States like these, and their terrorist allies, constitute an axis of evil, arming to threaten the peace of the world."

(Second State of the Union Address)

Essential Quotes

"I will not wait on events, while dangers gather. I will not stand by, as peril draws closer and closer. The United States of America will not permit the world's most dangerous regimes to threaten us with the world's most destructive weapons."

(Second State of the Union Address)

"To all the men and women of the United States Armed Forces now in the Middle East, the peace of a troubled world and the hopes of an oppressed people now depend on you. That trust is well placed."

(Address to the Nation on Military Operations in Iraq)

"We have no ambition in Iraq, except to remove a threat and restore control of that country to its own people."

(Address to the Nation on Military Operations in Iraq)

"There is only one force of history that can break the reign of hatred and resentment and expose the pretensions of tyrants and reward the hopes of the decent and tolerant. And that is the force of human freedom."

(Second Inaugural Address)

"America, in this young century, proclaims liberty throughout all the world and to all the inhabitants thereof. Renewed in our strength—tested, but not weary—we are ready for the greatest achievements in the history of freedom."

(Second Inaugural Address)

Further Reading

■ Articles

Balkin, Jack M. "*Bush v. Gore* and the Boundary between Law and Politics." *Yale Law Review* 110, no. 8 (June 2001).

Greenstein, Fred I. "George W. Bush and the Ghosts of Presidents Past." *Political Science and Politics* 34, no. 1 (March 2001).

Leffler, Melvyn P. "Think Again: Bush's Foreign Policy." *Foreign Policy* 144 (September–October 2004).

Reisman, W. Michael, and Andrew Armstrong. "The Past and Future of the Claim of Preemptive Self-Defense." *American Journal of International Law* 100, no. 3 (July 2006).

Rogoff, Kenneth. "Bush Throws a Party." *Foreign Policy* 141 (March–April 2004).

■ Books

Brady, David W. *Revolving Gridlock: Politics and Policy from Jimmy Carter to George W. Bush*. Boulder, Colo.: Westview Press, 2005.

Burke, John P. *Becoming President: The Bush Transition, 2000–2003*. Boulder, Colo.: Lynne Rienner, 2004.

Conley, Richard S., ed. *Transforming the American Polity: The Presidency of George W. Bush and the War on Terrorism*. Upper Saddle River, N.J.: Pearson/Prentice Hall, 2005.

Hilliard, Bryan, Tom Lansford, and Robert P. Watson, eds. *George W. Bush: Evaluating the President at Midterm*. Albany: State University of New York Press, 2004.

Jacobson, Gary C. *A Divider, Not a Uniter: George W. Bush and the American People*. New York: Pearson Longman, 2007.

Maranto, Robert, Doug Brattebo, and Tom Lansford, eds. *The Second Term of George W. Bush: Prospects and Perils*. New York: Palgrave Macmillan, 2006.

Woodward, Bob. *Bush at War*. New York: Simon & Schuster, 2002.

—*Tom Lansford*

Questions for Further Study

1. The Economic Growth and Tax Reconciliation Act reflected the belief of Bush and other conservatives that tax reduction would actually increase productivity on the part of the American people. Lower taxes, according to this view, would encourage individuals to earn more and increase government revenues. According to the opposing viewpoint, tax cuts favored the wealthy and lowered the amount of money the federal government received. Discuss these two viewpoints, both pro and con, and decide which is valid in your view. Cite previous examples—most notably, the tax cuts of John F. Kennedy in the 1960s and Ronald Reagan in the 1980s—and evaluate their effectiveness. Consider the Bush tax cuts in light of the increased government expenditures resulting from the war on terror and the economic crises of the 2000s.

2. For everyone old enough to remember September 11, 2001, that day is forever etched in memory. Most people can recall exactly where they were when they heard the news of the terrorist attacks and the subsequent events, culminating in the collapse of the World Trade Center towers. If you are old enough to remember that day, discuss your own reactions; if not, interview older people who do recall those events. How effective was Bush's address regarding the attacks? Evaluate his speech in terms of whether it struck the proper tone (sadness, anger, resolve, and so on) and included enough specifics in terms of actions the nation would take in response to those attacks. Compare with other presidential addresses in times of national crisis, most notably Franklin D. Roosevelt's message to the nation following the Pearl Harbor attacks.

3. Bush's second State of the Union address is often referred to as the "axis of evil" speech, because in it he identified three principal enemies of peace and freedom: Iran, Iraq, and North Korea, which he collectively named the "axis of evil." Critique his reasoning from a variety of perspectives. On the one hand, these three were all known for their harsh political systems, their support of terrorism, and their opposition to the United States. On the other hand, why did he name only these three rather than other notorious dictatorships, such as Cuba and Syria? In particular, was he right to include Iran, which, despite the fact that it is a hard-line Islamic state, actually opposed al Qaeda and the Taliban? Discuss the ways in which Iran, Iraq, and North Korea shared common aims and worked together, and the ways in which they differed and worked in opposition to one another (particularly Iran and Iraq, which fought a long war in the 1980s.)

4. Ever since the establishment of the Monroe Doctrine in 1823, subsequent presidents have had their own "doctrines" in which they outlined their principles for dealing with foreign threats. In his second State of the Union address, Bush presented what would come to be known as "the Bush Doctrine," whereby the United States would act preemptively against perceived threats. In other words, America would not wait to be attacked but would attack first, an idea brought into reality with the Iraq invasion. Consider the Bush Doctrine not only in terms of the many objections that have been raised against it but also in light of justifications for this position.

Document Text

Remarks on Signing the Economic Growth and Tax Relief Reconciliation Act

2001

Some months ago, in my speech to the joint session of Congress, I had the honor of introducing Steven Ramos to the Nation. Steven is the network administrator for a school district. His wife, Josefina, teaches at a charter school. They have a little girl named Lianna, and they're trying to save for Lianna's college education. High taxes made saving difficult. Last year they paid nearly $8,000 in Federal income taxes. Well, today we're beginning to make life for the Ramos' a lot easier. Today we start to return some of the Ramos' money and not only their money but the money of everybody who paid taxes in the United States of America.

Across the board tax relief does not happen often in Washington, DC. In fact, since World War II, it has happened only twice: President Kennedy's tax cut in the sixties and President Reagan's tax cuts in the 1980s. And now it's happening for the third time, and it's about time.

A year ago tax relief was said to be a political impossibility. Six months ago it was supposed to be a political liability. Today it becomes reality. It becomes reality because of the bipartisan leadership of the Members of the United States Congress, Members like Bill Thomas of California, Ralph Hall of Texas, Charles Grassley of Iowa, Max Baucus of Montana, Zell Miller of Georgia, John Breaux of Louisiana, Trent Lott of Mississippi and the entire leadership team in the Senate, and Denny Hastert of Illinois and the leadership team in the House of Representatives—some Democrats, many Republicans—who worked tirelessly and effectively to produce this important result.

I also want to pay tribute to the members of my administration who worked with Congress to bring about this day: Vice President Cheney, Secretary O'Neill, Director Daniels, and the team inside the White House of Andy Card and Larry Lindsey, Nick Calio, and their staffs.

With us today are 15 of the many families I met as I toured our country making the case for tax relief—hard-working Americans. I was able to talk about their stories and their struggles and their hopes, which made the case for tax relief much stronger than my words could possible convey. And I want to thank you all for coming.

And here at the White House today are representatives of millions of Americans, including labor union members, small-business owners, and family farmers. Your persistence and determination helped bring us to this day. The American people should be proud of your efforts on their behalf, and I personally thank you all for coming.

Tax relief is a great achievement for the American people. Tax relief is the first achievement produced by the new tone in Washington, and it was produced in record time.

Tax relief is an achievement for families struggling to enter the middle class. For hard-working lower income families, we have cut the bottom rate of Federal income tax from 15 percent to 10 percent. We doubled the per-child tax credit to $1,000 and made it refundable. Tax relief is compassionate, and it is now on the way.

Tax relief is an achievement for middle-class families squeezed by high energy prices and credit card debt. Most families can look forward to a $600 tax rebate before they have to pay the September back-to-school bills. And in the years ahead, taxpayers can look forward to steadily declining income tax rates.

Tax relief is an achievement for families that want the Government tax policy to be fair and not penalize them for making good choices, good choices such as marriage and raising a family. So we cut the marriage penalty.

Tax relief makes the code more fair for small businesses and farmers and individuals by eliminating the death tax. Over the long haul, tax relief will encourage work and innovation. It will allow American workers to save more on their pension plan or individual retirement accounts.

Tax relief expands individual freedom. The money we return, or don't take in the first place, can be saved for a child's education, spent on family needs, invested in a home or in a business or a mutual fund or used to reduce personal debt.

Document Text

The message we send today: It's up to the American people; it's the American people's choice. We recognize, loud and clear, the surplus is not the Government's money. The surplus is the people's money, and we ought to trust them with their own money.

This tax relief plan is principled. We cut taxes for every income-tax payer. We target nobody in; we target nobody out. And tax relief is now on the way.

Today is a great day for America. It is the first major achievement of a new era, an era of steady cooperation. And more achievements are ahead. I thank the Members of Congress in both parties who made today possible. Together, we will lead our country to new progress and new possibilities.

It is now my honor to sign the first broad tax relief in a generation.

Glossary

death tax:	estate taxes, or taxes on inheritances
marriage penalty:	a reference to the fact that some married couples actually pay higher taxes if they file their tax returns jointly rather than individually

George W. Bush with his parents, Barbara and George H. W. Bush, c. 1947

Address on the Terrorist Attacks of September 11

2001

Tonight we are a country awakened to danger and called to defend freedom. Our grief has turned to anger, and anger to resolution. Whether we bring our enemies to justice, or bring justice to our enemies, justice will be done....

On September the 11th, enemies of freedom committed an act of war against our country. Americans have known wars—but for the past 136 years, they have been wars on foreign soil, except for one Sunday in 1941. Americans have known the casualties of war—but not at the center of a great city on a peaceful morning. Americans have known surprise attacks—but never before on thousands of civilians. All of this was brought upon us in a single day—and night fell on a different world, a world where freedom itself is under attack.

Americans have many questions tonight. Americans are asking: Who attacked our country? The evidence we have gathered all points to a collection of loosely affiliated terrorist organizations known as al Qaeda. They are the same murderers indicted for bombing American embassies in Tanzania and Kenya, and responsible for bombing the USS *Cole* ....

The leadership of al Qaeda has great influence in Afghanistan and supports the Taliban regime in controlling most of that country. In Afghanistan, we see al Qaeda's vision for the world....

And tonight, the United States of America makes the following demands on the Taliban: Deliver to United States authorities all the leaders of al Qaeda who hide in your land. Release all foreign nationals, including American citizens, you have unjustly imprisoned. Protect foreign journalists, diplomats and aid workers in your country. Close immediately and permanently every terrorist training camp in Afghanistan, and hand over every terrorist, and every person in their support structure, to appropriate authorities. Give the United States full access to terrorist training camps, so we can make sure they are no longer operating.

These demands are not open to negotiation or discussion. The Taliban must act, and act immediately. They will hand over the terrorists, or they will share in their fate....

Our war on terror begins with al Qaeda, but it does not end there. It will not end until every terrorist group of global reach has been found, stopped and defeated.

Americans are asking, why do they hate us? They hate what we see right here in this chamber—a democratically elected government. Their leaders are self-appointed. They hate our freedoms—our freedom of religion, our freedom of speech, our freedom to vote and assemble and disagree with each other....

We are not deceived by their pretenses to piety. We have seen their kind before. They are the heirs of all the murderous ideologies of the 20th century. By sacrificing human life to serve their radical visions—by abandoning every value except the will to power—they follow in the path of fascism, and Nazism, and totalitarianism. And they will follow that path all the way, to where it ends: in history's unmarked grave of discarded lies....

Our response involves far more than instant retaliation and isolated strikes. Americans should not expect one battle, but a lengthy campaign, unlike any other we have ever seen. It may include dramatic strikes, visible on TV, and covert operations, secret even in success. We will starve terrorists of funding, turn them one against another, drive them from place to place, until there is no refuge or no rest. And we will pursue nations that provide aid or safe haven to terrorism. Every nation, in every region, now has a decision to make. Either you are with us, or you are with the terrorists. From this day forward, any nation that continues to harbor or support terrorism will be regarded by the United States as a hostile regime.

Our nation has been put on notice: We are not immune from attack. We will take defensive measures against terrorism to protect Americans. Today, dozens of federal departments and agencies, as well as state and local governments, have responsibilities affecting homeland security. These efforts must be coordinated at the highest level. So tonight I announce the creation of a Cabinet-level position reporting directly to me—the Office of Homeland Security....

We ask every nation to join us. We will ask, and we will need, the help of police forces, intelligence services, and banking systems around the world. The United States is grateful that many nations and many

Document Text

international organizations have already responded—with sympathy and with support. Nations from Latin America, to Asia, to Africa, to Europe, to the Islamic world. Perhaps the NATO Charter reflects best the attitude of the world: An attack on one is an attack on all....

I ask you to uphold the values of America, and remember why so many have come here. We are in a fight for our principles, and our first responsibility is to live by them. No one should be singled out for unfair treatment or unkind words because of their ethnic background or religious faith....

I ask your continued participation and confidence in the American economy. Terrorists attacked a symbol of American prosperity. They did not touch its source. America is successful because of the hard work, and creativity, and enterprise of our people. These were the true strengths of our economy before September 11th, and they are our strengths today.

And, finally, please continue praying for the victims of terror and their families, for those in uniform, and for our great country. Prayer has comforted us in sorrow, and will help strengthen us for the journey ahead....

After all that has just passed—all the lives taken, and all the possibilities and hopes that died with them—it is natural to wonder if America's future is one of fear. Some speak of an age of terror. I know there are struggles ahead, and dangers to face. But this country will define our times, not be defined by them. As long as the United States of America is determined and strong, this will not be an age of terror; this will be an age of liberty, here and across the world.

Great harm has been done to us. We have suffered great loss. And in our grief and anger we have found our mission and our moment. Freedom and fear are at war. The advance of human freedom—the great achievement of our time, and the great hope of every time—now depends on us. Our nation—this generation—will lift a dark threat of violence from our people and our future. We will rally the world to this cause by our efforts, by our courage. We will not tire, we will not falter, and we will not fail.

Glossary

covert: secret

ideologies: political belief systems; often used in reference to the most rigid or extreme of such systems

NATO Charter: a mutual defense treaty signed by the United States and several western European countries, thus forming the North Atlantic Treaty Organization in 1949

one Sunday in 1941: a reference to the bombing of Pearl Harbor by Japanese forces on December 7, 1941

piety: extreme religious devotion signified by strict observance of religious laws

resolution: determination

totalitarianism: a political system characterized by total control over every aspect of life and society

Second State of the Union Address

2002

We last met in an hour of shock and suffering. In four short months, our nation has comforted the victims, begun to rebuild New York and the Pentagon, rallied a great coalition, captured, arrested, and rid the world of thousands of terrorists, destroyed Afghanistan's terrorist training camps, saved a people from starvation, and freed a country from brutal oppression....

America and Afghanistan are now allies against terror. We'll be partners in rebuilding that country....

What we have found in Afghanistan confirms that, far from ending there, our war against terror is only beginning. Most of the 19 men who hijacked planes on September the 11th were trained in Afghanistan's camps, and so were tens of thousands of others. Thousands of dangerous killers, schooled in the methods of murder, often supported by outlaw regimes, are now spread throughout the world like ticking time bombs, set to go off without warning....

While the most visible military action is in Afghanistan, America is acting elsewhere. We now have troops in the Philippines, helping to train that country's armed forces to go after terrorist cells that have executed an American, and still hold hostages. Our soldiers, working with the Bosnian government, seized terrorists who were plotting to bomb our embassy. Our Navy is patrolling the coast of Africa to block the shipment of weapons and the establishment of terrorist camps in Somalia....

But some governments will be timid in the face of terror. And make no mistake about it: If they do not act, America will.

Our second goal is to prevent regimes that sponsor terror from threatening America or our friends and allies with weapons of mass destruction. Some of these regimes have been pretty quiet since September the 11th. But we know their true nature. North Korea is a regime arming with missiles and weapons of mass destruction, while starving its citizens.

Iran aggressively pursues these weapons and exports terror, while an unelected few repress the Iranian people's hope for freedom.

Iraq continues to flaunt its hostility toward America and to support terror. The Iraqi regime has plotted to develop anthrax, and nerve gas, and nuclear weapons for over a decade. This is a regime that has already used poison gas to murder thousands of its own citizens—leaving the bodies of mothers huddled over their dead children. This is a regime that agreed to international inspections—then kicked out the inspectors. This is a regime that has something to hide from the civilized world.

States like these, and their terrorist allies, constitute an axis of evil, arming to threaten the peace of the world. By seeking weapons of mass destruction, these regimes pose a grave and growing danger. They could provide these arms to terrorists, giving them the means to match their hatred. They could attack our allies or attempt to blackmail the United States. In any of these cases, the price of indifference would be catastrophic.

We will work closely with our coalition to deny terrorists and their state sponsors the materials, technology, and expertise to make and deliver weapons of mass destruction. We will develop and deploy effective missile defenses to protect America and our allies from sudden attack. And all nations should know: America will do what is necessary to ensure our nation's security.

We'll be deliberate, yet time is not on our side. I will not wait on events, while dangers gather. I will not stand by, as peril draws closer and closer. The United States of America will not permit the world's most dangerous regimes to threaten us with the world's most destructive weapons.

Our war on terror is well begun, but it is only begun. This campaign may not be finished on our watch—yet it must be and it will be waged on our watch....

My budget includes the largest increase in defense spending in two decades—because while the price of freedom and security is high, it is never too high. Whatever it costs to defend our country, we will pay.

The next priority of my budget is to do everything possible to protect our citizens and strengthen our nation against the ongoing threat of another attack. Time and distance from the events of September the 11th will not make us safer unless we act on its lessons. America is no longer protected by vast oceans. We are protected from attack only by vigorous action abroad, and increased vigilance at home....

Document Text

Homeland security will make America not only stronger, but, in many ways, better. Knowledge gained from bioterrorism research will improve public health. Stronger police and fire departments will mean safer neighborhoods. Stricter border enforcement will help combat illegal drugs. And as government works to better secure our homeland, America will continue to depend on the eyes and ears of alert citizens....

During these last few months, I've been humbled and privileged to see the true character of this country in a time of testing. Our enemies believed America was weak and materialistic, that we would splinter in fear and selfishness. They were as wrong as they are evil.

The American people have responded magnificently, with courage and compassion, strength and resolve. As I have met the heroes, hugged the families, and looked into the tired faces of rescuers, I have stood in awe of the American people....

For too long our culture has said, "If it feels good, do it." Now America is embracing a new ethic and a new creed: "Let's roll." In the sacrifice of soldiers, the fierce brotherhood of firefighters, and the bravery and generosity of ordinary citizens, we have glimpsed what a new culture of responsibility could look like. We want to be a nation that serves goals larger than self. We've been offered a unique opportunity, and we must not let this moment pass....

America will take the side of brave men and women who advocate these values around the world, including the Islamic world, because we have a greater objective than eliminating threats and containing resentment. We seek a just and peaceful world beyond the war on terror....

Our enemies send other people's children on missions of suicide and murder. They embrace tyranny and death as a cause and a creed. We stand for a different choice, made long ago, on the day of our founding. We affirm it again today. We choose freedom and the dignity of every life.

Steadfast in our purpose, we now press on. We have known freedom's price. We have shown freedom's power. And in this great conflict, my fellow Americans, we will see freedom's victory.

Glossary

anthrax:	a biological weapon used to spread a disease that causes acute ulcers and destroys vital organs
axis of evil:	reference to the Axis powers of World War II: Nazi Germany, Italy, Japan, and those aligned with them
coalition:	a group of allied nations or other parties
"Let's roll":	the rallying cry issued by passenger Todd Beamer in calling upon fellow hostages to fight back against the hijackers of United Airlines Flight 93 on September 11, 2001
nerve gas:	various chemical weapons that interrupt communication between nerves and organs in the human body, bringing about convulsions and eventual suffocation
weapons of mass destruction:	nuclear, biological, radiological, chemical, or other forms of weaponry capable of killing large numbers of people

Document Text

Address to the Nation on Military Operations in Iraq

2003

My fellow citizens, at this hour, American and coalition forces are in the early stages of military operations to disarm Iraq, to free its people and to defend the world from grave danger.

On my orders, coalition forces have begun striking selected targets of military importance to undermine Saddam Hussein's ability to wage war. These are opening stages of what will be a broad and concerted campaign. More than 35 countries are giving crucial support—from the use of naval and air bases, to help with intelligence and logistics, to the deployment of combat units. Every nation in this coalition has chosen to bear the duty and share the honor of serving in our common defense.

To all the men and women of the United States Armed Forces now in the Middle East, the peace of a troubled world and the hopes of an oppressed people now depend on you. That trust is well placed.

The enemies you confront will come to know your skill and bravery. The people you liberate will witness the honorable and decent spirit of the American military. In this conflict, America faces an enemy who has no regard for conventions of war or rules of morality. Saddam Hussein has placed Iraqi troops and equipment in civilian areas, attempting to use innocent men, women and children as shields for his own military—a final atrocity against his people.

I want Americans and all the world to know that coalition forces will make every effort to spare innocent civilians from harm. A campaign on the harsh terrain of a nation as large as California could be longer and more difficult than some predict. And helping Iraqis achieve a united, stable and free country will require our sustained commitment.

We come to Iraq with respect for its citizens, for their great civilization and for the religious faiths they practice. We have no ambition in Iraq, except to remove a threat and restore control of that country to its own people.

I know that the families of our military are praying that all those who serve will return safely and soon. Millions of Americans are praying with you for the safety of your loved ones and for the protection of the innocent. For your sacrifice, you have the gratitude and respect of the American people. And you can know that our forces will be coming home as soon as their work is done.

Our nation enters this conflict reluctantly—yet our purpose is sure. The people of the United States and our friends and allies will not live at the mercy of an outlaw regime that threatens the peace with weapons of mass murder. We will meet that threat now, with our Army, Air Force, Navy, Coast Guard and Marines, so that we do not have to meet it later with armies of fire fighters and police and doctors on the streets of our cities.

Now that conflict has come, the only way to limit its duration is to apply decisive force. And I assure you, this will not be a campaign of half measures, and we will accept no outcome but victory.

My fellow citizens, the dangers to our country and the world will be overcome. We will pass through this time of peril and carry on the work of peace. We will defend our freedom. We will bring freedom to others and we will prevail.

May God bless our country and all who defend her.

Glossary

conventions: agreements or rules

logistics: the organization, distribution, and operation of supplies and personnel

Second Inaugural Address

2005

For a half-century, America defended our own freedom by standing watch on distant borders. After the shipwreck of communism came years of relative quiet, years of repose, years of sabbatical—and then there came a day of fire....

There is only one force of history that can break the reign of hatred and resentment and expose the pretensions of tyrants and reward the hopes of the decent and tolerant. And that is the force of human freedom.

We are led, by events and common sense, to one conclusion: The survival of liberty in our land increasingly depends on the success of liberty in other lands. The best hope for peace in our world is the expansion of freedom in all the world....

So it is the policy of the United States to seek and support the growth of democratic movements and institutions in every nation and culture, with the ultimate goal of ending tyranny in our world.

This is not primarily the task of arms, though we will defend ourselves and our friends by force of arms when necessary. Freedom, by its nature, must be chosen and defended by citizens and sustained by the rule of law and the protection of minorities. And when the soul of a nation finally speaks, the institutions that arise may reflect customs and traditions very different from our own.

America will not impose our own style of government on the unwilling. Our goal instead is to help others find their own voice, attain their own freedom and make their own way.

The great objective of ending tyranny is the concentrated work of generations. The difficulty of the task is no excuse for avoiding it. America's influence is not unlimited, but fortunately for the oppressed, America's influence is considerable, and we will use it confidently in freedom's cause.

My most solemn duty is to protect this nation and its people from further attacks and emerging threats. Some have unwisely chosen to test America's resolve and have found it firm....

We will encourage reform in other governments by making clear that success in our relations will require the decent treatment of their own people. America's belief in human dignity will guide our policies. Yet, rights must be more than the grudging concessions of dictators; they are secured by free dissent and the participation of the governed. In the long run, there is no justice without freedom, and there can be no human rights without human liberty.

Some, I know, have questioned the global appeal of liberty—though this time in history, four decades defined by the swiftest advance of freedom ever seen, is an odd time for doubt. Americans, of all people, should never be surprised by the power of our ideals. Eventually, the call of freedom comes to every mind and every soul. We do not accept the existence of permanent tyranny because we do not accept the possibility of permanent slavery. Liberty will come to those who love it.

Today, America speaks anew to the peoples of the world:

All who live in tyranny and hopelessness can know: The United States will not ignore your oppression, or excuse your oppressors. When you stand for your liberty, we will stand with you.

Democratic reformers facing repression, prison or exile can know: America sees you for who you are—the future leaders of your free country.

The rulers of outlaw regimes can know that we still believe as Abraham Lincoln did: "Those who deny freedom to others deserve it not for themselves; and, under the rule of a just God, cannot long retain it."

The leaders of governments with long habits of control need to know: To serve your people you must learn to trust them. Start on this journey of progress and justice, and America will walk at your side.

And all the allies of the United States can know: We honor your friendship, we rely on your counsel, and we depend on your help. Division among free nations is a primary goal of freedom's enemies. The concerted effort of free nations to promote democracy is a prelude to our enemies' defeat....

History has an ebb and flow of justice, but history also has a visible direction set by liberty and the author of liberty.

When the Declaration of Independence was first read in public and the Liberty Bell was sounded in

Document Text

celebration, a witness said, "It rang as if it meant something." In our time it means something still.

America, in this young century, proclaims liberty throughout all the world and to all the inhabitants thereof. Renewed in our strength—tested, but not weary—we are ready for the greatest achievements in the history of freedom.

Glossary

author of liberty: God

pretensions: false claims

task of arms: something to be accomplished by military means

U.S. Senator Robert Byrd of West Virginia

Robert C. Byrd: Original Analysis

U.S. Congressman and Senator

1917–2010

Overview

Robert C. Byrd was born Cornelius Calvin Sale, Jr., in North Carolina in 1917. Adopted and raised by his aunt and uncle, Byrd grew up in the coalfields of West Virginia, where his father worked as a teamster, farmer, and coal miner. The Byrd family was poor, and Robert Byrd frequently did his homework by the light of oil lamps because their home had no electricity. After Byrd graduated from high school in 1934, he worked as a gas station attendant and a produce boy. After taking welding classes, he helped build cargo ships during World War II.

In 1946 Byrd ran for the West Virginia House of Delegates and won. While he was in the House of Delegates, he studied at Morris Harvey College (now the University of Charleston), at Concord College, and at Marshall College (now a university) but did not graduate. In 1950 he ran for a seat in the West Virginia Senate and won. Then, halfway through his Senate term, he ran for a seat in the U.S. House of Representatives and was elected in 1952. In 1953 Byrd began attending law school at American University in Washington, D.C., and finally earned his law degree in 1963. In the meantime, in 1958, he won the first of nine consecutive terms in the U.S. Senate.

Early in his political career, Byrd was known as a staunch conservative. Before he entered politics in 1946, he had been a member of the Ku Klux Klan (KKK) in West Virginia. Calling his membership in the organization a mistake, Byrd later claimed his youth and ambition led him to view the KKK as an outlet for his talents and political ambitions. Byrd stated that he had joined the group because it was strongly opposed to Communism and because its membership, made of local elites such as clergy, lawyers, doctors, and judges, supported traditional American values. He also stated that his membership was a reflection of the southern view of race and the fears and prejudices that existed at that time, though he also claimed that at no time did the Klan group to which he belonged preach hatred against blacks, Jews, and other such groups. Byrd maintained that he left the KKK in 1943, although his critics pointed to letters written in 1945 and 1946 that revealed Byrd's continued interest in the organization.

Throughout Byrd's congressional career, his former membership in the KKK led to sharp criticism when he voted on racial issues. Byrd fought against school desegregation in 1954 and held a fourteen-hour filibuster against the 1964 Civil Rights Act, which outlawed racial segregation in schools, public places, and employment. During these years he referred to the civil rights leader Martin Luther King, Jr., in highly disparaging terms. In 1967 he voted against the confirmation of Thurgood Marshall as the first black Supreme Court justice in U.S. history. Twenty-four years later he voted against the confirmation of the second black Supreme Court justice, Clarence Thomas.

Byrd remained a traditionalist. He always carried a copy of the U.S. Constitution in his pocket and often waved it on the Senate floor while he spoke. His strong defense of constitutional law resulted in his adamant opposition to proposed changes to the Constitution, such as line-item veto or balanced-budget amendments. Byrd opposed affirmative action, changes to the Social Security program, acceptance of gays into the military forces, and gay marriage. Yet he voted against the proposed federal marriage amendment (2006) that banned gay marriages, saying that it was unnecessary because states had the power to bar gay marriages. Despite his desire to protect the American flag, he also opposed the flag desecration amendment (2006), claiming that an amendment to the Constitution was not the way to protect the flag. Still, during his fifty years in the Senate, he became increasingly liberal, focusing on government spending for social programs that improved education and health care and voting for civil rights.

Byrd was a former defense hawk who voted in favor of President Lyndon B. Johnson's Gulf of Tonkin Resolution in August 1964. This resolution broadened presidential power to wage war without a formal declaration. Byrd, however, became the Senate's most outspoken critic of the 2003 Iraqi war. He believed that giving the president such broad authority to engage in war gave away power that belonged to the legislative branch of government. He insisted that Congress alone had the right to declare war under the U.S. Constitution and that presidential usurpation of that power, particularly under the administration of George W. Bush, disrupted the Constitution's system of checks and balances among the judicial, legislative, and executive branches of government.

Byrd's congressional career spanned numerous presidential administrations. On June 21, 2007, he became the first senator ever to cast eighteen thousand roll call votes in American history, and in November 2006 he was elected to an unprecedented ninth consecutive term in the U.S. Senate. Over the years, he served as majority leader, majority whip, minority leader, and president pro tempore of the Senate as well as on such key committees as the Senate Appropriations Committee, which he chaired.

Explanation and Analysis of Documents

Byrd's speeches before the Senate exhibited the oratorical skills of nineteenth-century statesmen, complete with flowery rhetoric and grand gestures. He recited poems; quoted historical figures, particularly the Roman statesman and orator Cicero; and frequently used parables from history and classical fairy tales to make his point; his use of the Danish writer Hans Christian Andersen's fairy story "The Emperor's New Clothes" is typical in this regard, and his line-item veto speech is replete with references to the French emperor Napoléon Bonaparte, the French philosopher Charles Montesquieu, the Spartan lawgiver Lycurgus, the Greek historian Polybius, the English historian Edward Gibbon, and others. Perhaps because of his oratorical skills, fellow senators tolerated his sometimes rhapsodic reflections on virtually any topic that came to his mind: Shakespeare, spring, Mother's Day, and a host of other topics. Well respected and highly influential, he also used his oratorical skills to address current issues, protect the constitutional power of the Senate, and maintain the integrity of the Constitution.

♦ Line-Item Veto Speech XIV

First brought before Congress in 1876, the line-item veto was meant to give the president of the United States the power to cut from legislation additional spending for individual or local projects in their home states that one or more members of Congress added to a bill. The line-item veto would allow presidents to eliminate such "pork barrel" legislation without having to veto the entire bill. Since 1876 the idea has reemerged in Congress approximately two hundred times in one form or another.

Under a line-item veto, Congress would pass spending or tax legislation that would then go to the president for approval. The president would sign the bill but have the power to "line out," or eliminate, funding for specific items he opposed. The president would then return the lined-out items to Congress. Congress could approve or disapprove of the president's rejection of those items by a simple majority. If Congress disapproved of the president's line-item vetoes, it would send a "bill of disapproval" containing the items back to the president, who could then choose to keep the expenditures or veto the disapproval bill. If vetoed, Congress would then have to approve the items the president vetoed, overriding the veto by a two-thirds majority.

Some legislators and others object to the line-item veto—a power held by governors in forty-three states—because they believe that it violates the presentment clause of the U.S. Constitution. This clause is found in Article I, Section 7, Clauses 2 and 3, and deals with the issue of legislative process. The relevant portion of the Constitution reads: "Every Bill which shall have passed the House of Representatives and the Senate, shall, before it becomes a Law, be presented to the President of the United States: If he approve he shall sign it, but if not he shall return it, with his Objections." In other words, those who oppose granting line-item veto power to the president believe that the legislative process outlined in the Constitution does not allow for the line-item veto.

In 1993 Byrd delivered a series of fourteen speeches against the line-item veto in the Senate. Byrd viewed the measure as dangerous: The executive branch could use the veto to force the legislative branch to agree with presidential initiatives or face presidential vetoes on congressional spending. Despite Byrd's arguments against the line-item veto, Congress passed the politically popular legislation, and President Bill Clinton signed it into law on April 9, 1996. Clinton used the line-item veto eighty-two times while he was in office. However, New York City appealed the use of the line-item veto to the U.S. Supreme Court. In *Clinton, President of the United States, et al. v. City of New York*, the city of New York claimed that Clinton had struck a legislative provision by which the U.S. Department of

Time Line

1917	November 20	■ Byrd is born Cornelius Calvin Sale, Jr., in North Wilkesboro, North Carolina.
1946	November 5	■ Byrd is elected to the West Virginia House of Delegates.
1950	November 7	■ Byrd is elected to West Virginia Senate.
1952	November 4	■ Byrd is elected to the U.S. House of Representatives.
1958	November 4	■ Byrd is elected to the U.S. Senate.
1993	October 18	■ Byrd delivers a speech in which he speaks out against the line-item veto—his fourteenth such speech on the topic.
October 2002–April 2004		■ Byrd delivers a series of twenty-seven speeches to the U.S. Senate concerning the war in Iraq.
2003	February 12	■ Byrd delivers his "we stand passively mute" speech, in which he cites numerous reasons for his opposition to the war in Iraq.
2003	October 17	■ Byrd delivers his "emperor has no clothes" speech, summarizing his belief that Iraq posed no imminent threat to the United States.

Health and Human Services relinquished its ability to collect $2.6 billion in health care benefits. The Supreme Court ruled on June 25, 1998, that the line-item veto was an unconstitutional violation of the separation of powers.

The hour-long line-item veto speeches, particularly the fourteenth, are perfect examples of Byrd's nineteenth-century style of oratory. Byrd linked the debate on the issue with the fall of the Roman Empire. An amateur historian, Byrd frequently referred to French philosopher Charles Montesquieu and Greek historian Polybius to examine the history of the Roman Empire, and to historians Edward Gibbon and William J. Durant to explain its decline. Byrd then links the decline of the Roman Empire to its failure to maintain a separation of power among the branches of government, thereby eliminating the necessary checks and balances needed to maintain a republic. Byrd claims, "Rome's fate was sealed by the one-by-one donations of power and prerogative that the Roman Senate plucked from its own quiver and voluntarily delivered into the hands, first, of Julius Caesar and then Octavian." He makes it clear that the U.S. Senate would be doing the same thing if it passed the line-item veto.

In this speech, Byrd discusses the parallels between the Roman Empire and the United States. Both republics emerged from virtuous, honest, and courageous people who valued family. Both had public officials who were dedicated to the cause of country and demonstrated responsibility and integrity without regard for personal gain. Both established national traditions and both had a sense of Manifest Destiny that led to quests to expand territorial frontiers. However, in later years, both republics faced an erosion of family and religious values, and family farms disappeared as the nations moved from a rural to an urban population. Territorial expansion led to military-industrial complexes that drained the nations of money and resources. More important, both suffered from public leadership that abandoned responsibility and integrity. Comparing Rome to America, Byrd said, "In the last century of the Republic, the old citizen soldiery and the old moral structure of integrity and dedication to the cause of country gave way to greed, graft, corruption, venality, and political demagoguery, much of which we see in our own time and in our own country." Byrd explains how each branch of government and the people were held accountable by a series of checks and balances and that when the balance of power shifted from one branch to another, it led to decline. Liberty, Byrd claims, can be maintained only through a balance of power. The Constitution states that Congress alone has the power and the responsibility to fund government, and Byrd is begging Congress not to abdicate that power to the executive branch as Rome did, or, like Rome, America would fail.

In 1997 several members of Congress, including Byrd, filed suit to have the Line Item Veto Act of 1996 declared unconstitutional. The case, *Gaines v. Byrd*, made its way to the U.S. Supreme Court, where, by a vote of seven to two, the Court ruled that the members of Congress did not have standing to maintain the suit; that is to say, the members of Congress could not show that the act imposed any kind of personal injury on them.

Byrd's critics would note that he had good reason for opposing the line-item veto. During his career in the Senate, he became known widely as the "pork barrel king" for having brought $3 billion in federal appropriations to his state through items that might very well have been eliminated under a line-item veto. Among the many projects in West Virginia funded by federal tax dollars, some fifty have Byrd's name on them, including, for example, the Robert C. Byrd Biotech Center, as well as schools, bridges, and highways. In his own defense, Byrd could point out that West Virginia has historically been a very poor state such that, for example, when he entered Congress, the state did not have a single mile of four-lane highway. Federal dollars have gone a long way to improving this situation.

♦ "We Stand Passively Mute" Speech

During his years in Congress, Byrd participated in numerous debates and votes on national security. He voted on issues pertaining to the cold war (1947–1991) and subsequent conflicts that resulted from America's attempt to contain Communism, such as the Korean War (1950–1953), the Cuban missile crisis (1962), and the war in Vietnam (1959–1975). He also made decisions on the intervention of the United States and the North American Treaty Organization in ethnic conflicts in Bosnia (1995) and Kosovo (1999) and America's invasion of Iraq during the Persian Gulf War (1991) to halt Saddam Hussein and Iraqi forces' invasion of Kuwait, an America ally. Of all of his votes in Congress, Byrd was most proud of his October 2002 vote against the war in Iraq. President Bush pushed for an invasion of Iraq after the destruction of the World Trade Center in New York City and the attack on the Pentagon by Islamic extremists on September 11, 2001. Bush maintained that under Hussein, Iraq supported and hid terrorists who were planning more attacks on America. Based on government intelligence, Bush insisted that terrorist networks were operating in Iraq and that Hussein's government was buying material to create weapons of mass destruction, including nuclear weapons. The United States bombed and invaded Iraq in March and April 2003 with the intention of toppling Saddam Hussein, capturing terrorists, confiscating weapons, and securing the Iraqi oil infrastructure. A vocal critic of the war and President George W. Bush's doctrine of preemptive action—that a nation has the right to attack another nation in the belief that it may be a future threat—Byrd delivered twenty-seven speeches to the U.S. Senate between October 2002 and April 2004 concerning the war in Iraq. In his speech on February 12, 2003, Byrd cites numerous reasons for his opposition to the war and expresses dismay at the Senate's tacit approval of it.

Byrd maintains that the decision to participate in this war was made hurriedly, without proper debate and without understanding the impact the war could have on both America and the world. He states that Bush's policies could slow down the economy by raising oil prices and increase the national deficit through military spending, humanitarian aid, and the rebuilding of Iraq. Communities could be less protected because increased military spending would limit the funding of local police departments and firefighters. Americans could become

increasingly fearful of another terrorist attack at home while also fearing for family members fighting abroad. In addition, the focus on Iraq could turn America's attention away from such issues as health care and the protection of American borders. He also warns that a disruption of oil production in the Middle East could raise prices, disturb the global economy, and create a worldwide recession. Byrd maintains that the administration and Congress failed to prepare for the impact military action in the Middle East could have on American allies, particularly Israel, Jordan, and Saudi Arabia. In addition, there were no debates on a plan for the removal of American troops or on the security of Iraq after troop withdrawal.

Byrd calls the war a "turning point in U.S. foreign policy." He claims that Bush's doctrine of preemption not only altered America's role as a "peacekeeper" but also led to fear, uncertainty, and mistrust in countries around the world. Byrd insists that this policy put some nations on the defensive and split our alliances with others, thereby threatening our national security. At the heart of Byrd's opposition to the war was his strong and forceful defense of the Constitution and what he regarded as President Bush's contempt for the constitutional balance of power. Under the Constitution, the power to declare war belongs to Congress. Byrd believed that Bush was usurping the power of the legislative branch and initiating policies that threatened civil liberties and denied American citizens their rights under the Constitution.

Ultimately, Byrd's efforts to halt the path to war were unavailing. In late 2002 he attempted to mount a filibuster to block passage of the resolution to go to war, but his effort was voted down. Accordingly, on October 11, 2002, the House of Representatives voted 296–133, and the Senate voted 77–23, to grant the president authorization to attack Iraq if Saddam Hussein failed to account for his weapons of mass destruction.

♦ "The Emperor Has No Clothes" Speech

One of Byrd's twenty-seven speeches on the Iraq War, referred to as "The Emperor Has No Clothes" speech, summarized his belief that there was no direct or imminent threat from Iraq. Byrd used Hans Christian Andersen's classic 1837 fairy tale to make his point. In the story, an emperor decks himself out in a suit of clothes thought to be visible only to those pure of heart and mind. All the townspeople exclaim over the beauty of the raiment as the emperor appears before them—except one child, who proclaims the truth of the emperor's nakedness.

On October 17, 2003, Byrd gave his speech prior to the Senate's vote on the Iraqi Supplemental Bill, an $87 billion presidential bill that would provide additional funding for the U.S. military in Iraq and for the reconstruction of the country. Continued military force, it was argued, would make Iraq more secure from outside terrorists groups and provide for the training of a new Iraqi military, and more funding was needed to rebuild needed public services such as electricity and water systems. Byrd pressed for improvements in the bill at least twelve times, calling for more accountability and congressional oversight of the money. Each time, President Bush garnered enough support to override Byrd's amendments to the proposed legislation.

In this speech, the "emperor" is President Bush, who, according to Byrd, promoted a war on the basis of something that was not there. Before the war, Bush claimed the war was necessary because Iraq had weapons of mass destruction, but no weapons of mass destruction were found during the months and years after the invasion. Bush also claimed that Iraqis were oppressed under Saddam Hussein's regime and that American troops would be seen as liberators, yet, Byrd insists, American troops were not welcomed with open arms. Despite the belief that Hussein's Iraq sponsored terrorism in America and was collecting materials from other countries to build nuclear weapons, Byrd says that no records were found to indicate that Hussein was involved in the terrorist attacks on September 11, 2001, and no evidence shows that he bought material to produce nuclear weapons from other nations. Bush told Americans that the conflict was over two months after the initial invasion while standing on the deck of an aircraft carrier, the USS *Abraham Lincoln*. Dressed in his "new" clothes, a flight suit worn by U.S. military pilots, Bush gave a speech in front of a large banner that proclaimed "Mission Accomplished." However, the mission was not over. The war dragged on, and, Byrd notes, more soldiers died after Bush declared the war over than during the invasion. Byrd claims that although the emperor knew nothing was there, he continued to insist Iraq was a threat to America. Since these threats, like the emperor's clothes, could be seen only by those who were "pure of heart," or patriotic, many Americans agreed with the "emperor."

Byrd maintains that by stirring up fears of imminent danger and denouncing those who did not believe in the danger as unpatriotic, Bush persuaded Americans to believe in something that was not there. He argues that in his arrogance Bush created a war based on falsehoods and that he lied to the American people as well as to America's allies throughout the world. Byrd ends the speech by comparing Bush's leadership to that of the Nazi Hermann Goering, the second man in Adolf Hitler's Third Reich, Germany's Fascist and racist government during World War II. Goering believed that leaders determined policy in any society and could always sway people to follow their policy by telling them they were being attacked and then denouncing pacifists for their lack of patriotism. Goering's belief led millions of innocent people to their deaths during the war. Byrd attracted widespread criticism for these remarks.

Once again, many of Byrd's criticisms of President Bush stemmed from his belief that Bush had little regard for the Constitution. He accuses Bush of trying to usurp the power of the Senate, particularly the power to declare war, and he insists that Bush abused the civil liberties of Americans as established in the Constitution through the creation and passage of laws such as the USA Patriot Act (October 26, 2001), a law that expanded the authority of U.S. law-enforcement agencies. Intended to provide agencies with widespread power to fight terrorism, the act authorized the search of telephone and e-mail communications and medical and financial records and redefined "terrorism" to include domestic terrorism.

Impact and Legacy

Throughout his career, Byrd emphasized the importance of education. In 1969 he initiated the Scholastic Recognition Award that provided savings bonds to thousands of high school valedictorians in West Virginia. In 1985 he authored and Congress approved a national merit-based scholarship program funded through the U.S. Department of Education. The Robert C. Byrd Honors Scholarship provides $1,500 in scholarship money to outstanding high school seniors across the nation. He also introduced legislation in 2002 that provided $50 million for the training of K–12 teachers in "traditional American history." Under the Teaching American History grants, primary and secondary school systems unite with universities and nonprofit organizations to provide increased knowledge and improved methodologies in teaching American history.

Byrd, as of 2008 one of the oldest and longest-serving members of the Senate, was labeled the "Guardian of the Senate." He gained wide respect for his knowledge of history, constitutional law and protocol, and senatorial procedures and prerogatives and for his steadfast defense of congressional power. Undoubtedly, Byrd was the last of the old-time orators to grace the floor of the Senate. His eloquent speeches acknowledged the importance of history and demonstrated how knowledge of the past was relevant to today's problems. In an age of conflicting interpretations of the Constitution and increasing infringements of power by one branch of the government over another, Senator Byrd established his place in history as one of the last defenders of the power of the Senate and a protector of the separation of powers called for in the Constitution. As such, Byrd will likely be remembered for his knowledge of and adherence to the principles of the nation's original founders.

Key Sources

The Robert C. Byrd Center for Legislative Studies, Shepherd University, Shepherdstown, West Virginia, promotes the study of the U.S. Congress and the Constitution. The center holds some of Byrd's papers and reading copies of many of his speeches. The majority of personal and professional information on Byrd comes from Byrd himself. Books Byrd authored include *Senate of the Roman Republic: Addresses on the History of Roman Constitutionalism* (1995), *We Stand Passively Mute: Senator Robert C. Byrd's Iraq Speeches* (2004), *Losing America: Confronting a Reckless and Arrogant Presidency* (2004), and *Robert C. Byrd: Child of the Appalachian Coalfields* (2005). He also authored a four-volume history of the U.S. Senate that includes *The Senate, 1789–1989: Addresses on the History of the United States Senate,* vol. 1 (1988); *The Senate, 1789–1989: Addresses on the History of the United States Senate,* vol. 2 (1991); *The Senate, 1789–1989: Historical Statistics, 1789–1992* (1993); and *The Senate, 1789–1989: Classic Speeches, 1830–1993* (1995). Byrd also recorded a record titled "U.S. Senator Robert Byrd: Mountain Fiddler (1978).

Essential Quotes

"It is my own sincere prayer … that the United States will not follow a course parallel to the Roman Republic into an inexorable decline and decadence."

(Line-Item Veto Speech XIV)

"But to turn one's frustration and anger into the kind of extremely destabilizing and dangerous foreign policy debacle that the world is currently witnessing is inexcusable from any Administration charged with the awesome power and responsibility of guiding the destiny of the greatest superpower on the planet."

("We Stand Passively Mute" Speech)

"The Emperor has no clothes. This entire adventure in Iraq has been based on propaganda and manipulation. Eighty-seven billion dollars is too much to pay for the continuation of a war based on falsehoods."

("The Emperor Has No Clothes" Speech)

Further Reading

Articles

Ashdown, G. G. "Marshall, Marbury, and Mr. Byrd: America Unchecked and Imbalanced." *West Virginia Law Review* 108, no. 3 (2006): 691–704.

Corbin, D. A. "Senator Robert C. Byrd, The 'Unsung Hero' of Watergate." *West Virginia Law Review* 108, no. 3 (2006): 669–690.

Michael, M. B. "The Power of History to Stir a Man's Blood: Senator Robert C. Byrd in the Line Item Veto Debate." *West Virginia Law Review* 108, no. 3 (2006): 593–606.

Books

Gould, Lewis. *The Most Exclusive Club: A History of the Modern United States Senate*. New York: Basic Books, 2006.

Harris, Fred R. *Deadlock or Decision: The U.S. Senate and the Rise of National Politics*. New York: Oxford University Press, 1993.

—*Connie Rice*

Questions for Further Study

1. In what ways did Byrd's positions and views later in life compare or contrast with those of his younger years—in particular, the period when he was involved with the Ku Klux Klan?

2. Discuss the many and varied historical references (primarily concerning ancient Sparta and Rome) in his line-item veto speech and how Byrd used them in support of his argument.

3. Assess the two speeches from 2003, both of which Byrd made in opposition to the Bush administration's war on terror. How effectively does he make his case? Compare and contrast his arguments with those of the administration, and evaluate the relative worth of both positions. Who is more right and who is more wrong and why?

Line-Item Veto Speech XIV

1993

Mr. President, this is the fourteenth in my series of speeches on the line-item veto, with particular reference to the Roman Republic and the Roman Senate. When I began this series of one-hour speeches on May 5, I spoke of Montesquieu, the eminent French philosopher and author who had greatly influenced the Founding Fathers with his political theory of checks and balances and separation of powers.hellip;

I have also stated a number of times that if we are to have a better appreciation and understanding of the U.S. Constitution—its separation of powers and checks and balances, and the power over the purse—then we should follow in Montesquieu's tracks and study Roman history as he did, and that is what we have been doing together during these past several months.

What have we acquired to pay us for our pains? What have we learned that can be applicable to our own time, our own country, and to the political questions of today concerning checks and balances and the control over the purse? Let us see.hellip;

Napoleon said, "Let my son often read and reflect on history. This is the only true philosophy." We have elected, therefore, as did Montesquieu, to look to Roman history for guidance.

Roman power derived from Roman virtue, basically; in other words, from great moral qualities. The average Roman, as we have noted, was simple, steadfast, honest, courageous, law-abiding, patriotic, and reverent, and his leaders were men of uncommon dedication and acumen.

From the earliest times, the Romans possessed a profound reverence for national tradition, a firm conviction of being the special object and instrument of destiny, and a strong sense of individual responsibility and obligation to that tradition and to the fulfillment of that destiny.hellip;

There spring to mind several parallels between the history of the Romans and the history of our own Republic, one such parallel being that the same old virtues which lent sturdiness and integrity to the early Romans, also gave stability and substance and strength and character to our own national life in the early years of its formation and development.

The Roman family was the cornerstone of the Roman social structure, and the family setting instilled in its members the self-discipline, the respect for authority, the veneration of ancestors, and the reverence for the gods that lent stability to Roman society and iron discipline to the Roman legions.

The Roman family unit was, indeed, a religious organization.hellip; Reverence and the idea of obligation—inherent in the Roman conception of the relation between gods and men—inevitably developed among the Romans a strong sense of duty, a moral factor of inestimable worth.

Mr. President, we have seen that same strong tradition of family and religious values prevalent in the formation and development of our own country, from colonial times down to the mid-twentieth century. The erosion of these values in America over the last thirty to forty years has signified a decline in the moral and spiritual strength of this nation, as it did in the Roman state.

We have seen in both the Roman and American psyches a sense of Manifest Destiny, and the same urge to extend territorial frontiers. We saw in the territorial expansion of the Roman city state what amounted to an overexpansion. We saw the drain that was placed upon Roman manpower, and the burden that was imposed upon the administration of the far-flung provinces. While, in our own case, territorial expansion has long since ceased, in recent years we have spent billions of dollars in space exploration, and we stand in danger of overextending our international commitments and our financial capability to sustain and underwrite them. hellip;

We have also drawn Roman and American parallels in the vanishing peasantry from the land and the decline in small family farms, the consequences of which have been increasing unemployment and crime and poverty in the cities, and a growing welfare dependence upon the state.

During the centuries of the early and middle Republic, public office in Rome could be obtained only through virtue, and brought with it no pay, no salary, no benefit other than honor, and the opportunity

Document Text

to prove one's self worthy of being preferred for further toils on behalf of the state.

In the last century of the Republic, the old citizen soldiery and the old moral structure of integrity and dedication to the cause of country gave way to greed, graft, corruption, venality, and political demagoguery, much of which we see in our own time and in our own country. The self-serving ambitions of Roman generals and politicians led to violence, civil wars, and military domination by standing armies made up of professional soldiers. In our own Republic today, the military-industrial complex, against which President Eisenhower warned, can pose a threat to the system.

Thus, Mr. President, there are sundry similarities between our own history and the history of the Romans.hellip;

Now, let us turn to the consideration of the Roman political system. In the Roman Republic, the political organization was complex, and it was also experimental, unlike that of Lycurgus, the Spartan lawgiver of the ninth century BCE.

Lycurgus united in his constitution all of the good and distinctive features of the best governments, so that none of the principal parts should unduly grow and predominate. But inasmuch as the force of each part would be neutralized by that of the others, neither of them should prevail and outbalance another. Therefore, the constitution should remain in a state of equilibrium.

Lycurgus, foreseeing by a process of reasoning whence and how events would naturally happen, constructed his constitution untaught by adversity. But, while the Romans would achieve the same final result, according to Polybius, they did not reach it by any process of reasoning but by the discipline of many trials and struggles.hellip;

Polybius viewed the Roman constitution as having three elements: the executive, the Senate, and the people, with their respective share of power in the state regulated by a scrupulous regard to equality and equilibrium.

Let us examine the separation of powers in the Roman Republic as explained by Polybius. The consuls—representing the executive—were the supreme masters of the administration of the government when remaining in Rome. All of the other magistrates, except the tribunes, were under the consuls and took their orders from the consuls. The consuls brought matters before the Senate that required its deliberation, and they saw to the execution of the Senate's decrees. In matters requiring the authorization of the people, the consuls summoned the popular meetings, presented the proposals for their decision, and carried out the decrees of the majority.

In matters of war, the consuls imposed such levies upon the allies as the consuls deemed appropriate, and made up the roll for soldiers and selected those who were suitable. Consuls had absolute power to inflict punishment upon all who were under their command, and had all but the absolute power in the conduct of military campaigns.

As to the Senate—we are talking about the separation of powers—hellip; it had complete control over the treasury and regulated receipts and disbursements alike.hellip;

The Senate also had jurisdiction over all crimes ... such as treason, conspiracy, poisoning, or willful murder, as well as controversies between and among allied states.hellip;

What part of the constitution was left to the people? The people participated in the ratification of treaties and alliances, and decided questions of war and peace. The people passed and repealed laws—subject to the Senate's veto—and bestowed public offices on the deserving, which, according to Polybius, "are the most honorable rewards for virtue."hellip;

How did the three parts of the state check and balance each other?hellip;

What were the checks upon the consuls, the executive? The consul—whose power over the administration of the government when in the city, and over the military when in the field, appeared absolute—still had need of the support of the Senate and the people. The consul needed supplies for his legions, but without a decree of the Senate, his soldiers could be supplied with neither corn nor clothes nor pay. Moreover, all of his plans would be futile if the Senate shrank from danger, or if the Senate opposed his plans or sought to hamper them. Therefore, whether the consul could bring any undertaking to a successful conclusion depended upon the Senate, which had the absolute power, at the end of the consul's one-year term, to replace him with another consul or to extend his command.

Even to the successes of the consuls on the field of battle, the Senate had the power to add distinction and glory, or to obscure their merits, for unless the Senate concurred in recognizing the achievements of the consuls and in voting the money, there could be no celebration or public triumph.

The consuls were also obliged to court the favor of the people, so here is the check of the people against

the consul, for it was the people who would ratify, or refuse to ratify, the terms of peace. But most of all, the consuls, when laying down their office at the conclusion of their one-year term, would have to give an accounting of their administration, both to the Senate and to the people. So, it was necessary that the consuls maintain the good will of both the Senate and the people.

What were the checks against the Senate? The Senate was obliged to take the multitude into account and respect the wishes of the people, for in matters directly affecting the senators—for instance, in the case of a law diminishing the Senate's traditional authority, or depriving senators of certain dignities, or even actually reducing the property of senators—in such cases, the people had the power to pass or reject the law in their assembly.

In addition, according to Polybius, if the tribunes imposed their veto, the Senate would not only be unable to pass a decree, but could not even hold a meeting. And because the tribunes must always have a regard for the people's wishes, the Senate stood in awe of the multitude and could not neglect the feelings of the people.

But as a counterbalance, what check was there against the people?hellip; According to Polybius, the people were far from being independent of the Senate, and were bound to take its wishes into account, both collectively and individually.hellip;

The Senate's ace card lay in its control over the purse strings. Also, the judges were selected from the Senate, at the time of Polybius, for the majority of trials in which the charges were heavy.hellip;

Polybius sums it up this way: "When any one of the three classes becomes puffed up, and manifests an inclination to be contentious and unduly encroaching, the mutual interdependency of all the three, and the possibility of the pretensions of any one being checked and thwarted by the others, must plainly check this tendency. And so the proper equilibrium is maintained by the impulsiveness of the one part being checked by its fear of the other."hellip;

The theory of a mixed constitution—that is what ours is, a mixed constitution with checks and balances, and separation of powers—hellip; had had its great measure of success in the Roman Republic. It is not surprising, therefore, that the Founding Fathers of the United States should have been familiar with the works of Polybius, or that Montesquieu should have been influenced by the checks and balances and separation of powers in the Roman constitutional system a clear element of which was the control over the purse, vested solely in the Senate in the heyday of the Republic.hellip;

Mr. President, in my presentations today and heretofore on this subject, I have drawn many parallels between our own Republic and the historical meanderings of that ancient Republic.hellip; It is my own sincere prayer, however, that the United States will not follow a course parallel to the Roman Republic into an inexorable decline and decadence.hellip;

Whereas Polybius wrote about the rise of the Roman Republic and its greatness, Gibbon wrote about the decline and fall of the Roman Empire, which followed on after the Republic collapsed.hellip;

Conversely, while Gibbon is acquainted with and recounts most of the evidences of Rome's decline that have nothing to do with Christianity—moral decadence, tyrannical emperors, barbarian incursions, the decline of the small family farms, the vanishing peasantry, the depletion of soils and accessible mineral resources, and the collapse of faith in the old gods—Gibbon treats these as being merely coincidental to Rome's decline.hellip;

Will Durant asserts that Rome was already in decline before Christianity emerged on the scene:

> "Decline in family life, rotting public and individual morality; the corrosion of discipline, patriotism, and the military esprit; abandonment of the land by the peasant classes, agricultural decline, deforestation; civil wars, class struggle, international warfare, praetorian intrigues and conspiracies, assassinations, violence, and civil disorders; bureaucratic despotism, economic, stifling taxes, and corruption in government; mad emperors, pestilences, and plague;...—all of these wore away the moral and spiritual and social underpinnings of the Roman state, and accelerated its plunge into hopeless impotence and eventual obscurity as a military power and territorial empire."hellip;

In short, Rome's fate was sealed by the one-by-one donations of power and prerogative that the Roman Senate plucked from its own quiver and voluntarily delivered into the hands, first, of Julius Caesar and then Octavian, and subsequently into the trust of the succession.hellip;

At the height of the Republic, the Roman Senate had been the one agency with the authority, the perspective, and the popular aura to debate, investigate, commission, and correct the problems that

Document Text

confronted the Roman state and its citizens. But the Senate's loss of will, and its eagerness to hand its responsibilities over to a one-man government—a man on a "white horse"—a dictator, and later an emperor, doomed Rome and predestined Rome's decline and ultimate fall.hellip;

Mr. President, in our own times we see the same problems, the same kinds of dilemmas that the hand of history wrote large upon Rome's slate, being written upon America's slate....

The solutions to these problems will be painful and will take time, perhaps years, to succeed.

This is not a truth that some people want to hear. Many would rather believe that quack remedies such as line-item vetoes and enhanced rescissions powers in the hands of presidents will somehow miraculously solve our current fiscal situation and eliminate our monstrous budget deficits....

Mr. President, let us learn from the pages of Rome's history. The basic lesson that we should remember for our purposes here is, that when the Roman Senate gave away its control of the purse strings, it gave away its power to check the executive....

This lesson is as true today as it was two thousand years ago. Does anyone really imagine that the splendors of our capital city stand or fall with mansions, monuments, buildings, and piles of masonry? These are but bricks and mortar, lifeless things, and their collapse or restoration means little or nothing when measured on the great clocktower of time. But the survival of the American constitutional system, the foundation upon which the superstructure of the Republic rests, finds its firmest support in the continued preservation of the delicate mechanism of checks and balances, separation of powers, and the control of the purse, solemnly instituted by the Founding Fathers. For over two hundred years, from the beginning of the Republic to this very hour, it has survived in unbroken continuity. We received it from our fathers. Let us as surely hand it on to our sons and daughters.

Glossary

the allies: nations under Rome's control

the check of the people against the consul: the legal power of the citizens to overrule their leaders by withdrawing their support

checks and balances ... separation of powers: features of the American constitutional system that prevent any one person or group from gaining power over all others in government

consuls: officials, selected by the Roman Senate to serve one-year terms, who led the Roman Republic

donations: losses

Gibbon: Edward Gibbon, writer of *Decline and Fall of the Roman Empire* who blamed the rise of Christianity for bringing about Rome's fall

Julius Caesar and then Octavian: Julius Caesar (100–44 BCE) ruled the Roman Republic until his murder, after which his nephew Octavian (63 BCE–14 CE) came to power as the first Roman emperor, renaming himself Augustus.

Glossary

levies:	taxes
Lycurgus:	a semilegendary figure credited with founding the city-state of Sparta; often used as an example of an honest leader
Manifest Destiny:	a term that refers specifically to the belief that expansion of America's frontiers is inevitable and desirable
military-industrial complex:	a term for the overall "business" of war, including both government agencies and civilian suppliers, first notably used by Dwight Eisenhower in his 1961 farewell address
Polybius:	a Greek historian (230–120 BCE) whose *Histories* discuss the Roman wars of conquest in the second century BCE
praetorian:	a reference to the Praetorian Guard, whose role as the Roman emperor's personal protectors gave them great influence in choosing leaders
receipts and disbursements:	funds coming in and funds to be paid out
rescissions:	acts for the rescinding, or reversal, of previous agreements
veto:	Latin for "I forbid," a term for the power of an executive, or leader, to overrule proposed legislation
Will Durant:	a popular American historian of the early to middle twentieth century

Byrd early in his Senate career

Document Text

"We Stand Passively Mute" Speech

2003

To contemplate war is to think about the most horrible of human experiences. On this February day, as this nation stands at the brink of battle, every American on some level must be contemplating the horrors of war.

Yet, this Chamber is, for the most part, silent—ominously, dreadfully silent. There is no debate, no discussion, no attempt to lay out for the nation the pros and cons of this particular war. There is nothing.

We stand passively mute in the United States Senate, paralyzed by our own uncertainty, seemingly stunned by the sheer turmoil of events. Only on the editorial pages of our newspapers is there much substantive discussion of the prudence or imprudence of engaging in this particular war.

And this is no small conflagration we contemplate. This is no simple attempt to defang a villain. No. This coming battle, if it materializes, represents a turning point in U.S. foreign policy and possibly a turning point in the recent history of the world.

This nation is about to embark upon the first test of a revolutionary doctrine applied in an extraordinary way at an unfortunate time. The doctrine of preemption—the idea that the United States or any other nation can legitimately attack a nation that is not imminently threatening but may be threatening in the future—is a radical new twist on the traditional idea of self defense. It appears to be in contravention of world-wide terrorism, making many countries around the globe wonder if they will soon be on our—or some other nation's—hit list. High level Administration figures recently refused to take nuclear weapons off of the table when discussing a possible attack against Iraq. What could be more destabilizing and unwise than this type of uncertainty, particularly in a world where globalism has tied the vital economic and security interests of many nations so closely together? There are huge cracks emerging in our time-honored alliances, and U.S. intentions are suddenly subject to damaging worldwide speculation. Anti-Americanism based on mistrust, misinformation, suspicion, and alarming rhetoric from U.S. leaders is fracturing the once solid alliances against global terrorism which existed after September 11.

Here at home, people are warned of imminent terrorist attacks with little guidance as to when or where such attacks might occur. Family members are being called to active military duty, with no idea of the duration of their stay or what horrors they may face. Communities are being left with less than adequate police and fire protection. Other essential services are also short-staffed. The mood of the nation is grim. The economy is stumbling. Fuel prices are rising and may soon spike higher.

This Administration, now in power for a little over two years, must be judged on its record. I believe that record is dismal....

In foreign policy, this Administration has failed to find Osama bin Laden. In fact, just yesterday, we heard from him again marshaling his forces and urging them to kill. This Administration has split traditional alliances, possibly crippling, for all time, international order-keeping entities like the United Nations and NATO. This Administration has called into question the traditional worldwide perception of the United States as well-intentioned peacekeeper. This Administration has turned the patient art of diplomacy into threats, labeling, and name calling of the sort that reflects quite poorly on the intelligence and sensitivity of our leaders, and which will have consequences for years to come.

Calling heads of state pygmies, labeling whole countries as evil, denigrating powerful European allies as irrelevant—these types of crude insensitivities can do our great nation no good. We may have massive military might, but we cannot fight a global war on terrorism alone. We need the cooperation and friendship of our time-honored allies as well as the newer found friends whom we can attract with our wealth. Our awesome military machine will do us little good if we suffer another devastating attack on our homeland which severely damages our economy. Our military manpower is already stretched thin and we will need the augmenting support of those nations who can supply troop strength, not just sign letters cheering us on.

The war in Afghanistan has cost us $37 billion so far, yet there is evidence that terrorism may already be starting to regain its hold in that region. We have not found bin Laden, and unless we secure the peace in Afghanistan, the dark dens of terrorism may yet again flourish in that remote and devastated land.

Pakistan as well is at risk of destabilizing forces. This Administration has not finished the first war against terrorism and yet it is eager to embark on

Document Text

another conflict with perils much greater than those in Afghanistan. Is our attention span that short? Have we not learned that after winning the war one must always secure the peace?

And yet we hear little about the aftermath of war in Iraq. In the absence of plans, speculation abroad is rife. Will we seize Iraq's oil fields, becoming an occupying power which controls the price and supply of that nation's oil for the foreseeable future? To whom do we propose to hand the reins of power after Saddam Hussein?

Will our war inflame the Muslim world resulting in devastating attacks on Israel? Will Israel retaliate with its own nuclear arsenal? Will the Jordanian and Saudi Arabian governments be toppled by radicals, bolstered by Iran which has much closer ties to terrorism than Iraq?

Could a disruption of the world's oil supply lead to a worldwide recession? Has our senselessly bellicose language and our callous disregard of the interests and opinions of other nations increased the global race to join the nuclear club and made proliferation an even more lucrative practice for nations which need the income?

In only the space of two short years this reckless and arrogant Administration has initiated policies which may reap disastrous consequences for years.

One can understand the anger and shock of any President after the savage attacks of September 11. One can appreciate the frustration of having only a shadow to chase and an amorphous, fleeting enemy on which it is nearly impossible to exact retribution.

But to turn one's frustration and anger into the kind of extremely destabilizing and dangerous foreign policy debacle that the world is currently witnessing is inexcusable from any Administration charged with the awesome power and responsibility of guiding the destiny of the greatest superpower on the planet. Frankly many of the pronouncements made by this Administration are outrageous. There is no other word.

Yet this chamber is hauntingly silent. On what is possibly the eve of horrific infliction of death and destruction on the population of the nation of Iraq—a population, I might add, of which over 50% is under age 15—this chamber is silent.... On the eve of what could possibly be a vicious terrorist attack in retaliation for our attack on Iraq, it is business as usual in the United States Senate.

We are truly "sleepwalking through history." In my heart of hearts, I pray that this great nation and its good and trusting citizens are not in for a rudest of awakenings.

To engage in war is always to pick a wild card. And war must always be a last resort, not a first choice. I truly must question the judgment of any President who can say that a massive unprovoked military attack on a nation which is over 50% children is "in the highest moral traditions of our country." This war is not necessary at this time. Pressure appears to be having a good result in Iraq. Our mistake was to put ourselves in a corner so quickly. Our challenge is to now find a graceful way out of a box of our own making. Perhaps there is still a way if we allow more time.

Glossary

calling heads of state pygmies:	reference to George Bush's scornful remark concerning North Korean dictator Kim Jong-Il, who wore platform shoes to make himself look taller
globalism:	the interconnectedness of most countries in a worldwide system of trade and communication
passively mute:	looking on in silence, incapable of taking action
preemption:	attacking another nation before it attacks, in the belief that it will do so eventually
proliferation:	the spread of nuclear arms and other weapons of mass destruction
sleepwalking through history:	the title of a 1992 book by the historian Haynes Johnson, subtitled *America in the Reagan Years*
this chamber:	the Senate

Document Text

"The Emperor Has No Clothes" Speech

2003

In 1837, Danish author, Hans Christian Andersen, wrote a wonderful fairy tale which he titled *The Emperor's New Clothes*. It may be the very first example of the power of political correctness. It is the story of the Ruler of a distant land who was so enamored of his appearance and his clothing that he had a different suit for every hour of the day.

One day two rogues arrived in town, claiming to be gifted weavers. They convinced the Emperor that they could weave the most wonderful cloth, which had a magical property. The clothes were only visible to those who were completely pure in heart and spirit.

The Emperor was impressed and ordered the weavers to begin work immediately. The rogues, who had a deep understanding of human nature, began to feign work on empty looms.

Minister after minister went to view the new clothes and all came back exhorting the beauty of the cloth on the looms even though none of them could see a thing.

Finally a grand procession was planned for the Emperor to display his new finery. The Emperor went to view his clothes and was shocked to see absolutely nothing, but he pretended to admire the fabulous cloth, inspect the clothes with awe, and, after disrobing, go through the motions of carefully putting on a suit of the new garments.

Under a royal canopy, the Emperor appeared to the admiring throng of his people—all of whom cheered and clapped because they all knew the rogue weavers' tale and did not want to be seen as less than pure of heart.

But, the bubble burst when an innocent child loudly exclaimed, for the whole kingdom to hear, that the Emperor had nothing on at all. He had no clothes.

That tale seems to me very like the way this nation was led to war.

We were told that we were threatened by weapons of mass destruction in Iraq, but they have not been seen.

We were told that the throngs of Iraqi's would welcome our troops with flowers, but no throngs or flowers appeared.

We were led to believe that Saddam Hussein was connected to the attack on the Twin Towers and the Pentagon, but no evidence has ever been produced.

We were told in 16 words that Saddam Hussein tried to buy "yellow cake" from Africa for the production of nuclear weapons, but the story has turned into empty air.

We were frightened with visions of mushroom clouds, but they turned out to be only vapors of the mind.

We were told that major combat was over but 101 [as of October 17] Americans have died in combat since that proclamation from the deck of an aircraft carrier by our very own Emperor in his new clothes.

Our emperor says that we are not occupiers, yet we show no inclination to relinquish the country of Iraq to its people.

Those who have dared to expose the nakedness of the Administration's policies in Iraq have been subjected to scorn. Those who have noticed the elephant in the room—that is, the fact that this war was based on falsehoods—have had our patriotism questioned. Those who have spoken aloud the thought shared by hundreds of thousands of military families across this country, that our troops should return quickly and safely from the dangers half a world away, have been accused of cowardice. We have then seen the untruths, the dissembling, the fabrication, the misleading inferences surrounding this rush to war in Iraq wrapped quickly in the flag....

The Emperor has no clothes. This entire adventure in Iraq has been based on propaganda and manipulation. Eighty-seven billion dollars is too much to pay for the continuation of a war based on falsehoods.

Taking the nation to war based on misleading rhetoric and hyped intelligence is a travesty and a tragedy. It is the most cynical of all cynical acts. It is dangerous to manipulate the truth. It is dangerous because once having lied, it is difficult to ever be believed again. Having misled the American people and stampeded them to war, this Administration must now attempt to sustain a policy predicated on falsehoods. The President asks for billions from those same citizens who know that they were misled about the need to go to war. We misinformed and insulted

Document Text

our friends and allies and now this Administration is having more than a little trouble getting help from the international community. It is perilous to mislead....

I cannot support the continuation of a policy that unwisely ties down 150,000 American troops for the foreseeable future, with no end in sight.

I cannot support a President who refuses to authorize the reasonable change in course that would bring traditional allies to our side in Iraq.

I cannot support the politics of zeal and "might makes right" that created the new American arrogance and unilateralism which passes for foreign policy in this Administration.

I cannot support this foolish manifestation of the dangerous and destabilizing doctrine of preemption that changes the image of America into that of a reckless bully.

The emperor has no clothes. And our former allies around the world were the first to loudly observe it.

I shall vote against this bill because I cannot support a policy based on prevarication. I cannot support doling out 87 billion of our hard-earned tax dollars when I have so many doubts about the wisdom of its use.

I began my remarks with a fairy tale. I shall close my remarks with a horror story, in the form of a quote from the book *Nuremberg Diaries*, written by G. M. Gilbert, in which the author interviews Hermann Goering:

"We got around to the subject of war again and I said that, contrary to his attitude, I did not think that the common people are very thankful for leaders who bring them war and destruction.

"...But, after all, it is the *leaders* of the country who determine the policy and it is always a simple matter to drag the people along, whether it is a democracy or a fascist dictatorship or a Parliament or a Communist dictatorship.

"There is one difference," I pointed out. "In a democracy the people have some say in the matter through their elected representatives, and in the United States only Congress can declare wars."

"Oh, that is all well and good, but, voice or no voice, the people can always be brought to the bidding of the leaders. That is easy. All you have to do is tell them they are being attacked and denounce the pacifists for lack of patriotism and exposing the country to danger. It works the same way in any country."

Glossary

unilateralism: a policy of taking action without consulting or considering the reactions of others

we were told in 16 words: reference to George W. Bush's statement, in his 2003 State of the Union speech, "The British government has learned that Saddam Hussein recently sought significant quantities of uranium from Africa."

weapons of mass destruction: nuclear, biological, radiological, chemical, or other forms of weaponry capable of killing large populations in a short time

yellow cake: a form of uranium that can be used for making nuclear weaponry

Calhoun photographed by Mathew Brady in 1849

John C. Calhoun: Original Analysis

U.S. Congressman, Senator, Vice President, and States' Rights Advocate

1782–1850

Overview

During his lifetime, John C. Calhoun was a larger-than-life figure; he was held almost in awe by many Americans. In his teens Calhoun displayed a voracious appetite for learning, poring over books and sucking up knowledge from wherever he could acquire it. At age fourteen, he became the manager of his family's farms and turned around his family's fortunes by making the farms profitable. Although he was from the backwoods of South Carolina, with little formal education, he earned admission to Yale College, where he cut a striking figure. He was six feet, two inches tall but was so thin that he seemed taller. He did not wear the stylish clothing of his rich classmates, seemingly oblivious to how his sturdy, rustic clothing and boots made him seem out of place. He spoke with a frontier twang that made him sound down-to-earth, a man of the people rather than part of southern aristocracy.

Even though he accomplished much in America's government—serving in the House of Representatives, in the Senate, as vice president in two separate administrations, and as a member of the cabinet—his modern reputation is dominated by his support for states' rights. He was heavily influenced by Thomas Jefferson's ideas about an agrarian democracy, in which people who were closely connected to the land would maintain American values of individual liberty, and he believed that such values were embodied in the U.S. Constitution, sometimes purposely and sometimes accidentally by the people who wrote the document and formed the United States. He viewed industrialization with suspicion; he believed that the agricultural production of slave states did much more to support the economy of the nation through the payments of tariffs and duties than did the machinery of the industries of other states. He believed that the formal institution of slavery was more honest than what he viewed as the industrial servitude of laborers in factories and mills. As an institution recognized by law, he argued, slavery put obligations on both slave and slave owner, including caring for slaves after they ceased to be able to work, whereas the slaves (as he viewed them) of free-state industries had no formal social contract and were left to starve and die homeless when their usefulness to industrialists ended. He was profoundly racist in his views. He believed that black Africans were inherently less capable of reasoning than were whites and that slavery actually enhanced the lives of black people by exposing them to the benefits of white American civilization.

If Calhoun's ill-informed views on ethnic groups had been all there were to his public career, his documents would have little to recommend themselves to modern people, but he was a wide-ranging thinker whose analyses of the Constitution and its effects on the everyday lives of Americans still resonate with the issues of modern times. For instance, his assessment of the Mexican-American War and its possible effects on America's future has found eerie echoes in wars that followed, even including the war in Iraq. Calhoun clung to the Constitution as if it were the only lifeboat in a sea of storms and sharks, and he cited it often as the key to holding the United States together; he believed that only with the states united as one nation could the civil rights of people be protected. It was his view that if any states succeeded in seceding from the United States, the protections of the Constitution would be lost for all Americans in all states and territories, and the experiment in self-government by the people would be lost to oppressive regimes in which the many labored for the comfort of a few. Thus, he resisted not only movements in New England to secede during the War of 1812 but also such movements even in his home state of South Carolina.

Calhoun believed that the United States was a truly revolutionary country, because the nation was, to his mind, a forthright rejection of Old World monarchies and aristocracies—a rejection of the notion that people were allowed to dominate others because of bearing hereditary aristocratic titles or because of having great wealth. His writings carry in them his defense of America's Constitution as a document intended to allow people to find their places in life based on their character. When he defends southern customs, he does so in the belief that the Constitution allows people in different places to pursue happiness in their own ways, without other people telling them what to do.

Thus, he was a champion of the civil rights of those in a minority, especially when a majority would try to impose its will on a minority. A government ruled strictly by a majority of its citizens would be a despotic government, because it would deny citizens the ability to pursue their own interests in whatever manner they might choose. To him, the issue of slavery epitomized the conflict between minority and majority, and the outcome of the conflict over slavery would be either despotism by a northern majority or a triumph of individual liberty for minorities throughout the United States. When read in chronological order, Calhoun's works reveal his growing belief that the original federal

government of the United States was being reshaped into a central government and that the change was creating conflict between states that otherwise would have no cause to abuse one another. His writings were often directed toward finding ways to preserve individual liberty while adjusting to social and economic changes that were moving America toward a society in which everyone was supposed to be like everyone else rather than allowing for a diversity of opinions and ways of life.

Calhoun distinguished between the words *federal* and *national* to convey his ideas about what was wrong with America's government and what needed to be fixed. In his speeches and writings, *federal* refers to the nation's government as originally conceived by the writers of the Constitution. That document created a federal government in which state laws dominated society. He believed that the best democracy exists when local people handle their own affairs without interference from a national government, such that being smaller makes states better able to provide for local self-governance than a centralized national government could. When he uses the word *national*, he is referring to a kind of government in which all laws and customs are imposed on citizens by a national majority seeking to make everyone like themselves; this sort of government would be as bad as an Old World monarchy, because when minorities are denied the opportunity to live as they please, everyone's liberty is at an end.

Explanation and Analysis of Documents

From the moment he entered public life, Calhoun was an impressive figure. When young members took control of the House of Representatives, Calhoun quickly became Speaker Henry Clay's floor leader and ably carried out his duties of persuasion among representatives in order to get legislation moved through committees and to votes. On December 12, 1811, he helped change the course of America with a speech that radically altered the balance of power in the House of Representatives, and he became a figure of national prominence. From that day onward, his speeches and writings were republished in newspapers; they were discussed in homes, businesses, legislatures, and even taverns. To Americans of his day, Calhoun was one of the most important politicians in the nation and one of the most important interpreters of the Constitution. He may have been the most important spokesman for the South.

♦ "On the Second Resolution Reported by the Committee on Foreign Relations"

Great Britain and France were at war, while America was a neutral country. Americans in general had profound dislike of the despotic regime in France and despised the regime in Great Britain. Great Britain declared an embargo on trade with France, but instead of just blockading French ports, it sent warships to blockade American ports, claiming that American ships might be bound for France. By 1811 Great

Time Line

1782	March 18	■ John Caldwell Calhoun is born in Abbeville, South Carolina.
1804		■ Calhoun graduates from Yale College.
1807		■ Calhoun graduates from Litchfield Law School, in Connecticut and opens a law practice in Abbeville.
1808		■ Calhoun is elected to the South Carolina legislature.
1810		■ Calhoun is elected to the U.S. House of Representatives, later becoming Speaker Henry Clay's floor leader.
1811	January 8	■ Calhoun marries his cousin Floride Colhoun.
	December 12	■ Calhoun delivers a speech entitled "On the Second Resolution Reported by the Committee on Foreign Relations" to the House of Representatives, advocating war against Great Britain and vaulting himself to national prominence.
1817		■ President James Monroe appoints Calhoun secretary of war.
1824		■ Calhoun is elected vice president of the United States by a wide margin in the Electoral College, while a three-way deadlock for president is decided in favor of John Quincy Adams by the House of Representatives.
1828		■ As Andrew Jackson's running mate, Calhoun is reelected vice president.
1830		■ President Jackson makes it publicly clear that he will use military force against any state that tries to secede from the United States.

Time Line

1831	July 26	■ The *New York Courier and Enquirer* publishes "On the Relation Which the States and General Government Bear to Each Other" (also known as the Fort Hill address), in which Calhoun argues that state governments are meant to serve as protectors of their citizens against unconstitutional acts of the federal government.
1832		■ Calhoun resigns as vice president and is elected a U.S. senator, representing South Carolina.
	November	■ Calhoun writes "To the People of the United States" to explain why South Carolina has the right to nullify federal laws.
1833		■ President Jackson prepares to use military force to compel South Carolina to obey federal laws, as South Carolina has tried to nullify federal laws that it believes damage its economy.
1837	February 6	■ Calhoun delivers his speech "On the Reception of Abolition Petitions" (also known as "Slavery a Positive Good") to the U.S. Senate.
1843		■ Calhoun leaves the Senate.
1844	April 1	■ President John Tyler appoints Calhoun secretary of state.
1845		■ Calhoun returns to serving as a U.S. senator.
1848	January 4	■ Calhoun delivers a speech entitled "On His Resolutions in Reference to the War with Mexico," taking a stance against the actions of President James Polk.
1850	March 4	■ Senator James Mason reads Calhoun's speech "On the Slavery Question" to the Senate, with Calhoun seated next to him, unable to stand or speak.
	March 31	■ Calhoun dies after an illness of several months.

Britain had seized more than one thousand American merchant ships and was impressing American seamen into the British navy, to serve as slaves, as Calhoun notes. The British blockade of American ports was bankrupting the country, because American goods could not be traded abroad and goods from abroad could not be imported—meaning that the federal government could collect no tariffs or other trade-related fees, which were the primary source of federal funding. The economies of agricultural and industrial states alike were collapsing, and people could not earn enough money to pay for the basics of life. Many politicians wanted to appease Great Britain, possibly by giving Maine to the British Empire.

Yet the House Committee on Foreign Relations delivered to the House of Representatives a recommendation that America prepare for war and demand reparations for the harm done by Great Britain. The response of many representatives was to point out that the resolution, if passed by the House, would be viewed by the British as a declaration of war and that America could not afford to fight the greatest military power on earth. On December 12, 1811, Calhoun rose to counter the arguments that opposed the recommendation of the Foreign Relations Committee. His speech struck the House like a thunderbolt. As Calhoun delivered it, his audience became ever more excited; what had been a depressed group became a group with a strong sense of direction, eager to go where Calhoun pointed. There was still a hard-fought battle before Calhoun's point of view won out and the House resolved to fight Great Britain, but from that day onward, Calhoun had followers of his own who regarded him as a great leader.

In this speech, Calhoun echoes the Declaration of Independence by trying to stir the emotions of his listeners as well as their minds. In so doing, he not only galvanized the House of Representatives but also reshaped how Americans thought of themselves. Instead of portraying America as a poor backwater in the world, he depicts America as a great nation, worth defending regardless of the expense, and Americans as a great people, worthy of standing among the greatest powers on earth. He urges the U.S. government not just to issue warnings to its oppressors but furthermore to take forceful action.

♦ "On the Relation Which the States and General Government Bear to Each Other"

This text, also known as the Fort Hill address, was written for publication, reaching print in the *New York Courier and Enquirer* on July 26, 1831. It contains Calhoun's ideas about how the states of the Union are supposed to be organized and how the Constitution was intended to delegate authority, among the branches of the federal government as well as between the federal government and the individual states. The key word in the document is *compact*. The term summarizes Calhoun's view of the proper relationship among the states and was an important concept in the debate over states' rights.

It was Calhoun's view that the Constitution created a compact among the states, whereas other Americans

believed that the Constitution created an inseparable bond among the states in which the federal government was preeminent. Calhoun's argument in "On the Relation Which the States and General Government Bear to Each Other" explains one of the principles that became one of the excuses used by some states to secede from the Union in 1861. In its essence, Calhoun's argument is that the Constitution created a compact among the states—that is, an agreement that each state had to abide by or the agreement would be broken. In his view, some free states were breaking the compact by refusing to return fugitive slaves to their owners, because the Constitution protected the property of citizens. By breaking the compact, the free states were creating a legitimate basis for secession from the Union by slave states.

Calhoun further states that he believes that the Constitution limited the federal government only to those powers specifically mentioned in it. All other powers, he argues, belong to the individual states. In fact, the states were intended to protect the rights of their citizens against oppression by the federal government, which might be swayed by a majority of the states to take civil rights away from citizens of other states. Thus, he believed that an individual state could nullify any federal law that did it harm. At the time, federal taxation was believed to unfairly target states that exported much of their agricultural output, and states such as South Carolina tried to declare those taxes null and void. This inspired one of the key breaks between Andrew Jackson and Calhoun, since Jackson was determined to use force to prevent states from nullifying federal laws.

♦ "To the People of the United States"

This address was written in November 1832 to explain why South Carolina sought to nullify certain federal laws. Therein, Calhoun expands on his idea that the U.S. government is the result of a compact among the states. He argues, in part, that individual states are better protectors of minorities than the federal government and therefore ought to be allowed to supersede federal laws with laws better suited to their local residents. In Calhoun's day, his arguments in favor of individual states being able to protect their people from federal laws that harm them were fought over in courts of law and in Congress, resulting in rulings in favor of the federal government's power to overrule state laws.

Calhoun's arguments that the United States was created as a compact shaped much of the debate over states' rights before the Civil War. His interpretation of history is that the British colonies of North America rebelled against Great Britain in order to liberate themselves individually and not collectively. That they eventually created a federal constitutional government was out of a need for taking collective action in such matters as foreign relations and war, and the writers of the Constitution carefully limited the federal government's powers so that individual states would be free to pursue their own ways of life. Calhoun argues that abolitionists were trying to end the limits on the federal government denoted in the Constitution and that if they succeeded, chaos would result in slave states because their individual social orders would be destroyed, as slavery was an integral part of their ways of life. He further argues that the compact would be broken the moment a majority of free staters in Congress combined with a free-state president to abolish slavery. It was his view that slavery was protected by the Constitution. His is a plea for a compromise on the issue of slavery, in order to save the Union, and he places the blame for the potential dissolution of the United States squarely on northern states.

♦ "On the Reception of Abolition Petitions"

From a modern perspective this 1837 speech before the U.S. Senate may be among the most embarrassing speeches ever delivered by an important American statesman, because of assertions that are not only racist but also often seem absurd. Yet this speech, also called "Slavery a Positive Good," was taken very seriously in its day, and much of Calhoun's reasoning became part of the defenses of the institution of slavery used by slave-state politicians until the end of the Civil War and by racial segregationists after the war. The underlying premise of the speech is that white-American civilization is superior to other civilizations and that people of other races are blessed even just by being exposed to white-American civilization. It is a premise that many, perhaps most, Americans would have agreed with in 1837.

Although Calhoun was a very well-read man, he had surprising gaps in his knowledge of cultures other than his own, and in "Slavery a Positive Good," his experience of other cultures seems very narrow—so narrow that he seems to be disingenuous when extolling the benefits slavery in America has had on those of African ancestry. His depiction of central Africa as a place of savagery does not jibe with the actual cultures of central Africa. His insistence that black Americans live better, happier lives than they would have lived in Africa seems out of touch with reality. There are two slightly mitigating aspects related to his argument. One is that he was devoted to his state of South Carolina, and his experiences with slavery derived primarily from that state. As Calhoun points out many times in his writings, each slave state had its own special customs. In the plantation regions of southern South Carolina, slaves outnumbered their white masters. The economy of the region could not have prospered without slaves being able to travel and conduct trade on behalf of their owners; this resulted in slaves of that region having more independence than elsewhere and in their being able to conduct commercial business of their own. Calhoun likely had these slaves in mind in this speech, rather than the ones in states where they were forbidden by law to be literate, where they could be whipped at an overseer's whim, or where they could be hung from trees in cages to starve to death for insubordination. The other slightly mitigating factor is Calhoun's juxtaposition of slavery with the abuses of workers in northern factories. His message that free states should clean up their

own cruelty toward the working class before decrying the abuses in the South had a powerful ring to it. Even so, he reveals a blindness toward the underlying moral issues that fueled outrage among abolitionists.

♦ "On His Resolutions in Reference to the War with Mexico"

This speech, with the title referring to the resolutions of President James Polk, is one of the most far-reaching and influential of Calhoun's speeches. By the time he delivered it on January 4, 1848, he had chosen to forsake his ambitions to become president in order to support unpopular political views that he viewed as important to preserving the Union. Furthermore, he had become a Jeremiah, warning of the impending doom of constitutional government if racial issues were to be left unsettled by Congress. The conquering of other countries, he argues in this document, would be disastrous for the other countries and disastrous for the rule of constitutional law in America. President Polk was openly imperialistic, plainly seeking to add the Mexican territories of New Mexico and Alta California to the United States, and he enjoyed broad popular support in America for the campaign against Mexico. Polk's arguments that the war was necessary for national security triumphed in Congress over Calhoun's objections that the war would result not in a democratic, constitutional government in Mexico but in an authoritarian government with few civil rights for the Mexican people. He was also worried that seizing vast Mexican territories would result in a multitude of new American citizens who knew nothing of America's democratic ways and whose elected congressional representatives could destroy American democracy by supporting dictatorial policies. His antiwar arguments are clouded by his racial prejudices, and readers must crawl through some absurd remarks about racial inferiority in order to discover the fundamental principles that Calhoun draws on to make his argument that America should not become an imperial power.

It may seem strange that the firebrand who directed the United States toward the War of 1812 should deliver an antiwar speech; it may seem as though Calhoun had changed his mind about armed conflict during the thirty-seven years between his advocating war against Great Britain and his opposing war against Mexico. Yet he was actually being consistent, because a theme uniting "On the Second Resolution Reported by the Committee on Foreign Relations" and "On His Resolutions in Reference to the War with Mexico" is the preservation of the Union. In the earlier speech, Calhoun insists that to preserve the Constitution and the liberties of American citizens, the federal government must protect them against crimes committed against them by the British. In 1848 he worries that the war against Mexico will result in fracturing the United States. In the new territories, he notes, issues such as whether new states and territories would allow or forbid slavery could prove divisive in the Union because of the debate over slavery. If people from slave states were to be forbidden to bring their slaves with them when settling in the newly captured territories, then the new states resulting from the territories would become politically part of the free states, increasing the South's concern that it would be treated unfairly by a Senate and a House of Representatives dominated by free staters. Thus, the acquisition of Mexican territory could propel the South to seceding.

♦ "On the Slavery Question"

This speech, delivered March 4, 1850, caused Calhoun's legend to continue to grow after his death less than a month later. He knew he was near death when he wrote it; when he went to the Senate to deliver it, he could barely stand and hardly speak, so he handed the speech to Senator James Mason, who read it to the Senate for him. The galleries were crowded with people who had come to hear what they believed would be Calhoun's last speech; even senators who opposed his views listened respectfully. While Mason delivered the speech, Calhoun sat, his face lined and hollowed with age and illness and his trademark great mane of white hair splashing from each side of his head. He looked the part of a biblical prophet, worn out from bearing too many burdens. The speech was his last significant attempt to end talk of states seceding from the Union and to preserve the rule of constitutional law.

Although this speech is known as "On the Slavery Question," it is not as narrow as the title implies. Calhoun's purpose is to enumerate the many grievances southern states have against the federal government and to explain how all of these grievances taken together are leading to secession, which would be a cataclysm that would end liberty for all Americans. He sees only tyranny resulting from secession and the civil war that would inevitably follow. The most important of the grievances he describes is taxation. Calhoun argues that southern states are taxed much more heavily than other states and that the taxes are spent more in the North than in the South, such that southern states are insufficiently benefiting from federal spending. The unfair taxation, he insists, impoverishes southern states. He asserts that this and other abuses by the federal government are the result of a perversion of the Constitution by politicians who have made Congress into a tyrannical organization that favors some states over others and who in the process have nearly destroyed the Constitution's protections of civil liberties throughout the nation. He pleads with his listeners to revisit the history of the Revolutionary War and the writing of the Constitution and relearn the lessons of the Founders of the United States; he expects that they would discover that the federal government was supposed not to rule people's lives but to shield those lives from government control. If the Constitution were to be understood by all as intended to restrict government's control over people's lives, secession and civil war could still be averted—although by 1850 Calhoun believed that war was inevitable, because people would not heed his warnings.

Impact and Legacy

When reading the many documents of Calhoun, covering more than forty years in politics, one is likely to notice a strain of pessimism in his thinking about America and the future. Even when he was in his first year at Yale College, his professors spoke of him as a future president of the United States. He stood his ground well in debates, and he was handsome, with thick hair, and had a deep, resonant voice that made it sound as though he spoke with the authority of profound wisdom. As he aged, the hollows in his face deepened; his eyes especially became arresting as they gazed out from deep under his brows. His hair grew white and unruly, making him appear to be a plain backwoodsman when he delivered his speeches. Many saw and heard him and believed he would be a great president, and he seems to have yearned for that office for most of his life. The closest he came was to be the overwhelming choice of the Electoral College for vice president in 1824. Yet Calhoun was torn between his ambition to become president and his fear that Americans would foolishly throw away their unique government in squabbles among different sections of the country. To become president, he would have needed to navigate America's political waters carefully. His 1811 speech "On the Second Resolution Reported by the Committee on Foreign Relations," delivered to the House of Representatives, elevated him to national prominence and made him a hero to most Americans, but he needed to steer clear of the issue of slavery if he hoped to win the support of free states when running for president. Although he hoped to be elected president, he chose what he believed to be the welfare of the nation over his own ambitions by warning repeatedly that disputes over the practice of slavery in the South could put an end to the United States. During much of his political career, he sought ways for all sides in the disputes over slavery to compromise in order to preserve the Constitution and individual liberty. His speech "Slavery a Positive Good" was delivered as a plea for compromise, and the sentiments in it and in his other speeches on the subject of compromise probably killed his chances to become president of the United States. During the last years of his life, he repeatedly predicted that the issue of slavery needed to be lastingly resolved or there would be a civil war.

Although Calhoun often said that secession from the United States would be disastrous for the states that seceded, his arguments for states' rights were used by secessionists to justify their actions. Similarly, his persistent insistence that problems between free states and slave states were caused by abolitionists rather than by slave owners was used by slave owners for propaganda that blamed secession on people outside the slave states rather than on the slave states themselves. His warnings that secession would be catastrophic were ignored, while his claim that the United States was a compact that could become void when any state violated the compact was used to give secession a constitutional justification, because free states that refused to return fugitive slaves to their masters were thought to have violated the Constitution. That he proved correct that secession by any states would result in a bloodbath probably would have given Calhoun no comfort.

In modern times, Calhoun's writings are included in college and law school courses about the Constitution and the history of constitutional law. His writings on race and slavery are considered not only distastefully racist but also outright absurd, as when he claims that slaves benefit from being slaves. On the other hand, his closely reasoned analyses of constitutional law are used in classes as examples of the divergent opinions of his day about how the Constitution was intended to organize the relationships between the federal and state governments.

Key Sources

A good selection of Calhoun's writings is found in *John C. Calhoun: Selected Writings and Speeches*, edited by H. Lee Cheek, Jr. (2003); a weakness for its use by students is that it lacks footnotes, thus leaving cross-references and allusions to contemporary events up to the reader to figure out. Calhoun's letters were published in *Correspondence of John C. Calhoun*, edited by J. Franklin Jameson (1900). A multivolume edition of Calhoun's works has been under way since 1959: *The Papers of John C. Calhoun*, edited by Robert L. Meriwether. *The Works of John C. Calhoun*, edited by Richard K. Crallé (1851, 1860–1870) may be found online at the Online Books Page (http://onlinebooks.library.upenn.edu/webbin/book/lookupname?key=Calhoun%2C%20John%20C.%20(John%20Caldwell)%2C%201782-1850).

Essential Quotes

"It is not for the human tongue to instil the sense of independence and honor. This is the work of nature; a generous nature that disdains tame submission to wrongs."

("On the Second Resolution Reported by the Committee on Foreign Relations")

Essential Quotes

"When we contend, let us contend for all our rights; the doubtful and the certain; the unimportant and essential. It is as easy to struggle, or even more so, for the whole as for a part."

("On the Second Resolution Reported by the Committee on Foreign Relations")

"It is no less the duty of the minority than a majority to endeavor to defend the country."

("On the Second Resolution Reported by the Committee on Foreign Relations")

"The great and leading principle is, that the General Government emanated from the people of the several States, forming distinct political communities, and acting in their separate and sovereign capacity, and not from all of the people forming one aggregate political community; that the Constitution of the United States is, in fact, a compact."

("On the Relation Which the States and General Government Bear to Each Other")

"We, then, hold it as unquestionable, that, on the separation from the Crown of Great Britain, the people of the several colonies became free and independent States, possessed of the full right of self-government; and that no power can be rightfully exercised over them, but by the consent and authority of their respective States, expressed or implied."

("To the People of the United States")

"We of the South will not, cannot surrender our institutions. To maintain the existing relations between the two races, inhabiting that section of the Union, is indispensable to the peace and happiness of both. It can not be subverted without drenching the country in blood, and extirpating one or the other of the races."

("Slavery a Positive Good")

"I hold that in the present state of civilization, where two races of different origin, and distinguished by color, and other physical differences, as well as intellectual, are brought together, the relation now existing in the slaveholding States between the two, is, instead of an evil, a good—a positive good."

("Slavery a Positive Good")

Essential Quotes

"War may be made by one party, but it requires two to make peace."

("On His Resolutions in Reference to the War with Mexico")

"I have, Senators, believed from the first that the agitation of the subject of slavery would, if not prevented by some timely and effective measure, end in disunion."

("On the Slavery Question")

"To destroy the constitution would be to destroy the Union."

("On the Slavery Question")

Further Reading

Books

Bartlett, Irving H. *John C. Calhoun: A Biography*. New York: W. W. Norton, 1993.

Cheek, H. Lee, Jr. *Calhoun and Popular Rule: The Political Theory of the Disquisition and Discourse*. Columbia: University of Missouri Press, 2001.

Coit, Margaret L. *John C. Calhoun: American Portrait*. Boston: Houghton Mifflin, 1950.

Current, Richard M. *John C. Calhoun*. New York: Washington Square Press, 1963.

Howe, Daniel Walker. *What Hath God Wrought: The Transformation of America, 1815–1848*. New York: Oxford University Press, 2007.

Marmor, Theodore R. *The Career of John C. Calhoun: Politician, Social Critic, Political Philosopher*. New York: Garland, 1988.

Niven, John. *John C. Calhoun and the Price of Union: A Biography*. Baton Rouge: Louisiana State University Press, 1988.

Spain, August O. *The Political Theory of John C. Calhoun*. New York: Bookman Associates, 1951.

—Kirk H. Beetz

Questions for Further Study

1. Compare and contrast the arguments Calhoun made in his 1811 and 1848 addresses on the possibility of war with Britain and Mexico, respectively. Whereas he stirred members of Congress to action, ultimately helping to pave the way for the War of 1812, more than three decades later he spoke just as effectively and vehemently against participation in what would become the Mexican-American War. Why did he consider the one military action justified, but not the other?

2. To what extent does Calhoun's argument against the Mexican-American War apply to the war in Iraq of the early 2000s? How are the situations similar and different? Consider, among other things, the nature of the

Questions for Further Study

leadership in Mexico and Iraq before the U.S. invasion, the degree to which each posed a threat to national security, and the respective nations' geographic proximity to areas of concern (Mexico being next door to the United States and Iraq close to such hotspots as Israel and Afghanistan).

3. Despite his greatness as a statesman, Calhoun is remembered today with mixed feelings due to the racist viewpoint that underlies numerous of his statements on slavery and other issues. For example, in his 1837 speech against the abolition of slavery, he made it clear that he believed white people to be superior to blacks, which meant that slavery was actually (to use phrasing from the alternate title of that speech) "a positive good." Likewise, in his 1848 argument against the Mexican War, he portrayed Mexicans as "utterly incompetent" and incapable of governing themselves. To what degree does his racism undercut the effectiveness of his arguments? In discussing this matter, keep in mind that his views were not different from those of most white Americans in his time.

4. Had Calhoun lived in the twenty-first century, he might have been described as the "poster boy" for states' rights. In the years leading up to the Civil War, itself a conflict in large part over states' rights, Calhoun was the leading spokesperson for the sovereignty of the individual states even as he sought to preserve the Union. Although national unity would ultimately triumph over states' rights, legitimate concerns over the independence of states have continued up to the present. Examine the arguments he made in his addresses "on the relation which the states and general government bear to each other" and "to the people of the United States." What are his best and most valid points? His weakest ones?

5. The career and legacy of John C. Calhoun is riddled with ironies. Chief among them was his adherence to slavery and states' rights even as he remained committed to upholding national union—beliefs that would ultimately prove irreconcilable. Much as he opposed secession, his writings would later provide justification to the secessionists whose movement culminated in the establishment of the Confederacy. Discuss these and other ironic aspects of Calhoun's work, including the fact that he is still respected as a constitutional scholar yet scorned for his racism.

"On the Second Resolution Reported by the Committee on Foreign Relations"

1811

"On the Second Resolution Reported by the Committee on Foreign Relations" (1811)

The extent, duration, and character of the injuries received; the failure of those peaceful means heretofore resorted to for the redress of our wrongs, are my proofs that it [war] is necessary. Why should I mention the impressment of our seamen; depredations on every branch of our commerce, including the direct export trade, continued for years, and made under laws which professedly undertake to regulate our trade with other nations; negotiation resorted to, again and again, till it is become hopeless; the restrictive system persisted in to avoid war, and in the vain expectation of returning justice? The evil still grows, and, in each succeeding year, swells in extent and pretension beyond the preceding. The question, even in the opinion and by the admission of our opponents is reduced to this single point. Which shall we do, abandon or defend our own commercial and maritime rights, and the personal liberties of our citizens employed in exercising them? These rights are vitally attacked, and war is the only means of redress.... It is not for the human tongue to instil the sense of independence and honor. This is the work of nature; a generous nature that disdains tame submission to wrongs....

When we contend, let us contend for all our rights; the doubtful and the certain; the unimportant and essential. It is as easy to struggle, or even more so, for the whole as for a part. At the termination of the contest, secure all that our wisdom and valor and the fortune of the war will permit. This is the dictate of common sense; such also is the usage of nations. The single instance alluded to, the endeavor of Mr. Fox to compel Mr. Pitt to define the object of the war against France, will not support the gentleman [John Randolph] from Virginia in his position. That was an extraordinary war for an extraordinary purpose, and was not governed by the usual rules. It was not for conquest, or for redress of injury, but to impose a government on France, which she refused to receive; an object so detestable that an avowal dared not be made.

Sir, I might here rest the question. The affirmative of the proposition is established. I cannot but advert, however, to the complaint of the gentleman from Virginia when he was first up on this question. He said he found himself reduced to the necessity of supporting the negative side of the question, before the affirmative was established. Let me tell the gentleman, that there is no hardship in his case. It is not every affirmative that ought to be proved. Were I to affirm, that the House is now in session, would it be reasonable to ask for proof? He who would deny its truth, on him would be the proof of so extraordinary a negative. How then could the gentleman, after his admissions, with the facts before him and the country, complain? The causes are such as to warrant, or rather make it indispensable, in any nation not absolutely dependent, to defend its rights by force. Let him, then, show the reasons why we ought not so to defend ourselves. On him lies the burden of proof....

The first argument of the gentleman which I shall notice, is the unprepared state of the country. Whatever weight this argument might have in a question of immediate war, it surely has little in that of preparation for it. If our country is unprepared, let us remedy the evil as soon as possible. Let the gentleman submit his plan; and if a reasonable one, I doubt not it will be supported by the House. But, Sir, let us admit the fact and the whole force of the argument. I ask whose is the fault? Who has been a member, for many years past, and seen the defenceless state of his country even near home, under his own eyes, without a single endeavor to remedy so serious an evil? Let him not say, "I have acted in a minority." It is no less the duty of the minority than a majority to endeavor to defend the country. For that purpose we are sent here, and not for that of opposition. We are next told of the expenses of the war; and that the people will not pay taxes. Why not? Is it from want of means? What, with 1,000,000, tons of shipping; a commerce of $100,000,000 annually; manufactures yielding a yearly product of $150,000,000; and agriculture of thrice that amount, shall we be told the country wants capacity to raise and support ten thousand or fifteen thousand additional regulars? No; it has the ability; that is admitted; and will it not have the disposition? Is not the cause a just and necessary one? Shall we then utter this libel on the people? Where will proof be found of a fact so disgraceful? It is answered; in the history of the country twelve or fifteen years ago.

Document Text

The case is not parallel. The ability of the country is greatly increased since. The whiskey-tax was unpopular. But on this, as well as my memory serves me, the objection was not to the tax or its amount, but the mode of collection. The people were startled by the number of officers; their love of liberty shocked with the multiplicity of regulations. We, in the spirit of imitation, copied from the most oppressive part of European laws on the subject of taxes, and imposed on a young and virtuous people all the severe provisions made necessary by corruption and long-practised evasions. If taxes should become necessary, I do not hesitate to say the people will pay cheerfully. It is for their government and their cause, and it would be their interest and their duty to pay. But it may be, and I believe was said, that the people will not pay taxes, because the rights violated are not worth defending; or that the defence will cost more than the gain. Sir, I here enter my solemn protest against this low and "calculating avarice" entering this hall of legislation. It is only fit for shops and counting-houses; and ought not to disgrace the seat of power by its squalid aspect. Whenever it touches sovereign power, the nation is ruined. It is too short-sighted to defend itself. It is a compromising spirit, always ready to yield a part to save the residue. It is too timid to have in itself the laws of self-preservation. It is never safe but under the shield of honor. There is, Sir, one principle necessary to make us a great people, to produce not the form, but real spirit of union; and that is, to protect every citizen in the lawful pursuit of his business. He will then feel that he is backed by the government; that its arm is his arm; and will rejoice in its increased strength and prosperity. Protection and patriotism are reciprocal. This is the way which has led nations to greatness.

Glossary

advert:	call attention to something, particularly a problem
the history of the country twelve or fifteen years ago:	a reference to the Whiskey Rebellion, a 1794 uprising in western Pennsylvania
impressment:	the act of forcing someone into labor or service
John Randolph:	leading figure in the "Old Republican" wing of the former Democratic-Republican Party, which opposed Calhoun's "National Republican" wing
Mr. Fox:	Charles James Fox (1749–1806), leading figure in the British parliament and chief opponent to William Pitt the Younger
Mr. Pitt:	William Pitt the Younger (1759–1806), British prime minister (1783–1801, 1804–1806)
professedly:	obviously; by clear statement or admission
regulars:	soldiers in a regular army—that is, a permanent, full-time military force
swells in extent and pretension:	grows in size and demands
the war against France:	Britain's opposition to Napoléon Bonaparte and his attempt to subdue all of Europe during the early 1800s

"On the Relation Which the States and General Government Bear to Each Other"

The question of the relation which the States and General Government bear to each other is not one of recent origin. From the commencement of our system, it has divided public sentiment. Even in the Convention, while the Constitution was struggling into existence, there were two parties as to what this relation should be, whose different sentiments constituted no small impediment in forming that instrument. After the General Government went into operation, experience soon proved that the question had not terminated with the labors of the Convention. The great struggle that preceded the political revolution of 1801, which brought Mr. Jefferson into power, turned essentially on it, and the doctrines and arguments on both sides were embodied and ably sustained; on the one [hand], in the Virginia and Kentucky Resolutions, and the Report to the Virginia Legislature; and on the other, in the replies of the Legislature of Massachusetts and some of the other States. These Resolutions and this Report, with the decision of the Supreme Court of Pennsylvania about the same time (particularly in the case of Cobbett, delivered by Chief Justice [Thomas] M'Kean, and concurred in by the whole bench), contain what I believe to be the true doctrine on this important subject. I refer to them in order to avoid the necessity of presenting my views, with the reasons in support of them, in detail....

The great and leading principle is, that the General Government emanated from the people of the several States, forming distinct political communities, and acting in their separate and sovereign capacity, and not from all of the people forming one aggregate political community; that the Constitution of the United States is, in fact, a compact, to which each State is a party, in the character already described; and that the several States, or parties, have a right to judge of its infractions; and in case of a deliberate, palpable, and dangerous exercise of power not delegated, they have the right, in the last resort, to use the language of the Virginia Resolutions, "*to interpose for arresting the progress of the evil, and for maintaining, within their respective limits, the authorities, rights, and liberties appertaining to them* ." This right of interposition, thus solemnly asserted by the State of Virginia, be it called what it may,—State-right, veto, nullification, or by any other name,—I conceive to be the fundamental principle of our system, resting on facts historically as certain as our revolution itself, and deductions as simple and demonstrative as that of any political or moral truth whatever; and I firmly believe that on its recognition depend the stability and safety of our political institutions....

Nearly half my life has been passed in the service of the Union, and whatever public reputation I have acquired is indissolubly identified with it. To be too national has, indeed, been considered by many, even of my friends, my greatest political fault. With these strong feelings of attachment, I have examined, with the utmost care, the bearing of the doctrine in question; and, so far from anarchical or revolutionary, I solemnly believe it to be the only solid foundation of our system, and of the Union itself; and that the opposite doctrine, which denies to the States the right of protecting their reserved powers, and which would vest in the General Government (it matters not through what department) the right of determining, exclusively and finally, the powers delegated to it, is incompatible with the sovereignty of the States, and of the Constitution itself, considered as the basis of a Federal Union. As strong as this language is, it is not stronger than that used by the illustrious Jefferson, who said, to give to the General Government the final and exclusive right to judge of its powers, is to make "*its discretion, and not the Constitution, the measure of its powers* ;" and that, "*in all cases of compact between parties having no common judge, each party has an equal right to judge for itself, as well of the infraction as of the mode and measure of redress.*" Language cannot be more explicit, nor can higher authority be adduced.

That different opinions are entertained on this subject, I consider but as an additional evidence of the great diversity of the human intellect. Had not able, experienced, and patriotic individuals, for whom I have the highest respect, taken different views, I would have thought the right too clear to admit of doubt; but I am taught by this, as well as by

Document Text

many similar instances, to treat with deference opinions differing from my own. The error may, possibly, be with me; but if so, I can only say that, after the most mature and conscientious examination, I have not been able to detect it. But, with all proper deference, I must think that theirs is the error who deny what seems to be an essential attribute of the conceded sovereignty of the States, and who attribute to the General Government a right utterly incompatible with what all acknowledge to be its limited and restricted character: an error originating principally, as I must think, in not duly reflecting on the nature of our institutions, and on what constitutes the only rational object of all political constitutions.

It has been well said by one of the most sagacious men of antiquity, that the object of a constitution is, to *restrain the government, as that of laws is to restrain individuals.* The remark is correct; nor is it less true where the government is vested in a majority, than where it is in a single or a few individuals in a republic, than a monarchy or aristocracy. No one can have a higher respect for the maxim that the majority ought to govern than I have, taken in its proper sense, subject to the restrictions imposed by the Constitution, and confined to objects in which every portion of the community have similar interests; but it is a great error to suppose, as many do, that the right of a majority to govern is a natural and not a conventional right, and therefore absolute and unlimited. By nature, every individual has the right to govern himself; and governments, whether founded on majorities or minorities, must derive their right from the assent, expressed or implied, of the governed, and to such limitations as they may impose.

Glossary

adduced:	brought forward for the purpose of making an argument
admit of:	permit or allow for
mode and measure:	type and degree
a natural and not a conventional right:	a right given by nature, not by law
parties:	viewpoints
political revolution of 1801:	the assumption of power in 1801 by Thomas Jefferson and the Democratic-Republican Party, marking a sharp break from the Federalist administration of John Adams
Virginia and Kentucky Resolutions:	policy statements, authored by Thomas Jefferson and James Madison in 1798, that affirmed states' rights against central government power

Document Text

"To the People of the United States"

1832

We, then, hold it as unquestionable, that, on the separation from the Crown of Great Britain, the people of the several colonies became free and independent States, possessed of the full right of self-government; and that no power can be rightfully exercised over them, but by the consent and authority of their respective States, expressed or implied. We also hold it as totally unquestionable, that the Constitution of the United States is a compact between the people of the several States, constituting free, independent, and sovereign communities; that the Government it created was formed and appointed to execute, according to the provisions of the instrument, the powers therein granted, as the joint agent of the several States; that all its acts, transcending these powers, are simply and of themselves, null and void, and that in case of such infractions, it is the right of the States, in their sovereign capacity, each acting for itself and its citizens, in like manner as they adopted the Constitution, to judge thereof in the last resort, and to adopt such measures not inconsistent with the compact as may be deemed fit, to arrest the execution of the act within their respective limits. Such we hold to be the right of the States, in reference to an unconstitutional act of the Government; nor do we deem their duty to exercise it on proper occasions, less certain and imperative, than the right itself is clear.

We hold it to be a very imperfect conception of the obligation, which each State contracted in ratifying the Constitution, and thereby becoming a member of the Union, to suppose that it would be fully and faithfully discharged, simply by abstaining, on its part, from exercising the powers delegated to the Government of the Union, or by sustaining it in the due execution of those powers. These are, undoubtedly, important federal duties, but there is another not less important, to resist the Government, should it, under color of exercising the delegated, encroach on the reserved powers. The duty of the States is no less clear in the one case than in the other; and the obligation as binding in the one as in the other; and in like manner the solemn obligation of an oath, imposed by the States through the Constitution, on all public functionaries, federal and State, to support that instrument, comprehends the one as well as the other duty; as well that of maintaining the Government in the due exercise of its powers, as that of resisting it when it transcends them.

But the obligation of a State to resist the encroachments of the Government on the reserved powers, is not limited simply to the discharge of its federal duties. We hold that it embraces another, if possible, more sacred; that of protecting its citizens, derived from their original sovereign character, viewed in their separate relations. There are none of the duties of a State of higher obligation. It is, indeed, the primitive duty, preceding all others, and in its nature paramount to them all; and so essential to the existence of a State, that she cannot neglect or abandon it, without forfeiting all just claims to the allegiance of her citizens, and with it, her sovereignty itself. In entering into the Union, the States by no means exempted themselves from the obligation of this, the first and most sacred of their duties; nor, indeed, can they without sinking into subordinate and dependent corporations. It is true, that in ratifying the Constitution, they placed a large and important portion of the rights of their citizens, under the joint protection of all the States, with a view to their more effectual security; but it is not less so, that they reserved, at the same time, a portion still larger, and not less important, under their own immediate guardianship; and in relation to which, the original obligation, to protect the rights of their citizens, from whatever quarter assailed, remained unchanged and unimpaired. Nor is it less true, that the General Government, created in order to preserve the rights placed under the joint protection of the States, and which, when restricted to its proper sphere, is calculated to afford them the most perfect security, may become, when not so restricted, the most dangerous enemy to the rights of their citizens, including those reserved under the immediate guardianship of the States respectively, as well as those under their joint protection; and thus, the original and inherent obligation of the States to protect their citizens, is united with that which they have contracted to support the Constitution; thereby rendering it the most sacred of all their duties to watch over and resist the encroachments of the Government; and on the faithful performance of which, we solemnly believe the duration of the Constitution and the liberty and happiness of the country depend.

Document Text

But, while we hold the rights and duties of the States to be such as we have stated, we are deeply impressed with the conviction, that it is due to the relation existing between them, as members of a common Union, and the respect which they ought ever to entertain towards the Government ordained to carry into effect the important objects for which the Constitution was formed, that the occasion to justify a State in interposing its authority, ought to be one of necessity; where all other peaceful remedies have been unsuccessfully tried; and where the only alternative is, interposition on one side, or oppression of its citizens, and imminent danger to the Constitution and liberty of the country on the other; and such we hold to be the present.

That the prohibitory, or protective system, which, as has been stated, is embraced in the acts which we have declared to be unconstitutional, and therefore null and void, is, in fact, unconstitutional, unequal, and oppressive in its operation on this, and the other staple and exporting States, and dangerous to the Constitution and liberty of the country, and that (all other peaceful remedies having been tried without success) an occasion has occurred, where it becomes the right and duty of the State to interpose its authority to arrest the evil within its limits, we hold to be certain; and it is under this deep and solemn conviction, that we have acted.

Glossary

delegated:	authorized
from whatever quarter assailed:	from whatever direction they are attacked
reserved powers:	constitutional rights of the states, which include all those powers not specifically delegated to the federal government
sovereign:	self-governing
under color of:	while pretending or claiming to be

"On the Reception of Abolition Petitions"

1837

The peculiar institution of the South that, on the maintenance of which the very existence of the slave-holding States depends, is pronounced to be sinful and odious, in the sight of God and man; and this with a systematic design of rendering us hateful in the eyes of the world with a view to a general crusade against us and our institutions. This, too, in the legislative halls of the Union; created by these confederated States, for the better protection of their peace, their safety, and their respective institutions; and yet, we, the representatives of twelve of these sovereign States against whom this deadly war is waged, are expected to sit here in silence, hearing ourselves and our constituents day after day denounced, without uttering a word; for if we but open our lips, the charge of agitation is resounded on all sides, and we are held up as seeking to aggravate the evil which we resist. Every reflecting mind must see in all this a state of things deeply and dangerously diseased.

I do not belong … to the school which holds that aggression is to be met by concession. Mine is the opposite creed, which teaches that encroachments must be met at the beginning, and that those who act on the opposite principle are prepared to become slaves. In this case, in particular, I hold concession or compromise to be fatal. If we concede an inch, concession would follow concession, compromise would follow compromise, until our ranks would be so broken that effectual resistance would be impossible. We must meet the enemy on the frontier, with a fixed determination of maintaining our position at every hazard.… We are now told that the most effectual mode of arresting the progress of abolition is, to reason it down; and with this view it is urged that the petitions ought to be referred to a committee. That is the very ground which was taken at the last session in the other House, but instead of arresting its progress it has since advanced more rapidly than ever. The most unquestionable right may be rendered doubtful, if once admitted to be a subject of controversy, and that would be the case in the present instance. The subject is beyond the jurisdiction of Congress; they have no right to touch it in any shape or form, or to make it the subject of deliberation or discussion.…

As widely as this incendiary spirit has spread, it has not yet infected this body, or the great mass of the intelligent and business portion of the North; but unless it be speedily stopped, it will spread and work upwards till it brings the two great sections of the Union into deadly conflict.…

They who imagine that the spirit now abroad in the North, will die away of itself without a shock or convulsion, have formed a very inadequate conception of its real character; it will continue to rise, and spread, unless prompt and efficient measures to stay its progress be adopted. Already it has taken possession of the pulpit, of the schools, and, to a considerable extent, of the press; those great instruments by which the mind of the rising generation will be formed.

However sound the great body of the non-slave-holding States are at present, in the course of a few years they will be succeeded by those who will have been taught to hate the people and institutions of nearly one-half of this Union, with a hatred more deadly than one hostile nation ever entertained towards another. It is easy to see the end. By the necessary course of events, if left to themselves, we must become, finally, two people. It is impossible under the deadly hatred which must spring up between the two great sections, if the present causes are permitted to operate unchecked, that we should continue under the same political system. The conflicting elements would burst the Union asunder, powerful as are the links which hold it together. Abolition and the Union cannot co-exist. As the friend of the Union I openly proclaim it, and the sooner it is known the better. The former may now be controlled, but in a short time it will be beyond the power of man to arrest the course of events. We of the South will not, cannot surrender our institutions. To maintain the existing relations between the two races, inhabiting that section of the Union, is indispensable to the peace and happiness of both. It can not be subverted without drenching the country in blood, and extirpating one or the other of the races. Be it good or bad, it has grown up with our society and institutions, and is so interwoven with them, that to destroy it would be to destroy us as a people. But let me not be understood as admitting, even by implication, that the existing relations between the two races in the slaveholding States is an evil: far otherwise; I hold it to be a good, as it has thus far proved itself to be to both, and will

Document Text

continue to prove so if not disturbed by the fell spirit of abolition. I appeal to facts. Never before has the black race of Central Africa, from the dawn of history to the present day, attained a condition so civilized and so improved, not only physically, but morally and intellectually. It came among us in a low, degraded, and savage condition, and in the course of a few generations it has grown up under the fostering care of our institutions, reviled as they have been, to its present comparatively civilized condition. This, with the rapid increase of numbers, is conclusive proof of the general happiness of the race, in spite of all the exaggerated tales to the contrary....

I hold that in the present state of civilization, where two races of different origin, and distinguished by color, and other physical differences, as well as intellectual, are brought together, the relation now existing in the slaveholding States between the two, is, instead of an evil, a good—a positive good. I feel myself called upon to speak freely upon the subject where the honor and interests of those I represent are involved. I hold then, that there never has yet existed a wealthy and civilized society in which one portion of the community did not, in point of fact, live on the labor of the other.

Glossary

abroad:	widespread
at every hazard:	at all costs
peculiar institution:	a term often used for the practice of slavery; "peculiar" meaning unusual, distinct, or individual
reason it down:	talk it over

"On His Resolutions in Reference to the War with Mexico"

1848

I, then, opposed the war, not only because it might have been easily avoided; not only because the President [James K. Polk] had no authority to order a part of the disputed territory in possession of the Mexicans to be occupied by our troops; not only because I believed the allegations upon which Congress sanctioned the war untrue; but from high considerations of policy because I believed it would lead to many and serious evils to the country, and greatly endanger its free institutions. But, after the war was declared, by authority of the Government, I acquiesced in what I could not prevent, and which it was impossible for me to arrest; and I then felt it to be my duty to limit my efforts to give such direction to the war as would, as far as possible, prevent the evils and danger with which it threatened the country and its institutions. For this purpose, at the last session, I suggested to the Senate the policy of adopting a defensive line; and for the same purpose I now offer these resolutions....

What is the object of a vigorous prosecution of the war? How can it be successful? I can see but one way of making it so, and that is, by suppressing all resistance on the part of Mexico, overpowering and dispersing her army, and utterly overthrowing her Government. But if this should be done; if a vigorous prosecution of the war should lead to this result, how are we to obtain an honorable peace? With whom shall we treat for indemnity for the past and security for the future? War may be made by one party, but it requires two to make peace. If all authority is overthrown in Mexico, where will be the power to enter into negotiation and make peace? Our very success would defeat the possibility of making peace. In that case the war would not end in peace, but in conquest; not in negotiation, but in subjugation; and defeat, I repeat, the very object you aim to accomplish,—and accomplish that which you disavow to be your intention, by destroying the separate existence of Mexico, overthrowing her nationality, and blotting out her name from the list of nations,—instead of leaving her a free. Republic, which the President has so earnestly expressed his desire to do.

If I understand his message correctly, I have his own authority for the conclusion to which I come. He takes very much the same view that I do, as to how a war ought to be prosecuted vigorously, and what would be its results, with the difference as to the latter resting on a single contingency, and that a remote one. He says that the great difficulty of obtaining peace results from this, that the people of Mexico are divided under factious chieftains, and that the chief in power dare not make peace, because for doing so he would be displaced by a rival. He also says, that the only way to remedy this evil and to obtain a treaty, is to put down the whole of them, including the one in power, as well as the others. Well, what then? Are we to stop there? No. Our generals are, it seems, authorized to encourage and to protect the well disposed inhabitants in establishing a republican government. He says they are numerous, and are prevented from expressing their opinions and making an attempt to form such a government, only by fear of those military chieftains. He proposes, when they have thus formed a government, under the encouragement and protection of our army, to obtain peace by a treaty with the government thus formed, which shall give us ample indemnity for the past and security for the future. I must say I am at a loss to see how a free and independent republic can be established in Mexico under the protection and authority of its conquerors. I can readily understand how an aristocracy or a despotic government might be, but how a free republican government can be so established, under such circumstances, is to me incomprehensible. I had always supposed that such a government must be the spontaneous wish of the people; that it must emanate from the hearts of the people, and be supported by their devotion to it, without support from abroad. But it seems that these are antiquated notions, obsolete ideas, and that free popular governments may be made under the authority and protection of a conqueror.

But suppose the difficulties surmounted, how can we make a free government in Mexico? Where are the materials? It is to be, I presume, a confederated government like their former. Where is the intelligence in Mexico for the construction and preservation of such a government? It is what she has been aiming at for more than twenty years, but so utterly incompetent are her people for the task, that it has been a complete failure from first to last. The great

Document Text

body of the intelligence and wealth of Mexico is concentrated in the priesthood, who are naturally disinclined to that form of government; the residue, for the most part, are the owners of the haciendas, the larger planters of the country, but they are without concert and destitute of the means of forming such a government. But if it were possible to establish such a government, it could not stand without the protection of our army. It would fall as soon as it is withdrawn.

If it be determined to have a treaty, it would be a far preferable course, it appears to me, to abstain from attacking or destroying the government now existing in Mexico, and to treat with it, if indeed it be capable of forming a treaty which it could maintain and execute.

Glossary

factious chieftains:	warring minor leaders
haciendas:	large estates in which peasants labor for a rich master
indemnity:	protection from prosecution or punishment
suppose the difficulties surmounted:	even if those problems were overcome

George Peter Alexander Healy's 1851 painting of Calhoun on exhibit at City Hall in Charleston, South Carolina

"On the Slavery Question"

I have, Senators, believed from the first that the agitation of the subject of slavery would, if not prevented by some timely and effective measure, end in disunion. Entertaining this opinion, I have, on all proper occasions, endeavored to call the attention of both the two great parties [Democrats and Whigs] which divide the country to adopt some measure to prevent so great a disaster, but without success. The agitation has been permitted to proceed, with almost no attempt to resist it, until it has reached a point when it can no longer be disguised or denied that the Union is in danger. You have thus had forced upon you the greatest and the gravest question that can ever come under your consideration—How can the Union be preserved?

To give a satisfactory answer to this mighty question, it is indispensable to have an accurate and thorough knowledge of the nature and the character of the cause by which the Union is endangered.... What is it that has endangered the Union?

To this question there can be but one answer, that the immediate cause is the almost universal discontent which pervades all the States composing the Southern section of the Union. This widely-extended discontent is not of recent origin. It commenced with the agitation of the slavery question, and has been increasing ever since. The next question, going one step further back, is—What has caused this widely diffused and almost universal discontent?...

What is the cause of this discontent? It will be found in the belief of the people of the Southern States, as prevalent as the discontent itself, that they cannot remain, as things now are, consistently with honor and safety, in the Union. The next question to be considered is—What has caused this belief?

One of the causes is, undoubtedly, to be traced to the long-continued agitation of the slave question on the part of the North, and the many aggressions which they have made on the rights of the South during the time....

But we are just at the close of the sixth decade, and the commencement of the seventh. The census is to be taken this year, which must add greatly to the decided preponderance of the North in the House of Representatives and in the electoral college. The prospect is, also, that a great increase will be added to its present preponderance in the Senate, during the period of the decade, by the addition of new States.... The prospect then is, that the two sections in the Senate, should the efforts now made to exclude the South from the newly acquired territories succeed, will stand, before the end of the decade, twenty Northern States to fourteen Southern (considering Delaware as neutral), and forty Northern Senators to twenty-eight Southern. This great increase of Senators, added to the great increase of members of the House of Representatives and the electoral college on the part of the North, which must take place under the next decade, will effectually and irretrievably destroy the equilibrium which existed when the Government commenced....

The next [reason] consists in adopting a system of revenue and disbursements, by which an undue proportion of the burden of taxation has been imposed upon the South, and an undue proportion of its proceeds appropriated to the North; and the last is a system of political measures, by which the original character of the Government has been radically changed....

It is well known that the Government has derived its revenue mainly from duties on imports. I shall not undertake to show that such duties must necessarily fall mainly on the exporting States, and that the South, as the great exporting portion of the Union, has in reality paid vastly more than her due proportion of the revenue; because I deem it unnecessary, as the subject has on so many occasions been fully discussed. Nor shall I, for the same reason, undertake to show that a far greater portion of the revenue has been disbursed at the North, than its due share; and that the joint effect of these causes has been, to transfer a vast amount from South to North, which, under an equal system of revenue and disbursements, would not have been lost to her....

The result of the whole of these causes combined is that the North has acquired a decided ascendency over every department of this Government, and through it a control over all the powers of the system. A single section governed by the will of the numerical majority, has now, in fact, the control of the Government and the entire powers of the system. What was once a constitutional federal republic, is now converted, in reality, into one as absolute as that of the

Document Text

Autocrat of Russia, and as despotic in its tendency as any absolute government that ever existed.

As, then, the North has the absolute control over the Government, it is manifest, that on all questions between it and the South, where there is a diversity of interests, the interest of the latter will be sacrificed to the former, however oppressive the effects may be....

I refer to the relation between the two races in the Southern section, which constitutes a vital portion of her social organization. Every portion of the North entertains views and feelings more or less hostile to it....On the contrary, the Southern section regards the relation as one which cannot be destroyed without subjecting the two races to the greatest calamity, and the section to poverty, desolation, and wretchedness; and accordingly they feel bound, by every consideration of interest and safety, to defend it....

It is a great mistake to suppose that disunion can be effected by a single blow. The cords which bound these States together in one common Union, are far too numerous and powerful for that. Disunion must be the work of time. It is only through a long process, and successively, that the cords can be snapped, until the whole fabric falls, asunder. Already the agitation of the slavery question has snapped some of the most important, and has greatly weakened all the others....

The cry of "Union, Union—the glorious Union!" can no more prevent disunion than the cry of "Health, health glorious health!" on the part of the physician, can save a patient lying dangerously ill. So long as the Union, instead of being regarded as a protector, is regarded in the opposite character, by not much less than a majority of the States, it will be in vain to attempt to conciliate them by pronouncing eulogies on it.

Besides this cry of Union comes commonly from those whom we cannot believe to be sincere. It usually comes from our assailants. But we cannot believe them to be sincere; for, if they loved the Union, they would necessarily be devoted to the constitution. It made the Union, and to destroy the constitution would be to destroy the Union.

Glossary

Autocrat of Russia:	the Russian czar, whom Calhoun cites as an example of a dictator
close of the sixth decade:	at the time of this address, sixty years since the first U.S. census, in 1790
conciliate:	appease
duties:	taxes
revenue and disbursements:	income and expenses

Andrew Carnegie, American businessman and philanthropist.

Andrew Carnegie: Original Analysis

1835-1919

Investor, Iron and Steel Magnate, Philanthropist, Pacifist

Overview

Andrew Carnegie was born November 25, 1835 in Dunfermline, Scotland; he and his family sailed to the US in 1848. Carnegie would remain connected to Scotland all his life, valuing the culture, landscape and folklore. The family moved to the area outside Pittsburgh, where Carnegie became a messenger boy for the O'Reilly Telegraph Company in 1850. After he taught himself Morse code, he graduated to becoming a telegraph operator. Finally he caught the eye of Thomas Scott, a superintendent for the Pennsylvania Railroad's Pittsburgh Division. Carnegie became his private secretary and telegraph operator, while Scott became Carnegie's mentor. Scott taught him to invest his $35 a week salary in stocks; when the stocks paid off in a dividend, Carnegie was hooked. It was the first money he had ever made without working for it – rather, his intelligence and Scott's advice had earned him a profit. From then on, Carnegie's future plotted itself out in finance, ownership and investment, as opposed to physical labor.

Scott moved up in the Pennsylvania Railroad corporate hierarchy, and in 1859 the board of trustees appointed Carnegie his successor as superintendent of the Pittsburgh Division. Carnegie invested his salary shrewdly, and by the end of the Civil War he was able to quit the railroad to concentrate on building his investments in the oil industry, bonds, ironworks and bridge building. In 1868, however, right as he became a well-known figure in the industrial world, Carnegie wrote himself a remarkable memorandum, one that he would save for the rest of his life.

Thirty-three and an income of 50,000$ per annum. By this time two years I can so arrange all my business as to make no effort to increase fortune, but spend the surplus each year for benevolent purposes. Cast aside business forever except for others.

In the memo, Carnegie plotted out the purposes of his fortune for the rest of his life. As he saw it, the goal of having all this money was to get an education, cultivate intellectual friendships, take care of the poor and generally "choose that life which will be the most elevating in its character." He considered his own pursuit of money "the worst sort of idolatry" and intended to give it up soon because it "must degrade me beyond hope of permanent recovery." His intention was to quit working in 1870 at age 35; like many things he wrote in the memo, he would not do that. Yet he would save it for a reason, and its sentiments, if not its actual dictates, would determine his goals from that time onward.

His major going concern at the time was the Keystone Bridge Company, which he had founded in 1865. In an effort to control the industry which produced the iron beams his company used to make bridges, Carnegie bought up a pair of rival iron mills outside Pittsburgh to form the Union Mills. Traveling to England in 1872, he saw the new Bessemer steel-making process and decided that steel would soon replace iron as the construction material of the future. Thus began the Carnegie Steel Company, the company that made him famous. Carnegie Steel pioneered the use of molds and chemical alloys to shape steel to fit its consumers' needs. While other businesses shrank when not able to sell product, Carnegie prepared for when the economy improved, and it paid off; his competitive tactics built Carnegie Steel into one of the world's most powerful businesses. His policy was what he called "verticality": to control the process of making steel, he wanted to control the iron ore mines, the plants that produced steel, the railroads that used steel rails, the companies that made railroad engines, the products that rolled on the rails, and anything else that either contributed to the making of steel or its utility as a product.

One such product was coke, de-carbonated coal which was used in the Bessemer process to reduce any impurities that made the steel brittle. The US' prime producer of coke was the Frick Coke Company, owned by Henry Clay Frick. The two men met in New York City in 1881, and Carnegie soon offered Frick a share in Carnegie Steel in return for half control over Frick's company. Carnegie and Frick became partners in 1884, building profits as a team by protecting each other's investments. Carnegie made Frick the chairman of his company in 1889, and Carnegie Steel was able to buy up a number of its Pittsburgh-centered rivals. At that point Carnegie Steel was earning $4.5 million in annual profits.

In 1892, the Carnegie Steel plant at Homestead, outside Pittsburgh, was in the midst of labor strife. The Amalgamated Association of Iron and Steel Workers union's contract was about to expire and the workers agitated for material improvements in conditions and salary. Carnegie, on his way to Scotland for his annual vacation, told Frick, his CEO, to "take care of" the union, meaning Carnegie wanted the strife ended on his terms. Frick took this to mean he had a free hand in handling the union, and regular telegrams from Carnegie encouraging Frick's actions in stonewalling the union convinced Frick he was doing

the right thing. Frick shut the plant down when the contract terminated on June 30 1892, locking out the workers and erecting fortifications around the works. The workers armed themselves and surrounded the fortifications, intending to keep any strikebreakers out. Frick then hired armed guards from the Pinkerton Agency to force the workers to leave. On July 6, the guards and workers fired on each other in a bloody battle for control of the plant; nine men were killed in the worst violence in American labor history to that time.

This was not what Carnegie had in mind. He blamed Frick for misunderstanding his orders; however, throughout the conflict he had telegraphed his support to Frick repeatedly. It was Carnegie that the public blamed for the violence, and despite his determination to be seen as a responsible employer, Carnegie would never live down the battle at Homestead. When Frick attempted to take control of Carnegie Steel in 1899 and 1900, Carnegie's anger and disgust led him to reconsider his career. He ousted Frick and sold his interest in Carnegie Steel to JP Morgan for $480 million. By March 1901, Morgan had formed the United States Steel Corporation out of Carnegie's holdings, and Carnegie, now retired at age 65, was the richest man in the world.

Retirement meant that Carnegie could finally devote his fortune to fulfilling the purposes of his 1868 memo. He was religious by upbringing and philosophical by nature, and despite having only four years of schooling in his life, he was a self-taught intellectual and was respected by many prominent intellectual friends as such. He wrote "The man who dies… rich, dies disgraced", and he had already been involved in many philanthropic projects, mostly the endowment of libraries, the building of public baths and the donation of pipe organs to churches. Now he intended to give away his entire fortune. He built public libraries all over the United States, Canada and Britain. He established pension funds for his workers, built universities and funded professors and their research, and especially provided museums and galleries for the cultural betterment of the people of Pittsburgh, his original American home. Once he came to realize that his investments were making him profits faster than he could give away his fortune, he established the Carnegie Corporation as a philanthropic institution to give it all away once he died.

As war scares began to rise in Europe in the early twentieth century, Carnegie increasingly devoted his intellect, money and energies to the project of peace. He wrote numerous books and articles and endowed the Carnegie Endowment for International Peace to promote the resolution of conflict between states. When the international community agreed to establish a World Court in the interest of pursuing human rights and international justice, Carnegie built the court a home at The Hague in the Netherlands. He called for summit meetings of the major powers of the day, particularly the US, Britain and Germany, to talk out diplomatic differences as opposed to resorting to war. It all went for naught when Europe embarked on the Great

Time Line

1835	November 25	■ Andrew Carnegie born in Scotland
1848		■ Carnegie moves to the United States and settles outside Pittsburgh
1850		■ Begins work for the O'Reilly Telegraph Company
1852		■ Becomes secretary for Thomas Scott of the Pennsylvania Railroad
1859		■ Carnegie appointed superintendent for the Pennsylvania Railroad
1861-1865		■ American Civil War; Carnegie's investments make him rich
1868		■ Writes memorandum to self on giving away wealth
1872		■ Carnegie travels to Britain to see workings of Bessemer steel-making process; foundation of the Carnegie Steel Company
1884-1899		■ Carnegie establishes business partnership with Henry Clay Frick
1889		■ Frick becomes chairman of Carnegie Steel
1892	April	■ Carnegie leaves for Scotland
	July	■ Homestead strike
	July 6	■ "Battle of Homestead"
1899-1900		■ Frick attempts takeover of Carnegie Steel
1901	January	■ Carnegie sells Carnegie Steel to JP Morgan
	March	■ Morgan forms US Steel; Carnegie becomes world's richest man

Time Line		
1901-1919		■ Peak period of Carnegie's philanthropy
1908		■ Foundation of Carnegie Corporation to give away fortune
1914-1918		■ Great War (First World War)
1919	August 11	■ Andrew Carnegie dies

War in 1914. According to Carnegie's wife, the war broke Carnegie's heart, especially in that it made crossing the Atlantic too dangerous, keeping him away from his beloved Scotland. He died in August 1919, soon after the Peace of Paris had concluded.

Explanation and Analysis of Documents

Despite his lack of formal education, Carnegie was a learned man, reading voraciously and using his wealth as an opening to intellectual and political society. He counted many of the leading British political and religious figures of the late nineteenth century as his friends, including prime minister William Gladstone, philosopher and educator Matthew Arnold, journalist W.T. Stead and novelist Rudyard Kipling. He himself produced eight books and numerous journal articles over the course of his life on varied subjects, all of which he covered with intelligence and erudition. *Triumphant Democracy* (1886), in which Carnegie compared the functions of American democracy favorably to the parliamentary system and national strife in British politics, sold 70,000 copies. Carnegie was not just wealthy – he was influential.

The philosopher Carnegie most admired was Herbert Spencer, a man who considered Carnegie one of his best American friends. Spencer was the original "social Darwinist", a thinker who adapted Charles Darwin's theory of evolution to the development of human society – Spencer coined the term "survival of the fittest". He believed that in a properly operating capitalist society, certain people were better designed to rise to the top of that society and accumulate wealth. Upon meeting each other, Spencer informed Carnegie that Carnegie was the best example of Spencer's ideas that existed; to a man like Carnegie, who was troubled by the accumulation of wealth, such words were, as he put it, "my true source of comfort".

Carnegie did not simply let this idea lie softly on his conscience, however; he intended to use it. In 1889, he published two articles entitled "Wealth" that were collected with several other related essays and published as *The Gospel of Wealth* (1901).

♦ "Wealth" (June 1889)

Carnegie states his thesis immediately: "The problem of our age is the proper administration of wealth, so that the ties of brotherhood may still bind together the rich and poor in harmonious relationship." His example of how far western civilization has advanced since that time is a comparison with the Sioux peoples, then housed on a miserable reservation near Wounded Knee, South Dakota. Certainly, in their poverty they were all equals, from the chiefs to the lowest of members of the tribe. But a year later, in 1890, many of the Sioux would be massacred by US soldiers in fear of the Ghost Dance movement, a provocative but peaceful religious sect that awaited the disappearance of all white men from North America. This might not have been the best comparison Carnegie could make between societies that distribute wealth well and those that do not.

Nevertheless, Carnegie's point is that wealth and wealthy people are constructive for the whole of society, so long as the benefits of their wealth are made available to all. He calls on the memory of "Maecenas", Gaius Cilnius Maecenas, a Roman aristocrat and soldier who patronized poets and artists like Horace and Virgil and made them well-known to Roman society. Carnegie sees this as the purpose of wealth: to uplift the society in which it was accumulated.

Often, Carnegie simply updates the arguments in Adam Smith's *Wealth of Nations* (1776), the foundational text of capitalism. Smith argues that those who succeed at business employ others to make more products and expand their profits, and improve their products to be competitive, thus benefiting society as a whole. Carnegie notes, "it insures the survival of the fittest in every department. ...It is a law, as certain as any of the others named, that men possessed of this peculiar talent for affairs, under the free play of economic forces, must, of necessity, soon be in receipt of more revenue than can be judiciously expended upon themselves; and this law is as beneficial for the race as the others." As a result, he is able to dismiss the idea that socialism, anarchy or communism is a better way to organize society. To do otherwise – to organize a society that looks like the 18th century philosopher Emanuel Swedenborg's conception of heaven as a place where all angels work for each other – is to overthrow society and human nature itself.

Carnegie refers often to the perceived inadequacies of socialism and communism to solve the problems of poverty. In 1889, when he wrote "Wealth", socialism was becoming popular in the United States and Britain, though not of the Marxist variety. In the US, farmers had organized into a series of political units that would later become the Populist Party; amongst other issues, they advocated for public ownership of railroads and an income tax, both perceived as ways of redistributing wealth to the poor. In Britain, the Fabian Socialists called for workers' ownership of the means of production, and state-sponsored efforts to redistribute wealth from rich to poor. Such movements alarmed Carnegie because he believed they were misguided efforts to improve society that would instead result in its impoverishment, as he repeats all through the essay. To Carnegie,

Spencer's teachings argued that a society organized properly along the lines of social Darwinism would be naturally capitalist.

Thus, Carnegie asks: "What is the proper mode of administering wealth after the laws upon which civilization is founded have thrown it into the hands of the few?" To Carnegie, there are three ways – to give it all to family descendants, to give it away after one dies, or to give it away before one dies. The first method is that of aristocrats and monarchs, who simply hoarded their wealth in land and ended up left behind in the growth of capitalism. Waiting until death to distribute wealth means that a rich man is essentially sitting on resources that could better his community, and gives Carnegie the impression that "Men who leave vast sums in this way may fairly be thought men who would not have left it at all, had they been able to take it with them" – a rather damning indictment of such men's motivations. Carnegie even approved of estate taxes as a method of forcing contributions of wealth on the rich.

In Carnegie's opinion, the only proper way to administer wealth was in one's own lifetime. The purpose of wealth was to use it in a fashion that would allow others to discover their own design, to allow people to achieve the best that they could with their own lives. Those among society's self-starters should get the opportunity to use the tools that a rich man's wealth could provide them in health, education, taste and moral uplift. As such, they would work and earn their way into comfort and perhaps wealth themselves, and society's riches would be better distributed. He provides two examples – of the donation of the American industrialist Peter Cooper to create the Cooper Union for the Advancement of Science and Art in New York City, and of former New York governor Samuel Tilden's bequeath of $5 million to the city of New York to found a public library.

Carnegie starts his conclusion by asserting that wealthy people need not be Christ-like to be good; the example he uses is of Leo Tolstoy, the most famous Russian novelist of the day. Like Carnegie, Tolstoy took a personal vow to give away all of the wealth he had received from the profits of his novels and his aristocratic lifestyle; unlike Carnegie, he believed that the proper way to do this was to live a life of poverty like Jesus had. Carnegie's entire point is that the wealthy need to do what they do best – get rich – in order to better their fellow man: one needs to work for the riches in order to give them away. Rather the man of wealth should live a modest lifestyle, take care of his family's needs and comforts, and give away the rest of his profits to intelligent public uses, to the approval and betterment of the community in which he lives.

The key element in giving away wealth is to do it intelligently. As examples here, Carnegie holds up Peter Cooper of the Cooper Union (again), Enoch Pratt, who gave funds to build a free library in Baltimore, Charles Pratt (no relation) who established the Pratt Institute in Brooklyn – a similar educational body to the Cooper Union – and Leland Stanford, founder of Stanford University. In another article published in the *North American Review*, Carnegie gave readers a list of "the best fields of philanthropy", of which there were seven. At the top were universities and scientific research, libraries (Carnegie's favorite, due to his background), hospitals and medical schools, parks, concert halls, public baths and lastly, churches.

To Carnegie, these men and others like them are the hope of humanity in the western world. They know what to do with their wealth, and when to do it; and should more follow their example, the world will be a better place. Should they not, Carnegie indicts them with his famous statement, "The man who dies thus rich dies disgraced." Such is, as he terms it in the end, "the true Gospel concerning Wealth".

♦ "Americanism versus Imperialism" (January 1899)

From the time he wrote his memo to himself, in 1868, Carnegie was privately interested in the cause of international peace, though he did not dedicate resources to the cause of peace until he retired. When he did, however, peace became an obsession for Carnegie as the European states lurched toward war in the early twentieth century. He built the Pan American Union building in Washington DC, the World Court in The Hague, established the Carnegie Endowment for International Peace, and courted world leaders – the last chapter of his autobiography is about Kaiser Wilhelm II of Germany, a man he hoped would aid the cause. The beginning of the Great War in 1914 dashed those hopes.

The event that seemed to galvanize his interest in peace was the Spanish-American War of 1898-1899. Cuba had been a Spanish colony since the time of Columbus, but in the latter half of the nineteenth century, the Cubans agitated for independence and gained the sympathy of many Americans. Another three-century old Spanish colony, the Philippines, held far less interest for the American public, but its potential as an American naval base near the vast market of China attracted the attention of some American politicians and military leaders. In 1896, Filipino revolutionaries took up arms against the Spanish, but by December 1897 they had run out of arms and money and their leaders had been exiled to Hong Kong.

In January 1898, Cubans finally rebelled against their Spanish overlords; the US battleship *Maine* was sent to Havana to protect any Americans caught in the fighting. In February, the *Maine* exploded and sank in Havana's harbor, likely from an overheated boiler. Yet the loss of the *Maine* was a perfect fabricated excuse for imperial-minded Americans to call for war with Spain, to free Cuba and the Philippines. In April 1898, the US declared war, despite President McKinley's wariness over the entire affair. US forces quickly defeated the Spanish forces in Cuba and a US naval squadron stationed in Hong Kong hurried off to the Philippines with the Filipino revolutionary leadership in tow. By August 1898 the war was effectively over and Cuba and the Philippines were on their way to independence.

Or so it was believed. In reality there was some debate about whether to annex Cuba as a state, and Manila's

usefulness as a naval base was raised once again in the White House and Congress. This debate apparently awakened Carnegie's interest, and he wrote an article for the *North American Review* in January 1899 about his opinion of the possibility of the US' acquisition of the Philippines as a colony. As usual in his writings, he left little for the reader to ponder about that opinion: the first sentence reads,

"For several grave reasons I regard possessions in the Far East as fraught with nothing but disaster to the Republic."

The reason Carnegie opposed US colonialism in east Asia was his fear of war in the region. The Chinese and Japanese governments had just fought a war in 1894 and 1895. When the Japanese expected to be ceded territory in Manchuria after the war, the western powers, led by Russia, forced them to leave, and then occupied Chinese cities themselves as safe ports of economic entry. The British Empire maintained control of Hong Kong and held a concession in Shanghai; American and German merchants lived under their own laws in other Chinese cities. Carnegie outlined the military forces present or headed to east Asia at that moment as proof of the potential for war – a war in which the US would not have the military leverage, according to his numbers, to buy the neutrality of its rivals, the way the others could count on the neutrality of Britain.

Here Carnegie seems to reveal his roots in business. Indeed, another industry, business or corporation might not have the means monetarily on hand to prevent, say, a buyout or the loss of assets. Having money and other resources immediately available to outflank rivals was the essence of good business, especially Carnegie's. But when he listed the troops and ships each state brought to the field of conflict, he saw those available numbers as something of an equivalent to money: if a power could not match a rival ship to ship, man to man, it stood no chance of competition.

As an argument against war and imperialism, Carnegie's heart was in the right place, but his planning was not. At that very moment, in 1899, the British Conservative government of Lord Salisbury was negotiating its way out of the building of an isthmian canal in Central America, and the German navy was carefully picking its way through the Caribbean, both out of fear of the power of the US – not in military numbers but in industrial capacity. As Carnegie himself would live to see in the Great War, the US had a limitless ability to field soldiers and supplies – not immediately, but for a sustained period in the future. He was correct to see the Spanish-American War as a sideshow to European conflicts, but the idea that the US could not hope to match the military power of the British or German Empires was somewhat myopic.

Carnegie's belief was that the United States could not build an empire without the friendship of the British government – an idea that Carnegie did not consider wise. Interestingly, his based his reticence on the opinion of a friend of his, Bishop Henry C. Potter, a well-known Anglican bishop in New York City, who said the US would become the "catspaw of Britain" – a mere tool of their imperial policy – if the US started its own colonial empire. Both Carnegie and Potter were members of the St. Andrew's Society, a club for Scotsmen in America; the club was notable for its friendliness to the British Empire, above and beyond its connection to Scotland. Clearly, despite his Anglophilia, Carnegie took pride in adopted country's independence in international affairs and, like Potter, would not give it up regardless of allies. In fact, Carnegie referred to an alliance between the US, Britain and Japan as "humiliating" for its obvious deference to the British Empire's naval power in the colonized world.

Why? For one thing, Carnegie considered military and diplomatic alliances fleeting. In particular he noted the Franco-Russian Alliance of 1894, which he considered to be directed against Britain. Actually, the treaty was signed to protect each state from a land-based German invasion, though French forces had held a tense stand-off with a British army at Fashoda in the Sudan less than a year earlier. He also believed that Italy, as a member of the Triple Alliance with Germany and Austria-Hungary, was allied against France; in reality, the Italians were considered hopelessly unreliable by the other signatories from the moment the treaty was concluded. He believed Britain and Germany were on the verge of war over German meddling in the Cape Colony, South Africa, where the German government provided weapons for the Dutch Afrikaaner residents of the Transvaal to fight against their British enemies. In point of fact, the rapprochement he mentions between the two governments was far more fleeting than their enmity – Britain would eventually join France (1904) and Russia (1907) in the Triple Entente directed against Germany. Each of these alliances was more permanent than Carnegie believed. They would last for another fourteen years, and become the basis for the division between states that defined the Great War.

This points up what would become Carnegie's major weakness as a negotiator for peace. While he had plenty of money and clout to direct at getting diplomats and politicians to listen to his ideas and applaud them, he did not have good judgment for the motivations of international actors – he considered the belligerent Kaiser Wilhelm of Germany one of the two great peacemakers in the world before 1914, along with President Woodrow Wilson – nor did he have a good eye for future diplomatic arrangements. Throughout this article and other writings he produced in the era between 1900 and 1914, he repeatedly guessed wrong as to who or what might best bring peace about.

Meantime, at the moment, in 1899, Carnegie believed the US had the potential to become a major imperial power, but it lacked the ambition and the interest in developing a navy within the next twenty years to match that of Britain. He refers to "The author of 'A Look Ahead,'", a reference to himself. "A Look Ahead" (1893) was an article that called for a closer relationship between the US and Britain as the "Anglo-Saxon races", a common cause at the time. What he begs to define at the moment is his disdain for any kind of formal alliance between the two powers. He did not want to enter into any arrangement by which the US might be

pitted against other friends like Russia or France, or any international situation where any state in the world might fear the US. It was not as if Britain and the US might ever go to war; in a Venezuelan border dispute between 1895 and 1899, the British government of Lord Salisbury submitted to international arbitration as dictated by the US, largely in an effort to get along. To avoid going to war with other powers, the US could find leverage in any international dispute by closing its ports to foreign trade, thus crippling the European economies. The building of any armed force, army or navy, to allow the US to hold colonies "by the sole power of our unlorded will" was too much of a price for Americans to pay.

So what should be done with the spoils of war in the Philippines and Cuba? The McKinley administration claimed to want to bring Cuba to "Free and Independent" government. Carnegie expected that the Cubans would ask for annexation and that the US government would turn them down; instead, in 1901 the Platt Amendment to an Army Appropriations Act set the terms for Cuba's independence on unequal terms of trade with the US, and President McKinley signed it. In Carnegie's opinion, the US had no reason not to offer "Free and Independent" government to the Philippines as well, since their people had fought for it too and would be too difficult to suppress as a result. Again, his hope was dashed – the US instead embarked on an expensive war of suppression that cost 4000 American lives and lasted five years.

The self-proclaimed social Darwinist Carnegie had a surprising faith in the ability of people around the world to govern themselves, a faith not shared by most western intellectuals at the time. He saw people in rural India, the Afridis, as being far from western standards of civilization, yet they had a mode of local government; there was no reason Filipinos might not do the same. If the setting up of government was accompanied by violence, "in which nation are these absent?" To his credit, he saw Americanism – in the respect that it was defined by men's ability to govern themselves – as being incompatible with imperialism, in the end.

♦ *The Autobiography of Andrew Carnegie*, Chapter XVIII: "Problems of Labor"

Being from an impoverished background, Carnegie sympathized with the industrial worker's existence in the nineteenth century – always worried about unemployment, afraid of sickness, unable to retire or take time off. Carnegie was thus inclined to accept the idea of unions in his mills. In 1886, he published essays in *Forum* magazine arguing that unions made it easier to negotiate collectively with his workers, cost nothing and provided leadership for workers that could be consulted and could communicate to the membership in order to improve production. Carnegie had a very good reputation with his workers in the 1870s and 1880s as a result.

In 1889, however, Carnegie's much-admired plant supervisor was scalded in a blast furnace accident, and died in the hospital. Frick became the chairman of Carnegie Steel in 1889, and he was known to be a much less empathetic employer. Some historians suggest that Frick's hire was meant to provide a buffer between Carnegie and the workers, that Carnegie did not find it possible to stand up to his workers' demands and needed someone who was tougher than himself to deal with the growing costs of labor. Regardless, Carnegie's reputation suffered immensely after the 1892 "battle of Homestead"; he became thought of as just another "robber baron". He never lived down the strife at Homestead, but in his autobiography, published in the year after his death, he addressed his relationship with his workers in a chapter.

A good introduction to his attitude toward them can be found in the quote about women by the playwright JM Barrie, author of "Peter Pan", which Carnegie uses to describe workers – "Dootless the Lord made a' things weel, but he left some michty queer kinks in women." While Carnegie valued the average man's work ethic and morality, as a collective, they were difficult to deal with. Chapter XVIII is a catalogue of stories Carnegie tells of his negotiations with his workers, in which he tries to come across as a bemused parent, outsmarting his children's efforts to wheedle concessions out of him. Always in his memory, Carnegie demands gentlemanly standards and behavior. In the first anecdote, he actually shushes his foreman, Captain Bill Jones, when a worker claims not to understand a wage agreement and Jones questions the worker's credibility. Later the same worker orders his "spalpeens" – an Irish term for "rascals" – back to work and becomes a trusted manager of men.

At issue was Carnegie's method of setting wages: on a sliding scale based on the price he could get for steel on the market. That way, if the price of steel went up and Carnegie Steel made a profit, the workers benefited as well as the managers and owners; if the price fell, the workers would understand the need for a wage cut. Under Jones, Carnegie set a safety net for any wage cut at $25 per ton of steel – if Carnegie Steel got less than that price, wages for the workers would still stay the same. However, in 1887 the price of steel dropped so low that Frick and Carnegie reset the safety net at $22 a ton. Here, Carnegie remembers a work stoppage at his Edgar Thomson plant where he entertained a workers' delegation sent to negotiate with him in New York; his combination of generous hosting of the workers in the city and his intractable stance on the resetting of the sliding scale again won the day. He later outsmarted the union by insisting that all of his workers at Edgar Thomson sign the sliding scale agreement, as opposed to just the union leaders, so no one could later claim a misunderstanding that would be the basis for a strike. In a comical overplaying of Carnegie's self-regard as a negotiator, he recalled that one of the leaders turned to another and whispered, "By golly, the jig's up!"

In a further negotiation, Carnegie cut off a "bully" amongst the workers by demanding that the man take off his hat in the presence of gentlemen; in another, Carnegie punned a joke about "taking a man's job", claiming that his sense of humor transformed the negotiations. He noted

further concessions willingly made to workers to make their lives easier by giving salaries every two weeks, setting up a company cooperative store, and providing them with cheap coal to heat their houses. Finally he gets to the matter he really wants to expose – "Had the Homestead men been our own old men, instead of men we had to pick up, it is scarcely possible that the trouble there in 1892 could have arisen." He is trying to claim that the Homestead workers were new to his employ. The plant had been bought nine years earlier, and while many of its workers had been made redundant due to new equipment, plenty were still in place who had worked for Carnegie Steel since the plant had been acquired. In some respects, he undermines his own depiction of the strike when he says that he traveled to the mill later in 1892 and met with "many of the old men who had not been concerned in the riot", who told him "Mr. Carnegie, it wasn't a question of dollars. The boys would have let you kick 'em, but they wouldn't let that other man stroke their hair." New workers likely would not have such an opinion of an unknown owner.

Impact and Legacy

Andrew Carnegie was a critical figure in the history of American business, politics and intellectual culture. Like other successful businessmen of the late nineteenth century, he pursued profit with ruthless efficiency, on occasion at the expense of the welfare of his employees. Unlike those other businessmen, he was not a mere "robber baron" – he pursued profit with a purpose. He had an ideological, even spiritual goal in mind for his wealth, well-defined reasons why he in particular should accumulate that wealth, and he put in place a strategy to give it away in the best interests of his society as he saw it.

Key Sources

Many of Carnegie's papers are collected in the Library of Congress; as yet they are not digitized, and many of his letters are located in British archives. However, all of his books and articles are readily available in any major library system in the United States; "Wealth" for example, is found in the online journal library JSTOR.org. A good selection of his writings is compiled in the *The Andrew Carnegie Reader*, as edited by Carnegie expert Joseph Wall. Some of his letters are collected in the US Steel Corporation Archives, in an underground archive outside Butler, Pennsylvania. There are smaller numbers of his papers in the New-York Public Library.

Essential Quotes

It is a law, as certain as any of the others named, that men possessed of this peculiar talent for affairs, under the free play of economic forces, must, of necessity, soon be in receipt of more revenue than can be judiciously expended upon themselves; and this law is as beneficial for the race as the others."

("Wealth")

I would as soon leave to my son a curse as the almighty dollar.

("Wealth")

[T]he man who dies leaving behind many millions of available wealth, which was his to administer during life, will pass away "unwept, unhonored, and unsung," no matter to what uses he leaves the dross which he cannot take with him. Of such as these the public verdict will then be: "The man who dies thus rich dies disgraced."

("Wealth")

Essential Quotes

My experience is that you can always rely upon the great body of working-men to do what is right, provided they have not taken up a position and promised their leaders to stand by them. But their loyalty to their leaders even when mistaken, is something to make us proud of them. Anything can be done with men who have this feeling of loyalty within them. They only need to be treated fairly.

(*Autobiography*, Chapter XVIII)

There have been many incidents in my business life proving that labor troubles are not solely founded upon wages. I believe the best preventive of quarrels to be recognition of, and sincere interest in, the men, satisfying them that you really care for them and that you rejoice in their success.

(*Autobiography*, Chapter XVIII)

For several grave reasons I regard possessions in the Far East as fraught with nothing but disaster to the Republic.

("Americanism versus Imperialism")

Imperialism implies naval and military force behind; moral force, education, civilization, are not the backbone of Imperialism; these are the moral forces which make for the higher civilization, for Americanism—the foundation for Imperialism is brutal physical strength, fighting men with material forces, warships and artillery.

("Americanism versus Imperialism")

Two questions are submitted to the decision of the American people: First—Shall we remain as we are, solid, compact, impregnable, republican, American; or, Second—Shall we creep under the protection, and become, as Bishop Potter says, "the catspaw" of Britain, in order that we may grasp the phantom of Imperialism?

("Americanism versus Imperialism")

Further Reading

■ Books

Krass, Peter. *Carnegie*. Hoboken, NJ: John Wiley & Sons, 2002.

Livesay, Harold C. *Andrew Carnegie and the Rise of Big Business*. New York: Pearson Longman, 2007.

Nasaw, David. *Andrew Carnegie*. New York: Penguin Press, 2006.

Standiford, Les. *Meet You in Hell: Andrew Carnegie, Henry Clay Frick, and the Bitter Partnership That Transformed America*. New York: Three Rivers Press, 2005.

■ Web Sites

Tweedale, Geoffrey. "Carnegie, Andrew (1835–1919)". *Oxford Dictionary of National Biography*, Oxford University Press. 2004 http://www.oxforddnb.com/view/article/32296 (accessed August 29, 2016).

Questions for Further Study

1. How has Carnegie's "Gospel of Wealth" had an impact on wealthy people in the United States? Who in modern American society seems to pursue a similar philosophy? What legacy do you think the "Gospel of Wealth" has had in American life?

2. The Homestead strike stained Carnegie's legacy irreparably. Many people assumed after it that, for whatever his statements otherwise, his only interest was in making money and keeping it, whatever the cost to his workers. Hopefully his life and ideas make it seem to be otherwise. Yet there are some easily noticed clues in his discussion of his negotiations with his workers that he did not take them as seriously in negotiations as, say, his business rivals or social equals. What were some of those clues?

3. Carnegie was one of the first wealthy Americans to use his wealth to establish a platform for himself as a commentator on current events. Who has picked up that platform since his time? Why and how?

"Wealth"

1889

The problem of our age is the proper administration of wealth, so that the ties of brotherhood may still bind together the rich and poor in harmonious relationship. The conditions of human life have not only been changed, but revolutionized, within the past few hundred years. In former days there was little difference between the dwelling, dress, food, and environment of the chief and those of his retainers. The Indians are to-day where civilized man then was. When visiting the Sioux, I was led to the wigwam of the chief. It was just like the others in external appearance, and even within the difference was trifling between it and those of the poorest of his braves. The contrast between the palace of the millionaire and the cottage of the laborer with us to-day measures the change which has come with civilization.

This change, however, is not to be deplored, but welcomed as highly beneficial. It is well, nay, essential for the progress of the race, that the houses of some should be homes for all that is highest and best in literature and the arts, and for all the refinements of civilization, rather than that none should be so. Much better this great irregularity than universal squalor. Without wealth there can be no Mæcenas. The "good old times " were not good old times. Neither master nor servant was as well situated then as to-day. A relapse to old conditions would be disastrous to both--not the least so to him who serves--and would Sweep away civilization with it. But whether the change be for good or ill, it is upon us, beyond our power to alter, and there fore to be accepted and made the best of. It is a waste of time to criticise the inevitable.

It is easy to see how the change has come. One illustration will serve for almost every phase of the cause. In the manufacture of products we have the whole story. It applies to all combinations of human industry, as stimulated and enlarged by the inventions of this scientific age. Formerly articles Were manufactured at the domestic hearth or in small shops which formed part of the household. The master and his apprentices worked side by side, the latter living with the master, and therefore subject to the same conditions. When these apprentices rose to be masters, there was little or no change in their mode of life, and they, in turn, educated in the same routine succeeding apprentices. There was, substantially social equality, and even political equality, for those engaged in industrial pursuits had then little or no political voice in the State.

But the inevitable result of such a mode of manufacture was crude articles at high prices. To-day the world obtains commodities of excellent quality at prices which even the generation preceding this would have deemed incredible. In the commercial world similar causes have produced similar results, and the race is benefited thereby. The poor enjoy what the rich could not before afford. What were the luxuries have become the necessaries of life. The laborer has now more comforts than the landlord had a few generations ago. The farmer has more luxuries than the landlord had, and is more richly clad and better housed. The landlord has books and pictures rarer, and appointments more artistic, than the King could then obtain.

The price we pay for this salutary change is, no doubt, great. We assemble thousands of operatives in the factory, in the mine, and in the counting-house, of whom the employer can know little or nothing, and to whom the employer is little better than a myth. All intercourse between them is at an end. Rigid Castes are formed, and, as usual, mutual ignorance breeds mutual distrust. Each Caste is without sympathy for the other, and ready to credit anything disparaging in regard to it. Under the law of competition, the employer of thousands is forced into the strictest economies, among which the rates paid to labor figure prominently, and often there is friction between the employer and the employed, between capital and labor, between rich and poor. Human society loses homogeneity.

The price which society pays for the law of competition, like the price it pays for cheap comforts and luxuries, is also great; but the advantage of this law are also greater still, for it is to this law that we owe our wonderful material development, which brings improved conditions in its train. But, whether the law be benign or not, we must say of it, as we say of the change in the conditions of men to which we have referred: It is here; we cannot evade it; no substitutes for it have been found; and while the law may be sometimes hard for the individual, it is best for the

race, because it insures the survival of the fittest in every department. We accept and welcome therefore, as conditions to which we must accommodate ourselves, great inequality of environment, the concentration of business, industrial and commercial, in the hands of a few, and the law of competition between these, as being not only beneficial, but essential for the future progress of the race. Having accepted these, it follows that there must be great scope for the exercise of special ability in the merchant and in the manufacturer who has to conduct affairs upon a great scale. That this talent for organization and management is rare among men is proved by the fact that it invariably secures for its possessor enormous rewards, no matter where or under what laws or conditions. The experienced in affairs always rate the MAN whose services can be obtained as a partner as not only the first consideration, but such as to render the question of his capital scarcely worth considering, for such men soon create capital; while, without the special talent required, capital soon takes wings. Such men become interested in firms or corporations using millions ; and estimating only simple interest to be made upon the capital invested, it is inevitable that their income must exceed their expenditures, and that they must accumulate wealth. Nor is there any middle ground which such men can occupy, because the great manufacturing or commercial concern which does not earn at least interest upon its capital soon becomes bankrupt. It, must either go forward or fall behind: to stand still is impossible. It is a condition essential for its successful operation that it should be thus far profitable, and even that, in addition to interest on capital, it should make profit. It is a law, as certain as any of the others named, that men possessed of this peculiar talent for affair, under the free play of economic forces, must, of necessity, soon be in receipt of more revenue than can be judiciously expended upon themselves; and this law is as beneficial for the race as the others.

Objections to the foundations upon which society is based are not in order, because the condition of the race is better with these than it has been with any others which have been tried. Of the effect of any new substitutes proposed we cannot be sure. The Socialist or Anarchist who seeks to overturn present conditions is to be regarded as attacking the foundation upon which civilization itself rests, for civilization took its start from the day that the capable, industrious workman said to his incompetent and lazy fellow, "If thou dost net sow, thou shalt net reap," and thus ended primitive Communism by separating the drones from the bees. One who studies this subject will soon be brought face to face with the conclusion that upon the sacredness of property civilization itself depends--the right of the laborer to his hundred dollars in the savings bank, and equally the legal right of the millionaire to his millions. To these who propose to substitute Communism for this intense Individualism the answer, therefore, is: The race has tried that. All progress from that barbarous day to the present time has resulted from its displacement. Not evil, but good, has come to the race from the accumulation of wealth by those who have the ability and energy that produce it. But even if we admit for a moment that it might be better for the race to discard its present foundation, Individualism,--that it is a nobler ideal that man should labor, not for himself alone, but in and for a brotherhood of his fellows, and share with them all in common, realizing Swedenborg's idea of Heaven, where, as he says, the angels derive their happiness, not from laboring for self, but for each other,--even admit all this, and a sufficient answer is, This is not evolution, but revolution. It necessitates the changing of human nature itself a work of oeons, even if it were good to change it, which we cannot know. It is not practicable in our day or in our age. Even if desirable theoretically, it belongs to another and long-succeeding sociological stratum. Our duty is with what is practicable now ; with the next step possible in our day and generation. It is criminal to waste our energies in endeavoring to uproot, when all we can profitably or possibly accomplish is to bend the universal tree of humanity a little in the direction most favorable to the production of good fruit under existing circumstances. We might as well urge the destruction of the highest existing type of man because he failed to reach our ideal as favor the destruction of Individualism, Private Property, the Law of Accumulation of Wealth, and the Law of Competition; for these are the highest results of human experience, the soil in which society so far has produced the best fruit. Unequally or unjustly, perhaps, as these laws sometimes operate, and imperfect as they appear to the Idealist, they are, nevertheless, like the highest type of man, the best and most valuable of all that humanity has yet accomplished.

We start, then, with a condition of affairs under which the best interests of the race are promoted, but which inevitably gives wealth to the few. Thus far, accepting conditions as they exist, the situation

can be surveyed and pronounced good. The question then arises, --and, if the foregoing be correct, it is the only question with which we have to deal, --What is the proper mode of administering wealth after the laws upon which civilization is founded have thrown it into the hands of the few ? And it is of this great question that I believe I offer the true solution. It will be understood that fortunes are here spoken of, not moderate sums saved by many years of effort, the returns on which are required for the comfortable maintenance and education of families. This is not wealth, but only competence which it should be the aim of all to acquire.

There are but three modes in which surplus wealth can be disposed of. It call be left to the families of the decedents; or it can be bequeathed for public purposes; or, finally, it can be administered during their lives by its possessors. Under the first and second modes most of the wealth of the world that has reached the few has hitherto been applied. Let us in turn consider each of these modes. The first is the most injudicious. In monarchical countries, the estates and the greatest portion of the wealth are left to the first son, that the vanity of the parent may be gratified by the thought that his name and title are to descend to succeeding generations unimpaired. The condition of this class in Europe to-day teaches the futility of such hopes or ambitions. The successors have become impoverished through their follies or from the fall in the value of land. Even in Great Britain the strict law of entail has been found inadequate to maintain the status of an hereditary class. Its soil is rapidly passing into the hands of the stranger. Under republican institutions the division of property among the children is much fairer, but the question which forces itself upon thoughtful men in all lands is: Why should men leave great fortunes to their children? If this is done from affection, is it not misguided affection? Observation teaches that, generally speaking, it is not well for the children that they should be so burdened. Neither is it well for the state. Beyond providing for the wife and daughters moderate sources of income, and very moderate allowances indeed, if any, for the sons, men may well hesitate, for it is no longer questionable that great suns bequeathed oftener work more for the injury than for the good of the recipients. Wise men will soon conclude that, for the best interests of the members of their families and of the state, such bequests are an improper use of their means.

It is not suggested that men who have failed to educate their sons to earn a livelihood shall cast them adrift in poverty. If any man has seen fit to rear his sons with a view to their living idle lives, or, what is highly commendable, has instilled in them the sentiment that they are in a position to labor for public ends without reference to pecuniary considerations, then, of course, the duty of the parent is to see that such are provided for ?fl moderation. There are instances of millionaires' sons unspoiled by wealth, who, being rich, still perform great services in the community. Such are the very salt of the earth, as valuable as, unfortunately, they are rare; still it is not the exception, but the rule, that men must regard, and, looking at the usual result of enormous sums conferred upon legatees, the thoughtful man must shortly say, "I would as soon leave to my son a curse as the almighty dollar," and admit to himself that it is not the welfare of the children, but family pride, which inspires these enormous legacies.

As to the second mode, that of leaving wealth at death for public uses, it may be said that this is only a means for the disposal of wealth, provided a man is content to wait until he is dead before it becomes of much good in the world. Knowledge of the results of legacies bequeathed is not calculated to inspire the brightest hopes of much posthumous good being accomplished. The cases are not few in which the real object sought by the testator is not attained, nor are they few in which his real wishes are thwarted. In many cases the bequests are so used as to become only monuments of his folly. It is well to remember that it requires the exercise of not less ability than that which acquired the wealth to use it so as to be really beneficial to the community. Besides this, it may fairly be said that no man is to be extolled for doing what he cannot help doing, nor is he to be thanked by the community to which he only leaves wealth at death. Men who leave vast sums in this way may fairly be thought men who would not have left it at all, had they been able to take it with them. The memories of such cannot be held in grateful remembrance, for there is no grace in their gifts. It is not to be wondered at that such bequests seem so generally to lack the blessing. -

The growing disposition to tax more and more heavily large estates left at death is a cheering indication of the growth of a salutary change in public opinion. The State of Pennsylvania now takes--subject to some exceptions--one-tenth of the property left by its citizens. The budget presented in the British Parliament the other day proposes to increase the death-duties; and, most significant of all, the new tax

is to be a graduated one. Of all forms of taxation, this seems the wisest. Men who continue hoarding great sums all their lives, the proper use of which for public ends would work good to the community, should be made to feel that the community, in the form of the state, cannot thus be deprived of its proper share. By taxing estates heavily at death the state marks its condemnation of the selfish millionaire's unworthy life.

It is desirable; that nations should go much further in this direction. Indeed, it is difficult to set bounds to the share of a rich man's estate which should go at his death to the public through the agency of the state, and by all means such taxes should be graduated, beginning at nothing upon moderate sums to dependents, and increasing rapidly as the amounts swell, until of the millionaire's hoard, as of Shylock's, at least

"_____ The other half

Comes to the privy coffer of the state."

This policy would work powerfully to induce the rich man to attend to the administration of wealth during his life, which is the end that society should always have in view, as being that by far most fruitful for the people. Nor need it be feared that this policy would sap the root of enterprise and render men less anxious to accumulate, for to the class whose ambition it is to leave great fortunes and be talked about after their death, it will attract even more attention, and, indeed, be a somewhat nobler ambition to have enormous sums paid over to the state from their fortunes.

There remains, then, only one mode of using great fortunes; but in this we have the true antidote for the temporary unequal distribution of wealth, the reconciliation of the rich and the poor--a reign of harmony--another ideal, differing, indeed, from that of the Communist in requiring only the further evolution of existing conditions, not the total overthrow of our civilization. It is founded upon the present most intense individualism, and the race is projected to put it in practice by degree whenever it pleases. Under its sway we shall have an ideal state, in which the surplus wealth of the few will become, in the best sense the property of the many, because administered for the common good, and this wealth, passing through the hands of the few, can be made a much more potent force for the elevation of our race than if it had been distributed in small sums to the people themselves. Even the poorest can be made to see this, and to agree that great sums gathered by some of their fellow-citizens and spent for public purposes, from which the masses reap the principal benefit, are more valuable to them than if scattered among them through the course of many years in trifling amounts.

If we consider what results flow from the Cooper Institute, for instance, to the best portion of the race in New York not possessed of means, and compare these with those which would have arisen for the good of the masses from an equal sum distributed by Mr. Cooper in his lifetime in the form of wages, which is the highest form of distribution, being for work done and not for charity, we can form some estimate of the possibilities for the improvement of the race which lie embedded in the present law of the accumulation of wealth. Much of this sum if distributed in small quantities among the people, would have been wasted in the indulgence of appetite, some of it in excess, and it may be doubted whether even the part put to the best use, that of adding to the comforts of the home, would have yielded results for the race, as a race, at all comparable to those which are flowing and are to flow from the Cooper Institute from generation to generation. Let the advocate of violent or radical change ponder well this thought.

We might even go so far as to take another instance, that of Mr. Tilden's bequest of five millions of dollars for a free library in the city of New York, but in referring to this one cannot help saying involuntarily, how much better if Mr. Tilden had devoted the last years of his own life to the proper administration of this immense sum; in which case neither legal contest nor any other cause of delay could have interfered with his aims. But let us assume that Mr. Tilden's millions finally become the means of giving to this city a noble public library, where the treasures of the world contained in books will be open to all forever, without money and without price. Considering the good of that part of the race which congregates in and around Manhattan Island, would its permanent benefit have been better promoted had these millions been allowed to circulate in small sums through the hands of the masses? Even the most strenuous advocate of Communism must entertain a doubt upon this subject. Most of those who think will probably entertain no doubt whatever.

Poor and restricted are our opportunities in this life; narrow our horizon; our best work most imperfect; but rich men should be thankful for one inestimable boon. They have it in their power during their lives to busy themselves in organizing benefactions from which the masses of their fellows will derive

Document Text

lasting advantage, and thus dignify their own lives. The highest life is probably to be reached, not by such imitation of the life of Christ as Count Tolstoi gives us, but, while animated by Christ's spirit, by recognizing the changed conditions of this age, and adopting modes of expressing this spirit suitable to the changed conditions under which we live ; still laboring for the good of our fellows, which was the essence of his life and teaching, but laboring in a different manner.

This, then, is held to be the duty of the man of Wealth: First, to set an example of modest, unostentatious living, shunning display or extravagance; to provide moderately for the legitimate wants of those dependent upon him; and after doing so to consider all surplus revenues which come to him simply as trust funds, which he is called upon to administer, and strictly bound as a matter of duty to administer in the manner which, in his judgment, is best calculated to produce the most beneficial results for the community--the man of wealth thus becoming the mere agent and trustee for his poorer brethren, bringing to their service his superior wisdom, experience and ability to administer, doing for them better than they would or could do for themselves.

We are met here with the difficulty of determining what are moderate sums to leave to members of the family; what is modest, unostentatious living; what is the test of extravagance. There must be different standards for different conditions. The answer is that it is as impossible to name exact amounts or actions as it is to define good manners, good taste, or the rules of propriety ; but, nevertheless, these are verities, well known although undefinable. Public sentiment is quick to know and to feel what offends these. So in the case of wealth. The rule in regard to good taste in the dress of men or women applies here. Whatever makes one conspicuous offends the canon. If any family be chiefly known for display, for extravagance in home, table, equipage, for enormous sums ostentatiously spent in any form upon itself, if these be its chief distinctions, we have no difficulty in estimating its nature or culture. So likewise in regard to the use or abuse of its surplus wealth, or to generous, freehanded cooperation in good public uses, or to unabated efforts to accumulate and hoard to the last, whether they administer or bequeath. The verdict rests with the best and most enlightened public sentiment. The community will surely judge and its judgments will not often be wrong.

The best uses to which surplus wealth can be put have already been indicated. These who, would administer wisely must, indeed, be wise, for one of the serious obstacles to the improvement of our race is indiscriminate charity. It were better for mankind that the millions of the rich were thrown in to the sea than so spent as to encourage the slothful, the drunken, the unworthy. Of every thousand dollars spent in so called charity to-day, it is probable that $950 is unwisely spent; so spent, indeed as to produce the very evils which it proposes to mitigate or cure. A well-known writer of philosophic books admitted the other day that he had given a quarter of a dollar to a man who approached him as he was coming to visit the house of his friend. He knew nothing of the habits of this beggar; knew not the use that would be made of this money, although he had every reason to suspect that it would be spent improperly. This man professed to be a disciple of Herbert Spencer; yet the quarter-dollar given that night will probably work more injury than all the money which its thoughtless donor will ever be able to give in true charity will do good. He only gratified his own feelings, saved himself from annoyance,—and this was probably one of the most selfish and very worst actions of his life, for in all respects he is most worthy.

In bestowing charity, the main consideration should be to help those who will help themselves; to provide part of the means by which those who desire to improve may do so; to give those who desire to use the aids by which they may rise; to assist, but rarely or never to do all. Neither the individual nor the race is improved by alms-giving. Those worthy of assistance, except in rare cases, seldom require assistance. The really valuable men of the race never do, except in cases of accident or sudden change. Every one has, of course, cases of individuals brought to his own knowledge where temporary assistance can do genuine good, and these he will not overlook. But the amount which can be wisely given by the individual for individuals is necessarily limited by his lack of knowledge of the circumstances connected with each. He is the only true reformer who is as careful and as anxious not to aid the unworthy as he is to aid the worthy, and, perhaps, even more so, for in almsgiving more injury is probably done by rewarding vice than by relieving virtue.

The rich man is thus almost restricted to following the examples of Peter Cooper, Enoch Pratt of Baltimore, Mr. Pratt of Brooklyn, Senator Stanford, and others, who know that the best means of benefiting the community is to place within its reach the ladders upon which the aspiring can rise--parks,

Document Text

and means of recreation, by which men are helped in body and mind; works of art, certain to give pleasure and improve the public taste, and public institutions of various kinds, which will improve the general condition of the people ;--in this manner returning their surplus wealth to the mass of their fellows in the forms best calculated to do them lasting good.

Thus is the problem of Rich and Poor to be solved. The laws of accumulation will be left free ; the laws of distribution free. Individualism will continue, but the millionaire will be but a trustee for the poor; intrusted for a season with a great part of the increased wealth of the community, but administering it for the community far better than it could or would have done for itself. The best minds will thus have reached a stage in the development of the race iii which it is clearly seen that there is no mode of disposing of surplus wealth creditable to thoughtful and earnest men into whose hands it flows save by using it year by year for the general good. This day already dawns. But a little while, and although, without incurring the pity of their fellows, men may die sharers in great business enterprises from which their capital cannot be or has not been withdrawn, and is left chiefly at death for public uses, yet the man who dies leaving behind many millions of available wealth, which was his to administer during life, will pass away "unwept, unhonored, and unsung," no matter to what uses he leaves the dross which he cannot take with him. Of such as these the public verdict will then be : "The man who dies thus rich dies disgraced."

Such, in my opinion, is the true Gospel concerning Wealth, obedience to which is destined some day to solve the problem of the Rich and the Poor, and to bring ' Peace on earth, among men Good-Will."

Americanism versus Imperialism

1899

For several grave reasons I regard possessions in the Far East as fraught with nothing hut disaster to the Republic. Only one of these, however, can now be considered—the dangers of war and of the almost constant rumors and threats of war to which all nations interested in the Far East are subject. There is seldom a week which does not bring alarming reports of threatened hostilities, or of new alliances, or of changes of alliances, between the powers arming for the coming struggle. It is chiefly this Far Eastern question which keeps every shipyard, gunyard, and armor yard in the world busy night and day, Sunday and Saturday, forging engines of destruction. It is in that region the thunderbolt is expected; it is there the storm is to burst.

It is only four years since Japan defeated China and had ceded to it a portion of Chinese territory, the fruits of victory. Then appeared upon the scene a combination of France, Russia and Germany, which drove Japan out of China. Russia took part of the spoils for herself, and Germany later took territory near by. Japan got nothing. Britain, the most powerful of all, stood by neutral. Had she decided to defend Japan, the greatest war ever known would have been the probable result; the thunderbolt would have fallen. Were the question to be decided to-day, it is now considered probable that Britain would support Japan.

Germany obtained a concession in China, and Britain promptly appeared, demanding that Germany should maintain the " open door" in all her Chinese territory; the same demand was made on Russia. Both perforce consented. The Far East is a mine of dynamite, always liable to explode.

Into this magazine the .United States proposes to enter and take a hand in the coming contest. It is obvious that what was done with Japan in regard to Chinese territory may be done with the United States in regard to her territory, the Philippines, and for the same reason, that the dictator is overwhelmingly strong and the victim helplessly weak.

The relative strength of the powers contending for Empire in the Far East is as follows: Great Britain has 80 first class ships of war, 581 warships in all; France has 50 first class warships, and a total of 403; Russia has 40 first class warships, 286 in all; Germany has 28 first class warships, a total of 216. Japan will soon rank with Germany, and be stronger there because close to the scene of action.

The United States proposes to enter into the zone of danger with 18 first class, and a total of 81 ships. These would hardly count as half that number, however, owing to her greater distance from the battle ground. Russia is 8,000 miles, the other Europeans about '9,000 miles from it. The United States is from 15,000 to 17,000 miles distant via the Cape and via the Straits; the route via Europe is about 12,000 miles, but that would be impracticable during war time, as the American ships going via Europe would pass right into the trap of their European enemies.

The armies of the European nations are as follows: Germany's army on a peace footing numbers 562,352 men, on a war footing 3,000,000 (and a large addition ordered); France's army on a peace footing, 615,413, on a war footing, 2,500,000; Russia's, on a peace footing, 750,944, on a war footing, 2,512,143. All Frenchmen and Germans over 20, and all Russians over 21 years of age, are subject to military service. They are, in fact, first soldiers, then citizens.

It is obvious that the United States cannot contest any question or oppose any demand of any one of its rivals which secures the neutrality of the other powers, as France, Germany and Bussia did that of Britain. She cannot stand alone. What the Saturday Review says here is true:

"Let us be frank and say outright that we expect mutual gain in material interests from this rapprochement. The American Commissioners at Paris are making their bargains, whether they realize it or not, under the protecting naval strength of England, and we shall expect a material quid pro quo for this assistance. We expect the United States to deal generously with Canada in the matter of tariffs, and we expect to be remembered when the United States comes into possession of the Philippine Islands, and above all we expect her assistance on the day, which is quickly approaching, when the future of China comes up for settlement, for the young imperialist; has entered upon a path where it will require a strong friend, and a lasting friendship between the two nations can be secured not by frothy sentimentality

on public platforms, but by reciprocal advantages in solid material interests."

Bishop Potter has recently stated that we must become the "catspaw of Britain," if we venture into the arena, and that is true. By Britain's neutrality, and by that alone, were we permitted to take the Philippines at all from Spain. But for that, France, Germany and Bussia never would have stood aloof, and the price demanded President McKinley has had to pay—the " open door," which secures the trade of our possessions for Britain. Nothing more significant has occurred than the statement of Senator Davis, Chairman of the Senate Committee upon Foreign Belations, whose ability, influence and position are alike commanding. He says:

"I favor a treaty of alliance including the United States, Great Britain and Japan; for the protection of all their interests north of the equator. The rest of the world would have a wholesome fear, synonymous with re spect, for us."

We may assume after this that it is true, that,—just as we were allowed by Britain to take the Philippines from Spain, so our position in the East depends upon her continued support or alliance—rather a humiliating position, I should say, for the Republic. But let us see about alliances. Can we depend upon an alliance? National combinations change with alarming rapidity in Europe. France and Britain allied, fought the Crimean War; they took Sebastopol as we took Manila. Their flags waved together there, but they did not consider that that fact gave them the right to demand territory. To-day Russia and France are in firm alliance against Britain and other nations. Germany fought Austria; to-day they are in the Triple Alliance together, Italy allied with France fought the Battle of Solferino; to-day Italy is a member of the Triple Alliance against France. Europe is a kaleidoscope, where alliances change, dissolve, recombine and take other forms with passing events. During the past week the bitter enmity which recently existed between Germany and Britain, owing to German interference in the Transvaal, is changed, and it is announced that "they see together upon many points and expect to co-operate more and more in the future." This morning the question is: Shall France and Germany combine for some common ends? This would have been considered remarkable a short time ago, but statesmen will remember that Germany and France did combine with Russia to drive Japan out of China. There is no alliance, not even the most apparently incongruous, that cannot be made, and that will not be made, to meet the immediate interests or ambitions of nations. Senator Davis seems to rest satisfied with an alliance for his country with Britain and Japan. If he had an alliance today, it might not be worth the paper it was written upon tomorrow.

I say, therefore, that no American statesman should place his country in any position which it could not defend, relying only upon its own strong right arm. Its arm at present is not much to depend upon; its 81 ships of war are too trifling to be taken into account; and as for its army—what are its 56,000 regulars ? Its volunteers are being disbanded. Both its Navy and its Army are good for one thing only—for easy capture or destruction by either one of the stronger powers. It is the protection of Britain, and that alone, upon which we have to rely—in the Far East—a slender thread indeed. Upon the shifting sands of alliances we are to have our only foundation.

The writer is not of those who believe that the Republic cannot make herself strong enough to walk alone, and to hold her own, and to be an imperial power of herself, and by herself, and not the weak protege of a real imperial power. But, in order to make herself an imperial power she must do as imperial powers do—she must create a navy equal to the navy of any other power. She must have hundreds of thousands of regular troops to cooperate with the navy.

If she devoted herself exclusively and unceasingly to creating a navy equal to that of Britain, for instance, which is what she will need, if she is not to be at the mercy of stronger powers, that will be the work of more than twenty years, building twenty warships per year; hitherto our navy has added only six per year. In order to get the men to man these ships, she must take the means to educate them. That she can do this there is no question; that the American either on sea or land is at least equal to the man of any other nation cannot be gainsaid. More than this, I know the American workman, especially the mechanic, to be the most skillful, most versatile, in the world—and victories at sea depend as much upon the mechanic below as upon the gunner on deck, and American gunners have no equals. It was no surprise to me that the American warships sunk those of Spain without loss. I spent last winter abroad in the society of distinguished men of European nations who congregate at Cannes. The opinion was universally held by them that for a time the Spanish Navy would be master over us, although it was admitted the superior resources of the United

Document Text

States must eventually ensure victory. I said then that, whenever any warships in the world met those of the American Navy, the other worships would go to the bottom—for two reasons; first, our ships were the latest and their equipment was the best, and, second, I knew the kind of men who were behind the guns. If ever the Republic falls from her industrial ideals and descends to the level of the war ideals of Europe she will be supreme. I have no doubt of that. The man whom this stimulating climate produces is the wiriest, quickest, most versatile of all men, and the power of organization exists in the American in greater perfection than in any other. But what I submit is that at present the Republic is an industrial hive, without an adequate navy and without soldiers; that she therefore must have a protector; and that if she is to figure in the East she cannot be in any sense an imperial power at all. Imperialism implies naval and military force behind; moral force", education, civilization, are not the backbone of Imperialism; these are the moral forces which make for the higher civilization, for Americanism—the foundation for Imperialism is brutal physical strength, fighting men with material forces, warships and artillery.

The author of "A Look Ahead," which first appeared in this Review, is not likely to be suspected of hostility to the coming together of the English-speaking race. It has been my dream, and it is one of the movements that lie closest to my heart. For many years the United flag has floated from my summer home in my native land, the Stars and Stripes and the Union Jack sewn together—the first of that kind of flag ever seen. That flag will continue to fly there and the winds to blow the two from side to side in loving embrace. But I do not favor a formal alliance, such as that desired by Senator Davis. On the contrary, I rely upon the "alliance of hearts," which happily exists to-day. Alliances of fighting power form and dissolve with the questions which arise from time to time. The patriotism of race lies deeper and is not disturbed by waves upon the surface. The present era of good feeling between the old and the new lands means that the home of Shakespeare and Burns will never be invaded without other than native-born Britons being found in its defence. It means that the giant child, the Republic, is not to be set upon by a combination of other races anti pushed to its destruction without a growl coming from the old lion which will shake the earth. But it should not mean that either the old land or the new binds itself to support the other in all its designs, either at home or abroad, but that the Republic shall remain the friend of all nations and the ally of none; that, being free to-day of all foreign entanglements, she shall not undertake to support Britain, who has these to deal with. Take Russia for instance. Only last year leading statesmen were pushing Britain into a crusade against that country. They proposed to prevent its legitimate expansion toward the Pacific—legitimate, because it is over coterminous territory, which Russia can absorb and Russianize, keeping her empire solid. She knows better than to have outlying possessions open to attack. Russia has always been the friend of the United States. When Lord Palmerston, Prime Minister of Great Britain, proposed to recognize the South, Russia sent her fleet to New York. Russia sold us Alaska; we have no opposing interests to those of Russia; the two nations are the only two great nations in the world, solid, compact, impregnable, because each has developed only coterminous territory, upon which its own race could grow. Even in the matter of trade with Russia, our exports are increasing with wonderful rapidity. Shiploads of American locomotives, American steel bridges and American electrical machinery for her leave our shores. Everything in which our country is either supreme or becoming supreme goes to Russia. Suppose Britain and Russia clash in the Far East and we have an alliance with Britain, we are at war against one of our best friends.

The sister Republic of France and our own, from her very beginning, have been close friends. The services France rendered at the Revolution may be, but should never be, forgotten by the American. That some interests in France sympathized with Spain was only natural. The financial world in France held the Spanish debt. The religion of France is the religion of Spain. The enemies of the French Republic sided with the monarchy. But this can be said without fear of contradiction, that those who govern France stood the friends of our Republic, and that our enemies in France were also the enemies of the French Government. An alliance with Britain and Japan would make us a possible enemy of France. I would not make an alliance which involved that. I would make no alliance with any power under any circumstances that can be imagined; I would have the Republic remain the friend of all powers. That has been her policy from the beginning, and so it should remain.

When "the world shall have a wholesome fear synonymous with respect for us," as Senator Davis desires, it will not be a good day for the Republic. Adherence to Washington's desire seems better to

me—that we should be the "friends of all nations"—a wholesome friendship instead of a "wholesome fear."

Reference has been made to possible difference arising between the protector and its ward, but I do not wish to be understood as entertaining the belief that actual war is probable between them. Far from this, my opinion is that actual war will never exist again between the two branches of the English-speaking race. Should one have a grievance, the other would offer Arbitration, and no government of either could exist which refused that offer. The most powerful government ever known in Britain was that of Lord Salisbury, when President Cleveland rightfully demanded Arbitration in the Venezuelan case. As is well known, Mr. Gladstone's government had agreed to Arbitration. Lord Salisbury, upon coming into power, repudiated that agreement. Lord Salisbury denied President Cleveland's request, and what was the result? Some uninformed persons in the -United States believe that he was compelled to withdraw his refusal and accede to President Cleveland's request by the attitude of the United States. That was only partially true. The forces in Britain supporting -Lord Salisbury compelled him to reverse his decision. This is an open secret. Those nearest and next to him in power who sided with President Cleveland could be named; but the published cables are sufficient. The heir and the next heir to the throne cabled "that they hoped and believed the question would be peacefully settled." That behind this cable was the Queen herself, always the friend of the Republic, need not be doubted.

The idea of actual war between Great Britain and the Republic can be dismissed as something which need not be taken into account; but what is to be feared is this: the neutrality of Britain—even to-day desired by other powers—in ease her ward gave her offence, or was as she supposed, ungrateful, and did not make full return for the protection accorded to the weakling, as we have said. It did not require the active hostility of Great Britain to thwart Japan and push her out of her possessions, but simply her decision not to interfere on Japan's behalf. Had Japan had satisfactory advantages to offer to Britain, she might have had Britain's support. It is the satisfactory bargain that alliances are founded upon in Europe; every European nation has its price, and every one of them has something which the other covets. Prance could give Britain a free hand in Egypt, Germany could concur in Britain's acquisition of Delagoa Bay and end her troubles in the Transvaal. This is something Britain dearly covets. Russia could give Britain a desired frontier in India. These nations have all co-related interests and desires, and no man can predict what alliances will be broken and what made—it is all a matter of self-interest. The United States has not this position. She has little desirable to offer in exchange for alliance, and in all probability she would be sacrificed for the aims of her strong rivals—at least she might be, being herself powerless.

When a statesman has in his keeping the position and interests of his country, all speculation as to the future fruition of ideas of what should be or what will one day rule the world, and of the "good day coming" when the pen shall supersede the sword, and of all the noble hopes and aspirations for a better future, must be resolutely dismissed. It is not with things as they are to be in the future, but with things as they are in the present, that it is his serious duty to deal. The dream, in which no one perhaps indulges more than the writer, of the union of the English-speaking race, even that entrancing dream must be recognized as only a dream. The "Parliament of Man, the Federation of the "World," we know is to come. The evolutionist has never any doubt about the realization of the highest ideals from the operation of that tendency within us, not ourselves, which makes for righteousness. But he is no statesman—he is only a dreamer—who allows his hopes to stand against facts, and he who proposes that the United States, as she stands to-day, shall enter into the coming struggle in the Far East, depending upon any alliance that can be made with any or all of the powers, seems unsuited to shape the policy or deal with the destinies of the Republic.

Just consider her position, solid, compact, impregnable; if all the naval forces were to combine to attack her what would be her reply? She would fill her ports with mines, she would draw her ships of war behind them, ready to rush out as favorable opportunities might offer to attack. But she would do more than this in extremity; she would close her ports—a few loaded scows would do the business—and all the powers in the world would be impotent to injure her seriously. The fringe only would be troubled; the great empire within would scarcely feel the attack.

The injury she would inflict upon the principal powers by closing her ports would be much more serious than could be inflicted upon her; because non-exportation of food-stuffs and cotton would mean famine and distress to Britain and injure her to

Document Text

a greater degree than loss in battle. Even in France and in Germany the results of non-exportation would be more serious than the effects of ordinary war. It would only be a matter of a short time until the powers recognized how futile was their attempt to injure seriously this self-contained Republic, whose estate here lies secure within a ring fence.

The national wealth would not grow as fast during the blockade, but that is all. Our foreign trade would suffer, but that is a trifle, not more than four per cent, of our domestic commerce. No expert estimates the annual domestic exchanges of the people at less than fifty thousand millions of dollars; those of exports and imports have never yet reached quite two thousand millions. The annual increase of domestic exchanges is estimated to be just about equal to the total of all our Foreign Trade, Imports and Exports combined. Labor would be displaced, but the new demand upon it caused by the new state of affairs would employ it all. We should emerge from the embargo without serious injury. So much for the impregnability of the Republic. Today Fortune rains upon her. For the first time in her history, she has become the greatest exporting nation in the world, even the exports of Britain being less than hers. Her manufactures are invading all lands, commercial expansion proceeds by leaps and bounds; New York has become the financial centre of the world. It is London no more, but New York, which is today the financial centre. This, however, is not yet to be claimed as permanent, but it promises to become so ere long, unless the Republic becomes involved in European wars through Imperialism. Labor is in demand at the highest wages paid in the world; the Industrial supremacy of the world lies at our feet. Two questions are submitted to the decision of the American people: First—Shall we remain as we are, solid, compact, impregnable, republican, American; or, Second—Shall we creep under the protection, and become, as Bishop Potter says, "the catspaw," of Britain, in order that we may grasp the phantom of Imperialism ?

If the latter be the choice, then it is submitted that we must first begin quietly to prepare ourselves for the new work which Imperialism imposes.

We need a large regular army of trained soldiers. There is no use trying to encounter regular armies with volunteers—we have found that out. Not that volunteers would not be superior to the class of men we shall get to enlist simply for pay in the regular army, if they would enlist there and be trained, but because they are not trained. Thirty-eight thousand more men are to be called for the regular army; but it is easy "to call spirits from the vasty deep "—they may not come. The present force of the army is 62,000 men by law; we have only 56,000, as the President tells us in his message. Why do we not first fill up the gap, instead of asking for legislation to enlist more? Because Labor is well employed and men are scarce in some States to-day; because men who now enlist know for what they are wanted, and that kind of work is not what American soldiers have been asked to perform hitherto. They have never had to leave their own country, much less to shoot down men whose only crime against the Republic was that they too, like ourselves, desired their country's independence and believed in the Declaration of Independence—in Americanism. The President may not get the soldiers he desires, and whom he must have if he is not to make shipwreck of his Imperialism. There is very grave reason to doubt whether the army can he raised even to one hundred thousand men without a great advance in pay, perhaps not without conscription.

But surely before we appear in the arena in the Par East we must have a large regular army.

The second indispensable requirement is a navy corresponding, at least in some degree, to the navies of the other powers interested in the East. We can get this in twenty years, perhaps, if we push matters, but this means building twenty ships a year. The securing of men trained to man them will be as difficult a task as the building of the ships.

When we have armed ourselves thus, but not till then, shall we be in a position to take and hold territory in the Far East "by the sole power of our unlorded will," as we should hold it, or not hold it at all. To rush in now, without army or navy, trusting to the treacherous shifting foundation of anybody's "protection," or "neutrality," or "alliance," is to court defeat, and such humibiation as has rarely fallen to the lot of any nation, even the poorest and most madly or most foolishly governed. It is not good sense.

This ends the subject upon which I undertook to write, but there remains the practical question: What shall we do with the Philippines? These are not ours, unless the Senate approves the Treaty; but, assuming that it will, that question arises.

The question can best be answered by asking another: What have we promised to do with Cuba? The cases are as nearly parallel as similar cases usually are. We drove Spain out of both Cuba and the Philippines. Our ships lie in the harbors of both. Our

flag waves over both. To Cuba the President in his message renews the pledge given by Congress—she is to be aided to form a "Free and Independent Government, at the earliest possible moment."

The magic words "Free and Independent" will be accepted by the people of Cuba and our soldiers hailed as deliverers. So well assured of this is our government, that only one-half the number of troops intended for Cuba are now to be sent there.

Even if we were tempted to play false to our pledge, as the enemies of the Republic in Europe predict we shall, the aspirations of a people for Independence are seldom quenched. There are a great number of Americans, and these of the best, who would soon revolt at our soldiers being used against the Cubans fighting for what they had been promised. The latest advices I have from Cuba are from a good source. This necessity is not likely to arise. Cuba will soon form a government, and, mark my prediction, she will ask for annexation. The proprietors of Cuba who will control the new government, and many Americans who are becoming interested with them in estates there, will see to this. "Free sugar " means fortune to all. Will the United States admit Cuba ? Doubtful. But Cuba need not trouble us very much. There is no "Imperialism " here—no danger of foreign wars.

Now why is the policy adopted for the Island of Cuba not the right policy for the Philippine Islands? General Schofield states that 30,000 troops will be required there, as we.may have to "lick them." What work this for Americans ! General Miles thinks 25,000 will do. If we promised them what we have promised Cuba, half the number would suffice, as with Cuba—probably less—and we should be spared the uncongenial task of shooting down people who were guiltless of offence against us.

If we insist "the slaves are ours because we bought them," and fail to tell them we come not as slave drivers, but as friends to assist them to Independence, we may have to "lick them" no doubt. It will say much for the Filipinos if they do rebel against "being bought and sold like cattle." It would be difficult to give a better proof of their fitness for self government,

Cuba is under the shield of the Monroe doctrine; no foreign interference is possible there. Place the Philippines under similar conditions until they have a stable government, when eight millions of people can be trusted to protect themselves. The truth is that none of the powers would risk the hostility of eight millions of people, who had tasted the hope of Independence. "Free and Independent " are magical words, never forgotten, and rarely unrealized.

Only one objection can be made to this policy. They are not fit to govern themselves. First, this has not been proved. This was said of every one of the sixteen Spanish Republics as they broke away from Spain; it was said even of Mexico within this generation; it was the belief of the British about ourselves. There is in the writer's opinion little force in the objection. In the Far East I have visited the village communities in India, to find even there a system of self-government dating back for two thousand years. In no country, not even the most backward, are not to be found government and "orders and degrees " of men.

The head men of tribes and others of lesser authority are often selected by the members. In the wild lands of the Afridis—a tribe in India which has just baffled seventy thousand soldiers, native and British, the largest army ever assembled there—there is a system of self-government, and a rigid one. Human societies cannot exist without establishing, as a rule, peace and order in greater or less perfection.

The Filipinos are by no means in the lowest scale—far from it—nor are they much lower than the Cubans. If left to themselves they will make mistakes, but what nation does not? Riot and bloodshed may break out—in which nation are these absent? Certainly not in our own; but the inevitable result will be a government better suited to the people than any that our soldiers and their officers could ever give.

Thus only can the Republic stand true to its pledges, that the sword was drawn only in the cause of humanity and not for territorial aggrandizement, and true to the fundamental principles upon which she rests: "that government derives its just powers from the consent of the governed"; "that the flag, wherever it floats, shall proclaim the equality of the citizen"; "one man's privilege every man's right"—"that all men are created equal," not that under its sway part only shall be citizens with rights and part only subjects without rights—freemen and serfs, not all freemen. Such is the issue between Americanism and Imperialism.

The Autobiography of Andrew Carnegie, Chapter XVIII: "Problems of Labor"

1920

I SHOULD like to record here some of the labor disputes I have had to deal with, as these may point a moral to both capital and labor.

The workers at the blast furnaces in our steel-rail works once sent in a "round-robin" stating that unless the firm gave them an advance of wages by Monday afternoon at four o'clock they would leave the furnaces. Now, the scale upon which these men had agreed to work did not lapse until the end of the year, several months off. I felt if men would break an agreement there was no use in making a second agreement with them, but nevertheless I took the night train from New York and was at the works early in the morning.

I asked the superintendent to call together the three committees which governed the works—not only the blast-furnace committee that was alone involved, but the mill and the converting works committees as well. They appeared and, of course, were received by me with great courtesy, not because it was good policy to be courteous, but because I have always enjoyed meeting our men. I am bound to say that the more I know of working-men the higher I rate their virtues. But it is with them as Barrie says with women: "Dootless the Lord made a' things weel, but he left some michty queer kinks in women." They have their prejudices and "red rags," which have to be respected, for the main root of trouble is ignorance, not hostility. The committee sat in a semicircle before me, all with their hats off, of course, as mine was also; and really there was the appearance of a model assembly.

Addressing the chairman of the mill committee, I said:

"Mr. Mackay" (he was an old gentleman and wore spectacles), "have we an agreement with you covering the remainder of the year?"

Taking the spectacles off slowly, and holding them in his hand, he said:

"Yes, sir, you have, Mr. Carnegie, and you haven't got enough money to make us break it either."

"There spoke the true American workman," I said. "I am proud of you."

"Mr. Johnson" (who was chairman of the rail converters' committee), "have we a similar agreement with you?"

Mr. Johnson was a small, spare man; he spoke very deliberately:

"Mr. Carnegie, when an agreement is presented to me to sign, I read it carefully, and if it don't suit me, I don't sign it, and if it does suit me, I do sign it, and when I sign it I keep it."

"There again speaks the self-respecting American workman," I said.

Turning now to the chairman of the blast-furnaces committee, an Irishman named Kelly, I addressed the same question to him:

"Mr. Kelly, have we an agreement with you covering the remainder of this year?"

Mr. Kelly answered that he couldn't say exactly. There was a paper sent round and he signed it, but didn't read it over carefully, and didn't understand just what was in it. At this moment our superintendent, Captain Jones, excellent manager, but impulsive, exclaimed abruptly:

"Now, Mr. Kelly, you know I read that over twice and discussed it with you!"

"Order, order, Captain! Mr. Kelly is entitled to give his explanation. I sign many a paper that I do not read—documents our lawyers and partners present to me to sign. Mr. Kelly states that he signed this document under such circumstances and his statement must be received. But, Mr. Kelly, I have always found that the best way is to carry out the provisions of the agreement one signs carelessly and resolve to be more careful next time. Would it not be better for you to continue four months longer under this agreement, and then, when you sign the next one, see that you understand it?"

There was no answer to this, and I arose and said:

"Gentlemen of the Blast-Furnace Committee, you have threatened our firm that you will break your agreement and that you will leave these blast furnaces (which means disaster) unless you get a favorable answer to your threat by four o'clock to-day. It is not yet three, but your answer is ready. You may leave the blast furnaces. The grass will grow around them before we yield to your threat. The worst day that labor has ever seen in this world is that day in which it dishonors itself by breaking its agreement. You have your answer."

The committee filed out slowly and there was silence among the partners. A stranger who was coming in on business met the committee in the passage and he reported:

"As I came in, a man wearing spectacles pushed up alongside of an Irishman he called Kelly, and he said: 'You fellows might just as well understand it now as later. There's to be no d——d monkeying round these works.'"

That meant business. Later we heard from one of our clerks what took place at the furnaces. Kelly and his committee marched down to them. Of course, the men were waiting and watching for the committee and a crowd had gathered. When the furnaces were reached, Kelly called out to them:

"Get to work, you spalpeens, what are you doing here? Begorra, the little boss just hit from the shoulder. He won't fight, but he says he has sat down, and begorra, we all know he'll be a skeleton afore he rises. Get to work, ye spalpeens."

The Irish and Scotch-Irish are queer, but the easiest and best fellows to get on with, if you only know how. That man Kelly was my stanch friend and admirer ever afterward, and he was before that one of our most violent men. My experience is that you can always rely upon the great body of working-men to do what is right, provided they have not taken up a position and promised their leaders to stand by them. But their loyalty to their leaders even when mistaken, is something to make us proud of them. Anything can be done with men who have this feeling of loyalty within them. They only need to be treated fairly.

The way a strike was once broken at our steel-rail mills is interesting. Here again, I am sorry to say, one hundred and thirty-four men in one department had bound themselves under secret oath to demand increased wages at the end of the year, several months away. The new year proved very unfavorable for business, and other iron and steel manufacturers throughout the country had effected reductions in wages. Nevertheless, these men, having secretly sworn months previously that they would not work unless they got increased wages, thought themselves bound to insist upon their demands. We could not advance wages when our competitors were reducing them, and the works were stopped in consequence. Every department of the works was brought to a stand by these strikers. The blast furnaces were abandoned a day or two before the time agreed upon, and we were greatly troubled in consequence.

I went to Pittsburgh and was surprised to find the furnaces had been banked, contrary to agreement. I was to meet the men in the morning upon arrival at Pittsburgh, but a message was sent to me from the works stating that the men had "left the furnaces and would meet me to-morrow." Here was a nice reception! My reply was:

"No they won't. Tell them I shall not be here to-morrow. Anybody can stop work; the trick is to start it again. Some fine day these men will want the works started and will be looking around for somebody who can start them, and I will tell them then just what I do now: that the works will never start except upon a sliding scale based upon the prices we get for our products. That scale will last three years and it will not be submitted by the men. They have submitted many scales to us. It is our turn now, and we are going to submit a scale to them.

"Now," I said to my partners, "I am going back to New York in the afternoon. Nothing more is to be done."

A short time after my message was received by the men they asked if they could come in and see me that afternoon before I left.

I answered: "Certainly!"

They came in and I said to them:

"Gentlemen, your chairman here, Mr. Bennett, assured you that I would make my appearance and settle with you in some way or other, as I always have settled. That is true. And he told you that I would not fight, which is also true. He is a true prophet. But he told you something else in which he was slightly mistaken. He said I could not fight. Gentlemen," looking Mr. Bennett straight in the eye and closing and raising my fist, "he forgot that I was Scotch. But I will tell you something; I will never fight you. I know better than to fight labor. I will not fight, but I can beat any committee that was ever made at sitting down, and I have sat down. These works will never start until the men vote by a two-thirds majority to start them, and then, as I told you this morning, they will start on our sliding scale. I have nothing more to say."

They retired. It was about two weeks afterwards that one of the house servants came to my library in New York with a card, and I found upon it the names of two of our workmen, and also the name of a reverend gentleman. The men said they were from the works at Pittsburgh and would like to see me.

"Ask if either of these gentlemen belongs to the blast-furnace workers who banked the furnaces contrary to agreement."

The man returned and said "No." I replied: "In that case go down and tell them that I shall be pleased to have them come up."

Document Text

Of course they were received with genuine warmth and cordiality and we sat and talked about New York, for some time, this being their first visit.

"Mr. Carnegie, we really came to talk about the trouble at the works," the minister said at last.

"Oh, indeed!" I answered. "Have the men voted?"

"No," he said.

My rejoinder was:

"You will have to excuse me from entering upon that subject; I said I never would discuss it until they voted by a two-thirds majority to start the mills. Gentlemen, you have never seen New York. Let me take you out and show you Fifth Avenue and the Park, and we shall come back here to lunch at half-past one."

This we did, talking about everything except the one thing that they wished to talk about. We had a good time, and I know they enjoyed their lunch. There is one great difference between the American working-man and the foreigner. The American is a man; he sits down at lunch with people as if he were (as he generally is) a gentleman born. It is splendid.

They returned to Pittsburgh, not another word having been said about the works. But the men soon voted (there were very few votes against starting) and I went again to Pittsburgh. I laid before the committee the scale under which they were to work. It was a sliding scale based on the price of the product. Such a scale really makes capital and labor partners, sharing prosperous and disastrous times together. Of course it has a minimum, so that the men are always sure of living wages. As the men had seen these scales, it was unnecessary to go over them. The chairman said:

"Mr. Carnegie, we will agree to everything. And now," he said hesitatingly, "we have one favor to ask of you, and we hope you will not refuse it."

"Well, gentlemen, if it be reasonable I shall surely grant it."

"Well, it is this: That you permit the officers of the union to sign these papers for the men."

"Why, certainly, gentlemen! With the greatest pleasure! And then I have a small favor to ask of you, which I hope you will not refuse, as I have granted yours. Just to please me, after the officers have signed, let every workman sign also for himself. You see, Mr. Bennett, this scale lasts for three years, and some man, or body of men, might dispute whether your president of the union had authority to bind them for so long, but if we have his signature also, there cannot be any misunderstanding."

There was a pause; then one man at his side whispered to Mr. Bennett (but I heard him perfectly):

"By golly, the jig's up!"

So it was, but it was not by direct attack, but by a flank movement. Had I not allowed the union officers to sign, they would have had a grievance and an excuse for war. As it was, having allowed them to do so, how could they refuse so simple a request as mine, that each free and independent American citizen should also sign for himself. My recollection is that as a matter of fact the officers of the union never signed, but they may have done so. Why should they, if every man's signature was required? Besides this, the workmen, knowing that the union could do nothing for them when the scale was adopted, neglected to pay dues and the union was deserted. We never heard of it again. [That was in 1889, now twenty-seven years ago. The scale has never been changed. The men would not change it if they could; it works for their benefit, as I told them it would.]

Of all my services rendered to labor the introduction of the sliding scale is chief. It is the solution of the capital and labor problem, because it really makes them partners—alike in prosperity and adversity. There was a yearly scale in operation in the Pittsburgh district in the early years, but it is not a good plan because men and employers at once begin preparing for a struggle which is almost certain to come. It is far better for both employers and employed to set no date for an agreed-upon scale to end. It should be subject to six months' or a year's notice on either side, and in that way might and probably would run on for years.

To show upon what trifles a contest between capital and labor may turn, let me tell of two instances which were amicably settled by mere incidents of seemingly little consequence. Once when I went out to meet a men's committee, which had in our opinion made unfair demands, I was informed that they were influenced by a man who secretly owned a drinking saloon, although working in the mills. He was a great bully. The sober, quiet workmen were afraid of him, and the drinking men were his debtors. He was the real instigator of the movement.

We met in the usual friendly fashion. I was glad to see the men, many of whom I had long known and could call by name. When we sat down at the table the leader's seat was at one end and mine at the other. We therefore faced each other. After I had laid our proposition before the meeting, I saw the leader pick up his hat from the floor and slowly put it on his head, intimating that he was about to depart. Here was my chance.

"Sir, you are in the presence of gentlemen! Please be so good as to take your hat off or leave the room!"

My eyes were kept full upon him. There was a silence that could be felt. The great bully hesitated, but I knew whatever he did, he was beaten. If he left it was because he had treated the meeting discourteously by keeping his hat on, he was no gentleman; if he remained and took off his hat, he had been crushed by the rebuke. I didn't care which course he took. He had only two and either of them was fatal. He had delivered himself into my hands. He very slowly took off the hat and put it on the floor. Not a word did he speak thereafter in that conference. I was told afterward that he had to leave the place. The men rejoiced in the episode and a settlement was harmoniously effected.

When the three years' scale was proposed to the men, a committee of sixteen was chosen by them to confer with us. Little progress was made at first, and I announced my engagements compelled me to return the next day to New York. Inquiry was made as to whether we would meet a committee of thirty-two, as the men wished others added to the committee—a sure sign of division in their ranks. Of course we agreed. The committee came from the works to meet me at the office in Pittsburgh. The proceedings were opened by one of our best men, Billy Edwards (I remember him well; he rose to high position afterwards), who thought that the total offered was fair, but that the scale was not equable. Some departments were all right, others were not fairly dealt with. Most of the men were naturally of this opinion, but when they came to indicate the underpaid, there was a difference, as was to be expected. No two men in the different departments could agree. Billy began:

"Mr. Carnegie, we agree that the total sum per ton to be paid is fair, but we think it is not properly distributed among us. Now, Mr. Carnegie, you take my job—"

"Order, order!" I cried. "None of that, Billy. Mr. Carnegie 'takes no man's job.' Taking another's job is an unpardonable offense among high-classed workmen."

There was loud laughter, followed by applause, and then more laughter. I laughed with them. We had scored on Billy. Of course the dispute was soon settled. It is not solely, often it is not chiefly, a matter of dollars with workmen. Appreciation, kind treatment, a fair deal—these are often the potent forces with the American workmen.

Employers can do so many desirable things for their men at little cost. At one meeting when I asked what we could do for them, I remember this same Billy Edwards rose and said that most of the men had to run in debt to the storekeepers because they were paid monthly. Well I remember his words:

"I have a good woman for wife who manages well. We go into Pittsburgh every fourth Saturday afternoon and buy our supplies wholesale for the next month and save one third. Not many of your men can do this. Shopkeepers here charge so much. And another thing, they charge very high for coal. If you paid your men every two weeks, instead of monthly, it would be as good for the careful men as a raise in wages of ten per cent or more."

"Mr. Edwards, that shall be done," I replied.

It involved increased labor and a few more clerks, but that was a small matter. The remark about high prices charged set me to thinking why the men could not open a coöperative store. This was also arranged—the firm agreeing to pay the rent of the building, but insisting that the men themselves take the stock and manage it. Out of that came the Braddock's Coöperative Society, a valuable institution for many reasons, not the least of them that it taught the men that business had its difficulties.

The coal trouble was cured effectively by our agreeing that the company sell all its men coal at the net cost price to us (about half of what had been charged by coal dealers, so I was told) and arranging to deliver it at the men's houses—the buyer paying only actual cost of cartage.

There was another matter. We found that the men's savings caused them anxiety, for little faith have the prudent, saving men in banks and, unfortunately, our Government at that time did not follow the British in having post-office deposit banks. We offered to take the actual savings of each workman, up to two thousand dollars, and pay six per cent interest upon them, to encourage thrift. Their money was kept separate from the business, in a trust fund, and lent to such as wished to build homes for themselves. I consider this one of the best things that can be done for the saving workman.

It was such concessions as these that proved the most profitable investments ever made by the company, even from an economical standpoint. It pays to go beyond the letter of the bond with your men. Two of my partners, as Mr. Phipps has put it, "knew my extreme disposition to always grant the demands of labor, however unreasonable," but looking back upon my failing in this respect, I wish it had been greater—much greater. No expenditure returned such dividends as the friendship of our workmen.

Document Text

We soon had a body of workmen, I truly believe, wholly unequaled—the best workmen and the best men ever drawn together. Quarrels and strikes became things of the past. Had the Homestead men been our own old men, instead of men we had to pick up, it is scarcely possible that the trouble there in 1892 could have arisen. The scale at the steel-rail mills, introduced in 1889, has been running up to the present time (1914), and I think there never has been a labor grievance at the works since. The men, as I have already stated, dissolved their old union because there was no use paying dues to a union when the men themselves had a three years' contract. Although their labor union is dissolved another and a better one has taken its place—a cordial union between the employers and their men, the best union of all for both parties.

It is for the interest of the employer that his men shall make good earnings and have steady work. The sliding scale enables the company to meet the market; and sometimes to take orders and keep the works running, which is the main thing for the workingmen. High wages are well enough, but they are not to be compared with steady employment. The Edgar Thomson Mills are, in my opinion, the ideal works in respect to the relations of capital and labor. I am told the men in our day, and even to this day (1914) prefer two to three turns, but three turns are sure to come. Labor's hours are to be shortened as we progress. Eight hours will be the rule—eight for work, eight for sleep, and eight for rest and recreation.

There have been many incidents in my business life proving that labor troubles are not solely founded upon wages. I believe the best preventive of quarrels to be recognition of, and sincere interest in, the men, satisfying them that you really care for them and that you rejoice in their success. This I can sincerely say—that I always enjoyed my conferences with our workmen, which were not always in regard to wages, and that the better I knew the men the more I liked them. They have usually two virtues to the employer's one, and they are certainly more generous to each other.

Labor is usually helpless against capital. The employer, perhaps, decides to shut up the shops; he ceases to make profits for a short time. There is no change in his habits, food, clothing, pleasures—no agonizing fear of want. Contrast this with his workman whose lessening means of subsistence torment him. He has few comforts, scarcely the necessities for his wife and children in health, and for the sick little ones no proper treatment. It is not capital we need to guard, but helpless labor. If I returned to business to-morrow, fear of labor troubles would not enter my mind, but tenderness for poor and sometimes misguided though well-meaning laborers would fill my heart and soften it; and thereby soften theirs.

Upon my return to Pittsburgh in 1892, after the Homestead trouble, I went to the works and met many of the old men who had not been concerned in the riot. They expressed the opinion that if I had been at home the strike would never have happened. I told them that the company had offered generous terms and beyond its offer I should not have gone; that before their cable reached me in Scotland, the Governor of the State had appeared on the scene with troops and wished the law vindicated; that the question had then passed out of my partners' hands. I added:

"You were badly advised. My partners' offer should have been accepted. It was very generous. I don't know that I would have offered so much."

To this one of the rollers said to me:

"Oh, Mr. Carnegie, it wasn't a question of dollars. The boys would have let you kick 'em, but they wouldn't let that other man stroke their hair."

So much does sentiment count for in the practical affairs of life, even with the laboring classes. This is not generally believed by those who do not know them, but I am certain that disputes about wages do not account for one half the disagreements between capital and labor. There is lack of due appreciation and of kind treatment of employees upon the part of the employers.

Suits had been entered against many of the strikers, but upon my return these were promptly dismissed. All the old men who remained, and had not been guilty of violence, were taken back. I had cabled from Scotland urging that Mr. Schwab be sent back to Homestead. He had been only recently promoted to the Edgar Thomson Works. He went back, and "Charlie," as he was affectionately called, soon restored order, peace, and harmony. Had he remained at the Homestead Works, in all probability no serious trouble would have arisen. "Charlie" liked his workmen and they liked him; but there still remained at Homestead an unsatisfactory element in the men who had previously been discarded from our various works for good reasons and had found employment at the new works before we purchased them.

Birthplace of Andrew Carnegie in Dunfermline, Scotland

Salmon Portland Chase (13 January 1808 – 7 May 1873) **was an American politician and jurist who served as United States Senator from Ohio and the 23rd Governor of Ohio; as U.S. Treasury Secretary under President Abraham Lincoln; and as the sixth Chief Justice of the United States Supreme Court. by Mathew Brady.**

Salmon P. Chase: Original Analysis

Governor, U.S. Senator, and Sixth Chief Justice of the United States

1808–1873

Overview

Salmon Portland Chase emerged over the course of his career as one of the most effective antislavery advocates in pre–Civil War politics. Driven by a desire for high office that even his allies found unnerving, Chase served as U.S. senator, governor of Ohio, U.S. treasury secretary, and, finally, as chief justice of the United States. Along the way, however, Chase consistently advocated for the cause of abolition and racial equality in the United States. He appeared on the national scene in the 1840s as a leader of the antislavery Liberty Party and a lawyer for fugitive slaves and the people who harbored them. In the 1840s and 1850s he articulated an influential narrative portraying the Constitution as a fundamentally antislavery document that had been distorted by a corrupt Slave Power. This narrative became part of the core of the new Republican Party's ideology in the 1850s. Although he never managed to parley his influence into a presidential nomination, Chase maneuvered himself into positions where he could force his commitments to abolition and racial equality into the center of antebellum politics and beyond. In so doing, he helped transform antislavery from a marginal political force in the 1840s to a dominant (and successful) one by the 1860s.

Explanation and Analysis of Documents

Chase dedicated his career to the ambitious pursuit of high office and the idealistic goals of abolition and equal rights for all Americans. The three documents that follow illustrate both aspects of his career as he moved from being a relatively obscure lawyer and state-level politician arguing against the constitutionality of the Fugitive Slave Law of 1793 to U.S. senator warning his constituents about dangers of a Slave Power and then to chief justice of the United States adjudicating the constitutionality of secession and Reconstruction policy.

♦ Reclamation of Fugitives from Service

Chase's career as a major antislavery figure began when he moved to Cincinnati, Ohio, in 1830. Within a few years of his arrival, Chase had established a successful legal practice, had become active in the city's political circles, and had thrown himself into a range of reform causes. By the mid-1830s those causes included abolition—the immediate end to slavery in the United States—and Chase made his contribution by defending fugitives fleeing to Ohio from southern border states. He had not picked an easy battle. Under Article 4, Section 2, of the Constitution, the so-called fugitive slave clause, masters and their agents held a right to track down runaway slaves in free states such as Ohio and take them back to the South. Congress had affirmed that right in a 1793 statute and even gave it more teeth by imposing stiff penalties on those who aided fugitives during their escape. Chase's challenge would become more daunting after 1842, when the U.S. Supreme Court ruled that the Fugitive Slave Law of 1793 was constitutional. In 1847 Chase asked the Court to revisit that decision in *Jones v. Van Zandt*, in which he defended a person accused of harboring fugitive slaves. His brief, which he later published under the title *Reclamation of Fugitives from Service*, made little headway with the justices, but it did present an analysis of the Constitution as a fundamentally antislavery document that would become highly influential in northern political circles.

Jones dealt with the question of harboring fugitives, and much of the brief involved Chase's effort to convince the justices (ultimately unsuccessfully) that his client had harbored no fugitives within the meaning of the Fugitive Slave Law. Chase, however, reaches beyond that issue and argues that the 1793 law violated both the Revolutionary generation's commitment to liberty and a proper understanding of the Constitution itself. Chase first has to convince the Court to reject its ruling in *Prigg v. Pennsylvania*, which upheld the Fugitive Slave Law of 1793. He notes that the justices in that case disagreed sharply as to why the law was constitutional. "In no former case," Chase asserts, "has so great a diversity of views marked the reasonings by which the several judges of this Court have reached their respective conclusions." Such division of opinion undermined the ruling's authority. "The decision," Chase notes, "has failed to command the assent of the profession, especially in the nonslaveholding states." And among nonlawyers, *Prigg* was "so repugnant to the feelings of all classes of men in the north and northwest … that it encounters, at this moment, a degree of jealousy and hostility beyond all former precedent."

Such hostility, Chase implies, came about because the Fugitive Slave Law departed from the original antislavery intent of America's founding. Reviewing the historical record, Chase argues that all parties involved in forming the U.S. government understood that "the practice of slaveholding was inconsistent with the principles on which that

government was to be founded." The Continental Congress's first act "contained a clause, by which the delegates pledged themselves and their constituents to discontinue, wholly, the traffic in slaves." Two years later, that body issued the Declaration of Independence and "and in that solemn appeal to God and Mankind, chose to put their cause upon the solid foundation of equality of rights among men." Every state adopted the Declaration of Independence, and in so doing committed themselves to antislavery principles. "It is not going too far ... to hold this declaration to be an authentic promulgation of the common law of the Union in respect to the inviolability and inalienability of personal liberty, and inconsistent with the longer continuance of slavery in any of the States."

Further proof of the Revolutionary generation's antislavery commitments came from the Northwest Ordinance (1787), which organized the territory that eventually became the states of Illinois, Indiana, Ohio, Michigan, and Wisconsin. The ordinance contained a clause prohibiting the introduction of slavery in the territory. "By that great instrument the Congress of the Confederation dedicated that immense national domain to liberty forever, and thus, by one illustrious act, manifested its own sincerity, and furnished a precedent for national action, in all future cases of like nature." This antislavery sentiment, Chase insists, extended throughout the Union. By 1787, only seven states had not taken steps to end slavery, and some of them—notably Maryland and Virginia—displayed an interest in emancipation. Thus, when the Constitutional Convention met in 1787 there was no expectation that "slavery would be a permanent institution of any state." The framers, Chase notes, deliberately excluded "all recognition of the rightfulness of slaveholding, and all national sanction to the practice." The word "slave" never appeared in the document. Although there were some clauses that obliquely referred to slavery, "not one of them refers to slavery as a national institution, to be upheld by national law." Rather, the national government sought to discourage slavery "by the powerful influence of example and recommendation."

This analysis ran counter to the Court's constitutional interpretation, which assumed, rightly or wrongly, that slavery was a legitimate institution and considered the clauses recognizing slaveholding to be the product of fundamental compromises that made the Union possible. Chase simply dismisses that position as a wrong. A pro-slavery reading of the document, he writes, was "a pernicious parasite ... which, planted by ... the constitutional oak, by other hands than those of the Founders ... , has twined itself around the venerable tree, and now displays its poisonous fruits and foliage from every branch." A proper reading of the document, he insists, would demonstrate the incompatibility between slavery and the Constitution. The Constitution recognized no slaves; it recognized only persons, although those persons may have been "bound to service" in the language of the fugitive slave clause or "imported" in the clause dealing with the slave trade. All persons, regardless of status, received constitutional protections that the

Time Line

1808	January 13	■ Salmon P. Chase is born in Cornish, New Hampshire.
1829		■ Chase is admitted to the bar in the District of Columbia.
1835		■ Chase embraces abolitionism.
1837		■ Chase conducts his first legal defense for a fugitive from slavery.
1841		■ Chase joins the Liberty Party.
1847		■ In his brief in *Jones v. Van Zandt,* Chase challenges the constitutionality of the Fugitive Slave Law of 1793 before the U.S. Supreme Court. He later publishes his brief under the title *Reclamation of Fugitives from Service.*
1848	August	■ Chase helps form the Free-Soil Party.
1849	March 4	■ Chase becomes a U.S. senator and joins opposition to the Compromise of 1850, a series of laws passed to balance sectional rivalries arising from slavery.
1854	January 19	■ Chase publishes "Appeal of the Independent Democrats in Congress to the People of the United States"; that year he leads opposition to the Kansas-Nebraska Act and helps form the Republican Party.
1856	January 14	■ Chase becomes governor of Ohio.
1860		■ Chase emerges as a contender for the Republican Party's presidential nomination.
1861	March 7	■ Chase becomes Treasury secretary for President Abraham Lincoln.

Time Line		
1864	December 15	■ Chase becomes chief justice of the United States.
1868	March–May	■ Chase presides over the impeachment trial of President Andrew Johnson.
1869	April 12	■ Chase rejects secession's constitutionality in his decision in *Texas v. White*.
1873	May 7	■ Chase dies in New York City.

Fugitive Slave Law violated. Contrary to the Fifth Amendment, the 1793 law deprived alleged fugitives of their Fourth and Fifth Amendment rights by subjecting them to seizing them unlawfully and depriving them of due process.

This law, Chase writes, threatens everyone. A person acting under the provisions of this act need not limit himself to African Americans. Any person could be defined as a servant and swept up under the law. Surely an act that would sanction such abuses must be unconstitutional. None of these arguments, however, swayed the Court, and the justices likewise found unpersuasive Chase's suggestions that Congress possessed no power to legislate on the subject of fugitive slaves or that the common law remedy of replevin, which Court used to explain the masters' right to reclaim alleged fugitives, was outdated and unsuited to American conditions. Justice Levi Woodbury, speaking for the Court, took note of the lengthy brief and then dismissed it in a paragraph.

Despite his loss, Chase introduced a number of arguments that would become highly influential off the Court. His portrayal of the Constitution as a fundamentally antislavery document, an interpretation that many historians find questionable, appealed to politicians attracted to antislavery but leery of arguments put forth by such abolitionists as William Lloyd Garrison or Wendell Phillips that portrayed the Constitution as essentially pro-slavery. Chase's contention that the federal system had lost sight of its original commitment to antislavery and needed to be placed back on track would become a staple of Republican Party ideology in the 1850s. So would his contention that a sinister force was bending the Constitution in pro-slavery directions. In the late 1840s, however, these ideas had not yet captured the imagination of the public. But Chase's advocacy of them made him an important figure in the Free Soil movement, which he used to launch himself into the U.S. Senate, where he would wait for another issue to propel his ideas forward.

♦ "Appeal of the Independent Democrats in Congress to the People of the United States"

The issue Chase would use to advance his ideas came in 1854, when Senator Stephen Douglas of Illinois began pushing a piece of legislation to organize the Kansas and Nebraska territories as part of his larger effort to secure a transcontinental rail line that would run through his home state. Douglas's effort to get the law through Congress required the support of southern legislators, who had their own ideas about where a rail line should run. As a concession to them, Douglas's bill repealed the antislavery provision of the Missouri Compromise—an agreement struck in 1820 between northern and southern legislators that allowed Missouri to enter the Union as a slave state in exchange for closing to slavery all the other federal territory (then held) that lay north of 36°30′ latitude (Missouri's southern border). Douglas's concession potentially opened all this territory to slavery and violated what Chase considered to be a sacred agreement between the slave and free states (although he had earlier criticized the compromise as a capitulation to the South). Interpreting this legislation as an act of pro-slavery aggression, Chase, together with his antislavery colleagues Senator Charles Sumner and Representatives Joshua R. Giddings, Edward Wade, Gerrit Smith, and Alexander DeWitt, published their "Appeal of the Independent Democrats in Congress to the People of the United States" and articulated the threat facing the North's citizens. The "Appeal," which some historians have characterized as one of the most successful works of political propaganda in American history, restated themes that had appeared in Chase's *Reclamation of Fugitives from Service* but did so in a way emphasizing that the expansion of slavery would strangle the free states.

Chase describes the pending Kansas-Nebraska bill as an imminent threat. He describes the bill "as a gross violation of a sacred pledge," and declares it "as part and parcel of an atrocious plot to exclude from a vast unoccupied region, immigrants from the Old World and free laborers from our own States, and convert it into a dreary region of despotism, inhabited by masters and slaves." Pro-slavery legislators sought a huge region—"larger, by thirty-three thousand square miles, than all the existing free states excluding California." And that region, moreover, had historically been considered as reserved to the free states by a great sectional compromise. Now, Douglas's bill offered to open this territory to slavery "in flagrant disregard of sound policy and sacred faith."

The breach of faith occurred because the Kansas-Nebraska bill permitted the extension of slavery in violation of what Chase considered to be the original policy of the United States. The Northwest Ordinance had set out the principles of nonextension in the 1780s, although Congress failed to adhere to them in 1803 when it refused to abolish slavery in the territory acquired in the Louisiana Purchase and in 1812 when it allowed Louisiana to join the Union as a slave state. The Missouri Compromise constituted a restoration of the original policy. Missouri petitioned Congress

in 1818 to enter the Union as a slave state, and opponents of the petition overcame fierce opposition in the House of Representatives to pass a measure that would gradually abolish slavery in the new state and close the federal territories to slavery. The measure then failed to pass the Senate, but at the next session Congress reached the compromise and established the 36°30′ line. This compromise represented a sectional agreement. President James Monroe's cabinet, which included such prominent southern politicians as William Wirt of Virginia, William Crawford of Georgia, and John C. Calhoun of South Carolina, gave the compromise written support. Northern members of Congress, Chase continues, would have never dropped their opposition to Missouri's admission without the prohibition on the extension of slavery.

But the North gained little from this arrangement. Three slave states—Louisiana, Missouri, and Arkansas—had emerged in the territory south of the 36°30⊠ line, but only a single free state—Iowa—had emerged in the northern portion. The free states, Chase writes, upheld their end of the agreement, but the slave states, which had nothing more to gain from the compromise, now sought repeal. Acquiescing to southern demands would amount to an act of dishonor, and Chase predicts dire consequences if the bill were to pass. Indeed, the railroad sought by Douglas might never be built. The presence of slavery would drive free laborers away, for "labor cannot be respected where any class of laborers is held in abject bondage." The exclusion of the free states' "energetic and intelligent masses" would defeat American's original vision of this territory. "Patriotic statesmen … anticipated … a free, industrious, and enlightened population," consisting of "freedom-loving emigrants from Europe, and energetic and intelligent laborers of our own land," who would together "extract abundant treasures of individual and public wealth" from the territorial soil. If Congress allowed "the blight of Slavery" to "cover the land," such developments would not take place. Free laborers simply would not migrate to the region. "Freemen, unless pressed by a hard and cruel necessity, will not, and should not, work beside slaves."

Of course, the threat posed by this act extended well beyond the territories of Kansas and Nebraska. The bill formed part of an effort to impose slavery throughout the Union. Chase describes the bill as "a bold scheme against American Liberty, worthy of an accomplished architect of ruin." If the bill passed, slave territory would stretch from Texas's southern border to Canada, and new free states and territories such as California and Oregon would be cut off from their counterparts to the east. That division went to the crux of the plan:

It is hoped … by compelling the whole commerce and the whole travel between the East and West to pass for hundreds of miles through a slaveholding region … and by the influence of a Federal Government controlled by a Slave Power, to extinguish Freedom and establish Slavery in the States and Territories of the Pacific, and subjugate the whole country to the yoke of a slaveholding despotism.

This bill demanded fierce resistance. Giving in would destroy the cause of liberty and justice, which was what the Union had stood for since its founding. Chase and his fellow signatories here vow to fight and to persist even in defeat because "the cause of human freedom is the cause of God."

The arguments presented in the "Appeal" helped transform American politics in the 1850s. Part of that transformation resulted from Chase's impeccable timing. He had asked Douglas, the bill's sponsor, to delay debate so that he could study the text, but his request was primarily a pretext for him to buy time to allow publication of the "Appeal" to be the opening shot in the debate. The "Appeal" also employed new political tactics by framing issues in terms of moral absolutes and by denouncing supporters of slavery as inherently evil men who could not be trusted. Douglas's bill was not poor policy; it was a "violation of a sacred pledge," part of "an atrocious plot," and "a bold scheme against American Liberty." Douglas and those who helped him craft the bill were "architect[s] of ruin" connected to a "Slave Power" determined to force slavery into the federal territories and even into California.

This argument—that a conspiracy of corrupt politicians would stop at nothing to expand slavery throughout the Union and would respect no agreement that stood in their way—would become an article of faith for the new Republican Party, which organized in the wake of the debate over the Kansas-Nebraska Act. Later events such as the Supreme Court's *Dred Scott* decision (1857), which held the Missouri Compromise to be unconstitutional, and the debate over the Lecompton Constitution (1857), Kansas's second attempt at a constitution, which tried to force Kansas into the Union as a slave state over the wishes of its inhabitants, convinced a majority of northern voters that Chase and his colleagues were right. Indeed, Chase advanced his political career considerably during this period as he moved from the Senate to the governorship of Ohio, emerged as a contender for the Republican presidential nomination in 1856 and 1860, served as President Abraham Lincoln's Treasury secretary through most of the Civil War, and then became chief justice of the United States.

♦ *Texas v. White*

As chief justice, Chase found himself as a referee for the Union's partisan and sectional struggles rather than a participant. When he presided over President Andrew Johnson's impeachment trial, for example, Chase insisted—to the point of alienating many of his once-close Republican allies—that the Senate follow judicial procedures rather than legislative ones that would have put Johnson at a disadvantage. Chase also had the opportunity to provide judicial oversight of Reconstruction—the process by which the rebelling southern states rejoined the Union. The chief justice had numerous disagreements with Congress's

handling of particular aspects of Reconstruction policy. He maneuvered his Court, however, in a manner that allowed it to affirm generally the goals of Radical Reconstruction—stringent policies with regard to the rebellious South after the Civil War advocated by the so-called Radical Republicans—while leaving troublesome particulars to the discretion of Congress. In so doing, Chase helped to cement the abolition of slavery and to create a foundation for the legal recognition of racial equality. *Texas v. White*, a case that superficially had nothing to do with these issues, illustrates how he did so.

Texas v. White involved a dispute over bonds that had been issued by the United States to Texas during the 1850s and then sold to third parties so that the state could fund its war effort against the Union. Before secession, Texas law mandated that these bonds could not be sold without the endorsement of the governor. The bonds in question lacked his signature, but Texas had changed its law shortly after it had left the Union, and the bonds had been sold in conformity with the new policy. The Court needed to decide which was the legitimate procedure. Before it could do so, the Court had to solve a jurisdictional problem because secession raised the question of whether Texas had remained a state within the meaning of the Constitution. Chase answered that Texas did indeed remain a state, and he did so in a manner that affirmed Congress's authority to reconstruct the southern states.

Despite its secession, Chase argues, Texas never ceased being a state. When it joined the United States in 1845, Texas entered "an indissoluble relation," binding it to "all the obligations of perpetual union, and all the guaranties of republican government in the Union." The state's decision was final, and the bond between Texas and the United States could not be broken except by mutual consent or by revolution. The state opted for the latter and failed. Consequently, "the ordinance of secession … and all the acts of her legislature intended to give effect to that ordinance, were absolutely null." But secession did alter the relationship between the state's government and the United States: "The government and the citizens of the State, refusing to recognize their constitutional obligations, assumed the character of enemies, and incurred the consequences of rebellion." Those actions required the federal government to assume the duties of putting down the rebellion and "of re-establishing the broken relations of the State with the Union." Fulfilling that duty compelled the president and Congress to create a temporary government for the state. Doing so was a pressing need because the war had shattered the rebellious government's ability to function and because the "great social change" wrought by emancipation demanded that new governments include recently freed African Americans as constituent members.

Chase at this point affirms the federal government's authority to reconstruct the South by viewing the Constitution's provision guaranteeing every state a republican government in the context of emancipation. At the end of the war, "the new freemen necessarily became part of the people, and the people … constituted the State." This newly constituted body politic required a republican government that represented its interests, and the Constitution's guarantee clause mandated that one be provided. That clause, however, gave the federal government wide discretion over the precise means used to carry out the guarantee. The only "essential" requirements were "that the means must be necessary and proper for carrying into execution the power conferred … and that no acts be done … which [are] either prohibited or unsanctioned by the Constitution." Because he construed the clause so broadly, Chase had no need to inquire closely into the specifics of Reconstruction policy. His view encompassed both the relatively conciliatory plans of Presidents Lincoln and Johnson as well as the more punitive ones advocated in Congress. His Court need not make a choice, and it avoided inserting itself into the central political issues of the late 1860s. At the same time, Chase affirms the unconstitutionally of secession—which meant that the owners of the bonds in question were not legitimate holders—and he makes the inclusion of freedmen in the polity a basic premise of a properly constituted republican government. With that ruling, Chase introduced into constitutional law ideas that would have never been thought possible by Supreme Court justices two decades before.

Impact and Legacy

Although Chase never achieved all his goals—he did not become president, and the nation's commitment to racial equality proved weak in the nineteenth century—Chase did help make emancipation possible in the United States. His persistence allowed him to carry forward a set of ideas that the Supreme Court could essentially dismiss as foolish in the 1840s and transform them into an organizing force for the Republican Party a few years later. The success of his party propelled Chase into positions from which he and his allies could transform those ideas into policy, and by the time of his death in 1873, Chase could claim that he had come a long way toward restoring the Founders' vision of the Constitution, as he understood it.

Key Sources

The Library of Congress houses the Salmon P. Chase Papers, but major research libraries often own microfilm versions. John Niven and his associate editors have recently published many of his papers in the five-volume *The Salmon P. Chase Papers* (1993–1998), which features his journals and correspondence from 1823 to 1873.

Essential Quotes

"It was the original policy of the government of the United States, to prohibit slavery, in all territory subject to its exclusive jurisdiction, and to discountenance it by the moral influence of its example and declarations, in the states and districts over which it had no legislative control."

(*Reclamation of Fugitives from Service*)

"Every where we see the clearest evidence of deliberate purpose, to exclude all recognition of the rightfulness of slaveholding, and all national sanction to the practice, from every provision of the constitution."

(*Reclamation of Fugitives from Service*)

"The Union was formed to establish justice and secure the blessings of liberty. When it fails to accomplish these ends it will be worthless, and when it becomes worthless it cannot long endure."

("Appeal of the Independent Democrats in Congress")

"Shall a plot against humanity and Democracy, so monstrous, and so dangerous to the interests of Liberty throughout the world, be permitted to succeed?"

("Appeal of the Independent Democrats in Congress")

"When, therefore, Texas became one of the United States, she entered into an indissoluble relation.… The union between Texas and the other States was as complete, as perpetual, and as indissoluble as the union between the original States. There was no place for reconsideration, or revocation, except through revolution, or through consent of the States."

(*Texas v. White*)

"The Union of the States never was a purely artificial and arbitrary relation. It began among the Colonies, and grew out of common origin, mutual sympathies, kindred principles, similar interests, and geographical relations."

(*Texas v. White*)

Further Reading

■ Articles

Gerteis, Louis S. "Salmon P. Chase, Radicalism, and the Politics of Emancipation, 1861–1864." *Journal of American History* 60, no. 1 (June 1973): 42–62.

Maizlish, Stephen E. "Salmon P. Chase: The Roots of Ambition and the Origins of Reform." *Journal of the Early Republic* 18, no. 1 (Spring 1998): 47–70.

Roseboom, Eugene H. "Salmon P. Chase and the Know Nothings." *Mississippi Valley Historical Review* 25, no. 3 (December 1938): 335–350.

■ Books

Blue, Frederick J. *Salmon P. Chase: A Life in Politics*. Kent, Ohio: Kent State University Press, 1987.

Foner, Eric. "Salmon P. Chase: The Constitution and the Slave Power." In *Free Soil, Free Labor, Free Men: The Ideology of the Republican Party before the Civil War*. New York: Oxford University Press, 1970.

Hyman, Harold M. *The Reconstruction of Salmon P. Chase*: In Re Turner *and* Texas v. White. Lawrence: University Press of Kansas, 1997.

Lurie, Jonathan. *The Chase Court: Justices, Rulings, and Legacy*. Santa Barbara, Calif.: ABC-CLIO, 2004.

Niven, John. *Salmon P. Chase: A Biography. New York: Oxford University Press, 1995.*

Potter, David M. *The Impending Crisis: 1848–1861*. New York: Harper and Row, 1976.

—Austin Allen

Questions for Further Study

1. What evidence does Salmon Chase marshal to support his claim that the Revolutionary War generation and the nation's founders were opposed to slavery? How does his view differ from that of many other abolitionists at the time?

2. Chase cleverly casts his antislavery appeals in ways that suggest to white northerners that slavery and proslavery agitation were a threat to them, not just to African Americans. Locate these types of appeals in the documents and explain Chase's reasoning.

3. To what extent did Chase's views and their forceful expression contribute to the formation of the Republican Party?

4. Post-Civil War Reconstruction in the South was highly controversial, pitting those who wanted vengeance against the South—or at least wanted to adopt stringent policies with regard to the South—against those who wanted to take a more lenient, forgiving policy. On which side of this divide did Chase fall? What arguments did he use to assert the federal government's authority in the postwar South?

5. Compare and contrast Chase's arguments in opposition to slavery with those of William Lloyd Garrison.

6. Contrast Chase's views regarding the extension of slavery with those of Sam Houston in his speech supporting the Compromise of 1850 and in his speech opposing the Kansas-Nebraska Act.

Reclamation of Fugitives from Service

I now reach the gravest and most momentous question in this important controversy:

Is the act of 1793 repugnant to the Constitution of the United States?

I am met at the threshold, by the objection, that this question has already received the full consideration and final decision of this Court, and is no longer an open question. But, with the greatest deference, I submit that no single decision of any tribunal, however exalted, upon a question of such high consequence as this, should be regarded as absolutely final and conclusive....

The precise question before this Court, in the memorable case of *Prigg v. Pennsylvania,* was this:... Does the Constitution of the United States ... confer on the masters of fugitive servants, the right, in person or by their agents, to retake them by force, in any state to which they may have escaped, and convey them out of such state to that from which they fled, without process or judicial sanction; and are all laws of the states to prevent kidnapping or abduction by private force, unconstitutional and void in their application to such cases? The court held that the master of a fugitive slave may pursue and recapture him, and convey him out of the state in which the seizure is made, without complying with the provisions of the act of Congress or of the state laws on the subject, and that all state legislation making such seizure and abduction penal, is unconstitutional and void.

It may be doubted, indeed, whether this decision can be quite consistent with the affirmation of the constitutionality of the act of 1793....

No question, therefore, as to the constitutionality of that act was necessarily before the court in the *Prigg* case. Its constitutionality was indeed, affirmed; by some of the judges, as the exercise of a power vested exclusively in Congress; by others, as the exercise of a power concurrent in Congress and in the state Legislatures....

In no former case, I think, has so great a diversity of views marked the reasonings by which the several judges of this Court have reached their respective conclusions. Perhaps, also, it is not too much to say, that the decision of the majority, both as to the right of recaption under the constitution, and as to the constitutionality of the act of Congress, has failed to command the assent of the profession, especially in the nonslaveholding states....

It is quite certain, also, as I think, that the right of reclamation, converted by the decision into a right of recaption, has not been fortified, but, on the contrary, seriously impaired by it. The right is placed, by the opinion of the court, upon a ground, so repugnant to the feelings of all classes of men in the north and northwest ... that it encounters, at this moment, a degree of jealousy and hostility beyond all former precedent....

I proceed, without further delay, to state the proposition which I shall endeavor to maintain. It is this: The act of Congress of February, 1793, so far as [it] relates to fugitives from service, is unconstitutional and void....

I insist, first, that the provisions of the act of 1793 are repugnant to several positive provisions of the Constitution.

In order to obtain a clear understanding of this matter, it will be necessary to advert to the circumstances of the country, and the state of public opinion, at the time of the adoption of the Constitution....

It is thought, by some, that a leading object in the formation of the Federal Constitution was to secure to the citizens of the slaveholding states their rights of property in slaves. But what is there in the history of the country, or of the Constitution, to warrant such an opinion? On the contrary, does not that history prove that it was the clear understanding of all parties concerned in the establishment of the National Government, that the practice of slaveholding was inconsistent with the principles on which that government was to be founded?...

The very first act of the first Congress of the Confederation—the memorable non-importation, non-consumption and non-exportation agreement of that illustrious body—contained a clause, by which the delegates pledged themselves and their constituents to discontinue, wholly, the traffic in slaves....

Two years afterwards the Declaration of Independence was promulgated. No one will be willing to say that its language was not carefully considered, or that the patriot statesmen, who put their names to it, were hypocrites who sought to delude

the world by empty flourishes of rhetoric. It will be admitted that they were earnest men, who meant what they said. Well, these men, at that solemn moment, and in that solemn appeal to God and Mankind, chose to put their cause upon the solid foundation of equality of rights among men.... It is not going too far, in my poor judgment, to hold this declaration to be an authentic promulgation of the common law of the Union in respect to the inviolability and inalienability of personal liberty, and inconsistent with the longer continuance of slavery in any of the States....

When the war of the revolution terminated in the recognized independence of the republic, the Congress issued an address to the states.... In the conclusion of this address, I find this passage ... "Let it be remembered, finally, that it has ever been the pride and boast of America, that the rights for which she contended, were the rights of human nature." Whatever else may be said of this, it cannot be denied that it proves, beyond controversy, that the Declaration was intended to assert the right to liberty, not as vested in a part of mankind only, but as inseparable from human nature itself....

If any man be disposed to reproach the fathers of the republic with inconsistency and hypocrisy, in not giving practical effect to their declarations in favor of liberty and the rights of human nature, let him turn to the Ordinance of 1787, and be silent. By that great instrument the Congress of the Confederation dedicated that immense national domain to liberty forever, and thus, by one illustrious act, manifested its own sincerity, and furnished a precedent for national action, in all future cases of like nature. By a single provision, the slavery, then existing in the territory, was abolished, and its future introduction was forever prohibited. And thus the Congress directly asserted, what it had before often indirectly declared, that slavery was incompatible with "the fundamental principles of civil and religious liberty," which constitute the basis of American Government.

These several national acts, it seems to me, supply conclusive proof that it was never intended that the American Nation, should be, in any sense, or in any degree, implicated in the support of slavery: but, on the contrary, that it was the original policy of the government of the United States, to prohibit slavery, in all territory subject to its exclusive jurisdiction, and to discountenance it by the moral influence of its example and declarations, in the states and districts over which it had no legislative control.

Nor is there, as it seems to me, any room for doubt that it was the general expectation, at that time, that slavery, under the influence thus exerted, would disappear from the legislation and the polity of every state, at no very distant period....

Such was the state of opinion at the time the constitution was framed; and the pages of Mr. Madison's report of the Debates in the Constitutional Convention are full of proofs of its influence upon the proceedings of that body. Every where we see the clearest evidence of deliberate purpose, to exclude all recognition of the rightfulness of slaveholding, and all national sanction to the practice, from every provision of the constitution. Mr. Madison, himself, declared that it was "wrong to admit in the constitution the idea, that there can be property in men." Neither the word "slave," nor the word "slavery," nor any term equivalent to either, is to be found in the instrument; and the exclusion of these words, is a most emphatic censure of the practice represented by them....

It is quite true that the constitution contains several clauses which were designed to refer to slaves; but not one of them refers to slavery as a national institution, to be upheld by national law. On the contrary, every clause, which ever has been, or can be construed as referring to slavery, treats it as the creature of state law, and dependent, wholly, upon state law, for its existence and continuance. Under the constitution ... the national government ... pledged ... to exert its legitimate authority to exclude it [slavery] from all national territories, and to discourage it elsewhere, by the powerful influence of example and recommendation.

A different doctrine has sprung up and found favorers since; but that doctrine is not the constitution. It is a pernicious parasite, rather, which, planted by the side of the constitutional oak, by other hands than those of the Founders of the Republic, and nurtured with malignant care, has twined itself around the venerable tree, and now displays its poisonous fruits and foliage from every branch....

I call upon this honorable court to restore the true construction of the charter of our union, by stamping with its decisive disapprobation, every attempt to introduce into it, what its framers studiously excluded from it, a sanction to "the idea that there can be property in men."

Glossary

advert:	turn attention to
Debates in the Constitutional Convention:	James Madison's chronicles of the Constitutional Convention's deliberations
disapprobation:	disapproval
inalienability:	the state of being incapable of being taken away
inviolability:	the state of being secure from violation
Mr. Madison:	James Madison (1751–1836), fourth U.S. president
non-importation, non-consumption and non-exportation agreement:	refusal by the colonists to import or consume goods from abroad and to export goods to Britain and its colonies; essentially a trade boycott
polity:	a politically organized unit; a nation
recaption:	seizure; recovery; usually used to refer to retaking property from another who holds it illegally

"Appeal of the Independent Democrats in Congress to the People of the United States"

1854

Shall Slavery be permitted in Nebraska?...

At the present session a new Nebraska bill has been reported by the Senate Committee on Territories, which, should it unhappily receive the sanction of Congress, will open all the unorganized Territories of the Union to the ingress of slavery.

We arraign this bill as a gross violation of a sacred pledge; as a criminal betrayal of precious rights; as part and parcel of an atrocious plot to exclude from a vast unoccupied region, immigrants from the Old World and free laborers from our own States, and convert it into a dreary region of despotism, inhabited by masters and slaves.

Take your maps, fellow citizens, we entreat you, and see what country it is which this bill gratuitously and recklessly proposes to open to slavery....

This immense region, occupying the very heart of the North American Continent, and larger, by thirty-three thousand square miles, than all the existing free States excluding California,... the bill now before the Senate, without reason and without excuse, but in flagrant disregard of sound policy and sacred faith, purposes to open to slavery.

We beg your attention, fellow-citizens, to a few historical facts:

The original settled policy of the United States, clearly indicated by the Jefferson proviso of 1784 and the Ordinance of 1787, was non-extension of slavery.

In 1803 Louisiana was acquired by purchase from France....

In 1818, six years later, the inhabitants of the Territory of Missouri applied to Congress for authority to form a State constitution, and for admission into the Union. There were, at that time, in the whole territory acquired from France, outside of the State of Louisiana, not three thousand slaves.

There was no apology, in the circumstances of the country, for the continuance of slavery. The original national policy was against it, and not less the plain language of the treaty under which the territory had been acquired from France.

It was proposed, therefore, to incorporate in the bill authorizing the formation of a State government, a provision requiring that the constitution of the new State should contain an article providing for the abolition of existing slavery, and prohibiting the further introduction of slaves.

This provision was vehemently and pertinaciously opposed, but finally prevailed in the House of Representatives by a decided vote. In the Senate it was rejected, and—in consequence of the disagreement between the two Houses the bill was lost.

At the next session of Congress, the controversy was renewed with increased violence. It was terminated at length by a compromise. Missouri was allowed to come into the Union with slavery; but a section was inserted in the act authorizing her admission, excluding slavery forever from all the territory acquired from France, not included in the new State, lying north of 36 deg. 30 min....

The question of the constitutionality of this prohibition was submitted by President Monroe to his cabinet. John Quincy Adams was then Secretary of State; John C. Calhoun was Secretary of War; William H. Crawford was Secretary of the Treasury; and William Wirt was Attorney-General. Each of these eminent gentlemen—three of them being from the slave states—gave a written opinion, affirming its constitutionality, and thereupon the act received the sanction of the President himself, also from a slave State.

Nothing is more certain in history than the fact that Missouri could not have been admitted as a slave State had not certain members from the free States been reconciled to the measure by the incorporation of this prohibition into the act of admission. Nothing is more certain than that this prohibition has been regarded and accepted by the whole country as a solemn compact against the extension of slavery into any part of the territory acquired from France lying north of 36 deg. 30 min, and not included in the new State of Missouri....

It is a strange and ominous fact, well calculated to awaken the worst apprehensions and the most fearful forebodings of future calamities, that it is now deliberately proposed to repeal this prohibition, by implication or directly—the latter certainly the manlier way—and thus to subvert the compact, and allow slavery in all the yet unorganized territory....

Document Text

What will be the effect of this measure ... upon the proposed Pacific Railroad?... Two of the principal routes ... traverse this territory. If Slavery be allowed there, the settlement and cultivation of the country must be greatly retarded. Inducements to the immigration of free laborers will almost be destroyed....

From the rich lands of this large Territory, also, patriotic statesmen have anticipated that a free, industrious, and enlightened population will extract abundant treasures of individual and public wealth. There, it has been expected, freedom-loving emigrants from Europe, and energetic and intelligent laborers of our own land, will find homes of comfort and fields of useful enterprise. If this bill shall become a law, all such expectation will turn to grievous disappointment. The blight of Slavery will cover the land. The Homestead Law, should Congress enact one, would be worthless there. Freemen, unless pressed by hard and cruel necessity, will not, and should not, work beside slaves. Labor cannot be respected where any class of laborers is held in abject bondage. It is the deplorable necessity of Slavery, that to make and keep a single slave, there must be a slave law; and where slave law exists; labor must necessarily be degraded....

It is of immense consequence, also, to scrutinize the geographical character of this project.... It will sever the East from the West ... by a wide slaveholding belt of the country, extending from the Gulf of Mexico to British North America. It is a bold scheme against American liberty, worthy of an accomplished architect of ruin.... It is hoped, doubtless, by compelling the whole commerce and the whole travel between the East and the West to pass for hundreds of miles through a slaveholding region ... and by the influence of a Federal Government controlled by the Slave Power, to extinguish Freedom and establish Slavery in the States and Territories of the Pacific, and subjugate the whole country to the yoke of a slaveholding despotism. Shall a plot against humanity and Democracy, so monstrous, and so dangerous to the interests of Liberty throughout the world, be permitted to succeed?

We appeal to the people. We warn you that the dearest interests of freedom and the Union are in imminent peril. Demagogues may tell you that the Union can be maintained only by submitting to the demands of slavery. We tell you that the Union can only be maintained by the full recognition of the just claims of freedom and man. The Union was formed to establish justice and secure the blessings of liberty. When it fails to accomplish these ends it will be worthless, and when it becomes worthless it cannot long endure.

We entreat you to be mindful of that fundamental maxim of Democracy—EQUAL RIGHTS AND EXACT JUSTICE FOR ALL MEN. Do not submit to become agents in extending legalized oppression and systematized injustice over a vast territory yet exempt from these terrible evils.

We implore Christians and Christian ministers to interpose. Their divine religion requires them to behold in every man a brother, and to labor for the advancement and regeneration of the human race.

Whatever apologies may be offered for the toleration of slavery in the States, none can be offered for its extension into Territories where it does not exist, and where that extension involves the repeal of ancient law and the violation of solemn compact. Let all protest, earnestly and emphatically, by correspondence, through the press, by memorials, by resolutions of public meetings and legislative bodies, and in whatever other mode may seem expedient, against this enormous crime.

For ourselves, we shall resist it by speech and vote, and with all the abilities which God has given us. Even if overcome in the impending struggle, we shall not submit. We shall go home to our constituents, erect anew the standard of freedom, and call on the people to come to the rescue of the country from the domination of slavery. We will not despair; for the cause of human freedom is the cause of God.

S. P. Chase

Charles Sumner

J. R. Giddiugs

Edward Wade

Gerritt Smith

Alexander De Witt

Glossary

arraign:	to accuse of being inadequate or faulty
British North America:	Canada
demagogues:	leaders who gain power through false claims and by appealing to prejudices
ingress:	entrance
Homestead Law:	a law that would grant land to settlers for free or on easy terms
Old World:	Europe
pertinaciously:	stubbornly

Texas v. White

1869

Did Texas … cease to be a State? Or, if not, did the State cease to be a member of the Union?

It is needless to discuss, at length, the question whether the right of a State to withdraw from the Union for any cause, regarded by herself as sufficient, is consistent with the Constitution of the United States.

The Union of the States never was a purely artificial and arbitrary relation. It began among the Colonies, and grew out of common origin, mutual sympathies, kindred principles, similar interests, and geographical relations. It was confirmed and strengthened by the necessities of war, and received definite form, and character, and sanction from the Articles of Confederation. By these the Union was solemnly declared to "be perpetual." And when these Articles were found to be inadequate to the exigencies of the country, the Constitution was ordained "to form a more perfect Union." It is difficult to convey the idea of indissoluble unity more clearly than by these words. What can be indissoluble if a perpetual Union, made more perfect, is not?

But the perpetuity and indissolubility of the Union by no means implies the loss of distinct and individual existence, or of the right of self-government by the States. Under the Articles of Confederation each State retained its sovereignty, freedom, and independence, and every power, jurisdiction, and right not expressly delegated to the United States. Under the Constitution, though the powers of the States were much restricted, still, all powers not delegated to the United States, nor prohibited to the States, are reserved to the States respectively, or to the people. And we have already had occasion to remark at this term, that "the people of each State compose a State, having its own government, and endowed with all the functions essential to separate and independent existence," and that "without the States in union, there could be no such political body as the United States." Not only, therefore, can there be no loss of separate and independent autonomy to the States, through their union under the Constitution, but it may be not unreasonably said that the preservation of the States, and the maintenance of their governments, are as much within the design and care of the Constitution as the preservation of the Union and the maintenance of the National government. The Constitution, in all its provisions, looks to an indestructible Union, composed of indestructible States.

When, therefore, Texas became one of the United States, she entered into an indissoluble relation. All the obligations of perpetual union, and all the guaranties of republican government in the Union, attached at once to the State. The act which consummated her admission into the Union was something more than a compact; it was the incorporation of a new member into the political body. And it was final. The union between Texas and the other States was as complete, as perpetual, and as indissoluble as the union between the original States. There was no place for reconsideration, or revocation, except through revolution, or through consent of the States.

Considered therefore as transactions under the Constitution, the ordinance of secession, adopted by the convention and ratified by a majority of the citizens of Texas, and all the acts of her legislature intended to give effect to that ordinance, were absolutely null. They were utterly without operation in law. The obligations of the State, as a member of the Union, and of every citizen of the State, as a citizen of the United States, remained perfect and unimpaired. It certainly follows that the State did not cease to be a State, nor her citizens to be citizens of the Union. If this were otherwise, the State must have become foreign, and her citizens foreigners. The war must have ceased to be a war for the suppression of rebellion, and must have become a war for conquest and subjugation.

Our conclusion therefore is, that Texas continued to be a State, and a State of the Union, notwithstanding the transactions to which we have referred. And this conclusion, in our judgment, is not in conflict with any act or declaration of any department of the National government, but entirely in accordance with the whole series of such acts and declarations since the first outbreak of the rebellion.

But in order to [secure] the exercise, by a State, of the right to sue in this court, there needs to be a State government, competent to represent the State in its relations with the National government, so far as least as the institution and prosecution of a suit is concerned.

And it is by no means a logical conclusion, from the premises which we have endeavored to establish, that the governmental relations of Texas to the Union remained unaltered. Obligations often remain unimpaired, while relations are greatly changed. The obligations of allegiance to the State, and of obedience to her laws, subject to the Constitution of the United States, are binding upon all citizens, whether faithful or unfaithful to them; but the relations which subsist while these obligations are performed, are essentially different from those which arise when they are disregarded and set at nought. And the same must necessarily be true of the obligations and relations of States and citizens to the Union. No one has been bold enough to contend that, while Texas was controlled by a government hostile to the United States, and in affiliation with a hostile confederation, waging war upon the United States, senators chosen by her legislature, or representatives elected by her citizens, were entitled to seats in Congress; or that any suit, instituted in her name, could be entertained in this court. All admit that, during this condition of civil war, the rights of the State as a member, and of her people as citizens of the Union, were suspended. The government and the citizens of the State, refusing to recognize their constitutional obligations, assumed the character of enemies, and incurred the consequences of rebellion.

These new relations imposed new duties upon the United States. The first was that of suppressing the rebellion. The next was that of re-establishing the broken relations of the State with the Union. The first of these duties having been performed, the next necessarily engaged the attention of the National government.

The authority for the performance of the first had been found in the power to suppress insurrection and carry on war; for the performance of the second, authority was derived from the obligation of the United States to guarantee to every State in the Union a republican form of government. The latter, indeed, in the case of a rebellion which involves the government of a State, and for the time excludes the National authority from its limits, seems to be a necessary complement to the former.

Of this, the case of Texas furnishes a striking illustration. When the war closed there was no government in the State except that which had been organized for the purpose of waging war against the United States. That government immediately disappeared. The chief functionaries left the State. Many of the subordinate officials followed their example. Legal responsibilities were annulled or greatly impaired. It was inevitable that great confusion should prevail. If order was maintained, it was where the good sense and virtue of the citizens gave support to local acting magistrates, or supplied more directly the needful restraints.

A great social change increased the difficulty of the situation. Slaves, in the insurgent States, with certain local exceptions, had been declared free by the Proclamation of Emancipation; and whatever questions might be made as to the effect of that act, under the Constitution, it was clear, from the beginning, that its practical operation, in connection with legislative acts of like tendency, must be complete enfranchisement. Wherever the National forces obtained control, the slaves became freemen. Support to the acts of Congress and the proclamation of the President, concerning slaves, was made a condition of amnesty by President Lincoln, in December, 1863, and by President Johnson in May, 1865. And emancipation was confirmed, rather than ordained, in the insurgent States, by the amendment to the Constitution prohibiting slavery throughout the Union, which was proposed by Congress in February, 1865, and ratified, before the close of the following autumn, by the requisite three-fourths of the States.

The new freemen necessarily became part of the people, and the people still constituted the State; for States, like individuals, retain their identity, though changed to some extent in their constituent elements. And it was the State, thus constituted, which was now entitled to the benefit of the constitutional guaranty.

There being then no government in Texas in constitutional relations with the Union, it became the duty of the United States to provide for the restoration of such a government. But the restoration of the government which existed before the rebellion, without a new election of officers, was obviously impossible; and before any such election could be properly held, it was necessary that the old constitution should receive such amendments as would conform its provisions to the new conditions created by emancipation, and afford adequate security to the people of the State.

In the exercise of the power conferred by the guaranty clause, as in the exercise of every other constitutional power, a discretion in the choice of means is necessarily allowed. It is essential only that the means must be necessary and proper for carrying into

Document Text

execution the power conferred, through the restoration of the State to its constitutional relations, under a republican form of government, and that no acts be done, and no authority exerted, which is either prohibited or unsanctioned by the Constitution.

It is not important to review, at length, the measures which have been taken, under this power, by the executive and legislative departments of the National government.

Glossary

exigencies:	crises; urgent situations
President Johnson:	Andrew Johnson (1808–1875), president of the United States following Abraham Lincoln

The first issue of $1 notes in 1862 as legal tender, featuring Chase. National Numismatic Collection, National Museum of American History.

César Chávez — speaking at the Delano UFW–United Farm Workers rally in Delano, California, June 1972.

César Chávez: Original Analysis

Civil Rights Activist and Labor Union Organizer

1927–1993

Overview

César Estrada Chávez was born to the children of Mexican immigrants in a small Arizona town in 1927. He experienced discrimination from an early age. In school his teachers punished him for speaking Spanish, and his classmates teased him because of his ethnicity. At age ten he moved with his family to California, where they and hundreds of thousands of others sought work as migrant laborers. After serving in the U.S. Navy for two years during World War II, Chávez returned to California. In 1952 he began working for the Community Service Organization, where he gained his first experiences working with striking agricultural workers. In 1962 he left the Community Service Organization and formed the National Farm Workers Association (NFWA).

In September of 1965 Chávez and the NFWA gained national attention as a result of the Delano grape strike, when workers associated with the Agricultural Workers Organizing Committee (AWOC) walked off their jobs on the farms of area grape growers, demanding wages equal to the federal minimum wage. A week later, the NFWA joined the strike, which lasted for five years. As spokesperson for the strike, Chávez articulated the so-called Plan of Delano, outlining the strikers' goals. From that time forward he became known as an inspiring public speaker. In March 1966 he and his supporters began a march to Sacramento, California, which ultimately led to growers' concessions to the NFWA's demands—the first union contract between growers and farmworkers in U.S. history. Also as a result of the strike, the NFWA joined the AWOC to become the United Farm Workers Organizing Committee (UFWOC). In 1968 Chávez engaged in a fast during a strike, to impress upon the UFWOC membership the necessity of a continued commitment to nonviolence. From 1969 to 1970 Chávez and the UFWOC organized a nationwide boycott of table grapes, which persuaded most California grape growers to sign contracts with the union.

In the 1970s farmworkers began to lose ground, and by the 1980s Chávez and his union found themselves battling a more conservative government, opposed to union gains and favoring laissez-fair economic policies. In his 1984 speech to the Seventh Constitutional Convention of the union, which had by then become the United Farm Workers of America (UFW), he cast the struggle as a larger issue of civil rights. That year he also began to focus on the negative effects of pesticides on farmworkers; in June he called for a boycott of grapes in an effort to stop growers from using pesticides. By 1986 the boycott was universally called the "wrath of grapes boycott," and Chávez was delivering his "wrath of grapes" speech at public rallies across the country. Although the grapes boycott brought national attention and support to the battle against pesticide use, the UFW never achieved significant legislation to protect workers against dangerous chemicals. Chávez died of natural causes on April 29, 1993.

Explanation and Analysis of Documents

Chávez emerged as a leader in an era of civil rights activism. He was both inspired by and inspirational to other major civil rights activists in the 1960s and beyond. He was distinct from most other civil rights leaders, however, in that his foremost concern was the rights of laborers. He frequently spoke to large crowds, and his speeches were designed to motivate the audience. He played upon people's emotions, often providing stories of individual suffering to put a face on the farmworkers he defended. He also frequently used religious themes in his speeches, presenting his followers as morally right and their opponents as amoral and money hungry. He furthermore insisted that the success of the farmworkers' struggle was preordained. Three speeches from throughout Chávez's career as a labor organizer and civil rights activist illustrate his commitment to the struggle of agricultural laborers and Chicanos: the Plan of Delano, his address to the UFW's Seventh Constitutional Convention; and the Wrath of Grapes Boycott speech.

♦ The Plan of Delano

In the spring of 1965 two strikes broke out among farmworkers in California. The first was a single farm uprising, in which the NFWA helped gain a wage increase for the striking laborers but failed to get the grower to recognize the union. The second was an AWOC strike of grape pickers in the Coachella Valley, where growers also conceded a wage increase but refused to recognize the union. As the fruit-picking season progressed, many migrant laborers moved farther north, following the crops. They found that the wage increase they had gained as a result of the spring strikes did not persist as they moved from farm to farm. On September 8, 1965, the AWOC organized workers from eight farms in the town of Delano to strike. The AWOC leadership asked Chávez and the NFWA to join the strike.

The NFWA endorsed the strike on September 16—Mexican Independence Day—and Chávez quickly became their spokesperson.

Chávez collaborated with the young Chicano playwright Luis Valdez on the Plan of Delano. They intended for the plan to be read at each of the stops on the march from Delano to Sacramento that Chávez and strikers began in March 1966. The title purposefully alluded to the "Plan de Ayala," the statement of goals presented by the early-twentieth-century Mexican revolutionary hero Emiliano Zapata. Throughout the document Chávez emphasizes that the strike is a struggle shared by impoverished people of many ethnicities. He frequently refers to Mexican cultural symbols and Mexican history, however, and presents the strike as part of a more general struggle for Chicano civil rights.

The Plan of Delano begins by stating the strikers' goal. The striking workers, according to Chávez, were fighting for their "liberation" through reform related to their working conditions. Chávez incorporates religious language in his explanation, claiming that the march is a "pilgrimage" engaged in to perform "penance" for farmworkers' past failure to publicly present their plan to improve their lives and working conditions. Chávez also explains the farmworkers' struggle in the context of American secular traditions. He emphasizes the right of farmworkers to demand improvements as workers in the United States and uses language that purposefully alludes to famous American political treatises. Chávez continues by historicizing the strike in the context of the long-term exploitation of Chicanos. He notes that California Valley growers have exploited Chicano agricultural laborers for generations. Their labor, says Chávez, has made farmers wealthy while Chicano laborers have remained in a cycle of agricultural work that passes from generation to generation. He recognizes that the march to Sacramento is part of a longer struggle for justice that Chicanos have already begun and will continue even after the strike.

Chávez then details the six propositions that constitute the plan. First, he defines the struggle as a "social movement" and explains that its participants are willing to make sacrifices, including dying, to see its goals accomplished. He also states that the strikers are committed to nonviolence. He then quotes Benito Juárez, Mexico's first indigenous president. Chávez directs the quotation to the ranchers and others who do not support the strikers. It translates to "Respect for another's right is the meaning of peace."

In the second proposition Chávez requests the support of politicians and the government, reminding listeners that the U.S. government is also supposed to protect the strikers. He blames the debased condition of farmworkers on legislators who have favored the interests of farmer owners over those of their laborers. Chávez argues that although legislators knew about the exploitation of agricultural laborers, they ignored the workers' plight and regarded their conditions as unchangeable. Because politicians have not represented farmworkers, Chávez says, the workers will no longer turn to the politicians for help. Instead, leaders will

Time Line

1927	March 31	■ César Estrada Chávez is born near Yuma, Arizona.
1937		■ Chávez and his family move to California in search of work.
1952		■ Chávez begins working for the Community Service Organization.
1962	March 31	■ Chávez leaves the Community Service Organization and forms the National Farm Workers Association.
1965	September 16	■ On Mexican Independence Day, the National Farm Workers Association votes to join a grape pickers' strike in Delano, California.
1966		■ Chávez outlines the Plan of Delano at several stops during the march from Delano to Sacramento.
		■ The National Farm Workers Association merges with the Agricultural Workers Organizing Committee and changes its name to the United Farm Workers Organizing Committee.
		■ California grape growers agree to National Farm Workers Association demands, resulting in the first union contract between growers and farmworkers in U.S. history.
1968	February 14	■ Chávez begins a twenty-five-day fast to demonstrate the significance of nonviolent tactics.
1969	May 10	■ Chávez and the United Farm Workers Organizing Committee launch a national boycott of all table grapes; as a result of the boycott, most grape growers sign contracts with the union.

Time Line

1972		■ The United Farm Workers Organizing Committee becomes an independent affiliate of the American Federation of Labor–Congress of Industrial Organizations; its name is changed to United Farm Workers of America.
	May 11	■ Chávez begins a twenty-five-day fast to protest an Arizona law banning farmworkers from striking or boycotting.
1984	June 12	■ Chávez initiates a grape boycott in response to policies initiated under California's governor George Deukmejian that had contributed to the loss of UFWOC members' union contracts and led to their firing and blacklisting as well as physical intimidation.
	September	■ Chávez addresses the United Farm Workers of America at their Seventh Annual Convention.
1986		■ Chávez delivers his "wrath of grapes" speech at public rallies across the nation.
1988	August 16	■ Chávez begins the final fast of his life, which lasts thirty-six days and draws attention to the suffering of workers and children affected by pesticides.
1993	April 23	■ Chávez dies in San Luis, Arizona, of natural causes at age sixty-six.

emerge from among the farmworkers themselves, and these leaders will understand the conditions endured by farmworkers and voice their concerns from governmental office.

Third, Chávez explains the religious element of the struggle. He states that the movement is nondenominational and that to demonstrate as much, the strikers carry symbols of Christianity and Judaism as well as images of the Virgin of Guadalupe, the patron saint of Mexico. The Virgin of Guadalupe had long been associated with the struggles of common people in Mexico; Mexican reformers and revolutionaries had marched under her banner since before independence from Spain. Chávez then quotes Leo XIII, the nineteenth-century pope who insisted upon protections for laborers.

In the fourth proposition Chávez describes agricultural laborers' suffering. He notes that the strikers have endured the awful conditions of farm labor as well as the knowledge that the government protects the wealthy at the expense of the poor. All future suffering, Chávez states, would occur as a result of the struggle to eradicate the conditions that farmworkers have historically faced. He stresses the necessity of endurance and encourages strikers to embrace the hardships with which the exploitative labor system had presented them.

The fifth proposition stresses the necessity for unity among farm laborers. Chávez argues that the strikers are not engaged in a race-specific movement. Although the majority of strikers (and agricultural laborers in California in general) were Mexican and Filipino, Chávez argues that the current strike represents the struggle of all poor people. He likens the conditions faced by agricultural laborers in California to those faced by farm laborers of various ethnicities throughout the United States. In order to succeed, Chávez says, the strikers need the support of all farmworkers. He then describes farm owners' attempts to keep laborers powerless by dividing them. One key tactic employers have used, Chávez states, is offering nonunion contracts. Only through collective bargaining would agricultural laborers make any concrete gain.

In the final proposition of the plan, Chávez reiterates the tactic he and his followers planned to use to enact change: striking. The struggle of agricultural laborers, which Chávez calls revolutionary, resembles the Mexican Revolution because poor people sought basic human rights in both cases. Unlike the Mexican Revolution, however, Chávez points out that the struggle of agricultural laborers would be nonviolent. He then stresses agricultural laborers' desire for dignified change. They did not want charity or the benevolence of farm owners. In contrast, Chávez argues, they simply want the basic rights that should be accorded to free men. They wanted the same rights as other laborers in the United States, including fair wages and safe working conditions. He insists that regardless of opposition, the agricultural laborers' struggle would continue either until the movement achieved its goals or its participants died trying to achieve them.

In closing, Chávez states that throughout the Southwest, farmworkers were continuing to organize. He says that the march to Sacramento would ignite further labor agitation among agricultural laborers, who would be inspired when they saw what had happened in California. He insists that the "liberation" of farmworkers is imminent and calls for the continuation of the strike and the struggle for farmworkers' rights more generally.

♦ Address to the Seventh Constitutional Convention of the United Farm Workers of America

By the 1980s the political climate in the United States had veered sharply to the right. Chávez found himself fighting not only the traditional problems faced by farmworkers but also a conservative movement that sought to roll back the gains made by agricultural laborers in the previous two decades and to implement new laissez-faire economic policies. In 1982 George Deukmejian was elected governor of California, aided by over $1 million in contributions from agribusiness. Under his governorship the farm labor board stopped enforcing laws that protected agricultural workers. Many farmworkers also lost their UFW contracts. When Chávez addressed the UFW's Seventh Constitutional Convention in September 1984, he provided an overview of the new obstacles the movement faced. Chávez describes Republican president Ronald Reagan and Republican Deukmejian as "the enemies of the poor and the working classes." He then lists the multiple ways that, in his view, Reagan, Deukmejian, and their supporters have wronged working people of color. These include unfair housing practices, tax cuts to the wealthy, a proposition to force migrant workers to carry state-issued identification cards, and reduction of aid and unemployment for the poor and working class.

The 1984 address is characteristic of how Chávez's speeches evolved after the 1960s. He connects the struggle of farmworkers to the struggle of people of color for civil rights more generally. He recognizes that racial oppression and class oppression are implemented and supported by the same groups, and therefore that the fight against both should be waged simultaneously. He also considers the struggle of farmworkers from more of an international perspective. He states that they are part of a struggle shared with the oppressed peoples of Central America, who in the 1980s suffered under dictatorial regimes. From Chávez's point of view, the oppressive circumstances in both cases largely resulted from Reagan's policies, because the Reagan administration had funded (and in some cases brought to power) the Central American dictatorships. Chávez then describes the accomplishments made by farmworkers as a result of unionization. He argues that farmworkers are losing some of their hard-earned protections and rights because Deukmejian and his allies refuse to recognize the right of farmworkers to organize. He says that UFW members have been victims of blacklisting, physical violence, and exploitation; they have also been denied the right to bargain as a collective unit.

All this led to Chávez's central concern: encouraging opposition to California Propositions 39 and 41. Proposition 41 advocated severely cutting welfare benefits, which Chávez saw as an attack on poor people in general. Under Proposition 39 legislative and congressional district boundaries would be redrawn. According to Chávez, Proposition 39 was explicitly designed to disempower Chicanos and farmworkers. Proposition 39 was a desperate effort on behalf of agribusiness and Deukmejian to return to the recent past, when they held complete political control and could subjugate farmworkers without fear of recourse. But the agricultural laborers would never allow a return to that time, according to Chávez. He describes the moral superiority of farmworkers, particularly when compared with the moral bankruptcy of agribusiness owners. He also expresses the hope that farm laborers' children would enter professions, hold political office, and ensure the long-term protection of agricultural laborers.

The crowd at the UFW's Seventh Constitutional Convention responded to Chávez's address with characteristic adulation. His argument apparently was either in keeping with or able to influence the opinions of California voters in general, because two months later they defeated both Proposition 39 and Proposition 41.

♦ Wrath of Grapes Speech

In the 1970s and 1980s Chávez increasingly focused on the negative effects that pesticides had on the health and well-being of workers. On June 12, 1984, he called for a boycott of grapes in an effort to force growers to stop using dangerous pesticides on their crops. In 1986 UFWOC began to refer to the boycott as the "wrath of grapes boycott." In 1988 the union produced a documentary film demonstrating the negative effects of pesticides on workers and consumers. In addition, Chávez delivered his speech explaining the boycott at public rallies and meetings across the country. His audience frequently comprised people sympathetic to his cause, including labor activists and consumers' rights groups. During the sixteen-year boycott that followed, he regularly spoke about the necessity of continuing to boycott grapes.

He opens his 1986 speech by impressing upon his audience the gravity of the issue. Human lives, he points out, were at stake. Understanding the dire consequences of the use of pesticides, one million Americans had begun boycotting grapes. He urges others to join them. Chávez goes on to explain the history of the struggle against the use of pesticides. As a result of the grape boycott declared during the Delano strike of 1966, agricultural laborers had established contracts that banned the use of three types of dangerous chemicals on crops. He states that under Governor Deukmejian, laws protecting workers and consumers against pesticides were being ignored, despite the fact that the Environmental Protection Agency had classified pesticide pollution as the gravest issue it faced. Chávez points out that the agency has reported that pesticides were to be found in both food products and water supplies and that farmworkers and consumers were therefore in danger of the health problems associated with pesticides, including cancer and birth defects.

Chávez then provides details about pesticides used in farming and their effects on the human beings exposed to them. To impress upon his audience how truly egregious the use of pesticides was, he gives specific examples of farmworkers and their family members who have been directly affected by them. Chávez asks the audience to consider the plight of these victims and to prevent future suffering by boycotting grapes. He then lists the goals he hopes to

attain through the boycott. They include a ban on certain pesticides, a program to test grapes for poisonous residues before they can be sold, fair workers' elections, and good-faith bargaining. Chávez asks that the audience support the cause by boycotting grapes and by contributing money. He closes by noting that the use of pesticides in grape growing is poisoning all Americans and that only a united opposition to the practice would allow them to protect themselves.

Impact and Legacy

In many respects Chávez resembled the other civil rights leaders of the 1960s and 1970s. Like Martin Luther King, Jr., Chávez remained concerned with racism throughout his life. Also like King, he was inspired by the nonviolent teachings of Mohandas Gandhi, the early-twentieth-century leader of the independence movement in India. He remained committed to nonviolent action throughout his career, even when militant organizations such as the Black Panther Party for Self-Defense and the Brown Berets captured the support of many people of color. Unlike many other civil rights activists, however, Chávez did not exclusively focus on the battle against racism. While he understood that the subordinate status of Chicanos was rooted in American racism, he fought for the rights of agricultural laborers in general. Both the NFWA and the UFW were always diverse organizations. Chávez's first allegiance was to the farmworker, regardless of ethnicity. Chávez was therefore important as both a labor leader and a Chicano activist. His most concrete gains pertained to laborers. Chávez was one of the first individuals to organize agricultural laborers at a state and, later, national level. He was arguably the most effective organizer ever to unionize agricultural workers. Under his leadership, farmworkers formed their first serious union, gained admission to the American Federation of Labor–Congress of Industrial Organizations, got their first union contracts, and negotiated safety standards.

Although Chávez's accomplishments as a Chicano leader were less tangible, they were no less significant. In the 1950s, when most Chicano community organizations focused on urban areas, Chávez expanded the struggle to rural Chicanos. He was also the first Chicano leader to gain national attention. His leadership of the UFW helped draw attention to the plight of Chicanos in general. His actions, words, and strategies had a serious impact on the Chicano community—especially in their emphasis on having Chicanos themselves represent their communities. His commitment to nonviolent action has likewise shaped Chicano activism. The largest protest gatherings of the 2000s have been May Day marches in major cities across the United States. The style of the marches and the use of nonviolent action to draw attention to civil rights issues have their roots in Chávez's activism. The religious element of Chávez's speeches also echoes in the voices of many contemporary Latino activists.

Chávez's legacy is also apparent in the continued work of the UFW. Despite a decrease in membership in the 1980s, the UFW rebounded and increased its membership in the 1990s. It also broadened its focus, facilitating landmark contracts for agricultural laborers working with a variety of fruit and vegetable crops. After 2000 the UFW also saw the passage of laws stipulating new protections for agricultural workers, including restrictions in the use of pesticides. The UFW remains a significant political force today. Tangible tributes to Chávez's legacy exist across the United States, especially in the Southwest. Many cities and towns have public murals and statues that commemorate him. Major cities, such as Los Angeles and San Francisco, have named streets in his honor, and California has made March 31, his birthday, a holiday. In 1994, Helen Chávez accepted in her late husband's name the Medal of Freedom from President Bill Clinton.

Key Sources

The United Farm Workers Collection held at the Walter P. Reuther Library's Archives of Labor and Urban Affairs at Wayne State University in Detroit, Michigan, contains a variety of manuscripts related to UFW action and history. Some of them are available as downloadable PDF files through the library's Web site at http://www.reuther.wayne.edu/collections/alua.html. The extensive César Chávez Collection Papers, which span 1947 to 1990, are also at the Reuther Library but do not offer online access. The California Department of Education has a Web site dedicated to Chávez, including an extensive set of primary sources. It can be found at http://Chávez.cde.ca.gov/researchcenter/.

Essential Quotes

"We know all of these towns of Delano, Madera, Fresno, Modesto, Stockton and Sacramento, because along this very same road, in this very same valley, the Mexican race has sacrificed itself for the last hundred

years. Our sweat and our blood have fallen on this land to make other men rich."

(The Plan of Delano)

"We are ready to give up everything, even our lives in our fight for social justice. We shall do it without violence because that is our destiny. To the ranchers, and to all those who oppose us, we say, in the words of Benito Juarez, 'EL RESPETO AL DERECHO AJENO ES LA PAZ.'"

(The Plan of Delano)

"The strength of the poor is also in union. We know that the poverty of the Mexican or Filipino worker in California is the same as that of all farm workers across the country, the Negroes and poor whites, the Puerto Ricans, Japanese, and Arabians; in short, all of the races that comprise the oppressed minorities of the United States. The majority of the people on our Pilgrimage are of Mexican descent, but the triumph of our race depends on a national association of all farm workers."

(The Plan of Delano)

"President Reagan is a man with a very special sense of religion. Reagan sees a proper role for government and a proper role for God. It's very simple: Reagan's government helps the rich and God helps the rest of us."

(Address to the Seventh Constitutional Convention of the United Farm Workers)

"Our enemies are responsible for the brutal murder of thousands of dark-skinned, Spanish-speaking farm workers through their military support of blood-thirsty dictators in Central America. The men, women and children who have been slaughtered committed the same crimes we have committed—they wanted a better life for themselves and their families—a life free from hunger and poverty and exploitation."

(Address the Seventh Constitutional Convention of the United Farm Workers)

Essential Quotes

"History and inevitability are on our side. The farm workers and their children—and the Hispanics and their children—are the future in this state. And corporate growers are the past."

(Address to the Seventh Constitutional Convention of the United Farm Workers of America)

"What we do know absolutely is that human lives are worth more than grapes and that innocent looking grapes on the table may disguise poisonous residues hidden deep inside where washing cannot reach."

(Wrath of Grapes Speech)

"My friends, the wrath of grapes is a plague born of selfish men that is indiscriminately and undeniably poisoning us all. Our only protection is to boycott the grapes and our only weapon is the truth. If we unite we can only triumph for ourselves, for our children and for their children."

(Wrath of Grapes Speech)

Further Reading

Articles

Garcia, Richard A. "César Chávez: A Personal and Historical Testimony." *Pacific Historical Review* 63, no. 2 (May 1994): 225–233.

Gordon, Robert. "Poisons in the Fields: The United Farm Workers, Pesticides, and Environmental Politics." *Pacific Historical Review* 68, no. 1 (February 1999): 51–77.

Stavans, Ilan. "Reading César." *Transition* 9, no. 4 (2000): 62–76.

Books

Ferriss, Susan, Ricardo Sandoval, and Diana Hembree. *The Fight in the Fields: Cesar Chavez and the Farmworkers Movement*. New York: Harcourt Brace, 1997.

Griswold del Castillo, Richard, and Richard Garcia. *Cesar Chavez: A Triumph of Spirit*. Norman: University of Oklahoma Press, 1995.

Hammerback, John C., and Richard J. Jensen. *The Rhetorical Career of Cesar Chavez*. College Station: Texas A&M University Press, 1998.

Houle, Michelle. *Cesar Chavez*. San Diego, Calif.: Greenhaven Press, 2003.

Web Sites

"United Farm Workers History." United Farm Workers Web site. http://www.ufw.org. Accessed on November 3, 2008.

—*G. Mehera Gerardo*

Questions for Further Study

1. Examine Chávez's style of making his arguments. What are its best and worst features?
2. In what ways does the Plan of Delano speech draw on common Mexican themes, and in what ways does it appeal to a larger movement of agricultural and other workers?
3. In his speeches and other writings, Chávez tended to use the language of bitter struggle, referring to foes as "enemies" and depicting the conflict between farmworkers and the combined forces of government and agribusiness as a battle of good versus evil. Find examples of this rhetoric, and discuss whether you think it was appropriate or too strong—or not strong enough.
4. Research the news events and other items referenced by Chávez in his Wrath of Grapes speech—reports of corruption, chemical poisoning, and innocent victims. Could some of these things reasonably be interpreted in a manner other than the way Chávez did? Why or why not?

Document Text

The Plan of Delano

1966

PLAN for the liberation of the Farm Workers associated with the Delano Grape Strike in the State of California, seeking social justice in farm labor with those reforms that they believe necessary for their well-being as workers in these United States.

We the undersigned, gathered in Pilgrimage to the capital of the State in Sacramento in penance for all the failings of Farm Workers, as free and sovereign men, do solemnly declare before the civilized world which judges our actions, and before the nation to which we belong, the propositions we have formulated to end the injustice that oppresses us.

We are conscious of the historical significance of our Pilgrimage. It is clearly evident that our path travels through a valley well known to all Mexican farm workers. We know all of these towns of Delano, Madera, Fresno, Modesto, Stockton and Sacramento, because along this very same road, in this very same valley, the Mexican race has sacrificed itself for the last hundred years. Our sweat and our blood have fallen on this land to make other men rich. This Pilgrimage is a witness to the suffering we have seen for generations.

The Penance we accept symbolizes the suffering we shall have in order to bring justice to these same towns, to this same valley. The Pilgrimage we make symbolizes the long historical road we have traveled in this valley alone, and the long road we have yet to travel, with much penance, in order to bring about the Revolution we need, and for which we present the propositions in the following PLAN:

1. This is the beginning of a social movement in fact and not in pronouncements. We seek our basic, God-given rights as human beings. Because we have suffered—and are not afraid to suffer—in order to survive. We are ready to give up everything, even our lives, in our fight for social justice. We shall do it without violence because that is our destiny. To the ranchers, and to all those who oppose us, we say, in the words of Benito Juarez, "EL RESPETO AL DERECHO AJENO ES LA PAZ."
2. We seek the support of all political groups and protection of the government, which is also our government, in our struggle. For too many years we have been treated like the lowest of the low. Our wages and working conditions have been determined from above, because irresponsible legislators who could have helped us have supported the rancher's argument that the plight of the Farm Worker was a special case. They saw the obvious effects of an unjust system, starvation wages, contractors, day hauls, forced migration, sickness, illiteracy, camps and sub-human living conditions, and acted is if they were irremediable causes. The farm worker has been abandoned to his own fate—without representation, without power—subject to mercy and caprice of the rancher. We are tired of words, of betrayals, of indifference. To the politicians we say that the years are gone when the farm worker said nothing and did nothing to help himself. From this movement shall spring leaders who shall understand us, lead us, be faithful to us, and we shall elect them to represent us. WE SHALL BE HEARD.
3. We seek, and have, the support of the Church in what we do. At the head of the Pilgrimage we carry LA VIRGEN DE LA GUADALUPE because she is ours, all ours, Patroness of the Mexican people. We also carry the Sacred Cross and the Star of David because we are not sectarians, and because we ask the help and prayers of all religions. All men are brothers—sons of the same God; that is why we say to all men of good will, in the words of Pope Leo XIII, "Everyone's first duty is to protect the workers from the greed of speculators who use human beings as instruments to provide themselves with money. It is neither just nor human to oppress men with excessive work to the point where their minds become enfeebled and their bodies worn out." GOD SHALL NOT ABANDON US.
4. We are suffering. We have suffered, and we are not afraid to suffer in order to win our cause. We have suffered unnumbered ills and crimes in the name of the law of the land. Our men, women, and children have suffered not only the basic brutality of stoop labor, and the most obvious injustices of the system; they have also suffered

Document Text

the desperation of knowing that that system caters to the greed of callous men and not to our needs. Now we will suffer for the purpose of ending the poverty, the misery, and the injustice, with the hope that our children will not be exploited as we have been. They have imposed hungers on us, and now we hunger for justice. We draw our strength from the very despair in which we have been forced to live. WE SHALL ENDURE.

5. We shall unite. We have learned the meaning of UNITY. We know why these United States are just that—united. The strength of the poor is also in union. We know that the poverty of the Mexican or Filipino worker in California is the same as that of all farm workers across the country, the Negroes and poor whites, the Puerto Ricans, Japanese, and Arabians; in short, all of the races that comprise the oppressed minorities of the United States. The majority of the people on our Pilgrimage are of Mexican descent, but the triumph of our race depends on a national association of all farm workers. The ranchers want to keep us divided in order to keep us weak. Many of us have signed individual "work contracts" with the ranchers or contractors, contracts in which they had all the power. These contracts were farces, one more cynical joke at our impotence. That is why we must get together and bargain collectively. We must use the only strength that we have, the force of our numbers. The ranchers are few; we are many. UNITED WE SHALL STAND.

6. We will strike. We shall pursue the REVOLUTION we have proposed. We are sons of the Mexican Revolution, a revolution of the poor seeking bread and justice. Our revolution will not be armed, but we want the existing social order to dissolve; we want a new social order. We are poor, we are humble, and our only choice is to strike in those ranches where we are not treated with the respect we deserve as working men, where our rights as free and sovereign men are not recognized. We do not want the paternalism of the rancher, we do not want the contractor; we do not want charity at the price of our dignity. We want to be equal with all the working men in the nation; we want a just wage, better working conditions, a decent future for our children. To those who oppose us, be they ranchers, police, politicians, or speculators, we say that we are going to continue fighting until we die, or we win. WE SHALL OVERCOME.

Across the San Joaquin Valley; across California, across the entire Southwest of the United States, wherever there are Mexican people, wherever there are farm workers, our movement is spreading like flames across a dry plain. Our PILGRIMAGE is the MATCH that will light our cause for all farm workers to see what is happening here, so that they may do as we have done. The time has come for the liberation of the poor farm workers.

History is on our side.

MAY THE STRIKE GO ON! VIVA LA CAUSA!

Glossary

Benito Juarez:	founder of the Mexican state, who led the country from 1858 to 1872
day hauls:	an arrangement whereby workers are hired at dawn and paid at dusk, usually without documentation or legal rights
EL RESPETO AL DERECHO AJENO ES LA PAZ:	Respect for another's right is the meaning of peace
forced migration:	a situation in which workers are forced to keep moving simply to keep up with their jobs
LA CAUSA:	a term, meaning simply "the cause," for the overall movement of migrant farm workers led by Chávez
LA VIRGEN DE LA GUADELUPE:	a highly important local religious symbol, commemorating what many believe was the appearance of the Virgin Mary in Mexico City in 1531

Glossary

Mexican Revolution:	a series of uprisings between 1910 and 1928 that generally resulted in the increase and spread of social, political, and economic rights under the Mexican state
paternalism:	a system based on the belief that the powerful minority in control is operating in the best interests of the majority
Pope Leo XIII:	leader of the Roman Catholic Church from 1878 to 1903, who sought to modernize the faith by incorporating themes of social justice
race:	ethnic group, as opposed to "race" in the sense of an anthropological group distinguished by particular physical features
sectarians:	believers in separation between religious faiths
speculators:	investors and business owners interested only in profit, without regard for morality
stoop labor:	work that requires constant bending of the back and knees and other physical exertions

Address to the Seventh Constitutional Convention of the United Farm Workers of America

1984

There is a shadow falling over the land, brothers and sisters, and the dark forces of reaction threaten us now as never before.

The enemies of the poor and the working classes hold power in the White House and the governor's office.

Our enemies seek to impose a new Bracero program on the farm workers of America. They seek to return to the days—before there was a farm workers union—when our people were treated as if they were agricultural implements instead of human beings.

Our enemies seek to hand over millions of dollars in government money to segregated private colleges that close their doors to blacks and other people of color.

Our enemies have given the wealthiest people the biggest tax cuts in American history at the same time they have increased taxes for the poor and working people.

They have created a whole new class of millionaires while forcing millions of ordinary people into poverty.

President Reagan is a man with a very special sense of religion.

Reagan sees a proper role for government and a proper role for God. It's very simple: Reagan's government helps the rich and God helps the rest of us.

Our enemies want all of us to carry identification cards issued by the government which only we will be forced to produce to get a job, to apply for unemployment insurance, to keep from being deported by the border patrol.

Our enemies have created the P.I.K. give-away program to give away millions of dollars in cash money to the richest corporate growers in America for not growing crops.

While unemployment benefits for farm workers are cut and while food and medical care for the poor are reduced.

Our enemies are refusing to enforce the nation's fair housing laws, which protect black and brown people from discrimination.

Our enemies are refusing to enforce the laws that protect working people on the job from unsafe conditions which cause injuries and take lives.

Our enemies are responsible for the brutal murder of thousands of dark-skinned, Spanish-speaking farm workers through their military support of bloodthirsty dictators in Central America. The men, women and children who have been slaughtered committed the same crimes we have committed—they wanted a better life for themselves and their families—a life free from hunger and poverty and exploitation.

The same dark forces of reaction which dominate the government in Washington also dominate the government in Sacramento.

Governor Deukmejian is a lackey of Ronald Reagan. They collect their money from the same reactionary interests; their decisions are made by the same slick public relations men. They attack working people, minority people, and poor people with the same fervor.

Farm workers are not the only people who have suffered under Deukmejian. But Deukmejian has taken a terrible toll in human suffering among the farm workers of this state.

The law that guarantees our right to organize helped farm workers make progress in overcoming injustice.

At companies where farm workers are protected by union contracts we made progress

Against child labor.

Against miserable wages and working conditions.

Against sexual harassment of women workers.

Against favoritism and discrimination in hiring and employment.

Against dangerous pesticides which poison our people.

Where we have organized, these injustices soon pass into history.

But under Deukmejian, the law that guarantees our right to organize no longer protects farm workers. It doesn't work anymore!

Instead of prosecuting growers who break the law, Deukmejian's men give them aid and comfort. Instead of enforcing the law as it was written against those who break it, Deukmejian invites growers who ignore their farm workers' rights by seeking relief from the governor's appointees.

Document Text

What does all this mean for you and for other farm workers?

It means that the right to vote in free elections is a sham!

It means that the right to talk freely about the union among your fellow workers on the job is a cruel hoax.

It means the right to be free from threats and intimidation by growers is an empty promise.

It means the right to sit down and negotiate with your employer as equals across the bargaining table—and not as peons in the fields—is a fraud.

It means that 6,300 farm workers who are owed $72 million in back pay because their employers broke the law are still waiting for their checks.

It means that 36,000 farm workers who voted to be represented by the UFW in free elections are still waiting for contracts because their employers won't bargain in good faith.

Are these make-believe threats? Are these exaggerations?

Ask your friends and co-workers who are waiting for the money they are owed from the growers.

Ask your friends and co-workers who are waiting for the growers to bargain in good faith and sign contracts.

Ask your friends and co-workers who've been fired from their jobs because they spoke out for the union.

Ask your friends and co-workers who've been threatened with physical violence because they support the UFW.

Ask the family of Rene Lopez, the young farm worker from Fresno who was shot to death last year because he supported the union … because he spoke out against injustice … because he exercised his rights under the law.

Farm workers are not the only people who have suffered under Deukmejian. And they are not the only people who are under attack by the dark forces of reaction.

Millions of dollars have been spent to place propositions on the November election ballot for the people of California to vote on.

The dark forces of reaction have placed Proposition 41 on the ballot. It will reduce the welfare benefits poor people in California receive by 40 percent.

The Republicans want to give poor people—women and children living in poverty—a 40 percent cut in their support money as a Christmas present this December.

There is another proposition on the ballot this November. Proposition 39, the Deukmejian Reapportionment Initiative.

Proposition 39 would redraw the boundary lines for legislative and congressional districts.

The existing reapportionment law that sets the current boundary lines was passed by the Democrats in the legislature. It represents a great victory in the long struggle for more political power by Hispanics and other minority people.

Deukmejian wants to redraw the boundary lines because he wants to get rid of the friends we have in the Legislature and in Congress—friends who vote to defend the interests of farm workers and other working people.

Deukmejian wants to redraw the lines so Mexican people will be split apart into many small communities—so our political strength will not be felt—so we will be forced to vote only for reactionary politicians who back Deukmejian.

The same Deukmejian who is working to deny a better life to farm workers is also working to deny all Hispanics in California the right to full participation in the political process.

Deukmejian and the corporate growers who are paying [to promote] Proposition 39 want to redraw the lines to send more of our enemies to Sacramento. The Western Growers Association has already given $50,000 to the Deukmejian Reapportionment Initiative. And growers continue to support Proposition 39 with their money and influence.

But brothers and sisters, the dark forces of reaction also want to pass Proposition 39 because they are afraid of us!

Deukmejian and the growers have looked into the future and the future is ours!

History and inevitability are on our side. The farm workers and their children—and the Hispanics and their children—are the future in this state. And corporate growers are the past.

The monumental growth of Hispanic influence in California means increased population; increased social and economic power; and increased political influence.

Those politicians who ally themselves with corporate growers are in for a big surprise. They want to make their careers in politics—they want to hold power 20 and 30 years from now.

But 20 and 30 years from now—in Modesto, in Salinas, in Fresno, in Bakersfield, in the Imperial Valley, and in many of the great cities of California—those

Document Text

communities will be dominated by farm workers and not by growers.

By the children and grandchildren of farm workers and not by the children and grandchildren of growers.

Look at the values we cherish! Look at the things they hold dear!

We came from big families; they keep down the size of their families. We take pride in our children. They take pride in the money they make.

The growers have money and everything it buys. We have people and numbers. We'll see who triumphs in the end.

The day will come when we're the majority, when our children are the lawyers and the doctors and the politicians—when we hold political power in this state.

These trends are part of the forces of history that cannot be stopped. No governor and no organization of rich growers can resist them for very long. They are inevitable.

Once change begins, it cannot be stopped. You cannot uneducate the person who has learned to read.

You cannot humiliate the person who feels pride.

You cannot oppress the people who are not afraid anymore.

Our people are on the move. Our day is coming. It may not come this year. It may not come during this decade. But it will come, someday!

And when that day comes, we shall see the fulfillment of that passage from the book of Matthew in the New Testament, "That the last shall be first and the first shall be last."

Our duty is clear. We must stand up and defend our rights as free men and women. We must defeat Proposition 39! We must unite with our Hispanic brothers and sisters who don't work in the fields by joining together in this noble crusade.

For 21 months we have taken all the abuse and injustice Governor Deukmejian can dish out. He has attacked us where it hurts the most.

He has deprived us of our rights under the law.

He has taken away the ability of many of us to provide for our families.

He has tried to deny us the dignity that can only be ours in a union that we build and control.

Now it is our turn to fight back. It's our turn to strike a blow for all Hispanics in California by defeating Proposition 39.

Glossary

a new Bracero program:	a new program harking back to the original Bracero program, which provided cheap Mexican labor to U.S. farms during the 1940s
P.I.K:	the Payment-In-Kind program, whereby the U.S. Department of Agriculture sought to raise the value of crops by reducing supply—that is, paying farmers not to grow them
reactionary:	one who reacts against progressive social ideas by calling for extreme conservatism and a return to the past

Wrath of Grapes Speech

1986

I am speaking to you about our Wrath of Grapes Boycott. Because I believe our greatest court, the court of last resort, is the American people. And I believe that once you have taken a few moments to hear this message you will concur in this verdict along with a million other North Americans who are already committed to the largest grape boycott in history. The worth of humans is involved here.

I see us as one family. We cannot turn our backs on each other and our future. We farm workers are closest to food production. We were the first to recognize the serious health hazards of agriculture pesticides to both consumers and ourselves.

20 years ago over 17 million Americans united in a grape boycott campaign that transformed the simple act of refusing to buy grapes into a powerful and effective force against poverty and injustice. Through the combined strengths of a national boycott, California farm workers won many of the same rights as other workers—the right to organize and negotiate with growers.

But we also won a critical battle for all Americans. Our first contracts banned the use of DDT, DDE, Dieldrin on crops, years before the federal government acted.

20 years later, our contracts still seek to limit the spread of poison in our food and fields, but we need your help once again if we are to succeed.

A powerful self-serving alliance between the California governor and the 14 billion dollar agricultural industry has resulted in a systematic and reckless poisoning of not only California farm workers but of grape consumers throughout our nation and Canada.

The hard won law enacted in 1975 has been trampled beneath the feet of self-interest. Blatant violations of California labor laws are constantly ignored. And worst of all, the indiscriminate and even illegal use of dangerous pesticides has radically increased in the last decade causing illness, permanent disability and even death.

We must not allow the Governor of California and the selfish interests of California grape growers to threaten lives throughout North America.

We have known for many years that pesticides used in agriculture pollute the air, earth and water, contaminate animals and humans and are found in the tissue of newborn infants and mothers' milk. This March, the *New York Times* reported that the Environmental Protection Agency finally considers pesticide pollution its most urgent problem, noting virtually everyone is exposed to pesticides.

The Environmental Protection Agency experts have warned that

No. 1— Pesticide residue is being found in a growing number of food products.

No. 2— Some poisons registered for use in the last 30 years cause cancer, mutations and birth defects.

No. 3— Most chemicals on the market have insufficient and sometimes fraudulent test results.

No. 4— Underground water supplies of 23 states are already tainted and farm workers suffer some pesticide induced illness in alarming numbers.

Consumers must be alerted now that no one can actually define or measure so called safe exposure to residual poison that accumulates in the human body as environments differ and each person's tolerance is unique.

What might be safe statistically for the average healthy 40 year old male, might irreparably harm an elderly consumer, a child, or the baby of a pregnant mother.

What we do know absolutely is that human lives are worth more than grapes and that innocent looking grapes on the table may disguise poisonous residues hidden deep inside where washing cannot reach.

Let me share the frightening facts with you. Last July the *New York Times* and national television reported that nearly 1,000 California, Pacific Northwest, Alaskan, and Canadian consumers became ill as the result of eating watermelons tainted with the powerful insecticide Aldicarb, labeled the most acutely toxic pesticide registered in the United States.

Yet Aldicarb cannot be legally used on watermelons.

In June local agriculture officials quarantined fields in Delano, California grape ranches because residues of the pesticide Orthene were found in the vineyards, yet Orthene cannot be legally used on table grapes.

And a new study shows pesticides used in growing may be responsible for the illness of over 300,000 of the nation's 4 million farm workers.

Document Text

But of the 27 legal restricted toxic poisons currently used on grapes, at least 5 are potentially as dangerous or more hazardous to consumers and grape workers than deadly Aldicarb and Orthene.

Here are 5 major threats to your health that cling to the California table grapes.

Parathion and Phosdrin—are highly poisonous insecticides, similar to nerve gas, and are responsible for the majority of deaths and serious poisoning of farm workers. They cause birth defects and are carcinogens.

Captan—a proven cancer causing and birth defect producing agent. (Fungicide)

Dinoseb—a highly toxic herbicide that has caused worker deaths.

Methyl Bromide—a more potent mutagen (an agent affecting genetic material) than mustard gas and is highly poisonous and [a] proven carcinogen.

Statistics and news articles do not relate the real cost, the human anguish that originates from poisons on our food. They do not tell the tragedies I personally learn of daily.

How can I explain these chemicals to 3 year old Amalia Larios who will never walk, born with a spinal defect due to pesticide exposure of her mother?

What statistics are important to Adrian Espinoza—7 years old and dying of cancer with 8 other children—whose only source of water was polluted with pesticides?

What headlines can justify the loss of irrigator Manuel Anaya's right hand, amputated due to recurrent infection from powerful herbicides added to the water he worked with in the fields?

How do we comfort the mothers of maimed and stillborn infants, the parents who watch their teenage children sicken or die?

What report can be cited at the hospital beds I visit, at growing numbers of wakes I attend?

What court will hear the case of 32 year old Juan Chaboya, murdered by deadly chemicals in the freshly sprayed fields outside San Diego, his dead body dumped by the growers 45 miles away at a Tijuana clinic? What excuse for justice will we offer his 4 children and his widow if we do nothing?

Now is the time for all of us to stand as a family and demand a response in the name of decency. Too much is at stake. This is a battle that none of us can afford to lose because it is a fight for the future of America. It is a fight we can win and it is a fight that everyone can join.

Add your voice to our demands of decency as we call for

No. 1—A ban on the 5 most dangerous pesticides used in grape production—Parathion, Phosdrin, Dinoseb, Methyl Bromide and Captan

No. 2—A joint UFW/grower testing program for poisonous residues on grapes sold in stores with the results made public.

No. 3—Free and fair elections for farm workers to decide whether to organize and negotiate contracts limiting the use of dangerous poisons in the fields.

No. 4—Good faith bargaining.

Until these demands of decency are met we will carry the message of the Wrath of Grapes Boycott from state to state. 10 years ago, 12% of the country boycotted grapes and the growers were forced to accountability. California Governor Deukmejian and agribusiness cannot withstand the judgment of outraged consumers who refused to purchase their tainted products. Every month over 1 million grape consumers like yourselves receive our message across North America. State and federal law makers, mayors and city councils, religious and labor leaders, students and senior citizens, mothers and fathers, rich and poor, concerned individuals in every walk of life have endorsed the Wrath of Grapes Boycott. With their commitment and their donations, they in turn have reached out to their friends and relatives to help bind the foundation of a growing coalition of decency.

Now I am reaching out to you for help because consumers and farm workers must stand together as one family if we are to be heard. I am not asking you to give up wine or raisins. I am asking you to give us your commitment and valuable support.

I am asking you to join us now and be counted to join the growing family of individuals who will boycott grapes until the demands of decency have been met.

And hard as it is for me to ask for money, I am asking you to contribute to the cause—$100, $50, $15, whatever you can afford. Whatever you would have spent on grapes this year. Insure that every week 1 million more consumers will know the truth.

You have my personal pledge that every cent of your contributions will be spent on the Wrath of Grapes Campaign bringing this message into every home in America because this message is the source of our combined strength

My friends, the wrath of grapes is a plague born of selfish men that is indiscriminately and undeniably poisoning us all. Our only protection is to boycott the grapes and our only weapon is the truth. If we unite we can only triumph for ourselves, for our children and for their children. We look forward to hearing from you soon.

Glossary

agribusiness:	the entire complex of large corporations involved in agriculture
DDT:	a pesticide, developed in 1874, whose effect on the environment led to its banning in the United States during the 1970s
mustard gas:	various highly dangerous sulfur compounds used (most notoriously in World War I) as a lethal form of chemical warfare and so named because it is said to smell like horseradish or mustard
mutations:	changes in genetic information, including those caused by exposure to particular chemical compounds
nerve gas:	various chemical weapons that interrupt communication between nerves and organs in the human body, bringing about convulsions and eventual suffocation
residual:	accumulated as a residue, or a portion left over after its original source has vanished
Wrath of Grapes:	a name that plays on that of John Steinbeck's book *The Grapes of Wrath*, a highly influential 1939 novel about migrant laborers in California

This historic building is the Santa Rita Center (also known as Santa Rita Hall). **It is where Cesar Chavez began his 24-day hunger strike on May 11, 1972.**

Shirley Chisholm, future member of the U.S. House of Representatives (D-NY), announcing her candidacy. By Thomas J. O'Halloran, U.S. News & World Reports.

Shirley Chisholm: Original Analysis

U.S. Congresswoman and Presidential Candidate

1924–2005

Overview

Shirley Anita St. Hill was born in Brooklyn in 1924 to West Indian parents. She graduated from Girls High School and Brooklyn College and later earned a master's degree in education from Columbia University. After working as a day-care teacher, she became a supervisor of day-care centers for New York City. During the 1950s Chisholm entered Democratic politics and supported rising African American candidates. In 1964 she was elected to represent Bedford-Stuyvesant in the New York State Assembly. Four years later, she became the first African American woman elected to the U.S. House of Representatives. Outspoken and independent, she campaigned with the slogan, "Fighting Shirley Chisholm—Unbought and Unbossed." In the assembly and in Congress she championed the rights of women, children, and minorities and was a vocal opponent of the Vietnam War.

In January 1972 Chisholm announced that she was seeking the Democratic presidential nomination. Her candidacy was enthusiastically embraced by feminist activists but did not gain the backing of top party leaders, including many African American men. Because she lacked money and organization, her presidential bid was viewed as a largely symbolic effort. One of the most dynamic and colorful public speakers of her era, she was in demand as a lecturer, especially on college campuses. After serving seven terms in Congress, she announced in 1982 that she would not seek reelection. In retirement, she continued to lecture widely and taught politics and women's studies at Mount Holyoke College. She died in Ormond Beach, Florida, in 2005.

Explanation and Analysis of Documents

Chisholm was never afraid to speak her mind. She championed the underdog against the privileged, was a critic of the establishment, and became an eloquent spokeswoman for reform. Her public career was fueled by anger at the dismissive treatment she received at the hands of political leaders. Despite her strong record as an organizer and advocate, male colleagues seldom took her seriously. Chisholm often claimed that she met with more discrimination being a woman than she did being black. At a time when the women's movement was beginning to gain national recognition, Chisholm emerged as one of its most prominent leaders. Her political career, especially her presidential candidacy, was an effort to convince the country that women deserved an equal voice in government.

♦ Speech in Favor of the Equal Rights Amendment

Shirley Chisholm was an ardent supporter of equal rights for women. By tradition, newly elected members of the House of Representatives were supposed to silently defer to their elders, but Chisholm was never one to sit quietly while important issues were being debated. In one of her first speeches in Congress she urged her colleagues to pass the Equal Rights Amendment. This amendment, which had been introduced in Congress every year since 1923, stated simply, "Equality of rights under the law shall not be denied or abridged by the United States or any state on account of sex." The civil rights movement had successfully lobbied for the extension of equal rights to African Americans and won legislation banning discrimination based on race. Women activists believed that they were entitled to similar legal protection. The National Organization for Women made passage of the Equal Rights Amendment one of its top priorities. With the growth of the women's movement in the late 1960s, support for the amendment blossomed and by 1970, when Chisholm delivered her speech, it appeared on the verge of adoption.

In this speech to the House of Representatives, Chisholm outlines the main reasons for supporting this historic measure. Its passage, she maintains, would reflect a continuing commitment to the principle of equality before the law enshrined in the Constitution. While prejudice based on religion or political beliefs had long been condemned and racial prejudice had increasingly come under attack, many Americans still viewed gender bias as "normal, natural, and right." It was time to extend equal opportunities to the nation's largest minority group. Enacting the Equal Rights Amendment would undermine the legal basis for the "most subtle, most pervasive, and most institutionalized form of prejudice"—bias against women. Chisholm concedes here that adopting this amendment would not eradicate prejudice against women, just as racial prejudice did not vanish after the 1964 Civil Rights Act became law, but in her view this fact could not be used to justify inaction.

Chisholm saw the constitutional guarantee of due process under the law as a powerful legal reason for supporting the amendment. In this speech she points to state laws that mandated differential treatment for men and women, including statutes denying college admission to women, excusing them from jury service, restricting their business

dealings, and imposing unequal penalties for crimes. Measures such as these would be canceled by ratification of the Equal Rights Amendment. Another form of discrimination rendered invalid would be labor laws limiting the number of hours women could work and weights they could lift on the job. Addressing arguments raised by opponents of the amendment, Chisholm assures her listeners that any negative effects of cancellation of these laws would be minimal. She points out that Title VII of the 1964 Civil Rights Act already prohibited employment discrimination based on race, color, religion, sex, and national origin. Direct economic costs from adoption of the amendment likewise would be insignificant. The benefits for women would be considerable; they would enjoy increased access to better-paying jobs in industry as well as improved opportunities for vocational training and graduate education.

The amendment's indirect effects, however, would likely be much greater. Chisholm argues that legislative hearings calling attention to the pervasive discrimination against women would lead to changed attitudes of parents, educators, and employers. This, in turn, would elevate career aspirations of girls and young women, as would support for these loftier goals by their families and teachers. In the long run, these improved attitudes would greatly enhance the economic opportunities open to American women. Women were not the only potential beneficiaries of the amendment; men also would benefit. They would no longer be the only people required to perform military duty under the Selective Service Act. Women would have the same obligation to participate in the national defense. Fathers would enjoy greater rights to child custody after divorce because working mothers would have to share responsibility for child support.

Another category of legislation requiring unequal treatment of men and women was that intended to safeguard female workers. Chisholm here rejects the notion that women need special treatment. If workplace conditions are dangerous for females, she asks, are they not also dangerous for men? Both genders deserve the same protection. Some people insisted that women should be governed by different standards because they are physically weaker than men. Chisholm refutes this argument as well. She notes that there is considerable overlap in the abilities of the sexes; many women are as strong as or stronger than their male co-workers. She argues that they should not be arbitrarily banned from certain occupations because of their gender. Laws limiting the number of hours women can work do not help them, she contends, but they impose economic hardship on those who need overtime pay to support their families.

The basic principle at stake in the debate over the Equal Rights Amendment is clear to her: "Artificial distinctions between persons must be wiped out of the law." Because these provisions rested on "outmoded" and "pre-scientific" beliefs about the abilities of women, they could no longer be tolerated. In the Declaration of Independence, Thomas Jefferson wrote the immortal words "all men are created equal." He and the other Founders did not believe that women were entitled to the same political rights as men. But today, Chisholm argues, this old-fashioned reasoning could no longer be used to deny equality to female citizens. Just as beliefs about racial inferiority had been rejected in favor of human equality, it was time to extend full rights to women. She urges her congressional colleagues to complete the march toward equal citizenship begun nearly two hundred years earlier.

Time Line

1924	November 30	■ Shirley Anita St. Hill is born in Brooklyn, New York.
1946		■ Chisholm graduates from Brooklyn College.
1964	November 3	■ Chisholm is elected to the New York State Assembly from Brooklyn.
1968	November 5	■ Chisholm is elected to the U.S. House of Representatives from Brooklyn.
1970		■ Chisholm helps form the Congressional Black Caucus.
	August 10	■ Chisholm delivers a speech in support of the Equal Rights Amendment.
1971	July	■ Chisholm is among the founders of the National Women's Political Caucus.
1972	January 25	■ Chisholm announces her candidacy for the Democratic presidential nomination.
1974	June 17	■ Chisholm delivers a speech, "The Black Woman in Contemporary America," at a symposium at the University of Missouri–Kansas City.
1982	February 10	■ Chisholm announces that she will not seek reelection to Congress.
2005	January 1	■ Chisholm dies in Ormond Beach, Florida.

♦ Announcement of Candidacy for the Democratic Nomination for President

Shirley Chisholm was not the first woman to seek the presidency. In the nineteenth century Victoria Woodhull and Belva Lockwood ran under the banner of the Equal Rights Party. Senator Margaret Chase Smith sought the Republi-

can presidential nomination in 1964. None of these candidates, however, attracted as much attention as Chisholm did. She had been a member of Congress for only four years when she decided to run for president. Ordinarily, such a junior representative would not contemplate running for the highest office in the land, but nothing about Chisholm was ordinary. Her candidacy made history as she became the first African American to contest for a major party's presidential nomination.

On a cold January night, standing before a cheering crowd inside Brooklyn's Concord Baptist Church, she boldly announced that she would seek the Democratic presidential nomination. From the beginning, she signaled that hers would not be a typical political campaign. She did not intend to run as a black candidate or as a woman candidate; she hoped to be seen as the candidate of the American people. In her speech she acknowledges that this would be an uphill battle. Without the support of special-interest groups, backing from established political bosses, or endorsements from big-name celebrities, she was a decided underdog. She promises that hers will be a different kind of campaign. Her candidacy symbolized the dawning of a new era in American politics. The system of constitutional democracy extended the promise of freedom and liberty to all people, and she pledges to use her candidacy to realize this promise.

A large part of Chisholm's motivation for running was her disgust with the administration of the incumbent president, Richard M. Nixon. In her speech she unleashes a blistering attack on his record. In Chisholm's view, instead of bringing the American people together, as he had promised in his 1968 campaign, Nixon exploited divisions of region, race, and age for partisan advantage. She characterizes Nixon's administration as just "another smooth exercise in political manipulation, deceit and deception, callousness and indifference to our individual problems and a disgusting playing of divisive politics." She accuses Nixon of acting on the basis of political expediency rather than addressing urgent human needs facing the nation.

Because of his record of broken promises, Chisholm declares that Nixon did not deserve a second term. Voters, she says, should replace him with a leader who could be trusted, one who would be responsive to the needs of all the American people. Chisholm clearly believed that she could furnish that leadership. She based her confidence on the wisdom, talent, and energy of the American people, which gave her the courage to speak out for change. With her candidacy she offered a brand of leadership that did not blindly follow public opinion but possessed the boldness and vision to build a strong and just society. In her announcement she proclaims her faith that the majority of American voters will be able to look past her gender and skin color. If they did, they would choose her based on her proven intelligence, character, and ability. Chisholm restates her conviction that Americans were ready to break with the past and adopt a new approach to government.

Chisholm offers herself as an alternative to the incumbent. As president, she notes, she would encourage citizens to work for a cleaner environment rather than spying on their activities as Nixon did. She would encourage young people to speak out and organize for peaceful change rather than ignoring their protests. She would work to limit campaign contributions by wealthy donors rather than fighting against these controls. She would not make policy decisions based on calculation of political costs. Chisholm's vision for a new America pictured a land where poor people would have as much influence as the wealthy; where violence and war would be banished; where poverty and discrimination did not exist; where medical care, employment, and decent housing would be available for all; where people would work together to clean up the environment and rebuild their neighborhoods; where all Americans would enjoy the opportunity to realize their full human potential. Chisholm concludes by appealing to all who shared her values, especially the young people who had protested at the 1968 Democratic convention as well as those who were alienated from the political system and felt neglected, ignored, or forgotten. She urges them to join her campaign to "reshape our society and regain control of our destiny."

♦ "The Black Woman in Contemporary America"

In 1974 Chisholm was invited to speak at a two-week symposium at the University of Missouri in Kansas City on the topic of black women in contemporary America. As the nation's most visible female African American leader and as one with a long history of advocacy for women's causes, Chisholm was the logical choice to deliver the keynote address. Drawing on a lifetime of personal experience as well as her twenty years of political involvement, she was well prepared to tackle this subject. Her starting point was the emasculation of the African American male during the years when slavery was prevalent in the South. Because black men were unable to provide for their children and protect their homes and because marriage was not recognized and men could be sold away from their families, black women were forced to take on nontraditional roles. Out of necessity, they developed the strength, perseverance, and tenacity to sustain their dependents. These attributes were often mistakenly described as *matriarchy* by such white social scientists as Daniel Patrick Moynihan, whose 1965 report, *The Negro Family: The Case for National Action*, was widely condemned by African American scholars and activists for its negative portrayal of the black family.

Rather than depicting black men and women as rivals in a contest for domination, Chisholm asserts that black women possessed valuable skills that could complement male contributions; each had vital abilities needed in the struggle for black liberation. Some leaders of black nationalist organizations suggested that African American women needed to step aside to allow men to claim their rightful place at the head of the family and community institutions. Chisholm rejects this proposal as a scapegoating technique; she emphasizes the need for both sexes to work together. Black women with skills and education could not be expected to retire from the scene and sit on the sidelines. This waste of badly needed talent would weaken rather than strengthen

the African American cause. Only by working side by side would the common goal of liberation be achieved; only by participating in the struggle as equal partners with men would black women realize their full potential.

Chisholm next reviews the tensions between the mostly white women's liberation movement and African American women—an issue that troubled many feminists. Many of the disagreements between these two groups had their roots in differences in their class composition. The issues of most importance to working-class black women were not always the same as those that motivated middle-class white women. Controversies over symbolic questions, such as the exclusion of women from certain cocktail lounges or the use of the title "Ms." instead of "Mrs." were of little concern to blacks, who were preoccupied with issues of economic survival. However, this did not mean that black women rejected all proposals made by white feminists; in some areas their interests coincided. For example, the nationalization of day-care services, a cause that Chisholm championed, would be a great benefit for both black and white mothers and would be supported by working women of both races. By advocating policies and programs that directly addressed the needs of their community, African American women could act as a valuable pressure group within the largely white women's movement.

Chisholm asserts in her address that many black women had come to realize they had to be freed from traditional women's roles if they were going to contribute fully to the cause of black liberation. In the past, black women had been expected to stay in the background and let men monopolize positions of prominence. The civil rights movement was a case in point. Strong black women were the foundation of the movement, supplying a majority of the participants and organizing grassroots protests, but male chauvinism caused men to claim nearly all of the leadership positions and keep women out of the public spotlight. A few, such as Coretta King and Betty Shabazz, enjoyed celebrity because of the prominence of their husbands (Martin Luther King, Jr., and Malcolm X, respectively), but the list of African American women in the civil rights movement is much longer. Ida Wells, Mary McLeod Bethune, Mary Church Terrell, Daisy Bates, and Diane Nash all made important contributions to the southern freedom struggle but rarely received the recognition they deserved.

Chisholm claims that black women suffered a double discrimination because of their color and gender; for that reason, their problems could not be lumped together with those faced by white women. Neither the black movement nor the women's movement had been sensitive to this heavy burden. Thus, black women had had to cultivate attitudes and organizations to address their own unique issues. Their experience in the civil rights movement had produced a better understanding of the workings of the political system as well as the confidence to embark on new forms of political participation. This, she observes, had led to their growing interest in politics. Younger women were emerging as a force for change and demanding their rightful place in American society.

In the past, cultural norms had relegated black women to a minor role in politics and discouraged them from seeking elective office. As women and as members of the black lower class, they had been systematically disenfranchised. In the present, however, a fundamental change was under way. The liberation movement that had begun in the late 1960s had helped black women realize that their well-being was directly tied to the success of contests for political power. This was especially true in urban centers, where they daily confronted the issues most critical to the black community. Chisholm was encouraged by evidence from such areas as New York City, where black mothers had been at the forefront of movements to eliminate poverty and injustice. Rising poverty levels and minimal public assistance threatened the welfare of black families. Black women had a moral obligation to their children. They had no choice; they had to take a more active role in government. Chisholm notes that this movement to the center stage of politics should not be viewed as a threat to men; it was a question of survival. Black women, she says, must fully commit themselves to political struggle to assure their children a brighter future.

Chisholm concludes by urging the black women in her audience to "stand up and be counted." Americans, she observes, are hung up on questions of gender. These hang-ups have historical roots that prevent black men and women from working together effectively. She cites her career as an example of what is possible if people ignore criticism and squarely face difficult issues. She encourages everyone to look beyond differences of race and gender, to forget tradition and convention. Only by being true to their God and their consciences, she says, will they be able to create the kind of nation that will allow them to reach their full potential.

Impact and Legacy

In an era when women are commonly seen as heads of state and well represented among U.S. governors, representatives, and senators, it is easy to forget that for much of the twentieth century it was rare to see a woman holding an important political office. The same could be said about the absence of African Americans in high government positions before the 1970s. The dramatic surge in the number of female and African American officeholders in the last third of the twentieth century was made possible by the energy and dedication of such farsighted activists as Shirley Chisholm.

Chisholm was a pioneer and trailblazer. She went places no African American woman had gone before, and her accomplishments opened doors for hundreds of women who followed in her footsteps. She pursued a career in politics, building a reputation as a relentless grassroots campaigner at a time when blacks and women were effectively barred from higher office. Her most significant contribution was as a role model and source of inspiration for younger protégées. In the forty years after she first took her

seat in Congress, more than twenty other African American women were elected to the House of Representatives. Chisholm realized that she had no realistic chance of winning the presidency in 1972, but she ran to call attention to issues that no other candidate addressed and to pave the way for others. The emergence of Barack Obama and Hillary Clinton as the leading contenders for the Democratic presidential nomination in 2008 was due, in part, to Chisholm's pioneering effort.

Chisholm's name is not associated with any major legislation. Her unwillingness to "play ball" with the entrenched political leadership limited her legislative effectiveness. She was not a person who suffered injustice in silence. Her vocal condemnation of the discrimination she encountered did not win friends among her fellow representatives. When named to the Agriculture Committee at the beginning of her first term in Congress, Chisholm loudly complained that the position was irrelevant to the needs of her urban district and eventually received a better assignment. This display of insubordination, however, did not endear her to the "old boys" who controlled the House of Representatives and the Democratic Party.

The Equal Rights Amendment, for which she fought so doggedly, never became law. After passing in the House in 1971 and the Senate in 1972, it encountered a well-organized "Stop ERA" movement led by the conservative activist Phyllis Schlafly. The amendment died after being ratified by thirty-five states, three short of the necessary three-fourths required for adoption. Similarly, Richard Nixon, whom Chisholm so fiercely condemned, won a second term in 1972 by a wide margin before resigning in disgrace two years later.

Chisholm's presidential campaign was hampered from the start by lack of funds and the unwillingness of male political leaders to take her candidacy seriously. She was bitterly disappointed by the failure of some prominent feminists and African American congressmen to back her run for the White House. She was supported by the National Organization for Women but not by the Congressional Black Caucus, an organization she helped to create. The Black National Political Convention, meeting that summer in Gary, Indiana, also refused to endorse her. In the twelve primary contests in which she campaigned, she gained only twenty-eight pledged delegates. At the 1972 Democratic convention in Miami she received 152 first-ballot votes for the nomination eventually won by Senator George McGovern.

Chisholm was a passionate advocate for the powerless—for children, women, minorities, and the poor. She opposed the Vietnam War and worked to end the military draft. She sponsored legislation to provide federally supported day care and to extend the minimum wage to domestic workers. Opponents accused her of being hopelessly idealistic and unable to compromise, but everyone knew that Shirley Chisholm would fight with all her strength for the causes she believed in.

Key Sources

Shirley Chisholm's papers are housed in the Rutgers University Center for American Women and Politics. Oral history interviews can be found at the Moorland-Spingarn Research Center of Howard University and the Library of Congress's Archive of Folk Culture. Chisholm wrote two books, *Unbought and Unbossed* (1970), about her early political career, and *The Good Fight* (1973), recounting her presidential bid. A documentary film, *Chisholm '72: Unbought and Unbossed* (2004), was broadcast on the PBS P.O.V. series.

Essential Quotes

Essential Quotes

"The argument that this amendment will not solve the problem of sex discrimination is not relevant. If the argument were used against a civil rights bill, as it has been used in the past, the prejudice that lies behind it would be embarrassing. Of course laws will not eliminate prejudice from the hearts of human beings. But that is no reason to allow prejudice to continue to be enshrined in our laws—to perpetuate injustice through inaction."

(Speech in Favor of the Equal Rights Amendment)

Essential Quotes

"Artificial distinctions between persons must be wiped out of the law. Legal discrimination between the sexes is, in almost every instance, founded on outmoded views of society and the pre-scientific beliefs about psychology and physiology. It is time to sweep away these relics of the past and set further generations free of them."

(Speech in Favor of the Equal Rights Amendment)

"I am not the candidate of black America, although I am black and proud. I am not the candidate of the women's movement of this country, although I am a woman, and I am equally proud of that. I am not the candidate of any political bosses or fat cats or special interests. I stand here now without endorsements from many big name politicians or celebrities or any other kind of prop. I do not intend to offer to you the tired and glib clichés, which for too long have been an accepted part of our political life. I am the candidate of the people of America. And my presence before you now symbolizes a new era in American political history."

(Announcement of Candidacy for the Democratic Nomination for President)

"The black woman lives in a society that discriminates against her on two counts. The black woman cannot be discussed in the same context as her Caucasian counterpart because of the twin jeopardy of race and sex which operates against her, and the psychological and political consequences which attend them. Black women are crushed by cultural restraints and abused by the legitimate power structure. To date, neither the black movement nor women's liberation succinctly addresses itself to the dilemma confronting the black who is female. And as a consequence of ignoring or being unable to handle the problems facing black women, black women themselves are now becoming socially and politically active."

("The Black Woman in Contemporary America")

"In the face of the increasing poverty besetting black communities, black women have a responsibility. Black women have a duty to bequeath a legacy to their children. Black women have a duty to move from the periphery of organized political activity into its main arena."

("The Black Woman in Contemporary America")

Further Reading

Articles

Gallagher, Julie. "Waging 'The Good Fight': The Political Career of Shirley Chisholm, 1953–1982." *Journal of African American History* 92, no. 3 (2007): 393–416.

Books

Duffy, Susan. *Shirley Chisholm: A Bibliography of Writings by and about Her*. Metuchen, N.J.: Scarecrow Press, 1988.

Web Sites

"Shirley Chisholm." National Women's Hall of Fame Web site. http://www.greatwomen.org/women.php?action=viewone&id=39.

—*Paul T. Murray*

Questions for Further Study

1. Using Chisholm's impassioned and well-reasoned speech in favor of the Equal Rights Amendment as a point of departure, discuss the reasons why the legislation ultimately failed to garner sufficient nationwide support. What are Chisholm's best and worst arguments, and what might be some of her opponents' most valid and effective counterarguments?

2. As the first African American to vie for presidential nomination on the ticket of a major party, what advice might Chisholm give to America's first black president, Barack Obama? Using her writing and verbal style as your guide, write a letter to Obama from Chisholm.

3. Research figures of the past that Chisholm references when discussing the black woman in contemporary America: Katherine Cleaver, Ida Wells, Mary McLeod Bethune, Mary Church Terrell, Daisy Bates, and Diane Nash. In what way might their careers, and particularly their speeches and writings, have influenced Chisholm?

Document Text

Speech in Favor of the Equal Rights Amendment

1970

Mr. Speaker, House Joint Resolution 264, before us today, which provides for equality under the law for both men and women, represents one of the most clear-cut opportunities we are likely to have to declare our faith in the principles that shaped our Constitution. It provides a legal basis for attack on the most subtle, most pervasive, and most institutionalized form of prejudice that exists. Discrimination against women, solely on the basis of their sex, is so widespread that it seems to many persons normal, natural and right.

Legal expression of prejudice on the grounds of religious or political belief has become a minor problem in our society. Prejudice on the basis of race is, at least, under systematic attack. There is reason for optimism that it will start to die with the present, older generation. It is time we act to assure full equality of opportunity to those citizens who, although in a majority, suffer the restrictions that are commonly imposed on minorities, to women.

The argument that this amendment will not solve the problem of sex discrimination is not relevant. If the argument were used against a civil rights bill, as it has been used in the past, the prejudice that lies behind it would be embarrassing. Of course laws will not eliminate prejudice from the hearts of human beings. But that is no reason to allow prejudice to continue to be enshrined in our laws—to perpetuate injustice through inaction.

The amendment is necessary to clarify countless ambiguities and inconsistencies in our legal system. For instance, the Constitution guarantees due process of law, in the 5th and 14th amendments. But the applicability of due process of sex distinctions is not clear. Women are excluded from some State colleges and universities. In some States, restrictions are placed on a married woman who engages in an independent business. Women may not be chosen for some juries. Women even receive heavier criminal penalties than men who commit the same crime. What would the legal effects of the equal rights amendment really be? The equal rights amendment would govern only the relationship between the State and its citizens—not relationships between private citizens. The amendment would be largely self-executing, that is, and Federal or State laws in conflict would be ineffective one year after date of ratification without further action by the Congress or State legislatures.

Opponents of the amendment claim its ratification would throw the law into a state of confusion and would result in much litigation to establish its meaning. This objection overlooks the influence of legislative history in determining intent and the recent activities of many groups preparing for legislative changes in this direction.

State labor laws applying only to women, such as those limiting hours of work and weights to be lifted would become inoperative unless the legislature amended them to apply to men. As of early 1970 most States would have some laws that would be affected. However, changes are being made so rapidly as a result of title VII of the Civil Rights Act of 1964, it is likely that by the time the equal rights amendment would become effective, no conflicting State laws would remain.

In any event, there has for years been great controversy as to the usefulness to women of these State labor laws. There has never been any doubt that they worked a hardship on women who need or want to work overtime and on women who need or want better-paying jobs, and there has been no persuasive evidence as to how many women benefit from the archaic policy of the laws. After the Delaware hours law was repealed in 1966, there were no complaints from women to any of the State agencies that might have been approached.

Jury service laws not making women equally liable for jury service would have to be revised. The selective service law would have to include women, but women would not be required to serve in the Armed Forces where they are not fitted any more than men are required to serve. Military service, while a great responsibility, is not without benefits, particularly for young men with limited education or training.…

What would be the economic effects of the equal rights amendment? Direct economic effects would be minor. If any labor laws applying only to women still remained, their amendment or repeal would provide opportunity for women in better-paying jobs in manufacturing. More opportunities in public vocational and graduate schools for women would also tend to open up opportunities in better jobs for women.

Document Text

Indirect effects could be much greater. The focusing of public attention on the gross legal, economic, and social discrimination against women by hearings and debates in the Federal and State legislatures would result in changes in attitude of parents, educators, and employers that would bring about substantial economic changes in the long run.

Sex prejudice cuts both ways. Men are oppressed by the requirements of the Selective Service Act, by enforced legal guardianship of minors, and by alimony laws. Each sex, I believe, should be liable when necessary to serve and defend this country. Each has a responsibility for the support of children.

There are objections raised to wiping out laws protecting women workers. No one would condone exploitation. But what does sex have to do with it? Working conditions and hours that are harmful to women are harmful to men; wages that are unfair for women are unfair for men. Laws setting employment limitations on the basis of sex are irrational, and the proof of this is their inconsistency from State to State. The physical characteristics of men and women are not fixed, but cover two wide spans that have a great deal of overlap. It is obvious, I think, that a robust woman could be more fit for physical labor than a weak man. The choice of occupation would be determined by individual capabilities, and the rewards for equal works should be equal.

This is what it comes down to: artificial distinctions between persons must be wiped out of the law. Legal discrimination between the sexes is, in almost every instance, founded on outmoded views of society and the pre-scientific beliefs about psychology and physiology. It is time to sweep away these relics of the past and set further generations free of them....

The time is clearly now to put this House on record for the fullest expression of that equality of opportunity which our founding fathers professed. They professed it, but they did not assure it to their daughters, as they tried to do for their sons.

The Constitution they wrote was designed to protect the rights of white, male citizens. As there were no black Founding Fathers, there were no founding mothers—a great pity, on both counts. It is not too late to complete the work they left undone. Today, here, we should start to do so.

Glossary

due process of law: the principle, guaranteed in the Fifth and Fourteenth Amendments, that an individual accused of a crime has a right to be formally charged and tried

pre-scientific beliefs: old-fashioned prejudices, based primarily on tradition or superstition rather than actual experience

ratification: the process whereby proposed amendments become law, as prescribed in Article V of the Constitution

Announcement of Candidacy for the Democratic Nomination for President

1972

I stand before you today as a candidate for the Democratic nomination for the Presidency of the United States of America.

I am not the candidate of black America, although I am black and proud.

I am not the candidate of the women's movement of this country, although I am a woman, and I am equally proud of that.

I am not the candidate of any political bosses or fat cats or special interests.

I stand here now without endorsements from many big name politicians or celebrities or any other kind of prop. I do not intend to offer to you the tired and glib clichés, which for too long have been an accepted part of our political life. I am the candidate of the people of America. And my presence before you now symbolizes a new era in American political history.

I have always earnestly believed in the great potential of America. Our constitutional democracy will soon celebrate its 200th anniversary, effective testimony, to the longevity to our cherished constitution and its unique bill of rights, which continues to give to the world an inspirational message of freedom and liberty....

Fellow Americans, we have looked in vain to the Nixon administration for the courage, the spirit, the character and the words to lift us. To bring out the best in us, to rekindle in each of us our faith in the American dream. Yet all we have received in return is just another smooth exercise in political manipulation, deceit and deception, callousness and indifference to our individual problems and a disgusting playing of divisive politics. [Pitting] the young against the old, labor against management, north against south, black against white. The abiding concern of this administration has been one of political expediency, rather than the needs of man's nature.

The president has broken his promises to us, and has therefore lost his claim to our trust and confidence in him. I cannot believe that this administration would ever have been elected four years ago, if we had known then what we know today. But we are entering a new era, in which we must, as Americans, must demand stature and size in our leadership—leadership which is fresh, leadership which is open, and leadership which is receptive to the problems of all Americans.

I have faith in the American people. I believe that we are smart enough to correct our mistakes. I believe that we are intelligent enough to recognize the talent, energy, and dedication which all Americans including women and minorities have to offer. I know from my travels to the cities and small towns of America that we have a vast potential, which can and must be put to constructive use in getting this great nation together. I know that millions of Americans, from all walks of life, agree with me that leadership does not mean putting the ear to the ground to follow public opinion, but to have the vision of what is necessary and the courage to make it possible, building a strong and just society, which is rich in its diversity and is noble in its quality of life.

I stand before you today, to repudiate the ridiculous notion that the American people will not vote for qualified candidates, simply because he is not white or because she is not a male. I do not believe that in 1972 the great majority of Americans will continue to harbor such narrow and petty prejudice.

I am convinced that the American people are in a mood to discard the politics and political personalities of the past.

I believe that they will show in 1972 and thereafter that they intend to make individual judgments on the merits of a particular candidate, based on that candidate's intelligence, character, physical ability, competence, integrity, and honesty. It is, I feel, the duty of responsible leaders in this country to encourage and maximize, not to dismiss and minimize such judgment.

Americans all over are demanding a new sensibility, a new philosophy of government from Washington. Instead of sending spies to snoop on participants on Earth Day, I would welcome the efforts of concerned citizens of all ages to stop the abuse of our environment. Instead of watching a football game on television, while young people beg for the attention of their President concerning our actions abroad, I would encourage them to speak out, organize for peaceful change, and vote in November. Instead of blocking efforts to control huge amounts of money given political candidates by the rich and

Document Text

the powerful, I would provide certain limits on such amounts and encourage all people of this nation to contribute small sums to the candidates of their choice. Instead of calculating political cost of this or that policy, and of weighing in favors of this or that group, depending on whether that group voted for me in 1968, I would remind all Americans at this hour of the words of Abraham Lincoln, "A house divided cannot stand."

We Americans are all fellow countrymen. One day [we shall be] confronting the judgment of history in our country. We are all God's children and a bit of each of us is as precious as the will of the most powerful general or corporate millionaire. Our will can create a new America in 1972, one where there is freedom from violence and war at home and abroad; where there is freedom from poverty and discrimination; where there exists at least a feeling that we are making progress and assuring for everyone medical care, employment, and decent housing; where we more decisively clean up our streets, our water, and our air; where we work together, black and white, to rebuild our neighborhoods and to make our cities quiet, attractive, and efficient; and fundamentally where we live in the confidence that every man and every woman in America has at long last the opportunity to become all that he was created of being, such as his ability.

In conclusion, all of you who share this vision, from New York to California, from Wisconsin to Florida, are brothers and sisters on the road to national unity and a new America. Those of you who were locked outside of the convention hall in 1968, those of you who can now vote for the first time, those of you who agree with me that the institutions of this country belong to all of the people who inhabit it. Those of you who have been neglected, left out, ignored, forgotten, or shunned aside for whatever reason, give me your help at this hour. Join me in an effort to reshape our society and regain control of our destiny as we go down the Chisholm Trail for 1972.

Glossary

Chisholm Trail: a famous "road" of the Old West, a north-south route between the cattle yards of Texas and the rail yards of Kansas

Document Text

"The Black Woman in Contemporary America"

1974

Ladies and gentlemen, and brothers and sisters all—I'm very glad to be here this evening. I'm very glad that I've had the opportunity to be the first lecturer with respect to the topic of the black woman in contemporary America. This has become a most talked-about topic and has caused a great deal of provocation and misunderstandings and misinterpretations. And I come to you this evening to speak on this topic not as any scholar, not as any academician, but as a person that has been out here for the past twenty years, trying to make my way as a black and a woman, and meeting all kinds of obstacles.

The black woman's role has not been placed in its proper perspective, particularly in terms of the current economic and political upheaval in America today. Since time immemorial the black man's emasculation resulted in the need of the black woman to assert herself in order to maintain some semblance of a family unit. And as a result of this historical circumstance, the black woman has developed perseverance; the black woman has developed strength; the black woman has developed tenacity of purpose and other attributes which today quite often are being looked upon negatively. She continues to be labeled a matriarch. And this is indeed a played-upon white sociological interpretation of the black woman's role that has been developed and perpetrated by Daniel Moynihan and other sociologists.

Black women by virtue of the role they have played in our society have much to offer toward the liberation of their people. We know that our men are coming forward, but the black race needs the collective talents and the collective abilities of black men and black women who have vital skills to supplement each other.

It is quite perturbing to divert ourselves on the dividing issue of the alleged fighting that absorbs the energies of black men and black women. Such statements as "the black woman has to step back while her black man steps forward" and "the black woman has kept back the black man" are grossly, historically incorrect and serve as a scapegoating technique to prevent us from coming together as human beings—some of whom are black men and some are black women.

The consuming interests of this type of dialogue abet the enemy in terms of taking our eyes off the ball, so that our collective talents can never redound in a beneficial manner to our ethnic group. The black woman who is educated and has ability cannot be expected to put said talent on the shelf when she can utilize these gifts side by side with her man. One does not learn, nor does one assist in the struggle, by standing on the sidelines, constantly complaining and criticizing. One learns by participating in the situation—listening, observing and then acting.

It is quite understandable why black women in the majority are not interested in walking and picketing a cocktail lounge which historically has refused to open its doors a certain two hours a day when men who have just returned from Wall Street gather in said lounge to exchange bits of business transactions that occurred on the market. This is a middle-class white woman's issue. This is not a priority of minority women. Another issue that black women are not overly concerned about is the "M-S" versus the "M-R-S" label. For many of us this is just the use of another label which does not basically change the fundamental inherent racial attitudes found in both men and women in this society. This is just another label, and black women are not preoccupied with any more label syndromes. Black women are desperately concerned with the issue of survival in a society in which the Caucasian group has never really practiced the espousal of equalitarian principles in America.

An aspect of the women's liberation movement that will and does interest many black women is the potential liberation, is the potential nationalization of daycare centers in this country. Black women can accept and understand this agenda item in the women's movement. It is important that black women utilize their brainpower and focus on

issues in any movement that will redound to the benefit of their people because we can serve as a vocal and a catalytic pressure group within the so-called humanistic movements, many of whom do not really comprehend the black man and the black woman.

An increasing number of black women are beginning to feel that it is important first to become free as women, in order to contribute more fully to the task of black liberation. Some feel that black men—like all men, or most men—have placed women in the stereotypes of domestics whose duty it is to stay in the background—cook, clean, have babies, and leave all of the glory to men. Black women point to the civil rights movement as an example of a subtle type of male oppression, where with few exceptions black women have not had active roles in the forefront of the fight. Some, like Coretta King, Katherine Cleaver, and Betty Shabazz, have come only to their positions in the shadows of their husbands. Yet, because of the oppression of black women, they are strongest in the fight for liberation. They have led the struggle to fight against white male supremacy dating from slavery times. And in view of these many facts it is not surprising that black women played a crucial role in the total fight for freedom in this nation. Ida Wells kept her newspaper free by walking the streets of Memphis, Tennessee, in the 1890s with two pistols on her hips. And within recent years, this militant condition of black women, who have been stifled because of racism and sexism, has been carried on by Mary McLeod Bethune, Mary Church Terrell, Daisy Bates, and Diane Nash.

The black woman lives in a society that discriminates against her on two counts. The black woman cannot be discussed in the same context as her Caucasian counterpart because of the twin jeopardy of race and sex which operates against her, and the psychological and political consequences which attend them. Black women are crushed by cultural restraints and abused by the legitimate power structure. To date, neither the black movement nor women's liberation succinctly addresses itself to the dilemma confronting the black who is female. And as a consequence of ignoring or being unable to handle the problems facing black women, black women themselves are now becoming socially and politically active.

Undoubtedly black women are cultivating new attitudes, most of which will have political repercussions in the future. They are attempting to change their conditions. The maturation of the civil rights movement by the mid '60s enabled many black women to develop interest in the American political process. From their experiences they learned that the real sources of power lay at the root of the political system. For example, black sororities and pressure groups like the National Council of Negro Women are adept at the methods of participatory politics—particularly in regard to voting and organizing. With the arrival of the '70s, young black women are demanding recognition like the other segments of society who also desire their humanity and their individual talents to be noticed. The tradition of the black woman and the Afro-American subculture and her current interest in the political process indicate the emergence of a new political entity.

Historically she has been discouraged from participating in politics. Thus she is trapped between the walls of the dominant white culture and her own subculture, both of which encourage deference to men. Both races of women have traditionally been limited to performing such tasks as opening envelopes, hanging up posters and giving teas. And the minimal involvement of black women exists because they have been systematically excluded from the political process and they are members of the politically dysfunctional black lower class. Thus, unlike white women, who escape the psychological and sociological handicaps of racism, the black woman's political involvement has been a most marginal role.

But within the last six years, the Afro-American subculture has undergone tremendous social and political transformation and these changes have altered the nature of the black community. They are beginning to realize their capacities not only as blacks, but also as women. They are beginning to understand that their cultural well-being and their social well-being would only be affirmed in connection with the total black struggle. The dominant role black women played in the civil rights movement began to allow them to grasp the significance of political power in America. So obviously black women who helped to spearhead the civil rights movement

Document Text

would also now, at this juncture, join and direct the vanguard which would shape and mold a new kind of political participation.

This has been acutely felt in urban areas, which have been rocked by sporadic rebellions. Nothing better illustrates the need for black women to organize politically than their unusual proximity to the most crucial issues affecting black people today. They have struggled in a wide range of protest movements to eliminate the poverty and injustice that permeates the lives of black people. In New York City, for example, welfare mothers and mothers of schoolchildren have ably demonstrated the commitment of black women to the elimination of the problems that threaten the well-being of the black family. Black women must view the problems of cities such as New York not as urban problems, but as the components of a crisis without whose elimination our family lives will neither survive nor prosper. Deprived of a stable family environment because of poverty and racial injustice, disproportionate numbers of our people must live on minimal welfare allowances that help to perpetuate the breakdown of family life. In the face of the increasing poverty besetting black communities, black women have a responsibility. Black women have a duty to bequeath a legacy to their children. Black women have a duty to move from the periphery of organized political activity into its main arena.

I say this on the basis of many experiences. I travel throughout this country and I've come in contact with thousands of my black sisters in all kinds of conditions in this nation. And I've said to them over and over again: it is not a question of competition against black men or brown men or red men or white men in America. It is a question of the recognition that, since we have a tremendous responsibility in terms of our own families, that to the best of our ability we have to give everything that is within ourselves to give—in terms of helping to make that future a better future for our little boys and our little girls, and not leave it to anybody....

And I stand here tonight to tell to you, my sisters, that if you have the courage of your convictions, you must stand up and be counted. I hope that the day will come in America when this business of male versus female does not become such an overriding issue, so that the talents and abilities that the almighty God [has] given to people can be utilized for the benefit of humanity.

One has to recognize that there are stupid white women and stupid white men, stupid black women and stupid black men, brilliant white women and brilliant white men, and brilliant black women and brilliant black men. Why do we get so hung-up in America on this question of sex? Of course, in terms of the black race, we understand the historical circumstances. We understand, also, some of the subtle maneuverings and machinations behind the scenes in order to prevent black women and black men from coming together as a race of unconquerable men and women.

And I just want to say to you tonight, if I say nothing else: I would never have been able to make it in America if I had paid attention to all of the doomsday-criers about me. And I want to say in conclusion that as you have this conference here for the next two weeks, put the cards out on the table and do not be afraid to discuss issues that perhaps you have been sweeping under the rug because of what people might say about you. You must remember that once we are able to face the truth, the truth shall set all of us free.

In conclusion, I just want to say to you, black and white, north and east, south and west, men and women: the time has come in America when we should no longer be the passive, complacent recipients of whatever the morals or the politics of a nation may decree for us in this nation. Forget traditions! Forget conventionalisms! Forget what the world will say whether you're in your place or out of your place. Stand up and be counted. Do your thing, looking only to God—whoever your God is—and to your consciences for approval.

Glossary

Daniel Moynihan: assistant secretary of labor in the administrations of John F. Kennedy and Lyndon B. Johnson in the 1960s and writer of a study called *The Negro Family: The Case for National Action,* which raised controversy by associating the economic problems of the black underclass with the disintegration of family structures

nationalization: placement under the control of the national, or federal, government

Portrait of Chisholm by Kadir Nelson in the Collection of the U.S. House of Representatives

Portrait of Henry Clay by Matthew Harris Jouett, 1818

Henry Clay: Original Analysis

U.S. Congressman, Senator, and Presidential Candidate

1777–1852

Overview

Henry Clay was born in Virginia in 1777. After earning a law license in 1797, he relocated to Lexington, Kentucky. He quickly gained a reputation as an adept trial lawyer, which led him into local politics. Elected to the state legislature in 1803, he interrupted his service to act as a defense counsel for the former vice president Aaron Burr in his trial for treason. After serving as speaker of the Kentucky House and filling out two unexpired terms in the U.S. Senate, Clay was elected to the U.S. House of Representatives and became its Speaker in 1811. Clay's charismatic personality and dramatic speaking style made him a natural leader. As the guiding force behind the so-called war hawks in Congress, Clay helped spur the United States into the War of 1812. He went on to serve as a peace commissioner in 1814, helping to negotiate the Treaty of Ghent.

Clay used his leadership position in the House to advance what he called his "American System," which included protective tariffs for manufacturers and federally funded support for roads, canals, and other internal improvements. His vision for the United States emphasized unity among the regions. Though he was a slaveholder, he did not champion southern interests against national ones. His role in shaping the Missouri Compromise in 1820 strengthened his stature as a conciliator between the North and South. In addition, Clay sought to promote American ideals of democracy abroad and advocated the recognition of newly formed nations in South America.

Despite his great political skills and large national following, Clay was repeatedly frustrated in his attempts to win the presidency. In 1824 he ran for the White House for the first time, coming in last in a four-way contest that was decided ultimately in the House of Representatives. When Clay swung his support to the victorious John Quincy Adams, charges of corrupt bargaining were raised by the supporters of Andrew Jackson, the candidate who had received the most popular votes. The charges only intensified after Adams selected Clay as his secretary of state. Adams's presidency never recovered from these charges, which damaged Clay's career as well. After Jackson defeated Adams in 1828, Clay entered the U.S. Senate and became Jackson's chief antagonist, particularly in the fight over the rechartering of the United States Bank. He lost to Jackson in the contest to become the presidential nominee of the National Republican Party in 1828. Clay's next move was to help organize the Whig Party, which soon emerged as the main opposition to Jackson's Democratic Party.

Clay declined to run against Martin Van Buren for the presidency in 1836 and then unsuccessfully sought the Whig nomination in 1840. But in 1844, with his Whigs united behind him, Clay launched another campaign for the presidency. His chances against the lesser-known Democrat James K. Polk were damaged after he seemed to hedge on the issue of annexing Texas to the Union. Clay was defeated and he retired from the Senate. After losing the 1848 Whig presidential nomination to General Zachary Taylor, Clay announced his intention to leave politics for good. He changed his mind and returned to the Senate a year later. Although he was in declining health, Clay decided to use his still-formidable influence to end the dispute over the extension of slavery into territory acquired by the United States after the Mexican-American War. Speaking for hours before packed Senate galleries, he predicted a long and bloody civil war if his compromise proposals were not adopted. After initially failing to pass as a package, the Compromise of 1850 was finally voted into law as separate bills. Clay's last act of service helped to delay the outbreak of civil war. After a long decline, Clay died in Washington, D.C., on June 29, 1852.

Explanation and Analysis of Documents

Friends and foes alike agreed that Clay was an exceptionally gifted orator. His richly toned voice and dramatic gestures made his speeches memorable ones, whether he was addressing Congress or speaking to crowds of voters. Certain themes—especially love of country and a desire to ease regional tensions—remained throughout his fifty-year career in politics. Whether urging support for U.S. troops during the War of 1812, advocating recognition for new South American nations, or seeking to make peace between the North and South, he reaffirmed his belief in the ideals of American independence and democracy. His boldness as a partisan warrior is captured in his denunciation of President Jackson's withdrawal of federal deposits from the Bank of the United States. His political skills—sometimes applied with too much cleverness—are displayed in his so-called Raleigh Letter regarding the annexation of Texas.

♦ Speech on the Bill to Raise an Additional Military Force

When Clay took his seat in the U.S. Senate in 1806, a series of incidents between the United States and Great Britain was beginning to point toward war. Britain's conflict with French forces under Napoléon Bonaparte had led Britain to violate U.S. neutrality in a number of ways. Britain's impressments of American sailors and its blockade of French ports were particularly offensive. Clay's attempts to rouse American opinion against the British only increased after his election as Speaker of the House in 1811. He and other members of the congressional war hawks' faction began to anticipate military action, including suppression of Britain's Native American allies and the conquest of Canada. Clay supported President James Madison after the latter requested a declaration of war against Britain on June 1, 1812; for his part, Madison seriously considered making Clay (who lacked any military experience) the commander of the American forces. A series of American defeats put supporters of the war on the defensive. Despite his lack of confidence in Madison's leadership, Clay offered a vigorous response to the president's critics on January 8, 1813. The immediate cause of the speech was to support a bill for reinforcing the army. But Clay ranged far beyond this point to refute a host of charges that had been made by the Massachusetts congressman Josiah Quincy in a scathing speech three days earlier.

After a few introductory remarks, Clay reviews the seemingly contradictory arguments of those who have opposed President Madison's policies. He accuses these critics of "tacking with every gale, displaying the colors of every party" in order to advance their drive for political power. He then concentrates on the charge made by Quincy that Madison has shown favoritism toward France during its struggle with Britain. With rising fervor, Clay ridicules the idea that the administration has been under French influence, though he acknowledges that there are Americans "foolish and credulous enough to believe it." He proceeds to express outrage over attacks upon the character of Thomas Jefferson, Madison's predecessor in the White House. In hailing Jefferson as a champion of liberty, Clay sneers at the attacks by the former president's foes as "the howlings of the whole British pack set loose from the Essex kennel." This is a reference to a group of pro-British Federalist Party members who were accused of favoring the secession of New England from the Union.

Continuing his speech on the House floor the following day, Clay stresses the theme of a united national interest in opposing the British. Responding to an earlier speech by the New York representative Harmanus Bleecker, he notes that it is not strange that southern and western congressmen would fight to protect American sailors, even though their constituents seemingly have little direct interest at stake. "Whenever the sacred rights of an American freeman are assailed, all hearts ought to unite and every arm should be braced to vindicate his cause," Clay declares. He goes on to insist that all Americans should recognize the value in taking Canada from the British.

Time Line

1777	April 12	■ Henry Clay is born in Hanover County, Virginia.
1803		■ Clay is elected to the Kentucky legislature.
1806		■ Clay is appointed to serve out an unexpired U.S. Senate term.
1811		■ Clay is elected to the U.S. House of Representatives and is elected Speaker.
1813	January 8	■ Clay delivers a speech defending President James Madison's war policies.
1814		■ Clay serves as a member of the U.S. Peace Commission at Ghent, Belgium.
1820	May 10	■ Clay delivers a speech supporting the recognition of South American republics.
1824		■ Clay runs unsuccessfully for the presidency.
1825		■ Clay becomes secretary of state under President John Quincy Adams.
1831		■ Clay is elected to the U.S. Senate.
1832		■ Clay loses his bid for the presidential nomination to Andrew Jackson.
1844	April 17	■ Clay publishes a letter opposing immediate annexation of Texas.
	November	■ Clay loses the presidency to James K. Polk.
1849	January	■ Clay is elected to the U.S. Senate for the final time.
1850	January 29	■ Clay delivers a speech introducing his Compromise Resolutions.
1852	June 29	■ Clay dies in Washington, D.C.

Clay reviews the events of the war, acknowledging America's setbacks while praising the heroism of its troops. He frankly admits that while the navy is well organized and disciplined, the army has been lacking in sound leadership. Battles fought at Brownstown (an early skirmish near Detroit) and Queenstown (an unsuccessful assault on a British position across the Niagara River) proved American courage, even if they did not make good tactical sense. He cites General William Hull's surrender to the British at Detroit on August 15, 1812, as a "disgrace" to American honor but claims that Madison's administration cannot be held responsible. He quickly moves on to list a series of "brilliant exploits" by U.S. forces, including General Samuel Hopkins's attacks upon the Indian allies of the British along the Wabash and Illinois rivers and the capture and destruction of enemy ships by Lieutenant JesseD. Elliott on Lake Erie.

As Clay builds toward the conclusion of his speech, he reviews the underlying causes of the war and stresses the need for the country to stand behind its troops. Seizure and destruction of American property, support for Indian raids, and impressments of U.S. sailors are among the wrongs of the British he cites. Madison's administration, he insists, has sought peace, only to be rebuffed time and again. Clay specifically mentions the repeated efforts of the American diplomat Jonathan Russell to secure an armistice with Britain. These efforts are contrasted with the dubious peace proposals made by the British admiral Sir John Warren. The British foreign secretary, Lord Castlereagh, would "laugh at our simplicity" if we accepted his government's misleading offers to end the war, Clay says. If the administration has made an error, it has been in the direction of conceding too much to the enemy. "An honorable peace is attainable only by an efficient war," Clay states firmly. America will succeed if it keeps its nerve and is favored by Divine Providence. Closing in a dramatic call for unity, Clay declares that if the American cause must fail, "let us fail like men, lash ourselves to our gallant tars [sailors], and expire together in one common struggle."

Clay's final remarks brought many of his listeners to tears. His speech received much favorable attention across the country and helped bolster support for Madison's administration. The War of 1812 dragged on with neither American nor British forces achieving a clear-cut victory. After both countries agreed to begin peace negotiations, Madison appointed Clay as one of five commissioners representing the United States. The American and British negotiators met in Ghent, Belgium, from June through December 1814. The peace treaty that resulted settled none of the problems that caused the war. But Clay, like many of his fellow citizens, felt that the war had reaffirmed America's independence and deepened its sense of national unity.

♦ Speech on South American Independence

The movement for self-government among the Spanish colonies in South America gained momentum following the end of the Napoleonic Wars. Clay was in the forefront of American leaders who favored recognizing the new governments on the continent, both for idealistic and practical reasons. As early as 1813 he expressed the view that South America's political future was of greater importance to the United States than the political future of Europe. Clay grew frustrated with President James Monroe, who favored a cautious approach to South America that avoided antagonizing Spain, with whom the United States was negotiating over the acquisition of Florida. On May 9, 1820, Monroe sent a special message to Congress condemning Spain for attempting to link the ceding of Florida to a declaration that the United States would abandon the right to recognize the new South American governments. Despite this expression of outrage, the president's statement did not go far enough for Clay. The following day, he introduced a House resolution to send a diplomatic representative to one or more of the new South American states.

After discussing preliminary matters, Clay states that his latest resolution in support of the new governments is as important as any matter before the House. In his view, Monroe admitted that his South American policy had failed; the United States had followed Spain's wishes, whether any principles have been conceded or not. American recognition of the new governments should have occurred two years earlier, when it was most needed. Since then, the South American states continued to show their viability as free republics. In the manner that France came to the aid of Britain's rebellious American colonies, the U.S. government, he thinks, should not wait until the rest of the world recognized the Spanish American states before extending the hand of friendship toward them.

With his characteristic passion, Clay goes on to envision a commercial system linking North and South America. Banking and manufacturing would necessarily be centered in the United States, while the southern nations would supply a rapidly expanding market with their goods. "Our enterprise, industry and habits of economy" will ensure that the United States will never fare the worse in competition with its southern neighbors, he says. By twenty-first-century standards, Clay's views toward South America seem condescending and chauvinistic; in his own time, though, they were probably as liberal-minded as any held by a U.S. political leader.

Moving beyond economic self-interest, Clay gives another reason to forge an early alliance with South America: self-defense against Europe. A shared love of self-government unites the United States with the new republics against the despots of the Old World. The South American rebels have embraced U.S. ideals, even though the U.S. government has refused to aid them. Their desire to model their institutions upon our own will only increase if we recognize their freedom, Clay insists.

Clay plays upon patriotic feelings by declaring that the United States should not wait for the approval of European powers before recognizing its new neighbors. From there, he addresses the claim that the South American states are not ready for independence. Clay asserts boldly that, in some ways, these nations are ahead of the United States.

He specifically notes that Grenada (Colombia), Venezuela, and "Buenos Ayres" (Argentina) have abolished slavery—though he quickly adds that he is not advocating that the United States do the same. His point is that "circumstances" allowed these nations to reach the point where they have been able to emancipate their slaves. Clay makes the case that the South American states have fully secured their independence and are creating enlightened societies within their borders. With these facts established, there is no reason to delay diplomatic recognition. To conclude, Clay mentions that he will be retiring from the House in the near future. Whether his resolution passes or fails, he at least takes pride in attempting to help the South American people. By alluding to the vast population the continent will contain in the future, he reminds the House that the United States ignores the new southern republics at its own peril.

Despite Clay's efforts, the House ultimately turned down a motion to send a minister to South America. Monroe refused to change his position of neutrality toward Spain and its rebel colonies; even the settlement of the Florida question in February 1821 failed to bring a shift in policy. Finally, in March 1822, Congress voted in favor of recognition of the new nations with Monroe's approval. Clay's views on hemispheric trade proved to be ahead of their time. By the close of the nineteenth century, the U.S. secretary of state James G. Blaine and President William McKinley were outlining an economic alliance between North and South America rooted in Clay's ideas.

♦ Letter to the Editors of the *Washington National Intelligencer on Texas Annexation*

As Clay grew older, his views on American expansion were tempered by a desire to avoid conflict. The request by the Republic of Texas to be annexed to the Union in July 1836 threatened to reignite the controversy over slavery, settled (at least temporarily) by the Missouri Compromise in 1821. In addition, Mexico still claimed sovereignty over its former territory, raising the possibility of war between the United States and its southern neighbor if annexation took place. As the debate began to intensify, Clay met with the former president Martin VanBuren in the spring of 1842. It was widely believed at the time that the two old rivals agreed not to make Texas an issue in the forthcoming presidential contest. When President John Tyler signed an annexation treaty with Texas on April 12, 1844, Clay could no longer avoid speaking out. During a campaign stop in Raleigh, North Carolina, on April 17, he attempted to clarify his views by composing a letter intended for publication in the *Washington National Intelligencer*.

Clay begins by expressing his reluctance to discuss the issue at all. The failure of previous efforts to annex Texas had convinced him that a majority of the American people no longer favored doing so. In fact, he claims to have been surprised that President Tyler had reopened the question the previous fall. Clay is still dubious about the amount of support for annexation and implies that Americans with a financial stake in the Texas Republic have been attempting to influence public opinion. Still, the signing of the treaty has made the topic unavoidable. Clay then proceeds to sum up the basic theme of the letter: Texas should not be annexed as conditions stood.

The United States was entitled to possession of Texas by the terms of the Louisiana Purchase, Clay says. This was not acted upon; instead, the Monroe administration essentially traded any claim on Texas for the right to acquire Florida in its 1819 treaty with Spain. Though he opposed these terms at the time, Clay states that they must stand now, even though Spain no longer governed Texas. He adds that the United States should be careful if it seeks to reacquire its lost territory.

After a further review of recent events, Clay discusses the current situation. He states plainly that he is not willing to go to war with Mexico over Texas, for both pragmatic and moral reasons. The former war hawk of 1812 now regards "all wars as great calamities" and considers "union, peace, and patience" to be his country's greatest need at present. Fighting a supposedly weak Mexico may not be as easy as some expect, he says. Damage to U.S. maritime commerce and possible intervention by European powers on the side of Mexico could result from an ill-considered war.

Stressing the theme of peace further, Clay asserts that keeping harmony within the present United States is far more important than adding a new state. He alludes to his reputation as the Great Pacificator (earned for his help in crafting the Missouri Compromise) as he stresses the need to "eradicate prejudices" and "produce general contentment" among his nation's people. Specifically, he addresses the fear that the annexation of Texas would upset the sectional balance between slave and free states. He warns that the attempt by one region to gain dominance over another by acquiring new territory would threaten the Union's existence. If Texas were acquired to tilt the balance of power toward the South, then the North might seek to absorb Canada to advance its own interests—an example not without irony, considering Clay's own desire to add Canada to the Union more than thirty years earlier. Clay also expresses concern over the assumption of Texas's financial obligations by the United States.

In Clay's view, the best outcome for the United States would be for both Texas and Canada to become independent republics. These two countries would influence each other favorably and become natural allies with the United States in any struggle with a European power. As sovereign nations, Texas and Canada would be free to adopt laws that suited their particular needs. He notes that Texas's constitution was superior to that of the United States in some ways. (With these comments, Clay may be indirectly referring to rumors that Britain had made efforts to persuade Texas to prohibit slavery in exchange for British protection of its sovereignty.)

Clay devotes his letter's final sentences to summing up his arguments against annexation. Lack of broad public support and a negative impact upon national unity are cited as key reasons for his opposition. But the crucial factor is the attitude of Mexico. By stressing his desire to avoid war,

Clay implies that he might be willing to consider annexing Texas if conditions were different. Significantly, he does not say that he personally opposes admitting Texas to the Union as a slave state. By separating his personal feelings about Texas from the conditions of the moment, Clay avoids directly offending those on either side of the issue.

Clay believed that his "Raleigh Letter" would satisfy his supporters and effectively remove Texas as an issue from the campaign. But the situation changed when the pro-annexation Democrat James Polk defeated VanBuren for his party's presidential nomination. Fearing movement toward Polk in the South, Clay wrote a pair of letters to an editor in Tuscaloosa, Alabama, in July that stated his personal desire to see Texas annexed under the right conditions. This shift in emphasis further complicated his position and alienated some of his northern supporters. Clay went on to lose to Polk narrowly in November, with the defection of antislavery voters in New York and other states a probable contributing cause. It is worth noting that Clay's assessment of the Texas issue in the "Raleigh Letter" turned out to be largely accurate. As a campaign document, however, its accuracy was irrelevant next to what it showed about the political drawbacks of his tendency toward moderation and compromise.

♦ Remarks on the Compromise of 1850 Resolutions

As Clay had predicted, tensions between the United States and Mexico over the annexation of Texas led to war in 1845. Mexico's defeat in 1848 resulted in the American acquisition of thousands of miles of western territory, which revived questions about the expansion of slavery. The debate became especially heated in Congress, where antislavery and pro-slavery factions used increasingly hostile language and threatened disunion. Although he was seventy-three years old and in fragile health, Clay took the lead in fashioning a legislative package that would attempt to solve a number of interrelated issues. On January 29, 1850, he introduced his compromise resolutions to the Senate.

Clay begins by calling his proposals a cordial settlement of all subjects of controversy between the free and the slave states on the subject of slavery. He then proceeds to read and comment upon his eight resolutions; these deal with the admission of California as a free state, the organization of new territories without reference to slavery, the settlement of the border dispute between Texas and New Mexico, the payment of the Texas public debt, the maintenance of slavery and the abolition of the slave trade in the District of Columbia, the strengthening of fugitive slave laws, and the acknowledgment of the legality of the slave trade between the slaveholding states. Some of these resolutions, Clay admits, reaffirm existing laws rather than calling for new ones. They are intended to remind Congress that certain basic principles need to be adhered to.

In the remarks that follow, Clay makes an emotional appeal for the passage of his resolutions, emphasizing that they represent "no sacrifice of any principle... by either party." Partisans on both sides of the issue are asked to restrain their feelings for the good of national harmony. He acknowledges, though, that he is asking antislavery northerners to make the greatest concessions. Clay still urges them to accept compromise in the name of patriotism. The North can afford to be generous because of its larger population, he says. As the numerically weaker section, the South needs to be guaranteed protection for its property and social structure. Moreover, the North's belief in the principles of "humanity and philanthropy" (in other words, opposition to slavery) is, in Clay's view, an "abstraction," something removed from the everyday lives of its people. Northerners face no risk of sacrifice in holding such a view—it is "a sentiment without danger... without loss," he says.

Using dramatic language, Clay tries to make northerners feel the fears of the South through visual images. Though he does not spell out in detail what lies behind these fears, he is most likely referring to the threat of slave uprisings inspired by northern abolitionist activities. Justifiably or not, southerners viscerally feel this threat to be a "storm" endangering their homes and families. Painting a picture of destruction, Clay invites his audience to "behold... that dwelling-house now wrapped in flames" and see "those women and children who are flying from the calamitous scene." He notes that northern wives and children do not face similar dangers. (It is worth stating that no major slave insurrections had occurred since Nat Turner's Rebellion in 1831, twenty years earlier. Still, the possibility seemed very real to many slaveholders.) Summing up this line of argument, Clay makes a stark comparison between the "sentiment" of the North and the vital, life-and-death interests of the South.

Before closing, Clay mentions a gift he had received earlier that day. A well-wisher had presented him with a fragment of George Washington's coffin—a relic that he now holds in his hand. Clay hopes it will cause his colleagues to "beware, to pause, to reflect, before they lend themselves to any purposes which shall destroy that Union which was cemented by his [Washington's] exertions and example." On this reverently patriotic note, he asks that his resolutions be given a fair consideration. Clay's resolutions became the basis of a legislative package dubbed the Omnibus Bill, which was defeated after seven months of debate. However, Senator Stephen A. Douglas of Illinois quickly revived the proposals as separate bills and secured their passage. As it turned out, the Compromise of 1850 was more of a truce between hostile forces than a long-lasting agreement. Clay died before the outcome of his proposals could be fully known.

Impact and Legacy

It is fair to say that Clay's favored mode of expression was oratory. Typically, his speeches were at least partially improvised; much of what he said does not survive in manuscript form. Largely self-educated, Clay lacked the scholarly background of his Senate peers Daniel Webster and JohnC. Cal-

houn. Conversely, his words convey an emotional intensity lacking in the coldly logical works of his more cultured rivals. From the beginning to the end of his long career, Clay adhered to a unionist vision that transcended the concerns of his native South. He advocated a financial and manufacturing system that would bind the United States closer together; looking further, he foresaw the Western Hemisphere as an integrated economic unit. While he personally opposed slavery and predicted its eventual demise, he subordinated any desire to abolish it to the greater good of preserving the Union.

Clay's enemies viewed him as a shallow adventurer desperate to advance his own interests. As a politician, he sometimes made reckless moves and frequently failed to attain his goals, most spectacularly in his attempts to reach the White House. Few of his proposals actually became law at the time he advocated them, though his ideas influenced a host of more successful statesmen, most notably Abraham Lincoln. Clay's most enduring legacy may be as an advocate for national unity and economic expansion during a time of rising political turmoil and sectional jealousy.

Key Sources

Clay's papers are scattered among numerous university and historical society collections. The Henry Clay Family papers at the Library of Congress are available on microfilm. Many diaries, letters, and other writings are housed at Ashland, the Henry Clay estate (now a National Historic Landmark) in Lexington, Kentucky. *The Papers of Henry Clay, 1797–1852*, 11 volumes (1959–1992), is the standard compilation of his works. Also valuable is *Works of Henry Clay*, 10 volumes (1904). The Web site of Ashland (http://henryclay.org/hc.htm)—the Henry Clay estate—offers a useful overview of Clay's life and career.

Essential Quotes

"Whenever the sacred rights of an American freeman are assailed, all hearts ought to unite and every arm should be braced to vindicate his cause."

(Speech on the Bill to Raise an Additional Military Force)

"We are told that England is a proud and lofty nation that disdaining to wait for danger, meets it half way. Haughty as she is, we once triumphed over her, and if we do not listen to the councils of timidity and despair we shall again prevail. In such a cause, with the aid of Providence, we must come out crowned with success; but if we fail, let us fail like men, lash ourselves to our gallant tars, and expire together in one common struggle, fighting for seamen's rights and free trade."

(Speech on the Bill to Raise an Additional Military Force)

"Our Institutions … now make us free; but, how long shall we continue so, if we mould our opinions on those of Europe? Let us break these commercial and political fetters; let us no longer watch the nod of any European politician; let us become real and true Americans, and place ourselves at the head of the American system."

(Speech on South American Independence)

Essential Quotes

"This Republic, with the exception of the People of South America, constitute[s] the sole depository of political and religious freedom: and can it be possible … that we can remain passive spectators of the struggle of those People to break the same chains which once bound us?"

(Speech on South American Independence)

"I regard all wars as great calamities, to be avoided, if possible, and honorable peace as the wisest and truest policy of this country. What the United States most need are union, peace, and patience."

(Letter to the Editors of the *Washington National Intelligencer* on Texas Annexation)

"I conceive that no motive for the acquisition of foreign territory would be more unfortunate, or pregnant with more fatal consequences, than that of obtaining it for the purpose of strengthening one part against another part of the common Confederacy."

(Letter to the Editors of the *Washington National Intelligencer* on Texas Annexation)

"The plan is founded upon mutual forbearance, originating in a spirit of reconciliation and concession; not of principles, but of matters of feeling."

(Remarks on the Compromise of 1850 Resolutions)

"Sir, look at the storm which is now raging before you, beating in all its rage pitilessly on your family. They are in the South. But where are your families, where are your people, senators from the free States? They are safely housed, enjoying all the blessings of domestic comfort, peace, and quiet, in the bosoms of their own families."

(Remarks on the Compromise of 1850 Resolutions)

Further Reading

■ Books

Baxter, Maurice G. *Henry Clay and the American System*. Lexington: University Press of Kentucky, 1995.

Eaton, Clement. *Henry Clay and the Art of American Politics*. Boston: Little, Brown, 1957.

Holt, Michael F. *The Rise and Fall of the American Whig Party: Jacksonian Politics and the Onset of the Civil War*. New York: Oxford University Press, 1999.

Peterson, Merrill D. *The Great Triumvirate: Webster, Clay, and Calhoun*. New York: Oxford University Press, 1987.

Remini, Robert V. *Henry Clay: Statesman for the Union*. New York: W. W. Norton, 1991.

Van Deusen, Glyndon G. *The Life of Henry Clay*. Boston: Little, Brown, 1936.

■ Web Sites

"Clay, Henry," Biographical Directory of the United States Congress Web site. http://bioguide.congress.gov/scripts/biodisplay.pl?index=C000482.

Lincoln, Abraham. "Eulogy on Henry Clay." Miller Center of Public Affairs Web site. http://millercenter.org/scripps/archive/speeches/detail/3487.

—Barry Alfonso

Questions for Further Study

1. From the vantage point of nearly two hundred years, the War of 1812 survives in the history books in the shadow of larger conflicts such as the Civil War and the two world wars of the twentieth century. At the time, however, the causes for war with Britain seemed compelling to many Americans. Summarize those causes as stated by Henry Clay.

2. Foreign relations were complex for the United States in the early nineteenth century, particularly considering that the nation was still in its infancy. What were the major foreign policy issues the United States faced in these years? How did the nation resolve them or attempt to do so? What were some of the major interests the United States felt compelled to protect?

3. Clay seemed eager to wage war with Britain in 1812 but was reluctant to wage war with Mexico over Texas in the 1840s. What do you believe accounted for the difference in his attitude?

4. Henry Clay believed that sectional rivalry over the issue of slavery could eventually lead to civil war. He died in 1852, some nine years before the Civil War broke out. How do you believe he would have reacted to the Civil War had he lived? Would he have felt vindicated that his predictions came true, or would he have been dismayed that such was the case?

5. Compare and contrast Sam Houston's speech supporting the Compromise of 1850 and Henry Clay's remarks on the Compromise of 1850 resolutions.

Speech on the Bill to Raise an Additional Military Force

1813

Considering the situation in which this country is now placed—in a state of actual war with one of the most powerful nations on the earth—it may not be useless to take a view of the past, of various parties which have at different times appeared in this country, and to attend to the manner by which we have been driven from a peaceful posture. Such an inquiry may assist in guiding us to that result, an honorable peace, which must be the sincere desire of every friend to America. The course of that opposition, by which the administration of the government had been unremittingly impeded for the last twelve years, was singular, and, I believe, unexampled in the history of any country. It has been alike the duty and the interest of the administration to preserve peace. Their duty, because it is necessary to the growth of an infant people, their genius, and their habits. Their interest, because a change of the condition of the nation brings along with it a danger of the loss of the affections of the people. The administration has not been forgetful of these solemn obligations. No art has been left unessayed; no experiment, promising a favorable result, left untried to maintain the peaceful relations of the country....

Is the administration for negociation? The opposition is tired, sick, disgusted with negociation. They want to draw the sword and avenge the nation's wrongs. When, at length, foreign nations, perhaps, emboldened by the very opposition here made, refused to listen to the amicable appeals made, and repeated and reiterated by administration, to their justice and to their interests—when, in fact, war with one of them became identified with our independence and our sovereignty, and it was no longer possible to abstain from it, behold the opposition becoming the friends of peace and of commerce. They tell you of the calamities of war—its tragical events—the squandering away of your resources—the waste of the public treasure, and the spilling of innocent blood. They tell you that honor is an illusion! Now we see them exhibiting the terrific forms of the roaring king of the forest. Now the meekness and humility of the lamb! They are for war, and no restrictions, when the administration is for peace. They are for peace and restrictions, when the administration is for war. You find them, sir, tacking with every gale, displaying the colors of every party, and of all nations, steady only in one unalterable purpose, to steer, if possible, into the haven of power.

During all this time the parasites of opposition do not fail by cunning sarcasm or sly in[n]uendo to throw out the idea of French influence, which is known to be false, which ought to be met in one manner only, and that is by the lie direct. The administration of this country devoted to foreign influence! The administration of this country subservient to France! Great God! how is it so influenced? By what ligament, on what basis, on what possible foundation does it rest? Is it on similarity of language? No! we speak different tongues, we speak the English language. On the resemblance of our laws? No! the sources of our jurisprudence spring from another and a different country. On commercial intercourse? No! we have comparatively none with France. Is it from the correspondence in the genius of the two governments? No! here alone is the liberty of man secure from the inexorable depotism which everywhere else tramples it under foot. Where then is the ground of such an influence? But, sir, I am insulting you by arguing on such a subject. Yet, preposterous and ridiculous as the insinuation is, it is propagated with so much industry, that there are persons found foolish and credulous enough to believe it....

Next to the notice which the opposition has found itself called upon to bestow upon the French Emperor, a distinguished citizen of Virginia, formerly President of the United States, has never for a moment failed to receive their kindest and most respectful attention. An honorable gentleman from Massachusetts (Mr. Quincy), of whom I am sorry to say it becomes necessary for me, in the course of my remarks, to take some notice, has alluded [to him] in a remarkable manner. Neither his retirement from public office, his eminent services, nor his advanced age, can exempt this patriot from the coarse assaults of party malevolence. No, sir, in 1801, he snatched from the rude hands of usurpation the violated constitution of his country, and *that* is his crime. He preserved that instrument in form, and substance, and spirit, a precious inheritance, for generations to come, and for *this* he can never be forgiven. How impotent is party rage directed against him! He is not

more elevated by his lofty residence, upon the summit of his own favorite mountain, than he is lifted, by the serenity of his mind, and the consciousness of a well spent life, above the malignant passions and the turmoils of the day. No! his own beloved Monticello is not less moved by the storms that beat against its sides than he hears with composure, if he hears at all, the howlings of the whole British pack set loose from the Essex kennel! When the gentleman to whom I have been compelled to allude shall have mingled his dust with that of his abused ancestors, when he shall be consigned to oblivion, or if he lives at all, shall live only in the treasonable annals of a certain junto, the name of Jefferson will be hailed as the second founder of the liberties of this people, and the period of his administration will be looked back to as one of the happiest and brightest epochs in American history. I beg the gentleman's pardon; he has secured to himself a more imperishable fame....

The honorable gentleman from New York (Mr. Bleecker), in the very sensible speech with which he favored the committee, made one observation that did not comport with his usual liberal and enlarged views. It was that those who are most interested against the practice of impressment did not desire a continuance of the war on account of it, whilst those (the southern and western members) who had no interest in it, were the zealous advocates of the American seaman. It was a provincial sentiment unworthy of that gentleman. It was one which, in a change of condition, he would not express, because I know he could not feel it. Does not that gentleman feel for the unhappy victims of the tomahawk in the Western country, although his quarter of the union may be exempted from similar barbarities? I am sure he does. If there be a description of rights which, more than any other, should unite all parties in all quarters of the Union, it is unquestionably the rights of the person. No matter what his vocation; whether he seeks subsistence amidst the dangers of the deep, or draws it from the bowels of the earth, or from the humblest occupations of mechanic life: whenever the sacred rights of an American freeman are assailed, all hearts ought to unite and every arm should be braced to vindicate his cause.

[Another representative] sees in Canada no object worthy of conquest. According to him, it is a cold, sterile, and inhospitable region. And yet, such are the allurements which it offers, that the same gentleman apprehends that, if it be annexed to the United States, already too much weakened by an extension of territory, the people of New England will rush over the line and depopulate that section of the Union! That gentleman considers it honest to hold Canada as a kind of hostage, to regard it as a sort of bond, for the good behaviour of the enemy. But he will not enforce the bond. The actual conquest of that country would, according to him, make no impression upon the enemy, and yet the very apprehension only of such a conquest would at all times have a powerful operation upon him! Other gentlemen consider the invasion of that country as wicked and unjustifiable. Its inhabitants are represented as unoffending, connected with those of the bordering states by a thousand tender ties, interchanging acts of kindness, and all the offices of good neighborhood; Canada, ... innocent! Canada unoffending! Is it not in Canada that the tomahawk of the savage has been moulded into its death-like form? From Canadian magazines, Malden and others, that those supplies have been issued which nourish and sustain the Indian hostilities? Supplies which have enabled the savage hordes to butcher the garrison of Chicago, and to commit other horrible murders? Was it not by the joint cooperation of Canadians and Indians that a remote American fort, Michilimackinac, was fallen upon and reduced, [while the garrison was] in ignorance of a state of war? But, sir, how soon have the opposition changed. When administration was striving, by the operation of peaceful measures, to bring Great Britain back to a sense of justice, they were for old-fashioned war. And now that they have got old-fashioned war, their sensibilities are cruelly shocked, and all their sympathies are lavished upon the harmless inhabitants of the adjoining provinces. What does a state of war present? The united energies of one people arrayed against the combined energies of another—a conflict in which each party aims to inflict all the injury it can, by sea and land, upon the territories, property and citizens of the other, subject only to the rules of mitigated war practised by civilized nations. The gentlemen would not touch the continental provinces of the enemy, nor, I presume, for the same reason, her possessions in the W. Indies. The same humane spirit would spare the seamen and soldiers of the enemy. The sacred person of his majesty must not be attacked, for the learned gentlemen, on the other side, are quite familiar with the maxim, that the king can do no wrong. Indeed, sir, I know of no person on whom we may make war, upon the principles of the honorable gentlemen, but Mr. Stephen, the celebrated author of the orders in council, or the board of admiralty, who authorise and regulate the practice of impressment!

Document Text

The disasters of the war admonish us, we are told, of the necessity of terminating the contest. If our achievements upon the land have been less splendid than those of our intrepid seamen, it is not because the American soldier is less brave. On the one element organization, discipline, and a thorough knowledge of their duties exist, on the part of the officers and their men. On the other, almost every thing is yet to be acquired. We have however the consolation that our country abounds with the richest materials, and that in no instance when engaged in an action have our arms been tarnished. At Brownstown and at Queenstown the valor of veterans was displayed, and acts of the noblest heroism were performed. It is true, that the disgrace of Detroit remains to be wiped off. That is a subject on which I cannot trust my feelings, it is not fitting I should speak. But this much I will say, it was an event which no human foresight could have anticipated, and for which administration cannot be justly censured. It was the parent of all the misfortunes we have experienced on land. But for it the Indian war would have been in a great measure prevented or terminated; the ascendency on lake Erie acquired, and the war pushed perhaps to Montreal. With the exception of that event, the war, even upon the land, has been attended by a series of the most brilliant exploits, which, whatever interest they may inspire on this side of the mountains, have given the greatest pleasure on the other. The expedition under the command of Gov. Edwards and Colonel Russell, to lake Pioria, on the Illinois, was completely successful. So was that of Captain Craig, who it is said ascended that river still higher. General Hopkins destroyed the Prophet's town. We have just received intelligence of the gallant enterprise of Colonel Campbell. In short, sir, the Indian towns have been swept, from the mouth to source of the Wabash, and a hostile country has been penetrated far beyond the most daring incursions of any campaign during the former Indian war. Never was more cool deliberate bravery displayed than that by Newnan's party from Georgia. And the capture of the Detroit, and the destruction of the Caledonia, (whether placed to our maritime or land account) for judgment, skill, and courage on the part of Lieutenant Elliott, has never been surpassed....

What cause, Mr. Chairman, which existed for declaring the war has been removed? We sought indemnity for the past and security for the future. The orders in council are suspended, not revoked; no compensation for spoliations, Indian hostilities, which were before secretly instigated, now openly encouraged; and the practice of impressment unremittingly persevered in and insisted upon. Yet administration has given the strongest demonstrations of its love of peace. On the 29th June, less than ten days after the declaration of war, the Secretary of State writes to Mr. Russell, authorising him to agree to an armistice, upon two conditions only, and what are they? That the orders in council should be repealed, and the practice of impressing American seamen cease, those already impressed being released. The proposition was for nothing more than a *real* truce; that the war should in fact cease on *both* sides. Again on the 27th July, one month later, anticipating a possible objection to these terms, reasonable as they are, Mr. Monroe empowers Mr. Russell to stipulate in general terms for an armistice, having only an informal understanding on these points. In return, the enemy is offered a prohibition of the employment of his seamen in our service, thus removing entirely all pretext for the practice of impressment. The very proposition which the gentleman from Connecticut (Mr. Pitkin) contends ought to be made has been made. How are these pacific advances met by the other party? Rejected as absolutely inadmissible, cavils are indulged about the inadequacy of Mr. Russell's powers, and the want of an act of Congress is intimated. And yet the constant usage of nations I believe is, where the legislation of one party is necessary to carry into effect a given stipulation, to leave it to the contracting party to provide the requisite laws. If he failed to do so, it is a breach of good faith, and a subject of subsequent remonstrance by the injured party. When Mr. Russell renews the overture, in what was intended as a more agreeable form to the British government, Lord Castlereagh is not content with a simple rejection, but clothes it in the language of insult. Afterwards, in conversation with Mr. Russell, the moderation of our government is misinterpreted and made the occasion of a sneer, that we are tired of the war. The proposition of Admiral Warren is submitted in a spirit not more pacific. He is instructed, he tells us, to propose that the government of the United States shall instantly recall their letters of marque and reprisal against British ships, together with all orders and instructions for any acts of hostility whatever against the territories of his Majesty or the persons or property of his subjects. That small affair being settled, he is further authorised to arrange as to the revocation of the laws which interdict the commerce and ships of war of his Majesty from the harbors and waters of the United States. This messenger of peace comes with one

Document Text

qualified concession in his pocket, not made to the justice of our demands, and is fully empowered to receive our homage, the contrite retraction of all our measures adopted against his master! And in default, he does not fail to assure us, the orders in council are to be forth-with revived. Administration, still anxious to terminate the war, suppresses the indignation which such a proposal ought to have created, and in its answer concludes by informing Admiral Warren, "that if there be no objection to an accommodation of the difference relating to impressment, in the mode proposed, other than the suspension of the British claim to impressment during the armistice, there can be none to proceeding, *without the armistice,* to an immediate discussion and arrangement of an article on that subject." Thus it has left the door of negociation unclosed, and it remains to be seen if the enemy will accept the invitation tendered to him. The honorable gentleman from North Carolina (Mr. Pearson) supposes, that if Congress would pass a law, prohibiting the employment of British seamen in our service, upon condition of a like prohibition on their part, and repeal the act of non-importation, peace would immediately follow. Sir, I have no doubt if such a law were passed, with all the requisite solemnities, and the repeal to take place, Lord Castlereagh would laugh at our simplicity. No, sir, administration has erred in the steps which it has taken to restore peace, but its error has been not in doing too little but in betraying too great a solicitude for that event. An honorable peace is attainable only by an efficient war. My plan would be to call out the ample resources of the country, give them a judicious direction, prosecute the war with the utmost vigor, strike wherever we can reach the enemy, at sea or on land, and negotiate the terms of a peace at Quebec or Halifax. We are told that England is a proud and lofty nation that disdaining to wait for danger, meets it half way. Haughty as she is, we once triumphed over her, and if we do not listen to the councils of timidity and despair we shall again prevail. In such a cause, with the aid of Providence, we must come out crowned with success; but if we fail, let us fail like men, lash ourselves to our gallant tars, and expire together in one common struggle, fighting for *"seamen's rights and free trade ."*

Glossary

Castlereagh:	Robert Stewart, Viscount Castlereagh (1769–1822), the British foreign secretary during the War of 1812
Essex kennel:	a reference to the so-called Essex junto, a group of merchants and lawyers from Essex County, Massachusetts, who were scheming to secede from the Union
impressment:	the practice of seizing men and forcing them to serve in the military
letters of marque:	official government warrants authorizing a person to search or seize the property belonging to a foreign party, often issued in reprisal against a foreign nation and to privateers against the merchant shipping of another nation
magazines:	here, a reference to stores of arms
Monticello:	the name of Thomas Jefferson's estate in Virginia
Mr. Quincy:	Boston congressman Josiah Quincy (1772–1864), at the time a U.S. congressional representative, whose motion to impeach President Thomas Jefferson was rejected by Congress
Prophet's town:	Prophetstown, a city in Illinois associated with the Indian leader Tecumseh
Russell:	Jonathan Russell (1771–1832), U.S. chargé d'affaires in London at the outbreak of the War of 1812
tacking with every gale:	a seafaring phrase suggesting that viewpoints change depending on the situation
W. Indies:	West Indies

Speech on South American Independence

1818

The proposition to recognize the Independent governments of South America offers a subject of as great importance as any which could claim the deliberate consideration of this House.

[Henry Clay] then went on to say, that it appeared to him the object of this government, heretofore, had been, so to manage its affairs, in regard to South America, as to produce an effect on its existing negociations with the parent country. The House were now apprized, by the Message from the President, that this policy had totally failed; it had failed, because our country would not dishonor itself by surrendering one of the most important rights incidental to sovereignty. Although we had observed a course towards the Patriots, as Mr. Gallatin said in his communication read yesterday, greatly exceeding in rigor the course pursued towards them either by France or England; altho', also, as was remarked by the Secretary of State, we had observed a neutrality so strict that blood had been spilt in enforcing it…still, Spanish honor was not satisfied, and fresh sacrifices were demanded of us. If they were resisted in form, they were substantially yielded by our course as to South America. We will not stipulate with Spain not to recognize the Independence of the South; but we nevertheless grant to her all she demands.…

Two years ago, Mr. C. said, would, in his opinion, have been the proper time for recognizing the independence of the South. Then the struggle was somewhat doubtful, and a kind office on the part of this government would have had a salutary effect. Since that period, what had occurred? Any thing to prevent a recognition of their independence, or to make it less expedient? No; every occurrence tended to prove the capacity of that country to maintain its independence. … There was a time, he said, when impressions are made on individuals and nations, by kindness towards them, which last forever…when they are surrounded with enemies, and embarrassments present themselves. Ages and ages may pass away, said Mr. C. before we forget the help we received, in our day of peril, from the hands of France. Her injustice, the tyranny of a despot, may alienate us for a time; but, the moment it ceases, we relapse into a good feeling towards her. Do you mean to wait, said Mr. C. until these Republics are recognized by the whole world, and then step in and extend your hand to them when it can no longer be withheld? … What would I give, exclaimed Mr. Clay, could we appreciate the advantages which may be realized by pursuing the course which I propose! It is in our power to create a system of which we shall be the centre, and in which all South America will act with us. In respect to commerce, we should be most benefitted: this country would become the place of deposit of the commerce of the world. Our citizens engaged in foreign trade were at present disheartened by the condition of that trade: they must seek new channels for it…and none so advantageous could be found, as those which the trade with South America would afford. Mr. C. took a prospective view of the growth of wealth, and increase of population of this country and of South America. That country had now a population of upwards of eighteen millions. The same activity of the principle of population would exist in that country as here. Twenty-five years hence its population might be estimated at thirty-six millions; fifty years hence, at seventy-two millions. *We* now have a population of ten millions. From the character of our population, we must always take the lead in the prosecution of commerce and manufactures. Imagine the vast power of the two countries, and the value of the intercourse between them, when we shall have a population of forty millions, and they of seventy millions! In relation to South America, the people of the United States will occupy the same position as the people of New England do to the rest of the United States. Our enterprize, industry, and habits of economy, will give us the advantage in any competition which South America may sustain with us, &c.

But however important our early recognition of the Independence of the South might be to us, as respects our commercial and manufacturing interests, was there not another view of the subject, infinitely more gratifying? We should become the centre of a system which would constitute the rallying point of human freedom against all the despotism of the Old World. Did any man doubt the feelings of the South towards us? In spite of our coldness towards them, of the rigor of our laws, and the conduct of our officers, their hearts still turned towards us, as to their brethren; and he had no earthly doubt, if our

Document Text

government would take the lead and recognize them, that they would become yet more anxious to imitate our Institutions, and to secure to themselves and to their posterity the same freedom which we enjoy. … Our Institutions, said Mr. C. now make us free; but, how long shall we continue so, if we mould our opinions on those of Europe? Let us break these commercial and political fetters; let us no longer watch the nod of any European politician; let us become real and true Americans, and place ourselves at the head of the American system.…

Two questions only, Mr. Clay argued, were necessarily preliminary to the recognition of the independence of the People of the South: first, as to the fact of their independence; and, secondly, as to their capacity for self government. On the first point, not a doubt existed. On the second, there was every evidence in their favor. They had fostered schools with great care; there were more newspapers in the single town of Buenos Ayres (at the time he was speaking) than in the whole kingdom of Spain. He never saw a question discussed with more ability than that in a newspaper of Buenos Ayres, whether a federative or consolidated form of government was best.…

With regard to the form of his proposition, Mr. C. said, all he wanted was to obtain an expression of the opinion of the house on this subject; and whether a Minister should be authorized to one or the other of these governments, or whether he should be of one grade or of another, he cared not. This Republic, with the exception of the People of South America, constituted the sole depository of political and religious freedom: and can it be possible, said he, that we can remain passive spectators of the struggle of those People to break the same chains which once bound us? The opinion of the friends of Freedom in Europe is, that our policy has been cold, heartless, and indifferent towards the greatest cause which could possibly engage our affections and enlist our feelings in its behalf.

Mr. C. concluded by saying that, whatever might be the decision of this house on this question, proposing shortly to go into retirement from public life, he should there have the consolation of knowing that he had used *his* best exertions in favor of a People inhabiting a territory calculated to contain as many souls as the whole of Christendom besides, whose happiness was at stake, and which it was in the power of this government to do so much towards securing.

Glossary

Buenos Ayres:	Buenos Aires, a city in Argentina
Gallatin:	Albert Gallatin (1761–1849), U.S. senator, diplomat, and secretary of the treasury
Old World:	Europe
Secretary of State:	John Quincy Adams

Letter to the Editors of the *Washington National Intelligencer* on Texas Annexation

1844

Subsequent to my departure from Ashland, in December last, I received various communications from popular assemblages and private individuals, requesting an expression of my opinion upon the question of the Annexation of Texas to the United States. I have forborne to reply to them, because it was not very convenient, during the progress of my journey, to do so, and for other reasons. … To the astonishment of the whole nation, we are now informed that a treaty of annexation has been actually concluded, and is to be submitted to the Senate for its consideration. The motives for my silence, therefore, no longer remain, and I feel it to be my duty to present an exposition of my views and opinions upon the question, for what they may be worth, to the public consideration. I adopt this method as being more convenient than several replies to the respective communications which I have received.

I regret that I have not the advantage of a view of the treaty itself, so as to enable me to adapt an expression of my opinion to the actual conditions and stipulations which it contains. Not possessing that opportunity, I am constrained to treat the question according to what I presume to be the terms of the treaty. If, without the loss of national character, without the hazard of foreign war, with the general concurrence of the nation, without any danger to the integrity of the Union, and without giving an unreasonable price for Texas, the question of annexation were presented, it would appear in quite a different light from that in which, I apprehend, it is now to be regarded.

The United States acquired a title to Texas, extending, as I believe, to the Rio del Norte, by the treaty of Louisiana. They ceded and relinquished that title to Spain by the treaty of 1819, by which the Sabine was substituted for the Rio del Norte as our western boundary. … When the treaty was laid before the House of Representatives, being a member of that body, I expressed the opinion, which I then entertained, and still hold, that Texas was sacrificed to the acquisition of Florida. We wanted Florida; but I thought it must, from its position, inevitably fall into our possession; that the point of a few years, sooner or later, was of no sort of consequence, and that in giving five millions of dollars and Texas for it, we gave more than a just equivalent. But, if we made a great sacrifice in the surrender of Texas, we ought to take care not to make too great a sacrifice in the attempt to re-acquire it.…

Annexation and war with Mexico are identical. Now, for one, I certainly am not willing to involve this country in a foreign war for the object of acquiring Texas. I know there are those who regard such a war with indifference and as a trifling affair, on account of the weakness of Mexico, and her inability to inflict serious injury upon this country. But I do not look upon it thus lightly. I regard all wars as great calamities, to be avoided, if possible, and honorable peace as the wisest and truest policy of this country. What the United States most need are union, peace, and patience. Nor do I think that the weakness of a Power should form a motive, in any case, for inducing us to engage in or to depreciate the evils of war. Honor and good faith and justice are equally due from this country towards the weak as towards the strong. And, if an act of injustice were to be perpetrated towards any Power, it would be more compatible with the dignity of the nation, and, in my judgment, less dishonorable, to inflict it upon a powerful instead of a weak foreign nation.…

I do not think that Texas ought to be received into the Union, as an integral part of it, in decided opposition to the wishes of a considerable and respectable portion of the Confederacy. I think it far more wise and important to compose and harmonize the present Confederacy, as it now exists, than to introduce a new element of discord and distraction into it. In my humble opinion, it should be the constant and earnest endeavor of American statesmen to eradicate prejudices, to cultivate and foster concord, and to produce general contentment among all parts of our Confederacy. And true wisdom, it seems to me, points to the duty of rendering its present members happy, prosperous, and satisfied with each other, rather than to attempt to introduce alien members, against the common consent and with the certainty of deep dissatisfaction.…

It is useless to disguise that there are those who espouse and those who oppose the annexation

Document Text

of Texas upon the ground of the influence which it would exert, in the balance of political power, between two great sections of the Union. I conceive that no motive for the acquisition of foreign territory would be more unfortunate, or pregnant with more fatal consequences, than that of obtaining it for the purpose of strengthening one part against another part of the common Confederacy. Such a principle, put into practical operation, would menace the existence, if it did not certainly sow the seeds of a dissolution of the Union. It would be to proclaim to the world an insatiable and unquenchable thirst for foreign conquest or acquisition of territory. For if to-day Texas be acquired to strengthen one part of the Confederacy, tomorrow Canada may be required to add strength to another....

Should Texas be annexed to the Union, the United States will assume and become responsible for the debt of Texas, be its amount what it may. What it is, I do not know certainly; but the least I have seen it stated at is thirteen millions of dollars. And this responsibility will exist, whether there be a stipulation in the treaty or not expressly assuming the payment of the debt of Texas. For I suppose it to be undeniable that, if one nation becomes incorporated in another, all the debts, and obligations, and incumbrances, and wars of the incorporated nation, become the debts, and obligations, and incumbrances, and wars of the common nation created by the incorporation....

In the future progress of events, it is probable that there will be a voluntary or forcible separation of the British North American possessions from the parent country. I am strongly inclined to think that it will be best for the happiness of all parties that, in that event, they should be erected into a separate and independent Republic. With the Canadian Republic on one side, that of Texas on the other, and the United States, the friend of both, between them, each could advance its own happiness by such constitutions, laws, and measures, as were best adapted to its peculiar condition. They would be natural allies, ready, by co-operation, to repel any European or foreign attack upon either. Each would afford a secure refuge to the persecuted and oppressed driven into exile by either of the others. They would emulate each other in improvements, in free institutions, and in the science of self-government. Whilst Texas has adopted our constitution as the model of hers, she has, in several important particulars, greatly improved upon it.

Although I have felt compelled, from the nature of the inquiries addressed to me, to extend this communication to a much greater length than I could have wished, I could not do justice to the subject, and fairly and fully expose my own opinions in a shorter space. In conclusion, they may be stated in a few words to be, that I consider the annexation of Texas, at this time, without the assent of Mexico, as a measure compromising the national character, involving us certainly in war with Mexico, probably with other foreign Powers, dangerous to the integrity of the Union, inexpedient in the present financial condition of the country, and not called for by any general expression of public opinion.

Remarks on the Compromise of 1850 Resolutions

Remarks on the Compromise of 1850 Resolutions (1850)

Mr. President, you have before you the whole series of resolutions, the whole scheme of arrangement and accommodation of these distracting questions, which I have to offer, after having bestowed on these subjects the most anxious, intensely anxious, consideration ever since I have been in this body. How far it may prove acceptable to both or either of the parties on these great questions, it is not for me to say. I think it ought to be acceptable to both. There is no sacrifice of any principle, proposed in any of them, by either party. The plan is founded upon mutual forbearance, originating in a spirit of reconciliation and concession; not of principles, but of matters of feeling. At the North, sir, I know that from feeling, by many at least cherished as being dictated by considerations of humanity and philanthropy, there exists a sentiment adverse to the institution of slavery.

Sir, I might, I think—although I believe this project contains about an equal amount of concession and forbearance on both sides—have asked from the free States of the North a more liberal and extensive concession than should be asked from the slave States. And why, sir? With you, gentlemen senators of the free States, what is it? An abstraction, a sentiment—a sentiment, if you please, of humanity and philanthropy—a noble sentiment, when directed rightly, with no sinister or party purposes; an atrocious sentiment—a detestable sentiment—or rather the abuse of it—when directed to the accomplishment of unworthy purposes. I said that I might ask from you larger and more expansive concessions than from the slave States. And why? You are numerically more powerful than the slave States. Not that there is any difference—for upon that subject I can not go along with the ardent expression of feeling by some of my friends coming from the same class of States from which I come—not that there is any difference in valor, in prowess, in noble and patriotic daring, whenever it is required for the safety and salvation of the country, between the people of one class of States and those of the other. You are, in point of numbers however, greater; and greatness and magnanimity should ever be allied.

But there are other reasons why concession upon such a subject as this should be more liberal, more expansive, coming from the free than from the slave States. It is, as I remarked, a sentiment, a sentiment of humanity and philanthropy on your side. Ay, sir, and when a sentiment of that kind is honestly and earnestly cherished, with a disposition to make sacrifices to enforce it, it is a noble and beautiful sentiment; but, sir, when the sacrifice is not to be made by those who cherish that sentiment and inculcate it, but by another people, in whose situation it is impossible, from their position, to sympathize and to share all and every thing that belongs to them, I must say to you, senators from the free States, it is a totally different question. On your side it is a sentiment, without sacrifice, a sentiment without danger, a sentiment without hazard, without peril, without loss. But how is it on the other side, to which, as I have said, a greater amount of concession ought to be made in any scheme of compromise?

In the first place, sir, there is a vast and incalculable amount of property to be sacrificed, and to be sacrificed, not by your sharing in the common burdens, but exclusive of you. And this is not all. The social intercourse, habit, safety, property, life, every thing is at hazard, in a greater or less degree, in the slave States.

Sir, look at the storm which is now raging before you, beating in all its rage pitilessly on your family. They are in the South. But where are your families, where are your people, senators from the free States? They are safely housed, enjoying all the blessings of domestic comfort, peace, and quiet, in the bosoms of their own families.

Behold, Mr. President, that dwelling-house now wrapped in flames. Listen, sir, to the rafters and beams which fall in succession, amid the crash; and the flames ascending higher and higher as they tumble down. Behold those women and children who are flying from the calamitous scene, and with their shrieks and lamentations imploring the aid of high Heaven. Whose house is that? Whose wives and children are they? Yours in the free States? No. You are looking on in safety and security, while the conflagration which I have described is raging in the slave States, and produced, not intentionally by you, but

Document Text

produced from the inevitable tendency of the measures which you have adopted, and which others have carried far beyond what you have wished.

In the one scale, then, we behold sentiment, sentiment, sentiment alone; in the other property, the social fabric, life, and all that makes life desirable and happy.…

But, sir, I find myself engaged much beyond what I intended, when I came this morning from my lodgings, in the exposition with which I intended these resolutions should go forth to the consideration of the world. I can not omit, however, before I conclude, relating an incident, a thrilling incident, which occurred prior to my leaving my lodgings this morning.

A man came to my room—the same at whose instance, a few days ago, I presented a memorial calling upon Congress for the purchase of Mount Vernon for the use of the public—and, without being at all aware of what purpose I entertained in the discharge of my public duty to-day; he said to me: "Mr. Clay, I heard you make a remark the other day, which induces me to I suppose that a precious relic in my possession would be acceptable to you." He then drew out of his pocket, and presented to me the object which I now hold in my hand. And what, Mr. President, do you suppose it is? It is a fragment of the coffin of Washington—a fragment of that coffin in which now repose in silence, in sleep, and speechless, all the earthly remains of the venerated Father of his country. Was it portentous that it should have been thus presented to me? Was it a sad presage of what might happen to that fabric which Washington's virtue, patriotism, and valor established? No, sir, no. It was a warning voice, coming from the grave to the Congress now in session to beware, to pause, to reflect, before they lend themselves to any purposes which shall destroy that Union which was cemented by his exertions and example. Sir, I hope an impression may be made on your mind such as that which was made on mine by the reception of this precious relic.

And, in conclusion, I now ask every senator, I entreat you gentlemen, in fairness and candor, to examine the plan of accommodation which this series of resolutions proposes, and not to pronounce against them until convinced after a thorough examination. I move that the resolutions be read and received.

Glossary

inculcate: to teach by repeated instruction

Mount Vernon: George Washington's estate in Virginia

View of Henry Clay's law office (1803-1810), **Lexington, Kentucky**

Gubernatorial portrait of Grover Cleveland by Eastman Johnson

Grover Cleveland: Original Analysis

Twenty-second and Twenty-fourth President of the United States

1837–1908

Overview

Grover Cleveland was born in New Jersey in 1837 but moved to New York as a youth. A lifelong Democrat, he was elected sheriff of Erie County, New York, in 1870 and then mayor of Buffalo. Cleveland established a reputation as a reformer and was elected governor in 1882. He won his party's nomination in 1884 and was elected president. Cleveland lost in the 1888 election, but he won a second term in 1892, becoming the only president in U.S. history to serve nonconsecutive terms. During his first term Cleveland endeavored to curb the power of special interests within Congress. His second term was marred by a severe economic crisis and a national dispute over the annexation of Hawaii. He declined to run for a third term in 1896 and instead retired from public life. Cleveland died on June 24, 1908.

In 1884 Cleveland was the first Democrat elected president since the Civil War. He entered office determined to reform national politics, and he issued a record number of vetoes, often to defeat bills that catered to special interests. He viewed the presidency as a public trust that required his utmost devotion and duty. A plain man, Cleveland was uncomfortable with the trappings of his office. He became the first president to be married in the White House when he wed Frances Folsom in 1886. Cleveland was extremely hardworking and impressed both admirers and detractors with his energy and zeal. He strongly resisted congressional efforts to constrain presidential power. Cleveland's actions helped strengthen the office of chief executive and established the foundation of the modern presidency.

Many of Cleveland's major domestic initiatives had limited success in his first term. He strongly favored free trade and lower tariffs, but he was unable to reform the nation's tariff system. He also failed to repeal currency laws that undermined the value of the dollar. During his second term a major depression caused widespread unemployment and stagnant economic growth. Cleveland worked to prevent the collapse of the dollar and protect the nation's gold reserves. His support of gold-backed currency put him at odds with westerners within his own party who supported silver. He took strong action against labor unrest, including the use of federal troops to quell labor protests.

In foreign policy Cleveland was a staunch anti-imperialist. He supported a free-trade agreement with Hawaii but opposed annexation of the island kingdom. The president resisted congressional efforts to involve the United States in the ongoing Cuban revolution. He thought that the United States should be neutral in the conflict, although he endorsed eventual Cuban independence from Spain. Cleveland also opposed German efforts to create a sphere of influence over the Solomon Islands. He used the Monroe Doctrine as a justification for intervening in a boundary dispute between Great Britain and Venezuela. Cleveland threatened military action as a way to pressure the British, who eventually agreed to arbitration. His policies reflected ongoing splits within the Democratic Party on foreign policy, economics, and social issues. The divisions within the party prompted Cleveland to retire after his second term.

Explanation and Analysis of Documents

Cleveland was an honest and forthright president during a period marked by scandal and political patronage. His rapid political success was the result of his reputation as a reformer willing to oppose elites and special interest groups. He was not a great orator (during the 1884 presidential campaign he gave only two speeches), but he had a strong moral code that was reflected in his public statements and papers. Cleveland crafted his public messages to emphasize his image as a reformer. Five documents—his first inaugural address; his letter to a local Democratic club on the importance of principles over political spoils; his message to the special session of Congress on the nation's economic crisis; a statement on his opposition to the annexation of Hawaii; and his final annual message to Congress, on U.S. neutrality in the Cuban crisis—provide insight into his political philosophy and the way in which he addressed the most pressing issues of his day

♦ First Inaugural Address

During the presidential race in 1884 Cleveland campaigned as a progressive reformer who would reorient national politics to minimize the power and influence of elites and special interests. The Republican Party selected the former secretary of state James D. Blaine as its presidential candidate. Many reformist Republicans, known as "mugwumps," saw Blaine as corrupt, and his nomination alienated many within the party. Cleveland sought to attract the mugwumps by emphasizing his reputation as an honest politician and his record as a reformer. In one of the closest elections in U.S. history he defeated Blaine by a margin of just over twenty-five thousand votes.

In his inaugural address Cleveland seeks to differentiate himself from previous chief executives and reaffirm his intention to reform national politics. He pledges to follow a "just and unstrained construction of the Constitution" and dutifully discharge his office. The incoming president also pledges to be a good and honest steward of public funds and calls upon the American people to keep a "vigilant watch and close scrutiny" over public servants and make "a fair and reasonable estimate of their fidelity and usefulness." Cleveland specifically promises to review the manner in which the federal government managed public lands in the West. He further promises that his foreign policy will emphasize neutrality and that he will oppose imperialism as well as unrestricted immigration. Cleveland concludes with an assurance that he will undertake civil service reform.

Once in office, Cleveland worked to implement his pledges. He rejected the prevailing spoils system under which past presidents had filled public offices with supporters and influential party members. Instead, Cleveland retained a significant number of Republican appointees even though this angered many in the Democratic Party who hoped to gain lucrative government appointments. He used the 1883 Pendleton Civil Service Act to convert a number of federal positions from being presidential appointments to new, merit-based civil service jobs. Cleveland also reduced the overall size of the federal government and eliminated a number of positions, many of which had been created with the sole purpose of rewarding party members and supporters.

During his tenure Cleveland faced a hostile Congress. The Republican Party controlled the Senate, and many expenditure bills were passed that Cleveland opposed because he believed they were designed to benefit special interests or individuals. He vetoed more bills than any other president up to that time. Most of the measures were pension bills that would have granted government benefits to those who had served during the Civil War. Many involved requests that had been rejected by the federal Bureau of Pensions, but the affected individuals had then appealed to their congressman or senator. In line with his inaugural promise to "closely limit public expenditures to the actual needs of the Government," Cleveland also vetoed a popular measure that would have provided $10,000 to farmers in Texas in 1887 after a drought devastated areas of the state. He argued that nothing in the Constitution granted the government the authority to use public funds to provide economic assistance to private citizens unless there was a compelling national need. Cleveland ordered a review of public lands in the West that had been granted to railroads. The railroads had originally been given rights to vast tracts of land in exchange for building new rail lines, but in many cases the companies had failed to construct the promised lines. As a result of the inquiry more than eighty-one million acres was restored to federal control.

Foreign policy under the first Cleveland administration followed the parameters laid out in the president's inaugural address. Cleveland withdrew a treaty that would have allowed the United States access to develop areas of the Congo, and he declined to pursue efforts to build a canal across Nicaragua. Under Cleveland the United States and Great Britain negotiated a long-standing fisheries dispute in the North Atlantic (although the Senate rejected the treaty). The administration did pledge to protect Samoa (where the United States had established a small naval base in 1878) from German colonialism and persuaded the German government to resolve any disputes related to the islands through an international conference.

Time Line

1837	March 18	■ Grover Cleveland is born in Caldwell, New Jersey.
1863		■ Cleveland becomes assistant district attorney in Erie County, New York.
1871	January 1	■ Cleveland is inaugurated sheriff of Erie County.
1881		■ Cleveland wins election as mayor of Buffalo, New York.
1882		■ Cleveland is elected governor of New York.
1884	November 4	■ Cleveland is elected president of the United States.
1885	March 4	■ Cleveland delivers his first inaugural address.
1890	December 4	■ Cleveland's letter to an Ohio Democratic Club calls for clean politics.
1892	November 8	■ Cleveland is again elected president of the United States.
1893	August 8	■ Cleveland calls a special session of Congress to deal with the nation's economic crisis.
	December 18	■ Cleveland sends Congress a message opposing the annexation of Hawaii.
1896	December 7	■ Cleveland delivers his annual message to Congress, in which he advocates U.S. neutrality in the Cuban revolution.
1908	June 24	■ Cleveland dies in Princeton, New Jersey.

Cleveland was unable to reform the nation's tariff system. He favored lower tariffs, an unpopular position especially in the industrial areas of the North. Tariffs dominated the 1888 presidential election. The Republican candidate, Benjamin Harrison, adopted a staunch protectionist platform. Cleveland won the popular balloting but lost in the electoral college, 233 to 168.

♦ "Principles above Spoils" Letter

After he left office, Cleveland joined a private law firm in New York. Initially the former president remained out of the public eye and declined to criticize Harrison or his policies. However, Cleveland continued to be active behind the scenes in Democratic politics, and there was a general expectation that he would seek the presidency again in 1892. In 1890 a financial panic initiated an economic depression. In addition, the Republicans had enacted the 1890 McKinley Tariff, which raised taxes on imports to their highest level in U.S. history. As a result, the Democrats swept the 1890 midterm congressional elections, winning eighty-six new seats while the Republicans lost ninety-three and the small Populist Party gained eight. In the aftermath of the congressional balloting, Cleveland launched his bid to replace Harrison.

On December 4, 1890, Cleveland sent a letter to a celebration in Canton, Ohio, of the Democratic victory. In the document he reminds his fellow Democrats that the American people were voting as much against Republicans as they were voting for Democrats and that it was incumbent upon the party to demonstrate that they were different from the Republicans. Cleveland notes that the victory occurred because of the support of many "who are not to be considered as irrevocably and under all circumstances members of our party."

Cleveland urges Democrats to ensure that in the party's conduct "principles touching the public welfare shall be placed above spoils." He also warns against using the party's newfound political power for personal gain. He wanted to make sure that the American people identified the Democrats as the party of reform—and the former president as the leader of the reform movement.

♦ Special Session Message to Congress on the Economic Crisis

Several elements in the Democratic Party opposed Cleveland's renomination for president in 1892, including protectionists who favored high tariffs and those who disagreed with the former president's opposition to the government's silver policy, a major issue of the era. However, Cleveland won his party's nomination on the first ballot at the convention in Chicago and defeated Harrison in the general election, with 46 percent of the popular vote and 277 electoral votes to Harrison's 43 percent and 145 electoral votes.

Soon after Cleveland was inaugurated, the country experienced a deep economic crisis, the Panic of 1893. The downturn started when a large number of railroads and banks failed. For instance, twelve banks in Denver failed in one day in July 1893, and by the end of the month, 377 businesses had failed and 435 mines had closed in Colorado, a state heavily dependent on silver mining. These closures left more than forty-five thousand Coloradans out of work. These failures were the result of a decline in the value of silver following the passage in 1890 of the Sherman Silver Purchase Act, which required the U.S. Treasury to buy large quantities of silver and use the metal on parity with gold in backing paper money. In 1890 the value of silver was just over $1 per ounce, but by 1893 it had declined to 62 cents per ounce. As the value of silver fell, mine owners across the nation cut workers, which led to labor unrest. Throughout the country other businesses also laid off employees, and unemployment grew dramatically, rising to 19 percent nationwide.

Cleveland responded by calling a special session of Congress in August 1893. The president had long criticized the Sherman Silver Act and believed that Congress needed to repeal it immediately in order for the United States to remain solvent. In one of the most important statements of his political career, Cleveland opened the session with a strident, yet detailed call for action. His message argues that the current financial crisis was not the result of a lack of natural resources or problems with the nation's manufacturing base. Instead, the president blames the depression on silver speculation that was driven by the Sherman Act. Inflation and currency depreciation prevented banks and other financial firms from lending money, and this lack of credit further hurt business and the agricultural sector. According to the president, "Surviving corporations and individuals are content to keep in hand the money they are usually anxious to loan, and those engaged in legitimate business are surprised to find that the securities they offer for loans, though heretofore satisfactory, are no longer accepted."

In explaining the damage inflicted on the economy by the Sherman Silver Act, Cleveland says that the requirement for gold and silver to be treated equally as strategic monetary reserves prevented the secretary of the treasury from taking action to stop the dramatic decline in the value of silver. The silver act committed the government to purchase 4.5 million ounces of silver per month—twice what the Treasury Department had previously acquired each month. As the government stocks of silver grew and there was a corresponding increase in the amount of money in circulation, silver's value declined. Meanwhile, the silver act's provision that paper currency could be redeemed in either gold or silver led to a steep reduction in the nation's gold reserves as individuals, corporations, and foreign governments demanded payment in gold rather than silver. The result, as Cleveland notes in his address, was that from 1890 to 1893 "gold coin and bullion in our Treasury decreased more than $132,000,000, while during the same period the silver coin and bullion in the Treasury increased more than $147,000,000." By 1893 the nation's gold reserves had fallen below $100 million, leading many to believe that the government was on the verge of financial collapse.

Proponents of silver often credited the precious metal as more representative of the character of the United States than gold. They asserted that gold was too closely identified with the monarchies of Europe. Cleveland argues that gold remained the standard currency by which world trade was denominated. The president contends that the use of silver by the United States undermined its economic status among its trade partners. Cleveland closes his message to Congress by asserting that the Sherman Silver Act had produced three years of economic problems and must be repealed. He also pledged that he would call another special session to deal with tariff reform in September.

Despite widespread support for the repeal of the silver measure, Cleveland faced significant opposition from within his party. He had to work with Republicans to secure the repeal of the Sherman Silver Act. Even after the House passed a measure to rescind the act, debate continued in the Senate, which finally approved the House measure by a vote of forty-eight to thirty-seven, on October 30, 1893. The repeal saved the nation's currency and set the stage for a gradual economic recovery. Nonetheless, it devastated the economies of silver-producing states in the West, including Colorado and Nevada. State militias had to be deployed to quell labor unrest. Cleveland believed that the nation's economy would rebound by itself, but many wanted his administration to increase government spending on roads or other infrastructure as a means to create more jobs. In April 1894 Joseph A. Coxey led a group of unemployed, known as Coxey's Army, to Washington to protest the administration's inaction. They were arrested on the day they arrived outside the Capitol. In June, Cleveland dispatched federal troops to force an end to a strike against the Pullman Company after a federal court ordered the workers to return to their jobs. These actions undermined Cleveland's popularity with working-class Americans and labor groups.

♦ Message to Congress on Hawaiian Sovereignty

In the midst of this economic crisis, Cleveland faced a difficult issue in foreign relations. In the final days of the Harrison administration in early 1893, American planters in Hawaii had overthrown the islands' monarchy and signed a treaty of annexation with the United States. Cleveland opposed the manner by which the Americans had seized control of the islands. Shortly after his inauguration, he withdrew the annexation treaty from the Senate and dispatched former Georgia congressman James Henderson Blount to Hawaii to conduct an investigation. Blount's subsequent report condemned the actions of the Americans in Hawaii, including the U.S. representative John L. Stevens. Cleveland feared that the Hawaiian example could mark a new age of imperialism for the United States and usher in an era of territorial expansion in which the nation would behave like the imperial powers of Europe. Privately, he also questioned the actions of the preceding administration for signing the annexation treaty in the last few days before it left office.

Based on Blount's report and his own personal inclinations, Cleveland sought a restoration of the Hawaiian monarchy. However, negotiations between Queen Liliuokalani and the pro-American government failed. In December 1893 Cleveland sent a message to Congress asking the legislature to develop a solution. In his message Cleveland stresses that the provisional pro-American government was not broad-based, nor was it representative of the people. He notes that "it did not appear that such provisional government had the sanction of either popular revolution or suffrage." Cleveland declares that past instances of U.S. territorial expansion stood in "marked contrast with the hasty recognition of a government openly and concededly set up for the purpose of tendering to us territorial annexation" of Hawaii.

The president's message outlines the chronology of the fall of the monarchy. He mentions a number of illicit actions taken by U.S. officials and expresses his belief that the provisional government would not have acted without support from those representatives. He informs Congress of his sincere hope that the past would be buried, and that the restored Government would "reassume its authority as if its continuity had not been interrupted." However, he also notes that the deposed queen was unwilling to grant clemency to those who had participated in her overthrow. As a result, U.S.-backed talks had failed to yield a compromise.

Cleveland's message met with mixed results. A significant faction in Congress supported the annexation of the Hawaiian Islands. Just as Cleveland had not been able to craft a compromise between the monarchy and the provisional government, the legislature was not able to develop a resolution. Instead, it produced the Morgan Report (named after Senator John Tyler Morgan of Alabama), which exonerated the Americans who participated in the coup. This was followed by a Senate resolution that tacitly accepted the status quo. It rejected the restoration of the monarchy and the proposed annexation and called for the United States to adopt a policy of noninterference in the islands. The status of Hawaii would be determined by Cleveland's successor, William McKinley, when the Senate approved a new annexation treaty in July 1898.

♦ Fourth Annual Message to Congress

Soured by U.S. actions in Hawaii, Cleveland feared that some in the United States might use an ongoing revolt against Spanish rule in Cuba as an excuse to prompt U.S. intervention. Anti-Spanish sentiment in the United States was inflamed by the brutal policies used to suppress the rebellion. A growing number of politicians and newspapers called for military intervention or at least support for the rebels, who were often depicted as freedom fighters seeking to overthrow colonial rule. The Cuban issue cut across party lines, with many Democrats, especially southern Democrats, in favor of annexation, while western Republicans tended to oppose U.S. intervention in the fighting.

Cleveland sincerely opposed U.S. intervention, which he believed would be an excuse for annexation of Cuba.

Through most of his administration he held to a policy of strict neutrality. On June 12, 1895, he even signed a statement of neutrality in the conflict. In April 1895 he authorized Secretary of State Richard Olney to initiate mediation with Spain in an effort to end fighting; however, Spain withdrew from the talks after two months. In his fourth and final annual message to Congress, Cleveland explains his preference for nonintervention and the reasons behind his policy.

Cleveland discounts the possibility of offering recognition to the rebels, since they did not have a formal governmental structure. He indicates a willingness to purchase Cuba "if there were any evidence of a desire or willingness on the part of Spain to entertain such a proposal." The president firmly rejects the idea of military intervention to end the conflict. Cleveland's message contains some of the president's strongest anti-imperialist language. He declares that the country did not need to acquire additional territory: "Its own ample and diversified domains satisfy all possible longings for territory, preclude all dreams of conquest, and prevent any casting of covetous eyes upon neighboring regions, however attractive." Cleveland also states his belief that the United States was a nation that traditionally did not use force to expand. Instead, he writes, the United States was "the most pacific of powers and desires nothing so much as to live in amity with all the world." While such a sentiment was not entirely correct, given the willingness of past administrations to use force against Native Americans or during the Mexican War, it reflects Cleveland's view of the way the nation should conduct its foreign policy.

Cleveland does explain that although he did not think it proper for the United States to intervene at the time, circumstances could change and compel the nation to take more forceful action. The president notes that "we may be drawn into such an unusual and unprecedented condition as will fix a limit to our patient waiting for Spain to end the contest, either alone and in her own way or with our friendly cooperation." This statement was perceived as a warning to Spain that the country needed to take measures to resolve the conflict quickly and that the longer fighting continued, the more likely it was that a future administration would be pulled into the conflict. Cleveland also states plainly that if it became clear that Spain no longer had effective control of the island, then the United States would consider recognizing a new government in Cuba. Following the address, Cleveland continued to seek a negotiated settlement between Spain and the Cuban rebels. In one of his last acts, he had a U.S. envoy suggest that Spain offer Cuba some form of limited autonomy, a proposal that the Spanish government initially rejected but put into place a year later.

Impact and Legacy

By 1896 Cleveland's standing within the Democratic Party had seriously eroded. Despite his reputation as a reformer and honest politician, his opposition to silver and his use of troops to suppress labor unrest had alienated him from the more liberal wing of the party. Eastern Democrats tried to persuade him to run for a third term, but he declined. Democrats choose William Jennings Bryan as their candidate in the 1896 election. Bryan was defeated in that and two subsequent elections, but the silver faction dominated party politics for the next decade. Nonetheless, Cleveland remained the leader of the conservative Democrats, who launched an unsuccessful effort to persuade him to run for the presidency in 1904.

Cleveland was not a great orator, and even his written messages lack the eloquence of other contemporary politicians. However, he took pains to communicate his stance on issues and to explain his policies in great detail. Cleveland did not necessarily lead the nation on the major issues of his day, but his writings and policies reflected the contemporary values and ideals of American politics. His emphasis on principle above party and his opposition to the spoils system would form part of the progressive creed that helped reform U.S. politics in the early years of the twentieth century.

Cleveland's writings on anti-imperialism reflect the long-standing preference in U.S. foreign policy to avoid interference with other regimes or to acquire territory by force. His documents and messages set forth the belief that the United States was a peaceful nation and would resort to force only if given no other option. Cleveland's support for the gold standard may be one of his most enduring legacies. His second term marked the beginning of the end of silver as a competitive alternative to gold for the nation's currency. Above all, Cleveland's honesty and efforts at reform marked him as one of the leaders of a new era of U.S. politics.

Key Sources

The Library of Congress contains the largest collection of Grover Cleveland's documents, including official papers, letters, and even documents from the president's work with the Association of Life Insurance Presidents. This eighty-seven-thousand-piece collection is available on microfilm through many major research libraries. The Grover Cleveland Library has an extensive collection of the president's speeches and documents that cover his political career both in New York and the White House and information on his early life, available online through the library's web site at http://www.groverclevelandlibrary.org/. The best collection of Cleveland's letters is Allan Nevins's *Letters of Grover Cleveland, 1850–1908* (1934). George F. Parker's *Writings and Speeches of Grover Cleveland* (1892) and Albert Bergh's *Letters and Addresses of Grover Cleveland* (1888) provide letters and documents that are unavailable elsewhere. The Miller Center of Public Affairs (http://millercenter.org/academic/americanpresident/cleveland) provides information on Cleveland's administration and policies.

Essential Quotes

"He who takes the oath today to preserve, protect, and defend the Constitution of the United States only assumes the solemn obligation which every patriotic citizen—on the farm, in the workshop, in the busy marts of trade, and everywhere—should share with him."

(First Inaugural Address)

"Those who are selected for a limited time to manage public affairs are still of the people, and may do much by their example to encourage, consistently with the dignity of their official functions, that plain way of life which among their fellow-citizens aids integrity and promotes thrift and prosperity."

(First Inaugural Address)

"The people demand reform in the administration of the Government and the application of business principles to public affairs."

(First Inaugural Address)

"I am convinced that our duty to those who have trusted us consists in pushing on continually and vigorously the principles in the advocacy of which we have triumphed, and thus superseding all that is ignoble and unworthy."

("Principles above Spoils" Letter)

"Whatever else the people have a right to expect from Congress, they may certainly demand that legislation condemned by the ordeal of three years' disastrous experience shall be removed from the statute books as soon as their representatives can legitimately deal with it."

(Special Session Message to Congress on the Economic Crisis)

Essential Quotes

"Surely under our Constitution and laws the enlargement of our limits is a manifestation of the highest attribute of sovereignty, and if entered upon as an Executive act, all things relating to the transaction should be clear and free from suspicion."

(Message to Congress on Hawaiian Sovereignty)

"The United States has, nevertheless, a character to maintain as a nation, which plainly dictates that right and not might should be the rule of its conduct."

(Fourth Annual Message to Congress)

"Until we face the contingencies suggested or the situation is by other incidents imperatively changed we should continue in the line of conduct heretofore pursued, thus in all circumstances exhibiting our obedience to the requirements of public law and our regard for the duty enjoined upon us by the position we occupy in the family of nations."

(Fourth Annual Message to Congress)

Further Reading

■ Books

Brodsky, Alyn. *Grover Cleveland: A Study in Character*. New York: St. Martin's, 2000.

Graff, Henry F. *Grover Cleveland*. New York: Times Books, 2002.

Jeffers, H. Paul. *An Honest President: The Life and Presidencies of Grover Cleveland*. New York: Morrow, 2000.

Welch, Richard E., Jr. *The Presidencies of Grover Cleveland*. Lawrence: University Press of Kansas, 1988.

—*Tom Lansford*

Questions for Further Study

1. Compare and contrast the vision for the Democratic Party presented in Cleveland's speeches to that of the party today. Consider, for instance, the stance on immigration expressed in the next-to-last paragraph of his first inaugural address, his warnings in the "principles above spoils" letter, or the opening paragraphs of his speech on the economic crisis, in which he blames government and not business.

2. Discuss the differences between the two leading figures in the Democratic Party of the 1890s, William Jennings Bryan and Cleveland himself. Pay special attention to their stands on the principal issues of the day: free silver, protectionism, and overseas intervention in areas such as Cuba and Hawaii.

3. To people familiar with the economic crisis of 2008, Cleveland's speech on the economic crisis of 1893 seems eerily familiar. Compare and contrast the two crises from a number of angles: the principal units of value involved (silver in the first case, housing in the second), the causes in terms of both government and private action, and the government response to the situation. What might people in 2008 have learned from events 115 years in the past?

4. Critique the various viewpoints to the question of Hawaiian sovereignty, beginning with Cleveland's statements in his message to Congress on that issue. On the other hand, consider the stances of those who disagreed with him: Hawaiian nationalists, as represented by the queen; the leaders of the revolt against the Hawaiian government, who sought to become part of the United States; and the legislators who, in opposition to Cleveland, called for U.S. intervention in this and other conflicts.

First Inaugural Address

1885

In the discharge of my official duty I shall endeavor to be guided by a just and unstrained construction of the Constitution, a careful observance of the distinction between the powers granted to the Federal Government and those reserved to the States or to the people, and by a cautious appreciation of those functions which by the Constitution and laws have been especially assigned to the executive branch of the Government.

But he who takes the oath today to preserve, protect, and defend the Constitution of the United States only assumes the solemn obligation which every patriotic citizen—on the farm, in the workshop, in the busy marts of trade, and everywhere—should share with him. The Constitution which prescribes his oath, my countrymen, is yours; the Government you have chosen him to administer for a time is yours; the suffrage which executes the will of freemen is yours; the laws and the entire scheme of our civil rule, from the town meeting to the State capitals and the national capital, is yours. Your every voter, as surely as your Chief Magistrate, under the same high sanction, though in a different sphere, exercises a public trust. Nor is this all. Every citizen owes to the country a vigilant watch and close scrutiny of its public servants and a fair and reasonable estimate of their fidelity and usefulness. Thus is the people's will impressed upon the whole framework of our civil polity—municipal, State, and Federal; and this is the price of our liberty and the inspiration of our faith in the Republic.

It is the duty of those serving the people in public place to closely limit public expenditures to the actual needs of the Government economically administered, because this bounds the right of the Government to exact tribute from the earnings of labor or the property of the citizen, and because public extravagance begets extravagance among the people. We should never be ashamed of the simplicity and prudential economies which are best suited to the operation of a republican form of government and most compatible with the mission of the American people. Those who are selected for a limited time to manage public affairs are still of the people, and may do much by their example to encourage, consistently with the dignity of their official functions, that plain way of life which among their fellow-citizens aids integrity and promotes thrift and prosperity.

The genius of our institutions, the needs of our people in their home life, and the attention which is demanded for the settlement and development of the resources of our vast territory dictate the scrupulous avoidance of any departure from that foreign policy commended by the history, the traditions, and the prosperity of our Republic. It is the policy of independence, favored by our position and defended by our known love of justice and by our power. It is the policy of peace suitable to our interests. It is the policy of neutrality, rejecting any share in foreign broils and ambitions upon other continents and repelling their intrusion here. It is the policy of Monroe and of Washington and Jefferson—"Peace, commerce, and honest friendship with all nations; entangling alliance with none."

A due regard for the interests and prosperity of all the people demands that our finances shall be established upon such a sound and sensible basis as shall secure the safety and confidence of business interests and make the wage of labor sure and steady, and that our system of revenue shall be so adjusted as to relieve the people of unnecessary taxation, having a due regard to the interests of capital invested and workingmen employed in American industries, and preventing the accumulation of a surplus in the Treasury to tempt extravagance and waste.

Care for the property of the nation and for the needs of future settlers requires that the public domain should be protected from purloining schemes and unlawful occupation.

The conscience of the people demands that the Indians within our boundaries shall be fairly and honestly treated as wards of the Government and their education and civilization promoted with a view to their ultimate citizenship, and that polygamy in the Territories, destructive of the family relation and offensive to the moral sense of the civilized world, shall be repressed.

The laws should be rigidly enforced which prohibit the immigration of a servile class to compete with American labor, with no intention of acquiring citizenship, and bringing with them and retaining habits and customs repugnant to our civilization.

Document Text

The people demand reform in the administration of the Government and the application of business principles to public affairs. As a means to this end, civil-service reform should be in good faith enforced. Our citizens have the right to protection from the incompetency of public employees who hold their places solely as the reward of partisan service, and from the corrupting influence of those who promise and the vicious methods of those who expect such rewards; and those who worthily seek public employment have the right to insist that merit and competency shall be recognized instead of party subserviency or the surrender of honest political belief.

Glossary

capital:	financial goods that can be used to generate additional money
civil rule:	rule by elected civilians, rather than military figures or other traditional authority figures
civil-service:	referring to government employment, typically nonelective, within the executive branch
exact tribute:	take taxes or other funds
he who takes the oath today:	Cleveland himself
polity:	the overall political makeup of a nation
polygamy in the Territories:	a reference to the practice among Mormon men, in areas with a large population of Mormons, of having several wives
prudential economies:	careful use of financial resources
republican:	referring to a government by elected officials rather than kings or others who impose their rule by force
sanction:	authority
wards:	persons under care and protection

Document Text

"Principles above Spoils" Letter

1890

I thank you for the invitation I have just received to meet with the members of the Young Men's Democratic Club at Canton to rejoice over the last Democratic victory. I am sorry to say that it will be impossible for me to be present on the occasion you contemplate, but I hope that it will be full of enthusiasm and congratulation.

And yet may I not suggest one sober thought which should constantly be in our minds. Our late success is, of course, the triumph of Democratic principles, but that success was made possible by the co-operation of many who are not to be considered as irrevocably and under all circumstances members of our party. They trusted us and allied themselves with us in the late struggle because they saw that those with whom they acted politically were heedless of the interests of the country and untrue to the people. We have still to convince them that Democracy means something more than mere management for party success and a partisan distribution of benefits after success. This can only be done by insisting that in the conduct of our party principles touching the public welfare shall be placed above spoils, and this is the sentiment of the masses of the Democratic Party to-day. They are disinterested and patriotic and they should not be misrepresented by the tricks of those who would not scruple to use the party name for selfish purposes.

I do not say that there is danger of this, but I am convinced that our duty to those who have trusted us consists in pushing on continually and vigorously the principles in the advocacy of which we have triumphed, and thus superseding all that is ignoble and unworthy. In this way we shall place our party on solid ground and confirm the people in the hope that we strive for their welfare, and, following this course, we shall deserve and achieve further success.

Glossary

the last Democratic victory: the 1890 elections, held about a month before Cleveland's speech, which dramatically and decisively overturned Republican control of the House

scruple: hesitate as a result of moral concerns

Special Session Message to Congress on the Economic Crisis

Our unfortunate financial plight is not the result of untoward events nor of conditions related to our natural resources, nor is it traceable to any of the afflictions which frequently check national growth and prosperity. With plenteous crops, with abundant promise of remunerative production and manufacture, with unusual invitation to safe investment, and with satisfactory assurance to business enterprise, suddenly financial distrust and fear have sprung up on every side. Numerous moneyed institutions have suspended because abundant assets were not immediately available to meet the demands of frightened depositors. Surviving corporations and individuals are content to keep in hand the money they are usually anxious to loan, and those engaged in legitimate business are surprised to find that the securities they offer for loans, though heretofore satisfactory, are no longer accepted. Values supposed to be fixed are fast becoming conjectural, and loss and failure have invaded every branch of business.

I believe these things are principally chargeable to Congressional legislation touching the purchase and coinage of silver by the General Government.

This legislation is embodied in a statute passed on the 14th day of July, 1890, which was the culmination of much agitation on the subject involved, and which may be considered a truce, after a long struggle, between the advocates of free silver coinage and those intending to be more conservative.

Undoubtedly the monthly purchases by the Government of 4,500,000 ounces of silver, enforced under that statute, were regarded by those interested in silver production as a certain guaranty of its increase in price. The result, however, has been entirely different, for immediately following a spasmodic and slight rise the price of silver began to fall after the passage of the act, and has since reached the lowest point ever known. This disappointing result has led to renewed and persistent effort in the direction of free silver coinage.

Meanwhile not only are the evil effects of the operation of the present law constantly accumulating, but the result to which its execution must inevitably lead is becoming palpable to all who give the least heed to financial subjects.

This law provides that in payment for the 4,500,000 ounces of silver bullion which the Secretary of the Treasury is commanded to purchase monthly there shall be issued Treasury notes redeemable on demand in gold or silver coin, at the discretion of the Secretary of the Treasury, and that said notes may be reissued. It is, however, declared in the act to be "the established policy of the United States to maintain the two metals on a parity with each other upon the present legal ratio or such ratio as may be provided by law." This declaration so controls the action of the Secretary of the Treasury as to prevent his exercising the discretion nominally vested in him if by such action the parity between gold and silver may be disturbed. Manifestly a refusal by the Secretary to pay these Treasury notes in gold if demanded would necessarily result in their discredit and depreciation as obligations payable only in silver, and would destroy the parity between the two metals by establishing a discrimination in favor of gold.

Up to the 15th day of July, 1893, these notes had been issued in payment of silver-bullion purchases to the amount of more than $147,000,000. While all but a very small quantity of this bullion remains uncoined and without usefulness in the Treasury, many of the notes given in its purchase have been paid in gold. This is illustrated by the statement that between the 1st day of May, 1892, and the 15th day of July, 1893, the notes of this kind issued in payment for silver bullion amounted to a little more than $54,000,000, and that during the same period about $49,000,000 were paid by the Treasury in gold for the redemption of such notes.

The policy necessarily adopted of paying these notes in gold has not spared the gold reserve of $100,000,000 long ago set aside by the Government for the redemption of other notes, for this fund has already been subjected to the payment of new obligations amounting to about $150,000,000 on account of silver purchases, and has as a consequence for the first time since its creation been encroached upon.

We have thus made the depletion of our gold easy and have tempted other and more appreciative nations to add it to their stock. That the opportunity we have offered has not been neglected is shown by the large amounts of gold which have been recently drawn from our Treasury and exported to increase the financial strength of foreign nations. The excess

Document Text

of exports of gold over its imports for the year ending June 30, 1893, amounted to more than $87,500,000.

Between the 1st day of July, 1890, and the 15th day of July, 1893, the gold coin and bullion in our Treasury decreased more than $132,000,000, while during the same period the silver coin and bullion in the Treasury increased more than $147,000,000. Unless Government bonds are to be constantly issued and sold to replenish our exhausted gold, only to be again exhausted, it is apparent that the operation of the silver-purchase law now in force leads in the direction of the entire substitution of silver for the gold in the Government Treasury, and that this must be followed by the payment of all Government obligations in depreciated silver.

At this stage gold and silver must part company and the Government must fail in its established policy to maintain the two metals on a parity with each other. Given over to the exclusive use of a currency greatly depreciated according to the standard of the commercial world, we could no longer claim a place among nations of the first class, nor could our Government claim a performance of its obligation, so far as such an obligation has been imposed upon it, to provide for the use of the people the best and safest money.

If, as many of its friends claim, silver ought to occupy a larger place in our currency and the currency of the world through general international cooperation and agreement, it is obvious that the United States will not be in a position to gain a hearing in favor of such an arrangement so long as we are willing to continue our attempt to accomplish the result single-handed....

Whatever else the people have a right to expect from Congress, they may certainly demand that legislation condemned by the ordeal of three years' disastrous experience shall be removed from the statute books as soon as their representatives can legitimately deal with it.

It was my purpose to summon Congress in special session early in the coming September, that we might enter promptly upon the work of tariff reform, which the true interests of the country clearly demand, which so large a majority of the people, as shown by their suffrages, desire and expect, and to the accomplishment of which every effort of the present Administration is pledged. But while tariff reform has lost nothing of its immediate and permanent importance and must in the near future engage the attention of Congress, it has seemed to me that the financial condition of the country should at once and before all other subjects be considered by your honorable body.

I earnestly recommend the prompt repeal of the provisions of the act passed July 14, 1890, authorizing the purchase of silver bullion, and that other legislative action may put beyond all doubt or mistake the intention and the ability of the Government to fulfill its pecuniary obligations in money universally recognized by all civilized countries.

Glossary

chargeable to: to be blamed on

free silver coinage: the right to coin U.S. dollars in silver as well as gold, an issue that dominated the politics of Cleveland's time

gold reserve: gold held by federal reserve banks as a means of maintaining economic stability

Government bonds: essentially an I.O.U. from a government, which sells the bonds to investors with a promise to redeem them at a certain time and at a certain interest rate

parity: equality

the silver-purchase law now in force: the Sherman Silver Purchase Act of 1890, which was repealed in 1893

tariff: taxes on imports

Treasury notes: securities sold to investors by the federal government to finance its activities

your honorable body: Congress

Message to Congress on Hawaiian Sovereignty

1893

When the present Administration entered upon its duties the Senate had under consideration a treaty providing for the annexation of the Hawaiian Islands to the territory of the United States. Surely under our Constitution and laws the enlargement of our limits is a manifestation of the highest attribute of sovereignty, and if entered upon as an Executive act, all things relating to the transaction should be clear and free from suspicion. Additional importance attached to this particular treaty of annexation, because it contemplated a departure from unbroken American tradition in providing for the addition to our territory of islands of the sea more than two thousand miles removed from our nearest coast.

These considerations might not of themselves call for interference with the completion of a treaty entered upon by a previous Administration. but it appeared from the documents accompanying the treaty when submitted to the Senate, that the ownership of Hawaii was tendered to us by a provisional government set up to succeed the constitutional ruler of the islands, who had been dethroned, and it did not appear that such provisional government had the sanction of either popular revolution or suffrage. Two other remarkable features of the transaction naturally attracted attention. One was the extraordinary haste—not to say precipitancy—characterizing all the transactions connected with the treaty. It appeared that a so-called Committee of Safety, ostensibly the source of the revolt against the constitutional Government of Hawaii, was organized on Saturday, the 14th day of January; that on Monday, the 16th, the United States forces were landed at Honolulu from a naval vessel lying in its harbor; that on the 17th the scheme of a provisional government was perfected, and a proclamation naming its officers was on the same day prepared and read at the Government building; that immediately thereupon the United States Minister recognized the provisional government thus created; that two days afterwards, on the 19th day of January, commissioners representing such government sailed for this country in a steamer especially chartered for the occasion, arriving in San Francisco on the 28th day of January, and in Washington on the 3rd day of February; that on the next day they had their first interview with the Secretary of State, and another on the 11th, when the treaty of annexation was practically agreed upon, and that on the 14th it was formally concluded and on the 15th transmitted to the Senate. Thus between the initiation of the scheme for a provisional government in Hawaii on the 14th day of January and the submission to the Senate of the treaty of annexation concluded with such government, the entire interval was thirty-two days, fifteen of which were spent by the Hawaiian Commissioners in their journey to Washington.

In the next place, upon the face of the papers submitted with the treaty, it clearly appeared that there was open and undetermined an issue of fact of the most vital importance. The message of the President accompanying the treaty declared that "the overthrow of the monarchy was not in any way promoted by this Government," and in a letter to the President from the Secretary of State also submitted to the Senate with the treaty, the following message occurs: "At the time the provisional government took possession of the Government buildings no troops or officers of the United States were present or took any part whatever in the proceedings. No public recognition was accorded to the provisional government by the United States Minister until after the Queen's abdication and when they were in effective possession of the Government buildings, the archives, the treasury, the barracks, the police station, and all the potential machinery of the Government." But a protest also accompanied said treaty, signed by the Queen and her ministers at the time she made way for the provisional government, which explicitly stated that she yielded to the superior force of the United States, whose Minister had caused United States troops to be landed at Honolulu and declared that he would support such provisional government.

The truth or falsity of this protest was surely of the first importance. If true, nothing but the concealment of its truth could induce our Government to negotiate with the semblance of a government thus created, nor could a treaty resulting from the acts stated in the protest have been knowingly deemed worthy of consideration by the Senate. Yet the truth or falsity of the protest had not been investigated.

Document Text

I conceived it to be my duty therefore to withdraw the treaty from the Senate for examination, and meanwhile to cause an accurate, full, and impartial investigation to be made of the facts attending the subversion of the constitutional Government of Hawaii and the installment in its place of the provisional government. I selected for the work of investigation the Hon. James H. Blount, of Georgia....

Our country was in danger of occupying the position of having actually set up a temporary government on foreign soil for the purpose of acquiring through that agency territory which we had wrongfully put in its possession. The control of both sides of a bargain acquired in such a manner is called by a familiar and unpleasant name when found in private transactions. We are not without a precedent showing how scrupulously we avoided such accusations in former days. After the people of Texas had declared their independence of Mexico they resolved that on the acknowledgment of their independence by the United States they would seek admission into the Union. Several months after the battle of San Jacinto, by which Texan independence was practically assured and established, President Jackson declined to recognize it, alleging as one of his reasons that in the circumstances it became us "to beware of a too early movement, as it might subject us, however unjustly, to the imputation of seeking to establish the claim of our neighbors to a territory with a view to its subsequent acquisition by ourselves." This is in marked contrast with the hasty recognition of a government openly and concededly set up for the purpose of tendering to us territorial annexation....

Actuated by these desires and purposes, and not unmindful of the inherent perplexities of the situation nor of the limitations upon my power, I instructed Minister Willis to advise the Queen and her supporters of my desire to aid in the restoration of the status existing before the lawless landing of the United States forces at Honolulu on the 16th of January last, if such restoration could be effected upon terms providing for clemency as well as justice to all parties concerned. The conditions suggested, as the instructions show, contemplate a general amnesty to those concerned in setting up the provisional government and a recognition of all its bona fide acts and obligations. In short, they require that the past should be buried, and that the restored Government should reassume its authority as if its continuity had not been interrupted. These conditions have not proved acceptable to the Queen, and though she has been informed that they will be insisted upon, and that, unless acceded to, the efforts of the President to aid in the restoration of her Government will cease, I have not thus far learned that she is willing to yield them her acquiescence. The check which my plans have thus encountered has prevented their presentation to the members of the provisional government, while unfortunate public misrepresentations of the situation and exaggerated statements of the sentiments of our people have obviously injured the prospects of successful Executive mediation.

Glossary

the enlargement of our limits:	the expansion of U.S. territory
it became us:	it was in our best interests
Minister Willis:	Albert Shelby Willis (1843–1897), U.S. representative from Kentucky
the Queen:	Lili'uokalani (1838–1917), last Hawaiian monarch, who reigned for slightly less than two years between January 1891 and January 1893
sovereignty:	self-rule

Fourth Annual Message to Congress

1896

These inevitable entanglements of the United States with the rebellion in Cuba, the large American property interests affected, and considerations of philanthropy and humanity in general have led to a vehement demand in various quarters for some sort of positive intervention on the part of the United States. It was at first proposed that belligerent rights should be accorded to the insurgents—a proposition no longer urged because untimely and in practical operation dearly perilous and injurious to our own interests. It has since been and is now sometimes contended that the independence of the insurgents should be recognized; but imperfect and restricted as the Spanish government of the island may be, no other exists there, unless the will of the military officer in temporary command of a particular district can be dignified as a species of government. It is now also suggested that the United States should buy the island—a suggestion possibly worthy of consideration if there were any evidence of a desire or willingness on the part of Spain to entertain such a proposal. It is urged finally that, all other methods failing, the existing internecine strife in Cuba should be terminated by our intervention, even at the cost of a war between the United States and Spain—a war which its advocates confidently prophesy could neither be large in its proportions nor doubtful in its issue.

The correctness of this forecast need be neither affirmed nor denied. The United States has, nevertheless, a character to maintain as a nation, which plainly dictates that right and not might should be the rule of its conduct. Further, though the United States is not a nation to which peace is a necessity, it is in truth the most pacific of powers and desires nothing so much as to live in amity with all the world. Its own ample and diversified domains satisfy all possible longings for territory, preclude all dreams of conquest, and prevent any casting of covetous eyes upon neighboring regions, however attractive....

It should be added that it can not be reasonably assumed that the hitherto expectant attitude of the United States will be indefinitely maintained. While we are anxious to accord all due respect to the sovereignty of Spain, we can not view the pending conflict in all its features and properly apprehend our inevitably close relations to it and its possible results without considering that by the course of events we may be drawn into such an unusual and unprecedented condition as will fix a limit to our patient waiting for Spain to end the contest, either alone and in her own way or with our friendly cooperation.

When the inability of Spain to deal successfully with the insurrection has become manifest and it is demonstrated that her sovereignty is extinct in Cuba for all purposes of its rightful existence, and when a hopeless struggle for its reestablishment has degenerated into a strife which means nothing more than the useless sacrifice of human life and the utter destruction of the very subject-matter of the conflict, a situation will be presented in which our obligations to the sovereignty of Spain will be superseded by higher obligations, which we can hardly hesitate to recognize and discharge. Deferring the choice of ways and methods until the time for action arrives, we should make them depend upon the precise conditions then existing; and they should not be determined upon without giving careful heed to every consideration involving our honor and interest or the international duty we owe to Spain. Until we face the contingencies suggested or the situation is by other incidents imperatively changed we should continue in the line of conduct heretofore pursued, thus in all circumstances exhibiting our obedience to the requirements of public law and our regard for the duty enjoined upon us by the position we occupy in the family of nations.

A contemplation of emergencies that may arise should plainly lead us to avoid their creation, either through a careless disregard of present duty or even an undue stimulation and ill-timed expression of feeling. But I have deemed it not amiss to remind the Congress that a time may arrive when a correct policy and care for our interests, as well as a regard for the interests of other nations and their citizens, joined by considerations of humanity and a desire to see a rich and fertile country intimately related to us saved from complete devastation, will constrain our Government to such action as will subserve the interests thus involved and at the same time promise to Cuba and its inhabitants an opportunity to enjoy the blessings of peace.

Glossary

entanglements:	probably a reference to important speeches by both George Washington and Thomas Jefferson warning against "entangling [foreign] alliances"
internecine:	within a group or country
rebellion in Cuba:	the fight of Cuban nationalists off and on since 1868 for independence from Spain
sovereignty:	independent rule

An early, undated photograph of Grover Cleveland

Official portrait of Secretary of State Hillary Clinton.

Hillary Rodham Clinton: Original Analysis

1946-

Secretary of State, Senator (NY), and Presidential Candidate

Overview

Hillary Rodham was born in Chicago on October 26, 1947; she lived most of her young life in Park Ridge, Illinois, a Chicago suburb. She was politically active from an early age. Hillary attended Wellesley College, and as its valedictorian, she was chosen to give the commencement address at her own graduation ceremony in 1969. In response to the preceding speech, given by Senator Edward Brooke of Massachusetts, that condemned student protests, Rodham threw away the addresss she had planned to give, and istead, challenged Brooke's viewpoint, stating "For too long, our leaders have viewed politics as the art of the possible. And the challenge now is to practice politics as the art of making what appears to be impossible possible." *Life* magazine published the speech and profiled Rodham, recognizing heras "a voice of her generation."

In the fall of 1969, she entered Yale Law School along with classmates who went on to significant positions in the government including future Secretary of Labor Robert Reich and future Supreme Court Justice Clarence Thomas. It was here that she met Bill Clinton, a student from Arkansas whose dedication to activist liberal politics mirrored her own. As a student, she worked for the Children's Defense Fund as well as participating on the staff of the House Judiciary Committee investigating the Watergate scandal. In 1974, after the investigation ended, she moved to Fayetteville, Arkansas, and married Bill Clinton in 1975, but did not take his last name as her own.

In a southern state with conservative cultural norms, Bill Clinton's political career was a more practical pursuit for the couple, so Hillary Rodham agreed to subordinate her own ambitions for his. He became Attorney General for Arkansas in 1976 and won the governorship in 1979. She took a position at the Rose Law Firm in Little Rock and was quickly promoted to partner. The couple struggled to maintain a balance between their public and private lives. Hillary's outspoken feminism rankled the Arkansas public, and there were rumors that Bill might be having affairs. Shortly after daughter Chelsea was born in 1980, Bill lost his bid for reelection as governor, forcing the couple to rethink their approach to politics. Hillary Rodham, in particular, had to learn to compromise her principles with her public presentation. She took Bill's last name, reworked her appearance to look more conservative, and helped manage her husband's successful 1983 bid to regain the governorship.

As First Lady of Arkansas, Hillary Rodham Clinton was unusually active while maintaining a focus on issues that the Arkansas voting public would recognize as being stereotypically feminine—children's health, education, better medical care for poor people. She contributed to Bill's positive political profile and his five-term run as successful governor. In 1992 he decided to run for president.

Yet again, the couple's private lives clashed with their public personae. Women came forward to accuse Bill of having multiple affairs. Though Hillary won sympathy in defending her husband from the accusations, her statements that she would not simply "stand by her man like Tammy Wynette" or that she was not the sort of First Lady who might have "stayed home, baked cookies and had teas" turned off many conservatives, making her a magnet for controversy in her own right. Worse, an old investment in a failed land deal from 1979, referred to as Whitewater, became the first of several investigations into the Clintons' relationships and finances. The Whitewater controversy pitted the couple's desire for privacy against the public's natural curiosity about the honesty of their chosen political representatives. The Republican Party capitalized on the conflict with every opportunity that was presented to them.

Nevertheless, Bill Clinton was elected president of the United States in 1992 and again in 1996.

First Lady Hillary Rodham Clinton's initial foray into policymaking in Washington was a failure. Bill appointed her as the director of his administration's Task Force on National Health Care Reform making her the first First Lady in American history to serve in such a powerful official capacity. Hillary toured the country and spoke to people about their health care issues and then, working in secret, drew up a proposal for mandatory health care available to all Americans. The plan, once release, was greeting with public and political distaste, and in 1994, the Clinton administration gave up on passing the plan as a bill.

Once again, Hillary Rodham Clinton had to learn to change her image to meet the expectations of a voting public. As she had as Arkansas's First Lady, she concentrated on health and childcare issues, under the banner of her much-quoted, "it takes a village to raise a child" statement. She became a voice in favor of women's rights, traveling the country and the world, and eventually saw her approval ratings climb. Following her testimony in the Whitewater investigation in 1996, she was exonerated of any wrongdoing. Her positive image increased yet again during the scandal that erupted when Bill Clinton was accused of having an affair with a White House intern, Monica Lewinsky. Her

grace under fire, even as her husband was tried by Congress for lying under oath, gained her public support, even when she accused the politicians and investigator behind the Lewinsky scandal as being a part of a "vast right-wing conspiracy.", Hillary capitalized on public sentiment and when Bill left office in 2000, , she was able to pursue her own political ambitions for the first time. She ran for and won the office of senator from New York State.

As a senator, Clinton was both active and opinionated. She was conspicuously present at the World Trade Center site after the terrorist attack of September 11, comforting victims and praising clean-up efforts. On the other hand, she voted in 2002 to give the Bush administration the prerogative to invade Iraq, a vote she later came to regret. She was reelected by a wide margin in 2006, and decided to try for the presidency in 2008 but was outpolled in a close electoral contest by her fellow senator, Barack Obama. Upon Obama's election to the presidency, she agreed to become his Secretary of State, an excellent way to prepare herself for a future election campaign once Obama left office.

Hillary Rodham Clinton the diplomat, in the eyes of most balanced observers, was a qualified success. She got along well with the president, her former rival, but Obama made it clear that he intended to direct foreign policy from the White House and that she would not be the final arbiter in decision-making. Nevertheless, she maintained a strong profile. She traveled to Haiti to help direct American disaster relief efforts after an earthquake and stood up to North Korean dictator Kim Jong-Il when he threatened war with South Korea. In 2010 and 2011, she worked with the president to send a Navy SEAL team to kill the terrorist leader Osama bin Laden, and then welcomed the Arab Spring, as several Arab peoples rose up to overthrow longstanding dictatorships. One of those dictatorships was in Libya. Muammar al-Qaddafi himself was captured and killed, and in the chaos that followed the fall of his government, four State Department workers were killed in the US embassy in the city of Benghazi, including the ambassador to Libya. Secretary Clinton was blamed for lax security and poor planning and had to testify before Congress about how the embassy attack went down.

Clinton resigned the secretary-ship in 2013 and decided to run for president in 2016. Despite a hard-fought primary battle with Senator Bernie Sanders of Vermont, she won the Democratic nomination and excited many Americans with the possibility that she might become the United States' first female president, but she was still dogged by controversy. As Secretary of State, she ignored advice to have a separate, private email address to conduct her personal affairs, and the internet vigilante group WikiLeaks collected her deleted emails and published thousands of them, uncovering instances where she conducted diplomatic business over the open server. An FBI investigation accused her of "extreme carelessness, ' but cleared her of actual wrongdoing in July of 2016, but speculation the

Time Line

1947	October 26	■ Hillary Rodham born in Chicago
1965-69		■ Attends Wellesley College
1969	May	■ Graduates from Wellesley and delivers commencement address
1969-73		■ Attends Yale Law School
1975		■ Marries Bill Clinton
1979-81		■ Bill Clinton Governor of Arkansas; Hillary Rodham First Lady
1980		■ Bill Clinton defeated for re-election
1981		■ Hillary Rodham takes the last name Clinton
1983-92		■ Bill Clinton Governor of Arkansas again, Hillary Rodham Clinton First Lady
1992		■ Bill Clinton runs for president
1992	January	■ Appearance on *60 Minutes* to discuss Bill Clinton's alleged affairs
1992	November	■ Bill Clinton elected President of the United States; Hillary Rodham Clinton First Lady
1993		■ Hillary Clinton named head of task force on health care reform
1994		■ Health care initiative fails
1995-99		■ Monica Lewinsky scandal
1996		■ Whitewater investigation concluded
1996	November	■ Bill Clinton re-elected President of the United States
2000-08		■ Serves as US Senator from New York
2002		■ Votes "Yes" on Senate Iraq War Resolution

Time Line		
2008		■ Runs for president, loses Democratic nomination to Senator Barack Obama
2009-2013		■ Serves Obama Administration of US Secretary of State
2015		■ Testimony before Senate about attack on US embassy in Libya
2016		■ Runs for president
2016	July	■ Wins Democratic nomination
	November	■ Loses general election to Republican Donald Trump

Clintons were corrupt, devious and dishonest continued. This speculation may have cost her the general election of November 2016, in which she won the popular vote but was still defeated based on electoral college votes by Republican Donald Trump in one of the most stunning upsets in American electoral history.

Explanation and Analysis of Documents

A nearly constant issue for both Clintons, and particularly Hillary Rodham Clinton, was that public believed that they were "shady," whether due to dishonesty, ambition, imperiousness, or any number of other motivations. Bill Clinton gained the derogatory nickname "Slick Willie," and during the 2016 election campaign, Donald Trump continued to address his opponent as "Corrupt Hillary."In point of fact, no accusations of corruption or immorality leveled at the Clintons has ever held up upon investigation, except for Bill Clinton's lie about his affair with Monica Lewinsky, which could be considered a venal, rather than a mortal, political sin.

Hillary Rodham Clinton's accusations of a "vast right-wing conspiracy" against her family thus had a certain level of merit—conservatives and Republicans took every opportunity to make political capital out of any accusation against the couple. The contrast between the Clinton's next major Democratic presidential couple, Barack and Michelle Obama, is hard to ignore; the Obamas seemed unscathed by accusations of untruthfulness or self-serving political motives. The reasons behind Hillary Rodham Clinton being perceived as untrustworthy are complex. Sexism played a role; the fact that Hillary Rodham Clinton was an ambitious, well-traveled, and well-informed political operative simply rubbed many Americans the wrong way. Her passion to maintain a private life and be a private person even while attempting take on one of the most public positions in the world certainly contributed to the problem as well, and may have prompted attacks on her as a politician meant to tip her up and fall afoul of the law, or at least standard governmental ethics.

The 2015 Senate investigation of the assault on the US embassy in Benghazi, Libya, was one such occasion. When the Libyan people rose up in revolt against their dictator, Muammar al-Qaddafi, in February 2011. Secretary Clinton appointed Ambassador J. Christopher Stevens to maintain a permanent embassy in the city of Benghazi in an effort to identify responsible political groups that might help establish a future democratic regime. Once Qaddafi was killed and the regime came to an end, the CIA focused on terrorist groups looking to exploit the temporary anarchy in Libya to advance their agenda and tried to track down international leaders of terrorist groups in the process. This made the embassy a focus of terrorist activity, and on September 11, 2012, an attack on the embassy in Benghazi resulted in the death of Ambassador Stevens, one of his State Department employees, and two CIA operatives. Immediately, Republicans in the Senate alleged that Secretary Clinton's security detail in Benghazi was lax, and a Senate investigation followed. Secretary Clinton was given an opportunity to make an opening statement to the Senate at the hearings, during which she spent more time lamenting the loss of the operatives in Benghazi and calling for bipartisan support for US diplomacy that she did defending her conduct.

♦ Opening Statement to the Benghazi Hearing, October 11, 2015

Secretary Clinton opens by expressing her admiration for the US government employees killed in Benghazi: Ambassador Chris Stevens, State Department operative Sean Smith, and CIA operatives Glen Doherty and Tyrone Woods. She describes Stevens as a friend, outlines his mission of peace in Benghazi and notes that the Libyan people themselves lamented his death, as proof of their recognition of his benign role. She also gives brief descriptions of the other three men.

Then she goes on to discuss the hazards of diplomatic life. She notes that, as Secretary, she maintained 70,000 diplomats and that some of them—diplomats in Iraq, Afghanistan, Mexico, Haiti and Libya, a motley collection of states—died in service, to her regret. Here, she is making the point that she takes responsibility for her government charges as well as implying that deaths in other foreign countries did not always prompt investigations on the part of the Senate, a point she returns to in her statement. She also refers to investigation by "an Accountability Review Board, seven prior congressional investigations, multiple news organizations and …law enforcement and intelligence

agencies." This may or may not be a subtle reference to the redundancy of the Senate investigation.

Secretary Clinton then states that she has three observations as to how the State Department can move forward from this tragedy. The first is that the United States' leadership in the world must not falter. State Department personnel have died in the line of duty before, sixty-five of them since the 1970s; there have been more than a hundred attacks on American diplomatic installations in the same period. Yet the United States' role in the world is to stand up in dangerous places for the values of human rights and democracy, and if it does not, extremist groups will exploit the void. Ambassador Stevens particularly understood that need, according to Clinton, and went to Libya to stand up for those principles.

Her second observation, proceeding from the first, is that diplomatic personnel need protection around the world because of the danger of standing up for American principles in a dangerous world. She cites further examples of diplomatic personnel being killed in previous administrations—the terrorist attacks on the US embassy and a Marine barracks in Beirut, Lebanon in 1983; the al-Qaeda bombings of east African embassies in 1998; and the destruction of the World Trade Center on September 11, 2001. Much of her point again seems to be that this has happened to previous administrations, which does not absolve her of responsibility, but does beg the question as to why only she has had to answer to the Senate, since similar accusations were not made at the hearings directed at the earlier tragedies.

She then discusses the accountability review board, a congressional organization that had met several times since the 1980s over problems with diplomatic security. She makes the point that the only two times its deliberations have been made public were with the bombings in Kenya and Tanzania and now with Benghazi – both occasion on which she and her husband were seen as being responsible for security. The board offered 29 recommendations for changes and Secretary Clinton agreed to all of them. But she asserts that "no administration can do it alone", and then asks for bipartisan Congressional support for security initiatives and in US foreign policy, her third observation. She states that "We need leadership at home to match our leadership abroad, leadership that puts national security ahead of politics and ideology." She cites examples of her own efforts to cross the aisle in the Senate to get Senatorial support for diplomatic issues in Russia and Myanmar and challenges the senators with the following: "Despite all the previous investigations and all the talk about partisan agendas, I'm here to honor those we lost and to do what I can to aid those who serve us still."

While it might appear that Secretary Clinton was displaying unwarranted paranoia with her charges of a "vast right-wing conspiracy," she had excellent reason to fear that Republican senators were really out to smear her reputation. A few weeks before her testimony, Republican congressman Kevin McCarthy let slip to a Fox TV interviewer that the panel was intended to call Clinton's veracity into question and cut into her popularity ratings ahead of the 2016 election; Representative Richard Hanna, another Republican admitted that Clinton's bid for the presidency triggered the investigation, largely in the interest of discrediting her, costing the American taxpayer "millions of dollars and tons of time."

Impact and Legacy

In November 2016, Hillary Rodham Clinton's future was unclear; at 69 years old when the presidential campaign ended, she was at an age where a further drive for the presidency in 2020 seemed remote. The constant taint of scandal that followed her, real or imagined, would surely be remembered. Yet her lifetime of public service should be remembered too, as well as the fact that she inspired millions of women around the United States and the globe to pursue their ambitions, whatever the obstacles. In every political role she played—lawyer, First Lady, health care task force director, senator, Secretary of State—her dedication to the public good and her desire to lead was remarkable, even in the face of the often-sexist opposition of an American public determined to resist her as a leader.

Key Sources

Little Rock, Arkansas is the home of the William J. Clinton Presidential Library and Museum, which holds the papers of the former president and husband of Hillary Rodham Clinton that have been declassified. The Library of Congress holds other correspondence related to the Clintons' time in the White House. Yet the best primary source related to the life of Hillary Rodham Clinton today is her memoir, *Living History*, published in 2003. It is certainly the best source to start from in describing her early life and her time as the First Lady of the United States. In 2015, she followed it up with a memoir on her first presidential run and her time as Secretary of State, called *Hard Choices*.

Essential Quotes

"The terrorist attacks at our diplomatic compound and later, at the CIA post in Benghazi, Libya, on September 11, 2012, took the lives of four brave Americans, Ambassador Chris Stevens, Sean Smith, Glen Doherty and Tyrone Woods. I'm here to honor the service of those four men."

"I would like to share three observations about how we can learn from this tragedy and move forward as a nation. First, America must lead in a dangerous world, and our diplomats must continue representing us in dangerous places.... [Second, w]e have a responsibility to provide our diplomats with the resources and support they need to do their jobs as safely and effectively as possible.... Finally,... [w]e need leadership at home to match our leadership abroad, leadership that puts national security ahead of politics and ideology."

"We should debate on the basis of fact, not fear. We should resist denigrating the patriotism or loyalty of those with whom we disagree. So I'm here. Despite all the previous investigations and all the talk about partisan agendas, I'm here to honor those we lost and to do what I can to aid those who serve us still."

Further Reading

Books

Allen, Jonathan and Amie Parnes. *HRC: State Secrets and the Rebirth of Hillary Clinton*. New York: Crown Publishers, 2014.

Bernstein, Carl. *A Woman in Charge: The Life of Hillary Rodham Clinton*. New York: Alfred A. Knopf, 2007.

Kornblut, Anne. *Notes from the Cracked Ceiling: Hillary Clinton, Sarah Palin, and What It Will Take for a Woman to Win*. New York: Crown Books, 2009.

Maraniss, David. *First in His Class: A Biography of Bill Clinton*. New York: Simon and Schuster, 1995.

Morris, Roger. *Partners in Power: The Clintons and Their America*. New York: Henry Holt, 1996.

Sheehy, Gail. *Hillary's Choice*. New York: Random House, 1999.

Web Sites

Frontline. "The Choice: 2016". Directed by Michael Kirk. Written by Michael Kirk & Mike Wiser. PBS, September 27, 2016 http://www.pbs.org/wgbh/frontline/film/the-choice-2016/ [accessed 10 November 2016].

—David Simonelli

Questions for Further Study

1. Secretary Clinton subtly questioned the ethics of the Senate investigation by comparing it implicitly with earlier, un-investigated incidents in American diplomacy where US officials were killed. At the same time, she openly admitted her responsibility for the safety of her diplomats and asked the senators for help in making that safety more effective. How do you think her earlier experiences with the political questioning of her ethics contributed to this defense?

2. Do you think Hillary Clinton's continued efforts to maintain secrecy or privacy contributed to the need for an investigation? Why or why not?

Hillary Rodham during university years.

Document Text

Opening Statement Benghazi Hearing

2015

GOWDY: The chair thanks the gentleman from Maryland.

Madam Secretary, you are recognized for your opening statement.

CLINTON: Thank you Mr. Chairman, Ranking Member Cummings, members of this committee.

The terrorist attacks at our diplomatic compound and later, at the CIA post in Benghazi, Libya, on September 11, 2012, took the lives of four brave Americans, Ambassador Chris Stevens, Sean Smith, Glen Doherty and Tyrone Woods.

I'm here to honor the service of those four men. The courage of the Diplomatic Security Agency and the CIA officers who risked their lives that night. And the work their colleagues do every single day all over the world.

I knew and admired Chris Stevens. He was one of our nation's most accomplished diplomats. Chris' mother liked to say he had "sand in his shoes," because he was always moving, always working, especially in the Middle East that he came to know so well.

When the revolution broke out in Libya, we named Chris as our envoy to the opposition. There was no easy way to get him into Benghazi to begin gathering information and meeting those Libyans who were rising up against the murderous dictator Gadhafi. But he found a way to get himself there on a Greek cargo ship, just like a 19th- century American envoy.

But his work was very much 21st-century, hard-nosed diplomacy.

CLINTON: It is a testament to the relationships that he built in Libya that on the day following the awareness of his death, tens of thousands of Libyans poured into the streets in Benghazi. They held signs reading, "Thugs don't represent Benghazi or Islam," "Sorry, people of America, this is not the behavior of our Islam or our prophet," "Chris Stevens, a friend to all Libyans."

Although I didn't have the privilege of meeting Sean Smith personally, he was a valued member of our State Department family. An Air Force veteran, he was an information management officer who had served in Pretoria, Baghdad, Montreal and the Hague.

Tyrone Woods and Glen Doherty worked for the CIA. They were killed by mortar fire at the CIA's outpost in Benghazi, a short distance from the diplomatic compound. They were both former Navy SEALs and trained paramedics with distinguished records of service including in Iraq and Afghanistan.

As secretary of State, I had the honor to lead and the responsibility to support nearly 70,000 diplomats and development experts across the globe. Losing any one of them, as we did in Iraq, Afghanistan, Mexico, Haiti and Libya, during my tenure was deeply painful for our entire State Department and USAID family and for me personally. I was the one who asked Chris to go to Libya as our envoy. I was the one who recommended him to be our ambassador to the president.

After the attacks, I stood next to President Obama as Marines carried his casket and those of the other three Americans off the plane at Andrews Air Force Base. I took responsibility, and as part of that, before I left office, I launched reforms to better protect our people in the field and help reduce the chance of another tragedy happening in the future.

What happened in Benghazi has been scrutinized by a non-partisan hard-hitting Accountability Review Board, seven prior congressional investigations, multiple news organizations and, of course, our law enforcement and intelligence agencies. So today, I would like to share three observations about how we can learn from this tragedy and move forward as a nation.

First, America must lead in a dangerous world, and our diplomats must continue representing us in dangerous places. The State Department sends people to more than 270 posts in 170 countries around the world. Chris Stevens understood that diplomats must operate in many places where our soldiers do not, where there are no other boots on the ground and safety is far from guaranteed. In fact, he volunteered for just those assignments.

He also understood we will never prevent every act of terrorism or achieve perfect security and that we inevitably must accept a level of risk to protect our country and advance our interests and values. And make no mistake, the risks are real. Terrorists have killed more than 65 American diplomatic personnel since the 1970s and more than 100 contractors and locally employed staff.

Document Text

Since 2001, there have been more than 100 attacks on U.S. diplomatic facilities around the world. But if you ask our most experienced ambassadors, they'll tell you they can't do their jobs for us from bunkers. It would compound the tragedy of Benghazi if Chris Stevens' death and the death of the other three Americans ended up undermining the work to which he and they devoted their lives.

We have learned the hard way when America is absent, especially from unstable places, there are consequences. Extremism take root, aggressors seek to fill the vacuum and security everywhere is threatened, including here at home. That's why Chris was in Benghazi. It's why he had served previously in Syria, Egypt, Saudi Arabia and Jerusalem during the second intifada.

Nobody knew the dangers of Libya better. A weak government, extremist groups, rampant instability. But Chris chose to go to Benghazi because he understood America had to be represented there at that pivotal time. He knew that eastern Libya was where the revolution had begun and that unrest there could derail the country's fragile transition to democracy. And if extremists gained a foothold, they would have the chance to destabilize the entire region, including Egypt and Tunisia. He also knew how urgent it was to ensure that the weapons Gadhafi had left strewn across the country, including shoulder-fired missiles that could knock an airplane out of the sky, did not fall into the wrong hands. The nearest Israeli airport is just a day's drive from the Libyan border.

Above all, Chris understood that most people in Libya or anywhere reject the extremists' argument that violence can ever be a path to dignity or justice. That's what those thousands of Libyans were saying after they learned of his death. And he understood there was no substitute for going beyond the embassy walls and doing the hard work of building relationships.

Retreat from the world is not an option. America cannot shrink from our responsibility to lead. That doesn't mean we should ever return to the go-it-alone foreign policy of the past, a foreign policy that puts boots on the ground as a first choice rather than a last resort. Quite the opposite. We need creative, confident leadership that harnesses all of America's strengths and values, leadership that integrates and balances the tools of diplomacy, development and defense.

And at the heart of that effort must be dedicated professionals like Chris Stevens and his colleagues who put their lives on the line for a country, our country, because they believed, as I do, that America is the greatest force for peace and progress the world has ever known. My second observation is this. We have a responsibility to provide our diplomats with the resources and support they need to do their jobs as safely and effectively as possible. After previous deadly attacks, leaders from both parties and both branches of government came together to determine what went wrong and how to fix it for the future.

That's what happened during the Reagan administration, when Hezbollah attacked our embassy and killed 63 people, including 17 Americans, and then in a later attack attacked our Marine barracks and killed so many more. Those two attacks in Beirut resulted in the deaths of 258 Americans.

It's what happened during the Clinton administration, when Al Qaida bombed our embassies in Kenya and Tanzania, killing more than 200 people, wounding more than 2,000 people and killing 12 Americans.

And it's what happened during the Bush administration after 9/11.

Part of America's strength is we learn, we adapt and we get stronger.

CLINTON: After the Benghazi attacks, I asked Ambassador Thomas Pickering, one of our most distinguished and longest serving diplomats, along with Admiral Mike Mullen, the former chairman of the Joint Chiefs of Staff -- appointed by President George W. Bush -- to lead an accountability review board.

This is an institution that the Congress set up after the terrible attacks in Beirut. There have been 18 previous accountability review boards. Only two have ever made any of their findings public -- the one following the attacks on our embassies in East Africa, and the one following the attack on Benghazi.

The accountability review board did not pull a single punch. They sound systemic problems and management deficiencies in two State Department bureaus. And the review board recommended 29 specific improvements. I pledged that by the time I left office, every one would be on the way to implementation and they were.

More Marines were slated for deployment to high-threat embassies. Additional diplomatic security agents were being hired and trained. And Secretary Kerry has continued this work.

But there is more to do and no administration can do it alone. Congress has to be our partner, as it has been after previous tragedies. For example, the accountability review board and subsequent investigations have recommended improved training for our

Document Text

officers before they deploy to the field. But efforts to establish a modern joint training center are being held up by Congress. The men and women who serve our country deserve better.

Finally, there is one more observation I'd like to share. I traveled to 112 countries as secretary of state. Every time I did, I felt great pride and honor representing the country that I love. We need leadership at home to match our leadership abroad, leadership that puts national security ahead of politics and ideology. Our nation has a long history of bipartisan cooperation on foreign policy and national security. Not that we always agree, far from it, but we do come together when it counts.

As secretary of state, I worked with the Republican chairman of the Senate Foreign Relations Committee to pass a landmark nuclear arms control treaty with Russia. I worked with the Republican leader, Senator Mitch McConnell, to open up Burma, now Myanmar, to democratic change. I know it's possible to find common ground because I have done it. We should debate on the basis of fact, not fear. We should resist denigrating the patriotism or loyalty of those with whom we disagree. So I'm here. Despite all the previous investigations and all the talk about partisan agendas, I'm here to honor those we lost and to do what I can to aid those who serve us still.

My challenge to you, members of this committee, is the same challenge I put to myself. Let's be worthy of the trust the American people have bestowed upon us. They expect us to lead, to learn the right lessons, to rise above partisanship and to reach for statesmanship. That's what I tried to do every day as secretary of state and it's what I hope we will all strive for here today and into the future.

Thank you.

Davy Crockett by William Henry Huddle, 1889

Davy Crockett: Original Analysis

Politician, Soldier

1786-1836

Overview

Davy Crockett was an American folklore hero, a real person whose myths – largely of his own creation – transcended his real life, which was eventful in and of itself. David Crockett was born on August 17, 1786 on what was then the recently-settled frontier of eastern Tennessee. He had a hard childhood, apprenticed to a cruel cattle driver from whom he ran away, and he was beaten by his father for skipping school. Living on his own, he worked odd jobs, and when he married at the age of twenty in 1806, he began working a farm near his parents' homestead in the Smoky Mountains. Five years later, though, he picked up his wife and two sons and moved to the border of what was then the Mississippi Territory, settling on the border of what is today Alabama.

At the time of his move, the new United States was involved in the War of 1812, a war with the British and several native American nations. Crockett enlisted as a volunteer, serving under Tennessee's famous general Andrew Jackson in battles against the Creek and Seminole Indians. He rose to the rank of lieutenant in the Franklin County militia by 1815. Like the rest of Tennessee's volunteer army, Crockett fought periodically in the Mississippi Territory, then went home between campaigns. His first wife died after giving birth to a daughter, and Crockett remarried soon after; he then moved his family westward into territory captured from the Creeks, in Lawrence County, Tennessee in 1817.

As a new white settler, with a military pedigree besides, Crockett had immediate status as a leader in the county. He served as a justice of the peace and a town commissioner, and was promoted to colonel in the county militia. Yet his mythical image really began to grow when he ran for a seat in the Tennessee State Legislature in 1821. Campaigning – especially in an era with no media available where his voice could be heard – meant that Crockett had to create a readable personality for himself, so people he had never seen before would vote for him on reputation alone. He was an excellent storyteller, claiming in one of his campaigns that he was "fresh from the backwoods, half-horse, half-alligator, a little touched with the snapping turtle; can wade the Mississippi, leap the Ohio, ride upon a streak of lightning, and slip without a scratch down a honey locust [tree]". He exaggerated his already considerable skills as a hunter of wild game and played up his connections to Tennessee hero Andrew Jackson, and won election twice to the legislature. He moved on to the US House of Representatives in 1827 and 1829, at the same time Jackson assumed the presidency. It only enhanced Crockett's reputation when he broke with Jackson over the Indian Removal Bill that led to the Trail of Tears in the 1830s. He lost his seat in 1831, but regained it in 1833 and maintained his status as a defender of native Americans in Congress.

Crockett was hardly a prominent congressman, though. More important was the fact that all of his campaign mythmaking could be put to work making him money and building his fame too. A playwright named James Kirke Paulding wrote a play on a commission to make an American frontiersman the center of the action. The resulting play, *The Lion of the West*, had a character named Nimrod Wildfire whom Paulding based on Crockett's stories about himself. The play was a massive New York hit in 1831 and 1832, and Crockett himself brought the play to Washington DC so he could see it before its company moved on to London. Then one James Strange French, an author otherwise lost to history, published *Sketches and Eccentricities of Colonel David Crockett of West Tennessee*, also to popular acclaim. In response, Crockett himself published his autobiography, allegedly to set the record straight about his life but likelier because he wanted to cash in on the publicity. Finally, in 1835, anonymous authors in Nashville came out with *Davy Crockett's Almanack, of Wild Sports in the West, and Life in the Backwoods*. Claiming to be written by Crockett himself, the *Almanacks* became famous for their homespun-sounding stories written in dialect about Crockett's racing other men while tied to a wildcat, fighting bears, wolves and catfish all at the same time, his wife and kids wrestling alligators and other tall tales. Britain had King Arthur and Robin Hood as emblems of chivalry, Spain had El Cid as the image of piety, and now the US had Davy Crockett, the embodiment of the frontiersman, the masthead of his *Almanack* urging Americans to "Go Ahead." The *Crockett Almanacks* came out twice a year for more than twenty years, solidifying Crockett's place in American folklore.

In the same year, 1835, Crockett planned to run for president to oppose Jackson's handpicked candidate, Martin Van Buren. To his apparent surprise, however, he was defeated in his reelection to Congress by Adam Huntsman, a one-legged lawyer. Disenchanted with politics, Crockett famously told a barroom crowd in Memphis, "Since you have chosen to elect a man with a timber toe to succeed me, you may all go to hell and I will go to Texas."

His hope was to make his fortune in Texas as a land agent and possibly revive his political career.

At the time, Texas was the northern frontier of Mexico, and the Mexican government was recruiting US farmers to come and settle the fertile farmland there – except without recourse to the institution of slavery, which the Mexican constitution forbade. The clash between southern US farmers and Mexicans became irreconcilable very quickly. Within two months of Crockett's arrival, the new settlers in Texas were in revolt against the Mexican government, and Crockett arrived at the Alamo outside San Antonio in February 1836. He joined Colonel William B. Travis in defense of the fort, and died there on March 6 1836. Even his death sprouted legends – while eyewitness accounts had him bayoneted and shot by Mexican soldiers after the fort surrendered, stories grew that he had fought until his bullets ran out, and then clubbed enemy soldiers with his rifle until cut down by bullets.

Explanation and Analysis of Documents

As with any number of politicians in the US throughout its history, Crockett allowed his early career as a soldier to establish his credentials as a patriot. In his case, he served as a scout in Andrew Jackson's army fighting against the Creek and Seminole Indians in Alabama and Florida.

The Creek War started in part because the Creek people were divided over their relationship with the European settlers. Half believed they should adopt European lifestyles as farmers, the others (known as "Red Sticks" because of their symbolic holding up of red sticks to vote for war) adhered to the defiance of the British-allied native chieftain Tecumseh, who believed in his brother's prophecy that all white men would soon be driven out of North America. The Red Sticks split from the rest of the Creeks and went to Pensacola to collect military supplies from the Spanish governor of Florida, with a letter from a British general vouching for their friendliness to the British and Spanish empires in North America. In response, a Mississippi militia attacked a Creek settlement at Burnt Corn Creek in southern Alabama, a preemptive strike that led to the Red Sticks declaring war on the US. In fear of the Red Sticks, locals in southern Alabama – white settlers, African-American slaves and Creeks who opposed the Red Sticks' cause – hastily erected Fort Mims, a stronghold near Mobile, Alabama. In August 1813, the Red Sticks sacked the fort and massacred the inhabitants. General Andrew Jackson and his soldiers determined to find the Red Sticks and punish them, and Davy Crockett joined this campaign.

A Narrative of the Life of David Crockett of the State of Tennessee – chapter V

Crockett opens this chapter of his autobiography (written in 1833) by stating that he believes his story may well get him elected president after Jackson finishes his term in 1836, a good example of his ambitions. The Creeks (only later does he distinguish between the Red Sticks and the rest) had provoked a war, in his opinion, and he felt a surge of bravery that overwhelmed his wife's efforts to keep him at home – after all, if every able man did not fight, the Creeks would come and kill women and children.

Upon mustering in Winchester, Crockett and the other sixty-day volunteers were addressed by Francis Jones, whom

Time Line

1786	August 17	■ David Crockett born
1806		■ First marriage
1811		■ Crockett moves to southern Tennessee
1813-1815		■ Creek War (part of the War of 1812); Crockett serves under Andrew Jackson
1817		■ Remarries; moves to frontier of western Tennessee
1821		■ Elected to Tennessee State Legislature
1827-1831		■ Elected to the US House of Representatives; Andrew Jackson president (Crockett becomes political opponent of Jackson)
1831		■ *The Lion of the West* produced in New York; character of Nimrod Wildfire based on Crockett
1832		■ James Strange French writes *Sketches and Eccentricities of Colonel David Crockett of West Tennessee*
1833		■ Crockett publishes his own autobiography; reelected to US House
1835-1856		■ *Davy Crockett's Almanack* published
1835	November	■ Crockett loses election to Adam Huntsman and begins moves to Texas
1836	January	■ Arrives in Texas
	February	■ Arrives at Alamo outside San Antonio
	March 6	■ Killed in battle

Crockett later notes would be a member of the House of Representatives, like himself. Soon after, Crockett was chosen out of the militia to join Major John Gibson (later a Lieutenant Colonel) on a scouting party across the Tennessee River. Crockett chose a teenager, George Russell, as his partner on the trip, and despite Gibson's misgivings over bringing a youngster into potential battle, Crockett's ornery nature was not to be trifled with. This is one of many times where Crockett notes that his "wrathy" nature impressed the people around him, a part of the mythmaking process.

Within a short period of time, Gibson gave Crockett command of half the men and they split up the party to scout a wider area. Crockett's party lost contact with Gibson, and Crockett determined to find the Creeks himself. He and his men arrived at the camp of a group of friendly Creeks, where they met with two slaves. The slaves had been taken by the Red Sticks and, having just escaped, they were "trying to get back to their masters again". The fact that they knew the Creek language makes it clear that Crockett's account of their status as recent kidnap victims was likely wrong. Translating, they told Crockett that if he stayed with the tribe, the Red Sticks would massacre the lot; Crockett's response is classic – "if one would come that night, I would carry the skin of his head home to make me a mockasin."

Sure enough, the Red Sticks came near the encampment, intending to hunt down Andrew Jackson's army and destroy them. While Creeks, slaves and soldiers alike quailed in fear, Crockett himself led his men back to the original army base back across the Tennessee River, sixty-five miles away, to warn Jackson. They rode overnight under dangerous circumstances, and arrived back at camp the next morning. There, Crockett reported to Major Gibson's superior, Colonel John Coffee, Andrew Jackson's most able officer and later, Jackson's negotiator with the Choctaw Indians for their removal from the southeastern United States in what would be called the Trail of Tears. Coffee was a man whom Crockett held in low esteem, because he did not take Crockett's reports on the danger of the Red Sticks seriously – until Major Gibson arrived and told the same story. Crockett remarks that he saw such class-based discrimination as "one of the hateful ways of the world", possibly an appeal to the poorer voters in the US in favor of his credentials as a "man of the people".

Later, Crockett and the rest of Jackson's army moved back into Alabama and slaughtered 186 Creek men, women and children at Tallushatchee. Crockett reenlisted in September 1814 and was a member of Jackson's army as it fought nearby Creeks and Seminoles in northern Florida. By 1815 he had been elected as a lieutenant in Tennessee's 32nd Militia.

A Narrative of the Life of David Crockett of the State of Tennessee – *chapter XI*

In 1821, Crockett was elected to the state legislature in Tennessee, and his storytelling abilities became essential to his campaigns. He related a tale in his autobiography from the period after his first term in Nashville. He set out westward in what was then the Tennessee territory to find a new home out on the frontier, where his family could live in relative isolation and where animals for hunting were plentiful. It says much for the fluid nature of European-native relations at the time that the old fighter against the Creek Red Sticks counted it as an asset that there were many Chickasaw tribes living in the region. Crockett in general proved to be open-minded in his relations with native Americans, and would later oppose Jackson's efforts to remove the Cherokees of southeastern Tennessee from their lands.

Crossing the Obion River proved to be a dangerous adventure, Crockett using all of his skills as a frontiersman in cutting down branches and trees to keep himself, his son and another youth from being carried away downstream. Finally the three arrived at the cabin of his prospective "neighbor", Mr. Owens. Owens's wife took care of Crockett's son and Owens offered Crockett a swig of whiskey. Upon warming and drying up, Crockett and his teenaged companion planned to board a boat and leave his son in the care of the Owenses while Crockett sailed down river to collect his family. Yet a "harricane" and the river's low water level meant their departure would be delayed. By "harricane", Crockett may have been referring to a lot of things. That area of the Mississippi River's course had just experienced a series of earthquakes centered in New Madrid, Missouri in 1811 and 1812; the region is also subject to tornadoes, and occasionally hurricanes will wear out their energies moving up river from Louisiana. Crockett seems to use the term to apply to the area on the Obion where he found damaged trees resulting from whatever natural disaster had occurred there.

While waiting for the river to rise, Crockett and the men from the boat erected a cabin to settle in once he returned with his family, and filled it with supplies. Crockett also proved his talents as a marksman by hunting for deer and elk to pay for his passage. Crockett proves in this passage that he considered his abilities as a huntsman to be his most saleable quality. He goes into detail on the animals he hunted, their numbers ("six that day"), how they died ("up he tumbled") and his efficiency in preparing them. One might easily guess that a candidate for governmental office who detailed such adventures would be seen as a man in tune with his constituency.

Finally, after crawling through painful underbrush to return to the boat, Crockett and the other men collected some of Crockett's kills and moved up the river. Crockett returned to his cabin with a helper to begin sowing corn. He shot more deer and bears alike, collected his family and served out his term in the legislature before settling beside the Obion for good.

In the winter of 1822, Crockett went up the Obion to collect a keg of gunpowder from his brother-in-law. There was snow on the ground, and crossing the river was treacherous – here, Crockett's talent for tall tales was on full display. He managed to wade through the freezing cold river on logs and carry his gun with him without getting it wet; his quick death from hypothermia was more likely than his ability to survive this harrowing ordeal. Another log later

flipped him into the water, yet he managed to hold his gun and a change of clothes out of the water so he could change into them on the other side (one imagines Crockett writing this passage while considering the limits of the credulity of his readers). Despite frozen feet, he made it to his brother-in-law's house, and killed two deer besides.

In terrible weather, Crockett set out to return to his meat-less family, "or die a-trying". Carrying his powder keg, he started across the frozen river and fell in the ice; instead of getting out, he simply chopped his way across with a tomahawk until he returned to a familiar spot and made his way across. He even considered chasing down a bear which he believed had fallen through the ice himself. But, since he never found the bear – who, as it turned out, did not exist, since it was his farm helper who had fallen through the ice looking for Crockett – nothing distracted Crockett from his efforts to follow the trail home to his family, powder and all.

Impact and Legacy

Crockett's impact came far less from this autobiography and more from the stories Americans told about him after his death. In the immediate era after 1836, the *Crockett Almanacks* took his huntin', fishin', fightin' lifestyle and embellished it to the point of humor. A century after the *Almanacks* ceased publication, Davy Crockett became a Cold War emblem of American individualism and toughness for the Disney Corporation, with Fess Parker playing Crockett as a simple, soft-spoken, coonskin-cap-wearing hero with an exemplary morality. In *The Alamo* (1960), John Wayne took on the role of the larger-than-life Tennesseean. Davy Crockett has proven, over two centuries, to be an example of an American's ability to be anyone they choose to be, particularly in a country with frontiers where European-style civilization was fleeting.

Key Sources

The New-York Historical Society has a full collection of the *Davy Crockett Almanacks*, digitized and available for the general reader. His autobiography is likewise available in digitized form at Archive.org, and is easily found in many libraries under different titles. The original title is *A Narrative of the Life of David Crockett of the State of Tennessee*, another title being *Davy Crockett's Own Story as Written by Himself: The Autobiography of America's Great Folk Hero*. A recent book, *David Crockett in Congress : The Rise and Fall of the Poor Man's Friend* is an edited collection of Crockett's letters, speeches and campaign literature. It is compiled by James R. Boylston and Allen J. Wiener. This may be the best source for his letters since they appear to be scattered all over the country; another source is the Shackford book listed below.The best bibliography of primary and secondary materials is Miles Tanenbaum, "Following Davy's Trail: A Crockett Bibliography," in *Crockett at Two Hundred: New Perspectives on the Man and the Myth*, ed. Michael A. Lofaro and Joe Cummings (1989).

Essential Quotes

...[A]s military men are making so much fuss in the world at this time, I must give an account of the part I took in the defence of the country. If it should make me president, why I can't help it; such things will sometimes happen; and my pluck is, never "to seek, nor decline office."

(Chapter V)

While we remained at the spring, a Major Gibson came, and wanted some volunteers to go with him across the Tennessee river and into the Creek nation, to find out the movements of the Indians. He came to my captain, and asked for two of his best woodsmen, and such as were best with a rifle. The captain pointed me out to him, and said he would be security that I would go as far as the major would himself, or any other man.

(Chapter V)

Essential Quotes

... [T]hey were very much alarmed, for the "red sticks," as they called the war party of the Creeks, would come and find us there; and, if so, we should all be killed. I directed him to tell them that I would watch, and if one would come that night, I would carry the skin of his head home to make me a mockasin.

(Chapter V)

Having returned from the Legislature, I determined to make another move, and so I took my eldest son with me, and a young man by the name of Abram Henry, and cut out for the Obion. I selected a spot when I got there, where I determined to settle; ... . It was a complete wilderness, and full of Indians who were hunting. Game was plenty of almost every kind, which suited me exactly, as I was always fond of hunting.

(Chapter XI)

To pay for these, I agreed to go with the boat up the river to their landing place. ... In the morning I started about daylight, intending to kill a deer, ...[and] I had gone but a little way before I killed a fine buck, and started to go back to the boat; but on the way I came on the tracks of a large gang of elks, and so I took after them. I had followed them only a little distance when I saw them, and directly after I saw two large bucks. I shot one down, and the other wouldn't leave him; so I loaded my gun, and shot him down too. I hung them up, and went ahead again after my elks.

(Chapter XI)

Further Reading

■ Books

Kanon, Tom. *Tennesseans at War 1812-1815: Andrew Jackson, the Creek War, and the Battle of New*

Orleans. Tuscaloosa, AL: University of Alabama Press, 2014.

Levy, Buddy. *American Legend: The Real-Life Adventures of David Crockett*. New York: G. P. Putnam's

Sons, 2005.

Lofaro, Michael A. and Joe Cummings, editors. *Crockett at Two Hundred: New Perspectives on the Man*

and the Myth. Knoxville, TN: University of Tennessee Press, 1989.

Shackford, James Atkins. *David Crockett: The Man and the Legend*, edited by John B. Shackford. Lincoln,

NE: University of Nebraska Press, 1994.

Wallis, Michael. *David Crockett: The Lion of the West*. New York: WW Norton and Co., 2011.

Williams, Paul. *Jackson, Crockett and Houston on the American Frontier: From Fort Mims to the Alamo, 1813-1836*. Jefferson, NC: McFarland & Company, Inc., Publishers, 2016.

Web Sites

Answering the Call: Tennesseans in the War of 1812. Tennessee State Library and Archives. 2014 http://share.tn.gov/tsla/exhibits/1812/index.htm [accessed August 28, 2016].

Lofaro, Michael A. "Crockett, David." *The Handbook of Texas Online* http://www.tshaonline.org/

handbook/online/articles/fcr24 [accessed August 28, 2016].

Falzone, Catherine. "Davy Crockett Almanacs". From the Stacks: The New-York Historical Society and

Museum. June 19, 2012 http://blog.nyhistory.org/davy-crockett-almanacs/ [accessed August 28, 2016].

Kanon, Tom. "Brief History of Tennessee in the War of 1812". Tennessee Secretary of State: History and Genealogy http://sos.tn.gov/products/tsla/brief-history-tennessee-war-1812 [accessed August 28, 2016].

—*David Simonelli*

Questions for Further Study

1. What role does the frontier play in Americans' image of themselves? Davy Crockett, Daniel Boone, Brigham Young, and mythical figures like Zorro and Paul Bunyan all embody similar qualities as men of the American frontier. What are those qualities and how do they contribute to how Americans think of what it means to be American?

2. From descriptions of Davy Crockett and his life, what was the media like in the early nineteenth century in the US? What "sold" to voters, book buyers and readers, farmers and other members of the general public? How was Davy Crockett's "brand" conveyed to people, before his death and then after it?

3. Crockett's life is exceedingly exaggerated, but it also has a solid grounding in reality. What was important to a settler on the Tennessee frontier when he and his family found a place to put up a home? What was the frontiersman's relationship with the local native population like? In his storytelling, how did Crockett's tales appeal to other frontiersmen – what did he exaggerate as qualities that would appeal to them as voters?

A NARRATIVE OF THE LIFE OF DAVID CROCKETT OF THE STATE OF TENNESSEE: CHAPTER V

1834

I WAS living ten miles below Winchester when the Creek war commenced; and as military men are making so much fuss in the world at this time, I must give an account of the part I took in the defence of the country. If it should make me president, why I can't help it; such things will sometimes happen; and my pluck is, never " to seek, nor decline office."

It is true, I had a little rather not; but yet, if the government can't get on without taking another president from Tennessee, to finish the work of "retrenchment and reform," why, then, I reckon I must go in for it. But I must begin about the war, and leave the other matter for the people to begin on.

The Creek Indians had commenced their open hostilities by a most bloody butchery at Fort Minims. There had been no war among us for so long, that but few, who were not too old to bear arms, knew any thing about the business. I, for one, had often thought about war, and had often heard it described; and I did verily believe in my own mind, that I couldn't fight in that way at all; but my after experience convinced me that this was all a notion. For when I heard of the mischief which was done at the fort, I instantly felt like going, and I had none of the dread of dying that I expected to feel. In a few days a general meeting of the militia was called for the purpose of raising volunteers; and when the day arrived for that meeting, my wife, who had heard me say I meant to go to the war, began to beg me not to turn out. She said she was a stranger in the parts where we lived, had no connexions living near her, and that she and our little children would be left in a lonesome and unhappy situation if I went away. It was mighty hard to go against such arguments as these; but my countrymen had been murdered, and I knew that the next thing would be, that the Indians would be scalping the women and children all about there, if we didn't put a stop to it. I reasoned the case with her as well as I could, and told her, that if every man would wait till his wife got willing for him to go to war, there would be no fighting done, until we would all be killed in our own houses; that I was as able to go as any man in the world; and that I believed it was a duty I owed to my country. Whether she was satisfied with this reasoning or not, she did not tell me; but seeing I was bent on it, all she did was to cry a little, and turn about to her work. The truth is, my dander was up, and nothing but war could bring it right again.

I went to Winchester, where the muster was to be, and a great many people had collected, for there was as much fuss among the people about the war as there is now about moving the deposites. When the men were paraded, a lawyer by the name of Jones addressed us, and .closed by turning out himself, and enquiring, at the same time, who among "us felt like we could fight Indians? This was the same Mr. Jones who after wards served in Congress, from the state of Tennessee. He informed us he wished to raise a company, and that then the men should meet and elect their own officers. I believe I was about the second or third man that step'd out; but on marching up and down the regiment a few times, we found we had a large company. We volunteered for sixty days, as it was supposed our services would not be longer wanted. A day or two after this we met and elected Mr. Jones our captain, and also elected our other officers. We then received orders to start on the next Monday week; before which time, I had fixed as well as I could to go, and my wife had equip'd me as well as she was able for the camp. The time arrived; I took a parting farewell of my wife and my little boys, mounted my horse, and set sail, to join my company. Expecting to be gone only a short time, 1 took no more clothing with me than I supposed would be necessary, so that 'if I got into an Indian battle, I might not be pestered with any unnecessary plunder, to prevent my having a fair shake with them. We all met and went ahead, till we passed Huntsville, and camped at a large spring called Beaty's spring. Here we staid for several days, in which time the troops began to collect from all quarters. At last we mustered about thirteen hundred strong, all mounted volunteers, and all determined to fight, judging from myself, for I felt wolfish all over. I verily believe the whole army was of the real grit. Our captain didn't want any other sort; and to trv them he several times told his men, that if any of them wanted to go back home, they might do so at any time, before they were regularly mustered into the service. But he had the honour to command all his men from first to last, as not one of them left him.

Document Text

Gen'l. Jackson had not yet left Nashville with his old foot volunteers, that had gone with him to Natchez in 1812, the year before. While we remained at the spring, a Major Gibson came, and wanted some volunteers to go with him across the Tennessee river and into the Creek nation, to find out the movements of the Indians. He came to my captain, and asked for two of his best woods men, and such as were best with a rifle. The cap tain pointed me out to him, and said he would be security that I would go as far as the major would himself, or any other man. I willingly engaged to go with him, and asked him to let me choose my own mate to go with me, which he said I might do. I chose a young man by the name of George Russell, a son of old Major Russell, of Tennessee. I called him up, but Major Gibson said he thought he hadn't beard enough to please him, he want ed men, and not boys. I must confess I was a lit tle nettled at this; for I know'd George Russell, and I know'd there was no mistake in him; and I didn't think that courage ought to be measured by the beard, for fear a goat would have the preference over a man. I told the major he was on the wrong scent; that Russell could go as far as he could, and I must have him along. He saw I was a little wrathy, and said I had the best chance of knowing, and agreed that it should be as I wanted it. He told us to be ready early in the morning for a start; and so we were. We took our camp equipage, mounted our horses, and, thirteen in number, including the major, we cut out. We went on, and crossed the Tennessee river at a place called Ditto's Landing; and then traveled about seven miles further, and took up camp for the night. Here a man by the name of John. Haynes overtook us. He had been an Indian trader in that part of the nation, and was well acquainted with it. He went with us as a pilot. The next morning, however, Major Gibson and myself concluded we should separate and take different directions to see what discoveries we could make; so he took seven of the men, and I five, making thirteen in all, including myself. He was to go by the house of a Cherokee Indian, named Dick Brown, and I was to go by Dick's father's j and getting all the information we could, we were to meet that evening where the roads came together, fifteen miles the other side of Brown's. At old Mr. Brown's I got a half blood Cherokee to agree to go with me, whose name was Jack Thompson. He was not then ready to start, but was to fix that evening, and overtake us at the fork road where I was to meet Major Gibson. I know'd it wouldn't be safe to camp right at the road; and so I told Jack, that when he got to the fork he must holler like an owl, and I would answer him in the same way; for I know'd it would be night before he got there. I and my men then started, and went on to the place of meeting, but Major Gibson was not there. We waited till almost dark, but still he didn't come. We then left the Indian trace a little distance, and turning into the head of a hollow, we struck up camp. It was about ten o'clock at night, when I heard my owl, and I answered him. Jack soon found us, and we determined to rest there during the night. We staid also next morning till after breakfast: but in vain, for the major didn't still come.

I told the men we had set out to hunt a fight, and I wouldn't go back in that way; that we must go ahead, and see what the red men were at. We started, and went to a Cherokee town about twenty miles off; and after a short stay there, we pushed on to the house of a man by the name of Radcliff. He was a white man, but had married a Creek woman, and lived just in the edge of the Creek nation. He had two sons, large likely fellows, and a great deal of potatoes and corn, and, indeed, almost every thing else to go on; so we fed our horses and got dinner with him, and seemed to be doing mighty well. But he was bad scared all the time. He told us there had been ten painted warriors at his house only an hour before, and if we were discovered there, they would kill us, and his family with us. I replied to him, that my business was to hunt for just such fellows as he had described, and I was determined not to go back until I had done it. Our dinner being over, we saddled up our horses, and made ready to start. But some of my small company I found were disposed to return. I told them, if we were to go back then, we should never hear the last of it; and I was determined to go ahead. I knowed some of them would go with me, and that the rest were afraid to go back by themselves; and so we pushed on to the camp of some of the friendly Creeks, which was distant about eight miles. The moon was about the full, and the night was clear; w r e therefore had the benefit of her light from night to morning, and I knew if we were placed in such danger as to make a retreat necessary, we could travel by night as w r ell as in the day time.

We had not gone very far, when we met two negroes, well mounted on Indian ponies, and each with a good rifle. They had been taken from their owners by the Indians, and were running away from them, and trying to get back to their masters again. They were brothers, both very large and likely, and

could talk Indian as well as English. One of them I sent on to Ditto's Landing, the other I took back with me. It was after dark when we got to the camp, where we found about forty men, women, and children.

They had bows and arrows, and I turned in to shooting with their boys by a pine light. In this way we amused ourselves very well for a while; but at last the negro, who had been talking to the Indians, came to me and told me they were very much alarmed, for the "red sticks," as they called the war party of the Creeks, would come and find us there; and, if so, we should all be killed. I directed him to tell them that I would watch, and if one would come that night, I would carry the skin of his head home to make me a mockasin. When he made this communication, the Indians laughed aloud. At about ten o'clock at night we all concluded to try to sleep a little; but that our horses might be ready for use, as the treasurer said of the drafts on the United States' bank, on certain "contingences," we tied them up with our saddles on them, and every thing to our hand, if in the night our quarters should get uncomfortable. We lay down with our guns in our arms, and I had just gotten into a dose of sleep, when I heard the sharpest scream that ever escaped the throat of a human creature. It was more like a wrathy painter than any thing else. The negro understood it, and he sprang to me; for tho' I heard the noise well enough, yet I wasn't wide awake enough to get up. So the negro caught me, and said the red sticks was coming. I rose quicker then, and asked what was the matter? Our negro had gone and talked with the Indian who had just fetched the scream, as he come into camp, and learned from him, that the war party had been crossing the Coosa river all day at the Ten islands; and were going on to meet Jackson, and this Indian had come as a runner. This news very much alarmed the friendly Indians in camp, and they were all off in a few minutes. I felt bound to make this intelligence known as soon as possible to the army we had left at the landing; and so we all mounted our horses, and put out in a long lope to make our way back to that place. We were about sixty-five miles off. We went on to the same Cherokee town we had visited on our way out, having first called at Radcliff's, who was off with his family; and at the town we found large fires burning, but not a single Indian was to be seen. They were all gone. These circumstances were calculated to lay our dander a little, as it appeared we must be in great danger; though we could easily have licked any force of not more than five to one. But we expected the whole nation would be on us, and against such fearful odds we were not so rampant for a fight.

We therefore staid only a short time in the light of the fires about the town, preferring the light of the moon and the shade of the woods. We pushed on till we got again to old Mr. Brown's, which was still about thirty miles from where we had left the main army. When we got there, the chickens were just at the first crowing for day. We fed our horses, got a morsel to eat ourselves, and again cut out. About ten o'clock in the morning we reached the camp, and I reported to Col. Coffee the news. He didn't seem to mind my report a bit, and this raised my dander higher than ever; but I knowed I had to be on my best behaviour, and so I kept it all to myself; though I was so mad that I was burning inside like a tarkiln, and I wonder that the smoke hadn't been pouring out of me at all points.

Major Gibson hadn't yet returned, and we all began to think he was killed; and that night they put out a double guard. The next day the major . got in, and brought a worse tale than I had, though he stated the same facts, so far as I went. This seemed to put our colonel all in a fidget; and it convinced me, clearly, of one of the hateful ways of the world. When I made my report, it wasn't believed, because I was no officer; I was no great man, but just a poor soldier. But when the same thing was reported by Major Gibson !! why, then, it was all as true as preaching, and the colonel believed it every word.

He, therefore, ordered breastworks to be thrown up, near a quarter of a mile long, and sent an express to Fayetteville, where General Jackson and his troops was, requesting them to push on like the very mischief, for fear we should all be cooked up to a cracklin before they could get there. Old Hickory-face made a forced march on getting the news; and on the next day, he and his men, got into camp, with their feet all blistered from the effects of their swift journey. The volunteers, therefore, stood guard altogether, to let them rest.

A Narrative of the Life of David Crockett of the State of Tennessee: Chapter XI

1834

HAVING returned from the Legislature, I determined to make another move, and so I took my eldest son with me, and a young man by the name of Abram Henry, and cut out for the Obion. I selected a spot when I got there, where I determined to settle; and the nearest house to it was seven miles, the next nearest was fifteen, and so on to twenty. It was a complete wilderness, and full of Indians who were hunting. Game was plenty of almost every kind, which suited me exactly, as I was always fond of hunting. The house which was nearest me, and which, as I have already stated, was seven miles off, and on the different side of the Obion river, belonged to a man by the name of Owens; and I started to go there. I had taken one horse along, to pack our provision, and when I got to the water I hobbled him out to graze, until I got back; as there was no boat to cross the river in, and it was so high that it had overflowed all the bottoms and low country near it.

We now took water like so many beavers, not withstanding it was mighty cold, and waded on. The water would sometimes be up to our necks, and at others not so deep; but I went, of course, before, and carried a pole, with which I would feel along before me, to see how deep it was, and to guard against falling into a slough, as there was many in our way. When I would come to one, I would take out my tomahawk and cut a small tree across it, and then go ahead again. Frequently my little son would have to swim, even where myself and the young man could wade; but we worked on till at last we got to the channel of the river, which made it about half a mile we had waded from where we took water. I saw a large tree that had fallen into the river from the other side, but it didn't reach across. One stood on the same bank where we were, that I thought I could fall, so as to reach the other; and so at it we went with my tomahawk, cutting away till we got it down; and, as good luck would have it, it fell right, and made us a way that we could pass.

When we got over this, it was still a sea of water as far as our eyes could reach. We took into it again, and went ahead, for about a mile, hardly ever seeing a single spot of land, and sometimes very deep. At last we come in sight of land, which was a very pleasing thing; and when we got out, we went but a little way, before we came in sight of the house, which was more pleasing than ever; for we were wet all over, allmighty cold. I felt mighty sorry when I would look at my little boy, and see him shaking like he had the worst sort of an ague, for there was no time for fever then. As we got near to the house, we saw Mr. Owens and several men that were with him, just starting away. They saw us, and stop'd, but looked much astonished until we got up to them, and I made my self known. The men who were with him were the owners of a boat which was the first that ever went that far up the Obion river; and some hands he had hired to carry it about a hundred miles still further up, by water, tho' it was only about thirty by land, as the river is very crooked.

They all turned back to the house with me, where I found Mrs. Owens, a fine, friendly old woman; and her kindness to my little boy did me ten times as much good as any thing she could have done for me, if she had tried her best. The old gentleman set out his bottle to us, and I concluded that if a horn wasn't good then, there was no use for its invention. So I swig'd off about a half pint, and the young man was by no means bashful in such a case; he took a strong pull at it too. I then gave my boy some, and in a little time we felt pretty well. We dried ourselves by the fire, and were asked to go on board of the boat that evening. I agreed to do so, but -left my son with the old lady, and my self and my young man went to the boat with Mr. Owens and the others. The boat was loaded with whiskey, flour, sugar, coffee, salt, castings, and other articles suitable for the country; and they were to receive five hundred dollars to land the load at M'Lemore's Bluff, beside the profit they could make on their load. This was merely to show that boats could get up to that point. We staid all night with them, and had a high night of it, as I took steam enough to drive out all the cold that was in me, and about three times as much more. In the morning we concluded to go on with the boat to where a great harricane had crossed the river, and blowed all the timber down into it. When we got there, we found the river was falling fast, and concluded we couldn't get through the timber without more rise; so we drop'd down opposite Mr. Owens' again, where they determined to wait for more water.

Document Text

Milestone Documents

The next day it rained rip-roriously, and the river rose pretty considerable, but not enough yet. And so I got the boatsmen all to go out with me to where I was going to settle, and we slap'd up a cabin in little or no time. I got from the boat four barrels of meal, and one of salt, and about ten gallons of whiskey.

To pay for these, I agreed to go with the boat up the river to their landing place. I got also a large middling of bacon, and killed a fine deer, and left them for my young man and my little boy, who were to stay at my cabin till I got back; which I expected would be in six or seven days. We cut out, and moved up to the harricane, where we stop'd for the night. In the morning I started about daylight, intending to kill a deer, as I had no thought they would get the boat through the timber that day. I had gone but a little way be fore I killed a fine buck, and started to go back to the boat; but on the way I came on the tracks of a large gang of elks, and so I took after them. I had followed them only a little distance when I saw them, and directly after I saw two large bucks. I shot one down, and the other wouldn't leave him; so I loaded my gun, and shot him down too. I hung them up, and went ahead again after my elks. I pursued on till after the middle of the day be fore I saw them again; but they took the hint before I got in shooting distance, and run off. I still pushed on till late in the evening, when I found I was about four miles from where I had left the boat, and as hungry as a wolf, for I hadn't eaten a bite that day.

I started down the edge of the river low grounds, giving out the pursuit of my elks, and hadn't gone hardly any distance at all, before I saw two more bucks, very large fellows too. I took a blizzard at one of them, and up he tumbled. The other ran off a few jumps and stop'd; and stood there till I loaded again, and fired at him. I knock'd his trotters from under him, and then I hung them both up. I pushed on again; and about sunset I saw three other bucks. I down'd with one of them, and the other two ran off. I hung this one up also, having now killed six that day. I then pushed on till I got to the harricane, and at the lower edge of it, about where I expected the boat was. Here I hollered as hard as I could roar, but could get no answer. I fired off my gun, and the men on the boat fired one too; but quite contrary to my expectation, they had got through the timber, and were about two miles above me. It was now dark, and I had to crawl through the fallen timber the best way I could; and if the reader don't know it was bad enough, I am sure I do. For the vines and briers had grown all through it, and so thick, that a good fat coon couldn't much more than get along. I got through at last, and went on near to where I had killed my last deer, and once more fired off my gun, which was again answered from the boat, which was still a little above me. I moved on as fast as I could, but soon came to water, and not knowing how deep it was, I halted and hollered till they came to me with a skiff. I no\v got to the boat, without further difficulty; but the briers had worked on me at such a rate, that I felt like I wanted sewing up, all over. I took a pretty stiff horn, which soon made me feel much better; but I was so tired that I could hardly work my jaws to eat.

In the morning, myself and a young man started and brought in the first buck I had killed; and after breakfast we went and brought in the last one. The boat then started, but we again went and got the two I had killed just as I turned down the river in the evening; and we then pushed on and overtook the boat, leaving the other two hanging in the woods, as we had now as much as we wanted.

We got up the river very well, but quite slowly; and we landed, on the eleventh day, at the place the load was to be delivered at. They here gave me their skiff, and myself and a young man by the name of Flavius Harris, who had determined to go and live with me, cut out down the river for my cabin, which we reached safely enough.

We turned in and cleared a field, and planted our corn; but it was so late in the spring, we had no time to make rails, and therefore we put no fence around our field. There was no stock, however, nor any thing else to disturb our corn, except the wild varments, and the old serpent himself, with a fence to help him, couldn't keep them out. I made corn enough to do me, and during that spring I killed ten bears, and a great abundance of deer. But in all this time, we saw the face of no white person in that country, except Mr. Owens' family, and a very few passengers, who went out there, looking at the country. Indians, though, were still plenty enough. Having laid by my trap, I went home, which was a distance of about a hundred and fifty miles; and when I got there, I was met by an order to attend a call-session of our Legislature. I attended it, and served out my time, and then returned, and took my family and what little plunder I had, and moved to where I had built my cabin, and made my trap.

I gathered my corn, and then set out for my Fall's hunt. This was in the last of October, 1822. I found bear very plenty, and, indeed, all sorts of game and wild varments, except buffalo. There was none of them. I hunted on till Christmass, having supplied

my family very well all along with wild meat, at which time my powder gave out; and I had none either to fire Christmass guns, which is very common in that country, or to hunt with. I had a brother-in-law who had now moved out and settled about six miles west of me, on the opposite side of Rutherford's fork of the Obion river, and he had brought me a keg of powder, but I had never gotten it home. There had just been another of Noah's freshes, and the low grounds were flooded all over with water. I know'd the stream was at least a mile wide which I would have to cross, as the water was from hill to hill, and yet I determined to go on over in some way or other, so as to get my powder. I told this to my wife, and she immediately opposed it with all her might. I still insisted, telling her we had no powder for Christmass, and, worse than all, we were out of meat. She said, we had as well starve as for me to freeze to death or to get drowned, and one or the other was certain if I attempted to go.

But I didn't believe the half -of this; and so I took my woolen wrappers, and a pair of mockasins, and put them on, and tied up some dry clothes and a pair of shoes and stockings, and started. But I didn't before know how much any body could suffer and not die. This, arid some of my other experiments in water, learned me something about it, and I therefore relate them.

The snow was about four inches deep when I started; and when I got to the water, which was only about a quarter of a mile off, it look'd like an ocean. I put in, and waded on till I come to the channel, where I crossed that on a high log. I then took water again, having my gun and all my hunting tools along, and waded till I came to a deep slough, that was wider than the river itself. I had crossed it often on a log; but, behold, when I got there, no log was to be seen. I knowed of an island in the slough, and a sapling stood on it close to the side of that log, which was now entirely under water. I knowed further, that the water was about eight or ten feet deep under the log, and I judged it to be about three feet deep over it. After studying a little what I should do, I determined to cut a forked sapling, which stood near me, so as to lodge it against the one that stood on the island, in which I succeeded very well. I then cut me a pole, and crawled along on my sapling till I got to the one it was lodged against, which was about six feet above the water. I then felt about with my pole till I found the log, which was just about as deep under the water as I had judged. I then crawled back and got my gun, which I had left at the stump of the sapling I had cut, and again made my way to the place of lodgement, and then climb'd down the other sap ling so as to get on the log. I then felt my way along with my feet, in the water, about waist deep, but it was a mighty ticklish business. However, I got over, and by this time I had very little feeling in my feet and legs, as I had been all the time in the water, except what time I was crossing the high log over the river, and climbing my lodged sapling.

I went but a short distance before I came to another slough, over which there was a log, but it was floating on the water. I thought I could walk it, and so I mounted on it; but when I had got about the middle of the deep water, some how or somehow else, it turned over, and in I went up to my head I waded out of this deep water, and went ahead till I came to the high-land, where I stop'd to pull of my wet clothes, and put on the others, which I had held up with my gun, above the water, when I fell in. I got them on, but my flesh had no feeling in it, I was so cold. I tied up the wet ones, and hung them up in a bush. I now thought I would run, so as to warm myself a little, but I couldn't raise a trot for some time; indeed, I couldn't step more than half the length of my foot. After a while I got better, and went on five miles to the house of my brother-in-law, having not even smelt fire from the time I started. I got there late in the evening, and he was much astonished at seeing me at such a time. I staid all night, and the next morning was most piercing cold, and so they persuaded me not to go home that day. I agreed, and turned out and killed him two deer; but the weather still got worse and colder, instead of better. I staid that night, and in the morning they still insisted I couldn't get home. I knowed the water would be frozen over, but not hard enough to bear me, and so I agreed to stay that day. I went out hunting again, and pursued a big he-bear all day, but didn't kill him. The next morning was bitter cold, but I knowed my family was without meat, and I determined to get home to them, or die a-trying.

I took my keg of powder, and all my hunting tools, and cut out. When I got to the water, it was a sheet of ice as far as I could see. I put on to it, but hadn't got far before it broke through with me; and so I took out my tomahawk, and broke my way along before me for a considerable distance. At last I got to where the ice would bear me for a short distance, and I mounted on it, and went ahead; but it soon broke in again, and I had to wade on till I came to my floating log. I found it so tight this time, that I know'd it couldn't give me another fall, as it was frozen in with the ice. I crossed over it without much difficulty, and worked along till I got to my lodged sapling, and my

Document Text

log under the water. The swiftness of the current prevented the water from freezing over it, and so I had to wade, just as I did when I crossed it before. When I got to my sapling, I left my gun and climbed out with my powder keg first, and then went back and got my gun. By this time I was nearly frozen to death, but I saw all along before me, where the ice had been fresh broke, and I thought it must be a bear straggling about in the water. I, there fore, fresh primed my gun, and, cold as I was, I was determined to make war on him, if we met. But I followed the trail till it led me home, and I then found it had been made by my young man that lived with me, who had been sent by my distressed wife to see, if he could, what had become of me, for they all believed that I was dead. When I got home I was'nt quite dead, but mighty nigh it; but I had my powder, and that was what I went for.

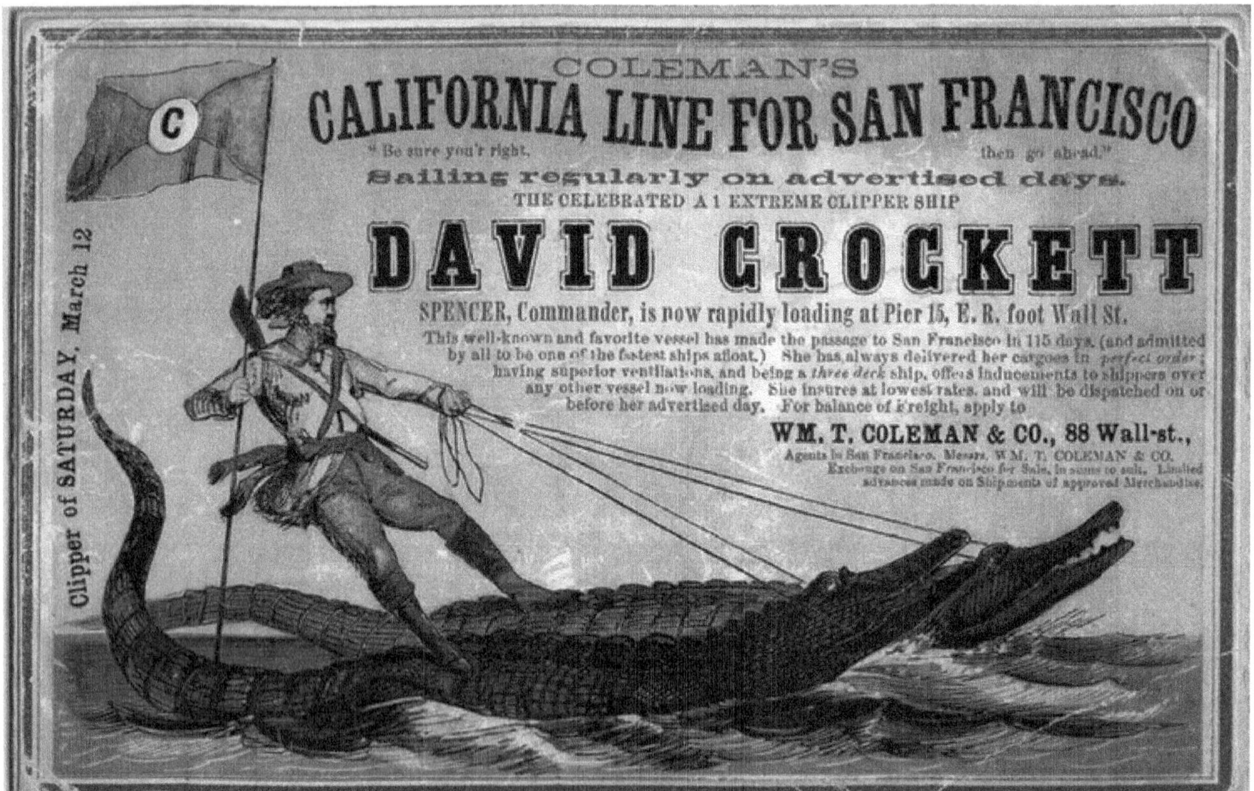

David Crockett clipper ship card, By G.F. Nesbitt & Co., printer,

Official White House photo of President Bill Clinton, President of the United States by Bob McNeely, The White House.

Bill Clinton: Original Analysis

Forty-second President of the United States

1946–

Overview

William Jefferson Blythe III was born in Hope, Arkansas, on August 19, 1946, three months after his father, William Jefferson Blythe, Jr., had died in an automobile accident. His mother, Virginia, remarried to a local automobile salesman, Roger Clinton, in 1950 and shortly thereafter changed young William's last name to Clinton. Bill Clinton graduated from Georgetown University in 1968 and was awarded a Rhodes Scholarship to Oxford University; he earned a law degree from Yale University in 1973.

Clinton was elected attorney general of Arkansas in 1976 and became governor of the state two years later. Although he lost his reelection bid in 1980, he successfully regained the governorship in 1982, holding the position until his election to the presidency in 1992. Campaigning on a platform of change and optimism during a period of economic decline, public dissatisfaction with government, and an electoral shift toward the political center, Clinton defeated the Republican incumbent, George H. W. Bush, and the independent candidate, Ross Perot. In January 1993 Clinton gave his inaugural address to the nation, establishing the political tone and agenda for his administration.

Clinton's first term ended with mixed results. The revolutionary efforts put forth by Clinton and his wife, Hillary Rodham Clinton, to reform health care failed, and investigations into the Clintons' past real-estate dealings and allegations of improper firings in the White House travel office beleaguered the administration. However, Clinton accomplished two of his most important priorities. He signed the North American Free Trade Agreement (NAFTA) in December 1993 and the Personal Responsibility and Work Opportunity Reconciliation Act, which implemented sweeping reforms to the nation's welfare system, in August 1996.

Although the Democrats lost both houses of Congress to the Republicans in the 1994 midterm elections, Clinton won reelection in 1996 against the Republican candidate, Bob Dole. However, Clinton's second term was derailed by the Monica Lewinsky scandal. Called to testify in the sexual harassment case brought by Paula Jones against the president, Lewinsky, an intern in the White House, became a public figure when her testimony revealed that she and the president had had an intimate relationship, though Clinton had publicly denied it. Clinton then testified before a grand jury investigation and admitted to the affair in a televised broadcast, but he denied that he had asked Lewinsky to lie. On September 9, 1998, the independent counsel Kenneth Starr sent Congress a report listing possible impeachable offenses against the president, including perjury and obstruction of justice. When the report was made public two days later, Clinton acknowledged that he had "sinned" at the annual White House prayer breakfast with religious leaders. He was impeached by the House of Representatives, but the Senate acquitted him on February 12, 1999.

George W. Bush defeated Vice President Al Gore in the bitterly contested 2000 presidential election, and Bill Clinton gave his farewell address to the nation on January 18, 2001. Out of office, he published his memoir, *My Life*, in 2004 and dedicated the William J. Clinton Presidential Center on November 18 of that year. Clinton actively campaigned for his wife's bid for the 2008 Democratic presidential nomination. He set up his own nonprofit foundation, which has funded a number of programs, including the Clinton Global Initiative, aimed at addressing poverty, the problem of limited access to health care, and religious and ethnic violence.

Explanation and Analysis of Documents

Bill Clinton entered the presidency in 1992 promising change and renewal to a recession-wracked nation just entering the post–cold war era. As the economy recovered while tensions in the former Soviet Union and elsewhere exploded into violence, Clinton sought to garner support for often controversial policy decisions through the message of positive change. Shadowed by scandal, Clinton's presidency saw unprecedented public involvement in the chief executive's personal life. Five public documents convey not only the consistent message of change and renewal but also the controversial nature of the Clinton presidency: his first inaugural speech, his remarks upon signing NAFTA and upon signing welfare reform, his speech to the annual White House prayer breakfast following his testimony regarding the Lewinsky matter, and his farewell address.

♦ First Inaugural Address

Clinton's victory in the 1992 presidential election was noteworthy in that he both defeated an incumbent and ended twelve years of Republican domination of the White House. Although in early 1991 George H. W. Bush had led the successful effort to repel Iraq's invasion of neighboring Kuwait, while the decades-long cold war had ended with the

dissolution of the Soviet Union in late 1991, the American public was pessimistic about the future of the nation. The collapse of the Soviet Union resulted in the birth of new republics, fueling long-standing ethnic and religious tensions in the region that exploded into violence in Yugoslavia. As America sank into economic recession, many feared that the country had lost its edge to technologically superior nations in Asia. Believing that the country was headed in the wrong direction, the public sought change. Campaigning with a message that he would fight for middle-class Americans, Clinton won with 43 percent of the popular vote.

Clinton was known for his oratorical skills, and his first inaugural address illustrates his talent for crafting a speech. Throughout the address, he develops the theme of the linkage between change and renewal. He begins with a reference to the season in which his inauguration takes place, winter, and uses spring as a metaphor for America's rebirth. The oppositions of winter and spring and of dark and light extend to current events; the cold war era was a winter of "shadows," whereas the new, post-Soviet era was being "warmed by the sunshine of freedom."

Clinton portrays change as a positive factor, not something to be feared. He compares the modern technological world with that of George Washington's era, pointing out that change offers enhanced opportunity but also requires determination. Using major historical events such as the Great Depression and the Civil War as examples, Clinton reminds his audience that America has a history of overcoming challenges through bold action and re-creating itself for the better in the process.

Clinton makes very calculated references to past presidents in this speech. He invokes Washington to contrast the modern world with the past. Also mentioned are Thomas Jefferson and Franklin Roosevelt, two prominent Democratic presidents. Jefferson's election in 1800 is often referred to as the "revolution of 1800" because of his difference from his predecessors, Washington and John Adams. Unlike Washington and Adams, whose constituencies consisted of the American upper class, Jefferson appealed to small farmers, independent businessmen, and other nonelites with his message of democratic values. Roosevelt, who presided over the New Deal programs during the Great Depression, ushered in massive changes in American views on poverty and on the government's role in providing a safety net for its people in times of economic upheaval. Although he does not specifically name him, Clinton alludes to John F. Kennedy with his statement that Americans must stop "expecting something for nothing from our Government." One of Kennedy's most famous statements was a remark made in his own 1961 inaugural address: "Ask not what your country can do for you—ask what you can do for your country."

The program that Clinton espouses for renewal involves the revitalization of democracy at home and of a sense of obligation for the nation's international responsibilities. In addition to the domestic challenges of economic inequality and recession, he points to the constantly changing political landscape that was already characterizing the post–cold

Time Line

1946	August 19	■ William Jefferson Blythe is born in Hope, Arkansas.
1968	June	■ Clinton graduates from Georgetown University with a bachelor of science in international affairs.
1976	November	■ Clinton is elected attorney general of Arkansas.
1978	November	■ Clinton is elected governor of Arkansas.
1992	November 3	■ Clinton is elected president of the United States.
1993	January 20	■ Clinton gives his inaugural address.
	December 8	■ Clinton signs the North American Free Trade Agreement.
1994	November 8	■ Democrats lose control of Congress in the midterm elections.
1996	August 22	■ Clinton signs the Personal Responsibility and Work Opportunity Reconciliation Act, instituting welfare reform.
	November 5	■ Clinton is reelected to a second term in office.
1997	December 17	■ Monica Lewinsky is subpoenaed by Paula Jones in her sexual harassment lawsuit against President Clinton.
1998	January 26	■ Clinton publicly states, "I did not have sexual relations with that woman, Miss Lewinsky."
	September 11	■ Clinton gives his remarks at the annual White House breakfast with religious leaders, in which he acknowledges, "I have sinned."
	December 19	■ Clinton is impeached by the House of Representatives on charges of perjury and obstruction of justice.
1999	February 12	■ Clinton is acquitted by the Senate of perjury and obstruction of justice.
2001	January 18	■ Clinton delivers his farewell speech, ending his service as president.

Time Line		
2004	June 22	■ Clinton publishes his memoirs, *My Life.*
	November 18	■ The William J. Clinton Presidential Center, Clinton's presidential library, is dedicated in Little Rock, Arkansas.
2005	February 1	■ United Nations Secretary-General Kofi Annan appoints Clinton as envoy for tsunami recovery following the devastating Indian Ocean tsunamis of December 2004.
2007	September 4	■ Clinton publishes *Giving: How Each of Us Can Change the World.*

war world. Clinton mentions AIDS, which had reached epidemic proportions in America, and the increasingly complex situation created by the breakup of the former Soviet Union into independent nations. As Clinton points out, the post-Soviet world was perhaps "more free," but it was certainly unstable, as arms dealers rushed into newly formed republics to supply them with weapons, adding fuel to the fires of smoldering ethnic and religious tensions. Russia demanded new access to American markets for weapons and sought the freedom to sell to adversaries of America as well. Serbia, part of the former Yugoslavia, had stockpiled enough weapons to continue the systematic slaughter of Bosnian Muslims in a program of "ethnic cleansing." Although the cold-war terror of mutually assured destruction had ended, new terrors were replacing it, and Clinton calls on Americans to serve as leaders in the new world order their nation had helped create.

Clinton ends his speech with a reference to the looming twenty-first century, a mark in time he used repeatedly in speeches and other documents to remind his audiences to look to the future with optimism. Interestingly, he invokes religious text, quoting from the King James Bible version of Paul's letter to the Galatians. Clinton also contrasts the joy of the mountaintop with the valley, a place of service. There are numerous biblical mountaintop revelations, including Moses' reception of the Ten Commandments and Jesus' transfiguration before the apostles; from the mountaintop, they are called on to return to serve God in the difficult realm of the valley. Clinton continues his biblical borrowing with a reference to trumpets, which are used to call people to battle, to announce the presence of angels or God, or to sound some other call to action. By invoking this religious imagery, Clinton lends a moral tone to his inaugural address. He also displays his knowledge of texts; a well-read man, Clinton often quotes from or draws on diverse sources, ranging from fiction to historical writings to scripture, in his various documents.

Clinton's inaugural address set the agenda and tone for his administration and effectively positioned him as a world leader. Known as a charismatic, if rather long-winded, public speaker, he carefully designed this speech to convey a focused message of change and renewal to an audience weary of the status quo and ready for a trumpet call to action.

♦ Remarks on Signing the North American Free Trade Agreement

President George H. W. Bush negotiated NAFTA, a landmark treaty to remove trade barriers between the United States, Mexico, and Canada. Clinton supported NAFTA during his campaign despite the fact that most Americans, particularly unionized labor, opposed the agreement because they believed that it would cost the nation jobs. The Texas billionaire Ross Perot, who ran as an independent candidate in the 1992 election, warned voters of a "giant sucking sound" that would accompany the loss of U.S. jobs to Mexico if NAFTA were to be enacted. Once elected, Clinton negotiated a series of side agreements to address his own NAFTA-related concerns regarding the maintenance of labor and environmental standards and cooperation in fighting drug trafficking.

Clinton delivered remarks on NAFTA during the signing ceremony. Early in the speech he mentions the side agreements, commenting that the treaty is about "social progress as well as economic growth." Mired in a recession, the nation could ill afford a loss of jobs; Clinton thus highlights the job-creation power of NAFTA. In keeping with his vision of an America that takes seriously its responsibilities to the global community, he also emphasizes the positive impacts, both economic and social, for the world.

Renewal and change are two themes that appear constantly in Clinton's documents, particularly those produced during his first term in office. Here, he compares NAFTA to other historic agreements, arguing that this, like the end of World War II, is a moment to "remake the world." Clinton references a number of important people and institutions. At the 1944 Bretton Woods conference, the forty-five Allied nations formed the World Bank and the International Monetary Fund to help stabilize currencies and rebuild Europe after the war. The 1947 Marshall Plan, named after Secretary of State George C. Marshall, was a far-reaching program of economic aid to Europe that included the ratification of the General Agreement on Tariffs and Trade, which reduced trade barriers between the United States and seventeen western European nations. Angered by the increased American influence that the Marshall Plan represented, Joseph Stalin implemented the Berlin blockade, preventing any traffic between Soviet-controlled East Germany and the West. In response, in 1949 the United States, Canada, and ten European countries formed the North Atlantic Treaty Organization (NATO), a mutual defense agreement by which all members agreed to defend an attack against any one member. Secretary of State Dean Acheson, of Harry Truman's second administration, played a prominent role in creating both the Marshall Plan and NATO. Senator Arthur Vandenberg, a Republican, authored the Vandenberg Resolution, a 1948 document that argued for regional alliances

for defensive purposes, such as the forthcoming NATO. By invoking all of this history, Clinton places NAFTA on the same level as these institutions designed to provide for worldwide security and prosperity. He also sets a precedent for American leadership in global affairs.

In keeping with his themes of renewal and change, Clinton emphasizes the different nature of the world after the cold war. Whereas Truman and Acheson dealt with "the grim certitude of the contest with communism," Clinton and his audience must face the "exuberant uncertainty" of international markets. Capitalism has prevailed, but it presents "promise and perils." Following World War II, America faced a world of oversupply; as productive capacity that had been used to build military equipment was converted to peacetime production, many wondered if there would be enough demand for all of the goods that American manufacturers were churning out. The Marshall Plan solved this problem by creating a vast overseas market for U.S. goods. With America "once again" facing a problem of overproduction, Clinton offers NAFTA as a solution. Just as the cold war institutions achieved their objectives so well, so, too, would NAFTA. New worlds require new solutions and new institutions.

Signing NAFTA turned out to cost Clinton and the Democrats. Opposition to the agreement carried into the 1994 midterm elections, in which Democrats lost control of both the House of Representatives and the Senate. The agreement remains controversial, with pundits arguing that it has had both positive and negative impacts on the global economy as well as on the U.S. job market, the environment, and labor standards. Clinton's remarks illustrate the controversial nature of this landmark legislation. Reminding his audience of the recently ended cold war, he establishes a historical precedent for American economic and defensive alliances while reiterating his administration's recurring themes of renewal, change, and global responsibility.

♦ Remarks on Signing the Personal Responsibility and Work Opportunity Reconciliation Act

Welfare reform was one of Clinton's campaign promises in 1992, but most of his first year in office was spent in a futile effort to revamp the nation's health-care system. Following the Democratic losses in the 1994 midterm elections, welfare reform resurfaced as an important agenda item. Increasingly conservative, most American voters believed that it was time to limit government spending on social programs. Popularized by President Ronald Reagan, the image of the "welfare queen," the single mother who abused the system, symbolized the perceived corruption and inefficiencies of public assistance.

In his remarks Clinton points out that the profile of a welfare aid recipient has changed since the program's inception. In 1935 Franklin Delano Roosevelt created Aid to Dependent Children, which covered mostly children of families headed by widows. By the 1960s the typical welfare recipient was a divorced, unwed, or deserted single mother. What had been designed as a minor program for a small, select group of needy children had expanded to a government subsidy serving well over ten million people by the 1970s. In addressing the shortcomings of welfare, Clinton is careful to fault the system rather than welfare recipients, removing the stigma associated with the "welfare queen." He describes those receiving aid as "trapped" within a system over which they have no control and as exiled "from the entire community of work" that provides meaning to Americans. Clinton invokes Robert F. Kennedy, who made urban poverty the centerpiece of his 1968 presidential campaign. In reminding Americans of a previous fight against poverty, Clinton emphasizes the need to change the system itself rather than blame those who are caught within it.

Clinton comments that the bill is "far from perfect." The Republican-controlled Congress sent welfare reform bills to the White House in 1994 and 1995, and Clinton vetoed both of them because of cuts in Medicare, Medicaid, school lunch and food stamp programs, and aid to immigrants and because they did not address the issue of child care. The Personal Responsibility and Work Opportunity Reconciliation Act replaced direct federal aid with block grants to states, which would administer their own aid programs. As Clinton notes, the new law directed substantial funds toward child care. In addition, it provided the states with incentives to move people off of the welfare rolls and into jobs; recipients have a five-year lifetime cap on benefits, and states may impose work and other behavioral requirements on those receiving assistance, such as limiting family size. While preserving many of the benefits that the original Republican bills cut, the act reduced funds for child nutrition and food stamps and denied benefits to noncitizens. Clinton expresses his concern that, without these benefits, some of the working poor would perhaps be unable to remain in the workforce, defeating the purpose of the legislation.

Returning to the important themes of change and renewal, Clinton invokes here the chance to "recreate the Nation's social bargain with the poor" through a new beginning. He also puts the onus for the legislation's success on politicians, business, and the general public rather than on the welfare recipients themselves. Drawing attention to the bitter bipartisan nature of Washington politics following the 1994 congressional election, Clinton repeatedly emphasizes that welfare cannot be a political matter. Republicans and Democrats alike will have to work together to ensure that reform takes place, and the private sector will also have to help with job creation.

It is no accident that Clinton uses "responsibility" several times in his remarks on signing the Personal Responsibility and Work Opportunity Reconciliation Act. Echoing the title of the legislation, he underlines the ways in which welfare reform encourages responsible behavior on the part of aid recipients, such as meeting child support obligations, finding jobs, and being responsible parents and citizens. Yet he emphasizes that the entire nation has responsibilities as well: to provide jobs, to ensure adequate support systems for those on welfare, and to cease bipartisan bickering. By stressing responsibility, Clinton not only reassures

his audience that the new law represents true reform but also reminds them that they must play a role in change and renewal as well.

♦ Remarks at Annual Prayer Breakfast

Clinton addressed the 1998 annual prayer breakfast at the White House just as the details of the Lewinsky scandal became public. Monica Lewinsky, an intern who worked for a brief time at the White House, was subpoenaed to testify in Paula Jones's sexual harassment lawsuit against the president. Rumors began circulating in the media of a sexual relationship between Clinton and Lewinsky. In January 1998 Clinton publicly denied any sexual relationship or that he had asked Lewinsky to lie in her testimony in the Jones case. Although the Jones case was dismissed, the independent prosecutor, Kenneth Starr, pursued his investigation into perjury and obstruction of justice, and, in exchange for immunity, Lewinsky testified that she and Clinton had had a sexual relationship, although he had not told her to lie. On August 17, Clinton testified before a grand jury investigating the case, and he went on television that same day to admit that he had had an "inappropriate relationship" with Ms. Lewinsky.

Facing a room full of religious representatives as well as political leaders from around the world on September 11, 1998, Clinton made the embarrassing scandal the centerpiece of his address. His apology of August 17 was judged by many to be insincere; in this speech, Clinton agrees that he "was not contrite enough" and confesses that he has "sinned." Much of his emphasis is thus on the recognition of his own moral failings and on his repentance, or determination to rectify the damage he has done. Given that the venue is a prayer breakfast, it is not surprising that Clinton uses the language of sin, repentance, and forgiveness to apologize for an extramarital affair.

Although he speaks as a repentant sinner, Clinton also uses the voice of the statesman, walking the line between private and public throughout this address. It is interesting to note how, while he acknowledges the impact of the scandal on the nation, he distinguishes between healing the country and healing himself. In part, this reinforces the validity of his repentance; Clinton states that he "cannot move beyond or forget" what has happened but that the nation must. In his critique of the Starr investigation, Clinton repeatedly argued that the prosecutor had stepped beyond appropriate boundaries, invading into private matters. Here, his separation of his own long-term healing process from the nation's need to move on quickly reinforces the idea that the Lewinsky matter was a private one that unfortunately became public. However, Clinton also states that "good can come of this for our country as well as for me and my family," now linking the personal with the public. He holds himself up as a lesson in the potential for redemption, as a message of forgiveness through repentance. If the health of the president is symbolic of the health of the body politic, then Clinton's embodiment of positive change becomes an object lesson in second chances.

The Lewinsky scandal is for many the most memorable event of Clinton's two terms in office. His speech at the annual prayer breakfast provides insight into both Clinton the man and Clinton the politician. In the address he portrays himself on the one hand as a contrite sinner before a religious audience, on the other as a statesman forced to publicly acknowledge his own private, personal shortcomings before other dignitaries.

♦ Farewell Address

In his last address to the public as president, Clinton highlights his administration's achievements and recommends three specific areas for future action after he leaves office. As with virtually all of his documents, this speech is highly structured and builds on the major themes of change, leadership for the future, and global responsibility.

Clinton congratulates the American public on preparing for the twenty-first century, pointing to the nation's "dramatic transformation," "renewal," and focus on the future. These were themes from his first days in office; here he takes a celebratory tone to note the accomplishments of the past eight years. Clinton mentions several specific policy achievements, including economic expansion and the reduction of the federal deficit that occurred under his administration. The Family and Medical Leave Act of 1993 was an early piece of legislation allowing employees to take unpaid leaves of absence for health reasons or to tend to an ailing relative or child. The Personal Responsibility and Work Opportunity Reconciliation Act reformed the federal welfare system, capping benefits at five years and providing a number of incentives for aid recipients to find employment and support their children. Pell grants, loans to underprivileged college students, increased under the Clinton administration, and interest rates on federally subsidized student loans were cut substantially. With strong support from Vice President Al Gore, the administration emphasized environmental protection, including the addition of land to the National Parks System.

Clinton's three recommendations for the future emphasize fiscal responsibility, global security and social responsibility, and tolerance at home. Clinton inherited a budget deficit of $290 billion in 1992 and left office with a budget surplus. As he did in his remarks on signing NAFTA, Clinton notes the double-edged sword of the global economy; it provides opportunity but also the seeds for economic inequality, terrorism, and environmental destruction. Last, Clinton refers to America's "coat of many colors," a reference to the garment worn by Joseph, son of Jacob in the Old Testament; the phrase is often used to symbolize diversity. Clinton believed that America had much to accomplish in the area of race relations; his last message to Congress, entitled "The Unfinished Work of Building One America," centers on recommendations to end racial discrimination in education, the legal system, health care, and economic opportunities.

Clinton's farewell address outlines his concerns for America's future, essentially calling for a continuation of his own policies as detailed in the first part of his speech. Fiscal responsibility, global leadership, and social justice

were linchpins of Clinton's policy decisions; he calls for these guiding principles to continue in the next administration, framing his own legacy within the confines of this very brief speech.

Impact and Legacy

Historians continue to debate the legacy of Clinton's presidency. Politically, his administration marked an important shift to the center for the Democratic Party. Disenchanted with government programs that seemed to have failed, the American public looked to alternatives to traditional solutions such as welfare. Clinton's agenda of renewal and revitalization represented a substantive change in Democratic policy and philosophy. Many in his own party criticized this shift; Clinton's welfare reform package and NAFTA, in particular, met with strong objections within the Democratic Party. Republicans, too, found much to quarrel with, particularly the Clintons' first-term attempt at health-care reform. The fact that his presidency was so polarizing is evidence of the centrist nature of his political agenda.

Clinton also left his personal stamp on the office of chief executive. A charismatic speaker and very strong personality, he and his wife brought energy and optimism to the White House; Hillary's involvement in policy decisions, particularly health-care reform, earned the first couple both scorn and admiration. Through his personal style and communication skills, Clinton conveyed genuine concern for his audience during public appearances and exhibited a remarkable ability to connect with the public. This aspect of his personality explains in part why most Americans continued to approve of his performance in office despite the Lewinsky scandal and subsequent impeachment proceedings.

Key Sources

Clinton's papers are contained in the William J. Clinton Presidential Library and Museum in Little Rock, Arkansas, and are accessible online (http://www.clintonlibrary.gov). Several of Clinton's speeches are available online through the William J. Clinton Foundation (http://www.clintonfoundation.org). The American Presidency Project also has many of Clinton's writings and oral addresses available online (http://www.presidency.ucsb.edu). In 2004 Clinton published his autobiography, *My Life*, which provides extensive detail from his life before and during his presidency. He also authored *Between Hope and History: Meeting America's Challenges for the 21st Century* (1996), in which he summarizes his first term in office, and *Giving: How Each of Us Can Change the World* (2007), which profiles several notable philanthropists and activists for social change.

Essential Quotes

"Today, a generation raised in the shadows of the cold war assumes new responsibilities in a world warmed by the sunshine of freedom but threatened still by ancient hatreds and new plagues."

(First Inaugural Address)

"Our democracy must be not only the envy of the world but the engine of our own renewal."

(First Inaugural Address)

"The grim certitude of the contest with communism has been replaced by the exuberant uncertainty of international economic competition. And the great question of this day is how to ensure security for our people at a time when change is the only constant."

(Remarks on Signing the North American Free Trade Agreement)

Essential Quotes

"Today we are ending welfare as we know it. But I hope this day will be remembered not for what it ended but for what it began: a new day that offers hope, honors responsibility, rewards work, and changes the terms of the debate so that no one in America ever feels again the need to criticize people who are poor on welfare."

(Remarks on Signing the Personal Responsibility and Work Opportunity Reconciliation Act)

"I don't think there is a fancy way to say that I have sinned."

(Address to the Annual Prayer Breakfast)

"You, the American people, have made our passage into the global information age an era of great American renewal."

(Farewell Address)

Milestone Documents

Further Reading

♦ Books

Campbell, Colin, and Bert A. Rockman, eds. *The Clinton Presidency: First Appraisals*. Chatham, N.J.: Chatham House Publishers, 1996.

Hamilton, Nigel. *Bill Clinton: An American Journey*. New York: Random House, 2003.

Harris, John F. *The Survivor: Bill Clinton in the White House*. New York: Random House, 2005.

Schier, Steven E., ed. *The Postmodern Presidency: Bill Clinton's Legacy in U.S. Politics*. Pittsburgh: University of Pittsburgh Press, 2000.

Shields, Todd G., Jeannie M. Whayne, and Donald R. Kelley, eds. *The Clinton Riddle: Perspectives on the Forty-second President*. Fayetteville: University of Arkansas Press, 2004.

♦ Web Sites

"William J. Clinton." White House Web site. http://www.whitehouse.gov/history/presidents/bc42.html.

—*Karen Linkletter*

Questions for Further Study

1. In his first inaugural address, Clinton strikes a highly optimistic tone, even as he discusses challenges facing America at the time. Do you think this optimism was justified, and did subsequent events warrant this optimism? Comment on the imagery Clinton uses, for example, the comparison of a nation to a family in his statement that "we must provide for our Nation the way a family provides for its children."

2. In supporting free trade in general and NAFTA in particular, Clinton found himself at odds with many in the Democratic Party, particularly labor unions and their supporters, who saw international competition as a threat to their wages. In fact, arguments over NAFTA made for some strange bedfellows, with Patrick Buchanan and Ralph Nader—leading figures of the extreme right and left, respectively—joining the opposition to NAFTA, while moderate Republicans and Democrats generally supported the agreement. Argue for or against NAFTA and the principles it represents. In doing so, critique Clinton's arguments: for instance, his claim that protectionism in the post-World War I era helped bring about the Great Depression.

3. By the 1990s, most Americans were in agreement that welfare needed reforming. Outside the political extremes of left and right, there was a consensus that government entitlement programs had not succeeded and needed to be reduced but that some type of safety net should remain in place for those least fortunate. Discuss Clinton's principles for welfare reform as expressed in his remarks on signing the Personal Responsibility and Work Opportunity Reconciliation Act. Think about points of agreement as well as objections that could be raised by liberals and conservatives.

4. Clinton and his supporters often referred to the Monica Lewinsky affair as a personal matter that had unfortunately become public owing to an abuse of power by the independent counsel Kenneth Starr and others, notably congressional Republicans. This, along with his efforts to apologize for wrongdoing, is an underlying theme of Clinton's comments at the White House prayer breakfast in September 1998. Consider this argument from a number of standpoints. Was Starr abusing his power, and did Republicans pursue the matter because they wanted to limit Clinton's effectiveness as president? Is an affair between a president and a White House intern truly a private matter? Would it have been treated as such had Clinton been an ordinary chief executive, rather than president of the United States?

5. Using his farewell address as a beginning point, consider Clinton's legacy as president. Examine the achievements he notes in the address and evaluate his successes. Then look at the less attractive aspects of his legacy, as claimed by his opponents. Many of these involve the Lewinsky scandal, which should be considered not only with regard to how it affected the Clinton administration directly but also in light of its impact on matters of sexual harassment and equality in the workplace. Might the scandal have exerted a much larger negative influence, inasmuch as Osama bin Laden and al Qaeda made their first appearance on the world stage in the fall of 1998 by bombing two U.S. embassies in Africa?

First Inaugural Address

1993

My fellow citizens, today we celebrate the mystery of American renewal. This ceremony is held in the depth of winter, but by the words we speak and the faces we show the world, we force the spring, a spring reborn in the world's oldest democracy that brings forth the vision and courage to reinvent America. When our Founders boldly declared America's independence to the world and our purposes to the Almighty, they knew that America, to endure, would have to change; not change for change's sake but change to preserve America's ideals: life, liberty, the pursuit of happiness. Though we marched to the music of our time, our mission is timeless. Each generation of Americans must define what it means to be an American....

Today, a generation raised in the shadows of the cold war assumes new responsibilities in a world warmed by the sunshine of freedom but threatened still by ancient hatreds and new plagues. Raised in unrivaled prosperity, we inherit an economy that is still the world's strongest but is weakened by business failures, stagnant wages, increasing inequality, and deep divisions among our own people.

When George Washington first took the oath I have just sworn to uphold, news traveled slowly across the land by horseback and across the ocean by boat. Now, the sights and sounds of this ceremony are broadcast instantaneously to billions around the world. Communications and commerce are global. Investment is mobile. Technology is almost magical. And ambition for a better life is now universal.

We earn our livelihood in America today in peaceful competition with people all across the Earth. Profound and powerful forces are shaking and remaking our world. And the urgent question of our time is whether we can make change our friend and not our enemy. This new world has already enriched the lives of millions of Americans who are able to compete and win in it. But when most people are working harder for less; when others cannot work at all; when the cost of health care devastates families and threatens to bankrupt our enterprises, great and small; when the fear of crime robs law-abiding citizens of their freedom; and when millions of poor children cannot even imagine the lives we are calling them to lead, we have not made change our friend.

We know we have to face hard truths and take strong steps, but we have not done so; instead, we have drifted. And that drifting has eroded our resources, fractured our economy, and shaken our confidence. Though our challenges are fearsome, so are our strengths. Americans have ever been a restless, questing, hopeful people. And we must bring to our task today the vision and will of those who came before us. From our Revolution to the Civil War, to the Great Depression, to the civil rights movement, our people have always mustered the determination to construct from these crises the pillars of our history. Thomas Jefferson believed that to preserve the very foundations of our Nation, we would need dramatic change from time to time. Well, my fellow Americans, this is our time. Let us embrace it.

Our democracy must be not only the envy of the world but the engine of our own renewal. There is nothing wrong with America that cannot be cured by what is right with America. And so today we pledge an end to the era of deadlock and drift, and a new season of American renewal has begun.

To renew America, we must be bold. We must do what no generation has had to do before. We must invest more in our own people, in their jobs, and in their future, and at the same time cut our massive debt. And we must do so in a world in which we must compete for every opportunity. It will not be easy. It will require sacrifice, but it can be done and done fairly, not choosing sacrifice for its own sake but for our own sake. We must provide for our Nation the way a family provides for its children.

Our Founders saw themselves in the light of posterity. We can do no less. Anyone who has ever watched a child's eyes wander into sleep knows what posterity is. Posterity is the world to come: the world for whom we hold our ideals, from whom we have borrowed our planet, and to whom we bear sacred responsibility. We must do what America does best: offer more opportunity to all and demand more responsibility from all. It is time to break the bad habit of expecting something for nothing from our Government or from each other. Let us all take more responsibility not only for ourselves and our families but for our communities and our country.

Document Text

To renew America, we must revitalize our democracy. This beautiful Capital, like every capital since the dawn of civilization, is often a place of intrigue and calculation. Powerful people maneuver for position and worry endlessly about who is in and who is out, who is up and who is down, forgetting those people whose toil and sweat sends us here and pays our way. Americans deserve better. And in this city today there are people who want to do better. And so I say to all of you here: Let us resolve to reform our politics so that power and privilege no longer shout down the voice of the people. Let us put aside personal advantage so that we can feel the pain and see the promise of America. Let us resolve to make our Government a place for what Franklin Roosevelt called bold, persistent experimentation, a Government for our tomorrows, not our yesterdays. Let us give this Capital back to the people to whom it belongs.

To renew America, we must meet challenges abroad as well as at home. There is no longer a clear division between what is foreign and what is domestic. The world economy, the world environment, the world AIDS crisis, the world arms race: they affect us all. Today, as an older order passes, the new world is more free but less stable. Communism's collapse has called forth old animosities and new dangers. Clearly, America must continue to lead the world we did so much to make....

Today we do more than celebrate America. We rededicate ourselves to the very idea of America, an idea born in revolution and renewed through two centuries of challenge; an idea tempered by the knowledge that, but for fate, we, the fortunate, and the unfortunate might have been each other; an idea ennobled by the faith that our Nation can summon from its myriad diversity the deepest measure of unity; an idea infused with the conviction that America's long, heroic journey must go forever upward.

And so, my fellow Americans, as we stand at the edge of the 21st century, let us begin anew with energy and hope, with faith and discipline. And let us work until our work is done. The Scripture says, "And let us not be weary in well doing: for in due season we shall reap, if we faint not." From this joyful mountaintop of celebration we hear a call to service in the valley. We have heard the trumpets. We have changed the guard. And now, each in our own way and with God's help, we must answer the call.

Thank you, and God bless you all.

Glossary

"let us not be weary in well doing": a quote from Galatians 6:9, meaning "Don't stop doing what you know is right"

Document Text

Remarks on Signing the North American Free Trade Agreement

1993

Milestone Documents

In a few moments, I will sign the North American free trade act into law. NAFTA will tear down trade barriers between our three nations. It will create the world's largest trade zone and create 200,000 jobs in this country by 1995 alone. The environmental and labor side agreements negotiated by our administration will make this agreement a force for social progress as well as economic growth. Already the confidence we've displayed by ratifying NAFTA has begun to bear fruit. We are now making real progress toward a worldwide trade agreement so significant that it could make the material gains of NAFTA for our country look small by comparison.

Today we have the chance to do what our parents did before us. We have the opportunity to remake the world. For this new era, our national security we now know will be determined as much by our ability to pull down foreign trade barriers as by our ability to breach distant ramparts. Once again, we are leading. And in so doing, we are rediscovering a fundamental truth about ourselves: When we lead, we build security, we build prosperity for our own people.

We've learned this lesson the hard way. Twice before in this century, we have been forced to define our role in the world. After World War I we turned inward, building walls of protectionism around our Nation. The result was a Great Depression and ultimately another horrible World War. After the Second World War, we took a different course: We reached outward. Gifted leaders of both political parties built a new order based on collective security and expanded trade. They created a foundation of stability and created in the process the conditions which led to the explosion of the great American middle class, one of the true economic miracles in the whole history of civilization. Their statecraft stands to this day: the IMF and the World Bank, GATT, and NATO.

In this very auditorium in 1949, President Harry Truman signed one of the charter documents of this golden era of American leadership, the North Atlantic Treaty that created NATO. "In this pact we hope to create a shield against aggression and the fear of aggression," Truman told his audience, "a bulwark which will permit us to get on with the real business of Government and society, the business of achieving a fuller and happier life for our citizens."

Now, the institutions built by Truman and Acheson, by Marshall and Vandenberg, have accomplished their task. The cold war is over. The grim certitude of the contest with communism has been replaced by the exuberant uncertainty of international economic competition. And the great question of this day is how to ensure security for our people at a time when change is the only constant.

Make no mistake, the global economy with all of its promise and perils is now the central fact of life for hard-working Americans. It has enriched the lives of millions of Americans. But for too many those same winds of change have worn away at the basis of their security. For two decades, most people have worked harder for less. Seemingly secure jobs have been lost. And while America once again is the most productive nation on Earth, this productivity itself holds the seeds of further insecurity. After all, productivity means the same people can produce more or, very often, that fewer people can produce more. This is the world we face.

We cannot stop global change. We cannot repeal the international economic competition that is everywhere. We can only harness the energy to our benefit. Now we must recognize that the only way for a wealthy nation to grow richer is to export, to simply find new customers for the products and services it makes. That, my fellow Americans, is the decision the Congress made when they voted to ratify NAFTA.

Glossary	
GATT:	General Agreement on Tariffs and Trade, an effort to regulate international commerce that led to the formation of the World Trade Organization in 1995
our three nations:	the United States, Canada, and Mexico
protectionism:	an effort to "protect" the industries in one's own nation by putting up trade barriers to discourage foreign competition
trade barriers:	efforts to discourage international trade, for instance by imposing high tariffs (taxes) on imports
trade zone:	an area, usually crossing national boundaries, in which trade restrictions and tariffs are reduced so as to encourage the exchange of goods and services

Clinton ran for President of the Student Council while attending the School of Foreign Service at Georgetown University.

Remarks on Signing the Personal Responsibility and Work Opportunity Reconciliation Act

1996

What we are trying to do today is to overcome the flaws of the welfare system for the people who are trapped on it. We all know that the typical family on welfare today is very different from the one that welfare was designed to deal with 60 years ago. We all know that there are a lot of good people on welfare who just get off of it in the ordinary course of business but that a significant number of people are trapped on welfare for a very long time, exiling them from the entire community of work that gives structure to our lives.

Nearly 30 years ago, Robert Kennedy said, "Work is the meaning of what this country is all about. We need it as individuals, we need to sense it in our fellow citizens, and we need it as a society and as a people." He was right then, and it's right now. From now on, our Nation's answer to this great social challenge will no longer be a never-ending cycle of welfare; it will be the dignity, the power, and the ethic of work. Today we are taking an historic chance to make welfare what it was meant to be: a second chance, not a way of life.

The bill I'm about to sign, as I have said many times, is far from perfect, but it has come a very long way. Congress sent me two previous bills that I strongly believe failed to protect our children and did too little to move people from welfare to work. I vetoed both of them. This bill had broad bipartisan support and is much, much better on both counts.

The new bill restores America's basic bargain of providing opportunity and demanding, in return, responsibility. It provides $14 billion for child care, $4 billion more than the present law does. It is good because without the assurance of child care it's all but impossible for a mother with young children to go to work. It requires States to maintain their own spending on welfare reform and gives them powerful performance incentives to place more people on welfare in jobs. It gives States the capacity to create jobs by taking money now used for welfare checks and giving it to employers as subsidies as incentives to hire people. This bill will help people to go to work so they can stop drawing a welfare check and start drawing a paycheck.

It's also better for children. It preserves the national safety net of food stamps and school lunches. It drops the deep cuts and the devastating changes in child protection, adoption, and help for disabled children. It preserves the national guarantee of health care for poor children, the disabled, the elderly, and people on welfare—the most important preservation of all.

It includes the tough child support enforcement measures that, as far as I know, every Member of Congress and everybody in the administration and every thinking person in the country has supported for more than 2 years now. It's the most sweeping crackdown on deadbeat parents in history. We have succeeded in increasing child support collection 40 percent, but over a third of the cases where there's delinquencies involve people who cross State lines. For a lot of women and children, the only reason they're on welfare today—the only reason—is that the father up and walked away when he could have made a contribution to the welfare of the children. That is wrong. If every parent paid the child support that he or she owes legally today, we could move 800,000 women and children off welfare immediately.

With this bill we say, if you don't pay the child support you owe we'll garnish your wages, take away your driver's license, track you across State lines, if necessary, make you work off what you pay—what you owe. It is a good thing, and it will help dramatically to reduce welfare, increase independence, and reinforce parental responsibility.

As the Vice President said, we strongly disagree with a couple of provisions of this bill. We believe that the nutritional cuts are too deep, especially as they affect low-income working people and children. We should not be punishing people who are working for a living already; we should do everything we can to lift them up and keep them at work and help them to support their children. We also believe that the congressional leadership insisted on cuts in programs for legal immigrants that are far too deep.

These cuts, however, have nothing to do with the fundamental purpose of welfare reform. I signed this bill because this is an historic chance, where Republicans and Democrats got together and said, we're going to take this historic chance to try to recreate the Nation's social bargain with the poor. We're going

Document Text

to try to change the parameters of the debate. We're going to make it all new again and see if we can't create a system of incentives which reinforce work and family and independence. We can change what is wrong. We should not have passed this historic opportunity to do what is right.

And so I want to ask all of you, without regard to party, to think through the implications of these other non-welfare issues on the American people, and let's work together in good spirits and good faith to remedy what is wrong. We can balance the budget without these cuts. But let's not obscure the fundamental purpose of the welfare provisions of this legislation, which are good and solid and which can give us at least the chance to end the terrible, almost physical isolation of huge numbers of poor people and their children from the rest of mainstream America. We have to do that.

Let me also say that there's something really good about this legislation: When I sign it, we all have to start again, and this becomes everybody's responsibility. After I sign my name to this bill, welfare will no longer be a political issue. The two parties cannot attack each other over it. Politicians cannot attack poor people over it. There are no encrusted habits, systems, and failures that can be laid at the foot of someone else. We have to begin again. This is not the end of welfare reform; this is the beginning. And we have to all assume responsibility. Now that we are saying with this bill we expect work, we have to make sure the people have a chance to go to work. If we really value work, everybody in this society—businesses, nonprofits, religious institutions, individuals, those in government—all have a responsibility to make sure the jobs are there....

Today we are ending welfare as we know it. But I hope this day will be remembered not for what it ended but for what it began: a new day that offers hope, honors responsibility, rewards work, and changes the terms of the debate so that no one in America ever feels again the need to criticize people who are poor on welfare but instead feels the responsibility to reach out to men and women and children who are isolated, who need opportunity, and who are willing to assume responsibility, and give them the opportunity and the terms of responsibility.

Glossary

garnish:	withhold part of a person's wages as a means of satisfying existing creditors
subsidies:	types of government economic assistance

Document Text

Remarks at Annual Prayer Breakfast

1998

First, I want to say to all of you that, as you might imagine, I have been on quite a journey these last few weeks to get to the end of this, to the rock bottom truth of where I am and where we all are. I agree with those who have said that in my first statement after I testified I was not contrite enough. I don't think there is a fancy way to say that I have sinned.

It is important to me that everybody who has been hurt know that the sorrow I feel is genuine: first and most important, my family, also my friends, my staff, my Cabinet, Monica Lewinsky and her family, and the American people. I have asked all for their forgiveness.

But I believe that to be forgiven, more than sorrow is required—at least two more things: First, genuine repentance—a determination to change and to repair breaches of my own making—I have repented; second, what my Bible calls a "broken spirit"; an understanding that I must have God's help to be the person that I want to be; a willingness to give the very forgiveness I seek; a renunciation of the pride and the anger which cloud judgment, lead people to excuse and compare and to blame and complain.

Now, what does all this mean for me and for us? First, I will instruct my lawyers to mount a vigorous defense, using all available appropriate arguments. But legal language must not obscure the fact that I have done wrong. Second, I will continue on the path of repentance, seeking pastoral support and that of other caring people so that they can hold me accountable for my own commitment.

Third, I will intensify my efforts to lead our country and the world toward peace and freedom, prosperity, and harmony, in the hope that with a broken spirit and a still strong heart I can be used for greater good, for we have many blessings and many challenges and so much work to do.

In this, I ask for your prayers and for your help in healing our Nation. And though I cannot move beyond or forget this—indeed, I must always keep it as a caution light in my life—it is very important that our Nation move forward.

I am very grateful for the many, many people, clergy and ordinary citizens alike, who have written me with wise counsel. I am profoundly grateful for the support of so many Americans who somehow through it all seem to still know that I care about them a great deal, that I care about their problems and their dreams. I am grateful for those who have stood by me and who say that in this case and many others, the bounds of privacy have been excessively and unwisely invaded. That may be. Nevertheless, in this case, it may be a blessing, because I still sinned. And if my repentance is genuine and sustained, and if I can maintain both a broken spirit and a strong heart, then good can come of this for our country as well as for me and my family.

The children of this country can learn in a profound way that integrity is important and selfishness is wrong, but God can change us and make us strong at the broken places. I want to embody those lessons for the children of this country, for that little boy in Florida who came up to me and said that he wanted to grow up and be President and to be just like me. I want the parents of all the children in America to be able to say that to their children.

Document Text

Farewell Address

2001

My fellow citizens, tonight is my last opportunity to speak to you from the Oval Office as your President. I am profoundly grateful to you for twice giving me the honor to serve, to work for you and with you to prepare our Nation for the 21st century....

This has been a time of dramatic transformation, and you have risen to every new challenge. You have made our social fabric stronger, our families healthier and safer, our people more prosperous. You, the American people, have made our passage into the global information age an era of great American renewal.

In all the work I have done as President—every decision I have made, every executive action I have taken, every bill I have proposed and signed—I've tried to give all Americans the tools and conditions to build the future of our dreams in a good society with a strong economy, a cleaner environment, and a freer, safer, more prosperous world.

I have steered my course by our enduring values: opportunity for all, responsibility from all, a community of all Americans. I have sought to give America a new kind of Government, smaller, more modern, more effective, full of ideas and policies appropriate to this new time, always putting people first, always focusing on the future.

Working together, America has done well. Our economy is breaking records with more than 22 million new jobs, the lowest unemployment in 30 years, the highest homeownership ever, the longest expansion in history. Our families and communities are stronger. Thirty-five million Americans have used the family leave law; 8 million have moved off welfare. Crime is at a 25-year low. Over 10 million Americans receive more college aid, and more people than ever are going to college. Our schools are better. Higher standards, greater accountability, and larger investments have brought higher test scores and higher graduation rates. More than 3 million children have health insurance now, and more than 7 million Americans have been lifted out of poverty. Incomes are rising across the board. Our air and water are cleaner. Our food and drinking water are safer. And more of our precious land has been preserved in the continental United States than at any time in 100 years.

America has been a force for peace and prosperity in every corner of the globe. I'm very grateful to be able to turn over the reins of leadership to a new President with America in such a strong position to meet the challenges of the future.

Tonight I want to leave you with three thoughts about our future. First, America must maintain our record of fiscal responsibility...

Second, because the world is more connected every day, in every way, America's security and prosperity require us to continue to lead in the world. At this remarkable moment in history, more people live in freedom than ever before. Our alliances are stronger than ever. People all around the world look to America to be a force for peace and prosperity, freedom and security.

The global economy is giving more of our own people and billions around the world the chance to work and live and raise their families with dignity. But the forces of integration that have created these good opportunities also make us more subject to global forces of destruction, to terrorism, organized crime and narcotrafficking, the spread of deadly weapons and disease, the degradation of the global environment.

The expansion of trade hasn't fully closed the gap between those of us who live on the cutting edge of the global economy and the billions around the world who live on the knife's edge of survival. This global gap requires more than compassion; it requires action. Global poverty is a powder keg that could be ignited by our indifference.

In his first Inaugural Address, Thomas Jefferson warned of entangling alliances. But in our times, America cannot and must not disentangle itself from the world. If we want the world to embody our shared values, then we must assume a shared responsibility....

Third, we must remember that America cannot lead in the world unless here at home we weave the threads of our coat of many colors into the fabric

Document Text

of one America. As we become ever more diverse, we must work harder to unite around our common values and our common humanity. We must work harder to overcome our differences, in our hearts and in our laws. We must treat all our people with fairness and dignity, regardless of their race, religion, gender, or sexual orientation, and regardless of when they arrived in our country—always moving toward the more perfect Union of our Founders' dreams.

Glossary

entangling alliances: agreements that unduly restrict one's freedom of action

narcotrafficking: production, sale, and transport of drugs

1861: Jefferson Davis by Mathew Brady.

Jefferson Davis: Original Analysis

U.S. Congressman and Senator and President of the Confederate States of America

1808–1889

Overview

To contemporary students of American history the name of Jefferson Davis is permanently linked with his role as president of the Confederate States of America. To Americans of the 1850s, however, Davis was a prominent member of the U.S. Senate and a significant figure in American politics. Known for his polished oratory, he was a hero of the Mexican-American War and served with distinction as secretary of war under President Franklin Pierce. Davis, as the leader of the southern cause and extoller of states' rights in the Congress, framed many of the political issues leading up to the Civil War. His leadership as Confederate president shaped the course of the Civil War, and his incarceration after the conflict laid the foundations for the image of the tragic but noble heroes of the South. Davis became the quintessential unreconstructed Confederate. His tenacious belief in the righteousness of the Confederate cause had a strong impact on the way in which the South dealt with defeat.

Davis was born on June 3, 1808, in Christian County (now Todd County) on a site that has since become a part of Fairview, Kentucky; he moved with his parents to southwestern Mississippi in 1810. In 1824 he entered the U.S. Military Academy at West Point, graduating in 1828 twenty-third in a class of thirty-three. After a brief and somewhat lackluster military career, Davis resigned from the army in 1835. In 1845 he was elected to the U.S. House of Representatives, his first political office.

In 1846 Davis resigned his seat in the House to lead a Mississippi unit in the Mexican-American War, during which he won recognition for heroism. Upon his return to civilian life, he was elected to the U.S. Senate and served until 1853, when he became secretary of war. In January 1856 Davis was again elected to the Senate, where he became the primary spokesperson in Congress for states' rights and the southern cause. A lifelong Democrat, Davis was a strong defender of slavery, its expansion into the territories, and the superiority of the white race, but he was also known as a benevolent master to the slaves on his plantation. By 1860 he was one of the largest slave owners in Mississippi; the 113 slaves who labored on his cotton plantation brought him not only financial wealth but also status as member of the plantation class. He served in the Senate until his resignation on January 21, 1861, twelve days after Mississippi seceded from the Union.

On the issue of secession, Davis hoped to save the Union if constitutionally possible. He did not see this belief as inconsistent with his support of states' rights and the compact theory of the Union: the theory that the nation was formed through a compact of states that retained their sovereign status and could constitutionally secede. Davis was not associated with the "Fire-eaters," the extreme pro-slavery politicians of the South. The vociferous voices of the Fire-eaters in support of the cause of the South in the late 1850s, and specifically during the crucial days leading to the election of 1860, did much to increase tensions between the sections and was a significant factor in the formation of the Confederate States of America. Fire-eaters saw the Republican victory of 1860 as evidence that the North would immediately attempt to abolish slavery, and they were instrumental in urging South Carolina to pass articles of secession in December 1860. As evidence of his moderate position, Davis believed that even with the election of Abraham Lincoln, the South could work out a solution to the conflicts over the issue of slavery, and he continued to seek an amicable solution up until the secession of his native Mississippi.

After he was officially notified that the Mississippi legislature had voted to secede from the Union, Davis resigned from the Senate. As a military hero and standard-bearer of the southern cause, Davis was a leading choice for president of the new Confederate States of America. He was a reluctant candidate for the office, however, and would have preferred a military post. As president of the Confederacy, he faced the daunting task of forming a central government from a group of states that had left the Union asserting their states' rights; at the same time he had to finance and fight a war against an enemy with superior industrial and military strength. In addition, Davis suffered from ill health during much of his presidency; many historians argue that this further limited his effectiveness as a chief executive. His critics portrayed him as an ideologue who lacked political skills and was prone to micromanaging the war. During and after the war, they placed much of the blame for the southern defeat on Davis.

After the surrender of General Robert E. Lee on April 9, 1865, Davis attempted to maintain his government while on the run, hoping to reestablish it west of the Mississippi. On May 10, 1865, he was arrested by federal troops. He was taken to Fortress Monroe, Virginia, and was ultimately charged with treason, a charge that the U.S. government never successfully prosecuted. In response, Davis sought a trial, holding that secession was not treason—a position that he would maintain for the rest of his life.

After the war Davis devoted most of his remaining years to asserting that states' rights, not slavery, had been the cause of the Civil War and to explaining why secession was constitutional. Plagued with financial problems, he ultimately retired to write his memoirs on the Gulf Coast as the guest of a wealthy Confederate widow in Mississippi. He never sought a pardon, maintaining that even in light of the suffering brought on by the war he would do the same things all over again. In 1881 he published his memoirs, *The Rise and Fall of the Confederate Government*, which was essentially a defense of arguments regarding secession and the validity of the Confederate cause. Davis died on December 6, 1889, in New Orleans.

Explanation and Analysis of Documents

To fully understand Davis and his importance during the critical period of the American Civil War, it is important to place him in the context of the time in which he lived and understand what led him and millions of other Americans to support the Confederate cause. For most of the 1850s Davis was the spokesperson for the southern cause in the Senate and a strong supporter of states' rights. The resolution he offered the Senate on February 20, 1860, represents a last-ditch effort on his part to unequivocally assert the southern cause, articulating positions from which the South would not retreat. These demands marked the death knell of Democratic unity, setting forth demands that were unacceptable to northern Democrats. Upon notification of the vote of the Mississippi legislature that the state formally seceded from the Union, Davis had to make a choice between his state and the Union. He also realized that any hope of an amicable solution was over. His resignation speech demonstrates why he chose to side with his state. Unlike other Civil War generals and politicians, who quickly published memoirs of the war, Davis waited until 1881 to speak. His preface to *The Rise and Fall of the Confederate States* reiterates many of the basic beliefs Davis held before the war. A common theme that flows through all three documents is that of states' rights, echoing the beliefs of millions of Americans who gave primary allegiance to their states and denied the supremacy of the federal government. The preface also demonstrates Davis's lifelong faith in the compact theory of the Union and his undying support for the Confederate cause, even after its military defeat by the North, and establishes him as the quintessential unreconstructed Confederate.

♦ Resolutions to the U.S. Senate on the Relations of States

Slavery and its expansion into the territories were at the center of political discourse in the United States for much of the 1850s. Tensions between the North and the South were enhanced by numerous factors, including the enforcement of a more stringent Fugitive Slave Law, enacted in 1850; the 1857 Supreme Court decision in the *Dred Scott* case, which held that Congress had no constitutional pow-

Time Line

1808	June 3	■ Jefferson Davis is born in Fairview, Kentucky.
1845	November 4	■ Davis is elected to the U.S. House of Representatives from Mississippi.
1847	August 10	■ Davis is elected to the U.S. Senate by the Mississippi legislature.
1853	March 7	■ Davis is sworn in as secretary of war in the administration of Franklin Pierce.
1856	January 16	■ Davis is reelected to the Senate.
1860	February 20	■ Davis offers his resolutions to the Senate on the relations of states.
1861	January 9	■ Mississippi secedes from the Union.
	January 21	■ Davis delivers his farewell address and resigns from the Senate.
	February 4	■ A provisional Confederate government is organized in Montgomery, Alabama.
	February 9	■ Davis is unanimously elected president of the Confederate States of America.
1864	April 9	■ General Robert E. Lee surrenders at Appomattox, ending the Civil War.
1865	May 10	■ Davis is arrested by U.S. Army troops.
1867–1869		■ Legal proceedings against Davis on charges of treason make their way through the courts.
1869	February 15	■ The treason case against Davis is dismissed by the U.S. government.
1881	June 3	■ *The Rise and Fall of the Confederate Government* is published.
1889	December 6	■ Davis dies in New Orleans, Louisiana.

er to exclude slavery in the territories; and the raid on Harpers Ferry by John Brown in October 1859.

The resolutions offered by Davis in the Senate in February 1860 were not an attempt to make law, nor did they suggest any legislative action. As the preeminent spokesperson of southern Democrats, Davis sought to firmly state the position of the South on key issues, most important of which was congressional protection of slavery in the territories, in anticipation of the upcoming presidential election. Davis's position contradicted that of the Illinois senator Stephen A. Douglas, the prospective presidential nominee of the northern wing of the Democratic Party, who supported popular sovereignty, or the right of residents of the territories to make their own decisions about slavery. Critics accused Davis of attempting to dictate the platform for the upcoming Democratic Party convention, but it could also be argued that Davis was seeking to prevent Douglas and his followers from precipitating conditions that would cause the South to secede.

The resolutions clearly demonstrate the division between northern and southern Democrats over slavery, including slavery in the territories; in many ways they sounded the death knell for Democratic Party unity in the 1860 election. Although they were subsequently debated and minor revisions made, the resolutions did not come to a vote in the Democratic caucus until after the Democratic National Convention in Charleston, South Carolina, held from April 23 to May 3, 1860. As front-runner, Douglas failed to receive the needed two-thirds majority, and the convention adjourned. On May 25 the resolutions were passed by a Democratic majority in the Senate. The convention reconvened in June in Baltimore, Maryland. With many delegates storming out in protest, Douglas ultimately received the nomination of the party. The southern wing of the Democratic Party met separately and nominated John C. Breckenridge, adopting many of the tenets of Davis's resolutions. This split in the Democratic Party virtually assured the election of the Republican candidate, Abraham Lincoln.

The first resolution asserts the validity of the compact theory of the union, arguing that by accepting statehood the several states did not abandon their sovereignty and that if the states found the actions of the federal government unacceptable, they could secede. It goes on to state that any interference by other states, the federal government, or individuals with "domestic institutions"—a euphemism for slavery—is a violation of the provisions of the Constitution and could result in the breakup of the Union. The second resolution states that Negro slavery is a vital institution in fifteen slaveholding states and that no matter what northerners thought about the institution, their opinions and feelings did not justify an attack on slavery. This was a direct attack on the abolitionist movement in the North.

At the heart of the document is the proposition set forth in the fourth resolution, which states that neither Congress nor a territorial legislature possesses the power under the Constitution to deprive a citizen of the right to take his property in slaves into federal territory. It proposes that if the judicial and executive branches of government fail to protect the property rights of slave owners, which southerners saw as guaranteed by the Constitution, it was incumbent on the Congress to pass appropriate legislation to do so. Finally, the resolution declares that the so-called personal liberty laws passed by a number of northern states that attempted to subvert the enforcement of the Fugitive Slave Law of 1850 violated the Constitution and were abhorrent to the South.

An understanding of the resolutions is important to an appreciation of the political climate that led up to the election of 1860. The resolutions show Davis's political influence outside the Senate and his involvement in party politics and demonstrate not only his importance as a spokesperson for the South but also the uncompromising position of the South regarding the maintenance of the institution of slavery, which was so vital to its economic and social existence.

♦ Farewell Address to the U.S. Senate

The sectional conflicts that faced the nation for much of the 1850s culminated in the election of Abraham Lincoln as president on November 6, 1860. The clouds of dissent that gathered over the North and the South as a result of slavery, its expansion, and states' rights cast a long shadow that portended secession and civil war. On December 20, 1860, South Carolina formally seceded from the Union. Although Davis, a moderate on the issue of secession, hoped to test it in the courts or through some constitutional means, on January 5, 1861, he joined senators from other slaveholding states in a resolution stating that as soon as possible their states should set up the necessary convention to organize a confederacy of the seceding states. On January 9, 1861, the Mississippi legislature voted to secede from the Union. Davis received notice of the act of secession while he was on his sickbed suffering from dyspepsia and neuralgia. His condition was so serious that doctors thought that he would be unable to speak.

On his final walk to the Senate, Davis knew that he was entering for the last time the chamber that he loved and had worked in for more than a decade. With the effects of his illness clearly visible to the crowded Senate gallery, Davis bid farewell to the U.S. Senate. The act of the Mississippi legislature had forced him to make a choice between loyalty to his state and loyalty to the Union. To Davis the choice was plain. Holding back tears, Davis made it clear that he was not hostile or bitter. In choosing his state, he recognized that his desire to preserve the Union was no longer viable, that reconciliation between North and South was impossible.

In the third paragraph of the speech he draws the distinction between nullification and secession, pointing out that the two are incompatible. By invoking the doctrine of nullification, a state declares null and void particular laws passed by the federal government but stays within the Union. But, Davis argues, when the national government violates the constitutional rights of the citizens of the individual states, specifically their constitutional right to

maintain their property rights in their slaves and carry that property into the territories, it becomes impossible for the states to remain within the Union, and secession is the only recourse.

With carefully chosen words, Davis states that his functions in the Senate are terminated. He closes by offering an apology for any wrongs that he may have done and bids a final adieu. At the close of his speech Davis sat down to thunderous applause from both northerners and southerners and to the tears of many in the audience.

♦ Preface to *The Rise and Fall of the Confederate Government*

At the end of the Civil War, Davis was one of the most hated men in the United States. He was seen in the North as the instigator of the war that had cost more than 620,000 lives and in the South as the man who bore the blame for southern defeat. But as he languished in a federal prison for 720 days and the legal proceedings charging him with treason dragged on, the image of Davis changed, and sympathy for him began to increase. In 1866, while Davis was still a prisoner, one of the physicians who attended him during his incarceration, Dr. John J. Craven, published *The Prison Life of Jefferson Davis*. The work describes the deplorable conditions in which Davis lived and the poor state of his health. Although Craven was listed as the author, the work was really written by Charles G. Halpine, a popular writer and Democratic operative who sought to gain sympathy for Davis and the southern cause by demonstrating the cruel treatment David received at the hand of his Republican-backed military captors. The work did much to make Davis a tragic hero and influenced public opinion regarding leniency toward Davis and other former Confederates. Although Davis had been severely criticized during the war, incarceration helped to endear him to the South and create an image of him as the martyr of the Confederacy.

Ironically, Davis detested *The Prison Life of Jefferson Davis* not only because of its many inconsistencies and errors but also for the image it created of him. He did not see himself as a tragic hero and did not accept defeat. Davis believed that he had acted legally and constitutionally in 1861, and if he had been right in 1861 in his position that secession was not treason, the same was true after the war. He saw himself as a patriot who stood up for the cause of the South and fought a war of self-defense to protect the sovereign rights of the State of Mississippi, not to protect slavery.

Believing both in the righteousness of his cause and that Davis had been maligned by Craven's book, Varina Davis urged her husband to write an account of his life and the war immediately after his release from prison. For unknown reasons Davis declined. In the 1870s many Confederate generals and politicians did write their memoirs, determined to tell the Confederate side of the story and prevent the history of the war from being written by the North, but Davis continued to remain silent. By December 1873 rumors circulated that Davis was, in fact, working on his memoirs, but it was not until 1876 that he actually entered into an agreement with a publishing company to commence work on the project. Coincidentally, this is the same year that many historians use to mark the end of Reconstruction in the South. Davis would spend the next four years on the work.

Davis admits in the preface that the work was written under difficult circumstances. Amid the massive destruction of the South, he had lost most of his books and papers, so it was hard to retell the story in detail. What Davis ultimately published in 1881 was, as he acknowledges, meant to present the southern side of the war. Rather than producing a personal history of the Confederacy, Davis devoted much of the two-volume work to the legal arguments regarding the validity of the Confederate cause. While there are some accounts of military actions, the emphasis of the work, as Davis points out in the first sentence of the preface, is a defense of his position more than a history of the conflict. Section 2 of the work, "The Constitution," is arguably the best available exposition of the compact theory of the Constitution. However, Davis's work is not an easy book to read, a fact that was reflected in its slow sales and lack of popular appeal. It is essentially the brief that Davis would have presented had he been given the opportunity to stand trial on charges of treason. His purpose was to vindicate his position and to prove himself right and the North wrong.

The Rise and Fall of the Confederate Government remains a monument to Davis's tenacity and determination to vindicate the cause of the South. He rejects the terms *rebellion* and *treason* in reference to the Confederate cause. He argues that the war was not fought to protect slavery but rather to protect states' rights. The book, which covers more than twelve hundred pages, was not a financial success, and the national press took little notice of it. Although it is read in its entirety by only the most serious scholars, the essential arguments made by Davis and the tenor of the work can be gleaned from the preface.

Impact and Legacy

There is little debate that the Civil War was the pivotal event of American history. While its causes were many, Davis did much to structure the political discourse and events leading up to the conflict, to influence its course, and to shape its place in American history. In February 1860, as the sectional conflicts between the North and the South heightened, Davis made the demands of his region clear. In his resolutions to the Senate, he told the national Democratic Party the minimum that southern Democrats would accept in a party platform for a presidential candidate in 1860. Davis resigned from the Senate in January 1861 because he had to stand up for the principles in which he believed. Although the North and the South would soon be engaged in a military conflict, throughout his farewell speech Davis maintained a level of nobility that in many ways laid the foundation for the later claims made by the

creators of the myth of the Lost Cause, who portrayed the cause of the South as noble and the Confederate leaders as exemplars of old-fashioned chivalry.

The antebellum writings and speeches of Davis provide insight into the southern perspective at the time the Civil War and promote a better understanding of the nature of the sectional conflicts that led to the Civil War. Davis's memoirs demonstrate the tenacity of both the southern cause and the man who maintained an undying devotion to the Confederacy and suggests the manner in which southerners sought to shape the history of the Civil War.

The legacy of Jefferson Davis lives on. A review of any map of the southern states will demonstrate a significant number of highways and monuments dedicated to his memory. Although Davis was adamant throughout his life that he did not want a pardon, in 1978 a bill restoring his citizenship was introduced by Senator Trent Lott of Mississippi. With little opposition, the bill was passed and then signed by President Jimmy Carter. In 1998 the State of Mississippi dedicated the Jefferson Davis Presidential Library and Museum. Mississippi allocated more than $10 million for the project and, with the help of additional private funds, built a repository housing many of Davis's papers and records as well as other artifacts and historical materials of the Confederate States of America.

Key Sources

The Papers of Jefferson Davis is a documentary editing project based at Rice University in Houston, Texas, that has more than one hundred thousand Davis documents. Originally initiated by the noted Civil War historians Frank E. Vandiver and Allan Nevins, the collection is supported by the National Historical Publications and Records Commission of the State of Mississippi and the Davis family. The Web site (http://jeffersondavis.rice.edu/) provides a complete chronology of Davis's life and an extensive bibliography. In addition, it features a significant number of important Davis documents online. There are also papers available at the Museum of the Confederacy, in Richmond, Virginia; the National Archives in Washington, D.C.; the Mississippi Department of Archives and History; and the Louisiana Historical Association Collection of Jefferson Davis Papers at Tulane University. Davis's biographer William J. Cooper, Jr., edited a collection of Davis papers entitled *Jefferson Davis: The Essential Writings* (2003). The most complete collection of Davis papers, *Jefferson Davis, Constitutionalist: His Letters, Papers, and Speeches* (10 vols., 1923) were edited by Dunbar Rowland. Davis's book *The Rise and Fall of the Confederate Government* is available in a modern edition put out by Da Capo Press (1990).

Essential Quotes

"Any intermeddling by any one or more States, or by a combination of their citizens, with the domestic institutions of the others, on any pretext, whether political, moral, or religious, with the view to their disturbance or subversion, is in violation of the Constitution."

(Resolutions to the U.S. Senate on the Relations of States)

"Negro slavery, as it exists in fifteen States of this Union, composes an important portion of their domestic institutions."

(Resolutions to the U.S. Senate on the Relations of States)

"I am sure I feel no hostility toward you, Senators from the North.... I wish you well.... I carry with me no hostile remembrance."

(Farewell Address to the U.S. Senate)

Essential Quotes

"The object of this work has been from historical data to show that the Southern States had rightfully the power to withdraw from a Union into which they had, as sovereign communities, voluntarily entered."

(Preface to *The Rise and Fall of the Confederate Government*)

"To those who knew that the Union was formed for specific enumerated purposes, and that the States had never surrendered their sovereignty it was a palpable absurdity to apply to them, or to their citizens when obeying their mandates, the terms 'rebellion' and 'treason.'"

(Preface to *The Rise and Fall of the Confederate Government*)

Further Reading

♦ Articles

Nichols, Roy F. "United States vs. Jefferson Davis, 1865–1869." *American Historical Review* 31(January 1926): 266–284.

♦ Books

Cashin, Joan E. *First Lady of the Confederacy: Varina Davis's Civil War*. Cambridge, Mass.: Belknap Press of Harvard University Press, 2006.

Cooper, William J., Jr. *Jefferson Davis, American*. New York: Knopf, 2000.

———. *Jefferson Davis and the Civil War Era*. Baton Rouge: Louisiana State University Press, 2009.

Davis, Varina. *Jefferson Davis: Ex-President of the Confederate States of America—A Memoir by His Wife*. 1890. Reprinted with an introduction by Craig L. Symonds. Baltimore: Nautical and Aviation Publishing Company of America, 1990.

Davis, William C. *Jefferson Davis: The Man and His Hour*. New York: HarperCollins Publishers, 1991.

Hattaway, Herman, and Richard E. Beringer. *Jefferson Davis: Confederate President*. Lawrence: University Press of Kansas, 2002.

—*C. Ellen Connally*

Questions for Further Study

1. The Confederacy, of which Davis was not only president but an enduring symbol, was based on a paradox in that it attempted to create a united central government for a group of states who had left the Union precisely because they demanded the right to operate as separate sovereignties. This paradox would undermine his effectiveness as a leader, yet Davis himself embraced it in his "resolutions on the relations of states." For example, he rejected the principle of popular sovereignty, or the right of citizens in the western territories to decide for themselves whether they would allow slavery within their borders, yet claimed that the people of the slaveholding states had a right to choose their own course. Discuss the contradictions in this and other positions expressed by Davis in the 1860 resolutions. Do you think he was aware of the conflict in his viewpoints? If so, how did he attempt to resolve the apparent contradictions?

2. In his farewell address to the U.S. Senate, Davis distanced himself from the principle of nullification—the idea that states had the right to simply refuse to enforce or abide by federal law. Yet he firmly embraced the right of secession, which itself provided the occasion for his speech: since his state of Mississippi was leaving the Union, he was too—departing the Senate for a new role in the Confederacy. How well does he establish a distinction between nullification and secession? Is such a distinction justified?

3. Quoting Thomas Jefferson, Davis in his farewell address to the Senate noted that "no man was born … booted and spurred to ride over the rest of mankind." Yet he went on to defend not only the practice of slavery but also the idea that blacks are inferior to whites. While this viewpoint is offensive to modern people, it was common among white people of Davis's time, not only in the South. On what basis did he justify his support for liberty and equality on the one hand and slavery and racism on the other?

Document Text

Resolutions to the U.S. Senate on the Relations of States

1860

1. *Resolved,* That in the adoption of the Federal Constitution, the States adopting the same acted severally as free and independent sovereignties, delegating a portion of their powers to be exercised by the Federal Government for the increased security of each, against dangers *domestic* as well as foreign; and that any intermeddling by any one or more States, or by a combination of their citizens, with the domestic institutions of the others, on any pretext, whether political, moral, or religious, with the view to their disturbance or subversion, is in violation of the Constitution, insulting to the States so interfered with, endangers their domestic peace and tranquility—objects for which the Constitution was formed—and, by necessary consequence, serves to weaken and destroy the Union itself.

2. *Resolved,* That negro slavery, as it exists in fifteen States of this Union, composes an important portion of their domestic institutions, inherited from their ancestors, and existing at the adoption of the Constitution, by which it is recognized as constituting an important element of the apportionment of powers among the States; and that no change of opinion or feeling on the part of the non-slaveholding States of the Union in relation to this institution can justify them or their citizens in open and systematic attacks thereon, with a view to its overthrow; and that all such attacks are in manifest violation of the mutual and solemn pledges to protect and defend each other, given by the States, respectively, on entering into the constitutional compact which formed the Union, and are a manifest breach of faith and a violation of the most solemn obligations.

3. *Resolved,* That the union of these States rests on the equality of rights and privileges among its members, and that it is especially the duty of the Senate, which represents the States in their sovereign capacity, to resist all attempts to discriminate either in relation to person or property, so as, in the Territories—which are the common possession of the United States—to give advantages to the citizens of one State which are not equally secured to those of every other State.

4. *Resolved,* That neither Congress, nor a Territorial Legislature, whether by direct legislation or legislation of an indirect and unfriendly nature, possess the power to annul or impair the constitutional right of any citizen of the United States to take his slaver property into the common Territories; but it is the duty of the Federal Government there to afford for that, as for other species of property, the needful protection; and if experience should at any time prove that the judiciary does not possess power to insure adequate protection, it will then become the duty of Congress to supply such deficiency.

5. *Resolved,* That the inhabitants of an organized Territory of the United States, when they rightfully form a constitution to be admitted as a State into the Union, may then, for the first time, like the people of a State when forming a new constitution, decide for themselves whether slavery, as a domestic institution, shall be maintained or prohibited within their jurisdiction; and if Congress shall admit them as a State, "they shall be received into the Union with or without slavery, as their constitution may prescribe at the time of their admission."

6. *Resolved,* That the provision of the Constitution for the rendition of fugitives from service or labor, "without the adoption of which the Union could not have been formed," and the laws of 1793 and 1850, which were enacted to secure its execution, and the main features of which, being similar, bear the impress of nearly seventy years of sanction by the highest judicial authority, have unquestionable claim to the respect and observance of all who enjoy the benefits of our compact of Union; and that the acts of State Legislatures to defeat the purpose, or nullify the requirements of that provision, and the laws made in pursuance of it, are hostile in character, subversive of the Constitution, revolutionary in their effect, and if persisted in, must sooner or later lead the States injured by such breach of the compact to exercise their judgment as to the proper mode and measure of redress.

Mr. DAVIS. Mr. President [Vice President John C. Breckinridge], I have presented these resolutions not for the purpose of discussing them, but with a view to get a vote upon them severally, hoping thus, by an expression of the deliberate opinion of the Senate, that we may reach some conclusion as to what is the present condition of opinion in relation to the principles there expressed. The expression even of

Document Text

the resolutions is, to a great extent, not new. The first and second are substantially those on which the Senate voted in 1837–38, affirming them then by a very large majority. I trust opinion to-day may be as sound as it was then. There is also an assertion of an historical fact, which is drawn from the opinion of Judge Story, in the decision of the ruling case of Prigg *vs.* the Commonwealth of Pennsylvania. It was my purpose to rest the propositions contained in these resolutions upon the highest authority of the land, judicial as well as other; and if it be possible to obtain a vote on them without debate, it will be most agreeable to me. To have them affirmed by the Senate without contradiction, would be an era in the recent history of our country which would be hailed with joy by every one who sincerely loves it. I ask that the resolutions may be printed, and be made a special order, for the purpose which I have indicated, for such day as the Senate may choose to name. I have no choice as to time, having no wish to discuss the resolutions, unless it shall be necessary by remarks which shall be made by others. I therefore would like any one to suggest a time when it will be probably agreeable to the Senate to take them up for consideration. Next Wednesday is suggested. I ask, then, that the resolutions may be printed for the use of the Senate, and made the special order for Wednesday next, at half past one o'clock.

Glossary

John C. Breckenridge: vice president to James Buchanan, southern Democratic candidate for the presidency (1860), general and later secretary of war under the Confederacy

rendition of fugitives from service or labor: the turning over of escaped slaves to their captors or masters

severally: individually

sovereignties: self-ruling governments

take his slaver property into the common Territories: move his slaves into the territories of the West, which had not yet become states

Farewell Address to the U.S. Senate

1861

I rise, Mr. President [John C. Breckinridge], for the purpose of announcing to the Senate that I have satisfactory evidence that the State of Mississippi, by a solemn ordinance of her people in convention assembled, has declared her separation from the United States. Under these circumstances, of course my functions are terminated here. It has seemed to me proper, however, that I should appear in the Senate to announce that fact to my associates, and I will say but very little more. The occasion does not invite me to go into argument; and my physical condition would not permit me to do so if it were otherwise; and yet it seems to become me to say something on the part of the State I here represent, on an occasion so solemn as this.

It is known to Senators who have served with me here, that I have for many years advocated, as an essential attribute of State sovereignty, the right of a State to secede from the Union. Therefore, if I had not believed there was justifiable cause; if I had thought that Mississippi was acting without sufficient provocation, or without an existing necessity, I should still, under my theory of the Government, because of my allegiance to the State of which I am a citizen, have been bound by her action. I, however, may be permitted to say that I do think she has justifiable cause, and I approve of her act. I conferred with her people before that act was taken, counseled them then that if the state of things which they apprehended should exist when the convention met, they should take the action which they have now adopted.

I hope none who hear me will confound this expression of mine with the advocacy of the right of a State to remain in the Union, and to disregard its constitutional obligations by the nullification of the law. Such is not my theory. Nullification and secession, so often confounded, are indeed antagonistic principles. Nullification is a remedy which it is sought to apply within the Union, and against the agent of the States. It is only to be justified when the agent has violated his constitutional obligation, and a State, assuming to judge for itself, denies the right of the agent thus to act, and appeals to the other States of the Union for a decision; but when the States themselves, and when the people of the States, have so acted as to convince us that they will not regard our constitutional rights, then, and then for the first time, arises the doctrine of secession in its practical application.

A great man who now reposes with his fathers, and who has been often arraigned for a want of fealty to the Union, advocated the doctrine of nullification, because it preserved the Union. It was because of his deep-seated attachment to the Union, his determination to find some remedy for existing ills short of a severance of the ties which bound South Carolina to the other States, that Mr. [John C.] Calhoun advocated the doctrine of nullification, which he proclaimed to be peaceful, to be within the limits of State power, not to disturb the Union, but only to be a means of bringing the agent before the tribunal of the States for their judgment.

Secession belongs to a different class of remedies. It is to be justified upon the basis that the States are sovereign. There was a time when none denied it. I hope the time may come again, when a better comprehension of the theory of our Government, and the inalienable rights of the people of the States, will prevent any one from denying that each State is a sovereign, and thus may reclaim the grants which it has made to any agent whomsoever.

I therefore say I concur in the action of the people of Mississippi, believing it to be necessary and proper, and should have been bound by their action if my belief had been otherwise; and this brings me to the important point which I wish on this last occasion to present to the Senate. It is by this confounding of nullification and secession that the name of a great man, whose ashes now mingle with his mother earth, has been invoked to justify coercion against a seceded State. The phrase "to execute the laws," was an expression which General Jackson applied to the case of a State refusing to obey the laws while yet a member of the Union. That is not the case which is now presented. The laws are to be executed over the United States, and upon the people of the United States. They have no relation to any foreign country. It is a perversion of terms, at least it is a great misapprehension of the case, which cites that expression for application to a State which has withdrawn from

the Union. You may make war on a foreign State. If it be the purpose of gentlemen, they may make war against a State which has withdrawn from the Union; but there are no laws of the United States to be executed within the limits of a seceded State. A State finding herself in the condition in which Mississippi has judged she is, in which her safety requires that she should provide for the maintenance of her rights out of the Union, surrenders all the benefits, (and they are known to be many,) deprives herself of the advantages, (they are known to be great,) severs all the ties of affection, (and they are close and enduring,) which have bound her to the Union; and thus divesting herself of every benefit, taking upon herself every burden, she claims to be exempt from any power to execute the laws of the United States within her limits.

I well remember an occasion when Massachusetts was arraigned before the bar of the Senate, and when then the doctrine of coercion was rife and to be applied against her because of the rescue of a fugitive slave in Boston. My opinion then was the same that it is now. Not in a spirit of egotism, but to show that I am not influenced in my opinion because the case is my own, I refer to that time and that occasion as containing the opinion which I then entertained, and on which my present conduct is based. I then said, if Massachusetts, following her through a stated line of conduct, chooses to take the last step which separates her from the Union, it is her right to go, and I will neither vote one dollar nor one man to coerce her back; but will say to her, God speed, in memory of the kind associations which once existed between her and the other States.

It has been a conviction of pressing necessity, it has been a belief that we are to be deprived in the Union of the rights which our fathers bequeathed to us, which has brought Mississippi into her present decision. She has heard proclaimed the theory that all men are created free and equal, and this made the basis of an attack upon her social institutions; and the sacred Declaration of Independence has been invoked to maintain the position of the equality of the races. That Declaration of Independence is to be construed by the circumstances and purposes for which it was made. The communities were declaring their independence; the people of those communities were asserting that no man was born—to use the language of Mr. Jefferson—booted and spurred to ride over the rest of mankind; that men were created equal—meaning the men of the political community; that there was no divine right to rule; that no man inherited the right to govern; that there were no classes by which power and place descended to families, but that all stations were equally within the grasp of each member of the body-politic. These were the great principles they announced; these were the purposes for which they made their declaration; these were the ends to which their enunciation was directed. They have no reference to the slave; else, how happened it that among the items of arraignment made against George III was that he endeavored to do just what the North has been endeavoring of late to do—to stir up insurrection among our slaves? Had the Declaration announced that the negroes were free and equal, how was the Prince to be arraigned for stirring up insurrection among them? And how was this to be enumerated among the high crimes which caused the colonies to sever their connection with the mother country? When our Constitution was formed, the same idea was rendered more palpable, for there we find provision made for that very class of persons as property; they were not put upon the footing of equality with white men—not even upon that of paupers and convicts; but, so far as representation was concerned, were discriminated against as a lower caste, only to be represented in the numerical proportion of three fifths.

Then, Senators, we recur to the compact which binds us together; we recur to the principles upon which our Government was founded; and when you deny them, and when you deny to us the right to withdraw from a Government which thus perverted threatens to be destructive of our rights, we but tread in the path of our fathers when we proclaim our independence, and take the hazard. This is done not in hostility to others, not to injure any section of the country, not even for our own pecuniary benefit; but from the high and solemn motive of defending and protecting the rights we inherited, and which it is our sacred duty to transmit unshorn to our children.

I find in myself, perhaps, a type of the general feeling of my constituents towards yours. I am sure I feel no hostility to you, Senators from the North. I am sure there is not one of you, whatever sharp discussion there may have been between us, to whom I cannot now say, in the presence of my God, I wish you well; and such, I am sure, is the feeling of the people whom I represent towards those whom you represent. I therefore feel that I but express their desire when I say I hope, and they hope, for peaceful relations with you, though we must part. They may

Document Text

be mutually beneficial to us in the future, as they have been in the past, if you so will it. The reverse may bring disaster on every portion of the country; and if you will have it thus, we will invoke the God of our fathers, who delivered them from the power of the lion, to protect us from the ravages of the bear; and thus, putting our trust in God and in our own firm hearts and strong arms, we will vindicate the right as best we may.

In the course of my service here, associated at different times with a great variety of Senators, I see now around me some with whom I have served long; there have been points of collision; but whatever of offense there has been to me, I leave here; I carry with me no hostile remembrance. Whatever offense I have given which has not been redressed, or for which satisfaction has not been demanded, I have, Senators, in this hour of our parting, to offer you my apology for any pain which, in heat of discussion, I have inflicted. I go hence unencumbered of the remembrance of any injury received, and having discharged the duty of making the only reparation in my power for any injury offered.

Mr. President, and Senators, having made the announcement which the occasion seemed to me to require, it only remains to me to bid you a final adieu.

Glossary

adieu: French for "farewell"

arraignment: formal or legal accusation

a great man who now reposes with his fathers: a reference to John C. Calhoun, vice president and senator, who had died in 1860

John C. Breckenridge: vice president to James Buchanan, southern Democratic candidate for the presidency (1860), general and later secretary of war under the Confederacy

lion… bear: a reference to the British and the U.S. government, respectively

nullification: refusal by a U.S. state to enforce the laws of the federal government

ordinance of her people in convention assembled: a formal and legal statement by the people of Mississippi, speaking through their elected representatives

unshorn: without being reduced

a want of fealty: a lack of loyalty

Document Text

PREFACE TO *THE RISE AND FALL OF THE CONFEDERATE GOVERNMENT*

1881

The object of this work has been from historical data to show that the Southern States had rightfully the power to withdraw from a Union into which they had, as sovereign communities, voluntarily entered; that the denial of that right was a violation of the letter and spirit of the compact between the States; and that the war waged by the Federal Government against the seceding States was in disregard of the limitations of the Constitution, and destructive of the principles of the Declaration of Independence.

The author, from his official position, may claim to have known much of the motives and acts of his countrymen immediately before and during the war of 1861–65, and he has sought to furnish material for the future historian, who, when the passions and prejudices of the day shall have given place to reason and sober thought, may, better than a contemporary, investigate the causes, conduct, and results of the war.

The incentive to undertake the work now offered to the public was the desire to correct misapprehensions created by industriously circulated misrepresentations as to the acts and purposes of the people and the General Government of the Confederate States. By the reiteration of such unappropriate terms as "rebellion" and "treason," and the asseveration that the South was levying war against the United States, those ignorant of the nature of the Union, and of the reserved powers of the States, have been led to believe that the Confederate States were in the condition of revolted provinces, and that the United States were forced to resort to arms for the preservation of their existence. To those who knew that the Union was formed for specific enumerated purposes, and that the States had never surrendered their sovereignty it was a palpable absurdity to apply to them, or to their citizens when obeying their mandates, the terms "rebellion" and "treason"; and, further, it is shown in the following pages that the Confederate States, so far from making war or seeking to destroy the United States, as soon as they had an official organ, strove earnestly, by peaceful recognition, to equitably adjust all questions growing out of the separation from their late associates.

Another great perversion of truth has been the arraignment of the men who participated in the formation of the Confederacy and who bore arms in its defense, as the instigators of a controversy leading to disunion. Sectional issues appear conspicuously in the debates of the Convention which framed the Federal Constitution, and its many compromises were designed to secure an equilibrium between the sections, and to preserve the interests as well as the liberties of the several States. African servitude at that time was not confined to a section, but was numerically greater in the South than in the North, with a tendency to its continuance in the former and cessation in the latter. It therefore thus early presents itself as a disturbing element, and the provisions of the Constitution, which were known to be necessary for its adoption, bound all the States to recognize and protect that species of property. When at a subsequent period there arose in the Northern States an antislavery agitation, it was a harmless and scarcely noticed movement until political demagogues seized upon it as a means to acquire power. Had it been left to pseudo-philanthropists and fanatics, most zealous where least informed, it never could have shaken the foundations of the Union and have incited one section to carry fire and sword into the other. That the agitation was political in its character, and was clearly developed as early as 1803, it is believed has been established in these pages. To preserve a sectional equilibrium and to maintain the equality of the States was the effort on one side, to acquire empire was the manifest purpose on the other. This struggle began before the men of the Confederacy were born; how it arose and how it progressed it has been attempted briefly to show. Its last stage was on the question of territorial governments; and, if in this work it has not been demonstrated that the position of the South was justified by the Constitution and the equal rights of the people of all the States, it must be because the author has failed to present the subject with a sufficient degree of force and clearness.

In describing the events of the war, space has not permitted, and the loss of both books and papers has prevented, the notice of very many entitled to consideration, as well for the humanity as the gallantry of our men in the unequal combats they fought. These numerous omissions, it is satisfactory to know, the official reports made at the time and the subsequent

Document Text

contributions which have been and are being published by the actors, will supply more fully and graphically than could have been done in this work.

Usurpations of the Federal Government have been presented, not in a spirit of hostility, but as a warning to the people against the dangers by which their liberties are beset. When the war ceased, the pretext on which it had been waged could no longer be alleged. The emancipation proclamation of Mr. Lincoln, which, when it was issued, he humorously admitted to be a nullity, had acquired validity by the action of the highest authority known to our institutions—the people assembled in their several State Conventions. The soldiers of the Confederacy had laid down their arms, had in good faith pledged themselves to abstain from further hostile operations, and had peacefully dispersed to their homes; there could not, then, have been further dread of them by the Government of the United States. The plea of necessity could, therefore, no longer exist for hostile demonstration against the people and States of the deceased Confederacy. Did vengeance, which stops at the grave, subside? Did real peace and the restoration of the States to their former rights and positions follow, as was promised on the restoration of the Union? Let the recital of the invasion of the reserved powers of the States, or the people, and the perversion of the republican form of government guaranteed to each State by the Constitution, answer the question. For the deplorable fact of the war, for the cruel manner in which it was waged, for the sad physical and yet sadder moral results it produced, the reader of these pages, I hope, will admit that the South, in the forum of conscience, stands fully acquitted.

Much of the past is irremediable; the best hope for a restoration in the future to the pristine purity and fraternity of the Union, rests on the opinions and character of the men who are to succeed this generation: that they may be suited to that blessed work, one, whose public course is ended, invokes them to draw their creed from the fountains of our political history, rather than from the lower stream, polluted as it has been by self-seeking place-hunters and by sectional strife.

THE AUTHOR.

Glossary

arraignment:	formal or legal accusation
asseveration:	declaration
the author:	Davis himself
nullity:	an act that has no legal force or validity
pseudo-philanthropists:	persons who falsely claim to be helping others
sovereignty:	self-rule

Wedding photograph of Jefferson Davis and Varina Howell, 1845

Eugene V. Debs photo portrait.

Eugene V. Debs: Original Analysis

Labor Activist and U.S. Presidential Candidate

1855–1926

Overview

Eugene Victor Debs was a trade union leader, orator, and frequent Socialist Party candidate for the presidency of the United States. He was born in Terre Haute, Indiana, in 1855. While working his way up through the hierarchy of the Brotherhood of Locomotive Firemen, an important railroad union, he was elected city clerk in Terre Haute in 1879. He also served one term in the Indiana state legislature in 1885. In 1893 Debs cofounded the American Railway Union (ARU), an industrial union that, unlike most exclusive railroad brotherhoods of the era, admitted railroad workers of all skill levels. As the leader of that organization, Debs led the infamous Pullman strike of 1894.

The Pullman strike was an effort to organize workers at the Pullman Palace Car Company of Pullman, Illinois. As part of the strike, ARU members nationwide decided to boycott all trains that carried the company's famous sleeping cars in an effort to force them to recognize the union. As a result, rail traffic stopped nationwide. In response, railroad companies deliberately placed mail cars on trains with Pullman Palace Cars in order to encourage government intervention in the dispute. The legal injunction issued by a federal judge in response to the boycott essentially shut down the strike and destroyed the union. In 1895 Debs was convicted of interfering with the mail as a result of his refusal to abide by that injunction. Debs's political views were greatly affected by the Socialist literature he read during his short stay in jail. Indeed, this incarceration would prove to be the pivotal point of his entire life.

Upon his release Debs announced his conversion to Socialism. He also changed career paths from being a trade union leader to being a political leader. Debs would serve as a Socialist Party presidential candidate five times: 1900, 1904, 1908, 1912, and 1920. His best showing occurred in 1912 when he came close to garnering a million votes. That was 6 percent of the total votes cast in that election. In 1918 Debs was convicted of sedition for a speech he had given in Canton, Ohio, earlier that year. Debs had to run his final campaign for president as a protest candidate from his jail cell. A famous campaign button from 1920 read "For President—Convict No. 9653." Between elections Debs toured the country giving speeches and writing articles that critiqued the American capitalist system and championed the cause of Socialism. Debs died in 1926 at the age of seventy.

Debs represented a vision of Socialism in America that got lost in the anti-Communist hysteria of the cold war era. His political beliefs, though Socialist, were grounded in American ideals like justice, equal rights, and Christianity. Debs's willingness to go to prison for the causes he championed greatly increased his appeal and the popularity of his ideas. While many other figures in American Socialism were immigrants from European countries like Germany, where Socialism was more in the mainstream, Debs attracted native-born Americans to the Socialist cause. His success as a politician came as the result of hundreds of thousands of Americans entertaining the possibility of radical change in American life in an era when the adverse effects of industrialization had made them unhappy with the existing political system.

Explanation and Analysis of Documents

Eugene Debs was a master at making what might look today like radical political ideas seem as American as apple pie. A student of history as well as politics, Debs regularly invoked the memory of the Founding Fathers to make his policy suggestions seem more acceptable. Motivated by an unyielding sense of justice, he often tried to shame authorities to do what he thought was right. Whether addressing audiences at a labor rally or on the campaign trail, Debs invariably came back to a sharp critique of the American political system, touting the virtues of his brand of Socialism. His goal as a politician was not necessarily to win elections but instead to inspire listeners by his own example and to win converts to the Socialist cause. In a country with no Socialist legacy—unlike many European countries where Socialism was established—it is really quite remarkable that Debs had any success at all as a politician. That success was due in no small part to the power of Debs's oratory and prose.

♦ "Liberty"

Eugene Debs's fame began during his prison term following the Pullman strike. Countless people sought his opinion during his imprisonment. Since the jail was actually just a room in a local sheriff's house and his jailer gave him and the other ARU leaders imprisoned with him an incredible degree of freedom, Debs had the opportunity to read

and to communicate with the outside world through correspondence and newspaper interviews. Upon his release, many newfound fans were excited to hear what he had to say about the modern world, especially about the government that had incarcerated him. While Debs had resisted adopting the Socialist label before his imprisonment, his embrace of the term at this juncture was extremely fortunate for the American Socialist movement. It not only gained a famous adherent, but it now also had its most eloquent spokesperson.

The speech begins with a tactic that was already a hundred years old when Debs used it, connecting modern labor struggles with the fight of the Patriots during the American Revolution. The idea was that modern workers struggled against the oppression of their employers in the same way that the American colonists fought the oppression of the British. Historians now call this concept "artisan republicanism." Since Debs believed that taking on rich corporations was a patriotic American thing to do, this tactic suited him well. He connects the American Revolution directly to his case later in the speech by equating his personal liberty to political liberty in the United States. At one point he even quotes the Revolutionary leader Patrick Henry, whose cry "Give me Liberty or give me death!" certainly fits the themes of Debs's career.

Debs also persuaded people to entertain his views by connecting his politics to the teachings of the Bible, and he does this often in this speech. Debs relates the battle between liberty and slavery to the battle between good and evil in the world and suggests, as the Bible does, that the fate of humanity hangs in the balance. Christian imagery supplies the structure of Debs's vision of citizenship. More important, like Saul, who would become the apostle Paul after a conversion experience on the road to Damascus, Debs uses this occasion to suggest that in jail he had seen the light. Such Christian imagery served as a way for Debs to explain his ideals and inspire others to see the world as he now saw it.

This speech is also important for understanding Debs's sense of justice and his willingness to take on what he deemed unjust laws. Debs makes no apologies for violating the injunction that led to his arrest. Indeed, in the course of his speech he directly attacks the judge and the institutions that supported him. This is in line with his readiness to criticize government in general whenever it supported corporations over the rights of its own citizens. Debs deftly elevates the Constitution at the same time that he criticizes the forces he sees as a threat to the rights contained in that document. His main goal here is to rescue American liberty from domination by the forces of monopoly, a major political issue during this era.

♦ "How I Became a Socialist"

In this article, Debs does his best to convey that he had always been a kind of Socialist, even though he had explicitly rejected that label for his political ideas before his imprisonment in 1895. His goal in this piece is to suggest

Time Line

1855	November 5	■ Debs is born in Terre Haute, Indiana.
1870	May 23	■ Debs begins working on railroads.
1875	February 27	■ Debs becomes a charter member of the new Terre Haute, Indiana, local of the Brotherhood of Locomotive Firemen.
1893	June 20	■ Debs and forty-nine others form the American Railway Union with Debs as leader.
1895	May 27	■ The U.S. Supreme Court issues its decision in *In Re Debs*, which validates the injunction that led to Debs's conviction for interfering with the mails.
	November 22	■ Upon his release from prison, Debs announces his new belief in Socialism.
1902	April	■ Debs writes "How I Became a Socialist" for the *New York Comrade*.
1905	June 29	■ Debs speaks before the founding convention of the Industrial Workers of the World.
1912	November 5	■ Debs garners 901,551 in the year's presidential election, the best showing, in percentage terms, of his five candidacies.
1918	June 16	■ Debs delivers speech in Canton, Ohio, which will lead to his conviction under the Sedition Act.
1920	Fall	■ Debs conducts his final presidential campaign from the Atlanta Federal Penitentiary.
1921	December 21	■ President Warren Harding pardons Debs and twenty-three other political prisoners effective Christmas Day.
1926	October 20	■ Debs dies in Elmhurst, Illinois.

that people like him who saw aspects of class conflict all around them but did not understand Socialism would come to embrace the movement once Socialists like Debs taught them to understand the world. Here he describes his own education in the hope that others might follow along his same path.

In the early sections of the essay, Debs conveys his enthusiasm for organizing his fellow members of the working class as a sign of his growing class consciousness. At that point in his life, he thought organization alone was enough to redress the many wrongs that management inflicted upon labor. , Debs explains that unlike other labor leaders of that era, he helped organize the ARU because he thought that all railroad men would do best standing together rather than separated into unions organized by skill. This is an implied contrast to the American Federation of Labor, an umbrella organization for unions that was just getting started around the time that Debs first gained prominence in the labor movement. Despite his comparatively broad view of organized labor's potential base, Debs's vision remained limited to what he could do in support of the trade union movement.

Then came the Pullman strike. "In the gleam of every bayonet and the flash of every rifle," Debs writes, " *the class struggle was revealed*." This justifiably famous line not only supports the idea that the Pullman strike converted Debs to Socialism but also helps explain his reasons for supporting Socialism. Since the federal army kept the exploitation of Pullman workers going, ordinary people had to be able to control the state so that it could support their cause rather than the goals of giant corporations. To Debs, then, labor and politics were inseparable. He could not help the working class without entering politics.

This philosophy is in sharp contrast to the predominant labor union philosophy of that era. The American Federation of Labor, led by Samuel Gompers, believed in what Gompers called "pure and simple unionism." This meant that trade unions should worry about raising the wages and improving the working conditions of their members, and absolutely nothing else. Unions that followed this philosophy ignored politics because politics took time and resources away from their core purpose—helping their members. This debate was sometimes referred to as the "political question" within union circles. However, by the time of his death in 1924, Gompers came around to Debs's point of view on this issue even if he never adopted Debs's radical positions.

♦ Speech to the Founding Convention of the Industrial Workers of the World

The Industrial Workers of the World (IWW, or Wobblies) was (and continues to be to this day) one of the most radical political organizations ever developed on American soil. Nominally a trade union, its actual goal was a revolution that would place the working class in control of the means of production. While the group offered little detail about the aftermath of this revolution, its efforts at achieving this goal resulted in the development of many new tactics for the American labor movement. For example, the IWW pioneered the organization of all workers regardless of race or class, a tactic that Debs had advocated since the Pullman strike. One way in which the IWW gained sympathy for its cause was to hold free-speech struggles, campaigns for the right to air its message rather than campaigns over the message itself. Obviously, after the injunction that ended the Pullman strike, Debs sympathized with this tactic too. It was no surprise, then, that Debs came to the founding convention of the IWW in Chicago and addressed the gathering.

To clear the way for the IWW, Debs dismisses the existing labor movement as a mouthpiece for employers. "The trades-union movement is today under the control of the capitalist class," he told his sympathetic audience of radicals. "It is preaching capitalist economics. It is serving capitalist purposes." In Debs's view, the small number of actual workers represented by the delegates in the hall did not matter so much as that the union formed there got its message right. According to Debs, workers would flock to a union like this upon its creation. Enlightened self-interest demanded that workers stand shoulder to shoulder in opposition to their bosses. Debs uses the term "fakir" to mean a particular kind of con man who says one thing but does another. The IWW, by aligning itself clearly with the most downtrodden members of society, was not going to swindle anyone.

With respect to the political question, Debs calls on the delegates to align their organization closely with his own Socialist Party. By doing so, they would bring about triumph on both the economic and political fields. Most of his passion goes into suggesting a broad outline of how the IWW should be organized. He expresses his belief that it should be a union of ordinary workers, the so-called rank and file. He also believed that it should be uncompromising and, appropriately for an economic philosopher like Debs, that it should appeal to the intelligence of American workers rather than to their prejudices. In the latter respect, he faulted other unions for what they had done, for example, with respect to keeping African Americans from joining their organizations.

The IWW was not as successful as Debs had hoped. Opposition from frightened employers and attacks on the patriotism of its leaders during World War I kept the IWW from growing beyond a regional phenomenon in a limited number of industries. Strains in the relationship between Debs and the organization later kept him from playing a big part in the history of the Wobblies beyond delivering this speech at the group's inception. In fact, Debs let his membership lapse during the mid-1910s. However, the outbreak of World War I united Debs and the IWW in opposing the conflict. The government crackdown on those who opposed the war shortly after it began led to the near destruction of the Wobblies when most of its leaders were indicted and jailed. Eugene V. Debs eventually met the same fate.

♦ Antiwar Speech

Debs began a speaking tour because the Socialist press that he had depended upon to distribute his writings was wiped out by government censorship. In 1917 and 1918 America passed the Espionage and Sedition Acts, which made expressing spoken and written opposition to both the war and the government that waged it a federal crime. Debs knew he was risking his already failing health and his freedom by speaking out. He toured anyway. The words that Debs spoke at Nimisilla Park in Canton, Ohio, before twelve hundred people were little different from the ones he had spoken at earlier stops on his tour. What made this speech different was the presence of a government stenographer and the willingness of the local U.S. attorney, E.S. Wertz, to prosecute Debs (against the advice of Wertz's superiors) for what he said.

Much of the speech deals with specific controversies, like the case of the jailed trade unionist Tom Mooney, that do not resonate down to this day, but there are many passages in the text that demonstrate Debs's ability to inspire. For example, near the beginning of the speech, Debs jokes openly about the possibility of getting arrested. Indeed, he suggests that he would rather be arrested than remain silent about the injustice around him. His willingness to speak under threat of arrest was undoubtedly as important in inspiring his listeners as any particular phrase he spoke that day. Notably, much of the speech is devoted to attacks not just on the government but also on Wall Street. He attacks Wall Street for greed and shortsightedness in the exploitation of its employees. Debs is arguing that the worse conditions get, the better Socialism will do. In fact, Debs suggests that the triumph of Socialism in America is near, an argument that might have seemed strange at a time when Socialists and Socialism had been largely silenced by government repression.

In the speech, Debs repeats his long-standing critique of the two-party system. He calls both the Democratic and Republican parties corrupt, presumably because of their mutual embrace of the war. He recommends organizing along industrial lines, meaning workers from all skill levels, just as the ARU had done. He then suggests that joining the Socialist Party is the political equivalent of industrial organization. If your union embraces the working class, he suggests, your political party should too. While the positions of the Socialist Party were unpopular at the time, Debs argues that a brighter day would come as long as his listeners remained true to themselves.

It is also worth noting that Debs defended the IWW during his speech, despite his differences with the organization. "Let me say here that I have great respect for the I.W.W.," he told the crowd. "Far greater than I have for their infamous detractors." This is an excellent illustration of how the Left came together in the face of a common enemy, in this case the Wilson administration. In September 1917, months before Debs spoke, the U.S. Justice Department had simultaneously raided forty-eight IWW meeting halls across the country, arresting 165 leaders. While this did not destroy the organization entirely, it certainly rendered it incapable of effectively opposing the war. The example of the Wobblies could not have been far from Debs's mind when he spoke in Canton. That Debs spoke there (and elsewhere beforehand) is a testament to his courage.

In his two-hour speech, Debs made no direct reference to World War I, which raged in Europe at the time. Instead, he attacks war in general, most notably in this famous passage: "The master class has always declared the wars; the subject class has always fought the battles. The master class has had all to gain and nothing to lose, while the subject class has had nothing to gain and all to lose—especially their lives." That quotation is nothing but an eloquent way of associating military warfare with class warfare, a point that has been made many times since. Unfortunately for Debs, the government and much of the public were unwilling to accept any public opposition to a conflict that was, in fact, fairly unpopular compared with other wars throughout American history. Simply pointing out that different social classes are affected differently by war was enough to get Debs arrested.

As was the case after the Pullman strike, Debs did not deny the charges against him. "I wish to admit the truth of all that has been testified to in this proceeding," he told the jury that eventually convicted him. "I would not retract a word that I have uttered that I believe to be true to save myself from going to the penitentiary for the rest of my days" (Debs, p. 434). Indeed, Debs refused to mount any defense at all. Although he was convicted, he did not die in prison or even serve his entire ten-year sentence. Combat in World War I ended in 1918, but the United States did not sign a peace treaty to end the war formally until after Warren Harding became president in 1921. With peace officially at hand, Harding pardoned Debs and other political prisoners who had opposed the war, effective that Christmas. Debs was in poor health before he ever went to jail. His time in prison undoubtedly accelerated his decline.

Impact and Legacy

Eugene V. Debs was undeniably the most important Socialist leader in American history. His many articles and speeches demonstrate his involvement in nearly every important political debate between factions of the American Left during this era. From the nature of the American working class to how the Left should respond to World War I, Debs's analysis often won the day among his colleagues and brought greater attention to their causes. Even more important than his leadership as a Socialist was his role as the most significant oppositional voice of his time. Debs lived at a time when the free speech clause of the First Amendment had not been reinforced by later U.S. Supreme Court decisions. For him to speak out against capitalist oppression and the government policy that supported that oppression took a tremendous amount of courage, since he constantly faced arrest. His variety of home-grown

Socialism almost single-handedly made this movement viable in the United States.

Unfortunately for Debs's historical reputation, all things Socialist or Communist were widely dismissed as anti-American with the onset of the cold war. Even his Americanized version of Socialism fell far out of favor. Nevertheless, many of the principles Debs championed, like justice and equality, can be separated from his Socialism and remain relevant in a political climate that still frowns upon Socialism of any kind. More important, Debs's willingness to express unpopular opinions during a time of war might serve as an inspiration to those who oppose modern government policies, such as the war in Iraq, but who fear the backlash such a stand might generate. Whether Debs's collected writings can play such a role depends upon the willingness of readers to take his arguments at their merits and see past the political label that he adopted. Indeed, the fact that almost a million Americans were not once but twice willing to vote for a presidential candidate as radical as Eugene V. Debs ought to serve as a reminder that Socialism might not be as alien to American political culture as some modern political observers believe.

Key Sources

The Eugene V. Debs Papers are in Cunningham Library at Indiana State University in Terre Haute. Perhaps the best collection of the kinds of Socialist newspapers in which Debs wrote is at the State Historical Society of Wisconsin in Madison. However, there are many good anthologies of Debs's speeches and writings. *Debs: His Life, Writing, and Speeches* was compiled by the Socialist newspaper *Appeal to Reason* in 1908. The archives of the American Socialist Party, for which Debs served as standard bearer, are at the William R. Perkins Library of Duke University in Durham, North Carolina. The "Address to the Jury" is in *Writings and Speeches of Eugene V. Debs* (1948).

Essential Quotes

"Liberty is not a word of modern coinage. Liberty and slavery are primal words, like good and evil, right and wrong; they are opposites and coexistent."

("Liberty")

"In the gleam of every bayonet and the flash of every rifle the class struggle was revealed."

("How I Became a Socialist")

"We know that without solidarity nothing is possible, that with it nothing is impossible."

(Speech to the Founding Convention of the Industrial Workers of the World)

"I would be ashamed to admit that I had risen from the ranks. When I rise it will be with the ranks, and not from the ranks."

(Antiwar Speech)

"I would rather a thousand times be a free soul in jail than to be a sycophant and coward in the streets."

(Antiwar Speech)

Essential Quotes

"The master class has always declared the wars; the subject class has always fought the battles. The master class has had all to gain and nothing to lose, while the subject class has had nothing to gain and all to lose—especially their lives."

(Antiwar Speech)

"It is only necessary to label a man 'I. W. W.' to have him lynched.... War makes possible all such crimes and outrages."

(Antiwar Speech)

Further Reading

Articles

Burns, David. "The Soul of Socialism: Christianity, Civilization and Citizenship in the Thought of Eugene Debs." *Labor* 5 (Summer 2008): 83–116.

Books

Brommel, Bernard J. *Eugene V. Debs: Spokesman for Labor and Socialism*. Chicago: Charles H. Kerr, 1978.

Ginger, Ray. *The Bending Cross*. New Brunswick, N.J.: Rutgers University Press, 1949.

Molloy, Scott. "Debs, Eugene V." In *Encyclopedia of the American Left*, 2nd. ed., ed. Mari Jo Buhle, Paul Buhle, and Dan Georgakas. New York: Oxford University Press, 1998.

Salvatore, Nick. *Eugene V. Debs: Citizen and Socialist*. Urbana: University of Illinois Press, 1982.

—Jonathan Rees

Questions for Further Study

1. Evaluate Debs's Socialist interpretation of history as a class struggle. To what extent did he borrow these ideas from Karl Marx and other Socialists, and to what extent were they his own? Does he making a convincing analysis? Why or why not?

2. Both Debs and Jane Addams wrote about the 1894 Pullman strike, of which Debs was a leader. As major figures in the Progressive movement of the time, the two certainly had plenty of ideas in common—both advocating, for example, a military-style approach to their movements for social justice—but they diverged on many points. Debs, after all, was a committed Socialist, while Addams remained a member of the Republican Party—as were a number of activists of that time. Compare and contrast their discussions of the strike, noting the areas in which they most agree and disagree.

3. In presenting a viable vision for Socialism in America, Debs faced a great challenge: A nation built on individualism had never been particularly receptive to Socialist ideas. Yet in his antiwar speech he uses the language of self-fulfillment, which sounds much more like Thomas Jefferson than Karl Marx: "That is your supreme need—to find yourself—to really know yourself and your purpose in life." How effectively did Debs manage to draw together Socialism and Americanism? What are his strongest and weakest arguments for a Socialist America?

4. Debs's speech to the Industrial Workers of the World makes reference to numerous recent strikes: "the textile workers at Fall River ... the subway employees in the city of New York ... the stockyard's employees here in Chicago ... the strike of the teamsters now in progress." Research these events and discuss the role and response of Debs and others in the workers' movement of the time. Were these, as Debs viewed most strikes, a case of good versus evil, workers versus capitalists? Or are there other factors to consider in evaluating what happened?

"Liberty"

1895

Manifestly the spirit of '76 still survives. The fires of liberty and noble aspirations are not yet extinguished. I greet you tonight as lovers of liberty and as despisers of despotism. I comprehend the significance of this demonstration and appreciate the honor that makes it possible for me to be your guest on such an occasion. The vindication and glorification of American principles of government, as proclaimed to the world in the Declaration of Independence, is the high purpose of this convocation.

Speaking for myself personally, I am not certain whether this is an occasion for rejoicing or lamentation. I confess to a serious doubt as to whether this day marks my deliverance from bondage to freedom or my doom from freedom to bondage. Certain it is, in the light of recent judicial proceedings, that I stand in your presence stripped of my constitutional rights as a freeman and shorn of the most sacred prerogatives of American citizenship, and what is true of myself is true of every other citizen who has the temerity to protest against corporation rule or question the absolute sway of the money power. It is not law nor the administration of law of which I complain. It is the flagrant violation of the constitution, the total abrogation of law and the usurpation of judicial and despotic power, by virtue of which my colleagues and myself were committed to jail, against which I enter my solemn protest; and any honest analysis of the proceedings must sustain the haggard truth of the indictment....

Dismissing this branch of the subject, permit me to assure you that I am not here to bemoan my lot. In my vocabulary there are no wails of despondency or despair. However gloomy the future may appear to others, I have an abiding faith in the ultimate triumph of the right....

Liberty is not a word of modern coinage. Liberty and slavery are primal worlds, like good and evil, right and wrong; they are opposites and coexistent....

The theme tonight is personal liberty; or giving it its full height, depth and breadth, American liberty, something that Americans have been accustomed to eulogize since the foundation of the Republic, and multiplied thousands of them continue in the habit to this day because they do not recognize the truth that in the imprisonment of one man in defiance of all constitutional guarantees, the liberties of all are invaded and placed in peril. In saying this, I conjecture I have struck the keynote of alarm that has convoked this vast audience....

Strike the fetters from the slave, give him liberty and he becomes an inhabitant of a new world. He looks abroad and beholds life and joy in all things around him. His soul expands beyond all boundaries. Emancipated by the genius of Liberty, he aspires to communion with all that is noble and beautiful, feels himself allied to all higher order of intelligence and superstition, a new being throbbing with glorious life....

It is in no spirit of laudation that I aver here tonight that it has fallen to the lot of the American Railway Union to arouse workingmen to a sense of the perils that environ their liberties.

In the great Pullman strike the American Railway Union challenged the power of corporations in a way that had not previously been done, and the analyzation of this fact serves to expand it to proportions that the most conservative men of the nation regard with alarm.

It must be borne in mind that the American Railway Union did not challenge the government. It threw down no gauntlet to courts or armies—it simply resisted the invasion of the rights of workingmen by corporations. It challenged and defied the power of corporations. Thrice armed with a just cause, the organization believed that justice would win for labor a notable victory; and the records proclaim that its confidence was not misplaced.

The corporations, left to their own resources of money, mendacity and malice, of thugs and ex-convicts, leeches and lawyers, would have been overwhelmed with defeat and the banners of organized labor would have floated triumphant in the breeze.

This the corporations saw and believed—hence the crowning act of infamy in which the federal courts and the federal armies participated, and which culminated in the defeat of labor....

From such reflections I turn to the practical lessons taught by this "Liberation Day" demonstration. It means that American lovers of liberty are setting in operation forces to rescue their constitutional liberties from the grasp of monopoly and its mercenary

Document Text

hirelings. It means that the people are aroused in view of impending perils and that agitation, organization, and unification are to be the future battle cries of men who will not part with their birthrights and, like Patrick Henry, will have the courage to exclaim; "Give me liberty or give me death!"

I have borne with such composure as I could command the imprisonment which deprived me of my liberty. Were I a criminal; were I guilty of crimes meriting a prison cell; had I ever lifted my hand against the life or the liberty of my fellowmen; had I ever sought to filch their good name, I would not be here. I would have fled from the haunts of civilization and taken up my residence in some cave where the voice of my kindred is never heard. But I am standing here without a self-accusation of crime or criminal intent festering in my conscience, in the sunlight once more, among my fellowmen, contributing as best I can to make this "Liberation Day" from Woodstock prison a memorial day.

Glossary

the haggard truth of the indictment:	the ugly truth, as Debs sees it, behind the circumstances of his and others' imprisonment following the Pullman Strike
threw down no gauntlet:	presented no challenge
usurpation:	taking control from legitimate authority

"How I Became a Socialist"

On the evening of February 27, 1875, the local lodge of the Brotherhood of Locomotive Firemen was organized at Terre Haute, Ind., by Joshua A. Leach, then grand master, and I was admitted as a charter member and at once chosen secretary. "Old Josh Leach," as he was affectionately called, a typical locomotive fireman of his day, was the founder of the brotherhood, and I was instantly attracted by his rugged honesty, simple manner and homely speech. How well I remember feeling his large, rough hand on my shoulder, the kindly eye of an elder brother searching my own as he gently said, "My boy, you're a little young, but I believe you're in earnest and will make your mark in the brotherhood." Of course, I assured him that I would do my best....

My first step was thus taken in organized labor and a new influence fired my ambition and changed the whole current of my career. I was filled with enthusiasm and my blood fairly leaped in my veins. Day and night I worked for the brotherhood. To see its watchfires glow and observe the increase of its sturdy members were the sunshine and shower of my life. To attend the "meeting" was my supreme joy, and for ten years I was not once absent when the faithful assembled....

Through all these years I was nourished at Fountain Proletaire. I drank deeply of its waters and every particle of my tissue became saturated with the spirit of the working class. I had fired an engine and been stung by the exposure and hardship of the rail. I was with the boys in their weary watches, at the broken engine's side and often helped to bear their bruised and bleeding bodies back to wife and child again. How could I but feel the burden of their wrongs? How the seed of agitation fail to take deep root in my heart?

And so I was spurred on in the work of organizing, not the firemen merely, but the brakemen, switchmen, telegraphers, shopmen, track-hands, all of them in fact, and as I had now become known as an organizer, the call came from all sides and there are but few trades I have not helped to organize and less still in whose strikes I have not at some time had a hand.

In 1894 the American Railway Union was organized and a braver body of men never fought the battle of the working class.

Up to this time I had heard but little of Socialism, knew practically nothing about the movement, and what little I did know was not calculated to impress me in its favor. I was bent on thorough and complete organization of the railroad men and ultimately the whole working class, and all my time and energy were given to that end. My supreme conviction was that if they were only organized in every branch of the service and all acted together in concert they could redress their wrongs and regulate the conditions of their employment. The stockholders of the corporation acted as one, why not the men? It was such a plain proposition—simply to follow the example set before their eyes by their masters—surely they could not fail to see it, act as one, and solve the problem....

The skirmish lines of the A. R. U. were well advanced. A series of small battles were fought and won without the loss of a man. A number of concessions were made by the corporations rather than risk an encounter. Then came the fight on the Great Northern, short, sharp, and decisive. The victory was complete—the only railroad strike of magnitude ever won by an organization in America.

Next followed the final shock—the Pullman strike—and the American Railway Union again won, clear and complete. The combined corporations were paralyzed and helpless. At this juncture there were delivered, from wholly unexpected quarters, a swift succession of blows that blinded me for an instant and then opened wide my eyes—and in the gleam of every bayonet and the flash of every rifle *the class struggle was revealed* . This was my first practical lesson in Socialism, though wholly unaware that it was called by that name.

An army of detectives, thugs and murderers were equipped with badge and beer and bludgeon and turned loose; old hulks of cars were fired; the alarm bells tolled; the people were terrified; the most startling rumors were set afloat; the press volleyed and thundered, and over all the wires sped the news that Chicago's white throat was in the clutch of a red mob; injunctions flew thick and fast, arrests followed, and our office and headquarters, the heart of the strike, was sacked, torn out and nailed up by the "lawful" authorities of the federal government; and

Document Text

when in company with my loyal comrades I found myself in Cook County jail at Chicago with the … press screaming conspiracy, treason and murder, and by some fateful coincidence I was given the cell occupied just previous to his execution by the assassin of Mayor Carter Harrison, Sr., overlooking the spot, a few feet distant, where the anarchists were hanged a few years before, I had another exceedingly practical and impressive lesson in Socialism.…

The Chicago jail sentences were followed by six months at Woodstock and it was here that Socialism gradually laid hold of me in its own irresistible fashion. Books and pamphlets and letters from socialists came by every mail and I began to read and think and dissect the anatomy of the system in which workingmen, however organized, could be shattered and battered and splintered at a single stroke.…

The American Railway Union was defeated but not conquered—overwhelmed but not destroyed. It lives and pulsates in the Socialist movement, and its defeat but blazed the way to economic freedom and hastened the dawn of human brotherhood.

Glossary

Chicago's white throat was the clutch of a red mob:	sarcastic comparison of the city to a woman (white, at that) in danger in from "reds," or Socialists
the class struggle:	fundamental conflict between the workers (proletariat) and business owners (capitalists)
Fountain Proletaire:	an expression, apparently of Debs's own coinage, that used the French adjectival format (noun followed by adjective) and presented the struggle of industrial workers as an opportunity to gain wisdom and grow
grand master:	a master craftsman, a leading figure in many local union bodies
Great Northern:	the Great Northern Railway
homely:	down home
watches:	shifts at work
where the anarchists were hanged a few years before:	a reference to the place of execution of four men out of eight charged for their alleged roles in the Haymarket riot in Chicago on May 4, 1886

Document Text

Speech to the Founding Convention of the Industrial Workers of the World

1905

Fellow Delegates and Comrades:

As the preliminaries in organizing the convention have been disposed of, we will get down to the real work before this body....

In taking a survey of the industrial field of today, we are at once impressed with the total inadequacy of working-class organization, with the lack of solidarity, with the widespread demoralization we see, and we are bound to conclude that the old form of pure and simple unionism has long since outgrown its usefulness; that it is now not only in the way of progress, but that it has become positively reactionary, a thing that is but an auxiliary of the capitalist class.

They charge us with being assembled here for the purpose of disrupting the union movement. It is already disrupted, and if it were not disrupted we would not behold the spectacle here in the very city of a white policeman guarding a black scab, and a black policeman guarding a white scab, while the trade unions stand by with their hands in their pockets wondering what is the matter with union labor in America. We are here today for the purpose of uniting the working class, for the purpose of eliminating that form of unionism which is responsible for the conditions as they exist today.

The trades-union movement is today under the control of the capitalist class. It is preaching capitalist economics. It is serving capitalist purposes. Proof of it, positive and overwhelming, appears on every hand. All of the important strikes during the textile workers at Fall River, that proved so disastrous to those who engaged in it; the strike of the subway employees in the city of New York, where under the present form of organization the local leaders repudiated the local leaders and were in alliance with the capitalist class to crush their own followers; the strike of the stockyard's employees here in Chicago; the strike of the teamsters now in progress—all, all of them bear testimony to the fact that the pure and simple form of unionism has fulfilled its mission, whatever that may have been, and that the time has come for it to go.

The American Federation of Labor has numbers, but the capitalist class do not fear the American Federation of Labor; quite the contrary. The capitalist papers here in this very city at this very time are championing the cause of pure and simple unionism. Since this convention met there has been nothing in these papers but a series of misrepresentations. If we had met instead in the interest of the American Federation of Labor these papers, these capitalist papers, would have had their columns filled with articles commending the work that is being done here. There is certainly something wrong with that form of unionism which has its chief support in the press that represents capitalism; something wrong in that form of unionism whose leaders are the lieutenants of capitalism; something wrong with that form of unionism that forms an alliance with such a capitalist combination as the Civic Federation, whose sole purpose it is to chloroform the working class while the capitalist class go through their pockets. There are those who believe that this form of unionism can be changed from within. They are very greatly mistaken. We might as well have remained in the Republican and Democratic parties and have expected to effect certain changes from within, instead of withdrawing from those parties and organizing a party that represented the exploited working class. There is but one way to effect this great change, and that is for the workingman to sever his relations with the American Federation and join the union that proposes upon the economic field to represent his class, and we are here today for the purpose of organizing that union. I believe that we are capable of profiting by the experiences of the past. I believe it is possible for the delegates here assembled to form a great, sound, economic organization of the working class based upon the class struggle, that shall be broad enough to embrace every honest worker, yet narrow enough to exclude every fakir....

I am satisfied that the great body of the working class in this country are prepared for just such an organization. I know, their leaders know, that if this convention is successful their doom is sealed. They can already see the hand-writing upon the wall, and so they are seeking by all of the power at their command to discredit this convention, and in alliance with the cohorts of capitalism they are doing what they can to defeat this convention. It may fail in its mission,

Document Text

for they may continue to misrepresent, deceive and betray the working class and keep them in the clutches of their capitalist masters and exploiters.

They are hoping that we will fail to get together. They are hoping, as they have already expressed it, that this convention will consist of a prolonged wrangle; that such is our feeling and relations toward each other that it will be impossible for us to agree upon any vital proposition; that we will fight each other upon every point, and that when we have concluded our labors we will leave things in a worse condition than they were before.

If we are true to ourselves we will undeceive those gentlemen. We will give them to understand that we are animated by motives too lofty for them in their baseness and sordidness to comprehend. We will give them to understand that the motive here is not to use unionism as a means of serving the capitalist class, but that the motive of the men and women assembled here is to serve the working class by so organizing that class as to make their organization the promise of the coming triumph upon the economic field and the political field and the ultimate emancipation of the working class.…

Let me say in closing that you and I and all of us who are here to enlist in the service of the working class need to have faith in each other, not the faith born of ignorance and stupidity, but the enlightened faith of self-interest. We are in precisely the same position; we depend absolutely upon each other. We must get close together and stand shoulder to shoulder. We know that without solidarity nothing is possible, that with it nothing is impossible.

And so we must dispel the petty prejudices that are born of the differences of the past, and I am of those who believe that, if we get together in the true working-class spirit, most of these differences will disappear, and if those of us who have differed in the past are willing to accord to each other that degree of conciliation that we ourselves feel that we are entitled to, that we will forget these differences, we will approach all of the problems that confront us with our intelligence combined, acting together in concert, all animated by the same high resolve to form that great union, so necessary to the working class, without which their condition remains as it is, and with which, when made practical and vitalized and renewed, the working class is permeated with the conquering spirit of the class struggle, and as if by magic the entire movement is vitalized, and side by side and shoulder to shoulder in a class-conscious phalanx we move forward to certain and complete victory.

Glossary

American Federation of Labor:	a mainstream labor group, which later joined with the Congress of Industrial Organizations to become the modern AFL-CIO
the capitalist class:	the business owners, whom Debs saw as the historic enemies of the working class
Civic Federation:	the National Civic Federation, another rival labor group at the time
class-conscious phalanx:	a group of soldiers for the cause of class warfare between the workers and capitalists
combination:	corporation
fakir:	a term derived from a word in the Hindi language of India referring to a type of holy man, but also—with emphasis on its similarity to the English "faker"—used derisively
lieutenants:	persons who carry out the orders of their superiors
reactionary:	one who reacts against progressive social ideas by calling for extreme conservatism and a return to the past
scab:	a worker who goes to work when others are striking
working class:	industrial workers, also known as the proletariat

Antiwar Speech

1918

Comrades, friends and fellow-workers, for this very cordial greeting, this very hearty reception, I thank you all with the fullest appreciation of your interest in and your devotion to the cause for which I am to speak to you this afternoon.

To speak for labor; to plead the cause of the men and women and children who toil; to serve the working class, has always been to me a high privilege; a duty of love....

I realize that, in speaking to you this afternoon, there are certain limitations placed upon the right of free speech. I must be exceedingly careful, prudent, as to what I say, and even more careful and prudent as to how I say it. I may not be able to say all I think; but I am not going to say anything that I do not think. I would rather a thousand times be a free soul in jail than to be a sycophant and coward in the streets....

If it had not been for the men and women who, in the past, have had the moral courage to go to jail, we would still be in the jungles....

There is but one thing you have to be concerned about, and that is that you keep foursquare with the principles of the international Socialist movement. It is only when you begin to compromise that trouble begins. So far as I am concerned, it does not matter what others may say, or think, or do, as long as I am sure that I am right with myself and the cause. There are so many who seek refuge in the popular side of a great question. As a Socialist, I have long since learned how to stand alone. For the last month I have been traveling over the Hoosier State; and, let me say to you, that, in all my connection with the Socialist movement, I have never seen such meetings, such enthusiasm, such unity of purpose; never have I seen such a promising outlook as there is today, notwithstanding the statement published repeatedly that our leaders have deserted us. Well, for myself, I never had much faith in leaders. I am willing to be charged with almost anything, rather than to be charged with being a leader. I am suspicious of leaders, and especially of the intellectual variety. Give me the rank and file every day in the week. If you go to the city of Washington, and you examine the pages of the Congressional Directory, you will find that almost all of those corporation lawyers and cowardly politicians, members of Congress, and misrepresentatives of the masses—you will find that almost all of them claim, in glowing terms, that they have risen from the ranks to places of eminence and distinction. I am very glad I cannot make that claim for myself. I would be ashamed to admit that I had risen from the ranks. When I rise it will be with the ranks, and not from the ranks....

They tell us that we live in a great free republic; that our institutions are democratic; that we are a free and self-governing people. This is too much, even for a joke. But it is not a subject for levity; it is an exceedingly serious matter....

Wars throughout history have been waged for conquest and plunder. In the Middle Ages when the feudal lords who inhabited the castles whose towers may still be seen along the Rhine concluded to enlarge their domains, to increase their power, their prestige and their wealth they declared war upon one another. But they themselves did not go to war any more than the modern feudal lords, the barons of Wall Street go to war. The feudal barons of the Middle Ages, the economic predecessors of the capitalists of our day, declared all wars. And their miserable serfs fought all the battles. The poor, ignorant serfs had been taught to revere their masters; to believe that when their masters declared war upon one another, it was their patriotic duty to fall upon one another and to cut one another's throats for the profit and glory of the lords and barons who held them in contempt. And that is war in a nutshell. The master class has always declared the wars; the subject class has always fought the battles. The master class has had all to gain and nothing to lose, while the subject class has had nothing to gain and all to lose—especially their lives.

They have always taught and trained you to believe it to be your patriotic duty to go to war and to have yourselves slaughtered at their command. But in all the history of the world you, the people, have never had a voice in declaring war, and strange as it certainly appears, no war by any nation in any age has ever been declared by the people.

And here let me emphasize the fact—and it cannot be repeated too often—that the working class who fight all the battles, the working class who make the supreme sacrifices, the working class who freely shed their blood and furnish the corpses, have never yet

Document Text

had a voice in either declaring war or making peace. It is the ruling class that invariably does both. They alone declare war and they alone make peace....

If war is right let it be declared by the people. You who have your lives to lose, you certainly above all others have the right to decide the momentous issue of war or peace....

The heart of the international Socialist never beats a retreat.

They are pressing forward, here, there and everywhere, in all the zones that girdle the globe. Everywhere these awakening workers, these class-conscious proletarians, these hardy sons and daughters of honest toil are proclaiming the glad tidings of the coming emancipation, everywhere their hearts are attuned to the most sacred cause that ever challenged men and women to action in all the history of the world. Everywhere they are moving toward democracy and the dawn; marching toward the sunrise, their faces all aglow with the light of the coming day. These are the Socialists, the most zealous and enthusiastic crusaders the world has ever known. They are making history that will light up the horizon of coming generations, for their mission is the emancipation of the human race. They have been reviled; they have been ridiculed, persecuted, imprisoned and have suffered death, but they have been sufficient to themselves and their cause, and their final triumph is but a question of time.

Do you wish to hasten the day of victory? Join the Socialist Party! Don't wait for the morrow. Join now! Enroll your name without fear and take your place where you belong. You cannot do your duty by proxy. You have got to do it yourself and do it squarely and then as you look yourself in the face you will have no occasion to blush. You will know what it is to be a real man or woman. You will lose nothing; you will gain everything. Not only will you lose nothing but you will find something of infinite value, and that something will be yourself. And that is your supreme need—to find yourself—to really know yourself and your purpose in life.

You need at this time especially to know that you are fit for something better than slavery and cannon fodder. You need to know that you were not created to work and produce and impoverish yourself to enrich an idle exploiter. You need to know that you have a mind to improve, a soul to develop, and a manhood to sustain....

To turn your back on the corrupt Republican Party and the still more corrupt Democratic Party—the gold-dust lackeys of the ruling class—counts for still more after you have stepped out of those popular and corrupt capitalist parties to join a minority party that has an ideal, that stands for a principle, and fights for a cause. This will be the most important change you have ever made and the time will come when you will thank me for having made the suggestion....

There are few men who have the courage to say a word in favor of the I.W.W. I have. Let me say here that I have great respect for the I.W.W. Far greater than I have for their infamous detractors.... It is only necessary to label a man "I.W.W." to have him lynched as they did Praeger, an absolutely innocent man. He was a Socialist and bore a German name, and that was his crime. A rumor was started that he was disloyal and he was promptly seized and lynched by the cowardly mob of so-called "patriots."

War makes possible all such crimes and outrages. And war comes in spite of the people. When Wall Street says war the press says war and the pulpit promptly follows with its Amen. In every age the pulpit has been on the side of the rulers and not on the side of the people. That is one reason why the preachers so fiercely denounce the I.W.W....

Political action and industrial action must supplement and sustain each other. You will never vote the Socialist republic into existence. You will have to lay its foundations in industrial organization. The industrial union is the forerunner of industrial democracy. In the shop where the workers are associated is where industrial democracy has its beginning. Organize according to your industries! Get together in every department of industrial service! United and acting together for the common good your power is invincible.

When you have organized industrially you will soon learn that you can manage as well as operate industry. You will soon realize that you do not need the idle masters and exploiters. They are simply parasites. They do not employ you as you imagine but you employ them to take from you what you produce, and that is how they function in industry. You can certainly dispense with them in that capacity. You do not need them to depend upon for your jobs. You can never be free while you work and live by their sufferance. You must own your own tools and then you will control your own jobs, enjoy the products of your own labor and be free men instead of industrial slaves.

Organize industrially and make your organization complete. Then unite in the Socialist Party. Vote as you strike and strike as you vote.

Your union and your party embrace the working class. The Socialist Party expresses the interests, hopes and aspirations of the toilers of all the world.

Glossary

bore a German name, and that was his crime:	reference to the widespread paranoia of the time regarding Germans and eastern Europeans, seen by many to be terrorists and spies
class-conscious:	aware of one's role in what Debs saw as the historic struggle between the workers and the capitalists
comrades:	a term used at the time by a wide spectrum on the far left to indicate brotherhood in the international workers' movement
industrial democracy:	a system of government whereby the workers act as a single union and thereby effectively control the government
proletarians:	industrial workers
sycophant:	someone who plays up to the rich and powerful

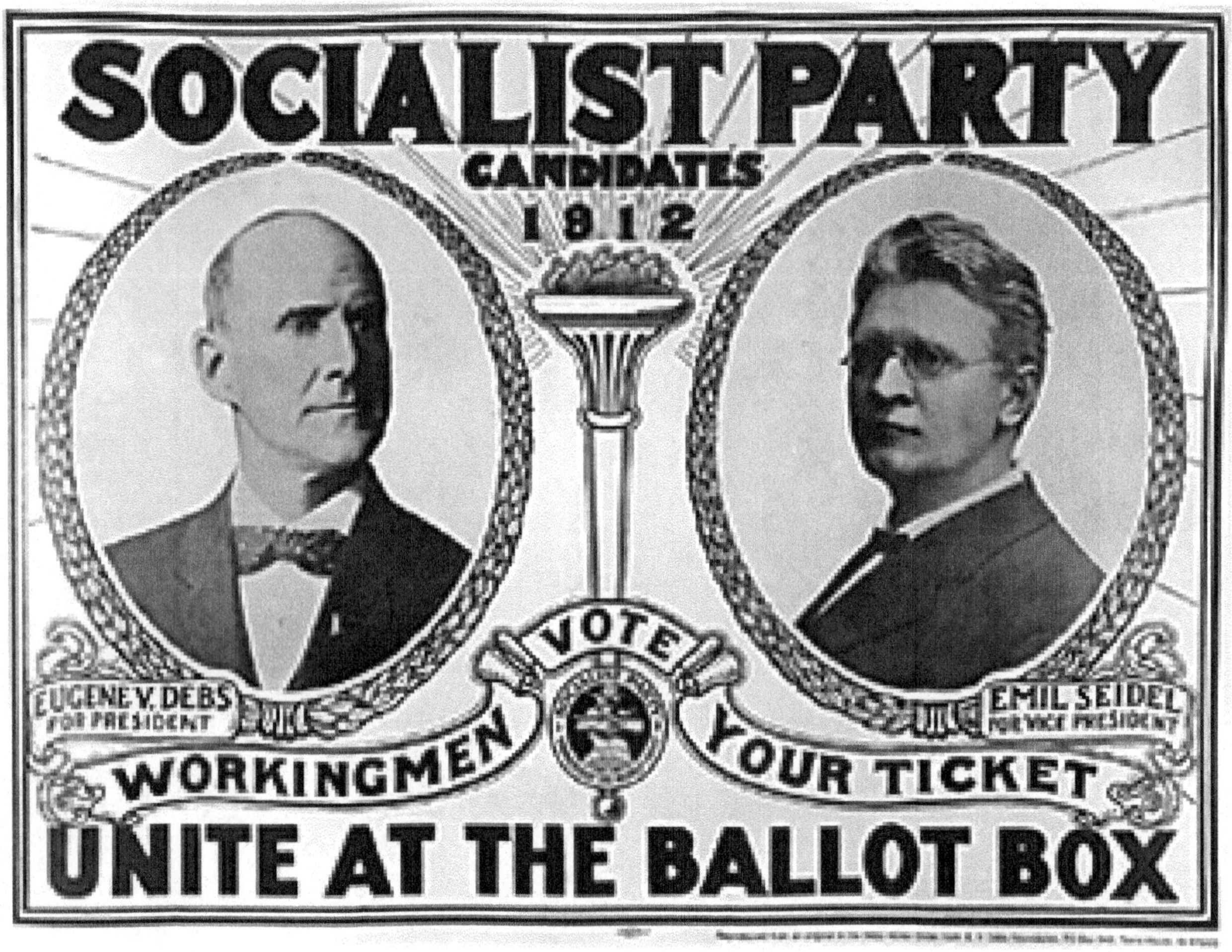

Campaign poster from his 1912 Presidential campaign, featuring Debs and Vice Presidential candidate Emil Seidel

Dirksen played a key role in passage of the 1964 Civil Rights Act.

Everett Dirksen: Original Analysis

U.S. Congressman and Senator

1896–1969

Overview

Everett McKinley Dirksen was born in Pekin, Illinois, in 1896. He fought in World War I, participated in a series of business ventures upon his return from Europe, and won a place on the Pekin City Council in 1926. After losing his first bid for a seat in the U.S. House of Representatives in 1930, Dirksen won the first of eight consecutive elections to Congress as a Republican in 1932. Forced by illness to retire from the House in 1948, Dirksen successfully challenged the incumbent Democratic senator from Illinois in 1950 to win a seat in the U.S. Senate. Dirksen's Republican colleagues elected him minority leader of the Senate in 1959, a post he held until his death on September 7, 1969.

Dirksen achieved prominence and influence as leader of the Senate Republicans during the presidential administrations of the Democrats John F. Kennedy and Lyndon B. Johnson. Although the Republicans were outnumbered two to one in the Senate during the 1960s, Senate rules in those years gave Dirksen and his colleagues in the minority great influence over legislation. Dirksen used his leadership position, his reputation for mastery of the legislative process, and his powers of persuasion to help Kennedy and Johnson pass such landmark acts as the 1963 Nuclear Test Ban Treaty, the Voting Rights Act of 1965, and the Civil Rights Act of 1968. The remarks he delivered on June 10, 1964, as Senate debate on the pending Civil Rights Act of 1964 ended, were widely credited with swinging enough Republican votes to ensure the passage of the bill. Dirksen was equally proud of his skill at keeping undesirable legislation off the books. He once explained, when asked in an interview what his most important accomplishment was, "Well, if I had to put it in the large, probably it would be my endeavors to stop legislation that was not in the public interest. Because I have followed the old precept of Gibbon, the great historian, who said 'Progress is made not so much by what goes on the statute book but rather by what is kept off and what is not put on'" (*ABC's Issues and Answers*).

Even outside the capitol, Dirksen's eloquence earned him celebrity status; in 1967 his patriotic recording *Gallant Men: Stories of American Adventure* won a Grammy Award. His practice of announcing the arrival of spring every year became a Washington tradition. Of his speaking style, Dirksen once explained to a reporter, "I always *extemporize.* I love the *diversions*, the *detours*. Without notes you may digress. You may dart. After you've taken on an interrupter, you don't have to flounder around the piece of paper, trying to find out where the hell you were" (qtd. in Shalit, p. 27). As such, full texts of Dirksen's remarks are relatively rare. But it is possible to identify the broad themes—freedom, the importance of the individual, the role of government, the primacy of the Constitution, and the role of Congress—from the notes and drafts he composed.

Explanation and Analysis of Documents

Dirksen appreciated the power of language more than do most people. He read widely in the classics throughout his life and practiced public speaking from an early age. In his high school yearbook (1913) his classmates called him "the man of many words" and someone who suffered hopelessly from "big worditus." Oratorical skill served Dirksen well, however, when he reached the pinnacle of his power in the U.S. Senate. As the leader of the minority party, he understood his responsibility to articulate the Republican message forcefully, consistently, and dramatically. In the days before cable television and the twenty-four-hour news cycle, Dirksen stood out as a master of the spoken word; his speeches attracted national press coverage. Five documents authored by Dirksen in the last years of his life illustrate the range of his interests, the fullness of his vocabulary, and the power of his words to persuade: his definition of "freedom," his reflections on his life influences and the permanence of change as he neared his seventh decade, his description of the foundations of good government, the draft of his remarks on behalf of the Civil Rights Act of 1964, and, finally, his celebration of the changing seasons and the arrival of spring.

♦ Observations on His Sixty-eighth Birth Anniversary

The year 1964 would prove pivotal in the nation's history. One of the first social events of the year was the celebration of Everett Dirksen's birthday on January 4, something of a tradition in the nation's capital. Four days later, Lyndon Johnson, the new president following the assassination of John F. Kennedy in November 1963, alerted the nation to his plans for an ambitious legislative agenda in his first State of the Union address. He called upon Congress to pass civil rights legislation, enact a tax cut, declare "all-out war" on human poverty and unemployment, address the health needs of older citizens, reform the transportation

system, improve the distribution of foreign aid, and build more homes, schools, libraries, and hospitals "than any single session of Congress in the history of our Republic." The president commanded Congress to "demonstrate effective legislative leadership by discharging the public business with clarity and dispatch, voting each important proposal up, or voting it down, but at least bringing it to a fair and final vote" (Johnson, pp. 112–113). Dirksen, who bore the leadership mantel for the thirty-three Republicans in the Senate, understood and accepted the challenge. Although the Republicans were outnumbered by the sixty-seven Democrats, their support would prove crucial to the passage of the cornerstones of what would become Johnson's Great Society initiatives.

Dirksen's birthday remarks of 1964 hint at the political action that would come. He begins by describing the state of the nation in 1896, the year of his birth. He notes the relatively modest cost of government in that year before highlighting a handful of developments from over the following five years. Dirksen draws from this recounting a lesson: "History moves in parallels or it repeats after a certain pattern." The situations in 1964 involving Hawaii, Puerto Rico, the Philippines, Cuba, and China seem to Dirksen to confirm his interpretation of history. But if history has patterns, the senator from Illinois also accepts that change is eternal. His is an optimistic view of the world. "One thing is certain," he proclaims. "Progress is the steadfast undramatic application of human life upon what is here." Dirksen believes that progress occurs in small steps that play out over time; he refers to "a time for every thing and a season for every purpose," from Ecclesiastes. This view informed his approach to legislation and to his leadership role in the Senate.

At this point in his remarks, Dirksen changes gears, using his birthday to reflect upon the influences in his life. He counts friendships—"the right friend with the right advice"—as a key to sustaining one's faith. He proceeds through some crucial aspects of his life: his decision to stay in school, his chance to go to West Point, his passion for culture and the performing arts, the challenge of ambition, the frustrations of public service, and his battle with illness. In these remembrances, it is possible to see some of Dirksen's essential qualities, such as his faith and religious conviction. He believes that all things are possible if one believes them to be, that fidelity to conscience trumps public criticism, that admitting to error is no flaw, and that friends will "help steer the bark of life out of the shadows and into the sunlight."

♦ Good Government Award Acceptance Speech

The American Good Government Society selected Dirksen to receive its Good Government Award in April 1964 during the height of the Senate filibuster on what would become the Civil Rights Act of 1964. The timing provides necessary context for understanding the tenor of the senator's remarks. The month began with Dirksen proposing forty amendments to the civil rights bill before the Senate in an

Time Line

1896	January 4	■ Everett McKinley Dirksen is born in Pekin, Illinois.
1914		■ Dirksen enrolls at the University of Minnesota.
1917		■ Dirksen leaves the university to enlist in the U.S. Army and is commissioned overseas, eventually becoming a second lieutenant in the 328th Field Artillery, 19th Balloon Corps.
1926		■ Dirksen is elected commissioner of finance for the city of Pekin.
1930		■ Dirksen is defeated in the Republican primary for the Illinois Sixteenth Congressional District seat.
1932		■ Dirksen wins election to the U.S. House of Representatives.
1943		■ More than thirty members of the House endorse Dirksen for the 1944 Republican nomination for president of the United States.
1948		■ Suffering from an eye ailment, Dirksen does not run for reelection to the House.
1950		■ Dirksen defeats the majority leader Scott W. Lucas for a seat in the U.S. Senate.
1957		■ Senate Republicans elect Dirksen as minority whip.
1959		■ Dirksen is elected Senate minority leader.
1963		■ Dirksen leads Republicans to support the Nuclear Test Ban Treaty.
1964	January 4	■ On the occasion of his sixty-eighth birthday, Dirksen talks about the influences on his life.
	April 30	■ Dirksen accepts the Good Government Award from the American Good Government Society.

Time Line

	June 10	■ On the Senate floor, Dirksen delivers the final speech before the vote to end the filibuster on the pending Civil Rights Act of 1964.
1965		■ Dirksen emphasizes "freedom" as a theme in his remarks.
		■ Dirksen leads Republicans to support the Voting Rights Act of 1965.
1968		■ Dirksen chairs the platform committee for the Republican National Convention.
1969	March	■ Dirksen delivers his annual message about the coming of spring.
	September 7	■ Dirksen dies following surgery at Walter Reed Army Hospital.

attempt to craft a bill that would attract support from liberal and conservative members of his party. There ensued much consternation among not only Republicans but also Democrats and the various interest groups backing the administration's version of the legislation. Dirksen held constant meetings, working piecemeal to strike the necessary compromise. He explained midmonth, "I have a fixed Pole Star to which I am pointed. This is, first, to get a bill; second, to get an acceptable bill; third, to get a workable bill; and finally, to get an equitable bill" (qtd. in MacNeil, p. 234).

Public pressure escalated, and much of it was directed at Senate minority leader Dirksen. African American interest groups, such as the National Association for the Advancement of Colored People and the Leadership Conference on Civil Rights, used protest demonstrations to attempt to speed Dirksen to act and accept the administration's bill unchanged. He refused to do so. By his own count, Dirksen received about a thousand letters per day dealing with civil rights. He was visited in his office by delegation upon delegation, some of which were, in his word, "imperious," demanding that the bill travel through the Senate unchanged—to which he responded that, as a legislator, his job was to perfect the measure. Meanwhile, negotiations involving Dirksen, his Republican colleagues, Senate Democrats, and the White House continued around the clock.

Against this backdrop, Dirksen accepted the Good Government Award and used the occasion to expound on the essence of good government. He expresses his basic optimism "that in our own land at least that government is good" because it respects the Constitution, respects the people it serves, observes the golden rule in foreign affairs, does not give in to unwise emotion, "exaults the dignity of man," stands firm for right and equal justice, and reveres the blessings of liberty as a legacy for future generations. He warns against the "arrogance of power and authority." Perhaps mindful of the tense situation facing the country at the time, Dirksen asserts that "courtesy and good manners are the plant food which nurture trust and confidence on the part of the people." He then addresses directly the public pressure surrounding the civil rights debate. He is fearful that "organized emotion" accounting only for the interests of a single group will threaten "the whole national interest." He calls on government to resist group pressure: "An unreasoning multitude can charge down first one extreme path and then another and this can lead to evil results." Dirksen concludes by restating his faith in the wisdom and power of the individual to preserve freedom. He wonders, "What then is the last best hope of good government here and elsewhere?" The simple answer is that it "lies in the hearts, the minds, and the souls of men who have been summoned" to serve in office. "The individual," he reasons, "is still the foundation stone of good government and the hope of social, political and economic progress."

♦ "An Idea Whose Time Has Come" Speech

The date June 10, 1964, may have marked the height of Everett Dirksen's influence and the moment of his highest achievement. The Senate had been debating the civil rights bill since March, as those opposed to the legislation had prevented an up-or-down vote by filibustering. Senate rules permitted such unlimited debate; the only way to end a filibuster required sixty-seven senators to invoke cloture—the limitation of debate. The majority Democrats were split on the matter, with southerners leading the filibuster, such that without Republican support the bill would never come to a vote. For weeks on end, Dirksen had labored to modify the bill so that his Republican colleagues would join northern Democrats to end the debate and pass the bill.

Precisely at 10:00am on June 10 the Senate was called to order. The gallery was packed, and 150 people lined the walls of the Senate chamber. All one hundred senators were present. After the logging of 534 hours, 1 minute, and 51 seconds, debate on the Civil Rights Act of 1964 was about to end. Dirksen had the last word. Understanding the importance of the event, Dirksen had worked carefully to craft his remarks. The basis for his three-thousand-word address that June morning was a quote from Victor Hugo, the nineteenth-century French author and human rights activist, who is said to have written, "There is one thing stronger than all the armies in the world; and that is an idea whose time has come." For Dirksen, passing the civil rights bill had become a moral responsibility whose time had come, and, he insists, "it will not be denied or resisted." In these notes, Dirksen supplies examples of other ideas, other public policy challenges, whose times had come—the Pure Food and Drug Act, civil service reform, and women's

suffrage among them. He then charts the contributions to the nation's war efforts by black Americans. Dirksen's references to the numbers of black professionals seem quaint, even racially tinged, in today's terms; even more so is the reference to "docile and tractable" "natives" who threw off the yoke of imperialism in their "yearning for independence and equality." But Dirksen, whose record in support of civil rights legislation could not be challenged, was no racist. Of the civil rights matter facing the nation, he intones, "It is here. It is on our doorstep. It will not go away. It is a challenge which must be met." He concludes in his notes, "Our problem as legislators is to deal with it realistically, fairly, equitably, practically and in the context of the rights of all citizens."

♦ Definition of Freedom

The meaning of freedom preoccupied Dirksen throughout his public career. His personal notebooks contain scores of entries on what freedom means, what threatens it, and how it should be protected. By the mid-1960s, at which time this version of his definition was written, his notion of freedom ultimately extended beyond the conventional view that freedom was, simply but profoundly, an inalienable, God-given right of all people. More than that, for Dirksen freedom "is a moral climate in which the greatest, truest freedom obtains when men are unconscious of freedom." Put differently, freedom fully occurs only when people do not fear the loss of it; in a sense, they should be able to take freedom for granted. Dirksen proceeds to enumerate the essential elements of such a moral climate, among them the freedoms to worship, to voice criticisms of men and government, to feel secure at home, to achieve prosperity by the dint of hard work, to respect others and feel respected by them, and to make mistakes and accept the results. He also acclaims flexibility to not conform and a shared sense of responsibility to maintain freedom "against the intense collective forces which are today at work to destroy it." Alas, the reader is left without the crescendo, what is "perhaps more important than any other thing"—Dirksen's notes end before the thought is complete.

♦ Final Spring Address

Beginning in the early 1960s, Dirksen took to the Senate floor annually to promote the adoption of the marigold as the nation's floral emblem. Although he was unsuccessful in persuading the Senate to pass the necessary enabling legislation, the occasion developed into a harbinger of seasonal change—and it afforded Dirksen the chance to wax eloquent (and theatrical) on two of his favorite themes: gardening and the arrival of spring as a time of rebirth and regeneration. The senator's last speech on the subject came in March 1969, only six months before his untimely death. He recorded a draft of the speech in a notebook.

After quoting the poet Percy Bysshe Shelley and contemplating the snow outside, Dirksen ruminates on plans for his garden as winter begins to fade. He catalogs the virtues of all manner of blossom, from impatiens to snapdragons. His fondness for language comes through in the word portrait he paints of tulips—"those stately soldiers in dark red who defy the elements and come nosing out of the soil almost as soon as Nature relents and permits the balmy breezes and the warm sun to kiss the earth into action." For Dirksen, spring serves as a metaphor for rebirth, as he reveals in asking a question from the book of Job, "If a man die, shall he live again?" Most certainly, opines Dirksen—as surely as the arrival of spring. Near the end, he imparts a larger meaning: "Let Kings and Emperors, Presidents and Senators permit highly important matters [to] furrow their brows. There must be a little time to draw back and think just a little about the noblest creations from the hand of a generous Creator—the endless variety of flowers."

Impact and Legacy

If Everett M. Dirksen is to be remembered, it will be for the influence he exercised in leading the Republicans in the U.S. Senate through the ambitious and far-reaching legislative agenda of the remarkable decade of the 1960s. In no small measure his influence derived from his use of language and the power of his speech. He was an orator whose freewheeling style allowed him to weave personal stories, humor, and historical asides as well as whimsy on every subject imaginable into speeches of profound substance. A 1962 *Time* cover story captured his essence:

He speaks, and the words emerge in a soft, sepulchral baritone. They undulate in measured phrases, expire in breathless wisps. He fills his lungs and blows word-rings like smoke. The sentences curl upward.... Now he conjures moods of mirth, now of sorrow. He rolls his bright blue eyes heavenward. In funeral tones, he paraphrases the Bible ... and church bells peal. 'Motherhood,' he whispers, and grown men weep. 'The Flag,' he bugles, and everybody salutes. (p. 27)

History does not recognize legislative leaders, particularly leaders of the minority party, on a par with presidents. Yet Dirksen merited much commendation during his years in Congress. Without him there might have been no Nuclear Test Ban Treaty of 1963, no Civil Rights Act of 1964, and no Voting Rights Act of 1965. Also significant was Dirksen's strong support of President Lyndon Johnson in the conduct of the Vietnam War. He demonstrated that a determined minority could work with the majority to meet the public policy challenges of the day and that grace, civility, and friendship could characterize the partnership. Upon learning of Dirksen's death, President Richard Nixon stated, "Everett Dirksen was one of a kind—and a remarkably likable man. To politics and government he brought a dedication matched by few and a style and eloquence matched by no political leader in our time. He had his greatest moments as the leader of the loyal opposition. In the history of that role in the Congress, he had unequaled influence and accomplishment" (Nixon, p. 707).

Key Sources

The papers of Everett M. Dirksen reside at the Dirksen Congressional Center in Pekin, Illinois. The collection includes documents, photographs, films, tapes, books, and artifacts. The bulk of the material relates to Dirksen's career in the Senate, with scattered references to the years before. The center's Web site offers information about the senator (http://www.dirksencenter.org/print_emd_features.htm) and includes an online guide to his collection (http://www.dirksencenter.org/print_collections_dirksen.htm), some of which is digitized. Dirksen was writing a memoir at the time of his death; covering his life up until his election to the Senate in 1950, it was published in 1998 as *The Education of a Senator*. The Senate Historical Office included the text of Dirksen's speech of June 10, 1964, as one of forty-six historically significant speeches in Robert C. Byrd, ed., *The Senate, 1789–1989*, vol. 3, *Classic Speeches, 1830–1993* (1994). Dirksen was interviewed by Edward P. Morgan for *ABC's Issues and Answers* on July 3, 1966. The transcript is among the Everett M. Dirksen Papers.

Essential Quotes

"One thing is eternal. That is change. One thing is certain—progress is the steadfast undramatic application of human life upon what is here."

(Observations on His Sixty-eighth Birth Anniversary)

"Service is the essence of one's labors and efforts in the public domain."

(Good Government Award Acceptance Speech)

"Good government calls for devotion to the Constitution."

(Good Government Award Acceptance Speech)

"In the whole American scheme the dignity of man and the divinity of human personality are the very foundation stones of our destiny as a free people."

(Good Government Award Acceptance Speech)

"Whether men serve by appointment or by election to public office, it is they who finally determine whether government is good, sound, just and prudent. If they succumb to the lures of public office, if they are venal and self-centered, if they are cynical, if they are cowardly in the face of challenge, if principle means nothing, then indeed are the hopes for good government rendered to ashes."

(Good Government Award Acceptance Speech)

"The idea of equal opportunity to vote, to secure schooling, to have public funds equitably spent, to have public parks and playgrounds

Essential Quotes

equally accessible, to have an equal opportunity for a livelihood without discrimination, to be equal before the law—the hour for this idea has come and it will not be denied or resisted."

("An Idea Whose Time Has Come" Speech)

"Our problem as legislators is to deal with it [civil rights legislation] realistically, fairly, equitably, practically and in the context of the rights of all citizens."

("An Idea Whose Time Has Come" Speech)

"All this and so much more with the Resurrection of Spring. Could the Resurrection have come in any season except Spring? It makes me think of the age-old question which Job in his misery propounded to his friends, 'If a man die, shall he live again?' Surely he will for the earth becomes vital all over again with Spring."

(Final Spring Address)

"But it is something more than a right. It is a moral climate in which the greatest, truest freedom obtains when men are unconscious of freedom."

(Definition of Freedom)

Further Reading

■ Articles

Fonsino, Frank. "Everett McKinley Dirksen: The Roots of an American Statesman," *Journal of the Illinois State Historical Society* 76 (Spring 1983): 17–34.

"The Leader." *Time*, September 14, 1962. Available online. Time Web site. http://www.time.com/time/magazine/article/0,9171,874437,00.html.

Shalit, Gene. "Everett McKinley Dirksen: A Mighty Minority of One," In *Look* (July 26, 1966): 26–30.

■ Books

Dirksen, Louella, with Norma Lee Browning. *The Honorable Mr. Marigold: My Life with Everett Dirksen*. Garden City, N.Y.: Doubleday, 1972.

Hulsey, Byron C. *Everett Dirksen and His Presidents: How a Senate Giant Shaped American Politics*. Lawrence: University Press of Kansas, 2000.

Loomis, Burdett. "Everett M. Dirksen: The Consummate Minority Leader." In *First among Equals: Outstanding Senate Leaders of the Twentieth Century*, ed. Richard A. Baker and Roger H. Davidson, Washington, D.C.: Congressional Quarterly, 1991.

Johnson, Lyndon B. "Annual Message to the Congress on the State of the Union." *Public Papers of the President: Lyndon B. Johnson* Washington, D.C.: U.S. Government Printing Office, 1965.

MacNeil, Neil. *Dirksen: Portrait of a Public Man*. New York: World Publishing Company, 1970.

Nixon, Richard. "Statement on the Death of Senator Everett McKinley Dirksen of Illinois" In *Public Papers of the President: Richard Nixon*. Washington, D.C.: U.S. Government Printing Office, 1971.

Schapsmeier, Edward L., and Frederick H. Schapsmeier. *Dirksen of Illinois: Senatorial Statesman*. Urbana: University of Illinois Press, 1985.

—*Frank H. Mackaman*

Questions for Further Study

1. Although the legislative success of the civil rights movement is usually credited to Democrats, the truth is more complicated. Many southern Democrats of the time opposed an end to segregation, and much of the key civil rights legislation might have failed without the support of Republicans such as Dirksen. Discuss the Republican role in the passage of the Civil Rights Act of 1964, with a special emphasis on Dirksen's speech "An Idea Whose Time Has Come."

2. Critique the "definition of freedom" Dirksen offers in the document of that name. Is it true, as he says, that "the greatest, truest freedom obtains when men are unconscious of freedom"? What about the other principles he puts forth in the second paragraph, in which he discusses freedom "in more concrete terms"? How did Dirksen's definition of freedom develop over time?

3. Consider the flower imagery in Dirksen's final spring address. With regard to the marigold, his choice for the national floral emblem, he establishes a direct political metaphor between the flower and the United States itself. But what about some of the other varieties mentioned—for instance, tulips or snapdragons? Examine specific qualities of those plants and discuss what sorts of political comparisons he might have made with regard to them.

Observations on His Sixty-eighth Birth Anniversary

1964

The year was 1896. The Time was January 4. That day I came into this world. I had only three problems—how to strategically get a big toe in my mouth, how to operate a non-nuclear milk bottle, and how to dispose of wind on the stomach without alka seltzer. My father christened me McKinley and my twin brother after the great Speaker Thomas Reed.

In that year, total expenditures were slightly over 500 million and revenues enough more to provide a surplus of 45 million. The public debt even after the War with Spain was only 1 and ¼ Billion.

At age 10 months, McKinley defeated Bryan. At age ONE gold was discovered in Alaska; at age TWO we went to war with Spain and by Treaty of Paris we secured Guam, Philippines, Puerto Rico, Cuba was evacuated, Hawaii was annexed the following year, and an open door with China was proclaimed. At age FIVE we put down the Boxers in China and Major Walter Reed and his associates conquered yellow fever. When I was FIVE, McKinley was assassinated.

History moves in parallels or it repeats after a certain pattern.

Hawaii is a state in the Union; Puerto Rico is struggling for status; the Philippines are independent; CUBA is back on the front page; the great hulk of CHINA is stirring; mankind still struggles for PEACE. We went to the gold standard when I was FIVE. We went off in 1934 when I was 38. Somehow the same problems recur over and over as if mankind were on a treadmill.

There were depressions before McKinley; there have been depressions since. There were wars before him; there have been wars since his day. There were dictators before him and a brutal one—General Weyler—during the war with Spain. There have been dictators since. Each generation has its devils. Only the names seem to change. Consider China, the Soviet Union, the Communist Bloc, the Latin nations and see how closely this pattern is followed.

One thing is eternal. That is change.

One thing is certain—progress is the steadfast undramatic application of human life upon what is here. The atom has been here since the dawn of Time. Only in our generation was it fractured and put to work.

There is a time for every thing and a season for every purpose. When we forget this, our efforts often prove fruitless and abortive.

What then is LIFE'S greatest asset? It is the steadfast friendship of friends who come at an appointed time to sustain one's faith. In every period, the right friend with the right advice is there.

What made me not only stay in school but want to stay in school when it was fashionable to drop out after eighth grade? It was my mother.

Who urged me always to make my own decisions, such as the one which confronted me after high school—to go or not to go to West Point and become a soldier? It was my mother.

Who told me to hark to Paul's admonition to Timothy, when the latter was wearying of his work? Paul wrote to him, "Let no man despise thy youth." It was an older brother.

Who sustained my interest in culture and in the performing arts? It was an inseparable high school classmate.

Who persuaded me that "If thou canst believe, all things are possible to him that believeth"? It was a country preacher with an Oxford accent.

Who was most instrumental in finding the right road? My wife, of course, but there was still another. He was a clerk in a haberdashery.

Who sustained me to follow a bold course and let the chips fall where they would? Those same two.

Who caused me to cast my first vote as I did in the House of Representatives and reap an avalanche of mail and messages threatening my political extinction just as I was started on a Federal political career. It was an ass't cashier in a bank who as I left for Washington for the first time, said to me, "It will not be nearly so important how you vote when you go down to the Big League but rather why you voted as you did."

Who provided the shoulder on which to weep when I was frustrated and could not see the sun? It was the building manager where I had my office, and my wife.

Who sustained me in my course when I thought I was right but contemporary opinion thought I was wrong? It was my wife.

Document Text

Who could and did persuade me when I was wrong and also persuaded me to back up? It was a member of my staff.

Who sustained me in dark hours with an unrelenting fidelity? One was a customers man in a brokerage firm; another was onetime a Greek taxi driver; still a third was one old enough to be my father for whom I had once performed a slight favor without hope or thought of recompense.

Who sustained me when confronted with a decision whether to have or not to have an eye removed? It was the Big, Unfailing Friend in the Sky.

Always and always and always, if one will be meek, there is an unfailing friend at just the right time to help steer the bark of life out of the shadows and into the sunlight.

Glossary

ass't:	assistant
At age 10 months, McKinley defeated Bryan:	a reference to the election of 1896, held when Dirksen was less than a year old, which saw the victory of William McKinley over William Jennings Bryan
Boxers:	members of a Chinese secret society that in 1900–1901 attempted to drive foreigners out of China, a rebellion put down by forces from the United States and seven other nations
General Weyler:	Valeriano Weyler Nicolau (1838–1930), Spanish military governor of Cuba in the 1890s who is said to have coined the term *concentration camp*
gold standard:	a system in which the value of a nation's currency is tied to that of gold, a principle abandoned by the United States in the early 1930s
have an eye removed:	reference to the fact that during the late 1940s Dirksen suffered from an eye ailment but refused a physician's suggestion that he have the eye surgically removed
"If thou canst believe, all things are possible …":	a statement made by Jesus and quoted in Mark 9:23
"Let no man despise thy youth":	a quote from the apostle Paul's advice to his young associate Timothy in 1 Timothy 4:12
There is a time for every thing and a season for every purpose:	loose rendition of a quote from Ecclesiastes 3:1
Thomas Reed:	Speaker of the House (1889–1891, 1895–1899) and a fierce opponent, within the Republican Party, of William McKinley

Document Text

Good Government Award Acceptance Speech

1964

I am grateful for the honor which you bestow upon me tonight and can only humbly hope that in modest measure I may through my public service have merited this expression of trust and esteem.

The Award after all symbolizes service to my constituency, my country, and to mankind. Service is the essence of one's labors and efforts in the public domain.

I am signally and doubly honored that the distinguished Majority Leader of the United States Senate should be present tonight to make the Award. Nothing could compliment me more than that he should take time from his busy schedule and share in this ceremony.

The very nature and title of the Award at once raises a question as to what constitutes good government. On this occasion one may very appropriately say that in our own land at least that government is good; it cherishes and practices a strict respect for the Constitution which brought this very government into being; it through its officers and agents maintains a wholesome and respectful regard for the people from whom government derives its power; it exhibits courtesy and good manners in all of its dealings with the people at home and the nations abroad; it is not moved to hasty and ill-advised action by the emotions of any given moment; it in the language of the ancient law shows restraint and does not follow a multitude to do evil; it charts a course calculated to be beneficial now and in the future to all of its citizens; it exaults the dignity of man and the dignity of human personality; it observes the golden rule in all of its dealings with other governments in the family of nations; it stands firm for right and for equal justice under the law; it is ever mindful that the blessings of liberty spring from the everlasting covenant between the instant generation and those generations who have gone before and those who will come after our day and time. This is indeed a king sized order in an unstable and feverish world.

All too often we take our Constitution and its vast and rewarding benefits for granted. It is the oldest written Constitution in this entire world. It is the product of a benign destiny and of inspired man. Its durability is the very rock of our salvation. Its flexibility has carried us through every storm in the life of the Republic. Its wisdom is a thing of magic and without it and without those dedicated people who gave it force and flesh in other days who shall say what our destiny might have been. Good government calls for devotion to the Constitution.

The arrogance of power and authority so easily besets many persons in high places and how easy it is for an attitude of mind to develop which treats the very people who are this government and who are the fountainhead of all power as if they were servants and not masters in the house of government.

Courtesy and good manners are the plant food which nurture trust and confidence on the part of the people and ever fortifies the hope that good government among us shall never perish.

Organized emotion can become a potent force in shaping public policy whether in the foreign or domestic realm. Too often this force takes account only of the interest of the group for whom benefits are sought and not the whole national interest. More and more good government for all of the people requires that group pressures be resisted and group demands be very closely screened. An unreasoning multitude can charge down first one extreme path and then another and this can lead to evil results. This is not the road to good, sound, durable government. It can be achieved only by a dispassionate consideration of the well-being of all of the people.

In the whole American scheme the dignity of man and the divinity of human personality are the very foundation stones of our destiny as a free people.

In some quarters these attributes are regarded with cynical amusement, yet without a proper regard for this exaulted station of man how can there be good government in its best sense and how can we effectively employ our resources, talents and ideals in the cause of a free world?

Liberty is being extinguished or fenced in in so many areas of the world and all too often the schemes to impair human freedom are successful, for in exchange for their liberties people are lured by a mess of material pottage.

The real shining hallmark of good government is a decent and wholesome respect for the people's liberties and to truly serve the cause of good government means a constant and dedicated effort to preserve freedom.

Document Text

So as one surveys the nations of the world and the state of mankind, as one contemplates the intranquility and friction, as one assesses the relentless assault upon man's freedom, as one takes thought of the fears which abound in so many people as they behold their own government, one must conclude that perhaps good government is an exception rather than the rule.

What then is the last best hope of good government here and elsewhere? The answer is simple indeed. It lies in the hearts, the minds, and the souls of men who have been summoned either to appointive or elective office to give to government at every level durable purposes, attainable ideals, wholesome administration and devoted effort.

Whether men serve by appointment or by election to public office, it is they who finally determine whether government is good, sound, just and prudent. If they succumb to the lures of public office, if they are venal and self-centered, if they are cynical, if they are cowardly in the face of challenge, if principle means nothing, then indeed are the hopes for good government rendered to ashes.

The individual is still the foundation stone of good government and the hope of social, political and economic progress.

Glossary

inspired man:	humanity under the influence and inspiration of God
Majority Leader of the Senate:	Mike Mansfield of Oklahoma
a mess of … pottage:	a reference to Genesis 25:29–34, in which Esau gave up his birthright as firstborn son in exchange for a meal of lentil stew offered by his brother, Jacob
venal:	capable of being bribed

"An Idea Whose Time Has Come" Speech

1964

It is said on the night he died, Victor Hugo made this closing entry in his diary: "There is one thing stronger than all the armies in the world; and that is an idea whose time has come." Later it was put in more dramatic form: "Greater than the tread of mighty armies is an idea whose hour has come." This is the issue with which we have been wrestling for months. There will be continued resistance for one reason or another. There will in some quarters be a steadfast refusal to come to grips with what seems an inevitable challenge which must be met. The idea of equal opportunity to vote, to secure schooling, to have public funds equitably spent, to have public parks and playgrounds equally accessible, to have an equal opportunity for a livelihood without discrimination, to be equal before the law—the hour for this idea has come and it will not be denied or resisted.

It is not the first time that an idea has pushed aside contemporary thinking and moved to the top. Long years ago in this Senate, the idea of a Pure Food & Drug Act was resisted in language which today sounds quaint. But it would not be denied. Long years ago, the Civil Service and merit system was decried and opposed but the shot which took the life of President Garfield suddenly opened the way and it would not be denied. Long years ago, even President Wilson thought that a Federal Child Labor Act was absurd but it would not be resisted. Long years ago, suffrage for women was regarded with genuine amusement but it would not be stopped. Even as these challenges faced the Senate in other days, so now we are faced with an idea whose hour has come.

What then are the forces which conspired to bring this idea to fruition in our day and time? There are many and perhaps we have failed to re-examine history with proper perspective. Let us go back to an orientation point.

June 28th, 1964, is an anniversary date. It will be so to millions but perhaps they have forgotten. It was just fifty years before on that date that the Archduke Ferdinand of Austria went to visit the newly acquired province of Bosnia. The people were sullen and angry. His journey took him and his morganatic wife to the little town of Sarajevo where he paid his respects at the city hall. Shortly thereafter, while entering his motorcar, a young man suddenly appeared with a pistol in his hand. He fired but two shots. Both proved fatal and the archduke and his wife died almost instantly.

The news was duly recorded on the front page but to us it made little impression at the time. Life was so sweet and delightful, so tranquil and diverting. Mary Pickford was then America's movie sweetheart and Maude Adams, Laurette Taylor and Ethel Barrymore were charming audiences over the land. Jack Johnson retained his heavyweight title and Billy Sunday was doing then what Billy Graham does now. The Underwood Tariff bill was the top political issue of the day and Champ Clark was Speaker of the House. There were 50,000 flivvers on the highway and it was the year that Ford announced the $5 eight hour day and that one could buy a Ford in any color so long as it was black. Mexico was in turmoil, Woodrow Wilson was in the White House and it was the first year for the Federal income tax.

But the ghost of Sarajevo was to haunt us. Soon, the Legions began to roll toward national frontiers, there were charges and countercharges and Europe was in the grip of conflict. The Kaiser's submarines were soon to prowl the seven seas and torpedo vessels in his efforts to humble Britain. As destiny would have it the Falaba, the Gulflight and the Lusitania were to become the victims of a torpedo and in the inevitable surge of events, Woodrow Wilson stood before a tense Congress and asked for a Declaration of war.

That war was to see millions of young Americans, white and non-white, don uniforms in the cause of Democracy. The record shows that 473,000 young negroes served in World War I, many of whom saw overseas service. There they were to observe that there was no color line and no discrimination and they were to return ultimately and bring those observations with them. That was nearly a half-century ago. Those young men, if alive, are in the sixties. Many of them are fathers and grandfathers and surely, as is the nature of a soldier, they were to recite their adventures to their children and grandchildren and not the least of their recitals would deal with the complete equality which they enjoyed abroad in uniform.

But 23 years after the armistice which concluded hostilities in World War I, came Pearl Harbor and

once more a generation of young Americans marched to the four corners of the earth to halt the march of Fascism and the liquidation of human freedom. A total of 16,112,566 Americans served in that struggle and of that number 1,611,000 were negroes.

There came in our time an effort to dominate the little country of Korea.... At the time, it was deemed nothing more than a policing action. But the cemeteries in Asia attest to its magnitude in blood and treasure. Before we were through, 5,700,000 young men served in that police action and 570,000 were negroes.

It is interesting that in every one of these conflicts, 10% of the men in uniform were colored.

But those who served in World War I are not only fathers but grandfathers. In places where they served, they noted the lack of discrimination on account of color and so the story must obviously have been told and retold to children and grandchildren.

The men of color—and women also—who served in World War II have become the fathers and mothers of families. They served in areas all over the world and particularly in countries where color was no bar and discrimination was unknown. Their children are the young negroes of today and from the lips of fathers and mothers, they have heard the story of non-discrimination elsewhere except in the land which sent them forth to fight for freedom and a free world.

All this has been a part of the incubation of an idea, more powerful than armies, whose time has come.

But other things have happened. There was a time with the negro was not particularly considered as a professional man. His role in life was generally accepted as a manual worker, a porter, a stevedore, a truck driver, a section hand on a railroad. But times have changed.

Today there are 2440 negro lawyers and judges and 4996 negro doctors; today there are 4193 negro engineers in all lines of engineering; today there are 2341 negro dentists and 3614 accountants; today there are 122 negro architects and 81 aviation pilots and navigators; today there are 325 negro actors and 1886 artists and art teachers; today there are 5869 negro college professors and instructors and 90,286 negro elementary school teachers; today there are 33,581 negro instructors in secondary schools and an additional 8272 not listed in these classifications. These are trained, educated people who for years have been contemplating the question of equality, freedom and discrimination and their thinking has assisted in the incubation of the idea whose time has come.

There are other factors which have contributed to this long inexorable process of incubation and gestation. Consider Africa, long the happy hunting ground of colonialism. But a generation ago, there one found the Belgians in the Congo, the French in northern and central Africa, the British in southern Africa, the Portuguese in south west Africa, Spain in northern Africa, the Germans in central Africa.

The natives took account of the living standards which freedom and industrial development could provide for a people. Docile and tractable as they were under the direction of the white empire builders from over the world, the yearning for independence and equality began to stir in the souls of even illiterate people. The throb of nationalism advanced from a hope to a murmur. The murmur became louder and soon expressed itself in a demand. The demand reached a crescendo and became stronger than the white man's soldiers and it would not be stayed. It became an idea whose time had come and today, what was so often referred to as The Dark Continent is in the main a continent of independent Republics holding the balance of power in the General Assembly of the United Nations. These and many other factors have quietly and almost imperceptibly nursed an idea whose time has come, the idea of freedom, equality before the law and equality of opportunity.

It is here. It is on our doorstep. It will not go away. It is a challenge which must be met. To think in terms of old forms is futile. To think provincially in terms of a state where the problem and the challenge has not reached substantial political dimensions is to ignore the overall challenge itself and what it means to our common country. We deal not with some economic platitude or with an abstruse unrevealing plank in a political platform. We deal with a throbbing idea whose time has come.

It has penetrated the conscience of the clergy and insinuated itself into the sense of fair play of the youth of the land. It has broken down the barriers in labor organizations and a host of other groups. Its time has come.

Our problem as legislators is to deal with it realistically, fairly, equitably, practically and in the context of the rights of all citizens.

Glossary

Archduke Ferdinand:	Franz Ferdinand, heir to the throne of the Austro-Hungarian Empire, who was assassinated on June 28, 1914, marking the start of World War I
color line:	a policy of politically, socially, or economically separating whites from nonwhites
colored:	though considered racially insensitive today, a term referring to black people that was common at the time
the Falaba, the Gulflight and the Lusitania:	three civilian ships, all carrying Americans, sunk by the Germans before the United States entered World War I
flivvers:	a slang term for cars in the early years of the automotive age
the Kaiser:	Wilhelm II, Germany's ruler during World War I
morganatic:	referring to a marriage between a person of noble or royal birth and a commoner, who agrees not to share any titles or properties or pass those on to their children
negro:	though considered racially insensitive today, a term for African Americans considered appropriate, even progressive, in 1964
platitude:	a statement that is neither original nor particularly meaningful, often intended for the purpose of hiding rather than revealing truth
policing action:	the official description of the Korean conflict (1950–1953), which did not involve an actual declaration of war by the United States
the shot which took the life of President Garfield:	reference to the shooting of James A. Garfield on July 2, 1881, and his death on September 19
stevedore:	someone whose job is to load and unload ships

Document Text

Definition of Freedom

ca. 1965

I have skimmed through book after book on the subject of liberty and freedom. They deal with the history, the evolution, the philosophical basis, the fruits, and the hopes of freedom. They compare civilizations, analyze the political, social and economic aspects of freedom and finally conclude as did Thomas Jefferson in the Declaration of Independence that it is an inalienable, God-given right of all men. But it is something more than a right. It is a moral climate in which the greatest, truest freedom obtains when men are unconscious of freedom.

But to put it in more concrete terms, freedom is a moral climate in which … men write … and speak even critically if so disposed of their fellow men and their government; a climate in which men without hesitation and without fear of penalty may praise or assail their government for its achievements or failures; a climate in which man feels secure in his own home against unauthorized or unjustified [intrusions]; a climate in which incentive and ambition flourishes and he can by his own efforts enrich himself while providing goods and services which enrich his fellow men and expand their enjoyment of living; a climate in which he is free to choose what and where to buy, what to eat and wear, where and when to work or not to work; a climate in which he may pursue his own good, in his own way so long as he accords that same freedom to all others; a climate in which he is free to make mistakes in judgment and accept the results of those mistakes; a climate in which the property he may accumulate through his own frugality and diligence is secure against seizure and trespass except through due legal process; a climate in which his conduct and behavior is not made to conform to some collective pattern; a climate in which he is aware of his duty to maintain that freedom against the intense collective forces which are today at work to destroy it.

Glossary

inalienable: not to be taken away

made to conform to some collective pattern: forced to fit in with everyone else, as in an authoritarian or totalitarian society

obtains: exists or comes to pass

Document Text

Final Spring Address

1969

Long ago the poet Shelley wrote, "O, Wind, If Winter comes, can Spring be far behind?" It takes a careless spirit to write that. It was written on March 1. I look out the window and it is snowing. Four inches of snow already lie on the earth's bosom. It's the white, wet type that clings to the branches and transforms the outdoors into a winter Disneyland. Small matter. Before me on the desk are a half dozen seed catalogues. With them is a chart of the garden areas to be seeded and planted. Here then is a feast for the eyes, the mind, the soul. If only one could get results to even reasonably approximate what the seed catalogue artist has depicted.

First off, there is a shady spot which gets virtually no sun. Obviously, it's a place for the blue ageratum and for impatiens. They do quite well in full shade and what a color combination they really are. Then the humble nasturtium which grows most anywhere with half a chance. It's not a truly showy creation but as cut flowers they are indeed a comfort to the soul.

Come now to the tulips—those stately soldiers in dark red who defy the elements and come nosing out of the soil almost as soon as Nature relents and permits the balmy breezes and the warm sun to kiss the earth into action. How good that they come so early in the Spring. The daffodils, narcissus are not far behind if at all. They can pop their gorgeous yellows before one really expects it and they add such a joyous note to early Spring.

But away from the catalogues for a moment to think of some other things. It's time to prune back the tea roses, cut away the dead wood and make ready for the grandeur of the roses in all colors. Is there anything more beautiful but in thinking about flowers? I continue to class the rose as a shrub rather than a flower. The same goes for the azaleas and camellias.

Where do we put the stately snapdragons that stand like gorgeous sentinels and withstand … the bugs. The garden closest the roadway is best. Every passerby can enjoy them and what exquisite cut flowers they are for all occasions. The zinnias must have full sun. Somehow, more than any other flower, they drink in the bright sunlight and heat and transform them into deep, majestic colors. Peach, salmon, deep red, yellow, ivory—you name it and the zinnia produces it with their huge, many-petaled heads. But they should have some edging. That is not a difficult problem. The petunia is just the dish—singles and doubles, plain blue, white, crimson, peppermint stick, candy stripe in vast variety. How hardy they are and how determined they are not to be outdone by anything in the flowery kingdom.

A momentary detour to look at the climbing roses. They wintered well but they must be tied up. What a rare diversion that will be. But here are the clematis, both regular and hybrid. How dead they seem. But wait a little for the caress of Spring and suddenly there they are—red, blue, and white. All this and so much more with the Resurrection of Spring. Could the Resurrection have come in any season except Spring? It makes me think of the age-old question which Job in his misery propounded to his friends, "If a man die, shall he live again?" Surely he will, for the earth becomes vital all over again with Spring. But I must not forget the marigold. For ten years I have sought to persuade Congress to adopt the marigold as our National floral emblem. Some prefer the rose … or the carnation or the petunia or the violet or the daffodil or some other bloom. But the marigold is native to this hemisphere, grows in every one of the 50 states, evidences a robustness against the elements, bugs, heat and weather unequaled by any other flower. Let Kings and Emperors, Presidents and Senators permit highly important matters [to] furrow their brows. There must be a little time to draw back and think just a little about the noblest creations from the hand of a generous Creator—the endless variety of flowers. Was it not the Galilean who said, "Consider the lilies of the field, how they grow; they toil not, neither do they spin: And yet I say unto you, that even Solomon in all his glory was not arrayed like one of these." And the flowers are there for every man, woman and child for the asking.

Glossary

careless:	carefree
"Consider the lilies of the field ...":	a reference to Jesus' words in Matthew 6:28
furrow their brows:	take on a facial expression suggesting worry or stress
the Galilean:	Jesus (of Nazareth, in the Galilee)
"If a man die, shall he live again?":	a quote from Job 14:14
Job:	principal figure in the Old Testament book by that name
Shelley:	the poet Percy Bysshe Shelley (1792–1822), whose "Ode to the West Wind" Dirksen quotes

Senators Mike Mansfield (left) and Dirksen conversing in 1967. By White House Photographic Office.

Stephen Arnold Douglas by Mathew Brady.

Stephen A. Douglas: Original Analysis

U.S. Congressman, Senator, and Presidential Candidate

1813–1861

Overview

Stephen Arnold Douglas was born in Brandon, Vermont, in 1813. In his early years he lived in upstate New York, where his father practiced as a physician. Up to the age of fourteen, Douglas received an excellent education at the private Canandaigua Academy but was plunged into poverty by the death of his father. He was apprenticed to a cabinetmaker by his mother, who could not support him in any other way. As soon as he could, he moved west to find better opportunities, as so many Americans did throughout the nineteenth century, and settled in Illinois, which was then on the frontier. Douglas spent the school year of 1833 to 1834 as a teacher while studying law; he was admitted to the bar the following summer and immediately began to practice law. He also set out on his political career, becoming a district attorney that same year (at age twenty-one). He traveled a meteoric course through the political ranks of the Illinois government, as a state legislator (1836), secretary of state (1840), and associate justice of the Illinois Supreme Court (1841). Then he moved on to Washington, D.C., first as a U.S. representative (1843) and next as senator (1847). (Senators at that time were elected by state legislatures.) Douglas was called the "Little Giant," which referred to both his small stature (five feet, four inches) and his vast political abilities and influence. He seems to have had some natural instinct for politics. He was a master at reaching political compromise that both sides found advantageous, without ever revealing his own political agenda or revealing it only after the fact. To Douglas, impassioned political discourse that broadcast the speaker's feelings was a distasteful and self-indulgent display.

As a congressman, Douglas became chairman of the House Committee on the Territories and chair of the same committee in the Senate in 1847. At the time, this was the most powerful committee in Congress because it controlled the vast unorganized western territories that had entered the United States through the Louisiana Purchase, the Mexican-American War (1846–1848), and the Oregon Treaty with Great Britain (1846), which included about two-thirds of the land area of the continental United States. It also controlled the future disposition of what was already one of the most contentious issues in America, the question of slavery. Douglas was to take the lead role in trying to resolve sectional rivalry between slave and free states in the Compromise of 1850 and finally through the doctrine of popular sovereignty, which meant letting each territory decide for itself, in the Kansas-Nebraska Act of 1854.

Douglas's great rival, Abraham Lincoln, represented a less compromising position on slavery, although, before the Civil War, even he did not envision doing more in the foreseeable future than limiting the spread of slavery outside the states where it already existed. Douglas won reelection to the Senate over Lincoln in 1859 precisely because he supported a compromise position that the Illinois legislature believed would not heighten already strained national tensions. However, Douglas's propensity for compromise threw the presidential election to Lincoln in 1860. Douglas managed to become the Democratic nominee, but his refusal to support a platform that forced slavery on all the territories (in line with the *Dred Scott* decision of the Supreme Court in 1857) split the convention, with the result that southern Democrats ran the sitting vice president, John Breckinridge, as a second Democrat candidate. The split meant that Douglas carried electoral votes only from New Jersey and Missouri and that Lincoln was elected by a majority in the Electoral College, but with only 40 percent of the popular vote. Douglas lived until June 1861 but was repulsed by the extreme southern position that finally resulted in secession and the Civil War. In the end he supported Lincoln's decision to preserve the Union by military force.

Explanation and Analysis of Documents

Douglas represents the height of traditional rhetoric. He was able to speak for three hours or more using forms and styles of speaking and gesturing going back to the Greeks and Romans. People came to see Douglas not only because of his political importance but also because he was a great performer. He lived in an age when communication was face to face between men (women as yet played no role in politics) with no media intervening. He spoke to and held in rapt attention crowds of thousands with no microphones, no teleprompter, no giant video screens, and often in the open air, without even the acoustics of a lecture hall to support his voice. As a consequence, his audience—quite different from the modern American electorate—was attuned to the subtle nuance of his discourse and was entertained by his turns of phrase and rhetorical invention. He was as adroit at answering questions from the audience as in delivering his prepared remarks. As a speaker, Douglas tended

toward agitation and aggression, with unusually violent and provocative gestures. Douglas gave more than four thousand speeches in his career. They built his career for him, for he had no family or other political connections to speak of, only the power to influence men's minds through his words.

♦ Speech Defending the Compromise of 1850

Douglas's career was haunted by the specter of slavery. He rightly saw that sectional disagreement about slavery was the most divisive factor in American politics and felt compelled to work out one compromise after another to calm the dispute. He was in a unique position to become the prime mediator between the factions. Although Illinois was ostensibly a free state, in reality, slaves who had lived in the Illinois Territory before statehood and their descendants could still be owned in Illinois, and a number of salt mines in southern Illinois had the right to use and import slaves, at the same time that the state's constitution excluded free blacks. Also, contradictorily, while he was a senator from the free state of Illinois, Douglas had, through marriage to his first wife, Martha Martin, gained ownership of a large slave plantation in Mississippi, which was the source of his vast private wealth.

Douglas's personal view was that what Congress did about slave territories did not matter, since as a practical fact most of the immigrants to the West would come from northern or free states and the climatic conditions of the West would not support plantations or the slave agricultural system. Douglas was content to see slavery continue in the fifteen states where it existed, since it had support of the people of those states, but he did not wish for it to expand. He rarely spoke bluntly about these matters. In his view, the eventual adoption of his policies was inevitable, and it was much better to mollify the delicate honor of the South by maintaining the hope or even the illusion that slavery might not only be maintained but also expanded. In Douglas's mind the Constitution did not allow the prohibition or repeal of slavery, since it had clearly permitted slavery and made provision to count slaves for purposes of determining the number of seats accorded to the states in the House of Representatives (at the rate of three-fifths of a free citizen) and since it had outlawed importation of new slaves beginning twenty years after its ratification, among other clauses. But it said nothing about extending the role of the federal government in regulating slavery or about how slavery would be treated in newly acquired territories.

The Missouri Compromise of 1820 had limited slavery to the southern part of the Louisiana Territory, below the parallel 36°30' north (the southern border of Missouri), and kept the balance of free and slave states at twelve each, not allowing either to dominate the Senate. This balance had been kept up to 1850, at which point there were fifteen free and fifteen slave states. But after 1848 and the incorporation of Texas and vast territories from Mexico, the matter had to be addressed again. The compromise that Douglas and the South Carolina senator John Calhoun worked out,

Time Line

1813	April 23	■ Stephen A. Douglas is born in Brandon, Vermont.
1835		■ Douglas becomes the state's attorney in Morgan County, Illinois.
1836		■ Douglas is elected to the Illinois state legislature.
1840		■ Douglas is appointed as Illinois secretary of state.
1841		■ Douglas is appointed to the Illinois Supreme Court.
1843		■ Douglas goes to Congress as a representative from Illinois.
1847		■ Douglas is elected to the U.S. Senate.
1850		■ Douglas engineers the Compromise of 1850, which attempted to limit the spread of slavery to certain geographic areas of the United States.
	October 23	■ Douglas delivers a speech justifying the Compromise of 1850 to the citizens of Chicago.
1853		■ Douglas is reelected as senator from Illinois.
1854		■ Douglas sponsors the Kansas-Nebraska Act, which attempted to settle the question of the expansion of slavery by popular sovereignty, allowing each territory to decide the matter for itself.
1858	August 21	■ Douglas begins a series of debates with Abraham Lincoln, his opponent for reelection to the Senate.
1859		■ Douglas is reelected as senator from Illinois.
1860		■ Douglas runs for president as the nominee of the Democratic Party but is defeated by the Republican Lincoln.
1861	June 3	■ Douglas dies at his residence in Chicago, Illinois.

and which was approved by Congress and the president, had five provisions: 1) California was admitted as a free state, shifting the balance in favor of free states. 2) Slaves could be held, but not bought or sold, in the District of Columbia. 3) The New Mexico and Utah territories were to be admitted under the principle of popular sovereignty. 4) A new fugitive slave act was passed. 5) Texas, until recently an independent country, was compensated monetarily for giving up its rights in the Territory of New Mexico (necessary to obtain the votes of Texas legislators).

Douglas was the architect of popular sovereignty, which he viewed as the key to the continued peaceful existence of the United States. It meant that the territories where it was applied would decide for themselves whether to become slave or free states when they wrote their constitutions prior to statehood. This appeased the South because it apparently granted the possibility of unlimited expansion of slave states in the future, calming the slave states about the imbalance caused by the admission of California as a free state. But, in practice, Douglas believed popular sovereignty meant the end of the expansion of slavery, since he did not believe any of the territories would voluntarily become slave states; this would, in turn, satisfy even the most extreme northern concerns about slavery.

As soon as news of the Compromise of 1850 reached the city of Chicago, "transmitted, by lightning, upon the wires," as Douglas put it—referring to the newly invented telegraph—both the city council and a mass meeting of Chicago citizens denounced the Fugitive Slave Act. They asserted that it "violates the Constitution of the United States and the Law of God" and that Douglas and the rest of the Illinois congressional delegation who voted for it were not only traitors but also Benedict Arnolds and Judas Iscariots, and they instructed the Chicago police and city prosecutors to do nothing to enforce it. On the third day, Douglas addressed the citizens and succeeded in getting them to reverse their opinion and vote to repeal their hasty declarations.

He pointed out that from a logical point of view, their actions had been almost a reductio ad absurdum, a nearly laughable caricature, based not on the actual content of the legislation but on a number of popular and nearly hysterical misconceptions and straw men (in rhetoric, a proposition that one's enemies do not actually hold but which one nevertheless argues against as though they did, in order to discredit them). Northern opposition to slavery had two causes: economic, in that northern workers feared their wages would fall in competition with slave labor (although, in fact, very few slave owners used their slaves in industry), and ethical, the belief that slavery was unjust and morally wrong. In the 1840s and 1850s only a small minority of northerners were radical abolitionists determined to end slavery altogether. Most opponents of slavery at that time, including Abraham Lincoln, merely wanted to see it contained within its then-current geographic and economic limits. But the southern reaction, Douglas informs his audience, was that "in some of the Southern States, special sessions of the Legislatures are being called for the purpose of organizing systematic and efficient measures of resistance to the execution of the laws of the land, and for the adoption of DISUNION as a remedy." That is, even at the early date of 1850, the slave states were threatening to leave the Union (as eleven southern states would in 1861, starting the Civil War) not over the provisions of the bills but driven by their baseless fears that the North, through the Compromise of 1850, was forcing the complete abolition of slavery on them. The threat was made not because the North was indeed forcing this issue but because it was the thing the southern states feared the most.

Conversely, northerners, and particularly the people and government of Chicago, were not reacting to the actual legislation of the Compromise either. They were reacting on the basis of their fear of the so-called Slave Power. Southerners wanted to protect what they saw as their justified economic interest in slavery and were not so much interested in extending their plantation system to the West as in providing political protection for their millions of dollars (in today's money, billions of dollars) of capital in the form of slaves. The only way they had been able to do this reliably was to maintain parity with the North in the Senate (that is, to keep the same number of slave as free states). But as northerners saw it, the conspiracy of wealthy plantation owners that represented the Slave Power was constantly working behind the scenes to extend slavery to every part of America. (The preponderance of southern presidents and Supreme Court justices throughout the 1840s and 1850s, the war with Mexico, and similar facts were often offered as proof of this conspiracy.) "For these contradictory reasons, the people in both sections of the Union are called upon to resist the laws of the land and the authority of the Federal Government, by violence, even unto death and disunion. Strange and contradictory positions!"

In fact, as Douglas pointed out, no southerner would want to send gangs of slave catchers to falsely kidnap free blacks, as many in Chicago feared, because that would be the surest way to stir up support for abolition. Instead, the Fugitive Slave Act reformed older legislation and added a new class of magistrates to enforce it justly. The right to capture fugitive slaves did not come from the Compromise of 1850 or any other law but from the Constitution itself. Convinced by this argument, the Chicago Council repealed its hasty enactment.

♦ First Speech of the Lincoln-Douglas Debates

In the eight years since the Compromise of 1850, sectionalism and the crisis over slavery had worsened. Douglas's 1850 efforts at compromise had, in fact, only exacerbated the conflict for the reasons Douglas had mentioned in Chicago—essentially each side's fear of the other, however irrational he considered those fears to be. In 1854 he had made another attempt to calm things with the Kansas-Nebraska Act, which extended popular sovereignty to all U.S. territories, abolishing the geographic limit on slavery enshrined in the Missouri Compromise. This act was interpreted by

many as another triumph of the Slave Power. It was directly responsible for the creation of the Republican Party—a party dedicated to at least limiting slavery—as a replacement for the moribund Whigs and a new rival to the Democrats. It led to a state of near anarchy in what was called Bleeding Kansas, with numerous acts of terrorism committed by both pro-slavery and antislavery partisans in an attempt to influence the referendum on the state constitution. In fact, in the "house divided" speech, delivered by Lincoln at Springfield on June 16, 1858, in which he formally announced his candidacy as a Republican for Douglas's Senate seat, Lincoln concluded that the most drastic actions would be necessary to fight the Slave Power.

Douglas's doctrine of popular sovereignty (which Lincoln mocked as "squatter sovereignty," emphasizing how ridiculous he considered it to allow small, isolated groups of people to decide larger moral questions affecting the whole nation) was, in Lincoln's view, a relatively minor problem compared with the *Dred Scott* decision. In that famous 1857 case, the Supreme Court refused, on the ground that it lacked jurisdiction, to hear the appeal from the Missouri Supreme Court of the slave Dred Scott, who claimed that his long residence in free territories had abolished his status as a slave. The refusal to hear the case ought to have ended the matter, but President James Buchanan, himself a southerner, conferred with southern justices and brought pressure to bear on one of the northern justices to influence the southern chief justice, Roger Taney, to produce a decision that effectively ended all federal and state limitation of slavery and extended it not only to the territories but also to the free states. After this, in his second debate with Lincoln, Douglas was forced to admit that the only way a state could prohibit slavery under this ruling was by a kind of civil disobedience, refusing to use its police power to support the claims of slave owners requesting return of their human property. This actually quite radical (and desperate) suggestion by Douglas was recalled by southerners during the 1860 presidential campaign and doomed Douglas's chances of election, splitting the Democratic Party and ensuring Lincoln's triumph.

Douglas and Lincoln agreed to hold a series of six debates at various cities across Illinois throughout the late summer and fall of 1858 leading up to the elections for the state legislature. Senators were still elected by the state legislatures rather than by direct election, and the only hope Lincoln had of winning was to change the balance in the predominantly Democratic Illinois House and Senate. Inasmuch as Lincoln had electrified the nation with his "house divided" speech to begin the campaign and was challenging the most powerful U.S. senator and the one most directly responsible for the extension of slavery (in reality or possibility), the debates were closely followed by the entire country and set the stage for the presidential election of 1860 between the same two candidates.

Douglas begins his speech by asking Lincoln to reaffirm his support for the 1854 Republican platform, which—while radical enough in seeking to prohibit the spread of slavery to any of the territories and prohibiting the interstate sale of slaves—did not actually seek to end slavery. Douglas's reading of the platform drew cheers from the crowd in northern Illinois, but he says that his object is to make Lincoln's positions absolutely clear, "when I trot him down to lower Egypt." This refers to southern Illinois, called Egypt to this day because of the confluence of the Ohio and Mississippi rivers (near the cities of Cairo, Illinois, and Memphis, Tennessee). Egypt was a region whose inhabitants had strong cultural contact and affinity with the South and generally favored slavery. This type of argument, playing regions of Illinois off against one another, show how important the details of practical politics were to Douglas in contrast to Lincoln, who indeed was happy to alienate those who disagreed with his principled views. Douglas points out that Lincoln expanded these absolute views in his "house divided" speech, quoting Lincoln as saying, "I believe this government *cannot endure permanently half slave and half free*." Douglas, in contrast, does not see this at all. For him the essence of democratic American government is compromise and toleration, and he firmly believes that each region not only can but also must be left to its own devices, so long as these devices do not violate the Constitution, which clearly permits slavery.

Douglas's appeal on the issue of slavery is frankly racist. He baits Lincoln by referring to his party as "the Black Republican Party." Douglas unashamedly held racist views himself and assumed the same of his audience. Indeed, it would be a very exceptional individual in the mid-nineteenth century who did not hold racist views. Even Lincoln, in the second debate, admitted that to a remarkable extent he agreed with Douglas on this issue:

> I agree with Judge Douglas that he [the negro] is not my equal in many respects, certainly not in color, perhaps not in intellectual and moral endowments; but in the right to eat the bread without the leave of any body else which his own hand earns, he is my equal and the equal of Judge Douglas, and the equal of every other man. (qtd. in Sparks, p. 399)

Douglas directly appeals to irrational racist fear in his audience. He asks them,

> Do you desire to turn this beautiful State into a free negro colony, in order that when Missouri abolishes slavery she can send one hundred thousand emancipated slaves into Illinois, to become citizens and voters, on an equality with yourselves? If you desire negro citizenship, if you desire to allow them to come into the State and settle with the white man, if you desire them to vote on an equality with yourselves, and to make them eligible to office, to serve on juries, and to adjudge your rights, then support Mr. Lincoln.

Douglas quite clearly expresses his views on race equality when he states that he believes blacks should never be accepted as citizens or granted voting rights, and further,

> I believe this Government [the United States] was made on the white basis. I believe it was made by white men, for the benefit of white men and their posterity forever, and I am in favor of confining citizenship to white men, men of

European birth and descent, instead of conferring it upon negroes, Indians, and other inferior races.

As a practical matter, both Lincoln and Douglas expressed the view in the 1850s that free blacks ought to, in most cases, be deported to Africa. In the case of this one particular issue, essentially the nature of race, Douglas's love of compromise and his support for the expression and toleration of minority rights in America disappear when he discussed compromise and rights outside the white community. For him no other political community existed. Ideas about race only began to change in the rush of the rapidly approaching Civil War and would assume their modern form only through a long and bitter historical progress. Even today the older, irrational views endorsed by Douglas have not entirely disappeared.

Impact and Legacy

Douglas valued above all else the right of free men to determine their own form of government. Since men would naturally disagree, and the rule of the majority would be as tyrannical as any other absolute rule, he saw the key to every level of government within the United States as being compromise and local determination of local manners, whether it be by a city, a county, or a state. Popular sovereignty embodied Douglas's idea of decentralizing power to the advantage of every applicable majority. His entire career was devoted to working out compromise between the increasingly irreconcilable northern and southern sections, between freedom and slavery. Although it would have been impossible for him to view it in these terms until after the fact, he worked to prevent the Civil War. His natural desire for order, his disgust at extreme and polarizing rhetoric, and his own considerable rhetorical and political skill made him a natural leader of the Senate when only a disinterested voice could have maintained balance between the ever more hostile sections. It sometimes seems as if his politics were dictated by his sense of decorum. But in his very last days, after the Civil War had begun, he recognized that the deep nature of the division, and acts such as the *Dred Scott* decision, had made war inevitable, and he finally supported the North as acting in the best interest of the Union once compromise had become impossible. With the possibility gone of conciliating the South, Douglas's wavering on the subject of slavery, which had split the Democratic Party in 1860, shifted at last to steady resolve against it.

Douglas's views on race seem extreme and irrational today, but they were in no way exceptional at the time and, on a scale measuring a true belief in equality, were not so very far from Lincoln's. In any case, as Douglas himself maintained, his personal views did not in the least enter into a matter that was to be judged solely by the Constitution and the will of the people. Those were the forces that dictated the realities of his world.

Key Sources

Douglas gave over four thousand political speeches. Those made in Congress are contained in the *Congressional Globe* and the *U.S. Serial Set*, which printed the deliberations of committees (predecessors to the *Congressional Record*), and in national newspapers or those of the locale where Douglas gave them. The two largest manuscript collections of Douglas's papers are housed at the University of Chicago (http://www.lib.uchicago.edu/e/spcl/excat/douglasint.html) and in a smaller collection at Illinois State Historical Society in Springfield. Robert W. Johannsen edited Douglas's letters in a volume titled simply *Letters* (1961). The texts of the Lincoln-Douglas debates (1858) are widely available, for example, in the facsimile edited by Edwin Erle Sparks: *The Lincoln-Douglas Debates of 1858* (1908). The Stephen A. Douglas Association (http://www.stephenadouglas.org/home/) maintains an archive of selected speeches, letters, and other documents relevant to Douglas.

Essential Quotes

"We have fallen on evil times, when passion, and prejudice, and ambition, can so blind the judgments and deaden the consciences of men, that the truth cannot be seen and felt."

(Speech Defending the Compromise of 1850)

"You would not care a farthing about the new law, or the old law, or any other law, or what provisions it contained, if there was a hole in it big enough for the fugitive to slip through and escape."

(Speech Defending the Compromise of 1850)

Essential Quotes

"We must stand by the Constitution of the Union, with all its compromises, or we must abolish it, and resolve each State back into its original elements. It is, therefore a question of Union or Disunion."

(Speech Defending the Compromise of 1850)

"Revelation has not furnished us with a constitution."

(Speech Defending the Compromise of 1850)

"Why can it not exist divided into Free and Slave States? Washington, Jefferson, Franklin, Madison, Hamilton, Jay, and the great men of that day, made this Government divided into Free States and Slave States, and left each State perfectly free to do as it pleased on the subject of slavery. Why can it not exist on the same principles on which our fathers made it?"

(First Speech of the Lincoln-Douglas Debates)

"I would never consent to confer the right of voting and of citizenship upon a negro."

(First Speech of the Lincoln-Douglas Debates)

"I believe that this new doctrine preached by Mr. Lincoln and his party will dissolve the Union if it succeeds. They are trying to array all the Northern States in one body against the South, to excite a sectional war between the Free States and the Slave States, in order that the one or the other may be driven to the wall."

(First Speech of the Lincoln-Douglas Debates)

Further Reading

■ Articles

Clinton, Anita. "Stephen Arnold Douglas—His Mississippi Experience." *Journal of Mississippi History* 50 (1988): 56–88.

Pratt, Harry E. "Stephen A. Douglas, Lawyer, Legislator, Register and Judge: 1833–1843." *Lincoln Herald* part I, 51 (December 1949): 11–16; part II, 52 (February 1950): 37–43.

■ Books

Crocker, Lionel George, ed. *An Analysis of Lincoln and Douglas as Public Speakers and Debaters*. Springfield, Ill.: Charles C. Thomas, 1968.

Good, Timothy S. *The Lincoln-Douglas Debates and the Making of a President*. Jefferson, N.C.: McFarland, 2007.

Huston, James L. *Stephen A. Douglas and the Dilemmas of Democratic Equality*. Lanham, Md.: Rowman and Littlefield, 2007.

Johannsen, Robert Walter. *Stephen A. Douglas*. Oxford, U.K.: Oxford University Press, 1973.

Morris, Roy. *The Long Pursuit: Abraham Lincoln's Thirty-Year Struggle with Stephen Douglas for the Heart and Soul of America*. New York: HarperCollins, 2008.

Sparks, Edwin Earle, ed. *The Lincoln-Douglas Debates of 1858*. Springfield: Illinois State Historical Library, 1908.

—*Bradley A. Skeen*

Questions for Further Study

1. In the middle of his speech defending the Compromise of 1850, Douglas makes a sweeping set of assessments regarding history and societies, maintaining that "when any race of men have shown themselves so degraded … as to be utterly incapable of governing themselves, they must … be governed by others." White Western society, he claims, is much more advanced than others, and therefore its people are deserving of self-rule. What evidence or conditions does he cite in favor of his arguments? What other explanations for the dominance of whites over the rest of the world might one put forward? (For example, the ethnobotanist Jared Diamond offers a fascinating analysis of this situation in his best-seller *Guns, Germs, and Steel*.)

2. Evaluate Douglas's logic regarding the issue of slavery as presented in both speeches. What are his principal arguments, and what about his position might have made the most sense to a white northerner of the time? On the other hand, what are some of his most questionable points? For instance, do you agree with his assertion that slaveholders had a reason to respect the rights of freed slaves? Why or why not?

3. Douglas has been cited for his talent for compromise, an ability that brought him far in the tense years leading up to the Civil War. In these two documents, how does he display that spirit of compromise, or what today would be called "bipartisanship"? Where did his desire for peace end and his convictions about the Constitution and law begin—or, more specifically, what caused him to change his position on slavery, aligning with his old foe Abraham Lincoln, on the eve of the war?

Speech Defending the Compromise of 1850

The agitation on the subject of Slavery, now raging through the breadth of the land, presents a most extraordinary spectacle. Congress, after a protracted session of nearly ten months, succeeded in passing a system of measures, which are believed to be just to all parts of the Republic, and ought to be satisfactory to the People. The South has not triumphed over the North, nor has the North achieved a victory over the South. Neither party has made any humiliating concessions to the other. Each has preserved its honor, while neither has surrendered an important right or sacrificed any substantial interest. The measures composing the scheme of adjustment are believed to be in harmony with the principles of justice and the Constitution. And yet we find that the agitation is re-opened in the two extremes of the Union with renewed vigor and increased violence. In some of the Southern States, special sessions of the Legislatures are being called for the purpose of organizing systematic and efficient measures of resistance to the execution of the laws of the land, and for the adoption of DISUNION as a remedy. In the Northern States, municipal corporations, and other organized bodies of men, are nullifying the acts of Congress, and raising the standard of rebellion against the authority of the Federal Government. At the South, the measures of adjustment are denounced as a disgraceful surrender of Southern rights to Northern abolitionism. At the North, the same measures are denounced with equal violence, as a total abandonment of the rights of freemen to conciliate the slave power. The Southern disunionists repudiate the authority of the highest judicial tribunal on earth, upon the ground that it is a pliant and corrupt instrument in the hands of Northern fanaticism. The Northern nullifiers refuse to submit the points at issue to the same exalted tribunal, upon the ground that the Supreme Court of the United States is a corrupt and supple instrument in the hands of the Southern slave-ocracy. For these contradictory reasons, the people in both sections of the Union are called upon to resist the laws of the land and the authority of the Federal Government, by violence, even unto death and disunion. Strange and contradictory positions! Both cannot be true, and I trust in God neither may prove to be. We have fallen on evil times, when passion, and prejudice, and ambition, can so blind the judgments and deaden the consciences of men, that the truth cannot be seen and felt. The people of the North, or the South, or both, are acting under a fatal delusion. Should we not pause, and reflect, and consider, whether we, as well as they, have not been egregiously deceived upon the subject?…

It is a far more important and serious matter, when viewed with reference to the principles involved, and the consequences which may result. The Common Council of the city of Chicago have assumed to themselves the right, and actually exercised the power, of determining the validity of an act of Congress, and have declared it void upon the ground that it violates the Constitution of the United States and the Law of God!…

I will now examine briefly the specific grounds of objection urged by the Council against the Fugitive Slave Bill, as reasons why it should not be obeyed. The objections are two in number: first, that it suspends the writ of habeas corpus in time of peace, in violation of the Constitution; secondly, that it abolishes the right of trial by jury.…

But I maintain …, that the writ of habeas corpus is applicable to the case of the arrest of a fugitive under this law, in the same sense in which the Constitution intended to confer it, and to the fullest extent for which that writ is ever rightfully issued in any case. In this I am fully sustained by the opinion of Mr. Crittenden, the Attorney General of the United States. As soon as the bill passed the two houses of Congress, an abolition paper raised the alarm that the habeas corpus had been suspended. The cry was eagerly caught up, and transmitted, by lightning, upon the wires, to every part of the Union, by those whose avocation is agitation.…

My object is to arrive at the truth to repel error and dissipate prejudice—and to avoid violence and bloodshed.

[Explaining that the main purpose of the new Fugitive Slave Law is to reform the bodies of judicial officers that enforce it] The Southern members [of Congress] voted for it for the reason that it was a better law than the old one—better for them, better for us, and better for the free blacks. It places the execution of the law in the hands of responsible officers

Document Text

of the government, instead of leaving every man to take the laws into his own hands and to execute it for himself. It affords personal security to the claimant while arresting his servant and taking him back, by providing him with the opportunity of establishing his legal rights by competent testimony before a tribunal duly authorized to try the case, and thus allay all apprehensions and suspicions, on the part of our citizens, that he is a villain, attempting to steal a free man for the purpose of selling him into slavery. The slaveholder has as strong a desire to protect the rights of the free black man, as we have, and much more interest to do so; for he well knows, that if outrages should be tolerated under the law, and free men are seized and carried into slavery, from that moment the indignant outcry against it would be so strong here, and every where, that even a fugitive from labor could not be returned, lest he might also happen to be free. The interest of the slaveholder, therefore, requires a law which shall protect the rights of all free men, black or white, from any invasion or violation whatever.…

The real objection is not to the new law,hellip; but to the Constitution itself. Those of you who hold these opinions, do not mean that the fugitive from labor shall be taken back. That is the real point of your objection. You would not care a farthing about the new law, or the old law, or any other law, or what provisions it contained, if there was a hole in it big enough for the fugitive to slip through and escape. Habeas corpuses—trials by jury—records from other States—pains and penalties, the whole catalogue of objections, would be all moonshine, if the negro was not required to go back to his master. Tell me, frankly, is not this the true character of your objection? [Here several gentlemen gave an affirmative answer. Mr. DOUGLAS said he would answer that objection by reading a portion of the Constitution of the United States. He then read as follows:] "No person held to service or labor in one State, under the laws thereof, escaping into another, shall, in consequence of any law or regulation therein, be discharged from such service or labor, BUT SHALL BE DELIVERED UP on the claim of the party to whom such service or labor may be due." This,… is the supreme law of the land, speaking to every citizen of the Republic. The command is imperative. There is no avoiding—no escaping the obligation, so long as we live under, and claim the protection of, the Constitution. We must yield implicit obedience, or we must take the necessary steps to release ourselves from the obligation to obey. There is no other alternative. We must stand by the Constitution of the Union, with all its compromises, or we must abolish it, and resolve each State back into its original elements. It is, therefore a question of Union or Disunion.…

The divine law is appealed to as authority for disregarding our most sacred duties to society. The City Council have appealed to it, as their excuse for nullifying an act of Congress; and a committee embodied the same principle in their resolutions to the meeting in this hall last night, as applicable both to the Constitution and laws. The general proposition that there is a law paramount to all human enactments—the law of the Supreme Ruler of the Universe—I trust that no civilized and Christian people is prepared to question, much less deny. We should all recognise, respect, and revere the divine law. But we should bear in mind that the law of God, as revealed to us, is intended to operate on our consciences, and insure the performance of our duties as individuals and Christians. The divine law does not prescribe the form of government under which we shall live, and the character of our political and civil institutions. Revelation has not furnished us with a constitution—a code of international law—and a system of civil and municipal jurisprudence. It has not determined the right of persons and property—much less the peculiar privileges which shall be awarded to each class of persons under any particular form of government. God has created man in his own image, and endowed him with the right of self-government, so soon as he shall evince the requisite intelligence, virtue, and capacity, to assert and enjoy the privilege. The history of the world furnishes few examples where any considerable portion of the human race have shown themselves sufficiently enlightened and civilized to exercise the rights and enjoy the blessings of freedom. In Asia and Africa, we find nothing but ignorance, superstition, and despotism. Large portions of Europe, and America, can scarcely lay claim to civilization and Christianity; and a still smaller portion have demonstrated their capacity for self-government. Is all this contrary to the laws of God? And if so, who is responsible? The civilized world have always held, that when any race of men have shown themselves so degraded, by ignorance, superstition, cruelty, and barbarism, as to be utterly incapable of governing themselves, they must, in the nature of things, be governed by others, by such laws as are deemed applicable to their condition. It is upon this principle alone, that England justifies the form of government she has established in the Indies, and for some of her other colonies—that Russia justified herself in holding her serfs as slaves,

and selling them as a part of the land on which they live—that our Pilgrim Fathers justified themselves in reducing the negro and Indian to servitude, and selling them as property—that we, in Illinois and most of the Free States, justify ourselves in denying the negro and the Indian the privilege of voting, and all other political rights—and that many of the States of the Union justify themselves in depriving the white man of the right of the elective franchise, unless he is fortunate enough to own a certain amount of property. These things certainly violate the principle of absolute equality among men, when considered as component parts of a political society or government, and so do many provisions of the Constitution of the United States, as well as the several States of the Union. In fact, no government ever existed on earth in which there was a perfect equality, in all things, among those composing it and governed by it. Neither sacred nor profane history furnishes an example. If inequality in the form and principles of government is therefore to be deemed a violation of the laws of God, and punishable as such, who is to escape? Under this principle all Christendom is doomed, and no Pagan can hope for mercy! Many of these things are, in my opinion, unwise and unjust, and, of course, subversive of Republican principles; but I am not prepared to say that they are either sanctioned or condemned by the divine law. Who can assert that God has prescribed the form and principles of government, and the character of the political, municipal, and domestic institutions of men on earth? This doctrine would annihilate the fundamental principle upon which our political system rests. Our forefathers held that the people had an inherent right to establish such Constitution and laws for the government of themselves and their posterity, as they should deem best calculated to insure the protection of life, liberty, and the pursuit of happiness; and that the same might be altered and changed as experience should satisfy them to be necessary and proper. Upon this principle the Constitution of the United States was formed, and our glorious Union established. All acts of Congress passed in pursuance of the Constitution, are declared to be the supreme laws of the land, and the Supreme Court of the United States is charged with expounding the same. All officers and magistrates, under the Federal and State Governments—executive, legislative, judicial, and ministerial—are required to take an oath to support the Constitution, before they can enter upon the performance of their respective duties. Any citizen, therefore, who, in his conscience, believes that the Constitution of the United States is in violation of a "higher law," has no right, as an honest man to take office under it, or exercise any other function of citizenship conferred by it. Every person born under the Constitution owes allegiance to it; and every naturalized citizen takes an oath to support it. Fidelity to the Constitution is the only passport to the enjoyment of rights under it. When a Senator elect presents his credentials, he is not allowed to take his seat until he places his hand upon the Holy Evangelist and appeals to his God for the sincerity of his vow to support the Constitution. He, who does this, with a mental reservation or secret intention to disregard any provision of the Constitution, commits a double crime—is morally guilty of perfidy to his God and treason to his country! If the Constitution of the United States is to be repudiated upon the ground that it is repugnant to the divine law, where are the friends of freedom and Christianity to look for another and a better? Who is to be the prophet to reveal the will of God and establish a Theocracy for us? Is he to be found in the ranks of Northern Abolitionism, or of Southern Disunion; or is the Common Council of the City of Chicago to have the distinguished honor of furnishing the chosen one? I will not venture to inquire what are to be the form and principles of the new government or to whom is to be intrusted the execution of its sacred functions; for, when we decide that the wisdom of our revolutionary fathers was foolishness, and their piety wickedness, and destroy the only system of self-government that has ever realized the hopes of the friends of freedom, and commanded the respect of mankind, it becomes us to wait patiently until the purposes of the Latter Day Saints shall be revealed unto us. For my part, I am prepared to maintain and preserve inviolate the Constitution as it is, with all its compromises, to stand or fall by the American Union, clinging with the tenacity of life to all its glorious memories of the past, and precious hopes of the future.

[Mr. DOUGLAS then secured the repeal of the previous day's enactment of the City Council.]

Glossary

Christendom:	countries in which Christianity was dominant—making them, in the view of Douglas and others at that time, synonymous with "the civilized world"
Common Council of the city of Chicago:	the Chicago city government in general
the fugitive from labor:	a runaway slave
the Holy Evangelist:	the Bible
Latter Day Saints:	not specifically a reference to Mormons, but instead ridiculing those who claim to speak for God
measures of adjustment:	attempts at compromise
ministerial:	rather than being a fourth branch of government, a term referring generally to members of the executive branch other than the president
moonshine:	nonsense
municipal corporations:	city governments
Pagan:	a worshipper of many gods, usually nature-based deities, rather than one god
peculiar:	particular
Republican principles:	a term referring not to a political party but to the rule of law and the protection of liberties
the right of the elective franchise:	the right to vote
Theocracy:	religious rule
writ of habeas corpus:	reference to the legal right of an accused person not to be held or detained without the opportunity of being formally charged for specific crimes

Document Text

First Speech of the Lincoln-Douglas Debates

1858

LADIES AND GENTLEMEN: I appear before you to-day for the purpose of discussing the leading political topics which now agitate the public mind. By an arrangement between Mr. Lincoln and myself, we are present here to-day for the purpose of having a joint discussion, as the representatives of the two great political parties of the State and Union, upon the principles in issue between those parties; and this vast concourse of people shows the deep feeling which pervades the public mind in regard to the questions dividing us....

My object in reading these resolutions was to put the question to Abraham Lincoln this day, whether he now stands and will stand by each article in that creed and carry it out. I desire to know whether Mr. Lincoln to-day stands, as he did in 1854, in favor of the unconditional repeal of the Fugitive Slave law. I desire him to answer whether he stands pledged to-day, as he did in 1854, against the admission of any more Slave States into the Union, even if the people want them. I want to know whether he stands pledged against the admission of a new State into the Union with such a Constitution as the people of that State may see fit to make. I want to know whether he stands to-day pledged to the abolition of slavery in the District of Columbia. I desire him to answer whether he stands pledged to the prohibition of the slave trade between the different States. I desire to know whether he stands pledged to prohibit slavery in all the Territories of the United States, North as well as South of the Missouri Compromise line. I desire him to answer whether he is opposed to the acquisition of any more territory, unless slavery is prohibited therein. I want his answer to these questions. Your affirmative cheers in favor of this Abolition platform is not satisfactory. I ask Abraham Lincoln to answer these questions, in order that, when I trot him down to lower Egypt, I may put the same questions to him. My principles are the same everywhere. I can proclaim them alike in the North, the South, the East, and the West. My principles will apply wherever the Constitution prevails and the American flag waves. I desire to know whether Mr. Lincoln's principles will bear transplanting from Ottawa to Jonesboro? I put these questions to him to-day distinctly, and ask an answer. I have a right to an answer, for I quote from the platform of the Republican party, made by himself and others at the time that party was formed, and the bargain made by Lincoln to dissolve and kill the old Whig party, and transfer its members, bound hand and foot, to the Abolition party, under the direction of Giddings and Fred Douglass...

Having formed this new party for the benefit of deserters from Whiggery, and deserters from Democracy, and having laid down the Abolition platform which I have read, Lincoln now takes his stand and proclaims his Abolition doctrines. Let me read a part of them. In his speech at Springfield to the Convention which nominated him for the Senate, he said:—

In my opinion it will not cease until a crisis shall have been reached and passed. 'A house divided against itself cannot stand.' I believe this government *cannot endure permanently half slave and half free.* I do not expect the Union to be dissolved,—I do not expect the house to fall; *but I do expect it will cease to be divided* . It will become all one thing, or all the other. Either the opponents of slavery *will arrest the further spread of it,* and place it where the public mind shall rest in the belief *that it is in the course of ultimate extinction,* or its advocates *will push it forward till it shall become alike lawful in all the States,*—old as well as new, North as well as South.

["Good," "Good," and cheers.]

I am delighted to hear you Black Republicans say "good." I have no doubt that doctrine expresses your sentiments, and I will prove to you now, if you will listen to me, that it is revolutionary and destructive of the existence of this Government. Mr. Lincoln, in the extract from which I have read, says that this Government cannot endure permanently in the same condition in which it was made by its framers,—divided into Free and Slave States. He says that it has existed for about seventy years thus divided, and yet he tells you that it cannot endure permanently on the same principles and in the same relative condition in which our fathers made it. Why can it not exist divided into Free and Slave States? Washington, Jefferson, Franklin, Madison, Hamilton, Jay, and the great men of that day, made this Government divided into Free States and Slave States, and left each State perfectly free to do as it pleased on

the subject of slavery. Why can it not exist on the same principles on which our fathers made it? They knew when they framed the Constitution that in a country as wide and broad as this, with such a variety of climate, production, and interest, the people necessarily required different laws and institutions in different localities. They knew that the laws and regulations which would suit the granite hills of New Hampshire would be unsuited to the rice plantations of South Carolina, and they therefore provided that each State should retain its own Legislature and its own sovereignty, with the full and complete power to do as it pleased within its own limits, in all that was local and not national. One of the reserved rights of the States, was the right to regulate the relations between master and servant, on the slavery question. At the time the Constitution was framed, there were thirteen States in the Union, twelve of which were slaveholding States and one a Free State. Suppose this doctrine of uniformity preached by Mr. Lincoln, that the States should all be free or all be slave had prevailed, and what would have been the result? Of course, the twelve slaveholding States would have overruled the one Free State, and slavery would have been fastened by a Constitutional provision on every inch of the American Republic, instead of being left, as our fathers wisely left it, to each State to decide for itself. Here I assert that uniformity in the local laws and institutions of the different States is neither possible nor desirable. If uniformity had been adopted when the Government was established, it must inevitably have been the uniformity of slavery everywhere, or else the uniformity of negro citizenship and negro equality everywhere.

We are told by Lincoln that he is utterly opposed to the Dred Scott decision, and will not submit to it, for the reason that he says it deprives the negro of the rights and privileges of citizenship. That is the first and main reason which he assigns for his warfare on the Supreme Court of the United States and its decision. I ask you, are you in favor of conferring upon the negro the rights and privileges of citizenship? Do you desire to strike out of our State Constitution that clause which keeps slaves and free negroes out of the State, and allow the free negroes to flow in, and cover your prairies with black settlements? Do you desire to turn this beautiful State into a free negro colony, in order that when Missouri abolishes slavery she can send one hundred thousand emancipated slaves into Illinois, to become citizens and voters, on an equality with yourselves? If you desire negro citizenship, if you desire to allow them to come into the State and settle with the white man, if you desire them to vote on an equality with yourselves, and to make them eligible to office, to serve on juries, and to adjudge your rights, then support Mr. Lincoln and the Black Republican party, who are in favor of the citizenship of the negro. For one, I am opposed to negro citizenship in any and every form. I believe this Government was made on the white basis. I believe it was made by white men, for the benefit of white men and their posterity forever, and I am in favor of confining citizenship to white men, men of European birth and descent, instead of conferring it upon negroes, Indians, and other inferior races.

Mr. Lincoln, following the example and lead of all the little Abolition orators, who go around and lecture in the basements of schools and churches, reads from the Declaration of Independence that all men were created equal, and then asks, How can you deprive a negro of the equality which God and the Declaration of Independence awards to him? He and they maintain that negro equality is guaranteed by the laws of God, and that it is asserted in the Declaration of Independence. If they think so, of course they have a right to say so, and so vote… What rights and privileges are consistent with the public good? This is a question which each State and each Territory must decide for itself; Illinois has decided it for herself. We have provided that the negro shall not be a slave, and we have also provided that he shall not be a citizen, but protect him in his civil rights, in his life, his person and his property, only depriving him of all political rights whatsoever, and refusing to put him on an equality with the white man. That policy of Illinois is satisfactory to the Democratic party and to me; and if it were to the Republicans, there would then be no question upon the subject. But the Republicans say that he ought to be made a citizen, and when he becomes a citizen he becomes your equal, with all your rights and privileges. They assert the Dred Scott decision to be monstrous because it denies that the negro is or can be a citizen under the Constitution… I would never consent to confer the right of voting and of citizenship upon a negro;… Mr. Lincoln and the Republican party set themselves up as wiser than these men who made this Government, which was flourished for seventy years under the principle of popular sovereignty, recognizing the right of each State to do as it pleased. Under that principle, we have grown from a nation of three or four millions to a nation of about thirty millions of people; we have crossed the Allegheny mountains and filled up the whole Northwest, turning the prairie into a

Document Text

garden, and building up churches and schools, thus spreading civilization and Christianity where before there was nothing but savage barbarism. Under that principle we have become, from a feeble nation, the most powerful on the face of the earth; and if we only adhere to that principle, we can go forward increasing in territory, in power, in strength, and in glory until the Republic of America shall be the North Star that shall guide the friends of freedom throughout the civilized world. And why can we not adhere to the great principle of self-government, upon which our institutions were originally based? I believe that this new doctrine preached by Mr. Lincoln and his party will dissolve the Union if it succeeds. They are trying to array all the Northern States in one body against the South, to excite a sectional war between the Free States and the Slave States, in order that the one or the other may be driven to the wall.

Glossary

the Abolition party, under the direction of Giddings and Fred Douglass:	a reference sarcastically suggesting that the new Republican Party will have at its helm the former slave Frederick Douglass as well as Joshua Giddings, an abolitionist who represented Ohio in Congress
Northwest:	not the Pacific Northwest but the northwestern corner of the nation in his time—that is, Minnesota and adjoining states
Ottawa to Jonesboro:	two towns in Illinois
popular sovereignty:	the principle that citizens in the territories had the right to decide for themselves, on a state-by-state basis, whether to allow slavery within their borders
revolutionary:	opposed to the authority of the Constitution

Forcing Slavery Down the Throat of a Freesoiler An 1856 cartoon depicts a giant "Free Soiler" being held down by James Buchanan and Lewis Cassstanding on the Democratic platform marked "Kansas", "Cuba" and "Central America". Franklin Pierce also holds down the giant's beard as Douglas shoves a black man down his throat. By John L. Magee (c.1820–c.1870).

Associate Justice William O Douglas by Harris & Ewing.

William O. Douglas: Original Analysis

Supreme Court Justice

1898–1980

Overview

William O. Douglas was one of the more idiosyncratic and naturally contrarian justices ever to serve on the Supreme Court. In his more than thirty-six years on the bench, Douglas authored 531 dissents, more than any other justice. His legal philosophy was strongly influenced by Underhill Moore, his professor at Columbia Law School and one of the most prominent of the legal realists, and by Louis D. Brandeis, the justice whose place Douglas took on the Supreme Court. From these two, he learned to draw upon sources as varied as poetry, sociology, agricultural reports, or his own intuition and to use these sources to justify his decisions, reflecting the realist belief that "real world" information needed to be considered in rendering legal decisions rather than relying exclusively on legal precedent. Douglas was known as a liberal throughout his tenure on the Court. In the 1930s he strongly supported President Franklin Roosevelt's New Deal program, the legislative and governmental reorganization measures aimed at alleviating the Great Depression. He also was generally a consistent civil libertarian, though he grew into that role haltingly during World War II.

Douglas is often said to have been an ecologist before there was such a thing, and his love of nature and the unspoiled wilderness was evident in several notable opinions in major Supreme Court cases. Washington's William O. Douglas National Wilderness is named in his honor, in recognition of his efforts on behalf of the environment. Spending so much time in the outdoors sharpened Douglas's appreciation for unspoiled nature, which he maintained for the remainder of his life, intervening personally to save the Chesapeake and Ohio Canal from being turned into a highway and prompting some of Douglas's more controversial opinions on behalf of environmental concerns.

Douglas was born on October 16, 1898, in Maine, Minnesota, the son of Julia Fisk Douglas and the Reverend William Douglas. Following her husband's death in 1904, Julia moved the family to Yakima, Washington, where she purchased a small home before losing much of the family's money in a failed land investment. Growing up poor and working odd jobs from the age of seven on, Douglas developed an appreciation for hard work and a strong sense of class justice that later expressed itself in his belief that all citizens should be entitled to the rights and privileges afforded the wealthy. Douglas went to nearby Whitman College, where he graduated in 1920. After spending time teaching, he enrolled at Columbia Law School in 1922. Douglas took on several jobs at Columbia, including assisting with the compilation of case law books, a task for which he was unqualified. The intellectual vigor he employed in the task was indicative of the engagement with which an interested Douglas would approach problems on the bench.

After graduating from Columbia, Douglas floated through several positions over the next decade, including two stints at a Wall Street law firm and positions on both the Columbia and Yale faculties. There he developed more fully his appreciation for legal realism, which he had first encountered as a student at Columbia. This belief that the law as traditionally practiced was too distant from "real life" and needed to be supplemented with empirical studies from other disciplines, such as sociology, psychology, and economics, strongly influenced Douglas's legal thought process, which in turn influenced his decisions on the Supreme Court. He was appointed to the Supreme Court in 1939, after serving as chairman of the Securities and Exchange Commission.

Douglas's approach and his willingness to sidestep judicial precedent in coming to his decisions made him a frequent—and sometimes justified—target of critics, who charged him with judicial activism. Douglas would set several records while on the bench, including the longest tenure. Throughout that time, he was the most consistently liberal justice, the steadiest civil libertarian, and the justice most willing to rule against corporate interests in favor of individuals or the environment. Nonetheless, he is widely viewed as having done liberal causes as much harm as good because he relied more on his own views in formulating his legal opinions than on case law precedents or an articulated legal philosophy. As a result, his impact was more limited than it otherwise could have been, and he left behind no theoretical legacy that succeeding justices could follow.

Explanation and Analysis of Documents

In Douglas's years on the bench, a variety of cases came before the Supreme Court that fundamentally affected American public life and the concepts of individual and civil rights. His long tenure was also marked by major international conflicts, such as World War II, the cold war, and the Vietnam War, as well as major domestic movements,

notably the civil rights movement. The opinions in *Dennis v. United States, Mapp v. Ohio, Griswold v. Connecticut, Sierra Club v. Morton*, and *Furman v. Georgia* demonstrate his judicial priorities—protection of civil and individual rights, including the right to privacy; near-absolute deference to the First Amendment; and environmental protection—and show how he sought to fit his opinions to what he saw as the social reality that underlay the question. Douglas addresses these cases not just from within the narrow confines of case-law precedent but also from what he saw as the social ramifications of the particular questions contested in the cases.

♦ *Dennis v. United States*

Although Douglas would come to be known as a committed civil libertarian, his early years on the Court showed a man trying to come to grips with the legal problems he encountered and find a way to reconcile the needs of the state with the rights of the individual. During World War II, he frequently joined majority opinions that favored the government at the expense of individuals and civil liberties. Two examples are *Minersville School District v. Gobitis* (1940), which upheld mandatory flag-saluting laws against a religious liberty challenge, and *Korematsu v. United States* (1944), which upheld the constitutionality of laws and ordinances banning Japanese Americans from areas deemed militarily sensitive.

At the same time, however, Douglas was revising his position and coming more and more to hold a strongly pro–civil liberties viewpoint. In *West Virginia v. Barnette*, a second flag-salute case, he voted with the majority to overturn *Gobitis*. Douglas continued to refine his position with regard to civil liberties throughout the end of the 1940s and into the 1950s, becoming a particularly vociferous advocate of the right to free speech, which he defended at great length in several of his books, including *The Right of the People* (1958) and *Points of Rebellion* (1970).

One of Douglas's most famous dissents came in 1951 in *Dennis v. United States*. Eugene Dennis and ten others had been convicted for teaching Communist doctrine, specifically works by Karl Marx and Friedrich Engels, Vladimir Lenin, and Joseph Stalin. The lower courts held that the defendants were guilty of violating the Smith Act, which made it illegal to willfully conspire to teach or to advocate the violent overthrow or other forced destruction of the federal government. The majority affirmed, finding that the Smith Act did not violate the First or Fifth Amendments and that the petitioners' actions constituted a "clear and present danger" to the government of the United States. The Court thus upheld the convictions.

Douglas disagreed and wrote a scathing dissent from the majority's opinion. For him, there was a fundamental difference between speech and action, particularly where sedition was concerned. Actions, according to Douglas, can always be punished, but the First Amendment protects speech in and of itself until speech becomes action. The right to free speech is not absolute, he notes, but the

Time Line

1898	October 16	■ William Orville Douglas is born in Maine, Minnesota.
1920		■ Douglas graduates from Whitman College, Walla Walla, Washington.
1925	June 3	■ Douglas graduates from Columbia Law School.
1925–1927		■ Douglas works for the New York City law firm of Cravath, De Gersdorff, Swaine and Wood.
1925–1929		■ Douglas serves on the law faculty at Columbia Law School.
1929–1934		■ Douglas serves as professor of law at Yale Law School.
1935	December 20	■ President Franklin Roosevelt offers Douglas a seat on the Securities and Exchange Commission.
1937	September 21	■ Douglas is voted chairman of the Securities and Exchange Commission.
1939	April 17	■ Douglas is sworn in to his seat on the Supreme Court, replacing Louis D. Brandeis.
1951	June 4	■ Douglas writes a dissent in *Dennis v. United States*.
1954	March 20–27	■ Douglas walks the length (184.5 miles) of the Chesapeake and Ohio Canal to protest plans to turn it into a highway; the publicity generated causes the plans to be discarded.
1961	June 19	■ Douglas concurs in *Mapp v. Ohio*.
1965	June 7	■ Douglas delivers the opinion of the court in *Griswold v. Connecticut*.
1972	April 19	■ Douglas dissents in *Sierra Club v. Morton*.
	June 29	■ Douglas concurs in *Furman v. Georgia*.
1975	November 12	■ Douglas retires from the Supreme Court.
1980	January 19	■ Douglas dies in Washington, D.C.

question of when freedom of speech could be infringed upon should be treated as a cost-benefit analysis. If the cost of permitting the speech outweighs the benefit to the people, then that speech could be regulated. If not, it must stand unmolested. Douglas argues that questions of free speech must be considered in light of the credibility of the threat posed. If advocacy of the violent overthrow of the government presents a credible threat to the government, then that speech may be suppressed; if it does not pose a credible threat, then the speech must be permitted.

Douglas quotes Thomas Jefferson in support of the free marketplace of ideas and declares that Communism has been discussed within this marketplace and found wanting. Dennis and his cohorts stood no chance of recruiting others to their cause and thus presented no legitimate danger to the state. He is careful not to disregard the threat that the USSR and Communism posed on the international scene. The Soviet Union does pose an international threat, he maintains, but Communism as an ideology within the United States does not, because it lacks credibility as an idea. Douglas argues in his dissent that the right of Dennis and like-minded individuals to teach Communist doctrine should be upheld as a basic freedom; he does, however, also mention his belief that teaching Communism will reveal to others the "ugliness" of the doctrine and further undermine its ideological credibility.

That decided, Douglas turns to what he saw as the heart of the question—the nature of the teacher rather than the content taught. He questions the majority's claim that it was not the teaching of Communist doctrine that was illegal but the fact that the defendants had conspired against the government. If these books are to remain on shelves, if they are not to be thrown to the flames, as they would be in the Soviet Union, Douglas wonders, why can they not be freely used in teaching? Even though these books advocate the violent overthrow of the U.S. government, Douglas says, they would not be prohibited from classroom use by law. Douglas faults the majority for implying that the distinction hinges on whether the teacher believes in the creed; presumably, if the material were taught by someone demonstrably opposed to the creed, it would be permitted. This, he says, is an unconstitutional abridgment of free speech, since it holds that speech is only free conditionally, depending on the viewpoints of the speaker. As Douglas warns in his dissent, this interpretation is "dangerous to the liberties of every citizen."

♦ *Mapp v. Ohio*

In 1957 Cleveland police, responding to a tip, knocked on Dollree Mapp's door and demanded entry, believing that Mapp harbored a suspect in a bombing case. Mapp called her attorney and refused to open the door before he was served with a search warrant. An officer broke glass in the door to open it. When Mapp demanded to see the warrant, a piece of paper was waved in her face. Mapp grabbed the paper and stuffed it down her dress, whereupon an officer retrieved it from her dress and handcuffed her. Mapp was forced upstairs handcuffed while officers searched her house, turning up several "pornographic" materials in a basement footlocker. Mapp was convicted of possession of obscene material on the basis of the evidence seized during the warrantless search.

After the Ohio Supreme Court upheld her conviction, Mapp appealed to the Supreme Court, which voted six to three in her favor, finding that all evidence discovered during an illegal search was excluded from judicial proceedings. This ruling had been the case in federal courts for decades, but it had not yet become the rule in state courts. *Mapp* overturned provisions in *Wolf v. Colorado* (1948), which held that although Fourth Amendment protections against unlawful searches and seizures applied to the states because of the due process clause of the Fourteenth Amendment, the states were not bound by the federal rule excluding all evidence obtained in unlawful seizures. *Mapp* extended the exclusionary rule to all courts.

Douglas joined the majority's opinion, which stated that the exclusionary rule must be extended if Fourth Amendment protections are extended to the states. After all, the majority reasoned, it does little good to protect citizens from unlawful searches and seizures if evidence so obtained is admissible in court. He goes further than the majority did, however, and provides several explicit reasons for his siding with the majority. First, Douglas never trusted the capacity of organizations to police themselves. If the exclusionary rule were not extended to state courts, he argues, homeowners are left with only two options: They can file trespassing charges against the officers, or they must trust in the willingness of law enforcement to bring charges against the offending officer. Douglas notes that a trespass charge is a meaningless remedy and dismisses the idea that law enforcement would police itself in such a manner. Besides, he says, neither of these remedies will release from prison a person convicted on the basis of illegally obtained evidence.

Douglas also states that this case demonstrates the "casual arrogance" of unrestrained law enforcement, a theme that he drives home narratively in constructing his concurrence. Somewhat unusually for a concurring opinion, he delivers a fairly lengthy retelling of the facts of the case, repeatedly mentioning that the search was "lawless" and using vivid language to describe the altercation between the police and the homeowner. Douglas's point in going into such detail was to support the legal argument with an emotional one, that is, that power in any form cannot be trusted if it is not restrained. This distrust of power stemmed not only from his acute class consciousness and his awareness of the simple rule that powerful individuals and organizations have a way of circumventing the law but also from a lesson he had learned while serving on the Securities and Exchange Commission in the 1930s. For Douglas, power always required checks, without which liberty cannot be preserved. Concurring here with the majority, he continued throughout the 1960s to side with the majority in decisions aimed both at expanding the civil rights of the accused and limiting the power of law enforcement, a line

of decisions that culminated in *Miranda v. Arizona* (1966), which resulted in the declaration of numerous formal rights of arrestees, including the right to have an attorney present while being questioned by police.

♦ *Griswold v. Connecticut*

In 1961 Estelle Griswold, executive director of the Planned Parenthood League of Connecticut, and Dr. C. Lee Buxton, a doctor and professor at Yale Medical School, were arrested and convicted of breaking an 1879 Connecticut law that prohibited provision of contraceptive devices, medicines, or advice, including to married couples. The pair appealed their conviction to the Supreme Court, which decided by a vote of seven to two in their favor, striking down the Connecticut law and establishing a constitutional right to privacy among married couples.

Griswold is Douglas's most controversial opinion, and his most enduring. It is frequently cited as a case of judicial activism, a charge somewhat buoyed by the fact that three concurring opinions were filed along with Douglas's majority opinion, all of which disagreed with Douglas as to the extent of the right of privacy and where that right is located. Douglas's language is also particularly esoteric, finding the right to privacy in the "penumbras" (implications) created by the "emanations" of certain rights specifically articulated in the Bill of Rights.

Despite its esoteric language, however, *Griswold* represents a crystallization of Douglas's thought process with regard to privacy, a subject on which he had been writing for several years by this point. In 1958 Douglas published *The Right of the People*, a collection of lectures he gave at Franklin and Marshall College in the spring of 1957. In "The Right to Privacy," he states that citizens have the right to privacy in matters of religion, of conscience, and within their own home. In language foreshadowing the *Griswold* decision, he argues that "penumbras" of the Bill of Rights render these rights implicit, even though privacy is not mentioned explicitly.

These penumbras form the basis for Douglas's articulation of the right to privacy in *Griswold*. In this opinion, Douglas defines marriage as an "association" and argues that because the Supreme Court had already found a right to privacy in associations, marriage was likewise protected. Douglas also found that the Third Amendment's prohibition against forced quartering of soldiers, the Fourth Amendment's protection against unreasonable searches and seizures, the Fifth Amendment's self-incrimination clause, and the Ninth Amendment's provision that rights not specifically named are reserved to the people combine to create a broad constitutional right to privacy. Douglas is especially concerned with the right to privacy in one's own home and cites the Court's decision in *Mapp v. Ohio*, with which he concurred, as having created a right to privacy that the current decision upholds.

Douglas's opinion in *Griswold* is not without its irony, however. At the same time that Douglas was in the process of divorcing his third wife before marrying a woman more than forty years his junior, which provoked a fair amount of controversy, Douglas writes that marriage is an intimate, sacred association, one that ideally will endure. Despite what his personal critics said about his decision, and despite the charges of judicial activism that the decision provoked, *Griswold* was a monumental decision, which provided the basis for later watershed cases. *Eisenstadt v. Baird* (1972) extended Griswold's holding to unmarried couples; *Roe v. Wade* (1973) used Justice John Marshall Harlan II's "due process privacy" argument from his concurrence in *Griswold* in striking down laws prohibiting abortion; and *Lawrence v. Texas* (2003) relied on *Griswold* in finding a right to privacy in consensual sex between adults. Although it is still a controversial matter, the right to privacy articulated in *Griswold* continues to be an important judicial idea. *Griswold* also demonstrates the limits of Douglas's lasting influence, however, for while Douglas declared the broader right to privacy, it was Harlan's "due process" right to privacy that provided the lasting theoretical support for later cases.

♦ *Sierra Club v. Morton*

If *Griswold* is Douglas's most famous opinion, *Sierra Club v. Morton* is his most infamous. The U.S. Forest Service had approved the Walt Disney Corporation's plans to develop a $35-million ski resort in Mineral King Valley, California, adjacent to Sequoia National Park. The Sierra Club sued to prevent the development, and the Supreme Court ruled that the club, a "membership corporation," lacked standing and thus could not bring the suit. The majority opinion, written by Potter Stewart, indicated, however, that a member of the club who would be injured by the development, such as losing hunting, hiking, or other recreational habitat, could bring suit. Such a suit was subsequently brought, and the development was never undertaken; Mineral King was made a part of Sequoia National Forest in 1978.

Douglas's approach was somewhat different from Stewart's. Douglas, who had strongly dissented from a decision not to hear a case involving the spraying of the pesticide DDT over Long Island neighborhoods, had been waiting more than a decade to stand up and help the environment from the bench. Seizing the opportunity, he wastes no time in getting to the root of the matter, the question of standing, or who has the right to bring a case before the court. His solution is simple: The problem of standing can be solved by granting standing to inanimate objects that are affected by development and despoliation, namely, the environment, whether local or general. In this way, anyone could bring a suit on behalf of the environment, whether affected individuals, as the majority allows, or special interests, as the majority disallows—thus denying the Sierra Club standing, that is, the right to file suit in the case.

Douglas's opinion is not as peculiar as it seems at first blush; it addresses what he considers two critical problems with the majority's decision. First, although the majority grants affected individuals the right to sue on behalf of a particular locale, Douglas sees a perceptual problem in adjudicating just who is adversely affected by development

plans. Whether the particular local environment is necessary to sustain life, or whether it is simply a beautiful recreational area, which individuals can rightly claim to be adversely affected? Although he resided three thousand miles from his beloved Cascades, Douglas certainly would have felt that he had the standing to bring a lawsuit to stop development in that mountain range, but would others agree, noting that he lived on the other side of the continent and was, at best, a frequent visitor to the location? Would a California hiker who had completed the Appalachian Trail be perceived as having the standing to sue to stop development of a site in Pennsylvania? Granting the inanimate objects standing, permitting anyone to bring suit on their behalf, Douglas avers, solves the problem of deciding which individuals truly are injured by the proposed action. The greater environmentalist ethic, as he terms it, can be advanced and protected in the courts.

Douglas's opinion also notes that other inanimate objects are granted standing in other types of cases. Ships, he points out, have been considered as persons in previous cases, and corporations are considered as persons for legal purposes. This same right, Douglas says, should be extended to waterways, landscapes, and even the air in areas that may be polluted or otherwise damaged by development. He argues that the natural objects that form the heart of America's beauty are not adequately protected by considering them part of the "public interest." While Congress theoretically has the power to act in their defense, he reminds us that the Congress is too "remote" from the problem. This is doubtless a loaded term. Congress is geographically remote from many of the vistas that could be developed. Moreover, given Douglas's distrust of power and the effect of wealth on the machinery of democracy, he clearly perceives Congress as remote from understanding the necessity of acting on behalf of the natural interests. Granting the inanimate natural objects standing solves this problem and offers them protection that Congress cannot.

♦ *Furman v. Georgia*

One of the most monumental and controversial decisions in history, the three cases that made up the *Furman v. Georgia* decision declared that capital punishment, as then practiced, amounted to an unconstitutional violation of the Eighth Amendment's prohibition on cruel and unusual punishments. The decision, which caught the nation by surprise, was so contested within the Supreme Court that nine separate opinions were filed. Five justices—Douglas, William Brennan, Thurgood Marshall, Potter Stewart, and Byron White—agreed that the death penalty as administered was unconstitutional, though for different reasons; none of the five signed any other's concurring opinion. Four justices—Chief Justice Warren Burger, Harry Blackmun, Lewis Powell, and William Rehnquist—found that the death penalty as administered was compatible with the Eighth Amendment and dissented from the majority's opinion.

Douglas's opinion is typically far-ranging, extending its consideration to the development of English law back to the Norman conquest of 1066. He notes that the English Bill of Rights (1689), from which the Eighth Amendment derives its language, was intended to prohibit discriminatory application of harsh penalties. He further states that the United States had a history of including prohibitions against cruel and unusual punishments in state constitutions and other legally determinative documents prior to the adoption of the Bill of Rights in 1791. Douglas argues, however, that this history is unhelpful in determining what constitutes a cruel or unusual punishment, the question at the center of *Furman*.

For Douglas, the term *cruel and unusual* clearly refers to punishments deemed "barbaric," but he goes further and states that it is cruel and unusual to apply the death penalty disproportionately to minorities or social outcasts. This is a critical insight and one that he bases on the findings of the President's Commission on Law Enforcement and the Administration of Justice, which found that the death penalty was disproportionately imposed on the poor, on African Americans, and on "unpopular groups," groups that Douglas had been defending from the bench for several decades. In driving the point home, he makes sure to mention that each of the defendants in the three cases under consideration was black and that the victims were white. Douglas also wonders whether anyone can find a wealthy person in American history who was executed for his or her crimes or whether the execution rolls were exclusively populated by those from lower economic classes.

On January 21, 1972, after hearing oral arguments in *Furman*, the nine justices convened to discuss the case among the entire assembled Court, the only time they would do so during their deliberations, speaking in order of seniority. Chief Justice Warren Burger explained that he did not see a constitutional problem with the death penalty and would vote to uphold the sentences. Douglas, speaking second as the longest-serving member of the Court, declared that he did not believe that the death penalty as applied passed constitutional muster and that he would vote against it. In so doing, he was the first justice to cast a vote against the death penalty in *Furman*. By addressing the issue of the racial disparities in application, as Douglas did in that conference and at length in his opinion, he stood far ahead of his colleagues on the bench. Although Brennan and Marshall declared their belief that the death penalty violated the Eighth Amendment and thus was unconstitutional in all cases, neither of them considered the racially discriminatory application of the penalty in their opinions. Neither did White or Stewart, both of whom wrote in concurrence on the basis of the capriciousness with which the death penalty was arbitrarily applied. Only Douglas was willing to look at the facts surrounding the use of the death penalty and declare his opposition based on the inequitable application of the penalty based on race. This discrimination was for him "incontestable," and he declares that any penalty

that can be shown to be discriminatorily applied, whether on the basis of the defendant's race, religion, social position, class or wealth, is inherently cruel and unusual and thus unconstitutional.

Impact and Legacy

In *Of Men and Mountains*, Douglas writes of a friend good-naturedly criticizing him for appearing to sleep during a hearing. Not true, Douglas is said to have replied, adding that he was fishing in the Cascades. This is an apt metaphor for his legacy. As a former law clerk put it, he had a unique capacity to take one to the top of the mountain and show the view. His detractors always felt that he was looking too far away from where he was. Both are correct, and Douglas's legacy is decidedly mixed.

On the negative side, Douglas was uniformly successful in alienating and making enemies of virtually everyone around him. He estranged himself from his two children so completely that neither bothered to tell him when their mother, his first wife, died. He was difficult to work with on the Supreme Court, continually antagonizing fellow justices and believing himself to be attacked by them, which both contributed to and stemmed from his natural predilection toward working alone. His critics were also correct in noticing that Douglas always had his eye on the next mountain, even aspiring to the presidency. His aspirations frequently had him politicking on his own behalf or inveighing on others to push his name onto a ticket. Douglas was Roosevelt's second choice for the vice presidency in 1944, Harry Truman's first choice in 1948, and reportedly Lyndon Johnson's first choice in 1960. For much of his first two decades on the bench, he served as a Supreme Court justice while openly trying to leave the bench, which demonstrated a lack of commitment to his position and, to his critics, a lack of earnestness in how he approached weighty constitutional problems.

Further, Douglas excelled in grandstanding and in making himself the center of spectacle and controversy. Always acting on the principle that all publicity was good publicity, he took virtually any opportunity to garner attention in the press, such as his affecting an impromptu press conference while being rescued from a near-fatal mountainside horseback riding accident in 1949. Additionally, Douglas wrote more books than any other Supreme Court justice, and the frequency with which he wrote brought a great deal of unwanted attention to the Court. He added to the controversy by publishing some of his writings in *Evergreen* magazine, which was infamous for frequently printing photographs of topless women, and in *Playboy*. The future president Gerald R. Ford attacked Douglas on moral grounds for writing for both of these publications.

At the same time, not all of Douglas's grandstanding can be fairly derided; despite the brash, abrasive way in which he often acted, he was willing to stand up for what he believed was right, even when he knew that he would do so alone. In 1953 Douglas issued a judicial order staying the execution for treason of Julius and Ethel Rosenberg, for which he was himself accused of treason. He saw his colleagues on the Court unite to overturn his order and allow the execution to go forward. In 1973, while on vacation in Washington, he reinstated a lower court's order to stop the bombing of Cambodia, thus officially bringing the Vietnam War to a halt for six hours, the time it took for the other eight justices to overturn his order unanimously and allow the bombing campaign to proceed. As his concurring opinion in *Furman* and dissenting opinion in *Dennis* demonstrate, Douglas often was willing to speak plainly and bluntly about the injustices he saw.

Douglas was undeniably a legal visionary. This gift—his ability to see consequences that lay ahead and articulate the problems and his decisions accordingly—was at times also a liability, as he often lacked the patience necessary to negotiate intermediate steps and chose instead to opine based on the reality he saw down the road rather than on the reality presented by the cases at hand. Instead of adjudicating in accordance with judicial precedent, he adjudicated on principle and insight; as a result he limited his own legal legacy. Unlike Hugo Black or Felix Frankfurter, justices remembered for the theoretical legacies they left, and unlike William Brennan, remembered for his dexterity in dealing with legal doctrine, Douglas is remembered primarily for individual opinions. The bulk of these opinions demonstrate that his opinions consistently defended the rights of the poor, of minorities, and of unpopular segments of society against entrenched wealth and power, particularly the police and the state.

Ultimately, Douglas's place in history is debated. He was an uncompromising defender of civil rights, free speech, privacy, and the belief that all citizens, regardless of wealth or social standing, deserve the same rights and privileges as the wealthy. At the same time, however, he has been described as having harmed his causes more than he helped them, owing to his confrontational style and his willingness to go it alone rather than compromise and seek support from others. His most obvious legacy rests in the pieces of wilderness that his efforts preserved for posterity, but the eminent civil libertarian left his mark on constitutional jurisprudence as well.

Key Sources

The William O. Douglas Papers at the Library of Congress is the single largest collection of Douglas's writings and material, with extensive holdings extending back to his time at Columbia Law School. The Oyez Project (http://www.oyez.org), an online Supreme Court archive, has links to Douglas's opinions (http://www.oyez.org/justices/william_o_douglas/opinions/); in some cases, audio recordings are available. A prolific author, Douglas left a large body of writings. Prominent among them are *The Right of the People* (1958) and *Points of Rebellion* (1969), both of

which contain writings vital to understanding Douglas's political and judicial thought processes. His two autobiographies, *Go East, Young Man: The Early Years* (1974) and *The Court Years, 1939–1975* (1980), contain his firsthand account of his career. *Of Men and Mountains* (1950) is Douglas's best-known naturalist work and is useful for his explanations of the ways in which his exposure to the wilderness shaped him. *Nature's Justice: Writings of William O. Douglas* (2000), edited by James M. O'Fallon, is an excellent volume of Douglas's major writings.

Essential Quotes

"We then start probing men's minds for motive and purpose; they become entangled in the law not for what they did, but for what they thought; *they get convicted not for what they said, but for the purpose with which they said it."*

(*Dennis v. United States*)

"Free speech has occupied an exalted position because of the high service it has given our society. Its protection is essential to the very existence of a democracy."

(*Dennis v. United States*)

"As stated in the Weeks *case, if evidence seized in violation of the Fourth Amendment can be used against an accused, 'his right to be secure against such searches and seizures is of no value, and … might as well be stricken from the* Constitution*.'"*

(*Mapp v. Ohio*)

"Would we allow the police to search the sacred precincts of marital bedrooms for telltale signs of the use of contraceptives? The very idea is repulsive to the notions of privacy surrounding the marriage relationship."

(*Griswold v. Connecticut*)

"Marriage is a coming together for better or for worse, hopefully enduring, and intimate to the degree of being sacred. It is an association that promotes a way of life, not causes; a harmony in living, not political faiths; a bilateral loyalty, not commercial or social projects."

(*Griswold v. Connecticut*)

Essential Quotes

"The critical question of 'standing' would be simplified and also put neatly in focus if we fashioned a federal rule that allowed environmental issues to be litigated before federal agencies or federal courts in the name of the inanimate object about to be despoiled, defaced, or invaded by roads and bulldozers, and where injury is the subject of public outrage."

(*Sierra Club v. Morton*)

"It would seem to be incontestable that the death penalty inflicted on one defendant is 'unusual' if it discriminates against him by reason of his race, religion, wealth, social position, or class, or if it is imposed under a procedure that gives room for the play of such prejudices."

(*Furman v. Georgia*)

"One searches our chronicles in vain for the execution of any member of the affluent strata of this society."

(*Furman v. Georgia*)

Further Reading

■ Books

Ball, Howard, and Phillip J. Cooper. *Of Power and Right: Hugo Black, William O. Douglas, and America's Constitutional Revolution*. New York: Oxford University Press, 1992.

Bosmajian, Haig A. *Justice Douglas and Freedom of Speech*. Metuchen, N.J.: Scarecrow Press, 1980.

Countryman, Vern. *The Judicial Record of Justice William O. Douglas*. Cambridge, Mass.: Harvard University Press, 1974.

Murphy, Bruce Allen. *Wild Bill: The Legend and Life of William O. Douglas*. New York: Random House, 2003.

Simon, James F. *Independent Journey: The Life of William O. Douglas*. New York: Harper and Row, 1980.

Urofsky, Melvin I., ed. *The Douglas Letters: Selections from the Private Papers of Justice William O. Douglas*. Bethesda, Md.: Adler and Adler, 1987.

—*Anthony Santoro*

Questions for Further Study

1. Compare and contrast the arguments on free speech (even for anti-American causes) that Douglas makes in *Dennis v. United States* with those of William Brennan on the Texas flag-burning case four decades later. How did the two justices' reasoning processes align with one another, and how did they differ?

2. In *Griswold v. Connecticut*, Douglas raises the issue of a "right to privacy," a powerful legal concept that would influence decisions on abortion and other social issues. How does he justify a "right to privacy" when this is not spelled out in the Constitution? Is there sufficient evidence in the document to infer such a right, as Douglas did? Why or why not?

3. Do you agree or disagree with Douglas's position, expressed in his *Sierra Club v. Morton* opinion, that inanimate objects can in some cases possess legal standing? Discuss his arguments and examples, along with any others you might find in current events, and consider what limits there should be for such an interpretation.

Dennis v. United States

1951

[Douglas dissent]

If this were a case where those who claimed protection under the First Amendment were teaching the techniques of sabotage, the assassination of the President, the filching of documents from public files, the planting of bombs, the art of street warfare, and the like, I would have no doubts. The freedom to speak is not absolute; the teaching of methods of terror and other seditious conduct should be beyond the pale along with obscenity and immorality. This case was argued as if those were the facts. The argument imported much seditious conduct into the record. That is easy, and it has popular appeal, for the activities of Communists in plotting and scheming against the free world are common knowledge. … Petitioners, however, were not charged with a "conspiracy to overthrow" the Government. They were charged with a conspiracy to form a party and groups and assemblies of people who teach and advocate the overthrow of our Government by force or violence and with a conspiracy to advocate and teach its overthrow by force and violence. It may well be that indoctrination in the techniques of terror to destroy the Government would be indictable under either statute. But the teaching which is condemned here is of a different character.

So far as the present record is concerned, what petitioners did was to organize people to teach and themselves teach the Marxist-Leninist doctrine contained chiefly in four books: Stalin, *Foundations of Leninism* (1924); Marx and Engels, *Manifesto of the Communist Party* (1848); Lenin, *The State and Revolution* (1917); *History of the Communist Party of the Soviet Union* (1939).

Those books are to Soviet Communism what *Mein Kampf* was to Nazism. If they are understood, the ugliness of Communism is revealed, its deceit and cunning are exposed, the nature of its activities becomes apparent, and the chances of its success less likely. That is not, of course, the reason why petitioners chose these books for their classrooms. They are fervent Communists to whom these volumes are gospel. They preached the creed with the hope that some day it would be acted upon.

The opinion of the Court does not outlaw these texts nor condemn them to the fire, as the Communists do literature offensive to their creed. But if the books themselves are not outlawed, if they can lawfully remain on library shelves, by what reasoning does their use in a classroom become a crime? It would not be a crime under the Act to introduce these books to a class, though that would be teaching what the creed of violent overthrow of the Government is. The Act, as construed, requires the element of intent—that those who teach the creed believe in it. The crime then depends not on what is taught, but on who the teacher is. That is to make freedom of speech turn not on what is said, but on the intent with which it is said. Once we start down that road, we enter territory dangerous to the liberties of every citizen.

There was a time in England when the concept of constructive treason flourished. Men were punished not for raising a hand against the king, but for thinking murderous thoughts about him. The Framers of the Constitution were alive to that abuse, and took steps to see that the practice would not flourish here. Treason was defined to require overt acts—the evolution of a plot against the country into an actual project. The present case is not one of treason. But the analogy is close when the illegality is made to turn on intent, not on the nature of the act. We then start probing men's minds for motive and purpose; they become entangled in the law not for what they did, but for what they thought; they get convicted not for what they said, but for the purpose with which they said it. …

Free speech has occupied an exalted position because of the high service it has given our society. Its protection is essential to the very existence of a democracy. … When ideas compete in the market for acceptance, full and free discussion exposes the false, and they gain few adherents. Full and free discussion even of ideas we hate encourages

the testing of our own prejudices and preconceptions. Full and free discussion keeps a society from becoming stagnant and unprepared for the stresses and strains that work to tear all civilizations apart.

Full and free discussion has indeed been the first article of our faith. We have founded our political system on it. It has been the safeguard of every religious, political, philosophical, economic, and racial group amongst us. We have counted on it to keep us from embracing what is cheap and false; we have trusted the common sense of our people to choose the doctrine true to our genius and to reject the rest. This has been the one single outstanding tenet that has made our institutions the symbol of freedom and equality. We have deemed it more costly to liberty to suppress a despised minority than to let them vent their spleen. We have above all else feared the political censor. We have wanted a land where our people can be exposed to all the diverse creeds and cultures of the world. …

The nature of Communism as a force on the world scene would, of course, be relevant to the issue of clear and present danger of petitioners' advocacy within the United States. But the primary consideration is the strength and tactical position of petitioners and their converts in this country. On that, there is no evidence in the record. If we are to take judicial notice of the threat of Communists within the nation, it should not be difficult to conclude that, as a political party, they are of little consequence. Communists in this country have never made a respectable or serious showing in any election. I would doubt that there is a village, let alone a city or county or state, which the Communists could carry. Communism in the world scene is no bogeyman; but Communism as a political faction or party in this country plainly is. Communism has been so thoroughly exposed in this country that it has been crippled as a political force. Free speech has destroyed it as an effective political party. It is inconceivable that those who went up and down this country preaching the doctrine of revolution which petitioners espouse would have any success … the doctrine of Soviet revolution is exposed in all of its ugliness, and the American people want none of it.

How it can be said that there is a clear and present danger that this advocacy will succeed is, therefore, a mystery. …

Free speech—the glory of our system of government—should not be sacrificed on anything less than plain and objective proof of danger that the evil advocated is imminent. On this record, no one can say that petitioners and their converts are in such a strategic position as to have even the slightest chance of achieving their aims.

The First Amendment provides that "Congress shall make no law … abridging the freedom of speech." The Constitution provides no exception. This does not mean, however, that the Nation need hold its hand until it is in such weakened condition that there is no time to protect itself from incitement to revolution. Seditious conduct can always be punished. But the command of the First Amendment is so clear that we should not allow Congress to call a halt to free speech except in the extreme case of peril from the speech itself. The First Amendment makes confidence in the common sense of our people and in their maturity of judgment the great postulate of our democracy. Its philosophy is that violence is rarely, if ever, stopped by denying civil liberties to those advocating resort to force. The First Amendment reflects the philosophy of Jefferson that it is time enough for the rightful purposes of civil government for its officers to interfere when principles break out into overt acts against peace and good order.

The political censor has no place in our public debates. Unless and until extreme and necessitous circumstances are shown, our aim should be to keep speech unfettered and to allow the processes of law to be invoked only when the provocateurs among us move from speech to action.

Vishinsky wrote in 1938 in *The Law of the Soviet State,* "In our state, naturally, there is and can be no place for freedom of speech, press, and so on for the foes of socialism."

Our concern should be that we accept no such standard for the United States. Our faith should be that our people will never give support to these advocates of revolution, so long as we remain loyal to the purposes for which our Nation was founded.

Glossary

the Act:	the state law under discussion in the case
alive to:	aware of
constructive treason:	treason defined by a particularly severe interpretation, or construction, of the law
hold its hand:	resist taking action
provocateurs:	persons who deliberately stir up unrest
seditious:	urging revolt
turn on intent:	revolve around the intentions of the party or parties involved
Vishinsky:	Andrey Vishinsky, one of the leading prosecutors in the Moscow show trials by which the Soviet dictator Josef Stalin liquidated most of his enemies in the 1930s

Mapp v. Ohio

1961

[Douglas concurrence]

Though I have joined the opinion of the Court, I add a few words. This criminal proceeding started with a lawless search and seizure. The police entered a home forcefully, and seized documents that were later used to convict the occupant of a crime.

She lived alone with her fifteen-year-old daughter in the second-floor flat of a duplex in Cleveland. At about 1:30 in the afternoon of May 23, 1957, three policemen arrived at this house. They rang the bell, and the appellant, appearing at her window, asked them what they wanted. According to their later testimony, the policemen had come to the house on information from "a confidential source that there was a person hiding out in the home who was wanted for questioning in connection with a recent bombing."

To the appellant's question, however, they replied only that they wanted to question her, and would not state the subject about which they wanted to talk.

The appellant, who had retained an attorney in connection with a pending civil matter, told the police she would call him to ask if she should let them in. On her attorney's advice, she told them she would let them in only when they produced a valid search warrant. For the next two and a half hours, the police laid siege to the house. At four o'clock, their number was increased to at least seven. Appellant's lawyer appeared on the scene, and one of the policemen told him that they now had a search warrant, but the officer refused to show it. Instead, going to the back door, the officer first tried to kick it in and, when that proved unsuccessful, he broke the glass in the door and opened it from the inside.

The appellant, who was on the steps going up to her flat, demanded to see the search warrant, but the officer refused to let her see it, although he waved a paper in front of her face. She grabbed it and thrust it down the front of her dress. The policemen seized her, took the paper from her, and had her handcuffed to another officer. She was taken upstairs, thus bound, and into the larger of the two bedrooms in the apartment; there she was forced to sit on the bed. Meanwhile, the officers entered the house and made a complete search of the four rooms of her flat and of the basement of the house.

The testimony concerning the search is largely nonconflicting. The approach of the officers; their long wait outside the home, watching all its doors; the arrival of reinforcements armed with a paper; breaking into the house; putting their hands on appellant and handcuffing her; numerous officers ransacking through every room and piece of furniture while the appellant sat, a prisoner in her own bedroom. There is direct conflict in the testimony, however, as to where the evidence which is the basis of this case was found. To understand the meaning of that conflict, one must understand that this case is based on the knowing possession of four little pamphlets, a couple of photographs, and a little pencil doodle—all of which are alleged to be pornographic.

According to the police officers who participated in the search, these articles were found, some in appellant's dressers and some in a suitcase found by her bed. According to appellant, most of the articles were found in a cardboard box in the basement; one in the suitcase beside her bed. All of this material, appellant—and a friend of hers—said were odds and ends belonging to a recent boarder, a man who had left suddenly for New York and had been detained there. As the Supreme Court of Ohio read the statute under which appellant is charged, she is guilty of the crime whichever story is true.

The Ohio Supreme Court sustained the conviction even though it was based on the documents obtained in the lawless search. For, in Ohio, evidence obtained by an unlawful search and seizure is admissible in a criminal prosecution, at least where it was not taken from the "defendant's person by the use of brutal or offensive force against defendant."… This evidence would have been inadmissible in a federal prosecution. For, as stated in the former decision,

"The effect of the Fourth Amendment is to put the courts of the United States and Federal officials, in the exercise of their power and authority, under limitations and restraints."…

It was therefore held that evidence obtained (which in that case was documents and correspondence) from a home without any warrant was not admissible in a federal prosecution.

We held in *Wolf v. Colorado* that the Fourth Amendment was applicable to the States by reason

Document Text

of the Due Process Clause of the Fourteenth Amendment. But a majority held that the exclusionary rule of the *Weeks* case was not required of the States, that they could apply such sanctions as they chose. That position had the necessary votes to carry the day. But, with all respect, it was not the voice of reason or principle. As stated in the *Weeks* case, if evidence seized in violation of the Fourth Amendment can be used against an accused, "his right to be secure against such searches and seizures is of no value, and ... might as well be stricken from the Constitution."

When we allowed States to give constitutional sanction to the "shabby business" of unlawful entry into a home ... we did indeed rob the Fourth Amendment of much meaningful force. There are, of course, other theoretical remedies. One is disciplinary action within the hierarchy of the police system, including prosecution of the police officer for a crime. Yet, as Mr. Justice [Frank] Murphy said in *Wolf v. Colorado,*

"Self-scrutiny is a lofty ideal, but its exaltation reaches new heights if we expect a District Attorney to prosecute himself or his associates for well meaning violations of the search and seizure clause during a raid the District Attorney or his associates have ordered."

The only remaining remedy, if exclusion of the evidence is not required, is an action of trespass by the homeowner against the offending officer. Mr. Justice Murphy showed how onerous and difficult it would be for the citizen to maintain that action, and how meager the relief even if the citizen prevails. The truth is that trespass actions against officers who make unlawful searches and seizures are mainly illusory remedies.

Without judicial action making the exclusionary rule applicable to the States, *Wolf v. Colorado,* in practical effect, reduced the guarantee against unreasonable searches and seizures to "a dead letter," as Mr. Justice [Wiley B.] Rutledge said in his dissent.

Glossary

appellant: the party appealing, or asking for a reconsideration of, a decision by a lower court

stricken: removed

the *Weeks* case: *Weeks v. United States* (1914), which the Court considered in making its *Wolf* ruling

Griswold v. Connecticut

1965

Appellant Griswold is Executive Director of the Planned Parenthood League of Connecticut. Appellant Buxton is a licensed physician and a professor at the Yale Medical School who served as Medical Director for the League at its Center in New Haven—a center open and operating from November 1 to November 10, 1961, when appellants were arrested.

They gave information, instruction, and medical advice to married persons as to the means of preventing conception. They examined the wife and prescribed the best contraceptive device or material for her use. Fees were usually charged, although some couples were serviced free....

The association of people is not mentioned in the Constitution nor in the Bill of Rights. The right to educate a child in a school of the parents' choice—whether public or private or parochial—is also not mentioned. Nor is the right to study any particular subject or any foreign language. Yet the First Amendment has been construed to include certain of those rights....

In *NAACP v. Alabama,* we protected the "freedom to associate and privacy in one's associations," noting that freedom of association was a peripheral First Amendment right.... In other words, the First Amendment has a penumbra where privacy is protected from governmental intrusion. In like context, we have protected forms of "association" that are not political in the customary sense, but pertain to the social, legal, and economic benefit of the members....

Those cases involved more than the "right of assembly"—a right that extends to all, irrespective of their race or ideology. The right of "association," like the right of belief, is more than the right to attend a meeting; it includes the right to express one's attitudes or philosophies by membership in a group or by affiliation with it or by other lawful means. Association in that context is a form of expression of opinion, and, while it is not expressly included in the First Amendment, its existence is necessary in making the express guarantees fully meaningful.

The foregoing cases suggest that specific guarantees in the Bill of Rights have penumbras, formed by emanations from those guarantees that help give them life and substance. Various guarantees create zones of privacy. The right of association contained in the penumbra of the First Amendment is one, as we have seen. The Third Amendment, in its prohibition against the quartering of soldiers "in any house" in time of peace without the consent of the owner, is another facet of that privacy. The Fourth Amendment explicitly affirms the "right of the people to be secure in their persons, houses, papers, and effects, against unreasonable searches and seizures." The Fifth Amendment, in its Self-Incrimination Clause, enables the citizen to create a zone of privacy which government may not force him to surrender to his detriment. The Ninth Amendment provides: "The enumeration in the Constitution, of certain rights, shall not be construed to deny or disparage others retained by the people."

The Fourth and Fifth Amendments were described in *Boyd v. United States* as protection against all governmental invasions "of the sanctity of a man's home and the privacies of life,"... the Fourth Amendment as creating a "right to privacy, no less important than any other right carefully and particularly reserved to the people."

We have had many controversies over these penumbral rights of "privacy and repose."... These cases bear witness that the right of privacy which presses for recognition here is a legitimate one.

The present case, then, concerns a relationship lying within the zone of privacy created by several fundamental constitutional guarantees. And it concerns a law which, in forbidding the use of contraceptives, rather than regulating their manufacture or sale, seeks to achieve its goals by means having a maximum destructive impact upon that relationship. Such a law cannot stand in light of the familiar principle, so often applied by this Court, that a

"governmental purpose to control or prevent activities constitutionally subject to state regulation may not be achieved by means which sweep unnecessarily broadly and thereby invade the area of protected freedoms [*NAACP v. Alabama*]."

Would we allow the police to search the sacred precincts of marital bedrooms for telltale signs of the use of contraceptives? The very idea is repulsive to the notions of privacy surrounding the marriage relationship.

We deal with a right of privacy older than the Bill of Rights—older than our political parties, older than

Document Text

our school system. Marriage is a coming together for better or for worse, hopefully enduring, and intimate to the degree of being sacred. It is an association that promotes a way of life, not causes; a harmony in living, not political faiths; a bilateral loyalty, not commercial or social projects. Yet it is an association for as noble a purpose as any involved in our prior decisions.

Glossary

appellant: the party appealing, or asking for a reconsideration of, a decision by a lower court

emanations: things that arise from a particular source

parochial: religious

penumbra: the halo or glow surrounding a source of light

SIERRA CLUB V. MORTON

1972

[Douglas dissent]

I share the views of my Brother BLACKMUN, and would reverse the judgment below.

The critical question of "standing" would be simplified and also put neatly in focus if we fashioned a federal rule that allowed environmental issues to be litigated before federal agencies or federal courts in the name of the inanimate object about to be despoiled, defaced, or invaded by roads and bulldozers, and where injury is the subject of public outrage. Contemporary public concern for protecting nature's ecological equilibrium should lead to the conferral of standing upon environmental objects to sue for their own preservation.... This suit would therefore be more properly labeled as *Mineral King v. Morton*.

Inanimate objects are sometimes parties in litigation. A ship has a legal personality, a fiction found useful for maritime purposes. The corporation sole—a creature of ecclesiastical law—is an acceptable adversary, and large fortunes ride on its cases. The ordinary corporation is a "person" for purposes of the adjudicatory processes, whether it represents proprietary, spiritual, aesthetic, or charitable causes.

So it should be as respects valleys, alpine meadows, rivers, lakes, estuaries, beaches, ridges, groves of trees, swampland, or even air that feels the destructive pressures of modern technology and modern life. The river, for example, is the living symbol of all the life it sustains or nourishes—fish, aquatic insects, water ouzels, otter, fisher, deer, elk, bear, and all other animals, including man, who are dependent on it or who enjoy it for its sight, its sound, or its life. The river as plaintiff speaks for the ecological unit of life that is part of it. Those people who have a meaningful relation to that body of water—whether it be a fisherman, a canoeist, a zoologist, or a logger—must be able to speak for the values which the river represents, and which are threatened with destruction.

I do not know Mineral King. I have never seen it, nor traveled it.... The Sierra Club, in its complaint alleges that "[o]ne of the principal purposes of the Sierra Club is to protect and conserve the national resources of the Sierra Nevada Mountains." The District Court held that this uncontested allegation made the Sierra Club "sufficiently aggrieved" to have "standing" to sue on behalf of Mineral King.

Mineral King is doubtless like other wonders of the Sierra Nevada such as Tuolumne Meadows and the John Muir Trail. Those who hike it, fish it, hunt it, camp in it, frequent it, or visit it merely to sit in solitude and wonderment are legitimate spokesmen for it, whether they may be few or many. Those who have that intimate relation with the inanimate object about to be injured, polluted, or otherwise despoiled are its legitimate spokesmen.

The Solicitor General ... takes a wholly different approach. He considers the problem in terms of "government by the Judiciary." With all respect, the problem is to make certain that the inanimate objects, which are the very core of America's beauty, have spokesmen before they are destroyed. It is, of course, true that most of them are under the control of a federal or state agency. The standards given those agencies are usually expressed in terms of the "public interest." Yet "public interest" has so many differing shades of meaning as to be quite meaningless on the environmental front. Congress accordingly has adopted ecological standards in the National Environmental Policy Act of 1969....

Yet the pressures on agencies for favorable action one way or the other are enormous. The suggestion that Congress can stop action which is undesirable is true in theory; yet even Congress is too remote to give meaningful direction, and its machinery is too ponderous to use very often. The federal agencies of which I speak are not venal or corrupt. But they are notoriously under the control of powerful interests who manipulate them through advisory committees, or friendly working relations, or who have that natural affinity with the agency which in time develops between the regulator and the regulated. As early as 1894, Attorney General [Richard] Olney predicted that regulatory agencies might become "industry-minded," as illustrated by his forecast concerning the Interstate Commerce Commission:

"The Commission ... is, or can be, made of great use to the railroads. It satisfies the popular clamor for a government supervision of railroads, at the same time that that supervision is almost entirely nominal. Further, the older such a commission gets to be, the more inclined it will be found to take the business and railroad view of things."

Document Text

Years later, a court of appeals observed,

"the recurring question which has plagued public regulation of industry [is] whether the regulatory agency is unduly oriented toward the interests of the industry it is designed to regulate, rather than the public interest it is designed to protect."

The Forest Service—one of the federal agencies behind the scheme to despoil Mineral King—has been notorious for its alignment with lumber companies, although its mandate from Congress directs it to consider the various aspects of multiple use in its supervision of the national forests.

The voice of the inanimate object, therefore, should not be stilled. That does not mean that the judiciary takes over the managerial functions from the federal agency. It merely means that, before these priceless bits of Americana (such as a valley, an alpine meadow, a river, or a lake) are forever lost or are so transformed as to be reduced to the eventual rubble of our urban environment, the voice of the existing beneficiaries of these environmental wonders should be heard.

Perhaps they will not win. Perhaps the bulldozers of "progress" will plow under all the aesthetic wonders of this beautiful land. That is not the present question. The sole question is, who has standing to be heard?

Those who hike the Appalachian Trail into Sunfish Pond, New Jersey, and camp or sleep there, or run the Allagash in Maine, or climb the Guadalupes in West Texas, or who canoe and portage the Quetico Superior in Minnesota, certainly should have standing to defend those natural wonders before courts or agencies, though they live 3,000 miles away. Those who merely are caught up in environmental news or propaganda and flock to defend these waters or areas may be treated differently. That is why these environmental issues should be tendered by the inanimate object itself. Then there will be assurances that all of the forms of life which it represents will stand before the court—the pileated woodpecker as well as the coyote and bear, the lemmings as well as the trout in the streams. Those inarticulate members of the ecological group cannot speak. But those people who have so frequented the place as to know its values and wonders will be able to speak for the entire ecological community.

Ecology reflects the land ethic; and Aldo Leopold wrote in *A Sand County Almanac* (1949), "The land ethic simply enlarges the boundaries of the community to include soils, waters, plants, and animals, or collectively: the land."

That, as I see it, is the issue of "standing" in the present case and controversy.

Glossary

adjudicatory processes:	proceedings involved in deciding a legal case
brother:	a term by which Supreme Court justices refer to one another
the corporation sole:	a business entity, sometimes treated as a "person" under the law
litigated:	argued within a legal context
mandate:	authorization
nominal:	in name only
standing:	the right to bring legal action
venal:	open to bribery

FURMAN V. GEORGIA

1972

[Douglas concurrence]

In these three cases the death penalty was imposed, one of them for murder, and two for rape. In each, the determination of whether the penalty should be death or a lighter punishment was left by the State to the discretion of the judge or of the jury. In each of the three cases, the trial was to a jury. They are here on petitions for certiorari which we granted limited to the question whether the imposition and execution of the death penalty constitute "cruel and unusual punishment" within the meaning of the Eighth Amendment as applied to the States by the Fourteenth. I vote to vacate each judgment, believing that the exaction of the death penalty does violate the Eighth and Fourteenth Amendments.

That the requirements of due process ban cruel and unusual punishment is now settled....

It has been assumed in our decisions that punishment by death is not cruel, unless the manner of execution can be said to be inhuman and barbarous. It is also said in our opinions that the proscription of cruel and unusual punishments "is not fastened to the obsolete, but may acquire meaning as public opinion becomes enlightened by a humane justice." A like statement was made in *Trop v. Dulles,* that the Eighth Amendment "must draw its meaning from the evolving standards of decency that mark the progress of a maturing society."

The generality of a law inflicting capital punishment is one thing. What may be said of the validity of a law on the books and what may be done with the law in its application do, or may, lead to quite different conclusions.

It would seem to be incontestable that the death penalty inflicted on one defendant is "unusual" if it discriminates against him by reason of his race, religion, wealth, social position, or class, or if it is imposed under a procedure that gives room for the play of such prejudices.

There is evidence that the provision of the English Bill of Rights of 1689, from which the language of the Eighth Amendment was taken, was concerned primarily with selective or irregular application of harsh penalties, and that its aim was to forbid arbitrary and discriminatory penalties of a severe nature:

"Following the Norman conquest of England in 1066, the old system of penalties, which ensured equality between crime and punishment, suddenly disappeared. By the time systematic judicial records were kept, its demise was almost complete. With the exception of certain grave crimes for which the punishment was death or outlawry, the arbitrary fine was replaced by a discretionary amercement. Although amercement's discretionary character allowed the circumstances of each case to be taken into account, and the level of cash penalties to be decreased or increased accordingly, the amercement presented an opportunity for excessive or oppressive fines.

"The problem of excessive amercements became so prevalent that three chapters of the Magna Carta were devoted to their regulation. Maitland said of Chapter 14 that, 'very likely, there was no clause in the Magna Carta more grateful to the mass of the people.' Chapter 14 clearly stipulated as fundamental law a prohibition of excessiveness in punishments:

"A free man shall not be amerced for a trivial offence, except in accordance with the degree of the offence, and for a serious offence, he shall be amerced according to its gravity, saving his livelihood; and a merchant likewise, saving his merchandise; in the same way, a villein shall be amerced saving his wainage, if they fall into our mercy. And none of the aforesaid amercements shall be imposed except by the testimony of reputable men of the neighborhood."

The English Bill of Rights, enacted December 16, 1689, stated that "excessive bail ought not to be required, nor excessive fines imposed, nor cruel and unusual punishments inflicted." These were the words chosen for our Eighth Amendment. A like provision had been in Virginia's Constitution of 1776, and in the constitutions of seven other States. The Northwest Ordinance, enacted under the Articles of Confederation, included a prohibition of cruel and unusual punishments. But the debates of the First Congress on the Bill of Rights throw little light on its intended meaning....

The words "cruel and unusual" certainly include penalties that are barbaric. But the words, at least when read in light of the English proscription against selective and irregular use of penalties, suggest that it is "cruel and unusual" to apply the death penalty—or

Document Text

any other penalty—selectively to minorities whose numbers are few, who are outcasts of society, and who are unpopular, but whom society is willing to see suffer though it would not countenance general application of the same penalty across the board....

There is increasing recognition of the fact that the basic theme of equal protection is implicit in "cruel and unusual" punishments. "A penalty ... should be considered unusually imposed if it is administered arbitrarily or discriminatorily." The same authors add that "[t]he extreme rarity with which applicable death penalty provisions are put to use raises a strong inference of arbitrariness." The President's Commission on Law Enforcement and Administration of Justice recently concluded:

"Finally, there is evidence that the imposition of the death sentence and the exercise of dispensing power by the courts and the executive follow discriminatory patterns. The death sentence is disproportionately imposed, and carried out on the poor, the Negro, and the members of unpopular groups."

A study of capital cases in Texas from 1924 to 1968 reached the following conclusions:

"Application of the death penalty is unequal: most of those executed were poor, young, and ignorant."...

"Seventy-five of the 460 cases involved codefendants, who, under Texas law, were given separate trials. In several instances where a white and a Negro were co-defendants, the white was sentenced to life imprisonment or a term of years, and the Negro was given the death penalty."

"Another ethnic disparity is found in the type of sentence imposed for rape. The Negro convicted of rape is far more likely to get the death penalty than a term sentence, whereas whites and Latins are far more likely to get a term sentence than the death penalty."

Warden Lewis E. Lawes of Sing Sing said:

"Not only does capital punishment fail in its justification, but no punishment could be invented with so many inherent defects. It is an unequal punishment in the way it is applied to the rich and to the poor. The defendant of wealth and position never goes to the electric chair or to the gallows. Juries do not intentionally favour the rich, the law is theoretically impartial, but the defendant with ample means is able to have his case presented with every favourable aspect, while the poor defendant often has a lawyer assigned by the court. Sometimes such assignment is considered part of political patronage; usually the lawyer assigned has had no experience whatever in a capital case."

Former Attorney General Ramsey Clark has said, "It is the poor, the sick, the ignorant, the powerless and the hated who are executed. One searches our chronicles in vain for the execution of any member of the affluent strata of this society. The Leopolds and Loebs are given prison terms, not sentenced to death.

"Jackson, a black, convicted of the rape of a white woman, was 21 years old....

"Furman, a black, killed a householder while seeking to enter the home at night....

"Branch, a black, entered the rural home of a 65-year-old widow, a white, while she slept and raped her, holding his arm against her throat....

"We cannot say from facts disclosed in these records that these defendants were sentenced to death because they were black. Yet our task is not restricted to an effort to divine what motives impelled these death penalties. Rather, we deal with a system of law and of justice that leaves to the uncontrolled discretion of judges or juries the determination whether defendants committing these crimes should die or be imprisoned. Under these laws, no standards govern the selection of the penalty. People live or die, dependent on the whim of one man or of 12."...

Those who wrote the Eighth Amendment knew what price their forebears had paid for a system based not on equal justice, but on discrimination. In those days, the target was not the blacks or the poor, but the dissenters, those who opposed absolutism in government, who struggled for a parliamentary regime, and who opposed governments' recurring efforts to foist a particular religion on the people. But the tool of capital punishment was used with vengeance against the opposition and those unpopular with the regime. One cannot read this history without realizing that the desire for equality was reflected in the ban against "cruel and unusual punishments" contained in the Eighth Amendment.

In a Nation committed to equal protection of the laws there is no permissible "caste" aspect of law enforcement. Yet we know that the discretion of judges and juries in imposing the death penalty enables the penalty to be selectively applied, feeding prejudices against the accused if he is poor and despised, and lacking political clout, or if he is a member of a suspect or unpopular minority, and saving those who by social position may be in a more protected position. In ancient Hindu law, a Brahman was exempt from capital punishment, and, under that law, "[g]enerally, in the law books, punishment increased in severity as social status diminished." We have, I fear, taken in practice the same position, partially as a

Document Text

result of making the death penalty discretionary and partially as a result of the ability of the rich to purchase the services of the most respected and most resourceful legal talent in the Nation.

The high service rendered by the "cruel and unusual" punishment clause of the Eighth Amendment is to require legislatures to write penal laws that are evenhanded, nonselective, and nonarbitrary, and to require judges to see to it that general laws are not applied sparsely, selectively, and spottily to unpopular groups.

A law that stated that anyone making more than $50,000 would be exempt from the death penalty would plainly fall, as would a law that in terms said that blacks, those who never went beyond the fifth grade in school, those who made less than $3,000 a year, or those who were unpopular or unstable should be the only people executed. A law which, in the overall view, reaches that result in practice has no more sanctity than a law which in terms provides the same.

Thus, these discretionary statutes are unconstitutional in their operation. They are pregnant with discrimination, and discrimination is an ingredient not compatible with the idea of equal protection of the laws that is implicit in the ban on "cruel and unusual" punishments.

Any law which is nondiscriminatory on its face may be applied in such a way as to violate the Equal Protection Clause of the Fourteenth Amendment. Such conceivably might be the fate of a mandatory death penalty, where equal or lesser sentences were imposed on the elite, a harsher one on the minorities or members of the lower castes. Whether a mandatory death penalty would otherwise be constitutional is a question I do not reach.

I concur in the judgments of the Court.

Glossary

absolutism: complete control by a ruler

according to its gravity: in connection to the seriousness of the case

amerced: fined or charged

Brahman: the highest-ranking group in the caste system of Hinduism

capital cases: cases involving a crime for which the defendant might, if proved guilty, be executed

caste: a rigid form of social class

certiorari: a demand by a higher court that a lower court release its records relating to a particular case

discretionary amercement: choice, on the part of the court, in setting fines

disparity: difference, usually with the implication that one individual or group has an unfair advantage over others

due process: the right to proper, fair, and impartial treatment in legal proceedings

fastened to the obsolete: tied to something that is or will soon be outmoded

inference of arbitrariness: the conclusion that justice is not being applied fairly

into our mercy: under our jurisdiction

the Leopolds and Loebs: a reference to Nathan Leopold and Richard A. Loeb, rich young men convicted of murdering fourteen-year-old Bobby Franks in Chicago in 1924

Magna Carta: the "Great Charter," signed by King John of England in 1215, which granted specific rights to citizens and required the king to obey the law

Glossary

Maitland:	English historian Frederic William Maitland
our decisions:	decisions that the Supreme Court has made as a whole, whether or not Douglas had a role in a particular case
patronage:	the exchange of support and favors for political or social advantage
saving his livelihood:	with the exception of his means for earning an income (for example, tools)
a term sentence:	a sentence to serve a particular number of years
vacate:	overrule, strike down
villein:	peasant
wainage:	carts and carriages

William O. Douglas Wilderness outside Yakima, Washington

Douglass circa 1847–52. By Samuel J. Miller; American, 1822-1888.

Frederick Douglass: Original Analysis

Civil Rights Activist, Newspaper Editor, and Orator

1818–1895

Overview

Heralded as one of the most significant civil rights activists of the nineteenth century, Frederick Douglass was born a slave in Talbot County, Maryland, on February 7, 1818. From the most humble of beginnings, Douglass rose to become a world-famous orator, newspaper editor, and champion of the rights of women and African Americans.

Known in his youth as Frederick Augustus Washington Bailey, Douglass spent his first twenty years in bondage, first on a plantation owned by Edward Lloyd IV and then in the shipbuilding city of Baltimore, Maryland. Although it was illegal for slaves to gain an education, Douglass learned to read and write with the aid of his master's wife and through his own ingenuity. During his time in Baltimore, he secured a copy of Caleb Bingham's *Columbian Orator*, a collection of speeches by famous orators and politicians. The experience gained from practicing these speeches led Douglass to develop a powerful oratorical style that later allowed him to hold sway with audiences around the world.

Douglass began his life in freedom on September 3, 1838, when at the age of twenty he fled Baltimore, boarded a train, and headed for freedom in the North. Settling in New Bedford, Massachusetts, he changed his last name to Douglass and subsequently became acquainted with the movement to abolish slavery. In 1841 he was invited to speak before an antislavery meeting at Nantucket, Massachusetts, and was soon hired as a lecturing agent for the Massachusetts Anti-Slavery Society. His lectures detailing his experience in slavery were so eloquent that some charged that Douglass was an imposter who could never have been enslaved. In response, in 1845 he penned the first of three autobiographies, *Narrative of the Life of Frederick Douglass*, quieting his critics by offering details of his life in slavery, including the name of his master, Thomas Auld. He also spoke critically of Auld's brother, Hugh, with whom Douglass had lived during many of his years in slavery. Following the publication of the *Narrative*, Hugh Auld purchased Douglass from his brother and determined to bring him back to slavery in Maryland. To escape capture, Douglass departed for an extended tour of Ireland and Great Britain following publication of the *Narrative* and, through his many lectures there, gained an international reputation as an orator and reformer. His British admirers paid Douglass's slave master $711.66, and he returned to the United States a truly free man in April 1847.

For the remainder of the antebellum years, Douglass fought tirelessly for the rights of African Americans, for the abolition of slavery, and for women's rights. In 1848 he attended the Seneca Falls Convention on women's rights, where he persuaded the gathering to support a resolution calling for women's right to vote. While he continued to lecture on behalf of the antislavery movement, Douglass's reform horizon expanded to include temperance and especially voting and civil rights for black Americans. In the period 1847 through 1861, he edited a succession of newspapers beginning with the *North Star*. In 1851 Douglass's activism took a more political turn, and he renamed his weekly *Frederick Douglass' Paper*; it became an important organ for the antislavery Liberty Party. Once the Civil War erupted in 1861, Douglass supported the Union war effort and acted as a recruiter for African American troops. Twice during the war he was invited to the White House to advise President Abraham Lincoln on the participation of blacks in the war effort.

Following the ratification of the Thirteenth Amendment in 1865, Douglass rejoiced in the official abolition of slavery in the United States. He turned his efforts toward gaining the vote for African American men through the Fifteenth Amendment and improving the condition of his fellow black Americans. He also benefited from continued loyalty to the Republican Party through appointment to several offices. Douglass moved his family to Washington, D.C., in 1872 to be nearer the center of political change and served briefly as president of the Freedman's Savings Bank in 1874. As Reconstruction came to a close, President Rutherford B. Hayes appointed Douglass U.S. marshal for the District of Columbia. This post was followed in 1881 by his appointment by President James A. Garfield to the lucrative position of recorder of deeds for the District, whereby Douglass received a commission from all land transactions recorded in the office. His prominence and knowledge of world events led President Benjamin Harrison to designate Douglass as resident minister and consul general to the nation of Haiti, a post he held from 1889 to 1891, through the controversial attempt of the United States to secure a naval base on the island. Although his ministry left him on poor terms with some in Washington, Haiti appointed Douglass commissioner of that nation's pavilion at the World's Columbian Exposition held at Chicago in 1893.

In his senior years Douglass remained active on the lecture circuit, commanding audiences with his fiery speeches. Although he lost support of some feminist followers in the debate over the Fifteenth Amendment when he rejected the inclusion of women in that bill, he regained their respect with his support for their suffrage movement late in his life. In fact, it was following an address before the International Council of Women on February 20, 1895, that Douglass collapsed and died at Cedar Hill, his home in the Anacostia neighborhood of Washington, D.C.

Explanation and Analysis of Documents

Key documents offer a glimpse of Douglass's life and career before and after the Civil War. The first selection is from the first of Douglass's three published autobiographies, *Narrative of the Life of Frederick Douglass*, which appeared in 1845. Intended as antislavery propaganda, the *Narrative* served the secondary purpose of verifying and documenting Douglass's life in slavery. Douglass's letter to his former slave owner, Thomas Auld, was penned ten years following his escape from slavery and was published in Douglass's weekly newspaper. Douglass's most famous oration, "What to the Slave Is the Fourth of July?," was delivered before a sympathetic audience of antislavery activists in Rochester, New York, on July 5, 1852. "Our National Capital," is a lengthy speech Douglass delivered at Baltimore, Maryland, just after his appointment as federal marshal for the District of Columbia. In it, Douglass is critical of the lack of progress made on the issue of racial equality in the years following the abolition of slavery and the Civil War.

♦ *Narrative of the Life of Frederick Douglass*

In the spring of 1845 Douglass's first autobiography, *Narrative of the Life of Frederick Douglass, an American Slave, Written by Himself*, was published by the Anti-slavery Office in Boston. In the 1840s firsthand narratives of slavery, world travels, and Native American captivity were more popular than fiction with the reading public in the United States. Although Douglass's recollection of his first two decades in slavery was not the first slave narrative to gain wide readership, it became the most popular and most enduring account of American slavery. The *Narrative* served two important purposes. First and foremost it was antislavery propaganda that aimed to reveal the horrors of slavery, and as such it outsold any other black autobiography appearing in print before the Civil War. More than 4,500 copies sold during its first four months in publication, and by 1848 it had been translated into German, French, and Dutch. During Douglass's tour of Ireland and Great Britain from 1845 to 1847, at least two Irish and four English editions were printed. As many as thirty thousand copies of the book were sold by 1853.

Besides adding his own story to the growing body of slave narratives, Douglass had a second and more personal reason for penning an account of his enslavement. While

Time Line

1818	February 7	■ Frederick Augustus Washington Bailey is born at Holme Hill Farm on Tuckahoe Creek in Talbot County, Maryland, as the slave of Aaron Anthony, overseer for Edward Lloyd IV.
1827	October 18	■ Following the death of his master, young Frederick becomes the property of Thomas Auld in the division of Aaron Anthony's estate in Saint Michaels, Maryland, and is sent to live with his new master's brother, Hugh Auld, in Baltimore.
1833	March	■ Frederick returns to Saint Michaels to live with Thomas Auld.
1834	January 1	■ Frederick begins a year as a hired laborer in the home of the notorious "Negro breaker" Edward Covey.
1836	April	■ After a failed escape attempt, Frederick is returned to Baltimore and the home of Hugh Auld.
1838	September 3	■ Borrowing the identification papers of a free black sailor, Frederick boards a train and escapes to the North. He adopts the name Frederick Douglass after a character in Sir Walter Scott's *Lady of the Lake*.
1841	August 12–13	■ Douglass addresses an antislavery meeting at Nantucket, Massachusetts; his firsthand account of slavery is so compelling that he is hired as a lecturing agent for the Massachusetts Anti-Slavery Society.
1845	May	■ Douglass publishes *Narrative of the Life of Frederick Douglass*, the first of three autobiographies, and then departs for an extended tour of Ireland and the United Kingdom because details in the book could lead to his recapture and return to slavery.

Time Line

1848	September 3	■ Douglass writes his letter "To My Old Master" on the tenth anniversary of his escape from slavery; it is published five days later.
1852	July 5	■ As a world-famous orator, Douglass delivers his most famous speech, "What to the Slave Is the Fourth of July?" at Rochester, New York.
1855	August	■ Douglass's second autobiography, *My Bondage and My Freedom,* is published.
1859	August 20	■ Near Chambersburg, Maryland, Douglass meets secretly with John Brown, an American abolitionist who advocates and practices armed insurrection as a means to abolish slavery. At this meeting, Douglass refuses to join Brown's raid on the federal arsenal at Harpers Ferry, Virginia.
1863	February–March	■ Douglass issues the call for "Men of Color, to Arms!" and acts as a recruiter for the Union Army.
	July	■ Douglass meets with Abraham Lincoln at the White House to advise the president on African American participation in the war effort.
1874	March	■ Douglass is appointed president of the Freedman's Savings Bank in Washington, D.C.
1877	March 18	■ The Senate confirms Douglass's appointment as U.S. marshal for the District of Columbia.
	May 8	■ Douglass delivers his controversial "Our National Capital" lecture at the Douglass Institute in Baltimore.
1881	January	■ Douglass's third autobiography, *Life and Times of Frederick Douglass,* is published, but few copies sell. An expanded edition appears in 1892.
	March	■ President James A. Garfield appoints Douglass recorder of deeds for the District of Columbia.
1889	July 1	■ President Benjamin Harrison appoints Douglass minister resident and consul general to Haiti.
1895	February 20	■ Douglass dies at Cedar Hill, his home in the Anacostia neighborhood of the District of Columbia.

on the antislavery lecture circuit, Douglass was sometimes charged with defrauding his audience. Some believed that one who spoke so eloquently could never have been enslaved. Douglass wrote the *Narrative* to dispel the skepticism of his critics, but he did so at great personal risk. Although the book appeared seven years after Douglass left slavery, he was legally still a fugitive who risked recapture and possible return to slavery by revealing the intimate details of his life in bondage. Douglass willingly placed his freedom in jeopardy, but only to a degree. He left the United States for an extended tour of Ireland and Great Britain, returning in April 1847 after British reformers supplied the funds to pay his slave master to grant his true freedom.

Douglass's *Narrative* begins with his earliest memories as the slave of Aaron Anthony, chief overseer of the wealthy Maryland planter Edward Lloyd IV, who may have been Douglass's father. During the division of Anthony's estate following his 1826 death, Douglass passed to Anthony's daughter, Lucretia Planner Anthony Auld, and her husband, Thomas Auld. Douglass spent his youth traveling between the household of Thomas Auld on Maryland's rural Eastern Shore and that of his brother, Hugh Auld, who lived in Baltimore. For the year 1834, sixteen-year-old Douglass was leased to a small farmer near Saint Michaels, Maryland. In areas of the Upper South, where crops were becoming increasingly diversified after 1820, slave leasing was a common means of earning extra income. Owners who held more slaves than they could employ on their farms leased their surplus workers to small farmers, businesses, or manufacturers. Besides supplying cash payment for slaves' labor, the practice of leasing slaves released owners from the burden of providing housing and food. Leasing was commonly conducted during the New Year holiday, and most lease contracts between owners and small farmers, industrialists, or even railroads were for an entire year's service.

In chapter 10 of the *Narrative*, Douglass gives a detailed account of his year as the leased slave of Edward Covey. Born about 1806, Covey managed to rise from humble beginnings as a tenant farmer to accumulate real estate

valued at $23,000 by 1850. Although he was a small farmer among the many great plantations in Talbot County, Maryland, Covey gained the reputation as a "slave breaker," which allowed him to negotiate lucrative lease arrangements with area planters eager to have their slaves taught appropriate behavior and discipline. Douglass's master, Thomas Auld, probably had in mind reducing the spirit of his young slave when he arranged the year-long lease with Covey for 1834. Before returning to Saint Michaels in March 1833, Douglass had spent several years in the Baltimore home of Hugh and Sophia Auld, and he had there learned to enjoy the quasi freedom of the urban environment. Although it was illegal, Douglass managed to learn to read and to interact with both slaves and the free black community. When he returned to rural Saint Michaels, he brought some of his urban ways with him and organized a short-lived Sabbath school for area slaves with the help of a local white man. Disbanded after only three meetings, the Sabbath school pointed to Douglass's audacity and likely led his master to seek out the help of the notorious "Negro breaker" Covey. However, instead of breaking Douglass's spirit and making him more fit for slavery, the year with Covey instilled in Douglass a desire to be free.

Douglass's struggle and eventual fight with Covey is one of the most enduring narrations of a master's cruelty and also one of the clearest descriptions of slave resistance. Covey expected Douglass to work alongside his other three leased slaves, performing general labor on his farm. Having spent much of his youth in Baltimore, Douglass was unaccustomed to field work and suffered whippings as a result of his incompetence. During Douglass's first week on the farm, Covey directed him to drive an oxen cart to gather a load of firewood. Because Douglass had no experience in driving a team of oxen, it seems likely that Covey had set Douglass to fail. When the cart turned over and the oxen scattered, Douglass managed to locate them but returned without the firewood. Covey then subjected him to the first of almost weekly beatings. Instead of meekly complying with Covey's demand that he strip off his clothing, Douglass refused, maintaining his dignity as best he could under the circumstances.

The repeated beatings and hard labor he endured under Covey's lash very nearly broke Douglass's spirit. The tide turned, Douglass notes, in August 1834 when Covey pushed him past the limit of his strength to tolerate this malicious treatment. On a hot August day, Douglass fell ill and collapsed while fanning wheat. The description of the events that follow left the readers of Douglass's *Narrative* with a chilling portrait of the evil nature of slavery and the indifference of slaveholders to the suffering of the enslaved. Instead of providing the ill Douglass with medical attention, Covey kicked him repeatedly and hit him in the head with a hickory slat removed from a nearby barrel. Ill, dazed, and in severe pain, Douglass sought the refuge of his owner, Thomas Auld, whom he believed would remove him from Covey's household once he learned of the latter's brutal behavior. Taking some five hours to cover the seven miles between Auld's home and the Covey farm, Douglass found no refuge with his master, who instead sent him directly back to Covey.

In his *Narrative* and in subsequent orations and writings, Douglass described what followed as the major turning point in his life as a slave. With his antislavery readers cheering him on, Douglass told of his resolve to no longer be the passive recipient of Covey's violent attacks. When Covey tried to beat Douglass the Monday following his ordeal, Douglass fought back, leaving the supposed "Negro breaker" embarrassed and in pain. Douglass finished the year in Covey's employ but was never beaten again. The fight with Covey rekindled Douglass's desire to be free. When he recounted these events in his speeches and autobiographies, he sought to restore agency to the enslaved population that northern antislavery audiences sometimes viewed as helpless victims.

♦ Letter "To My Old Master"

On the tenth anniversary of his escape from slavery, on September 3, 1848, Frederick Douglass penned a letter to his former slave master, Thomas Auld. The letter appeared in Douglass's weekly antislavery newspaper, the *North Star*, on September 8, 1848. Intended as antislavery propaganda and obviously for a wider reading audience, the letter offered Douglass an opportunity to expand on the details of his life in slavery. When Douglass's *Narrative* was published in 1845, he was still legally a fugitive, so his language was somewhat tempered. By 1848, however, Douglass was truly a free man and for a year had been acting as editor of his own antislavery newspaper. The letter to his former master allowed him to condemn all slaveholders through his attack on Auld. His words offered *North Star* readers a visualization of the horrors of slavery unlike any they had read in the past. "To My Old Master" is one of the most enduring critiques of slavery. It was reprinted in numerous contemporary newspapers and today is used by historians and educators to explore slavery from the perspective of those enslaved.

Douglass's "old master," Thomas Auld, was born in Saint Michaels, Maryland, where he learned the trade of shipbuilding. He worked for the wealthy planter Edward Lloyd IV and married Lucretia Anthony, the daughter of Douglass's first owner. As the captain of Lloyd's sloop, he was responsible for moving plantation crops to market in Baltimore. He later became a store owner in Saint Michaels and then retired to a nearby farm. In 1827 he inherited Douglass, along with ten other slaves, from the estate of his father-in-law, Aaron Anthony. Because he was not a farmer through most of his career, Auld did not have much use for all of his slave labor. As a result, he sent a youthful Douglass to live in the home of his brother, Hugh Auld, in the shipbuilding city of Baltimore. In 1833 Douglass was sent back to Thomas Auld's Saint Michaels home and then leased to a succession of farmers, including the notorious Edward Covey and later the kind William Freeland. Following a failed escape attempt in 1836, Douglass was returned

to Hugh Auld's care in Baltimore, but he remained the property of Thomas Auld.

The excerpt begins with Douglass describing the fear and trepidation he had felt on the day that he escaped from slavery. He remarks that his chances for success were small, but the reward, life as a free man, made the risk worth taking. Douglass then offers Auld his justification for running away. Because he was also writing for a northern antislavery audience, Douglass chastises Auld, condemning his slave master for failing to conclude on his own accord that slavery was morally wrong. He searches his memory for his earliest desire to be free of bonds and recalls that he had first resolved to run away at about the age of six. As in his autobiographies, Douglass shocks his readers with a vivid description of the beating of an enslaved woman that he had witnessed as a young child. He recalls himself cowering and weeping while the slave driver whipped the woman until her neck bled. To northern readers, this story was all the more real because Douglass was an eyewitness to the horrific beating and was forced to endure such experiences as a young boy. Unlike much antislavery propaganda, which arrived secondhand and without corroboration, Douglass's letter offered legitimate evidence of the ungodly behavior of slaveholders from a well-respected source. The letter moves on to explain to Auld how Douglass eventually came to believe that slavery was wrong and that he was justified in taking the freedom he was denied.

Although he was attacked for being critical of Christianity in his *Narrative*, to the point that he felt the need to add an appendix apologizing and clarifying his position, Douglass returns to questioning God and religion in his letter. He questions the rightness and goodness of a God who would make one race of men subservient to another. He then describes several events that led to his realization that slavery was not always a permanent condition for African Americans. As a boy he had heard several elders in the slave community talk of their relatives' capture in Africa and subsequent sale into slavery in the United States. He credited the successful escape of his Aunt Jinny and Uncle Noah with instilling in him the knowledge that the free states existed and a desire to get there someday. Returning to his chastisement of Auld, Douglass demands that his old master recognize his humanity and realize that he was justified in taking his freedom.

Douglass then shifts his discussion from the past to the present. He tells Auld about his life in freedom and his ability to earn his own money and to decide how to spend his time. Once he began to speak on the antislavery circuit, Douglass notes, Auld and his cruelty as a slave master often figured prominently in his lectures. Douglass regularly recounted on the lecture circuit and in his first autobiography how his master became even crueler once he gained religion, and Douglass makes reference to the low opinion northern abolitionists held of him and all slaveholders. Ominously, Douglass next turns to beg for the release of his four siblings, still held in bondage by Auld at Saint Michaels. He demands to know how Auld would feel if Douglass captured his own daughter and held her as his slave. By juxtaposing his own family's experience in slavery with the Auld's life in freedom, Douglass draws a powerful contrast and makes a strong argument against the justification for racial slavery. He concludes by telling Auld of his plans to make his former master the subject of future orations and editorials, but this letter is the main document featuring Auld as the center of Douglass's condemnation of slavery and slaveholders. Late in his life, just three years before Auld's death in 1880, Douglass returned to Saint Michaels, where he visited his old master and managed an awkward reconciliation.

♦ "What to the Slave Is the Fourth of July?" Speech

Douglass delivered his most famous speech on July 5, 1852, at Corinthian Hall in Rochester, New York, before a crowd of five hundred to six hundred people. Initially invited to offer the traditional annual Independence Day oration, Douglass demurred, choosing instead to speak the following day. Published versions of the address appeared in pamphlet form and in his own *Frederick Douglass' Paper*. The lengthy speech is one of the most enduring articulations of what it meant for African Americans to live within the United States without fully benefiting from participation in society and without full protection of the civil rights afforded white citizens. It offers a clear and compelling juxtaposition of slavery and freedom that touched everyone in the audience and thousands who read the oration in its printed version. The speech endures today because Douglass moved beyond a condemnation of slavery to adopt a hopeful tone, foreshadowing the day when African Americans would be invited to take part fully and freely in American society.

The speech begins with Douglass distancing himself from the heritage of the American Revolution. His audience was accustomed to July Fourth orations celebrating the Founding Fathers and the accomplishments of the Revolution, namely America's freedom from Great Britain. He casts himself in the role of outsider, reminding his audience that African Americans, particularly those in slavery, did not benefit from the Revolution and subsequent formation of a republican government for the new United States. Douglass argues that celebrating the legacy of American independence is intolerable while millions of blacks are held in bondage. Instead of making progress, he proclaims the dismal state of race relations and states that American commitment to slavery is stronger than ever.

The speech was delivered two years after the passage of the Fugitive Slave Act of 1850, which created special courts to adjudicate runaway cases and strengthened the legal position of slaveholders. In addition, the climate of race relations in the United States rarely allowed for recognition of the accomplishments, and indeed even the humanity, of people of color. He alludes to the inequality of southern justice, noting that dozens of crimes, including some very minor offenses, could result in the death penalty for African Americans. He rails against those who would deny the humanity of the slave. According to Douglass, the

persistence of southern legislation to restrict and confine slaves helped make his case that a slave is a man and as such should be allowed full participation in society. He points to the laws forbidding the teaching of slaves to read or write and dares his audience to find similar restrictions against another species.

The common language of republicanism and liberty often recounted on the Fourth of July provided Douglass with additional evidence to make his point about the incongruity of slavery and freedom in the United States. The Declaration of Independence, he proclaims, already presented the doctrine of natural rights. The heritage of the Revolution put forth the basic idea that all men are created equal and are the rightful owners of their own bodies. He notes, "There is not a man beneath the canopy of heaven that does not know that slavery is wrong for him." In the most powerful section of the speech, Douglass comments that for African Americans, Independence Day is a sham that serves only to point out the gross injustice of the United States. He argues that instead of acting as a beacon of republicanism and freedom, the existence of slavery makes the United States a nation of barbarism and hypocrisy.

♦ "Our National Capital" Lecture

Following the Civil War, Douglass rejoiced in the end of slavery and was optimistic that the Thirteenth Amendment abolishing the institution marked a new beginning that would bring equal rights and racial equality to the United States. A strong supporter of the Republican Party as the vehicle for such change, Douglass moved his family to Washington, D.C., in 1872, hoping to take an active part in the progress of his race. Taking up the editor's pen at the Washington weekly, the *New National Era*, in 1870, Douglass urged African Americans to practice self-reliance, to build their own culture, and to accumulate property. He took his own advice to heart, purchasing a large home in the Anacostia neighborhood of the District of Columbia.

As Reconstruction came to a close following the disputed presidential election of 1876, some African Americans began to question the Republican Party's commitment to racial equality. Douglass was not one of those critics, and his continued loyalty to the party of Lincoln led some to label him as a political "yes man." This criticism intensified in 1877, when President Rutherford B. Hayes appointed Douglass federal marshal for the District of Columbia. However, soon after his senate confirmation Douglass delivered an address at the Douglass Institute in Baltimore that was so controversial that citizens of the national capital circulated a petition demanding that President Hayes remove Douglass from his post as marshal. The speech was excerpted from an unpublished lecture Douglass had delivered in Washington the year before, but this time parts of the speech appeared in the Baltimore press and were reprinted in the Washington *National Republican* and the *New York Times*. Douglass clearly had no intention of lowering his voice on behalf of equality for African Americans. He was also highly critical of those who sought political favors from those holding influence in Washington.

The excerpt shows that Douglass's lecture was particularly critical of office seekers and the members of Congress who pandered to them. Demonstrating that he had not lost his independence of opinion or his willingness to speak his mind, Douglass argues that it was virtually impossible for a man to be elected to Congress without owing a debt to office or favor seekers. These, he maintains, followed the congressman, asking him to assist in finding the political creditor a civil service post or other position tied to the government. But, according to Douglass, anyone connected to the administration was liable to be beset with favor seekers. Douglass's own experience was mainly with African American office hunters who believed that his connection with the Hayes administration gave him the needed influence to secure a post. He was principally angry with whites who approached him seeking favors and proclaiming their ties to the antebellum antislavery movement.

The racist nature of the national capital also figured prominently in Douglass's address. In a voice that must have been dripping with irony, he maintains that the legacy of slavery in Washington left a residuum that he labeled the "black boy." Douglass asserts that African American men, whether young or old, were often called "boy" and relegated to demeaning forms of service work. Especially humiliating was the post–Civil War appearance of wrought-iron hitching posts for horses depicting the image of a young black boy. Douglass believed that the image contributed to the continued subservience of African Americans and demonstrated that although slavery had been officially abolished, attitudes toward blacks had changed little following the war. In opposition to the menial labor performed by African Americans in Washington, Douglass claims that the white clerks in the city's many government departments and offices did very little work. He states that once a young man gained a clerkship or other position in a government office, he worked no more than six hours per day and was "seldom fitted for anything else in life."

Publication of the most controversial sections of the speech allowed Douglass's words to resonate unpleasantly around the country. Many in Washington had embraced the compromise ending the enforcement of Reconstruction and were looking toward regional reconciliation between North and South. Yet here was Douglass, a minor federal appointee but also the most famous civil rights activist of his age, loudly condemning Washington for its political corruption and racist behavior. The general press consensus suggested that the critique was particularly stinging because it was delivered by Douglass. Had a white man offered the same words of condemnation, little attention would have been paid to them. Following the speech, Washington businessmen and lawyers began a petition drive for his removal as marshal. Fortunately for Douglass, President Hayes refused to comply.

Impact and Legacy

Frederick Douglass was the most prominent African American activist of the nineteenth century. Not only did he manage to survive slavery and live in freedom, but he also became an articulate critic of the institution and an active participant in the U.S. political system. From the most humble of beginnings Douglass rose to advise presidents of the United States on issues important to his race, and eventually he formally represented his country in the diplomatic corps. His is an important example of the American dream of overcoming obstacles and reaching one's goals. In addition to his important achievements, Douglass was a giant among the thinkers of his century. Because he was so articulate and prolific in his speeches, autobiographies, and editorials, Americans can today know Douglass and the world he inhabited. Douglass offers an important example that social distance does not have to be a deterrent to achieving greatness in America. He remains important in American history and contemporary culture because he moved beyond rejoicing in his personal freedom from slavery to dedicate his to life to the progress of his race and of his country.

Key Sources

An important source for Douglass's writings is the Frederick Douglass Papers held by the Library of Congress. The complete holdings have been digitized and are available through the Library's American Memory Web site at http://memory.loc.gov/ammem/doughtml/. Editors at the Frederick Douglass Papers project at Indiana University–Purdue University at Indianapolis are working to complete published scholarly editions of Douglass's autobiographies, speeches, and correspondence. Volumes now available through Yale University Press include five selected volumes of speeches found in *The Frederick Douglass Papers*, Series 1: *Speeches, Debates, and Interviews* (1979–1992) and two of three autobiography volumes in *The Frederick Douglass Papers*, Series 2: *Autobiographical Writings* (1999–2003). An older, but still valuable selected collection of Douglass's papers and writings comprises the five volumes edited by Philip S. Foner, *Life and Writings of Frederick Douglass* (1950–1955). In addition, numerous scholarly and popular editions of Douglass's three autobiographies—*Narrative of the Life of Frederick Douglass* (1845), *My Bondage and My Freedom* (1855), and *Life and Times of Frederick Douglass* (1881, 1892)—are readily available.

Essential Quotes

"However long I might remain a slave in form, the day had passed forever when I could be a slave in fact."

(*Narrative of the Life of Frederick Douglass*)

"I embraced the golden opportunity, took the morning tide at the flood; and a free man, young, active, and strong, is the result."

(Letter "To My Old Master")

"I intend to make use of you as a weapon with which to assail the system of slavery—as a means of concentrating public attention on the system, and deepening their horror of trafficking in the souls and bodies of men."

(Letter "To My Old Master")

"What, to the American slave is your Fourth of July? I answer: a day that reveals to him, more than all other days in the year, the gross injustice and cruelty to which he is the constant victim."

("What to the Slave Is the Fourth of July?" Speech)

Essential Quotes

"Fellow citizens above your national, tumultuous joy, I hear the mournful wail of millions! whose chains, heavy and grievous yesterday, are, today, rendered more intolerable by the jubilee shouts that reach them."

("What to the Slave Is the Fourth of July?" Speech)

"When white men wish my aid, they tell me wonderful things of what they or their fathers did in the abolition cause, when it cost something to be known as an abolitionist. Through this class I have learned that there were a great many more Under Ground Railroad Stations at the north than I ever dreamed of in the time of slavery and when I sorely needed one myself."

("Our National Capital" Lecture)

Further Reading

Books

Andrews, William L, ed.. *Critical Essays on Frederick Douglass*. Boston: G. K. Hall, 1991.

Blight, David W. *Frederick Douglass' Civil War: Keeping Faith in Jubilee*. Baton Rouge: Louisiana State University Press, 1989.

Colaiaco, James A. *Frederick Douglass and the Fourth of July*. New York: Palgrave Macmillan, 2006.

Martin, Waldo E. *The Mind of Frederick Douglass*. Chapel Hill: University of North Carolina Press, 1984.

McFeely, William S. *Frederick Douglass*. New York: W. W. Norton, 1991.

Myers, Peter C. *Frederick Douglass: Race and the Rebirth of American Liberalism*. Lawrence: University Press of Kansas, 2008.

Preston, Dickson J. *Young Frederick Douglass: The Maryland Years*. Baltimore: Johns Hopkins University Press, 1980.

Rice, Alan J., and Martin Crawford, eds. *Liberating Sojourn: Frederick Douglass and Transatlantic Reform*. Athens: University of Georgia Press, 1999.

Sundquist, Eric J., ed. *Frederick Douglass: New Literary and Historical Essays*. New York: Cambridge University Press, 1990.

—L. Diane Barnes

Questions for Further Study

1. The passage from *Narrative of the Life of Frederick Douglass* is from the author's experience, yet it reads like an exciting fictional story. Study Douglass's writing from the standpoint of literature, as opposed to a purely political work. How well does he tell his tale? Discuss his use of concrete images—actual physical "things" such as the hickory slat and the briars that cut him. What other stylistic techniques does he use to keep his audience engaged?

2. Analyze the thoughts and feelings that went into Douglass's letter to his former master. In what ways has he forgiven the man who caused him so much misfortune? How has he transcended, or moved above and beyond, the experience of slavery? On the other hand, look at the ways in which he clearly (and understandably) remained bitter and how he expressed this, particularly through sarcasm.

3. Near the end of "What to the Slave Is the Fourth of July?" Douglass says that "There is not a nation on earth guilty of practices more shocking and bloody than are the people of the United States at this very hour." As undeniably cruel as American slavery was—and Douglass's powerful words made that cruelty real and immediate to his listeners—it is important to remember that millions of people lived under brutal systems in other parts of the world. Compare and contrast American slavery with the situation of the serfs in Russia, peasants in China, or other downtrodden groups. Keep in mind the ideals of freedom underlying the American system—ideals to which Douglass refers throughout the speech—and how they create a sharp contrast between America's government and political systems that never claimed to represent freedom.

4. A figure of extreme controversy during the days of slavery, Douglass in 1877 found himself once again in conflict, as expressed in his "National Capital" lecture. This time, however, he was standing up not against slaveholders and other enemies but against many who claimed to be allies. Consider the similarities between this and other works, such as the "Fourth of July" speech, as well as the differences. In what ways might it actually have been more difficult for Douglass, whose work had played no small part in the abolition of slavery, to confront the problems of the United States after the abolition of slavery? How well does he make his points, both about the current situation and its past causes?

Narrative of the Life of Frederick Douglass

1845

I lived with Mr. Covey one year. During the first six months, of that year, scarce a week passed without his whipping me. I was seldom free from a sore back. We were often in the field from the first approach of day till its last lingering ray had left us; and at saving-fodder time, midnight often caught us in the field binding blades.

If at any one time of my life more than another, I was made to drink the bitterest dregs of slavery, that time was during the first six months of my stay with Mr. Covey. We were worked in all weathers. It was never too hot or too cold; it could never rain, blow, hail, or snow, too hard for us to work in the field. Work, work, work, was scarcely more the order of the day than of the night. The longest days were too short for him, and the shortest nights too long for him. I was somewhat unmanageable when I first went there, but a few months of this discipline tamed me. Mr. Covey succeeded in breaking me. I was broken in body, soul, and spirit. My natural elasticity was crushed, my intellect languished, the disposition to read departed, the cheerful spark that lingered about my eye died; the dark night of slavery closed in upon me; and behold a man transformed into a brute!

My condition was much worse, during the first six months of my stay at Mr. Covey's, than in the last six. The circumstances leading to the change in Mr. Covey's course toward me form an epoch in my humble history. You have seen how a man was made a slave; you shall see how a slave was made a man. On one of the hottest days of the month of August 1934, I broke down; my strength failed me; I was seized with a violent aching of the head, attended with extreme dizziness; I trembled in every limb. Finding what was coming, I nerved myself up, feeling it would never do to stop work. I stood as long as I could stagger to the hopper with grain. When I could stand no longer, I fell, and felt as held down by an immense weight.

Mr. Covey was at the house, about one hundred yards from the treading-yard where we were fanning. He left immediately, and came to the spot where we were. He hastily inquired what the matter was. Bill [Smith, a hired hand] answered that I was sick, and there was no one to bring wheat to the fan. I had by this time crawled away under the side of the post and rail-fence by which the yard was enclosed, hoping to find relief by getting out of the sun. He then asked where I was. He was told by one of the hands. He came to the spot, and, after looking at me awhile, asked me what was the matter. I told him as well as I could, for I scarce had strength to speak. He then gave me a savage kick in the side, and told me to get up. I tried to do so, but fell back in the attempt. He gave me another kick, and again told me to rise. I again tried, and succeeded in gaining my feet; but, stooping to get the tub with which I was feeding the fan, I again staggered and fell. While down in this situation, Mr. Covey took up the hickory slat with which [William] Hughes [another hired hand] had been striking off the half-bushel measure, and with it gave me a heavy blow upon the head, making a large wound, and the blood ran freely; and with this again told me to get up. I made no effort to comply, having now made up my mind to let him do his worst. In a short time after receiving this blow, my head grew better. Mr. Covey had now left me to my fate. At this moment I resolved, for the first time, to go to my master, enter a complaint, and ask his protection. In order to this, I must that afternoon walk seven miles; and this, under the circumstances, was truly a severe undertaking. I was exceedingly feeble; made so as much by the kicks and blows which I received, as by the severe fit of sickness to which I had been subjected. I, however, watched my chance, while Covey was looking in an opposite direction, and started for St. Michael's. I succeeded in getting a considerable distance on my way to the woods, when Covey discovered me, and called after me to come back, threatening what he would do if I did not come. I, disregarded both his calls and his threats, and made my way to the woods as fast as my feeble state would allow; and thinking I might be overhauled by him if I kept the road, I walked through the woods, keeping far enough from the road to avoid detection, and near enough to prevent losing my way. I had not gone far before my little strength again failed me. I could go no farther. I fell down, and lay for a considerable time. The blood was yet oozing from the wound on my head. For a time I thought I should bleed to death; and think now that I should have done so, but that the blood so matted my hair as to stop the wound. After lying there about three quarters of an hour,

I nerved myself up again, and started on my way, through bogs and briers, barefooted and bareheaded, tearing my feet sometimes at nearly every step; and after a journey of about seven miles, occupying some five hours to perform it, I arrived at master's store. I then presented an appearance enough to affect any but a heart of iron. From the crown of my head to my feet, I was covered with blood. My hair was all clotted with dust and blood; my shirt was stiff with blood. My legs and feet were torn in sundry places with briers and thorns, and were also covered with blood. I suppose I looked like a man who had escaped a den of wild beasts, and barely escaped them. In this state I appeared before my master, humbly entreating him to interpose his authority for my protection. I told him all the circumstances as well as I could, and it seemed, as I spoke, at times to affect him. He would then walk the floor, and seek to justify Covey by saying he expected I deserved it. He asked me what I wanted. I told him, to let me get a new home; that as sure as I lived with Mr. Covey again, I should live with but to die with him; that Covey would surely kill me; he was in a fair way for it. Master Thomas ridiculed the idea that there was any danger of Mr. Covey's killing me, and said that he knew Mr. Covey; that he was a good man, and that he could not think of taking me from him; that, should he do so, he would lose the whole year's wages; that I belonged to Mr. Covey for one year, and that I must go back to him, come what might; and that I must not trouble him with any more stories, or that he would himself get hold of me. After threatening me thus, he gave me a very large dose of salts, telling me that I might remain in St. Michael's that night, (it being quite late,) but that I must be off back to Mr. Covey's early in the morning; and that if I did not, he would get hold of me, which meant that he would whip me.

I immediately started for home; and upon entering the yard gate, out came Mr. Covey on his way to meeting. He spoke, to me very kindly, bade me drive the pigs from a lot near by, and passed on towards the church. All went well till Monday morning. Long before daylight I was called to go and rub, curry, and feed, the horses. I obeyed, and was glad to obey. But whilst thus engaged, whilst in the act of throwing down some blades from the loft, Mr. Covey entered the stable with a long rope; and just as I was half out of the loft, he caught hold of my legs, and was about tying me. As soon as I found what he was up to, I gave a sudden spring, and as I did so, he holding to my legs, I was brought sprawling on the stable floor. Mr. Covey seemed now to think he had me, and could do what he pleased; but at this moment—from whence came the spirit I don't know I resolved to fight; and, suiting my action to the resolution, I seized Covey hard by the throat; and, as I did so, I rose. He held onto me, and I to him. My resistance was so entirely unexpected, that Covey seemed taken all aback. He trembled like a leaf. This gave me assurance, and I held him uneasy, causing the blood to run where I touched him with the ends of my fingers. Mr. Covey soon called out to Hughes for help. Hughes came, and, while Covey held me, attempted to tie my right hand. While he was in the act of doing so, I watched my chance, and gave him a heavy kick close under the ribs. This kick fairly sickened Hughes, so that he left me in the hands of Mr. Covey. This kick had the effect of not only weakening Hughes, but Covey also. When he saw Hughes bending over with pain, his courage quailed.

He asked me if I meant to persist in my resistance. I told him I did, come what might; that he had used me like a brute for six months, and that I was determined to be used so no longer. With that, he strove to drag me to a stick that was lying just out of the stable door. He meant to knock me down. But just as he was leaning over to get the stick, I seized him with both hands by his collar, and brought him by a sudden snatch to the ground. By this time, Bill came. Covey called upon him for assistance. Bill wanted to know what he could do. Covey said, "Take hold of him, take hold of him!" Bill said his master hired him out to work, and not to help to whip me; so he left Covey and myself to fight our own battle out. We were at it for nearly two hours. Covey at length let me go, puffing and blowing at a great rate, saying that if I had not resisted, he would not have whipped me half so much. The truth was, that he had not whipped me at all. I considered him as getting entirely the worst end of the bargain; for he had drawn no blood from me, but I had from him. The whole six months afterwards, that I spent with Mr. Covey, he never laid the weight of his finger upon me in anger. He would occasionally say, he didn't want to get hold of me again. "No," thought I, "you need not; for you will come off worse than you did before."

This battle with Mr. Covey was the turning-point in my career as a slave. It rekindled the few expiring embers of freedom, and revived within me a sense of my own manhood. It recalled the departed self-confidence, and inspired me again with a determination to be free. The gratification afforded by the triumph was a full compensation for whatever else

Document Text

might follow, even death itself. He only can understand the deep satisfaction which I experienced, who has himself repelled by force the bloody arm of slavery. I felt as I never felt before. It was a glorious resurrection, from the tomb of slavery, to the heaven of freedom. My long-crushed spirit rose, cowardice departed, bold defiance took its place; and I now resolved that, however long I might remain a slave in form, the day had passed forever when I could be a slave in fact. I did not hesitate to let it be known of me, that the white man who expected to succeed in whipping, must also succeed in killing me.

Glossary

binding blades:	putting together stalks of corn leaves and other plants used in making fodder
brute:	animal
fan:	a machine for separating wheat and other grains from chaff, or material to be discarded
the hopper:	a funnel into which grains are placed for storage
meeting:	church services
salts:	medicine
saving-fodder time:	the end of the day, when slaves would gather up fodder, a mixture of corn leaves and other plants used for feeding livestock
striking off the half-bushel measure:	pushing away the wheat above the half-bushel line

Document Text

Letter "To My Old Master"

1848

Milestone Documents

THOMAS AULD—SIR:—I have selected this day on which to address you, because it is the anniversary of my emancipation; and knowing of no better way, I am led to this as the best mode of celebrating that truly important event. Just ten years ago this beautiful September morning, yon bright sun beheld me a slave—a poor degraded chattel—trembling at the sound of your voice, lamenting that I was a man, and wishing myself a brute. The hopes which I had treasured up for weeks of a safe and successful escape from your grasp, were powerfully confronted at this last hour by dark clouds of doubt and fear, making my person shake and my bosom to heave with the heavy contest between hope and fear. I have no words to describe to you the deep agony of soul which I experienced on that never-to-be-forgotten morning—(for I left by daylight.)—I was taking a leap in the dark. The probabilities, so far as I could by reason determine them, were stoutly against the undertaking. The preliminaries and precautions I had adopted previously, all worked badly. I was like one going to war without weapons—ten chances of defeat to one of victory. I embraced the golden opportunity, took the morning tide at the flood; and a free man, young, active, and strong, is the result.

I have often thought I should like to explain to you the grounds upon which I have justified myself in running away from you. I am almost ashamed to do so now, for by this time you may have discovered them yourself. I will, however, glance at them. When yet but a child about six years old, I imbibed the determination to run away. The very first mental effort that I now remember on my part, was an attempt to solve the mystery, Why am I a slave? and with this question my youthful mind was troubled for many days, pressing upon me more heavily at [some] times than others. When I saw the slave-driver whip a slave-woman, cut the blood out of her neck, and heard her piteous cries, I went away into the corner of the fence, wept and pondered over this mystery. I had, through some medium, I know not what, got some idea of God, the Creator of all mankind, the black and the white, and that he had made the blacks to serve the whites as slaves. How he could do this and be good, I could not tell. I was not satisfied with this theory, which made God responsible for slavery, for it pained me greatly, and I have wept over it long and often. At one time, your first wife, Mrs. Lucretia, heard me singing and saw me shedding tears, and asked of me the matter, but I was afraid to tell her. I was puzzled with this question, till one night, while sitting in the kitchen, I heard some of the old slaves talking of their parents having been stolen from Africa by white men, and were sold here as slaves. The whole mystery was solved at once. Very soon after this, my aunt Jinny and uncle Noah ran away, and the great noise made about it by your father-in-law, made me for the first time acquainted with the fact, that there were free States as well as slave States. From that time, I resolved that I would some day run away. The morality of the act, I dispose of as follows: I am myself; you are yourself; we are two distinct persons, equal persons. What you are I am. You are a man, and so am I.—God created both, and made us separate beings. I am not by nature bound to you, or you to me. Nature does not make your existence depend upon me, or mine to depend upon yours. I cannot walk upon your legs, or you upon mine. I cannot breathe for you, or you for me; I must breathe for myself, and you for yourself. We are distinct persons, and are each equally provided with faculties necessary to our individual existence. In leaving you, I took nothing but what belonged to me, and in no way lessened your means of obtaining an honest living. Your faculties remained yours, and mine became useful to their rightful owner. I therefore see no wrong in any part of the transaction. It is true, I went off secretly, but that was more your fault than mine. Had I let you into the secret, you would have defeated the enterprise entirely; but for this, I should have been really glad to have made you acquainted with my intention to leave.

Since I left you, I have had a rich experience. I have occupied stations which I never dreamed of when a slave. Three out of the ten years since I left you, I spent as a common laborer on the wharves of New Bedford, Massachusetts. It was there I earned my first free dollar. It was mine. I could spend it as I pleased. I could buy hams or herring with it, without asking any odds of anybody. That was a precious dollar to me. You remember when I used to make seven or eight, and even nine dollars a week in Baltimore,

Document Text

you would take every cent of it from me every Saturday night, saying that I belonged to you, and my earnings also.

I married soon after leaving you: in fact, I was engaged to be married before I left you; and instead of finding my companion a burden, she was truly a helpmeet. She went to live at service, and I to work on the wharf, and though we toiled hard the first winter, we never lived more happily. After remaining in New Bedford for three years, I met with Wm. Lloyd Garrison, a person of whom you have possibly heard, as he is pretty generally known among slaveholders. He put it into my head that I might make myself serviceable to the cause of the slave by devoting a portion of my time to telling my own sorrows, and those of other slaves which had come under my observation. This was the commencement of a higher state of existence than any to which I had ever aspired. I was thrown into society the most pure, enlightened and benevolent that the country affords. Among these, I have never forgotten you, but have invariably made you the topic of conversation—thus giving you all the notoriety I could do. I need not tell you that the opinion formed of you in these circles, is far from being favorable. They have little respect for your honesty, and less for your religion.

At this moment, you are probably the guilty holder of at least three of my own dear sisters, and my only brother in bondage. These you regard as your property. They are recorded on your ledger, or perhaps have been sold to human flesh mongers, with a view to filling your own ever-hungry purse.

The responsibility which you have assumed in this regard is truly awful—and how you could stagger under it these many years is marvellous. Your mind must have become darkened, your heart hardened, your conscience seared and petrified, or you would have long since thrown off the accursed load and sought relief at the hands of a sin forgiving God. How, let me ask, would you look upon me, were I some dark night in company with a band of hardened villains, to enter the precincts of your own elegant dwelling and seize the person of your own lovely daughter Amanda, and carry her off from your family, friends and all the loved ones of her youth—make her my slave—compel her to work, and I take her wages—place her name on my ledger as property—disregard her personal rights—fetter the powers of her immortal soul by denying her the right and privilege of learning to read and write—feed her coarsely—clothe her scantily, and whip her on the naked back occasionally; more and still more horrible, leave her unprotected—a degraded victim to the brutal lust of fiendish overseers who would pollute, blight, and blast her fair soul—rob her of all dignity—destroy her virtue, and annihilate all in her person the graces that adorn the character of virtuous womanhood? I ask how would you regard me, if such were my conduct? Oh! the vocabulary of the damned would not afford a word sufficiently infernal, to express your idea of my God-provoking wickedness. Yet sir, your treatment of my beloved sisters is in all essential points, precisely like the case I have now supposed. Damning as would be such a deed on my part, it would be no more so than that which you have committed against me and my sisters.

I will now bring this letter to a close, you shall not hear from me again unless you let me hear from you. I intend to make use of you as a weapon with which to assail the system of slavery—as a means of concentrating public attention on the system, and deepening their horror of trafficking in the souls and bodies of men. I shall make use of you as a means of exposing the character of the American church and clergy—and as a means of bringing this guilty nation with yourself to repentance. In doing this I entertain no malice towards you personally. There is no roof under which you would be more safe than mine, and there is nothing in my house which you might need for your comfort, which I would not readily grant. Indeed, I should esteem it a privilege, to set you an example as to how mankind ought to treat each other.

I am your fellow man but not your slave,

Frederick Douglass

Glossary

brute:	animal
chattel:	slave
helpmeet:	partner, in all senses; typically used to describe a spouse
live at service:	work as a maid or other domestic servant
took the morning tide at the flood:	took a particularly convenient opportunity when it arose
the vocabulary of the damned would not afford a word sufficiently infernal:	even people in hell could not imagine a word so horrible
with a view to filling your own ever-hungry purse:	with the idea of satisfying your bottomless greed
Wm. Lloyd Garrison:	American social reformer William Lloyd Garrison (1805–1879), who was publisher of the *Liberator*, a leading abolitionist periodical

Douglass argued against John Brown's plan to attack the arsenal at Harpers Ferry, painting by Jacob Lawrence.

Document Text

"What to the Slave Is the Fourth of July?" Speech

1852

Fellow citizens above your national, tumultuous joy, I hear the mournful wail of millions! whose chains, heavy and grievous yesterday, are, today, rendered more intolerable by the jubilee shouts that reach them. If I do forget, if I do not faithfully remember those bleeding children of sorrow this day, "may my right hand forget her cunning, and may my tongue cleave to the roof of my mouth"! To forget them, to pass lightly over their wrongs, and to chime in with the popular theme would be treason most scandalous and shocking, and would make me a reproach before God and the world. My subject, then, fellow citizens, is American Slavery.

I do not hesitate to declare with all my soul that the character and conduct of this nation never looked blacker to me than on this Fourth of July! Whether we turn to the declarations of the past or to the professions of the present, the conduct of the nation seems equally hideous and revolting. America is false to the past, false to the present, and solemnly binds herself to be false to the future. Standing with God and the crushed and bleeding slave on this occasion, I will, in the name of humanity which is outraged, in the name of liberty which is fettered, in the name of the Constitution and the Bible which are disregarded and trampled upon, dare to call in question and to denounce, with all the emphasis I can command, everything that serves to perpetuate slavery—the great sin and shame of America! "I will not equivocate, I will not excuse"; I will use the severest of language I can command; and yet not one word shall escape that any man, whose judgment is not blinded by prejudice, or who is not at heart a slaveholder, shall not confess to be right and just.

Must I undertake to prove that the slave is a man? That point is conceded already. Nobody doubts it. The slaveholders themselves acknowledge it in the enactment of laws for their government. They acknowledge it when they punish disobedience on the part of the slave. There are seventy-two crimes in the state of Virginia which, if committed by a black man (no matter how ignorant he be), subject him to the punishment of death, while only two of the same crimes will subject a white man to the like punishment. What is this but the acknowledgment that the slave is a moral, intellectual, and responsible being? The manhood of the slave is conceded.

It is admitted in the fact that the Southern statute books are covered with enactments forbidding, under severe fines and penalties, the teaching of the slave to read or to write. When you can point to any such laws in reference to the beasts of the field, then I may consent to argue the manhood of the slave. When the dogs in your streets, when the fowls of the air, when the cattle on your hills, when the fish of the sea and the reptiles that crawl shall be unable to distinguish the slave from a brute, then will I argue with you that the slave is a man!

For the present, it is enough to affirm the equal manhood of the Negro race. Is it not astonishing that, while we are plowing, planting, and reaping, using all kinds of mechanical tools erecting houses, constructing bridges, building ships, working in metals of brass, iron, copper and silver, and gold; that, while we are reading, writing, and ciphering, acting as clerks, merchants and secretaries, having among us lawyers, doctors, ministers, poets, authors, editors, orators, and teachers; that, while we are engaged in all manner of enterprises common to other men, digging gold in California, capturing the whale in the Pacific, feeding sheep and cattle on the hillside, living, moving, acting, thinking, planning, living in families as husbands, wives, and children, and, above all, confessing and worshipping the Christian's God, and looking hopefully for life and immortality beyond the grave, we are called upon to prove that we are men!

Would you have me argue that man is entitled to liberty? That he is the rightful owner of his own body? You have already declared it. Must I argue the wrongfulness of slavery? Is that a question for republicans? Is it to be settled by the rules of logic and argumentation, as a matter beset with great difficulty, involving a doubtful application of the principle of justice, hard to be understood? How should I look today, in the presence of Americans, dividing and subdividing a discourse, to show that men have a natural right to freedom? speaking of it relatively and positively, negatively and affirmatively? To do so would be to make myself ridiculous and to offer an insult to your understanding. There is not a man

Document Text

beneath the canopy of heaven that does not know that slavery is wrong for him.

What, am I to argue that it is wrong to make men brutes, to rob them of their liberty, to work them without wages, to keep them ignorant of their relations to their fellow men, to beat them with sticks, to flay their flesh with the last, to load their limbs with irons, to hunt them with dogs, to sell them at auction, to sunder their families, to knock out their teeth, to burn their flesh, to starve them into obedience and submission to their masters? Must I argue that a system thus marked with blood, and stained with pollution, is wrong? No! I will not. I have better employment for my time and strength than such arguments would imply.

What, then remains to be argued? Is it that slavery is not divine; that God did not establish it; that our doctors of divinity are mistaken? There is blasphemy in the thought. That which is inhuman cannot be divine? Who can reason on such a proposition? They that can may; I cannot. The time for such argument is past....

What, to the American slave is your Fourth of July? I answer: a day that reveals to him, more than all other days in the year, the gross injustice and cruelty to which he is the constant victim. To him, your celebration is a sham; your boasted liberty an unholy license; your national greatness, swelling vanity; your sound of rejoicing are empty and heartless; your denunciation of tyrants, brass-fronted impudence; your shouts of liberty and equality, hollow mockery; your prayers and hymns, your sermons and thanksgivings with all your religious parade and solemnity, are, to Him, mere bombast, fraud, deception, impiety, and hypocrisy a thin veil to cover up crimes which would disgrace a nation of savages. There is not a nation of savages. There is not a nation on earth guilty of practices more shocking and bloody than are the people of the United States at this very hour.

Go where you may, search where you will, roam through all the monarchies and despotisms of the Old World, travel through South America, search out every abuse, and when you have found the last, lay your facts by the side of the everyday practices of this nation, and you will say with that, for revolting barbarity and shameless hypocrisy, America reigns without a rival.

Glossary

brute:	animal
dividing and subdividing a discourse:	going over a point in great detail and with great thoroughness
flay their flesh with the last:	rip apart their skin by whipping it with a last, a foot-shaped block used by shoemakers
Him: God	
"I will not equivocate…":	from a famous speech by the abolitionist William Lloyd Garrison
jubilee:	anniversary; particularly the fiftieth, which in the Israel of the Old Testament marked a year for forgiving debts and freeing slaves
the manhood of the slave is conceded:	meaning that it is agreed that slaves are human
may my right hand …:	a quote from Psalm 137:5–6
republicans:	supporters of a political system in which leadership is decided by popular election, rather than by heredity or military force
unholy license:	highly dishonorable misuse or abuse

Document Text

"Our National Capital" Lecture

1877

It is commonly thought to be a nice and pleasant thing to be a member of Congress, but I think it would be difficult for a man to find any position more abundant in vexation. A man who gets himself elected to Congress can seldom do so without drawing after him to Washington a lively swarm of political creditors who want their pay in the shape of an office somewhere in the civil service. They besiege his house at all hours, night and day, break his bell wires before breakfast, and so crowd his doorway that, if he is in, he cannot get out without seeing them, and if he is out, he cannot get in without seeing them. They waylay him as he goes to his house and dog him to the very doors, and summon him to the cloak room or lobby after he may have been so fortunate as to have reached his seat in the House of Representatives.

In all this sort of vexation and trouble he must be too polite or too prudent to express the slightest sense of annoyance. If he would be a successful politician he must face it all with blandest suavity and the patience of a true martyr.

But members of Congress are not the only victims of this incessant, persistent and annoying importunity for help to get official positions. The hour a man takes up his abode in Washington, his relation to the administration is inquired into and ascertained. No neutrality is allowed him. He is instantly weighed, measured, and stamped and duly assigned to one of two classes; the class which is used by everybody, or the class that uses everybody.

Once let it get abroad that you are friendly to the administration, or worse still, that the administration is friendly to you, and you will at once find yourself a famous man. Smiling faces anxious to see you and to serve their country, will cluster and whirl about your pathway, like the ripe leaves of declining autumn. If you were never before aware of your greatness, you will be made aware of it now, as plainly as words can reveal it. Men will tell you of it oftener than you can muster face to hear it. You will be urged to sign papers, write letters, and go in person and urge the appointment of some one of your numerous friends and admirers, every day in the year, and if you do not *sign, write, and go,* you will be denounced as a cold and heartless man.

I have had, since residing in Washington, my full share of this kind of service. I am usually approached by the dark side of our fellow citizens. They have been told by somebody, somewhere, that if they can only get to Washington and find Douglass, they will be quite sure to get an office.

When white men wish my aid, they tell me wonderful things of what they or their fathers did in the abolition cause, when it cost something to be known as an abolitionist. Through this class I have learned that there were a great many more Under Ground Railroad Stations at the north than I ever dreamed of in the time of slavery and when I sorely needed one myself.

Just what becomes of this ever accumulating and ever dissolving cloud of place hunters, I cannot engage to tell.

I have already said that the people of Washington have no claim to superiority in the matter of material civilization. The evidence in support of this assertion is found in the evident neglect with which they have treated their natural advantages and opportunities for improvement.

Two causes must explain the destitution of energy, enterprise and industry which have made this fact possible.

1st the presence and natural influence of slavery.

2nd the overshadowing presence and example of the government.

Slavery has left a residuum in Washington which, for the want of a better name, I call "the black boy." Its influence seems to be in the air and few who reside for any length of time at the capital escape it. Every body is waited upon by the black boy, and every body wants the black boy to wait upon him. Age and size furnish no criterion as to the appropriateness of the name. The black boy may be old or young, large or small, tall or short, seven years or seventy years old, he is always according to the parlance of slavery, the black boy. Send for a mechanic to put a shingle on your roof; a plumber to mend your water pipe, or your gas pipe; or send to anybody else to do the smallest piece of work, and at his heels you will find the inevitable black boy. He is there to carry the tools, to tote the water, and to otherwise wait and tend on the *Boss.*

Document Text

When the wife of the humble mechanic in Washington goes to do her marketing, if only to buy a single head of cabbage or a half a peck of potatoes, like all the rest she must have the black boy to walk behind her and carry the basket. In some cases the black boy might, by an oriental, be mistaken for an object of worship, and he might be led to suspect that the people have placed these objects at their front doors, for adoration; but the iron black boy at the front door of a Washington gentleman is not there for religious purposes. He is simply planted there as hitching post for horses. In these black ragged iron images, barefooted and bareheaded, with one suspender over the shoulder, after the manner of the black boy in slavery, we may see the kind of Christian civilization which has flourished here. Next to the degradation of labor by slavery and the consequent discouragement of industry, stand example influence as illustrated in these figures. Governmental departments are also a standing temptation to win men from labor and industry. At three 'clock in the afternoon of the long summer's day, a multitude of well dressed, young gentlemen are seen emerging from the majestic marble structures known as the departments. These young men look like the lilies of the field that neither toil nor spin. They have worked six hours and their day[']s work is done.

Now a young man who comes here to engage in some industrial pursuit and to begin the business of life must be well stocked with energy, industry and manly ambition, if he is able to resist the desire to be arrayed like one of these, and ten chances to one, he does not resist. He compares his lot with that of the clerks and other officers in the departments; measures his ten hours of labor with their six, and finds his just four hours too long. Besides, the clerks are clean; he is soiled; the clerks look fresh and he is tired. He is disgusted by the contrast; sighs and seeks for office and, if he succeeds, that is about the last of him for any useful business or calling in the world. Men are worked upon by what they work upon, and when once a man finds himself fitted to a desk and stool, and becomes rooted and grounded into the routine of a Government Clerk, he is seldom fitted for anything else in life.

Glossary

abroad:	widely known
abundant in vexation:	having many troubles
the blandest suavity:	the most casual nonchalance
break his bell wires:	a reference to the mechanism of doorbells, important in the era before the telephone; the equivalent of "ringing his phone off the hook"
civil service:	government employment, typically nonelective, within the executive branch
dark side of our fellow citizens:	African Americans
furnish no criterion:	do not really matter
lilies of the field … arrayed like one of these:	sarcastic comparison of idle young men to the flowers spoken of by Jesus in Matthew 6:28–29
national capital:	a pun referring both to Washington, D.C., and to "capital" as money or another unit of value
oriental:	a person from an eastern country, the term referring here to someone unfamiliar with American culture
place hunters:	job seekers